D0536710

Marketing

Marketing

Canadian edition

▶ **Warren J. Keegan**
Pace University, New York City and Westchester

▶ **Sandra E. Moriarty**
University of Colorado at Boulder

▶ **Thomas R. Duncan**
University of Colorado at Boulder

▶ **Stanley J. Paliwoda**
University of Calgary

Prentice Hall Canada

Canadian Cataloguing in Publication Data

Main entry under title:

Marketing

Canadian ed.
Includes index.
ISBN 0-13-184185-8

1. Marketing. I. Keegan, Warren J.

HF5415.M37 1995   658.8   C94-932812-X

Prentice-Hall, Inc., Englewood Cliffs, New Jersey
Prentice-Hall International (UK) Limited, London
Prentice-Hall of Australia Pty. Limited, Sydney
Prentice-Hall Hispanoamericana, S.A., Mexico City
Prentice-Hall of India Private Limited, New Delhi
Prentice-Hall of Japan, Inc., Tokyo
Simon & Schuster Asia Private Limited, Singapore
Editora Prentice-Hall do Brasil, Ltda., Rio de Janeiro

ISBN 0-13-184185-8

Acquisitions Editor: Patrick Ferrier
Developmental Editor: Dawn du Quesnay
Production Editor: Valerie Adams
Production Coordinator: Deborah Starks
Permissions/Photo Research: Karen Taylor
Page Layout: Hermia Chung
Cover Design: Julie Fletcher
Cover Art: Vasily Kandinsky
        Dream Motion (Träumerisch Regung). March 1923
        Watercolour, India ink, and pencil on paper
        46.4 × 40 cm (18¼ × 15¾ inches)
        Solomon R. Guggenheim Museum, New York, Gift, Solomon R. Guggenheim, 1938.
        Photograph by David Heald © The Solomon R. Guggenheim Foundation, New York
        FN 38.258

Original U.S. edition published by Prentice-Hall Inc., Englewood Cliffs, New Jersey
© 1995, 1992 by Prentice-Hall Inc.

1 2 3 4 5   cc   99 98 97 96 95

Printed and bound in the United States of America

Brief Contents

Contents

PART 2 THE KNOWLEDGE BASE

xi

There was an old Moscow joke about the military parade passing in front of Brezhnev who was standing atop the Kremlin Wall. Wave upon wave of tanks and missiles went by and then, after a gap, along came a pink convertible with a man dressed in a loud suit waving energetically to the cheering crowd. Brezhnev immediately turned to his comrades for an explanation as to what this civilian was doing in a military parade. "Comrade Brezhnev, this is no mistake—you have no idea how much damage one marketing expert can do!"

Marketing as a discipline and body of thought was aptly summed up by Regis McKenna in a Harvard Business article: "Marketing is everything. Today, everything a company or organization does affects its relationship—either directly or indirectly—with its customers, it suppliers, its competitors.

Yet everyone thinks they know something about marketing and will attempt it without prior knowledge or set objectives.

Contemporary marketing is about *building relationships*. A product, service, brand, or corporation is successful only to the degree that it means something important to the people with whose lives it is linked. Customers, employees, shareholders, distributors, dealers, franchisees, retailers, competitors, neighbors, government leaders, and even members of the press—people we call *stakeholders* because they have a stake in the success of companies and brands—are involved with or affected by marketing programs. Thus we discuss relationship marketing not only as a way to build product-customer relations but as a way to create sustained and satisfying relationships between an organization and all its stakeholders.

Marketers today have the responsibility to treat customers as guests, suppliers as partners, employees as team members, and the earth and its environment as a fragile vessel that can carry us to a bountiful future or to ecological calamity, depending on how we manage our opportunities, and our sources.

GLOBAL IS EVERYWHERE

Marketers and companies who fail to recognize that they are now functioning in a global marketplace invite trouble and risk financial disaster. The marketing principles described in this book are as applicable in Tokyo as in London, in Montreal as in Dar Es Salaam. Markets are different, but the marketing discipline is universal.

Thirty years ago, a little German car made by Volkswagen (the "Beetle") began to open up the small-car market, becoming a marketing legend in its own time. Starting in the mid-1970s Japanese auto makers began acquiring significant shares of the small and medium-size automobile market in Canada and the United States (after the oil stock price increases instituted by the OPEC Cartel), edging out both domestic companies and Volkswagen, whose market share dropped from ten to less than one percent. Why did the market close for one small car and open for another? What did German and Japanese auto makers know about the North American market that domestic manufacturers failed to see? How do such major shifts in market share come about?

The auto industry, which is very important to Canada, is only one of the many industries whose future is enmeshed in global trends. The marketing stories of our time—both successes and failures—are often interlaced with international issues, and that is why this book draws on examples from around the world, as well as Canada, to incorporate a global focus throughout. Global concerns have been woven seamlessly into all the major discussions throughout the book. In these discussions we present both the complexities of international marketing—the necessary adjustments to differing cultures—as well as the universal principles and practices. Indexes to discussions of global issues and ethical issues may be found at the end of the book.

STRATEGY MEANS PLANNING

We believe the formulation of a marketing plan to be crucial to all marketing strategy. We have tried to make it easy for readers to follow the process of developing an effective marketing program, which starts with the marketing plan and continues with its implementation: In Chapters 2 and 3 we build the reader's understanding of the SWOT analysis with which the marketing planning process begins—the analysis of a company's internal strengths and weaknesses and external opportunities and threats. In Chapter 4 we outline the marketing planning process and, in an appendix, present an actual marketing plan that illustrates the chapter's discussions. In the remaining chapters of the book we show how the objectives and strategies determined in the planning process guide marketers from product development through marketing communication. Finally, Chapter 22's examination of the marketing audits shows how the evaluation of a marketing program is linked to the original plan.

THE CHALLENGE OF INTEGRATED MARKETING

In line with the concept that marketing is everything, the integrated approach to marketing holds that every decision in marketing is interrelated with other marketing and management decisions and sees all marketing mix strategies as interdependent. This emphasis on interrelationships may sometimes seem to threaten one function or aspect of the marketing mix, but in the long run it presents all marketers with a challenge. Advertising, for example, was long the dominant area of marketing communication for most packaged goods, but today marketers are beginning to rely more on sales promotion, direct marketing, and public relations. Shifts like this have a tremendous impact on all the marketing communication professions, but they also challenge marketers to make the most effective use of the forms of marketing communication available to them within the limitations of the marketing budget.

FEATURES

Marketing, Canadian Edition, offers a unique approach to the coverage of the theory and practice of marketing, as well as a number of special features.

A Concise, Contemporary Text: We hope we have accomplished our goal of giving the reader a succinct presentation, while at the same time presenting important new topics and up-to-date examples and stories.

A Video Case Program: We present one CBC video case per chapter, each carefully chosen to reflect the chapter content.

An Integrative Case Program: Three longer cases, whose discussions illustrate topics throughout the book, follow Chapter 22, and questions on each of these cases are found at the end of each chapter. The instructor has the option of using one or another of these cases in a given semester.

LEARNING AIDS

Chapter Objectives and Key Points Summaries. To help the student tie chapter objectives to the text material, we have frequently referred back to specific objectives in relevant portions of the text. In a further effort to facilitate the student's learning we have linked each objective with a corresponding entry in the summary section. We hope this approach will help students both locate heralded topics as they study the chapter and review these major subjects when they have finished reading it.

Opening and Closing Stories. Opening, "Think About It" stories attempt to engage students on a personal level, raising marketing issues that relate to the chapter topic but that also have current and direct impact on their own lives. For example, Chapter 1's opening story raises a topic close to the hearts of many Canadians sympathetic to the continued existence of our two national airlines. "Bottom Line Realities" stories, which close each chapter, address marketing problems of more general relevance and encourage students to think seriously about such issues as the impact on the environment of so-called disposable products and to answer specific questions or undertake exercises related to these issues.

When Is a Box Not a Box? Our "embedded boxes" are actually sections of the chapter text. They are designed to be read in sequence with the rest of the text; they are not optional reading. Like most "boxes," they are of several recurring types: "Risks and Gambles" sections offer accounts of risky marketing ventures, such as the current efforts to bring HDTV to market. "Behind the Scenes" sections present in-depth discussions of such subjects as the worldwide ISO 9000 certification program. "Open to Debate" sections explore controversial issues, such as the ethics of sophisticated modern methods of acquiring personal information about potential customers.

Chapter Discussion Questions. Each chapter is followed by a set of questions on topics covered in the chapter. Some questions help students review materials studied, others require students to extrapolate from what they have studied to hypothetical marketing situations, and still others offer applied projects and exercises.

Video Cases. At the end of each chapter is a video case that relates to the chapter topic and concludes with several discussion questions. These cases are based on CBC videos (described under "Supplements").

Integrative Cases. To reinforce the concept that all marketing functions are interrelated not only with all others but with all other aspects of a business, we present three longer, integrative cases—The Body Shop, Harley-Davidson, and the Millennium Power System—at the back of the book, immediately following Chapter 22. Each integrative case illustrates topics in every chapter, and to facilitate linking these cases with the chapters, we offer one or more questions on each case after the general chapter discussion questions.

Key Terms, Margin Definitions, and Glossary. All major terms are boldfaced at the their definitions in the text and highlighted in adjacent margin definitions. A glossary at the back of the book includes all terms and definitions.

"Careers in Marketing" and "Marketing-Data Analysis and Mathematics" Appendixes. The careers appendix describes actual jobs in marketing as well as current prospects on the job scene in various marketing fields. Brief profiles provided by "real-world" marketers describe actual marketing jobs and offer other information useful to those starting out in marketing. There is also an appendix on marketing data analysis and mathematics.

SUPPLEMENTS

Instructor's Manual: The Instructor's Manual is a comprehensive teaching resource that contains, for each text chapter, a concise summary of the chapter's content; a brief lecture outline; an extended teaching outline that summarizes text and case material for each reference; answers to chapter discussion questions and integrative case discussion questions; teaching notes for the chapter case; supplementary discussion questions and answers; and additional references.

Study Guide: The Canadian edition of the Study Guide, prepared by Deborah Lee Andrus of the University of Calgary, offers students practice test questions and applications projects. Answers are also provided for the questions, about half of which come from the Test Item File. Designed to increase the student's ability to apply the text material, applications projects for each chapter are generally based on the book's cases; there is at least one project for each of the book's three integrative cases. The applications projects are also referred to in the Instructor's Manual. A Computerized Study Guide is also available.

Test Item File: Prepared by Carolyn Guichon and Lynne Ricker of the University of Calgary, the Test Item File offers approximately 2500 items in essay-question, multiple-choice, and true-false format. The test bank, which covers both text and case material, taps all levels of difficulty with definitional, general comprehension, and applications questions. The Test Item File is also available on disk (IBM) through the Prentice Hall TestManager testing system.

Color Transparencies With Notes: A set of full-color transparencies to the U.S. Edition will be made available to qualified adopters of the text.

CBC/Prentice Hall Video Library: Prentice Hall Canada and the CBC have worked together to bring you the best and most comprehensive Canadian video package available in the college market, containing clips from such notable CBC programs as *Venture* and *Market Place*. Designed specifically to complement the text, this library is an excellent tool for bringing students into contact with the world outside the classroom. These programs have extremely high production quality, present substantial content, and are hosted by well-versed, well-known anchors, and have been chosen to relate directly to chapter content.

CBC ⊛

Financial Post Supplement: The *Financial Post* and Prentice Hall Canada have joined together in an exclusive arrangement to produce a student edition of the *Financial Post*, tailored to students of marketing. Through this program, the core subject matter provided in the text is supplemented by a collection of specially chosen, time-sensitive articles from one of Canada's most distinguished business newspapers. These articles demonstrate the vital, ongoing connection between what is learned in the classroom and what is happening in Canada and the world around us, and are updated annually. This supplement is shrinkwrapped free to the text.

The Financial Post

Personal Computer Applications Software: BRANDS™, by Randall G. Chapman of Boston University, is a marketing simulation game designed for use in the marketing principles course. With the instructor's guidance, students are able to apply their marketing knowledge and skills in realistic exercises. Forming teams, they manage the daily operations of firms competing within a single industry, making marketing decisions and dealing with the responses of a simulated marketplace.

ACKNOWLEDGEMENTS

We are grateful to Ian Bootle, VP International Marketing, Canadian Airlines for help with this text as well as for transparencies used. Similarly Jackie Stratton of Canadian Fracmaster loaned us their framed photograph of the presentation of their CABE for marketing excellence. Sue Cruickshank of the Shell Picture Library also helped out with illustrations. From Ireland we had support from Peter Boland of Ballygowan Spring Water Company, and from Edinburgh, Scotland, the Editor of the Scotland-on-Sunday supplied us with the "Soap Wars" photograph.

Many people contributed to this work. Special mention and thanks is due to Angie Driscoll who has just successfully defended her Ph.D. Her painstaking attention to detail and her ability to work long hours and forever remain critical of what was going on is remarkable. Her contribution has to be noted just in case it was not abundantly clear throughout this highly stressful production process!

Many companies and many individuals responded well when approached and sincere thanks are due to them. Special attention should be made to Karen McGhee, Royal Bank of Canada, Diana Higgins, CIBC, Lee Edwards (local franchisee, Holiday Inn Express Motels), and David Kyzebol of Westfair Foods, which owns Real Canadian Superstore and President's Choice and "no-name" brand lines. We are pleased also to have been able to include charities among our examples of the best Canadian marketing practices, and hope that this innovativeness will continue.

Finally, a word of recognition to the Prentice Hall team that helped bring this book to fruition including Pat Ferrier, Dawn du Quesnay, Valerie Adams, Paula Thiessen, and Karen Taylor.

We have tried here to represent some of the best of Canadian business marketing practice, but the above list omits many contributors. Nevertheless, we have sought to include as many of those as possible who responded so quickly when first approached. Your generosity made our work much easier and more meaningful to our student readership. We acknowledge our debt of gratitude to each one of you.

Stan Paliwoda
1995

WARREN J. KEEGAN

SANDRA E. MORIARTY

Warren J. Keegan, Professor of International Business and Marketing and Director of the Institute for Global Business Strategy at the Lubin School of Business, Pace University, is the founder of Warren Keegan Associates, Inc., a consulting consortium of experts in global strategic management and marketing.

A frequent speaker to business audiences, he is widely sought as an expert on global marketing and business to appear on national and global television. He is the Prodigy online international business expert and writes the weekly *Global Observer* commentary for International Business, a core feature of the Prodigy service.

Warren Keegan is the author or co-author of five books in addition to the present text: *Marketing Sans Frontiers; Advertising Worldwide; Global Marketing Management; Judgments, Choices, and Decisions: Effective Management Through Self-Knowledge;* and *Principles of Global Marketing* (forthcoming).

Experienced in business and government as well as academic teaching and research, he has served on the General Motors marketing staff; consulted with the Boston Consulting Group and Arthur D. Little; and served as both Assistant Secretary for Development Planning and Secretary of the Economic Development Commission of Tanzania.

Warren Keegan holds an M.B.A. and a D.B.A. from the Harvard Business School and is a former MIT Fellow in Africa. He has taught at INSEAD, in France; at the Stockholm School of Economics; at Emmanuel College of Cambridge University; and at the University of Hawaii. He is a former faculty member of Columbia University, Baruch College, George Washington University, and New York University.

Sandra E. Moriarty, Professor in the Integrated Marketing Program at the University of Colorado-Boulder, taught previously at the University of Kansas and at Michigan State University. Before moving into full-time teaching she owned her own public relations and advertising agency. Her current research interests include the analysis of changing marketing practices and the development of new theoretical approaches in the several fields of marketing communication.

In addition to the present text, she has written or co-written six books in the area of marketing communication: *The Creative Package, Creative Advertising, Advertising Principles and Practices, The ABCs of Typography,* and *How to Create and Deliver Winning Presentations.* She co-authored the latter book with Tom Duncan, to whom she is married. She is also the author of articles in scholarly and trade journals.

Sandra Moriarty presents frequent seminars and workshops on marketing communication to businesses and groups in the United States and in other countries around the world. Among the organizations she has addressed are Nestlé, Dentsu, BBDO-Europe, the Greek Advertising Association, and the International Advertising Association.

She holds degrees in journalism from the University of Missouri and Kansas State University, as well as a Ph.D. in instructional communication from Kansas State.

The Authors

THOMAS R. DUNCAN

STANLEY J. PALIWODA

Thomas R. Duncan, Director of the Integrated Marketing Communication graduate program at the University of Colorado-Boulder, is one of today's leading thinkers in integrated marketing and integrated marketing communications. He has taught marketing and marketing communication for over ten years, both in the United States and in England.

Before entering the academic world, he spent fifteen years in industry. He started his career in marketing research and account management at the Leo Burnett advertising agency in Chicago and went on to become Director of Marketing Services for a major division of Beatrice Foods and then Vice President of Marketing for Jeno's Frozen Foods. He continues to keep his hand in business by serving as a marketing consultant for such global companies as IBM, Allied Signal, Coors, Dentsu, and Nestlé as well as start-up, entrepreneurial companies.

Founder of the interdisciplinary integrated marketing program he now directs, Tom Duncan does extensive speaking throughout North America and has conducted seminars and workshops for marketing executives and educators in Japan, Malaysia, Greece, Canada, France, and Mexico.

In addition to numerous articles and academic presentations on marketing, he is author of *The Re-Integration of Marketing Communications* (forthcoming) and co-author of *How to Create and Deliver Winning Presentations.* He holds bachelor's and masters' degrees in advertising from Northwestern University and a Ph.D. from the University of Iowa.

Stanley J. Paliwoda, Professor and Chair of Marketing at the University of Calgary and Visiting Professor in Marketing at the Warsaw School of Economics, Poland, taught previously at UMIST (University of Manchester Institute of Science and Technology) England. He has worked in sales management and market research. His interests are primarily in international marketing, focusing on foreign market entry modes, business to business marketing strategy and marketing relationship management.

In addition to a number of articles in refereed journals, he is the author or co-author of ten books aside from this present one, including most recently *Business Opportunities in Eastern Europe,* Addison-Wesley/EIU Books, 1994; a forthcoming *International Marketing Reader,* Routledge, 1995 (with Dr. John K. Ryans Jr.); *Essence of International Marketing* with Prentice Hall, 1994, and *International Marketing* now in its second edition with Butterworth-Heinemann, 1993. He is the editor of *The Journal of East-West Business,* a refereed journal dealing with Eastern Europe and the Russian Republics, published by Haworth Press, New York.

He has a BA from the University of Ulster, a Master's degree from Bradford University, and a Ph.D. from Cranfield University, England, which also won him an Export Research prize. He was elected a Fellow of the Chartered Institute of Marketing (UK) in 1993 and is a professional member of the Institute of Export (UK) and former examiner for their International Marketing professional examinations. He is listed in a number of international directories including *Who's Who in the World.*

Marketing

Chapter 1

Marketing in a Global Society

AIRLINES ADAPT TO A NEW ENVIRONMENT

Between 1989 and 1994, the world's airlines lost record amounts of money. In 1995, a radically changed airline industry is finally emerging from crisis and struggling to return to profitability.

The crisis started when the Gulf War sent fuel prices soaring faster than airfares could keep up. At the same time, airlines began to realize how inefficiently they were operating and new low-cost, no-frills airlines were forcing big names to lower their fares. The situation was made worse by a recession and a spending hangover from the 1980s that grounded some airlines for good.

In Canada, airlines also faced industry deregulation and the entry of charter airlines into the market. It became more difficult to survive, let alone compete, and even harder

for an airline to distinguish itself from its competition. If fares, schedules, frequent flyer programs and the basic air transportation product are essentially the same, what sets one airline apart from another?

Canadian Airlines International is distinguishing itself by redefining the way it does business. In 1990, Canadian committed itself to service quality and refocused the company to listen to customers. Now what customers say they want provides direction for Canadian's products and services.

When business travelers said that on-time performance was their number one concern, Canadian launched a company-wide initiative to better its on-time performance. In less than two years, Canadian's process improvements boosted on-time performance from 93 percent to over 96 percent, the best of any major scheduled airline in Canada.

Canadian Airlines was also strengthened by the largest consensual restructuring in Canadian financial history. As part of the restructuring, more than 15,000 employees invested $200 million in the airline. Apart from its financial value, employee ownership also proved to be important to the airline's customers. This became the basis for a national advertising campaign which featured the tag line, "If your good name were riding on it, wouldn't you do what it takes to make a difference?" and an aircraft signed by hundreds of employees.

In 1995, Canadian will continue to serve more destinations in Canada than any other airline, fortify its position as Canada's primary carrier to Asia, and post its first annual profit of the decade.

This Canadian Airlines example shows that survival and success depend on a business's ability to be flexible and innovative and to respond with products and services which not only meet, but exceed, varied and changing customers' needs. ■

The problem facing Canadian Airlines and the rest of the airline industry illustrates a dilemma at the heart of marketing: How can a company offer products and services that consumers value and that serve their needs while at the same time maintaining a healthy operating base? In this chapter we will define marketing and its key concepts, explore its social and economic underpinnings, and explain why the marketing-driven philosophy has emerged as the most successful strategy for business. As we introduce you to these basic concepts of marketing, we'll involve you in the many problems and issues companies face as they search for innovative solutions to their marketing problems.

Throughout this book you'll read inside stories about the successes and failures of some products familiar to you and others that you may not have heard of. These stories illustrate the basic themes of this book—creating value and quality, building positive marketing relationships, understanding bottom-line realities, and examining marketing from a global viewpoint. We hope they will make the world of marketing—its principles, controversies, decisions and gambles—come alive for you.

WHAT IS MARKETING?

The term *marketing* has two principal meanings and so the first objective of this chapter asks you to distinguish between the them. Traditionally, marketing has been considered an upscale replacement word for *selling* without adding to its functions. In this sense, it is being misapplied. However, marketing in its correct sense, means a philosophy of business—a point of view that focuses the attention of the entire business on the customer and brings all the organization's resources and skills to bear on the task of understanding and meeting consumer needs. Firms which follow this philosophy are said to be "consumer driven." Throughout this book, when we refer to the *marketing concept,* we are speaking of the philosophy.

Most definitions of marketing, however, focus on the function of marketing. The official American Marketing Association definition articulates a broad view of the marketing function that has emerged in recent years to mirror the idea of a marketing philosophy of business management. In the AMA's *Dictionary of Marketing Terms*, **marketing** is "the process of planning and executing the conception, pricing, promotion, and distribution of ideas, goods, and services to create exchanges that will satisfy individual and organizational objectives."[1] Note that marketing's role is seen here as not only to price, promote, and distribute a product but also to plan and execute all the activities involved in the product's development. This is similar to the definition offered by the Chartered Institute of Marketing in the U.K.: "The management process which seeks to identify, anticipate and satisfy customer requirements properly." Marketing is a management function but has to be far-reaching in vision and includes other definitions. The CIM also emphasizes profitability.

When these criteria of the marketing function are seen in the broader context of a business philosophy, marketing is not just a function assigned to certain people within an organization, but a part of every employee's job. That is because the activities of every employee, and the results of every decision, affect the organization's pursuit of its goals as well as its corporate and brand image.

In this sense, marketing considerations drive an organization's total efforts. Regis McKenna, in his book *Relationship Marketing*, says that "marketing is everything and everything is marketing."[2] That is the philosophy we have adopted for this book: Every business activity has marketing implications, and every marketing decision affects the entire organization.

One of the most crucial tasks of marketing is to create a willingness to buy on the part of potential consumers who have been identified as able to buy your product or service. Through market research we can learn what consumers need and want (we will discuss this later), and this can lead us through various possible product alternatives to a prototype and through further market testing to new products and services. Finally by communicating the usefulness and desirability of this new product or service to customers, marketers *create value*.

According to the AMA dictionary, **value** represents the power of a good to command other goods, such as money, in an exchange. *Creating value*, then, means making a product especially desirable to consumers in various ways and for any number of reasons. The "ways" and "reasons" result from marketing decisions and strategies. By creating value, a company like J. Higby's (Exhibit 1-1) influences consumer demand for its product. Throughout this book you will see repeatedly the central importance to marketing of creating value for consumers.

Exhibit 1-1
"The First Frozen Yogurt with the Taste of Premium Ice Cream"

J. Higby's is a highly successful marketer through identifying and creating important values for its customers

exchange
A marketing transaction, often called a *sale*, in which a buyer gives something of value to a seller in return for goods or services.

market
A group of potential buyers who need and want a particular product and who are both willing and able to buy it.

MARKETS

The nature of an exchange and the market in which an exchange takes place are the subject of our second chapter objective. An **exchange** is a marketing transaction in which a buyer gives something of value to a seller in return for a product, which may be either a good, a service, a place, a personality, a concept, or an idea that the buyer values.

Because an exchange is often called a *sale*, marketing and selling are often confused. We need to distinguish clearly between them. *Selling* focuses on the firm and what it produces to sell, while *marketing* focuses on consumers and what they want to buy. Marketing includes a number of activities—research, strategic planning, product development, product management, pricing, distribution, and marketing communications—that make selling more efficient. That is, marketing helps a company identify what the consumer is most likely to buy and then makes it available. Advertising to target groups identified by market research also helps answer questions as to price levels and favored distribution channels.

Buyers At the most basic level, any place where an exchange occurs is referred to as a *market*. On another level, the word **market** is used to mean all the people or organizations who want or need a particular product and who are both willing and able to buy it. Yet there is more. We need to have some concept of the size of that market, how to penetrate it with distribution, and how potential customers may react to pricing and promotion strategies.

Some markets are based on *needs* that derive from people's work or life situations. For example, as you can see from Exhibit 1-2, Rubbermaid identified one consumer market as traveling salespeople who need an efficient and convenient way to store and access the papers and other items they use in their work. Similarly, Kimberly-Clark and other makers of disposable diapers have found in new parents a need-based consumer market—one that is currently fraught with controversy, as we will see in the "Pampering the Environment?" discussion at the end of the chapter.

Exhibit 1-2
A Proven Innovator

Rubbermaid is another company that has been particularly adept at identifying customer needs and devising ways to fulfill them.

Other markets, like those for small cars, are based more on people's preferences or *wants*. For example, although they may not need to drive a small car for economy, some consumers may simply prefer them. For Canadian Airlines or Air Canada, the business traveler market may be its largest but for both, its vacationer market makes up a significant portion of its revenues and an important strategic decision the airline must make is how much attention to devote to each of its various markets between business needs and vacationer wants.

A market may also be described with some limited degree of accuracy as a *mass market*, which means the people in it represent a wide variety of ages, incomes, and lifestyles. Snacks and soft drinks are typically sold to mass markets. Or a market may be defined as a **niche market**, which means it is small

niche market
A small, tightly defined group of customers who share certain characteristics that make them a target market for some specialized product.

and tightly constrained by certain characteristics. Cheerleaders, for example, are a niche market within the broader teenage market.

The buyer, one of the participants in the exchange, is the person who purchases and uses the goods, services, or ideas offered by an organization. A **customer** is the *buyer* of a product—often, in retail marketing, someone with whom a seller deals on a regular basis. A **consumer** is the *user* of the product, who may or may not be the buyer. In business, for example, purchasing agents buy products on behalf of technicians who actually use the products; in the private sphere, parents buy books for their children to use in their schoolwork. Despite this formal distinction, however, we often use the word *consumers* to mean both buyers and users.

Types of Markets Traditionally, we identify five types of markets: the consumer market, the industrial market, the government market, the institutional market and the international market. Here, we will focus on the first four. Note that all five may involve the use of intermediaries in the distribution channel. In a *consumer* market, people buy products and services for their own personal use or for the use of others in their households. When a mother buys Kellogg's Fruit Loops or when you buy a Prentice Hall textbook, both of you are functioning in the consumer market. When a firm buys products or services to use in its business—either in making products or in supporting its other business functions—it is operating in an *industrial* market. Canadian Airlines, for example, buys not only airplanes but also cleaning supplies to maintain its fleet, computers for billing and inventory control, and food products for its passengers.

The government market functions at several levels: municipal, provincial and federal. In terms of purchasing, procedures are different again. Usually tenders to bid are invited and sealed bids submitted by a certain date. It is usually also made clear that there is no obligation to accept the lowest tender. Frequently, political considerations enter into the final choice of supplier with government contracts.

Intermediaries (once called "middlemen") such as wholesalers, retailers, and other types of distributors buy finished goods and resell them to other businesses or to individuals. A manufacturer of eyeglass frames, for example, sells its frames to a wholesaler (reseller), who sells them to an optician (another reseller), who sells them to an individual customer. In an *institutional* market, the buyers of large quantities of products and services are neither individuals nor companies but institutions like hospitals and schools. Such organizations buy many sorts of goods, from furniture and electronic equipment to athletic supplies and books. They may buy on the basis of the lowest of three bids received if for a new purchase or for routine purchases on a frequent basis. There is the greatest distance possible here between the user and the purchaser.

The Marketplace A market may be defined, in many ways: geographically, demographically or psychographically, which means simply targetting people according to their known values, attitudes, beliefs and lifestyles. A geographical market may be Victoria, B.C., where an increasing population of older and retired people is creating demand for leisure-time products like gardening equipment and lawn furniture. Another geographic market is Eastern Europe, where, as we will see in Chapter 2, marketers need to adjust their promotional techniques to suit local needs and customs as there is little commonality across the region in terms of either disposable income, language, or tastes. No one would assume that all forty-year-olds share the same tastes. Why then should people share the same tastes because they happen to live together? It is nonsense. Only psychographic segmentation makes sense in this instance.

---

customer
The buyer of a product, often someone with whom a seller deals on a regular basis.

consumer
The user of a product.

One company can serve several or even all of these different categories of markets. Levi's, for example, markets in many different geographic regions. The company is a mass marketer in the sense that there is a youth market that differs little internationally and people of all ages wear its products, but it is also a niche marketer when it develops products for special markets, like tiny overalls for babies (socio-demographic segmentation) or special labels for special groups of people (psychographic segmentation).

Defining a target market can be crucial to a company's success. Even companies that don't market internationally find themselves caught up in global marketing because they face international competition at home. Thus your company may make sandals and market them only in your own region, but when your sales representative calls on the local shoe store owner, he or she will find that your product has to compete with sandals made in Mexico and the Far East, where labor costs are much lower.

In our view, marketing is *always* worldwide, first, because competition in most industries is now global, and second, because the basic principles of marketing are as applicable in Tanzania, Tasmania, Tbilisi, and Teotihuacán as they are in Toronto and Tuktoyaktuk. **Global marketing**, which is a theme of this textbook, means applying the fundamental concepts, tools, and practices of marketing on a worldwide basis and focusing an organization's resources and objectives on market opportunities worldwide. Throughout this book stories like the one that follows will emphasize our belief that although local conditions may require alterations in strategies and tactics, marketing principles are applicable in most all countries.

global marketing
Applying the fundamental concepts, tools, and practices of marketing on a worldwide basis and focusing an organization's resources and objectives on *both* international and domestic market opportunities.

RISKS AND GAMBLES
HONDA'S ROAD TO SUCCESS

At the end of World War II Japan was in a shambles and Soichiro Honda was destitute. His growing manufacturing business, which had made everything from piston rings to aircraft propellers, was wiped out. But his talent, confidence, and capacity for hard work were intact.

From the wartime rubble the self-taught forty-year-old engineer and mechanical tinkerer salvaged a few hundred small motors and adapted them to bicycles that he sold to buyers desperate for any kind of transportation. By 1948, with a mere $3,300 in capital, he was able to incorporate the Honda Motor Company, Ltd., and twelve years later Honda was the largest maker of motorcycles in the world.

In the 1960s, when consumers were becoming a little more affluent, Honda entered the automobile business. Its first few models were hardly memorable, but Honda persevered, and by the early 1970s, it had established itself as an important international auto maker. By the early 1990s, Honda ranked tenth among the world's auto manufacturers, and for three years—1989–1991—its Accord was the top selling car in Canada. Since then the Accord has been second only to Ford Taurus.

Clearly, Honda's original strategies were dictated by circumstance, but those early decisions set a pattern that the company has followed ever since: Find out what people want and offer them a simple, affordable, reliable product that satisfies that want. Honda did just that, first at home and then abroad.

THE PRODUCT

product
Any good, service, or idea that can be offered to a market and that satisfies consumer wants or needs.

goods
Tangible products that are grown, produced, or manufactured.

shopping goods
Relatively high-value branded products.

durable goods
Major high-priced purchases that last for three years or more.

consumables
Products purchased frequently and used up in a relatively short period of time.

service
Time and expertise provided or activities performed on the customer's behalf by an individual or firm.

The **product** sold in a marketing exchange is any tangible good, service, place, personality or idea that satisfies customers' needs or wants. All are found in both consumer and industrial markets—for example, both individuals and firms purchase computers, health services, and ideas such as support for charitable organizations—but products are marketed differently to consumers and industries. In marketing its computers to business customers, a company will stress time-saving and efficiency features, while in marketing to individuals it will emphasize convenience and personal applications.

Tangible products that are produced, grown, or manufactured are known as **goods**. The three major types of goods are durable goods, shopping goods, and consumables. **Shopping goods** are most commonly relatively high-value branded products. Since they are branded, direct comparisons can be made across retail outlets. In this category, the consumer is quite specific about what they are looking for, and this may be an Olympus camera or a Compaq computer. Since the product remains the same regardless of outlets where it is sold, only price will vary. The consumer will not readily accept substitutions in this category. **Durable goods** are high-ticket items such as major appliances, automobiles, and furniture—things that are generally expected to last three years or longer. Major appliances such as refrigerators, washers and dryers, and freezers are often termed "white goods" by retailers. **Consumables**, or nondurable goods, are used up fairly quickly and thus purchased frequently. Foods (cereal, fresh produce, soft drinks), packaged goods (shampoo, toothpaste, soap), and "soft goods" (apparel, textiles, linens) are consumables. These items are bought routinely and have their own possible substitutions in the mind of the consumer.

The second major type of product is **service**: the time, expertise, or activities of an individual or firm that does something for customers. Service is an increasingly important element in any product sale and is sometimes difficult to disentangle from the product itself. Banks and restaurants sell services; so do doctors, lawyers, accountants, hair stylists, and realtors. Canadian Airlines, which offers transportation, is also in the service category.

Marketers can promote *ideas*—philosophies, concepts, and points of view—just as well as goods and services. Insurance companies, for example, promote the idea that you should protect yourself against possible accidents and disasters, and political parties promote their political philosophies and the candidates who espouse them. Companies often market their corporate image—the idea for which the company stands. Businesses sometimes advocate positions on social issues. The Body Shop, for example, promotes the ideas of environmental and social responsibility. Canadian Airlines is a good example of bilingualism being put to work effectively in developing a corporate image. The logo for Canadian has an arrowhead where in English there would be an "a" and in French would be an "e." Having neither is a neutral position that will offend no one. Air Canada is able to surmount this problem totally as its name is the same in both French and English. The public is aware,

Promoting Ideas

Like many other major companies in the last several years, Shell Canada is adopting environmental goals, including its new program on sustainable development. Pictured is Shell Canada's Calgary Research Centre.

though, that Air Canada is based in Montreal and Canadian in Calgary so the issue of language and of predominant culture, if any, is a live one. Finally, organizations like the Canadian Heart and Stroke Foundation promote the idea that funding medical research can help find cures for life-threatening illnesses.

THE QUEST FOR PROFITS

The notion of profit is integral to the marketing function. Before a firm introduces a new product or offers a rebate on an existing one, marketing managers evaluate the impact of the projected change on costs, potential sales, and, most important, profits. This book is about how companies use marketing to help make a **profit**, which is the excess of revenues over costs. Indeed, it is the lack of profits that has driven airline companies to rethink their entire marketing programs. Note that profit may sometimes be measured in terms other than dollars: for nonprofit organizations, profit may mean more volunteers or more donations or changed public attitudes or behavioral change aimed at healthier lifestyles.

profit
The return that a company receives on a transaction after costs have been subtracted.

A young attorney learned the importance of profit one day when he was interviewed for a position with Maytag. The chairman of Maytag asked him if he knew what the company made. Having done an exceptional job of researching the firm, the lawyer promptly listed the major items in Maytag's product line, and even named a new product that was still in development. The chairman was impressed by the candidate's knowledge—particularly of the secret new product—but sternly corrected him: "No, young man, what we make here is a *profit*."

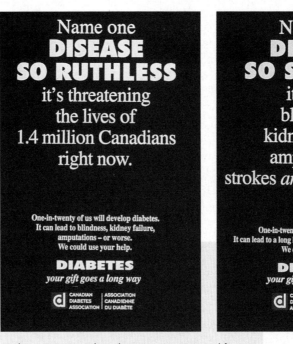
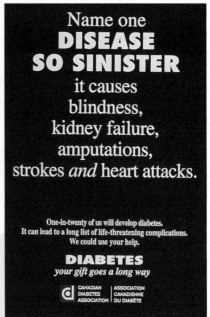

Nonprofit Marketing

Nonprofit organizations, like the Canadian Diabetes Association, face many of the same marketing problems as for-profit organizations. Effective and sincere advertisements, such as these two, are essential for a nonprofit organizations's success.

DYNAMICS OF THE MARKETPLACE

In highly competitive markets many companies struggle just to break even. A marketer needs to keep in mind the ways in which buyers and sellers interact economically in the marketplace, which is the third objective for this chapter. These transactions are ruled largely by economic concepts, like supply and demand and economies of scale, that will be familiar to those of you who have studied economics. Basic assumptions from economics form the very cornerstones of marketing. Marketing takes a different direction from economics in that it is not a science—it's about people who are our customers, suppliers, workforce and shareholders. Marketing provides the methods to evaluate the impact of different tastes, incomes, competition, and product differences in order to maximize customer value.

SUPPLY AND DEMAND

demand
The amount of a product consumers are willing to purchase at a particular price.

supply
The amount of a product producers are willing to provide at a particular price.

The market system depends on supply and demand. **Demand** is the amount of a product buyers are willing to purchase at a particular price. Considered alone, demand is like one hand clapping. The parallel economic concept is **supply**—the amount of a product producers are willing to offer for sale at a particular price.

Does demand or supply come first? Sometimes people demand or express a need for things they have never seen—like a cure for cancer. Often, however, a firm identifies a customer need or want that may or may not be recognized by consumers, designs a product to fill it, and then informs the consumer about it. Liquid soap and toothpaste in a pump were developed in this way. In these cases, the supply preceded the perceived need.

12

Needs and Wants The law of supply and demand rests on human needs and wants. A **need** is a real lack of something we consider necessary for living. This may be a physical item, such as clothing, food, or shelter, or an intangible, psychological quality, such as self-confidence. In contrast, **wants** are the ways society—and our individual tastes—lead us to fulfill our needs. To illustrate the difference, your thirst is a *need* that you may *want* to quench with mineral water, soda pop, or water.

American Standard's experience in the plumbing fixture business makes clear how important it is for marketers to distinguish between needs and wants. North Americans generally consider toilets a need, and for many years were satisfied with a simple high-quality white fixture. Until the early 1980s, American Standard lived up to its name—it was the number-one maker of plumbing fixtures in the continent. Since it was driven by engineers rather than marketers, however, the company failed to note an emerging consumer trend, the view of the bathroom as a decorator "living center." Marketing-driven competitor Kohler leapfrogged American Standard by offering high-quality plumbing fixtures in a selection of colors and styles that met consumers' fashion wants.

Consumer Demand Human needs and wants create demand. When a significantly large group of people focuses on a particularly compelling need or want, the result is *consumer demand* (assuming consumers' willingness and ability to pay).

Consumer demand may be either primary or selective. *Primary* demand is for a generic product, like rubber automobile tires. *Selective* demand is for a particular brand of product, such as consumers' choice of colorful Kohler bathroom fixtures over American Standard's plain white fixtures.

THE VALUE EQUATION

We've already said that marketing activities are designed to create value for customers. That creation of value, in turn, creates demand. Value marketing

need
A real lack of something that people consider necessary and desirable.

want
The manner in which individuals seek to satisfy a need; influenced by individual tastes and societal factors.

Nobody Buffets Buffett
Jimmy Buffett may not have been the top student in his marketing class, but what he studied must have sunk in. The owner of three major companies in wholly unrelated fields, Buffett is one of the 1990s' most successful marketers.

can be achieved in a number of ways: offer products that perform, give more than the customer expects, give guarantees, avoid unrealistic pricing, give the customer the facts, and build relationships.

The worth of any product to the buyer—its value—may be expressed in terms of money, participation, or affiliation (such as paying dues or volunteering time to an organization). For most goods and services, value is closely related to price. **Price** is the value put on a product by a seller or marketer; usually after conducting market research to test what customers will pay. While we use the word *price* in this equation, remember that for products like services and ideas, the "price" may be time spent, participation, personal sacrifice, or some other indication of what something is worth to you. Value in this sense is always a relationship between benefits received or anticipated from a product and the price paid for it. The **value equation** expresses this relationship:

$$value = \frac{benefits}{cost}$$

When you buy a product, you choose the brand that you think will give you the greatest benefit for the price you pay. Quality is assessed by customer perceptions. Colgate offers you a toothpaste that prevents cavities; the Red Cross and the Salvation Army offer you a feeling of having helped others. The price of the toothpaste is $1.89 plus a trip to the store. If the toothpaste is not perceived to be worth $1.89 and the effort it takes to buy it, then it is not a good value. The cost of the good feeling you get from the Red Cross or Salvation Army is a pint of your blood or time spent in doing volunteer work or donating used goods.

Price, of course, is only one part of the value equation. A firm can increase a consumer's valuation of a product not only by decreasing its price but also by bundling benefits in a package. Against Japanese automotive quality, American auto manufacturers seek to offer greater value. They bundle benefits such as ABS braking or air conditioning into a final price. Bundling makes it harder to unscramble different component parts of a final price and make comparisons. It also increases value to the manufacturer.

You cannot succeed only by slicing prices; delivering value profitably is an art. McDonald's survived the economic downturn of the early 1990s and watched its profits climb to record levels by linking lower prices with "Extra Value Meals," combination meals designed to coax adult customers and kids to spend a little more each visit.

These marketing efforts focus on adding value to the basic product, which is this chapter's fifth objective. Four factors generate **added value**: features, quality, exclusiveness, and image. *Features* are the details of the product offering, such as McDonald's "Extra Value Meals" and the benefits they offer to a consumer. With an increasingly competitive market for credit cards, the service component is emphasized in terms of creating a differential advantage. Thus, more flexibility, more acceptability world-wide, and special features unique to your card issuer, such as free air miles or rental car insurance or health insurance or goods breakage insurance, may be included. Even a low price guarantee is now being offered by Scotiabank so if you find the same product for less, you can claim a refund from Scotiabank. These competitive moves have driven credit card companies far from where they were when credit cards were first introduced. The basic core service of charging goods to a credit card is still there, but the range of additional services offered has proliferated. *Quality* means excellence, durability, or reliability. *Exclusiveness* means that a product is available to only a select few. A product's *image*, or the way it is perceived by consumers, may also be a concrete benefit (a larger size meal) or it can be something intan-

---

price
The statement of value put on goods or services by a seller.

value equation
An expression of value as the relationship between benefits and costs of a product to the consumer.

added value
Marketing's contribution to the value of a product, which may take the form of special features, extra quality, durability, or reliability.

gible (the macho image of the late Marlboro cigarette smoker). A pair of jeans is just a pair of jeans, but a pair of Guess? or Levi's is something special. That something special is the added value created by marketing.

Every decision in this marketing process creates value for the customer. The cumulative effect of this process is to increase the value of a product in its customer market but not necessarily its price.

The concept of *boundaryless marketing* is another current interpretation (see Figure 1-1) which eliminates demarcations between the marketing function and the other functional areas in a business, such as production and operations. This concept makes everyone in the organization responsible for marketing—from the receptionist who answers the telephone to the engineer who designs the product to the people in manufacturing who make it and those who work in after-sales services, such as repairs. All of these people, as well as those officially involved in "marketing," are important in marketing.

ECONOMIES OF SCALE

One of marketing's most important goals is to increase demand for products. Strong consumer demand for a product encourages firms to produce more of it. Increased production affects the value equation by altering price levels: production costs drop as more products are produced, so the price can also drop because the cost per unit decreases as initial start-up costs are spread across more units.

This effect, known as **economies of scale**, enables firms to reduce prices, while it increases profits and funds more new-product development and marketing activities—all of which further spurs consumption. Thus increased demand generates a circular process that leads to further increases in demand. Manipulating consumer demand, however, is just one way to effect economies of scale. Other methods include moving from mass production (stressing quantity) to customized and lean manufacturing (stressing quality and efficiency).

economies of scale
The principle that as the size of a production run grows, per-unit production costs decrease because of gains in efficiency.

Figure 1-1
The Value Chain and Boundaryless Marketing.

Marketing is more than just one link in the chain that builds customer value

because it affects every other link in the process.

© 1993 Warren Keegan Associates, Inc. Reprinted by permission.

15

Companies seek economies of scale because even small savings can give them an advantage over their rivals. Each time a company doubles its production, it can expect to achieve cost savings of around one third. Large companies, therefore, have different cost structures from small ones. Competitors are springing up all over the world today, making nearly every market a global one. Although 2 percent of the market in one country may not justify a company's production costs, over several countries it may be more than adequate.

How economies of scale affect prices is easiest to see with new products. Pocket calculators, VCRs, and personal computers are among the many products that were introduced to the market at a high price, which steadily dropped as sales increased and production efficiencies were achieved. Consider the cellular phone. In 1987 a standard car phone cost about $1,000, including installation, and a portable (battery-powered) phone cost twice as much. By 1990, the price of a standard car phone was down to under $299, and by early 1994 a cellular phone could be had for less than a hundred dollars (see Figure 1-2). The price is expected to fall even further with increased competition from Japanese, South Korean, and Finnish suppliers.

Why did the price fall so dramatically? Production costs generally represent 40 to 60 percent of a cellular phone's wholesale price. Because of the experience curve effect, these costs decline by up to 30 percent each time production volume doubles.

As many marketers in competitive markets become more and more specialized to reach more tightly defined *niche markets*, they are manipulating the supply-demand model. Specialization means fewer customers, but more refined products means increased demand within that smaller group. In today's world, companies following such a strategy need to sell in all available markets to earn a realistic payback. Global marketing is the method modest-sized companies use in niche markets to achieve economies of scale.

For example, Instron is a small American company that makes testing equipment. It spent two years and $1 million developing a ceramics testing machine for a Japanese client. Since ceramics is a specialized industry, the company was only able to recoup its development costs and earn a profit by selling six other machines in Japan, six each in the United States and continental Europe, three in the United Kingdom, and one each in Taiwan and China. That is not a large volume of sales, but the price on each machine was high enough to offset the initial costs and make a profit for Instron. The U.S. market alone was too small to allow Instron to spread the machine's develop-

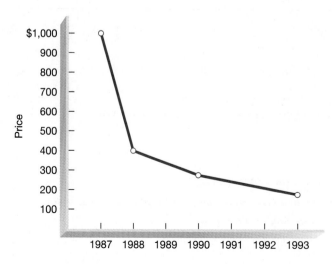

Figure 1-2
Cellular Phone Prices.

The cost of a cellular phone dropped 60 percent within the first year shown, and five years later these phones cost less than 20 percent of their original price. What accounts for such a rapid and steep price drop?

ment costs across enough units to achieve economies of scale; global marketing made that possible.[3]

EVOLUTION OF THE MARKETING PHILOSOPHY ●

Marketing is constantly evolving. That's the sign of a healthy and dynamic, but relatively new, field. It's hard to say exactly when marketing began, but it certainly began to take root with the Industrial Revolution which simultaneously created manufacturing efficiencies and surplus products. As marketing has evolved, so have different philosophies which are the subject of chapter objective number six.

Some historians of marketing trace a progression from the production-centered to the sales-oriented to the marketing-driven approach to marketing. The *production-centered* approach focuses on the invention and manufacture of products and is engineering-based. It grew out of the Industrial Revolution, which created a plethora of new products simultaneously for the first time in history, and it is still used by manufacturers concerned with engineering efficiencies and new-product development rather than customer desires. The *sales-oriented* approach arose when mass communication and mass distribution made it possible to offer a variety of new products to new markets. Personal selling was needed for products like encyclopedias and specialty brushes in order to convince consumers of their value and intensify demand. Firms like Avon, Amway, and Tupperware still use this approach. With alternatives available, customers, it was thought, could not be expected to buy of their own accord and so forceful personal selling techniques were devised and implemented to push people on an individual basis to purchase. This approach assumes that there is a plentiful supply of potential customers. Chances of repeat business are much slimmer because of the sales technique and because of the product being sold. Few will buy funeral insurance or encyclopedias twice but more importantly, will they even recommend them to others?

The *marketing-driven* approach arose after World War II, when it became possible to create more products than the market demanded and when consumer spending power suddenly increased substantially. The highly competitive nature of many markets led companies to identify people's needs and wants and then to fulfill them profitably. The hallmark of the marketing-driven philosophy is customer orientation. Products are developed to fill both *unmet* and *unrecognized* needs. The more thoroughly a company incorporates this concept into its philosophy, the more important the marketing function and customer satisfaction become.

Many firms are constantly changing their marketing strategies to keep pace with the evolving philosophies of marketing. For example, Choice Hotels, Canada's largest hotel chain, is changing its marketing strategy to meet consumer wants and needs. Apart from developing a brand identity for each hotel, building a loyal customer database for the chain underpins the changes in marketing strategy.

THE MARKETING CONCEPT

A consumer-oriented philosophy of business that stresses meeting consumer wants and needs is called the **marketing concept.** A good illustration of how this approach to marketing works is Honda's rise to prominence in the North American automobile market. Honda started by satisfying North American drivers' desire for fuel-efficient cars with the economical Civic in 1973. Then, when

marketing concept
The philosophy that marketing activities should focus on consumer needs and wants.

consumers' preferences changed to roominess, comfort, and performance, Honda brought out the Accord, which became one of the best-selling cars in Canada and the United States in the early 1990s. When consumers began to look for luxury in their cars, Honda introduced the Acura. Note that every change in Honda's product line was prompted by a changing consumer need.

A company can't develop a product that satisfies consumer needs simply by asking consumers what they want, as Bennett and Cooper warned in their article "The Misuse of Marketing."[4] Most of us can't articulate a need for something we have never thought of before. Meeting consumer needs requires sophisticated programs of research that provide insight into consumer problems and strong research and development programs (R&D) that spark true innovation.

The U.S. mail order company, Lands End Inc., of Dodgeville, Wisconsin, has radically altered its marketing approach—particularly in dealing with customers in Canada. In an attempt to keep Canadian customers satisfied, Lands End has set up a special unit to process Canadian orders fast and without surprises. After calculating duty at a flat rate and GST applicable to each order, "we then clear your order through Canada Customs and deliver it right to your door. No extra fees, no hassles," says Stephen Miles of Lands End.[5]

Marketing philosophy has changed over the years. Figure 1-3 compares the old "telling and selling" approach with the contemporary idea of focusing on the "marketing mix" and with the contemporary philosophy of "relationship marketing." In the early days of marketing, marketers focused exclusively on selling. That approach was succeeded by the idea of managing the *marketing mix*—all the elements outlined in the AMA definition that we introduced at the beginning of the chapter. In contemporary marketing, this now-traditional marketing-mix approach has evolved to the point where customers and marketers are partners, and the end result of marketing is a relationship that promotes long-term growth for the company and maximum satisfaction for the customer. This is called **relationship marketing.** Satisfying customers requires staying in touch with people's changing needs and ensuring the company's ability to fill those needs with new product lines and marketing strategies.

In cutting-edge marketing the marketing concept has been extended to integrate concern for customer satisfaction into *every* corporate function.

18
CHAPTER 1

relationship marketing
An approach to marketing in which a company endeavors to build continuing relationships with its customers that promote both the company's long-term growth and the customer's maximum satisfaction.

**Figure 1-3
Marketing Is
Everything.**
© Warren Keegan
Associates, Inc.
Reprinted by permission.

That is why you will find discussions of relationship building in many chapters of this book. In the next chapter, for example, we will explore how the concepts of quality, or excellence in products and the ways in which they are produced, and relationship building are interrelated. In Chapter 7 we will see that the demands of business-to-business buying and selling make the establishment of ongoing relationships between suppliers and purchasers exceedingly important. In Chapter 10 we will look at the special nature of the relationship between customers and the brand-name products to which they are often intensely loyal.

THE MARKETING MIX

Marketing-driven companies control and integrate a variety of complex business activities commonly referred to as the marketing mix, which is chapter objective number seven. In the traditional approach to marketing, the **marketing mix** is the set of tools and techniques—the product, its pricing and distribution, and its marketing communication—used by an organization to market its products at a profit.[6] (These elements of the marketing mix are sometimes called the **four P's:** product, pricing, place, and promotion.) Within these broad areas fall such specific marketing activities as product development and management, branding, packaging, pricing, physical distribution, personal selling, retailing, public relations, advertising, and sales promotion (see Figure 1-4). We will discuss all of these activities in subsequent chapters.

The "mix" part of the concept means that these separate elements must come together and be strategically coordinated. Designing the mix for a given target market involves creating the right combination of product features, pricing levels, distribution systems, and marketing communication to make the product more attractive to its market than competing products.

The research, planning, and strategic thinking that go into handling this activity is called *managing the marketing mix*. Effective marketing executives juggle the different aspects of the mix to maximize profitable sales. As you will see, the optimal marketing mix differs for each company and product; it depends on such factors as the firm's mission, management knowledge of the marketplace, sales and marketing objectives, and level of existing competition.

marketing mix
The tools and techniques for implementing the marketing of a product, sometimes referred to as the *four P's*.

four P's
The four major types of activities included in the marketing mix: activities revolving around the product's development; pricing; placement, or distribution; and promotion, or marketing communication.

Figure 1-4
The Marketing Mix

The four P's of the marketing mix subsume a number of important functions. Does it surprise you that promotion, or marketing communication, has a greater number of contributory functions than the other P's? Why or why not?

THE MARKETING PLAN

marketing plan
A document that summarizes a coordinated and focused program for managing the marketing mix in order to meet consumer needs at a profit for the company.

The **marketing plan** is a document that presents a coordinated and focused program in which all areas of the marketing mix work together to profitably meet consumer needs. You will see an outline of a marketing plan in Chapter 4, where we discuss these plans in greater detail. For the moment, the following excerpts from IBM's original personal computer marketing plan will give you an idea of how such plans work:

Strategy: Target managers and professionals, not hobbyists or technical specialists.

Product: Employ standard technology that's fairly easy to learn and use.

Price: Set prices at a reasonable level—not high enough to provide an umbrella for competitors but high enough to yield healthy profits.

Communication: Promote the product through personal sales by IBM's sales force to large customers and through heavy advertising stressing friendliness and broad applicability of the product.

Distribution: Distribute to major customers through the sales force and to individuals through independent full-service dealers.[7]

MARKETING ON A GLOBAL BASIS

As we have already pointed out, nearly every market is global today, and it is for this reason that we have integrated global issues and practices throughout the entire book. *Global marketing* is a fundamental concept in contemporary marketing, as chapter objective number eight makes clear. Two decades ago marketers spoke of *international* or *multinational* marketing, terms that reflected the patchwork approach to marketing outside the home country that was common then. Today an understanding of global marketing is essential for almost everyone in business—certainly for anyone in an industry that is already global, like automobiles, and in industries with the potential for globalization, like compact discs and bicycles.

It is not just large companies that are global. Instron Corporation, which was described earlier as a small company that makes testing instruments, is a global marketer despite its modest size. About 60 percent of its sales come from abroad and the company operates thirty-five offices in seventeen countries. Collectively, its employees speak forty-four languages.

How do companies market on a global basis? Are the principles which govern marketing in Nepal and Borneo the same as those that rule marketing in Canada? This question has been debated for almost thirty years and, as you will see in the next section, continues to provoke argument.

OPEN TO DEBATE

IS THE WORLD BECOMING HOMOGENIZED?

The issue of whether global markets are similar or different has sparked heated debate. On one side stands Theodore Levitt, who generated a storm of controversy in 1983 when he wrote in the *Harvard Business Review* that companies must learn to operate as though the world is one large

A Global Brand
Levi Strauss and Company may be the only truly global U.S.-based apparel maker—about 40 percent of its total revenues come from markets outside the United States. Although it gives its outside the United States manager leeway to respond to local market changes, Levi's protects its all-important brand identity and quality image by maintaining foreign operations as subsidiary companies.

market.[8] His contention is that consumer differences around the world are diminishing and companies should ignore superficial regional and national differences in favor of selling the same things in the same way everywhere.

Levitt argued that consumers around the world are motivated by the same desires for modernity, quality, and value. Furthermore, technology and standardized production have now made universal marketing programs feasible. To demonstrate his thesis, Levitt points to McDonald's on the Champs-Élysees in Paris and the Ginza in Tokyo, Coca Cola in Bahrain, Pepsi Cola in Moscow, and Revlon cosmetics, Sony televisions, and Levi's jeans everywhere.

The British journal *Marketing* weighed in on the other side of the debate in 1988: "Not even the mass-marketing Japanese demand complete subjugation to a single, world master plan." Polaroid's director of European marketing claims that "Successful cases of global marketing are very few and far between."[9]

Levitt recently modified his position, claiming that in 1983 he was being "deliberately provocative to awaken marketers to the possibilities offered by the similarities between markets." Others, however, have picked up Levitt's original banner. The Global Media Commission of the International Advertising Association calls global marketing a breakthrough marketing tool: "No longer will there be a different advertising campaign for each country and each language of the world. Increasingly, products and their marketing support systems will be truly global."

In fact, British Airways, a leading airline now linked with US Air, has standardized global advertising campaigns on the theory that the concerns of international business travelers are much the same, whatever their nationality. Do you agree? Do you think the same similarity holds in other product markets or do you think that in all markets basic similarities are likely to be matched by local differences?

BALANCING THE PERSPECTIVE

There is much evidence that real differences in customs and practices around the globe affect such basic things as product development. For example, one reason American car manufacturers have had such a hard time breaking into the Japanese market is that until recently they refused to offer cars with right-hand steering! Cultural and religious taboos also affect marketing decisions: few marketers would try to sell bikinis in Muslim countries or products made of cowhide in India.

Global marketing requires marketers to understand a variety of business and market environments and to conduct marketing activities in many different countries at the same time. Markets can differ dramatically from country to country in terms of language, currency convertibility, cultural attitudes, government regulations, and national customs. The marketer's task is further complicated by the fact that, as we saw in our discussion of airlines, international events outside a business's control can have a tremendous impact on it. CEO Gerry Pencer of Cott Corp, in Toronto, is taking retail branded pop into the global market. By spreading into the United States, Japan, Australia, the United Kingdom, South Africa and Spain, Pencer vows that Colt will be a $2 billion company by the year 2000.[10]

While the principles of marketing are universal, local differences will affect how they are applied. We also believe that global marketing is affected by certain social and environmental issues, some of which we discuss in the next section.

SOCIALLY RESPONSIBLE MARKETING ●

Companies are increasingly facing the need to develop corporate policies on pressing social and environmental issues, which is the point of chapter objective number nine. Business today is seen as part of the larger society, contributing to its problems, but also responsible for devising solutions to those problems. This idea, called *societal marketing,* is another step in the evolution of the marketing concept.

Many companies have adopted a societal marketing philosophy, an approach that holds that firms should compete in ways that maintain or improve the well-being of consumers and society. Even as they make a profit, companies must also be good citizens. Coquitlam, B.C.-based Kavanaugh Foods Ltd., for example, has developed a cereal package made from 100% recycled paper fibers and is printed in water-soluble ink. Ben and Jerry's Homemade, Inc., whose Vermont plant is hydro-powered and whose vans are solar-powered, maintains voter registration facilities in all its Vermont ice cream parlors. People who register get a free scoop. The company's suppliers include a bakery that employs the homeless and a group of black southern farmers who grow the peaches used in its Georgia Peach ice cream.

SOCIETY AND THE INDIVIDUAL

Concerned about the slipping quality of public education, many Canadian and U.S. businesses have donated time, products, and money to schools. Businesses now spend an estimated $1 billion a year on a vast array of school-related programs, including some 50,000 business-education partnerships. First Calgary Savings and Credit Union, for example, has established nine partnerships with local elementary schools.

Much of the pressure for socially responsible actions by businesses has come from their customers. The consumer movement, or **consumerism**,

consumerism
A movement seeking to protect consumers against dangerous products and unethical or deceptive business practices.

began in the 1960s as a protest against the marketing of dangerous products, unethical pricing practices, and deceptive advertising. Chief among the early leaders of the movement was Ralph Nader, whose best-selling *Unsafe at Any Speed* condemned General Motors' Corvair. Today Nader leads an influential citizen group that lobbies government legislators and regulators about unsafe and unethical business practices.

Consumerism has increased in recent years, particularly with respect to certain issues. The Center for Science in the Public Interest (CSPI), for example, has been in the forefront of both the antismoking campaign and the effort to curtail marketers' unsupported health claims for food products. Special-interest groups have become more action-oriented, boycotting the products of firms that violate ethical principles. The Council on Economic Priorities has sold 200,000 copies of a guide to "ethical shopping" that ranks the 170 manufacturers of 1,300 supermarket brands according to these companies' performance in areas such as donations to charity, advancement of women and minorities, protection of the environment, and policies on animal experimentation. Green-peace has effectively mounted an international campaign to boycott the paper products of McMillan-Bloedel who are logging in the highly contentious area of Clayoquot Sound on Vancouver Island, B.C., an area which had until recently, remained untouched for thousands of years.

THE ENVIRONMENT

Marketers have often been criticized for their products' effects on the environment. The design of some products, like automobiles, clearly contributes to air pollution. Manufacturers of plastic products and certain packaging materials that have an adverse affect on the environment have also been targeted by environmental groups. Aseptic juice boxes, disposable diapers, microwaveable foods, blister packaging, and solvent-based paints and wood treatments are all under fire.

According to a recent *Fortune* article, 75 percent of Americans say that a company's environmental reputation affects their buying decisions. *Business Week* reports that three-quarters of Americans believe that business needs to clean up its environmental act, but only 36 percent think it is doing so. And a study by an industrial design firm found that 75 percent of consumers surveyed were inclined to buy goods they perceived as environmentally sound—that is, made of recycled, recyclable, or biodegradable material. As the corporate environmental affairs director for Coca-Cola says, this is more than an "environmental movement." It is a pervasive change in attitudes: "our core values have changed."[11]

Firms are beginning to respond to these concerns. For example, Wal-Mart has announced its intention to curb its energy use to prevent pollution and has urged its suppliers to be good environmentalists. In 1992, a consortium of more than twenty major firms, including McDonald's, Coca-Cola, Sears, 3M, Dupont, UPS, and Safeway, launched a national campaign to encourage the companies they do business with to buy and use recycled materials and products (see also Exhibit 1-3). The National Packaging Protocol, endorsed by the Canadian Council of Ministers of the Environment in March 1990, aims to reduce packaging waste by 35 percent by 1996 and 50 percent by 2000. Under the proposed Canadian Industry Packaging Stewardship Initiative (CIPSI), the packaging industry will be accountable for the disposal and collection of its own products, paying varying levies according to the recyclability of its packaging to fund the development of secondary markets.[12]

Europeans are generally ahead of North Americans on environmental issues. For years the citizens of many European countries have been expressing their environmental concerns in the voting booth, and the Green Movement is a major international political force that brings environmental issues to the floor of many parliaments.

In recent years an important corporate strategy for many companies in Canada and the United States has become the development of such things as environmentally safer products, biodegradable packaging, and hazardous waste controls. Unfortunately, the occasional misuse of environmental claims as a sales gimmick has come to be resented. In the late 1980s many companies rushed to advertise "environmental benefits" of their products that were sometimes so remote as to be nonexistent, which has made consumers skeptical.

Promotional strategies that position a firm as enviromentally correct on one issue but ignore overall social responsibility can backfire. It doesn't help a cosmetics manufacturer to trumpet that its products are not tested on laboratory animals if an environmental group shows that its products are overpackaged. It is better to underclaim and overperform on environmental issues than to overclaim and be publically embarrassed.

MARKETING ETHICS

Ethics are closely related to social responsibility. In a field like marketing, *ethics* articulates the moral principles or values and the standards of conduct by which the profession is judged. Marketing is now seen to be in the front line of ethical behavior in business.[13]

Some companies have taken strong proactive measures. Phillips-Van Heusen, for instance has threatened to terminate orders from its apparel suppliers if they violate the company's ethical, environmental, and human rights code. Dow Chemical seeks assurances from its suppliers that they conform not just to local pollution and safety laws, but to the often tougher national standards as well.[14]

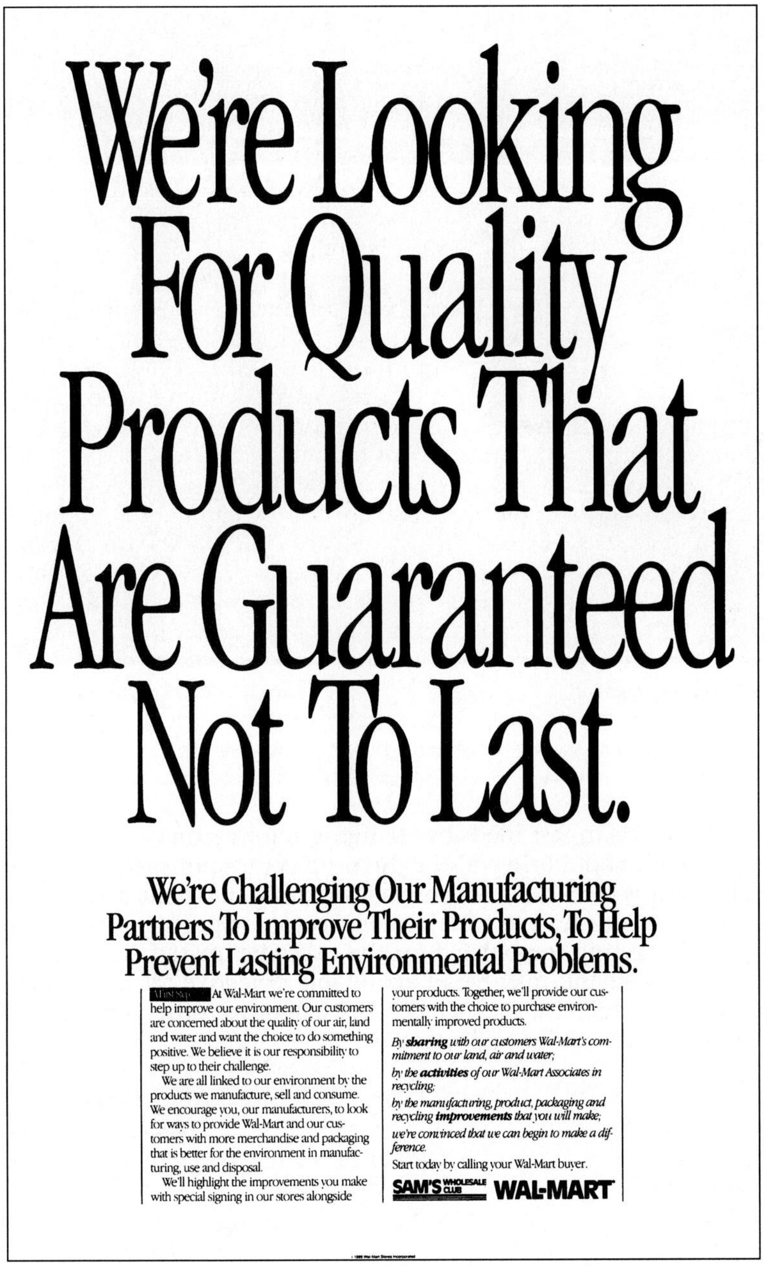

Exhibit 1-3
Support for Recycling

Wal-Mart has challenged the companies that manufacture the products sold in its stores to develop new ways to use recycled materials.

How should cigarettes and liquor be marketed? Cigarette manufacturers are being charged with artificially adding nicotine to low tar cigarette brands to enhance the addictive quality of the brand. This is an allegation based on conjecture. There are reportedly 500 compounds which can be used as cigarette additives, but it is not known which are being used in Canada and whether nicotine would be regarded as an additive even if added artificially since it is a natural derivative of tobacco.

What responsibility do food companies have to reformulate products to make them healthier? Many burger chains have responded to concerns about

DIAPER RECYCLING PLANT

cholesterol and fat levels in fast foods by changing the way they cook french fries and make shakes. Should they also lighten up on sodium and preservatives? Should billboards be banned for contributing to visual pollution?

All of these questions lead to a major question some people in our society are asking: Is marketing responsible for the excessive materialism in our culture? Stimulating demand may be an acceptable objective for marketing, but is it an acceptable objective for society? As we approach the new millennium, these ethical issues will be important.

BOTTOM LINE REALITIES

PAMPERING THE ENVIRONMENT?

Suppose you are the marketing manager for Kimberly-Clark's Huggies. You're locked in a pitched battle with Procter and Gamble for the $500-million-a-year disposable diaper market that's now dominated by P&G's Pampers. Your task is to figure out a long-term strategy for Huggies that is both competitively sound and environmentally sensitive.

As you may know, "disposable" is a misnomer. Because they are made largely of plastic, these diapers don't decompose. Indeed, some scientists estimate that they will remain in our landfills for anywhere from 100 to 500 years. Until a few decades ago, Canadian babies sported cotton diapers, each good for 100–150 washes. But the introduction of single-use diapers in 1961 seemed to offer benefits all around: Babies got drier bottoms, parents got greater convenience, and marketers found a new source of repeat purchases. Today the single-use, throwaway diaper enjoys 85 percent of the Canadian diaper market, up from 35 percent in 1975, whereas the cotton diaper has only 15 percent. Since the same pattern is developing in other countries, the problem of nonbiodegradable diapers is now global.[15]

Enormous resources are invested in these diapers. In Canada alone, the manufacture of single-use diapers consumes 18,000 tonnes of plastic and more than a million trees every year. And some 1.7 billion disposable diapers are trucked to the nation's landfills each year. Disposable diapers account for about 2 percent of municipal garbage. Costs of disposing of single-use diapers are levied on all citizens, whether or not they have babies.

What is to be done? Lawmakers in a number of American states have banned or are considering banning the sale of nonbiodegradable diapers. Many consumers have responded by returning to diaper services. Once considered a luxury, these services are now often seen as a bargain. Parents who had been spending $15 a week on single-use diapers found that diaper services cost only $9 to $12 a week. In terms of the environment, however, it's not an easy trade-off, for the energy consumed to heat the water needed to wash cotton diapers 100 to 150 times is considerable. And energy, of course, causes pollution.

Meanwhile, disposable-diaper makers are trying to come up with a truly biodegradable, nonchemical product. Because the costs of developing such a product are high, they anticipate charging a high price for these diapers, at least initially. Will parents care enough to pay the extra money? Apparently not, if American Enviro Products' experience is significant. The company recently brought out Bunnies diapers, which it claims will decompose in three to five years, and to date, it has had little success in marketing this higher-priced product. Moreover, rival companies like P&G have questioned whether the product is all it claims to be.

In an effort to be socially responsible, Procter & Gamble is underwriting pilot recycling programs that collect used diapers and separate them into pulp and plastic. The pulp is disposed of like other paper waste, and the plastic portions of the diapers are recycled into such products as plastic flower pots, park benches, trash bags, and building insulation. Recycling, however, is only available where facilities exist.

Other manufacturers have taken a more aggressive, less socially responsible approach in responding to the environmental threat to their business. In the U.S. Kimberly-Clark, for example, spearheaded lobbying efforts to defeat both a California bill to require warning labels and a Wisconsin proposal to tax disposables.

As the Huggies marketing manager, would you agree with your associates that fighting it out in the legislature is the way to go? Or would you propose some other solution of this critical problem? Outline a "white paper" (that's a statement of a company's position on an issue) for Kimberly-Clark. Begin by identifying all the options you can think of. Then present the arguments for each possible choice and discuss both the short-term and long-term implications of each option for the company and its customers. Conclude with a paragraph giving your recommendations. ▼

KEY POINTS SUMMARY ▼

1. Marketing is both a function and a philosophy of business. It is a set of steps and procedures professionals use to create exchanges that satisfy both a customer's and an organization's needs. Marketing is also a point of view that focuses all of the organization's attention on meeting consumer needs.

2. An exchange between a buyer and a seller, or a marketer, takes place in a market, defined as a group of individuals or organizations who share a common need, want, or problem and are able and willing to pay for a product that satisfies it. Markets may be large or small, and they may or may not be geographic in nature, but they can all be divided into five types: consumer, industrial, government, institutional, and international markets.

3. Basic economic principles underlie all marketing practices: First, the law of supply and demand states that as prices go up, people buy less and supply increases, and that, conversely, as prices go down, people buy more and supply diminishes. Second, a need is something we lack that we consider necessary; a want is something we lack but may not need. Companies operating with a marketing philosophy try to provide products that meet either a consumer need or want. Third, production costs drop as more products are produced and, therefore, the price can also drop because the costs per unit have decreased.

4. The value of anything is expressed in terms of its price—the value put on it by the seller and agreed to by the buyer. Value expresses the relationship between what you get from a product, called the *benefit,* and what you are willing to pay for it, called the *cost.* That relationship can be depicted as an equation: value = benefit/cost.

5. Marketing's contribution to a product, above and beyond the product's features, is called *added value.* Marketing creates and adds value by building consumers' perception of quality, exclusiveness, and brand image. Economies of scale also contribute added value by achieving price reductions through more efficient production.

6. Marketing has evolved from a production-oriented to a sales-oriented to a marketing-driven approach. The last approach is generally referred to as the *marketing concept* —the corporate philosophy that sees as the key to a firm's success the satisfaction of customers' needs and wants and the solution of customers' problems in a way that is profitable to the company. In contemporary business the marketing concept has come to include the notion of relationship marketing—the building of satisfying long-term relationships between buyers and sellers.

7. Marketers can implement the marketing concept by manipulating the major components of the marketing mix: product, price, distribution, and marketing communication, Successful marketing means finding the right mix of these four components.

8. Basic marketing principles are universal, but markets around the world exhibit cultural and other differences that marketers must take into account when mapping their global marketing strategies.

9. Enlightened marketers respond not only to consumer demands for specific products but also to the growing pressure from both individuals and societal groups to change business practices and products that are destructive to society, culture, or the environment.

DISCUSSION QUESTIONS ▼

1. How does the concept of exchange relate to marketing? What important principles of marketing are derived from the concept of an exchange? Explain the complexities of the exchange in marketing socially responsible products like Ben and Jerry's ice cream.

2. Explain the difference between needs and wants in terms of current airline marketing programs and describe your response to such programs.

3. Differentiate between the law of supply and the law of demand and explain how it affects the pricing of disposable and washable diapers. If you were the marketing director for a disposable diaper product, how would you manipulate demand? What could you do to manipulate demand for washable diapers?

4. Explain how economies of scale affect the price of both disposable and washable diapers.

28

5. Explain the marketing concept. How does it differ from the other major marketing philosophies? How does the Honda story illustrate the differing philosophies of marketing?

6. You are developing a marketing plan for friends who own a bicycle store near campus. Prepare to explain the marketing mix to them and identify the key areas they need to focus on in their marketing.

7. Select a firm for which you or some member of your immediate family has worked. How would you describe the firm's marketing philosophy? Explain your answer.

8. You have been named marketing manager for a chemical company that will be reprocessing plastics for recycling. Develop a memo outlining the kinds of social responsibility issues that you and your staff need to consider.

9. You are an environmentally concerned parent. Weigh the disadvantages of disposable diapers (landfill capacity and biodegradability) against those of washable diapers (energy costs, air pollution, and water usage). How would you make a decision you could live with?

Integrative Case • Discussion Questions

The Body Shop*

1. How does The Body Shop operation exemplify the marketing concept? How does it reflect the societal marketing concept?

2. When The Body Shop first got started was it facing global competition? What helped the firm expand?

3. Is Anita Roddick right that consumers are over-marketed? That they are "hyped out"? If so, what can marketers do about this?

Harley-Davidson

1. Analyze the way Harley-Davidson has added value to its product over the years.

The Millennium Power System

1. How does the Millennium system of batteries and chargers reflect the societal marketing concept?

2. From the point of view of both consumers and retailers, describe the value added by the Millennium battery/charger system.

*The three cases at the back of the book—"The Body Shop," "Harley-Davidson," and "The Millennium Power System"—illustrate topics discussed in all chapters of this book. Your instructor will tell you when to read a particular case and answer the discussion questions on it that appear at the end of each chapter.

● Chapter 2

Marketing, Quality, and the Organization

OBJECTIVES

AFTER COMPLETING THIS CHAPTER, YOU SHOULD BE ABLE TO:

1
IDENTIFY COMMON BUSINESS FUNCTIONS AND EXPLAIN WHY MARKETING MOVES FROM A FUNCTION TO AN OVERRIDING PHILOSOPHY IN MARKETING-DRIVEN COMPANIES

2
DESCRIBE HOW FIRMS STRUCTURE THEIR WORK RESPONSIBILITIES AND WHERE MARKETING FITS IN VARIOUS TYPES OF FIRMS

3
ANALYZE THE ADVANTAGES AND DISADVANTAGES OF CENTRALIZATION AND DECENTRALIZATION

4
UNDERSTAND THE CRITICAL FUNCTION OF COORDINATION AND EXPLAIN MARKETING'S ROLE IN COORDINATING ITS ACTIVITIES WITH OTHER BUSINESS FUNCTIONS

5
EXPLAIN THE ROLE AND RESPONSIBILITIES OF THE BRAND OR PRODUCT MANAGER

6
DISCUSS ORGANIZATIONAL PROBLEMS THAT OCCUR IN GLOBAL MARKETING PROGRAMS

7
DESCRIBE THE INTERNAL CORPORATE FACTORS THAT DELINEATE THE MARKETING FUNCTION

8
DISTINGUISH BETWEEN CORPORATE MISSION AND CORPORATE CULTURE AND DESCRIBE HOW BOTH AFFECT MARKETING PROGRAMS

9
EXPLAIN HOW QUALITY PROGRAMS INTERACT WITH MARKETING PROGRAMS

THE MARKETING ORGANIZATION

IBM makes computers—all kinds of computers—and owns big plants with many employees. GM makes cars—all kinds of cars—and it, too, owns big plants with many employees. IBM has a huge staff of sales representatives to sell computers and another large group of maintenance representatives

to service the computers. Similarly, GM has a large network of dealers to sell cars and service shops to repair the cars, as well as a finance company to provide loans to GM customers who want to buy cars. Both IBM and GM have been leaders in the marketplace throughout most of the 20th century, even models of management. As we approach the new millennium, however, both companies are in deep trouble.

If present trends continue, the leading companies in the 21st century will be firms like Dell Computer and Nike. What's the difference between them and IBM and GM? For one thing, Dell and Nike are examples of a new breed of organization—the *marketing organization*. Dell doesn't manufacture computers, nor does it bother with computer stores. It sells hardware made by other companies; it sells directly to its customers and it has a large staff of well-informed sales reps who can answer customers' questions. Nike doesn't make athletic shoes. It designs state-of-the-art shoes, has them made by other companies, and promotes them with advertising that is legendary. Both companies are expert marketers who have leveraged a core of knowledge and competence into dominance in their respective markets.

Like Dell and Nike, Taco Bell doesn't make the food for which it's become famous—it distributes it. One reason Taco Bell has become so dominant in the fast-food market is because it sells a tremendous volume of food from a very small facility that's not much larger than a counter. Taco Bell restaurants can be small because every job that is time- and space-intensive, like chopping lettuce and frying hamburgers, is jobbed out to suppliers; the only food related activity actually done at the restaurant is assembling the different products. Taco Bell focuses its efforts on promoting the product and then on managing the exchange at the counter.

Famous Amos cookies is yet another example of a marketing organization. This U.S. based company that sells cookies internationally *employs only sixteen people*. All the Famous Amos people do is manage the marketing; manufacturing, distribution, and sales are all outsourced. What Famous Amos has is a recipe and a small group of savvy people who understand that marketing is everything.

What's happening here? IBM, one of the most respected companies in the world with a rich heritage in creating advanced business machines, lost $16 billion between 1991 and 1993. Dell, an upstart company run by a brash twenty-seven-year-old, didn't even exist a decade ago, and today it is doubling its revenues annually. As part of its turnaround effort, IBM is changing its corporate style. It has lightened up on the white shirt/blue suit requirement and turned its sober corporate magazine *Think* into a tabloid that even uses occasional humor. Will IBM be the same company if it changes its corporate style? Would Dell's direct marketing approach better serve your needs than IBM's more traditional approach? ■

In this chapter we discuss two aspects of marketing and the organization. First, we talk about the marketing function and where it fits into the organization; then we review the internal factors within a corporation that impact the marketing program and become important internal variables to consider in developing a marketing plan. The focus of both discussions is on how internal strengths and weaknesses are analyzed, which is the foundation on which a marketing plan is built.

CORPORATE STRUCTURE

How marketing functions in a company depends on the way the company structures its business. Furthermore, how marketing operates within that structure can be considered a corporate strength or a weakness. For example, IBM departmentalizes its marketing activities, and employees involved in marketing operations may or may not be involved with other business planning efforts. Lack of coordination and inability to achieve a marketing-oriented philosophy may be important factors in IBM's current troubles.

In contrast, marketing-focused companies like Nike and Dell analyze every corporate activity both for its impact on marketing and for what marketing thinking can add to sharpen that business function. In order to better understand how marketing can be organized, let's first look at how companies are structured.

BUSINESS FUNCTIONS

In the traditional "management" model used by both IBM and GM, marketing is one of the business functions (Figure 2-1) and is the focus of the first objective for this chapter. Other important business functions are finance, legal, personnel, and production/manufacturing (operation in service businesses). The more marketing-oriented a company is, the higher the marketing man-

A. Traditional Model

| Finance | R&D | Marketing | Purchasing | Accounting | Manufacturing | Human Resources |

B. Marketing-Philosophy Model

Figure 2-1
Two Very Different Management Models

Invention at ITW

The Impulse power nailer is just one of ITW's 2,400 active patents. Highly decentralized, ITW encourages maximum creativity from its designers and fills as many market niches as it can find. "We try to sell where our competitors aren't," says one general manager.

organizations also benefit from economies of scale because the same materials—such as order forms and sales kits—can be used everywhere in the company in the same form. In recent years increased international competition and declining market shares for companies have led many North American firms to seek the greater flexibility of decentralized structures. It is easier for a decentralized company to move fast to enter a new market or to react quickly to changing local market conditions because there are fewer bureaucratic hindrances than in centralized organizations.

A company need not have self-sufficient units to be decentralized. Another form of decentralization is *consensus management*, which treats every employee's opinions as equal in decision making, in contrast to leader-based management, where the boss makes the decisions. This form of decentralization brings marketing thinking into all levels of decision making and introduces everyone in the company to the marketing philosophy. Compaq Computer, a leading supplier of IBM-compatible personal computers and a growth leader in both North American and overseas markets, has a consensus-management system. The Compaq approach uses product strategy teams, which include top management, engineering, and marketing participants. The groups meet eight to twelve hours a week to share market and technical information, as well as to review specific projects and to toss around ideas. The self-described "muscle car of computers" attributes much of its success to involving marketing in every aspect of its decision making.

Global Centralization Issues As we saw in Chapter 1, there is an ongoing debate in international marketing over the use of centralized marketing programs. Some companies believe competition, local practices, cultural differences, and consumer values are too varied to permit standardization of marketing programs and handle their products on a market-by-market basis. Other firms are developing unified global strategies for selected products that focus on the similarities among people rather than their differences. Neither approach is wrong. Some product categories are more suited to standardization than others, and some types of markets are more similar across cultural boundaries than other markets.

Procter & Gamble has found that today more and more products can be sold in a similar way around the world. Former CEO John Smale believes that although some habits and practices differ from country to country, many dif-

ferences are disappearing. He observes that, "Head & Shoulders shampoo has the same objective everywhere. So does Crest." Smale notes that what he terms a "world-class product" can be used in some form "almost around the world."[1] The challenge is to find the right balance between central and local control, centralizing some activities and localizing others. Strategic planning, for example, might be centralized, while advertising executions are often done locally.

COORDINATION AND MARKETING

An organization's overall corporate structure determines whether the marketing staff operates within a brand or product group or as a free standing department. Sometimes a separate marketing department functions as an umbrella group with a strong coordination responsibility. In other situations the coordination function is largely ignored and marketing is responsible for implementation. In production-driven companies, where marketing is a separate department or function, marketing people are typically called in late in the product-development process to handle such marketing service areas as advertising, packaging, and sales promotion.

Orchestrating the activities of other functions with marketing activities, the topic of chapter objective number four, is a major problem (see Exhibit 2-1). To give you an idea of just how complicated the coordination process is, we will consider typical interactions among a few of the functional areas that are particularly important to marketing.

Accounting Accounting oversees all budgets, including that of marketing. Every payroll and expense check for marketing personnel goes through accounting. Drawing on information from researchers, engineers, and others in the company, accountants also develop final cost projections for new products and production facilities. So accounting has extremely important input into sales forecasts, which are usually considered marketing's responsiblity to coordinate.

Exhibit 2-1
Cacophony or Concerto?

This is the first page of a three-page advertisement for IBM's file service that networks PCs so people can share information. It uses the common idea of separate business functions working separately to dramatize the coordination problems that occur when business functions aren't working "in concert."

Research and Development Marketing depends heavily on research and development which are two quite separate activities. R&D is the arm of the company responsible for solving product problems (such as improving taste, shelf life, or appearance), redesigning products, and suggesting new products. If R&D comes up with a significant product improvement, the product may virtually sell itself. On the other hand, if the competition comes out with a way to make a tastier crust for frozen pizza, it's up to R&D to match that development or the company's frozen pizzas won't be competitive. R&D's innovations can propel a product into market leadership, and its lack of innovation can cause a category leader to drop into second or third place. So R&D has a significant impact on the marketing program and marketing has to carefully coordinate its efforts with R&D.

Engineering and Design The engineering and product design department takes ideas and materials from R&D and other sources and designs products. The quality and creativity of a company's engineering and design are critical to product development. Unless there is fruitful coordination with marketing, however, products will not be optimally developed and marketed. AT&T's research and development department created the transistor, but it was Sony that saw the transistor's possibilities and opened up an entirely new product category by putting it into radios. Engineering and design also affect the pricing and promotion of a product because well-designed products are frequently less costly to produce and more likely to have features with high sales potential. Quality and value begin with design, so marketing is very much concerned with and involved in coordinating these activities.

Production Production is the manufacturing arm of a company. Its goal is always to build something cheaper and faster. Marketing decisions can have a tremendous impact on production. For example, a marketing manager might decide to have a package redesigned to use a lighter-weight cardboard that saves a penny a unit. But if the production line is slowed down because the new package tears more easily, then the savings in packaging cost may be eaten up by the loss in production efficiency.

Production also affects marketing. If you are developing a special promotion, you need to know whether manufacturing can handle the increased production. If there is a big order, will production be able to put on a third shift to take care of it, or will they need to schedule larger runs and warehouse the extra production? Quality is another area where manufacturing can hurt or help the marketing program. A quality image nurtured over years can be killed in months by the failure to find defects before the customer does and eliminate them.

Sales In the best-managed companies marketing and sales work side by side, but in many companies there is a gulf between the two. In the worst case, sales managers see brand managers as ivory-tower corporate climbers who know nothing about customers.

The chief cause of this rift is the short-term focus of sales personnel versus the long-term focus of marketers. For example, the sales staff may want to spend the entire promotional budget on short-term promotions that stimulate immediate sales, while the marketing team argues for spending on advertising to promote long-term image development. Other sources of irritation include the fact that marketing typically controls promotional budgets and timing, and sales staffs depend on marketing for samples and sales kits.

Whatever the source of tension, it is crucial that marketing and sales work together for the good of the whole firm. The sales staff must be informed about any change in any aspect of the marketing mix. If a package size changes, a coupon ad is rescheduled, or a discounted price is canceled, the sales force must be able to warn customers. Changes play havoc with sales literature, printed in advance but has to be kept up to date. Marketers who nurture good relations with sales gain much from their interaction, for sales representatives can give valuable feedback on how both the company's product and the competition are doing in the marketplace. Marketing guru Don Shultz says that salespeople must become relationship builders with their customers. He predicts that they will become more involved in identifying the product needs and the manufacturing process.[2]

Coordinating marketing activities with all these departments and functions is a complex and often difficult task. Doing it well is a definite strength and doing it poorly a definite weakness for any firm in a competitive marketplace. As one research team studying marketing coordination has observed, "political processes, jockeying for influence, conflicts, and communication difficulties" may all interfere with marketing decision making, particularly with the implementation of plans and programs.[3] The difficulties increase when an organization moves to international marketing and confronts the problem of cross-cultural differences.

ORGANIZING THE MARKETING FUNCTION ●

Even companies that practice the "marketing-is-everything" philosophy need special people to handle marketing planning as well as daily marketing activities. Because marketing is a relatively new field and because the marketing philosophy is changing the way many companies do business, there is little standardization of job titles and responsibilities from company to company. In addition to showing where the marketing function fits in a traditional management structure, the hypothetical organizational chart depicted in Figure 2-3 illustrates three different types of organizational schemes: organizing by functional area, by customer market, and by geographical market.

Coors is a good example of how a company's marketing organization changes as its market changes. Coors didn't feel the need for a marketing department until the 1970s because its beer sold so successfully on the basis of its Rocky Mountain "mystique." Since then, the beer category has become extremely competitive and Coors has had to fight for its share of the market and establish a comprehensive marketing program. In June 1993 it spun off 130 people from its marketing services department as a separate company named Integer, which brings the insights of both an internal staff function and an external consulting firm to its marketing strategy and programs. This type of radical restructuring, referred to as "reengineering," is something many companies are going through as they try to better fit their organization to the demands of the 21st century.

UPPER MANAGEMENT

Most marketing jobs fall into one of three categories: upper management, product and brand management, or marketing specialties. Top marketing executives in companies with a marketing philosophy usually carry such titles as vice president (VP) or executive vice president (EVP) of marketing, although in small businesses the company president may also be the top marketing executive.

A study of chief marketing executives in Fortune 500 companies found that they see their responsibilities (in order of descending importance) as: determining market strategy, identifying markets for both existing and new products, setting objectives, executing marketing plans, measuring competitive standing, and preparing long-range plans.[4] It should not be surprising that in this age of short-term thinking, long-range planning was last on the list.

Large companies have other upper-management marketing staff, including marketing directors and marketing managers, both of whom report to marketing VPs or EVPs or, in firms where marketing is not a vice presidential level function, to the top executive. Also considered to be at the upper-management level are directors of marketing services, who coordinate specific marketing activities such as packaging, sales promotion, and advertising.

Figure 2-3
Traditional
Organizational Chart

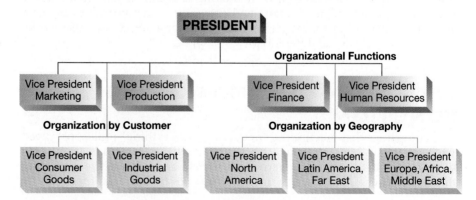

porate culture is based on a set of shared understandings (often unstated) and a subtle sense of agreement; it supports the feeling that everyone is working together toward the same goals. A firm's corporate culture is established by senior executives, many of them corporate founders like Henry Ford at Ford Motor Company and Thomas J. Watson Sr., who built IBM into a global giant by rallying his employees with the famous motto "T-H-I-N-K," which he had posted everywhere in corporate offices.

Corporate culture also reflects the company's "personality" expressed in such things as the degree of formality, office decor, the degree of warmth of personal relationships, rank and privilege, and style of dress. A corporate culture with negative aspects like restrictions on personal initiative often produces low productivity and employee resentment. An open culture can be a strength because it encourages entrepreneurship and risk taking; a closed culture can bog down operations with layers of bureaucracy and approval processes, and generate employee fear and distrust.

By hiring individuals who fit the corporate culture, senior executives strengthen that culture. Thus Compaq, which promotes a management style that includes consensus building, hires people who are team players, not individualists. Apple, on the other hand, is known for its independent-minded employees who do not hesitate to criticize the company, its managers, and their colleagues, despite the fact that they believe strongly in Apple's mission.

Management determines a corporate culture but it is employees who must maintain it. Because marketing success frequently depends on employees who are far removed from the central office, firms need an effective back-and-forth communication program that reaches all levels of employees with messages about the company's philosophy and the details of its marketing activities.[10]

Just as an individual may clash with a particular corporate culture, so may two firms that have merged find their cultures incompatible. In its early years

The Hand's-On Corporate Culture

The corporate culture at Hewlett-Packard Canada Ltd. stresses equality, openness, and group cohesiveness. Gord McLean, the Senior Vice-President of Finance and Administration, is a part of this culture. Note the name tag, which all employees wear.

Celestial Seasonings, purveyor of herbal teas, established a firmly New Age corporate culture. When the firm was purchased by Kraft Foods, Celestial Seasonings found itself mismatched. In 1988, frustrated by the more formal culture at Kraft, Celestial Seasonings' employees arranged to buy back their company.

Firms expanding globally must be prepared to cope with differences that arise as individuals of other nations attempt to fit themselves—and their operations—into the corporate culture. A study of corporate cultures that compared British and North American companies on "consumer closeness," corporate values, and market-oriented focus found that firms with similar corporate cultures responded similarly, regardless of their geographic location. This research also found that the best predictor of a strong corporate culture was a consumer orientation in which employees demonstrated pride in the quality of the firm's product and the firm valued the individual employee as a creator of quality.[11]

Risk Taking A major component of every corporate culture is its attitude toward risk taking and innovation. Traditionally, the tendency to take risks and to try new ideas has been characteristic of small start-up companies and counter to the long-time values of many big corporations. But as IBM found out, "too much time spent *thinking*, created bureaucracy and unending internal debates which paralyzed the company and made it painfully vulnerable to faster-moving competitors."[12] When managers are uncomfortable with risky new ideas, they may insist on a great deal of testing and reviewing by multiple management levels before making decisions, and lose competitive advantage in the process. Fear of risk also limits the vision of any company trying to reach a new level of productivity.

entrepreneur
A person with novel but often highly speculative project ideas who organizes, operates, and assumes the risk for a start-up business venture.

Consequently, **entrepreneurs**—people with novel but risky new ideas who are willing to start up and manage a new business—have preferred to operate outside the big corporations. Such individuals are usually comfortable with making decisions on the spot, which allows their companies to respond rapidly to changing situations. In the 1980s, however, the entrepreneurial spirit began sweeping through corporate offices. Many corporations set up *intrapreneur* programs—entrepreneurial activities under the corporate roof. Other big companies attempted to mimic smaller firms by reengineering themselves into small, highly decentralized business units whose managers were given greater flexibility and freedom.

For example, Chairman Jack F. Welch speaks of transforming General Electric into a "big-company/small-company hybrid," combining the large corporation's resources with the small company's agility: "We want the best of both," he explains, "a big company with the heart and hunger of a small one." Not surprisingly, some of the most successful big companies, including Johnson & Johnson, Hewlett-Packard, and AT&T, have reengineered themselves into groups of smaller companies and units. Hewlett-Packard, for example, has fifty independent business units, each with its own profit-and-loss responsibility and separate planning and support functions.

Short-Term Thinking In most firms risk taking is stymied by a habit of short-term thinking. The tensions between short-term goals oriented toward immediate profit and long-term goals aimed at building stakeholder relationships over time stem from corporate objectives and corporate philosophy. If top management pushes for shorter payout periods, less risk, more control, a higher level of profit, and higher return to shareholders, then marketing will find itself in a bind because its mission is to develop powerful brands and new products, and these activities take time. Although some marketing programs, such as sales promotions, operate in the short run, many marketing costs represent investment spending, the return on which extends over a long period. Research and development, new products, the development of a quality program, packaging, advertising, and guarantees all require long-term investments.

QUALITY PROGRAMS

Over the years no matter what went wrong with an item purchased by a customer, the local Eaton's store would cheerfully replace it free of charge and without question. In the early 1980s this promise was many Canadians' idea of quality. Today the philosophy that "doing it over can make up for the failure to do it right the first time" is not accepted. At cutting-edge companies, that philosophy has been replaced by the philosophy of "zero defects."

Managers are finally recognizing how much the "do-it-over" credo really costs. The typical North American factory spends *up to 25 percent* of its operating budget to find and fix its mistakes. By contrast, many Japanese companies pay such careful attention to production-process variables that their employees are able to identify problems before they happen and correct them on the line. This gives Japanese vendors of computer memory chips, for example, three times as many chips to sell as competitor companies from the same production run—which greatly reduces their costs and increases their competitive advantages. North American executives from Motorola and Xerox who toured Japanese facilities in the late 1980s found defect levels 500 to 1,000 times lower than in domestic electronics plants.[13]

How quality programs interact with marketing programs is the topic of our last chapter objective. Quality programs consist of more than just *quality control*, a topic that will be discussed in more detail in Chapter 11. Programs that maximize quality, like total quality management (TQM) and continuous quality improvement (CQI), are really directed at creating *customer satisfaction*, which is a topic in Chapter 12. Quality expert Joseph M. Juran defines quality programs this way: "Quality equals fitness of use by the customer," not conformance to specifications. He says a quality product is "free from deficiencies" and a gauge of quality is "the cost to make it right without excessive waste and rework."

For most companies, adopting the total quality approach demands a complete shift in corporate culture, with management and marketing leading the way. As the Hamilton/Avnet advertisement in Exhibit 2-4 points out, the TQM goal has become "the absolute requirement" for staying in the game in many industries. Quality programs are particularly important for marketing-driven companies because of their emphasis on customer satisfaction as well

Exhibit 2-4
Quality is the Bottom Line

Cutting-edge marketers have taken up the difficult quest for total quality, as this Hamilton/Avnet electronics firm indicates.

as on building positive relationships with **stakeholders**—any group or individual who can affect, or be affected by, an organization. These include employees, stockholders, suppliers, distributors, retailers, legislators and government officials, and people in the community. The quality philosophy is an important theme throughout this book. We explore the origins of the quality approach in the next section and will continue to develop the concept in many of the chapters that follow.

BEHIND THE SCENES — THE QUEST FOR QUALITY

The quest for quality that has been a dominant force in the global business community for over a decade got its start in Japan in the 1950s. The concept of **Total Quality Management**, or **TQM**, originated with U.S. management consultants like W. Edwards Deming and Joseph Juran who, unable to interest U.S. businesses in their ideas, found an eager audience among Japanese organizations that wanted to overturn their country's reputation for shoddy products.

Three decades later, U.S. businesses finally realized that they, too, had to master quality if they intended to remain competitive in the international marketplace. Seeing firms from other countries take over markets once dominated by U.S. industries alarmed the federal government. To help spur U.S. firms to meet powerful global competition and regain their place in world markets, the U.S. government established the Malcolm Baldrige National Quality Award, named for a former U.S. secretary of commerce and patterned after Japan's Deming Award.

TQM encourages open corporate environments where employees are encouraged to spot problems and speak up about them. At Saturn, for example, employees who let someone in management know about a problem, even if it prompts a recall, are rewarded rather than punished. Because its customers recognize that quality is an important part of corporate philosophy, the company has been able to weather difficult times, such as the 1993 recall of 80 percent of its cars to fix an electrical flaw.

TQM invites employee teams to help improve poor procedures and to polish corporate work habits so that a product achieves the highest possible level of excellence. Essentially, quality programs start at the bottom; they're not handed down from the top. Motorola, for example, winner of the first Baldrige Award in 1988, sponsors a worldwide competition within the corporation to encourage teams of workers to develop new procedures. The manufacturer estimates that ideas generated by its teams save the company about $2.2 billion annually.

Service industries and the service side of goods manufacture are also a source of inefficiency and customer complaints. Customers get just as

CANADA AWARDS FOR BUSINESS EXCELLENCE

THE MARK OF A LEADER
LE SCEAU D'EXCELLENCE

PROFILES OF EXCELLENCE 1993

angry at a delivery error or the rudeness of a sales clerk as they do at product defects.

Progressive companies are dragging their suppliers into the quality arena because they look at suppliers as extensions of their own factories. Motorola has put pressure on its suppliers by requiring that they apply for the Baldrige award in the U.S.A. or the CABE Award (Canadian Award for Business Excellence) within five years of becoming a supplier to them. In making demands of this sort, companies are shrinking their base of quality suppliers to a smaller number of reliable firms with whom they are building long-term relationships. Xerox, for example, slashed its supplier base from 3,000 to 350; Motorola went from 4,000 to 1,500.

Experts believe that quality programs begin with a corporate culture that will not stand for mediocrity and holds that any defect, no matter how small, is unacceptable. Such an approach leads to a philosophy of total customer satisfaction.

Quality has eight dimensions according to David Garvin of the Harvard Business School (see Table 2-2).

TABLE 2-2	**EIGHT DIMENSIONS OF QUALITY FROM A CUSTOMER'S PERSPECTIVE**

- Performance
- Features
- Reliability
- Conformance
- Durability
- Serviceability
- Aesthetics
- Perceived Quality

Source: David A Garvin, "Competing on the Eight Dimentions of Quality," *Harvard Business Review*, November–December, 1987, p. 101.

INTERNAL STRENGTHS AND WEAKNESSES

All the internal factors we've discussed—financial resources; type of leadership and ownership; corporate culture; technology; expertise; research and development; organizational structure, mission, and vision; risk taking; long-term thinking; and commitment to quality—have a decided impact on world-class marketing. These variables, which are listed in Table 2-3, can be either a fund of strength or a source of weakness for a company. Moreover, to a certain extent they control marketing either by enhancing marketing programs or by restructuring them.

If, for example, you work for a pharmaceutical company that has a patent on a widely used medicine, the product may virtually sell itself because it has few competitors. The patent is a major source of corporate strength. When the patent runs out and you face a number of competitors who are now able to offer essentially the same product, that puts extraordinary pressure on your cost structure to maintain your leadership position. An analysis of internal strengths and weaknesses, which is the first step in developing a marketing plan, uncovers such situations and assesses their importance.

To take another example, an organizational structure that treats marketing like a function and isolates it from the other functional areas will never be able to develop a "marketing-is-everything" philosophy. In those situations, marketing is a tool that is used to implement plans rather than a guide that gives direction to planning. The focus is then on marketing services—the tactical uses of advertising, sales promotion, price deals, and so forth, and the details of their implementation.

The weakness of such an approach is that it tends to miss valuable insights into customer needs and lacks the vision to see how various corporate activities add value to a product. Both insights into customer needs and vision are basic premises of the marketing philosophy. In today's competitive marketplace, the narrow view of marketing is often a very damaging weakness because competitors who take the broader view are more in tune with customer needs and far better able to marshall their corporate strengths to add value to their products.

TABLE 2-3	**INTERNAL CORPORATE FACTORS THAT AFFECT MARKETING**

The following factors can be either strengths or weaknesses and thus may either facilitate or limit the development and implementation of marketing programs. State-of-the-art technology, for example, may give R&D the freedom to create useful new products, whereas outmoded technology may make marketing's task very difficult.

Corporate financial resources
Technology
Type of ownership and leadership
Type of industry
Expertise of employees
R&D capabilities
Corporate mission and vision
Commitment to quality
Risk taking
Long-term thinking versus short-term thinking
Corporate culture
Organizational structure
Marketing's role in the organization

WESTERN BUSINESS VALUES IN EASTERN EUROPE

Just as fundamental marketing principles apply globally, so are basic organizational issues universal concerns. One of the biggest changes to hit Eastern Europe after the fall of the Berlin Wall was the introduction of hard-charging Western business values into what was a tightly controlled but low-productivity market system. Eastern workers, who had operated all their lives in a controlled environment that provided few incentives and little motivation, found they needed to learn a new work ethic, and basic business principles in order to be competitive.

In Hungary, for example, when GE entered into a joint venture with Tungsram, a light-bulb manufacturer, it found it had to explain the meaning of profit to the Hungarian company's managers. Unilever found a similar ignorance of basic business principles and productivity concepts in Poland when it purchased a laundry detergent factory there.[14]

And other companies setting up operations in countries undergoing the wrenching transformation to a market economy have also found deeply entrenched problems, from outdated plants to the lack of a distribution system to total ignorance of Western business methods and values. Many managers at Eastern European concerns have no understanding of the importance of efficient production and marketing techniques, and consequently no idea of how to make production more efficient and marketing more strategic.

GE also found that wages were low in Hungary—on the average, U.S. $3,000 per year—as was productivity. Furthermore, many practices were inefficient and the defect level was very high. When GE took over Tungsram, 18,000 people produced U.S. $3 million worth of light bulbs. By way of comparison, GE's other 18,000 employees in lighting operations outside Hungary produced six times as many bulbs. Tungsram employed 150 people just to stuff the 18,000 pay envelopes with cash because checking accounts are virtually unknown in Hungary.

For the buttoned-down managers of GE and Unilever, the

Spotlighting the Differences
GE and Tungsram managers inspect fluorescent bulbs coming off the line in a joint venture plant in Hungary.

solution to the quality problem seemed to be to import Western technology and cost-efficiency procedures and to inaugurate procedures designed to improve the abysmal productivity levels, eliminate inefficient job assignments, and lower the defect levels. But how much change is acceptable, or even desirable, in the name of modernization in these countries? Those 150 check stuffers, however inefficient their methods, had jobs. Improvements in efficiency can also raise unemployment levels.

As Unilever, GE, and other major Western marketers move into Eastern Europe, more instances of cultural conflict will undoubtedly arise. If you were working for one of these companies, how far would you go in centralizing marketing operations in corporate headquarters as opposed to allowing local managers who may not understand much about marketing run these programs? Is it possible—or even wise—to quickly introduce Western notions of efficiency, modernization, and quality control into these cultures? ▼

KEY POINTS SUMMARY ▼

1. In traditional organizations marketing is considered a business function along with such areas as production/manufacturing (operations in service companies), human resources, legal, and finance. In marketing-driven companies marketing is a philosophy, a way of doing business, that also relates to all of these other functional areas.

2. Work and responsibility in organizations can be organized into departments, divisions, or strategic business units. The most complex form of organization is the matrix system, which overlaps two patterns of reporting and control.

3. There are advantages and disadvantages to both centralized and decentralized structures. The trend today is toward decentralization because it makes it possible to react to changes quickly and to adapt to local market situations.

4. In companies with a strong marketing philosophy, the marketing department has the responsibility for coordinating its programs with other functional areas and implementing a marketing-is-everything corporate viewpoint. In situations where marketing is considered a separate function, marketing staff are typically responsible only for marketing service areas such as advertising, packaging, and sales promotion.

5. Product/brand managers control the total business and marketing efforts of a particular product, line of products, or brand, including profit and loss. They either direct or coordinate the activities of other marketing services, such as advertising, sales promotion, and packaging.

6. The primary organizational issues facing marketing personnel in global firms are the appropriate degree of centralization and how to manage conflicts between cultures.

7. Internal factors that affect marketing policies and practices include the company's financial resources, its type of ownership, its technology, the skill and experience of its management, the expertise of its staff, its research and development capabilities, its corporate culture, and its organization and structure.

8. The corporate mission statement formally defines the organization's business and reflects the firm's corporate culture and vision of what it aspires to be. Together, the mission and corporate culture—especially risk taking, long-term thinking, and commitment to quality—influence the functioning and structure of marketing operations in cutting-edge corporations.

9. A company with marketing myopia focuses on what it produces rather than on what its customers want and, as a result, loses sight of the business it's in.

10. Quality programs aim at providing the best possible products, value customer satisfaction, and build positive relationships with other stakeholders, such as employees, suppliers, distributors, and people in the community.

54

DISCUSSION QUESTIONS ▼

1. How can you determine the importance of the marketing function to a company? Find an article about a company that considers marketing very important and an article about another company that looks on marketing as a simple business function. Analyze the differences in the two approaches and their impact on other measures of success, such as market share, sales, profit, or whatever business measures are discussed in the articles.

2. Interview a local company that manufactures a product. Outline how its marketing program is organized relative to the other business functions. With which other areas in the company does marketing have the best relations? The worst relations? Why?

3. Find an article about a company that is moving to decentralize its business functions and marketing operations. What changes in the real world have influenced it to decentralize?

4. Interview a brand manager or marketing executive in two different local companies. Compare their job responsibilities and the way their marketing programs are organized.

5. Find an article about a company in an East European country that is moving to a market economy. Describe the internal factors affecting the development of marketing in that company and explain how they represent strengths and weakness of the firm.

6. In your business library review the collection of annual reports and assemble ten mission statements. Do any of the statements also seem to represent vision statements—that is, state the firm's long-term aspirations as well as its short-term goals? How believable are these statements?

7. Select a nonprofit organization in your community and describe its marketing operation. How would you describe its attitude toward marketing?

8. Is any company in your community involved in a quality program? Interview the marketing manager and determine how the quality program affects the company's marketing program. Is the manager satisfied with the interface? Why or why not?

9. Find a company that is organized along traditional functional lines. Write a proposal detailing the changes necessary to turn this company into an oganization that operates with a marketing-is-everything philosophy.

Integrative Case ● Discussion Questions

The Body Shop*

1. How has The Body Shop's high degree of centralization helped or hindered the firm's growth? Do you think this centralized style of management and marketing will prove a positive or a negative force in the future?

2. Is The Body Shop a global organization? Why or why not?

Harley-Davidson

1. In your judgment, is Harley-Davidson a centralized or a decentralized firm?

2. Write two mission statements for Harley—one for the firm at its founding and one for the firm today. Do these statements differ and, if so, why?

3. Would you write a global mission statement for Harley differently from the way you wrote a domestic one? Why or why not?

The Millennium Power System

1. Now that Ralston Purina owns both the Eveready and Millennium brands, how should the company stimulate competition between the brands? Should they use centralized or decentralized decison making?

2. Write a mission statement for the Millennium battery/charger system.

*The three cases at the back of the book—"The Body Shop," "Harley-Davidson," and "The Millennium Power System"—illustrate topics discussed in all chapters of this book. Your instructor will tell you when to read a particular case and answer the discussion questions on it that appear at the end of each chapter.

Flexibility May Destroy Those Dinosaurs

Investing in technology can be an important strategic advantage in today's changing business environment. Those companies, like Borland, IBM and Unisys, who are involved in providing technology alternatives to companies are facing new challenges in marketing their products. Their business customers are more sophisticated and more demanding concerning their computer equipment investments and the competitive advantages they provide.

Mainframe computers were once considered state-of-the-art. This is no longer the situation. As companies are becoming flatter and leaner to be competitive, they are expecting computer software and hardware manufacturers to respond to their needs. Mainframes supported the business environment at the time when there were long business planning cycles. Major investments in technology lasted five years. Today, it takes 18 months to two years for a technology to become outdated—the market is moving so fast.

This changing environment has placed incredible pressure on today's technology developers. Whether it is software, hardware, or peripheral devices, suppliers need to rethink their marketing strategies and how their customers have changed. More importantly, they need to understand how and why their customers are downsizing their computer investment. The business market is looking for computer systems which will allow them to be flexible and provide them with a competitive advantage in their own industries.

The computing industry is looking for ways to survive the chaos in their industry. Borland chose to compete on price, forcing a price war which has hurt a large number of software developers. Borland is one of those companies that has suffered from the price war. Business customers are not complaining, though, because they are reaping financial benefits.

Changes in marketing approaches are happening. Vendors of software and hardware have to change from merely selling to providing solutions for their customers. They are now learning to develop long-term relationships with their customers.

QUESTIONS

1. What is the difference between a market-driven company and a technology-driven company? What are the strengths and weaknesses of each?
2. Why have companies who are developing and manufacturing computer software and hardware had to change their approach to marketing? What role does the level of industry maturity play in this?
3. Is there evidence that computer vendors are market-driven? What role does the marketing function play in the rate of change of technology?

Source: This case was prepared by Deborah Andrus and is based on the *Venture* series episode "Computer Downsizing," first broadcast on December 5, 1993.

● Chapter 3

The External Marketing Environment

OBJECTIVES

AFTER COMPLETING THIS CHAPTER, YOU SHOULD BE ABLE TO:

1
EXPLAIN HOW OPPORTUNITIES AND THREATS IN THE EXTERNAL ENVIRONMENT FORCE COMPANIES TO CREATE VALUE FOR CUSTOMERS

2
IDENTIFY DIFFERENT ECONOMIC SYSTEMS AND COMPARE THEIR ABILITIES TO MEET THE NEEDS OF INDIVIDUAL AND INDUSTRIAL BUYERS

3
EXPLAIN THE CRITICAL IMPORTANCE OF THE COMPETITIVE ENVIRONMENT FOR MARKETING STRATEGY, INCLUDING WHY MARKET SHARE IS IMPORTANT, AND DESCRIBE FOUR COMPETITIVE INDUSTRY STRUCTURES

4
IDENTIFY THE EFFECTS OF LEGAL AND REGULATORY RESTRAINTS ON BUSINESS

5
OUTLINE THE WAYS IN WHICH THE SOCIO-ECONOMIC ENVIRONMENT SHAPES A FIRM'S EXTERNAL MARKETING ENVIRONMENT

6
UNDERSTAND HOW A CHANGING INDUSTRY ENVIRONMENT AFFECTS THE SUCCESS OF A COMPANY AND ITS PRODUCTS

7
DESCRIBE THE IMPACT OF TECHNOLOGICAL CHANGE ON A COMPANY AND ITS PRODUCTS

THINK ABOUT IT!

GLOBAL IS ALL AROUND YOU

One of the themes of this book is that marketing operates in a global environment. Even if you work for a company that markets only in your home country, chances are your company will be in competition with companies from foreign countries. And even if it's not dealing with international competition, then you may find that your company's raw materials or intermediate suppliers are from outside your country.

Test this out. Open your closet and go through the labels on your clothes, shoes, accessories, and anything else stored there. Make an inventory: how many clothing items, for example, were produced wholly in one country? Were they produced in your own country or a

foreign one? Check out your sporting goods. Where were your skis made? Your bicycle? Your running shoes? Your tennis racquet?

Do an inventory of the parts on your car. Check your Vehicle Identifica-

59

tion Number to determine where your car was assembled.

Having products made or assembled in a foreign country can sometimes be a marketing problem. Wal-Mart got into trouble for mismanaging its "home-town," "buy America" image when NBC investigated the company's clothing lines and found a number of items that were made in part or in whole in the Far East. Not only that, some of the factories identified allegedly used child and prison labor. Although such labor may not be frowned on in the countries Wal-Mart was dealing with, it is unacceptable to most North Americans. Do you think Wal-Mart was wrong to appeal to the "made in America" market while it was offering products for sale that were made in other countries? If you think the company was wrong, what should it to to correct its error?

Do you care if the products you buy are made in a foreign country? Do you think people should buy goods made abroad? What if these products are made using child or prison labor? Are these companies bringing jobs to poor people in developing countries or exploiting children or prisoners so that the company can offer a lower price than its competition? ■

THE EXTERNAL ENVIRONMENT ●

The world has undergone a remarkable transformation over the past fifty years. Thanks to modern technology, companies almost anywhere on earth can be in instant voice communication with each other in a matter of seconds. Supersonic jets make it possible to work until noon in Paris and have lunch with clients in New York.

This increased ability to communicate and to move goods and services, coupled with worldwide economic growth and rising productivity, has encouraged some companies to expand internationally. Afraid to be left behind, their competitors have also braved international waters. At the same time, the move toward privatization and deregulation at home and abroad has pushed whole industries that operate separate facilities in many countries to become truly global in their approach. For example, the deregulation and breakup of AT&T in the United States, the privatization of British Telecom in the United Kingdom, and the breakup of telephone monopolies in Canada are revolutionizing the telecommunications industry. For the first time, this industry is experiencing intense global competition.

DEFINING THE EXTERNAL MARKETING ENVIRONMENT

external marketing environment
All the forces outside a firm that may affect sales within a market and pose threats to marketers.

Those factors and forces *outside* the organization that affect both the firm's marketing opportunities and threats, controlling the environment in which marketing activities take place, are known collectively as the firm's **external marketing environment.** As shown in Figure 3-1, these outside factors are the people and organizations that directly determine a company's success: the

60

competition, customers, channels of distribution, and suppliers. Each of these elements is, in turn, affected by the economic, technological, legal and regulatory, political, industrial, and sociocultural environments set within larger environments that range from local and national to multinational and global. As we will see, changes in any of these types of environments may offer a company opportunities in the marketplace or challenges to its ability to prosper or even survive.

One of the most dramatic examples of the effect on an industry of changes in the multinational, political, and economic environments was provided by the so-called oil crisis of the early 1970s. Up to that time the North American consumer was in love with cars that were large and powerful. The fact that these cars used a great deal of gasoline was not important because gas was cheap and plentiful. Suddenly, however, actions of the Organization of Petroleum Exporting Countries (OPEC) led to drastic shortages in the supply and sharp increases in the price per gallon. Consumer preferences shifted overnight, as many car buyers began to perceive small, more fuel-efficient cars as offering the greater overall value. Because at that time large, high-horsepower cars were made primarily by North American companies and smaller, fuel-efficient cars were mostly made elsewhere, foreign manufacturers gained the competitive advantage over North American car makers.

OPPORTUNITIES AND THREATS

The oil crisis presented the North American automobile industry with both a threat to its existing policies and practices and an opportunity to create new value for consumers. For reasons that are still not entirely clear, the industry

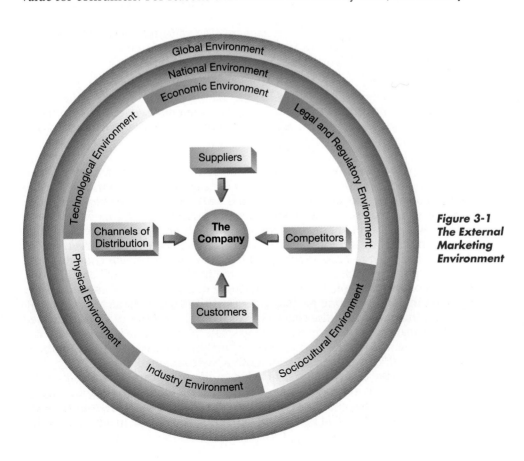

Figure 3-1
The External
Marketing
Environment

Topping Off Growth

In 1973 the oil-rich nations of the Middle East dramatically increased the price of crude oil on the world market. This action, combined with consumer countries' price and allocation controls, caused the price of oil to skyrocket from U.S.$4 to U.S.$40 per barrel (a 900 percent increase). However, when the free market reasserted itself in the 1980s, oil prices collapsed, and the oil companies, which had increased production to counter shortages in a time of peak prices, found themselves severely overextended. Many failed, and others were forced to merge.

misread the signals, and the Japanese and others gained the advantage. Let's look at some of the characteristics of opportunities and threats that the external environment offers to companies—the subject of the first chapter objective.

Recall that in Chapter 1, we said creating value for consumers is central to the marketing effort. An *opportunity* is a chance to create value for customers at a profit. Opportunities are of two general types:

1. The opportunity to create something new
2. The opportunity to improve an existing good or service by, for example, adding attractive and useful features or offering the product at a lower price

To paraphrase the old saying about a better mousetrap, if you are a marketer who creates value, the world will beat a path to your door. Mazda capitalized on an opportunity to create value with its Miata, introduced in 1989. It achieved instant success in a market that many said no longer existed in North America—small, inexpensive sports cars. Indeed, this market was small and shrinking: in 1989 it was only 1.2 percent of the overall market, half of what it had been in 1986. However, the overall car market was changing, and Mazda spotted the clues: more two-income families, maturing baby boomers with good incomes, older buyers with more discretionary income, and rising purchasing power among people under thirty. With the Miata, Mazda capitalized on the romance of the classic British sports cars of the 1950s and showed that the real reason nobody was buying small sports cars was that nobody was making them. Mazda's environmental analysis focused on the economic, socio-cultural, consumer, and competitive environments.

The Miata is an example of what a company can do when it tracks trends in the environment around it. It also highlights the importance of managing the value chain (see Chapter 1) in order to create customer value. Initially, Mazda planned to build only 20,000 Miatas a year in a single plant, a strategy that could give the car scarcity value and lead to a highly profitable niche for years. In its first year, however, Miata's dealers could not keep the car in stock and reported that it was selling for thousands of dollars over the sticker price. Mazda did not expand production, however; it stuck with its original plans. The initial demand surge proved temporary, confirming Mazda's estimate of its market.

Changes in external factors don't always have a positive effect on a company. Some changes may pose a *threat* to a firm's ability to create value for customers. Successful firms view such threats as warnings that they must take action. For example, the ever increasing power and declining cost of personal computer processor chips and memory have created a tremendous competitive challenge, not only for traditional large "mainframe" computer manufacturers, but for personal computer manufacturers as well. As the technology races ahead, product cycles become shorter and firms are constantly pressured to develop new products that will make their own existing lines obsolete. Unfortunately, the companies most apt to face threats from environmental change are the very firms least apt to be looking ahead at consumer trends and market changes.

Just as each of the internal factors we discussed in Chapter 2 can be either a strength or a weakness for a firm, the external factors we discuss in this chapter present either an opportunity or a threat. Let's look at each of these factors to see how they impact on marketing programs and activities.

THE ECONOMIC ENVIRONMENT ●

A business is surrounded by and dependent on an **economic environment**, or the economy in which it operates. This environment—which today is for almost all businesses not just the national economy, but the world—consists of forces that affect the production and availability of a product, the resources and raw materials needed to produce the product, and the willingness and ability of buyers to purchase it. Among these forces are the nation's rate of economic growth, its economic stability, its consumers' income level, its trade policies, and the value of its currency in the global market. All these economic aspects of the environment greatly influence marketing activities.

economic environment The economic factors and forces that affect both the production and availability of goods and services and the willingness and ability of buyers to purchase them; includes the economic system, factors of economic growth and stability, consumer income levels, and foreign exchange rates.

ECONOMIC SYSTEMS

All of the world's economies can be classified as either free-market, controlled-market, or mixed economic systems. These systems, the topic of chapter objective number two, are distinguished by how decisions are made about what to produce, who controls the resources for production, and how products are distributed.

In a **free-market system** private individuals and businesses own the resources used to produce goods. The market forces of demand and supply determine what quantity of a product will be produced and how the product will be distributed. In this free-market, or capitalistic, system the basic rule of the game is that the market (consumers) decides which companies and products will be successful and which will not. Government's only role in a pure free-market system is to ensure a level playing for national companies. The free-market system—which characterizes all the world's high-income countries—provides the greatest opportunity and challenge for marketing because it puts the customer in charge of deciding what and how much will be produced. For an example of a product whose design and marketing have been strongly influenced by the economic environment, see Exhibit 3-1.

free-market system An economic system in which private individuals or businesses own the resources needed to produce goods and consumer demand determines what will be produced and how products will be distributed.

centrally planned system
A failed economic system in which the government controls all production and markets.

mixed economic system
A system combining elements of the free-market and centrally planned systems.

Enthusiasm for free-market systems has grown throughout the world in recent years. From 1989 the countries of Eastern Europe and the former USSR each turned to the free market system and away from the central planning system under which they had lived for four decades or more. In a **centrally planned system**, the government owns and controls all resources of production, decides how much of various products to make, and largely determines who will receive the goods and services produced. Because the government controls all resource decisions, marketing has virtually no role to play in this system. Today only Cuba and North Korea continue to rely primarily on a system of government control and planned resource allocation.

In fact, there are no "pure" free-market or controlled-market systems in the world; in most countries a **mixed economic system** prevails. Japan is a capitalist country whose growth has been driven by private enterprise, but the Japanese government has played a major role in encouraging the growth of key industries. China is officially a communist country whose government in recent years has permitted private ownership and market allocation, and whose ruling patriarch, Deng Xiaoping, has said to the people: "To get rich is glorious!" By imposing taxes and spending public monies, all nations to some degree control the allocation of resources. Although theoretically in democracies the taxpayers' wishes are served by their elected representatives, taxpayers are rarely consulted about whether or not they wish to support a particular government program.

ECONOMIC COOPERATION

One of the most important trends in the world today is the movement toward greater international economic cooperation through multilateral trade negotiations such as the General Agreement on Tariffs and Trade (GATT). GATT is a pact of over 100 countries that have agreed to negotiate trade agreements with one another on a so-called most-favored-nation basis: that is, members agree to extend the terms of any agreement that two or more of them reach to all other signatories of the pact.

One of the most important forms of international economic cooperation in the past two decades has been regional economic integration. The most advanced expression of this is in Europe, where twelve West European countries (Belgium, Denmark, France, Germany, Greece, Ireland, Italy, Luxembourg, The Netherlands, Portugal, Spain, and The United Kingdom) have formed the European Union, (EU, formerly the European Community). EU members are committed to removing all barriers to the free movement of goods, services, people, and money across their national boundaries and also to the harmonization of social policy and business law practice. The aim is not only to create a single market but also to unite Europe monetarily, politically, and culturally. What sets the EU apart from other instances of economic cooperation is that the member countries of the community have actually given up part of their sovereignty and have agreed to be bound by the majority decisions of the community. This unique organization has been described as *supranational* because it derives its power not from the ongoing consent of its member countries to particular actions but rather from the treaty by which each country has bound itself.

Today a business establishment in any member country has the right to conduct business anywhere else in the EU. There is a single external tariff, and within the community there are no tariff barriers. It is the goal of the EU to create a single currency by the year 2000 to eliminate the last barrier to the free movement of goods and services. The countries of central and eastern Europe are eager to join the European Union, and, many believe, will someday be admitted. To date four have associate member status and two, Hungary and Poland, have applied for full membership, which is likely before the end of the decade.

In 1993, after a hard-fought battle, the Canadian government approved the North American Free Trade Agreement (NAFTA), eliminating barriers to trade and investment among Canada, the United States, and Mexico. Proponents argued vigorously that the agreement will open up new export market opportunities in Mexico for the United States and Canada, while opponents contended just as vigorously that it will lead to the outflow of capital and jobs from the United States and Canada to Mexico, where labor costs are much lower. Actually, NAFTA is far less ambitious than the European Union in that there are no provisions for monetary, political, or cultural union, and it only involves three nations. Nevertheless, it is considered an important step toward future agreements that may also include much of South America as well.

Similar regional agreements in the Pacific and other areas of the world, and the continued commitment to GATT negotiations by most of the advanced and developing nations, are making the world a much smaller place. Today, nearly every country is part of the world trading system, and that system is becoming more and more open. This means both greater opportunity and greater challenge for marketers the world over.

ECONOMIC GROWTH AND DEVELOPMENT

A nation's economic health has a major impact on marketing in that country. Most economies have three basic, interlinked goals: strong economic growth, stable prices, and high employment. Where a nation stands with respect to each of these goals directly affects the marketing of products.

Economic growth is an increase in a nation's **gross national product (GNP)**, which is the value of all goods and services that a nation produces for world (that is, both domestic and foreign) markets. Dividing a country's GNP by its population gives us average GNP per capita, a measure that is useful in

gross national product (GNP)
The value of all goods and services produced by factors of production owned by a country's citizens, regardless of where the goods and services are produced. GNP is differentiated from gross domestic product (GDP), which is the value of all goods and services produced by factors of production within a country.

GATT and the U.S. Movie Industry

One of the major issues in the GATT (General Agreement on Tariffs and Trade) talks late in 1993 was European opposition to the flow of U.S. films, television programs, and other audiovisual technology into their marketplace. Although American representatives pointed out that many U.S. films are international productions, directed, produced, and acted by people from different countries, European directors feared their industry might be buried by Hollywood's sheer output. U.S. trade negotiators, for their part, hoped to abolish France's 11 percent tax on every admission ticket to a U.S. film.

comparing the wealth of one country with that of others. Table 3-1 shows per capita GNP figures for the ten wealthiest countries although national wealth per head of the population does not approximate to personal disposable income or the ability or willingness to buy.

In Figure 3-2 you can see how the GNP has grown in Canada in the twentieth century. A pattern in which alternating periods of growth and decline are repeated is known as a *business cycle*. Marketing activities are clearly affected by a nation's rate of economic growth; changes in growth rates represent threats to some marketers and opportunities for others.

During a recession like those of 1975, 1982, and 1991, spending on consumer durables such as major appliances and automobiles slows. A **recession** is a period of little or no economic growth in which unemployment levels rise and the rate of increase in income and purchasing power slows. More serious is a **depression**, a period of economic contraction in which consumer income and purchasing power actually decline. The most severe depression of modern times was the worldwide Great Depression of the 1930s.

The business cycle has a definite impact on consumer behavior. In Canada during the recession years of the early 1990s, sales of private-label products—"brands" that are up to 50 percent cheaper than national brands—soared as budget-conscious consumers bought more generic paper, food, and tobacco products. In Europe, where unemployment levels were much higher during this same period, thrifty consumers bought private label and store

recession
A period of economic contraction with minimal economic growth.

depression
A period of economic contraction in which consumer income and purchasing power decline.

TABLE 3-1	PER CAPITA GNP FOR THE TOP 10 COUNTRIES WORLDWIDE, 1993		
	Countries	**Per Capita GNP (in U.S. dollars)**	**% of Switzerland's GNP**
1	Switzerland	$34,591	100.00
2	Luxembourg	33,487	96.81
3	Japan	28,949	83.69
4	Sweden	26,364	76.22
5	Finland	25,635	74.11
6	Norway	25,235	72.95
7	Germany	24,702	71.41
8	Denmark	24,664	71.30
9	United States	23,518	67.99
10	Canada	22,162	64.07

Source: Keegan, Warren J., *Global Income and Population 1933, and Projected Growth to 2020,* Institute for Global Business Strategy, Pace University, 1993.

brands at double the rate of North American consumers.

Real economic growth and prosperity should not be confused with the nominal growth of wages and prices of goods brought on by inflation. **Inflation**, an increase in prices that results from an imbalance of supply and de-

inflation
An increase in the price levels of available goods and services caused by an imbalance of supply and demand.

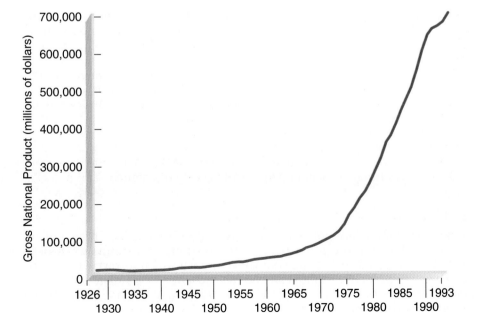

Figure 3-2
Canada's Gross National Product at Market Prices since 1926 (in millions of dollars)

Source: Canadian Economic Observer: Historical Statistical Supplement, 1993/1994, p. 8.

mand, occurs when wages and prices of goods rise without a commensurate rise in productivity. If prices increase 10 percent while productivity increases by only 5 percent, for example, the inflation rate is 5 percent. The 10 percent increase in nominal output is actually only a 5 percent real increase.

Inflation rates vary widely from nation to nation and sometimes within the same nation from period to period. After reaching double-digit levels in the 1970s, inflation slowed in North America in the 1980s, in part because oil prices fell. Some nations, however, struggle with chronic high inflation. In Brazil, for example, the rate of inflation ranged from 400 to 1800 percent between 1987 and 1992, and was expected to exceed 2000 percent for 1993! At mid-1993 prices were rising at a rate of 37 percent per month. Among the developed nations of the world, present-day Germany and Japan are noted for their low rates of inflation. The price stability and prosperity of these countries are the product of governmental economic policies and productive, globally competitive economies.

One of the most serious concerns in the high-income countries today is the persistence of high unemployment through periods of economic growth. Figure 3-3 shows the link between unemployment and the business cycle in Canada since World War II. Note that unemployment remained high for more than a year after the recessions of the early 1980s and the early 1990s.

INCOME AND PURCHASING POWER

disposable income
The balance of income that individual consumers have left after paying taxes.

purchasing power
The potential ability of consumers to buy goods and services at the prices recommended by marketers.

discretionary income
Money which consumers have left after paying taxes and covering essential personal and household expenditures.

foreign exchange rate
The price at which one currency may be exchanged for another.

Inflation and recession are important concerns of marketers because both affect consumers' income, especially their disposable income. **Disposable income** is what people have left of the money earned from work or from interest on their investments after payment of taxes. Disposable income is a measure of consumers' **purchasing power**—that is, the amount of money consumers have available to buy products or services at the prices recommended by marketers. When income increases faster than prices, consumers have abundant purchasing power but when prices rise faster than income (as in an inflationary period), purchasing power falls.

Also of interest to marketers is **discretionary income**—money consumers have left after paying taxes and necessary household costs. Discretionary income, which is used for such "nonessentials" as videotapes and CDs, extra clothing, or vacation trips, is not evenly distributed.

FOREIGN EXCHANGE RATES

When consumers buy goods and services in global markets, their buying power depends on foreign exchange rates. A country's **foreign exchange rate** is the amount in another country's currency which its own unit of currency will trade for. For example, if you can exchange 2 Canadian dollars for 1 pound sterling (£) or 1 Canadian dollar for 50 pence, the exchange rate can be expressed in one of two ways:

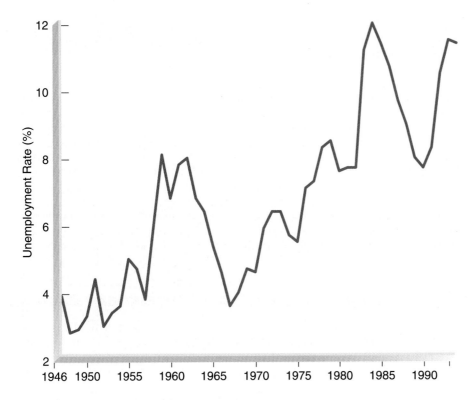

Figure 3-3
Unemployed as a
Percentage of the
Labor Force
1946–1993

Source: Canadian
Statistical Review: Historial
Summary, 1970, Statistics
Canada, p.50; *Canadian*
Economic Observer,
Historial Statistical
Supplement, Statistics
Canada, 1943/1994,
p. 36.

£1 = $2 Cdn
or
$1 Cdn = 50 pence

At that exchange rate, how much would a machine tool that sells for $40,000 cost a U.K. buyer? The formula:

$$\frac{40{,}000 \text{ (price in Cdn \$)}}{x \text{ (price in £ sterling)}} = \frac{2 \text{ (\$ Cdn)}}{1 \text{ (£ sterling)}}$$

$$2x = 40{,}000$$
$$x = 20{,}000, \text{ or } £20{,}000$$

What happens when the exchange rate changes? If the pound gets stronger so that £1 can be traded for Cdn $2.5 and the machine tool still costs Cdn $40,000 , you will pay only £16,000:

$$\frac{40{,}000 \text{ (price in Cdn \$)}}{x \text{ (price in £ sterling)}} = \frac{2.5 \text{ (\$ Cdn)}}{1 \text{ (£ sterling)}}$$

$$2.5x = 40{,}000$$
$$x = 16{,}000, \text{ or } £16{,}000$$

The brand manager responsible for machine tool sales in the United Kingdom will be very happy with this change, because the Canadian products are now much more competitively priced. But the change in exchange rates also means that Canadians who want to buy British-made products have to pay 25 percent more than they did before. When a country has a strong currency, imported goods are less expensive, but that country's exports become more expensive for foreign consumers. A weak currency has the opposite effect: It makes imports more expensive for the country, but gives its exporters a price advantage on the world market.

Companies that fail to respond promptly to fluctuations in the value of their home-country currency risk losing market share in competitive global markets. Strong companies protect against exchange rate fluctuations by setting prices according to multiple factors, including competition, marketplace objectives, price elasticity of demand, and the company's long-term plans for penetrating a market (see Chapters 16 and 17). For example, as the yen appreciated in value from 360 to the U.S. dollar in the 1970s to a little over 100 to the dollar in the early 1990s, Japanese companies protected their market share in the United States by reducing their prices in yen. Instead of passing on the full impact of a stronger yen to foreign buyers, Japanese firms accepted smaller profit margins and concentrated on reducing costs and increasing quality to make their goods attractive. As we see next, however, the newly developing economy of Russia is not yet in a position to make this kind of adjustment.

BEHIND THE SCENES
IS THERE A MARKET IN RUSSIA?[1]

Are the Russians as poor as many authorities claim? A recent book by Andrei Illarionov, Richard Fay, and Peter Orszag suggests otherwise. According to this trio of advisers to the Russian government, the citizens of the new Russia are better off than we have been led to suppose.

As of mid-1993, the average Russian wage was 23,500 rubles per month, a mere U.S. $25 at the prevailing exchange rate. This equates to an annual salary of U.S. $300, lower than the annual wage in all but the very poorest countries of the world. For a nation that recently held superpower status, these numbers are startling indeed. How can we explain them?

For starters, what is left out of all simple calculations based on foreign exchange rates is the actual purchasing power of the currency at home—the ability of that currency to buy goods and services domestically. The purchasing power of the Russian ruble in Russia is much greater than that implied by the current foreign exchange rate. One reason for the difficulty in comparison is that many essential goods are so inexpensive in Russia that they are virtually free. In Moscow, for example, 98 percent of the private individual's cost for gas, heating, and electricity is subsidized by the city government.

In the old (communist) Russia there were severe shortages of food even when people had the money to pay for it. Today Russians have consumer options they never had before, even though many goods, including food, are quite expensive for the average person. In short, it does not appear that Russian living conditions are any worse today—in some cases, at least, they may be considerably improved.

Anyone who stands on a Moscow sidewalk for a while—and one of your authors has done this—will notice a surprising number of BMWs and Mercedes cruising by. Clearly there is a sizeable dollar economy operating in the country that does not show up in the official statistics. Who are the people who can afford these expensive cars and other luxury items? According to recent articles by Aslund and Galuszka, they are "Russia's newly rich *biznezmen*, a small group of wheeler-dealers who often operate in dollars . . . entrepreneurs, people importing and exporting metals, oil, chemicals, minerals—whatever." They are also criminals of the ordinary variety, for Russia has a powerful underworld. And some former Communist bosses have been able, through very shady means, to get cheap money to back their new entrepreneurial enterprises.

Still, what about the "little people"? In Moscow today you can step under the familiar yellow arch and buy a Big Mac in either rubles or dollars. Whatever currency you use, this now-global fast food will cost half of what you would pay in Canada. Nevertheless, if you compare the purchasing power of the average Russian to that of the average Canadian, you will see why the Big Mac is still a rare treat for most Russians.

So, is there a market for U.S., Canadian, and other foreign products in Russia or not? Yes there is, but it is small, and there are major political risks for any investor. Former U.S. Ambassador Robert Strauss once remarked: "If I were a young man with one million dollars to invest and wanted to make a lot of money, I'd invest it in Russia. And if I had ten million dollars to invest, I'd still invest one million in Russia." If you were a marketing manager for consumer goods, would you move into the Russian market today? What information might you want to gather before making such a move?

Rolls is Rolling Now in Moscow

Rolls-Royce opened its first showroom in Moscow in the summer of 1993. Potential customers wearing evening dress sipped cocktails and moved around the floor to live Dixieland, admiring shiny new Rollses and Bentleys ranging in price from U.S. $145,000 to more than U.S. $300,000. The dealers who opened the franchise had done their market research by standing on a Moscow street corner watching luxury cars go by—and there were a lot. When they saw no Rollses, Peter G. Terian and his partners knew they had a chance to win market share.

THE COMPETITIVE ENVIRONMENT

A free-market economy depends on competition to motivate firms to create greater value for their customers. The *competitive environment*, the subject of chapter objective number three, includes all of the firms that vie with one another by offering products and services to the same consumers or target markets. Competition is good for consumers because it makes firms eager to please with new products and reasonable prices. But why does competition persist?

MARKET SHARE

market share
The percentage of the total market held by a particular company or brand.

Competition is a struggle for **market share,** or the percentage of the total market held by a particular company, type of company, or brand. As noted in chapter objective three, market share has an important effect on a firm's external marketing environment. Because there is more than one type of market, when we discuss market share we need to define what market we're talking about. For example, in the early 1990s Philips had the second largest share of Europe's second largest electronics market, but only a tiny share of the world personal computer market. Electrolux, the Swedish appliance company, has a leading share of the European major appliance market, but it runs a distant third behind General Electric and Whirlpool in the same market in North America.

As industries globalize, the important market is the *global market*. RCA learned this too late. The company long believed it was a leader in the television business because it had the largest share of the North American television market. It failed to notice that it was a distant third in the world market until it was overcome by foreign competition and went out of business.

Many companies have adopted strategies intended to achieve world leadership in their industries. In the early 1980s, under the leadership of Jack Welch, General Electric articulated a strategy of being number one or number two in the *world* in every business it was in. For every business that did not make that grade, Welch said, "We are going to fix it, sell it, or close it."[2] He was determined to avoid the blindsiding possible when a company has a strong home country position in an emerging global industry.

COMPETITIVE STRUCTURE

Looking at the market shares of the various firms in an industry enables us to determine the competitive structure of that industry, which is the topic of the second half of chapter objective number three. The four main types of competitive structures are monopoly, oligopoly, perfect competition, and monopolistic competition. As you can see from Table 3-2, these structures are distinguished by the number of competing companies they include, the amount of market share each holds, and their ability either singly or in collaboration to influence prices.

monopoly
A competitive structure characterized by a single seller in a market.

Monopoly   A government or private **monopoly** exists when there is only one seller in a market. Your electric and gas company, for example, holds the total market for these needed utilities in your area. Unless regulated by the government, a monopoly firm has an absolute influence on price. The products of monopolists always cost somewhat more than these same products would if produced in a highly competitive market.

An example of a near-monopoly is Monsanto's NutraSweet, which currently accounts for most of the North American market for noncaloric sweeteners. (This market will soon become more competitive because NutraSweet's patent is running out.) Marketing activities for private monopolies such as

TABLE 3-2   INDUSTRY STRUCTURE

Type of Structure	Monopoly	Oligopoly	Monopolistic Competition	Perfect Competition
Number of sellers	1	Few	Many	No limit
Barriers to entry	Absolute	High	Moderate	Low
Nature of product	Few substutites	Open	Differentiated	Homogeneous, no differences
Market share/seller	100%	High	Low	Fragmented
Influence on price	Absolute	High	Lower	Low
Examples	Electric & gas public utilities; PTTs*	Automobile, detergent telephone companies (Bell Canada, AGT, Sprint)	Jeans, soft drinks cigarettes	Commodity markets: wheat, oxide glycol

*PTTs = Postal and Telecommunications Organizations.

power utilities are usually directed toward reassuring the public that the company is worthy of its trust and support. The gas industry, for example, promotes natural gas as a clean, plentiful source of energy, and the nuclear power industry promotes the idea that nuclear energy is more reliable than imported oil.

Oligopoly An **oligopoly** is a competitive environment with only a few sellers, each of whom has a substantial market share and considerable influence on prices. Most industries are oligopolies. For example, the infant formula market in North America is dominated by Abbott Laboratories and Bristol-Myers, both of which employ large numbers of sales representatives to call regularly on pediatricians and other physicians who treat infants. These firms have won the allegiance of physicians, who tend to stick with the tried-and-true. Carnation and Gerber have both tried to break into the infant formula market by marketing directly to new parents, but so far have had little success, because it is almost always a physician who recommends a particular formula to parents.

The North American—and, increasingly, worldwide—soft drink market is dominated by Coca Cola and Pepsi Cola, whose flagship brands hold the lion's share of the dark-cola market. These companies also market a line of clear sodas and fruit-flavored drinks. Niche-market companies can prosper in the soft drink category, but none has ever come close to challenging the dominance of these two industry leaders. In Canada, Lyons Tetley Canada currently controls 48 percent of the iced tea market and is marketing aggressively to prevent its market leadership position from weakening.

The marketing communication of an oligopoly leader often focuses on differentiating the good or service offered from the competition, while the challengers typically focus on service or price. Avis, for instance, relied for years on the slogan, "We try harder" to capitalize on its number two position in the car rental industry, while Sprint in its challenge to Bell Canada has relied more

oligopoly
A competitive environment in which each of a small group of sellers has substantial market share and influence on price.

73

and more on price as the differentiating weapon in an industry where most consumers do not perceive a quality difference between competitive offerings.

Perfect Competition When a market contains so many competitors that none of them can achieve an advantage over the others in terms of price, quality, or size, there is said to be **perfect competition**. Examples of perfectly competitive markets are those for agricultural products and chemical commodities. To flour companies buying raw materials, winter wheat is pretty much winter wheat. To a feedstock purchaser, oxide glycol is oxide glycol. When the price of winter wheat changes, it changes for all buyers. When the price of oxide glycol goes down in Hong Kong, it goes down worldwide.

Monopolistic Competition The extremes of perfect competition and true monopoly are relatively rare. Most businesses operate in a state of **monopolistic competition**, an industry structure that combines characteristics of monopolies and perfect competition. Like perfectly competitive markets, these "imperfectly" competitive markets have many sellers, and like monopoly markets, monopolistically competitive markets allow sellers to influence price to some degree. Sellers in these markets gain share influence by differentiating their products from the essentially very similar products of their competitors. Finding a way to make this differentiation is the heart of modern marketing—for example, marketers of jeans have managed to differentiate Levi's from Lees from Guess? from Calvins, and so on. Moreover, by narrowly defining its market, a monopolistically competitive firm could be said to have 100 percent of its targeted market.

THE PHYSICAL ENVIRONMENT

As the world population continues to increase, people are becoming concerned about their **physical environment**—the geologic, atmospheric, biological world in which they live. General interest in *ecology*, the study of the detrimental effects of modern civilization on the physical environment with a view toward prevention or reversal, has greatly increased. Marketers alert to these changes know that conservation of the physical environment is important for them, not only from the perspective of social responsibility, but also in terms of their success in the marketplace.

ENVIRONMENTAL CONCERN AND ECONOMIC DEVELOPMENT

In general, the lower a country's per capita income, the less concern it manifests about the physical environment. Visit any rapidly growing low- or lower-middle-income country like Mexico or China, and in the cities you will have a difficult and unpleasant time breathing. It is only when average income rises significantly and people are living better that they feel they can afford to take the measures necessary to protect their environment.

This raises an ethical issue: If a company headquartered in a high-income country is operating in a country like China or Mexico, should it adhere to the environmental standards that it must meet at home or should it adopt local practices that may include serious pollution of the air, water, and earth? If the foreign company chooses the ecologically correct course of action, it may be disadvantaged in the marketplace because its local competitors, who are not observing the higher standards, will have lower costs.

Because of the greater concern about the environment in high-income countries like Canada and the United States, companies operating in these countries often go beyond mere compliance with the law to create environ-

---

perfect competition
A competitive environment in which there are so many competitors that none holds an advantage over the others in price, quality, or size.

monopolistic competition
A competitive environment in which a reasonably large number of sellers compete on the basis of differentiated products.

physical environment
The geologic, atmospheric, and biological world in which we live.

mentally friendly products. For instance, The Body Shop (see "The Body Shop," Integrative Case at the end of the book) has positioned itself as concerned about ecological issues and its products as environmentally safe. This credo appeals to high-income customers and is thus an important part of The Body Shop's competitive advantage.

POLLUTION

Pollution is the contamination of soil, water, or atmosphere by the discharge of harmful substances from industrial or other facilities. Marketers have a great opportunity to create value for consumers with products and manufacturing processes that do not pollute the environment. Consider the issue of packaging: when marketers reduce the amount of material used in their packaging they lessen the waste that must be absorbed by the environment. For example, laundry detergents have been repackaged and sold in highly concentrated form, and many CD manufacturers have eliminated the large cardboard sleeve that was common.

A major source of environmental pollution, the gasoline-powered internal combustion engine, has been engineered to run cleaner, and oil companies have created cleaner-burning fuels for both automobiles and trucks. The nuclear power industry promotes nuclear power as more environmentally friendly than other power sources (see Exhibit 3-2). Manufacturers of air

Exhibit 3-2
The Environment First

This ad from the AECL tells us that its CANDU nuclear power system is not damaging to the environment. These nuclear plants emit no greenhouse gases and do not cause acid rain. As incomes rise, countries become more and more concerned about environmental issues—such as air quality—and the AECL markets its product according to these concerns.

conditioners and refrigerators have redesigned their products to eliminate the use of Freon, which is damaging to the biosphere.

Technology created the environmental pollution we confront today, and technology must become the principal instrument for cleaning up our environment. It is possible to have both a clean environment and a high standard of living, and marketers contribute to this goal by educating consumers and by giving them environmentally sound products.

THE LEGAL AND REGULATORY ENVIRONMENTS

Every country has legal and regulatory environments that are unique and constantly evolving. Exhibit 3-3 shows one country's sensitivity to this. Consider Europe. Many of the most significant European laws and regulations date back to the Treaty of Rome (1958), which laid the ground work for the European Union. The terms of this treaty removed many barriers to trade across national borders in Europe and provided for a common market among member nations.

Concern about competitiveness is one of the motivators behind legal and regulatory controls on business, the topic of the fourth chapter objective. The *legal environment* consists of laws passed by legislative bodies, judicial rulings on these laws, and long-standing customs. Table 3-3 lists major laws restricting business activities in Canada, and Table 3-4 lists some important court proceedings involving Canadian regulatory laws.

Government officials are also active in the *regulatory environment*. A number of municipal, provincial, and federal agencies enforce laws or set guidelines for ethical business conduct, and a wide variety of laws and regulations require firms to provide accurate information about their products or face stiff penalties. The professional association of state attorneys general reviews possibly misleading advertising in a number of industries, including the airline, pork, and cigarette industries.

Nongovernmental agencies, trade associations, self-regulating industry groups, and groups of concerned citizens also help to regulate the behavior of businesses. An example of **self-regulation** or the policing of an industry by an entity made up of the industry members, is the Better Business Bureau (BBB). This nationwide organization formed by business and industry provides consumers with information about local businesses and serves as an arbitrator when consumers have complaints about its member businesses. The BBB helped to establish the National Advertising Review Council (NARC), the self-regulatory arm of the advertising industry that is regarded as its most comprehensive and effective investigator.

On the other side of the fence, a number of consumer groups have been formed to pressure business and industry to police its products. The Parents' Music Resource Center (PMRC), for example, has pressured the recording industry to place warning labels on albums, compact discs, and cassettes containing profane language or sexually explicit lyrics. PMRC has also persuaded some retailers not to stock certain albums in their stores because of cover art or lyric content. Regardless of how they originate, laws and regulations concerning business have three basic goals: to ensure free competition, to protect consumers, and to preserve business property.

One way in which the legal-regulatory environment can affect marketing is by the imposition of special taxes on certain products. Most high-income countries have relatively high "sin" taxes on cigarettes and alcohol both to raise revenue and to discourage people from smoking and drinking.

self-regulation
Activities on the part of an industry to police itself.

THE RULES, REGULATIONS AND CUSTOMS OF 130 COUNTRIES AROUND THE WORLD AREN'T FOREIGN TO US. Most of AIG's 34,000 people are native to the lands in which they work. So they have a deep understanding of local laws, practices and traditions. They know how to design insurance products specifically for their own markets and can respond quickly to changing conditions and customer needs. Together they form a unique network of service capabilities. Because the quality of our services to clients is a product of the number and experience of our people. And that is something no one else can match in this fast-changing world.

AIG WORLD LEADERS IN INSURANCE AND FINANCIAL SERVICES.
American International Group, Inc., Dept. A, 70 Pine Street, New York, NY 10270.

Exhibit 3-3
Marketing Your Knowledge and Experience

Understanding local laws and rules is essential for business success in any country. AIG, a global insurance and financial services company, markets itself as having special expertise in local business regulations because in every country in which it maintains offices it employs local personnel.

TABLE 3-3	REGULATORY LEGISLATION IN CANADA

The Competition Act became law in Canada in June 1986, and represents a major overhaul of the former Combines Investigation Act. The Competition Act contains both criminal and non-criminal provisions. Criminal offences include conspiracy, bid rigging, discriminatory and predatory pricing, price maintenance, and misleading advertising or deceptive marketing practices. Prosecutions are brought before criminal courts where strict rules of evidence apply. Non-criminal reviewable matters include mergers, abuse of dominant position, refusal to deal, consignment selling, exclusive dealing, tied selling, market restriction and delivered pricing. These matters when referred by the Director of Investigation & Research, are reviewed by the Competition Tribunal under non-criminal law standards.

The Director is responsible for enforcing the Competition Act in a fair, effective and timely manner. The Director is Head of the Federal Bureau of Competition policy, part of Consumer & Corporate Affairs Canada. Violations of the criminal provisions of the Act are prosecuted by the Attorney General of Canada.

TABLE 3-3	REGULATORY LEGISLATION IN CANADA (CONTINUED)

Part VI: Criminal Offences

Conspiracy has been a criminal offence under Canada's competition law since the original legislation was passed in 1889. Penalties now include a fine of as much as $10 million or up to 5 years imprisonment, or both. Any conspiracy, agreement or arrangement that would, if implemented, lessen competition unduly by, for example, fixing prices or preventing new competitors from entering the market, is a criminal offence.

Bid Rigging: an agreement between parties whereby one or more bidders will refrain from submitting bids in response to a call for tenders, or bids are submitted which have been arranged between parties.

Price Discrimination & Predatory Pricing exists when a supplier charges different prices to competitors who purchase similar volumes of an article. Predatory pricing infractions fall into two categories. The first is selling products in one region of Canada at prices lower than in another region (after taking into account transportation costs) for the purposes of lessening competition substantially or eliminating a competitor. The second is selling products at unreasonably low prices for the same purpose.

Price Maintenance: an attempt by suppliers to influence upward prices charged by those supplied, or to discourage price reduction, by agreement, threat or promise. It is also illegal to refuse to supply a product or to discriminate against any other person because of their low pricing policy. Likewise, it is illegal to attempt to induce a supplier to engage in price maintenance.

Misleading Advertising or Deceptive Marketing Practices: Representations which are false or misleading in a material respect are prohibited. Unsubstantiated performance and durability claims, misleading warranties and misrepresentations as to regular price fall into this category.

Promotional contests are subject to the Act. The person conducting a promotional contest must ensure disclosure of the number and approximate value of any prizes offered. There must also be disclosure of any facts known to the advertiser that substantially affect the chances of winning. Distribution of prizes must not be unduly delayed. Selection of participants or distribution of prizes must be made on the basis of skill or at random.

The Act also prohibits double ticketing (where the higher of two prices marked on the product is charged), pyramid selling, sale above advertised price and bait and switch selling (when a product is advertised at a bargain price, but a reasonable supply of it is not available).

Part VII: Non-Criminal Reviewable Matters

Mergers: A merger is essentially the acquisition of one or more business entities by another. The Act applies to every merger in Canada (large or small) even if it involves foreign owned or controlled companies.

Companies are obliged to notify the Bureau of a proposed merger when two thresholds are met. The parties (or any affiliates) must have total assets in Canada or gross annual revenues from sales in, from or into Canada over $400 million. As well, the value of the assets to be acquired or gross revenues from sales generated by those assets must exceed $35 million. In the case of corporate amalgamation, the second threshold is $70 million.

Following notification, the parties are required to wait either seven or twenty one days before completing the transaction. The Director conducts an examination during this period to determine if the proposal raises any competition concerns.

Abuse of Dominant Position. Examples of such behavior would include:
(i) acquisition of a customer who would otherwise be available to a competitor to impede a competitor's entry into the market.
(ii) use of product brands on a temporary basis to discipline or eliminate a competitor;
(iii) purchase of products to prevent the reduction of existing price levels; and
(iv) selling articles at a price lower than the acquisition cost to discipline or eliminate a competitor.

For this provision to apply, one or more persons must substantially control a class of business in Canada. They must be engaged in or currently engaging in, anti-competitive acts having the effect of preventing or lessening competition substantially.

TABLE 3-3   REGULATORY LEGISLATION IN CANADA
(CONTINUED)

Refusal to Deal: The Tribunal may issue an order if it finds a party is substantially affected or precluded from carrying on business due to its inability to obtain adequate supplies of a product because of insufficient competition among suppliers.

Consignment Selling is the practice of supplying products to a dealer who only pays for what sells and is permitted to return unsold products without penalty. The Tribunal must find that the practice was introduced to control the price at which a dealer supplies the product or to discriminate between consignees and other dealers.

Exclusive Dealing: Exclusive dealing is the practice of a supplier requiring or inducing a customer to purchase products primarily from him/her or to refrain from dealing in another product.

Tied Selling is a practice whereby a supplier requires a customer to acquire a second product from him/her as a condition of being granted a supply of the first product or the supplier requires the customer to refrain from distributing, in conjunction with the tying product, another product not manufactured by that supplier.

Market Restriction is a practice whereby a supplier of a product, as a condition of supplying the product, requires the customer to offer the product in a defined geographical market only or the supplier extracts a penalty if the customer breaches this condition.

The key factor about exclusive dealing, tied selling and market restriction is that the practice will only be challenged if it has a substantial impact on competition.

Delivered Pricing is the practice of refusing a customer delivery of an article on the same trade terms as other customers in the same location.

Specialization Agreements typically involve a situation where two parties manufacture the same two articles and each agrees to discontinue producing one article in order to individually specialize in the production of the other.

Source: An Overview of Canada's Competition Act, Director of Investigation & Research, Ministry of Supplies & Services Canada, 1993.

TABLE 3-4   COURT PROCEEDINGS

June 25, 1991: IFA Intercontinental Fine Arts Ltd. was fined $100,000 following a conviction for making misleading representation regarding art prints.

Sept. 4, 1991: 139834 Canada Inc., carrying on business as Distribution Copie Centrale/Distribution Copy Central, was fined $120,000 for misleading telephone solicitations promoting the sale of photocopier toner.

Jan. 22, 1992: Donald Mercer Cormie was convicted of making a misleading statement in the Principal Group's 1985 Annual Review. He was fined $500,000—the highest fine ever against an individual under the Act.

Sept. 6, 1991: Canadian Oxygen Limited and Union Carbide Canada Ltd. pleaded guilty to conspiring to fix the price of compressed gases sold or supplied in bulk liquid form, and were fined $700,000 and $1.7 million respectively. On September 13, 1991, Canadian Liquid Air Ltd. and Liquid Carbonic Inc. pleaded guilty to similar charges and were fined $1.7 million each. On October 18, 1991, two corporate executives pleaded guilty in relation to their roles in the conspiracy and were fined $75,000 each. A fifth company Air Products Canada Ltd. pleaded guilty on October 25, 1991, and was fined $200,000.

Source: Annual Report for the year ended March 31, 1992, Director of Investigation & Research, Minister of Supply & Services Canada, 1992.

Cigarette manufacturers are now required by law to display warning messages on their products (see Exhibit 3-4), but in early 1994 cigarette taxes dropped in some Canadian provinces in an effort to stem the tide of cigarette smuggling from the United States. Based on the Canadian experience, it is estimated that an additional tax of about $2.00 a pack (which would bring the retail price up to about $4.00 a pack in the United States) would result in a 25 percent decline in smoking in the United States. Even so, the additional tax would increase the total spending on cigarettes, and the increase would go to the government in the form of tax revenue. Why do you think the U.S. government has been so reluctant to raise this tax? Why do you think that some Canadian provinces have lowered tobacco tax while others have not?

ENSURING COMPETITION

With the explosive growth of many industries in the United States after the Civil War companies grew larger and larger. In 1890, concerned about the power of these huge firms to drive out smaller competitors and to reap exces-

Exhibit 3-4
From Endorsement to Warning

Today, when all cigarette packs sold in Canada carry a statement such as "Cigarettes cause strokes and heart disease," "Cigarettes cause cancer," and "Smoking can kill you," it is hard to believe that tobacco companies like the manufacturer of Camels once advertised their products as not only endorsed but enthusiastically used by physicians.

sive profits, the U.S. government took its first major step toward curbing such behavior by passing the Sherman Act. Over the next seventy-five years other laws strengthened this act.

Antitrust enforcement varies, to some degree, according to whether the political environment is pro- or antibusiness. Thus, the 1980s saw widespread corporate mergers and buyouts and a lessening of governmental control. Nonetheless, in the U.S.A. Coca Cola was denied permission to acquire Dr. Pepper, and Pepsi Cola failed in its bid to acquire Seven-Up from Philip Morris because of the U.S. Justice Department's concerns about potential monopoly situations.

PROTECTING CONSUMERS

Many laws are designed to protect consumers from unethical marketing practices. In Canada, Consumer and Corporate Affairs, established in 1967, creates and enforces regulations that protect consumer interests. Consumer and Corporate Affairs' legislation has five main objectives. First, to protect consumers against dangerous products, legislation such as the Food and Drugs Act, The Hazardous Products Act, and the Motor Vehicle Safety Act have been established. Second, acts such as the Weights and Measures Act and The Competition Act are designed to protect the consumer against fraudulent practices, such as misleading advertising. Third, Consumer and Corporate Affairs protects consumers against unscrupulous contracts which contain unreasonable terms. Fourth, the Consumer Packaging and Labelling Act aims to ensure the consumer better access to information. Finally, community legal service clinics and provincial legal aid provide consumers with advice and access to conflict resolution agencies.[3]

In the United States, the Clayton Act (1914) and the Robinson-Patman Act (1936) forbid certain pricing policies, and the Federal Trade Commission Act (1914) and the Wheeler-Lea Act (1938) mandate truthfulness in advertising. Some laws are industry specific, like the Federal Cigarette Labeling and Advertising Act of 1965, which requires cigarette manufacturers to put health warnings on their product. Congress created a number of government agencies to enforce all these laws: the Federal Trade Commission (FTC), the Food and Drug Administration (FDA), the U.S. Department of Agriculture (USDA), the Federal Communications Commission (FCC), and the Environmental Protection Agency (EPA).

These agencies regulate marketing activities in the areas of antimonopoly (antitrust) and consumer protection. For example, the FTC, which was created in 1914, has broad enforcement powers over a wide range of marketing activities. It can issue complaints, consent decrees (administrative orders in which an individual or organization consents to limit its activity in the way spelled out in the decree), and cease-and-desist-orders to organizations whose marketing activities are alleged to violate the law in some way. The FDA oversees a drug-testing program designed to ensure that drugs are both safe for human consumption and effective before they are marketed. The FCC is in charge of issuing licences to broadcasters, who are required to meet certain standards of community responsibility.

The European Union presents a particularly challenging environment for the global marketer. In principle, Europe is a single market. In practice, the harmonization of regulations in EU member countries is taking the "Eurocrats" a long time to accomplish. Consider the homey matter of breakfast food. The Dutch, like many North Americans, spread jam on bread or toast for breakfast, and therefore usually prefer smooth jam. The French, however, like to eat jam out of a jar with a spoon, and therefore prefer lumpy jam. These minor cultural eccentricities can present some sticky problems to anyone wanting to sell jam in both the Netherlands and France. The Eurocrats have been trying to set jam standards since 1959, and the issue isn't as petty as it might seem. For example, sulfur dioxide coolant was once used to preserve the fruit that goes into jam. Countries like the Netherlands and Germany, which import most of their fruit, naturally wanted liberal standards; Italy, however, wanted to minimize the use of chemical additives. Fortunately, advances in refrigeration technology had solved this particular problem by the mid-1980s.

Considering that it took nearly twenty-five years to break this logjam, the Eurocrats decided their had to be a better way to regulate the thousands of other products, both consumer and industrial, that are marketed in the European Union. Around 1985, the European Commission, the EU organization responsible for the implementation of the treaty agreements, made a breakthrough: It decided that each nation could sets its own health and safety standards and that any product satisfying those standards could test itself on a relatively open market. Take tractor seats. "For twenty years," says one commission official, "we beavered away trying to define the perfect tractor seat. We finally abandoned that, and we've found the market produces a lot of fine tractor seats."

The result is that numerous national trade regulations remain intact. For example, spaghetti can be made from several types of wheat, but Italy requires it to be made of durum wheat (which happens to be prevalent in the country). Taking advantage of its right to set its own health standards, France demands more Vitamin B_1 in Gatorade than Italy does and won't let Coca-Cola put Nutrasweet in Diet Coke marketed in France.

PRESERVING BUSINESS PROPERTY

Governments seek to encourage invention by issuing patents to inventors that give them the right to control the use of their inventions. Similarly, copyright law protects computer software and literary, artistic, and musical productions by giving the holder of the copyright the exclusive right to reproduce, publish, and sell the copyrighted material for a certain number of years. Finally, firms may trademark a brand name or symbol or both and thereby gain the exclusive right to use these names or images commercially. We will discuss such government protection for business in greater detail in Chapter 10.

DEREGULATION AND PRIVATIZATION

During the 1980s national leaders like Brian Mulroney, Ronald Reagan, and Margaret Thatcher sought to reduce the regulation of many industries. The **deregulation,** or relaxation or elimination of regulations and laws governing such industries as communications, airlines, and banking, created both new opportunities and new problems for marketers and consumers.

One form of deregulation that has become popular throughout the world in recent years is **privatization**, or the transfer of government-owned and controlled major enterprises to private owners. In the United Kingdom, for instance, the state-owned telephone monopoly British Telecom was sold to the public and is now a private company. The French are actively planning to privatize state-owned companies like Renault, the auto and truck manufacturer.

The greatest movement toward privatization today is in Eastern Europe and the former USSR (now called the Commonwealth of Independent States), where for decades every large enterprise was state-owned. After the collapse of socialism there was almost universal agreement that economic success would

deregulation
The practice of relaxing or eliminating laws and regulations governing specific industries.

privatization
The conversion of a government-owned firm to private ownership.

be impossible without private ownership and a free market. The countries of the former Soviet bloc are now undertaking the enormous task of transferring enterprises from state to private ownership.

Before the deregulation of long-distance phone services in Canada, long-distance traffic was provided by an agreement between the domestic carriers (Bell Canada, AGT, Sask Tel, MTS, B.C. Tel) and Teleglobe Canada (then a Crown corporation). Today these one-time monopolies must compete with companies such as Sprint Canada, Unitel, Telnet, and STN in the long-distance market, and, as a result, long-distance rates have come down. In the United States in 1982, AT&T, or "Ma Bell," agreed to split off the "Baby Bells"—its seven regional telephone networks—as separate companies, thus relinquishing its control of local telephone service as well. The regionals are now engaged in all sorts of businesses—from cable-TV ventures to equipment manufacturing—which has made this industry much more dynamic than it was in the sleepy era of regulation.

Deregulation has had costs in other industries. The Canadian and American airline industries, for example, have gone through a brutal period since being deregulated and the effects can be clearly seen in the damaging battle between Air Canada and Canadian Airlines for market share. In the United States, deregulation encouraged new entrants into the business and spectacular price wars that eventually demolished some of the oldest airlines, like Pan Am. Of all the new entrants, perhaps the most dramatic in its rise and fall was People Express. Begun in the early 1980s, People Express marketed itself as a very low cost, "no frills" airline. This combination was very successful in attracting people who travel for personal reasons, but could not make a dent among business travelers, who prize reliability and comfort. This failure led to People's eventual bankruptcy, but by that time its pioneering low-price policy had had a tremendous effect on the market. In this new environment airline ticket prices on many routes are cheaper than they were under regulation, but on routes where there is little competition prices are often higher.

As more airlines responded to market opportunities with price-cutting, weaker rivals charged that the price cutters were engaging in predatory pricing. What is the difference between predatory and aggressive proconsumer pricing? According to the U.S. Supreme Court, a plaintiff charging a competitor with predatory pricing must show that the competitor's pricing practice would ultimately cause prices to rise, thus compensating the alleged predator for slashing prices in the first place.[4]

The behavior of deregulated businesses has prompted charges of unfair competition and calls for reregulation in other industries. Heading the list of industries that will probably see more regulation in the future is North American banking. Banking deregulation in the 1980s was not accompanied by the lifting of federal deposit insurance for depositors, which would have been politically impossible. The effect was that managers at a number of savings and loan associations and commercial banks used federally insured deposits to rush into risky investment areas now open to them in the hope of reaping very high profits. When the Canadian and U.S. economies—particularly the real estate market—declined in the late 1980s, they took a number of these financial institutions, and the taxpayers (remember the deposit guarantees), down with them. In 1994 the U.S. federal government was still spending taxpayer dollars to clean up the huge mess. Given this costly experience, government regulators are expected to play a major role in the banking market in the years to come.

Marketers attempt to influence factors in both the legal and regulatory environments that affect their activities through lobbying. Companies and industry groups hire lobbyists to represent their interests to federal, state, and local officials. For example, the automobile industry has lobbied U.S. Congress for years to relax federal pollution controls and mileage requirements established by the Environmental Protection Agency for the nation's automobiles. On the other hand, sensitive to the growing concern about the quality of our environment, other industries are marketing a number of environmentally safer products.

TRADE POLICY

The increasingly global nature of business has forced the governments of many countries to reexamine their trade policies. National trade policies can help or hurt globalizing companies because by discouraging or encouraging certain types of trade they affect both these companies' opportunities and their threats.

Imposing tariffs, duties, and import/export quotas discourages free trade, but such measures are popular with companies (and workers) that are losing domestic market share to foreign competitors. Pressure from the U.S. auto industry, for example, led to the adoption of voluntary export quotas by Japanese manufacturers and encouraged them to set up manufacturing and assembly operations in the United States that would employ American workers. By establishing plants in North America, these Japanese companies have moved toward creating transnational as opposed to national enterprises.

THE SOCIOCULTURAL ENVIRONMENT

Laws and regulatory agencies are just one aspect of society's effect on business. Social institutions—economic, family, education, government, and religious—interact to form a culture, a common set of beliefs, attitudes, values, and behavior. We will discuss the roots of these societal elements in greater detail in Chapter 6. But first let's see how the combination of institutions and beliefs that make up the **sociocultural environment** affect marketing activities, the topic of the fifth chapter objective.

With increasing travel and faster communications, many national attitudes toward style in such things as clothing, music, and food and drink are becoming international, even universal. This internationalization of culture has moved very quickly, thanks to the multinational companies that have capitalized on opportunities to extend their products into global markets. Coke and Pepsi, Levi Strauss, Kentucky Fried Chicken, IBM, and Apple are just a few companies breaking down cultural distinctiveness by their expansion into new world markets.

Differences do remain, however, and international marketers must adapt to these differences to be successful. Any attempt to reach a foreign market requires a combination of tough-mindedness and generosity: the tough-mindedness to put aside the marketer's own cultural ways temporarily, and the generosity to accept and appreciate other ways of life and points of view. The international marketer needs both these attitudes to recognize diversity and understand how others' attitudes, beliefs, and values shape their behavior in the marketplace and, in turn, are shaped by the marketplace.

DEMOGRAPHICS

Marketers need to take account of the demographic changes that occur within cultural frameworks, usually rather gradually. The **demographic environment** includes such measurable characteristics of the population as size, geographic location, age, gender, race, income, and education. As you

sociocultural environment
The beliefs, attitudes, values, and social institutions of the society and culture in which marketing activities take place.

demographic environment
Objective, measurable population characteristics such as size, geographic location, age, gender, race, income, and education.

will see in Chapters 6 and 8, marketers often use demographics to identify customers and markets.

In the developed, postindustrial countries, for example, low birth rates have combined with increasing life expectancy to create a rapidly expanding market of upper-age adults. Marketers have already begun to develop and sell products aimed at this market—for example, travel packages, "adult community" housing, financial services, and so on. The increase in the percentage of single adults and single parents also affects marketing strategies. Manufacturers of products ranging from autos to furniture target the young singles market. This is an especially attractive market segment because it has a lifetime of spending ahead of it. Other marketers have pitched their appeal to an "attitudinal" market.

THE INDUSTRY ENVIRONMENT ●

Like trends in the larger society, changes in the **industry environment**— the character of the industry to which a particular firm belongs—may call for changes in marketing strategy. There are major differences in marketing products in such industries as cigarettes, cosmetics, fast food, health care, paper goods, soft drinks, and transportation.

In planning marketing programs, marketers must answer several questions. How big is the industry and is it growing or contracting? Is it healthy or in trouble? Compiling statistics on various dimensions of industry size and importance, as is done in Table 3-5, can be useful in answering such questions. We can also investigate whether the prices of industry stocks are moving up or down, whether prices for and costs of producing a good or service are rising or falling, and whether innovations such as robotics are having an impact on costs and product quality.

Some industries go through a period of skyrocketing growth followed by a long drought. The do-it-yourself moving industry, for example, had a decade of growth, then hit a sluggish market in the late 1980s. Farm-related industries were hurt by an agriculture slump that continued throughout the 1980s, but they hope to turn the corner in the 1990s. The on-line interactive computing service industry, on the other hand, has not had a downturn so far; it is growing at a compound rate of 25% per annum.

A company's success is directly related to its industry environment. If it is in a "bad" industry, one that is serving markets in the mature stage of the product life cycle and that is overpopulated by companies offering relatively undifferentiated products, it will do poorly no matter how good its management. It is axiomatic that when good management faces a bad industry, the bad industry always wins. Conversely, in a "good" industry, where the demand for products is strong and there are significant barriers to entry, even average managers will look like geniuses.

To illustrate "good" and "bad" industries, let's compare the cable TV industry with the textile industry. Fortunes have been made in cable TV, although no one would argue that cable management has been in any way exceptional. On the other hand, fortunes have been lost in the textile industry because no management team in a high-income/high-wage country, however talented or dedicated, has been able to overcome the bad economics of this industry. While cable television is a growth market with massive barriers to entry (most cable systems operate as a monopoly in their served markets), the textile industry serves a mature market and there are almost no barriers to entry for firms from all over the world, including companies in low-wage countries.

industry environment
The character of the industry of which a particular firm is a member.

TABLE 3-5	THE TOP 50 COMPANIES IN CANADA, 1992

Sales rank	The Corporate Canadian Business	Sales ($MIL)	Net income ($MIL)	Performance ratios Profit Margin %	Debt/ Equity	Return on Inv. Cap. %
1.	BCE Inc. (management holding co.)	20,784.0	1,390.0	6.7	0.70	11.3
2.	General Motors of Canada Ltd. (automobiles)	18,347.8	−72.0	−0.4	0.09	−3.0
3.	Ford Motor Co. of Canada Ltd. (automobiles)	14,443.1	−363.8	−2.5	0.50	−53.8
4.	George Weston Ltd. (grocery stores, bakeries)	11,599.0	48.0	0.4	0.58	3.8
5.	Imasco Ltd. (tobacco, restaurants, drug stores)	9,957.2	380.4	3.8	0.64	12.4
6.	Alcan Aluminum Ltd.* (mining & processing)	9,654.0	−142.3	−1.5	0.54	−2.6
7.	Chrysler Canada Ltd. (automobiles)	9,453.8	−48.6	−0.5	0.04	−4.3
8.	Loblaw Cos. Ltd. (grocery stores)	9,261.6	79.8	0.9	0.59	8.2
9.	Imperial Oil Ltd. (oil & gas)	9,127.0	195.0	2.1	0.34	2.9
10.	Canadian Pacific Ltd. (management holding co.)	8,963.6	−487.3	−5.4	1.12	−7.8
11.	Noranda Inc. (mining, pulp & paper, oil & gas)	8,643.0	79.0	0.9	1.19	1.9
12.	Northern Telecom Ltd. (telecommunications equip.)	8,408.9	548.3	6.5	0.28	13.3
13.	Brascan Ltd. (management holding co.)	8,094.0	−113.4	−1.4	0.48	−5.0
14.	Bell Canada (telecommunications)	7,862.8	1,006.1	12.8	0.66	11.7
15.	Seagram Co. Ltd.* (spirits, wine, juice)	7,734.8	−1,141.0	−14.8	0.52	−18.3
16.	Thomson Corp.* (newspaper publishing)	7,600.0	211.0	2.8	1.08	5.5
17.	Ontario Hydro (electric utility)	7,143.0	204.0	2.9	4.55	3.1
18.	Hydro-Québec (electric utility)	6,807.0	724.0	10.6	3.08	7.2
19.	IBM Canada Ltd. (information systems)	6,759.0	1.0	0.0	—	—
20.	Univa Inc. (food distribution)	6,701.6	32.5	0.5	1.07	7.2
21.	Power Corp. of Canada[1] (financial services, communications)	6,181.5	152.3	2.5	0.28	6.8
22.	Hudson's Bay Co. (department stores)	5,152.2	116.7	2.3	0.67	8.9
23.	Oshawa Group Ltd. (food wholesaler & retailer)	5,011.4	41.8	0.8	0.04	6.3
24.	Petro-Canada (oil & gas)	4,718.0	9.0	0.2	0.33	0.3
25.	Shell Canada Ltd. (oil & gas, petroleum products)	4,547.0	80.0	1.8	0.43	2.7
26.	Noranda Forest Inc. (lumber products)	4,478.0	−88.0	−2.0	2.33	−7.8
27.	John Labatt Ltd. (brewing, entertainment)	4,404.0	101.0	2.3	0.43	6.8
28.	Bombardier Inc. (aircraft, parts & vehicles)	4,388.3	132.8	3.0	0.58	11.1
29.	Canada Safeway Ltd. (grocery stores)	4,357.7	45.5	1.0	3.96	27.7
30.	Canadian National Railway Co. (rail transport)	4,051.5	−1,005.2	−24.8	0.67	−40.4
31.	Sears Canada Inc. (department stores, mail order catalogue)	3,957.7	−90.9	−2.3	0.85	−10.5
32.	Amoco Canada Petroleum Co. Ltd. (oil & gas)	3,826.0	−608.0	−15.9	—	—
33.	Canada Post Corp. (postal service)	3,804.5	−127.5	−3.4	0.10	−9.7
34.	TransCanada PipeLines Ltd. (natural gas transmission)	3,757.5	328.7	8.7	1.45	12.2
35.	Air Canada (air transport)	3,501.0	−454.0	−13.0	7.74	−143.7
36.	Inco Ltd.* (mining & metals)	3,252.3	−22.9	−0.7	0.65	−1.1
37.	Canadian Tire Corp. Ltd. (auto parts, hardware retailer)	3,221.9	72.3	2.2	0.39	6.3
38.	Moore Corp. Ltd.* (forms, labels, information services)	3,092.0	−2.9	−0.1	0.02	−0.2
39.	Mitsui & Co. (Canada) Ltd. (dry goods, chemical sales)	3,045.0	4.9	0.2	0.50	8.4
40.	MacMillan Bloedel Ltd. (lumber, pulp & paper)	3,039.3	−48.8	−1.6	1.05	−3.4
41.	Nova Corp. of Alberta (gas & pipelines)	3,027.0	164.0	5.4	1.19	7.0
42.	Jim Pattison Group of Cos. (holding co.)	2,917.0	—	—	—	—
43.	Molson Cos. Ltd. (diversified)	2,904.3	126.2	4.3	0.52	13.7
44.	PWA Corp. (air transport)	2,877.0	−543.0	−18.9	—	—
45.	Onex Corp. (holding co.)	2,816.1	13.5	0.5	1.54	4.1
46.	Maple Leaf Foods Inc. (food processing)	2,751.0	72.5	2.6	0.05	7.7
47.	McCain Foods Ltd. (frozen foods)	2,741.7	—	—	—	—
48.	Honda Canada Inc. (automobiles)	2,722.2	—	—	—	—
49.	Crownx Inc. (health care facilities)	2,571.3	−19.6	−0.8	—	−6.9
50.	Quebecor Inc. (publishing & printing)	2,535.6	87.3	3.4	0.83	13.6

* Figures converted from U.S. dollars
[1] Figures fully consolidated as of Jan. 1, 1992

Source: *Canadian Business*, June 1993.

THE TECHNOLOGICAL ENVIRONMENT ●

Product categories and even the industry in which a firm operates may change as a result of technological changes. *Technology* is the application of scientific knowledge to human activities. The **technological environment** consists of those forces of innovation that contribute to improvements in the way human beings and machines accomplish tasks. Innovative modern technologies are responsible for such things as computer chips, fiber optics, satellites, and lasers.

Today the world's dominant nations and corporations are masters not of land and machines, but of ideas and technology. Sound marketing requires becoming part of the technological revolution, joining the drive for "modernity" that has revolutionized world markets. As one philosopher of marketing has put it:

> A powerful force drives the world toward a converging commonalty, and that force is technology. Almost everyone, everywhere wants all the things they've heard about, seen, or experienced via the new technologies.[5]

The enormous increase in the speed of travel—almost 20,000 times from the mid-nineteenth-century pony express to the nuclear rocket—gives us a feel for the rapidly accelerating rate of development since the Industrial Revolution. The pace of technological change in some industries has been downright astonishing in recent years, especially in the computer industry. The cost of computer logic devices falls at the rate of 25 percent per year and the cost of memory by 40 percent per year. Computational speed has increased by a factor of 200 in twenty-five years. In the same period the cost, energy consumption, and size of computers of comparable power have decreased by a factor of 10,000. If the aircraft industry had evolved as spectacularly as the computer industry has over the past quarter of a century, a Boeing 767 would cost $500 today and it would circle the globe in twenty minutes on five gallons of fuel.[6]

EFFECTS OF TECHNOLOGICAL CHANGE

Technological advances can create new patterns of living and open up entirely new markets—which is good news for some companies and bad news for others. As one author notes, "once a new technology rolls over you, if you're not part of the steamroller, you're part of the road."[7] The facsimile (fax) machine, introduced in the late 1970s, was known many years before. The Science Museum in London, England, has a very early facsimile machine which is in working condition but for generations was regarded only as a curiosity and not as a commercializable technology. However, since then it has become clear that it offers companies the benefits of increased speed and efficiency in both external and internal communication. That's good news for the companies (mostly Japanese) that seized the opportunity to manufacture and market fax machines, but it's been bad news for both Canada Post and overnight mail services such as Federal Express. Advertisers can take pleasure in the fact that cable TV and backyard satellite dishes now bring more channels, more programs, and more commercials into homes than ever before. This technology also permits advertisers to identify even more viewer traits and thus to run ads in front of the best potential audience. The problem is that many TV viewers are using technological advances such as remote controls to "zap" commercials instead of watching them.

87

THE EXTERNAL MARKETING ENVIRONMENT

TECHNOLOGY AND THE FUTURE

In the offing are not only exciting advances in computers and other individual technologies but also tremendous opportunities resulting from the combination of these technologies. Researchers at the Media Lab of the Massachusetts Institute of Technology envision the convergence of innovations in three previously distinct industries—broadcast and motion pictures, print and publishing, and computers—that will result in "personalized" newspapers and television programming that correspond precisely to subscribers' individual wants and needs.

Remember, though, that just because such things as a "personal newspaper" and "personal television" are possible does not mean they will automatically sell. There is a vast difference between technological possibilities and market opportunities. As we have seen, a market opportunity is created by a need or want backed up with the ability to pay. Markets exist when people or organizations with money decide that something is valuable and worth paying for. Many technologies either do not fill market needs or wants—for example, the video telephone, which so far has failed in the marketplace—or are too expensive to satisfy them.

BOTTOM LINE REALITIES

HOW SHALL WE DRIVE THE INFORMATION HIGHWAY?

One of the most important external factors affecting marketing is the fast-changing area of new technology. Technological innovations are affecting how products are designed, developed, distributed, and promoted. Current developments in the area known as the "information highway" or "the electronic superhighway" are also bringing into play most of the important factors in marketing's external environment: government, major companies, technology, the financial community, and the public interest.

A high-speed superhighway for data would do for the flow of information what the transcontinental railroad and highway programs did for the flow of transportation. The proposed information highway is a land-based system linked by satellite communication that will operate on a network of fiber-optic cable and digital compression switchers accessed by computers to deliver words, pictures, sounds, and music—the conventional elements of newspapers, television, movies, radio, and recordings. In addition, the highway will allow users to access libraries and to transmit all forms of business communication, from manufacturing diagrams, construction blueprints, and marketing plans

to data banks like *InfoGlobe* report, catalogs, and all the transactions of stock exchanges around the world.

The technology to put this highway into operation already exists, but there is much controversy over who is going to control it and who is going to both invest in and profit from it. Will the information highway be government-sponsored or private? Major telephone, computer, and cable companies are already operating pieces of the system.

It's staggering to imagine all the information that could be transmitted with the convergence of telephone, fax machines, computers, and television. Without doubt, the information highway will radically transform the way business is conducted. But how will this electronic highway affect the day-to-day world of marketing? Polish off your crystal ball and come up with some ideas about how your life as a marketing manager, when the information highway is in place, will differ from the life of today's marketing manager.▼

KEY POINTS SUMMARY ▼

1. The marketing environment is constantly changing, offering new threats and new opportunities that call for constant monitoring and assessment by marketers.

2. Economic systems determine how decisions are made about what to produce, who controls resources for production, and how products are distributed. Whatever the economic system—free-market, government-controlled, or mixed—it seeks growth and stability, which are the basis of income, purchasing power, and foreign exchange rates.

3. The competitive environment is determined by the number of competitors, their influence on price, and the relative ease with which new competitors can enter an industry. Market shares of firms in an industry are an important measure of its competitive structure. The major types of industry structure are monopoly, oligopoly, perfect competition, and monopolistic competition.

4. The major goals of legal and regulatoy restraints on business are to ensure fair competition, protect consumers from unethical or hazardous practices and products, preserve business property, and protect a nation's industries while encouraging trade with other countries.

5. The sociocultural environment affects business and marketing activities through the demographic characteristics of a population and its mix of beliefs, attitudes, values, and cultural practices.

6. A company's threats and opportunities are directly related to changes in its industry environment. It is easy to be successful in a "good" industry and impossible to succeed in a "bad" industry.

7. The technological environment consists of innovations that improve the ways in which human beings and machines accomplish tasks. Technology interacts with the other elements of the external environment to create new opportunities and threats for companies.

DISCUSSION QUESTIONS ▼

1. How do the economic, legal and regulatory, and social environments differ from one another? How do they affect one another?

2. What are the advantages of privatization? What are the disadvantages?

3. How do monopolies, oligopolies, monopolistically competitive, and perfectly competitive firms differ in the number of firms involved, their control over price, and ease of entry into the market?

4. Which of the goals of legal and regulatory restrictions on businesses do you think is most important? Why?

5. Use government publications or other sources to determine key economic indicators in the most recent calendar year for which figures are available. For example: What is the rate of inflation? What is the value of the Canadian dollar relative to the U.S. dollar, the yen, the deutsche mark, and other world currencies? What impact have changes in important economic factors had on marketing activities both in Canada and in the rest of the world?

6. Would privatization be attractive if government monopolies were marketing-oriented? Why or why not?

7. Interview someone in marketing at a company near your home town. What external factors most affect the company's marketing program?

8. Select an industry that you find interesting. Identify some major changes that have occurred in the last ten years in the environment surrounding that industry and describe how these changes have affected industry marketing activities.

Integrative Case • Discussion Questions

The Body Shop*

1. Evaluate the impact that the economic, competitive, sociocultural, and global environments have had on The Body Shop. Have these forces been positive or negative?

Harley-Davidson

1. What kind of competitive structure is the domestic motorcycle market? How does this structure affect pricing in the motorbike market?

2. How has the legal and regulatory environment affected the motorcycle industry?

The Millennium Power System

1. How may the current economic, legal and regulatory, and sociocultural environments facilitate or hinder sales of rechargeable batteries?

2. How might the changing demographics of North American society affect the demand for rechargeable batteries?

*The three cases at the back of the book—"The Body Shop," "Harley-Davidson," and "The Millennium Power System"—illustrate topics discussed in all chapters of this book. Your instructor will tell you when to read a particular case and answer the discussion questions on it that appear at the end of each chapter.

Guru Review:
The External Environment

The competitive business environment is comprised of everything outside of the organization including the knowledge base it must draw upon, the nature of its products, customers, and competitors, its geographic setting, and the political climate in which it must operate. How effectively an organization responds to environment changes will not only dictate the firm's chances of survival, but ultimately, the degree to which a firm prospers and grows, demonstrating the ability to continuously offer superior value to customers.

However, responding effectively to the competitive environment is an increasingly difficult proposition, as environmental turbulence, hostility, diversity, complexity, and dynamism are escalating in both magnitude and intensity as the competitive nature of markets evolve. Customer needs and wants and competitor's strategies change rapidly as critical elements of the competitive environment. Failure to adapt rapidly to these changes, or even the failure to accurately predict and be adequately prepared to meet them, can mean the quick death of an organization in today's business world.

Businesspeople of all backgrounds are urgently attempting not only to keep up with the pace of change in the competitive environment, but also proactively pursue some form of crystal ball to gaze into, in hopes of predicting the future. Firms can no longer be content to keep pace with competitors; rather, they must continually attempt to leap ahead of the competition in order to garner an adequate share of the consumer dollar. Once the consumer is won, the organization must then fight against competitors to retain that customer's loyalty, all the while looking to the marketplace, and the future, for potential consumers. It's truly "dog eat dog" in today's competitive business environment!

The necessity of environmental adaptation has given rise to an entire industry based on providing expert insight into present and future competitive environments. A whole new class of "business gurus" have emerged in the past decade, all attempting to peddle their versions of the future, or their analysis of, and solutions to, the current competitive situation. Multitudes of businesspeople are willing to pay hundreds of dollars to listen to these gurus for a short time in the hope that they will shed some faint ray of insight previously unheard, which may then be applied to their own competitive situation.

The irony, as Tom Peters (perhaps the best-known of the business gurus) admits, is that "there are no experts." No business expert or guru can accurately predict the future, or convincingly arrive at the definitive answer to the challenge of competing effectively in today's rapidly changing business environment.

Peters's open admission of this fact while conducting his $450.00 seminars only serves to highlight the critical importance businesspeople attach to their ability to respond to the evolving business environment. Highly seasoned, often very successful businesspeople are willing to pay significant sums of money in the sheer hope of catching some glimpse of the competitive future, and perhaps seize upon some small pearl of wisdom related to managing that same future effectively.

QUESTIONS

1. Which environmental forces do you consider to have the greatest impact on the marketing effectiveness of the firm? How can the firm respond effectively to these forces?

2. Should the marketing department in the organization be responsible for tracking environmental changes? If not the marketing department, then who?

3. How does technological change impact the formulation of the organization's marketing strategy in terms of implementing this same strategy?

4. Can you suggest a number of effective ways to monitor competitors' marketing strategies? What are the most efficient methods? The most cost-effective?

Source: The case was prepared by Byron Osing and is based on the *Venture* series episode entitled "Guru Review," which was first broadcast on May 15, 1994.

● Chapter 4

Marketing Strategy and Planning

OBJECTIVES

AFTER COMPLETING THIS CHAPTER, YOU SHOULD BE ABLE TO:

1
UNDERSTAND HOW THE CORPORATE MISSION, LONG-RANGE PLAN, AND BUSINESS PLAN RELATE TO THE MARKETING PLAN

2
UNDERSTAND HOW PLANNING MODELS HELP CORPORATIONS SET FINANCIAL GOALS AND MANAGE THEIR STRATEGIC BUSINESS UNITS

3
DISTINGUISH BETWEEN THE PROCESS OF PLANNING AND THE MARKETING PLAN

4
DESCRIBE THE FIVE MAJOR STEPS IN THE MARKETING PLANNING PROCESS

5
EXPLAIN HOW ANALYZING STRENGTHS AND WEAKNESSES, AND OPPORTUNITIES AND THREATS, CONTRIBUTES TO A SWOT ANALYSIS

6
DISCUSS THE FOUR STRATEGIC MARKETING DECISIONS THAT HAVE TO BE MADE BEFORE THE MARKETING MIX CAN BE DETERMINED

7
DESCRIBE THE STRATEGIC OPTIONS FOR A COMPANY MOVING INTO GLOBAL MARKETING

8
EXPLAIN HOW THE KEY ELEMENTS OF THE MARKETING MIX SUPPORT THE MARKETING OBJECTIVES AND STRATEGIES

9
OUTLINE THE MANAGEMENT TASKS INVOLVED IN CONTROLLING AND COORDINATING MARKETING ACTIVITIES

RECHARGING FOR THE MILLENNIUM

The year 2001 ushers in a new millennium, and it promises to be a challenging time for businesses. One brand that is maneuvering for a position in this new marketplace is Millennium rechargeable batteries. If ever a brand needed smart, well thought-out marketing plans, it is Millennium, for it has to overcome two major marketing challenges.

First, Millennium did not enter the market until 1990, after four well-known brands—Eveready, General Electric, Panasonic, and Radio Shack—had already introduced and established lines of rechargeable batteries. Many marketing experts believe that if you are not one of the top three brands in a market, it will be very difficult for you to maintain profitability, let alone to grow. Millennium is an intrepid David facing

four Goliaths. And newer competitors like Rayovac are also fighting for market share.

Second, rechargeables represent only a small percentage of all batteries sold. Just 25 percent of households have ever purchased rechargeable batteries, so they simply are far from the most popular way to power things that require batteries. Millennium sees this low penetration as more of an opportunity than a threat because the company believes this product category is in its infancy. It proposes to help expand the rechargeable battery category and expects to grow as the category itself grows.

One of the primary reasons only a minority of households use rechargeables is that their retail price is about four times higher than the price of disposable batteries. Moreover, in order to reactivate these batteries, it is necessary to have a recharging unit, which runs anywhere from $10 to $30. Even though rechargeables can be used over and over and the recharging unit is normally a one-time purchase, the high initial outlay for the unit may discourage many potential customers.

Think about the last time you bought batteries for your Walkman, flashlight, or camera. Were they rechargeable? Did you even consider rechargeables? If you are like the majority of consumers, you probably bought regular batteries without giving the decision much thought.

Now think about what Millennium would have to do to get you not only to think about buying rechargeable batteries the next time your Walkman dies but to buy its brand! If you were the director of marketing for Millennium, how would you go about convincing someone to buy rechargeable Millennium batteries? What would your marketing plan include? ■

P lanning is a systematic process. This chapter explains how companies use planning to organize both their corporate and their marketing activities. More specifically, it discusses the process of marketing planning and the major components of a marketing plan.

CORPORATE PLANNING ●

To help demonstrate planning, the marketing plan for Millennium, the company we have just described, is presented as an appendix to this chapter. You'll want to spend some time familiarizing yourself with the Millennium marketing plan because we'll refer to it often throughout the book as we show you how all the marketing-mix elements fit together. By way of background, it began as a product line within the Gates Rubber Company, making products for other companies, which placed their own brand names on the batteries. After seeing the rechargeable market continue to grow through the 1980s, Gates decided in 1990 to give this product line, which includes chargers as well as rechargeable batteries, its own brand name—Millennium. Then in 1993 it sold the Millenium product line to the Eveready division of the Ralston Purina company.

Before we get into the details of a marketing plan, we'll take a look at corporate planning in general so that you will appreciate the way marketing plans relate to other organizational planning efforts, the topic of chapter objective number one.

LONG-RANGE PLANNING, STRETCH, AND LEVERAGE

A large, well-run organization has a long-range corporate plan that is prepared by top management and driven by its vision of where and what it wants the organization to be in the future. Long-range planning and this vision can include such goals as becoming the leader in a particular product category, achieving global distribution of the firm's products, and entering a new-product category. Long-range plans, which usually look ahead three to five years, are important for all businesses, regardless of their size. All long-term goals relate in some way to the marketplace. Although they are corporate goals, they mirror marketing's concerns, which is why cutting-edge companies are said to be operating with a "marketing-is-everything" philosophy. For example, the executives, at Kmart Canada have been heavily involved in developing a new strategy aimed at successfully competing against giant discount stores such as Wal-Mart and Zellers. According to Don Beaumont, president of Kmart Canada, increasing competition has been "a call to action for our total organization."[1]

In forward-thinking companies the long-range plan articulates both "stretch" and "leverage." These are new and powerful views of business planning that deliberately create a chasm between ambition and resources in order to force growth.[2] *Stretch* means reaching way beyond where the company is, committing to new objectives that demand a great deal of growth. *Leverage* means building on resources and moving beyond present company strengths to a new level of competence. CNN, British Airways, Sony, and Harley Davidson all displaced competitors with deeper pockets through stretch and leverage. Their secret: greater ambition than their rivals and the ability to find less resource intensive ways to achieve their goals. These companies brought aspiration and ambition to planning. McCaw Cellular Communications company, for example, had $5 billion in debt and never had positive earnings when it was acquired by AT&T for $12.6 billion in 1993. Craig McCaw, the company's founder and chairman, had long been one of the leaders of the cellular industry. With limited resources, but with great ambition and vision, he stretched to launch a strategy of building the largest cellular phone company in the United States by leveraging his ideas with borrowed money.

At the opposite end of the corporate spectrum is the Unisys case. James Unruh became chairman at this $8 billion company in the early 1990s when it was on the verge of bankruptcy. The previous management, however visionary, had not produced cash flow. By strategically leveraging the long-time relationships Unisys had built over the years with its customers and suppliers, and by stretching his personal and corporate credibility to the limit, Unruh was able to stop the cash hemorrhaging and save the company.[3]

STRATEGIC BUSINESS UNITS

In large corporations like Gates and Ralston Purina, top management reevaluates its long-range plan every year, and a major part of this reevaluation is looking at each *strategic business unit* (SBU) and deciding which ones warrant more financial support and resources and which ones need less. An SBU, you will recall from Chapter 2, is a division of a company—usually a product line or a brand—large enough to be considered a separate profit center. Top management also decides which SBUs, if any, should be shut down or sold off (as Gates did with Millennium) and whether the company should start or buy other business units that could help it meet its long-range goals (as Ralston did when it bought Millennium).

As you can see, a primary purpose of long-range planning is managing all the various businesses or product lines that a corporation owns. Large corporations typically have a large "portfolio" of business units, but even small companies can have several product lines that are managed as separate businesses. A number of planning models and theories are available to help large corporations manage these "portfolios" of business units, the topic of the second chapter objective. Three of the best known models for **portfolio analysis** are the BCG matrix, the McKinsey-GE model, and the diversification risk matrix. Each of these models seeks to assess needs, allocate resources, and spread risk across the firm's SBUs so that all units help achieve corporate objectives. These model-driven analyses help managers at all levels make decisions that affect marketing as well as the other corporate functions.

The BCG Product Portfolio Matrix   This widely used portfolio analysis model was developed in the 1970s by the Boston Consulting Group and is based on several assumptions including the product life cycle and the experience curve which states that cost savings of around one third can be achieved each time production is doubled. By emphasising relative market share, the BCG Matrix is saying that there is an important difference between a market situation where everyone is equal at 33.3% and one where one company has 33.3% but the closest rival has 66.6%. Basically, the cost structure of the two companies will be quite different, a point that escapes many when they start to adopt a pricing strategy of following the market leader. The BCG Matrix usefully examines products in their market setting. A similar matrix could also be drawn for corporate customer accounts. The BCG approach enables top management to rate various SBUs within their corporation according to growth rate and share of market. This model, depicted in Figure 4-1, classifies each SBU in one of four categories: stars, cash cows, question marks, and dogs.

- A *star* has a high market share in a high-growth market. Stars are heavy cash users and require substantial investment to sustain the demands of rapid growth. A good example of a *star* is Millennium, which is now number one in the fast-growing rechargeable category.

- A *cash cow* has a high market share in a mature market. Such SBUs as Marlboro (part of the Philip Morris company) generate substantial cash flows that can be used to finance the growth of stars as well as other activities like new product research and development.

- *Question marks* (sometimes called "problem children") have low market shares in high-growth markets. Since competitors have significantly, larger shares and stronger positions, it would require a large investment to transform a question mark into a star. That is why question marks are often candidates for divestiture. Converse, which for years had a major share in the athletic shoe category, became a minor brand lagging far behind Reebok and Nike in the 1980s, when this whole category reinvented itself and Converse stood still. Today the brand is a question mark that would need a huge cash infusion and savvy planning to recapture its star position.

- A *dog* has a low market share in a low-growth market. A dog may generate a moderate amount of cash, which can be used to maintain ongoing operations and market share without any drain on the corporation. Few of

portfolio analysis
The assessment of needs, allocation of resources, and balancing of risk across a corporation's separate business units so that all SBUs can contribute to the achievement of corporate objectives.

Relative Market Share

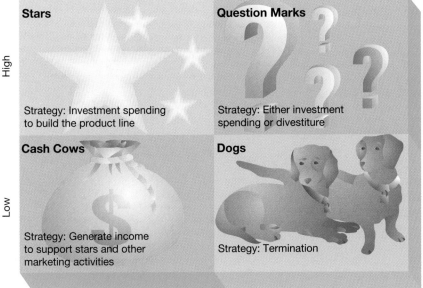

Figure 4-1
BCG Market Product
Portfolio Matrix

Stars

Strategy: Investment spending to build the product line

Question Marks

Strategy: Either investment spending or divestiture

Cash Cows

Strategy: Generate income to support stars and other marketing activities

Dogs

Strategy: Termination

the company's resources will be allocated to its growth, and at some point it may make more sense to close the business. Still, some dogs can be revived under a different organization. A Kentucky Fried Chicken retail store owned by the KFC corporation, for example, may not have enough sales to meet corporate objectives. To KFC, therefore, it is a dog. However, if the store is sold to an independent owner who has less overhead costs, it may be operated profitably.

Because of its simplicity, the BCG model has attracted a lot of attention. Some experts say it is *too* simple to be of much value as a planning tool. It requires all of the company's products to be categorized simply in four cells. There may be products which sit astride these boundary walls. Also, products can move. A question mark or a cash cow can become a dog. Likewise, if there is intense competition, a star can be sent crashing and terminated quickly. There is a time element that has to be taken into consideration.

The McKinsey-GE Model Developed by McKinsey (a management consulting company) and the General Electric Company, this model plots on one axis *industry attractiveness,* defined as potential for market growth based on overall market size and industry profitability, and on the other axis *business strength,* a firm's market share plus its profitability relative to the profitability of the industry as a whole (Figure 4-2). According to the GE-McKinsey model, SBUs that are assessed as medium or high in both industry attractiveness and business position are given the "green light" as top candidates for investment and growth strategies. SBUs in the medium/low or low cells present a "red light"; these are businesses or products that should be sold or repositioned. SBUs placed in the yellow ("proceed with caution") diagonal cells may be retained and improved on a selective basis. Obviously, this model gives more direction to the corporate planner than the BCG model does, and nine cells as opposed to four create more freedom of action.

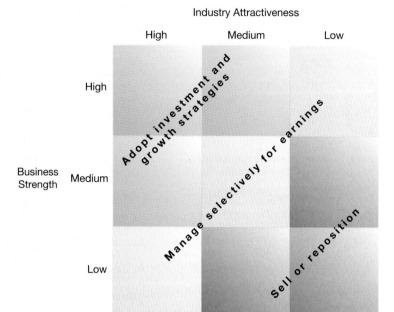

Figure 4-2
McKinsey-GE Model

Industry Attractiveness

High   Medium   Low

High

Business
Strength   Medium

Low

Adopt investment and growth strategies

Manage selectively for earnings

Sell or reposition

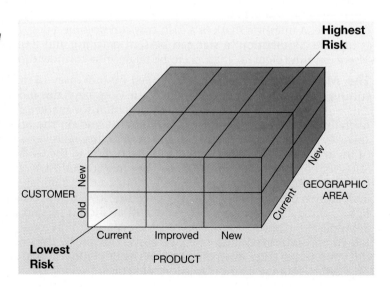

Diversification Risk Matrix The basic thrust of the BCG and GE models is to place more emphasis on more profitable units, and less emphasis on less profitable units. What neither model shows, however, is how an organization can grow if it doesn't have any product "stars." To acquire a star, firms generally must come up with a new product, a new market for an old product, or a new way of reaching an old market. In a global economy diversification is often a strategic growth strategy. The basic premise of the *diversification risk model* is: The greater the change, the greater the risk. As you can see in Figure 4-3, the strategy with the greatest risk is the one in which a company offers a *new* product to a *new* customer segment in a *new* geographical area.

Figure 4-3
Diversification Risk Model

Highest
Risk

New

CUSTOMER

Old

Current   Improved   New

Lowest
Risk

PRODUCT

New

Current

GEOGRAPHIC
AREA

Although these models—and the SBU concept itself—are used primarily by large corporations, the strategic planning concept on which they are based is of value regardless of the product category or organization's size. A local furniture retailer, for example, can analyze its business in terms of brands sold (Thomasville, Henredon, Drexel) or style of furniture (Early American, traditional, contemporary, art deco) and determine which is the most profitable and fastest growing—that is, which are the "stars" and which are the "dogs." The smart furniture retailer might draw up a long-range plan that says it wants 50 percent of its revenue to come from corporate sales and intends to be the number-one seller of contemporary furniture in its market area within three years.

THE BUSINESS PLAN

Guided by the long-range plan and the portfolio analysis of SBUs, each year top management lays out the firm's corporate financial objectives and allocation of resources in a written *business plan*.[4] Financial objectives include such things as return on investment (ROI), revenue, and profit objectives. Allocating resources means deciding what budget, staff, and other resources each functional area (production/operations, marketing, finance, human resources) will be given to accomplish its objectives.

Each functional area also develops its own plan (marketing does a marketing plan, production does a production plan, etc.) to explain what it will do to help the corporation accomplish its business plan. Table 4-1 depicts how these levels of planning activities relate. Although each functional area develops its own annual plan, these plans must be carefully coordinated. In companies operating with a "marketing-is-everything" philosophy, each functional

TABLE 4-1	LEVELS OF PLANNING RESPONSIBILITY	
Management Level	**Planning Responsibility**	**Manifested In**
Corporate	Corporate vision, mission, and strategic intent	Long-range plan Corporate objectives, strategies
	Organization of SBUs	Annual business plan Fiscal objectives
Business units	Product lines	Marketing plans
	Brands	Sales and share objectives
		Marketing strategies
Marketing-mix areas	Product development and pricing	Action plans Objectives, strategies
	Distribution Marketing communications	Tactics

strategic planning
The systematic setting of objectives and establishment of strategies that enable the organization to make operational decisions in the light of probable consequences over time.

objective
A goal; a statement of what the firm wants to accomplish.

strategy
A plan of action designed to accomplish a stated objective.

tactics
Specific short-term actions designed to accomplish longer-term objectives.

area integrates marketing concerns about relationships and customer needs into its own decision making.

The business plan and functional plans are developed annually and their results are stated in terms of objectives for a specified *fiscal year*. A fiscal year is a twelve-month period, but does not necessarily begin on January 1, as a calendar year does. A company whose high season is winter may, for example, choose a fiscal year of July 1 to June 30 so it can more effectively plan through its busy season.

The Sharper Image is a retail store that made a dramatic turnaround in its sales targets during the early 1990s. Known as the "yuppie toy store" during the go-go 1980s, it generated more than $208 million in sales in 1989, its best year ever. In 1990, however, it began the decade with $3.6 million in red ink. How did The Sharper Image reverse this decline? By a careful analysis of its target market and a brand new product merchandise strategy. The Sharper Image sells trends and the products that attract a market in the 1990s are entirely different from what sold in the 1980s.

STRATEGIC PLANNING

The process used to turn The Sharper Image around is called **strategic planning**, which is the consideration of current decision alternatives in light of their probable consequences over time.[5] In order to be useful, each plan needs to state specific objectives and strategies. An **objective** is *what* you want to accomplish. Objectives should be clearly defined in measurable terms. For example, one of Millennium's objectives is: "Increase share of market to 15% in North America by the end of the 1995 fiscal year," an objective specific enough to measure easily. Just as important as deciding what you want to accomplish is deciding *how* to do it—the **strategy**. Strategy encompasses all activities used to accomplish an objective. For example, two of the strategies Millennium will use to help accomplish its 15 percent share objective are:

◆ Penetrate hardware/home center, drug, and photo stores (distribution)

◆ Hire national expertise to strengthen Millennium's sales force (sales)

Each strategy should be accompanied by a *rationale*, which is a statement of the reason for doing something. The rationale provides the thinking behind each of the major recommended strategies. Before a marketing plan or any other major plan within an organization can be executed, it must have the approval of top management. Rationales help to "sell" these strategies to a company's top executives by explaining the logic that underlies their construction.

Once top management has agreed to objectives and strategies as laid out in a plan, the next step is to determine the tactics—how the plan will be executed. **Tactics** are short-term, specific actions designed to cumulatively accomplish the longer-term objectives. A Millennium tactic for "penetrating photo stores," for example, might be having a booth at the 1995 International Retail Photo show.

Some companies use bottom-up planning, which means top management depends heavily on input from the people below them, recognizing that they are closer to the organization's customers and competitors and therefore probably have a better idea of what is needed to build and nourish customer relationships. Bottom-up planning is particularly important in companies involved in quality management programs. Other companies use top-down planning, which means top management takes a more arbitrary approach to planning, basically setting long-term objectives and telling the various functions and divisions within the organization what they must do to accomplish these objectives. Top-down planning is typical of companies that have a strong visionary leader. Actually, most companies use a combination of bottom-up and top-down approaches to planning, but give more weight to one or the other method.

RISKS AND GAMBLES

PLAY IT SMART

How do you take a good idea and move it into the marketplace as a viable product? The U.S. giant AT&T and a tiny Colorado firm called Racom Systems are both working on the introduction of a "smart card," which is a miniature computer on a plastic card. It looks like a credit card, but it's capable of storing and processing the equivalent of several pages of information. It will be interesting to see who will win—would you bet on corporate know-how or entrepreneurship?[6]

The applications are endless. On one level, these cards are a fancy version of what we now call bank debit cards or mass transit passes. But they have the potential for more sophisticated uses: medical records could be stored on them; they could be used for electronic ticketing for travel, reservations, ski tickets, and events; a college student could use them to pay fees, buy books, pay for meals and library fines, purchase tickets to events, and even to store student transcripts. The problem is: How do you translate these applications into meaningful selling points?

Because it is an infant technology, both companies are making major investments in perfecting and marketing their respective products. But a lot of planning must be done before the smart cards will be viable in most markets. Although AT&T has been marketing its card in Europe since 1989, the card has made inroads there primarily as a telephone card. Racom launched its "In-Charge" card in the United States in 1993.

How would you build a market for the smart card in Canada? If you were developing a marketing plan for this product, what objectives and strategies would be important for its launch? Whom would you target? What elements of the marketing mix would be critical and in what ways?

THE MARKETING PLANNING PROCESS

If you were assigned the smart card business for Racom, you would start by developing a marketing plan. The purpose of marketing planning is either to develop the strategy for the launching of a new product like a smart card *or* to devise a strategy for protecting and strengthening existing brands, opening up new marketing opportunities, and anticipating and addressing competitive and other external "threats." Planning involves both a process and a document, as chapter objective three makes clear. "Disciplined marketing planning is a sequential, interlocking, step-by-step decision and action process."[7] The process leads to the creation of a **marketing plan**, a document that outlines the major decisions that will guide the company's marketing efforts for the coming year. In most companies the process of developing this marketing plan is the responsibility of the marketing department.

marketing plan
A document that outlines the major decisions formulated to guide a company's marketing efforts for a specified period of time.

As we walk you through this process, we will identify those elements that show up as sections in the formal marketing plan. Not everything you do in developing a plan goes into the final document. You review a lot more information, for example, than you report in the plan because some information turns out to be valueless in making final decisions and recommendations.

AN OUTLINE OF THE PLANNING PROCESS

The planning process, the topic of chapter objective four, varies from firm to firm (and by industry sector), depending on such things as the size of the organization, the product and/or brand life cycle, the competitiveness of the particular market, and the organization's marketing philosophy. The basic procedure, however, is fairly standard and leads to the primary decisions found in most marketing plans. In Appendix 4B "The Marketing Planning Process" we have outlined the basic process as it is most commonly followed. Here is an overview of the five-step marketing planning process:

1. *Corporate Directions:* Review the corporate mission statement and philosophy of business, long-term corporate objectives and short-term financial objectives, and the organization of the business units

2. *SWOT Analysis:* Identify the *s*trengths and *w*eaknesses of the firm and its product(s) as well as the *o*pportunities and *t*hreats in the marketing environment. The idea is to determine in what areas the organization can leverage its strengths and what it needs to do to correct its weaknesses, handle outside threats, and take advantage of opportunities in the marketplace.

3. *Marketing Objectives and Strategies*: Determine sales and share objectives first, and then the targeting, branding, positioning, and marketing-mix strategies that will help accomplish these objectives.

4. *Marketing Mix:* Determine objectives and strategies for each of the marketing tools—product, distribution, pricing, and marketing communications—and how they will work together to accomplish marketing objectives.

5. *Control and Evaluation Plans:* Identify and put in place measurements and control methods to monitor the plan as it is executed.

Appendix 4B gives you an in-depth look at all the varied considerations and decisions required in the marketing planning process. To help you see how this planning process translates into an actual marketing plan, we have begun each of the five major sections of "The Marketing Planning Process" with a paragraph that describes how these five general sets of activities are reported in a marketing plan document. In the last major section of this chapter, "The Marketing Plan," we present a detailed outline for such a document. Both the outline of the planning process in Appendix 4B and the outline of the actual marketing plan document are extremely important professional tools. Study them carefully, for they will help you to prepare a marketing plan if asked to do so for your employer, for your own company, or for a friend who is starting a new business.

In the rest of this chapter we will explain the marketing planning process in more detail, outlining the steps and thinking behind the type of decisions made in each major area. As we go along, we will indicate in what chapters of this textbook each area is discussed in depth.

CORPORATE DIRECTIONS ⬤

The first step in developing a marketing plan is understanding what the overall organizational goals are and how marketing can contribute to them. Most marketing plans are developed annually, so this discussion will be framed by the understanding that we are preparing an annual plan.

CORPORATE REVIEW

This part of the process has an internal focus. It starts with the corporate mission statement and its stretch and leverage dimensions, then proceeds to analyze how the firm's product (good or service) expresses and fulfills that mission. The long-term objectives and business plan are reviewed in terms of any particular corporate needs and strategies that might affect the firm's product, either directly or indirectly. For example, if last year the company downsized its corporate R&D department, that action might be analyzed this year in terms of its impact on the firm's ability to develop new products. The objective of this review is to determine where and how this year's marketing program can best contribute to the corporate mission and objectives.

SWOT ANALYSIS ⬤

Once the organization's goals and guidelines are understood, the next step is to review the conditions and situations that can positively or negatively affect marketing practices. For years this has been called a **situational analysis** but this would typically examine only strengths and weaknesses. Modern marketers have found that a **SWOT analysis,** the topic of the fifth chapter objective, provides a thorough understanding of these conditions and situations. This analysis has two basic parts: first, the organization's most important *internal* strengths and weaknesses are identified; then the *external* opportunities and threats facing the company in the marketplace are recognized and prioritized.[8]

1. **Strengths:** Competitive advantages that can provide leverage, allowing the organization to accomplish "more with less."
2. **Weaknesses:** Situations or conditions that, once recognized, can either be improved or compensated for in some way.
3. **Opportunities:** Marketplace situations or conditions that can make the organization's product/brand more acceptable or desirable if the proper link is made between these situations/conditions and the product.

situational analysis
A summary of the conditions and situations that can positively or negatively affect marketing objectives, strategies, and tactics.

SWOT analysis
An analysis of the strengths and weaknesses in a firm's internal environment and the opportunities and threats in its external environment.

4. Threats: External situations and conditions that can negatively affect marketing efforts. Although threats can seldom be controlled, they can be influenced if identified before they become too strong. By being aware of threats, the organization can often plan "around" them.

The outline of the marketing planning process in Appendix 4A is as comprehensive as we could make it, because it is a teaching model. The actual information needed for any one company or brand seldom includes everything in this outline. A new product, for example, requires a more extensive market review than an existing product does; on the other hand, an existing product has historical information that permits trend analysis. Note that the Millennium Marketing Plan in the appendix contains only those sections of our model outline that are relevant to the brand's particular situation.

INTERNAL STRENGTHS AND WEAKNESSES

This portion of the review focuses on the organization's own product lines, brands, and corporate resources, and as you can see from the outline, it compiles a lot of information. As Table 4-2 illustrates, strengths and weaknesses reside in the *internal* variables—those the organization can generally control. An example of a strength would be a company's expertise in metallurgy or medical research. A weakness might be distribution that is less broad than major competitors' (as is the case with Millennium).

This section of the SWOT analysis also focuses on the way the company's products differ from those of the competition, the way its sales trends differ from industry trends, and what strategies and tactics have and have not worked in the past for this brand. For example, if brand sales have exceeded

| TABLE 4-2 | SWOT ANALYSIS |

Internal Factors That May Be Strengths or Weaknesses (Can be controlled by the firm)	External Factors That May Present Opportunities or Threats (Cannot be controlled by the firm)
Mission, vision, business philosophy	Competitive environment
Corporate financial resources	Economic environment
Ownership and leadership	Legal and regulatory environment
Technological resources	Sociocultural environment
Staff expertise	Industry environment
R&D capabilities	Technological environment
Corporate culture	Physical environment
Commitment to quality	Global environment
Organizational structure	

industry average sales in one geographical area but lagged in another, further analysis is needed to explain the discrepancy. In Chapters 10 through 13 we discuss goods, services, new products, and branding—all of which describe the types of information compiled for a product or brand review.

EXTERNAL OPPORTUNITIES AND THREATS

This part of the SWOT analysis reviews the environments—competitive, economic, legal/regulatory, sociocultural, industry, technological, and global—that are likely to affect the firm's operations for good or ill. These external variables, which are usually beyond the firm's ability to control, were discussed in Chapter 3 and are listed in Table 4-2. *Opportunities* provide marketers with a way to create extra value for their products by taking advantage of relevant social concerns or trends. For example, environmental concerns have been an opportunity for Millennium since its batteries are reused rather than thrown away. Conversely, *threats* can hinder a firm. For example, an increase in oil prices forces trucking companies to pay more for fuel. The negative effect of a "threat," however, can often be reduced if the organization plans for it. Trucking companies can establish a pricing strategy that employs long-term contracts with a price-adjustment clause based on world-market crude oil prices.

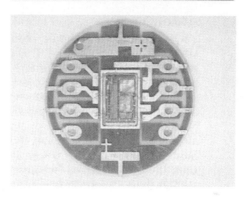

The Smart Card Chip

This tiny computer chip and the technology that makes it possible together have created a new category of business called "smart cards."

The smart card is an example of an innovation driven by technology. Implementation of the smart card system depends critically on the development of a national electronic infrastructure, (probably based on fiber optics) that will make it possible for users to access the card system's microprocessor the way people access their bank accounts today through an automated teller machine (ATM). Establishing that electronic highway, in turn, depends on political and regulatory decisions at the national level. These could turn out to be either opportunities or threats for smart card companies, depending on what decisions are made.

Product Category Review Every good or service belongs to a **product class or category**, which consists of all the products, or brands, against which it competes. Industries are often made up of several product categories. For example, lipstick and perfume are *categories* within the cosmetic industry. A product category review usually includes an analysis of categorywide sales trends. Typically, sales figures are reported in three ways: in numbers of units sold, in amount of dollars (or other relevant currency) earned, and in market share.

Sales are also examined by subproduct categories (for example, different package sizes, different flavors), by means of distribution (for instance, major chains, independent businesses), and by geographical areas. In the case of Millennium, in 1994 its dollar share of rechargeable battery and charger retail sales (the charger is a subcategory of battery sales) was 9 percent. The external

product class or category
The collection of branded products against which a particular product must compete.

environment also should be examined for trends or changes that may affect the product category positively or negatively. For example, society's growing concern about the environment has been a positive external factor for Millennium with its rechargeable system and a negative one for manufacturers of disposable batteries.

All these product category analyses culminate in a brand and category *sales forecast*. We discuss forecasting in Chapter 8.

Competitive Review The competitive review continues the category analysis by determining who are the market leaders and followers. This review seeks to identify the competitors' strengths, but even more importantly, it is looking for points of weakness that could give the organization a competitive advantage. Competitive analysis and its role in determining competitive advantage are discussed in Chapter 9. As mentioned earlier, when Millennium was first introduced, it went up against some marketing giants with strong financial resources. Although Millennium's budget and relative size were weaknesses, it compensated by being more flexible and more willing to take risks.

One way to compare competitors is in terms of market share, which you'll recall from Chapter 3, is determined by calculating the proportion or percentage of the total unit or total dollar sales for a product category achieved by the firm. The easiest way to think about market share is to picture a pie sliced into pieces of varying sizes. If one company gets a quarter of the pie, its market share is 25 percent. For example, if Malaysian Airlines carried 500,000 of the 2 million people who took trips last year from all the cities the airline served, it would have had a 25 percent market share in terms of numbers of units (trips). However, if the airline's average ticket price was higher than the price charged by the other airlines serving those cities, Malaysian's market share in terms of revenue dollars would be more than 25 percent.

Customer/Consumer Review Another important activity is the consumer review. Customers, both individuals and organizations, make the decision to buy or not to buy a brand. For new products without an existing group of customers, *consumers* in general are analyzed to determine levels of demand. This customer or consumer analysis also provides information for forecasting category and brand sales. For example, the question that Millennium must address is whether consumers care enough about environmental issues to change their buying habits and pay more initially to get into rechargeable batteries. We discuss consumer buying behavior in Chapter 6 and industrial buying behavior in Chapter 7.

The customer/consumer review also seeks to determine how much *demand* there is for this product and whether the demand is driven by consumers or by the trade (distributors and retailers). In addition, this review tries to identify the users, as well as the buyers and influencers, of products in the category, and how the users of individual brands differ in terms of demographics (age, gender, education, income) and psychographics (attitudes, values, beliefs, and lifestyles). Levels of product usage are very important in targeting, so the review tries to determine who are the heavy and light users. Another important insight comes from understanding the decision process the customer uses in purchasing this product. What are the critical factors and how is the brand selection made?

In addition to customers, other stakeholders (people who have a stake in the company) are important because they influence how people see the firm, its dealings, and its products. Government and regulatory officials, for example, can affect product development, as well as distribution and marketing communications. The financial community is important in terms of investment spending on such activities as R&D. The local community has some say over facilities and resources. Employees are also sources of communication as well as community ambassadors, and their enthusiasm is a great asset in the production and marketing of quality products. Most importantly, all of these stakeholders can also be customers.

PRIORITIZATION OF SWOTS

Once all the internal and external factors have been analyzed to determine to what extent each is a strength or a weakness, an opportunity or a threat, they need to be prioritized to identify the most important windows of opportunity and problem areas. These judgments are based on five criteria:

1. How significant are the weaknesses and threats?
2. How much time and money would it take to correct or address these?
3. How significant are the strengths and opportunities?
4. How much time and money are required to leverage the strengths and take advantage of the opportunities?
5. How immediate are the threats and opportunities?

The SWOT analysis also helps identify the situations that lead to competitive advantage. Particular attention should be given to "the areas of excellence that a company deliberately cultivates over time . . . to give it an edge in the marketplace, "[9] as well as those factors that create product differentiation, which Porter defines as "a product or service that is perceived industrywide as being unique."[10] A firm's *competitive advantage* (see Chapter 9) is its ability to do something better than its competition. For example, Millennium offers a lifetime warranty on its recharging units, something none of its competitors provide. Competitive advantage can be in any area of the marketing mix. A company may make a stronger sandpaper, price it lower than other brands, make it available in more places, or have an advertising campaign that is unusually memorable and persuasive. We'll have more to say about competitive advantage in Chapter 9.

A SWOT analysis is similar to an airline pilot's preflight check. The pilot goes through a long list of things that could affect the flight, making sure nothing is overlooked in this important review. Most good marketers develop an intuitive feel for determining what the priorities should be, just as good pilots develop an intuitive feel for when the plane is safe to take off. However, both good marketers and good pilots still go through the "preflight check" to make sure they haven't overlooked anything.

MARKETING OBJECTIVES AND STRATEGIES ●

The SWOT prioritization provides the direction for determining the marketing plan objectives and strategies and the marketing-mix objectives and strategies. This prioritization is thus the intellectual bridge between analysis and the plan.

MARKETING OBJECTIVES

The marketing objectives—sales and market share—are the bridge between the corporate plan objectives and those developed for the marketing mix. How all these sets of objectives dovetail is depicted in Figure 4-4.

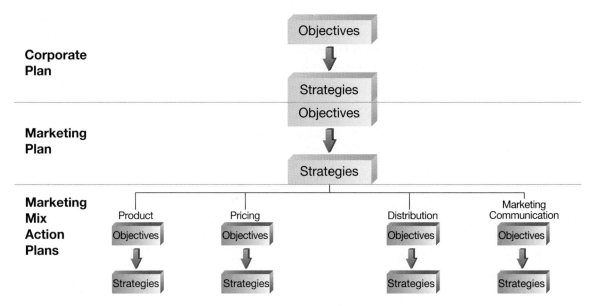

Figure 4-4
The Flow of Planning

As the text explains, at each corporate level, the strategies developed to achieve objectives become the objectives targeted by the next succeeding level.

Sales Objectives Before making specific planning decisions, a marketing planner sets the sales objective. In most organizations marketing and sales executives discuss their sales forecast with top management and out of these meetings comes a final sales objective. It is generally stated in terms of units (number of the product sold, however this is counted—cases, reams, boxes, or individual units) and currency (value of the units in dollars, yen, pounds, etc.). Millennium's 1995 sales dollar objective is $33 million, a 50 percent increase over 1994 (which was $22 million). As you can see in the Millennium Marketing Plan, sales objectives are set not only annually but also by quarter (January–March, April–June, and so on) as well as by region.

Market Share This sales objective is then stated as a market share, which is the percent of the total category owned by the product or brand. Millennium's market share objective for 1995, as stated in its Marketing Plan, is 12 percent, an increase of 33 percent over the previous year (when its objective was 9 percent).

The sales objective "number" (and market share) drives the rest of the planning process. Because this number affects so many aspects of the organization, in many companies it becomes so sacred that drastic measures are resorted to when it becomes clear the number will not be met. When Apple Computer's profits dropped in 1993, CEO John Sculley was asked to resign, thousands of employees were laid off, and cuts were made in many marketing programs.

MARKETING STRATEGIES

Strategic thinking is used to plan the handling of targeting, branding, and positioning. It is also used to identify windows of opportunity in the way markets are approached. These four strategic marketing decisions are the subject of chapter objective six. Together with the SWOT analysis, they determine the marketing mix.

Targeting Strategy When marketers analyze, evaluate, and select **target markets**, they are identifying the groups of people who are most likely to

target market
The group of people with the most potential for purchasing or influencing the purchase of a given product.

110

purchase or to influence the purchase of a product. The strategy is to identify those groups who perceive the greatest value in the brand. In business-to-business selling, this is often a buying agent rather than the user of the product or service. In these cases, companies try to reach both the buying agents and the end users.

Another aspect of targeting involves deciding how much emphasis to put on the consumer and how much to put on the trade. Marketers use consumer-focused marketing—known as a **pull strategy**—when they are trying to create a demand for their products. A new flavor of cake mix, for example, may be something a consumer would notice in advertising and ask for in the store. When consumers ask for a product, they are "pulling" the product through the distribution process. Other goods are better sold using a **push strategy,** in which the trade—distributors, salespeople, dealers, and others—begins to stock, promote and sometimes promotionally price a new product to customers who haven't heard of it. To enhance sales of their flavored mineral water, Shoppers Drug Mart started offering a free bottle to every customer making a purchase in excess of $10. This allowed the custormer to move to the "trial" stage and perhaps make a decision as to whether to become a committed consumer of the product or not. Most products need both push and pull efforts; the marketing planner must decide whether to emphasize one approach over the other.

Targeting all the people in a market is rarely an efficient strategy, as you will read in Chapter 8, although some products can be more broadly mass marketed (Pepsi Cola) than others (bulldozers). Many successful products are designed either for **market segments** or for the *niche markets* we defined in Chapter 1: for example, computer technicians, working mothers, or people with allergies. Often several different targets will be identified within a market and prioritized as either primary or secondary in importance for this year's plan. For example, Millennium targets both consumers and trade (managers of stores). There may be different categories within those two areas that can be prioritized, such as heavy and light users and users of competitors' products.

The targeting plan may also consider stakeholders such as employees, who may need to be informed about how to sell a new product, company shareholders, and community leaders—all of whom may also be customers. Marketing research is the key tool used in making all these targeting decisions, as you will see in the next chapter.

Branding Strategy   On a simple level, branding is a means of identifying a product and making it stand out from its competitors by naming it and giving it a distinctive design. On a higher level, branding represents the link people have with the products they buy. All the things that connect a person to a product—past experiences buying and using it, the advertising, the product and package design, the logo, and so forth—merge into a brand image. Brands, like people, have personalities and people's relationships with their favorite brands are built on their liking this personality or image.

The development of brands like Marlboro or McDonald's and the maintenance of their imagery are very important strategically. It can take years to establish a brand image, so it is important not to change the branding each year. Rather, assuming the brand image has been successful, the goal is to reinforce it. The positive associations created over time through experiences with a brand create *brand equity*, which is what a brand is worth in the long term; we discuss brand equity in Chapter 10.

Branding gets complicated when you have products with multiple tiers of brand identifications—for example, the Ford Bronco. Both Ford and Bronco have their own brand images; product line—or rather, brand extensions—often create these complex situations. Frango Mint, for example, is a

---

pull strategy
A marketing strategy that stimulates customer demand by communicating directly with potential customers, leading them to seek out and purchase a product and to pull it through the marketing channel.

push strategy
A marketing strategy that emphasizes product distribution and that creates an incentive for retailers and other distributors to sell or "push" a product to customers.

market segment
A group of customers who make up a subcategory within a larger target market.

brand name used by Marshall Fields for its chocolates, brownies, cookies, and liqueur. All of the products carry just the one name. In contrast, Red Zinger, Sleepytime, and Morning Thunder are all distinctive names for teas carried by Celestial Seasonings, which is a distinctive name in its own right. The strategy lies in deciding how they work together and which image to emphasize in what situations. Against this strategy, Sony uses simply its name on all its equipment.

Positioning Strategy   For established brands, especially those that have been doing well, it is important to maintain the product's position. *Positioning* means establishing the way a brand ranks or compares to the competition *in customers' minds*. For example, when people think of cars, Mercedes ranks higher than Honda on prestige but lower than Honda on economy. Thus Mercedes can be said to have a status position and Honda an economical position. Positioning is based both on a brand's own characteristics and marketing strategy and on its competitors' characteristics and strategies.

Although a position is an established place that a brand holds in the customer's mind relative to competing brands, marketers can influence a position by focusing all the "messages" sent by the different elements in the marketing mix. For example, a new item that has a contemporary design and a relatively high price (compared to the other brands against which it is competing) and that is elegantly packaged and distributed in only specialty stores will probably be thought of—that is, positioned in consumers' minds—as an upscale, quality product. Positions, like brand images, take years to establish, so changing a position is also a major undertaking. Of course, if a position isn't working or no longer adequately represents a brand's competitive advantage, it may need to be changed. In the case of a new product, obviously a position must be created.

Millennium has two positions: one for consumers—"the power to last a lifetime"—which is a durability position, and one for the trade—"one brand fits all"—which conveys the idea that the Millenium line includes all battery sizes and satisfies all consumer needs. In 1995 Millennium will make a special effort to strengthen both of these positions and to benefit from the synergy that the overlap between consumer and trade promotion can provide. For example, in-store displays will be designed to contain all the various product-line items, which will better serve the retailers, but they will be printed with the consumer message, which will attract potential buyers' attention. In Chapter 9 we explore positioning strategies in greater depth.

Market Strategies   Windows of opportunity for market growth can be created through four strategies: market penetration, market development, market expansion, and market diversification (see Table 4-3).

◆ The *market penetration* approach calls for increasing sales in the existing geographic distribution areas by getting current customers to buy more or by getting users of competitors' brands to switch to your brand. This is a highly competitive approach that often involves intense pricing and sales promotion and aggressive distribution activities.

◆ The *market development* approach identifies consumer or business segments that aren't currently being served by the product. Baby shampoo, for example, can be sold to adults for their own use, particularly if they have sensitive skin.

◆ The *market* or *category expansion* strategy develops variations on a product, such as offering it in different sizes or flavors or in new packaging. Another useful tactic is a **line extension**—adding new products within a family of related products that all carry the same brand identification. A

line extension
Adding new related products to an existing brand line.

TABLE 4-3   MARKET-GROWTH STRATEGIES

Strategy	Focus
•Market Penetration: Sell quantity	Emphasizes distribution, pricing, promotion
•Market Development: Find new segments	Emphasizes targeting markets
•Market Expansion: Develop new products	Emphasizes product development, line extensions
•Market Diversification: Move into new categories	Emphasizes mergers, takeovers, buyouts, and startups

good example of this is producing single-serving cans of soups and vegetables to accommodate the growing number of single adults.

◆ *Market diversification* involves either entering a different product category or subcategory or a new geographic market, or going after new consumer targets. Diversification spreads corporate risk over a number of categories. For example, when Millennium entered the highly competitive battery business, it knew it was going up against several major, established brands and it immediately diversified into battery chargers. Another example of diversification is the recent move by Philip Morris into the food industry. For years, Philip Morris sold only tobacco products; then anticipating that public pressure against smoking would eventually cut its profits from tobacco products, the company acquired Kraft General Foods, Miller Beer, and Jacobs Suchard, the Swiss chocolate maker.

International Strategies Another important market approach uses an international strategy, the topic of the eighth chapter objective. Marketing in foreign countries imposes some special requirements, and companies that undertake it must decide if they will approach their international operations differently from their domestic operations. There are several alternatives open to a firm looking for windows of opportunity in international markets: it can extend its domestic plan, adapt that plan, or create an entirely new plan. In most cases, international marketers use a fourth option, which is to combine two or three of these strategies.

Extending the Domestic Plan Companies using this approach go into the international market with essentially the same product, price, marketing communications, and distribution strategies they are using at home. Extension is a good choice when the category is established in the foreign market and a similar, local product already exists. For example, if Lever is entering the Thai market with a dishwashing soap it already markets in other

---

Going Light on Line Extension

In the late 1980s Frito-Lay, a division of PepsiCo, went on a new-product binge, introducing such failures as Stuffers cheese-filled snacks and Rumbles granola nuggets. When operating profits dropped by 13 percent, Frito took advantage of a special corn oil and a reduced-oil cooking process to create new light snacks as extensions of such existing lines as Doritos, Ruffles, and Cheetos cheese puffs. By 1989, operating profits had jumped 26 percent.

113

areas of the world, it will probably decide to introduce the product by extending a standard marketing plan if the Thai people are familiar with dishwashing soaps and know how to use and evaluate them.

Adapting the Domestic Plan When a company perceives significant differences in a foreign market, it may decide to adapt its marketing mix so as to increase the value of its product to foreign consumers. For example, electrical products like hair dryers and computers must be able to use local voltage and electrical outlets, which vary around the world. Although you may think the need for this sort of adaptation is so obvious it need not be mentioned, a surprising number of companies fail to realize it. North American auto makers, for example, have had a hard time exporting their products to many countries because they refused to make cars with right-hand steering. Lack of awareness or lack of coordination within the company are but partial excuses. In most cases, firms adapt some, but not all, of the elements of their marketing mix. For example, both Coke and Pepsi have adapted their products to respond to different degrees of sweetness preference in various foreign countries, and they have adjusted their prices to accommodate different income levels and competitive situations, even though their targeting, positioning, packaging, and marketing communication strategies are similar in many parts of the world.

Creating an Entirely New Marketing Plan This strategy involves studying world markets and creating a new marketing mix to serve world market needs. It can start with the market need and work back to the product design, or it can start with the product and work forward to the markets of the world. Whatever the starting point, the launch of a new product designed to compete in global markets must be based on a marketing strategy that targets the world and not just one domestic or foreign market. For example, the Sony Walkman was designed for sale in the world market, and it was launched simultaneously all over the globe.

As we said earlier, most companies use a combination of these approaches. When Millennium expanded into South America, for example, its marketing communications had to be adapted since the word "power" had different meanings there than here. In distribution, it had to develop a whole new strategy, which involved working through distributors. Its packaging, however, has remained basically the same, with the exception that the words were translated.

MARKETING-MIX STRATEGY

There are many different marketing tools in the marketing mix—pricing, product, distribution, and all the various types of marketing communication—and the marketing plan determines how and to what extent each of these tools will be used to support marketing objectives and strategies—the topic of the eighth chapter objective. For example, in determining the marketing mix, a company could decide to emphasize (put more money into) sales promotions and deemphasize (reduce the amount of money going into) advertising. Think of the marketing plan as a cake. The differences in the look and taste of various cakes come from the differences in cake mixes or proportions of ingredients used.

The marketing mix is driven by the results of the SWOT analysis. For example, an external opportunity may be identified in the area of distribution because it was found that main competitors had little distribution in convenience stores. Once the objectives and strategies have been determined for each area of the marketing mix, the marketing plan then outlines specific *tactics*—or *action plans*—for carrying out the strategies (in this example, how to get greater distribution in convenience stores).

One of Millennium's major strategies for reaching its $33 million sales objective is increased market penetration, which, as we have seen, is the most competitive marketing strategy. To support this marketing strategy, the company's *distribution objective* is to escalate North American distribution to achieve a category share of 15 percent; its *marketing communication objective* is to create a 25 percent level of brand awareness among the target audience in North America through the use of a highly visible advertising campaign; and its *pricing objective* is to price the product 5 percent lower than last year in key markets. In order to make a profit at this lower price, it may be necessary to redesign the manufacturing process and find new sources of raw materials. As a result, the company's *product objective* might be to reduce product costs by 10 percent through manufacturing changes.

THE PRODUCT

Product-related variables such as ingredients and warranties are critically important for product quality as well as for differentiating a product in the marketplace. In service industries variables related directly to the service provided—such as the way in which employees are selected, trained, and supported—are critical. Chapters 11 to 13 discuss goods, services, and the development of new products. Keep in mind that marketers can add value to a product by adding *features* to it. Adding a microprocessor chip to the smart card gave it a significantly greater amount of memory than the old debit cards could offer in their magnetic strips.

Packaging can be both a product feature that adds value and an important aspect of marketing communication. For example, orange juice was long sold in cardboard cartons that couldn't be resealed and were awkward to handle. Then Tropicana introduced a 96-ounce plastic container for its premium, fresh-squeezed orange juice. The new design, with its screw-on cap and jug-style container, was promoted in terms of its ease and convenience. You will see other examples of how packaging methods can serve marketing strategies when we discuss packaging in the product chapters (Chapters 11–13) and in the marketing communication chapters (Chapters 18–21).

DISTRIBUTION

Making sure that a product is easily accessible to consumers can enhance its value in their eyes. As the Steelcase ad in Exhibit 4-1 illustrates, getting a product to the customer sometimes demands more than just unloading a crate. If a firm's distribution objective is to introduce its brands in the Northeast, the people responsible for distribution need to determine what they must do to make sure the product is available in that area. The company may have to contract with a trucking company and lease warehouse space in order to make the product available. The complex practices and issues of distribution are covered in Chapters 14 and 15.

Holiday Inn Worldwide has a branding strategy which divides its hotels into four categories or brands: (1) Crowne Plaza Hotels and Resorts; (2) Holiday Inn Select Hotels geared for the business traveler; (3) Holiday Inn Hotel and Suites which will have a minimum of 10% suites and the remainder will be traditional guest rooms; and (4) Holiday Inn Express, introduced in 1990, which offers economically priced packages for travelers seeking only the basics. Here is the Holiday Inn Express located in Calgary.

PRICING

If value is defined by the relationship between benefits and price (Chapter 1), shouldn't dropping the price add to the value of a product in consumers'

TABLE 4-5 — A MARKETING PLAN OUTLINE

EXECUTIVE SUMMARY

I. Corporate Directions

II. The SWOT Analysis

III. Marketing Objectives and Strategies
   A. Targeting
   B. Branding
   C. Positioning

IV. The Marketing-Mix Action Plans
   A. Product
   B. Distribution
   C. Pricing
   D. Marketing Communication

V. Budget and Calendar

VI. Evaluation Plan

and presents a coordinated and focused program for managing the marketing mix to meet customer needs at a profit for the company. Just as the list on page 104 reviewed the marketing planning process for you, Table 4-5 shows you the key sections of a marketing plan. You'll see this brief outline fleshed out with real-world data when you examine Millennium's actual marketing plan in Appendix 4A. You will also see that Millennium, like many other companies and brands, doesn't follow this outline exactly, nor does it include every section that the outline suggests. For starters, Millennium doesn't present an "executive summary," which is a synopsis, or an abstract, of the marketing plan. Some people find such brief overviews very helpful; others do not.

A marketing plan has three important purposes:

1. It provides *a disciplined approach to allocating corporate resources.*

2. It is *a blueprint for action.* It coordinates and focuses the activities of everyone—within the organization and outside it—who is involved in the marketing effort. It helps ensure that everyone works toward the same end and uses resources in the most effective and efficient way.

3. It serves as *a measuring stick.* Having established measurable objectives, management can use sales analyses and other types of research to determine if the objectives are being met—if the firm's resources are being wisely spent. A good marketing plan provides for intermediate checkpoints so that strategies and tactics can be adjusted if the objectives are not being met.

IMPLEMENTATION

Planning is an important step, but the actual implementation of the plan is handled over a period of time—usually a year—by a variety of people and departments. Just as a typical corporation has various functional areas (marketing, production or operations, finance, human resources, legal), the marketing function (and plan) has various subparts represented by the marketing-mix areas: product development, distribution, pricing, sales, advertising, sales promotion, packaging, and public relations. These areas are guided by *action plans* that drive the actual implementation of the marketing plan on a day-to-day basis.

Action plans are task specific and dominated by tactics and details. For example, a local soft-drink bottler may have a merchandising plan for a special fall promotion that involves a contest for drivers, posters for retail outlets, and advertisements for customers. All the details for this special event must be planned, cost-estimated, scheduled, and assigned to people or companies who will handle the production of the materials. Other aspects of implementation include the production of tactical materials like advertisements, merchandising pieces, and sales kits. Furthermore, meetings have to be held to keep all the people involved in the various aspects of the marketing mix informed and working together.

COORDINATION AND INTEGRATION

The success of marketing planning is dependent upon the ability of the marketing manager to coordinate functions, people, budgets, timing, and activities. Coordination is the secret to both creating a plan and implementing it. For example, if it's decided that a packaging change is one of the strategies for accomplishing the objective of "making our product more contemporary looking," production changes must be scheduled and advertising must be updated to reflect the changes. Failure to carefully coordinate action plans can result in chaos.

When Campbell Soup Company introduced Le Menu premium frozen dinners, it launched the product before company engineers had designed some of the equipment necessary to fill round dinner plates (till then a rectangular shape had been used for most frozen foods). Initial demand for the product was so strong that extra plant personnel had to be hired to fill the plates using ice cream scoops and gloved hands. Because this led to higher than anticipated labor costs, profits on early sales were minimal.

At the highest level, successful marketing planning is *integrated marketing*—the coordination of all marketing-related activities throughout the firm to produce a synergy. *Synergy* means that the impact of the integrated marketing plan is greater than the effect of each function carried out independently. Think of an orchestra: when all the musicians are playing from the same arrangement, the sound is much better than when each musician plays whatever he or she feels like playing. Although integrated marketing sounds like common sense, in many large organizations it is often difficult to coordinate marketing efforts for several reasons: pressures to make decisions often don't allow time to talk to other departments; people in each area tend to feel that their function is the most important and are therefore unwilling to compromise on dates or activities; department heads often have large egos that prevent interaction with other departments.

Checkout scanners at Wal-mart send real-time sales data, via the Wal-mart Satellite, back to their suppliers' factories. These factories cut lead time which allows Wal-mart to turn inventory faster. As a result, logistics' costs evaporate & prices remain low.[11]

There is a practical reason for integrating the functions in planning: they overlap. For example, everything an organization does sends a message. If your product is displayed by mass merchandisers like Kmart or Zellers, people will perceive your brand in a different way than they would if it were distributed in Birks. The price of a brand also sends a message, as does its physical appearance. Similarly, the atmosphere in which a service is performed or delivered may have as much to do with the client's or customer's perception of that service as the service itself. Finally, integrated marketing also means that all corporate functions (for example, production or finance) work together with a single overall objective of building strong, long-term customer relationships at a profit to the firm.

Successful implementation of a marketing plan requires the commitment of every individual who interacts with any aspect of the marketing mix, including all marketing staff. Those who have the most to gain or lose from the product's success or failure should be the people most involved in the planning process. Representatives of top management should also be in on drawing up the marketing plan because their participation will defuse fears that the plan may clash with the corporate mission or corporate culture.[12]

SOUP THE WORLD OVER

Campbell's Soup, with its ubiquitous red-and-white cans that are an enduring symbol of Americana, intends to become a global marketer—to transform itself from an insular American soup company into a global force in food. By the year 2000, the company wants no less than half of Campbell's $6.3 billion revenues to come from outside the United States. That objective will take some doing, for foreign sales in 1993 accounted for less than 26 percent of the company's revenues.[13]

What strategies is Campbell's using to accomplish this long-term corporate objective? One is expansion: Campbell's soup is being shipped to Asia, for example, where people consume vast quantities of soup. Along with expansion comes product reformulation: flavors are being redesigned to appeal to other palates. New Campbell's flavors include *flaki*, a peppery tripe soup for Poland, *watercress and duck-gizzard* for Hong Kong and China, and a *fiery crema de chile poblano* for Mexico.

Another strategy is acquisition and diversification. In 1992 and 1993 the company set its sights on Australia's Arnotts Ltd., a $485 million company that is a household name throughout Australia. Campbell's already owned one-third of Arnotts' stock, so it seemed like a natural marriage. Unfortunately Arnotts didn't agree, and the cherubic Campbell's Kids were portrayed in the Australian press as bare-knuckled street brawlers. Campbell's finally prevailed in the battle, boosting its share of Arnotts' stock to 58 percent.

Unfortunately for Campbell's global ambitions, food products are one of the most difficult product lines to market worldwide because tastes are decidedly cultural. Furthermore, Campbell's faces formidable competitors in the global market: CPC, which markets Knorrs powdered soups everywhere, and H. J. Heinz already have a strong presence.

Analysts say, however, that Campbell's doesn't have much choice but to go global because its sales have hit a ceiling in North America. Moreover, canned soup, the company's mainstay, has been losing ground to fresh and frozen foods, which are more in tune with a health-conscious marketplace. Campbell's other

120

product lines, such as Swanson frozen foods and Pepperidge Farm cookies, are in tough competitive markets with few growth opportunities. Campbell's has already gone through a restructuring, and a new president in the early 1990s slashed operating costs by closing or selling twenty U.S. plants.

Campbell's seems to think that global growth is the key to survival. Do you agree? What other changes in strategies and objectives will Campbell's have to make to achieve a global presence? ▼

KEY POINTS SUMMARY ▼

1. Most well-run companies have a *long-range plan* that is prepared by top management for a period of three to five years and is driven by the organization's vision and goals for the future. Top management also lays out the firm's corporate financial objectives and allocation of resources annually in a written *business plan*. Marketing plans are designed in support of these corporate plans and to dovetail with their objectives.

2. In setting financial goals and deciding which divisions warrant more financial support and resources and which need less, corporations often find it useful to use one of several models that put responsibility for profits on the firm's SBUs. These models are the BCG Market Growth Matrix, the McKinsey-GE model, and the diversification risk matrix.

3. Marketing planning involves both a process—a sequential, interlocking set of decisions—and a document—a *marketing plan* that outlines the major decisions that will guide the company's marketing efforts for the coming year. In most companies the process of developing this marketing plan is the responsibility of the marketing department.

4. The five steps involved in marketing planning are (1) analyzing corporate directions; (2) analyzing the firm's SWOTs (strengths, weaknesses, opportunities, threats); (3) setting marketing objectives and strategies; (4) developing the marketing mix; and (5) planning the control and evaluation activities. They are also the major sections in most marketing plans.

5. The SWOT analysis, which is based on a thorough review of the business (corporation, product category, competition, customers, and products), identifies the internal strengths and weaknesses of the company as well as its external threats and opportunities are identified. Windows of opportunity are identified through market analysis and analysis of competitive advantage.

6. Four key planning decisions that guide marketing strategy are: (1) identifying and prioritizing target audiences; (2) analyzing branding; (3) reconfirming or revising brand positioning; and (4) identifying the market approach that provides the greatest window of opportunity. These four strategic decisions, along with the SWOT analysis, provide the basis for determining the marketing mix.

7. Global firms may penetrate new international markets by extending the current marketing plan to a new market, adapting that plan for the local market, devising an entirely new plan, or using a combination of these approaches.

8. The marketing-mix objectives and strategies divide up the responsibility of achieving overall marketing objectives among the pricing, distribution, product development, and marketing communications areas. Each of these functional areas determines its own objectives and strategies. The tactics are spelled out as action plans, which are the detailed plans that make implementation of the marketing plan possible.

9. Firms control and coordinate the varied marketing activities through scheduling, budgeting, forecasting, and evaluating the success of the plan at specified intervals.

DISCUSSION QUESTIONS ▼

1. Why do you think Gates sold the Millennium product line to Eveready and why do you think Eveready bought it? What corporate strategies are represented by this deal? What do you think will be the impact of the new ownership on Millennium? If you were the marketing manager for Millennium, what impact would this ownership change have on your marketing plan?

2. Find four products that fit into the four positions on the BCG matrix. Have any of these products moved from one position to another within the matrix in recent years?

3. What are the two aspects of integrated marketing and why are they important? If you were marketing manager for Millennium, what would you add to the marketing plan in order to strengthen the company's integrated marketing program?

4. Which aspect of the SWOT analysis do you think is the hardest to complete? Why? Is there any section of the Millennium Marketing Plan that you think requires more information? Why?

5. Develop a SWOT analysis for the smart card.

6. Which should come first in marketing strategy: identification of target market, development of the product, or establishment of objectives? Why?

7. Explain the difference between push and pull strategies. Analyze how these two strategies should work for Millennium.

8. What impact should Campbell's Soup's global market strategy have on its marketing mix? Analyze each element of the market mix and explain what this new strategy will mean to that area. Draw up a list of task-oriented action plans that might be needed to implement this corporate strategy.

9. You have been hired by the Millennium division of Eveready to develop a marketing plan for a niche market—teenagers of both high school and college age. Explain what changes would need to be made in each section of the current Millennium Marketing Plan in order to reach this new market.

Integrative Case ● Discussion Questions

The Body Shop*

1. If you had been Anita Roddick's banker in 1976, how would you have evaluated her proposed business in terms of the GE industry attractiveness/business strength matrix?

2. Perform two SWOT analyses for Roddick's business, one as of April 1976, and one for the 1990s.

3. How do you think customers of The Body Shop will react to the firm's AIDS campaign? How will the larger public respond?

Harley-Davidson

1. How has Harley-Davidson diversified? Does this diversification spread the firm's risk?

2. What do you see as Harley's current (internal) weaknesses? Its (external) opportunities?

3. Has Harley extended its domestic marketing plan to foreign markets or has it adapted the plan to suit conditions in individual countries?

*The three cases at the back of the book—"The Body Shop," "Harley-Davidson," and "The Millennium Power System"—illustrate topics discussed in all chapters of this book. Your instructor will tell you when to read a particular case and answer the discussion questions on it that appear at the end of each chapter.

The Millennium Power System Battery

1. What are Millennium's strengths and weaknesses vis-à-vis competitors such as GE and Panasonic?

2. In BCG terminology, the Millennium system (as part of Ralston Purina) and Eveready rechargeable brand of batteries appears to be a _____. Defend your answer.

3. How well does the Millennium product group match with its target market?

Taking a Risk or Playing it Safe

Two men in Guelph were marketing almost identical products but using totally different strategies. One of them, an engineer, had invented a wagon to pull behind a bike. His neighbor, a former sales executive with a large corporation, was helping develop the marketing plan, and was intending to become a partner. In many ways, this is the perfect complement of skills for an entrepreneurial venture. Not in this case though.

The North American market for this product category is 140,000 units per year at an average cost of $500. The WIKE Wonder Wagon has lots of advantages over any similar product already in the marketplace, and has a much lower price point. The engineer wanted to licence the production to his neighbor and sit back to collect royalties. The neighbor felt he already had a stake in developing the product and wanted a partnership. They also had disagreements over the strategy to use to get the product to market, and each went his own direction with his version of the product. Problem is, each of their versions was almost identical.

The engineer/inventor mounted a small manufacturing operation in his home. He tinkered with the design for his WIKE, making only 10–12 units a week. He only wanted to sell 500 units at local farmers' markets in the first year, establish a need, and then sell the rights to someone else to take a product to the national level. He was also very cautious about claiming that the product can be used for carrying kids, in spite of the fact that all the local customers told him they wanted to use it for that purpose, and stores told him that that's the main usage for these types of wagons. In every respect, he kept it small because he was unwilling to take any kind of risk. He didn't even believe in his product enough to resist discounting an already low price.

The sales type decided to go national right away with his Wonder Wagon, and set up a fairly major manufacturing operation. A key decision was the addition of a 5-point harness so the wagon could be used to transport kids. He did in-store presentations to independent bicycle shop buyers who loved it because it made customers happy and gave them a larger profit margin. He even offered to help them out with co-op advertising dollars. Somehow he became a corporate sponsor for an annual bike race in Vancouver, with major exposure to both the public and dealers. He then landed significant orders from national retailers and benefits from the exposure generated by their advertising budgets. Good results came from this strategy, in part because of the willingness to take some risks.

QUESTIONS

1. What are the advantages of each strategy?
2. What is the likely outcome of each strategy?

Source: This case was prepared by Ray Friedman and is based on the *Venture* series episode "Buggy Wars," which was first broadcast on June 26, 1994.

124

Millennium Marketing Plan

[**Authors' note:** To make the wealth of material in Millennium's Marketing Plan more manageable, we have for the most part reproduced only those portions that relate to Millennium's major sellers: rechargeable batteries (also referred to as *round cells*) and battery chargers (*chargers*). There are some references to the company's other products—for example, rechargeables for camcorders and for cordless and cellular telephones—but these occur mostly in material of market share. For proprietary reasons, the numbers in this plan have been slightly altered. In making these changes, however, we have maintained the relationships between numbers.]

I. MILLENNIUM SBU DIRECTIONS

A. PHILOSOPHY OF BUSINESS

Our 1995 Marketing Plan definitely reflects the **imagination and purpose** that embody the spirit of the Millennium brand. Your team efforts, individual contributions, talents, and imaginations have taken an unknown brand to the pinnacle of market leadership in an extremely competitive category. All this has been made possible because of our focus on total customer satisfaction for retailers and "the ultimate customer," the consumer.

B. LONG-TERM CORPORATE OBJECTIVES

- Grow and maintain category leadership
- Achieve a 15% share of the total rechargeable market by 1996
- Achieve a 25% share of the round-cells/charger category by 1996

C. FINANCIAL OBJECTIVES

- Generate $6.2 million profit
- Increase gross margins in 1995 to 43%

II. SWOT ANALYSIS

A. INTERNAL STRENGTHS AND WEAKNESSES

1. **Corporate Strengths:** The Brand's new corporate parent, Ralston Purina, brings financial resources and market knowledge to Millennium. Its Eveready SBU has been a help in increasing Millennium's distribution.

   Corporate Weaknesses: At the same time that Eveready has been of help, it also competes for internal resources.

2. Product/Brand

a. Round cells: AA, C, D, AAA, 9V

Strengths:

◆ 50% longer runtime than other rechargeables
◆ First rechargeable battery with a lifetime replacement guarantee
◆ Affordable rapid-charge convenience
◆ Millennium has the highest consumer satisfaction ratings on every attribute compared to the other major brands. When rating their "overall satisfaction," Millennium purchasers are significantly more satisfied than users of other products in the industry.

Weaknesses:

◆ Millennium has the lowest annual average number of rechargeable batteries purchased.
◆ Millennium also has the lowest share of toy and flashlight/lantern usage of any of the major brands. (This is consistent with Millennium's in-store position in consumer electronics departments with its key accounts.)

b. Chargers: Charge Man, 3-hour, 4-position, 6-hour, 4-position, 1-hour, 4AA

Strengths:

◆ Promotional $9.95 price point
◆ Affordable 3-hour system
◆ First affordable ($19.95) 1-hour charger

c. 1994 Sales by quarter, by product category (see below)

Product	1 Qtr	2 Qtr	3 Qtr	4 Qtr
Round Cells/ Chargers	61.5%	52.2%	45.6%	45.8%
Camcorder Power Packs	34.6	45.1	48.0	47.2
Cordless Phone Packs	3.0	1.7	3.4	4.0
Hobby Packs	1.0	7.0	1.0	1.2
Cellular Power Packs	0.0	0.3	1.9%	1.9

d. Distribution

[See Exhibits 1 and 2.]

Strengths:

◆ Strong base in discount and drug chains
◆ Potential leveraging of Eveready distribution channels
◆ Potential to leverage support from Eveready sales force in opening up new geographic areas

e. Brand image. In a study of retailers, Millennium was rated number one vs. GE, Eveready, Panasonic, and Saft in the following categories:

- High quality
- Value for the money
- Good delivery
- Advertising and promotion
- Innovative products
- Marketing assistance

[*See Exhibit 3.*]

f. Consumer brand positioning. The Millennium Power System represents the optimal consumer choice for rechargeable battery power, offering added-value products with the highest quality available, thereby ensuring and complementing the enjoyment and use of portable/cordless and leisure electronic products in the household.

Strengths:

- Presents the brand in a leadership light
- Stresses consumer value and product quality
- Addresses and links the use of Millennium products to emotional satisfaction
- Accentuates the "mission" of the brand and focuses directly on it, owning a position in the consumer's mind

| EXHIBIT 1 | CURRENT NATIONAL DISTRIBUTION OF CLASS BY TRADE |

Class of Trade	# of Accounts	Total Sales Counters
Consumer Electronics	183	1,499
Mass Merchant/Discount	11	2,285
Department Stores	12	259
Catalog Showroom	7	725
Distributors	90	3,165
Photo Chain	33	86
Mail Order	10	NA
Hardware	15	90
Other	37	66
SALES COUNTER TOTAL	398	8,175

Exhibit 2
U.S Round-Cell/
Charger Market: Sales
by Distribution
Channel

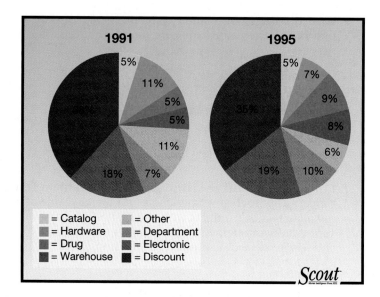

Exhibit 3
Millennium Positive
Aspect Profile All
respondents (Base: 239).

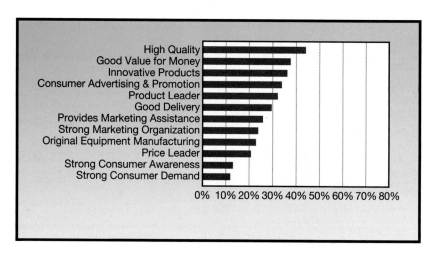

◆ Utilizes round-cell lifetime replacement guarantee as an "umbrella" over all product lines, communicating quality, credibility, reusability and durability

g. Trade positioning. The Millennium Power System is the only nationally advertised, promoted brand of rechargeable power products that addresses both the retailer's diverse customer base and the varied battery-powered products merchandised throughout their stores, thereby offering retailers the profitable advantage of partnering with one focused supplier instead of many.

Trade Positioning Taglines:

"We're Leading the Charge in Rechargeables"

"One Brand Fits All"

Trade Positioning Strengths:

◆ Presents the brand in a leadership light

◆ Addresses the retailer's customer base and product profiles

- Emphasizes the advantages of a "national brand": advertising, promotion, consumer awareness and purchase intent
- Stresses the importance and profitability of partnership
- Accentuates the "mission" of the brand and focuses directly on it: owning a position in the retailer's mind

h. Round-cell positioning. Millennium Power Cells represent a sound economic and convenient alternative to throwaway batteries.

Strengths (of positioning):

- Lowers the price-value negative perception of rechargeables
- Offers Millennium a competitive mental angle with the consumer
- Gives Millennium a "sharp hook" in the marketplace
- Breaks through the "clutter" in the industry
- Adds economic and performance credibility to the product

i. RapidCharger positioning. Millennium RapidChargers, through advanced (patented) technology, offer consumers economic and convenient fast charging (6 hours, 3 hours and 1 hour) at affordable retail prices.

Strengths:

Satisfaction ratings of battery chargers all measured on seven attributes.

Millennium's satisfaction ratings are significantly higher than the industry for five of these:

- Reduces the need for disposable batteries
- Length of time to recharge batteries
- Overall satisfaction
- The average recharge time for the industry was 6 hours in 1993; Millennium's average is the lowest (4 hours) and GE's is the highest (9 hours)
- Millennium and Panasonic have a significantly higher number of rechargeable battery purchases with a charger

Weaknesses:

- Six in ten households have the capability to charge more than four round cells, but Millennium's largest charger only holds four cells. This fact supports Millennium's introduction of the eight-position charger.
- Millennium purchasers listed "Length of time to recharge batteries" significantly more than the industry and "Charges a variety of battery sizes" and "Well-known brand" significantly less

B. EXTERNAL OPPORTUNITIES AND THREATS

1. Product Category Review for Rechargeable Round Cells and Chargers

a. Market size 1994

- Total retail sales $210 million
- Total sales to dealers (wholesale) $111 million

b. Opportunities

◆ Environmental concerns continue to be discussed
◆ New products/technologies in appliances and batteries
◆ Environmental legislation will proliferate
◆ Emerging products projected for increased household penetration (cellular, computer, mobile office, etc.)
◆ A divergent market rapidly moving toward a convergent opportunity
◆ Consumer demographics and product distribution "mainstreaming"
◆ Aftermarket dominated by appliance original equipment manufacturers—but moving long term to battery brands

c. Threats

◆ Early 1990s category growth slowed to 5–10%
◆ No new "appliance" product categories to drive consumption
◆ Lack of consumer promotions on rechargeables by all brands

d. Recharger market overview

◆ Of those who own battery chargers, three-quarters of the households own one charger unit and one-quarter own two.
◆ The share of chargers purchased with a 3-hour recharge time has been increasing each quarter, while the share whose recharge time is more than 3 hours has been decreasing.
◆ Top reasons for purchasing a brand of charger are:
  —convenience of having charged batteries whenever needed
  —reduces the need for disposable batteries
  —charges a variety of battery sizes
◆ Over 80% of all charger purchases also include a purchase of rechargeable batteries.
◆ The research has continued to show a trend that when more charger-position capacity exists in a household, more rechargeable round cells are in use in the household. In 1993, half of the households with a capacity to charge less than five round cells owned less than five rechargeables. More than one-third of the households with a capacity to charge more than six round cells owned more than sixteen rechargeables.

2. Competitor Analysis

a. Competing products' major opportunities and threats

EVEREADY

Threats	Opportunities
◆ Brand-name recognition	◆ Only offer round cells/chargers
◆ Large, direct sales force	◆ Nonmanufacturer
◆ Consumer advertising	◆ Focused on alkaline growth

GENERAL ELECTRIC/SANYO

Threats	Opportunities
◆ Brand-name recognition	◆ No consumer/trade promotion
◆ Large, direct sales force	◆ Confusion on dual brand

- ◆ "Semi"-full product line
- ◆ High-quality product

- ◆ Lack of commitment from GE-Sanyo

PANASONIC

Threats

- ◆ Price
- ◆ Packaging
- ◆ Recognized CE brand
- ◆ High-quality product

Opportunities

- ◆ Only offer round cells/chargers
- ◆ No formal marketing strategy

SAFT

Threats

- ◆ "Full" product line
- ◆ Price

Opportunities

- ◆ No consumer awareness
- ◆ Little/no consumer promotions
- ◆ No product advantages
- ◆ Weak sales force

b. Sales and market shares

- ◆ GE's unit volume share has decreased each quarter from 37% in Q492 (4th quarter of 1992) to 20% in Q393.
- ◆ Eveready now has the largest share (23%).
- ◆ Panasonic's share has been fluctuating each quarter, but is now tied with GE.
- ◆ Millennium, which recently overtook Radio Shack, has increased each quarter to 16% in Q393. Radio Shack is now at 12% share.

[*See Exhibits 4–12.*]

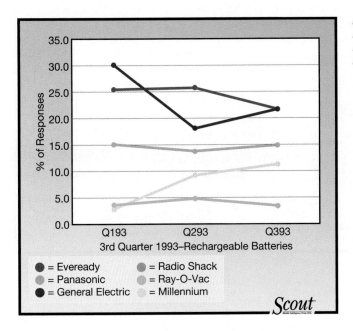

Exhibit 4
Rechargeable
Batteries: Brand Share
by Dollar Volume

**Exhibit 5
Battery Charger Units:
Brand Share by Dollar
Volume**

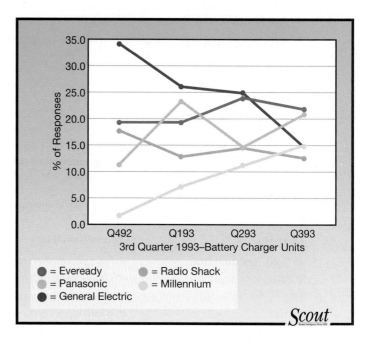

**Exhibit 6
Rechargeable Battery
Market Brand Share
by Distribution
Channel, 1993**

*Source: Millennium
Estimate*

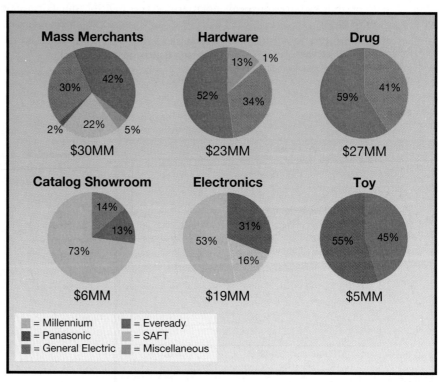

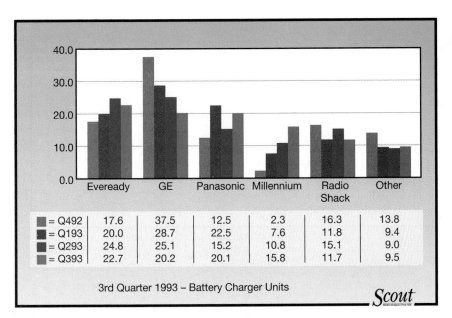

Exhibit 7
Brand Share by Unit
Volume

	Eveready	GE	Panasonic	Millennium	Radio Shack	Other
= Q492	17.6	37.5	12.5	2.3	16.3	13.8
= Q193	20.0	28.7	22.5	7.6	11.8	9.4
= Q293	24.8	25.1	15.2	10.8	15.1	9.0
= Q393	22.7	20.2	20.1	15.8	11.7	9.5

3rd Quarter 1993 – Battery Charger Units

Scout

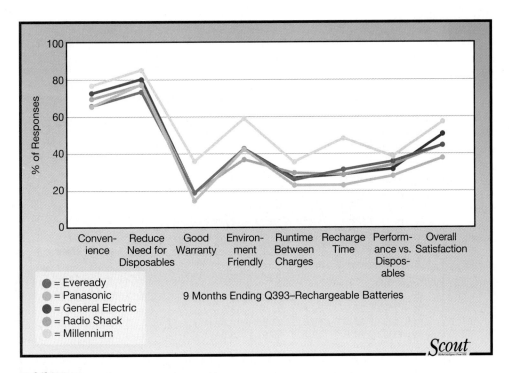

9 Months Ending Q393–Rechargeable Batteries

● = Eveready
● = Panasonic
● = General Electric
● = Radio Shack
● = Millennium

Scout

Exhibit 8
Overall Satisfaction
Ratings (Percent Who
Are Extremely
Satisfied)

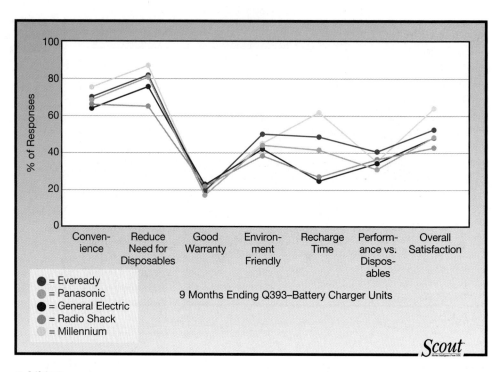

Exhibit 9
Overall Satisfaction
Ratings (Percent Who
Are Extremely
Satisfied)

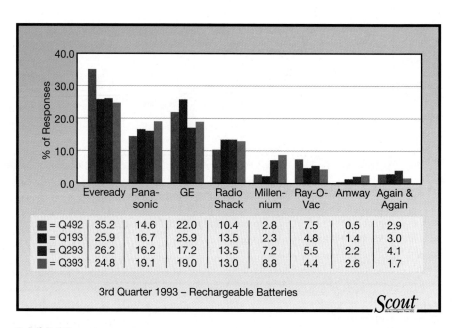

Exhibit 10
Brand Share by Unit
Volume

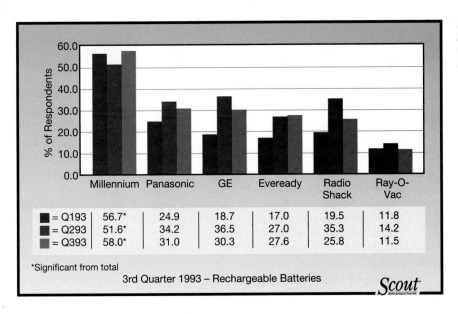

Exhibit 11
Purchased Charger
with Batteries by
Brand

	Millennium	Panasonic	GE	Eveready	Radio Shack	Ray-O-Vac
■ = Q193	56.7*	24.9	18.7	17.0	19.5	11.8
■ = Q293	51.6*	34.2	36.5	27.0	35.3	14.2
■ = Q393	58.0*	31.0	30.3	27.6	25.8	11.5

*Significant from total

3rd Quarter 1993 – Rechargeable Batteries

Scout

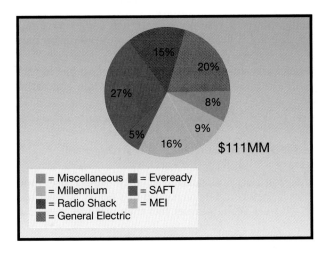

Exhibit 12
U.S. Retail
Rechargeable Battery
Market for Round
Cell/Chargers, 1993

■ = Miscellaneous   ■ = Eveready
■ = Millennium   ■ = SAFT
■ = Radio Shack   ■ = MEI
■ = General Electric

135
MILLENNIUM
MARKETING
PLAN

3. Customer/Consumer Analysis

◆ Profile of typical rechargeable battery user is:
  —male
  —children in household
  —upper Income
  —higher Education
  —under 55 years old
  —likely to be a heavy user of disposable batteries
◆ One-quarter of all households indicate usage of rechargeable batteries. Ownership skews:
  —more male than female (32.9% vs. 22.1%)

—upper income (31.2% for $50K+ vs. 19.1% for $25K or less)

—among households with children (31% vs. 27%)

◆ Direct relationship between incidence of rechargeable battery usage and increasing income of household:

—for households with incomes less than $35K ($35,000), the incidence is well below 25%

—for households with incomes over $50K, the incidence is 33% or greater

◆ Higher use with higher levels of education. Incidence is above average for households with college-educated adults, the highest among those with postgraduate degrees.

◆ Usage of rechargeable batteries increases as size of household increases. One-person households report an incidence of 18.3% vs. 33% for those with households of 5+. The greatest incidence of rechargeable battery usage is among households with children between 6 and 17 years of age.

◆ Usage of rechargeable batteries differs slightly by geographic region. The regions of the greatest incidence are:

—Mountain (31.2% usage)

—Pacific (29.4% usage)

—New England (28.5% usage)

◆ Average household purchased 2.7 rechargeable batteries in the past 2 years. In households that presently use rechargeables, 80% have purchased batteries in the last 3 years, compared to only 44% who have bought chargers.

◆ Attitudes towards rechargeables: As would be expected, there are dramatic differences in attitudes towards rechargeables when comparing users and nonusers.

—71% of users indicate that they "like" rechargeables vs. 9% for nonusers.

—66% of users feel they are a better value than disposable vs. 16% for nonusers.

—18% of the nonusers indicated that they would use more rechargeables if they could be recharged in 3 hours. Almost half the people who use rechargeables feel they perform as well as disposable batteries.

[See Exhibits 13–15.]

◆ Approximately one third of households own a Walkman, with incidence skewing dramatically toward younger and upper income households.

◆ The average household purchases approximately 16 disposable batteries per year.

◆ Use of disposable batteries is dramatically greater among families with children than among those without.

◆ Current users of rechargeable batteries appear to be quite satisfied (findings of the Clarion Study):

—71% indicate they "really" like them

—66% feel they are a better value than disposables

—45% feel that they perform as well as disposables

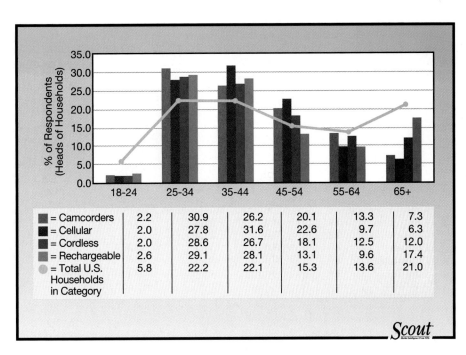

**Exhibit 13
Percentage of
Rechargeable
Purchases by
Age of
Purchasers**

*From 2nd quarter
Screener data &
follow-up ques-
tionnaires. National
Demographics and
Lifestyles*

	18-24	25-34	35-44	45-54	55-64	65+
■ = Camcorders	2.2	30.9	26.2	20.1	13.3	7.3
■ = Cellular	2.0	27.8	31.6	22.6	9.7	6.3
■ = Cordless	2.0	28.6	26.7	18.1	12.5	12.0
■ = Rechargeable	2.6	29.1	28.1	13.1	9.6	17.4
● = Total U.S. Households in Category	5.8	22.2	22.1	15.3	13.6	21.0

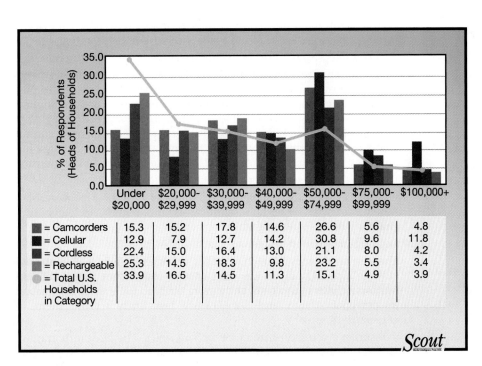

	Under $20,000	$20,000-$29,999	$30,000-$39,999	$40,000-$49,999	$50,000-$74,999	$75,000-$99,999	$100,000+
■ = Camcorders	15.3	15.2	17.8	14.6	26.6	5.6	4.8
■ = Cellular	12.9	7.9	12.7	14.2	30.8	9.6	11.8
■ = Cordless	22.4	15.0	16.4	13.0	21.1	8.0	4.2
■ = Rechargeable	25.3	14.5	18.3	9.8	23.2	5.5	3.4
● = Total U.S. Households in Category	33.9	16.5	14.5	11.3	15.1	4.9	3.9

**Exhibit 14
Percentage of Rechargeable Purchases by Income of Purchasers**

*Data from 2nd quarter Screener data & follow-up questionnaires. National
Demographics and Lifestyles*

**Exhibit 15
Percentage of
Rechargeable
Purchases by
Education of
Purchasers**

*Data from 2nd
quarter Screener
data & follow-up
questionnaires.
U.S. house-
hold date from
1980 Census.
National Demo-
graphics and
Lifestyles*

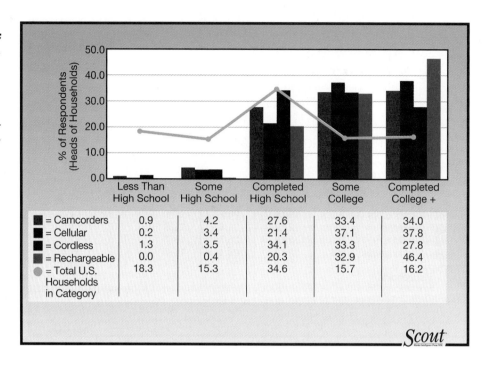

	Less Than High School	Some High School	Completed High School	Some College	Completed College +
■ = Camcorders	0.9	4.2	27.6	33.4	34.0
■ = Cellular	0.2	3.4	21.4	37.1	37.8
■ = Cordless	1.3	3.5	34.1	33.3	27.8
■ = Rechargeable	0.0	0.4	20.3	32.9	46.4
● = Total U.S. Households in Category	18.3	15.3	34.6	15.7	16.2

Scout

◆ The preliminary evidence from the Clarion Study indicates that incremental volume would be generated in the rechargeable category if more people were aware of the availability of 3-hour charging.

◆ Seven is the average number of rechargeable batteries purchased.

Since most of the profit in this industry is generated by the rechargeable batteries and not the charger, the number of rechargeables purchased is very important. Panasonic has consistently had the highest average number of rechargeables purchased, but since they are only available in Sam's Wholesale Club, Panasonic's profit margin is considerably less than other competitors'. The average number purchased has remained steady at roughly seven rechargeable batteries for the industry.

◆ One-third purchase charger with rechargeables.

Overall, one-third of purchasers buy a charger with their rechargeables. Millennium purchasers are significantly more likely to purchase a charger with their rechargeables.

◆ Rechargeable battery usage.

The top three uses of rechargeables are toys, personal stereos, and cassette/tape/CD players (all with 35% of respondent usage). Millennium purchasers are significantly more likely to use their rechargeables in personal stereos and significantly less likely to use them in camera/flash units.

◆ Consumer evaluation criteria for rechargeables. The most important of the eight consumer satisfaction attributes are:

—convenience of having charged batteries whenever needed

—reduces the need for disposable batteries

◆ Future use:

—over one-half of purchasers said they will use rechargeable batteries more often

—Millennium purchasers are significantly more likely to use rechargeables more often (almost three-quarters)

—85% percent of rechargeable battery purchasers said rechargeables reduced the number of disposable batteries they purchased

C. PRIORITIZED SWOT FINDINGS

1. Strength

◆ Trend of strong increases in annual sales

2. Weakness

◆ Not in several major chains

3. Opportunities

◆ Continued concern about environmental issues
◆ Category leader

4. Threats

◆ Established battery brands becoming more aggressive with their rechargeables

III. MARKETING OBJECTIVES AND STRATEGIES ●

A. SALES

1. Sales objectives

◆ Total sales budget: $33 million; sales goal: $36,000 million
◆ Quarterly sales objectives:

1st Quarter	13.2%
2nd Quarter	20.2%
3rd Quarter	28.4%
4th Quarter	38.2%

◆ Product sales-mix objectives:

Camcorder Power Packs	37.5%
Round Cells/Chargers	50.0%
Cordless Phone Packs	2.7%
Hobby Packs	1.8%
Cellular Phone Packs	6.4%
Miscellaneous	1.6%

[See Exhibits 16–17.]

◆ Close two major national accounts and four regional mass merchants (e.g. Kmart, Ace, Home Depot, Toys "R" Us, Circuit City, Silo, Walgreens, Eckerd, Cotter).

[See Exhibit 18.]

2. Sales Strategies

◆ Develop and implement class of trade program strategies to penetrate key regional and national target accounts.
◆ Build upon/nurture "current customer" and "class successes."

	1994 Sales Total	1995 Sales Budget*	1995 Sales Goal**	Optimal Sales Increase 1994 to 1995
EXHIBIT 16 **1995 REGIONAL SALES BUDGET SUMMARY**				
East	$3.7	$5.6	$6.2	$2.5
Central	$2.1	$5.5	$5.9	$3.8
West	$6.3	$9.5	$9.9	$3.6
National Account Manager, Central	$3.8	$5.3	$6.2	$2.4
National Account Manager, East	$4.3	$6.1	$6.8	$2.5
Fulfillment	$1.0	$1.0	$1.0	$0.0
TOTAL	$21.2	$33.0	$36.0	$14.8

*In many companies, the term *sales budget* is used to mean *sales forecast*.

**The figures in this column represent an application of the notion of *stretch* (see "Long Range Planning, Stretch, and Leverage" in this chapter) to budgeting. As you can see, these goals are well above the projected sales figures in column 2.

Exhibit 17
Millennium 1994 Sales Analysis

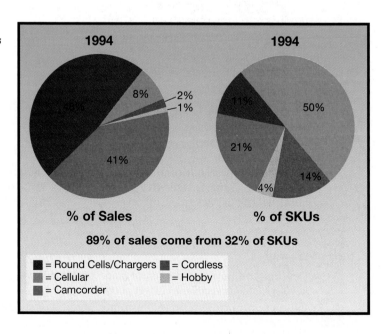

1994 — % of Sales

1994 — % of SKUs

89% of sales come from 32% of SKUs

■ = Round Cells/Chargers   ■ = Cordless
■ = Cellular   ■ = Hobby
■ = Camcorder

EXHIBIT 18   1995 KEY TARGET ACCOUNTS: EAST/WEST/CENTRAL REGIONS

Account Name	# Stores	Manufacturers' Sales Representatives	Product Lines—Competitive Brands Carried	Key City Advertising ($K)	Adv./Promo Vehicles	Avg. % Operating Income	1995 Sales Budget ($M)	Annual Sales Goal ($M)*
Target	465	Select	Round Cells—Eveready Camcorder—NONE	$200	Adv./displ./merch. Sidekick display	25%	$1,000	$2,000
Sears	865	Levitt/Harris	Round Cells—Eveready Camcorder—Dual Voltage	$200	Seasonal promo/flyer; Merch. display	30%	$1,000	$4,000
Bradlees	134	House of Reps.	Round Cells—GE	$200	Biweekly rotos Coupon book/merch.	30%	$1,000	$1,250
Toys "R" Us	262	Trent	Round Cells—Eveready	$50	Color flyers In-store merch.	30%	$500	$2,000
Circuit City	192	Legato	Round Cells—SAFT Camcorder—SAFT	$100	5-color flyers	35%	$1,000	$3,000
Lowes	115	Kyle Ford	Round Cells—GE	$20	Buy sidekick space Adv./promotion	30%	$350	$750
Lechmere	20	House of Reps.	Round Cells—GE	$40	12 roto ads; Merch.	35%	$200	$400
Kmart	2300	Nat'l. Acct.	Round Cells—GE Camcorder—Ambico	$100	Color roto Merch. display	35%	$1,000	$5,000
Pay-n-Save	126	Rittenhouse	Round Cells—GE Phone Packs—Gemini	$25	Ad support Merch. Display	25%	$150	$500
TOTALS	2,124			$1,010		16.3%**	$6,200	$18,900

*As in "1995 Regional Sales Budget Summary" table, this column represents goals based on *stretch.*
**Percent of all accounts represented by key accounts.

- ◆ Venture into "unfamiliar waters": penetrate hardware/home center, drug, and photo trade channels.
- ◆ Hire national account expertise to accelerate successes.

B. TARGETING STRATEGY

1. Trade Target—Major Discount, Drug, Photo, and Food Chains

2. Consumer Target—Heavy Disposable Battery Users Who Are:

- ◆ Adults 25–44
- ◆ Household incomes of $55K+
- ◆ Parents
- ◆ College graduates

C. BRANDING STRATEGY

1. Single-Tiered, Maintain Millennium Brand, and Relate to Eveready Only at the Trade Level

2. Strengthen Current Brand Image

D. POSITIONING STRATEGY: MAINTAIN CURRENT POSITIONING

- ◆ Consumer: **"The Power to Last a Lifetime"**
- ◆ Trade: **"One Brand Fits All"**

Brand positioning synergy: The synergy between Millennium consumer and trade positionings offers countless messaging opportunities to reach individuals, not mass markets.

E. GLOBAL MARKETING STRATEGY

- ◆ Continue to expand in South America and Asia.
- ◆ Use same positioning and brand strategy, but localize executions.
- ◆ Maintain graphic style and "power bolt" border.
- ◆ Make full use of an integrated marketing communications strategy during introduction and brand building.
- ◆ Put distribution focus on electronic retailers.

IV. MARKETING MIX ●

A. PRODUCT

1. Objectives

- ◆ Establish product management leadership and category expertise.
- ◆ Establish Millennium as the product and information "source" for rechargeable category segments.
- ◆ Develop differentiated/added-value new products.

2. Strategies

- ◆ Offer differentiated, value-added products that appeal to both the consumer and the trade.

- Accentuate product features and benefits identified through marketing research.
- Establish a competitive mental angle in the minds of consumers and the trade with every product line.
- Continue to introduce new products that offer a consistent family-line extension.
- Reinforce the brand's commitment to quality in every product and communicate "quality" to the consumer.
- Strive for preemptive features and benefits in every product and position product lines to capitalize on these "hooks" in the marketplace.

B. DISTRIBUTION

1. Distribution Objectives
- Escalate North American distribution
- Double 1994 counter displays to 16,000
- Double product line exposure in at least half of top 50 accounts

2. Distribution Strategies
- Leverage "One Brand Fits All" trade positioning
- Sell "cost effectiveness" of having one supplier supply all types
- Sell strengths of consumer marketing communications program

C. PRICING

1. Pricing Objectives
- Increase round cells price 3%
- Increase sealed lead camcorder batteries price 5%

2. Pricing Strategies
- Offer 2% 30, net 45 standard terms
- Special terms available with written authorization from senior management

D. MARKETING COMMUNICATIONS

1. Trade Advertising Programs

a. Trade advertising objectives
- Reinforce Millennium positioning of "One brand fits all."
- Reinforce the image within the trade of Millennium as the dominant brand in rechargeable batteries.
- Target key decision makers (corporate officers, buyers, and merchandise managers) involved in the following retail categories:
  —mass merchandise/discount stores
  —catalog
  —electronics
  —photo camera
- Create national awareness of the Millennium Power System throughout the year.

◆ Provide a supplemental emphasis in regional headquarter markets as needed.

b. Trade advertising strategies

◆ Maintain a leadership presence in the leading trade publications encompassing the target audience nationally.

◆ Select issues which are editorially appropriate, covering the product category and/or important trade shows.

◆ Utilize a combination of spreads and full pages to create a dominant image for Millennium.

◆ Employ a combination of traditional and nontraditional media to reach target audiences.

◆ Support sales effort by pinpointing key account headquarter markets.

◆ Support with dominant presence in major industry trade shows.

◆ Ensure that Millennium's recognized standards in appearance and message are maintained both domestically and internationally.

c. Trade advertising tactics

◆ Maintain advertising schedules in trade magazines serving target segments:
   —HFD
   —TWICE
   —Discount Store News
   —Dealerscope Merchandising/First of the Month
   —Photo Trade News
   —Photo Business

◆ Use existing inventory of ads and supplement with ads to communicate new products and programs.

◆ Purchase television and newspaper on a calling-card basis as a unique way to support the sales effort in key account headquarters markets.

◆ Continue to be the dominant rechargeable battery exhibitor in major trade shows:
   —Consumer Electronics Show (summer and winter)
   —Photo Marketing Association (February)
   —International Mass Market Retailers (May)
   —National Hardware Show (August)

◆ Begin design and procurement of a new trade show booth to debut at Winter Consumer Electronics Show '95.

[*See Exhibit 19.*]

2. Trade Promotional Programs

a. Trade promotional objectives

◆ Support the sales/distribution effort.

b. Trade promotional strategies

◆ Continue to unify strategy around a "One Brand Fits All" positioning with additional incentives equating to increased battery sales throughout the entire brand. The 1995 Millennium trade programs will offer retailers:

—*simplified* buying programs that feature one standard program for all product lines. Each account will receive published program discounts when product is ordered and shipped during specified periods.

—*lucrative* advertising and merchandising allowances that will be tied directly to dollar volume to incite dealers to advertise and merchandise during key battery retail periods of the year.

—*aggressive* selling strategy specific to Millennium Rapidchargers that offers retailers an aggressive invoice price on chargers in conjunction with a lucrative consumer rebate that enables the retailer to advertise at "hot" after-rebate price to consumers.

c. Trade promotion tactics

◆ Standardized for all classes of trade:
—Promotional Claim Form
—Meet Competition Form
◆ Contract programs must be authorized by senior management.

Key City Promotions

Funds reserved solely for incremental advertising, merchandising, promotional, and placement activity with key local, regional, and national accounts. Programs must be authorized by senior management.

Stocklifts:

In 1995, all approved stocklifts will be charged against sales by sales representative firm, by region. Programs to follow policy and must be approved by senior management.

Buying Programs

Off-Invoice:	10% any order over $1,000
	5% during buy period
Allowance:	10% Advertising
	5% Merchandising
Terms:	2% 30 net 45 days

Buy Periods

Period I	Dates: 1/4/95–4/3/95 (13 weeks)
Period II	Dates: 5/3/95–7/31/95 (12 weeks)
Period III	Dates: 9/6/95–12/18/95 (16 weeks)

(All purchase orders must request ship dates during BUY PERIODS to receive discounts. Back-ordered product will receive OFF-INVOICE discount when shipped.)

◆ Millennium Advantage Program—Another "FIRST" for Millennium Power System

The Millennium Advantage Program is the first comprehensive buying system to address retailers' needs for the entire rechargeable category. The Advantage Program takes the complexity out of product selection, merchandising, and promotion of rechargeables while helping the retailer focus on increasing sales and profits.

Exhibit 19
Millennium 1995 Trade Advertising Effort

Element	January				February				March				April				May					June				July					August				September				October					November				December			
	2	9	16	23	6	13	20	27	6	13	20	27	3	10	17	24	1	8	15	22	29	5	12	19	26	3	10	17	24	31	7	14	21	28	4	11	18	25	2	9	16	23	30	6	12	20	27	4	11	18	25
HFD		F			F	F				F				F			F			F			F			F	F			F			F			F				F					F				F		
TWICE	S		F		F				F				F				F		F			S	F			F				S	S		F			F			F		F				F				F		
Dealerscope		S			F				F									F				F									F					F			F		F			F				F		
First of the Month		S			F				F									F				F											F			F			F		F			F				F		
Discount Store News	S	R			F	R		S	R		S	R	R	R			F	S				F	R	R		F	R				F	R	R		F			R	F	R	R		F	R	R			F	R		
Photo Business						F					F								F				F					F				F				F				F									F		
Photo Trade News											F																						F																		
PMA Show (PTN)					F												*																*																		
IMRA Show (DSN)					*																																														
Hardware Show																																																			

S = Two-page spread
F = Full Page
R = Rateholder

* = Show Dailies/Page
Shading = Consumer Electronic
Show Editorial

Presented in a step-by-step, modular guidebook, the Millennium Advantage Program offers retailers a simple, direct plan for product selection, merchandising, promotion, consumer research, advertising and new trends in the rechargeable category. What gives the Advantage Program its strength is the fact that retailers choose among a myriad of tools to custom-fit the dynamics of their business.

The Millennium Advantage Program Guidebook is easy to use and illustrated throughout with colorful diagrams, plan-o-grams, product photography, merchandising suggestions, and advertising/promotional guidelines and opportunities. The Advantage Program also includes a system for customizing an array of offerings to meet the needs of each individual retailer. Other highlights include the latest innovations in rechargeable merchandising, retailer advertising, and plan-o-gram suggestions for each store or individual department. Ideas for cross-merchandising rechargeables with the products they power also are demonstrated, along with other merchandising tips such as product mix, displays, space allotments, and key selling seasons.

3. Trade In-Store Merchandising Programs

a. Merchandising objectives

◆ Increase sales volume of Millennium products at point-of-sale through proper display of product for consumer selection and purchase.

◆ Provide plan-o-gram assistance to key accounts to encourage consistent merchandising across market segments and regions.

◆ Encourage usage of secondary displays through utilization of existing plan-o-gram space at retail and providing merchandising alternatives for Millennium products.

b. Merchandising strategies and tactics

◆ Cross-Reference Module

A new consumer-targeted cross-reference display module will be available in mid-1994 to provide Millennium retailers with "the next level" of cross-reference assistance to their customers. This new display allows customers to check cross-reference information independently of sales assistance wherever the module is displayed.

◆ Four-Sided Spinner Countertop Display

Increased efficiency in full-line merchandising of Millennium power products will be possible with the new sided spinner rack scheduled to be available in 3rd Qtr 1995. This display will be intended for secondary location display of Millennium products.

◆ Charge Man Merchandiser

The 12-pack corrugated Charge Man merchandiser is actively being shipped to customers. Future plans may include transitioning this corrugated shipper to become the standard packaging configuration for Charge Man—encouraging placement of this promotional item in multiple locations at retail.

◆ Millennium Advantage Program—Retail Training Kit

A retail training kit, distributed to retailers at store level, was designed and developed to assist retail salespeople responsible for selling Millennium Power System products to consumers. The kit contains a training video, two updated cross-reference guides, and two useful pocket calendars that include Millennium selling tips.

◆ Plan-O-Gram Layout

Based on consumer and trade research, recommend that RapidChargers be relocated at the top of Millennium displays at point-of-sale. This approach places chargers at eyelevel and communicates their importance in the rechargeable system. And it translates the "razor/razorblade" theory to the retail floor—encouraging the sale of power cells to fill charging positions and electronic products. While this concept was introduced in 1993, actual implementation is just beginning to take place. Communication of this new concept, coupled with the new RapidCharger pricing strategy being implemented by the sales force will create an environment capable of placing increased numbers of chargers in consumers' hands—and therefore an opportunity to keep those chargers filled with Millennium Power Cells.

◆ Power Center "Systematic" Approach

A "system approach" presentation of rechargeable products continues to be imperative for consumer understanding of the product line, and thus for sell-through.

◆ Cross-Merchandising

Cross-merchandising rechargeable power products with the applications/devices best suited for their use helps consumers understand the accessory value of rechargeables over alkaline batteries.

◆ Millennium Advantage Program—Retail Training Kit

The video aids in developing selling skills and knowledge of rechargeable products and provides clear, easy-to-understand educational information for department managers and their retail salespeople. It features product benefits, usage information, and important selling tips and covers the full line of Millennium rechargeable products.

In addition, follow-up training tapes will be produced to maintain consistent sales knowledge at store levels as the Millennium product line progresses.

◆ Dual-Purpose (Round-Cell or Camcorder/Cellular) Countertop Display

The existing round-cell/camcorder countertop display will remain in the Millennium merchandiser lineup in 1995. Still a clean, "systematic" display fixture for either the round-cell product line or the camcorder/cellular product lines, it can be hung within existing pegboard displays at retail, a communicated necessity by many Millennium dealers.

◆ Secondary Displays

Allocation and distribution of Millennium countertop merchandisers will be modified in 1995 to target their use as secondary displays only. Primary, preferred placement of Millennium Power System components is on in-store plan-o-gram diagrams. This promotes long-term vendor buying commitments by creating a more difficult environment for change to a competitive product line.

◆ Product-Mix Recommendation

Product mix of Millennium rechargeable products should continue to be as follows:

AAs	60%
Cs	15
Ds	15
AAAs	5
9V	5

◆ Merchandising Assistance

Millennium marketing continues to offer merchandising assistance to key retail accounts such as Sears, Caldor, and Venture Stores. These requests are welcomed as they provide us the unique opportunity to directly affect the presentation of Millennium products to our ultimate customer—the consumer.

Backed by various levels of consumer and trade research and marketing expertise, the merchandising philosophies applied to our plan-o-gram suggestions are more often than not embraced with enthusiasm by our customers. When implemented at point-of-sale, feedback has been positive and can be used to strengthen the philosophy for other accounts.

Presentations are prepared and offered to retailers, along with marketing research and trending information to drive the sale of Millennium Power products through tried-and-true merchandising techniques.

In addition to account-specific assistance in plan-o-gramming, the Millennium Advantage Program provides several suggestions and templates capable of providing adequate assistance to most small- to mid-sized retail accounts.

◆ Plan-o-gram Examples

Following are several examples of plan-o-grams [Authors' note: guides to setting up retail displays] that have been completed and presented to Millennium's key accounts. Included are:

Power Center ....Trade Show Demonstration

Cross-Merchandising ....Trade Show Demonstration

Sears ....Presented and accepted

Caldor ....Presented and accepted

Venture ....Presented

[See Exhibits 20–21.]

4. Consumer Advertising Programs

a. Consumer advertising objectives

◆ Continue to establish Millennium as the consumer's brand of choice in the rechargeable category.

◆ Create 25% unaided brand awareness in North America among battery users.

◆ Continue to build consumer awareness of Millennium.

◆ Provide advertising support for the trade.

◆ Stimulate product trial.

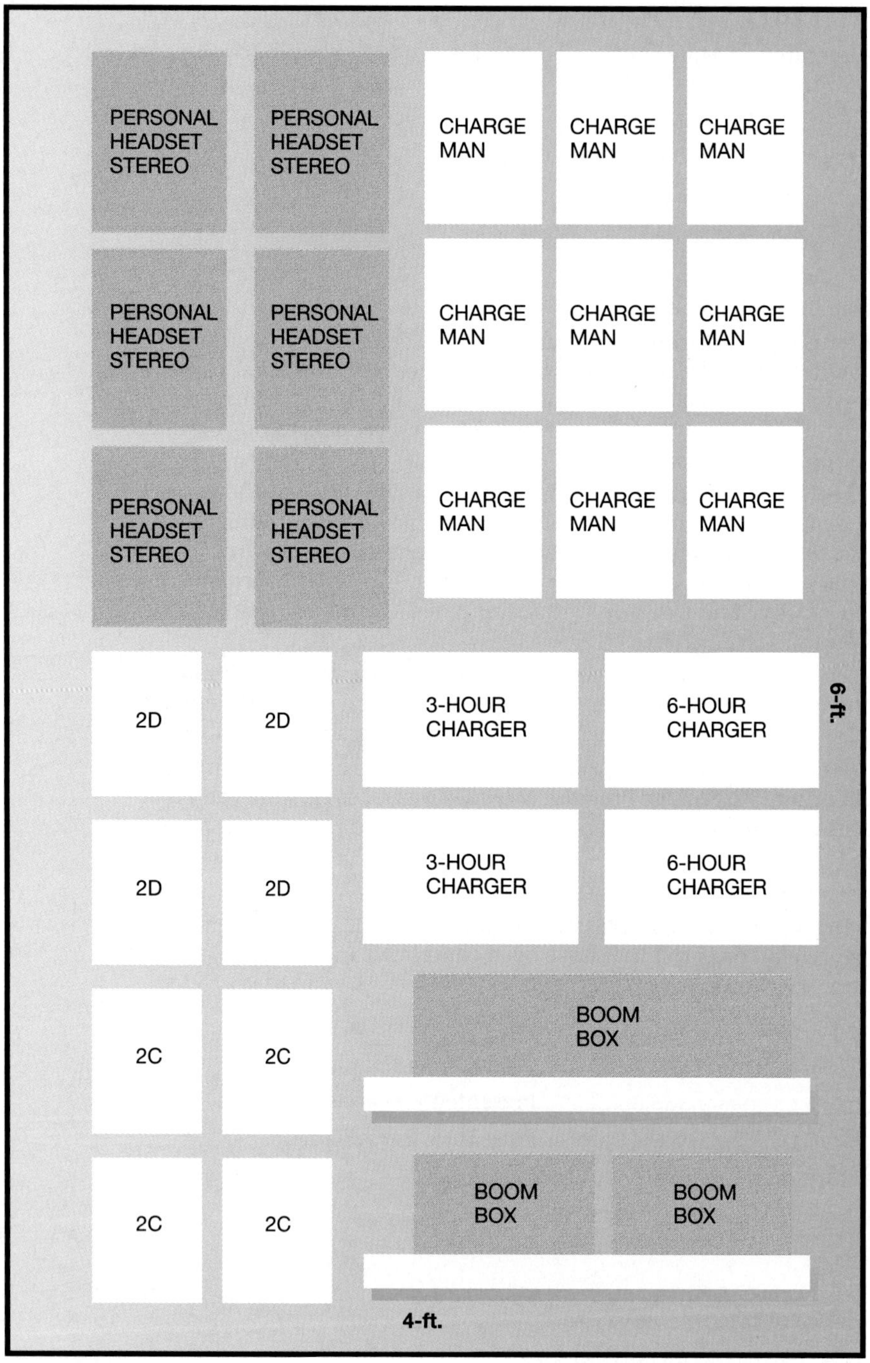

PERSONAL HEADSET STEREO	PERSONAL HEADSET STEREO	CHARGE MAN	CHARGE MAN	CHARGE MAN
PERSONAL HEADSET STEREO	PERSONAL HEADSET STEREO	CHARGE MAN	CHARGE MAN	CHARGE MAN
PERSONAL HEADSET STEREO	PERSONAL HEADSET STEREO	CHARGE MAN	CHARGE MAN	CHARGE MAN

6-ft.

2D	2D	3-HOUR CHARGER	6-HOUR CHARGER
2D	2D	3-HOUR CHARGER	6-HOUR CHARGER
2C	2C	BOOM BOX	
2C	2C	BOOM BOX	BOOM BOX

4-ft.

Exhibit 20
Plan-o-Gram:
Charge Man/Walkman
C & D/Boom Boxes

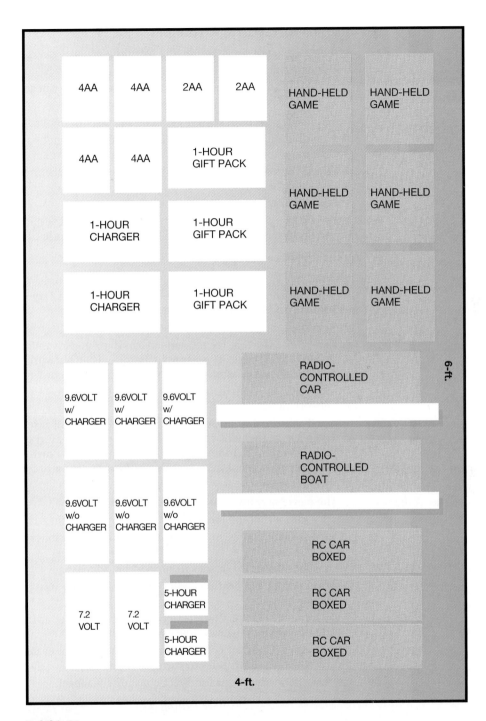

Exhibit 21
Plan-o-Gram:
AA/Games
RC Packs/RC Vehicles

b. Consumer advertising strategies

◆ Increase overall consumer media spending.

◆ Use national media that will:

—position Millennium as a "key player" in the category

—provide an impactful presence

—allow for both consumer and trade promotional support

◆ A combination of network TV, national cable TV, network radio, and national print is recommended to meet our objectives.

◆ Presell the consumer while concentrating our efforts on the key holiday selling season.

◆ Begin application of specific advertising.

◆ Use ongoing consumer research to better define the target audience and understand the messages that best reach this audience.

c. Consumer advertising tactics

◆ Network TV

Will consist of a reprise of the 1994 Thanksgiving Day event of NFL Football and the Thanksgiving Day Parade.

◆ National cable

A 6-week effort is recommended to start in November and carry through Christmas. The Family Channel, USA Network, A&E, CNN, and Nickelodeon would be considered for the schedule. A total of 25–30 announcements/week will be scheduled.

◆ Network radio

A full-sponsorship position within Fox NFL Football is recommended. The package includes sponsorship of 33 regular season games and 12 playoff games, including the Super Bowl and Pro Bowl. Four (4) 30's per game plus opening and closing billboards are part of this package.

◆ National print

The national print effort would take two forms:

—support of the Fox NFL sponsorship via tune-in ads in *USA Today*

—targeted magazine titles to support toy applications–specific message

—consumer magazines to support brand message

A total of 12 publications will be included in the buy preceding the holiday period.

◆ Continue to extend the research base on consumer attitudes and behavior relative to the rechargeable category:

—use NDL Scout consumer monitoring study to evaluate trends in consumer attitudes to batteries (ongoing)

—use focus groups for direct consumer feedback

[*See Exhibit 22.*]

5. Consumer Promotional Programs

a. Consumer promotion objectives

◆ Increase sell-through and exposure of the Millennium product line while maintaining brand and product positioning by introducing

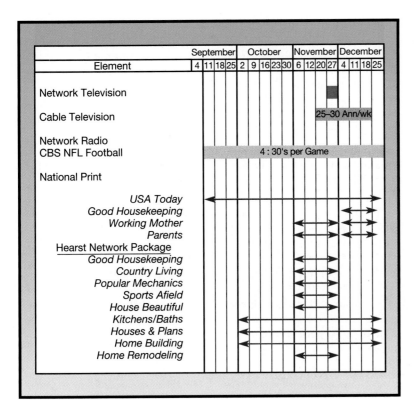

**Exhibit 22
Millennium 1995
Consumer Media
Schedule**

creative and innovative promotional programs that have measurable results.

b. Consumer promotion strategies

◆ Increase sell-through of Millennium RapidChargers by offering competitive market pricing and an on-pack rebate offer.

◆ Build and maintain brand loyalty using direct-mail promotional offers.

◆ Position Millennium for product-line expansion at key retailers by offering exciting and creative promotions that differentiate us from competitors.

◆ Work with key retailers to develop and customize regional promotional programs that drive sell-through and strengthen the dealer-brand relationship.

c. Consumer promotion tactics

◆ Millennium RapidCharger™ Rebate Program—a $3.00 national rebate on all Millennium RapidChargers (with the exception of ChargeMan).

The $3.00 rebate offer will be communicated to the customer via an "I-POP" coupon on the front of our RapidCharger packaging. In addition to the $3.00 rebate, Millennium consumers will receive bounce-back "Compare & Save" coupons with rebate offers on other Millennium products. This program will be in effect from April 1995 through February 1996.

◆ Millennium Compare & Save™ Programs

In-Store Program: Millennium will continue its Compare & Save™ in-store program, which invites consumers to compare and save by using rechargeable batteries. As part of this program, we will offer consumers in-store rebates on the following product categories:

—$5.00 off any Millennium Camcorder/Cellular Pack

—$12.00 off any 2 Millennium Camcorder/Cellular Packs

—$1.00 rebate on any Millennium Round Cells, Phone Packs, or Hobby Packs

◆ Continuity Direct-Mail Program: Consumers who receive a rebate on Millennium RapidChargers, and who send in their product registration cards, will receive rebate offers with a value of $20 on other Millennium products. The rebate offers consist of the following:

—4 coupons for $1.00 each on Millennium Round Cells

—1 coupon for $5.00 on any Millennium Camcorder Pack

—1 coupon for $5.00 on any Millennium Cellular Pack

—1 coupon for $5.00 on any Millennium Cellular Accessory

—1 coupon for $1.00 on any Millennium Cordless Phone pack

Rationale for Direct-Mail Program:

—maintain brand loyalty on future purchases of rechargeable batteries

—thank our customers for purchasing Millennium products and offer them rebates on all Millennium products

—position Millennium as the "one brand that fits all" for consumers' power needs

—help drive sell-through of Millennium products at retail

—allow us to build and maintain a consumer database for future promotional offers and market research

—differentiate Millennium in the marketplace as the brand that is doing more to drive sell-through than any of its competitors, thus reinforcing our dealer ties

◆ *Playskool Electronics Co-Promotion:* Millennium will become the "official rechargeable battery" of Playskool Electronics in 1995. This program will consist of the following:

(1) Millennium package violator on 1.2 million pieces of selected Playskool Electronic toys, including Kids First Walkie Talkie, Hipster Personal Stereo, Cassette recorder with Microphone, Talk N' Play Interactive Tape Player, Kid Keys Electronic Keyboard, Little Strummer Guitar.

(2) The Millennium and Playskool logos will appear in select Millennium and Playskool Electronics advertisements during the

1995 calendar year with respect to the products contained in this joint promotional effort.

◆ Millennium will include a promotional insert inside the packages of the selected Playskool Electronics. This brochure will inform parents of the potential savings by using Millennium Rechargeable batteries and include a $20.00 rebate offer on Millennium Chargers and Round Cells.

[*See Exhibit 23.*]

6. Public Relations Program

Millennium's 1995 national public relations programs are publicity driven to build brand visibility in targeted consumer and trade media. Consumer publicity initiatives create a predisposition to report on the category and Millennium. Product publicity and category features are primary communications tools. Continued education, relationship building, and interaction are critical to building consumer media relations.

Trade publicity initiatives maximize relationships with key trade editors to increase the frequency and depth of coverage. Millennium must be positioned as not only the category leader, but also as a resource to offer expert commentary on industry issues.

a. Marketing PR Objectives

◆ Enhance and expand national print and broadcast media access.

◆ Secure targeted brand and category coverage over 12 months.

◆ Achieve media reciprocity.

◆ Build the marketing database.

◆ Deliver monthly coverage in one or more key books.

◆ Sustain and expand relationships and coverage opportunities with key trade books.

◆ Provide publicity and promotional materials to support sales personnel.

◆ Target consumer and trade publicity vehicles and messages to reinforce key account relationships and predispose new account acquisition.

b. Marketing PR strategies

◆ Target and pitch consumer print and trade media by relevant columns, departments, sections, and audience profiles.

◆ Employ spokespersons to achieve primary broadcast media coverage.

◆ Weight consumer article pitching to support key Q4/Q1 (winter) sales cycle.

◆ Use rechargeable category story line as primary "pitch point" with consumer media.

◆ Tie consumer and trade pitch lines to product-line sales/merchandising objectives.

◆ Create "expert source" commentary opportunities in consumer and trade media.

EXHIBIT 23   MILLENNIUM 1995 CONSUMER
PROMOTIONAL EXPENSE ESTIMATES

Playskool Electronics

Promotional Fee	$190,000	
Estimated Rebate Redemption	$18,480	
(1.2MM × .1% × $15.40)		
Artwork	$7,000	
TOTAL		**$215,480**
Gross Impressions	22,000,000	
(Violater, Millennium, Playskool Advertising)		
Cost per Thousand	$9.80	

Millennium RapidCharger Rebate Program

I-POP Printing	$7,792	
Redemption (140K x 2% x $3.40)	$9,520	
TOTAL		**$17,312**

Millennium Compare & Save Programs

In-store:		
Printing of Coupons/Counter Cards	$20,000	
Estimated Redemption	$15,000	
Mail Program:		
Printing of Coupon Books (200K)	$24,400	
Mailing of Coupon Books/Fulfillment	$52,000	
Redemption (200K x 4% x $1.40 x 5)	$56,000	
(200K x 1% x 5.40 x 3)	$32,500	
TOTAL		**$199,900**

Millennium Cordless Phone Pack Promotion

Calling Card	$1,670	
Color Separations	$495	
Counter/Peg Cards Printing	$3,260	
Rebate Pads (25,000/50 sheets)	$5,228	
Redemption (250,000 x 2% x $3.75)	$18,750	
TOTAL		**$29,403**
Promotional Program Total		***$462,095***

◆ Consistently reinforce cost savings, convenience, and environmental messages to consumer media.

◆ Identify multiple consumer and trade media spokespersons.

◆ Develop a brand and select retailer case histories to use in pitching Millennium profiles to trade media.

◆ Consistently reinforce category-leader, one-brand-fits-all, value-added, and sales-support messages to trade publications.

◆ Pitch stories based on target consumer and trade publications' editorial calendars.

◆ Use trade and consumer article reprints to merchandise and reinforce publicity to key accounts and prospects.

◆ Produce collateral materials to educate retailers and reinforce selling messages.

◆ Equip sales personnel with information and materials that add true value to vendor relationships.

◆ Develop crisis/contingency plans that contain and manage product and manufacturing issues having potential negative impact on sell-through.

c. Marketing PR Tactics

◆ Media relations
Establish and maintain ongoing dialogue with target consumer and trade media. Develop and pitch story lines to these media (consumer media pitching based on publicity planning calendar).

◆ Product sales support publicity
Develop story lines based on product introductions, seasonal selling strategies, national promotions, category growth, and other relevant topics.

◆ Direct-response publicity
Research and write six press releases reporting on product-related trends and issues. Each release will offer the 800 telephone number and Taking Charge brochure.

◆ "Garbologist" media tour
A six-market broadcast and print media tour based on the environmental benefits of rechargeables and featuring the nation's foremost authority on garbage as Millennium's spokesperson.

◆ "Dadgets" media tour
A six-market broadcast and print media tour based on rechargeable-powered gift ideas for Father's Day (June).

◆ Power Preview '95

A New York media event designed to secure coverage in holiday issues of national consumer magazines. Editors are introduced to the hottest battery-powered products for the holidays, based on retail buyers' predictions (June 2).

◆ "Hidden Costs" holiday media tour

An eight-market broadcast and print media tour based on holiday shopping and the "real" cost of battery-powered holiday gifts. The USA Shopping Survey will be conducted to determine shopping plans and trivia.

◆ Industry Issues and Insight Roundtable

Co-sponsor a symposium with a target trade magazine to discuss issues critical to the rechargeable industry and position Millennium as the expert source for the category.

◆ Ad Campaign Publicity

Seek publicity for Millennium's advertising campaign among targeted national, regional, and local advertising/marketing media.

◆ Media Spotlight on Millennium Reprints

Reproduce and highlight key media clips with brand and product messages for the sales force to use with their contacts.

◆ Key Account Relations

Secure local market print and broadcast publicity through media tours or other efforts in home-office cities of key and target accounts.

◆ MAP Update Newsletter

Produce a quarterly newsletter with useful and timely information to help customers and the sales force sell Millennium products.

[*See Exhibit 24.*]

7. Packaging

a. Charge Man

Marketing has designed and recommended a new packaging configuration change in 1995 that will further increase sales of the CH2AA-BP. Packaging the Charge Man in its own 12-pack corrugated merchandising shipper should increase Charge Man's chances of receiving placement at checkout counters and other key secondary locations throughout stores. These additional locations will offer "impulse" buying opportunities to Charge Man never before enjoyed in the rechargeable category, especially during the important 4th quarter selling season.

b. RapidCharger

New 4-color "lifestyle" packaging will appear at retail in 1995 on both the new 8-Position, 6-Hour and the existing 4-Position, 3-Hour RapidChargers. The new packaging offers improved presentation of the product on

EXHIBIT 24

12 MONTHS OF MILLENNIUM NATIONAL PRODUCT PUBLICITY

January	February	March	April
Sticker Shock: ◆ Holiday gifts have dead batteries. ◆ *Emphasize cost savings of rechargeables.*	**"Dead" of Winter:** ◆ Rechargeable power means never being stuck with another dead battery. ◆ *Emphasize rechargeables' convenience.*	**Spring Cleaning:** ◆ Clean out throwaway batteries. ◆ *Emphasize stop throwing away money, time, and batteries.*	**Future Shock:** ◆ "Earth Day" focus. ◆ *Emphasize environmental benefits of rechargeables.*

May	June	July	August
Cellular Feature: ◆ Focus on cellular products. ◆ *Emphasize rechargeable benefits for mobile phones.*	**"Dadgets":** ◆ Father's Day gift buying focus. ◆ *Features "Gadget Guru" promoting rechargeables as a gift idea for Dad.*	**Successful Summer Vacations:** ◆ How to make your camcorder work for you. ◆ *Tips on operation, battery usage, and camcorder features.*	**Budget Beaters:** ◆ New ways to cut costs in your home. ◆ *Emphasize rechargeables by comparing product benefits to throwaways.*

September	October	November	December
Power Play: ◆ Battery-powered gadgets at sporting events. ◆ *Emphasize rechargeable use at sporting events (in headset stereos, portable TVs, cameras, and camcorders).*	**Battery Horror Stories:** ◆ How to avoid a throwaway battery nightmare. ◆ *Emphasize use of rechargeables by comparing product benefits to throwaways.*	**Ready for the Holidays:** ◆ Rechargeables are a perfect Christmas gift. ◆ *Gift guide coverage of Millennium products.*	**Hidden Cost of Toys:** ◆ Favorite holiday gifts include hidden costs. ◆ *Focus on cutting costs by using rechargeables.*

the front panel and highlights "ideal uses" application photography on the back panel. This new packaging concept should improve Millennium's point-of-sale presentation of the charger product line.

c. Recycling logo additions

Meeting requirements issued by PRBA (Portable Rechargeable Battery Association) will require that all Millennium power cell and power pack labels receive the addition of a recycling logo and the statement "NICKEL-CADMIUM (or SEALED LEAD-ACID) RECHARGEABLE BATTERY. MUST BE RECYCLED OR DISPOSED OF PROPERLY." Label artwork for all SKUs affected by this requirement are in the process of being modified. All new SKUs requiring label artwork will be created to meet the requirement.

d. International support

Production of packaging artwork in support of international introduction requirements (Latin America/Far East/European Union) is continuing to be developed as needed.

8. Trade Show Plan

a. Objectives

- ◆ Continue to create a leading share-of-mind presence at selected industry trade shows.
- ◆ Coordinate planning and activities (exhibit modifications, moving, special services, housing, etc.) to ensure that all aspects of trade show experience go smoothly.
- ◆ Generate significant awareness of Millennium among relevant trade show attendees, especially electronic executives.
- ◆ Create a dominant presence for Millennium.

b. Strategies

- ◆ Utilize a combination of print, broadcast, transit, and outdoor (airport videos).
- ◆ Schedule dominant creative advertisement in Consumer Electronic Show issues with bonus distribution, in addition to the show daily package.
- ◆ Reinforce the print campaign with morning television scheduled to reach the target audience preparing to leave for the Convention Center.
- ◆ Display the Millennium message en route to the convention via shuttle bus advertising and airport video walls.
- ◆ Place dominant-sized ads in show issues of trade publications.
- ◆ Place Millennium ads in premier positions in show dailies for presence on the showroom and in hotel lobbies.
- ◆ Be where the competition isn't.
- ◆ Generate additional exposure through off-premise advertising.

c. Tactics: Participate in the following shows:

- ◆ 1995 Winter Consumer Electronics Show
  January—Las Vegas, Nevada

◆ 1995 Consumer Electronics Show
June—Chicago, Illinois
◆ 1995 National Hardware Show
August—Chicago, Illinois
◆ Other trade shows and industry events

The Marketing Communications Department will provide support for other trade shows and industry events as needed. Although not exhibiting at these events, we will maintain some presence, either through the pop-up exhibit, a hospitality suite or some other means. So far, events that have been identified are PMA and IMRA.

[*See Exhibits 25–28.*]

Element	Thursday 16-Feb.	Friday 17-Feb.	Saturday 18-Feb.	Sunday 19-Feb.
Photo Trade News Daily				
Full-Page 4C	░	░	░	
Television				
Local and Cable TV 6 AM–10 AM	▓	▓	▓	▓

Exhibit 25
Millennium
Photo Marketing
Association
Trade Effort

Element	Sunday 30-April	Monday 1-May	Tuesday 2-May
Wall Street Journal			
Regional Edition Pg.B/W		░	
Spectra Vision			
Hotel Cable TV 6 AM-10 AM	▓	▓	▓
Discount Store News–IMRA Daily	░	░	░

Exhibit 26
Millennium
International Mass
Retailers Association
Trade Effort

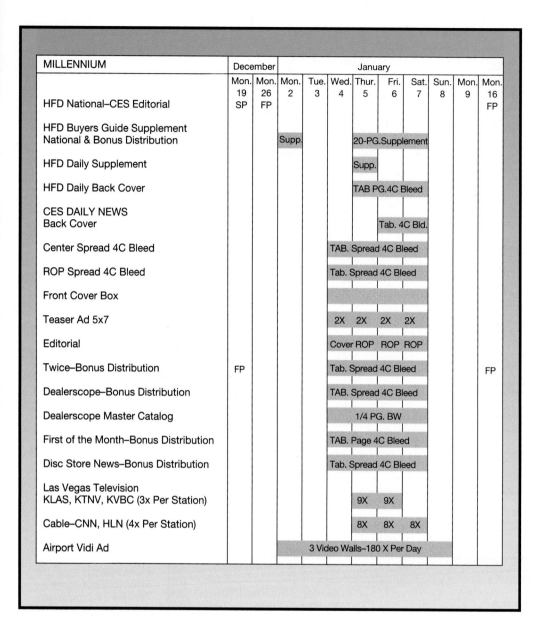

MILLENNIUM	December		January								
	Mon. 19	Mon. 26	Mon. 2	Tue. 3	Wed. 4	Thur. 5	Fri. 6	Sat. 7	Sun. 8	Mon. 9	Mon. 16
HFD National–CES Editorial	SP	FP									FP
HFD Buyers Guide Supplement National & Bonus Distribution			Supp.			20-PG. Supplement					
HFD Daily Supplement						Supp.					
HFD Daily Back Cover						TAB PG. 4C Bleed					
CES DAILY NEWS Back Cover								Tab. 4C Bld.			
Center Spread 4C Bleed						TAB. Spread 4C Bleed					
ROP Spread 4C Bleed						Tab. Spread 4C Bleed					
Front Cover Box											
Teaser Ad 5x7					2X	2X	2X	2X			
Editorial					Cover	ROP	ROP	ROP			
Twice–Bonus Distribution	FP					Tab. Spread 4C Bleed					FP
Dealerscope–Bonus Distribution						TAB. Spread 4C Bleed					
Dealerscope Master Catalog						1/4 PG. BW					
First of the Month–Bonus Distribution						TAB. Page 4C Bleed					
Disc Store News–Bonus Distribution						Tab. Spread 4C Bleed					
Las Vegas Television KLAS, KTNV, KVBC (3x Per Station)						9X	9X				
Cable–CNN, HLN (4x Per Station)						8X	8X	8X			
Airport Vidi Ad				3 Video Walls–180 X Per Day							

Exhibit 27
Consumer Electronics
Show

Element	May Mon. 8	June Wed. 1	Thurs. 2	Fri. 3	Sat. 4	Sun. 5
CES Daily News Package						
Center Spread		███	███	███	███	
Back Cover		███	███	███	███	
Front Cover Box		███	███	███	███	
Teaser Ads		2X	2X	2X	2X	
Editorial		Cover	ROP	ROP	ROP	
HFD Daily			Back Cover			
HFD Bonus Distribution			4C Spread			
TWICE Bonus Distribution			4C Spread			
Disc. Store News–Bonus Distribution			4C Page			
Dealerscope–Bonus Distribution			4C Page			
In-Hotel TV			███			
Building Projection			███			
CES Show Planner	Cover 4					
Consumer Guide Book						Cover 4
Chicago White Sox				Box		

Exhibit 28
Millennium Consumer
Electronics Show Trade
Effort

MILLENNIUM
MARKETING
PLAN

Appendix 4B

The Marketing Planning Process

I. CORPORATE DIRECTIONS ●

The analysis of the marketing situation begins with an understanding of the corporate environment within which the marketing program operates. The planner reviews everything that gives direction to the marketing plan such as the corporate mission and philosophy of business, as well as corporate financial objectives and business unit structure. Because most company managers are familiar with these issues, they need not be discussed in detail. The plan will try to link up to those elements in the corporate review that are most relevant to the current year's marketing program.

A. Corporate Overview, Objectives and Strategies
    1. Mission statement/vision/philosophy of business
    2. Long-term corporate objectives
    3. Financial objectives (return on investment, profit, share price)
    4. Organization and responsibilities of business units

II. SWOT ANALYSIS ●

Corporate guidelines provide the overall direction for the marketing plan. Information about each of the major internal and external areas is then analyzed in order to identify the most important **strengths, weaknesses, opportunities,** and **threats** facing the company and brand. Once these are prioritized, they, along with organization's objectives, drive the actual marketing plan.

A. Internal Strengths and Weaknesses
    1. Corporate
        a. Research and development capabilities
        b. Staff expertise
        c. Facilities, resources
        d. Financial position
    2. Products and brands
        a. Sales and share trend vs. category by region, channel, subcategories, season
        b. Sales forecast (optimistic, realistic, pessimistic)
        c. Proforma which sets out the costs and revenues
        d. Brand awareness, trial, and repeat purchases by major markets vs. key competitors
        e. Brand development index (BDI) for major markets
        f. Major distribution channels, key accounts
        g. Description of customer databases, accessibility, past use
        h. Share of retail shelf facings in key retailers vs. competition
        i. Brand positioning, creative strategy

NOTE: SOME OF THE FOLLOWING TERMS ARE A BIT TECHNICAL, BUT THEY WILL BE DEFINED AND DESCRIBED IN DETAIL IN SUBSEQUENT CHAPTERS.

164

    j. History of marketing communications spending, share of media voice

    k. Pricing history and current strategy

    l. Profile of sales organization (direct, brokers, sales regions)

    m. Location of plants, sales offices

    n. Anticipated changes (new products, new territories, changes in distribution channels, changes in promotional strategies, etc.)

B. External Opportunities and Threats

  1. Product category review

    a. Market size in product units and dollars or other currency

    b. Sales by major wholesalers, distributors, retailers

    c. Sales trends by year, region, product subcategories, unit sizes, major channels

    d. Category sales forecasts

    e. Category development index (CDI) for major markets

    f. Stage in product life cycle

    h. Social, economic, and regulatory changes affecting category

  2. Competitor review

    a. Competing products' major strengths and weaknesses

    b. Sales and market-share trends by region, distribution channel, subcategories

    c. Brand position, creative strategies

    d. History of marketing communications spending

    e. Pricing trends and strategies

    f. Profile of sales organization (direct, brokers, sales regions)

    g. Location of plants, sales offices

    h. Anticipated changes (new products, new territories, changes in distribution channels, changes in promotional strategies, etc.)

  3. Customer/consumer review

    a. Profile of intermediary purchasers, purchase influencers, users (identification of past primary and secondary targets)

    b. Buyer description: demographic, psychographic, usage (heavy, medium, light), Standard Industrial Code (SIC)

    c. Average purchase frequency and quantity

    d. Product usage trends; Brand selection/buying decision process

    e. Prioritization of all points of contact between customer and brand or company

    f. Prioritization of brand/corporate stakeholders

    g. Demand analysis

  4. Relevant social, economic, legal/regulatory, and technological trends and changes

C. Prioritizing SWOT Findings

  1. Identify which of the above are sources of major internal strengths and weaknesses, external opportunities and threats

  2. Prioritization—what factors are the most necessary to address during the next year and the most likely to offer significant opportunities for growth?

III. MARKETING OBJECTIVES AND STRATEGIES ●

Marketing objectives must dovetail with and support the business plan and long-range plan. Measurable marketing objectives are developed, along with the strategies to accomplish them. These key decisions, which guide the marketing mix are spelled out and justified in the marketing plan.

A. Sales Objectives
   1. Number of units by product category and geographical area
   2. Currency (dollars, yen, francs) by product category and geographical area
   3. Share of market (percentage)

B. Targeting Strategy
   1. Customer analysis and strategies
      a. Primary (buyers, users, key influencers) or secondary
      b. Heavy and light users, nonusers, competitor's users
   2. Trade analysis and strategies
   3. Balance between push (trade) and pull (consumer) strategies
   4. Other stakeholders

C. Branding Strategy
   1. Single- or multiple-tiered levels of brands
   2. Brand and line extensions
   3. Brand image: establish, change, or strengthen

D. Positioning Strategy
   1. Establish
   2. Change
   3. Confirm and strengthen

E. Global Marketing Strategy
   1. Extending domestic plan
   2. Adapting domestic plan
   3. Creating new plan

IV. MARKETING MIX ●

Each element of the marketing mix has its own objectives and strategies that must dovetail with the overall marketing objectives and strategies and with each other. Tactical implementation of planning decisions at this level through development of task-specific action plans makes it possible to accomplish the marketing objectives. Different areas are important at different times and in different situations; not all marketing plans have all areas.

A. Product
   1. Objectives
      a. Ingredient/operational changes
      b. Line extensions/deletions
      c. Cost adjustments
   2. Strategies and rationales
   3. Tactical "action plans"

B. Distribution
   1. Objectives
      a. All-commodity volume (ACV)—i.e., volume of market penetration
      b. Geography
      c. Shelf facings
      d. Channel additions/deletions/improvements
   2. Strategies and rationales
   3. Tactical "action plans"

C. Pricing
   1. Objectives
      a. Regional, international
      b. Margins
      c. Increase cash flow
      d. Balance sales fluctuations
      e. Respond to competitive change
   2. Strategies and rationales
   3. Tactical "action plans"

D. Marketing Communications
   1. Objectives
      a. Personal selling (new accounts, growth in current accounts, strengthen customer relationships)
      b. Advertising (increase brand awareness, increase brand knowledge, position brand)
      c. Sales promotion (increase trial and/or repeat purchase, add value to product)
      d. Consumer/trade merchandising (in-store programs, banners, signs, displays, etc.)
      e. Public relations (increase message credibility, reach hard-to-reach targets and other stakeholders)
      f. Direct response (conduct product test, bypass wholesaler and retailer, build relationships with current customers)
      g. Packaging (reach customer at point-of-purchase, reinforce purchase decision, differentiate brand, cross-promote other brands)
      h. Event sponsorships ("involve" customers and prospects, reinforce positioning)
      i. Trade shows and exhibits
   2. Strategies and rationales
   3. Tactical "action plans"

E. Marketing-Mix Strategy
   1. Balance interaction of product, distribution, pricing, marketing communications
   2. Driven by the competitive advantage

V. CONTROL AND EVALUATE

Scheduling and budgeting are designed to control and coordinate the implementation activities. Evaluation is used throughout and at the end of the year to determine if the plan is being followed and objectives are being met. Marketing plans usually spell out the schedule and budget, and most include an evaluation section.

A. Scheduling and Timing (Calendar of Events)

B. Budgeting
   1. By brand, region, and functional activity
   2. Risk analysis

C. Evaluation
   1. Tracking studies (awareness, trial, repeat)
   2. Test programs (product, price, marketing communications)

Chapter 5

Marketing Information and Research

THINK ABOUT IT!

PILLSBURY LOST SOME OF ITS DOUGH

Companies like Ford and Coca-Cola have provided valuable case studies on how *not* to do market research and how *not* to read the findings of such research. The failure of the Edsel and of New Coke have made marketing history. Unfortunately, the kinds of errors in marketing research that underlay these major disasters are not that unusual, and when they occur they are usually followed by a bloodbath of red ink on a company's balance sheet.

Pillsbury, an experienced marketer with a good record of new-product introductions, was badly shaken when it introduced Oven Lovin' Cookie Dough, a product that should have been a winner. An exten-sion of Pillsbury's already successful cookie dough line, the new product was packaged in a reusable, albeit somewhat more expensive plastic container and loaded with Hershey's chocolate chips, Reese's Pieces, and Brachs candies. Oven Lovin' was supported by an extensive advertising campaign

and some 200 million coupons, and within months of its launch, it was available in 90 percent of U.S. supermarkets.

Sales were brisk at first so the spending

appeared to be paying off. But soon after launch sales plunged precipitously, and within two years the product was pulled from the market. The problem: Penny-pinching shoppers didn't think the newly packaged product was worth 20 cents more than the company's conventional tube of dough, especially as it contained 20 percent less dough than the old containers.

How did Pillsbury come to misread consumers? Some analysts say that in its eagerness to bring the product to market, the company cut corners on marketing research and launched Oven Lovin' nationally without testing consumer response to price and volume levels. The fast launch is being used more and more by cost-conscious marketers, but it's a practice that can backfire. Before putting Oven Lovin' into supermarkets nationwide, should Pillsbury have had its researchers determine what price consumers were willing to pay for this new product—assuming they liked it well enough to drop it into their shopping carts—and whether they would buy it again?

These insights are not easy to come by. Consider your own experience of food sampling in a supermarket. If you don't like a product, do you tell the company representative? If you do like it, do you say how much you'd be willing to pay for it? Gauging the honesty of consumers' responses takes considerable skill. Pillsbury hasn't said how much it lost on Oven Lovin', but the figure was doubtless in the millions. ■

This chapter describes the various methods of research marketers use to try to get useful information, accurate answers, and insights into consumers' attitudes and behaviors—all of which are needed in order to make intelligent strategic marketing decisions.

WHAT IS MARKETING RESEARCH?

Marketing research is the essential information-gathering process that underlies intelligent and effective marketing decision making. According to the American Marketing Association, marketing research

marketing research
A systematic process of identifying the information needs of marketing decision makers, designing and implementing procedures for gathering and analyzing relevant data, and reporting research findings.

links the consumer, customer, and public to the marketer through information—information used to identify and define marketing opportunities and problems; generate, refine, and evaluate marketing actions; monitor marketing performance; and improve understanding of marketing as a process. Marketing research determines the information needed for these purposes, specifies and implements the data collecting process, and interprets and communicates results.[1]

We can define **marketing research** more simply as the systematic process of identifying the information needs of marketing decision makers, designing and implementing procedures for gathering and analyzing relevant information, and then communicating research findings to the appropriate people.

The marketing research process may use formal scientific methods or informal forms of investigation. However it is carried out, marketing research has two major goals: to find ways to improve all elements in the marketing mix; and to reduce the uncertainty—and thus the risk—of a business venture, whether that venture is the introduction of a new product (like Pillsbury's Oven Lovin' Cookie Dough), a new advertising campaign for an existing product, the opening of a new sales territory, or some other high-risk marketing activity. Accurate marketing research reduces risk by giving managers the information they need to make sound decisions. Exhibit 5-1, a promotional piece for research findings on a particular market, is an example of the kind of information marketers seek.

MARKETING INFORMATION

Marketing research addresses virtually every aspect of a firm's operations. Today more than ever managerial decision making at all levels relies on obtaining, understanding, and using marketing information to create value for customers.

This need for knowledge in every aspect of a business has led to the development of the marketing information system, which is the first type of system referred to in objective one of this chapter. The **marketing information system** (usually known as **MIS** but also sometimes referred to as **MkIS**) is an integrated, company-wide program for collecting, storing, and retrieving internal and external information used in marketing decision making.

Actually, every marketing information system is part of a larger system called a *management information system* (also abbreviated MIS), which is the second type of system referred to in objective one of this chapter. Management information systems are organized systems of people, equipment, and procedures responsible for gathering, analyzing, classifying, evaluating, recording, and disseminating relevant and timely information throughout a company. Computers in the corporate MIS manipulate databases to answer questions for in-house clients such as top management, marketing, sales, marketing research, and R&D.

Tombstone Pizza began as a frozen convenience item used in small taverns. When the company expanded its customer base to include large supermarkets, it found it needed a better information system to support its new marketing strategy. As business grew rapidly, Tombstone identified several deficiencies in its reporting systems:

1. It had no provision for acquiring detailed sales information on cash customers.

2. Its sales reporting was based solely on product shipped from the plant; it took no account of outlet purchases.

3. The company's route salespeople were allowed to give discounts on individual sales without furnishing Tombstone with information about which customers received discounts and on what product varieties.

4. Headquarters was receiving little information on how effectively Tombstone was penetrating existing market areas.

5. The company's estimates of its market share were inaccurate because they were based on outside data sources that monitored warehouse activity.[2]

marketing information system (MIS or MkIS) An integrated company-wide information program that collects, stores, and processes both internal and external data to provide appropriate staff with the information they need to make valid marketing decisions.

Exhibit 5-1
Research for Sale

*Mediamark Research is an
independent company that
does research on particular
markets and sells the findings
to client companies. This is a
report on one of Mediamark's
studies of the Affluent
Market. What marketers
would be interested in this
information?*

The Affluent Market!

Presenting Mediamark's Upper Deck Report. Not just a reflection. The affluent market as it actually is.

The affluent. Are you really going to find them at the polo club, sipping cognac after a couple of chukkers?

The truth is, the affluent of the 90's are quite different from the stereotypes. In fact, you're more likely to find them watching a game show than a horse show.

Mediamark's Upper Deck Report is the only study of the affluent to go beyond the stereotypes and offer a wealth of actionable data about today's diverse, unconventional high-income consumers.

Tracking the affluent: six years of trendable data

Mediamark Research is *the* authority on upscale consumers and has offered a study of the affluent market every year since 1983. Each year we report on the demographics (more than 60 measures), product and service usage (more than 450 categories) and media preferences (250 magazines plus newspapers, broadcast TV, cable, and radio) of this

Well Feathered Nests. *Households with at least one high income earner with children present. The best educated segment. The ones most likely to rent automobiles, to fly on business trips, and to purchase business suits.*

Nanny's in Charge. *Households with two or more earners, none high income, with children present. The largest households among all segments. The ones most likely to purchase electric blenders, food processors and dishwashers.*

sought-after population group.

If you want to know how luxury car purchases are trending, the Upper Deck can give you the answer. Is wine consumption among the affluent up or down? Check the Upper Deck.

It is, quite simply, the definitive upscale market database for the most affluent society on earth.

Defining the affluent: who they are and who they're not.

There may be as many ways to define the affluent as there are studies about them. But only Mediamark's Upper Deck Report offers a consistent, inflation-proof definition that allows for reliable comparisons with the population at large.

Using household income figures for the entire nation, we select the top ten percent (or upper decile) for the Upper Deck Report. That way, we can be sure we are always getting a representative sample of the affluent, regardless of inflation or changes in income distribution.

In 1983, when our first report was published, the Upper Deck segments had current household incomes of $47,806 and above. Today, that figure has increased to $62,400.

A study in reliability

Data in the Upper Deck Report are collected from nearly 6,000 affluent consumers over a two-year period, using the most statistically reliable research techniques.

Our sample is "turned over" every year, and is large enough to ensure reliable projections. In 1989, the sample size for the Upper Deck Report is 5,950. For the $75,000-and-up income earners, the Upper Deck sample is a sizeable 3,296.

One of the greatest strengths of the Upper Deck study is

The Good Life. *person employed employed. Most have retired from consumers of liq*

Tombstone's new MIS not only monitors discounting and pricing but also details sales by product variety so regional taste distinctions are highlighted. Moreover, route salespeople now use the MIS reports to help retail customers identify their most efficient purchase levels. The system has clearly revealed to managers not only that sales are growing but also that profitability is up in specified areas and in particular types of retail outlets. Like most companies, Tombstone has found that the more usable information it obtains on its business activities, the more responsive it can be to strategic opportunities.

The key word here is *usable,* for firms sometimes find themselves overwhelmed by rapidly accumulated data that they are hard pressed to assimilate. New technologies like **electronic data interchange (EDI)**—an interactive electronic network that enables manufacturers to share information with suppliers, distributors, and retailers—are creating more data than individual marketers can handle. Some companies now have a *chief information officer (CIO)* who is responsible for compiling data in ways that are most useful to busy managers. This new position is often of high rank on the organization chart, right up there with the CEO (chief executive officer) and CFO (chief financial officer).

electronic data interchange (EDI)
An interactive electronic network that connects manufacturers with suppliers, distributors, and retailers so they can share information.

our high survey response rate—66.5% for the top income stratum in 1989 as compared to around 50% (or considerably less) for other upscale market reports. For a group that is traditionally hard to reach, the Upper Deck Report represents an unusually solid base for decision-making.

Targeting the affluent: a matter of perspective

When you set your sights on the affluent you have to be able to look at them in comparison to the rest of the population. What, other than having higher incomes, sets them apart?

And, just as importantly, how can you be sure your comparisons are valid?

They will be—if they're drawn from a single source. All Upper Deck respondents are drawn from Mediamark's National Survey of American Consumers. They provide the same information as the rest of our respondents. They are visited by the same interviewers, using the same questionnaires. Their responses are coded and analyzed by the same methods.

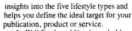

No Strings Attached.
Households with at least one high income earner and no children. The largest income group among women. The biggest investors in money market funds and common or preferred stock.

Not one upscale market, but five.

In 1983, when Mediamark first began to study this market, we made an interesting discovery: affluent households are not all alike.

In fact, there are *five* types of affluent households, each possessing a unique consumer profile of its own. And only Mediamark's Upper Deck Report can tell you who they are and what they're buying.

New! Lifestyle analysis section

An exclusive feature of the 1989 Upper Deck Report is a new lifestyle analysis section highlighting the differences between affluent market segments. This provides quick, accessible

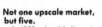

Affluent households with no or the head of household not members are 55 and older and n the workforce. The heaviest quors and champagne.

insights into the five lifestyle types and helps you define the ideal target for your publication, product or service.

• In *Well Feathered Nest* households, one in three women are homemakers, as opposed to *Nanny's in Charge* households where almost all of the women work.

• Most *Good Life* households are in the South and West while other affluent segments are concentrated in the Northeast and Pacific Southwest.

• Selling first class travel? Target the *No Strings* group. You'll be surprised to find that they're much more likely to pack up and go than *Good Life* households.

Learn the Lifestyles of the Rich and You'll be Famous

Why settle for a mere reflection of the affluent market when you can study it in depth—and make a name for yourself and your company with sharper marketing, better targeting and bigger sales. Call Mediamark Research and order the Upper Deck Report today.

Two Careers. *Two or more income earners, none high. Three out of four households have adult children contributing to household income. The segment most likely to have recently purchased a video cassette recorder or open a new checking and savings account.*

Managing Information

Management decisions are based on information, and the collection and management of information are the responsibilities of a marketing information system. An MIS is a process for developing a continuous flow of information: it contributes to decision making by producing structured summary reports on a regular schedule.

DATA AND INFORMATION VERSUS INSIGHT

The many people involved in marketing research have two basic functions: to collect data and to analyze those data to produce useful information. It's important to distinguish between these two. *Data*—facts, statistics, and observations—are the raw material. When assembled and properly analyzed, data become *information*—knowledge or intelligence about a situation or circumstance—that is critical to planning and decision making.

The challenge for planners is to derive real insight from data and information. Lisa Fortini-Campbell says that time and again marketers miss connecting with their customers, not because they lack information, but because they lack insight into their customers.[3] As you'll see in the next section, even firms as mighty as Coca-Cola sometimes stumble.

RISKS AND GAMBLES
RESEARCH THAT FIZZLED

You Can't Beat "Classic"

Had Coca-Cola introduced Coke II, its sweeter variety designed to do battle with Pepsi, as a brand extension like Cherry Coke, Coke II might have done better. But it may have done the brand a favor by getting Coke to rename its original drink "Classic."

Back in 1886 a druggist named John Pemberton concocted a new cola beverage for his soda-fountain customers. For ninety-nine years Pemberton's "7X" formula was the recipe for success at Coca-Cola, but in the 1980s the company's management began to feel its market erode under the onslaught of PepsiCola. Blind taste tests repeatedly showed that cola drinkers preferred Pepsi's slightly sweeter product. This was especially true of young people, the largest cola-drinking segment of the population, who were promotionally dubbed "the Pepsi generation."[4]

Like most large corporations, Coke turned to market research for a solution to its problem. About $4 million and 200,000 consumer blind taste tests later, one consistent finding emerged: Coke drinkers preferred the company's new, sweeter formula. Of the 110 million additional people asked to try the new cola, 80 million said they liked it enough to drink it again. Accordingly, management decided to dump the old formula and announce the birth of "New Coke."

The reaction was totally unexpected. Loyal Coke drinkers, initially stunned, began to fight for their product. They wrote angry letters, staged formal protests, and threatened lawsuits to force the retention of the "Real Thing" they had grown up with. Clearly they had formed an emotional attachment to Coca-Cola that went undetected by the company's marketing research. Two months after announcing the demise of the old formula, embarrassed company officials reintroduced its century-old formula as "Classic Coke."

Today New Coke has barely 1.5 percent of the market. Nevertheless, industry analysts point out, Coca-Cola has at least temporarily increased its shelf space and market share by offering two Cokes instead of one—proof, in their view, that a creative marketing effort can reap success from failure. In 1990 New Coke was repackaged as Coke II, and the product was launched nationally in 1992 after test marketing. Coke II thus continues the battle, although as yet it has only a tiny share of the market.

The case of New Coke underscores an important risk in modern marketing. Marketing research must be as objective as possible, but marketers must never forget that number crunching cannot substitute for insight into people's attitudes and behavior. Customer insight must inform modern marketing decision making.

ENVIRONMENTAL SCANNING

Successful marketing executives are constantly scanning the environment for information that will help them plan their marketing efforts. They have a passion for knowing everything there is to know about the industry in which their business operates, other players in that industry, the industry's consumers, and general marketplace trends. *Environmental scanning*, the topic of chapter objective two, can provide valuable insights into both existing and potential problems and opportunities. In its informal form, called *surveillance*, marketers keep their ears and eyes tuned for rumors, nuggets of information, and insights from other marketers' experiences.

The information gathered in the surveillance mode comes to managers who keep in touch. The more formal *search* mode of information scanning involves a deliberate attempt to learn more about a particular topic. It includes such investigations as reading trade publications and books, walking through stores to get a general sense of consumer behavior, and talking to sales representatives and members of the distribution chain either in person or by telephone (the latter technique is known as "desk research").

To see how this environmental scanning process works in actual practice, consider the activities of a small restaurant owner. In the course of seating people and handing them menus, the proprietor *views* a great many behaviors on the part of both customers and staff. As an owner who is concerned about the quality of service, she also *monitors*, or focuses specifically on, such things as whether servers smile at customers. To *investigate* customers' assessment of the quality of food served, the owner may stop at individual tables and ask people how they enjoyed their meals. Finally, the owner may commission formal *research* to reveal the market's demographics.

THE MARKETING RESEARCH PROCESS ●

The formal marketing research process, the subject of the third chapter objective, consists of five basic steps:

1. Identification of the research problem
2. Development of a research plan and methodology
3. Data collection
4. Analysis and interpretation of the data
5. Communication of the findings

We will consider each of these steps, which are depicted in Figure 5-1, in detail.

STEP 1: IDENTIFYING THE RESEARCH PROBLEM ●

Defining the problem—which may be either an opportunity or a threat—is the hardest part of the research process. There is an old saying that if you know the problem, you are half-way towards solving it. It requires clear thinking about precisely what information is necessary to make marketing decisions that will enable you to take advantage of what appears to be a business opportunity or to solve a particular business problem. If you fail to identify the problem, misidentify it, or assemble information that is unrelated to the decisions you need to make, then the rest of the process will be useless. No

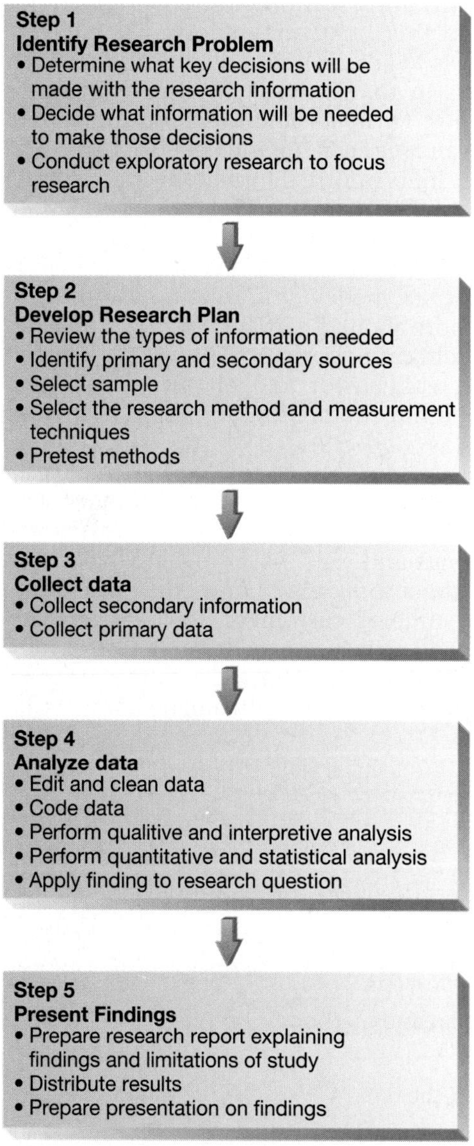

Step 1
Identify Research Problem
- Determine what key decisions will be made with the research information
- Decide what information will be needed to make those decisions
- Conduct exploratory research to focus research

Step 2
Develop Research Plan
- Review the types of information needed
- Identify primary and secondary sources
- Select sample
- Select the research method and measurement techniques
- Pretest methods

Step 3
Collect data
- Collect secondary information
- Collect primary data

Step 4
Analyze data
- Edit and clean data
- Code data
- Perform qualitive and interpretive analysis
- Perform quantitative and statistical analysis
- Apply finding to research question

Step 5
Present Findings
- Prepare research report explaining findings and limitations of study
- Distribute results
- Prepare presentation on findings

Figure 5-1
The Marketing Research Process

matter how good your data gathering, no matter how excellent your questionnaire, no matter how precise your statistical analysis, unless your efforts are directed at the real problem, you will end up with what may be a great solution—to the wrong problem!

It is extremely important at this stage not to confuse a problem with its symptoms. If sales or profits have fallen far below projections in one region, for example, the shortfall is not the problem—it is a *symptom* of the real problem. The real problem might be an increase in competitors' activity in the marketplace, poor cooperation on the part of retailers, or a decline in sales-force performance.

When you cannot easily determine the nature of the real problem, the best course may be exploratory research. *Exploratory research* seeks to clarify questions, not to obtain answers to specific research questions. Suppose sales have declined in a firm's Quebec division. To get a fix on the reason for the decline, marketers need some kind of historical perspective on the division's performance, and the best place to look for that would be in past sales data. Information on economic, political, competitive, and other external factors would probably also be useful. Looking at all of this information together might help marketers formulate specific questions that other forms of marketing research could then be used to answer.

Whether or not exploratory research is needed, the outcome of this first step in the marketing research process should be a statement of the basic problem to be explored. Identifying the problem, the first topic of chapter objective four, leads to a set of research questions or hypotheses. These questions will guide the rest of the marketing research process, beginning with the development of a research plan, which is alluded to in chapter objective four.

STEP 2: DEVELOPING A RESEARCH METHODOLOGY AND PLAN

Methodology, budget, and schedule all need to be decided upon and included in a *research plan*. This is a written document that communicates to all involved what types of information are needed, the primary and secondary sources of the information, the research methods and sampling procedures selected for the research, the pretest parameters, who is responsible for carrying out the study, and the timetables for the various research activities.

Depending on the goals of the research effort, marketers will select methodologies that are either quantitative or qualitative. **Quantitative research** methods focus on the collection of numerical data; they make extensive use of statistical analysis and produce tables and charts. **Qualitative research** methods are more interpretive and require more judgment on the part of researchers; they are used to search out underlying motives for the feelings and opinions respondents express.

Since formal marketing research costs the company both time and money, managers must decide early in the process whether an extensive research effort will pay off. They must weigh the time and cost of the research against the risk of making an uninformed decision. Pillsbury opted to introduce its new cookie dough without undertaking a full-blown research program, and its gamble probably cost it a lot more money than the company would have spent had it done the research necessary to evaluate the product relative to its price.

As Figure 5-2 illustrates, in the early stages of research you lower your risk rapidly because you acquire a lot of information quite quickly. If you continue to do research, however, the amount of additional information you acquire decreases and the rate at which you lower your risk slows greatly. Notice how the curve in Figure 5-2 flattens out, indicating that no matter how much

quantitative research
Research that seeks quantifiable data and usually employs some form of statistical analysis.

qualitative research
Research that typically uses open-ended data-collection methods in order to gain insight into consumers' motives and reasons.

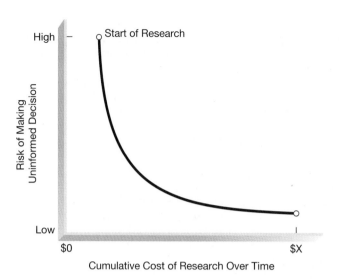

High — ○ Start of Research

Risk of Making
Uninformed Decision

Low ○

$0 $X

Cumulative Cost of Research Over Time

Figure 5-2
Risk and the Cost of
Information

178

more money you spend, you are not going to learn a great deal more. Some managers hide their refusal to make a decision by doing more and more research, continuing to spend money with little gain in insight. In the business this is known as *analysis paralysis*.

Perhaps the best way to assess how extensive your research should be is to look at the different options under consideration at the firm. If the company's actions will be the same no matter what the research findings, time and money can obviously be better spent in other ways. Thus planners often use a "backward approach." They start at the end of the marketing research process—with the envisioned goals, decisions, and actions—and work backward so that the ends of the endeavor shape the entire process.[5] To decide how extensive your research effort should be, then, you must review the type of information needed to make the key marketing decisions that you have identified in Step 1.

No matter what the magnitude or implications of the decisions managers will make based on research findings, the expense of marketing research is always a crucial consideration. The costs of marketing research vary widely, depending on the size of the study and the data-collection methods used. Top executives often suffer "sticker shock" when given a realistic estimate of research costs. It's in the subsequent discussion of what is critical to know, what is only "nice to know," and what lower-cost alternatives are available that managers earn their pay.

STEP 3: COLLECTING THE DATA

How much time, effort, and energy are expended on data collection depends on the specific research methods used. We discuss these methodological tools in the next major section of the chapter, "Data Collection Methodology." In this section we focus on the kinds of data that can be collected, the topic of chapter objective five, and the sources from which they can be obtained, the subject of chapter objective six.

Data sources may be primary or secondary. **Primary data** are derived from original research undertaken either by the firm itself or by a research company hired by the firm to address a specific problem. **Secondary data**

primary data
Data obtained from original research by the firm itself or by professional researchers hired by the firm.

secondary data
Published sources of information that are usually in the public domain but are often very general and lack timeliness. Government is the largest provider of such data.

are data that already exist, having been gathered for some other purpose. Secondary data can be culled from libraries, databanks, and reports from such sources as associations and trade publications. Whenever possible, marketing researchers try to use secondary data to save time and money, for the costs of accessing computer databases are generally lower than the costs of doing new research. We will look at this relatively inexpensive source of information first and then explore the use of primary data.

Secondary Data Government agencies at the federal, provincial, and local levels are the largest suppliers of secondary data in Canada. The *1993 Statistics Canada Catalogue* lists many reports that are available. Statistics Canada also publishes the *Market Research Handbook* each year which provides an overview of the economy, while the *Canadian Economic Observer* provides monthly updates. Specialist publications also available include *Canadian Social Trends* (annual); *Energy Statistics Handbook* with monthly updates; "Perspectives on Income and Labour" (quarterly); *Intercorporate Ownership 1992*, and when all else fails, the *Guide to Statistics Canada's Programs and Products*. Trade and industry associations also provide extensive industry information. The *Encyclopedia of Associations*, which is found in most libraries, gives brief descriptions of associations in many fields and lists their publications, including pamphlets, journals, and reports. Business publications such as *The Financial Times, The Financial Post, Canadian Business, Maclean's,* and *The Globe and Mail,* as well as *The Wall Street Journal, Business Week, Forbes,* and *Fortune,* often carry statistics of use to the marketing researcher; these kinds of publications are particularly good sources of industry and product-category data. In addition, many business-to-business marketers find it useful to subscribe to journals that report regularly on the industries to which they sell their products and to attend meetings of the professional associations that represent these industries. Reading such journals regularly and attending association meetings can provide the marketer with valuable insights into industry changes that may affect sales.

Since marketing research departments rarely have enough people to read through the countless government and trade publications available on a regular basis, they tend to use data banks, syndicated studies, and firms in the information industry to obtain secondary data. **Databases** are large, often computerized collections of information of all kinds, including industry statistics. Most small and mid-sized marketers access statistical and economic data banks through libraries, business schools, chambers of commerce, trade associations, and government agencies. Stock exchange and the news wire services provide more general databases. Companies and individuals may also subscribe to commercial computer services.

The database originated in the United States and has rapidly expanded into other parts of the world. In Europe, for example, marketing databases are being developed as the European Union (EU), formerly known as the European Community, moves toward a single market. The London Chamber of Commerce runs one of the United Kingdom's largest database access services, providing more than 1,000 individual databases to British companies that sell their products either domestically or throughout the EU. To cut the cost of acquiring information, the EU's Brussels-based executive arm is setting up major database networks for the use of member nations.[6]

Computerization of many data banks by such on-line services as LEXIS/NEXIS, Info Track, ABI Inform, New Product Announcements, Prompt, the F&S Index of Corporations and Industries, Compuserve, Mead Data Central, and Dialog Information Service has made secondary data far more accessible. One data bank that is useful for industry information, particularly on a

databases
Large, often computerized, collections of information.

global basis, is the National Trade Data Bank (NTDB), which references all U.S. government reports on trade. Some search programs are free; others charge for computer connect time. Some programs are restricted in scope, but others enable you to access a wide array of databases. Dialog, for example, offers instant access to more than 320 databases, including Dun & Bradstreet, Standard & Poor's, Moody's, Disclosure, @Predicasts, Trinet, McGraw-Hill, Reuters, API, UPI, Knight-Ridder, and government agencies.

There is hardly an industry today that isn't covered by one or more *syndicated studies*. These studies are termed "syndicated" because they are available to all firms that subscribe to the research services offering them. The Mediamark Research report featured earlier in this chapter (Exhibit 5-1) is an example of syndicated research. Almost 400 research companies, such as Business Communications Company, Business Trend Analysts, FIND/SVP, Mediamark, and Packaged Facts, publish studies that are available for a fee usually ranging from $400 to $3,000. Packaged Facts, for example, offers reports of research studies in such markets as bicycles, chocolate, energy drinks, ethnic cosmetics and hair care, health and natural foods, home medical testing, infant formulas, nonprescription contraceptives, oral hygiene, tabletop sweeteners, and wristwatches. Mediamark conducts a comprehensive annual survey of more than 20,000 consumers, then profiles them according to more than 60 characteristics and assesses their media exposure and product usage patterns.

If you look back at the Millennium Marketing Plan in Appendix 4A, you will see that it includes a great deal of information accumulated from secondary sources. In particular, Millennium used the Scout reports purchased from National Demographics and Lifestyle (NDL), a service that analyzes

Databases and Knowledge Workers

Like many other members of the organization, marketing researchers are "knowledge workers." As people who deal in data, they are the natural beneficiaries of new technological developments like this optical disk, which is capable of storing the contents of hundreds of file boxes and from which any piece of information can be called up instantly. At least one study has found, however, that the most productive companies spend less per employee on MIS than companies with just average productivity, which suggests that technology works best when error reduction and customer service get proper attention first.

clude a simple, clear, summation of the results of the research and of any limitations on those results (such as a sample that is too small for reliable conclusions to be drawn). If clients don't understand or trust research findings, or if they are too unimpressed by them, the research effort will have been wasted.

DATA COLLECTION METHODOLOGY ●

Primary data are never free. The costs vary according to the size of the sample studied, the amount of time allowed for data collection, and the data collection method used. We begin this section with a discussion of sampling techniques, the topic of chapter objective seven. Then we explore several data collection methods: observation; interviews; focus groups; surveys; panels; diaries and scanners; and experiments, including test marketing.

SAMPLING

A key decision that must be made before collecting primary data is what population will be studied. A **population** is a total group of people—such as teenaged boys, Chinese Canadians, or new parents—about whom marketers and researchers wish to know something. But marketing researchers can rarely afford to talk to *all* prospective buyers. For example, if the market for bar soap consists of adults nineteen years and older in North America and the European Union, there is no way that the Dial brand manager can afford to find out how *every one* of these people feels about an ad concept, package, and new product features.

Researchers solve this problem by interviewing a portion of the market—a **sample**—that is representative of the larger designated population. The sample must accurately reflect the attitudes, interests, and behaviors of the larger population, and to ensure that it does, it is carefully matched by certain key characteristics—age, gender, racial composition, education, and so forth—to the larger population. If the matching is accurate, researchers can use information obtained from the sample to draw valid conclusions regarding the whole population. In rare instances, usually when the population is quite small, a study will look at *all* individuals in that population; this type of study is called a *census*.

In selecting a sampling technique, marketing researchers must answer three questions:

1. *Who is to be surveyed?* Answering this question requires making a proper choice of population. The choice of a population is often constrained by such factors as: Who has the desired information? For example, if you want to investigate whether consumers are interested in widescreen television, you would probably want to limit the population to people who are owners of high-end electronics products, since they are the ones most likely to know enough to appreciate and pay for such an innovation. Another factor constraining population choice is: Who can be accessed with relative ease, as by phone book, street directories, membership directories, or other readily available lists? Finding people who are high-end electronics users could be difficult as there are not many directories that list these people.

2. *How many people should be surveyed?* Small samples cost less and usually take less time to study than large ones, but large samples tend to produce more accurate research results. The researcher must balance these

population
A defined group of people or organizations about which a researcher wants to know something.

185

MARKETING INFORMATION AND RESEARCH

sample
A portion of the population that the researcher selects for a particular study. A sample must be representative of the population from which it is drawn.

factors and determine a reasonable sample size given budget and accuracy requirements.

3. *How should the sample be chosen to assure its validity?*

Whenever possible, researchers prefer to use a *probability sample*—that is, one drawn according to precise rules that ensure that every key characteristic is matched in exactly the right statistical proportion to the population. This rigorous method of ensuring representativeness allows the researchers to generalize from findings in the sample to the larger population.

The size of the sample is one factor determining reliability. In general, the larger the sample, the more precise the data. This is especially true with small studies using the lowest ranges of sample size—say, below 100. Size, however, must be balanced against cost. With carefully defined probability samples, for example, national surveys can be conducted in Canada with as few as 2,000 respondents.

One type of probability sample, the **random sample**, involves selecting names at random from a list containing the names of all members of a population. For example, the phone book can be used to compile a random numbers list. Another type of probability sample, the **stratified sample**, divides a population into categories that mirror the percentages of people within those categories in the total population. A random selection method is then used to choose names from each category. For example, if the Dial brand manager knows that adults in the countries of the European Union make up 64 percent of his entire population, he will want 64 percent of the sample he chooses to be from the European Union; within this group as well as all others, survey respondents will be selected at random.

Sometimes the cost (in both time and money) of probability selection procedures forces researchers to use *nonprobability samples*, whose demographics are far less precisely matched to those of the larger population. Unfortunately, the lack of precision in the selection of nonprobability samples can affect the accuracy of findings and, in turn, the ability of researchers to make accurate predictions.

Nonprobability samples are accurate enough in some situations, however, such as diagnosing the communication problems in a piece of advertising copy or probing for why shoppers are not responding to a merchandise display. The two common forms of nonprobability samples are convenience samples and quota samples. A **convenience sample** selects the easiest people to find; for example, you might conduct a survey on pizza buyers by interviewing fellow students in your marketing class. A **quota sample** is very similar to a stratified sample in that its categories are designed to proportionally represent the total population. However, in this technique actual sampling is arbitrary, not random. A certain number of respondents are sought to complete a survey who meet certain citeria but their selection is more convenience-based than random.

OBSERVATION

Once researchers have selected their sample, they must collect their data. *Observation*, the first of the data-collection methods we discuss here, calls for a trained observer or some mechanical device that can watch and record the behaviors of actual buyers. Some observable buyer behaviors include the number of people who enter a mall, the amount of time customers spend at a counter, and the number of cars that pass a particular location within a given time period. Managers and marketing executives often perform observational research by doing *store checks*—that is, walking through stores and checking

---

random sample
A form of *probability* sample in which names are selected on a basis that ensures each name has an equal chance of selection.

stratified sample
A form of probability sample in which a population is divided into predetermined categories and then selected at random from within those categories.

convenience sample
A form of *nonprobability* sample in which the easiest people to find are selected.

quota sample
A form of *nonprobability* sample in which the population is divided into categories based on certain characteristics and then a number (quota) is assigned for each category that mirrors the percentages of people found in that category within the total population.

such things as the location and number of product packages facing the aisle on the shelves.

In the late 1980s a team of researchers conducted a formal nationwide study in which they used direct observation to determine how people interacted with products in their daily lives. For months they toured the country in a motor home loaded with a video recorder, a VCR monitor, two computers, an audio-tape recorder, and a refrigerator full of film. On this Consumer Behavior Odyssey the researchers' goal was to experience and record consumer behavior in many different settings. The four researchers on the study team were joined at various points by some twenty-four other researchers from various disciplines who spent two to four weeks traveling with the team. The Odyssey project generated more than 800 single-spaced pages of field notes, journals, and logs, more than 60 hours of video tape recordings; dozens of audio tapes; and 3,000 photographs. From these data the team developed some important consumer behavior themes, such as the effect of role transition on women as entrepreneurs and the carving out of private space in a home.[9]

The great advantage of the observational method of data collection is its realism: it reports on the real buying patterns of people, the true amount of exposure your product or brand is getting on the retailers' shelves, and the actual percentage of stores using your display materials. Moreover, the method is relatively inexpensive and simple. Its drawback is that it does not tell *why* the observed behavior occurred.

INTERVIEWS

One-on-one *in-depth interviews* give the researcher a chance to ask "why" questions and to explore the answers. There may be only ten official questions, but a good

The Push-Button Interview

In computer-assisted telephone interviewing (CATI) a console TV-like screen displays questions, answers, and interviewing directions. The console is connected to a computer that selects random-digit telephone numbers and processes survey information. After a phone number has been reached, each question appears on the screen in order and with number-coded answer categories; as each answer is given, the interviewer records it with the push of a button. Interviewer error is reduced because the computer prevents the omission of questions and rejects inconsistent or erroneous responses.

in-depth interviewer may find another twenty-five ways to probe: "Why do you say that?" or "Tell me why you feel that way." Personal interviews are conducted either door-to-door or by means of a store, street, or mall *intercept* technique. Researchers using the latter technique stop people who are shopping or in transit and ask them if they are willing to participate in a survey. Interviews are expensive, but they provide the best insights into how people relate to a product or brand.

In-depth interviewing requires patient probing. Consider an interview survey of fifty women conducted for Duncan Hines cake mix. The researchers knew that moistness was the hallmark of a good cake mix, but wondered how people tested a cake for moistness. After interviewers talked to respondents for two hours, one woman made a comment that turned out to be golden: "It's the fork. If you can pick up the extra crumbs off the plate—if they stick to the fork, then it's moist." That little nugget inspired a Duncan Hines television commercial with a fork demonstration that had great believability, according to Duncan Hines research.

FOCUS GROUPS

focus group
An in-depth group interview with a small number of people who engage in intensive conversation about a particular product or advertisement for a product.

In an in-depth *group interview*, a **focus group**—a small number of people representative of the target audience—is led by a trained moderator in discussing such things as a new product or an advertisement. Because the findings from just one group session may turn out to be skewed, researchers usually conduct three to four sessions with focus groups of eight to ten people each. These sessions are generally held in a conference room, and either an audio tape or a video tape is made of them. Typically, marketing staff and others watch the session from an adjoining room through one-way mirrored glass. As the moderator asks probing questions and tries to use group dynamics to elicit sponta-

Focusing on the Consumer

Focus groups are particularly useful for exploratory research, but they can also have more immediate value. These group interviews can identify problems in existing products, evaluate new products and features, examine the effectiveness of marketing communications, and reveal consumer perceptions and attitudes. As one company discovered, they can also be a source of creative ideas: a Campbell's Soup campaign slogan—"A warm hug from Campbell's"—was inspired by a consumer comment in a focus group.

188

Figure 5-4
**Outline for Millennium
Focus Group on
Energy Products**

Prepared for a focus

group to explore

market possibilities for

Millennium batteries

and battery chargers.

*Source: Millennium Power
Systems.*

(Prescreen to ensure that all participants use some type of battery-powered home appliance, entertainment device, etc. Half of group should use disposable batteries, half rechargeable batteries.)

Introduction

Explain research is being conducted for a company in the energy business. Tell participants there are no right or wrong answers, just their opinions. If observers are behind a one-way mirror, tell participants they are being observed. Also inform them that the session is being recorded (and video-taped, if that is being done also).

I. Lifestyle of Battery-User Households

    a. How many battery-powered devices are in your home?

    b. How are these used (by whom, frequency of use, etc.)?

    c. How often are batteries changed?

II. Battery Usage

    a. Who buys the batteries?

    b. At what type of store are they purchased?

    c. How often are batteries purchased? How many are bought on each purchase occasion?

    d. What type of batteries is purchased: disposable? rechargeable? Why?

III. Battery Performance

    a. Differences between rechargeable and disposable batteries (make sure discussion includes the following):

       —length of life

       —price

       —convenience

       —environmental concerns

    b. Why/why not use rechargeables?

IV. Brands of Rechargeables

    a. List all brands used (make sure Millennium is on list)

    b. Strengths/weaknesses of each brand

V. Recharging Units

    a. How many per household? How frequently used?

    b. Where located in house?

    c. Who is responsible for operating charger(s)?

    d. Differences between chargers? How selected?

    e. Brand comparison

VI. "Economics" Test: Have each person add up how much is spent each year on batteries, then compare cost of disposable versus rechargeable batteries.

    a. How surprised are users of disposable batteries by the difference in cost?

    b. Will this difference make them convert to rechargeables? If not, why not?

neous and candid comments (see Figure 5-4), the watchers send in notes to the moderator with suggestions for follow-up questions. The taped interview is then transcribed into a verbatim, (unedited) record of participants' comments.

Focus groups are useful in exploratory research because they encourage consumers to discuss the product and product category in everyday language. Marketers can thus get a better understanding of how the product fits into people's lives, how they use it, and what they think about it (if they do think about it). Focus group participants generally do not hesitate to tell you frankly that your product is of poor quality or that your advertising copy is badly conceptualized or written.

Focus group research can help firms sell to both private customers and industrial buyers. Hallmark, whose market is almost exclusively composed of individual consumers, relies heavily on consumer focus groups to evaluate ideas for its cards both before and after development. Reports on these sessions tell Hallmark why every card in a particular line did or didn't sell.

A supplier in the architectural/construction market decided to use focus groups to evaluate its industrial buyers' reception of a major new product. The company's product managers, who thought they knew their customers, got a shock when focus groups revealed that the product was incorrectly positioned, incorrectly priced, and essentially unwanted as it stood. By changing the price, package, and position of the product in keeping with focus group suggestions, the company wound up with a soaring success instead of a dismal failure. Focus groups are now starting to move into the computer laboratories where with the right kind of software and a closed network of say 30 terminals, responses can be generated quickly from fairly open questions. There is not the problem of anyone leading the discussion. Anything that emerges will be more consensual as a result.

SURVEYS

Probably the most common type of marketing research is survey research. *Surveys* obtain data from people by means of a *questionnaire*—a list of questions designed to elicit measurable data. Surveys can provide both *quantitative data,* (for example, How many respondents are aware of a product? How often do they use the product?) and *qualitative data,* (for example, Why do they use the product? When do they use it?).

These two types of data are the subject of the eighth chapter objective. Qualitative information comes from *open-ended* questions that encourage respondents to answer in their own words. Typical questions are: Why do you prefer one product over another? How do you go about acquiring product information? How do you make a product decision? Quantitative data come from structured, *closed-ended* questions that require respondents to give a yes or no answer, rate several possible answers by number, or choose one answer from a list of possible responses. The questionnaire shown in Figure 5-5 offers examples of both open-ended and closed-ended questions. Can you identify which are of one type, which the other?

Surveys are usually conducted either by mail or by telephone, but some are done face-to-face in the respondent's home or in a store or mall and some even by e-mail. Table 5-1 lists some of the advantages and disadvantages of these three survey techniques.

To analyze the results of quantitative surveys, researchers must first *code* the data—that is, give each answer category a number or indicator that can be tabulated. For instance, for a survey question asking the respondent's gender, answer categories might be coded 1 = female, 2 = male. Then respondents' answers are entered into a computer and tabulated, giving a total of so many male and so many female responses. When the answer categories are predetermined, as they are with all closed-ended questions, coding is relatively easy.

Amtrak conducted a survey intended to answer the question of how to get passengers to ride trains even though planes can get them to their destination faster and cars are more convenient. To determine what types of people were already riding the railroad and what they wanted out of their trip, Amtrak armed researchers with questionnaires and put them aboard its trains. These passenger surveys found out that business travelers are more concerned with comfort than with speed. They want to arrive on time, but consider

Household Telephone Calling Card Survey

1. Your name? _____

2. Age _____

3. Marital status _____

4. Income _____

5. Which, if any of the following telephone calling cards do you have?

   1. _____ Bell Canada   **2.** _____ Provincial phone company

   3. _____ Sprint Canada   **4.** _____ Others

6. How frequently do you use a calling card?

Infrequently   Very Frequently

      1   2   3   4   5   6   7

7. What do you think of the telephone calling card offered by Bell?

_____

8. Suppose your household were to select a telephone calling card. Please rate the importance of the following factors in selecting a card.

	Not Important				Very Important
a. Cost per call	1	2	3	4	5
b. Ease of use	1	2	3	4	5
c. Local and long distance charges included in the same bill	1	2	3	4	5
d. Rebates and discounts on calls	1	2	3	4	5
e. Quality of telephone service	1	2	3	4	5
f. Quality of customer service	1	2	3	4	5

9. How important is it for a telephone company to offer a calling card?

Not Important   Very Important

      1   2   3   4   5   6   7

10. Do you have children living at home? _____

Thank You For Your Help.

Figure 5-5
Sample Market Research Questionnaire

Source: Adapted from Naresh K. Malhotra, *Marketing Research: An Applied Orientation.*
Englewood Cliffs, N.J.: Prentice Hall, 1993, pp. 344–45.

	Mail	Phone	In Person[1]
TABLE 5-1 — SURVEY ADMINISTRATION METHODS			
Speed of collecting data	Usually slow; researcher cannot control	Fastest	Moderately fast
Cost	Lowest	Low to high	Highest
Length of questionnaire possible	Depends on incentive	Moderate	Long
Flexibility and versatility in interviewing	Low—standardized format	Moderate	High
Interviewer influence bias	None	Moderate	High
Response rate	Low to moderate	Moderate	High

[1]Includes door-to-door, in-store, and mall-intercept interviewing.

roomy seats and telephones more important. Vacationers, on the other hand, prize good food, service, and distractions such as movies and bingo. With the knowledge its researchers accumulated in this study, Amtrak was able to capitalize on its advantages over its competitors by making telephones available to every passenger and showing movies.

A number of innovative qualitative methods have been devised to help marketers gain deeper insights into consumer attitudes and behavior. With open-ended questions like those used in qualitative studies, however, it's much more difficult to group responses so you can identify patterns and generalize from the data. Moreover, as the next section suggests, qualitative research can raise ethical issues.

OPEN TO DEBATE

FINDING THE SWEET SPOT

Accumulating lots of data about consumers doesn't tell you much about how they *think* and that's what marketers need to know in order to develop strategies. As Fortini-Campbell explains in her book *Hitting the Sweet Spot*, "Finding a way to make your brand connect with your consumer is not easy. It demands that you go beyond just knowing who your consumer is to something deeper—understanding, respect, and empathy."[10] She identifies the *sweet spot* as the point where the product message connects with the consumer on a deep personal level.

In addition to the large number of qualitative research methods outlined in Fortini-Campbell's book, marketers and advertisers have developed innovative methods to better understand their customers at this deep level. BBDO uses a research method that asks people to profile the personality and product usage behaviors of other people based on a bank of photographic images. Marc Bourgery of Bloom FCA uses a method called *context analysis* that also employs photos—in this instance to develop "brandscapes," or wordless images of brands. The brandscapes are analyzed for what the images express to consumers. To gain insights into consumers for developing advertising strategies, Steve Verba, president of Wyse Advertising's research company, uses *semiotics*, which is the study of signs and symbols and how people derive meaning from them, as well as *neural network research* methods that look at how the brain makes connections between things.

Diagnostic Research International uses minimovies that plumb the emotional depths of consumers' relationships with the products they buy. One minimovie on motorcycle riders and their cerebral and visceral relationships with their Harley-Davidson bikes had H-D's top management mesmerized. It provided the platform for shaping everything from the content of the bike maker's advertising to customer relations to long-term international planning.[11]

These are nifty research methods for acquiring insight into consumer attitudes and behaviors, but are there ethical issues involved in probing this deeply into people's psyches? Carol Moog (who analyzes this type of research in her book *Are They Selling Her Lips?*) speculates that it may be indirectly responsible for identity problems in North Americans because the insights it yields are used to create marketing and advertising that set up impossible standards of beauty and physical fitness.[12] Should you as a marketer be concerned about the ethics of setting such disturbing standards? Do you care about the implications of using people's deepest needs and fears to get them to buy products?

Tracking Studies Research is an ongoing process in which information accumulates over time. Researchers monitor changes in the marketing situation by conducting **tracking studies**, surveys that monitor top-of-mind brand awareness, as well as trial and repeat purchases. For consumer goods, such studies usually take the form of phone surveys of selected households in which marketers check periodically on whether consumers are aware of a product's existence, whether they have tried it, and if so, whether they have bought it again or plan to do so. Tracking studies are also used as *brand diagnostics*: they help monitor such consumer perceptions as the quality of a brand (is it stable? slipping?) and the appropriateness of its price (too high? too low?)

It is often useful to establish *benchmarks* for purposes of comparisons when doing tracking studies. Suppose a marketing manager wants to track what happens to his or her brand's sales when a competitor runs ads with coupons. In order to determine if there is a dropoff in sales because of this competitive activity, the manager needs to have a benchmark level of sales.

PANELS, DIARIES, AND SCANNERS

To collect repeated data over time from the same sample of respondents, researchers use consumer *panels*—groups of people who are chosen because

tracking study
A survey that monitors top-of-mind awareness as well as trial and repeat purchases of a particular product or brand.

they represent certain characteristics of a target market. In their own homes panel members regularly complete questionnaires or keep *diaries* of particular purchasing and consumption behaviors. Members may be asked questions on a variety of topics, including past and planned household expenditures, regular exposure to various forms of media, recreation and leisure activities, and attitudes and opinions regarding social trends and contemporary issues. Panels are particularly useful for tracking change because you can ask members *why* they have changed their behavior or opinions.

To increase the accuracy of panel research and to make it easier for panelists to record their purchases, several companies now use **scanners**. These small hand-held computers are miniature versions of the supermarket scanner now in wide use; like them, they "read" the universal product codes (UPC) on products. Panelists "scan" their purchases and punch in price and other information on the scanner keyboard.

Supermarket scanners also offer marketers useful information and provide them with opportunities to expand their markets, as Exhibit 5-3 indicates. Armed with the information from these scanners, supermarkets are able to move into direct marketing by offering coupons and other special deals to targeted households with particular purchasing patterns. Combining purchasing data from store scanners with data from household consumer panels and sometimes other sources is one of the most exciting trends in marketing research. This information, known as **single-source data** because it describes a single household, helps marketers develop more effective marketing communications. The combination furnishes extensive data that can be converted into cause-and-effect explanations, which help marketers devise marketing-mix changes.[13]

One of the best-known single-source data firms, A. C. Nielsen Company, is famous for using a mechanical device to record consumer behavior—the *people meters* that track television viewing. While once "Nielsen families" had to write down in a diary what programs they watched, today an electronic device attached to the television set does the logging and family members merely punch in codes to indicate who is viewing at a given time—a much more reliable method.

EXPERIMENTS

Experimental methods are another way to test for cause-and-effect relationships. The researcher is looking to see if a change in a marketing *variable* (such as product features, price, availability, or advertising) will affect consumer behavior (such as trial or repeat purchase). In experimental research a *dependent variable* is some factor whose variations will let you analyze the impact of the *independent variables*—those factors in the marketing mix that you are testing, such as various ways to deliver a promotional message.

Researchers might want to know by how much sales will change (the dependent variable) if a product's price is raised by a certain percent (independent variable); or they might want to know if the redesign of a package (independent variable) will affect consumer preference (dependent variable). The researcher adjusts the marketing mix (the cause) while controlling other factors that could affect the experiment's results, and then measures the behavior change (the effect).

Experiments are sometimes conducted in artificial settings like laboratories or classrooms, but more often they take the form of *in-market* or *in-store testing*. Almost any marketing-mix variable can be field-tested by this method, though the most common test is of new products and pricing levels in consumer markets. For example, a major snack manufacturer used two sample groups of retail stores that were equivalent in type and location to test alter-

scanner
A hand-held computer (provided to members of the buying public on a shopping panel) that reads UPC bar codes on products and records other information about a sale.

single-source data
Information about individual household purchases often derived from a number of sources but notably from a combination of supermarket scanner data and household consumer panel data.

Exhibit 5-3
Getting to Know You

Collecting consumer information at the checkout counter can help retailers and manufacturers analyze purchasing patterns and do highly targeted promotions.

195

MARKETING
INFORMATION
AND RESEARCH

native price levels for a specific snack product. The only difference was that at the stores in group A the product was priced 10 percent higher than the regular price and at the stores in group B it was priced 20 percent higher than the regular price. Researchers found that the higher price level had almost no effect on sales of the snack—it merely increased profits.

Promotions are often tested in-store. Common promotion devices are special displays, instantly redeemable coupons, and on-pack premiums. Demonstrations in the store, combined with product samples and coupons, can be used to test the impact of the promotion on immediate and long-run sales.

Advertising can be tested in one or two markets to see what effect it has and to find any communication problems with the message before it is used in the overall market. Split-runs of television and newspaper ads permit the advertiser to compare different creative approaches to determine their selling power as well as the relative advantages of different media mixes.

Test Markets   Experimentation is valuable to marketing researchers and managers because it is the best way to find out whether a change in the marketing mix will have real impact. **Test marketing** is also a useful predictive tool that was perfected in the 1960s by major marketers like Procter & Gamble and Lever Brothers. In this form of field experimentation, one or two market sites are selected in which to test the response of retailers and consumers to a new product or new marketing strategy. From results obtained in the test market, researchers predict market share, distribution levels, and other things that should occur when the marketing effort rolls out into the larger marketplace.

Test marketing does have some serious disadvantages. It takes time, costs money, and may tip off competitors about a company's strategy. This fear of tipping off competitors is why Pillsbury elected not to do this kind of research for its Oven Lovin' cookie dough.

GLOBAL RESEARCH CONSIDERATIONS

As chapter objective number nine suggests, marketing research on a global scale is a complicated proposition. The two major challenges for global marketers are obtaining data that can be reliably compared across markets and adapting research techniques to local conditions.

To illustrate the nature of the first challenge, secondary data are often kept in different forms in different countries. Many third world nations may have very little secondary data available, and this is frequently highly inaccurate or inflated for political reasons. Even primary data collected in different nations may not be comparable if local researchers take different approaches to data collection and change the statistical base for collection. For example, age groups usually form the pattern set by national government statistical offices but there may be little standardization in this across countries. This is one benefit of the ECI if they are able to standardize market data collection.

The second challenge, however, sometimes makes taking a different approach to primary data collection unavoidable. For example, telephone surveys are very popular in North America because they make it easy to contact a cross section of the population. In developing countries, however, it is often only the wealthy who have phones. And in some countries phone calls from strangers are considered a serious violation of privacy, so would-be surveyors cannot get the answers they seek. However, in Eastern Europe the tradition is to use the telephone in business and certainly not mail. Whether the fax machine will succeed in this environment has yet to be seen. Meanwhile, answers have to be collected orally or not at all. Yet another hurdle is the need to translate questions into different languages and interpret and compare answers from different cultures.

Perhaps the most serious problem in global market research is the difference in cultures. Each national market has unique characteristics that must be taken into account when conducting and analyzing research. Especially creative marketing researchers are required to balance the need to fit the approach to the country against the need for data that can be usefully compared with data from other areas.

THE FINAL TALLY

Marketing research is as much an art as a science. To develop a marketing plan, marketing managers need useful information, accurate answers, and deep insights into the reasons behind consumers' attitudes and behaviors. The first problem is to find the right questions to ask, but even more difficult is knowing how to make sense of the answers. One of the obstacles researchers face in interpreting comments made in interviews and focus groups is that they are often overwhelmingly positive because participants, particularly in non-Western cultures, tend to be polite. Also, consumers everywhere find it difficult to evaluate a product based on limited experience—or a new product idea based on no experience at all.

No matter what research method you select, you must use it *objectively*, meaning the handling of the matter must be free of any kind of bias. You must also make sure the method *accurately* answers the research question and addresses the real problem that needs to be investigated. Finally, your research method must be *exhaustive* enough to investigate all the relevant dimensions of the problem and all relevant sources of answers without becoming impossibly expensive.

Unless these three criteria are met, you cannot be sure of the usefulness of the information you obtain from marketing research. Moreover, unless you estimate the cost of doing the research and compare that against the value of the information you're trying to get, you cannot be sure of the bottom-line value of your research.

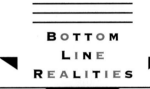

BOTTOM
LINE
REALITIES

A WORLD COLORED BY INFORMATION

Thanks to Benetton's up-to-the-minute information system, you can color this company's competitors green with envy. The key to the success of this family-run Italian firm that brings the latest fashions to markets all over the world is information that keeps the company ahead of fashion trends around the world.

Benetton uses a General Electric information network to plan manufacturing based on orders received and transferred continually to company headquarters in a small Italian town. Speed is of the essence in the fashion business. Traditionally,

the lead time between designing a sweater and getting it on a retailer's shelf was about six months—a long time in a very fast-changing market. Benetton's system has enabled the company to reduce the time from design to shipment from months to weeks.

Benetton bases its operations on information about its customers' preferences. In all its stores around the world, Benetton collects information on sales from *point-of-sales devices*—essentially, intelligent cash registers that record product information that is then instantly transmitted by satellite to company headquarters. There it is analyzed to determine such things as what colors and styles are the hot sellers. It's this instant information that

allows Benetton to maintain its position as a leader in fashion merchandising.

How does the system work? At Benetton headquarters, information about product choices in the field is relayed to designers, who then create sportswear on video screens based on their analysis of these fashion trends. The new-product designs are relayed by computer to computer-controlled knitting and cutting machines that deliver a finished product ready for distribution in a few hours.

An innovative "just-in-time" dyeing process gives Benetton another advantage. Benetton manufactures many of its products undyed. Then, as the company gets daily reports on which colors are selling and which are not, it orders batches dyed accordingly.

These information and manufacturing innovations have permitted Benetton to reduce the lead time between selling one sweater in Vancouver and replacing it with another to just a few weeks. As a result in-stock inventory is reduced and there is little need to mark down slow-moving items—a problem that plagues most companies in the fashion industry. Its instant information system allows Benetton to be a harbinger of the latest fashion trends and colors.

Benetton's system is essentially an MIS system. If you were hired by Benetton as a marketing consultant, what would you add to the company's research program to develop deeper insights into consumer fashion tastes and trends? What information would be useful for predicting fashion trends beyond the MIS data the Benetton system is already tracking?▼

KEY POINTS SUMMARY ▼

1. A marketing information system (MIS) combines a data-gathering system with a decision-support system to collect and convert data into information that managers can use to gain insight into marketing problems and challenges. A management information system (also abbreviated MIS) collects and manages information about a company.

2. Environmental scanning is a process of information acquisition that may be relatively informal (surveillance) or that may use formal investigation and research procedures (search).

3. The five steps in the marketing research process are: (1) identification of the research problem, (2) development of a research plan and methodology, (3) data collection, (4) analysis of the data, and (5) presentation of the findings.

4. Market research begins with the identification of a problem whose solution will enable managers to make the decisions needed to capitalize on a market opportunity or successfully combat a threat. Researchers must be careful to distinguish a problem's symptoms from the problem itself. Exploratory research may help identify problems that are not immediately apparent. Whether researchers select quantitative or qualitative methodologies in developing a research plan depends on the goals of the research. Researchers must decide whether to use primary or secondary-source data; if primary data are desired, researchers must choose specific research methods and sampling procedures. In all cases they must prepare a timetable for their research activities.

5. Primary data are developed through formal research methods by the firm or by outside consultants to answer marketing questions specific to the firm itself. Secondary data are data obtained by outside agencies for other purposes. Primary data are up to date and are precisely tailored to answer questions about the specific problem being studied but are costly and time-consuming to collect. Secondary data can be had almost immediately and at relatively low cost but are nonspecific and may be out of date.

6. Research methods used to collect primary data include observation; interviews and focus groups; surveys and tracking studies; panels, diaries, and scanners; experiments; and in-market testing. Methods used to obtain secondary data include searching data banks of various types, online database services, and syndicated studies.

7. The accuracy of primary research depends on how well the sample studied by the researchers represents the key characteristics of the total population. Probability sampling, as opposed to nonprobability sampling, increases the degree of this representativeness.

8. The data obtained from primary research methods may be either quantitative or qualitative, depending on the research goals and the format of the data-gathering instrument. Quantitative research makes extensive use of

statistical analysis; qualitative analysis requires considerable interpretation and judgment by the researchers, who probe reasons and opinions offered by consumers to gain insight into their behavior.

9. Performing marketing research on a global basis forces researchers to balance the need for techniques that are appropriate in each country against the need for data that can be reliably compared across different countries.

DISCUSSION QUESTIONS ▼

1. You have been asked to design a marketing information system for a local shoe store. What sorts of information will enable the store to manage its business more effectively, and how should this information be obtained?

2. You have been asked to conduct marketing research for your local public transportation authority. Outline the activities you would undertake in following each of the five basic steps in the marketing research process.

3. Go to your business library and make a list of all the computerized information services that provide the kinds of information you would find useful if you were working on a marketing plan for a museum, symphony orchestra, zoo, or other cultural or arts center in your locale.

4. Why do market researchers prefer probability to nonprobability samples? Why do they sometimes use nonprobability samples anyway? If you were conducting a tourism study for your state, how would you use the two types of sampling methods?

5. Compare and contrast any two primary data-collection methods described in this chapter in terms of their operation, and advantages and disadvantages.

6. You are marketing manager for a brand of cereal:

   a. Outline a program of environmental scanning to begin research on your product.

   b. What types of primary and secondary data would you want to obtain for your annual marketing plan? What are the advantages and disadvantages of each type of data you plan to collect?

   c. How can you use single-source data to analyze your company's marketing mix?

7. As manager for new product development in the area of laptop and notebook computers for a major computer company, what potential marketing problems would you want marketing research to address before bringing out a model for the world market?

8. Puffs tissue is considering the introduction of Puffs 2-ply toilet paper. Outline a research program that will help Puffs decide whether to add this product to its line.

9. A new bike shop is opening in a university town of 80,000.

   a. What kinds of informal research should the manager do?

   b. The manager hires you as a researcher. Develop a series of research questions that you need to answer.

   c. Draft a questionnaire that will provide answers for those research questions.

10. Federal Express has just appointed you vice president for marketing. Outline a research plan to obtain the information you need to develop a strategy for penetrating the Central European market.

Integrative Case ● Discussion Questions

The Body Shop*

1. The Body Shop does not conduct formal marketing research. What kinds of marketing data does the company have readily available, however, and how could they use it?

Harley-Davidson

1. What type of marketing research does Harley use? What are its advantages and disadvantages?
2. How could Harley select a random sample of owners to survey?

The Millennium Power System

1. Does the Millennium marketing plan seem appropriate given the results of their consumer research?

2. Millennium's market research indicated that its product had the highest customer satisfaction ratings in the industry. The data were collected by means of a postcard-sized questionnaire mailed to 15,000 households. What are the positive and negative aspects of this research technique?

3. Millennium's response rate was unusually high: of the 15,000 households targeted, 10,599, or 71 percent replied. What techniques do you think the researchers might have used to generate such a large response rate?

*The three cases at the back of the book—"The Body Shop," "Harley-Davidson," and "The Millennium Power System"—illustrate topics discussed in all chapters of this book. Your instructor will tell you when to read a particular case and answer the discussion questions on it that appear at the end of each chapter.

Voice Mail Hang-Ups

Voice mail. Just hearing those two words makes some people shudder. Voice mail is a vast electronic darkness, filled with twisting corridors and dead-end hallways. A place where real people have vanished and microchips have moved in. If you get trapped inside, you might well think that you'll never escape. Voice mail is becoming a lot more prevalent in business and government offices and like it or not, it's here to stay. As you Press 1 for service in English or Press 6 for information on store hours, you probably wonder if anyone ever answers the phone anymore.

Generally, voice mail can be useful tool if used properly. The idea behind voice mail is based on good intentions. Organizations that find they need to answer more inquiries than staff can handle often turn to voice mail as the solution. Those that introduce it to extend their customer service generally profit from it. Those who set it up as a cost-cutting measure, in order to avoid having a live human answer customer complaints and inquiries, generally do not set it up very well and antagonize a number of their customers.

No matter what the original motive, if a system is improperly designed, callers can wind up in "voice mail jail." And customers who end up there often end up looking for somewhere else to shop. In general, the impersonal nature of voice mail is enough to turn off many segments in the market. Marketers must not forget that a system that is better for the business could end up costing the caller more in either time or money.

All voice mail systems are programmed by computer specialists, but some "think like a marketer" and others don't. Marketers always keep customer needs first in mind. Programmers often think first of the technological restrictions. The programmers create a series of software commands that take the caller through a menu of choices that branches out as the caller gets closer to the destination. For example, a first choice that asks you to press 1 or 2 depending on whether you are calling about flight arrivals or departures, will then give more detailed choices such as which airport or which airline. The problem with most bad voice mail systems is the menu of choices it gives the caller. Some of the choices are misleading, and the choices often do not cover every opportunity, situation and option a caller may have. At the very least, one of the choices must always be the option to exit to a live operator.

One of the common applications for voice mail is to provide callers with recordings of repetitive information such as the availability of government programs. But what if the customer's need cannot be met by the limited menu options? Another common application of voice mail is to take customer orders or inquiries of a specific nature, such as the status of a student loan application. If you plan to use the latest in voice recognition software, can it distinguish a lot of different accents, or just a few basic ones?

A final request to all who use a voice mail message to keep callers informed of your whereabouts: Remember to update your message regularly. It is very annoying to get an inaccurate message on Thursday that was recorded on the previous Monday. And the messages that say "I'm either on the phone or away from my desk, but leave a message…" don't inspire confidence that I will get a reply. If you don't even know where you are, why do you expect me to leave a message?

201

QUESTIONS

1. In this case, what does it mean to "think like a marketer"?
2. In order to recognize customer needs, what types of research would you undertake?
3. Assume you are the marketing person at a local public swimming/fitness facility (or other similar place). You are deciding whether or not to install a voice mail system. Prepare a brief survey questionnaire that would give you valuable information to use in your decision making process. If you can actually administer the survey, do it. Otherwise, assume what the likely responses would have been.
4. Based on the answers to your survey, write the script for the system.

Source: This case was prepared by Ray Friedman and is based on the *Market Place* series episode "Voice Mail," which was originally broadcast on February 8, 1994.

202

Chapter 6

Consumer Buying Behavior

THINK ABOUT IT!

GENERATION X SEARCHES FOR AN IDENTITY

The people born 1964 and 1975—those who are "twentysomething"—have grown up in some fairly depressing societal conditions. Often called the "Generation X" because marketers are still searching for the right name (other labels are "the New Lost Generation," "baby busters," "the Bradys," "the Cable Generation," "latchkeys," "technobabies," and "mall rats"), these people came to maturity at a time when precocious sex and illicit drug use were widespread, an AIDS epidemic was in the making, an extended recession was putting family members and neighbors out of work, and nuclear annihilation was threatening civilization.[1] These *Xers*, who grew up in the shadow of the huge baby-boom generation, make up a viable, lucrative, and tar-

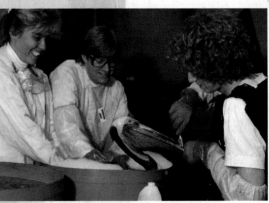

getable market, although one that is still searching for identification.

Schwinn a Winner Again?

For years the major bike manufacturer, Schwinn slipped in the late 1980s, in large part because it misinterpreted the mountain-bike craze as a fad. Mountain bikes, particularly popular with Generation Xers, now account for nearly 70 percent of all bikes sold in the North America. Schwinn began making a comeback, expecting in 1994 to make its first profit since 1989. Company executives visited Schwinn's loyal dealers, winning many of them back from competing bikes.

Some anthropologists have described nineties men and women as people who believe they can and must change both themselves and society in order to survive. The portrait that emerges from these studies is one of people who are media savvy but skeptical and alienated from the mainstream culture, which they feel has ignored them and created an array of problems that they will have to solve. Many Xers resent the baby boomers for a variety of evils, including running up the national debt, destroying the environment, and keeping all the good jobs for themselves.

In fact, not only do young people in their twenties confront the staggering national debt but Xers who left college in the 1990–1991 recession were burdened by twice as much debt as 1977 graduates and entered one of the worst job markets in over 30 years. No wonder some writers (Jeff Giles, "Generalizations X," *Newsweek*, June 6, 1994, 62–72) find twentysomethings more cautious and financially conservative than 20-years-olds in earlier years.

Generation X is a group that is incredibly difficult to reach with traditional media and marketing communication messages. Many of these people feel that advertising insults their intelligence, and little on television or in magazines holds any real meaning for them.

Perhaps the tendency attributed to young peo-

ple in their twenties to think that advertising "is all lies and hype" (Karen Ritchie quoted in Giles, "Generalizations," 70) helps explain the elusiveness of this group as a marketing target. Many Xers resent being bunched together, typed, and labeled. In fact, they are among the most diverse (racially and in other ways) of any generation to date. Indeed, many think "Generation X" is one big hype by boomer business people who see them "not as human beings but as disposable incomes in sneakers" (Giles, "Generalizations," 72).

If you are in your twenties, how would you portray your generation? If you belong to an older generation, talk with your younger classmates and try to get a clearer picture of this group. Now, as a marketer, how would you reach these people? And what would you say to them? ■

THE DYNAMIC CONSUMER MARKET ●

Today many companies confront a fragmented marketplace in which increasingly sophisticated consumers change their tastes and preferences seemingly overnight. As a result, marketers find themselves compelled to do constant research if they are to have a chance of drawing a bead on this moving target. David Nichol of President's Choice fame says that shoppers have changed. They have become tougher to reach and more sophisticated. They buy on the basis of value.[2]

Marketers also need theories about consumer behavior to organize what they know. They look for *trends* that apply, not just to the users of one particular product or brand, but to wide segments of the population as well. In this chapter we consider the attitudes and buying behavior of individual consumers. In the next we will discuss the rather different characteristics and decision-making processes of organizational buyers.

THE "BLACK BOX" MODEL OF CONSUMER BEHAVIOR

In addition to research into trends and changing consumer behaviors, studies over the years have provided information about more generalized patterns of consumer buying behavior. It is this information that establishes the basis for theories about how to identify who customers are, what factors influence their choices, and how they make buying decisions. In order to better understand consumer behavior, let's begin by looking at the basic model that is the topic of the first objective stated for this chapter.

Figure 6-1 shows the "black box" model of consumer buying behavior derived from the work of psychologist Kurt Lewin.[3] Lewin was interested in how someone's inner needs, thoughts, and beliefs interact with factors in the environment to produce that person's ultimate behavior. In the black box model of marketing, a variety of external and environmental factors influence individuals, who then process this information in the light of personal factors in their lives, and finally apply it to the decision-making process when considering whether to buy a particular item.

Figure 6-1
Black Box Model of Consumer Buying Behavior

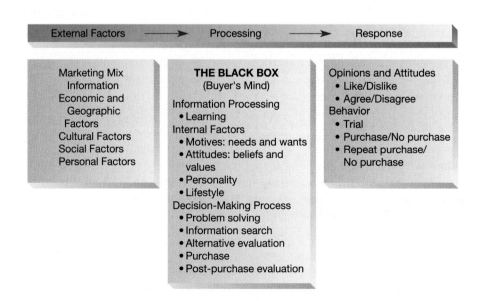

On the left of the figure is product information, which is derived from both personal experience and marketing communications. Marketing communications is an area of the marketing mix that will be discussed in more detail in Chapters 18–21. In this chapter we focus on the other important external influences that affect consumer behavior: economic, geographical, cultural, social, and personal factors.

It is the middle portion of Figure 6-1, which represents the consumer's internal processing, that gives the model its name. Psychologists often liken human reasoning to a "black box." We may perceive things going into a person's mind and other things emerging from that mind, but we can never know for sure just how the information that goes in turns into the idea or decision that comes out. If marketers could turn on a light inside that box, they would likely discover that the combination of internal individual factors (motives, attitudes, personality characteristics, and lifestyle factors) and individual modes of information processing leads to a decision-making process about products and brands.

On the far right of the model in Figure 6-1 are the responses buyers make after they have mentally processed information about the product or brand. Generally these responses appear as either opinions and attitudes (like/dislike, agree/disagree) or behaviors (trial, purchase, repeat purchase, or no purchase at all). Study Figure 6-1, for it gives an overview of this chapter's organization.

EXTERNAL INFLUENCES ON CONSUMER BEHAVIOR ●

Marketers are always interested in trends affecting consumers. Such things as technological change and economic downturns can pose threats as well as opportunities to the marketing program. The external areas that are the focus of the second objective for this chapter are economic and geographic, cultural, social, and personal factors that influence consumer behavior.

ECONOMIC AND GEOGRAPHIC FACTORS

The two major economic influences on consumer buying behavior are the state of the economy and the state of the individual's finances. Geographic factors have some influence here; as we saw in Chapter 3, some economic trends are determined by regional and national boundaries.

Markets cannot exist without *buying power*—that is, resources (especially money) that people can exchange for goods or services. Buying power depends in part on price levels, which shift with the economy. In times of inflation, when prices are rising, people living on fixed incomes (such as retirees) have less buying power. In a recession or a depression, when prices typically go down, buying power does also. Consumers who have lost their jobs can't afford even lower-priced items.

Historically, it is the blue-collar workers who have felt the effects of recessions most strongly. The downturn of the early 1990s, however, was very much a white-collar recession, and it imposed severe income constraints on some groups of consumers who were among the heaviest spenders in the 1980s. As you might expect, purchases of luxury items and other nonnecessities were most affected by this recent recession.

Marketers selling food and clothing are particularly concerned about the level of *disposable* income, which varies depending upon such economic factors as inflation and recession. Of more importance to marketers who sell products in the educational, leisure, and luxury categories is *discretionary* income, which determines purchasing power for such things as higher education and vacations, as well as luxuries like boats, second cars, and second homes. Typically, the amount of discretionary income is disproportionate: wealthier people have considerably more money to spend on nonessentials.

Unfortunately, in North America the gender factor significantly affects income levels. The average working woman's income is now about 71 percent of the average working man's, and although the gap has been slowly narrowing in recent years, the still-considerable discrepancy affects women's purchasing patterns, particularly single women's. This is an important factor for marketers who sell products to the women's market. Many upscale cosmetics firms, for instance, have developed budget-priced lines to extend their products down into the large, but generally poorer, market of single women.

On the international level, geography and economics are especially intertwined. Some of the fastest-growing economies in the world—and some of the wealthiest consumers—are in Asian countries such as Taiwan, Korea, Hong Kong, Singapore, and Malaysia. In Singapore, for example, the stock market foundered in 1993 because of what many Singaporeans considered dismal economic news: the economy had grown by only 5.8 percent—a growth rate that would have caused elation in most countries—instead of by the 8 percent this tiny country had come to expect.[4] International marketers are targeting these regions because the people living there have the discretionary income to purchase luxury products.

CULTURAL INFLUENCES

A **culture** is a way of living that distinguishes one group of people from another. Culture is learned and transmitted from one generation to the next. This "way of living" includes attitudes and values as well as accepted patterns of behavior, language, religion, education, class structure, and other social phenomena. Cultures can often be geographically defined—that is, certain groups, particularly ethnic and racial populations, tend to live in certain places. Within larger multicultural societies there are usually *subcultures* defined by such factors as age, religion, and ethnic origin. The senior market, for example, is a subculture defined by age. Subcultures offer excellent bases for identifying and targeting niche markets.

From a marketing perspective, culture is what determines *wants*—the way people define their needs. Wants are culturally based and are shaped by the environment in which we live and grew up. Do you eat the meat of dogs or horses? You might if you grew up in Korea or France, respectively, but probably not if you grew up in Canada or the United States.

Cultural Values Table 6-1 identifies some of the cultural values that affect consumer behavior. For example, Canada is a culture that values individual action in contrast to many Asian cultures, which value collective action and decision making. Advertising planners must take account of these values when developing message strategies. It may be inappropriate to use a hard-driving executive, particularly a woman executive, in ads for China, although that strategy might work fine in Canada. Which of the values in Table 6-1 apply to the culture in which you live and how do these values affect the types of products you buy?

Global Cultural Differences Differences in cultural values and changes in values over time and from nation to nation add to the complexity of global marketing. Although the need to adapt marketing plans to the culture or subculture may seem obvious, examples of marketers failing to do so are legion, especially in the global arena. Campbell's soups, for instance, failed in Brazil because Brazilian housewives do not like to serve soup that they cannot call

culture
A way of living that distinguishes one group of people from another. Culture is learned and transmitted from one generation to the next.

TABLE 6-1

CULTURAL VALUE DIMENSIONS THAT HELP DEFINE AND PREDICT CONSUMER BEHAVIOR

Interpersonal Values

Individual-Collective: Does the culture place more value on individual activity and initiative or on collective activity and conformity?

Adult-Child: Is family life organized primarily to meet the needs of the children or the needs of the adults?

Masculine-Feminine: Is social power vested principally in men or in women?

Competition-Cooperation: Does one gain success by excelling over others or by cooperating with them?

Youth-Age: Are wisdom and prestige assigned to the younger or the older members of the culture?

Societal Values

Cleanliness: To what extent is cleanliness pursued beyond the minimum needed for health?

Performance-Status: Is the culture's reward system based on performance or on inherited factors such as family and social class?

Tradition-Change: Does the culture value existing, or traditional, patterns of behavior more or less than new and innovative ways of doing things?

Risk Taking-Security: Are those who risk their established positions to overcome obstacles or achieve high goals admired more or less than those who do not take such risks?

Problem Solving-Fatalism: Are people encouraged to overcome all problems or to take a "what will be, will be" attitude?

Nature: Are nature and the environment regarded as something to be admired or obstacles to be overcome?

Self-Oriented Values

Active-Passive: Is a physically active approach to life valued more or less highly than a less active orientation?

Material-Nonmaterial: How much importance is attached to the acquisition of material wealth?

Hard Work-Leisure: Is the person who works harder than economically necessary admired more or less than the one who does not?

Postponed Gratification-Immediate Gratification: Are people encouraged to "save for a rainy day" or to "live for the moment"?

Sensual Gratification-Abstinence: To what extent is it acceptable to enjoy sensual pleasures such as sexual activity?

Humor-Serious: Is life to be regarded as a strictly serious affair or is it to be treated lightly?

Source: Adapted from Del I. Hawkins, Roger J. Best, and Kenneth A. Coney, *Consumer Behavior: Implications for Marketing Strategy*, 4th ed. (Homewood, Ill: BPI/Irwin, 1989), p. 50.

their own; they prefer to start with a dehydrated soup product and then add their own ingredients.

Sometimes, however, cultural differences are more myth than reality. Before Yamazaki-Nabisco began to sell Oreo cookies in Japan, the company

was told that the Japanese would not eat "black food." Pepsico was told that the Japanese would not drink its cola because it tasted medicinal, and an executive of another company was told that the Japanese would not eat pizza because they believed cheese tasted like soap. The companies went ahead and entered the Japanese market anyway. Oreos quickly became the number-one cookie in Japan, colas assumed the leadership role in soft drinks, and the country experienced a pizza craze.

Recall from Chapter 1 that Harvard's Theodore Levitt popularized the concept of global marketing with the theory that people around the world are growing more alike as a result of a common drive for modernity. Many marketers still contend that global businesses must pay particular attention to national and cultural differences. Others, however, focus their energies on consumers whose needs and preferences cross national boundaries, at least in regard to certain types of products.

The theory of *global stratification*[5] looks at the world as "layers" of specific consumer characteristics or roles that cross national boundaries. For example, new mothers constitute a group whose buying preferences are very similar regardless of their cultural differences. As Procter & Gamble, maker of Pampers, reminds us, "babies' bottoms are the same everywhere." Other groups with specific consumer characteristics that overcome national or cultural boundaries are teenagers, business travelers, and computer users. As you read the next section, consider the importance of targetting specific groups in Canada.

OPEN TO DEBATE

MULTICULTURAL MARKETING

Canada's subcultures are evident in cities where urban and suburban neighbourhoods are characterized by large populations of ethnic groups. Marketing organizations with growth plans, now and in the future, are paying greater attention to ethnic target markets. By 2001, members of visible minorities will comprise 45 percent of Toronto's population and 39 percent of Vancouver's population. Visible minorities in the whole of Canada will total 5.7 million people, about 17 percent of the projected population.

Asian-Canadians are a particularly attractive target. They generally arrive in Canada with cash to lay down on big-ticket items such as houses, appliances and cars. Once they are settled, usually in Toronto or Vancouver, they tend to earn more than other Canadians. The characteristics that make Asian-Canadians an attractive target to marketers are that they:

◆ Influenced more strongly by reference groups
◆ have an average household income of $52 800
◆ are starting young families (9 out of 10 immigrants are under 35 years of age)
◆ have an above-average education
◆ prefer owning to renting
◆ are status-conscious (e.g., they like prestige labels)
◆ pay with cash instead of credit

Among many companies that have successfully targeted the Chinese- and Asian-Canadians are Sun Life Assurance, Best Foods, and Simmons Canada. Here's a brief look at some of their marketing activity.

Sun Life Assurance Company launched a marketing strategy aimed directly at Toronto's Chinese community. Certain cultural differences were identified that influenced their marketing strategy (e.g., the importance and influence of parents and grandparents). The language barrier was overcome by developing promotional literature in Chinese. Also, new sales representatives of Chinese descent were hired. The company name was translated to become the Forever Bright Assurance Company. The plan was so successful—it generated $20 million in premiums the first year—that it was expanded to include Winnipeg and Vancouver the following year. Sun Life has since developed similar strategies for other ethnic groups.

Best Foods Canada Inc. targeted the Chinese communities in major Canadian cities with campaigns for Mazola Oil, Knorr soups, and Skippy peanut butter. Communications were in Chinese and packaging labels were trilingual (by law all package labels must be in English and French; in this case Chinese was added.) As a percentage of the company's business, the volume generated was insignificant, but it is a growth segment compared to other segments of the market. The company sees much greater potential in the future. The products were initially distributed in independent, specialty grocery stores, frequented by the Chinese, but plans are in place to expand distribution into mainstream supermarkets.

Simmons Canada Limited is a leader in the mattress market. Acting on a tip from sales clerks in a Toronto department store, Simmons discovered that Asians prefer extremely hard surfaces for sleeping. The company acted quickly and launched a line called Dr. Hard, using product design specifications obtained from an affiliated company in the Far East. The hard surface is formed from uniquely constructed layers of padding. The product was an immediate hit with the Asian target, and Simmons is forecasting that the new line could account for as much as 20 percent of company sales in the future.

In reaching ethnic targets, these three companies used foreign-language advertising in media that cater to ethnic communities. To meet the growing demand for ethnic advertising, a wide range of national and local media outlets have sprung up across the country. For example, *ChinaVision* is a national PayTV network in Canada; in Toronto, Channel 47 is a multicultural television station offering programming in a variety of languages; and in local markets there are numerous newspapers and magazines targeted at ethnic groups.[6]

SOCIAL INFLUENCES

"No man is an island," wrote the English poet John Donne in 1624. Every decision you make is in part a reaction to social influences—social role, social class, reference groups, and status.

Social Roles Social influences shape your **role**, the function or position and the set of actions related to it (including purchasing decisions) that you are expected to perform under certain circumstances. We learn to be students, parents, workers, bosses—and consumers—and this is a form of social learning, or *socialization*. From a marketing standpoint, social roles are important because each role carries with it a set of activities that relate to acceptance of products and services. New mothers, for example, are interested in baby food, diapers, and developmentally sound toys.

Socialization also teaches us responsibility and social consciousness, which means we are aware of the positive and negative aspects of our behaviors on society. Marketing that is concerned with a social responsibility role appeals to and is encouraged by this aspect of socialization.

Social Class How people are ranked by such factors as parental background, occupation, education, and source of income reveals a culture's *social class* structure.[7] Some societies, such as India, are highly stratified, with very clearly defined social classes that limit where people live, their work options and income potential, and their educational opportunities. In such societies, class is a function of birth and people have little opportunity to change their social position. Among other things, this significantly restricts the use of aspirational strategies in marketing.

In contrast, in North America people can move up (and down) the social scale fairly easily based on their accomplishments and accumulation of wealth. However, even in Canada and the United States there are some commonly accepted notions of class structure that affect how products are priced, positioned, distributed, and promoted. Demographers have identified seven categories of social class; these are summarized in Table 6-2.[8]

Reference Groups Any set of people whose outlook we use as a comparison for our own personal behavior is a **reference group**. The first and most important reference group is one's *family*. Indeed, the brand of soap a person buys long after having left home may well be the one his or her parents bought. The frequency with which people clean their cars is often based on how often their parents cleaned the family car.

Families also tend to go through *life cycles* with definable stages that bring new consumption patterns. Single people, for example, tend to have more discretionary income, as do "dinks" (for "double income-no kids," or

role
The set of actions (including purchasing decisions) that society expects an individual to perform under certain circumstances.

reference group
Any set of people whose views and behavior are modeled by others in developing their own attitudes and actions.

214
CHAPTER 6

TABLE 6-2   **SOCIAL CLASS DESCRIPTIONS**

1. *Upper Upper (less than 1 percent of the total population):* Members of this highest class—the social elite—come from old and usually well-known families and live on inherited wealth, although some also work at formal jobs.

2. *Lower Upper (about 2 percent):* These professionals and businesspeople often start life in the middle class but rise by virtue of their outstanding abilities and high earnings.

3. *Upper Middle (12 percent):* This class is made up of professionals, small-business owners, and corporate managers with comfortable incomes.

4. *Middle (32 percent):* The middle class is composed of both white- and blue-collar workers who earn what is an average salary for North Americans and who try to live "on the right side of town."

5. *Working Class (38 percent):* Made up largely of blue-collar workers, this largest of the social classes also includes people who earn average pay but opt for a "blue-collar" lifestyle.

6. *Upper Lower (9 percent):* These "working poor" perform unskilled labor and menial work for minimal wages.

7. *Lower Lower (7 percent):* The members of the lowest class dwell in poverty; they are unemployed and often on welfare.

Source: Adapted from Richard P. Coleman and Lee P. Rainwater, *Social Standing in America: New Dimensions of Class* (New York: Basic Books, 1978).

---

young two-income couples without children). Newlywed couples save to buy things for their new home. When their first child arrives, they are in the market for all sorts of products designed for babies. Millennium has found that the use of rechargeable batteries is dramatically greater among families with children—the next stage in the family life cycle—than in those without. Its ideal consumer market is a family with children between the ages of six and seventeen. "Empty nesters" whose children have left home often have more money to spend on things for their own enjoyment and a large sector of the populations in Canada and the United States is now moving into this group.

Three other types of reference groups influence people's buying behavior: membership, aspirational, and dissociative groups. *Membership* groups are those to which a person belongs. These can be primary, informal membership groups, such as friends, co-workers, and fellow students, or clubs, associations, church groups, and unions.

Aspirational groups are those that a person would like to join. For example, a young executive who hopes to rise in her company may join a country club and pattern her clothing, car, work habits, and values on those of upper management in an effort to be accepted into the latter group. In contrast, people generally avoid membership in groups they view as *dissociative*. A motorcyclist, for instance, may enjoy recreational cycling but not want to be perceived as a member of a motorcycle gang.

Reference groups have the greatest influence on consumer behavior when the product in question is seen as a luxury and its consumption is visible to others. For example, reference groups may strongly influence your choice of a vacation location but have little impact on your purchase of a mattress. Direct marketing companies like Tupperware and Mary Kay Cosmetics, which sell their merchandise at special parties, also depend on reference-group influence.

Almost every reference group has an *opinion leader*—someone to whom the others turn for advice and/or information. Because opinion leaders are perceived as expert, they have high credibility and thus great influence. In some instances, marketers have identified opinion leaders and targeted information to them on the theory that they are capable of influencing the larger market. Feick and Price have explored the opinion leader relationship in marketing and developed the concept of "marketing maven" to describe people who are information sources and actively involved in passing on marketplace news.[9]

Status Many of us have a deep-seated need to evaluate ourselves by comparing our accomplishments to those of others—in other words, we hold ourselves to a standard of achievement that is socially defined. *Status* is how we measure our position in society relative to other people, and *status symbols* are the products that we use as benchmarks in this comparison. A major motivation for the purchase of some products such as Mercedes cars and Rolex watches is not so much to use them as to own and display them for others to see.

This drive for status objects can lead to the phenomenon of *conspicuous consumption*, a phrase coined by social philosopher Thorstein Veblen nearly a century ago to describe the need to consume lavishly and publicly in order to be admired.[10] This craving to acquire goods to enhance social prestige is the basis for some social critics' concern about marketing; they fear that much marketing promotion inspires excessive *materialism* at the expense of concern for other people's welfare and the welfare of the environment.

PERSONAL FACTORS

Marketers need to accumulate as much personal information as they can about the people to whom they hope to sell their products so they will better understand what these consumers want and need, like and dislike. Consumers gather information, form attitudes, and make most of their purchasing decisions as individuals operating in their own idiosyncratic ways. But they also have personal characteristics—such as age, gender, ethnic background and race, and lifestyle—that make it possible for marketers to predict more generalized interests and buying patterns.

Gender It's trite but true that men and women, boys and girls, have different needs and use different products. Certain product categories such as jock straps and tampons are obviously useful to only one gender. Other products are simply perceived as masculine or feminine because of cultural beliefs and customs. In Canada, for example, skirts are a feminine item, while in Scotland kilts are traditionally worn by men. However, many cultural beliefs and hence product perceptions have been changing in North America, so women buying weight-lifting equipment and men purchasing hair spray are no longer considered unusual.

A major trend of interest to marketers is the increasing number of working women. In Canada, 45% of the labor force in 1992 was composed of women, and this proportion continues to rise. Since most single mothers (another growing category) also work outside the home, the population of working women has burgeoned in recent years.

Women who go to work have different needs from homemakers, such as briefcases and business suits. Marketers have also noted the increased numbers of men who are taking on household duties, such as shopping for food and doing housework. Moreover, because in dual-wage-earner households both men and women have less time and energy for housework, both are demanding more convenience foods, clothing and furnishings that are easier to care for, and—most important of all—reliable child care. At the same time, the higher household incomes in two-career families increase the market for luxury goods and services.

Age Age is important because the events you have lived through from the time of your birth to the present have had a considerable influence on the person you are today. Anthropologists use a technique called *cohort analysis* to identify generations of people with the same birth years and, presumably, core values. These scientists believe that the values we form between the ages of thirteen and twenty, together with the significant events that occur during that period, affect us for the rest of our lives. Knowing the formative attitudes of an *age cohort* is very valuable. At present marketers are looking particularly hard at identifying characteristics of the twentysomething group—people whose attitudes and values have been shaped by the complex upheavals of recent times. People's behaviors are also affected by their *stage in life*. Children, teenagers, young adults, the middle-aged, and senior citizens all have different needs and buying patterns, as the next section suggests.

BEHIND THE SCENES — TOURING THE GENERATIONS

Changes in the birth rate and in generational values since World War II have had a profound effect on marketers.[11] Let's take a tour of the generations to see what researchers have found out about people born in different decades.

Makers of infant food and clothing profited from the postwar "baby boom" (1946–1964) but faced difficult times during the "baby bust" that followed (1964–1976) because the birth rate dropped. They are now trying to cash in on the "boomlet" of babies born since 1984 to baby-boomer yuppies who postponed having children.

Although baby busters, who include Xers and their older siblings, are not as well off as their boomer predecessors or their parents, they are dedicated consumers who become brand conscious at a very early age. They want quality and they are willing to pay top dollar for it. Baby busters have to work harder to counter the effects of more frequent recessions, fewer job opportunities because of the large number of boomers in the job market, and a stingier government that has provided them with less educational and home financing support than their parents received.

The demographic cluster that contains the buster cohort—the eighteen-to-thirty-four-year-olds who have traditionally been the primary target of most marketers—is in a major decline. This so-called Bermuda

Triangle of marketing is expected to worry marketers till the end of the century.

With boomers making up about 40 percent of the population, the emphasis in much marketing has shifted to meeting the changing needs of this group as it grows older. For example, Walt Disney has added a Touchstone Films division to produce movies for this older group.

The over-forty baby boomer, the group for whom the term *yuppie* was originally invented, is particularly driven by possessions and has been since adolescence. Incidentally, this is the group that Millennium has found includes the most frequent buyers of rechargeable batteries, partly because it is so attracted to the electronic products (Walkmans, camcorders, and cellular phones) that benefit from rechargeables. However, as people age, possessions tend to mean less (this is true even for yuppies). When people turn fifty they become more service-oriented and believe life experiences are more important than having things. This makes them an important market for continuing education and travel.

The over-fifty category—the parents of the boomers—constitutes only one-quarter of the total population but has almost one-half of all disposable income. Many savvy marketers, like Land Rover (see the Range Rover ad in Exhibit 6-1), are beginning to go after this market. This is a new trend: in the past the fiftysomething group was a forgotten generation because marketers tended to target teenagers and the eighteen-to-thirty-four-year-olds.

This fiftysomething generation is unusual in another respect: it is a generation of caregivers. Many people in this group take care of both

Exhibit 6-1
Pleasure at Leisure

High-priced, status-laden products are targeted to the upper end of the baby-boomer market and to people in their sixties and older. These products are marketed on such features as comfort and classiness rather than on price competitiveness or safety concerns like child proofing.

It not only says you've arrived. It also says you'll get home.

RANGE ROVER

their aging parents and their young grandchildren if the latter's parents are working. After spending twenty years worrying about their own children, they got a break for a few years, and now look forward to spending another twenty years worrying about their parents. They find themselves putting Depends for their parents and Pampers for their grandchildren into the same grocery cart.

As an indication of how fast the senior market is growing, consider this: People aged sixty-five and older made up 10.7 percent of the Canadian population in 1986. By the year 2000, this group is expected to reach 13.5 percent of Canada's population.

This senior market is driving growth in leisure activities, vacations, and second homes, as well as in health care and retirement living programs.

Going for the Gray

Although the full impact of baby-boomer spending won't be felt until about 1997, some boomers will enter their fifties before that. Savvy marketers like Saatchi and Saatchi Advertising are well aware that the fiftysomething generation is not only wealthier than other groups in society but healthier than people their age have ever been. Old stereotypes about "senior citizens" are going out the window as marketers prepare to take advantage of the fact that over-fifty consumers already make more than 80 percent of leisure and travel expenditures and buy 50 percent of all domestic cars.

Ethnic Background and Race Another demographic shift of interest to marketers is the changing ethnic and racial makeup of countries and regions.

In Canada, the proportion of all Canadians with French as a mother tongue and home language has declined from 29% in 1951 to around 24% in the 1990s. The vast majority of people who are bilingual reside in Quebec and New Brunswick. According to 1991 Statistics Canada figures, 35% live in Quebec and 29.5% in New Brunswick. Ontario had 11% in 1991 but all other provinces are below 10%. In terms of ethnic origin for Canada as a whole, British and French links are still by far the most prevalent—21% British and 23% French, but note that 29% claim multiple origins.

Since the Canadian birthrate has been declining steadily since the mid-1960s, immigrants account for a major part of the increase in Canada's population. Most recent immigrants that have entered Canada have not been of Western-European background, but instead, from Asia and the Caribbean, and this trend has led to large Asian and Black communities, particularly in large Canadian cities.

In the 1991 census, 7 million people in Canada identified themselves as members of a single ethnic or mixed ethnic heritage other than British or French. The major groups are shown in Table 6-3.

The changing ethnic and racial composition of Canada is affecting how marketers position, distribute, and target products. Most major consumer goods companies now offer food, music, and other products aimed at different cultural groups and develop promotions in languages other than English and French. This trend will undoubtedly continue into the next century. Such

TABLE 6-3	MAJOR ETHNIC GROUPS IN CANADA OTHER THAN BRITISH OR FRENCH		
German	911,560	Portuguese	246,890
Italian	750,055	Jewish	245,840
Chinese	586,645	Black	224,620
Aboriginal	470,615	Filipino	157,250
South Asian	420,295	Greek	151,150
Ukranian	406,645	Arab	144,050
Dutch	358,185	Caribbean	94,395
Polish	272,810		

Source: 1991 Canadian Census.

lifestyle
An individual's set of values and tastes that determines the conduct of his daily life, as well as how time, energy, and money are allocated or spent.

practices are common in countries like Malaysia, which has a diverse population of Malays, Chinese, and Indians—all of whom have different languages, religions, and cultural values. Malaysia, in fact, is a case study in how to market products successfully in a multicultural environment.

Lifestyle Each of us has a **lifestyle**, a set of values and tastes that determines how we spend our time, energy, and money. (The Royal Bank ads in Exhibit 6-2 show that it recognizes the needs of people with different lifestyles.) Some people put their spare money into retirement funds; others buy big homes and expensive cars. Some look forward to relaxing during a beachside vacation, others never take a vacation at all. Some people enjoy active sports, others are dedicated spectators. All of these are differences in lifestyle. Adventure capitalists—such as North Vancouver's Rob Mulder, co-owner and founder of Roberts High Performance Sailboards—signify a new breed of entrepreneurs who have been able to turn their sporting pastimes into businesses that tap the world market for top-of-the-line recreational and leisure products.

With lifestyle information, marketers are better able to target their products and messages. They can create advertisements that depict settings and people with whom consumers identify. What other kinds of products would you market to people with the lifestyle implied in the Range Rover ad in Exhibit 6-1?

Increasingly, consumer product marketers are finding that consumer behavior varies more within than among countries because differences in consumer behavior often reside in lifestyles rather than in cultural differences. For example, business travelers have much the same needs, regardless of their nationality. So do new mothers in nearly every land. Moreover, universal systems of mass communication like CNN are producing universal consumption patterns. Teenagers across the world have become a universal cross-cultural niche market, listening to the same music, wearing the same fashions, and expressing many of the same attitudes—such as concern for the environment.

Exhibit 6-2
One Customer at a Time

In a new advertising campaign, the Royal Bank points out that it is Canada's largest bank because it treats its customers as individuals. It adapts its banking services to meet the needs of people of different ages, varying lifestyles, and so, varying needs.

221

Despite this trend, marketers must still keep cultural values in mind when deciding on global marketing communications. For example, in nations where literacy rates are still low, marketers may find magazine advertising unprofitable. In many Asian countries, where confrontation is frowned on, attempts to "hard-sell" a product may backfire. In many cultures, too, it is considered in bad taste to make negative statements about one's competitors in advertising.

THE BLACK BOX ●

Although external factors have a substantial effect on buying behavior, even more important are internal factors—those most personal aspects of our being, such as the way we process information and learn things, our needs and motives, our attitudes, beliefs, and values, and, of course, our personalities. These are the factors that cannot be observed because they reside deep in our minds, emotions, and psyches. Any good marketer is a student of consumer psychology, always trying to learn more about what goes on in that black box, the subject of the third chapter objective. We start our tour of the hidden mind with theories about how human beings make sense of things.

INFORMATION PROCESSING

The procedure by which we receive, interpret, and remember information is called **information processing**. This five-step process involving exposure, attention, comprehension, acceptance, and retention (memory) is the topic of chapter objective four.

The Process To begin with, you are *exposed* to something in the environment and you *perceive* it—that is, you take it into your awareness through one of your five senses in an operation that we call *perception*. Although you are exposed to countless stimuli every day, you pay *attention* to relatively few of them. You make use of *selective perception,* focusing on the objects or events that interest you most and letting that information into your awareness, while ignoring other things in the environment.

Next, you organize and interpret the stimuli you've allowed into your awareness in order to *comprehend* them. If the resulting information confirms something you already know or believe, you are more likely to *accept* it and store it in *memory* so that you can use it later in making decisions.

Suppose you go to a store looking for a coffee maker. Your selective perception will focus your attention on various coffee makers, and you will ignore most of the other products displayed in the appliance department. You may also read lists of the features possessed by various models of coffee makers in order to comprehend the options. You are most likely to accept the claims of the brand whose features fit your particular needs if you remember the brand's advertising or the comments of a friend who had a good experience with that brand.

Selection Different people exposed to the same stimuli interpret them differently because of what they choose to focus on and screen out. *Selective perception* is very individualistic; it is shaped by an individual's needs, motives, attitudes, beliefs, values, and prior learning.

Two related selection processes are also quite personal: In *selective distortion*, people try to make new information fit their old ideas about something. For example, you may remember that a computer you are interested in is on sale but misremember the advertised price, which was lower than the price

information processing
The procedure by which individuals receive, interpret, and retain information.

tag in the store, because you have already formed a positive opinion of the product and you are looking for reasons to justify your decision to buy it right now. Under the influence of *selective retention*, people are more apt to attend to and recall stimuli that confirm their previously held attitudes. For example, after you have purchased a car, you will likely be able to recall positive reviews of it because they confirm your decision, but may have trouble remembering negative comments.

LEARNING

Consumers learn when experience or information leads them to acquire new knowledge and alter their behavior. *Learning*, then, means a change in behavior or potential behavior owing to experience or knowledge. Here we look briefly at three theories of learning: classical conditioning, operant conditioning, and cognitive learning.

Classical and operant conditioning share the key principle of *conditioning*. Through being exposed to the repetition of certain events, or *stimuli*, and through responding to these stimuli repeatedly with certain behaviors, a person learns to associate these events with specific *responses*. In classical conditioning, a new response occurs because it is associated with a response already in the person's repertoire. In operant conditioning, a person learns a new response because it is paired with a reward.

Marketers use classical conditioning because of its power to build associations. Have you ever noticed that advertisements often use children and animals, even though they have no particular relevance to the product being advertised? This is because children and animals are associated with "warm, fuzzy feelings." In the ad in Exhibit 6-3, the product being touted is associated with the concept of having "quality time" with one's family. The marketer hopes that readers will transfer the positive feelings generated by this image to Pioneer sound systems.

Operant conditioning teaches people to associate certain behaviors with certain consequences. At the heart of this kind of learning are *rewards*. To increase the likelihood of people performing a desired behavior (such as buying your product or having a positive attitude about your firm), you reward them. Notice that in addition to warm associations, the Pioneer ad also promises dad "quality time" with his baby.

The third theory of learning, *cognitive learning,* is based on the notion that we also learn through problem solving and reasoning from information and past experiences. Marketers use the cognitive approach when they provide information that, in combination with our past knowledge, experiences, values, and goals, will help us to understand something better. The cognitive approach is especially appropriate when introducing new products to satisfy newly recognized needs. The Range Rover ad in Exhibit 6-1, for instance, helps you understand the car's durability as well as its quality.

Often associated with cognitive learning, *social learning* enables us to learn through the experiences of others by watching them and then *modeling* our behavior on theirs. Typically, our models are people we know (our parents are our first models) and/or admire (film stars and other prominent people). This form of learning is at the root of advertisements featuring testimonials from famous people.

INTERNAL FACTORS ●

As we noted in Chapter 1, all demand for goods and services is motivated by human needs (the feeling that something is lacking) and wants (the wish to

Exhibit 6-3
Music to Parent By

This Pioneer advertisement speaks to the new-style father who cherishes parenting. The ad uses the principles of association (linking the pleasures of parenting and good music) and cognitive learning (information provided in the blurb) to deliver its message.

hierarchy of needs
Abraham Maslow's five-level theory of needs in which the need at each successive level must be essentially fulfilled before the person will attempt to fulfill higher-level needs.

fulfill that lack). A sufficiently strong need will arouse a *motivation* to remedy the lack. In addition to motivation, marketers are concerned with *attitudes* and how they develop from beliefs and values. In this section we discuss these four factors, the focus of chapter objective five.

MOTIVATION: NEEDS AND WANTS

Consumer-behavior researchers have found psychologist Abraham Maslow's **hierarchy of needs** a particularly useful theory of motivation.[12] Maslow's theory, illustrated in Figure 6-2, is based on the assumption that human needs are arranged in a hierarchy of importance and that it is only when needs at lower levels have been largely satisfied that we can consider needs at the next level. Furthermore, according to Maslow, needs influence behavior only when they are *unsatisfied*. The only exception is self-actualization which continues to motivate because it can never be fully satisfied.

Figure 6-2
Maslow's Hierarchy of Needs

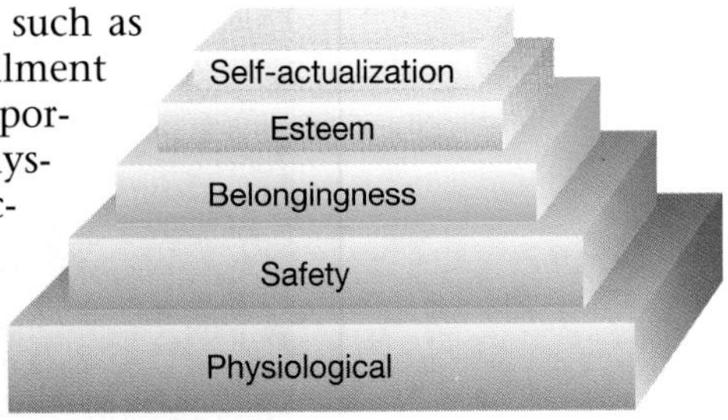

At the base of the hierarchy are *physiological needs*, such as for food, clothing, and shelter. In the sense that the fulfillment of these needs is fundamental to life, they are the most important. Next come *safety needs*, which are concerned with physical protection. *Belongingness needs*, such as for love and acceptance by other people, are third. At the fourth level, *esteem needs* lead the individual to strive for a sense of personal accomplishment and respect from others. Finally come *self-actualization needs*, or the craving for creativity and new ideas and challenges.

Self-actualization
Esteem
Belongingness
Safety
Physiological

To take a somewhat oversimplified example, suppose you're finished with school and out on your own. Once you have regular meals and a roof over your head, you can think about fulfilling your safety needs by buying a smoke alarm, extra locks, or insurance. The need to belong to a group may lead you to join clubs and, perhaps, to worry whether you'll "fit into" your new neighborhood. Once you've established your home, you may decorate it in ways that signal your status, thus giving evidence of your need for esteem. And if you've chosen to live in a geodesic dome in the middle of a suburban neighborhood of ranch-style houses, you may be expressing your need for self-actualization by daring to be different.

ATTITUDES: BELIEFS AND VALUES

Relatively enduring feelings of favorableness or unfavorableness toward an object, an idea, or a behavior are called *attitudes*. Attitudes, which are crucial elements in any buying decision, interact with belief systems and cultural values. A *belief* is a strongly held opinion—not always based on objective facts—about some attribute of an object, an idea, or a behavior. Beliefs often come in sets of related opinions referred to as a *belief system*. A *value* is a culturally determined belief that something—generally a principle or an idea—is intrinsically worthwhile (refer back to Table 6-1).

Marketers are interested in attitudes and the values and beliefs they represent because these are thought to influence consumption behaviors. You are more likely to buy a product in which you believe and about which you have a positive attitude than one that you do not believe in or like. Since attitudes are easier to change than beliefs or values, they are often the focus of marketing efforts to get consumers to buy. Marketers often talk about the need to "build positive attitudes" toward a product or to "change people's attitudes" about something.

Researchers have found some interesting changes in North American attitudes and lifestyles recently. One change is in eating habits: in addition to the rise in the habit of grazing at the refrigerator, a Louis Harris survey in 1993 revealed that North Americans are not eating as well or exercising as much as they did in the 1980s. On the other hand, the survey found that they have become very concerned about the presence of chemical additives in food and that represents a significant shift in attitudes, for North Americans had previously focused on the convenience, performance, status, or value of products.[13]

Marketing strategies that attempt to change attitudes—a difficult task at best—generally focus on one of two broad areas: changing the underlying belief or changing the importance the consumer places on it. Table 6-4 summa-

you are with the area in which the buying decision must be made and the higher the level of risk, the more likely it is that you will try to learn more about product features before you make a purchase.[16]

For example, having decided that you need your own computer, you will probably investigate a number of alternatives before making this relatively expensive and semi-permanent purchase. You may seek information from your past experiences—that is, your knowledge of computers that you have used—or you may search for information from external sources—say, friends' experiences, salespeople's advice, magazine articles, advertising, and other product literature.

The information search may be extensive, limited, or routine. If consumers lack experience in a particular area, they will usually engage in *extensive problem solving,* which means a lengthy information search. If they are more experienced, their problem solving will be more *limited* because they are already familiar with the options. As consumers rely more on what they know or feel and less on new information, evaluation is reduced until, eventually, the search becomes *routine.* Think of how many supermarket and drugstore purchases you make automatically, moving down the aisles and simply taking things mechanically from the shelves and putting them into your shopping cart or basket.

evoked set
In consumer purchase decision making, the relatively small set of alternatives that one actually considers in making a final choice.

inert set
In consumer purchase decision making, the set of alternatives about which one is neutral.

inept set
In consumer purchase decision making, the set of rejected alternatives.

STAGE 3: EVALUATION OF ALTERNATIVES

Purchase decisions often depend on the way the consumer evaluates the product and its features. Millennium's research has found, for example, that the most important of eight consumer-satisfaction indicators to its buyers are: (1) convenience and (2) reduces the need for disposable batteries.

In your search for a computer—a major purchase—you will probably assemble a *set* of possible choices. Consumer psychologists divide these choice sets into three categories: evoked, inert, and inept sets. The **evoked set** contains only those alternatives that you will actually consider in making your final choice.[17] Evoked sets tend to be small, often containing only four or five choices. Alternatives about which you are neutral—for example, Radio Shack computers, which are not available in your area—form your **inert set.** Rejected alternatives—for example, you may have decided against Apple Macintosh because you want an MS DOS computer—compose your **inept set.**

Because each of the alternatives in your evoked set is a "bundle of benefits" that yields different kinds of satisfactory solutions, you will probably make your final evaluation by rating the strong and weak points of each product and comparing the ratings in terms of the relative importance (salience) to you of each of those points.

STAGE 4: PURCHASE

At the fourth step, the actual purchase, we shift to the final column of *response* in the consumer behavior model depicted in Figure 6-1. Marketers are particularly concerned with behavioral responses like trial, purchase, and repeat purchase. Opinions and attitudes and comprehension are also important to marketers, for they measure the effectiveness of marketing communication, but the most important marketing response is obviously the decision to purchase or not to purchase.

Actually, purchase involves a set of decisions. If you decide to buy, you must also decide where to buy, when to buy, and how to pay. The marketing mix determines the availability of the product, the price you will have to pay for it, the amount of information you obtain from advertising, the incentive to purchase provided by sales promotions, and the help you can get from salespeople. Your own situational factors, such as deadlines you are working under (for example, the due date for your term paper), physical surroundings, the time of day, and your financial resources, are also important and may cause you to alter, postpone, or even rescind your decision.

STAGE 5: POSTPURCHASE EVALUATION

The moment you begin to use the product you have purchased you start to evaluate your selection. If the computer performs as expected, you will feel satisfied. If it fails to live up to expectations, you will feel dissatisfied. The things that please and/or vex you about the product will influence your future buying decision making. If you are generally satisfied with your purchase, you are likely to make repeat purchases, to become brand loyal, and to give positive testimonials about the product to your friends—that is, to become an opinion leader. But if you are dissatisfied, your response will almost certainly be not to repurchase and, on average, tell eight friends of your complaints.

One form of postpurchase evaluation is *buyer remorse*. This is an example of what psychologists call **cognitive dissonance**, an uncomfortable state of mind in which you experience conflict between some belief, attitude, or value and a particular action or set of actions you have taken. People may experience cognitive dissonance when they find that the product they have chosen to purchase has some unexpected drawbacks and that the rejected alternatives actually have more or better positive features. In essence, they are plagued by doubt: "Did I make the right decision?"[18]

High-Involvement Purchases Need Research

Although computers have come down considerably in price since the mid-1980s, they are still continuing to fall as both hardware and software appear to have a shelf life of only two years. Many consumers do a lot of research on the special features, strengths, and weaknesses of different brands of computers before making a purchase.

cognitive dissonance
Self-doubt which has crept in after the purchase of a high-value item is quite common. Advertisers of cars, for example, build reassurance into their advertisements which will be reread by new buyers.

Suppose you're not sure about the computer you bought. You might try to reduce dissonance by seeking information to support your decision—for example, by reading advertisements for your brand or by talking with people who made the same choice. Or you might try to avoid information that supports the alternative you rejected—for example, by throwing out, unread, promotional material that arrives in the mail. When cognitive dissonance is extremely intense, purchasers may try to reverse the unsatisfactory decision by returning or reselling the product they purchased.

Savvy marketers strive to reduce the likelihood that buyers will experience cognitive dissonance. Salespeople may assure buyers by emphasizing the store's return policy or the product's extended warranty. Many computer software and hardware firms offer technical "hotline" telephone numbers for consumers who experience difficulty using their purchases. And automobile dealers, most of whom have active *after-marketing* programs, often follow up sales with letters detailing the services they offer car owners. Home Team, a chain of appliance stores in New Zealand, provides a good example of efforts to prevent postpurchase regret. The stores offer at the time of purchase a 10-year buyback campaign, promising consumers "free appliances" if they purchased during the 10 weeks of promotion. If a customer purchases a refrigerator for $1000 in September 1992, The Home Team would buy the same refrigerator back in September 2002 for $1000.

VARIATIONS ON THE DECISION MODEL

Although the model we've discussed is very useful to marketers for understanding how consumers make major purchases, the lengthy five-stage process it describes applies to only some purchase decisions. In many cases, consumers shorten or even bypass the search and evaluation stages. Which stages the individual actually uses depends on the buyer's level of involvement in the purchase, perception of risks, and willingness to be an innovator—the three factors mentioned in the seventh chapter objective.

Level of Involvement   A consumer's level of **involvement** in a buying decision depends on how important the purchase is to that consumer. *High-involvement* purchases are generally of products that are expensive and/or reflect on the social status or self-image of the buyer; examples are automobiles, houses, jewelry, and ski equipment. In such situations consumers often engage in extensive search, evaluation, and problem solving, going through all five of the buying-decision stages. In contrast, with *low-involvement* products, such as chewing gum or paper clips, search and evaluation are minimal. The consumer either engages in random choice, buys one brand out of habit, or casually experiments by trying different brands.

Risk   An important element of your personality is your response to risk. **Perceived risk** is your view of the relationship between the benefits you think you will derive from purchasing a particular item versus the possible losses lurking in this product—you may not like it, it may not work as well as you thought it would, or it may not be worth the money.

Risk increases both as *uncertainty* increases and as the possible *consequences* become more important—for example, the purchase is high-priced or is something that has social visibility and will therefore reflect on your self-image. Taking friends to an unfamiliar expensive restaurant is a high-risk situation; stopping at McDonald's for breakfast on your way to work is a low-risk one.

Marketers attempt to reduce perceived risk by providing expert testimonials, obtaining endorsements such as the Good Housekeeping Seal of Approval, providing test-based proof of a product's performance, or by offering warranties, return privileges, or postpurchase services. The goal is to change the buyer's attitude so the purchase moves from being a high risk to a low risk.

Innovation   How experimental you are and how willing you are to be innovative also affect your decision making. An *innovation* is an idea, practice, or object perceived as new by an individual. In the classification system outlined by Rogers,[19] *innovators* are that 2.5 percent of the population who are risk takers by personality. They are sometimes also referred to as a "lunatic fringe." It is important to note that they do not constitute a market in themselves in view of their small size. Next to try something new are the *early adopters*, who make up 13.5 percent of the population and they are vitally important in having a product accepted. Their opinion is quite crucial as others look to early adopters as knowledgeable, well educated people who will have opinions. The biggest proportions of the population are identified as *early majority* and *late majority adopters*. The late majority are a different group again characterized as being skeptical and very careful with money. They only buy tried and tested products and shy clear of risk. Each group makes up 34 percent of the population. The *laggards*, roughly 16 percent, are the last to come on board but they too are different again in that they have no fixed income. This group includes students as well as senior citizens and no one therefore targets this group as they are very price conscious and so lack loyalty to any supplier.

By the time the late majority and the laggards—who together are 50 percent of the population—get around to trying something, it is no longer an innovation.

This classification system illustrates the point that innovations are not adopted rapidly or all at once in a social system. It is particularly important for marketers of new or trendy products to recognize this fact of life. Over time, too, the marketing message has to change as we come up against different groups of people who respond to different criteria.

BOTTOM LINE REALITIES

THE TREND TRACKERS

To keep their finger on the pulse of any given market, marketers do continuous research. Only solid information about consumer buying behaviors enables them to keep up with changes in the marketplace and make effective decisions about the many aspects of the marketing mix that create both willingness to buy and consumer satisfaction.

A new breed of market researcher known as a *trend forecaster* or *trend tracker* studies consumer groups like Xers and dinks and identifies consumer trends such as "mall jamming" (teenagers hanging around malls) and "cocooning"

(retreating from the harsh, unpredictable world into one's home). Trend trackers advise major marketers such as the consumer-product giants Procter & Gamble and Pepsico on changes in consumer attitudes and behaviors and what they mean to marketing programs.

Although less known to the public than widely published "futurists" like John Naisbett and Alvin Toffler, who specialize in geopolitical theorizing, consumer trend forecasters conduct a wide variety of marketing research studies and consult with some of the best-known companies. Faith Popcorn, president of BrainReserve, Inc., and author of the acclaimed *Popcorn Report*, was the first to identify the "cocooning" trend—which she interpreted as an increased interest in activi-

ties centered around home life. One result of her tracking was the increased attention by marketers to bathrooms as luxurious in-home spas.

Consumer research is critical to marketing because it is the only way to uncover consumer needs and wants, track attitudes, and evaluate the meaning of consumer behaviors. Trends are particularly difficult to predict, but without such information, marketers are working in the dark.

Can you think of any recent trends that marketers are using today in their strategies? What was the lag time between your noticing the trend and its showing up in marketing? What trends do you see emerging right now that affect your own population group? ▼

KEY POINTS SUMMARY ▼

1. In the consumer buying behavior model the *external factors* (marketing-mix information plus economic, cultural, social, and personal factors) influence how people make sense of things and process information. The *black box* where the processing occurs includes *information processing* procedures, *internal factors*, and the *decision-making process*. What comes out of the black box is a *response*, which can be opinions or behaviors.

2. Buying decisions are shaped initially by the way *external influences—economic* and *geographic* factors; *cultural* values and differences; *social* roles, class, and status; and *personal* factors such as age, gender, race, and lifestyle—interact with product information as the consumer moves into information processing.

3. In the "black box" information processing and learning interact first with internal influences, then with the five-step decision-making process. The black box is hidden in the mind; thus, unlike external influences, its factors and processes are impossible to observe.

4. *Information processing* describes how people make sense of marketing messages. First they are exposed to information (perception); then they select and attend to it, comprehend and accept it, and ultimately file it away in memory. If the process is completed, they have learned the information. Theories of *learning*, principally classical and operant conditioning

and cognitive learning theories, have taught marketers to use principles of association and reward strategies in marketing communications.

5. Developing insight into the *internal factors*—motivation (needs and wants), attitudes (beliefs and values)—helps marketers determine what strategies to use to reach and motivate individuals. Maslow's theory of the hierarchy of needs says that people are motivated to act first to satisfy fundamental physiological needs and then to fulfill more psychological needs—such as belongingness, esteem, and self-actualization.

6. The *decision-making process* used by consumers for many purchases involves five steps: problem recognition, information search, evaluation of alternatives, purchase, and postpurchase evaluation.

7. The decision-making process does not operate the same way in all situations. The level of involvement and perceived risk determines how much problem solving and information searching a consumer will do. In some situations, such as routine purchases and the purchase of low-involvement products, the decision-making process is considerably shortened. Also affecting the consumer decision-making process are individual differences in innovativeness: some people are more willing than others to try something new.

DISCUSSION QUESTIONS ▼

1. Explain what we know about what happens inside the "black box" of the consumer's mind and what we don't know.

2. Of economic, geographic, cultural, social, and personal factors, which most influenced your latest purchase over $20? Over $200?

3. Distinguish among attitudes, beliefs, and values, and give an example of each that affected a recent purchase you made.

4. How would you describe yourself in terms of culture, reference groups, role(s), and social class?

5. Talk with the marketing manager of a local business and then describe the ways that firm

is attempting to change attitudes in the marketing of its products.

6. Why are information processing and learning so important for understanding consumer behavior? Explain how you learned about the school you're now attending and how your information processing worked as you considered your educational alternatives.

7. Explain the steps in information processing, using the example of how you perceived and made sense of the Pioneer ad in Exhibit 6-3. Compare that process with what you went through to understand the Royal Bank ad (Exhibit 6-2).

8. Which step in the consumer decision-making process would you expect to take the longest? Why?

9. Compare the steps you would use in a buying decision process for an expensive pair of jogging shoes with the steps you would use for the choice of a new cereal.

10. You have been hired by a large marketing consulting company to conduct a study aimed at achieving a better definition of Generation X. Interview your friends and classmates and develop a profile of the twentysomething generation. What are their central concerns? What lifestyle changes do you think this group will bring to twenty-first century society? What label will you use in your report to describe this group?

Integrative Case • Discussion Questions

The Body Shop*

1. What reference groups and social factors help to explain the loyalty and enthusiasm of Body Shop customers?

2. How does The Body Shop attempt to affect consumer perceptions? How might selective exposure, selective attention, and selective retention work in The Body Shop's favor?

3. What kind of learning is Anita Roddick trying to stimulate? Is her approach typical of the cosmetics industry? Explain your answer.

4. Would you guess that brand loyalty is higher for Body Shop products than for other, competing products? Why or why not?

Harley-Davidson

1. Describe the lifestyle of the typical Harley owner. How involved are Harley owners with their bikes and with the Harley image?

2. How has the company affected consumer perception of the Harley through changes in product attributes and features? How have the media affected the perception of Harleys?

The Millennium Power System

1. Explain how situational, lifestyle, and social-class factors can affect consumers' battery-buying behavior.

2. How do the manufacturers of rechargeable systems try to stimulate brand loyalty?

3. What type of learning is illustrated by Danny's initial choice of the brand of battery he and his dad usually purchased? What type of learning do we see when Danny's father reads the Renewal System information and compares prices?

4. How does the Millennium System attempt to reduce perceived risk?

5. Which system will Danny and his dad buy if they want to reduce their initial investment? If they want to maximize their investment over the next five years?

6. Because of Millennium's emphasis on cross merchandising, their products are usually located in stores' electronics sections—away from displays of other batteries, which typically are set up near checkout counters. How do you think Millennium's location policy might affect consumers' information search and evaluation of rechargeable battery alternatives?

*The three cases at the back of the book—"The Body Shop," "Harley-Davidson," and "The Millennium Power System"—illustrate topics discussed in all chapters of this book. Your instructor will tell you when to read a particular case and answer the discussion questions on it that appear at the end of each chapter.

Too Much Choice: Consumer Buying Behavior

Drive down a main street in any city and notice that four gas stations are located at many intersections, one on each of the four corners. All are selling the same basic product lines, and service levels do not vary to any noticeable degree. How do you decide which station to pull into to fill up with gasoline? Do you really care which brand of gasoline you purchase, as it is really all the same anyway? How do these operations manage to survive, let alone earn a profit?

Walk into the nearest shopping mall with the intent of purchasing a piece of men's or ladies' apparel. You rapidly discover that there exist dozens of stores offering the category of product you are searching for, some very specialized, some offering a huge variety of products. Furthermore, you determine that, despite some cosmetic differences, the majority of the stores selling the product category you are interested in seem to be "clones" in many regards. How do you proceed? Do you shop with great determination, going from store to store intent on discovering the item offering the very best price or value? Do you simply purchase the first item you prefer, feeling that an extended effort is futile? Or do you leave the mall in disgust, feeling confused and frustrated?

Consumer decision-making is an increasingly complicated issue, and of critical importance as an element of an organization's overall marketing strategy. This is particularly valid as the competitive environment becomes increasingly hostile, with more direct competitors fighting for the same customer dollar, and consumers becoming highly sophisticated in their purchase behavior.

The result of these trends has been to render the consumer's decision-making environment extremely complex. Even the most sophisticated marketing organizations, such as Coca-Cola, admit that they are unsure as to exactly what the customer desires, or which marketing and advertising strategies are truly effective in attracting customers to their products and services. Marketer's general inability to pinpoint increasingly diverse consumer needs and wants has resulted in many organizations adopting a "shotgun" approach to many aspects of their marketing strategy, in the hopes of connecting with consumers. "Power walls" display hundreds of competing products for the consumer with hundreds of advertisements per day, and shopping malls are packed with dozens of retail clones all scrambling to reach for the same consumer dollar.

What is the result? Do consumers appreciate the greater range or product and service choices? Are the vast number of choices available confusing or even angering consumers? Has product/service differentiation come down to insignificant hair splitting in the mind of the consumer? How can we realistically know what consumers truly desire? If we cannot possibly know or even adapt to consumer's rapidly changing wants and needs, how can marketing organizations effectively adapt and offer continuous superior value to their customers? The issue of consumer buying behavior is indeed perplexing, interesting, and critical to marketing success.

234

QUESTIONS

1. Relate the marketing concept of differentiation to the consumer choice dilemma. Why are many retailers and other businesses failing in attempts to significantly differentiate themselves from their competitors?

2. How important is product or service branding when attempting differentiation? Do you think branding is increasing or decreasing in importance in the consumer decision making process? Why?

3. Do you think that a product line "shotgunning" approach is effective? What are your reasons? What do you think is the more effective approach, shotgunning or differentiation?

4. Do you think that "box" stores like Wal-Mart, which adopt a shotgun approach, offering customers fewer choices of a broad number of product categories generally out-compete specialty stores, which target highly specialized consumer segments? How could you measure and compare competitive performance?

Source: This case was prepared by Byron Osing and is based on the *Venture* series episode "Too Much Choice," which was first broadcast on November 28, 1993.

235

Chapter 7

Organizational Buying Behavior

OBJECTIVES

AFTER COMPLETING THIS CHAPTER, YOU SHOULD BE ABLE TO

1
COMPARE AND CONTRAST THE THREE ORGANIZATIONAL BUYING MARKETS AND EXPLAIN THE IMPORTANCE OF EACH

2
EXPLAIN HOW ORGANIZATIONAL BUYING BEHAVIOR DIFFERS FROM CONSUMER BUYING BEHAVIOR BY ANALYZING THE KEY FACTORS IN THE BUSINESS-TO-BUSINESS BUYING MODEL

3
IDENTIFY THE THREE TYPES OF BUYING SITUATIONS IN INDUSTRIAL MARKETS AND DIFFERENT BUYING PHASES

4
EXPLAIN THE BUYING CENTER AND DESCRIBE ITS MAJOR INFLUENCES ON ORGANIZATIONAL BUYERS

5
DESCRIBE HOW THE DECISION-MAKING PROCESSES USED BY RESELLER AND GOVERNMENT BUYERS DIFFER FROM THE PROCESS USED BY INDUSTRIAL BUYERS

MAKING A NATURAL DECISION

The products you as a consumer purchase have been produced through an involved process of industrial buying. Since manufacturers get their supplies, materials, and services from other companies, a number of purchase decisions go into the product you ultimately buy. Here's an example that illustrates how the buying decision chain works.

Marylou Marsh liked to buy natural products. In particular, she liked all-cotton fabrics made from organically grown cotton.[1] Finding this type of clothing was a challenge for her, so she and her husband, David, decided to start a company called EcoSport to manufacture it for people who also appreciated "organic clothes." At first this firm had a hard time finding even a bale of unbleached cotton, but now they are getting

calls from farmers who have switched to organic farming because, among other reasons, it's kinder to the soil.

Finding the resources for your product is the first step; selling the man-

237

ufactured product to retailers is the sometimes tricky next step in the chain of sales in business-to-business marketing. EcoSport started out supplying clothing to private-label marketers and environmental groups such as Greenpeace, which didn't have a purely unbleached cotton T-shirt in its catalog when EcoSport contact-ed it. EcoSport also sold to an odd combination of surf shops, natural food stores, and regular T-shirt shops.

The firm has seen an explosion in its distribution avenues, new products, and annual sales, which in 1993 reached more than US $3 million. As commonly happens with any specialty product, however, moving into the mainstream has meant that EcoSport must compete on price. Currently, an EcoSport T-shirt costs more than a regular cotton T-shirt. Do you think there is a demand for organically derived clothing? Will people who are environmentally concerned pay the extra price? Would it be worth it to you? ■

BUSINESS-TO-BUSINESS MARKETING ●

Like private consumers, whom we discussed in the last chapter, organizations—companies, institutions, associations, governments—need products and services in order to function. However, the types and quantities of products that organizations buy are often different from the ones consumers buy, and organizations use different methods of buying. As a result, the marketing programs of businesses that sell products to other businesses are often different from the programs of firms that sell to individual consumers, although, as you'll see, many basic concepts of marketing remain the same. These differences in buyer behavior and seller approach are the focus of this chapter.

One key difference between organizational and private consumer buying lies in the nature of the demand. The demand for organizational goods and services is described as **derived demand**—that is, it *derives*, or ultimately comes, from consumer demand for finished products. For example, if there were no consumer demand for clothing made of organically grown cotton, there would be no business market (stores) for EcoSport to serve.

Another example of derived demand is the Millennium rechargeable battery technology that is sold to other manufacturers for use in their products. Millennium's technology, called *IntelliLink*^{TM} (Exhibit 7-1), can be used in portable vacuums, camcorders, portable computers, cordless telephones, and cellular telephones that have their own built-in recharging units. If Motorola uses Millennium rechargeable battery units in its cellular telephones and Motorola's customers begin to demand fewer phones, the company's demand for Millennium's product will decline.

THE ORGANIZATIONAL MARKET

The organizational market is huge. At about $6 trillion annually, it's almost three times the size of the consumer market. Thus much more is bought and

derived demand
Demand in organizational markets that arises, or is derived from, demand in consumer markets.

238

FOR MANUFACTURERS OF RECHARGEABLE PRODUCTS:
What The IntelliLink™ System Can Do For You.

Many manufacturers of rechargeable products are facing a costly, unplanned redesign to meet the requirements of the "easily removable" legislation. Redesigning, retooling and manufacturing the redesigned products places a serious burden on the manufacturer. However, with the IntelliLink System, costs can be kept to a minimum and many other marketing benefits can also be derived.

MY PRODUCT CURRENTLY HAS A CUSTOMIZED, BUILT-IN RECHARGEABLE BATTERY. HOW CAN I COMPLY WITH THE "EASILY REMOVABLE" LAW AT A MINIMUM OF EXPENSE AND DESIGN TIME?

Standardizing your power design around the IntelliLink System offers many benefits. First, using standard AA, C and D IntelliLink batteries throughout your entire line of battery-powered products is less costly than custom-designing a new battery pack or system every time you introduce a new product. Once you adopt the IntelliLink System, your power design requirements are simplified forever. This will make future product development faster and cheaper.

WILL ALL MILLENNIUM BATTERIES HAVE THE SPECIAL INTELLILINK TERMINAL?

The IntelliLink terminal will be available on Millennium AA, C and D Power Cells. The Millennium Power System is Gates Energy Products' line of consumer rechargeables, currently available in over 3,500 retail locations nationwide.

WILL THE INTELLILINK TERMINAL ONLY BE AVAILABLE ON MILLENNIUM POWER CELLS?

The IntelliLink terminal will also be available on other well-known brands of rechargeable batteries in the near future. In addition, Gates Energy Products will consider private-labeling batteries for manufacturers who would like to incorporate the IntelliLink System into their products under their own brand name.

Printed on Recycled Paper

Exhibit 7-1
Recharging the Market

This page from Millennium's promotional literature describes the company's IntelliLink™ System, which is used by manufacturers to standardize the power systems in their various products.

sold from business to business than from business to consumer. Firms with business customers are successful if they are responsive to those customers' needs and if they can market performance and real product improvements. The Royal Bank ad in Exhibit 7-2 stresses the importance of marketing to businesses.

As noted in the first chapter objective, there are three primary types of organizational markets: industrial, reseller, and government/institutional markets. We will review each of these markets briefly here before considering them in more detail later in the chapter.

The Industrial Market Whenever an organization buys and uses goods and services to produce other goods and services that it then sells to other firms, it is part of the **industrial market**. For example, Canadian Foremost makes many types of all-terrain vehicles for use in many different applications. Canadian Foremost is both a buyer and a seller: it buys items like tires,

industrial market
The aggregate of all firms in an industrial sector which buy goods and services to produce other goods and services.

Exhibit 7-2
The Royal Bank Backs Businesses

This Royal Bank ad points out that it believes in adapting its services to meet the needs of business customers, such as entrepreneurs and small-business owners.

engines, seats, and formed sheet metal in order to make the vehicles it sells to other companies.

Of the three organizational markets, the industrial market is the largest and most diverse. With hundreds of thousands of North American firms producing all sorts of products that become components in yet other products, sales of goods and services in industrial markets exceed $3 trillion each year.

The **Standard Industrial Classification (SIC) system** categorizes firms according to the types of products they produce. The SIC system designates eleven major industrial divisions: agriculture, construction, finance, manufacturing, mining, public administration, retail trade, services, transportation, wholesale-trade, and a general or "nonclassifiable" category. An organization that falls within one of these major divisions is identified by a two-digit *major group* code that indicates the type of product it sells. Each major

Standard Industrial Classification (SIC) system
A system of classifying industries and firms according to the types of products they produce.

group is subdivided, with increasing specificity, into *industry groups, specific industries, product classes* (categories), and *products*, and each of these subgroup classifications adds a digit to the identifying code number. Thus, as Figure 7-1 illustrates, fabricated metals are designated major group number 34 within the manufacturing division; the industry group of cutlery and hand tools is identified by the number 342, the specific industry of hand and edge tools is coded 3423, and so on.[2]

Of particular interest to marketers are product classes (usually called product *categories*; see Chapter 4), which are major segments of a whole industry. Together, a firm's industry and product category code identify not only the nature of its product and the business it is in but its competition as well. The SIC system helps buyers to locate new suppliers and sellers to identify potential customers. For example, an aluminum processing company that needs new suppliers of aluminum ore can get an SIC report that lists all aluminum mining operations in a particular region of the country. Similarly, a seller of aluminum ore can request an SIC report containing the names of all aluminum fabricators within a certain area.

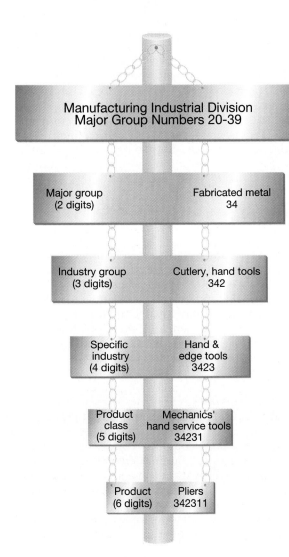

Figure 7-1
How the Standard Industrial
Classification (SIC) System Works

resellers
Organizations which buy goods and services and resell these products, without alteration, to end users, including both individuals and businesses.

The Reseller Market   The second type of organizational market is the reseller market. As we saw in Chapter 1, **resellers** are organizations that buy goods and services and resell them to so-called end users, who may be either private individuals or businesses; the latter include distributors and retailers. An office supply distributor in Halifax, Nova Scotia, for example, might buy desks and chairs from Superior Furniture Manufacturing, Inc., personal computers from IBM, copiers from Canon, and offset presses from A. B. Dick. This distributor, who is a *buyer in the reseller market*, then sells these products at a profit to local businesses. It may surprise you to learn that companies which provide temporary workers for offices and other spheres of business and industry are resellers too: they "buy" human resources—for example, secretaries, bookkeepers, accountants, receptionists, bank guards—and then hire these people out to organizations that need their skills. In all, the reseller market accounts for some $2 trillion in spending per year.

The Government/Institutional Market   The last of our three organizational markets, the *government and institutional market*, is composed of federal, provincial, and local governmental units and other public and private institutions. Purchases by governments and institutions come to nearly $900 billion annually.[3] In fact, the federal government is the nation's single largest customer. In order to carry out their functions, federal, provincial, and local governments have to buy goods and services: naval frigates, aircraft carriers, automobiles, computers, desks, chairs, garbage trucks—the list is almost endless.

Institutions like hospitals and universities also buy a wide variety of items for use in providing their goods or services to customers. Universities buy books, whiteboards, overhead projectors, copiers, athletic equipment, beds, desks, carpet, landscaping, and cleaning supplies as well as cleaning services. Hospitals buy such goods as pharmaceuticals, operating tables, X-ray equipment, waiting room furniture, and beds. Both types of organization may also purchase the services of telecommunication consultants, outside auditors, and security guards.

CONSUMER AND BUSINESS BUYER DIFFERENCES

Organizational markets differ from consumer markets in a number of significant ways. Two of the most important differences are in the buying process and the relationships which form between buyers and sellers. Firms selling to consumers generally think in terms of hundreds of thousands—if not millions—of customers. Although organizations buy in larger quantities than individual consumers do, there are far fewer of them and, therefore, fewer buyers for the business-to-business seller to target. This smaller pool of buyers poses both opportunities and problems for marketers, for these buyers are professional too.

Consider the case of Microsoft's computer software product Windows. In order to sell as many copies of this software as possible, Microsoft relies on large computer manufacturers such as IBM and Compaq to adopt it and provide copies to computer buyers. Compared to all the consumers who have personal computers in their homes, the large computer companies to whom Microsoft can sell Windows are only a handful. But if Microsoft impresses decision makers at IBM and/or Compaq, buyers within these firms will purchase huge quantities of the software. The opportunity for Microsoft is to grab a big market share with a few sales calls. The problem is to get the attention of the decision makers at big firms. You have to reach fewer people to sell a large volume in industrial markets, but those people are often hard to reach and even more difficult to convince.

Most of these business-to-business purchasers are known as the company's "buyers" or "purchasing agents," and they operate with established procurement policies and procedures. The objective for sellers in organizational buying is to get on the buyer's list of accepted vendors or sources and then to maintain that relationship over time. Many companies purchase routine items from an "approved vendor" list of three to five suppliers. Any supplier not on the list will have difficulty selling its products to the firm.

The Relationship Factor   In leading-edge marketing, the *relationship* between buyers and sellers is a crucial factor. This important aspect of the buying decision process is referred to in marketing literature as *relationship marketing*. Organizational buyers and sellers generally depend on each other much more than consumers depend on the businesses from which they buy. Indeed, organizational buyers and sellers with long-term relationships often work together as partners to develop and build a given product. The assistance of sales representatives is especially critical when products must be custom designed to fit an organizational buyer's unique needs. In long-term relationships—especially those involving very expensive products—sellers may work with buyers to set the specifications for such products. The concept of *partnering* is very important in many business-supplier relationships.

In Japan these types of strong corporate relationships are called *keiretsu*. In many instances, *keiretsu* is a financial relationship in which a group of mutually supporting companies own one another's shares. The *keiretsu* is like a contract that guarantees that each company in the group won't buy from a company that is competing with any member of the group. Many trade negotiators believe that *keiretsu* is the primary reason non-Japanese companies have such a difficult time selling in Japan. The Japanese counter that *keiretsu* is just a very efficient way of doing business.

The Quality Factor   In Chapter 2 we saw how important a culture of quality has become to leading-edge companies. It is particularly important at the business-to-business level, where long-term customer satisfaction is critical to business success. Relationship building is also a key tenet of the company-wide *quality* programs that operate under such labels as TQM (total quality management), TQC (total quality control), and CQI (continuous quality improvement). Firms buying parts they will use to assemble other products recognize that they need suppliers who will adhere to high-quality standards, a point being made in the Donnelley ad in Exhibit 7-3. After all, the quality of the finished product depends on the quality of every bit of labor and every piece of material that goes into it. For that reason, many companies competing in the U.S. government–sponsored Baldrige National Quality Award program require that their suppliers also participate in the competition.[4]

Creating and maintaining customer satisfaction is probably the strongest competitive advantage a firm can establish in business-to-business marketing, but this advantage is hard to achieve. In TQM programs it begins with a *customer satisfaction survey* that includes customer characteristics, essential needs, decision factors, and buying criteria, as well as marketing and communication strategies. The research can take any form: personal interviews, telephone interviews, focus groups, mail surveys, packing list surveys, or a combination of methods. Effective customer satisfaction programs often start with qualitative research that helps guide the design of the survey. An initial survey is then done to provide a *benchmark* or baseline against which future improvement can be measured.

Experts warn that such customer satisfaction surveys should not be undertaken without a commitment to continuous improvement, for firms that fail to follow through damage their credibility with customers. Unfortunately, these surveys rarely zero in on the specific operating problems that contribute to cus-

Exhibit 7-3
Monsters Don't Do
Quality

In this ad in
Publishers' Weekly
R. R. Donnelley offers
full-service book
production to
children's book
publishers. Do you
think the image of
Frankenstein was a
good choice to show
that using many
different suppliers can
create serious quality
control problems?

tomer dissatisfaction, so customers may view them as bland public relations devices designed to tell the company what it wants to hear.

The process of ensuring quality operations and products has been formalized in the international ISO 9000 series of certification programs. Wilkinson Steel Metals in Vancouver has applied for 1SO 9002 certification at nine plants. David Fazekas, Manager of facilities says that the reason for applying for ISO certification is that the company "found that more and more of our customers want to deal with ISO-approved suppliers."

BEHIND THE SCENES

THE ISO 9000 ADVANTAGE

For companies involved in quality programs, world-class certification of the excellence of their products and operations is now available. The International Standards Organization, which was set up in Europe in the mid-1940s, has since 1979 been offering the *ISO 9000* designation to firms that meet rigorous quality standards for performance, environmental preservation, on-the-job safety, and service to customers. The ISO 9000 "registration" is the culmination of a year-long investigation that covers technical, organizational, and managerial functions, and includes interviews with a company's clients. Once registered, a firm can expect follow-up evaluations every six months.

The Standards Council of Canada manages the ISO process, while the General Standards Board is accredited by the Standards Council of

Canada for ISO 9000. Although only about 600 Canadian companies are ISO-approved, a further 1000 are in the application process. ISO 9000 certification is required for many consumer and industrial products sold in the European Union and quality experts predict that it will be demanded by more and more trading partners around the world.[5]

Employee performance is critical to every company seeking this accreditation. Training, productivity, accuracy, cost effectiveness, and safety all contribute to employee performance, and it is the quality of all these components that must be documented in order for a firm to receive ISO 9000 certification. Documentation provides a formal statement of the way the firm is attempting to achieve and/or maintain its ideal level of employee performance. It summarizes two things: *This is how we do it* and *Is this the best way to do it?*

CULTURAL DIFFERENCES

Global buyer-seller relationships are often affected by an extremely important practice called *friendship first*. In many countries—including Japan, the Arab nations, and the nations of Latin America—the would-be seller of component parts or some other business product must first establish a friendship with the prospective buyer. Only then can business be discussed. This emphasis on friendship affects not only initial sales but also ongoing relations between buyer and seller. In nations where friendship first is a business rule, discontented buyers work out their problems personally with the sellers. In nations like Canada and the United States, however, where friendship first is *not* a business rule, disgruntled buyers are often quick to resort to lawsuits. Does it surprise you to learn that the United States has one lawyer for every 600 individuals, but that Japan has only one for every 12,000? What meaning might this have for marketers and exporters in the United States and Canada?

A MODEL OF BUSINESS-TO-BUSINESS BUYING

Although there are many similarities between the model of consumer buying behavior developed in the last chapter and the model of organizational buying behavior discussed in this section and illustrated in Figure 7-2, the many differences between these two types of buying make the business model quite distinct from the consumer one. These differences, the topic of chapter objective two, will be noted as we analyze each major component of the business-to-business buying model. Keep in mind that organizational buying decisions are often actually a series of many small decisions on such things as who has the highest-quality product, what firm can supply the optimal quantity for the company's needs, who offers the fastest and most reliable delivery, what firm gives the best overall service, and what company offers the most favorable payment terms. These kinds of decisions add up to the major decision of what to order and from whom.

EXTERNAL FACTORS

The product itself and other elements of the marketing mix are central to the organizational buying decision. As in consumer buying, the marketing-mix

Figure 7-2
A Model of Business-
to-Business Buying
Behavior

THE EXTERNAL ENVIRONMENT	THE BUYING ORGANIZATION	THE BUYER'S RESPONSE
Buying Situation **Marketing Mix** • Product/Branding • Price/Quality • Distribution • Marketing communication **Other Factors** • Competition • Cultural factors • Economic situation • Political climate • Technology	**Organizational Influences** • Corporate purchasing policies • Necessary approvals • Gatekeepers **Buying Center** Decision process Decision factors • Technical • Interpersonal • Personal	**Results of Buying Decision Process** **Purchase** • Quantity • Delivery • Payment terms • Service **No Purchase** • Postdecisional evaluation • Repeat purchase/ No purchase

straight repurchase
A type of buying situation in which a firm reorders the exact same item that it has routinely purchased in the past.

modified repurchase
A type of buying situation in which a firm makes some change to the specifications for a product that it has bought before.

factors are surrounded by other environmental factors, and all are embedded in a buying situation that affects the way the purchase is handled. Factors in the business-to-business marketing environment include many of the same variables identified in the consumer model.

In this section we discuss the buying situation first. Then we examine branding and marketing communication, two elements of the marketing mix that particularly affect the organizational buying situation. Finally, we review some product factors that are peculiar to organizational buying situations.

The Buying Situation Industrial buyers face three major types of buying situations, the subject of chapter objective three. In order of increasing complexity, these situations are straight repurchase, modified repurchase, and new purchase (see Figure 7-3).[6]

A firm makes a **straight repurchase**, also known as a *routine purchase*, when it reorders the very same item that it has bought in the past. Office supplies such as computer paper and janitorial supplies such as cleaning compounds, paper towels, and light bulbs are often straight repurchases. The firm follows a set routine for making these purchases, generally choosing from among so-called *in suppliers* who have a proven record of quality and service. *Out suppliers* usually must not only meet the same order specifications but offer an incentive such as a discount to get a foot in the door.

When a firm changes some of the specifications for a product it has bought before—say, insurance or a telephone system or some other system that is in place—it makes a **modified repurchase**.

When a company buys a good or service for the first time, whether this is a com-

The Greening of Business

Dare Foods of Kitchener, Ontario, is one of 26 companies supplied by Cultural Survival Enterprises. CSE focuses on developing trade opportunities for indigenous people in Brazil. From a nut processing plant in Xapuri, CSE annually ships $4.5 million worth of nuts, fruits, and oils from Brazil's endangered rain forest for use in products such as Dare Rainforest Cookies.

Straight Repurchase	Modified Repurchase	New Purchase
• Electricity, water, gas	• New cars, trucks	• Custom-built house or office
• Office supplies	• Consulting services	• Complex buildings, bridges, dams
• Gum, cigarettes	• Electrical components	• Installations (computers, other machinery)
• Bulk chemicals	• Computer terminal	• Weapons systems, space vehicles

ROUTINE *SOME NEW SPECS* *FULLY NEGOTIABLE*

Figure 7-3
Complexity of Purchase and the Buying Situation.

Source: Adapted from Ben M. Enis. Marketing Principles. 3rd ed. Copyright 1980 by Scott, Foresman and Company. Reprinted by permission.

puter or a health insurance plan, the transaction is known as a **new purchase**. If the product is expensive or highly technical, members of the organization involved in the buying decision generally gather as much information as they can about various alternatives since this decision also incorporates a high level of risk. Suppliers, or sellers, often work closely with buyers throughout the decision process. Since there is no experience with a seller in this situation, buyers will probably consider a number of suppliers.

Branding Although a product's entire marketing-mix strategy affects purchase decisions, branding is particularly important. The importance of branding in business-to-business buying rests more on the value of proprietary factors, such as patents, trademarks, and manufacturing know-how, and less on the advertising and promotional spending that are so important in consumer buying.[7] In organizational buying, branding is used to build a *reputation platform* that serves as a foundation for the continued maintenance of the buyer-seller relationship. The brand's reputation platform also serves as a springboard for salespeople in a new-purchase situation.

Marketing Communication Marketing communication is the second important marketing-mix factor in business-to-business buying. In consumer marketing, advertising is often the most efficient way to make the large number of potential customers aware of products. In contrast, in organizational buying, trade advertising is used to build a reputation platform for the product that will open the door for sales. Personal selling, however, is usually the most important means of communication between organizational buyers and sellers, and this is where relationship marketing really makes a difference.

Products Unlike consumers, organizations purchase many goods that they will use to create the products they sell. Few consumers have any use for *raw materials* such as the organic cotton that EcoSport uses in its clothing. Similarly, few consumers buy *components* like the silicon chips that go into personal computers or the laser that reads compact disks in a CD player. The products demanded by organizational buyers often have very precise technical specifications. Many suppliers of industrial products offer custom-built or specially designed products to fit other companies' specific needs. As you can see from the advertisement in Exhibit 7-4, in promoting its sweatshirts Lee emphasizes their printability, an important quality to a prospective purchaser who wants to imprint a logo.

Businesses also buy more high-cost items and services than private consumers do. Consumers may take twenty-five years or more to pay $100,000 to $200,000 for their largest purchase, a house. By comparison, oil refineries pay $50,000 to $100,000 periodically to remove carbon deposits from the

new purchase
A type of buying situation in which a firm purchases a good or service for the first time. As there is no prior experience to provide guidance, this is accompanied by a high level of risk.

247

ORGANIZATIONAL
BUYING
BEHAVIOR

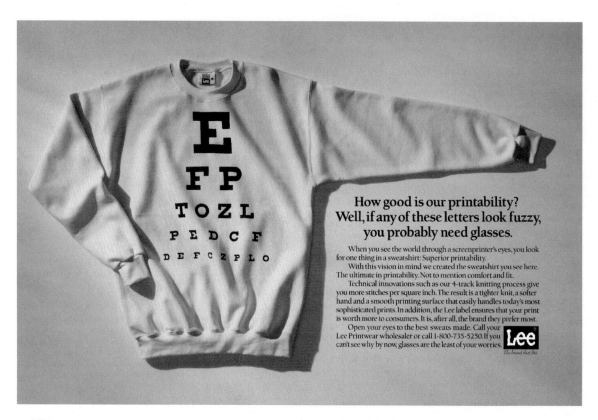

Exhibit 7-4
If You Can't See It It's Not Lee's

Lee supplies sweatshirts to firms that print logos and emblems on them. In addition to traditional aspects of sweatshirt quality such as comfort and fit, the fabric surface must accept screenprinting.

machinery they use to turn crude oil into various products. Even when buying ordinary supplies like paper, pens, and brooms, organizations buy in larger quantities than individuals do, partly because they have more people to supply and partly because they often receive discounts for buying in quantity.

THE BUYING ORGANIZATION

In the middle of the model depicted in Figure 7-2 is the buying organization, whose decision process is much more open to study than the "black box" of the consumer's mind. When you want to buy a new television, you need only consult your own wishes (and finances) and perhaps the people with whom you live. When an organization wants to buy a piece of machinery, many individuals may have to "sign off" on the decision. This larger number of decision makers reflects both the higher costs of many industrial products and the frequent need for broad expertise in judging their technical complexity.

For example, before buying Campagnolo's chain rings and sprockets for a line of racing bicycles, a purchasing agent may check Campagnolo's past performance as a supplier of cycle components. Was there ever a problem with a past order or shipment of vehicles, and, if so, how quickly did the Campagnolo's sales representative correct it? A plant maintenance manager may be involved in choosing the types of components, a financial officer may be required to approve funds for the purchase, and a product manager may be concerned with how the purchase will affect the cost of producing products on the manufacturing line.

Organizational Influences Buyers in organizations are often subject to constraints that do not affect individual consumers. Corporate buying policies have a major impact on all business buying decisions. For example, purchasing agents may be required to buy from the seller with the lowest price, assuming all other specifications are met. In response to foreign competition, some organizations may institute policies to "buy local" whenever possible.

The Eco-Store—a Calgary store that sells "environmental products" ensures that the raw materials it purchases are environmentally acceptable. And industrial buyers of built-in rechargeable batteries used in products like razors, power equipment, and telephones are subject to government mandates that batteries be "easily removable" so they can be separated from regular trash when the product wears out and is thrown away (see Exhibit 7-1).

In large organizations some buying decisions require the approval of so many people at so many different levels that the seller can encounter serious problems. A major purchase often begins at organization headquarters but must be approved at separate operating units. Trying to make a sale though these multiple levels is very difficult for a new or small firm and the problem is in identifying who these decision influencers may be. For example, a small start-up firm called Inter-ad developed a touch-screen store directory that enabled customers in a supermarket to get information on the location of specific products throughout the store simply by touching points on a video monitor. Executives at several supermarket chains liked the idea and authorized purchases of small numbers of these directories on an experimental basis. But selling enough machines to go into each of the hundreds of stores in any chain involved getting the approval of many people presiding over many different budgets. Inter-ad ultimately failed because it could not obtain all these approvals.

An additional problem involves information control. A *gatekeeper* is any participant in the buying process who regulates the flow of information from suppliers to others involved in the purchase decision. A purchasing agent who controls a sales representative's access to other people in the firm who influence a buying decision is considered a gatekeeper. A secretary who decides which suppliers will get appointments with the office manager is a gatekeeper. Salespeople often view gatekeepers as obstacles. Without them, however, buyers would be interrupted so much that they would be unable to do their jobs. However it is not all negative, a gatekeeper may also bring forward new product or new supplier information for consideration.

The Buying Center   The topic of chapter objective four, the **buying center** is not usually a formal structure within a company but something more like an ad hoc committee. The usual practice for a company that finds itself in need of a particular product is to assemble a group of people to make the buying decision; this buying center then dissolves after the decision is made. A few organizations, however, have *buying teams* that work together on a regular basis. For example, AT&T uses buying teams for items it purchases regularly, such as chemicals. The size of a buying center depends on both the firm and the buying situation. For example, for straight repurchase items, one person—often a purchasing agent—generally makes the decision.

The people involved in the buying center play different roles in the *decision process*. Some bring information and product expertise to the deliberations, others bring expertise in buying, and still others may make the final choice. And because the people who actually use a product are generally knowledgeable about which of its features are most important and what sorts of malfunctions are most common, these *users* are often included in the buying center. Thus if secretaries are the most frequent users of a copying machine, they may be asked to try out various copiers and comment on their features before the firm makes a purchase decision. Users may find that they need certain features, such as collating of long documents, but can live without others, such as double-sided copying.

buying center
may operate as a found or unfound group. Formally, the group of people assembled to make a particular buying decision in an organization. Informally this is a diffuse group of people who have particular influence over a particular buying decision.

TABLE 7-1	BEYOND TRANSACTIONS TO RELATIONSHIPS	

Transaction Marketing	Relationship Marketing
• Focus on single sale	• Focus on Customer Retention
• Orientation on product features	• Orientation on product benefits
• Short time scale	• Long time scale
• Little emphasis on customer service	• High customer service
• Limited customer commitment	• High customer commitment
• Moderate customer contact	• High customer contact
• Quality is primarily a concern of production	• Quality is the concern of all

Source: Theodore Levitt, *Harvard Business Review*

An alternative framework for undersanding the buyer-seller process is the Interaction Model (see Figure 7-4).

Negotiation Because of the complex technical nature of many industrial products, the high risk of purchase, and the number of individuals involved in the buying process, organizational buying decisions often take longer to make than consumer buying decisions do. Complex negotiations over price,

Business-to-Business Buying

Industrial buyers frequently obtain competitor and market information at trade shows, where businesses display and demonstrate their newest products. An entrepreneur like a professional photographer may make a purchase on the spot, whereas a representative of a large firm may gather material to share later with a buying center.

delivery, service, and contracts may slow the process. In selling an office facsimile machine (fax), for example, a sales representative may have to make multiple visits to a potential customer over an extended period before getting the order. Generally, the buying process lengthens in proportion to the amount of money to be spent. Keep in mind, however, that although organizational purchase negotiations are slower than consumer negotiations, the former are made less frequently because organizations negotiate long-term contracts for things they use often or in large quantities.

Rational Decision Making Usually organizational buying is said to be more rational than consumer buying because the decision to buy is based on needs for specific functions rather than on individual wants or impulses. For example, a buyer at a chemical plant may need several pipeline valves for installation in the plant and will ask such questions as: Can the valve withstand temperatures below freezing? What is the maximum pressure (pounds per square inch) the valve can withstand? However, committee decisions do not always reflect rationality and there is another side to this. Individuals may feel that they can make more adventurous decisions as part of a committee than they can as individuals.

Even when purchasing an item that is quite routine, like a cleaning solvent, organizational buyers will carefully examine different alternatives such as the strength of the cleaner, the number and types of materials with which it can be used, and the options for disposing of used solvent (most industrial cleaners are environmentally hazardous substances for which regulatory agencies may have set specific safety standards).

Buyers for organizations approach their task not only rationally, but professionally. Performance evaluations for purchasing agents are often based on how effectively they conduct negotiations with suppliers. Many buyers are members of the Purchasing Management Association of Canada (PMAC). The PMAC sponsors educational programs for buyers, including courses on pur-

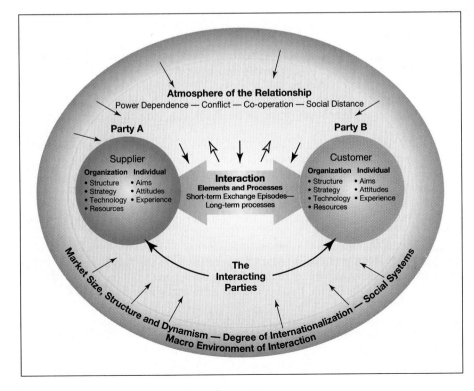

Figure 7-4
The Nature and Scope of Supplier-Customer Interaction.

Source: Peter W. Turnbull and Jean-Paul Valla, *Strategies for International Industrial Marketing,* Croom-Helm, London, p. 6.

chasing that lead to certification as a CPP, or certified professional purchaser. The CPP accreditation program is the only education program on purchasing and materials management in Canada which grants the CPP designation. Many companies pay for an employee to complete this certification program and promotions and raises may be influenced by a buyer's acquisition of the CPP certificate.

Decision Factors Like consumers, organizational buyers make decisions based on four important factors: price, performance (quality), service, and delivery time. Price is important because buyers do not want to pay more than an item is worth. In some companies purchasing agents are evaluated according to their skill in getting sellers to offer lower prices or a discount on items purchased.

Still, a supplier with the lowest price on an item will probably not get the order if the buyer has severe reservations about the product's performance. Buyers in the 1990s are looking for quality. If the price is low but the quality is also low, the price advantage may be more than canceled out by higher cost of service and replacements. There are other disadvantages to low-priced goods of poor quality. For instance, a valve that leaks may not only cost a chemical plant money to replace the valve as well as the lost chemicals but it may also leave the firm liable to huge fines from government environmental and safety inspectors.

Organizational buyers rely heavily on sales representatives for expert information about products. Pharmaceutical sales representatives, for example, must know at least as much about their line of prescription drugs as the doctors on whom they call. The sales rep must know how the drug works in the body, its possible side effects, and how it may interact with other drugs or medicines prescribed simultaneously. Similarly, sales representatives of firms like Boeing, which sells products of technological complexity to governments as well as to private customers, must have special training and knowledge.

Because the product information in business-to-business selling is often so technical, firms spend more money on mockups, trade shows, and product demonstrations than firms selling consumer products do. For example, Cessna spent $30 million to turn its headquarters in Wichita, Kansas, into an exhibition space where full-scale mockups of the planes in its Citation business jet line can be displayed. Clients can walk through the mockups to see what different interior layouts and designs look like. According to Cessna's director of marketing, when companies are spending between $3 million and $15 million for a plane, they want to be absolutely sure they are making the right decision.[9]

Ads in trade publications tend to offer more information than do ads for consumer products. Specific product details are often included, as well as some sort of direct-response method (a toll-free telephone number, a mail-in coupon) to enable buyers to gain more information. The Lee advertisement in Exhibit 7-4 is a good example of an ad that encourages inquiry.

Service is also very important in organizational buying. Organizational buyers often require some type of service guarantee from sellers. If a valve suddenly fails and causes a rupture in a pipeline, for example, it could shut down all or part of a chemical plant's operations, so the buyer needs a guarantee that the seller will fix or replace faulty valves within a day, a half day, or a certain number of hours, depending on how accessible the buyer's plant is to the seller.

Delivery can be crucial for organizational buyers. If a shipload of chemicals needed at a chemical plant is late, it can delay the production of an entire series of items that use that raw material as a component. Buyers cannot afford to have products delivered later than promised. The so-called just-in-

time delivery procedure that we will discuss in Chapter 15 is already a critical concept in retailing distribution and is becoming increasingly important in manufacturing.

OTHER ORGANIZATIONAL BUYERS ●

Resellers and institutional buyers are similar to industrial buyers in that all three are affected by environmental, organizational, and interpersonal factors. But resellers do have somewhat different concerns, and the buying decision process is often sharply different in government markets. These differences, the topic of the fifth chapter objective, are described in this section.

RESELLERS

Resellers buy products not for their own use but in order to sell them to someone else at a profit. Thus for resellers, problem recognition means determining the needs and wants of their customers. In seeking information about a product, resellers want to find out whether it will malfunction and make their customers unhappy. Their evaluations may focus heavily on a manufacturer's credit, delivery, and return policies because the reseller may not be able to offer such support to the end user.

In measuring postpurchase satisfaction, resellers ask: "Did it sell as easily as I thought, did I make as much profit as I intended, and are customers making repeat purchases?" rather than "Did it work the way I thought it would?" as a user might ask. In other words, resellers' concern with a product's performance is limited to how that affects the satisfaction of their own customers.

GOVERNMENT MARKETS

Selling to government agencies can be much more complex and time-consuming than selling to industrial customers because these agencies are public entities and accountable to the general public for their buying decisions. Marketers have to know which forms to use in order just to acquire information on buying requirements. Firms that are interested in selling to the government should also read the *Canada Gazette,* which is issued every Saturday by the Government Printing Office. This publication lists all government procurement notices to suppliers.

Many companies hire lobbyists when bidding on government contracts in the hope that lobbyists help level the playing field. "If there are many bids, the process declares the winner," says the head of government relations for one company. "But if it's a tie or there are silent political winds blowing, lobbyists are a real asset."[10]

Open-Bid Buying Government agencies often use what is called *open-bid buying.* The process begins when an agency publishes an announcement in the *Commerce Business Daily* (for federal agencies) or in local newspapers (for state and local agencies) notifying potential suppliers and giving specifications for the desired good or service. An interested supplier puts together a proposal, or **bid**, that explain how the product meets the specifications, price, delivery, and service requirements outlined. As a rule, the lowest-price bidder that meets all specifications is given the contract. Sometimes, however, the lowest bidder is passed over because of the poor quality of its products or services in the past. In addition, when a product is very expensive and very complex, like a bomber, governments use *negotiated purchasing,* in which the government agency concerned works closely with one or more bidding companies in order to develop the specifications and negotiate the contract.

bid
A proposal made by a seller to a buyer in which the seller offers a product that meets a set of formal specifications at a certain price.

The Canadian Patrol Frigate Project

One major government contract of recent years was for the Department of National Defence, who commissioned the construction of twelve new navy frigates. The prime contractor, Saint John Shipbuilding Limited, was responsible for ship design, construction, systems integration, quality assurance, tests and trials, material support, shore facilities, training, and all other services.

OUTSOURCING AND UNBUNDLING

Immediately after graduation you find a job developing a test marketing program for a marketer. Then the unthinkable happens: within a year they close down the program and let you go. Why?

Unfortunately for many new employees, there is a trend in business toward *outsourcing* specialized functions.[11] Your company may have decided that its test marketing program could be handled more efficiently, effectively, and cheaply by an outside firm that specializes in such work. In terms of the firm's corporate mission, the test market department became a luxury. In terms of organizational buying, such moves just set up more opportunities for outside contracting.

An example of a company that depends heavily on outsourcing is Taco Bell, which has become successful by focusing on providing fast food at the lowest possible price. Most of the hand work—for example, chopping lettuce and tomatoes, cooking meat, and shredding cheese—is contracted out to local food-handling companies.

Taco with Salsa

Taco Bell is saving time and money not only by outsourcing its food preparation but by computerizing its drive-through service. You give your order to the attendant, who enters it into a hand-held computer, and almost before you reach the pick-up window your food and beverages are ready.

Since Taco Bell doesn't have to hire staff or provide space in its tiny stores for these tasks, overhead is low and it can concentrate most of its resources on taking customers' orders and assembling their food items.

In another new practice called *unbundling*, an entire department is established as a separate company. For example, in some adver-

tising firms the media buying department is set up as a separate profit center.

Whatever they call it—outsourcing, subcontracting, or unbundling—more and more companies are shedding activities and defining their core business narrowly. The truth is that businesses can't afford the luxury of what used to be called *vertical integration*—handling all the activities in a chain of support businesses that ultimately produce a product or service.

Although you may think this leaves you out in the cold as a test marketing specialist, your line of work has not become obsolete. You may find a job with a firm that specializes in doing test marketing. Or, if you want to be an entrepreneur, you may consider founding a consulting firm that offers test marketing services. The work is still there, although business and industry are reconfiguring themselves so rapidly that it's sometimes hard to see where the jobs are. In what ways do you think this trend complicates the job of organizational buyers? ▼

257

KEY POINTS SUMMARY ▼

1. The industrial market includes all organizations that buy goods and services to use in the production of products that are then leased or sold to others. The reseller market is composed of all organizations that buy goods and services with the intention of selling these same unaltered products to others at a profit. The government/institutional market is composed of all federal, state, and local governments and public institutions.

2. The business-to-business buying model contains the same five basic steps as the consumer buying model. However, organizational buying differs from consumer buying in several ways: (1) organizational demand is often *derived* from consumer demand; (2) the products demanded may be more technically complex; (3) organizational buying decisions are more strictly rational than private consumer decisions; (4) organizational decisions are more complex and involve more people; (5) buyers and sellers often work together to refine the product; and (6) person-to-person sales are more important.

3. Industrial buyers engage in three types of purchases: straight repurchase, modified repurchase, and new purchase.

4. Decisions in organizations are made by the members of a buying center, who take on different roles in the decision process, such as user, influencer, buyer, and decision maker. The gatekeeper role is played by people who control access either to the decision makers or to information the seller needs. Corporate policies, factors in the marketing environment, and multiple levels of approvals also affect the buying decision.

5. Reseller buying differs from institutional buying in that resellers are ultimately concerned not so much with how a product performs as with how it sells. Government buying often follows formal bidding procedures but involves negotiated contracts for high-tech products.

DISCUSSION QUESTIONS ▼

1. Give an example of a good or service that would be purchased by an industrial buyer and describe how it might be bought and used. Do the same for a reseller and a government or institutional buyer.

2. What do you think is the most significant difference between organizational buyers and consumer buyers? Explain your answer.

3. Pick a product that might be purchased in an industrial market and explain how various members of a buying center for that product might affect the buying decision.

4. Which stage of the buying decision process normally takes the most time? Why?

5. How does open-bid buying work? Why does the federal government sometimes use negotiated contracts instead of regular bidding?

6. How might SIC data help a sales manager realign the sales territories of a firm's sales representatives?

7. Interview a purchasing agent at a local firm and report back on what role that person played in the buying decision for each of the following: a supply, a component part, a routine service, a major piece of equipment.

8. Select a product that might be purchased by an industrial market and trace the issues to be considered/decided at each stage in the buying decision process.

9. Describe the buying process that a university might go through in purchasing a new mainframe computer system. Who would be involved in the buying center? Describe possible activities of buying center members at various stages in the decision-making process.

10. Form a focus group (defined in Chapter 5) composed of your classmates. How many of them care about the fabric used in the clothes they buy? Is there a derived demand among this group for natural fabrics? Based on discussions in this focus group, do you think a company like EcoSport would find a market for its clothing in shops near your school?

11. Interview five recent graduates (people who graduated from college within the last three years) and ask them if they have encountered

the outsourcing phenomenon in their work. In what areas is work being contracted out? Have they come across any instances of unbundling, where entire departments have been cut out and set up as separate companies? Do they feel that their jobs are threatened by outsourcing? Why or why not?

Integrative Case ● Discussion Questions

The Body Shop*

1. How does The Body Shop's search for new suppliers differ from that of other, traditional cosmetic companies?

2. Industrial buying is usually considered to be highly rational. Would you say that is true at The Body Shop?

Harley-Davidson

1. Both Harley dealers and government agencies (police, military units) buy from Harley-Davidson. Describe the differences in the buying processes of these two types of buyers.

2. How do these two kinds of buyers differ in motivation?

The Millennium Power System

1. To what type of organizational buyer does Millennium sell? How might this type of buyer differ from a governmental buyer?

2. What are Millennium's organizational buyers' major criteria in choosing to purchase the Millennium Power System?

*The three cases at the back of the book—"The Body Shop," "Harley-Davidson," and "The Millennium Rechargeable Power System"—illustrate topics discussed in all chapters of this book. Your instructor will tell you when to read a particular case and when to answer the discussion questions on it that appear at the end of each chapter.

Flying High or a Nose Dive?

"**A**ll I have to do is get it from the Czech Republic, put the wings on it and sell it to somebody," said Joe Kane, partner in Zlin Aerospace. It sounds easy, but getting the Czech two-seater plane into the air in North America has been a three year struggle for the Ontario importer. It was exciting when Joe Kane and his partner Roy LoPresti entered into a joint venture with Moravan, a Czech Republic manufacturer. Before the tremendous changes in the eastern bloc took place, Moravan manufactured aerobatic planes for the Russian military.

Joe Kane is confident about the quality of the Zlin 242L, claiming that it handles like a Porsche. The manoeuverability is excellent. However, Zlin Aerospace has not been able to move the $2 million inventory they are currently storing due to problems with certification from the United States government. The Canadian government approved the plane and six planes have been sold and delivered in Canada. But, Kane is counting on the U.S. market for the majority of sales due to its size. They have sold a number of planes to U.S. customers, but they have not been able to deliver due to the lack of certification. Receiving certification will change the fate of the company. In the meantime, Zlin's reputation for being able to deliver is suffering.

Working with a company from the Czech Repulic has been both rewarding and frustrating. Moravan trusts Zlin implicitly, sending planes without payment or even a down payment. However, the language problems and cultural differences cause problems, particularly in the placing of special orders.

An important tool used by business-to-business marketers is the trade show. Zlin Aerospace took their two-seater to Florida to the Flying Show market, an industry trade show. It was important for U.S. flying school owners and buyers to see the product and try it out. It was at this trade show that Kane learned that speed is an important feature when flying school buyers consider purchasing aircraft.

Joe Kane believes in the product and is working to overcome problems of working with a supplier in a foreign country and exacting regulations enforced by the U.S. government.

QUESTIONS

1. Who are the buyers of the Zlin 242L? What type of a buying situation is it for them?
2. What is it that Zlin Aerospace needs to do in order to develop a better working relationship with its supplier, Moravan?
3. Why is it that Moravan behaves the way it does when dealing with their major customer, Zlin Aerospace?
4. What are the critical factors for successfully selling an aircraft such as the Zlin 242L?

Source: This case was prepared by Deborah Andrus and is based on the *Venture* series episode "Zlin Aerospace," which was first broadcast on June 19, 1994.

Chapter 8

Segmentation, Targeting, and Forecasting

OBJECTIVES

AFTER COMPLETING THIS CHAPTER, YOU SHOULD BE ABLE TO:

1
EXPLAIN THE FUNCTION OF SEGMENTATION AND TARGETING IN THE MARKETING PLAN

2
DESCRIBE THE MAJOR CRITERIA FOR SEGMENTING A MARKET

3
DISCUSS THE CRITERIA FOR MARKET SEGMENTATION IN INDUSTRIAL, OR BUSINESS-TO-BUSINESS, MARKETING

4
IDENTIFY THE CRITERIA FOR TARGETING SPECIFIC MARKETS AND DISCUSS TARGETING STRATEGIES

5
EXPLAIN THE PURPOSE OF FORECASTING AND DESCRIBE THE TOOLS AVAILABLE FOR MAKING MARKET FORECASTS

THINK ABOUT IT!

ARE *YOU* A MICROMARKET?

In an important form of contemporary marketing called *micromarketing,* marketers are focusing their efforts on smaller and smaller segments of the population. For example, some marketers are attempting to get their message to people by households or even individually.[1] Micromarketing is "up close and personal." As an article in *Business Week* puts it, "Rather than wagering big bucks in hopes of producing one boffo TV ad that will quickly boost sales, micromarketers spread their bets on many different efforts, each of which may pay off in small increments."[2]

Micromarketing is a hot new topic in sales meetings and conference rooms all over the world. This change in focus in marketing strategy from regions and cities to neighborhoods, households, and individuals is being driven by some very sophisticated techniques, including high-tech electronic scanning devices for gathering sales data. Information-service firms like Nielsen and Donnelley Marketing are now working on methods of combining

scanner data from stores with the information on population characteristics contained in Donnelley's Conquest database. Ultimately, this combination of information resources will enable marketers to target virtually every store customer as an individual consumer.

Meanwhile, another Donnelley—R. R. Donnelley and Sons, the largest printer in the United States—has developed the technology for printing virtually any single message on any single book or magazine page as it comes down the bindery line (ordinarily, printing and binding are two separate operations). As a result, a Donnelley client like *American Baby* magazine, with a circulation of 1.1 million, can now easily publish more than 100 versions of a given issue, each with different reading material and advertisements, and thus reach over 100 different market segments. This kind of printing capacity means a clothing company's advertisement can offer one reader a discount on lingerie while inviting that reader's next-door neighbor to save money on hunting jackets—and both pages can have the reader's name printed on them! This same technology, according to Donnelley, will certainly have an important impact on direct-mail advertising (see Chapter 20).

Checkout scanners like those in supermarkets have for several years been providing information about consumer buying behavior to marketers, who usually purchase such data from companies like Information Resource's BehaviorScan service. Like other contemporary technologies, these systems are becoming more sophisticated and capable of doing the sort of data gathering necessary for successful micromarketing.

What do you think of micromarketing? Are *you* a market? Do you *want* to be a market? Do you think micromarketing is a viable new avenue or a passing fad? The opposite which we all fear, is market fragmentation where there is such a plethora of products it is impossible to differentiate. ■

Discovering what people need and finding a way to fill those needs is what marketing is all about. In this chapter we consider how marketers are able to meet customers' needs more effectively by segmenting, or dividing, markets by identifying various individual and group characteristics and then marketing to, or targeting, the specific segments that seem most likely to provide a welcome audience for the product or service.

WHAT IS MARKET SEGMENTATION? ●

As we noted in Chapter 1, a market is a group of individuals and/or organizations who share a need that can be met by a specific product or service and who have the willingness and ability to pay for it. To stay in business and prosper, companies need to produce and sell goods and services that meet the needs of the market.

But markets differ. At one time, many businesspeople believed it was possible to engage in **mass marketing**—that is, to use the same marketing mix (product, price, distribution, and marketing communication) for everyone. Today, however, mass marketing is not possible. Even Coca Cola, which sells its original-formula Coke worldwide, now offers variations on the famous soft drink to appeal to different parts of the soft-drink market. After the false start we discussed in Chapter 5, New Coke has found its followers. Coca Cola also sells Diet Coke to weight watchers, Caffeine-Free Coke to people careful about their caffeine intake, Cherry Coke to sweet-drink lovers, and Sprite to noncola drinkers.

Instead of mass marketing, then, modern marketers seek to segment and target markets, which is the topic of our first chapter objective. **Segmentation** is the identification of groups of people who have common needs. **Targeting** means evaluating the various segments thus identified and selecting the segment or portion thereof that promises the best return on the firm's marketing investment. The process of segmenting and targeting focuses a firm on the most likely customers for its products. For example, the computer market includes everyone from individuals who would like to compute their taxes on a home computer to large firms looking for complex systems to handle corporate transactions. Clearly, no one machine can meet the needs of all the segments of this market. By positioning their notebook computers to meet the needs of one segment—people who travel in their work—Compaq, Apple, and other PC makers have been able to earn attractive returns.

Segmentation and targeting strategies were developed to enable marketers to fulfill consumer needs and wants more successfully and with greater cost effectiveness. Targeting specific groups is not only more efficient but also less expensive than trying to reach everyone. Segmentation and targeting allow marketers to match *specific* groups of consumer needs and preferences with *specific* marketing mixes.

Segmentation can be controversial, however. When a number of wine producers, including Gallo, began selling a fortified (high-alcohol-content) wine in small bottles, the product was a particularly big hit with skid row alcoholics. As you may imagine, Gallo found itself under serious attack for exploiting this segment of society.

As we noted in Chapter 1, a small, specialized market is called a *niche market*. The new-car market has a price range of $7,000 to $450,000; most cars are priced between $9,000 and $30,000. Cars priced above and below these points in a narrow range are in a niche—for example, one niche is cars priced under $9,000 and another is cars priced above $100,000.

Everyone is a member of many markets. For example, you might belong to the college student market, the eighteen-to-twenty-five-year-old market, the used-car-buyer market, the apartment-renters market, the bicycle market, and the fast-food-consumer market. Someone else might also be in the college student market, but in the thirty-five-to-fifty-year-old market, the new-car-buyer market, the single-family-home market, the motorcycle market, the vacation market, and the restaurant market.

Although segmentation is crucial in marketing, and seems a commonsense approach, we must point out a caveat to the would-be marketer. The downside of segmentation is that it is neither an easy process nor a clear-cut one, even among those with experience. One can't just sally out into the marketplace

mass marketing
Using the same marketing mix to sell the same product to a variety of people in a variety of geographic areas through a variety of outlets.

segmentation
Identifying groups of people who have common needs.

targeting
Focusing a marketing effort on a market group that has significant potential to respond.

Wrangling a Niche

Wrangler jeans targets a very specific niche market: over-thirty, small-town, blue-collar family men who love the outdoors. "Our audience lives in blue jeans," says the creative director of Wrangler's ad agency; "they wear them to work, then change into another pair at night."

and find groups of people wearing labels that identify them as members of a particular segment. Over an unknown period of time, segments will steadily erode to the point where they fade away. The "yuppies" did not survive into the recession of the early 90s. Studies suggest that consumers often flip-flop between different types of products as their moods and desires shift. So although marketing strategists use less guesswork today than they did years ago, planning segmentation and targeting strategies is still complex—and a good deal of it is highly intuitive. Segments have to meet five important criteria, therefore, to justify being called a segment. They require to be sizeable, measurable, accessible, able to buy and willing to buy the product in question. Without all five you have a hunch, not a segment.

AIMS OF MARKET SEGMENTATION

Market segmentation is one of the most powerful tools in marketing. It enables marketers to make decisions about resource allocation across the different segments which they presently service, as well as create awareness of change taking place that might give rise to a new product to meet a new demand. Timeliness is key but so, too, is product positioning and being able to target a group with the right style of advertising. How do we know? Only through research which then allows us to plan strategically to take advantage of timing or new product launches and relaunches for specific groups. Understanding the market is what this chapter is about—not just in terms of understanding market information but in how to apply this information and use it effectively in a strategic manner.

TYPES OF CONSUMER MARKET SEGMENTATION ●

In general, marketers segment markets according to personal, social, and environmental characteristics that fall into five broad categories—*demographics, geographics, psychographics, behavioral characteristics*, and *benefits sought*—and into subcategories within each of these areas. These criteria for segmenting a market, the topic of chapter objective two, are depicted in Figure 8-1. Which of these general categories and subcategories will be most appropriate for a marketer to use will vary according to both the product and the market.

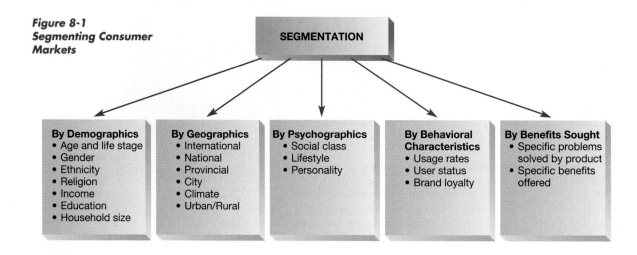

Figure 8-1
Segmenting Consumer Markets

SEGMENTATION

By Demographics
• Age and life stage
• Gender
• Ethnicity
• Religion
• Income
• Education
• Household size

By Geographics
• International
• National
• Provincial
• City
• Climate
• Urban/Rural

By Psychographics
• Social class
• Lifestyle
• Personality

By Behavioral Characteristics
• Usage rates
• User status
• Brand loyalty

By Benefits Sought
• Specific problems solved by product
• Specific benefits offered

As you study this section on market segmentation, keep in mind that while we discuss the characteristics of people in various groups, they are a market segment *only* when they share a common need that can be met by a marketer. If their needs cannot be met by a marketer, they are a just segment of the public, not a market segment.

DEMOGRAPHIC SEGMENTATION

The technique most commonly used to identify a market segment is *demographic segmentation*. **Demographics** are statistical measures of significant facts about a population, starting with its size and including such other characteristics as age, gender, housing, mobility, income, occupation, education, and geography.

To understand the relevance of demographic characteristics to marketing concerns, consider the impact of geography on the marketing mix. If there is a shift in population, a product's *promotion* and *distribution* methods may need to be changed—for example, if more people move to British Columbia, a company may need to establish more outlets in that area and begin to advertise in B.C. media. But that's not all: such a shift in relative population densities among regions of a country can signal a need to change the *product* itself. For example, as people move from colder to warmer climates, the demand for snowblowers will decrease and that for light clothing, raincoats, umbrellas, and air conditioners will increase.

Age and Life-Stage Segmentation
Age is an important demographic factor that affects other demographic factors like educational status, family status, and, to a certain extent, income. As we noted in Chapter 6, the fifty-plus market is booming all over the world because people are living longer and populations are becoming older; the oldest members of the huge baby boomer generation are about to enter this market. Reading these important social trends companies can now prepare themselves to launch innovative new leisure products and services for a senior market that makes up the bulk of the population and is largely retired. Early retirement and the transference of wealth from their parents will mean that this seniors group will have an unparalleled purchasing power compared to their predecessors. Also with fewer years left remaining to them, they may choose to be more adventurous as to how they spend this money.

Closely related to age is the stage at which people are in their life cycle. *Life-stage segmentation*, as developed by the J. Walter Thompson Advertising Agency and illustrated in Figure 8-2, assigns consumers to one of nine groups

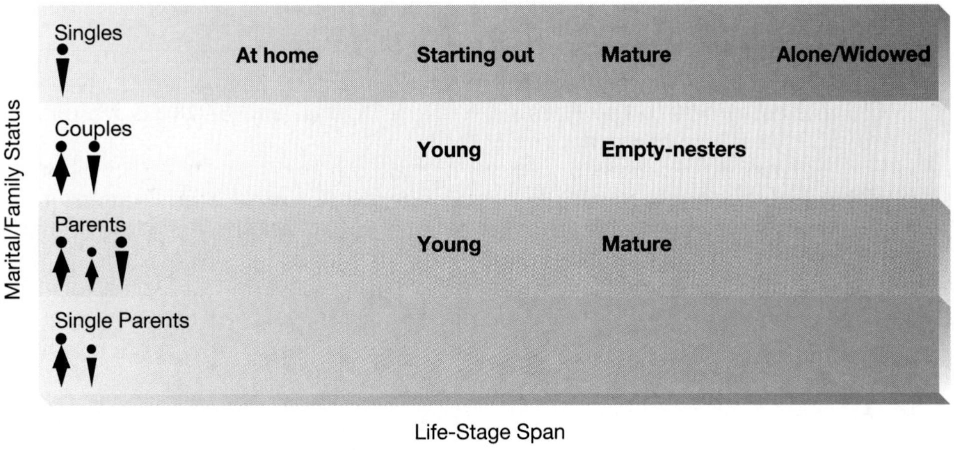

demographics
Statistical measures of a population in terms of such characteristics as age, life stage, gender, ethnicity, income, education, household size, and socioeconomic status.

267

SEGMENTATION, TARGETING, AND FORECASTING

*Figure 8-2
Life-Stage
Segmentation*

The baby is quicker than the eye. That's why Safety 1st makes more than 100 child safety products—from cord shorteners and drawer locks to VCR protectors and stove knob covers—all designed to help keep your kids out of trouble. Even when they're out of sight. **Safety 1st**

Exhibit 8-1
Follow That Child!

Safety 1st products are designed to appeal to one very specific segment of the population: young parents with small children who are fast crawling into toddlerhood.

based on the interaction of their life stage and marital and family status variables. Life-stage segmentation focuses on so-called watershed events in people's lives, like graduating from high school or college, marrying, or having a baby (see Exhibit 8-1). These are the "events that shape our values and attitudes," explains Peter Kim, director of JWT's consumer behavior department.[3]

People at the same life stage often share certain needs. For example, many recent college graduates require furnishings for their first apartment and the services of an employment agency, needs that are far less common among fifty-year-olds. But age and life stage are *not* the same. One couple in their forties may be *empty-nesters* whose children are grown and out of the home, while another may be the parents of a newborn. The products demanded by these two sets of middle-aged couples will differ greatly.

Gender Segmentation Because of the many differences in the needs of males and females, marketers often find it useful to segment markets along gender lines. For example, Procter & Gamble and a number of competitors have introduced gender-specific diapers. The superabsorbent materials are positioned differently in order to accommodate boys or girls. As P&G ads note: "There is a little difference between boys and girls and the way their diapers get wet."

At the same time, marketers have also recognized that gender differences are breaking down in many areas of life in North America, Western Europe, and Asia. Today men are more concerned about their appearance and less likely to reject a traditionally "female" product like hair spray. As women have moved into business offices and the professions, they have been buying business suits, briefcases, and cellular phones.

Ethnic and Religious Segmentation Most countries have subgroups whose religion and culture differ from those of the majority. Recognizing this, some companies have successfully used religious or ethnic segmentation to market their products. For example, kosher-food producers target that part of the Jewish population that is willing to pay a premium for such products. Segmenting along ethnic lines also affects marketing communications. For example, in Vancouver and Toronto, the influx of Chinese immigrants has led to the development of Chinese malls in British Columbia, a national cable TV business, and Chinese newspapers.

The Royal Bank, which has consistently ranked number one in serving the Asian population, partly attributes the success of its financial hotline for Chinese customers to the liberal use of the digits 3 and 8—digits which signify liveliness and prosperity respectively.

Segmenting markets on ethnic or religious bases can be tricky because individuals within a particular group often differ more from one another than they do from people in other groups. It can also be risky, as the marketer of a new cigarette targeted to African Americans discovered when it was accused of endangering the health of this group and was forced to withdraw the brand. Targeting a particular group can be an effective marketing tool, however, when the product or service genuinely meets that group's needs, as the case for this chapter shows.

Parlez-Vous Chinois?

Although in most parts of Canada, signs are usually printed in English, French, or both, in Agincourt, Ontario, many stores have their signs translated into Chinese—in order to reach the large Chinese population in that area.

Income and Educational Segmentation Because the ability to pay is a crucial criterion for membership in any market, income is often a very useful method of market segmentation. Some luxury items—such as five-carat diamond rings and Rolls-Royce automobiles—have very small, though highly profitable, high-income market segments. Other items—such as mobile homes and space heaters—appeal most strongly to people with limited incomes.

Income is often closely linked to educational level. (It is also linked to social class, as we will see in the next section.) However, regardless of their income, highly educated people are more likely to buy books and newspapers, to watch public television and listen to public radio, and to read publications like *Maclean's, The Financial Post,* and *The Globe and Mail.*

Socioeconomic Segmentation Socioeconomic segmentation links the two elements of income and social class. Alfred P. Sloan relied on socioeconomic segmentation when building General Motors after World War I. GM's automobiles were targeted to five socioeconomic segments and priced accordingly, from the lower-priced Chevrolet up through the Pontiac, the Oldsmobile, the Buick, and finally the top-of-the-line Cadillac (see Figure 8-3). For fifty years this market model may have worked well for GM, but in recent decades the tendency of auto buyers to choose on the basis of lifestyle rather than income or social class has made it obsolete.[4] Competition has increased

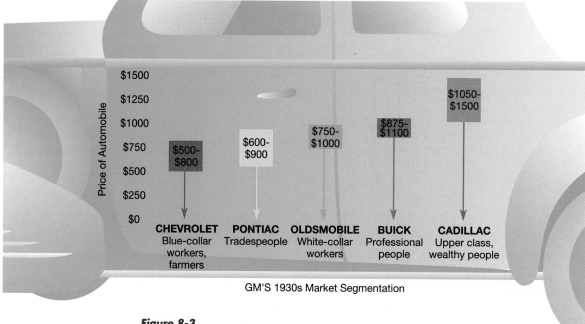

Price of Automobile

$1500					$1050-$1500
$1250					
$1000				$875-$1100	
$750	$500-$800	$600-$900	$750-$1000		
$500					
$250					
$0	CHEVROLET	PONTIAC	OLDSMOBILE	BUICK	CADILLAC

CHEVROLET	PONTIAC	OLDSMOBILE	BUICK	CADILLAC
Blue-collar workers, farmers	Tradespeople	White-collar workers	Professional people	Upper class, wealthy people

GM'S 1930s Market Segmentation

Figure 8-3
GM's 1930s Market Segmentation

with the number of new entrants particularly from Japan and consumers are comparing the value package being offered by each.

Household-Size Segmentation The average household in North America has been shrinking in size since the early 1960s, and this has had an effect on marketers because the number of people living in a home influences the household needs. Single people living alone and childless couples, for example, usually want smaller serving sizes of food products, while larger households appreciate the "family packs" of meats and poultry sold in supermarkets, often at a discount.

GEOGRAPHIC SEGMENTATION

Over the years marketers have learned to their sorrow that the same products and sales pitches that work beautifully in one place often bomb in others. The reason is simple: consumers' needs vary according to where they live. Geographic markets may be segmented by world region, nation, province, state, or city. Some of the factors that affect geographic marketing are climate, population density, and the urban or rural character.

International Markets World regions and nations are useful bases for segmentation. Differences between nations, including language, money, laws and regulations, competitive practices, and consumer preferences, generally require changes in the marketing mix. For example, a firm may need to modify its electrical products to ensure that they work on the local electrical system, set its prices in terms of the local currency, arrange distribution through local channels, and advertise in the local language.

North American companies selling in the Japanese market must revise the entire presentation of their products. Japanese consumers consider quality more important than price, and they have much sterner criteria of quality than North American and European consumers. Like the latter, the Japanese judge a product by its performance and overall appearance, but they also intensely scrutinize its fine detailing and packaging. Unless the product and its package *look* perfect, the Japanese will assume that it is inferior. Any flaw, no matter how slight, is a red flag. Meeting these standards may add to the price of a product, but the Japanese are more than willing to pay extra.

National Differences   Within any large country, there are major regional differences. In Canada, provincial differences have had a tremendous impact on the marketing of certain products. For example, Irwin Toys' Emilie and Blanche dolls are aimed specifically at French Canadians in Quebec. The legal climate of particular provinces can also affect marketing practices. The liquor laws across Canada make the retailing of liquor a provincial monopoly and the recycling of bottles and cans a legal necessity.

City-to-city differences are also important to marketers, including differences in climate, economic conditions, and even transportation systems. For example, people who live in Saint John's, Newfoundland, shop very differently from those in Toronto or Vancouver who spend much of their lives negotiating highways.

Climatic and Other Factors   Climate greatly influences the types of products demanded by consumers. People living in northern climates need down parkas and other cold-weather clothing, while loose white cottons that help the wearer stay cool are attractive to people living in tropical climates. Although many a Briton leaves for work every day with an umbrella in hand, a Saudi may not even own such an item.

Whether a location is urban or rural, its population density affects consumer needs. Urban consumers in densely populated cities need public water services—it would be impossible to install the individual wells and septic tanks common in rural areas. Urban dwellers can pick up groceries every night on their way home from work, while rural inhabitants who live miles from supermarkets shop much less frequently and therefore buy in larger quantities and prefer products that keep well.

Companies often segment a market by both geography and some other factor. For example, Ringling Brothers Circus identifies its markets in terms of geography and ethnic background. Some of the ninety cities the circus visits each year have local television stations; others do not. For those cities with television, Ringling uses a TV campaign backed by newspaper advertisements. For cities without television, it relies on billboards, signs, radio, and newspapers. Ringling's marketing strategy, built city by city, exemplifies the current trend toward localized marketing. Ringling also makes a special effort to reach groups who may be unfamiliar with the North American circus tradition, such as Hispanic and Vietnamese populations.

One aspect of geographic segmentation that appeals to marketers is the ease with which they can acquire this information and use it to compare sub-subsegments. Demographic information is usually easy to obtain, at least in developed countries. In Canada federal government publishes the *Census of Population* every five years. Local chambers of commerce, provincial governments, regional industrial commissions, and national development ministries are other good sources of information about consumer populations. Many United Nations publications offer statistical surveys of global demographics.

In the commercial sector many marketing research firms are excellent sources of information, and the periodicals *American Demographics* and *Sales and Marketing Management* both publish information on demographic trends and changes. Canadian systems such as *Conquest Canada* and *PC Census* provide data for many different consumer patterns based on the individuality of the postal code, which has on average between 14 and 17 people to a postal code. Other useful sources of information are the *category development index (CDI)* and *brand development index (BDI)*, which give marketers weighted information that facilitates comparing sales of a product from place to place.

Combining geographic and demographic information, a technique known as **geodemographics**, lets marketers segment by neighborhood, by lifestyle, or even by individual stores. For example, Sears "geocodes" its credit card customers by postal code in order to find its best customers and identify which segments are growing in size. These analyses can determine which merchandise is best suited to a particular store in a particular neighborhood.

geodemographics
A measure that combines geographic and demographic data to identify residents of a particular area with similar demographic traits.

PSYCHOGRAPHIC SEGMENTATION

psychographics
The study and classification of differing lifestyles, based largely on the analysis of people's attitudes, interests, and opinions.

Psychographics is a method of studying people's lifestyles, based largely on analyzing the general patterns of activities, interests, and opinions that they evidence. Two consumers can share the same demographic characteristics and yet be very different. For example, you may decide to take a sightseeing vacation in Paris, while your best friend, whose demographic makeup and income match your own, may prefer to get away from it all in a small cabin in the Rockies.

Most contemporary psychographic research looks at *activities* (work, hobbies, social events, entertainment, shopping, sports), *interests* (family, job, community, recreation, reading, watching TV), and *opinions* (about oneself, social issues, politics, business, economics, the future, specific products). Research that studies these three variables uses what are often called *AIO questionnaires* to solicit people's responses to statements like the following:

◆ I enjoy watching situation comedies on television.
◆ Comfort is more important to me than fashion.
◆ I do not participate in team sports.
◆ I think many product claims in advertising are exaggerated.

Social and Personal Characteristics   Psychographic data also let marketers segment consumers by social class, personality, or lifestyle characteristics. Consider the case of two neighboring families whose adults hold similar executive jobs and have roughly the same income. The family in one house is intellectual and likes art films and classical music, whereas the other family is action-oriented and prefers adventure movies and rock music. Each family thinks and feels differently about life and responds differently to products and services.

In Chapter 6 we noted some of the consumer differences among various social classes. Differences in *social class* usually translate into differences in perceptions, attitudes, and values. Since these differences influence important aspects of consumer behavior, many companies target specific social classes with their products or services.

As we saw in Chapter 6, *lifestyle* is a combination of many factors such as income, education, social class, personal preferences, beliefs, and values. The most famous lifestyle category of the 1980s was "yuppies"—young urban professionals, single or married, who live and work in urban areas and have considerable discretionary income and a taste for the good life. This segment, also described as "the tail end of the baby boom," has popularized such products as Audis, BMWs, Porsches, cellular phones, Cuisinarts, and Rolex watches. "Yuppie puppies"—the children of affluent baby boomers—generally enjoy a rich childhood as their parents rush to provide them with everything they could possibly need, and more.

Pacific Rim Yuppies

Many "yuppies" in the Pacific Rim area can well afford Porsches, as this scene at a Bangkok dealership suggests. A market of about a million strong in an arc that includes the cities of Singapore, Hong Kong, and Seoul as well, this group has a spending power that is 5 to 10 times that of most of their countrymen—and it is growing.

The singles market is usually regarded as both a lifestyle and a demographic category, but it includes widowed and divorced people as well as those who have never been married. Moreover, all three of these subcategories can be further segmented by gender. For example, divorced men tend to acquire new wardrobes, join health clubs, move into new apartments or houses, and buy dishes and curtains. Although marketers are more interested in the general single-people market, the divorced male is a particularly attractive subsegment because he usually faces a sudden need to upgrade his image and furnish a new household.

Segmentation can also be determined by *personality characteristics*. For example, marketers often differentiate people according to whether they make decisions on the basis of feeling or thinking. These two groups—which are based on Carl Jung's psychological typology (see Chapter 6)—respond differently to appeals: the "thinkers" want the facts, while the "feelers" want a relationship with the product. It's been suggested that IBM personal computers are for thinkers and Macintosh computers for feelers. Mac users love their Macs because they have formed an emotional relationship with the computer, while IBM users like their PCs because they do the job and are good value for the money.

An interesting set of personality characteristics was revealed in a study by the Illinois Lottery that found three primary segments in the lottery market: people who play for the thrill of winning; people who play for a sense of worth, convinced that their number is somehow special; and people who play because they think they're doing the smart thing by not passing up the opportunity to win.[5]

The VALS 2 Model To segment markets by psychographic criteria many marketers look to the Stanford Research Institute's Values and Life Styles (VALS) program which is based on a large survey of the population. Both large and small companies use VALS to identify market segments and develop marketing communication programs for them. In the new VALS 2 model consumers are defined by three self-orientations—to principles, status, or action—and by where they fall on the continuum called "resources," which includes intelligence, self-confidence, health, energy level, income, education, and eagerness to buy. As you can see from Figure 8-4, the resources dimension is split into two major levels: average to minimal and average to abundant. This two-variable design produces six basic categories and two additional groups that don't quite fit the basic dimensions. *Actualizers*, at the top of the diagram, have abundant resources and tend not to be bound to one self-orientation. *Strugglers*, at the bottom of the figure, have very few resources and thus are also hard to categorize in terms of the three orientations. Exhibit 8-2 addresses a segment of our society—those who are addicted to cigarettes and likely burdened with health problem—that might fall into the struggler category. Brief descriptions of the other six groups—the *fulfilleds*, *achievers*, *experiencers*, *believers*, *strivers*, and *makers*—are given in Figure 8-4.

BEHAVIOR SEGMENTATION

Behavior segmentation divides people into groups on the basis of how they behave with respect to a product—that is, whether or not they use it, how

Figure 8-4
The VALS 2 Psychographic Model.

Source: Adapted from George E. Belch and Michael A. Belch, Introduction to Advertising Promotion and Management. Homewood, Ill.: Irwin, 1990.

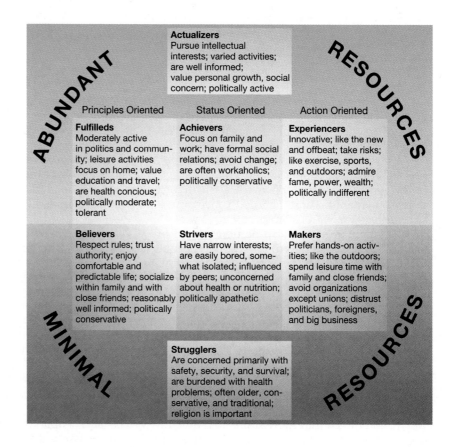

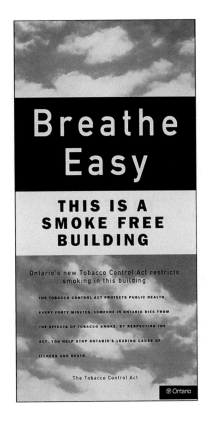

often they use it, how much of it they use, and how loyally. Marketers employ a **usage rate** to group people according to their purchase and use of a product. Consumer usage is most commonly categorized as heavy, medium, light, and nonusage. **User status** describes consumers in terms of their past, present, and possible future use of a product. Thus status categories include potential users, nonusers, ex-users, regulars, first-timers, and users of competitors' products.

Marketers often direct a certain product at people with specific behavioral patterns. For example, Coca-Cola's new OK brand soft drink is "for people with holes in their jeans," says Tom Pirk of the consulting firm Bevmark. Aimed at males aged 12 to 25 who want to debunk the norm, OK soda is described as post-modern, post-grunge, and post-apathy.[6]

People who buy the same brand over and over again—those who display *brand loyalty* (see Chapter 10)—are a product's most important segment. They are also the most difficult group for competitors to reach.

BENEFIT SEGMENTATION

A problem or a need can also suggest groups of users, such as people who want a portable computer or a cellular phone. They are not seeking out products. What they are seeking is solutions to their problems in product offerings. In addition, consumers can be grouped by their buying behavior as "searchers," "impulse buyers," and people who buy in quantity and stock up. Because such behaviors can provide important clues to what turns a consumer

usage rate
A measure of the amount and frequency with which a particular group of individual consumers buys and uses a specific product. Assesses whether they are light, heavy or committed loyal users to the brand in question.

usage rate
A measure of the amount and frequency with which a particular group of individual consumers buys and uses a specific product. Assesses whether they are light, heavy or committed loyal users to the brand in question.

into a prospect for a given product, it is important for marketers to understand them all when planning a segmentation strategy.

Finally, marketers can segment on the basis of the problem a product solves for consumers or the benefits it offers them—a strategy called **benefit segmentation**. In the 1920s, for example, athlete's foot was recognized as a health problem that was shared by many people and Absorbine Jr. was designed to solve it. Since that time, millions of bottles have been sold to consumers. Preparation H is a problem solver for that segment of the adult market that suffers from hemorrhoids. Many varieties of toothpaste are now on the market. Some are dispensed from a pump, others from the traditional tube; some whiten teeth and remove smoke stains; still others prevent cavities and help control the buildup of plaque. Some toothpastes are specially flavored to encourage children to brush their teeth. In each instance, the product tries to solve a problem or confer a benefit on the user. The value in use is a perception unique to the customer.

benefit segmentation
Segmenting a market based on the benefits people seek from a product or brand or the problem it solves.

TYPES OF INDUSTRIAL MARKET SEGMENTATION

Like consumer markets, industrial markets (see Chapter 7) can be segmented by such variables on organizational and industry sector characteristics as size, geography, and buyer behavior. Because the process uses many of the same variables, segmenting the industrial market is just as challenging as segmenting the consumer market. In our discussion of the criteria for industrial market segmentation—the third chapter objective—we will follow the outline presented in Table 8-1, which lists the categories and criteria most commonly used in this type of segmentation.

As in consumer markets, choosing the appropriate criteria for segmentation depends on both the product and the buyer. A firm selling concrete, for example, might worry about loyalty because it needs repeat customers. The end use of the concrete—bridges, highways, and buildings—could also be a key to segmenting the industrial concrete market if different uses call for different grades of concrete or require different delivery channels. Standard Industrial Classification (SIC) codes could then be meaningfully employed.

Behavior segmentation is often useful in the business software market. Business software is designed to help companies earn and save money by

---

TABLE 8-1	INDUSTRIAL SEGMENTATION CATEGORIES

1. Usage:
   - End use of product
   - Buyer
   - Loyalty

2. Benefits: Why is it being used?

3. Demographics:
   - Company size or sales level
   - Type of firm or organization

4. Geographic region located or served

5. Psychographics:
   - Corporate culture
   - Decision making

6. Behavior

making common tasks more efficient. Its four major segments, as defined by the Software Publishers Association, are word processing, spreadsheets, database programs, and graphics. Because a computer program's life span extends only until its next major revision, timing is particularly important. The market leader usually dominates the category until it undertakes a major upgrade, at which point a window of opportunity opens to the competition. A competitor may then make a technological change or advancement that allows it to leapfrog over the leader. The situation is roughly analogous to passing the lead race car driver while he is making a pit stop.

Benefits are just as important to industrial buyers as they are to consumers (see Exhibit 8-3). The computer market, for example, is segmented according to the nature of the work that various types of computers can facilitate: mainframes are fast and handle immense data banks; minicomputers and work stations are good for coordinating a network of terminals; personal computers provide computing power for individual users at a relatively low cost; computer-aided design (CAD) systems are used by engineers and architects for generating electronic blueprints. Even as this is written, the lines be-

Exhibit 8-3
The Timeless Taste of Tiffany's

A gift from Tiffany's enhances the giver's image of quality and timeless tradition, intangible benefits of considerable value to both industrial and private recipients.

tween these categories are being blurred by the appearance of more powerful processors and greater memory capacity together with improved network software and new applications software. There is convergence also between television and telephone systems bringing together a new world of communication and CD-rom players offering access to new and unlimited databases previously inaccessible to individuals and to small companies.

Industrial markets can also be identified as *major* or *minor* in terms of customer size or sales level. Major clients may buy large quantities and earn volume discounts. The type of organization—manufacturer, wholesaler, retailer, government, nonprofit—may also be an important factor in market segmentation. Both the size and type of firm are demographic factors. Geographic factors can have a significant impact on delivery of products; for example, market segments may be designated as in-the-city, in-the-country, or within-fifty-miles. Usage and user segmentation can likewise then be performed just as in consumer marketing.

Industrial segmentation may also consider psychographics, looking at such things as corporate culture (see Chapter 2). Whereas some companies are innovative and willing to experiment, others are more conservative. Some encourage flexibility in purchasing; others—especially governments—adhere to strict procedures. Because many industrial products are designed to meet specific industry requirements, industrial segments tend to be narrower than consumer segments.

NESTED APPROACH TO INDUSTRIAL MARKET SEGMENTATION ●

The psychological approach also is valid in industrial marketing when considering this not in terms of organizations but as a form of exchange between people in organizations. This then is the segmentation schema proposed by Bonoma and Shapiro (see Figure 8-5). Demographics give a broad description of the company and general customer size, location, needs and usage pat-

Figure 8-5
A "Nested Approach" to Industrial Market Segmentation

Source: Thomas V. Bonoma and Benson P. Shapiro, *Segmenting the Industrial Market,* Lexington, Mass, Lexington Books, 1983, p. 10.

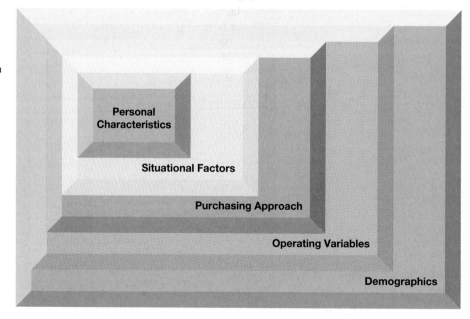

Personal Characteristics

Situational Factors

Purchasing Approach

Operating Variables

Demographics

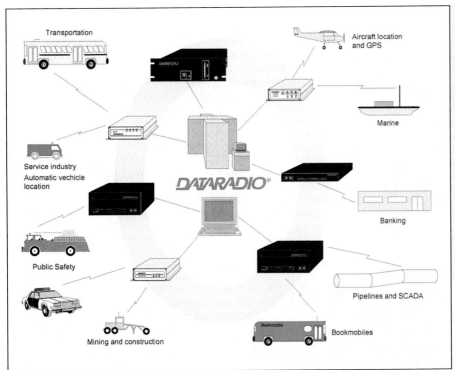

Niche Marketing in Industry

Montreal-based Dataradio Inc. designs and manufactures radio-based modem equipment used for banking terminals, dispatch systems for public safety (police, fire, ambulance), and utility systems (such as hydro and gas). The company markets and distributes 17 products throughout the world.

terns. Operating variables enable more precise identification of existing and potential customers within demographic categories, such as technology in manufacturing and of its product, product and brand use status, and customer capabilites. Purchasing approaches deal with the formal organization of the purchasing function, power structure, and the nature of buyer-seller relationships. Organizationally, a vendor with decentralized operations may find it difficult to meet centralized bumpy patterns. Power structures may shape or force directions in a particular way. Policies may be in place as to who they prefer to deal with or whether it is a free competitive budding situation. Situational factors include the urgency of fulfilling the order, size of order, and the nature and application of the product itself. Buyers' personal characteristics are also important as they make decisions albeit within an organizational framework. Segmentation is possible in terms of buyer-seller similarity, buyer motivation, individual perceptions and risk-management strategies.

TARGETING ●

Segmenting a market is just the starting point. The whole purpose of segmentation is to identify addressable markets and narrow the firm's focus to the most likely customers. Such narrowing calls for weighing the pros and cons for various market segments and selecting, or *targeting*, the best opportunities. Segmenting lets you consider a number of possible targets. Refining your segments, as Figure 8-6 suggests, can lead you to the target you want to aim for.

By identifying the most profitable prospects, targeting enables marketers to custom-design a marketing mix to provide the best return in sales. Distribution, for example, can be fitted to the geographical characteristics of the segment, and advertising messages can be delivered directly to typical customers rather than to a random mass audience.

Deciding on target markets means that a firm can count on specialized publications and other sources to help define a group as precisely as possible. For example, Hong Kong residents, like many other Asians, are just beginning to make use of credit cards. Research showed marketers that many Hong Kong women wanted cards of their own, reflecting their independent means, rather than the supplementary cards linked to those of their husbands or parents that they had long held. The Bank of Asia responded with MyCard, which also offers discounts at Hong Kong's most prestigious hair and fur salons, jewelers, and beauty products counters. The bank attracted more cardholders with its focused approach than it could with mass marketing.[7]

Targeting markets is a two-step process, as noted in chapter objective four. In this section we discuss how marketers compare the potential of various market segments, and then look at some of the ways in which, using these criteria, they select a targeting strategy.

CRITERIA FOR TARGETING

In deciding on target markets, marketers must review what they have learned about various market segments, giving particular consideration to three major issues: current and expected size of the segment, potential competition for the segment, and whether the target fits the firm's overall objectives.

Current and Expected Market Size How big is the market? Is it growing? Size and growth potential are important, but the biggest, fastest-growing market isn't always the best choice. Sometimes companies lack the resources to produce enough goods for or to fight off the larger number of competitors in big, fast-growing markets. Still, a market must be large enough to enable a company to make a profit. As we will see shortly, Soho Soda succeeded by targeting a rather small but growing segment of the soft-drink market—consumers seeking all-natural carbonated beverages.

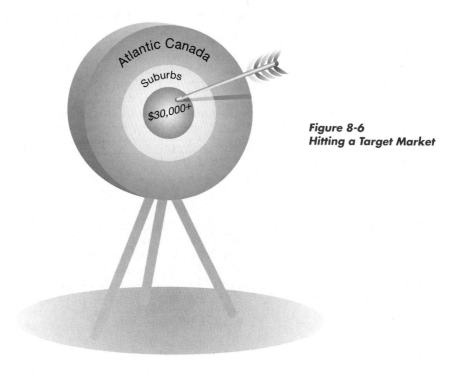

Figure 8-6
Hitting a Target Market

Potential Competition Strong competition is never a reason to avoid a market segment. Indeed, marketers must beware of markets in which there is no competition because this may be a red flag that there is no demand for the product or service. On the other hand, if a company correctly identifies a market for which there initially appears to be no visible demand, it can be a big winner because of the advantages that go to the first entrant into a new market.

BEHIND THE SCENES
WHEN A WATCH IS A SWATCH

If there *is* competition in a market, the question is whether or not the company can create a sustainable competitive advantage. Believing that he could achieve such an advantage for his Swiss Corporation for Microelectronics and Watchmaking, Swatch titan Nicolas Hayek engineered a spectacular comeback for the entire Swiss watch industry by consolidating hundreds of family-owned companies into a single efficient enterprise that successfully targeted what proved to be a number of lucrative markets. Today SMH is everywhere: Its brash and playful Swatch model, which sells for about $50, has become a pop culture phenomenon. It also dominates the luxury watch market with brands like Omega which retails for prices in the $1,000 to $20,000 range and Blancpain which produces luxury mechanical watches that sell for as much as $200,000 and up.

SMH is a vertically integrated fortress. It assembles all the watches it sells, and it builds most of the components for the watches it assembles. The company breaks two widely accepted rules in contemporary business: it has a product price range from $40 to $200,000 plus; and it designs and manufactures in Switzerland, the nation that has the highest per capita income in the world (a secretary in Switzerland makes more money than a chief engineer in Thailand). According to Hayek, low-wage countries can't compete with SMH on a cost basis because SMH holds labor costs to less than 15 percent of total costs. Even if the competition's employees work for nothing, SMH will still succeed because it is more creative and its labor costs are a small percentage of its total costs.

According to Hayek, several lessons can be drawn from SMH's success: First, it is possible to manufacture high-quality, high-value, large-market consumer products in high-wage countries at a low cost. Second, it is possible for one company to succeed in a number of target markets, each of which has very different tastes and spending power. And third, you can manufacture products for several quite different mass markets in countries like Switzerland, Canada or the United States only if you embrace the vigorous fantasy and imagination of your childhood and youth. True, the Swatch is a triumph of engineering, but it is more importantly a triumph of imagination.[8]

Compatibility with Firm's Objective If the market is big enough and competitors are scarce enough, companies must consider whether they can reach the target market effectively. If a firm pursues target markets that do not fit its overall goals, it will squander its energy and resources. Another question that must be answered is whether the firm can spend the money required to reach a given target market. Small firms may not be able to afford the national advertising necessary to reach some very large markets. Soho's founder, Sophia Collier, had *very* limited resources when she decided to launch her soft-drink company, so in the beginning she hired a small bottler to produce her soft drinks in one flavor—fruit punch—and distributed them to local stores and restaurants herself.

SELECTING A TARGET MARKET STRATEGY

After choosing a target market based on evaluations of the criteria we've discussed, the marketer must decide on the most suitable targeting strategy. Targeting strategies fall into three basic categories: undifferentiated marketing, concentrated marketing, and differentiated marketing.

undifferentiated marketing
An alternative term for *mass marketing.*

Undifferentiated Marketing **Undifferentiated marketing** is really mass marketing—the company uses the same marketing mix of product, price, distribution, and marketing communications for all potential buyers. As we noted at the start of this chapter, mass marketing means *not* segmenting, so by extension, it means *not* targeting. Although few markets still lend themselves to this approach, its appeal is clear: the firm can mass-produce the item (cutting production costs) and save the time, energy, and expense of segmenting and targeting. When undifferentiated marketing works, the payoffs can be as huge as the market itself. But only large firms serving large markets can afford the expenditures of mass marketing today. Coke and Pepsi have been good examples of undifferentiated marketers, serving large markets, spending huge amounts of money on marketing, and reaping huge profits. Both are moving now, however, into more segmented strategies.

concentrated marketing
Targeting just one or two market segments with the same marketing mix.

Concentrated Marketing In **concentrated marketing** a firm selects one or two market segments that it can reach with the same marketing mix and targets only those segments. This strategy is very popular with small firms for several reasons. First, it limits the resources necessary to produce and promote a product. Second, it allows firms to learn a great deal about a narrow market and to gain a strong market share that may withstand later competitive assaults. Third, it makes for very efficient marketing because there is no need to juggle multiple marketing plans. But concentrated marketing can be dangerous: if the bottom drops out of a narrow market or if competitors stream in, the concentrated marketer may have no place to go.

Almost every start-up company that succeeds is a concentrated marketer serving a well-defined segment. Boston Chicken, one of the first of the Rotisserie chicken chains, was a huge success because it defined a very specific market and did an excellent job of serving that market. The stock market liked Boston Chicken's strategy so much that on the first day the company's stock was issued to the public, its price rose from $20 to over $50 per share!

differentiated marketing
Identifying multiple market segments and developing a unique marketing mix for each.

Differentiated Marketing In **differentiated marketing**, a company targets multiple market segments and employs a unique marketing mix for each segment. A successful differentiated marketing strategy will create greater value for the customer and greater profit for the company; an unsuccessful one will lower customers' value and reduce profits. Success in differentiated marketing depends on the execution of the strategy; not surprisingly, the same company can be highly successful at one time and unsuccessful at another.

As we pointed out in discussing the socioeconomic method of market segmentation, General Motors was successful for half a century with its differentiated marketing strategy of targeting five different socioeconomic market segments. By the 1970s, however, markets were changing, and the old socioeconomic segmentation method no longer suited the automobile market. It was time to retarget the market using the newer segmentation technique based on lifestyle. But blinded by its long success with the old strategy, GM continued to do business as usual: as its former market segments disappeared, the business organization and the five product name plates serving these segments stayed in place. GM began losing market share steadily. The problem was GM's failure to understand that its market segments were now differentiated in an entirely different way. Successful auto companies still use differentiated marketing, but they base their market segments on lifestyle and benefit segmentation: for example, four-wheel drive, trucks, vans, sport coupes, compact economy, luxury sedans, and high-performance sports cars.

FORECASTING ●

Once marketers have determined what market segment they want to target, they must plan the marketing mix for that segment and develop their marketing plan. As you learned in Chapter 4, one of the most crucial elements in developing this plan is the prediction of how successful a company can be in its chosen market—the first topic of chapter objective five. Much of the work that goes into preparing the marketing plan consists of analyzing one's own and one's competitors' strengths, weaknesses, and actual performance. In order to perform these analyses, marketers have to try to *forecast* future events and potential sales.

In broad terms, **forecasting** is the estimation of future events by the analysis of hard data or, sometimes, by intuiting what is likely to happen. The interesting thing about the future is that it is our only field of power: the past is history. I may alter the records and lie about the past, but that does not change the past, for my actions only record a falsehood, not a fact. The future, in contrast, is a field of liberty because I am free to conceive of something that does not now exist. It is a field of power because I have the power to validate my conception. It is also a field of uncertainty because what will be cannot be verified in the same way as an accomplished fact.[9]

Forecasting attempts to answer the questions "When?" and "How much?" for the sales of products. Like a meteorologist's weather forecast, a business forecast tries to predict future events accurately enough to form a reasonable basis for present actions. Most daily activities of a company's employees and all marketing plans are based on some type of forecast. Indeed, the most important use of forecasting is in planning. When marketing managers identify alternatives and assess their impact, they are trying to forecast how events both within and outside the firm will affect each alternative and—even more importantly—what the outcome of each alternative will be. For example, pricing decisions are based on two forecasts: how the market will respond to price changes and how the competition will react.

There are two key forecasts: potential *demand* for a product category and potential *sales levels* for a company's product. These forecasts lead directly to the statement of corporate marketing objectives in the marketing plan. If forecasts based on analyses of company actions, competitors' responses, and consumer demand suggest that sales objectives will not be realized, then managers know that some critical unaccounted-for problem needs to be addressed by the marketing plan. Either other elements in the plan that influence demand—such as sales promotion and advertising—have to be changed

forecasting
The estimation of the future based either on the analysis of hard data or on expert judgment or opinion.

so that forecasted sales and the sales objectives agree, or objectives have to be lowered.

In order to develop more realistic insights into future market conditions and demand levels, experts recommend that marketers follow the five-step framework shown in Table 8-2.

TYPES OF FORECAST

Market demand is an estimate of the quantity of a product that would be bought by a targeted group of customers in a certain market area during a specific period of time, given a defined marketing environment and a defined marketing program. The broadest type of forecast estimate, market demand is also the least specific, for it is a function of many marketing conditions.

In estimating market demand, marketers try to determine *actual demand*, or sales by all suppliers of a particular product in a given period of time. This sounds like an easy number to obtain, but in many industries it is not known. Each company knows its own sales to resellers and to end users, but unless companies within the industry formulate some sort of cooperation agreement, none may know what the others have sold.

Market potential is an estimate of the unit sales by all suppliers of a given product during a given time period with a specified level of industrywide marketing activity. When making a market potential estimate, it is important to clearly specify the product. The potential market for seven-pound notebook computers with an average price of $2,000 is quite different from that for two-pound notebooks with an average price of $1,000. Market potential depends on all the elements of the external environment: economic, social, physical, political, legal and regulatory, technological, and competitive.

Companies estimating global market potential often base their determinations on the highest level of market penetration achieved in a national market. The U.S. soft-drink companies, for example, believe that the upper limit of sales in the global market is the per capita consumption of soft drinks in the United States.

TABLE 8-2	FORECASTING DEMAND: A SYSTEMATIC APPROACH
Step	**Example**
1. Define the market.	Solar heating.
2. Divide total industry demand into its major components.	Home heating, pool heating, industrial/commercial heating.
3. Identify the demand drivers and the factors that restrain demand.	Price of oil and natural gas. Higher prices stimulate demand, lower prices restrain demand.
4. Predict the driving and restraining force factors.	Oil prices are expected to remain stable for the next 5 years based on estimates of world demand and supply.
5. Calculate the forecast demand.	Demand for solar heating will be limited to unusual specialty applications until the price of oil rises above $20 a barrel in 1994 dollars.

The *market forecast* is an estimate of the number of units of a product that will be purchased from all suppliers in a given time period and of the prices at which these units will be purchased. It is based on assumptions about price levels and the quality and quantity of the marketing efforts of all the firms that are active in the market.

When the foregoing estimates of the performance of the market in general have been established, marketers can turn to preparing forecasts that relate solely to their own companies. **Sales potential** is the term given to the estimate of the maximum percentage of market potential that a company can expect to achieve, given certain assumptions about the market and the behavior of customers. In the **sales forecast** marketers try to pinpoint the amount of product that a company expects to sell during a specified period of time with a specified level of marketing activity and a specified marketing mix.

FORECASTING METHODS

There are a number of methods for forecasting market potential and sales. These tools, which are the second topic of chapter objective five, include judgment based on experience and intuition, surveys, time series analysis, and statistical demand analysis.

Judgment   One of the least expensive and quickest forecasting methods uses *judgment* and intuition. Since its effectiveness depends entirely on the skills and competence of the forecaster, this method is unscientific and very risky. Even an experienced executive with a superb track record as a forecaster may be wrong on a forecast—and disastrously so. Nevertheless, judgment is a common forecasting tool because it is cheap and fast and often does produce excellent results.

Surveys   The *survey*, a more objective method of forecasting, involves asking actual and potential customers about their purchase intentions. The disadvantage of this method is that the data it produces are not wholly reliable. In the first place, people often do not *know* what they will do, so many responses will turn out to be inaccurate. In addition, survey respondents are often influenced by the way in which a question is put, so their answers are invalid. In spite of these drawbacks, research organizations regularly carry out surveys of buyer intentions and turn the information into an index of purchase intentions that is then used to predict buyer behavior. Although the data are not wholly reliable, it is valuable to know the *direction* of change.

Time Series Analysis   *Time series analysis* uses historical purchasing behavior to infer what people will do in the future. Forecasters rely on four variations of this method: trend, cycle, seasonal, and erratic or random event analysis. *Trend analysis* looks for the pattern in historical sales data; marketers try to fit a statistical curve to the historical sales data. *Cycle analysis* looks at the pattern of rising and falling sales over time. *Seasonal analysis* searches for patterns in the levels of sales recorded at different times of the year. Finally, researchers must tease out and remove *random events* from the data because, by definition, such events are unique and unpredictable and thus cannot be used to establish predictable patterns.

Statistical Demand Analysis   Statistical analysis looks for the factors that explain demand. In *statistical demand analysis* demand is considered the dependent variable, and the marketer looks for the independent variables that explain variations in demand level. Although computer programs have made it easy to compute statistical analysis relationships, the marketer still must evaluate the value of estimates obtained. Statistical analysis will always find a

sales potential
The maximum percentage of market potential that a given firm can expect to achieve based on certain assumptions about the market and the behavior of customers.

sales forecast
An estimate of the total sales of a product that a company expects to achieve during a specified period of time with a specified marketing mix and a specified level of marketing activity.

"fit" between historical data and available independent variables. The problem with this "fit" is that it describes past relationships, and the forecaster is interested in the future. Statistical analysis is valuable and reasonably accurate if markets are stable. But when significant changes are occurring in the market—and significant change is pretty common today—such analysis will not provide an accurate prediction of the future.

Clearly, forecasting is a difficult and risky assignment. As you read the account of the changes Dell Computer recently made in its marketing program, ask yourself how the company might best have gone about forecasting future demand and sales.

DELL'S NEW "TECHNO" MARKET SEGMENTS

In the early years of personal computing, companies generally offered buyers a basic model to which they could then add whatever components and accessories they wished. Dell Computer, the company Michael Dell founded while he was still a student at the University of Texas in Austin, supplied components and accessories to computer owners. The company's great advantage was its ability to price under its higher-cost competitors because of its low overhead.

Dell's great insight was that the personal computer had become almost an essential commodity—as one Dell vice president put it, the PC was "one step above rice in the food chain." The company's marketing strategy was to build

the exact computer that each of its customers wanted. In taking the customer's order, Dell asked which components and accessories—for example, extra memory, additional drives, modems—the customer wanted added. Dell's big advantage was lower costs which translated into lower prices.

No success lasts forever, and in 1993 Dell hit a wall. Competitors had pushed down their costs and were meeting Dell on price. In addition, Dell was finding that the company's products simply didn't match the markets it was serving—as Sean Burke, Dell's product marketing director, put it, "Our products were in between our customers."[10]

Realizing it needed a new arrow in its quiver, the company decided to try using marketing segmentation and target marketing. Dell reasoned that it was serving essentially four types of customers:

- *Techno-teamers:* price-sensitive corporate buyers who were seeking primarily networking capabilities and reliability.
- *Techno-criticals:* corporate buyers of high-end (more expensive, higher-performance) computers who were seeking advanced features and enhanced productivity.
- *Techno-wizards:* individual buyers who wanted the latest and most sophisticated components.
- Technos-to-go: buyers who wanted a simple, affordable computer they could take out of the box, plug in, and use.

Dell believed it could bring its costs down and increase its marketing effectiveness by targeting these four segments of the personal computer market. Costs would decline because Dell would be able to build in popular features as the computers were being assembled rather than add them on after the order was received. Marketing effectiveness would improve because the company would be targeting real segments.

Do you think Dell's market segments make sense? Would you add any segments? Would you delete any? Which segment are *you* in? If you were advising Michael Dell, the company's founder and CEO, what would you suggest that he do to remedy slumping sales and earnings? ▼

KEY POINTS SUMMARY ▼

1. The purpose of segmenting and targeting is to focus marketing efforts on the customers most likely to buy a particular product or respond to a particular marketing mix. Marketers first segment markets into groups with some common characteristic and then target the section they feel is best suited to their overall goals and capabilities.

2. Marketers usually segment markets according to five broad classes of characteristics: demographic, geographic, psychographic, behavioral, and benefit. Demographic segmentation is based on such factors as age, life stage, gender, ethnicity, religion, income, education, socioeconomic status, and household size. Geographic segmentation takes into account international, national, regional, state, city, county, and even neighborhood differences. The chief variables in psychographic segmentation are social class, lifestyle, and personality; the VALS 2 model is often used in psychographic segmentation. Behavioral segmentation is generally based on usage rates, user status, or brand loyalty. Some markets are segmented on the basis of the specific benefits consumers seek or the problems they expect a product to solve.

3. Industrial markets, like consumer markets, can be segmented according to demographic variables (for example, size and type of firm), geo-graphic factors, psychographic variables (for example, corporate culture), behavioral variables (for example, innovations, timing of product introduction), and benefits (for example, the varying needs that a given product may fulfill for different firms).

4. When making a decision about targeting a market, firms must consider both the current and the anticipated size of the market; the nature of the competition and the likelihood that it can achieve a competitive advantage in the market; and whether, given its goals and resources, the firm can reach the market effectively. The primary targeting strategies are undifferentiated marketing, also known as "mass marketing"; concentrated marketing, sometimes called "niche marketing"; and differentiated marketing.

5. The purpose of forecasting is to predict the degree of success a firm can expect to achieve in marketing a particular product in a particular market segment during a specified period of time. In preparing market and sales forecasts, marketers estimate market demand, actual demand, market potential, and sales potential. Marketers can choose among several techniques for gathering forecast data; chief among these are use of the marketer's own judgment, surveys of buyers' intentions, time series analysis, and statistical demand analysis.

DISCUSSION QUESTIONS ▼

1. What are the key differences between mass marketing and segmented marketing?

2. Explain the five basic segmentation strategies. Give examples of each.

3. How are industrial markets segmented? Give an example for each major type of industrial segmentation.

4. What are the advantages and disadvantages of

undifferentiated, concentrated, and differentiated marketing?

5. Explain the difference between segmenting and targeting. Choose a product that you use often and describe these two processes as they may have entered into the firm's plan for marketing that product to you.

6. You are the marketing director for a company that sells tea. Your company has decided to begin selling in Quebec, where 20 percent of the consumers drink tea and 80 percent do not. Should your company target the users or nonusers?

7. You are the marketing manager for Whirlpool. How will changes in marketing, such as the breakup of the mass market, the practice of narrow targeting, and globalization, affect your industry? How will these changes affect Whirlpool's target marketing?

8. You are advising your athletic department on season ticket sales:

(a) Segment the Canadian Football League season ticket market. How many different groups can you identify? What are their key distinguishing characteristics? How do people in the market differ from those who are not in the market? Give each group a name.

(b) Which segment would you target for immediate attention? Assign priorities to all your segments and explain which ones are more important ultimately from a marketing viewpoint.

9. Interview a marketing manager for a local firm and report back on how that firm has segmented and targeted its market(s).

10. What is the difference between a market forecast and a sales forecast?

11. What methods do marketers use to forecast sales and market potential?

Integrative Case • Discussion Questions

The Body Shop*

1. What variables might be very useful in segmenting the market for The Body Shop?

Harley-Davidson

1. Describe the market segments to whom Harley sells. How do they differ?

2. There are Harley Owners Groups in Canada, the United States, and in Japan. How do the benefits sought by each of these groups differ?

The Millennium Power System

1. What segmentation bases did Millennium use in defining its final consumer target market?

*The three cases at the back of the book—"The Body Shop," "Harley-Davidson," and "The Millennium Power System"—illustrate topics discussed in all chapters of this book. Your instructor will tell you when to read a particular case and when to answer the discussion questions on it that appear at the end of each chapter.

Seniors Marketing: Segmentation, Targeting, and Forecasting

What does every marketer dream about when searching for a target market segment which can be successfully marketed to by the marketer's organization? First, the marketer loves to uncover a level of disposable income, and is willing to spend it. The marketer becomes more interested upon determining that the segment is very visible, can be exactly sub-segmented, and easily reached with a wide variety of marketing communications. The marketer becomes excited as it is realized that this particular market segment is growing in size, and will continue to do so for at least 20 years. The clincher comes when the marketer discovers that consumers comprising this market segment actually wish to be marketed to; clearly responding to having products and services specifically designed for them, and to having marketing communications not only communicate information to them, but acknowledge their very existence, and significance, to the world.

Is the "seniors market" or, using the term preferred by seniors, the "mature market" a marketer's dream segment come true? If so, how is it that Canadian marketer's have literally ignored the mature market for years? The Canadian seniors market, comprised of those individuals 50 years of age and over, is the only growing demographic market segment current existing in Canada, future growth being assured by the "graying" of the baby boomer market so prized by marketers. The senior's market currently comprises 30% of the entire Canadian population, 40% of the households, and most importantly, possesses 75–80% of the disposable income vied for by Canadian businesses each year. Seniors demonstrate a high disposable income not only because they are better savers, but because they have typically paid off their mortgages, and have no children to support or put through school. Furthermore, Canadian seniors are living longer, are in better health, and are more active than in the past.

Given the obvious visibility and attractiveness of the Canadian mature market, why have more Canadian marketers not generated products and services specifically tailored to the needs of seniors, or suitably modified existing products or services to render them attractive to seniors? It would appear that marketers in the United States have been on their toes, having paid due notice to the seniors market, generating a wide variety of products and services targeted specifically to the needs of the segment, including such offerings as cosmetics lines for seniors, seniors travel agencies and insurance firms, and of course, the large volume of pharmaceutical products targeted at seniors.

QUESTIONS

1. What possible demographic and psychographic sub-segments can you identify amongst the general seniors market segment?
2. What types of marketing communications could be most effectively utilized to reach the various target market sub-segments you have just identified?

289

3. Do you think it is possible to design global products and services aimed at seniors markets around the world? Can you offer any examples of products and services of this nature?
4. Why do you think Canadian marketers have largely ignored the mature market to date? What possible ethical complications can arise from marketing directly to seniors?

Source: This case was prepared by Byron Osing and is based on the *Venture* series episode "Seniors Marketing," which was first broadcast on April 10, 1994.

Chapter 9

Competitive Advantage and Positioning

DOES LOCATION MAKE A DIFFERENCE?

Author and competitive strategy expert Michael Porter argues that location makes a difference. If you were to draw up a map showing where the most successful companies in the world are sited, you would see that they are not randomly distributed. They are not located in the countries with the cheapest labor, but in the richest countries: the nations that make up the European Union (formerly known as the European Community or EC), the United States and Canada, and Japan. Why are so many successful companies located in these countries?

Porter uses a diamond analogy to explain why companies have competitive advantage. As Figure 9-1 shows, the four points of the diamond are: *company strategy, structure, and rivalry; demand conditions*, or the market; *related and supporting industries*; and *factor conditions*, or the basic elements of production—land, labor, and capital. Two variables, *government* and *chance*, affect competitive advantage by influencing the four points of the diamond.

Although government (the inner circle in Figure 9-1) does not directly create competitive advantage, through regula-

ANALYZING THE MARKETPLACE

In our discussion of the marketing plan in Chapter 4, we noted the need to analyze the competitive marketplace when doing the overall situation analysis. In this chapter we move a step further and outline competitive strategy alternatives based on an assessment of the market and the competitive situation. Crucial to success is identifying and ensuring your **competitive advantage**—the elements that make your product or services superior to your competitors' by virtue either of greater perceived value or lower price or a combination of both. No matter how good your company is, if there is another company that is better, that company will have the competitive advantage. In the highly competitive beer market, the value of the Molson brand slumped by 29 percent as the brand's operating profit dropped by 37 percent because of competition from discounted products.

competitive advantage
An advantage over the competition gained by offering either greater perceived value or a lower price or a combination of both.

As you will see when we discuss positioning toward the end of this chapter, skillfully positioning a product or service, both in the minds of consumers and in relation to competitive or alternative products and services, is one of the most important strategic parts of the marketing plan and one of the best ways to create competitive advantage.

In order to build competitive advantage, as noted in chapter objective one, you must identify and compare three factors: what customers want (market demand), your own product's strengths and weaknesses, and the strengths and weaknesses of your competition. Note how Citibank succeeds in implying its superiority in all three of these areas by emphasizing the second—its product's advantage—in the advertisement reproduced in Exhibit 9-1.

ADVANTAGE AND VALUE

Competitive advantage grows out of the *value* a firm creates for customers. In Chapter 1 we defined value as what something was worth to a buyer or the relationship of a benefit received to the cost paid. Because value is determined by individual consumers or groups of buyers in organizations, it is ultimately subjective—that is, a product's value is what people decide that product is worth. Competitive advantage therefore means that in some aspect important to customers a product has more value than a competitor's product has. In the 1950s Sony took the then-revolutionary transistor developed by AT&T's Bell Labs and made the first small, energy-efficient, truly portable radio. Its product had a major advantage over the furniture-size radios of the day.

Competitive advantage exists when the match between the competence of a company and the factors critical for success within the industry permits the firm to outperform its competitors.[1] There are two basic ways to gain a competitive advantage, and we will refer to these methods throughout this chapter. First, firms may pursue a strategy of low costs, which enables them to offer similar products (benefits) at lower prices than those charged by their competitors. This may only prove to be a short term advantage and may well lead to cultural price competition and early casualties. Second, firms may pursue a strategy of differentiation—that is, one of trying to convince customers that their products have unique benefits that offset their premium prices. Note that both of these strategies have the same effect: they increase the perceived benefits of the product but the second strategy proves more of a lasting advantage.[2] Another way to gain competitive advantage is to combine low costs and differentiation.

COMPETITOR ANALYSIS

In developing a competitive strategy, organizations must never lose sight of the competition. The amount of competitive challenge varies with the prod-

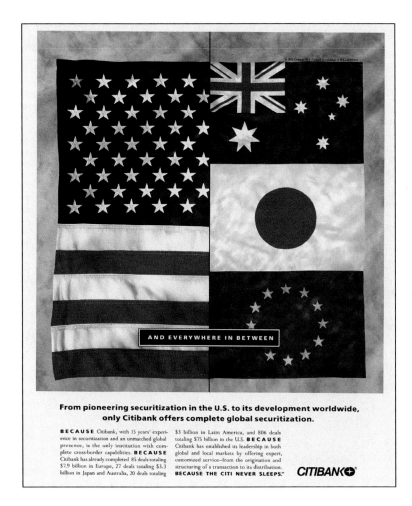

Exhibit 9-1
Global Extension

Citibank positions itself as a global leader in securitization (a form of debt-security investment, also known as "factoring") based on its fifteen years of experience after its "pioneering" entry into this market in the United States.

uct category. In mature markets, which by definition are not growing, one company's growth can occur only at another company's expense. Competition thus focuses on stealing someone else's market share. New competitors entering such markets which do not make a whole lot of sense may need to use a strategy of low price—often at the expense of short-term profit—simply to establish a beachhead.

In contrast, if a product category is new or has room for expansion, then everyone can grow. Any new industry or market offers this kind of opportunity: wireless communication is a growth industry, and rotisserie chicken is a growth niche in the fast-food industry. In the growth stage of a product's life cycle, competition focuses on getting share of an expanding market. Note that this kind of growth may not mean increased market share, but only increased sales volume—which can be quite profitable if it comes without having to lower price. But because market share is a percentage of the whole market for a product category, a company can't increase its own market share unless a competitor's share shrinks. Winners in the highly competitive global marketplace are companies that think market share rather than short-term profit. Indeed, success in such markets is often the result of sacrificing short-term profitability to achieve a long-term position of market dominance.

Who are your competitors? At the product level, marketers identify their competition as directly competing products—those within the same cate-

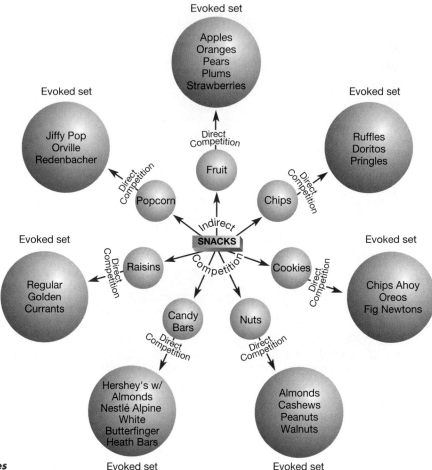

Figure 9-2
Competition and Categories

gory—and alternative products—those that consumers consider purchasing instead even though they are in a different category. These two types of competition are the topic of chapter objective two.

Consider Figure 9-2. If you are in the mood for a snack, what categories of products do you think of—fruit? salty snacks? cookies? You have just named some of the Snickers' marketing manager's indirect competition (see the inner circle in Figure 9-2). **Indirect competition** is made up of products in a different category from a firm's product but that are alternative purchase choices. **Direct competition** is made up of products in the same category as a firm's product. Thus, Snickers' direct competition is restricted to other candy bars—whether all candy bars or only those that contain chocolate depends upon how narrowly Snickers' marketing manager chooses to define the competition.

To draw a more detailed picture of the competition a brand faces, we can use the concept of the *evoked set*—that group of brands that comes to the consumer's mind when a purchase is being considered (see Chapter 6). For most types of consumer products, evoked sets are small, generally from three to six brands. So for candy bars, your evoked set might be Hershey's with Almonds, Nestlé's Alpine White, Heath Bars, and Butterfingers (in Figure 9-2's outer circle). If you are *brand loyal*, you have an evoked set of one: when you want a candy bar, you think only of Heath Bars, and that's all you buy. Research into

indirect competition
A term for products that are in a different category from a company's product but that serve as alternative purchase choices.

direct competition
Products or brands in the same category as a company's product.

consumers' evoked sets is crucial for planning competitive strategies for specific brands.

The concept of the evoked set also applies to industrial markets. Often companies have a list of approved brands on which they base the majority of their purchasing decisions.

Which of your competitors is most likely to challenge you, and on what basis? Does your product have any advantages over its competitors? For example, as Exhibit 9-2 shows, Compaq extols its computer's flexibility. If consumers perceive your product as more useful, more fun, of better quality, or (perhaps best of all) less expensive, then you have a competitive advantage based on that perceived difference.

COMPETITIVE ANALYSIS

Once you have identified the market's needs, your strengths and weaknesses, and your competition's strengths and weaknesses, you are ready to analyze the overall situation. **Feature analysis** is a structured approach in which you compare your product's features against the features of competing products and the needs and wants of consumers. This simple process based on the concept of consumer value involves the following steps:

1. Make a list of your product's features.

2. Rate how important each feature is to your target audience (using primary research—see Chapter 5). The relevant features will vary according to the product: taste, for example, is an important dimension for candy; styling and fit are important for jeans.

3. Evaluate how well your product and your competitors' products perform on these dimensions.

feature analysis
Comparing a product's features with the features of competing products and analyzing the perceived importance of each to consumers.

Exhibit 9-2
Differentiation Focus

One of the ways companies compete is through differentiation.
Compaq proclaims its notebook to be "untraditional."

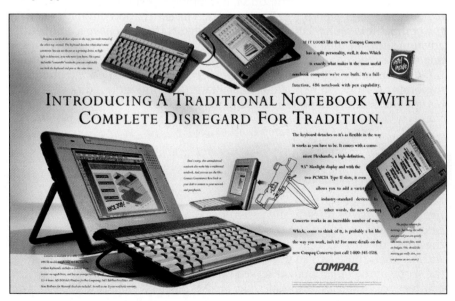

TABLE 9-1	FEATURE ANALYSIS: VCRs			
Feature	**Importance**	**Performance**		
		Your Brand	**Brand X**	**Brand Y**
Durability	9	9	6	5
Dual-tape capacity	5	4	9	6
Remote control	6	6	7	10
Price	10	7	7	9

parity product
A product that is equal in features, performance, and quality to its competition.

Your analysis will identify your strong features, your competitors' weak ones, and the saliency of all these features to your target market. Your competitive advantage lies in that area where you have *a strong feature that is important to the target and your competition is weak on that feature*. With a **parity product**—one whose features, performance, and quality are rated equal to those of competitive products—the competitive advantage might lie with perceptions, or the image values created by advertising.

Table 9-1 shows a hypothetical feature analysis for the VCR market. The features listed in the first column are those determined to be important by consumer research. The second column gives the importance rating assigned to each feature by consumers, and the last three columns provide ratings for your VCR and two of its competitors. (A 1–10 rating scale was used for this example, 10 being the highest rating.)

In using this chart for your feature analysis, you would evaluate how your product rates on the features most important to consumers (durability and price) and how those ratings compare to those received by your competitors. Looking at the two most important features, you note that you rank higher on durability than the other two brands, and equal to Brand X but lower than Brand Y on price. Furthermore, you see that on durability both of the competitors rank relatively low. This suggests that you have a competitive advantage in the area of durability. Brand X has a competitive advantage in dual-tape capacity and remote control, but these aren't very important features to consumers. Brand Y has a competitive advantage in price, which *is* an important feature. You conclude that Brand X is the more vulnerable competitor and Brand Y the more challenging.

TYPES OF COMPETITIVE ADVANTAGE

Michael Porter of Harvard University, whose "diamond" theory of competitive strategy we've already discussed, has developed a set of "generic" business strategies based on the two basic types of competitive advantage that are the topic of chapter objective three: *price* and *differentiation*. As Figure 9-3 shows, when these two sources of competitive advantage are combined with the scope of the target market served (narrow or broad), the result is four general types of strategies: *cost leadership, product differentiation, cost focus,* and *differentiation focus*. These "generic" strategies are based on the principle that achieving competitive advantage is the core of a superior marketing strategy. We treat the first two broad strategies separately here and combine the last two under "Narrow-Focus Advantage."

THE COST-LEADERSHIP ADVANTAGE

Cost leadership, the first business strategy referred to in chapter objective three, is based on a firm's position as the industry's low-cost producer in a broadly defined or mass market. The **cost-leadership advantage** allows a firm to offer lower prices—and therefore more value—to customers. For example, Japanese manufacturers in many industries have been the low-cost producers for many years. This leadership began in the 1960s and 1970s, when the Japanese yen was undervalued and Japanese labor costs were low, but it has been maintained more recently because of superior manufacturing methods and management.

Cost leadership, then, does not require cheap labor and/or an undervalued currency. It can also be gained or maintained by achieving economies of scale in manufacturing and marketing and by reducing the labor percentage of total manufacturing cost. Bic's volume production techniques, combined with its effective promotion and distribution, make it the cost and market-share leader in disposable pens, lighters, and razors. As a result of its high volume of production and sales, it enjoys further savings in manufacturing.

Cost leadership is a sustainable competitive advantage only if there are barriers preventing competitors from achieving the same low costs. In this era of rapid technological improvements in manufacturing, it is difficult for one firm to enjoy a cost advantage for very long. At one time, for instance, the Swiss had the low-cost advantage in watch production. Then the Japanese and other Asian producers reduced their production costs enough to wrest the advantage from the Swiss.

Swiss manufacturers fought back. Nicolas G. Hayek, a Swiss executive, engineered a comeback for Switzerland by merging the country's two giant watch manufacturers to form the Swiss Corporation for Microelectronics and Watchmaking (SMH). Hayek rejected the advice of experts who advise that companies should locate production in low-wage countries and committed SMH to manufacturing in Switzerland, the highest wage country in the world. Hayek is passionate about the principle that companies must manufacture and build in their home countries. Hayek puts it very simply: "We must build where we live."[3] With this commitment, the company focused upon labor. By designing a manufacturing process where labor accounts for less than 10% of total cost, there is nothing to stop SMH or any company from manufacturing in Switzerland, the most expensive country in the world. SMH's success is based upon two legs: one is its position as low cost producer, and the other is the creative design and marketing of SMH products. The company understands the watch business and dominates the watch as a fashion accessory business worldwide.

SMH took a risk by seeking to be the cost leader: some firms attempting the cost-leadership strategy have failed. Berkshire Hathaway, for example, did everything right to become one of the most efficient low-cost producers of textiles in the United States. Its strategy failed, however, because Berkshire could not compete with competitors in countries where wages are much lower.

Figure 9-3
Porter's "Generic" Strategies for Achieving Competitive Advantage

Source: Adapted from Michael E. Porter, Competitive Advantage: Creating and Sustaining Superior Performance (New York: The Free Press, 1985).

cost-leadership advantage
A strategy of gaining a competitive advantage by being an industry's lowest-cost producer.

Exhibit 9-3
Money Back Guarantee

Extending the warranty period is one way of attracting customers. Maytag here underlines its positioning as a trouble-free, long-life appliance maker.

There is only one refrigerator with a money-back guarantee until the year 2000. It is not the one you have now.

Introducing the refrigerator built like a Maytag, with a guarantee only The Dependability People would offer. Buy one now and if it's not working by the year 2000, we'll buy it back. See the new line of Maytag refrigerators at your dealer, now.

MAYTAG
THE DEPENDABILITY PEOPLE

THE PRODUCT-DIFFERENTIATION ADVANTAGE

product-differentiation advantage
A strategy of gaining a competitive advantage by offering products with unique customer benefits or features not available from competitors.

When a firm's product has unique customer benefits or features not available from competitors, it is said to have a **product-differentiation advantage**—the second business strategy referred to in chapter objective three. For example, a pet-boarding firm may differentiate its services by placing vacationing owners' pets in private homes rather than in fenced kennels. Private home care costs two to three times as much as traditional kennel care, but more and more people seem willing to pay the difference so their pets can have "all the comforts of home."

A classic example of differentiation is provided by Maytag washers. In the washing machine market the existence of many competing brands has led to lower prices and declining profit margins for many firms. But Maytag's differentiation is based on quality and reliability, which allows it to charge prices 15 percent higher than the competition while maintaining a high market share.[4] Note that this differentiation exists in the minds of consumers, not necessarily in the product. GE, for example, claims that its product quality is as good as Maytag's, but consumers still perceive Maytag's quality as higher.

Maytag has reinforced this consumer perception with a very successful series of advertisements. As Exhibit 9-3 shows, most North Americans can identify Maytag's famous "lonely repairman" who constantly sits idle because Maytag products never break down. But this ad campaign works only because it reinforces what consumers believe to be true and have heard from people owning Maytag machines.

Industrial buyers prize reliability even more, perhaps, than consumers because equipment breakdowns can halt production. Thus Caterpillar differentiates its earth-moving equipment on the basis of durability, global spare parts service, and a strong dealer network. The firm has a strong network of loyal dealers and offers guaranteed delivery of spare parts anywhere in the world within forty-eight hours.

THE NARROW-FOCUS ADVANTAGE

Cost-leadership and product-differentiation strategies are designed to make an impact on broad markets. By contrast, strategies to achieve a **narrow-focus advantage**—the third type of strategy referred to in chapter objective three—are designed to appeal to a narrowly defined target market by creating greater customer value for this segment through a better understanding of its needs and wants.

A narrow-focus strategy can be combined with either cost- or differentiation-advantage strategies. A cost focus means offering a narrow target market low prices, while a differentiation focus entails offering a narrow target market the perception of product uniqueness.

narrow-focus advantage
A strategy of gaining a competitive advantage by studying the needs and wants of a narrowly defined target market and creating greater customer value for it.

RISKS AND GAMBLES
NARROW-FOCUS STRATEGIES IN THE LUXURY AUTOMOBILE INDUSTRY[5]

A key question that has emerged in the fiercely competitive automotive industry of the 1990s is: How can a firm achieve competitive advantage in the market for luxury cars—highly profitable vehicles that sell for $40,000 (or U.S. $30,000).

The luxury market is highly segmented. In North America the Big Three have long dominated the low end of the market (under $40,000), while Mercedes and BMW have dominated the high end (over $40,000). In recent years, however, Honda's Acura division has successfully entered the low end of the luxury market, while Toyota's Lexus and Nissan's Infiniti have begun to challenge the high-end leaders.

Since its introduction in 1986 in the United States and 1987 in Canada, the Acura has enjoyed phenomenal success in North America. To avoid creating confusion about Acura's identity, the car is sold through independent Acura dealerships rather than through Honda's regular dealer system. With the Acura Legend featured at the top of the line, Acura models captured over 7 percent of the North American luxury car market in 1988—almost exactly the same as Mercedes-Benz. By the end of 1989, Acura's 300 dealers had sold nearly 400,000 cars.

How did Acura accomplish this stunning feat? By using *high value* as a tool for competitive entry. Acuras are marketed as cars of very high quality—a claim borne out by the fact that J. D. Powers & Associates, an independent automotive survey group, ranked Acura number one in its consumer satisfaction index for three consecutive years. What makes the honor so remarkable is that many Mercedes models, although outranked by Acura, sell for twice as much.

More recently, both Toyota and Nissan have entered the luxury car market using much the same strategy as Honda—that is, with totally new cars, engineered from the ground up, to be sold at specialized new dealerships across North America. Toyota spent six years developing its new luxury model, the Lexus, which sports a 32-valve V-8 engine and is touted by Toyota as a better-performing version of Mercedes and BMW models that cost twice as much. The target buyer for the Lexus LS is forty-three years old and has an annual household income of $100,000. When the Lexus was unveiled in the summer of 1989, the head of U.S. sales and marketing for BMW was unimpressed. Gunter Kramer accused the new car of having no tradition: "At this end of the market, a tradition of prestige is what brings in buyers," he said. In the long run, Toyota's success with the Lexus may hinge on its ability to create a new image from scratch. At present some of the car's body styling is borrowed from Mercedes.

Image is also a key issue for Nissan's new Infiniti line, headed by the Infiniti Q45. Nissan's introductory ads, which featured unusual zenlike images of nature rather than any information about Infiniti's high-performance capabilities, aroused some controversy. As one industry analyst put it: "What they've clearly been trying to do is develop an anticipation for the vehicle itself, and they're creating a mystery about it."

Existing market leaders have not taken the Japanese challenge lightly. German manufacturers have responded by lowering prices. BMW has stopped producing models with 4-cylinder engines—today's BMWs have either a 6- or an 8-cylinder engine. The Germans are banking on the premise that tradition and prestige—intangibles dependent on perception and image—will remain a competitive advantage in the upper end of the market.

Domestic car makers have responded to the foreign challenge in the luxury car market in different ways. First, Ford made major changes in its Lincoln Continental to compete against the Acura at the low end of the market. Then in 1989, in a bid to enter the high-end market against BMW and Mercedes-Benz, Ford paid U.S. $2.6 billion for Jaguar, the British manufacturer of classic sports and luxury cars. According to Ford of Europe Chairman L. Lindsay Halstead, the Jaguar acquisition fulfilled "a longtime strategic objective of entering the luxury car market in a significant way."

The Jaguar purchase is a questionable strategy. As one automotive analyst notes, "Jaguar's classy image is its most cherished possession," while, as Daniel Jones, professor of motor industry management at the University of Cardiff's Business School, observes, "the Ford name is synonymous with bread and butter." Will consumers buy a Jaguar from Ford?

Cost Focus Firms using a narrow cost-focus strategy offer lower prices than their competitors to tightly defined market segments. For example, Dell Computer and AST Research sell their IBM personal computer "clones" for much lower prices than IBM gets for its versions. Their strategy is to keep costs and overhead to a minimum so they can offer a significant price advantage to consumers. As Thomas Yuen, chief operating officer of AST, puts it, IBM has "too big an infrastructure to be competitive in pricing."[6]

Differentiation Focus Cray Research made a clear decision to differentiate narrowly when it decided to focus on the supercomputer market—which totals only $1.7 billion worldwide—and ignore the minicomputer market. Supercomputers, the most powerful computers available, cost between $5 million and $25 million; they have mostly scientific rather than commercial applications.

This narrow-differentiation strategy has enabled Cray to create value and competitive advantage in supercomputers, but the Cray story since the late 1980s illustrates the strategy's risks. In 1989 slumping demand for supercomputers forced Cray to lay off 400 employees—the first time such action was in the company's seventeen-year history—and drove its stock down over 100 points from its 1987 high. Cray has little choice but to maintain its chosen focus, however, because abandoning it would mean losing much of the power and leverage the company has acquired by serving a narrowly defined and demanding market. In 1990 Cray did enlarge its focus slightly by buying a company that makes "mini-supercomputers" that are nearly as powerful as Cray's computers but cost only half a million dollars.[7]

DEVELOPING A COMPETITIVE STRATEGY ●

In addition to competing at the product and brand levels, firms need a competitive strategy at the corporate level—that is, every company needs to decide where it will locate itself in relation to its competitors. Basically, it has two choices: it can aim to become (or remain) the market leader, or it can use a strategy of market following. These two basic strategies are the focus of the fourth chapter objective.

MARKET-LEADER STRATEGY

Observers generally define a firm as having the competitive advantage of **market leadership** if it has twice the overall market share of its closest competitor. Thus, as Figure 9-4 shows, the market leader might have 40 percent of the market, the number-two company 20 percent, and all others combined 40 percent.

Often the market leader is the firm that first penetrated a market and has held on to that leading position. Such market leaders include well-known global firms like 3M, Procter & Gamble, Hertz, Caterpillar, GE, Sony, Nintendo, Louis Vuitton, and Daimler Benz.

A **market challenger** can displace the market leader by means of an innovative marketing strategy and secure a leading position. The greatest dangers for a leader are complacency and fear of taking risks. Recognizing challengers' strengths is the prerequisite for beating them. For example, Hallmark Cards, the world's largest greeting card maker, reacted to inroads made by more offbeat card makers by forming its own Shoebox Cards division.

Regardless of how they gained market leadership, firms can only hold on to this position by maintaining a competitive advantage in one or more

market leadership
The competitive advantage enjoyed by a company that has twice the market share of its closest competitor and successfully defends that position against all competitors.

market challenger
A firm seeking to displace the market leader by means of an innovative marketing strategy.

**Figure 9-4
Competitive Advantage
and Market Share**

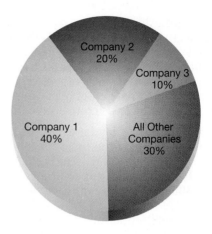

areas of the marketing mix. Superiority in *any* element of the marketing mix can constitute a *decisive point of advantage*: Thus the advantage may take the form of a significantly better product (including packaging), better marketing communications, better distribution, or a better price (lower in most cases, but not always). Note that the four topic heads in this section reflect the four P's of the marketing mix.

Voulez-Vous Vuitton?

The French firm of Louis Vuitton has long been a market leader in fine leather goods. New Yorkers who visit this 57th Street shop can choose from an array of expensive handbags, briefcases, luggage, and other items.

Product Leadership 3M has relied on strong and innovative **product leadership**—being first to launch an innovative product or to add new product features and benefits—to maintain its number-one position in adhesives and related products. Thanks in part to a system that rewards employees for new ideas with a piece of the profits, 3M develops about 200 new products every year. Two of its greatest successes have been a tape for mending broken bones and the ubiquitous Post-it notes, but as Exhibit 9-4 suggests, 3M's interests are broad.

Companies that do not remain innovative in their product offerings may find themselves displaced by market challengers. Before Sony launched the first home video-cassette recorder (VCR), the Betamax, in May 1975, the company had consented to share video-recording patents with Matsushita and JVC in the hope that all three companies could agree on a worldwide standard for a home-use VCR. Unfortunately, Sony was too insistent that the other companies adopt the Betamax technology with virtually no changes. Sony's competitors resisted on the grounds that there was a "basic inadequacy" in Sony's technology: the first home Betamax models could only

**Exhibit 9-4
Product
Leadership**

**3M
demonstrates
product
leadership by
addressing
health concerns.**

307

COMPETITIVE
ADVANTAGE AND
POSITIONING

Before creating our furniture stripper, we
considered people who don't even own furniture.

Your hobby shouldn't be hazardous to your family's health.

That's why we invented Safest Stripper™ paint and varnish remover. Unlike conventional strippers, it has no harmful fumes and won't hurt the skin. It's non-flammable and even cleans up easily with water.

But, this is just one example of our innovative thinking. We also invented Scotch-Brite™ Soft Scour!™ scrub sponges

for scratch-free cleaning. Post-it™ Brand removable notes to help busy people communicate effectively. And personal care products like Heat Comfort™ microwaveable hot packs to help relax muscles.

3M is constantly solving problems with breakthrough ideas for home, office, industry and health care. So that every day, in 135 countries around the world, people benefit from 3M products and services.

Innovation working for you™

3M

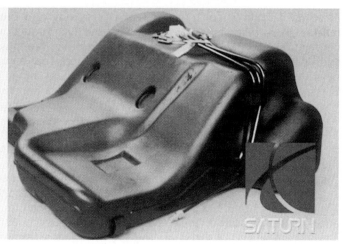

record for one hour. JVC and Matsushita quickly and quietly (without Sony's knowledge) improved the technology, and scarcely more than two years after the Betamax was launched, they introduced video-cassette recorders in a new VHS (video home system) format that could record for four hours—enough time to tape an entire football game. Today the Betamax is virtually obsolete.

price leadership
A strategy of gaining a competitive advantage by initiating a price change in a given product category and stimulating other companies to follow suit.

Price Leadership Some companies achieve a number-one position through **price leadership** that is based on their industry position as low-cost producer. For example, Intel and other winners in the integrated-circuits industry adopted the strategy of pricing aggressively to increase sales. They then managed the growth in production volume to drive their costs down so they could sell the expanded volume at a profit.

Service firms can also use price leadership as a competitive advantage. For example, Thrifty Rent-a-Car does not place its facilities in or even very near airport terminals in large cities. By avoiding the high property rental costs at airports, Thrifty saves enough money to pay for the shuttle buses it operates for its clients—and is still able to offer lower prices than other major rental agencies.

Market challengers often use low price as a wedge for entering a market and eroding the position of the market leader. Typically, the challenger offers a product that is just as good or even better than the leader's product—but at a lower price. The new offer is hard to refuse because it promises consumers more value. For example, in North America the Acura Legend, Lexus, and Infiniti sold, when they first appeared, for about half the price of a comparably sized Mercedes or BMW, the established German luxury cars they see as their competition.

Once market challengers become market leaders, they can raise their prices to increase their profits because the market has recognized the value of their product. By doing so, of course, they create a hole for future market challengers to drive through. One of the biggest mistakes that any leader can make is to assume that the *price cue* of a potential challenger is an indicator of the *overall value* of the challenger's offering—that is, that price signals the potential value of a product to the consumer, with a higher price indicating greater overall value, a lower price signaling lower overall value. The challenger must offer *something* to encourage customers to *switch,* and price is usually the single most compelling benefit in the consumer's mind. If the challenger is offering equivalent or greater value than the leader, customers will eventually become aware of this advantage. The balance of market power will then shift so that the challenger preempts the old leader and the new market leader then has an opportunity to raise prices.

Distribution Leadership Some companies gain competitive advantage by achieving **distribution leadership**—developing innovative or superior product distribution. In the United States Snap-On Tools has a competitive advantage based on distribution. The firm sells its tools right off its trucks, which make routine calls on many automotive garages around the nation.

Distribution can also help new firms in a market beat the market leader. A prime example is Wal-Mart, which has taken the discount crown from Kmart. Wal-Mart has a dual distribution advantage over Kmart: first, it got its foot in the door by opening stores in towns Kmart rejected as too small to be profitable; and second, its regional distribution centers keep its stores steadily supplied, even when demand for a product is higher than anticipated. The combination of concentrated purchasing, which gives it great bargaining leverage to obtain the lowest prices from suppliers, and low physical distribution costs gives Wal-Mart a significant cost advantage over its competition.

Marketing Communication Leadership Finally, marketing communication strategies can create market leadership. As we saw in Chapter 1, Nike owes its number-one status largely to its innovative advertising—a form of **marketing communication leadership.**

In the cosmetics industry Estée Lauder was able to take the number-one spot away from long-time market leader Revlon with an innovative sales-promotion strategy. Lauder pioneered the practice of giving customers special "bonus gifts" in return for making a purchase of a certain dollar amount. Today most cosmetics companies consider such premiums a necessary cost of doing business.

MARKET-FOLLOWING STRATEGY

When a company allows other firms to introduce innovative products and checks market response before changing its own products, it is known as a **market follower**. Although *following* is a notion that has negative connotations, there are successful and unsuccessful ways to be a market follower. *Proactive* market following is a strategy that can lead to great success and profitability, while *reactive* market following is indeed a negative business strategy.

Proactive Following The **proactive market follower** seeks competitive advantage by refining or improving on the market leader's innovations. A creative proactive follower learns from the leader's experience and quickly offers customers a product that is as good as or better than the leader's product—usually at a lower price.

Japan's Matsushita Industrial Electric Company is an excellent example of a proactive market follower. Matsushita's strategy of "creative followership" is based on the idea that leaders often take a beating getting a product introduced. As one observer notes: "Matsushita likes to come in second, after the trail has been blazed a little and you can see which way is safest." Matsushita's products are rarely the last word in the field, according to electronics buffs, but they have a way of arriving just when the larger public is ready to consider buying that particular item and the buffs have turned their attention to something newer. And they frequently come with a lower price than competing products, a few extra features, or both. The experts may not be dazzled, but the competition usually is.[8]

Reactive Following As the phrase suggests, the **reactive market follower** reacts to the leader's innovations by playing "catch-up" and cloning

---

distribution leadership
A strategy of gaining a competitive advantage through innovative or superior product distribution.

marketing communication leadership
A strategy of gaining a competitive advantage through innovative use of marketing communications.

309
COMPETITIVE ADVANTAGE AND POSITIONING

market follower
A firm that allows other firms to introduce innovations into the market and waits to verify market response before making any changes in its own marketing offerings.

proactive market follower
A firm that seeks competitive advantage by refining or improving on a market leader's innovations.

reactive market follower
A firm that "clones" the products of market leaders.

them. Unlike the proactive follower, the reactive follower does not have an explicit strategy for creating competitive advantage.

Wherever a company has lost market share and position, it is often because it is a reactive follower. In the telephone wars in Canada, AGT was a reactive follower of the pricing innovations of its long-distance competitors. Several months after the deregulation of phone services, AGT decided to "take off the gloves" and came out swinging with an aggressive campaign of advertising, direct mail, and telemarketing that was designed to win back lost customers with new products and pricing strategies. The initial response from some consumers to AGT's effort was poor because the company continued its reactive approach.

COMPETITIVE ADVANTAGE THROUGH INNOVATION

As you have seen, competitive advantages of all kinds often rest on innovation. Successful competitive strategies are also innovative. Writing in the *Harvard Business Review*, Gary Hamel and C. K. Prahalad note that "few competitive advantages are long-lasting. Keeping up with existing advantages is not the same as building new advantages. The essence of strategy lies in creating tomorrow's competitive advantages faster than competitors mimic the ones you possess today. An organization's capacity to improve existing skills and learn new ones is the most defensible competitive advantage of all."[9]

This approach is founded on the ideas of W. E. Deming, who insisted that a company must commit itself to constant improvement (what the Japanese call *kaizen)* in order to win out in a competitive struggle. For years Deming's message fell on deaf ears in North America, while the Japanese took his views to heart, even naming their most prestigious business award after him. Finally, however, North American manufacturers are starting to pay attention. So has the Canadian government, which now honors quality producers with the Canadian Award for Business Excellence.

BEHIND THE SCENES

TURNING QUALITY INTO COMPETITIVE ADVANTAGE[10]

Believe it or not, Japanese products were once renowned for their shoddiness. In fact, the label "Made in Japan" was virtually a guarantee of inferior quality until an American management theorist named W. Edwards Deming went to Japan to lecture on quality control in 1950. Committed to a human-relations model of management, Deming preached the gospel that management is above all *people* management, and people will do quality work if they are taught how to do it and are given the proper conditions for doing it.

Tom Peters, an adherent of Deming's human-relations philosophy and coauthor of the influential books *In Search of Excellence* and *A Passion for Excellence*, carries on Deming's "quality crusade" in today's increasingly competitive environment. Against managers who blame unions for the low quality of many U.S. products he quotes Ken Iverson, president of Nucor Corporation, a non-union American steel producer, on the relationship between productivity and labor:

> I've heard people say that Nucor is proof that unions per se have a negative impact on worker productivity. That's nonsense! That conveniently ignores vital questions like: What's the quality of direction being given the workers? Where are the resources the workers need to get the job done efficiently? Where's the opportunity for workers to contribute ideas about how to do the job better? The real impediment to producing a higher-quality product more efficiently isn't the workers, union or nonunion; it's management.

The Case for Positioning

Sri Lanka is still known as Ceylon when it comes to tea. Being recognized as a quality producer allows Dilmah to promote its Ceylon teas in upscale packaging.

In the 1950s, when the United States held unquestioned leadership in most industries, American manufacturers were not interested in hearing such Deming pronouncements as: "Henry Ford made great contributions, but his Model T was not a quality car." But when Deming insisted that companies must commit themselves to constant quality improvement in order to survive in an increasingly competitive environment, the Japanese listened carefully—and the rest, as they say, is history. "The father of the Japanese quality revolution" was for a long time largely ignored in his own country, but today his ideas are well known and highly respected in American management circles. When the editors of *Fortune* magazine surveyed American CEOs in 1990 about prospects for global competitiveness, they discovered a renewed emphasis on quality. "We have shaken off our lethargy," reported Grumman Aircraft's John O'Brien. "We are paying more attention to quality, and that has made us more competitive."

Deming, who declared that management is 90 percent of the quality problem, laid down the fourteen rules of thumb listed in Table 9-2 for managers who want to make quality a competitive tool.

COMPETITIVE INNOVATION

In addition to improving their own products, many firms have gained a competitive advantage by *disadvantaging* rivals through "competitive innovation." Hamel and Prahalad define competitive innovation as "the art of containing competitive risks within manageable proportions."[11] They identify four successful approaches to competitive innovation utilized by Japanese firms: *building layers of advantage, searching for loose bricks, changing the rules of engagement,* and *collaborating.*[12]

Layers of Advantage A company faces less risk in competitive encounters if it has a wide portfolio of advantages. Successful companies steadily build such portfolios by establishing layers of advantage, one on top of another. Consider the TV industry in Japan. By 1970, Japan was not only the world's largest producer of black-and-white TV sets but was well on its way to

| TABLE 9-2 | HOW TO MAKE QUALITY A COMPETITIVE TOOL |

1. Plan for the long term, not for the next month or year.

2. Never be complacent about the quality of your product.

3. Establish statistical control over your production processes and require your suppliers to do so as well.

4. Deal with the fewest number of suppliers—the best ones, of course.

5. Find out whether your problems are confined to particular parts of the production process or stem from the overall process itself.

6. Train workers for the job that you are asking them to perform.

7. Raise the quality of your line supervisors.

8. "Drive out fear."

9. Encourage departments to work closely together rather than to concentrate on departmental or divisional distinction.

10. Do not be sucked into adopting strictly numerical goals, including the widely popular formula of "zero defects."

11. Require your workers to do quality work, not just to be at their stations from 9 to 5.

12. Train your employees to understand statistical methods.

13. Train your employees in new skills as the need arises.

14. Make top managers responsible for implementing these principles.

Source: W. Edwards Deming, "Improvement of Quality and Productivity Through Action by Management," *National Productivity Review 1* (Winter 1981–1982):12–22.

becoming the leader in producing color sets. The main competitive advantage for such companies as Matsushita at that time was *low labor costs*.

Because they realized that cost advantages are often temporary, the Japanese added layers of *quality and reliability* advantages by building plants large enough to serve world markets. Much of this output did not carry the manufacturer's brand name. For example, Matsushita sold televisions to companies such as RCA, which put their own brand names on Matsushita products. The idea was simple: A product sold was a product sold, no matter whose label it carried.

To build the next layer of advantage, the Japanese spent the 1970s investing heavily in new marketing channels and branding to gain recognition. This strategy added yet another layer of competitive advantage: the *global brand franchise*—that is, a global customer base. By the late 1970s, channels and brand awareness were well enough established to support the introduction of new products that could benefit from global marketing—VCRs and photocopy machines, for example.

Loose Bricks The second approach to competitive innovation takes advantage of the "loose bricks" in the defensive walls of competitors who focus on a narrow market segment. For example, for many years, Harley Davidson concentrated its efforts on large motorcycles, so it was unconcerned when Honda entered the motorcycle market because Honda's first exports to the North America were bikes with small (50cc) engines. Managers at Harley weren't aware of—or didn't realize the significance of—Honda's experimental racing of larger bikes in Europe. But Honda used this activity to gain important experience in large-displacement engine design and technology. Harley was caught napping, and by 1983 Honda had over 50 percent of the U.S. market for motorcycles with 700cc engines or larger.

Harley responded to the competitive challenge by shamelessly copying Japanese lean manufacturing technology to get its quality up to world class standards (that is, up to Japanese standards). Harley's newfound quality, combined with its superior knowledge of what customers in its niche wanted, led to a dramatic comeback for Harley and a setback for Honda. By 1993, Harley had captured over 70 percent of the market for superheavyweight motorcycles and Honda was down to about 25 percent. Harley was able to make such an impressive comeback not only because it had deep strengths based upon its knowledge of what customers really wanted but also because its management was determined to survive and succeed. The will to succeed is a critical factor in creating competitive advantage.

Changing the Rules   The third approach to competitive innovation involves refusing to play by the rules set by industry leaders. For example, in the copier market, while Kodak was imitating the marketing strategies of Xerox, the leader in photocopiers, Canon wrote a new rulebook.

While Xerox built a wide range of copiers, Canon built standardized machines and components, reducing its manufacturing costs. While Xerox employed a huge direct sales force, Canon chose to distribute through office-product dealers. Since Canon designed serviceability as well as reliability into its products, it could depend on dealers for service rather than create a service network. Canon also decided to sell rather than lease its machines, freeing the company from the burden of financing a lease base. In another major departure, Canon targeted its copiers at secretaries and department managers rather than at the heads of corporate duplicating operations.[13]

The result? Since the late-1980s, Canon copiers have been outselling Xerox in both Canada and the United States. In Canada in 1993, Canon sold 28,902 copiers, compared to Xerox's 24,510.[14] Canon was also the first to introduce full-color copiers and copiers with "connectivity"—the ability to print images from sources such as video camcorders and computers. The Canon example shows how an innovative marketing strategy—with fresh approaches to product, pricing, distribution, and selling—can lead to an overall competitive advantage in the marketplace.

In another effort to change the rules—or at least to bend them—Mercedes-Benz and Nissan have offered lower-priced luxury automobile models (see Exhibit 9-5). The new models carry the name and get the same dealer service as the more expensive flagship models.

Collaboration   The final approach to competitive advantage involves using know-how developed by other companies. Such *collaboration* may take the form of licensing agreements, joint ventures, or partnerships. For example, Kmart Canada has a partnership with Rubbermaid Canada Inc., which in turn has a partnership program with Husky Injection Molding Inc. Another example is one of the legendary licensing agreements in modern business history: Sony's licensing of transistor technology from AT&T in the 1950s for $25,000. As you will see in the section that follows, this bargain gave Sony access to the transistor that allowed it to become a world leader in the manufacture and marketing of portable radios.

However and wherever a firm chooses to create competitive advantage, one fact remains clear. Competitive advantage is a "win-win" situation for producer and buyer. The producer stands to gain sales, earnings, and market share. The buyer gains a better product, better price, better distribution, or better marketing communication—in short, a better fulfillment of needs.

Exhibit 9-5
Competition Among Luxury Cars Heats Up

Offering an affordable luxury car model, Mercedes says it has the competitive advantage. Infiniti, also pushing a new lower-priced model, counters that if you buy an "affordable" model from another company, you may be treated like a second-class citizen.

RISKS AND GAMBLES

OF GOOD THINGS IN SMALL PACKAGES[15]

In March 1952, Masaru Ibuka, managing director and cofounder of Sony, made his first trip to the United States. While in New York, he learned that AT&T had decided to license a discovery made five years earlier at Bell Laboratories, AT&T's major research unit. The discovery was the transistor. Although the transistor may seem primitive today, it was revolutionary in the early 1950s. Smaller, sturdier, and less power-hungry than the vacuum tubes that were then an integral part of radios, tape recorders, and other professional electronic equipment, the transistor promised to make possible sophisticated electronic devices for casual everyday use. In fact, the transistor embodied the very goal that had led Ibuka to found his company in the first place—namely, making high technology available to the average consumer.

When Ibuka first encountered the transistor, he wanted to sign a licensing agreement with AT&T. First, however, Sony had to secure the approval of Japan's Ministry of International Trade and Industry (MITI) to pay the $25,000 required by AT&T of any licensee. Originally, MITI was not in an accommodating mood: it saw the deal as an unpromising combination of a fledgling company (Sony) with unproved technology. Moreover, Toshiba, Mitsubishi, and Hitachi—all bigger companies than Sony—were preparing to enter the transistor business with technical guidance from RCA. Why was Sony trying to go it alone?

Two years later, however, MITI gave in to Ibuka's insistence that Sony could make its licensing agreement with AT&T work. Ibuka then returned to the United States to learn about his new acquisition. He had already decided to use transistors to make radios that, as he put it, would be "small enough so each individual will be able to carry them around for his own use, with power that will enable civilization to reach even those areas that have no electric power yet."

When Ibuka mentioned the word "radio" at AT&T, however, he received a paternal lecture to the effect that while the transistor was a fascinating discovery, its near-term applications were limited. He was told that so far no one had been able to manufacture a transistor that could even come close to handling the high frequencies that a radio would require and was advised to try making hearing aids instead.

Ibuka remained determined about his goal (*gaman,* or persistence, has always been a highly valued quality in Japanese culture). Sony's engineers had already learned a great deal about improving high-frequency output, or yield, while developing a line of tape recorders. In fact, Sony already held a monopoly in the Japanese market for tape recorders—a cash cow product whose profits it was reinvesting in transistor research. After months of patient and expensive research, Sony engineers finally succeeded in making the necessary improvements in the yield of transistors.

By 1957, Sony was ready to announce the world's first pocket-size radio—the TR-63. Actually, it was a little larger than "pocket size," but Sony quickly solved that problem: it went into the shirt business solely to provide its salespeople with radio-size pockets with which to demonstrate its new product. The world, if not entirely fooled, was at least entranced. In the years that followed, Sony sold over a million of its "pocketables"—along with hundreds of thousands of transistorized models with AM/FM and dozens of other refinements. The company's dominance in the transistorized radio market was temporary—as almost every very successful new-product advantage is apt to be—but for two years Sony took pride in the fact that it had the portable radio market in its pocket.

POSITIONING AND
REPOSITIONING ●

Where there is no competition, there is no need for a positioning strategy. The more competitive the target market, however, the greater the need for a positioning strategy that will appeal to consumers and separate the product from its competitors.

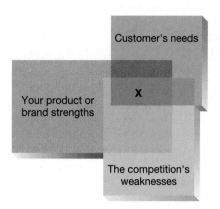

Figure 9-5
Identifying
Competitive
Advantage

positioning
The act of formulating a marketing mix that locates a product in the mind of the customer in relation to alternative products or services offered by competitors with the aim of achieving competitive advantage.

The term *positioning* first appeared in a 1969 article by Al Ries and Jack Trout in *Industrial Marketing*. In that article and later publications, Ries and Trout described the process whereby a firm attempts to cope with a larger, more established competitor's position in the minds of consumers.[16] Ries and Trout coined the term *positioning era* to describe the realization in the 1970s that a marketing campaign had to do more than just offer something for sale; if it was to be successful, it had to get the product into the minds of consumers.

Positioning, the topic of the fifth chapter objective, is the act of formulating a marketing mix that locates your product in the mind of the customer in relation to the products offered by your competitors so that your product achieves a competitive advantage. In Figure 9-5 the X identifies the location where a product is positioned most favorably vis-à-vis its competition. In a marketing plan the positioning statement is always written in terms of how *consumers* will see the product: it summarizes the *subjective* evaluation of the product in comparison to its competition. Rockport Shoes, for example, is positioned as "the leader of the walking fitness movement." Yahoon Supermarket in Vancouver positions itself as offering Canada's widest selection of oriental food. Curtis Mathes is trying to get back into the home entertainment market by resurrecting its successful 1970s strategy: positioning its products in the high-end home electronics market as "the most expensive television sets in America." Canadian beef producers are now positioning their product as a healthy part of a balanced diet, and are using Olympic athletes to underscore that idea (see Exhibit 9-6). Mercedes is positioned exclusively as a luxury car in North America, but in Europe it is positioned as a luxury car, taxi, and truck.

Positioning is an important exercise with a *new* product or brand. When Honda introduced its motorcycles into the North America, its advertising strategy centered around the message: "You meet the nicest people on a Honda." This message helped position Honda against Harley-Davidson's Hell's Angels image.

Repositioning is changing the position of an existing product or brand. Many of the examples in the rest of this section represent repositioning, which is often required if a product has never been clearly positioned—which may be true even if it has been on the market for years—if its original positioning has become obsolete, or if a new position will reach a larger market.

BASIC POSITIONING STRATEGIES

Essentially, marketers have only two strong choices in positioning their products versus the competition: they can go head-to-head against other firms in direct competition, or they can try to differentiate their own product—that is, make it unique so that it has no direct competition. Using either of these two fundamental approaches, firms select from among the six basic strategies that are the subject of the sixth chapter objective: they position their products by attributes or benefits, by quality/price, by use, by user, by product category, or by competitors.[17]

Attribute or Benefit The most frequently used positioning strategy exploits a particular product attribute, benefit, or feature. Economy, reliability, and durability are the most frequently used attributes in this strategy. For example, Volvos are known for their solid construction and durability in crashes.

Products can also be positioned using a combination of attributes. While Crest toothpaste became a leading brand by positioning itself on its

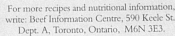
Exhibit 9-6
Positioning for Health

The Canadian Beef industry now positions its product as a healthy part of a balanced diet. To tie in the ideas of health and good nutrition, popular Canadian Olympic athletes (such as gold medalist Mark Tewkesbury) are used to endorse the product.

proven "cavity prevention" benefit, Aim toothpaste was positioned as being both pleasant tasting and cavity fighting, and Aquafresh was positioned as a cavity fighter that also provided the benefit of fresh breath. The danger is that using more than one attribute in a positioning strategy may confuse consumers.

Apple positioned its Macintosh as easy to set up and learn to use. The initial success of this strategy enabled Apple to charge premium prices, but when the competition adopted many of Apple's special features, this position lost its appeal although Apple still leads in connectivity of peripherals as it continues to make its own. This underlines an important principle in positioning: You can be certain that if you stand still, you are going to be overtaken by competitors.

Quality/Price It is useful to think of this strategy in terms of a continuum from high to low. Some marketers pursue a strategy of high fashion/quality at

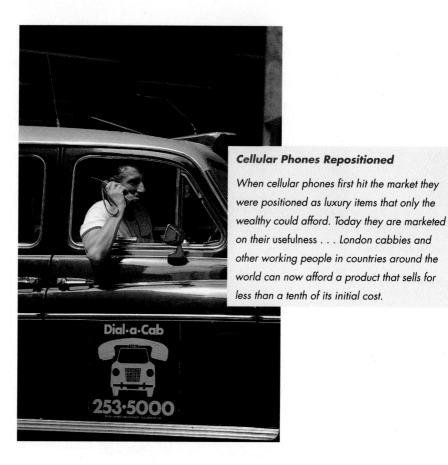

Cellular Phones Repositioned

When cellular phones first hit the market they were positioned as luxury items that only the wealthy could afford. Today they are marketed on their usefulness . . . London cabbies and other working people in countries around the world can now afford a product that sells for less than a tenth of its initial cost.

a high price, while others position their brands as offering good value (rather than "low quality") at a low price. In retailing, for example, department stores such as The Bay and Eaton's position themselves at the high end of the continuum, Sears falls below them, and discount stores such as Kmart and Zellers are still further down the scale.

Makers of imported vodka brands took advantage of a unique opportunity to position by quality/price. According to U.S. law, any substance labeled "vodka" must be a neutral spirit "without distinctive character, aroma, or taste." Imported vodkas are exempt from the law, however, and they do, in fact, taste different.[18] Marketers of vodka brands like Absolut and Stolichnaya have taken advantage of the exemption and successfully positioned their brands as premium products at double the price of "ordinary" vodka.

Use and User To stimulate consumption of products whose growth has slowed, marketers sometimes develop new ways for consumers to use a product. A classic example of this approach is Cow Brand baking soda. After years of being positioned as a baking product, baking soda was repositioned as a refrigerator deodorant. Shoppers were encouraged to pick up two boxes—one for the cupboard and one for the refrigerator. Other examples of positioning by use are A1 Steak Sauce (for hamburgers as well as steak) and orange juice ("It's not just for breakfast any more"). Positioning by use can also be a secondary positioning strategy aimed at increasing consumption on a seasonal basis. For example, Ralston's Chex cereals are positioned as a snack-mix food near the holidays.

Yet another strategy entails associating a product with a user or class of users, as we saw earlier in the case of Honda. More recently, Harley Davidson has successfully broadened its image to reach a new class of motorcycle enthusiasts: aging baby-boomer professionals.

Many beverage products are positioned or repositioned according to the user. Pepsico has attempted to change Mountain Dew's hillbilly image in order to expand consumption in urban areas. Mountain Dew traditionally appealed to rural youths and blue-collar young adults. New advertising features actor Patrick Swayze, and a new label features mountains, evergreens, and streams in an attempt to appeal to urban teenagers.

Product Category The objective of this strategy may be to get consumers to associate a particular product with a product category for which they have a positive image. For example, Folger's instant coffee positioned itself as tasting like freshly brewed coffee. Or the objective may be to get consumers to dissociate a product from a product category for which they have a negative image. GM's "This is not your father's Oldsmobile" campaign illustrates the second form of the strategy. Big American cars have traditionally been associated with people over fifty—not the thirty-five- to forty-four-year-olds GM sought as new customers. However, despite a high level of consumer awareness and recall (the campaign scored well in *Advertising Age* magazine's monthly poll of best-remembered ads), relatively few younger people bought Oldsmobiles—perhaps because despite GM's positioning claim, its Olds models were still being designed with older, traditional car buyers in mind.[19]

Competitors Positioning relative to competitors can succeed when a competitor is well known or has a well-established image. The most famous example of this strategy dates back to 1959, when Avis, the car rental company, began to use the daring advertising slogan "We're number two, but we try harder." It was then considered daring to acknowledge that a competitor was number one, but the campaign met with great success. By publicly stating that it was number two behind Hertz and making a promise, Avis linked the promise and its position in a way that gave the promise credibility. The logic of Avis's announcement was that the company tried harder *because* it was number two. Avis succeeded in separating itself from all the other car rental agencies and gained tremendous consumer recognition. Before Avis's novel positioning, there were Hertz and "all the rest." After the campaign, there were Hertz and Avis and *then* "all the rest."

TASKS OF POSITIONING

Regardless of the strategy employed, positioning must accomplish three basic tasks: it must define the product for customers; it must help customers remember the product; and it must communicate the product's attributes that are relevant to customers. Positioning begins with product definition. Pledge, for example, became a major marketing success when it realized that it was a dusting aid as well as a furniture wax. Defining a product is not as easy as it may seem, however.

Sometimes the positioning problem lies with defining the category. For example, when Apple introduced Newton, its personal digital assistant or PDA, the company decided to attempt to create a new software category that Apple could dominate. Apple's challenge was to get market acceptance for this new category, which few understood at the time of Newton's launch. The company's marketing focus was not on the Newton hardware, but rather on the PDA operating software.

Marketers must facilitate the customer's recall and evaluation. Try this simple test: Take out a piece of paper and write down all the brands of shampoo you can think of. Chances are you can't think of more than seven. The names you recalled are part of your *evoked set* (Figure 9-2) for shampoos—an exclusive club that marketers attempt to enter by positioning brands in your mind.

Positioning also reflects something Trout and Ries called "product ladders," a concept they developed to explain how products are evaluated against one another by consumers. Look at your list of shampoos and figure out your points of comparison—cleans better, smells better, leaves hair softer, is less damaging. Notice how some brands rank higher and some lower on these different features in your mind.

Although a position lies in the minds of consumers, it is generally the product's advertising, or *communications*, that establishes that positioning. Often positioning is achieved by exploiting a particular product attribute—Columbian coffee, for example, is positioned as the richest coffee in the world, Maytag points to the superior reliability built into Maytag appliances, and Avis emphasizes its customer service ("We try harder"). All of these positions were established through heavy advertising.

The attributes communicated may or may not reflect a real difference—the Maytag and Avis claims, for instance, are disputed by their competitors—but ultimately, the issue is decided in the consumer's mind. If a consumer firmly believes that Maytag is the most reliable washing machine, then General Electric's claims to the contrary are like the sound of a tree falling in a deserted forest.

perceptual map
A diagram that indicates how consumers rate various brands in terms of their most important decision-making criteria.

MAPPING PERCEPTIONS

Because a position is located in the mind of the consumer, positioning research has to grapple with questions about how people perceive products in a competitive situation. The most common type of analysis involves mapping product locations within consumers' "mental space." The result is a **perceptual map,** or diagram showing how consumers rate various brands and

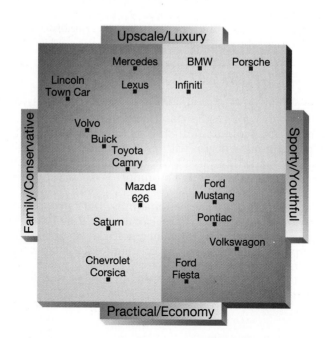

Figure 9-6
A Perceptual Map for Automobile Makes and Models

products in terms of their most important decision-making criteria.[20] Figure 9-6 is a perceptual map of automobiles in North America.

This type of analysis begins by determining the most relevant attributes of the product. If you have consumers rate your product and the competition on the two attributes most important to them you can then develop a two-dimensional perceptual map based on those ratings. For example, if you are evaluating the position of competing restaurants in the pizza category, you might have consumers rate the restaurants on such characteristics as price, ambiance, pizza quality, or service.

Perceptual maps are also useful when repositioning products whose position is unfocused or inappropriate. A perceptual map can show the differences between the product's current and desired positions. Repositioning a product requires a tremendous advertising effort. Miller beer and Marlboro cigarettes were both originally seen as women's products at a time when the women's market for cigarettes and beer was limited. Both were later repositioned as "macho" products for both sexes through extensive and costly advertising campaigns.

BOTTOM LINE REALITIES

WHEN DOING EVERYTHING WELL ISN'T ENOUGH

If we trace the evolution of the Honda Accord, we will see how Honda originally positioned this car in the market and the kind of customer it targeted. We will also see how Honda gained a competitive advantage and then lost it.

The first Accord was launched in 1976. It was a small, sporty coupe that sold for U.S. $3,995 and became instantly popular with the kind of buyers Honda was looking for—young singles, especially women. That year roughly 19,000 Accords were sold.

In 1977 and 1978 the original Accord was embellished with some luxury accessories, and its price rose sharply for the top-of-the-line LX version. The first Accord four-door sedan appeared in 1979, and the line was further expanded over the next few years—to four versions in 1981, with a top price of U.S. $9,950. That year sales rose to 172,557. Between 1976 and 1981, Honda carefully positioned the Accord to appeal to the affluent baby-boomer market by stressing quality, value, and stylishness—its marketing message was that the Accord was the car for thinking people.

A second-generation Accord appeared in 1982. Although somewhat larger and more stylish than its predecessor, it remained in the same price range. In succeeding years the Accord was upgraded with such equipment and amenities as a four-speed automatic transmission, a more powerful engine, and power windows.

A third-generation Accord followed in 1985. Again the car had grown more luxurious, featuring such advanced technology as a four-wheel, independent double-wishbone suspension. A coupe was added in 1989, when the Accord became one of the best-selling cars in North America.

With the fourth generation in 1990, the Accord tightened its grip on the biggest share of the largest segment of the automotive market. By this time, there were many repeat buyers who had, in a sense, grown up with the Accord. Honda had hooked this generation of buyers with the first Accord while it was young and continued to cultivate it as it grew older by providing high quality, style, performance, and value. By the time many of these consumers had reached middle-aged affluence, Honda was ready with the Acura, a higher-priced luxury car that targeted aging baby boomers.

End of story? Not quite! From 1989 through December

of 1992, Honda's Accord remained the best-selling car in the United States. In 1993, however, the number-one position was taken by Ford's Taurus. Sales of the Accord plunged 35 percent; the car did not even make the top five. What happened? The appreciation of the yen versus the U.S. dollar did not help: in mid-1993 the yen was up almost 20 percent against the U.S. dollar. But that only partially explains Honda's decline.

Honda's problem is competition: everyone else in the marketplace is getting better faster. Both North American and Japanese competitors' quality and dealer services are up, and many of Honda's competitors are offering what the market feels are more exciting cars. In targeting the mass market, Honda lost touch with its original customer base. New models were designed to satisfy a broad range of demographic groups and this led to products that excited no one. As one expert put it, the Accord "is one bland machine. It does everything well, but it doesn't excite."[21]

Honda was a very successful niche marketer that faltered when it targeted a broader market. Where did Honda go wrong? What do you think led to its setback in 1993? If you were a marketing consultant, how would you advise Honda to go about reclaiming its position and competitive advantage? ■

KEY POINTS SUMMARY ▼

1. Competitive advantage is achieved by creating more value than one's competition. It starts with an analysis of three factors: the market's needs, the firm's strengths and weaknesses, and competitors' strengths and weaknesses. Though value is based on a product's innate advantages, it is subjective in that it ultimately exists in the mind of the buyer.

2. Direct competition for a firm's products includes only those products within the same category as the firm's products. Indirect competition includes products in a variety of categories that function as alternative purchase choices.

3. Competitive advantage generally stems from cost leadership or product differentiation. In each of these areas a firm may employ one of three general business strategies: cost leadership (broad), product differentiation (broad), or a focus on a narrowly defined target market.

4. Firms may take or seek to take (challenge) a position of market leadership, or they may become market followers. Market leadership may derive from competitive advantages in any area of the marketing mix. Proactive market following can be profitable for firms, but reactive market following is not profitable in the long run.

5. Positioning a product, or getting consumers to associate the product with certain features and qualities that its competitors either lack or underemphasize, is particularly crucial in launching new products. Distinguishing a new product from tens or hundreds of competing brands requires finding the special way in which the product can be seen as unique or as fulfilling a newly recognized consumer need. Repositioning can also be extremely important when a product was incorrectly positioned at its launch, when its positioning has become outdated, or when marketers become aware of a wholly new market for the product. Positioning, when it is successful, can greatly enhance competitive advantage by means of a number of specific strategies.

6. Of the six major positioning strategies discussed here, emphasizing a particular attribute or benefit of a product is the most commonly used. Quality and price strategies are often used in interaction; for example, a high-quality, high-price product may attract one target audience, whereas a high-quality-for-low-price strategy may work with another. A third strategy focuses on devising new uses for existing products; a fourth attempts to address a group of potential users who share some specific need or want. Getting people to associate a product with an entire product category of which they have a positive image is a fifth positioning strategy. The sixth, used with great success in combating the rental-car industry leadership of Hertz, involves identifying a product as second only to the "number one" company; Avis's "We try harder," now belongs to marketing history.

DISCUSSION QUESTIONS ▼

1. How can a company measure its competitive advantage? How does a firm know if it is gaining or losing competitive advantage?

2. What are the advantages and disadvantages of being the market leader? Give three examples of market leaders other than those cited in this chapter.

3. What are the advantages and disadvantages of being the market challenger? the market follower? Give three examples of each of these strategies other than those cited in this chapter.

4. Give an example of each of the four major types of competitive advantage: cost leadership/narrow focus, cost leadership/broad focus, product differentiation/narrow focus, product differentiation/broad focus.

5. Which of the four innovation strategies discussed in the chapter would you expect to find used most often? Why?

6. Make a list of the brands in your evoked set for the following categories: athletic shoes, supermarkets, soft drinks.

7. If the president of your college called you in and asked how your school could create a competitive advantage for itself, what would you recommend? (Be sure to consider the costs as well as the benefits of your proposal.)

8. Describe the competitive situation for restaurants in your community—who competes with whom—and then analyze the various restaurants' points of competitive advantage.

9. Research a large company that does business on a global basis and describe its competitive advantages, its attitude toward market leadership/following, and whether its competitive focus is broad or narrow. Which of the innovation approaches discussed in this chapter does this firm appear to be taking?

10. Choose a local company and interview the manager about the firm's perception of its competitive situation. Does this company have a clear picture of its competitive advantages?

11. If you were the Pillsbury brand manager and were assigned to introduce a new product named Figurines, would you position it as a nutritional breakfast substitute and compete against other instant breakfast lines, or would you position it as a low-calorie snack and compete against granola bars?

Integrative Case ● Discussion Questions

The Body Shop*

1. How has The Body Shop's competitive advantage changed since 1976?

2. What is The Body Shop's competitive strategy?

Harley-Davidson

1. How does Harley position its heavyweight bikes?

2. Draw a perceptual map for Honda, BMW, and Harley heavyweight bikes. What should the vertical and horizontal axes be?

3. How has Harley established market leadership in the heavyweight bike category?

The Millennium Power System

1. Of what does Millennium's competitive advantage consist? Will they be able to sustain this advantage in the long run?

2. What is Millennium's competitive strategy (e.g., product leadership, price leadership). Should it continue to pursue this strategy?

*The three cases at the back of the book—"The Body Shop," "Harley-Davidson," and "The Millennium Power System"—illustrate topics discussed in all chapters of this book. Your instructor will tell you when to read a particular case and answer the discussion questions on it that appear at the end of each chapter.

Boots: Competitive Advantage

What do most individuals living outside of Canada picture when asked to describe their vision of the Canadian landscape? Typically, snow and ice, with the odd slab of back bacon thrown in. It seems that most of those foreign to Canada typically maintain a picture in their mind of a rugged, frozen landscape, complete with glaciers, dogsleds, and even the odd igloo.

While this stereotype may nag at those who wish to expound on the bounties of the Canadian nation and cultural mosaic, others have clearly adopted the Canadian cold weather cliché, and used it to bolster their competitive advantage in both domestic and foreign markets. While typical Canadian shoe store sales are comprised of only 20% of stock which originates in Canada, the vast bulk of this 20% is accounted for by boot sales. Canadian boot manufacturers have cultivated a distinct competitive advantage in the world boot market, not only for winter boots, but for a variety of product lines.

National identity has always played a significant role in consumer perceptions of the nature of products produced in various nations. The Swiss are famous for their watches and chocolate; the French for their food and wine; the Germans for exquisite automobiles; the Russians for vodka, caviar, and sable; the Japanese for high quality automobiles and technology-based products; and the Americans for being innovators in all product categories. Naturally, it falls that Canadians must be experts in products and services related to cold weather. Whether or not these categorizations are valid, the country of origin stereotype effects can be utilized to gain competitive advantage in the marketplace.

Canadian shoesellers and manufacturers realize that they cannot effectively compete against the low-production costs in the Far East, Brazil, or other emerging economies. Nor can they effectively compete against the perception that Italian-made shoes are the highest quality, or that American manufacturers produce the most innovative, high-tech running shoe. They have managed, however, to capitalize on the widely held perception that Canadian bootmakers are the embodiment of high quality, and are specialists in the manufacture of boots, particularly those designed to withstand the harsh Canadian environment.

Canadian bootmakers continue to capitalize on this perception, carving out niches in the world footwear market, as 30% of Canadian boot sales are now export-based. Canadian bootmakers continue to capitalize on their competitive image, developing broad lines of high quality boot products which are marketed at home and abroad. Popular boot lines produced by such manufacturers as Greb and Sorrel include winter boots, work boots, safety boots, military and police boots, casual boot lines, and others. Water-proofing and insulation are felt to be Canadians' forte around the globe. After all, Canadians must know something about protection from cold and moisture to have survived this long.

QUESTIONS

1. Do you think that the Canadian "country of origin" competitive advantage is sustainable?
2. What marketing strategies might be applied to assist in sustaining this advantage?

324

3. Define and explain market positioning and outline how Canadian boot products may be positioned in the mind of foreign consumers.
4. Using Porter's "Competitive Forces" model as a guide, what potential dangers might Canadian boot manufacturers face in the future?

Source: This case was prepared by Byrong Osing and is based on the *Venture* series episode "Boots," which was first broadcast on February 6, 1994.

Chapter 10

Brand Building and Relationship Marketing

HOW FRIENDLY ARE THOSE SKIES?

If you have traveled much in Canada, you probably have a certain image of or feeling about the brand Canadian Airlines International. You may even be a regular customer, someone marketers describe as *brand loyal*. Suppose that you call for information about a Canadian Airlines flight or take a trip on the airline. As a result of that trip or call, your overall perception of Canadian Airlines will probably change.

The extent of this change will depend on your experience. If your trip goes smoothly or the Canadian Airlines representative you talk to on the phone is pleasant and helpful, your good feelings about Canadian Airlines will be reinforced, strengthening your brand loyalty. But if your luggage gets lost, your flight is delayed, or the person on the phone can't answer your questions, your liking of Canadian Airlines will

decrease and you will probably be less brand loyal than before, and thus more likely to consider another airline for future trips.

Everything a company does sends a message.

327

benefits it promises. When brand images are strong, they can be used to enhance a person's self-image. A successful executive's choice in cars, like the cut of his or her suit, may reveal much about the image that the executive wants to project. Car brands make statements, not only about wealth, but about social class, taste, discernment, security, and style as well. As the case on Harley-Davidson points out, the Harley bike is an example of a product that once had a negative image associated with Hell's Angels and other outlaw types, but over the years Harley has evolved a very positive, upscale image of "individualism."

Brand images can only be determined by research. Research on the image of the Millennium rechargeable battery in both trade and consumer markets found that the brand's position was perceived as number one in the categories of quality, value for money, innovation, good delivery, advertising and promotion, and marketing assistance in comparison to competitors GE, Eveready, Panasonic, and Duracell. Despite these findings, Millennium's brand awareness is low because it is a new product and hasn't yet developed a strong image. The research told the company that its marketing strategy should focus on enhancing brand awareness with both trade and consumers.

Your brand selection can affect the way people perceive you. In a study of brand perception, subjects were shown two shopping lists that were identical, except that one list included a premium brand of coffee whereas the other contained an unknown brand. When the subjects were asked to describe the owners of each list, they described the person with the list containing the premium brand of coffee in a significantly more positive way than they did the person whose list included the unknown brand.

Brand Image and Slogans

The new slogan "There's a lot more for a lot less" has been developed to reflect the changes at Canadian Tire. Canadian Tire is in the business of satisfying customers' desire for value, a wide assortment of products and services, and everyday low prices.

MORE THAN A LOGO

The distinctive depiction of a manufacturer's brand name and/or symbol is called a **logo**. Retailers also often use logos on signs in front of their stores, and service companies usually put their logos on trucks, employees' uniforms, and stationery. *Logo* comes from the printing term *logotype,* meaning a single piece of wood or metal plate faced with a "signature" such as the name of a newspaper or a trademark. Exhibit 10-1 illustrates CIBC's new logos.

Although people frequently use the words *logo* and *brand* interchangeably because it is the logo that prompts them to think of the brand, technically they are not synonyms. A brand is much more than a logo because it contains all the personal associations that consumers have built up for the product. This is not to take away from the importance of the logo, however, for that is the primary cue that moves a brand from a customer's subconscious to conscious mind.

When you see or hear "Coke," what comes to your mind? Probably a memory of a cold liquid, a refreshing, sweet, pleasant drink. You may even "see" the logo in your mind—four white letters on a red background. Someone else hearing the word, however, may have negative thoughts, such as "too sweet," "too much bite," or "too fattening." This person "sees" the same logo that you do, but for him or her the brand is different. Think of the distinction this way—*a logo is on a product, a brand is in someone's head.*

This difference underlines a critical aspect of branding: a brand can be influenced but not controlled. A company can *control* its logo—change the typeface, colors, make it smaller or larger—but it can only *influence* its brand image.

A Promise   A brand is a promise. When you see McDonald's golden arches and drive in to get a hamburger, fries, and shake, you expect certain things— the products will satisfy you, the prices will be low compared to those in other restaurants, the facilities will be clean, the service will be quick, and the people behind the counter will be courteous. This *value promise* is a result of the interaction of all the elements of the marketing mix combined with your past experiences of McDonald's. Calvin Klein is a good example of a brand that owes its brand promise as much to strong image advertising as to product performance. Although one element of an image may play a more dominant role than others, all contribute to the value promise.

logo
The distinctive way in which a brand name is written, symbolized and incorporated in a design.

331

BRAND
BUILDING AND
RELATIONSHIP
MARKETING

Exhibit 10-1
A New Logo for CIBC

CIBC's new logo launched in June 1994 is designed to project a more unified, consistent identity that symbolizes its transformation into a broad-based financial services company. CIBC chairman Al Flood says "Having a strong visual identity is vital when an institution is involved in such a diverse range of activities."

Ideally, the value promise is a positive one, but in certain buying situations some brands can offer a negative promise. Zellers' positive value promise when you're buying underwear and kids' clothing may become negative when you are in the market for a wedding ring.

The value promise establishes a brand relationship that helps consumers in their product decision making. Branding is especially important with products that are of high value and involve a high-risk decision, as with low-involvement products. Choosing a computer is much more risky than choosing a brand of candy bar. When you are having the boss over for dinner, you are not likely to risk serving an unfamiliar or cheap brand of wine.

Brand knowledge is also helpful when buying decisions are difficult because of the complex nature of the product. Most people don't understand the technology behind their television sets or their cars, so they rely on brand images of quality engineering to guide their purchases.

BRANDING AND RELATIONSHIPS ●

The most important thing about a brand—and this is the focus of the second objective for this chapter—is that it represents the relationship that marketing has established with a customer. As Regis McKenna explains in his book *Relationship Marketing,* it means moving from being sales driven to being customer driven; from manipulating customers to involving them; from selling and telling to asking and satisfying. Relationship marketing represents a shift from "monologue to dialogue," with information flowing in both directions as a result of new technology that is transforming consumer choice and decision making. Asking "What is a successful brand but a special relationship?" McKenna explains that in a world where the customer has so many options, establishing a personal relationship is the only way to retain customer loyalty.[2] Successful brands, like those carried by Galeries Lafayette, have established very strong images, as well as relationships, with their customers.

People have unique relationships with almost all the brands they use, and these relationships continually change with direct and indirect exposure to the product and its company. As we discussed in the opening story, a brand is *psychologically fluid,* changing with every brand experience. Furthermore, the nature of a brand relationship differs from one person to the next because we all have individual sets of psychological filters—product criteria, level of product need, values, and usage situations—that determine how we interpret and integrate the messages a company sends out about its products. This is why marketing communication messages, as well as the rest of the things a company does (including such "small" things as how its people answer the phone), must be positive and consistent.

The *richness* of the brand image determines the quality of the relationship. An example is the difference between two American brands of hot dogs—Eckrich and Oscar Mayer. Although both are premium brands with high brand awareness in several markets in the central region of the United States, in focus groups set up to determine brand image and personality, the two differed greatly. When asked to describe Eckrich, responses came slowly and were along the lines of "clean plants," high "quality," and "strict." When asked about Oscar Mayer, however, the respondents' faces lit up, and the animated answers were "like your favorite uncle," "Santa Claus," "fun." Although it's nice to have a "quality" image, the Eckrich marketing people admitted they envied the richness of the responses Oscar Mayer evoked. It was obvious that many consumers had a much more emotional relationship with the Oscar Mayer brand.

Logo Chic

The flagship store of Galeries Lafayette has been a landmark in Paris since 1895 and a retailing legend for nearly as long. Unabashedly upscale, Galeries Lafayette is committed to fashionable brand-name products. The Paris store devotes whole floors to couturiers like Christian Dior and to cosmetic products by names like Estée Lauder and Chanel.

Relationships also have *strength*. Coke found that out in the mid-1980s when it dropped the classic formula and brought out the sweeter New Coke. Coke loyalists were so enraged that the embarrassed company brought back the original formula to sit side by side on supermarket shelves with the New Coke—which never became a big seller. Procter & Gamble made the same mistake when it dropped the original green version of Prell shampoo in 1991 and replaced it with a reformulated blue version. As P&G found out, there is often a bond between a brand and its customers, and marketers had better not underestimate the strength of that bond. P&G's vice president and general manager for hair care observed: "Yes, we were surprised at how strongly loyal green Prell users were," and P&G has since brought back green Prell.[3]

BRAND EQUITY

What successful relationship marketing does is develop **brand equity**, which is of value both to a company and to a brand's users. From the company's perspective, equity is the value attached to a brand because of the powerful relationship that has been developed between the brand and customers and other stakeholders over time. It can be thought of as the brand's "consumer franchise." Brand equity is not the same thing as brand image because equity goes far beyond physical elements and symbolism. It is often defined

brand equity
The goodwill value attached to a brand because of the relationship that has been developed with customers and other stakeholders over time.

in economic terms. As Marieke de Mooij says in her book *Advertising World-wide*, "brands are the most enduring assets companies possess."[4]

This set of assets can be thought of in terms of the *additional* cash flow achieved by successfully developing a brand association and establishing it as an *added value* for the underlying product or service. Brand equity represents "the incremental price that a customer will pay for a brand versus the price [the customer is willing to pay] for a comparable product without a brand name."[5]

In other words, most consumers will pay more for a brand name they trust than for a similar but unknown product. A well-known brand will earn more than its less visible competitors because it promises some kind of added value. The better known and accepted the brand name, the more added value—and thus the more equity—the brand has. Branding, if done well, can be a major competitive advantage as well as a significant contributor to profits.

Underlying this discussion is the assumption that brands—and the brand relationship—have value for consumers. As we said earlier, branding inspires confidence in consumers because it gives them a means of organizing their marketplace experiences. When consumers can label and define a product in terms of past experiences—positive or negative—they can more easily make a decision to buy or not to buy. Most consumers feel better about buying something they are familiar with, and consistent identification of a product is essential to true familiarity. On another level, consumers' feelings about themselves are often reflected in their product choices and the particular associations embedded for them in brand personalities. Thus brand names can contribute to self-image.[6]

Brand equity offers certain strategic benefits to companies. It is important for adding line extensions. Dupont has found that using its corporate brand name in advertising for its Stainmaster Carpet increases Stainmaster's market share by up to 200 percent.[7] When a product category has entered the decline stage of the product life cycle, strong brand equity can help a brand survive longer than its competitors. Likewise, in periods of economic downturn, brand equity provides a platform that keeps the brand profitably afloat long after competing products less identifiable to the buying public have begun to flounder.

The power of brand equity is especially important in international marketing, when a brand name known worldwide becomes a platform for market entry. Such global brands as Sony, Rolex, Mercedes-Benz, IBM, Nestlé, and Coke, by virtue of their global presence and worldwide recognition, have strong market shares in many different countries. Global brands, by definition, have international presence and visibility, and this "equity" makes it easier for them to expand. They are more likely to obtain the trade concessions from governments and to gain the financial and political respect necessary for building plants and setting up distribution facilities abroad.

Brand equity is also what enables branded products to charge premium prices. Most major brands are positioned as quality products, and most people are willing to pay more for a quality product they are familiar with, particularly if the brand has an image with which they would like to be associated. A perception of quality is thus a key factor in branding. A study of the strongest brands in the United States in terms of quality found Disney to be the top-rated brand, followed by Kodak, Hallmark, UPS, Fisher-Price, Levi's, Arm & Hammer, AT&T, and IBM. Because of their power, most of these brands are also respected around the world.

One market observer has stated: "World class brands lead the quality standard and avoid the price war."[8] In other words, the added value of branding also translates into a higher price level. Still, important brands like Marlboro and Kraft have found that they can only use their brand power to leverage price up to a point. If they go beyond that "acceptable" level, consumers will buy cheaper products. The challenge is to find the point where the premium price is still acceptable in exchange for the confidence and associations embedded in the brand.

Brand Life Cycle   Brands, like products, have life cycles. But unlike product life cycles, which are determined by shifts in customers' wants and needs, a *brand's life cycle* is mostly a result of the marketing mix. By changing the marketing mix—including the product itself—a brand's life cycle, especially in the maturity stage, can be greatly extended. McDonald's is a good example: McDonald's has changed its product offerings (adding breakfast, salads, kiddie meals, and regional food products) and its distribution methods (over a third of its business is now drive-through) from the original simple hamburger or cheeseburger, fries, shakes, and soft drinks available only across the counter. By these methods, the McDonald's brand has far outstripped its original menu.

The Value of a Brand   What is brand equity worth? The 1994 annual survey by U.S. magazine *Financial World* now rates Coca-Cola as the world's most valuable brand, knocking Marlboro into second place. Coca-Cola is now estimated to be worth just under U.S. $36 billion, compared to U.S. $33 billion for Philip Morris's Marlboro. Nestlé's Nescafe instant coffee is a distant third place, with a value of U.S. $11.5 billion.[9] A brand equity includes not only the value of the brand image but also (implicitly) the value of proprietary technologies, patents, trademarks, and other intangibles such as manufacturing know-how.

The value of a brand is well illustrated by an incident involving a former Coca-Cola CEO who was concerned about inconsistencies in the way the Coke trademark was being used. If a trademark is not consistently used exactly as it is registered, the courts will eventually refuse to protect it. Calling the bottlers and marketing people together, the CEO told them that even if the company lost all its trucks, all its employees, and all its bottling plants, it could still go into major banks anywhere in the world and borrow enough money to rebuild the entire company as long as it had exclusive rights to its trademark.

Although a company's stock price represents more than brand equity, when one of a company's brands gets into trouble, a change in brand equity can significantly affect the stock price. Foodmaker, Inc., owns Jack-in-the-Box (a fast-food hamburger chain) and Chi-Chi's (a chain of full-service Mexican restaurants). In February 1993 stories suddenly appeared in the U.S. media about people getting sick, even dying, after eating at Jack-in-the-Box restaurants. An investigation found that the food poisoning had been caused by undercooked, contaminated ground beef and the chain's relationship with its customers and other stakeholders—especially its stockholders and the financial community in general—was negatively affected. Foodmaker's stock lost nearly 40 percent of its value in less than a month, falling from a high of 14 to a low of 8.5.

BRANDING STRATEGIES ●

Branding is important to companies because product category leadership often depends on brand equity. In hotly contested product categories there are usually brands identified as "leaders." Research shows that ranking first, second, or third in brand dominance is a predictor of profitability. As a result, some companies, like Procter & Gamble, are divesting themselves of brands that don't rank in the top three.[10]

In this section we describe the various types of branding strategies, the topic of chapter objective three. But to understand the strategy of branding, you first need to understand the strategic alternatives to branding—generics and private brands.

GENERICS AND PRIVATE BRANDS

generic product
A product sold without a brand name, and using just a category label.

private brand
An exclusive brand that is made to the retailer's specifications.

A nonbranded product sold by its category label is known as a **generic product**. Generic products are usually more attractive to consumers during economic downturns. Some grocery stores have sections for generic brands, where you will find sugar, flour, cocoa mix, and dozens of other commodity products, all unbranded and identifiable by their plain packaging. Lower costs result from not having to promote the brand through advertisers or distinctive packaging. Loblaws began selling house brands in the late 1970s under the no-name banner.

Manufacturers also sell products to wholesalers or retailers who put their own private brand on the product. A **private brand**—also called a *private label*, *distributor's brand*, or *house brand*—is exclusive to one retailer or distributor; the product is made to the retailer's specifications. In North America private-label products are usually of the same or lesser quality than manufacturer's brands. In Europe, however, sometimes the opposite is true; some private labels, like those sold by the Sainsbury's supermarket chain in the United Kingdom, are considered higher in quality. In 1984, Loblaw's created its President's Choice line, which now has sales in the range of $500–$700 million per year.

Private labels are a popular strategy with retailers. For years (up until the introduction of its Brand Central) virtually everything sold by Sears carried one of its private labels, such as Kenmore or Craftsman. Whatever their label, all of Sears' products are made by a variety of outside manufacturers who supply the retailer with everything from detergent to major appliances.

Food chains like Dominion and Safeway also carry their "own" brands of high-volume products, such as bread, dairy products, and selected canned goods. Usually these products are not produced by the chains themselves but by outside suppliers and then labeled with the store's private brand. Some stores offer manufacturer's brand "knockoffs" such as the artificial sweetener Sweet Lite, which is made for Kmart and looks similar to the Sweet 'n Low label.

Private-label brands benefit both retailers and manufacturers. They enable retailers to offer customers an additional brand choice, one that is generally priced lower than national brands. This lower pricing reflects not only the lack of advertising and promotion costs but also savings realized by the retailer's control of product specifications. Private labels enable manufacturers to use their production capacity more efficiently. By making private brands as well as their own, they can keep production lines going for two or three shifts, thus spreading the cost of production equipment and facilities over more output. This gives them a lower cost base for each of their own branded items, allowing them to earn a higher profit per item and/or to offer a more competitive price against other national competing brands. For retailers there is also the financial incentive of profitability with private labels being seven times more profitable than standard brands. It is harder also for the consumer to compare price and quality, so satisfied customers will continue to return. According to Toronto-based A.C. Nielson, private and generic label products accounted for 19.5 percent of all grocery sales in Canada for the year ended October 17, 1992, up from 16 percent from a year earlier.

CORPORATE BRANDS

Among corporate brands, which still far outnumber private-label brands, a common strategy is to use the corporate name as a brand name. This strategy has been used successfully by Kodak, AT&T, and Fisher-Price. Sony is both a corporate name and a brand name, although its corporate name is more prominent than its product-line names, with the possible exception of Sony's Walkman radios. In effect, companies that brand "the corporation behind the product" believe their corporate name is more important than the product brands from a marketing standpoint.[11]

Multiple Brands Another strategy is to operate with *multiple brands* in a category. Procter & Gamble, the number-one advocate of the multiple-branding strategy, assigns distinctive brand names to products that are marketed to different market segments. For example, P&G markets both Pampers and Luvs brands in the disposable diaper category; in the bar soap category, it offers Ivory, Camay, Safeguard, Lava, Coast, and Zest. P&G uses a similar multiple-brand strategy in other categories like laundry soap and shampoo, where its brands compete with each other in order to extend the corporation's overall market share.

Multiple brands are expected to stand on their own, without a corporate identification. Note in the advertisement for Nestlé's brands depicted in Exhibit 10-2 that Nestlé's, like P&G, rarely uses its corporate name on its brands,

Exhibit 10-2
Nestlé's Family of Brands

In this ad, Nestlé is beginning to establish its many well-known brand names under the corporate identity of the Nestlé nest logo. Until this point, the brands have been marketed independently, whether they originated with Nestlé or were acquired from other companies.

ALL OVER THE WORLD THIS IS A SYMBOL FOR WARMTH, FAMILY AND SHELTER.

In 1867, a man named Henri Nestlé began to build a food company.

His name, which means "little nest," has since become synonymous with food, family and quality throughout the world.

Today, that symbol can be found on the back of many well-known products.

Great-tasting Nestlé brands that include Stouffer's, Contadina, Libby's, Taster's Choice, Hills Bros, Carnation and more.

AND NESTLÉ.

And thanks to an unparalleled international network of Nestlé research and development centers, you have our assurance the products we introduce in the future will be as good as the ones we make today.

It's also why this little bird's nest represents 125 years of Nestlé quality. As well as the very best.

Nestlé
Makes the very best.

other than its candy line. Instead, it focuses its branding on individual products such as Carnation, Taster's Choice, Nescafé, and Butterfinger. This policy of not using the corporate name is changing in Asia, where the corporate name is far more important than it is in North America.

Brand Extensions   A single brand name can be used to identify a family of products. For example, the Ivory brand name is used on a multiproduct line that includes laundry soap, hand soap, dishwashing soap, shampoo, and hair conditioner. Similarly, Lipton produces a variety of teas, soups, and other food products, Pillsbury has a broad family of baking products all marketed under that name, and Black & Decker uses a family brand name for its wide variety of tools and home appliances. This strategy leverages a brand image across new products when the parent brand (Ivory soap, Lipton tea) is well known and respected.

Tiered Branding   Some companies use two or three "tiers" of branding. For example, Kellogg's Product 19 and Dupont's Kevlar (a bullet-resistant fabric) are two-tiered brands that combine a corporate name with a brand name. In Exhibit 10-2 you can see an example of three-tiered branding in Carnation Coffeemate; the parent name Nestlé appears on the back of the package in small type. Another example of three-tiered branding is General Motors' Chevrolet Camaro.

Multitiered branding is used to leverage the corporate identity while at the same time developing a distinctive identity for a line of products. The strategic decision is to what extent each of the brands should be emphasized. Consider the case of GM's Saturn line of cars, which entered the market in 1990. GM knew that it could compete on the basis of quality and price with imported midsize cars. However, the negative image GM and the other domestic carmakers had accumulated from years of poor quality imagery put roadblocks in the way of the new project.

Although in talking to the financial community GM never hid its affiliation, the company decided to introduce Saturn without any direct reference in its consumer advertising to the corporate name. Rather than sell the car through existing GM dealers, the company set up separate Saturn showrooms and service facilities. The story of GM's Corvette is similar. Aware that its corporate name has little leverage as a maker of high-performance sports cars, GM has ensured that the Corvette nameplate stands on its own in consumer advertising.

GLOBAL BRANDS

When a firm uses the same name for essentially the same product worldwide, it is said to have a standardized branding strategy. A *global brand* is more than a single name for an identical or similar product. It implies the same basic personality, strategy, and positioning in world markets. Coca-Cola, Levi Strauss, Mercedes-Benz, and Sony are examples of brands that have made the transition from national to global brands; as Exhibit 10-3 illustrates, *Coca-Cola* is transcribed into the language of the country in which it is marketed.

When the same product has different brand names in different countries, it is sometimes called a *world product*. World products evolve naturally in companies that have long been multinational in orientation. Some multinational firms focus on adapting to local cultures and choose an "invented-here" name in each region for a product that is sold worldwide. Sometimes the different names are a result of mergers. Almost every company that has operated as a multinational has world products. Lever Brothers, for example, manufactures the same formula of detergent in several European countries, but sells it under different brand names, including Jif, Viss, and Cif.

**Japan is Enchanted by the
Disney Magic**

Tokyo Disneyland has already
surpassed the original Disney
theme parks in the United States in
attendance, and it provides a
striking contrast to the
disappointing response of
Europeans to the Disney park near
Paris. In Tokyo in 1993, 16
million visitors spent an average
of $85; in a similar period
EuroDisney lost nearly a billion
dollars. What happened? One
factor may be that EuroDisney
opened in 1992, in the midst of a
recession with both summer and
winter Olympic games, whereas
the Tokyo park opened in 1983 in
a strong economic period.

In recent years many established companies have been reevalu-
ating their world-product policies and converting world products to
global brands. Mars (a U.S.-based candy company) marketed the
Snickers candy bar as a world product with a different name in several regions. For example, it was called Marathon in Great Britain because Mars felt that Snickers was too close to the word *knickers*, which
is a British slang term for a woman's underpants. In light of the
rapidly emerging single market in Europe during the late 1980s, however, Mars decided to switch to a standardized global brand strategy.
To take advantage of the efficiency and leverage of a single name
worldwide, the Marathon name was replaced with the Snickers name
and logo in Great Britain and other markets.

339

THE BRAND-BUILDING PROCESS ●

Branding enables buyers to identify a product, remember it, and, if satisfied with its performance, seek it out again. Thus it makes shopping easier for the customer. Branding is a challenge for companies, however, for many companies do not start making a profit from a particular customer until that customer has purchased the good or service several times. This is because the company must build a brand relationship, which takes time and money. Most potential buyers must go through four steps before they become "brand loyal." First, they must become aware of, and recognize, the brand mark. Second, they must accept the claims made by the brand. Third, they must prefer the brand over its competitors. And fourth, they must take action by buying the brand repeatedly. Following is a more detailed discussion of these four steps—awareness, acceptance, preference, and action—which are the subject of the fourth chapter objective and depicted in Figure 10-2.

1. *Brand Recognition and Awareness.* Initially, branding involves linking product claims with a set of identification symbols such as a name, logo, product character or symbol, slogan, and package design. When a brand is recognized, the consumer has seen it before—either in advertising or in the marketplace—and is aware of having seen it before. A recognized brand is one that has successfully implanted its image in the customer's mind. Once this familiarity is created, the marketer hopes it will be reinforced through repeated positive experiences with the brand. While brand recognition means that the brand's identification system is working effectively, nonrecognition means that the brand is either unknown or the consumer is unaware of it. As Franzen and Holzhauer remark: "Unknown brands are dead. Dead brands are unknown."[12]

2. *Brand Acceptance.* The second important step in brand development is creating acceptance of the brand. Brand acceptance means that a brand's image is received favorably by consumers. Brand rejection means that consumers are either unreceptive to the image or unsatisfied with the product. If brand rejection is the result of an image problem, marketers will have to either change the brand's image or target a more receptive segment of the population.

   If the problem is rejection of the product itself, then either the product or the methods used to produce it will have to be changed. For example, if you go to a restaurant that is part of a fast-food chain you are unfamiliar with and the service is poor, you may conclude that poor service is a characteristic of the entire chain. Although the employees at this particular restaurant may just be having a bad day, your image of the chain will be colored by this one experience, and it may cause you to reject all restaurants that are part of this chain. Unless something changes—say, a friend recommends the same or another restaurant in the chain or the chain launches a new advertising campaign focusing on good service—you are unlikely to give this brand of restaurant a second chance.

3. *Brand Preference.* When consumers desire a specific brand, they have reached the stage of brand preference. This doesn't always mean they will buy the brand, however. Although a consumer may prefer an Omega watch, he may be able to afford only a Timex. Preference means that buyers would like to choose a particular brand rather than any of its competitors, because they have become convinced of its value. Dif-

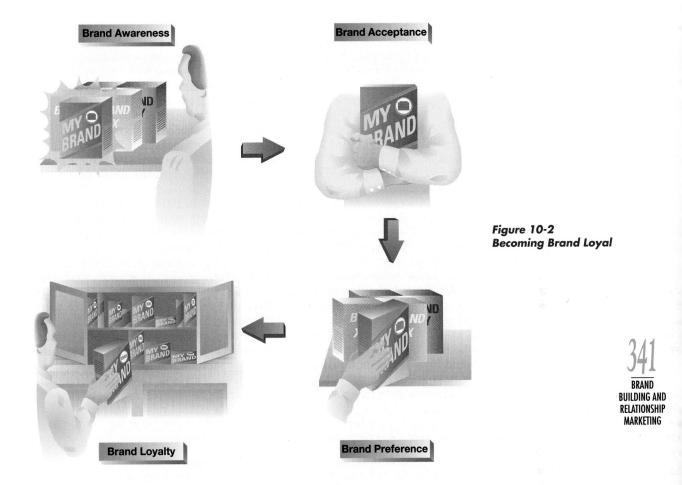

Brand Awareness

Brand Acceptance

Figure 10-2
Becoming Brand Loyal

Brand Loyalty

Brand Preference

ferentiating a brand from the competition is an important first step in creating brand preference.

4. *Brand Loyalty*. Branding adds value, but only over time. It generally takes years to develop a recognized brand and make it valued by a group of customers. According to Alan Gregg, from Decima research, consumers today are less loyal to national brands. In fact, less than 20 percent of shoppers know the brand when they enter the store. A stated or unstated marketing objective of nearly every company is to build *brand loyalty* (see our definition of this term in Chapter 6); that is, to ensure that customers will develop a relationship with the firm's product and buy that brand repeatedly. Canada's first world champion baseball team, the Toronto Blue Jays is being heavily marketed to gain loyalty.

Underlying the concept of brand loyalty is the reality of buyer choice. North Americans can now choose from among 572 different models of cars, vans, and trucks, up from 408 at the beginning of the 1980s. "For car marketers," a recent report observed, "it has become a much tougher battle to keep loyal customers from defecting to one of the new makes on the block." According to the survey, "the proliferation of choice is both liberating and confusing" for consumers, because "when consumers have so many choices, brand loyalty is much harder to maintain." Indeed, 53 percent of today's car buyers intend to switch brands.[13]

Car owners once moved up in quality within a family of models offered by their favorite dealers. For example, as we outlined in Chapter 9, GM had a forty-year segmentation strategy in which a young couple would start with GM's Chevrolet, move up to a Pontiac as they became more financially secure, then graduate to a Buick as they got older, and finally, after accumulating a substantial income, ratify their status with a Cadillac. That purchasing pattern has eroded in recent decades, however, mainly because the GM models lost their clear-cut images as a result of competition. Cadillac, for example, has moved down into Buick's market, while some Buicks now cost as much as some Cadillacs. Because each of GM's nameplates has been a separate profit center, each has expanded into the others' niches, with the result that none of the nameplates is as distinct as it once was.

Another problem for companies that invest heavily in building brands is that in recessionary times brand loyalty tends to decline. In the recession of the early 1990s, for example, there was a decline in consumer interest in status cars. Moreover, a 1993 study by Information Resources following the officially designated end of that recession found that consumers were still buying cheaper private-label and store brands, even in product categories that were traditionally resistant to economic downturns. Private labels had risen to 18.3 percent of all units sold in supermarkets, up from 16.4 in 1989.[14] Consumers also tend to trade down in terms of the outlets from which they purchase. For example, Wal-Mart and Kmart are now attracting more affluent customers who have become price-conscious as a result of economic times. They are still brand loyal but now find they can buy the same brand for less. These stores are now being termed "category-killers" as they are able to be price-competitive across a wide range of branded products.

ELEMENTS OF BRANDING

Many elements are involved in branding. The design of a trademark or logo, the use of a symbol, the creation of a brand character to represent the personality of the brand, the choice of a brand name, and the advertising used to convey this information are the most important elements of branding, and they are the topic of the fifth chapter objective.

BRAND NAMES

Marketers have many decisions to make regarding brand names. As we've said, names can identify a manufacturer, a line, or a product.

For many years after the end of World War II, the United States was the preeminent global marketer; such powerful brand names as IBM, Coca-Cola, and Marlboro were recognized worldwide. During this same period, European brands such as Nestlé, Unilever, and Mercedes were beginning to develop a global stance. In the last decade or so, we have seen the emergence of global brands from Asia, such as the widely respected Sony, Honda, and Hitachi. Japan is home to twenty-nine of the top fifty global advertisers in expenditures outside the United States.[15] With the European Union now implementing its single-market program, European brands may become even more powerful in the global marketplace as the East European countries become free-market economies.

Selecting Names After devising an overall strategy for its corporate brands, a firm must decide on specific brand names. Naming a product is a critical decision in new-product development. Every new product should have a name that will stand out and reflect positively on the product and company. Table 10-1 summarizes the characteristics of desirable brand names.

In the past, creating a name was relatively simple: staff within a company or at the company's ad agency would brainstorm until they came up with something notable. Brand names were often based on individuals, such as Ford, Hershey, and Sears and Roebuck, and in the fashion industry they still are: Liz Claiborne, Calvin Klein, and Ralph Lauren. Other names reflected aspirations, like the Great Atlantic & Pacific Tea Company (A&P), or geographic areas of service, like the Atchison, Topeka, and Santa Fe Railroad.

Today there are sophisticated companies that specialize in developing and testing brand names for firms to determine their potential effectiveness as product links, the associated meanings they would bring to the product, and their linguistic suitability. The NameLab company employs linguists and also uses computers that store some 6,000 morphemes—the basic prefixes, suffixes, and root words of which the English language is composed. NameLab staff meet with a client to discuss the positioning of the product or company, and then use the computer to produce combinations of morphemes based on the client's semantic and phonetic needs. When Nissan Motors asked NameLab to develop a name for a new small car that would help allay the public's fears about the dangers of small cars, NameLab came up with Sentra (from sentry). The Compaq computer firm reportedly paid NameLab about $30,000 to develop its name.

TABLE 10-1	WHAT'S IN A BRAND NAME?

A brand name should

- be simple

- be distinctive

- be meaningful

- be a verbal or sound associate of the product class

- be an emotional word (e.g., *Luvs*)

- elicit a mental image

- reflect the product's benefits, attributes, positioning, or use (e.g., *All*)

- give the product a "psychological label" and a symbolic basis for consumer interpretation

- have a connotative meaning that matches the desired brand positioning; (e.g., *Infiniti*)

- make use of repetitive sounds (e.g., *Coca-Cola*)

- make use of the characteristics of many morphemes and phonemes (the small, linguistic units of words) that facilitate communication of special meanings and have punch (e.g., *Compaq*, *Tide*, *Jif*)

Source: Adapted from Kim Robertson, "Strategically Desirable Brand Name Characteristics," *Journal of Consumer Marketing* 6 (Fall 1989): 61–70.

Meanings of Names   One problem with name selection is that you want a word or name that has a consistent meaning among most consumers—but so do many other companies. For example, about 7,500 products and services now use either "Light" or "Lite" in their names. This trend started in the early 1970s when Miller Brewing Company introduced its Lite beer. Today every major beer manufacturer has a "light" product. The word _light_ has also moved into such diverse categories as cheese, microwave popcorn, chips, desserts, and salad dressings.

Another problem is the lack of clear definition as to what terms like _light_ and _natural_ really mean. A number of American states sued Sara Lee for false advertising, contending that the company's "light" cheesecake had the same number of calories as the regular Sara Lee cheesecake. The company countered that it was using the term _light_ to connote a fluffier texture, not fewer calories, but it was forced to pull a "light" line off the market anyway. These kinds of problems are mushrooming as companies rush to introduce what we assume to be healthier versions of existing food and beverage products.

Unsuccessful names may be ones that carry meanings marketers _don't_ want associated with their product. For example, a Japanese professor found that he had to change the name of his government-sponsored research group—the Kinki Research Complex—in order to do business in the United States. In Japan the name _Kinki_ is widely used because of its historical significance; traditionally, it referred to the region around Osaka and Kyoto, a national center of culture and the former site of the emperor's palace. North Americans, however, heard the English word _kinky._

The word _diet_ can also pose problems even when correctly translated. In North America "diet" as adjective has come to mean "low-calorie." But in some countries "diet" connotes a medicinal or therapeutic product that must conform with local laws for pharmaceuticals. In some countries diet refers to a government assembly such as a parliament. As you can see from the photo on the facing page, Unitel had some trouble with its name—because the name was already registered elsewhere.

TRADEMARKS

trademarks
Legally registered symbols that a company has the exclusive right to use.

Names, characters, and brand marks (logos) can all serve as **trademarks**, which are distinctive symbols identified with a particular company or brand that are formally registered with the federal government in order to ensure the company's _exclusive right to their use._ Imagine the confusion and disappointment if just any company could put the Coke trademark on whatever type of beverage it wanted to make and sell. Consumers would have no idea what they were getting for their money.

The idea of trademarks dates back centuries to the simple signs or symbols that were used to identify the makers of such products as metal containers, glass, paper, shoes, and wine in cultures where most people couldn't read—a sign showing a shoe, for instance, signified that the person was a cobbler. During the Middle Ages members of craft guilds used individual "hallmarks" to regulate work by member artisans. If a certain product was not of good quality or didn't perform well, the guild could instantly tell who was responsible by checking the product's hallmark.

Modern trademarks include the rainbow-colored apple used by Apple Computer and the red wave and distinctive lettering used on the Coke can. All trademarks—whether they take the form of stylized typefaces or designs—are meant to remind people of the brand.

Trademark Protection   Under trademark laws, companies can obtain the exclusive rights to a name or symbol by registering it. The length of the regis-

We DiDN'T iNVENT the LoNG-DiSTANCE CARD.

We just mADe it BETTeR.

uniTEL

1 800 957 9000   PIN/NIP
924 000 6780 2345
J RAYMOND

INTERNATIONAL   891869 924 000 6780 3 50

(Up to 28% BETTeR AS A MATTeR OF FACT.)

tration processes varies from country to country. In Canada, registering with the Intellectual Property Office of Consumer and Corporate Affairs Canada can take as long as 24 months. As Figure 10-3 illustrates, some kinds of trademarks are easier to protect than others.

Just what constitutes trademark infringement can be a subtle question. Lotus Software, developers of the 1-2-3 spreadsheet program used by so many businesses, successfully sued to prevent a competitor from copying Lotus's on-screen appearance and command names. Although the court acknowledged that any product that didn't imitate Lotus would have great difficulty persuading 1-2-3 users to switch, it ruled that the copycat software did indeed infringe on the Lotus trademark and patent.

A firm can lose its trademark if it fails to protect its exclusive right to it. Otis Elevator, for example, no longer has the trademark it once held on the term *escalator*. More recently, Windsurfer lost its trademark protection by failing to take action against other users of the term. Xerox and Kleenex have long struggled to prevent their names from becoming generic terms for a category, for when that happens, the government may deem that a company has

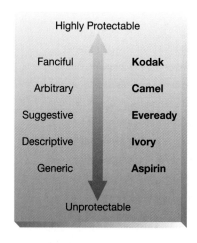

Highly Protectable

Fanciful	**Kodak**
Arbitrary	**Camel**
Suggestive	**Eveready**
Descriptive	**Ivory**
Generic	**Aspirin**

Unprotectable

Figure 10-3
How Protectable Are Trademarks?

Source: Adapted from Dorothy Cohen,
"Trademark Strategy," Journal of Marketing
50 (January 1986): 61–74.

given up exclusive use of its name. A study of product/category confusion found that consumers often confuse brand names with generic categories. The most commonly misperceived were: Band-Aids (61 percent of respondents), Kleenex (56 percent), Scotch Tape (52 percent), Xerox (49 percent), Q-Tips (48 percent) and Jell-O (42 percent).[16]

Companies with products that dominate categories and whose names are used generically must constantly fight to protect their brand names from this fate. Companies protect their brand names by using the generic category description after the trademarked name, such as Scotch® brand cellophane tape, Sanka® brand decaffeinated coffee, and Post-it® brand note pads. Notice also the careful use of the word *brand* after the trademark name. Most people are oblivious to these legal usages, but they are important in protecting brand names. For years, Xerox has run print ads like the one in Exhibit 10-4 to remind the world that its name is a registered trademark and should not be used as a general name for copy machines.

BEHIND THE SCENES

PROTECTING YOUR GOOD NAME

Formica's troubles began in 1978, when the company was put on notice that the U.S. Federal Trade Commission intended to cancel "Formica" as a trademark. The FTC argued that the word *formica* had entered the language as a generic name for decorative laminate and was therefore available for use by any company. The Formica Corporation, however, had invented laminate as a product in 1913 and had coined the Formica name. It believed that it was now being penalized for its success in getting Formica accepted as a brand.[17]

The battle was essentially a legal one. Early skirmishes were fought before the Trademark Trial and Appeals Board. Later rounds were fought in court. In addition, Formica mounted an extensive public relations campaign to generate grass-roots support for its position, sending letters to Congress and enlisting the support of customers, suppliers, and employees. Even the competition, to their credit, joined Formica's side. Speeches were given at influential trade meetings and before business and professional groups of all kinds. A special effort was made to get the active support of the company's employee union. Formica stated its position in some 970,000 booklets, pamphlets, speech reprints, and media articles. The company's attorney also solicited direct assistance from the nervous owners of other well-known trademarks. In short, Formica felt that it was fighting its trademark case for thousands of other businesses.

After many years the FTC finally retreated, but the Formica company is still cautious and no longer takes its trademark for granted. It continues to bolster its defenses with a comprehensive program for protecting the company's good name.

BRAND CHARACTERS

In addition to brand names, many firms use characters, either real or created, to personify a product. Orville Redenbacher, a popcorn perfectionist, and Frank Perdue, a specialist on chickens, are unusual because they are real people. The fictional Jolly Green Giant, on the other hand, is a cartoon character who communicates to children (as well as adults) that it's fun to eat vegetables. The kind but fictional "Betty Crocker" has been encouraging cooks since 1921. As Exhibit 10-5 shows, however, brand characters may need updating over the years, to evoke appropriate responses from new customers.

BRAND LICENSING

Legally protected logos, symbols, and characters must be licensed by the trademark holder before they can be used by other companies. In **brand licensing**, a company with an established brand "rents" that brand to other companies, allowing them to use its brand logo on their products. Brand licensing is a big business in North America, where designers like Gucci, Yves St. Laurent (YSL), and Pierre Cardin have licensed their brand names and initials for use on everything from fashion accessories to sunglasses, ties, linens, and luggage. The Disney company has licensed its cartoon characters and theme park symbols for use by other major marketers such as Delta Airlines and Chevrolet.

brand licensing
The practice whereby a company with an established brand "rents" it to another company.

XEROX

You can't Xerox a Xerox on a Xerox.

But we don't mind at all if you copy a copy on a Xerox copier.
In fact, we prefer it. Because the Xerox trademark should only identify products made by us. Like Xerox copiers and Xerox printing systems.
As a trademark, the term Xerox should always be used as an adjective, followed by a noun. And it's never used as a verb.
© 1991 XEROX CORPORATION. XEROX® is a trademark of XEROX CORPORATION.

Of course, helping us protect our trademark also helps you. Because you'll continue to get what you're actually asking for.
And not an inferior copy.

XEROX
The Document Company

Exhibit 10-4
Why Xerox Isn't a Generic Word for Copying

When a brand dominates a product category to the extent that its name gets used as a generic label, a trademark problem has been created. These brands must prove to the government that they are trying to maintain their exclusive use of the registered name, as Xerox demonstrates in this rather clever ad.

347

Exhibit 10-5
Updating Trade
Characters

Betty Crocker has been a trade character for more than seventy years. The problem with this type of symbol is that the character must be updated constantly to stay in tune with the times, and as we've pointed out in the text, consumers are often resistant to brand changes. In the case of Betty Crocker, the changes have been so subtle over the years that they have not caught the attention— or roused the ire—of most brand users.

franchising
The practice whereby a company permits its name, logo, design, and management systems to be used in establishing a new business.

Branding is also at the heart of franchising, another type of licensing. **Franchising** permits a person or company to use not only another company's brand name, logo, and corporate design but its management procedures and operations know-how as well. McDonald's, KFC, and Avis rental cars all derive large amounts of income from franchising their brand names and operations. In other words, the McDonald's Corporation doesn't own all the McDonald's restaurants you see, although it does tightly control how these franchisees operate their stores. Franchising is discussed in more detail in the retailing section of Chapter 15.

BRANDING AND THE
MARKETING MIX ●

As we said earlier in this chapter, because brands exist in people's heads, branding can be influenced but it can't be completely controlled. One of the primary methods of influencing branding, as indicated by the sixth chapter objective, is marketing communications. To convey the brand promise to potential buyers, marketers often use *image advertising* that dramatizes the benefits of the brand, and sometimes even the personalities and lifestyles of people with whom the marketer would like to have the product associated.

Good advertising can interpret product features into emotionally appealing benefits. For example, advertising has transformed Levi's 501 jeans from a product offering the generic benefit of sturdy denim to one with the emotionally appealing benefit of being stylishly attired. Advertising has made Levi's 501 into a fashion statement.

If you doubt the reality of such differences, try giving someone a watch in a Sears box and, at another time, a similar watch in a box that comes from Tiffany & Co. or Royal de Versailles jewelers. The entire experience of gift giving is influenced by the images associated with each of these different brands.[18]

Not all brands, however, have been built primarily by marketing communications. The Hershey brand was built on broad distribution and positive consumer experiences with the product itself. Hershey didn't even feel the need to do consumer advertising until the 1970s because it had such a strong image as a popular candy bar. Then there is L'Eggs panty hose, which owes virtually all of its brand image and success to its packaging. The way a product is priced also sends a message about the brand. For example, you can buy a bicycle for anywhere from $95 to $2,500. Chances are you won't buy the $95 one because that says "too cheap," just as to most of us the $2,500 price tag says "too expensive." We will look in greater detail at the messages each element of the marketing mix sends in the chapters that follow on distribution, pricing, and market communication.

BOTTOM LINE REALITIES

IS BRANDING DYING?

The marketing and advertising industries refer to April 2, 1993, as "Marlboro Friday." On that day Philip Morris lowered the price on its venerable Marlboro brand in order to compete with discount brands and private labels. As we've seen, one of the benefits of strong brand equity is that it allows the marketer to charge more than a physically similar good or service that has less brand equity can command. Marlboro had taken advantage of its brand equity over the years to gradually increase its price over the less established brands. Following Marlboro Friday, however, with its impli-

cations for branding's ability to leverage pricing, the marketing trade press and convention programs were full of articles and speeches predicting the death of branding. Brands were going out of business, it was said, because consumers were no longer brand loyal, and advertising agencies were therefore in deep trouble.

In a *New York Times* column, for example, the writer observed that "brand" was becoming the equivalent of a four-letter word on Wall Street. Advertising's leading executives at an American Association of Advertising Agencies (4As) meeting in 1993 made a plea to marketers to recognize the need for long-term brand building and advertising's role in

that process. For advertising executives, the fate of the branded product is a matter of survival. Several months earlier the 4As had joined with the Association of National Advertisers and nine other media organizations to form a group called the Coalition for Brand Equity, whose purpose is to make the case for increasing the value of brands—or stemming the loss of brand equity for ailing brands.[19]

Several factors have been at work in the decline of brands. One is the recent economic downturn that put price ahead of image in many consumer brand decisions. When consumers become more price conscious, companies have to resort to short-term efforts, such as sales and trade promotions, to achieve their sales objectives. When companies spend less on brand-building advertising and more on price promotions, their brands start to look like discount brands and their brand images deteriorate. And when store brands improve their quality and begin to advertise themselves, the difference between the two erodes.

Larry Light, head of the Coalition for Brand Equity, has said: "When brands die, we all die. Branding is the only basis for advertising. It's the only basis for promotion. It's the only basis for what we do." In a 1993 article he charged that brands "are being bargained, belittled, bartered, and battered." Light believes that current marketing practices are leading to "brand suicide."[20] According to Dave Aaker, author of the book *Managing Brand Equity*:

"Brand strategy is the key to business strategy."[21]

What do you think? Do brands seem less important to you, your family members, and your friends than they used to be? If brands further decline in importance, do you think that will be good or bad for consumers? Are store brands such as "President's Choice" now taking over as premium private label brands?▼

KEY POINTS SUMMARY ▼

1. Branding is a complex bundle of images and experiences. It creates an image of the product in the consumer's mind based on the sum of that individual's experiences with all aspects of a product, including its use, the personality conveyed in its marketing communications, its pricing, and where and how it is displayed.

2. Branding creates a long-term relationship with those people who loyally buy the product over and over again. This relationship is referred to as *brand equity*. The more well known a brand is and the more added value it contributes to a product, the higher its brand equity. Brand equity is a platform for adding line extensions, for international expansion, and for premium pricing.

3. Brand strategy involves, first, making a decision about whether to sell a product with a brand at all. The alternatives to branding are generic products (products sold by category labels) and private labels (products sold to retailers who put their name on the labels). If the manufacturer opts to sell the product with a brand, it must decide whether to use the company name (corporate branding) or to develop a different brand name.

4. The process of brand development includes four steps: recognition and awareness, acceptance, preference, and loyalty. That is, con-

sumers must become aware of the brand's image; find it to be a positive one; come to prefer it, refusing to accept substitutes; and demonstrate their loyalty by buying the product over and over again.

5. The important elements of branding are the brand name, the trademark or logo, the brand character, and the advertising used to convey all these. The brand name itself can reinforce the brand's positioning, calling up desirable qualities or allaying consumers' fears. Copyright and trademark laws protect brand names, characters, and symbols from infringement that could cause confusion with other brands thus strengthening the brand's relationship with customers. And because protected names and images can be used by other firms only through licensing agreements with the brand owner, advertising that uses the brand name or logo can effectively build or create brand relationships.

6. Brand building is supported by every element of the marketing mix, but marketing communication plays a particularly important role. Image advertising is frequently used as a tool in brand building because it transforms the experience of buying and using a brand and gives the brand personality.

DISCUSSION QUESTIONS ▼

1. What is branding? Why is branding a product important to a company? To customers?

2. What are private labels and why are they gaining in popularity?

3. How is relationship marketing related to branding?

4. Select a branded product in common use at your college and interview your classmates on their perception of that brand's personality.

5. From an issue of a major consumer magazine choose an ad you believe projects a very strong brand image. Discuss the image and the cues in the ad that communicate that image.

6. Choose a good or service you have used at least once but decided not to use again and explain where in the brand-building process you became turned off the product. What might the producer of that product do to get you to try that product again?

7. Look through a foreign (not American) magazine to find a global brand you are familiar with from its Canadian advertising. Has the producer altered its image/advertising for the market in the nation where this magazine is published?

8. Interview a marketing manager for a local firm and identify: (a) the brand image of the company's primary product (including its personality and the promise conveyed); (b) the stage in the brand-building process this product currently occupies; and (c) the ways in which the firm has protected this brand legally.

9. Analyze how consumers' attitudes toward products are formed and how they shift as a result of positive or negative experiences. Pick a service business, such as a restaurant or bank, and develop and summarize your classmates' attitudes toward that business. Plot your data on a chart and show in what directions attitudes shift as a result of different experiences. Does there seem to be a trend, either positive or negative for this service business?

10. Identify a product category within which you always buy a specific brand and another category within which the brand makes little difference to you. Explain where the difference lies. If familiar brands were to disappear in the category in which you normally buy by brand, what would that do to your decision making process? How would you feel?

Integrative Case ● Discussion Questions

The Body Shop*

1. What kind of brand is Body Shop Carrot Moisture Cream?

2. Describe the personality of The Body Shop brand. Does this brand meet the criteria for desirable brand names? Why or why not?

Harley-Davidson

1. What type of brand is Harley-Davidson?

2. Describe the Harley mystique.

3. Does Harley have a single image or multiple images? If a single image, how does it manage to appeal to multiple market segments? If Harley has multiple images, name them.

The Millennium Power System

1. The company that created the Millennium system produced private-label batteries before it launched Millennium. Why do you think it decided to introduce a nationally branded rechargeable battery?

2. Danny thought *Millennium* was a "cool" name. What advantages or disadvantages do you see in this brand name? What kind of image does it evoke?

*The three cases at the back of the book—"The Body Shop," "Harley-Davidson," and "The Millennium Power System"—illustrate topics discussed in all chapters of this book. Your instructor will tell you when to read a particular case and when to answer the discussion questions on it that appear at the end of each chapter.

Mary, Mary Quite Contrary

The gardening industry has been experiencing unprecedented growth over the past few years. There doesn't seem to be an end in sight for this $2 billion industry with forecasted growth expected at 5% a year. Why has there been an increase in this basically traditional, no-technology industry?

The population continues to change in their tastes and in their leisure activities. This changes traditional industries and also creates new ones. With a growing proportion of the Canadian population with more time for leisure activities, there is a large group turning to gardening. This is good for companies like Dominion Seed House, Vanhof & Blokker, and McKenzie Seeds.

These companies are among the major suppliers to the retail gardening shops and major department stores where consumers shop for their spring-time delights. Dominion Seed House is reaping benefits from the change in shopping habits as more and more shoppers are turning to catalogs for almost every type of product imaginable.

The gardening group is brand loyal. However, with unpredictable changes in color choice or flowers and the increasing variety of vegetables available, seed and bulb suppliers are at risk in a very risky business. Very few industries face the level of unpredictability with regard to fickle weather and the changing mood of consumers as this one, leaving seed and bulb suppliers often vulnerable with each spring planting season.

Due to the varied product mix selection, retailers are able to ride out a bad gardening season where seed and bulb suppliers can not. In Canada, there are some factors of taste which suppliers must react to. One year, bulbs in a certain color may not sell well even if they sold well a few years earlier. In Western Canada, gardeners prefer green beans while Eastern Canadians grow more yellow beans. Even the top pea can change at the drop of a hat.

New product development is an issue in this type of industry. Expanding a product line takes a great deal of ingenuity and perseverance on the part of the suppliers. Innovative marketing is important in this industry.

QUESTIONS

1. Why would there be a high level of brand loyalty in the gardening industry?
2. How does relationship marketing play a role in this industry? What does it take to gain a competitive advantage in the seed and bulb industry?
3. Relate what you know about branding strategies to this industry? How important is quality and image in this industry?

Source: This case was prepared by Deborah Andrus and is based on the *Venture* series episode "Garden Biz," which was first broadcast on March 27, 1994.

352

The Product: Goods

THINK ABOUT IT!

DOES PRODUCT PROLIFERATION CREATE HEADACHES?

Have you ever stood in the cold-remedy aisle at your local drugstore and tried to figure out which product you need for your cold? Do you want an antihistamine? A decongestant? How do you avoid getting one that will put you to sleep while you are driving or one that will keep you awake when you want to sleep? William Weilbacher, in his book, *Brand Marketing*,[1] tells a story about watching a couple try to buy aspirin. After studying eight versions of Bayer and reading the labels over and over again to try to figure out the differences, the couple finally gave up and bought the house brand.

The business section of most bookstores is full of books on how to "grow" a business, but Weilbacher's book unmasks the destructiveness of *product proliferation* carried to extremes. According to Weilbacher, in addition to creating consumer confusion, the proliferation of products and *line extensions* (related products sold under the same brand name) has made

it impossible to create the psychological value embodied in the great brands of the past—Kodak, Coca-Cola, Tide, Green Giant, Marlboro, BMW. His thesis is that we are drowning in unfathomable and largely insignificant product differences.

Do you agree? In your experience, have you been able to find exactly what you want? This is one benefit of information technology and micro-segmentation. Have you ever been baffled by the number of product choices? Or is choice so valuable to you that you regard excessive product proliferation as only a small nuisance of no great importance? How do you think most consumers feel about this issue? ■

In this chapter we consider the complexities of developing and marketing product "goods"; the next chapter focuses on the marketing of services and ideas. Although the distinction between products and services is important, keep in mind that there are many similarities between the two. For example, our discussion of "Product Objectives and Strategies" in the first section of this chapter in most instances applies equally to services and products. What sometimes makes a discussion of products and services confusing is the fact that although both are technically products, *product* is more often used interchangeably with the word *goods* than with *services*.

Another thing you need to keep in mind is that many businesses provide both products and services. Benetton, a noted clothing manufacturer, also serves customers in retailing its product through its own stores with carefully trained salespeople. McDonald's is considered by most people to be a service business, yet it makes the tangible products—hamburgers, fries, shakes, and so forth—it sells.

PRODUCT OBJECTIVES AND STRATEGIES ●

Product objectives direct the development of the product and the *product mix*—how many product variations will be offered and in what configurations. Product objectives may also focus on developing products with certain price points, quality levels, or appeal to niche markets. Strategies to achieve these objectives are usually cost driven and often involve changing specifications or materials to get a tougher, lighter, faster, cheaper, or more aesthetically pleasing product. They may involve manipulating the production schedule to better accommodate just-in-time ordering (see Chapters 14 and 15) or redesigning the product to meet shelf configurations that affect packaging.

In terms of marketing planning, it is necessary to consider the product's features and benefits in targeting and segmenting. To an important degree, a company's products define its business. Although making or manufacturing an industrial or packaged good is usually the responsibility of a company's production division (remember the other business functions we discussed in Chapter 2), this department must work closely with marketing (as we also emphasized in that chapter). It is marketing's responsibility to identify what customers want and what competitors are doing. Based on this information, the production people set up assembly lines, acquire raw materials, and handle all the other details needed to actually manufacture a product. This is an example of the *integrated marketing* process that was discussed in Chapter 2—marketing and production planning must be integrated if the company is to be successful.

PRODUCT FEATURES

Product **features** are the physical *attributes* and perceived service advantages that characterize a given product. Refer back to Chapter 2 to see how David Garvin of Harvard Business School lists eight different dimensions of quality. Among a car's most basic product features, for example, are its size and body styling, the power of its engine, and the gas mileage it gets. About to become almost as standard as these features, interestingly, is the cup holder. GM minivans seem to be the winner in the cup-holder war with one model that has fourteen, although Chrysler is adding more to its vans and luxury cars. The cup-holder war is more than a design fad. With people making longer commutes and fast-food drive-up windows gaining in popularity, cars are becoming fast food diners.

Industrial buyers also base their decisions on features. The German firm of Windmoller & Holscher makes high-quality flexible packaging machines with "extras" such as microprocessor controls and data storage programming. These features are important to manufacturers of goods, such as flashlights and kitchen utensils, that come mounted on cardboard within a tough plastic "bubble wrap."

Product features are important factors in buyer decision making. When buyers select a product, they base their decision partly on its positioning—its overall image and the way they perceive it versus competing products and how their peers will perceive them for buying it—and partly on its design. They compare *product features* and *perceived benefits* as well as brand images—the values created for the product by the marketing effort. Given equal availability of products and pricing, both physical elements and added values such as quality, design, warranties, services, and packaging are important.

For example, a watch sold as an upscale sportsman's watch should have a stainless steel casing and a stopwatch function and be shock resistant, waterproof, and antimagnetic. Timex has moved into this category with a line of products that has a different set of features. The Skiathlon comes with a thermometer, oversize control buttons (so that it can be operated easily with ski gloves or cold fingers), and two straps—an elastic one that fits over a heavy ski parka sleeve, and a lighter one to wear with thinner ski clothing or casual wear. Timex also makes the Ironman for triatheletes and those who take biking, running, or swimming very seriously; the Victory for sailboat racers; and the Aerobix for those partial to aerobic activities. In contrast, the "fun-fashion" watch market is dominated by Swatch, the Swiss firm that introduced fashion watches in bright colors and inventive graphics. All of these watches perform the same basic function of telling time, but their product features—and hence their value to consumers—differ radically (see Exhibit 11-1).

A product's added-value features often determine its image more than its functional features do. For example, the function of a tractor is to pull farm implements. All tractors do that. Buyer choices, however, are based both on the ability of the tractor to pull implements and on brand image and reputation as well as dealer reputation for service and support. The success of a product depends not only on its basic "hardware" but also on this surrounding "software"—including image, feel, and customer appeal added by marketing. The more competitive a category is—watches, for example, are highly competitive—the more these added-value elements influence the selection process. Rolex is sold much more on its image than on its physical features.

features
The distinctive physical characteristics and perceived service advantages of a product.

Exhibit 11-1
Watch That
Swatch!

Swatch has
always positioned
itself as a fashion
watch. In its new
lines it is empha-
sizing other fea-
tures, such as
water resistance
for this line of
deep-sea
watches.

PRODUCT BENEFITS

Most consumers choose a product on the basis of what the product will do for them—what the features mean in terms of *benefits* to the user. This distinction between features and benefits is the focus of the first chapter objective. Customers are not necessarily looking for products in a product search but for solutions to their problem. As Harvard's Ted Levitt points out, consumers (and industrial buyers) don't buy quarter-inch drill bits, they buy quarter-inch holes. The benefit is the hole—how smooth it is, how quickly it can be made, and how accurate it is. However, in order to ensure that customers get holes that are smooth, quick to make, and precisely one-quarter inch in diameter, a producer must focus on the tangible aspect of the drill bit: the type of metal used, the method of tempering, the distance between cutting edges—that is, on the whole tool-and-die operation. Find out what is the core benefit that the customer is seeking and provide it. Effective marketing, as shown in the next section, ensures that the product has the proper attributes and that these features are communicated in a way that demonstrates the benefits they provide. It is necessary to create products around customer problems and desired solutions and not simply the technology offered by the production department.

RISKS AND GAMBLES

FROM BENEFIT TO HEALTHY CATEGORY

One of the most unusual product-development stories in the history of modern marketing recounts how an unpopular health food served at a religious sanatorium became the leading brand in one of the most competitive and largest food categories in today's supermarkets.

In 1894 two brothers who owned and managed a sanatorium affiliated with the Seventh-Day Adventist Church made an interesting discovery. They had long been trying to get their guests to eat healthy foods such as ground grains. But the guests—wealthy people used to the good life—complained about the taste and texture of the brothers' "health foods." One of the brothers then tried running some day-old wheat dough through rollers. The resultant crispy flakes met with the approval of the sanatorium's clients, which spurred the brothers to try the same process with other grains.

By 1906, one of the brothers, Will Kellogg, was convinced there was a larger market for his corn flakes. He set up the Battle Creek Toasted Corn Flake Company to market the product, which soon became well known as Kellogg's Corn Flakes. His brother and former partner, John, a physician, objected that advertising the corn flakes violated medical ethics since it was being used as a health food at the sanatorium. Will apparently ignored him, and today Kellogg's is the world's largest marketer of cereals.

A postscript to this story is even more interesting. One of the guests who stayed at the Kellogg sanatorium soon after corn flakes were introduced was a fellow named C. W. Post—the founder and namesake of one of Kellogg's biggest competitors. Whatever the sanatorium did for his health, it clearly was an enormous benefit to his finances, for it gave him the idea to get in on the ground floor of the marketing of this new type of product.

PRODUCT DESIGN

Another factor that influences purchase decisions is *product design*, the way a product is created, engineered, styled, or fashioned. A successful design is both functional and aesthetically pleasing to the customer; these are the important factors alluded to in the second chapter objective.

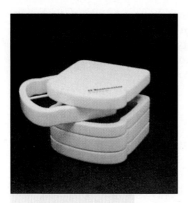

Product Architecture

Its form hardly looks like a toaster, but its design suggests a sense of liberation from the humdrum efficiency of the kitchen. Such advances as digital electronics, with computer chips replacing bulkier machinery, allow contemporary designers more freedom to experiment with "product architecture." For some goods, design is now a feature distinct from essentially functional features.

Design begins with the *function* of the product. For example, batteries must have positive and negative contact points; computers must have some means of entering information, processing it, and storing it. But the design of a product also must take account of consumer needs and aesthetics. Computer manufacturers, for example, are designing more and more powerful machines that are shrinking in size and becoming more sophisticated in styling. Since design involves functional, mechanical, technical, and aesthetic decisions, the people who develop products must be both engineers and artists.

One of the most dramatic illustrations of the importance of design aesthetics is the success of the Ford Taurus and Mercury Sable. The introduction of these innovatively styled cars in 1985 turned the Ford Motor Company around. Don Petersen, chairman of Ford at that time, put it into perspective: "Our products [had become] progressively worse until we hit rock bottom." As he explained, up to that point, financial, marketing, engineering, and production concerns had dictated the way new cars were developed at Ford, "choking off the creativity of the very people whose job it was to be creative . . . the industrial designers." Petersen came to believe that design is "a major strategic weapon."[2]

Designing a good product is only the beginning. Successful products are constantly improved as times and technology change. The Design Exchange ad in Exhibit 11-2 explains how innovations continue to modernize automobiles. Innovation in product design can also create a competitive advantage. The Bacho Ergo screwdriver, whose handle is shaped to allow workers to use both hands (as people usually do when handling a screwdriver) has won design prizes, been displayed in museums, and sold well.

Design Costs   Every marketing decision, including product design, must weigh the costs against the projected increase in revenue or market share. To design the next state-of-the-art 35mm camera, for example, will cost in excess of $10 million. Before Kodak or Canon undertakes this, it must forecast sales to show that the investment will be successful. Production processes are very complex, and one small change in a specification can create enormous cost increases. Every product designer needs a thorough understanding of a product's ingredients and production processes in order to be able to estimate production costs. Marketing managers, too, must be concerned about the production particulars detailed in Table 11-1.

Packaging   The package that contains the product has several functions: it provides protection, it facilitates transportation, and it conveys information about the product and its intended audience. The last, a communication function, will be discussed in detail in Chapter 19. In terms of marketing strategy, packaging is the most visible statement of a product's quality other than the product itself. Generic products, for example, may be signaled by their austere black-and-white package graphics but not always. Some stores however have more than one in-house brand of differing quality or value.

The packaging size is an important decision that supports targeting and segmenting strategies. Distribution channels are particularly concerned with the size, shipping, and stacking requirements of packages. One classic example of a strategically successful package is the egg-shaped container used for L'Eggs pantyhose. The novel product container must be displayed in its own stand, which increases the product's visibility.

The package itself can be an added value. For example, aseptic packaging created an entirely new category in the beverage market. Juices in aseptic boxes are portable, convenient, lightweight, healthy drinks—which turned out to be ideal for kids, campers, and other lunch toters, although they are a

Exhibit 11-2
Innovation and Design in the
Auto Industry

Innovation is the most
important factor in product
design, as this ad for Design
Exchange (DX) expresses.

problem for landfills. Many products promote the reusability of their containers, and some containers, such as liquor gift bottles and Avon bottles, are even considered collectibles.

Product Liability In designing goods, companies must always keep in mind the need to produce safe products. The issue of **product liability**—the reality that businesses are responsible for injuries or damage caused by their products—is a major concern of goods marketers. Consumer laws and rules issued by such regulatory agencies as Consumer and Corporate Affairs Canada, as well as regulations being passed by Consumer and Corporate Affairs Canada and the European Union, focus on consumer safety. When product failure or faulty design results in some kind of injury to the product user, the manufacturer is likely to be sued. Publicity about such legal actions and other kinds of product "scares" can quickly have a strong negative effect on sales and the brand's image.

In April 1993, for example, the U.S. National Highway Traffic Safety Administration requested that General Motors issue a voluntary recall of GM pickup trucks manufactured between 1973 and 1987 that had side-mounted gas tanks because some of these trucks had been exploding upon impact when involved in accidents. GM refused the request, just as it had refused suggestions made earlier that month by consumer safety advocates that it install a protective cage around these gas tanks. The cost of installing protective cages was estimated at $200 million, while a voluntary recall would have set the company back by $300 million to $1 billion. The publicity about GM's

product liability
The reality that firms are responsible for any damage or injuries caused by their products.

TABLE 11-1	PRODUCTION CONCERNS

1. *Raw Materials and/or Components* These are variable costs and can account for a significant portion of the price of a good; by knowing what ingredients and parts are used, the marketing manager can help make informed decisions on appropriate substitutions that will not have a negative impact on the product's marketing strategy. For example, if Häagen Dazs ice cream bars are positioned as upscale ice cream products, then production can't cut back on the use of high-quality—and more expensive—ingredients without damaging the product's image and position.

2. *Production Processes* A production line affects marketing costs in several ways: (a) *overhead*—the cost of machinery must be amortized over a period of time and applied to the product either directly or, more commonly, indirectly in the form of fixed overhead; (b) *labor costs*—these are determined by both the number of people needed and their skill levels (the higher the skill level, the higher the wage); (c) *speed*—determines how many products are produced per hour: the higher the speed of the production line, the more units over which labor and overhead costs can be spread. Before marketing directors request a product change that could affect the production process (such as in ingredients or packaging size), they must know the cost impact. Changes that add to production costs, either directly or indirectly, must be evaluated against the potential for increased sales or decreased costs in other areas.

3. *Research and Development* Companies, especially pharmaceutical makers like Eli Lilly and Company, frequently spend millions to develop a new product and refine old ones. These R&D costs must be recovered—a task that is accomplished by including them in the price of new products. Although equipment is often shown as an overhead cost, it must in the end be paid for by the consumer. Marketing may discover a certain consumer need, but the R&D cost of finding the answer to that need (such as the cure for cancer) may be prohibitive. Because there is no guarantee that R&D can do what it sets out to do, R&D spending is always a risk. The smaller the company, and the fewer products over which to spread R&D costs, the higher the R&D risk. (R&D is discussed in Chapter 13.)

4. *Quality Control* When we talk about a product's quality, we are referring to its degree of excellence in production and its lack of defects. The best quality results from a total commitment to quality throughout the design, production, and marketing of a product. If sales are being hurt because of poor design, product defects, or poor performance, marketing needs to talk to the responsible people in quality control and/or production to see what corrections can be made and at what cost.

adamant stance convinced many people that the company was more concerned about its profits than about its customers. So GM was not only fighting cases in court, it was also fighting to save its reputation.

GM had won three and lost four court cases on this issue by the middle of the spring of 1993. The auto maker would not disclose the number of out-of-court settlements it had made. In one case, however, GM was ordered to pay the family of a deceased motorist $105 million.

It is not enough that products be made safe, they must also be accompanied by instructions for safe use—which generally appear on the package. As is well known, pharmaceutical companies are required to state proper dosages and all known side effects of a drug's use on the package. Other manufacturers are voluntarily making every effort to prevent injuries in people who use their products. For example, a small industrial equipment company that produces gearboxes and control mechanisms for hydraulic lifts has sought help from visual communication consultants in designing and placing instructions and warning labels on its equipment. The company is trying to make every effort to prevent someone from being injured while operating the equipment. This *effort to educate* can also be a legal defense should the company ever be sued. Product liability suits as a result of production and design decisions are a legal concern. Helping to prevent such suits through product instruction is a marketing responsibility.

Global Product Design Function is an important factor in designing products for international markets. Consider the characteristics of a refrigerator. In industrialized countries the *primary functional purposes* of the refrigerator are to store frozen foods for weeks, preserve perishable foods between car trips to the supermarket, and keep bottled drinks cold for short-notice consumption. In many countries, however, frozen foods are not widely used and people shop daily, not weekly. The primary functions of the refrigerator in such countries are to store small quantities of perishable food for one day and to preserve leftovers for slightly longer periods. Given these needs, smaller refrigerators are adequate. But refrigerators have an important *secondary purpose* in some developing countries: they fulfill a need for prestige. In these countries there is demand for the largest models, which may be prominently displayed in the living room rather than in the kitchen.

Other product features that are important in international marketing are durability and service, quality, and method of operation. For example, in developing markets appliances are more likely to be reparable than in advanced countries, where the cost of labor makes repair expensive. A reparable appliance is a quality product in low-income markets, where high-priced products that are not built to be repaired are perceived as being of low quality.

Another important characteristic in the global market is *method of operation*. For example, the voltage and cycle requirements for an electrical appliance are important method-of-operation considerations in determining product design. The key for global marketers is to design a product with widely desired features that need only minor modifications to fit an individual country or culture.

PRODUCT QUALITY

Excellence in product design can contribute to a major competitive advantage—*product quality*. Product quality, the focus of chapter objective three, has two dimensions: production and use. For the producer, quality depends on how closely the manufacturing process adheres to specifications. For the buyer, quality is determined by how well products perform and how closely they match needs and wants. Buyers weigh the quality of a product against its price. A person buying a bicycle for occasional recreational use is generally less concerned about the quality of the bike's drive-chain system than someone who participates in competitive bike racing. The second buyer is much more likely to be willing to pay a higher price for higher quality.

Quality can be perceived in different ways. Caterpillar tractors have more breakdowns soon after purchase than Komatsu tractors. Komatsu's better performance is the result of more welding of parts. But this design and production difference makes Komatsu tractors more than twice as expensive as Caterpillars to repair when they do break down. Customers who most value reliability believe Komatsu has the higher quality, while those who focus on the cost of operation prefer Caterpillar.

Product quality is determined by a number of things: planning and design, raw materials used, production techniques, quality-control measures, and management philosophy. **Quality control** is the process of testing a product during its production to detect possible defects in the product itself

quality control
The process of testing products in production to detect and correct defects in structure or function.

or its operation. Although production managers for many companies continually work to reduce the number of defects, it is sometimes not economically feasible to aim for zero defects at every step in the production process. Although that is the objective of some quality control programs, some companies, however, use quality-control checkpoints where defects are either corrected or the product is discarded. Because some defects do not affect the primary function or performance of the product, companies in the china, cutlery, luggage, apparel, and other businesses sell products with minor quality problems as "seconds" in burgeoning "factory outlets."

Warranties and Guarantees An important intangible feature of many goods—especially durable goods—is some form of warranty that provides buyers with recourse should they get a defective product. A **warranty**, which benefits buyers by reducing their risk, is a formal statement of expected product performance that lists the types of services the manufacturer will provide if the buyer discovers defects or performance problems. Products protected by a warranty have to be returned to a manufacturer or designated repair center. A classic example of a firm whose warranty has made its business is Midas Mufflers. Midas promises to replace any muffler it installs for "as long as you own your car." Few people own cars long enough to cash in on this warranty, but the security it brings has meant success for Midas.

More general in scope than a warranty, a **guarantee** assures the buyer that the product can be returned if its performance is unsatisfactory. As we noted in Chapter 6, consumers don't like to take risks, and the more they pay for an item, the less they like to take chances. An unconditional money-back guarantee eliminates most of the consumer risk involved in a purchase and can give the seller an important competitive advantage. Eaton's, for example, has a policy of accepting any returns, regardless of the reason, and tries to make its customers feel comfortable with the return process. Eaton's then returns these items to the manufacturer for credit. Thus it is the manufacturers who are really taking responsibility for defects when stores have such a policy. If a manufacturer refuses to cooperate, a retail chain like Wal-Mart may stop carrying its products, a move that can seriously hurt the manufacturer's sales.

The Philosophy of Quality Increasingly, companies are recognizing that concern about quality cannot be limited to a few people in a quality-control department or to a reliance on a warranty program. Rather, it must be a constant preoccupation of employees at all levels in all aspects of production and marketing. *Total quality control* (TQC), a management philosophy developed by marketing theorist Armand Feigenbaum, requires a commitment to quality by everyone in the company and uses scientific methods to measure improvements in quality.

The world's foremost quality expert W. Edwards Deming, who is known for the Total Quality Management (TQM) approach, argued that quality must be built into a product; it cannot be vested in inspections designed to catch and correct problems after products are produced.[3] One way to do this is to institute *quality-improvement processes* (QIPs), corporate quality programs that encompass such diverse areas as statistical analysis of defects, delivery and service, customer relations, and employee communications. Companies as diverse as Xerox and Harley Davidson have QIP programs. QIP programs produce better products, but they are so demanding that they usually require changes in the entire corporate culture.[4]

To encourage companies to take quality seriously, the Canadian Award for Business Excellence is given annually to companies that best represent quality excellence in Canadian business. The CABE trophy was introduced in 1984 and is administered by the National Quality in Ottawa and by Industry Canada. Awards are made in the areas of Entrepreneurship, Environment, In-

warranty
A formal statement of expected product performance and of the manufacturer's liability for replacement or repair of defects.

guarantee
A general assurance that a product can be returned if its performance is unsatisfactory.

Exhibit 11-3
Quality Wins National Award

Calgary-based Canadian Fracmaster won the Canadian Award for Business Excellence in 1993. The organization is a privately owned company that provides services to the oil and gas industry. Known for quality, innovation, and skills in negotiating, the company expanded into the former Soviet Union and is now the largest foreign oil producer and exporter in Russia. Pictured are (left to right) Alfred H. Balm, Doug Ramsay, Donald Schurman, and Christina A. Gold.

dustrial Design, Innovation, Invention, Marketing, and Total Quality. Marketing winners include Canadian Fracmaster of Calgary (see Exhibit 11-3); Jean Coutu Groups of Longueil, Quebec; MBI Systems Inc. of Longueil, Quebec; Connaught Laboratories of North York, Ontario; Fountain Tire Ltd. of Edmonton; Grenico Inc. of Quebec; Classy Formal Wear Inc. of Montreal; Pursuit Fisheries (1987) Ltd.—A Division of Clearwater Fine Foods Inc. of Bedford, Nova Scotia; W.C. Wood Company Ltd. of Guelph, Ontario; JPL International Inc. of Saint-Laurent, Quebec; Datasym Inc. of Bedford, Ontario; and Koala Springs Canada Inc. of Concord, Ontario.

THE CLASSIFICATION OF GOODS ●

In order to plan the marketing of goods, you need to understand the differences between various types of goods, the subject of chapter objective four. Business analysts generally classify both consumer and industrial goods according to two criteria: how long the goods remain in use and who uses them. Table 11-2 summarizes both of these classifications and their subcategories.

PERIOD OF USE

Some products are bought frequently and used often; others are purchased infrequently and are used either seldom or over a long period of time. This dichotomy sets up a major difference in the way products are marketed.

consumables
Products of low value that are purchased frequently and that have a relatively short usage period.

Durables and Consumables Goods purchased frequently and used up rapidly are called **consumables**, as we said in Chapter 1. Examples are food, cleaning items, paper goods, and beverages, as well as *soft goods* such as apparel, linens, and textiles. Building brand loyalty is especially desirable when selling consumables; ads for these products typically focus on brand image. Packaging is so important to consumables that many household and personal-care products are sometimes called *packaged goods*. (In Europe these products are referred to as *fast-moving consumer goods*, or *FMCG*.) In contrast, *durable goods,* which we also defined in Chapter 1, are bought infrequently and used over an extended period of time. Examples are fountain pens, tractors, major appliances, furniture, and eye glasses. **Durables** are usually mar-

durables
Products that last over an extended period.

TABLE 11-2	**PRODUCT CLASSIFICATIONS**

A. Classification by Period of Use

1. *Durables:* high-ticket items that last for an extended period.
   a. *White goods:* major appliances
   b. *Soft goods:* products constructed of fabric and textiles

2. *Consumables:* products that are purchased frequently over a relatively short period of time
   a. *Packaged goods:* consumables that are distributed, displayed, and sold in a container

3. *Disposables:* products designed to be used for only a short period of time and then discarded

4. *Collectibles:* products that become part of a valued group and that collectors hope will increase in value

B. Classification by Buyer Orientation

1. *Convenience Products:* frequently purchased products, including commodity and inexpensive items; products that generally have little or no brand difference and are sold on price and availability
   a. *Staples:* regularly purchased consumer products
   b. *Impulse products:* convenience items purchased without much deliberation
   c. *Emergency products:* items needed urgently and generally unexpectedly at a particular time
   d. *Commodity products:* undifferentiated products sold on price and availability—can include supplies, raw materials, and parts

2. *Preference Products:* products that elicit high brand preference

3. *Shopping Products:* products that involve a lot of comparison shopping before a purchase decision is made—buyers take the time to "shop around" for a particular type of product or feature

4. *Specialty Products:* products that are unique in some physical way and valued for that distinctiveness

keted on the basis of their distinctive features, the value which they offer and the level of quality.

Disposables and Collectibles As consumers demand more convenience, a growing number of durable categories are having to include *disposable* products, which are inexpensive durables that have moved over to the consumable category. Examples are disposable razors and disposable contact lenses, butane cigarette lighters, and even some cameras. Consumers of disposables are often willing to pay more for the added convenience of these items. Disposables are generally marketed in the same way as consumables. Conversely, *collectibles*, such as rare coins, stamps, statuary, art, and various types of memorabilia, are often marketed like durables. Once merely a promotional feature to sell bubble gum to children, baseball cards are now big business. It's estimated that $500 million worth of baseball cards are traded each year.

OPEN TO DEBATE

IS DISPOSABILITY A PRODUCT FEATURE?

In 1989 food industry experts hailed aseptic boxes as the greatest technical achievement of the last fifty years (beating out frozen orange juice and the microwave). Food manufacturers began using these packages because of their features—thin layers of paper and plastic, which makes them both sturdy and lightweight, and the aluminum-foil lining which keeps light and oxygen from spoiling the contents. Unfortunately, progress in packaging turned out to be an environmental problem. Landfill operators claim that the layered materials are too hard to separate and that the aseptic boxes clog disposal sites.

The problem is much larger than disposable packaging. Landfill operators are searching the earth over for places to dump the accumulating trash that is becoming a turn-of-the-century nightmare. Car junkyards have been littering the landscape since the beginning of the century, and researchers have been working almost as long to discover what new products can be made from reclaimed rubber tires. And now computer disposal is becoming a serious problem.[5]

Some companies are taking more responsibility for the disposal problem. Carnation has converted its pet food cans to recyclable aluminum. Glad trash bags are now made of a new plastic supposed to decompose more quickly than their original plastic trash bags. Heinz has replaced its perennial dump

The Disposal Problem

Great inventions come to rest in waste management centers, where they can create great problems if no thought is given in product design to product disposal.

367

filler, the squeezable ketchup bottle, with one that can be more easily recycled. GE is collecting used high-performance plastics from local dumps to be ground down and reincarnated as ABX, a tough plastic that can withstand high temperatures and corrosive chemicals. Colgate-Palmolive, P&G, and the Dial Corporation are testing new packaging that uses refillable containers for detergents. P&G's Downy fabric softener refill is being repackaged as a concentrate in a milk carton.

Disposable products are a wonderful convenience for consumers. Whether Canadians and people in other developed nations will give up the convenience of nonrefillables for the sake of the environment remains to be seen.

BUYER ORIENTATION

Goods can be classified several ways, such as how long they last, their relative importance to buyers, and the amount of energy or effort needed to acquire them. The four categories of goods listed under the *B* heading in Table 11-2—*convenience, preference, shopping*, and *specialty*—are based on the notion of buyer orientation.

Murphy and Enis developed a model (Figure 11-1) that helps explain how buyer orientation combines with the three factors of risk, effort, and involvement to influence marketing activities. An understanding of these relationships can help marketers select the best strategy for selling each of these four categories of goods. *Effort* is the combination of money, time, and energy a buyer will expend to acquire a product: it encompasses the physical aspects of the buying process. *Risk* is buyer recognition that a product might not provide the benefits anticipated. *Involvement* refers to the amount of overall thought and concern invested; it encompasses the psychological aspects of the buying process. Knowing where a product fits in this model helps a marketer plan strategy. For example, knowing that chewing gum is a convenience product is equivalent to knowing that consumers will not go to great efforts to buy it. Therefore distribution should be extensive to minimize the effort the customer has to make to buy the product. On the other hand, knowing that buying a package of gum is not seen as high risk by the consumer, the marketer may decide on a selling proposition that is more emotional than rational.

As shown in Figure 11-1, customers, both consumer and business-to-business, generally put forth less effort to buy low involvement products; also, low involvement products are considered to be less risky to buy. Buying high involvement products, however, generally involves more effort and more risk. Take collectibles, for example: the "hunt" to find these is part of the buying experience, the risk of buying something at a high price that may soon lose its value is always present.

capital good
Expensive, long-lasting industrial good used in the production of other goods and services.

expense good
Inexpensive industrial good used regularly and rapidly.

Industrial goods have traditionally been divided into *capital goods* and *expense goods*. A **capital good** is expensive, long-lasting, and used to directly or indirectly produce other goods—an example is a machine used to grind wheat into flour. An **expense good** is relatively inexpensive and consumed regularly and rapidly. A good bought for individual use is a consumer good, but that same good—be it a light bulb, a computer, or a set of curtains—is an industrial (or business-to-business) product if purchased for use in a business. This focus on *use* is important to marketers because consumer and industrial buying behaviors differ (see Chapters 6 and 7), and so must the marketing efforts aimed at each of these groups.

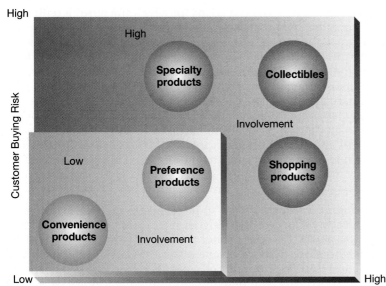

Figure 11-1
How Buyer Orientation
Determines Marketing Effort

*Source: Adapted from Patrick E.
Murphy and Ben M. Enis, "Classifying
Products Strategically,"* Journal of
Marketing *50 (1986): 24–42.*

Convenience Products Buyers give little thought to the buying decision when purchasing *convenience goods* because purchases of these low-priced, widely available products pose little risk and require little effort. We divide consumer convenience goods into *staples*, which are regularly purchased products such as fresh produce, flour, sugar, and toilet paper; *impulse items*, which are bought on the spur of the moment (almost all of the products you see while waiting in line at the supermarket are impulse items), and *emergency products*, which are "must-have-one-now" items such as mittens during the season's first snowstorm and flashlights during a power outage. Convenience goods generate little brand loyalty because consumers usually have acceptable substitutes.[6] Since buyers switch easily from one brand to another if the price is right, sales promotions are particularly important in marketing consumer convenience goods.

Industrial buyers also purchase convenience goods. The best example is **commodity goods**—undifferentiated products such as raw materials like gasoline and corn. When manufactured *parts* are undifferentiated, such as nails, they, too, can be considered convenience goods. So can supplies—computer paper, fuel for delivery trucks, and maintenance and repair items such as paint, floor wax, mops, and fan belts. Like consumer convenience goods, industrial convenience goods are marketed on the basis of price and availability. Supplies can be particularly competitive items, making cost and delivery very important.

commodity goods
Undifferentiated products, like raw materials, with little difference between supplier offerings, that are purchased frequently and in large quantities as consumables.

Preference Products Nondurables that involve slightly more effort and/or risk than convenience goods are called *preference goods*. Although these goods require low shopping effort and little involvement, buyers have high brand preference. In fact, the difference between convenience and preference products is primarily the power of branding: the customer has a good comfort level buying a particular brand because a good brand relationship has been established. The most common examples of customer preference products are in the packaged-goods industry—soft drinks, cookies and snack foods, toothpaste, and shampoo. Industrial preference goods include particular brands of such things as typewriter and computer printer ribbons and computer disks.

Shopping Products   Differentiated goods for which the buyer is willing to compare prices, quality, style, and other features are called *shopping goods*. Shopping goods are higher priced and less frequently purchased than convenience goods. Examples of consumer shopping goods are appliances, bedding, china, audio equipment, and fashion apparel. Consumers will often travel to several stores to make comparisons before they buy a shopping good. Advertising and personal sales, as well as packaging and product literature, are important in marketing shopping goods because of the need to increase brand knowledge and to emphasize product differences. Industrial shopping goods include equipment and specialized parts sold on the basis of distinctive features, such as modular office furniture, personal computers, and X-ray equipment. Since industrial shopping goods are relatively expensive and long-lasting, many people are usually involved in the buying decision.

Specialty Products   Products similar to preference goods but that involve higher risks (generally because of their higher price) and extra efforts to find are called *specialty products*. These products are generally characterized by high brand differentiation, high involvement on the part of the buyer, and (often) strong brand loyalty. Examples of consumer specialty goods are expensive perfumes, sports cars, and designer clothing. A consumer who has a strong brand preference for Oscar de la Renta perfume, Ralph Lauren Polo shirts, or a Prince tennis racquet is willing to make an extra effort to find and buy the desired brand. Advertising plays an important role in the preselling of specialty products, particularly those with strong emotional images or personality association. For example, Royal de Versailles jewelers uses strong emotional associations in its specialty jewelry advertisements, such as the "Celebration of Love" theme.

Industrial specialty goods include major capital goods like one-of-a-kind pieces of equipment, a six-color printing press, and an industrial robotic system. As you might expect, the buying process for industrial specialty goods is often long and complicated. A company that makes paper napkins may spend months considering whether to purchase a new napkin-folding machine from a company like C. G. Bretting, which virtually owns the market. Most of Bretting's machines sell for about $750,000. This may seem expensive for putting a few folds in a napkin, but the process demands a highly engineered piece of equipment for two reasons: first, the paper being folded is thin and difficult to handle; and second, the machine must be fast. Bretting's machines can fold 2,000 napkins per minute. This efficiency is important to most napkin manufacturers; they will go to great lengths to get the most efficient machine available since this will reduce their production costs.

PRODUCT ITEMS, MIXES, AND LINES ⬤

In the old days a salesperson would be asked: "What line are you in?" The question referred to the *line of goods* he or she specialized in selling. Today the question is more likely to be: "Who are you with?" Since modern salespeople often sell a range of products—representing a company's *product mix*—they are identified more by company affiliation than by product line.

stock-keeping units (SKUs)
Individual product items and their identifying inventory numbers.

STOCK-KEEPING UNITS (SKUs)

Manufacturers, intermediaries (sometimes called middlemen or resellers), and retailers alike keep track of inventories in terms of **stock keeping units**, or **SKUs**. These are individual product items: the 180-gram package of Miss

Vickie's Potato chips and the same brand's 55-gram package would have separate SKU numbers. For most consumer packaged goods and, increasingly, for industrial goods as well, the SKU is part of the **UPC (universal product code)**—the barcode or set of vertical bars printed on a package that is electronically scanned to total up your purchases at a store's cash register. These bar codes help you get through the checkout line quickly and, even more important, help retailers keep track of their inventory by recording every item sold. Some stores' inventory systems are so sophisticated that the system automatically places an order with the manufacturer of an item when the store's inventory of that item falls below a certain level.

Another advantage of the UPC coding system is that stores no longer have to put the price on each individual package because it is indicated at the point of purchase. To make a price change, the retailer simply enters the new price into the computer and changes the sign on the shelf. The latter is very important for customer relationships because when a retailer changes the price in the computer but fails to change it on the shelf, customers quickly complain and sometimes accuse the store of trying to trick them.

PRODUCT MIX AND LINES

The differences between product mix and product line are the focus of chapter objective five. Very few companies follow the pattern of McIlhenny's Tabasco Sauce and focus all their efforts on producing and selling just one product line. Many market a variety of product lines, often in completely different product categories. A company's **product mix** is the total of all the products it makes. Determining the product mix is a top-management decision because the more varied the product lines, the greater the need to coordinate production, distribution, and selling systems. For example, when P&G acquired the Fisher Nut company, it expanded its snack-food product mix. The purchase of this SBU (strategic business unit) was also a wise strategic move because it brought cost efficiencies to P&G, which was already buying peanuts for its Jif peanut butter. Table 11-3 identifies some of the advantages of having a varied product mix.

product mix The assortment of products and product lines available from a given manufacturer.

371

THE PRODUCT: GOODS

TABLE 11-3	PRODUCT-MIX OBJECTIVES

1. *Capitalize on Areas of Strength*   For example, Rubbermaid, Inc. (manufacturers of plastic household utility items), recently acquired Little Tikes Company, which makes toys. Using its strong distribution network and sales force, Rubbermaid has taken Little Tikes from a company operating out of an old barn to a $200 million-plus brand.

2. *Counter Seasonal Fluctuations*   Lipton spans the seasons by promoting the use of its dry soup mixes for dips (e.g., the famous California Onion Dip) during summer months. The Sun Tea concept and promotion were specifically developed by Lipton in the late 1970s for naturally brewing tea during warm weather months.

3. *Exploit Brand Name*   The Colgate-Palmolive Company, knowing that the name Colgate is well known and respected, has tested using it on a variety of new products, including over-the-counter drugs, aspirin, and shampoo. Black & Decker, which has established itself as a manufacturer of durable shop tools such as drills and sanders, decided in the 1980s to place its name on a line of small home appliances—today that line has sales of over $750 million a year. Extending a brand name to unrelated products, however, can be risky.

product line
A group of products that are related and similar in one or more ways and manufactured by the same company.

Most firms find that once they have a plant, production line, trained workers, established distribution channels, a sales force, and a certain level of brand awareness, it is profitable to use this integrated system to produce and market a line of products. All items in a product line usually (though not always) carry the same brand name, as in the case of a paper products manufacturer that makes paper towels, toilet paper, napkins, and disposable diapers. A **product line** is a group of products that are similar in: (1) product formulation; (2) production methods; (3) packaging; (4) channels of distribution; and/or (5) consumer targets. For example, Oscar Mayer's hot dogs make up a product line because: (1) the basic ingredients are the same; (2) all are made by grinding up the meat, adding the spices, and baking; (3) all are packaged in plastic, shrink-wrapped, airtight material; (4) all are sold primarily in food stores; and (5) the primary customers for all are families with children.

A company's product mix is described in terms of *width,* while its product lines are described in terms of *depth.* Width is the number or variety of product lines in the mix, and depth is the range of sizes, colors, flavors, and models that make up each product line.

In spite of the rather narrow product mix, the consumer product line for Millennium is extensive and deep, containing round cells in the AA, C, D, AAA, and 9V configurations; four different kinds of chargers; and four different types of battery packs for camcorders, cordless phones, cellular phones, and other hobby uses.

The width of product mixes varies from firm to firm. Colgate-Palmolive has a very broad width of products, ranging from Kick the Habit (a stop-smoking product) to Palmolive bar soap. By contrast, Oscar Mayer is considered to have a narrow width because it has only a few product lines—hot dogs, cold cuts, bacons, and meat specialities (such as meat spreads)—and they are all fairly similar in content and use. The advantage of having a broad width in a product mix is diversification, which helps maintain a strong base of sales even when one or two product categories slow down. The advantage of a narrow width is the ability to specialize—to establish expertise—in a certain product category, making your brand the standard for its product area.

Sometimes a firm overextends its product mix. The Daewoo Group, a Korean conglomerate, advertises that it's into everything "from A to Z." But in 1990 the Korean government told Daewoo and other conglomerates that they should focus on fewer products if they expect to get continued government support. In fact, it wants Daewoo to reduce its 915 subsidiaries to 90 because excessive conglomerate diversity has resulted in drawing resources away from products with the greatest potential. For example, Samsung, another conglomerate, has been investing in petrochemical operations and says it wants to build automobiles—yet both these industries already have too many members competing for customers, according to the Korean government.[7]

Although Oscar Mayer has a narrow product mix, its product lines are very deep. Its hot dog line, for example, contains several types—beef and pork, all beef, with cheese, extra long—packaged in different sizes—12 ounces, 16 ounces, 24 ounces, and 12 pounds (for institutional and deli use). The primary reason for having depth in a product line is consumer *segmentation.* As we saw in Chapter 8, segmentation lets firms give more satisfaction to specific groups of customers with particular needs—in this case, for different hot dog product sizes and tastes. For example, the 12-ounce package appeals to a single parent with one small child, while the 24-ounce size is more suited to a family with three teenagers.

At Lääst.
The Häagen-Dazs
of Frozen Yogurt.

+

Frozen yogurt inspired by

the world's finest ice cream.

Try delicious Peach, Vanilla

Strawberry, Chocolate, and

Vanilla Almond Crunch.

Made with all natural ingredi-

ents, 96% fat-free, it's the only

frozen yogurt good enough to

carry the Häagen-Dazs name.

Tääste the Passion.™

Also available in Häagen-Dazs shops.

Exhibit 11-4
Quality Breeds Quality

Häagen-Dazs was slower than some ice cream manufacturers to bring out frozen yogurt, but because of the brand's upscale, quality image, when the new product was launched it hit the ground running.

BRAND EXTENSIONS

Because of the economic advantages that a variety of product lines can offer a firm, companies often add new items under an existing brand name, a process called *brand* or *line extension*. The Häagen-Dazs frozen yogurt featured in the ad in Exhibit 11-4 is a brand extension of the company's original ice cream brand. The primary reason for such additions is to increase sales, counter a move by a competitor, or compensate for declining sales in a category in which the company is currently selling. For example, Alpo, a leading dog-food maker, is aware that more North Americans are now choosing cats for pets. In order to stay competitive in the $5.9 billion pet-food industry, Alpo knew it had to develop a cat-food line. The question it faced was whether it should create a new brand name for its cat food or use the Alpo brand name—in other words, extend the Alpo line. It chose the latter course.

Line extensions are usually variations in one or more of the following product features:

Flavor: Coke added Cherry Coke.

Package size: Campbell Soups now offers single-serving packages for the growing number of single consumers.

Price and quality: GEO is the smallest and least expensive car sold by Chevrolet.

Color: Reynolds created colored plastic wrap to sell alongside its traditional clear wrap.

Use or positioning: Swatch repositioned its watches as costume jewelry.

Added value: Tide with bleach is a multipurpose product that offers greater convenience.

Using established brand names for new product lines is a popular trend. Arm & Hammer, for example, has expanded the venerable baking-soda franchise into toothpaste, fabric softener sheets for dryers, and room deodorizers. Table 11-4 summarizes those situations in which a line extension is most likely to succeed. Line extensions are not always the answer, however. When Campbell entered the dry soup market using its famous red-and-white package and script logo, it never got the 25 percent market share it hoped for in this category dominated by Lipton. Sometimes when line extensions are not sufficiently successful, new products are discontinued, or melded into an existing product. For example, Proctor & Gamble in Canada is folding its Luvs line of diapers into the Pampers Trainers line because Pampers has a stronger name than Luvs.

A major potential danger with brand extensions is *cannibalization*: customers switch from your original product to your new one. If the new product merely steals sales and market share from the older one, the firm's total sales do not rise. There is actually a net loss in profits because the firm has incurred additional expenses for developing, introducing, and inventorying a new item or SKU. Cannibalization of Alka Seltzer by Alka Seltzer Plus is a classic case.

Cannibalization does have one positive aspect, however: customers who have switched from the firm's original product(s) to its new one may now be more satisfied (why else would they switch?). And more satisfied consumers are less likely to change to a competitor's brand. Cannibalization can also be a successful corporate strategy if it induces consumers to trade up to higher-priced items.

INTERNATIONAL EXPANSION

Sony (Japan), Nestlé (Switzerland), Johnson & Johnson (United States), Mercedes-Benz (Germany), and many other companies sell internationally. Many companies, however, sell only within their own national boundaries. An important question facing such companies in this era of globalization is whether they should attempt to market their products outside their own country. Although many things need to be taken into consideration when answering this question, the first is whether or not the firm's products are wanted or needed in other countries.

Some products made for a domestic market—such as vegemite and marmite, vegetable spreads loved by Australians and New Zealanders—are acquired tastes and have only a slim chance of succeeding elsewhere in the world. Others—such as the body spray Impulse that originated in South

| TABLE 11-4 | LINE-EXTENSION OBJECTIVES |

1. *Counter the Competition*
   Either anticipate or respond to a competitor's new product, such as P&G's need to counter Kimberly-Clark's disposable training pants that are worn like underwear but come with an absorbent lining.

2. *Provide Greater Consumer Satisfaction*
   Kellogg's offers a variety of flavors and types of cereals (sugar-coated, nutritional, fiber and fruit, and all-family) to try to satisfy every household's needs with Kellogg's brands. (Kellogg's knows, however, that cereal has one of the lowest levels of brand loyalty of all food items. What consumers are loyal to is a cereal menu—three to five cereals they consistently buy. For example, a single mother may buy two different kinds of cereals for herself and three other kinds for her two teenagers.)

3. *Take Advantage of Trends*
   In the 1980s, when consumers became more health- and weight-conscious, "light" products became popular. P&G thus added a light item to its Pringles line and Frito-Lay test-marketed a Doritos Light Nacho Cheese flavor (along with three other new light items). Coors Beer added a light formulation that grew quickly until, by 1989, it accounted for 60 percent of that brewer's sales. Another example is the success of Stouffer's Lean Cuisine, which combines upscale frozen entrees (great taste and convenience) with low calories (health).

4. *Use Extra Capacity*
   The more expensive production facilities are, the more important it is to maximize their use. Consider a company that has an annual equipment overhead expense of $1 million. If the plant only runs one shift and produces 1 million cases of the product a year, each case will have a $1.00 equipment-overhead charge. But if the plant could run three shifts and produce 3 million cases a year, the equivalent per-case charge would be only 33 cents—resulting in a more competitive price, more profit, or both.

5. *Increase Presence in the Market*
   A brand with only one or two items can get lost in the crowd. With over 20,000 items in larger supermarkets today, a brand needs several facings merely to be noticed on the shelf. Pepperidge Farms thus creates a "billboard" from the repetitiveness of its familiar package and design elements across many varieties of its cookies.

Africa—potentially have broad appeal. (Impulse has been "rolled out" and is now being sold throughout Europe and North America).

As local markets become more competitive, some manufacturers are finding that it is easier to expand internationally than to try to increase share in their native country. Other companies make a point of looking for highly successful "local" products and then copying them or buying the company that makes them and expanding the product into other countries. Finally, some companies have instructed their new-product development people to work only on products that will have international appeal. Examples of the last product strategy are the deodorant Naturel and the feminine hygiene product Always. Both were specifically developed as pan-European products, meaning it was intended from the beginning that they would be distributed and promoted throughout Europe.

Even though a local product may be quite profitable, limiting distribution to a single country means sacrificing a chance to develop an international competitive advantage through such headquarters services as marketing,

R&D, and production. In large corporations producing "local" brands may not even be cost effective. For example, at one time General Foods was in the chewing gum business in France, the ice cream business in Brazil, and the pasta business in Italy. Although each of these unrelated businesses was quite profitable in isolation, the scale of each was too small to justify management activities at headquarters. In cases like this, the corporate strategy is often to either expand the SBUs internationally or sell them off.

PRODUCT LIFE CYCLE ●

product life cycle
The set of stages through which a product or brand passes in the marketplace over time.

**Figure 11-2
The Product Life Cycle**

Source: Adapted from John E. Smallwood, "The Product Life Cycle: A Key to Strategic Marketing Planning," MSU Business Topics, Winter 1973, pp. 29–35.

Products, like people, have life cycles. The **product life cycle** describes the stages through which product categories pass as they "age" in the marketplace. Figure 11-2 shows the four stages: *product introduction, growth, maturity,* and *decline.* These stages, the focus of the sixth chapter objective, are affected by such things as demand (the size of the pool of prospective buyers), competition (the number and strength of companies selling similar products), and the resource/regulatory environment (technology, materials, systems, regulations).[8] Each life-cycle stage requires a different marketing strategy.

As you read the following descriptions of each life-cycle stage, keep in mind three characteristics of this product life cycle concept. First, product categories (such as soft drinks), subcategories (diet soft drinks), and specific brands (Diet A&W Root Beer) *each* have their own life cycles. It is not at all unusual for each of these to be at a different life-cycle stage at the same time. Thus while the soft-drink category was in the maturity stage, the subcategory

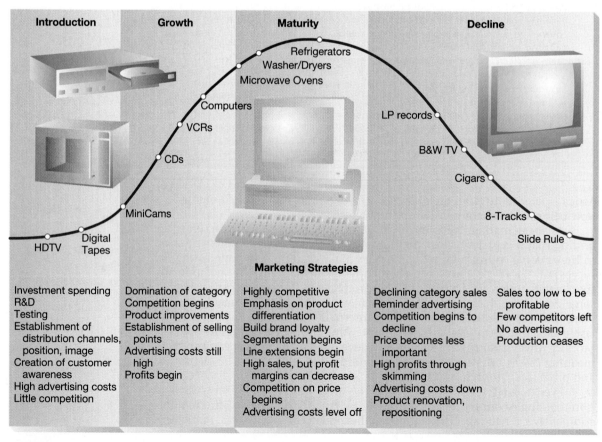

Introduction	Growth	Maturity	Decline

Marketing Strategies

Introduction	Growth	Maturity	Decline	
Investment spending	Domination of category	Highly competitive	Declining category sales	Sales too low to be
R&D	Competition begins	Emphasis on product	Reminder advertising	profitable
Testing	Product improvements	differentiation	Competition begins to	Few competitors left
Establishment of	Establishment of selling	Build brand loyalty	decline	No advertising
distribution channels,	points	Segmentation begins	Price becomes less	Production ceases
position, image	Advertising costs still	Line extensions begin	important	
Creation of customer	high	High sales, but profit	High profits through	
awareness	Profits begin	margins can decrease	skimming	
High advertising costs		Competition on price	Advertising costs down	
Little competition		begins	Product renovation,	
		Advertising costs level off	repositioning	

of diet soft drinks was in its growth stage, and Diet A&W Root Beer was in its introductory stage. Furthermore, a product category that is at one stage of the life cycle in one country may be at a very different stage in other countries.

Second, note that sales usually increase before profits do and sales will continue to rise even while profitability drops; significant profits are made in only two of the five stages—growth and maturity. Finally, a product *turnaround* can occur at almost any stage, restarting the cycle. Thus soft cheese spread (Cheese Whiz, for example) was in the decline stage when a product manager put a jar of it in his microwave at home and gave it a second life as a convenient hot cheese sauce that is widely used now for making nachos.

PROFITABILITY CURVE

Note that while the sales of the product in question are still increasing and entering the maturity stage, a strange thing happens to the profitability curve. The profitability curve can only start with sales so it starts later than the product life cycle but what is curious is that the profitability curve dips while product sales are still increasing. The explanation for this seeming contradiction is that profit per unit sold decreases after the introductory stage. Competitors are drawn in and will move products on the market. Inevitably the price falls and the profit margin per unit sold may fall also. It is a point to watch. There is little to be gained from acquiring ownership of an unprofitable product market. Serious questions about continuation may therefore have to be asked in the maturity stage and many competitors will withdraw or disappear. To be last in the market is supremely profitable, it is a niche.

PRODUCT INTRODUCTION

During the first stage of the product life cycle, marketing usually focuses on two activities: product introduction and refinement. HDTV (high-definition television) is a good example of a product currently in the *introduction stage*. The basic research and development (R&D) was completed in 1994, and it was possible to buy a HDTV set in a few stores, though sets were selling for a steep $20,000 and very few programs that took advantage of this new technology were being broadcast. Manufacturers of HDTV are steadily refining the technology, however, which will lower the price of a set and thus make it affordable to a larger group—which will, in turn, motivate the production of

The Product Life Cycle, Past and Future

Today, color television, launched by RCA in 1954, is in the mature stage of the product life cycle. With $6 billion in annual sales, it is a major category in the rapidly expanding electronics industry branching out now into home theater with multiple speakers strategically placed and a living space area and a very large high quality screen at the center. By contrast, its apparent heir, HDTV, is in the introduction stage. Currently available in only a few stores and selling for around $20,000, HDTV sets should come down to $700–$1,000 when the category reaches maturity. Most manufacturers of HDTV are either based in Japan or Europe.

more HDTV telecasts. For products that do not require a new technology or intensive R&D, such as a new brand of laundry detergent or a ball-point pen, the introductory stage is relatively short and there is little need for product refinement.

During the introductory stage sales are usually slow and profits nonexistent. The product pipeline is being filled—that is, the product has begun "flowing" through the distribution channels. Its positioning and brand image are being established in customers' minds, and the target markets are being confirmed (or, if necessary, redefined). Potential competitors are watching the new product's performance to see if it is worth their while to launch a competing product. Advertising and promotion are often at their highest levels; companies frequently spend nearly 50 percent of the brand's marketing communication budget during the first three months of the new product's launch.

If a brand in this stage has no competition, the company must bear the entire burden of educating consumers about the product category as well as of establishing its own brand image, as Apple did when it introduced the then new category of personal home computers. It must also find the *innovators* and *early adopters* we discussed in Chapter 6, the risk takers who will provide the initial buyer response. In a product category that is already growing or developed—such as the bicycle market—the marketer of the new product must focus on showing consumers how it is better than established products. Obviously, the greater physical competitive advantage a product has, the easier this is to do: "me-too" products often die quick deaths in the introduction stage. Some market observers estimate that nine out of ten new products fail.

GROWTH

Once distribution has begun and brand awareness is building, a product is in the *growth stage*. Examples of products in the growth stage today are CD players, cellular telephones, and notebook, sub-notebook and palmtop computers. Buyers, who are usually the *early majority* consumers described in the adoption process model presented in Chapter 6, are responding to the introductory advertising and promotion, as well as to the experiences and comments of *opinion leaders*. Profit per unit usually runs high because there are few competitors at this stage. But product improvements are now important to ensure that the brand will be able to compete with the new products starting to come onto the market who have the advantage of learning from the early entrants and so modifying new products prior to market launch.

MATURITY

The period during which the sales curve begins leveling off is called the *maturity stage*. Mature products include microwave ovens, television sets, and earth-moving equipment. Personal computers are in the maturity stage in developed countries, although they are still in the growth stage in other parts of the world. Most potential consumers of mature products have been identified and competitors are established. Buyers of mature products are the *late majority* adopters who are highly skeptical by nature and *laggards* who are generally on no fixed income. Brands with significant shares are now getting repeat purchases. Profit margins may be high for leading brands that have refined their operations to minimize production, distribution, and selling expenses. In highly competitive categories such as TV sets, brands other than the leaders generally have reduced their profit margins in order to offer a more competitive price.

Maturity is generally the longest stage in the product life cycle. The length of this stage for a specific product depends on what modifications its manufacturer makes to keep ahead of the competition and to meet changing consumer needs. It also depends on the viability of the product category as a whole. For example, the product categories of record players and eight-track tape players have been replaced by cassettes and CDs. This means that no matter how good a record player a company could make today, there would be little consumer interest in it.

DECLINE

This stage is the reverse of the growth period—sales of either the category or the brand decline. As category sales decline, brands begin to drop out because they can no longer make a profit. Sometimes there is enough residual business for one or two brands to last for years. Black-and-white televisions, mechanical typewriters, and telex machines are in the decline stage. Slowing—or even declining—sales growth does not always mean declining profits for all brands in the category. Demand for cigars, for example, has been declining for decades, yet a few remaining cigar manufacturers prosper. During the decline stage advertising and promotion have little effect since the few remaining customers buy only because they are loyal. Therefore, firms still selling during this stage can often minimize their marketing expenses and enjoy good profit margins for they are sitting on what the Boston Consulting Group calls "cash cows."

As a product category becomes obsolete, each brand has to decide when to stop production. Portable bonnet-style hair dryers and slide rules have disappeared from the market. Hand-operated washing machines and treadle sewing machines have also disappeared in the industrialized countries, although there is a growth market for them in less developed countries.

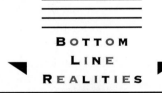

BOTTOM
LINE
REALITIES

TURNING AROUND A "HOG"

Because of their bulky size and the types of people that rode them, for years Harley-Davidson motorcycles were known as "hogs." Over the years this company has had a roller-coaster history: it's been a leader, a follower, and almost bankrupt. In the 1970s it lost leadership to imported motorcycles, especially those made in Japan by Honda, and in the early 1980s Harley found itself close to bankruptcy. The company managed to convince the U.S. government to grant it trade protection: import quotas were established in 1983 for the next five years in order to give the last remaining U.S. motorcycle maker a chance to survive. Harley then set about improving its image, its products, and its marketing strategies.

Harley was spending only one percent of its sales on engineering, which put it at a distinct disadvantage compared to its competitors with their superior German and Japanese manufacturing. That figure had to be increased immediately. Another facet of the old hog that had to change was its tendency to leak oil and to break down frequently. Recognizing that many potential buyers lacked the backyard-mechanic skills needed to keep the old hogs on the road, Harley moved to improve its cycles' quality and reliability.

The company instituted an employee involvement program and "quality circles" (an employee-motivated process of quality control copied from Japanese manufacturers) to improve product quality and a new inventory system to reduce inventory costs and shorten manufacturing times. The results were a 36 percent reduction in warranty costs, a 46 percent increase in defect-free motorcycles delivered to dealers, and a 50 percent increase in employee productivity. Harley also began to think about rider comfort for the first time in its history: it mounted the engines on its touring models on rubber to reduce vibration. New options were introduced, including stereo systems and helmet intercom systems, stores were remodeled, and a line of Harley clothing was bought out.

In 1987 Harley asked the government to withdraw the trade protection and met its foreign competitors with its engines roaring. Today the company is profitable. It dominates the U.S. super-heavy-weight market and is penetrating the global market (Harley is the number-one imported motorcycle in Japan). (For more on Harley-Davidson see the Integrative Case at the back of the book.) ▼

KEY POINTS SUMMARY ▼

1. Product features are those attributes that define a product, including both its functional components and its intangible "extras"; benefits are the values that a product's features create for the user.

2. Product design involves functional (engineering) and aesthetic considerations. It is a major strategic factor because innovations in product design can create competitive advantages, while poor product design can lead to loss of market share and even to product liability lawsuits.

3. Product quality derives from a total commitment to producing according to product specifications what customers need and want. At the production end, it is determined by such things as raw materials used, production techniques, quality-control measures, and management philosophy. At the consumer end, it is determined by how well the product performs for its price. There are various levels of quality; generally the higher the quality, the higher the price, because higher quality requires better raw materials and more precise production techniques.

4. Goods are classified by duration of use as durables, consumables, disposables, and collectibles. Both consumer and industrial goods can also be classified as convenience, specialty, shopping, and preference goods, depending on the risk, effort, and involvement of customers in the buying decision process.

5. The breadth of a firm's product mix refers to the assortment of product categories and product lines the firm markets. The depth of a product mix refers to the variety of items in a product line—that group of products that carry the same brand name and are similar in formulation, production, packaging, distribution, and consumer targets.

6. The four stages in the product life cycle are introduction, growth, maturity, and decline. Product categories, subcategories, and specific brands can each have their own life cycles.

DISCUSSION QUESTIONS ▼

1. If you bought a bicycle from a local store, would you expect to get a warranty or a guarantee? Explain the difference.

2. What is the difference between a high-quality and a low-quality product? How is quality determined and what are the quality considerations that affect marketing?

3. Give an example of a durable good and a consumable good and explain the difference in how they are marketed.

4. Distinguish among convenience, preference, shopping, and specialty goods and give an example of each—other than those in the text—for the consumer and the industrial markets.

5. Identify the four basic stages in a product's life cycle and give an example of a product that fits in each stage.

6. Think about your favorite car (either your own, your family's, or a friend's) and make a list of all its features. Which ones are distinctive? What are the benefits of these features to you? Which ones are the most important?

7. If you were marketing manager for a power tool, what product liability issues would concern you?

8. If you were the marketing manager for a frozen pizza producer, how might you improve your product's quality? For that matter, how would you *define* quality in frozen pizzas?

9. You are marketing manager for OfficeCrafts, a (hypothetical) company that makes quality office furniture. Develop a chart that explains your existing product mix and product lines. In what area might you propose a line extension? What are the pros and cons for your company in developing this line extension?

10. Interview the marketing manager for a local company and identify its primary products and where these products fall in the product life cycle.

11. Can you think of other categories besides over-the-counter drugs where product proliferation has become a serious problem? Do an aisle study in a discount store and identify those product categories that may be in product proliferation trouble. Choose one category and chart the number of products offered, the line extensions, and the distinctive features, if any, that the various brands offer.

12. Either from your own experience or from library research, identify a product that has accomplished the turnaround we described for Harley Davidson. What were the problems that produced the decline? How was the turnaround engineered?

Integrative Case • Discussion Questions

The Body Shop*

1. What types of goods does The Body Shop sell—convenience, shopping, or specialty?

2. What are the important features/attributes of The Body Shop products?

3. When The Body Shop adds Blue Corn hand lotion and toner to their product mix, is this a line extension or a new product?

4. In what stage of the product life cycle is The Body Shop?

Harley-Davidson

1. What type of good (e.g., convenience, shopping) is a Harley?

2. What are the important benefits of owning a Harley? of belonging to a Harley Owners Group?

3. Describe Harley-Davidson's product mix.

4. In North America, in what stage of the product life cycle are motorcycles? In developing countries in what stage are they? If they are in different stages, how may this affect the marketing of motorcycles?

The Millennium Power System

1. Why are Millennium's batteries of different sizes in different colors? Do you think the choice of colors was good or bad? If bad, how would you change them?

2. What is the depth of the Millennium charger line? the depth of its battery line? What is the width of Millennium's product mix?

3. In what stage of the life cycle are rechargeable battery systems? How should rechargeable systems be promoted and distributed in this stage?

4. Do you think Millennium's marketing plan is appropriate to its product's life-cycle stage? Why or why not?

*The three cases at the back of the book—"The Body Shop," "Harley-Davidson," and "The Millennium Power System"—illustrate topics discussed in all chapters of this book. Your instructor will tell you when to read a particular case and when to answer the discussion questions on it that appear at the end of each chapter.

Creating Bread:
The Staple of Life

Bread is bread; or is it? Would you pay $6 for a loaf of bread? If it is Manoucher bread you would. Manoucher Etmanen has changed the concept of breadmaking and added to the appeal of a new product category, Gourmet Food.

Canadians eat more than 900 million loaves of bread each year. That is about 30 loaves per person. Manoucher Etmanen came to Canada in the late 1970s from Iran and decided to make bread like nobody ever had. He developed a line of gourmet breads which appeal to customers who know their food and enjoy it, regardless of the cost.

Today, the sales of Manoucher Bread have reached $5 million. The secret of his success has been in the development of his unique bread dough recipes, all of which have been done in secret. The chemist for the organization is also the head of security. Competitiveness in this market is fierce and recipes must be protected in order to maintain a competitive advantage based on taste.

Adding to the popular herb bread line, the newest bread to be introduced to the market is the Mediterranean Sunset Bread. The ingredients are a mystery to all, even the consumer. But, the taste makes it a winner. Manoucher is counting on its success as he expands his business by exporting.

Manoucher is first tackling the British market before he takes on the rest of Europe, where the real test of his bread will happen. His first customers in England are Harrods, Selfridges, and Harvey Nichols, all retailers committed to the gourmet food consumer. Manoucher bread sells for $20 per loaf.

The real key to food selling is sampling, and Manoucher personally takes care of the customers of his major customers to ensure his product is being sold properly. Another important factor in selling bread internationally is the packaging. Again, Manoucher takes a personal interest in the appropriate packaging of his bread. It needs to be attractive yet protect the bread while it is in transit.

QUESTIONS

1. What type of good is bread? What type of good is Manoucher Bread?
2. What product life cycle would whole wheat bread be in? What product life cycle would Manoucher Bread be in? Why?
3. What are the features and benefits of Manoucher Bread? Why is this product a success?
4. What role does packaging play in the positioning of Manoucher bread?

Source: This case was prepared by Deborah Andrus and is based on the *Venture* series episode "Breadman," which was first broadcast on March 6, 1994.

383

Chapter 12

The Product: Services and Nonprofits

OBJECTIVES

AFTER COMPLETING THIS CHAPTER, YOU SHOULD BE ABLE TO:

1
DEFINE SERVICE SECTOR AND DISCUSS THE INTERSECTION OF GOODS AND SERVICES IN LIGHT OF THE GOODS-SERVICES CONTINUUM CONCEPT

2
DESCRIBE THE DIFFERENCES BETWEEN SERVICE PRODUCTS AND FACILITATING SERVICES

3
ANALYZE SERVICE QUALITY AND DESCRIBE HOW IT CONTRIBUTES TO CUSTOMER SATISFACTION AND RETENTION

4
EXPLAIN THE CONCEPT OF THE "SERVICE ATTITUDE"

5
EXPLAIN HOW THE MARKETING OF SERVICES DIFFERS FROM THE MARKETING OF GOODS

6
EXPLAIN HOW THE NONPROFIT SECTOR USES MARKETING

"WE'RE ONLY HERE TO SERVE YOU"

What is the one thing that irritates you the most about a bank? If you are like most people, it's standing in line. You may have had bad experiences with a teller or a loan officer that makes you dread all such encounters, but the number-one problem for most people is waiting in line. And the frustration you feel is intensified when you see lots of people working behind the counter but not serving customers. Even more frustrating is to see other employees happily talking among themselves while you and other customers stand waiting.

This isn't only a problem at banks, of course. You have to wait in line at all kinds of service providers—airline check-in desks, doctors' offices, even the service department at a car dealer. Do you often wonder why something called a "service department" makes the people it "serves" wait in line and endure other types of hassles like getting to and from

work without a car? And how about the phone call from the "service department" saying the mechanic couldn't get to your car today, so they need to hold it overnight ... as if their needs are so much more important than yours? The worst indignities that consumers have to endure usually come under the heading of "service."

Service businesses like banks, airlines, and even doctors have few ways of differentiating their products from competitors other than how they treat customers. Most banks, for example, offer the same types of products (loans, savings and checking accounts, mortgages) and similar rates and fees. Given their need to differentiate themselves, why haven't more service providers done something about the wait-in-line problem? ■

THE GOODS-SERVICE CONTINUUM

Although we focus in this chapter on firms whose primary product is a service, as we noted in Chapter 11, nearly all businesses have some service element. Thus it is useful to think of businesses, as the first objective for this chapter points out, as falling somewhere on a *continuum* like that depicted in Figure 12-1. In between those firms that are almost exclusively goods oriented and those that are almost exclusively services oriented are businesses that sell goods and provide services—and businesses that sell services as well as goods.

Restaurants, for example, while services-oriented, provide tangible "goods" like hamburgers and chicken dinners. Indeed, many service-oriented businesses provide a wide variety of goods. If you have ever been to a concert, play, theme park, zoo, or museum, you have probably made the drive home with tangible goods like records, clothing, and souvenirs.

By the same token, manufacturers and other businesses that focus on goods also sell services. Appliances and automobiles, for example, often come with extended service contracts. Sometimes the sale of these service contracts is almost as profitable as the sale of the goods themselves. The General Motors

**Figure 12-1
Goods-Service
Continuum**

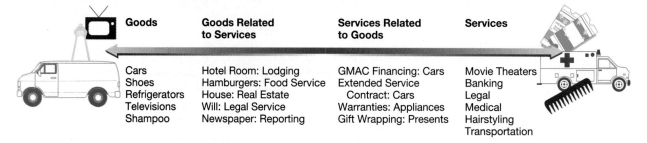

Goods	Goods Related to Services	Services Related to Goods	Services
Cars	Hotel Room: Lodging	GMAC Financing: Cars	Movie Theaters
Shoes	Hamburgers: Food Service	Extended Service	Banking
Refrigerators	House: Real Estate	Contract: Cars	Legal
Televisions	Will: Legal Service	Warranties: Appliances	Medical
Shampoo	Newspaper: Reporting	Gift Wrapping: Presents	Hairstyling
			Transportation

Thank you Molly Maid

I love coming home to a clean house ...

MOLLY MAID *more affordable than you think*

Acceptance Corporation, which finances cars for GM, is responsible for more than one-quarter of the parent company's total earnings. In fact, GMAC is the United States' largest single holder of consumer debt.[1]

Many manufacturing companies are finding whole new areas of growth by servicing needs related to the purchase and use of their goods. Called **aftermarketing**, this is another instance in which goods and services intersect. Fertilizer firms now contract to apply fertilizer for their customers, whether they are farmers with hundreds of acres or just plain homeowners. Gerber Products, well known for its baby food, is developing a chain of Gerber Day Care centers for working mothers and selling direct-mail life insurance to parents of newborns. Batesville Casket found few options for growth until it began selling funeral planning and insurance to families, using the funeral directors who distribute their caskets as sales agents.

Incidentally, this strategy gave Batesville Casket distributors a service product they could promote in a positive light.

Some marketers are seeing a shift in the importance of services, which they identify with the phrase *a product is a service.* In other words, the way the product performs is a service. If you buy a computer, the computer provides you with a service. Furthermore, product support—assistance, upgrades, maintenance—is an integral part of the physical product. With the spread of this philosophy, the service concept is becoming more and more critical to all areas of marketing.

Despite the overlap between goods and services, some firms are primarily engaged in service operations. We discuss this type of service first. Then we move on to the second meaning of the word *service*—the idea that service is critical not only to the sale but also to relationship marketing and to quality programs for all kinds of products. Finally, we discuss nonprofit organizations, many of which are service based, and their marketing programs and problems.

aftermarketing
The servicing by a company of a customer's needs related to the purchase and use of the company's product.

THE SERVICE SECTOR ●

When people hear the word *business*, manufacturers almost always come to mind. Certainly many of the nation's largest and most visible firms are goods producers. But in recent decades, economic growth has come primarily from the **service sector**—firms whose product is a service rather than a good. These services may be anything from financial services to transportation, selling real estate, food services, beauty and personal care, health care, repair and maintenance, entertainment, and professional services like accounting, law, medicine, and dentistry.

THE TWO TYPES OF SERVICE

There are two types of services: the basic *service product* and the *facilitating service*, which supports the service product. The **service product** is a task or action whose performance, by a seller, offers some benefit to a buyer. Canadian consumers spend more on service products than on durable and nondurable goods combined. The service sector accounts for almost three-fourths of the GDP or gross domestic product (the gross amount of products, both goods and services, produced within a particular country's national boundaries) of Canada and the United States and uses over three-fourths of the labor force.

The biggest areas of growth in the service sector are such high tech fields as computers and electronic communication. More than half of all service workers are in highly skilled professional occupations such as law, bank management, and computer programming. Nor are services restricted to consumer markets. Businesses hire accountants, lawyers, planners, researchers, advertising agencies, and consultants, including marketing consultants. In Canada, the total revenue generated from business service industries is $32.9 billion (see Table 12-1)

service sector
Those businesses and other organizations whose product is a service rather than a good.

service product
A task or action, usually performed by a seller, that offers some benefit to a buyer.

TABLE 12-1	TOTAL REVENUE FOR BUSINESS SERVICE INDUSTRIES IN CANADA (1989) IN MILLIONS OF DOLLARS
Employment Agencies and Personnel Suppliers	$2175.3
Computer Services	5510.7
Advertising Services	3184.1
Architectural, Engineering, Scientific Services	—
Other Business Services	7666.0
Machinery and Equipment Rental and Leasing Services	2913.4
Automobile and Truck Rental and Leasing Services	3058.8
Photographers	506.1
Other Repair Services	1468.7
Services to Buildings and Dwellings	2210.8
Travel Services	4222.0
Total (Millions of Dollars)	32,915.9

Source: Market Research Handbook, 1993–1994, Statistics Canada.

Retailing and government are considered to be in the service sector. In fact, government is a major employer of people in this sector. The number of people employed in government service industries in Canada is 717,300. Add this to the number employed in education (871,200) and in health and social services (1,133,700), and the total jumps to 2,722,200 employees. Government services at the local, provincial, and federal levels include education, law enforcement, and transportation facilities. Government agencies use marketing programs to promote such things as safety, good health, stamp collecting, public transportation, and home mortgage loans.

Although the service product is the basic service, the nature and quality of the facilitating service are often of prime importance in a customer's purchase decision. The **facilitating service** is an ancillary task or an act that enhances the value of the service product; it may be performed before or after the delivery of the basic service. For example, several airlines can fly you from Vancouver to Toronto at the same price, so you may choose an airline on such factors as scheduling, on-time arrivals, baggage handling, and food quality. Hotels will also compete for business by providing special services—the Sutton Place Grande Hotel Le Meridien in Toronto, for example, offers its guests in-room faxes and cordless telephone services. The same is true with goods. There are a number of models available in most auto categories, so your buying decision will often be based on your feelings about the salesperson, the reliability and trustworthiness of the service department, and the ease with which you can finance the car. The primary product is the car, but the facilitating services may be the tie-breaker in the purchase decision.

facilitating service
An activity or task performed by a seller in order to enhance the value of a service product.

GLOBAL SERVICES

In recent years the service sector of international business has also been growing rapidly. A few decades ago many people believed that services were rooted in national culture and thus were not exportable. This assumption has been proved wrong. Virtually any service is a candidate for globalization, though savvy marketers realize that marketing services internationally requires careful consideration of the differences among markets.

389

THE PRODUCT:
SERVICES AND
NONPROFIT

Exporting Services

Midas, which began in the U.S. in 1955, has grown into a huge network of auto-service across the United States, Canada, Australia, Mexico, and Panama. The first Canadian Midas was opened in Toronto in 1960, and now there are 240 Midas shops across Canada.

One difference among nations lies in the strength of the role played by services in the national economy. As a nation's GDP rises, so does the percentage of its production that is composed of services. The high-income regions of the world—Japan–Hong Kong–Singapore, North America, and Western Europe—all have strong and growing service sectors. This means greater competition among service firms and greater striving for differences that provide a competitive advantage. For example, as a country becomes more modern and developed, it attracts service from more international airlines.

CHARACTERISTICS OF SERVICE PRODUCTS

Services marketers must cope with such service characteristics as labor intensity, product intangibility, customer relationships, "perishability," and inseparability from the service provider. Quality is variable and standardization is difficult to achieve, due to fluctuating demand and the need to have a client relationship. Table 12-2 outlines some of the marketing problems these features generate and describes marketing strategies for overcoming them.

Intangibility Prudential Insurance sells peace of mind. Disney World sells entertainment, an escape into a fantasy world. A chic local restaurant sells ambiance and the royal feeling that comes from being waited on by several people. These are the *intangibles* of services. Although you can experience them, you cannot touch them. The goal of marketing communications strategies for services is to make them tangible—to dramatize their *benefits*. One insurance company commercial shows a young mother and child forced out of their beautiful home because "Dad" died without enough insurance—a very tangible loss.

It is the intangible nature of services that makes people concerned about their providers. For example, the U.S. banking crisis and savings and loan scandals of the 1980s and early 1990s left many Americans uneasy about the financial stability of the institutions where they banked. In Canada, recent instability and uncertainty in the insurance industry has left consumers unsure of their insurance coverage. In fact, concern about service providers and their qualifications is one reason that many professionals—ranging from beauticians and barbers to doctors, dentists, and lawyers—must be licensed to practice.

Customer Relationships Unlike goods, many services cannot be provided without the presence and cooperation of the customer. To get a home or office building designed, you must work with an architect, explaining your needs and wants. To get your teeth cleaned, you must go to the dentist and follow instructions to "open wide" and "rinse." Even when customers are not directly involved in the service (such as car repair), *relationships* between the service provider and customer are particularly important. The degree of customer contact is important because what is at stake here is the shell of the service provider in a market where there is great variety. To ensure customer loyalty means that you have to retain customers and you can only do this once you know your customers.

For example, Federal Express, the first service company to win the Baldrige Quality Award, is built on a commitment to reliable and fast delivery service. The company makes an explicit *promise* to its customers: "When it absolutely, positively has to be there overnight." Keeping that promise is essential to the relationship FedEx has established with its customers because FedEx—like a travel agent, stockbroker, or realtor—acts on behalf of a cus-

TABLE 12-2 PROBLEMS AND STRATEGIES IN SERVICES MARKETING

Feature	Marketing Problem Presented	Marketing Strategy
Intangibility	• Cannot easily be displayed • Cannot be protected with patents	• Stress tangible cues • Use personal sources • Stimulate word-of-mouth • Use postpurchase communications
Close Customer Relationship	• Customer involved in production • Service performance uses customer's time	• Focus on appearance of facility and employees • Stress employee courtesy • Use multisite locations • Don't keep people waiting in lines
Perishability	• Customer must be present • Value can be short-lived • Capacity is finite • Time periods may be limited • Cannot be inventoried	• Focus on convenience, saving time, fast service • Extend hours • Focus on competence and expertise • Predict fluctuations in demand • Manage capacity to balance supply and demand
Product Inseparable from Producer	• Harder to mass-produce product • Less efficient than goods production	• Need strong training programs, incentives • Focus on personal attention
Quality Variability	• Standardization hard to achieve • Hard to set up quality controls • Can only predict quality or determine it after service is performed	• Stress standardization and performance consistency • Focus on employee training programs, performance evaluations • Consider licensing and other forms of credential requirements

Source: Adapted from Valarie A. Zeithaml, A. Parasuraman, and Leonard L. Berry, "Problems and Strategies in Services Marketing," *Journal of Marketing 49* (Spring 1985): 33–46.

tomer. For this reason, relationship marketing is a major strategy practiced by FedEx.

To strengthen its customer relationships, in 1993 FedEx introduced the Powership program. Regular FedEx customers are given a computer loaded with special software; the customer only has to pay for a phone line to connect the computer to the local FedEx office. Using this computer, a customer can check on the status of all its FedEx shipments—whether they have left the local FedEx office, arrived in the destination city, or been received at their final destination (including the name of the person who actually received the item and at what time). This ability to check on a shipment's progress and easily confirm its arrival provides customers with peace of mind, a definite added value. With this added-value service, FedEx is building stronger customer relationships. Some experts speculate that this concept of relationship marketing is as important in the 1990s as the basic marketing concept was thirty years ago.[2]

Canadian Tire is another company dedicated to strengthening customer relationships. In January 1994, Canadian Tire launched a new credit card incorporating the new Options program. The Options program is designed as a customer loyalty program which rewards frequent shoppers with bonus points which can be redeemed for store purchases.

BEHIND THE SCENES
RITZ-CARLTON'S KEYS TO CUSTOMER RELATIONSHIPS

The Ritz-Carlton is in a class by itself when it comes to employee training. That is one of the principal reasons it became the first hotel to win the Baldrige Award and has the highest occupancy rates in the industry, even though it is one of the most expensive hotel chains.

All new employees attend a two-day orientation session. This is followed by 100 additional hours of training, daily inspections for appearance, and periodic performance reviews—through all of which there is an unrelenting emphasis on responsiveness to customers. To underscore the importance of the Ritz-Carlton's quality philosophy, the president and chief operating officer of the company conduct the orientation sessions at each new hotel.

Employees are told that they were not hired, they were selected; that they serve, but they are not servants; and that they are important members of an elite team that is always looking for ways to improve. For hotel guests, no detail is too small, no request too large. Service is more than a smile and a greeting. Employees are taught to escort guests when they ask for directions rather than just pointing the way. Furthermore, they are charged with taking personal responsibility for any guest's complaint and doing whatever needs to be done to see that it is resolved. Although employees are paid about the same as at other hotels, Ritz-Carlton recognizes exceptional performance with rewards like extra fully paid vacations. Consequently, employee turnover is much lower than at other luxury hotels.

Even though the hotel chain won the Baldrige Award, the jurors found seventy-five areas that needed improvement, which sets up new standards of quality for Ritz-Carlton to meet. The hotel's corporate director of quality is seeking to involve the hotel's suppliers in the quality-improvement effort. But the emphasis remains on Ritz-Carlton's own employees, and the new goals include giving them more decision-making authority.

Perishability When services require customers to be present, companies must consider these customers' time constraints. A tax assistance service that is open only nine to five Monday through Friday cannot serve the many people who work during those hours. Speedy service is also very important in many customer-present services, since people look on the amount of time they must spend to get services as a cost. One of the major reasons for the success of the quick-oil-change business is that it saves people time. In the fast-food industry a wait of more than 3 minutes is considered a "product defect."

Services that require customers to be present are said to be *perishable*. The potential income from empty theater seats is lost forever once the show is over. A plane that leaves London on its way to Rome with twenty-five empty seats forever loses the opportunity to sell those twenty-five seats, though the expenses for the flight are the same as they would have been had the plane been full (less twenty-five in-flight meals, which cost only a few dollars each).

Services are perishable in another sense: they cannot be provided ahead and inventoried. The only "inventory" that many service firms have is their staff time. Others do have inventory in the form of supplies needed to produce the service—rental car companies like Avis and Hertz, for example, store a number of cars. The more trained people a company can draw on to perform a service, or the more supplies it has on hand (such as cars), the more potential *capacity* it has. So it is possible to inventory services from the perspective of number of trained employees on call or cars available for rent.

Managers of services concentrate on **capacity management**—balancing the supply of staff with demand—because demand that cannot be met is often lost business, or nonrepeat business when customers are made to wait too long. This is the point that banks are missing when they make customers stand in long lines. One bank that took action on the problem is Toronto Dominion. The bank now offers $5.00 to every customer who has to wait in line for more than five minutes. To take another example, if a restaurant is full, some people will wait for seats, but others will move on to another restaurant. On the other hand, staffing up for demand that never materializes is a waste: if a restaurant doubles its serving area and staff but doesn't double its business, its extra costs will outweigh its extra income. Table 12-3 identifies six ways that businesses with perishability constraints balance demand.

Inseparability For most services, the perishable part of the marketing mix is *the performance of a task* by a person. Therefore the front-line employee is an essential part of the product.[3] One result of this characteristic is that service industries are often *labor intensive*: that is, labor costs are higher for a service company than they are for most goods producers. Labor costs at your local pizzeria are probably about 35 percent of the price of a meal—nearly four times the 8 to 10 percent labor cost involved in making a frozen pizza. At repair services for appliances, cars, watches, and similar items, labor costs are by far the largest component of the fee charged. While professional services are also labor intensive, hospitals and airlines have relatively low labor costs compared to their costs for facilities and equipment. Just as manufacturers of goods must pay close attention to the cost of labor and raw materials (variable costs), most service businesses scrutinize their labor versus other costs against the standard ratio for their industry. Table 12-4 ranks the labor intensiveness of various services.

When experienced service marketers enter low-income countries, they face special challenges related to the inseparability of a service from its employee-provider. Since many workers in low-income nations are not accus-

capacity management Balancing the number of staff in a service organization with the amount of demand for the organization's service.

TABLE 12-3	HOW SERVICE BUSINESSES BALANCE DEMAND

1. *Adjusting Prices* By offering its services at lower prices during low-demand periods, a service company can attract customers away from peak periods. Movie theaters frequently offer discounts for afternoon and weeknight showings because these are not very popular times for people to go to the movies. For example, some movie theaters in Calgary offer Tuesday night screenings for only $1.00 per ticket. Another pricing strategy is to sell an extended period service contract—such as a pest control service. Instead of just selling the service when people notice bugs, these businesses sell homeowners on having their home sprayed periodically. When customers agree to buy multiple visits, the per-visit price is reduced.

2. *Using Part-Time Employees* McDonald's, like many restaurants, finds people who only want to work a few hours a day and schedules them during high-demand periods such as mealtimes.

3. *Automating Performance* Over the years the soft-drink and snack industries have greatly expanded their sales by automating service delivery—for example, through vending machines. Automated developing equipment has reduced the time and expertise needed to develop film and has resulted in one-hour photo-finishing stores.

4. *Targeting Different Segments* Hospitals, realizing that there are no longer enough sick people to fill all their beds, are targeting healthy people. They are selling wellness programs to corporations, promising corporate customers that certain preventive procedures cause absenteeism and insurance costs to drop.

5. *Selling Complementary Services* Companies that contract with airlines to deliver lost luggage can balance their workload by offering small-package delivery service within their assigned area.

6. *Selling "Off-Season" Services* A lawn-care service can do snow removal during the winter.

tomed to working in service industries they are sometimes insensitive to the need to provide a service in a pleasant manner.

McDonald's faced an enormous challenge in this regard when it became the first fast-food firm to open operations in Russia. McDonald's credo is to offer "quality, service, cleanliness, and value." Suppliers had to be taught that only certain types and qualities of potatoes and meat were acceptable and they had to build the meat processing plant, the bakery, and even plant the very potatoes they would use in their operation. Restaurant workers had to be trained to be efficient, courteous, and, above all, friendly—most found the notion of smiling at customers bizarre at first. Workers also had to be trained to keep the store immaculately clean. As a result of this training program, McDonald's was received by Russians as an excellent value—despite higher prices and longer lines than at many other restaurants.

FACILITATING SERVICES ●

The competitive advantage in most service industries—like hotels, car rentals, airlines, and banking—as well as in many manufacturing industries—like au-

TABLE 12-4	LABOR INTENSITY OF SOME BROAD SERVICE GROUPS	

Electric utilities, gas, sanitation services	14.21
Communications	5.31
Amusement and Recreation	2.49
Hospitals:	
Teaching	1.59
For-profit	1.63
All other (e.g., community)	1.75
Auto and other repair	1.60
Transportation	1.27
Banking	1.20
Hotels	1.01

High Labor-Intensive Services	Capital-Labor Ratio
Securities and commodities brokers	0.15
Insurance agents and services	0.18
Business services (e.g., advertising, credit reporting, mailing and reproduction, building services, personnel supply, computer and data processing, management consulting and public relations)	0.42
Personal services (e.g., laundry, photo, beauty/barber shops, funeral services)	0.53
Wholesale trade	0.54
Retail trade	0.62

Source: Roger W. Schmenner, "How Can Service Businesses Survive and Prosper?" in *Managing Services: Marketing, Operations, and Human Resources,* ed. Christopher H. Lovelace (Englewood Cliffs, N.J.: Prentice Hall, 1988), p. 27.

tomobiles and computers—lies with the company that is perceived as providing the best package of facilitating services to support or enhance the sale. The promise of a service automatically creates a close relationship between a firm and its customers, so service-based marketing requires an especially high knowledge of customer needs and wants and a commitment to a customer orientation, or putting the customer first.[4] For example, Delta Hotels of Toronto are attempting to attract frequent business travelers with the "one minute guarantee or your room is free" check-in service. This program has been credited with increasing membership in the Delta privilege program by 34 percent in the first four months. Service quality that enhances customer satisfaction and quality controls are the focus of the third chapter objective.

SERVICE QUALITY

The crucial role of labor in both service products and facilitating services leads to greater quality *variability* than is found in goods production. Manufactured goods have tangible qualities that make it fairly easy to set up quality controls, but in many cases the quality of the service performance cannot be determined until *after* it is performed. To illustrate, if your grandfather needs to spend some time in a nursing home, you will want to find a place that will provide him with excellent care. However, you can only *predict* the level of care your relative will receive. You must select a home on the basis of care provided in the past—which assumes that programs and staff will remain unchanged. Because the service is performed by employees, you will use their appearance, attitude, language, and competence to judge what level of service they will provide.

The Service Attitude The manner in which a service is performed or the degree of effort that employees extend to make a customer's buying experience more satisfying is known as the **service attitude**. Service attitude, the topic of chapter objective four, is a major factor in the perception of quality for both goods and service industries. A survey in the early 1990s found that while consumers believe that service is improving in supermarkets and restaurants, they perceive it is getting worse at airlines, gas stations, and insurance companies.[5]

Service professionals are often rated quite low in service attitude. As one observer has noted: "Of all the sectors of the economy, the service professionals—medicine, law, architecture, and accounting—have the farthest to go in developing genuine client sensitivity. Unlike other fields, the education and professional culture of these areas suggests to them that they know what's best. This elitism makes it almost impossible for them to be client-oriented."[6] In recent years, however, as professions such as law and dentistry have become more competitive, their practitioners have had to show more sensitivity to their clients' needs (and often to become more aggressive in their marketing).

One of the brightest stars in the airline industry is Southwest Airlines, which has stayed financially successful by emphasizing the service attitude. This airline is concerned with more than just an attitude that focuses on customers. It encourages its employees to have fun and to make flying an enjoyable experience for everyone aboard, which adds a new dimension of value to service. The airline delegates authority to make decisions to its on-the-line employees, which gives them the confidence to take a flexible rather than a rigid, standardized approach to service.

Service attitudes differ from country to country. When TGI Friday's restaurant chain, known for its outgoing waiters and waitresses, began to expand into Europe, it faced the challenge of exporting a very North American service attitude. An executive of Whitbread, the giant British brewing and restaurant company that franchises Friday's in London, explained that the English have "missed out on the service culture. We have had to close that cultural gap." The London Friday's used a novel method to choose the right sort of employee: they held auditions in a West End theater and asked applicants to sing, dance, tell jokes, and act like TV talk-show hosts. In fact, to maintain that typical Friday's outgoing personality, employees do role-playing exercises in meetings prior to starting work. As one English waiter explained: "British people are a lot more backward about being forward."

Global Standards International marketers must be conscious of the fact that standards for "high-quality" service vary from country to country, although service quality is universally appreciated. The ad in Exhibit 12-1 illustrates how much importance one international telecommunication company attaches to service. Experts generally acknowledge that service standards in Japan are among the highest in the world. Japanese visitors to the North America are often shocked by the generally low level of competence and poor service attitude they see in lower-level employees in North American businesses.

We'll give you the kind of treatment you deserve.

PTT We make it our business to make you feel at home when your telecommunications needs take you to Europe. After all, hospitality has been a Swiss tradition for centuries.

We understand the natural fear of things foreign. So we've established Swiss Telecom North America—staffed with Americans—to act as your liaison with the PTT.

And on the other side of the Atlantic we'll serve as your agent in charting a course through the Continent's fast-changing telecommunications regulatory maze. Using our connections at other European administrations and our high-speed digital links,

we'll get your traffic anywhere it's going in Europe. Our recently expanded Leaseline Control Center in Berne makes it easy for you to get answers about the status of your network. It's staffed around the clock with people who know both engineering and English.

When you make Switzerland your hub, you're building your network on the most modern telecommunications infrastructure in Europe. And working with people to whom "Welcome" is not a foreign word.

SwissTelecom

To find out more, contact Tom Lamoureux, Swiss Telecom, N.A., Suite 902, 2001 L St. N.W., Washington, D.C. 20036. 1-800-966-1145.

Exhibit 12-1
Service Without
Boundaries

One of the problems in international business is dealing with overseas telecommunications. Here Swiss-Telecom suggests that not only is its business friendly to "foreigners" but also that it will take the initiative in solving customers' telecommunications regulatory problems in the new European Union.

The experience of a Japanese executive in the United States illustrates this point. Yoshiko Ito Schied purchased a headboard from Sears that was delivered to her apartment in a package. When she opened the package, she found that the headboard was damaged. She called the store and discovered that she was expected to contact the returns department and arrange for the return or the replacement of the headboard herself. She did as instructed, only to find herself waiting endlessly on the telephone line. After a while she decided to contact the person who had sold her the headboard, only to discover that he did not have the slightest interest in her anymore: his job apparently ended the moment he made the sale. She was amazed at this experience,

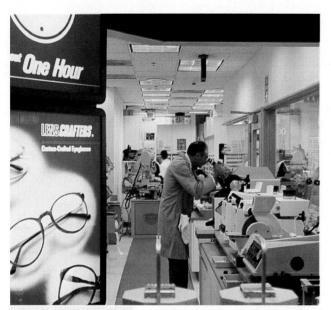

especially at the fact that the Sears salesman apparently felt no shame about selling an inferior product. Japanese sales clerks, according to Mrs. Schied and many Western visitors to Japan, typically take much more responsibility for creating customer satisfaction than the average North American sales clerk does.

CUSTOMER SATISFACTION

Satisfied customers are the goal of all marketing. In high-income countries consumer demand for quality service is higher than ever. Customer satisfaction isn't an end in itself, it's a necessity for repeat business. One study found that two-thirds of the customers who stop patronizing a business do so because of service problems. Because 65 percent of the average firm's business comes from its present customers, and because it can cost six to ten times as much to acquire a new customer as it does to retain an existing one, companies pay a high price when they lose a customer.[7] For example, it costs cellular telephone companies several hundred dollars to attract a new customer—a substantial loss if the customer then defects to another company or drops cellular phone service altogether.

A positive service attitude not only contributes to customer satisfaction and customer retention. It can be an important competitive advantage. The frustration of waiting in lines, the focus of this chapter's opening story, is really a time issue. Most customers have an idea of how long it should take to perform a given service, and they are not willing to be kept waiting much beyond that point. Banks have tried to deal with the waiting problem by making round-the-clock ATMs available at most of their locations. Unfortunately, in many cases, ATM service has turned out to be just another occasion for standing in line.

QUALITY CONTROL IN SERVICES

Quality control in the service sectors is difficult but possible, as proved by the increasing number of service companies winning the Canadian Award for Business Excellence. To manage and continually improve service quality requires three major steps: (1) *benchmarking*—identifying and measuring factors that affect customer satisfaction; (2) *employee training*—designing a plan to equip workers to better deliver quality services; and (3) *performance evaluation*—measuring the firm's performance against the benchmarks.

Benchmarks The first step toward delivering quality services is to find out what *customers* define as quality service. One team of researchers identified ten general determinants of quality in services marketing: accessibility, communication, competence, courtesy, credibility, reliability, responsiveness, security, understanding the customer, and such tangibles as physical facilities and appearance of personnel.[8] One of the few quality dimensions that service marketers can objectively measure is time, which happens to be one of the most important factors in customer satisfaction. How fast is the phone answered? How long does it take to respond to a customer's question? Other im-

Seeing is Believing

Whether or not Lenscrafters has read Randolph Hall's warning, in Queueing Methods for Services and Manufacturing, *that if businesses don't do something about the lines in which people often wait for service they will lose customers, it sells prompt and efficient optician service, both in print ads and on TV.*

portant but harder-to-measure factors are courtesy, empathy, and responsiveness. One example of perceived poor-quality service involves one of the Federal Government's departments. The department's new phone enquiry system has created many dissatisfied customers. After navigating their way around the phone system, customers may decide that they need to speak to a customer service representative. If a representative is not available to take a customer's call, the customer is disconnected from the phone system rather than being placed on hold until the next available representative can take the call, thus leaving the customer to repeatedly tackle the phone system until a representative becomes available.

Companies involved in the Baldrige, Deming, or Canadian Awards for Business Excellence (CABE) quality programs usually design their own research programs to assess their customers' level of satisfaction and then use these as benchmarks against which improvements are measured. The most important thing to understand is that the quality in service businesses is always defined from the customer's point of view. Rational or not, customers' impressions and experiences are what count.

BEHIND THE SCENES

TRACKING TRANSACTIONS

A pioneer in improving service quality, American Express systematically measures both customer satisfaction and employee performance worldwide. The company's tracking system, developed in the 1970s, measures service to individual credit card holders as well as to business customers, including both the retailers, restaurants, airlines, and other service providers that accept the AmEx card, and the corporations that have card programs for their employees.[9]

A monthly "service tracking report" compiles statistics on the performance of AmEx business units throughout the world as measured against more than 100 service quality factors. It especially tracks employee responsiveness, timeliness, and accuracy—factors that were isolated as important to consumers by customer research and analysis of mail and phone calls.

AmEx has operations in more than 300 countries. Each national unit prepares its own monthly performance report, including strategies for improvement based on the economy, laws, culture, and customer expectations in that country. The reports are consolidated and sent out to managers worldwide so that solutions to common problems can be shared. This performance tracking system is one of the elements that made AmEx a Baldrige Award winner. By the time the system had been in operation for three years, AmEx had improved the quality of its service delivery by 78 percent and reduced the cost of each transaction by 21 percent.

In addition to this monitoring effort, American Express encourages employee service quality through an annual "great performances" award for those who provide the highest levels of service. Altogether, the company has more than 100 programs for recognizing and rewarding employees who are particularly responsive to customers.

Employee Training   The second step in increasing the quality of service is to set up special training programs for employees. More than 200,000 companies have installed 800 toll-free customer service lines. The problem with this service, of course, is to make sure the calls are answered speedily by people who accurately respond to customers' questions. One of the most successful 800 customer service programs is the GE Answer Center, which has 230 operators answering calls around the clock. These operators deal with 20,000 callers a week at an annual cost of approximately $10 million. To ensure that this system runs smoothly, GE's operators are put through a training program and then continuously monitored by supervisors. GE says the payback—in terms of sales, profit, reduced usage of service warranties, and long-term goodwill—is many times the cost.

Millennium is one goods manufacturer that recognizes that the level of customer service at retail can positively or negatively affect consumer response to its products. Therefore the company provides training on rechargeable battery systems to retail sales clerks.

Using videos and classroom-type instruction, McDonald's does an excellent job of training new employees to prepare food, drinks, and wait on customers efficiently and with a smile. When these employees are first put to work, they are closely monitored by "trainers" who correct any procedural errors the trainees make. McDonald's even has new employees wear a badge that says "Trainee." The purpose of the badge is twofold: to remind new employees that they still have things to learn and to explain to customers why their orders may not be handled with normal McDonald's efficiency.

To get its employees to empathize with senior customers, one Pennsylvania bank asks employees to fill out deposit slips with Vaseline smeared on their glasses to simulate loss of vision and to count money with their fingers taped together to simulate arthritis. A resort hotel that caters to families makes employees act out the registration procedures that their customers must endure after traveling for many hours with children, hauling their luggage in and out of airports, renting a car, and arriving at their destination late and exhausted.

One Canadian company that stresses the importance of training is Fountain Tire. Founded in 1956 by Bill Fountain in Edmonton, the company presently has 86 stores, a sales turnover of $110 million which is growing at around 18% per annum for the last four years. Fountain Tire credits much of their success to training which is above the industry average and focuses on the customer service side as well as hard technical skills. President Brent Hesje says: "Until you convince people that training is an investment and not an expense, it doesn't work.

Service companies obviously have a vested interest in employees who have been put through a costly training process. Yet employee turnover is a nagging problem in the service industries. Higher wages and better working conditions help, but more creative solutions are sometimes more effective. A Burger King in Detroit, for instance, offered to pay the cost of tuition and books for employees attending either of two local community colleges. The strategy succeeded: the turnover rate dropped and the store's ratings for quality of service went up.

In addition to training, most quality programs include incentives to encourage employees to do their best work and to encourage stakeholders to respond to their research programs. American Airlines, for example, gives $25 travel certificates to customers who respond to a customer service survey.

Performance Evaluation The third step in quality control is *performance evaluation*. In the case of professional services, poor performance can result in the loss of a license to offer such services. Some service companies keep records on the number of compliments and complaints received on each employee. Others use incentive programs to motivate their staffs to do more than the acceptable minimum. Some retailers and manufacturers use "mystery shoppers"—trained research people hired to act like typical customers and record exactly how they are treated—in order to evaluate the quality of service at the point of purchase. Customer surveys also provide feedback to management about potential problems. All these types of controls are necessary since, as we pointed out earlier, services can only be evaluated after the fact.

Proper training and periodic performance evaluations should lead to *performance consistency*, or service that is predictable for consumers. Without standardization, each purchase carries a high level of consumer risk. As we explained earlier, consumers want to minimize their risk when spending their money and time. One reason for McDonald's global success is its consistency: whether you are in Montreal, Paris, Moscow, or a McDonald's-serviced train traveling from Hamburg to Munich, you get the same kind of service. Standardization of performance also helps firms like McDonald's control costs.

Because so many goods are similar, the service that accompanies a brand is often the deciding factor in a buying decision. With service products, of course, the quality of service is even more important. Customers are increasingly likely to defect to competitors who offer them higher-quality services. One method that some companies use to monitor their service quality is known as the SERVQUAL model. This model isolates five dimensions of service—tangibles (equipment, facilities, employee dress, visually appealing materials), reliability, responsiveness, assurance, and empathy—and measures the differences between customers' expectations in these areas and their actual experiences.[10] This model also identified five gaps in service delivery: between consumer expectation and management perception; between management perception and service quality specification; between service quality specifications and service delivery; between service delivery and external communications; and between perceived service and expected service.

SERVICES MARKETING
STRATEGY ●

The marketing mix and basic strategy decisions are essentially the same for services as for goods. There are, however, some small differences in the way the mix is planned to further relationship marketing and create customer satisfaction. These differences are the focus of the fifth chapter objective and the topic of this section.

TARGETING

Targeting is as important for services as for goods manufacturers. The ad in Exhibit 12-2 illustrates how a large bank is targeting small business-owners and entrepreneurs. We have already seen how the rising numbers of older

Exhibit 12-2
Service for Customers' Special Needs
This ad by the Bank of Montreal illustrates why a major bank is concerned with meeting the needs of small business owners and entrepreneurs. The bank encourages and supports entrepreneurs because they help the economy and ultimately provide benefits for all Canadians.

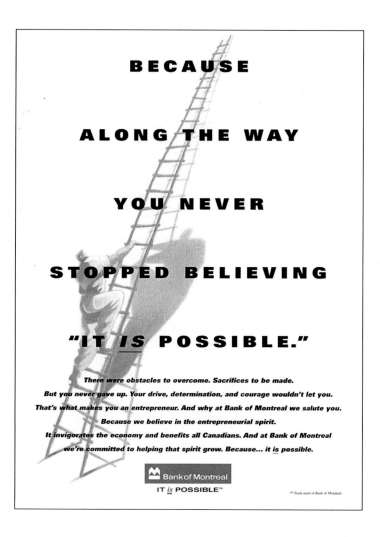

people are prompting marketers of all kinds to address this group's needs with specialized housing and health care products.

At the other end of the age spectrum, day-care chains are growing with astonishing speed because six out of ten mothers with preschoolers or school-age children work outside the home. Chains like Kinder-Care have capitalized on parental fears arising from stories of child abuse in locally owned day-care centers by providing a carefully organized program overseen by local, area, regional, and national supervisors. Concerned parents find it easier to leave their children in child-care programs of recognized quality. A new product for this age group is the "pay-for-play" centers, such as Discovery Zone and McDonald's Leaps and Bounds, that are springing up in shopping centers around the country.

THE MARKETING MIX

The typical service product is an activity, entertainment, or work performed on your behalf by someone else. Life insurance is a good example of a service product; you regularly pay money to a company so it will financially help support your family after you die. You could invest your own money and develop your own personal insurance program, but most people prefer to have

Innovations in Retail Service

Because young adults and families buy the most furniture, the Scandinavian retailer IKEA, which specializes in stylish but inexpensive furniture, targets its facilitating service efforts at this group. Child care, strollers, and even free diapers are available, as is the loan of an automobile roof rack for getting purchases from the store to the home. IKEA is the source of many service-oriented innovations that American retailers like Wal-Mart are now beginning to copy.

someone else handle this task. One of the interesting business changes in North America in the 1990s is the reconfiguration of the insurance industry. More and more of the large companies are transforming themselves into health-care providers by setting up their own health maintenance organizations (HMOs). This new product is thriving because North Americans are more concerned about financing their health than their death and because the cost of traditional-style health care escalated so much during the 1970s and 1980s.

As the insurance story illustrates, service providers strive for constant *product improvement.* In late 1992 the General Motors Corporation introduced a credit card with no annual fee that earned users up to $500 credit a year toward the purchase of a GM car. Five months later it announced a gold card for more affluent customers that had an annual fee but offered a higher credit line and a rebate of $1,000. Service industries also offer multiproduct lines. In the financial services area, for example, banks serve both corporations and individuals with a wide variety of products, including chequing accounts, savings accounts, credit cards, mortgages, financial planning, and auto loans.

Pricing   The bottom line is as important to a company selling services as it is to a firm selling goods. The difference is that the calculations needed to arrive at a price for a service are usually more complicated. Seven basic components affect service pricing: (1) the amount of *time* it takes to perform the service; (2) the *level of expertise* required; (3) the *level of customer convenience* (how long must the customer wait?); (4) *equipment and supplies* required; (5) *over-head* (is the service performed in home or at the provider's location?); (6) *pro-motional expenses*; and (7) *profit*.

Pricing strategies depend on the nature of the service. Carpenters, plumbers, and professionals such as lawyers and accountants often charge *hourly* rates. Dentists often charge a **set fee** for a specific procedure such as a root canal or a cleaning. Set fees are often based on a schedule of fixed charges for a number of specific activities. Telephone companies charge a *set fee plus extras*—a monthly rate plus long-distance charges, for example. Stockbrokers and real estate agents usually get a **commission**—a percentage of the cost of a transaction paid to a person or firm that provides a service. Health clubs charge a *membership rate* based on a set time period (one year, three years), not how often you use the facilities. Symphony orchestras and sports teams sell *subscriptions* for season tickets. Your college or university collects *periodic charges*, or fees, from you every semester or term.

Distribution

Delivery of a service can differ dramatically from the distribution of a manufactured good. In goods manufacturing, production is usually followed by distribution. Production in the service industry, usually referred to as *operations*, is often combined with delivery at retail outlets and other places of consumption. For example, you can't take a taxi ride without being *in* the taxi or get your hair cut without being *in* the salon or barbershop. In these instances, the customer visits the service "factory." When customers are part of the service, there are no physical channels or intermediaries in service distribution.

There are exceptions to this rule. Agents for an insurance company are intermediaries or "retailers," selling products that were designed and sent out

set fee
A charge for services rendered; a specific amount based on a schedule of charges for specific activities.

commission
A percentage of the cost of a transaction paid to an individual or firm instrumental in providing a service.

Your Friendly International Banker

International banking is a highly competitive service business, with billions of dollars changing hands every day. All the major Canadian banks, including Toronto Dominion (shown here in Hong Kong) successfully operate branches in foreign countries.

from the home office in another town or province. Hertz and Avis have outlets in airports and at different sites around town. Similarly, broadcasting and electronic transfer services use electronic networks to distribute their product. International banking uses the electronic information highway, whose ability to transmit global information fast contributes to a competitive advantage.

Regardless of the level of customer involvement, distribution strategy for most service industries must consider *convenience*. The number one reason for choosing a fast-food brand is convenience, so the closer the outlet is to a potential customer, the more apt the customer is to buy there. Thus many services opt for multiple sites (for example, branch banks).

As we pointed out earlier in this chapter, even though services are intangible, they can be inventoried. They can also be wholesaled. In the tourism industry, for example, tour arrangers buy blocks of seats on planes and rooms in hotels at "wholesale" prices and then pull from their inventory of transportation and lodging to sell packaged excursions and customized tours. Unlike inventories of goods, which are moved into a warehouse, the rooms and seats are just "set aside" in anticipation of their being used. But since, conceptually, warehousing is storing product to have on hand when needed, what the tour operator is doing is building inventory. The reason you usually see business and first class being advertised by the major international airlines is that many of the coach seats have already been sold to tour arrangers. These service providers use capacity management as a competitive strategy. They are able to offer "good prices" on their tours because they made deals with the hotels and airlines by buying large quantities.

Marketing Communication   The intangibility of services and the importance of the provider's reputation make image communication that focuses on service quality extremely important for marketing a service. For example, British Rail in the U.K. and Amtrak in the U.S. have fought negative images stemming from scheduling difficulties and problems with on-time performance. In the 1980s Amtrak rejuvenated its services by upgrading trains, improving on-time performance, and installing a state-of-the-art reservation system—and featured all of these improvements in an award-winning advertising campaign designed to upgrade its image, but British Rail has yet to overcome some of its difficulties, especially labor disputes, which cripple its service across the country.

Advertising is important, but it is not the only kind of communication used in services marketing. The current "burger war," for instance, is being fought with price promotions, tie-in special events, and public relations programs such as McDonald's Ronald McDonald Houses for families of hospitalized children.

Service marketers have to decide whether to promote the service or the service organization. This issue is complicated in an era of mergers, deregulation, and the blurring of distinctions between service firms. For example, Prudential used to be an insurance company, but after buying the financial-services company Bache, it became Prudential-Bache, an insurance and investment company. Because the famous rock—the "Rock of Gibraltar"—doesn't fit well with Bache, the company has had an identity problem in its image advertising.

Sales, of course, is on the front line of marketing communication in many service industries. In the 1990s, given the emphasis on diversity and international marketing, an important new topic is cultural sensitivity. As ethnic diversity is becoming more the norm, and as more people travel beyond their countries' borders, service employees are challenged to approach customers with cultural sensitivity.[11] In recognition of this fact, Canadian Airlines International's print advertisements for its Asian destinations (Hong

Kong, Taipei, Beijing, Tokyo, Nagoya, Shanghai, and Bangkok) now feature the name of each of the destinations written in the characters of the language of each country.

NONPROFIT MARKETING ●

Not-for-profit organizations (NFPs) use marketing to "sell" their services and ideas just as businesses use marketing to sell their goods, services, ideas, and images. As the NFPs have become more competitive, their marketing efforts, the focus of the sixth chapter objective, have grown more sophisticated. Today many nonprofit organizations sell goods as well as services. Zoos, museums, and symphonies, as we mentioned earlier, often have elaborate gift shops that take in thousands of dollars a year. The Metropolitan Museum of Art in New York, the Smithsonian, and many other museums also publish catalogs that they send to members and anyone else they think might make a purchase.

NONPROFIT OBJECTIVES

To support their overall mission, most well-run nonprofit organizations set up behavioral response or financial contribution goals. For example, *affiliation* and *participation* are objectives of organizations like churches (spiritual and temporal goals), labor unions (collective bargaining goals), political parties (candidate election goals), and special interest groups like Ducks Unlimited and the Sierra Club. *Recruitment* is an objective of clubs and the military, as well as universities vis-à-vis prospective students and their parents. The Canadian Museum of Civilization in Hull, Quebec, uses glossy publications to invite the public to become friends of the museum.

Nonprofits are also concerned with more traditional bottom-line objectives. *Contributions* are an objective of philanthropic groups and associations like the Red Cross and the Worldwide Wildlife Society, as well as of churches and political parties or of universities when they contact their members and alumni for donations. *Visits*, or attendance, is an objective of cultural centers, museums, zoos, theaters, and provincial tourism departments. *Attitude change* is an objective of public service groups such as the Ad Council, the Mormon Church, and the Friends of the Earth (Exhibit 12-3) when they sponsor public service advertising campaigns.

STRATEGY IN NONPROFIT MARKETING

Because people have only a limited number of hours in which they can volunteer, only a certain number of dollars they are willing to give away, and only one way to vote on a political issue, the nonprofit sector has become tremendously competitive. Hospitals, symphonies, zoos, foundations, charities, and churches compete both directly and indirectly for volunteers' time, money, and patronage. As they become more competitive, the NFPs are making more use of marketing research, positioning, and idea "packaging" and are thinking in terms of product-mix strategies.

Like commercial organizations, not-for-profit groups need to develop competitive advantages, target new audiences, polish their positions, and find unique niches. Like companies selling services, many nonprofits must "sell" their target audience an intangible. In order for Greenpeace to get people to donate to the organization, it must convince them that what Greenpeace believes in and is doing is worth supporting. Hospitals try to "sell" people on volunteering to read to patients, work in the gift shop, and take magazines and books around to patients. Some of the problems connected with NFPs include multiple objectives, public security, and non-market pressures.

Generating Response NFPs, just like businesses, need a cash flow to pay salaries, utilities, and rent, and purchase the materials they need to perform their particular services. Some of the group's budget may be generated internally by fees, memberships, and ticket sales. Other income comes from donations, grants, government contributions, and the sale of merchandise. An article in a trade journal for the nonprofit industry summarizes the four Ps of nonprofit marketing as: performing, pleading, petitioning, and praying.[12] Although the idea of "return" is quite different with NFPs in that they are promoting the goods of political candidates, unions, and charitable organizations, essentially NFPs are utilizing the same tools of market segregation, consumer research, concept development, communications, incentives, and exchange theory to maximize target group response.

In 1984 and 1985 heart-rending images of starving Ethiopians—particularly emaciated children with bulging eyes and distended stomachs—filled the media, spurring a tremendous outpouring of contributions dedicated to the alleviation of poverty and starvation in the Third World. By the end of the 1980s, however, donations to the Save the Children charity had fallen by 50 percent. The organization attributed the decline to "donor fatigue": people who had given financially in the past were so emotionally depleted by reports of horrors that they were now ignoring them and no longer contributing. The problem is complicated by the fact that North Americans are constantly besieged by stories of new crises—AIDS, homelessness, and "ethnic cleansing," to name a few.

As a result, marketing strategies for organized *fund-raising* campaigns have become quite sophisticated. Groups such as Save the Children are trying to target new audiences, use segmentation strategies, and develop other messages to replace the photographs of starving children, which aren't generating as much response as in the past. In hopes of attracting consistent donors, Save the Children is now targeting a new segment of the North American population—"yuppies with a conscience."

Recruiting Marketing is also gaining importance among NFPs that find themselves with "excess capacity." In the face of declining enrollments, universities and other types of private schools are trying to carve out distinctive positions for themselves in the educational market in order to compete more successfully for students.

**Exhibit 12-3
Selling a Cause**

Established in Canada in 1978, Friends of the Earth is an international nonprofit corporation with branches in 52 countries. The organization's main objective is promoting environment education and research for industry, government, and the general public.

407

INCREASING GIVING FROM UNIVERSITY ALUMNI

Many colleges and universities in Canada have experienced a reduction in provincial funding over the last several years. While these institutions have increased tuition fees charged to their students to offset most of the loss in provincial funding, increased emphasis has also been placed on private support. Such support may allow the institutions to enhance their programs or facilities and, more commonly, this support is being used to supplement operating funds available to the institutions.

Fund raising has focused on support from corporations, foundations and individuals especially through capital campaigns. Gifts from alumni, parents of current students and even the students themselves have become an increasingly important part of the university's private support.

The University of Calgary, for example, attracted $3 million in support from its alumni and $2.2 million in support from its undergraduate students as part of its successful "Building on the Vision" campaign which topped the $46 million mark in just three years.

Often, the decision on the part of alumni or students to provide a gift to a college or university's fund raising program is based on their experience with the institution. This can range from the level of involvement the individual had (involvement in clubs, societies, athletics or other student activities) the level of service they received from the institution and the quality of academic program in which they were or are enrolled. Negative experiences such as frustration with registration processes, confusion with class time tabling, or more day-to-day experiences such as lack of parking can have a negative impact on the desire to make a gift.

As our colleges and universities restructure and redefine their missions in response to changing social, economic, and demographic needs there is a greater focus on the student as customer. While the focus is not driven by the increase of private gifts from students and alumni, there is an understanding that greater satisfaction may have as one of its results increased support down the road. Faculty in the classroom are becoming increasingly aware of the correlation between student satisfaction and the general reputation of the university and its ability to attract private support. Consider your own response five years down the road from an approach from your alma mater for private support. Would you give? What factors would you take into consideration in determining the level of support you would be willing to provide? Would your satisfaction with the services you received while you were a student play an important role in your decision making? ▼

KEY POINTS SUMMARY ▼

1. The goods-services continuum includes services that sell goods and manufacturers that sell services. In some ways, the marketing of all goods includes some form of service (although not all services include some form of goods).

2. Service products are primary services—usually time, expertise, or actions performed by the seller for the buyer. The chief characteristics of service products are intangibility, close customer relationship, perishability, inseparability from the service provider, and quality variability. Facilitating services are support services offered to facilitate the purchase and use of the product.

3. Service quality focuses on customer satisfaction. It is highly dependent on the caliber of the employees performing the service. Quality control involves benchmarking, employee training, and regular performance evaluations.

4. Service attitude, the manner in which a service is performed, is most satisfying when it focuses on pleasing customers. It is a major factor in the customers' perception of the quality of both the service itself and the organization that provides the service.

5. Service marketing is much like the marketing of goods, although pricing is usually more complicated. The greatest difference is in delivery: since services are perishable, involve the customer, and cannot be separated from the service provider, there are usually no physical channels or intermediaries.

6. Not-for-profit groups use marketing to persuade people to affiliate with, participate in, be recruited by, contribute to, change attitudes about, or make visits to their organizations.

DISCUSSION QUESTIONS ▼

1. Using the concept of the goods-services continuum, describe the relationship between goods and services in marketing a car rental company and explain what services are important in the customer's decision-making process.

2. Select a service business in which the customer must be present for the service to occur. Outline a plan to help that company motivate its employees to be more cooperative and helpful toward customers.

3. Interview the marketing manager of a local service firm and then describe that firm in terms of: (1) its place on the goods-services continuum; (2) the degree to which its service is intangible and perishable; (3) the degree to which providing the service involves the customer; (4) the nature of the customer relationship the firm has built; (5) the firm's strategies and marketing mix.

4. What are the most common objectives of non-profit organizations? Give examples of objectives of organizations to which you, your family, or some of your friends belong. How effectively do these organizations achieve their objectives and what strategies do they use to do so?

5. You are the manager of a moderately priced East European hotel that would like to attract more West European and North American tourists, but is having a hard time doing so because the employees have a poor service attitude. Outline a plan for motivating your employees to understand and practice good customer service.

6. How does the marketing plan for Junior Achievement differ from the one for Millennium presented at the end of Chapter 4?

7. You have been hired by a local bank to improve its level of customer satisfaction. Outline the steps you would take in approaching this task. What key factors do you think would need improvement? Brainstorm some ideas for addressing these problem areas and increasing customer satisfaction.

8. Analyze the concept of customer satisfaction at your school. How does your school balance the demands for customer satisfaction with the need to maintain grading standards? Interview the head of your school's foundation or gift-giving office to determine what alumni regard as the most important factors in their relationship with the school. Write a report for the president on "Customer Satisfaction and Quality Education at (your school's name)."

The Body Shop*

1. How does The Body Shop create customer satisfaction?

Harley-Davidson

1. Do Harley dealers perform basic or facilitating services?

2. How has Harley attempted to improve dealer service?

3. What is the Harley dealer's biggest problem today and what can he do about it?

The Millennium Power System

1. If Millennium purchasers are more satisfied than purchasers of other systems, why are Millennium's sales fourth in the industry?

*The three cases at the back of the book—"The Body Shop," "Harley-Davidson," and "The Millennium Power System"—illustrate topics discussed in all chapters of this book. Your instructor will tell you when to read a particular case and when to answer the discussion questions on it that appear at the end of each chapter.

Mutual Mania

Does it appear to be a difficult proposition to market an intangible product or service, offering an unguaranteed and unpredictable benefit, to potential customers bearing high expectations of performance, given that they are typically trading-off significant levels of personal and financial risk in expectation of this benefit? While common sense may dictate that this would be a difficult task for any marketing guru, the hundreds of individuals lining up to be licensed to sell or trade mutual funds, easily the hottest selling investment vehicles in Canada for the past few years, do not seem to share in this sentiment.

Consumer expectations have been fuelled into an inferno by two years of exceptionally high growth in mutual fund markets, with many mutual funds returning 30–40 percent, and some funds loudly advertising returns of 70–80 percent. Rookie investors are jumping into the mutual fund market, plugging their RRSPs and life savings into mutual funds advertising high past-years' performance. Few of these inexperienced investors seem to realize that high returns typically call for a high degree of risk, and many mutual fund managers are biting their nails over potential customer dissatisfaction in the coming year. They realize that, as with any intangible product or service, customer satisfaction is largely based on at least meeting, and preferably exceeding all prior customer expectations. The dilemma is, what do you do when your own industry is largely responsible for raising customer expectations to a level that is deemed unrealistic?

Most Canadian mutual fund managers expect the worst. They feel that a market correction is imminent, and that small high-growth companies have been largely saturated with mutual fund capital investment, leaving only the large, slow-growing companies seeking additional investment. Mutual fund managers and sellers are scrambling in attempts to judiciously reduce customer performance expectations, and at the same time, reduce the possibility of a mass panic sell-off of stock, which could devastate the industry. However, trying to convince inexperienced rookie investors to adopt a long-term perspective is not a simple manner, given the performance of mutual funds in the past several years.

Mutual fund managers are trying harder than ever to form long-term relationships with their customers based on trust, as convincing rookie investors to adopt a long-term investment perspective requires that a strong element of mutual trust exists. In the long run, both the industry and its customers would be best served by a smoothing of buying and selling patterns. But how do you cool customers off once you have heated them up with your marketing efforts and previous track record, without risking permanently turning them off to your product or service offered?

QUESTIONS:

1. What unique difficulties might you experience when marketing an intangible product or service?
2. Why is "relationship marketing" an important element of marketing intangible products or services?
3. Can you think of ways to compensate for a lack of product or service tangibility in your marketing efforts?

413

4. Make a list of common intangible products and services that you have recently seen marketed? Can you see any common marketing obstacles that they share? Are there any unique common marketing possibilities that you can identify?

Source: This case was prepared by Byron Osing and is based on the *Venture* series episode "Mutual Mania," originally broadcast on January 30, 1994.

● Chapter 13

New Products

ARE "FRANKENFOODS" GOOD FOR YOU?

The success of *Jurassic Park* has brought new scares to the table as consumers worry about genetically engineered food—giant tomatoes and "the zucchini that ate Chicago." Foes of biotechnology— the altering of plants, animals, or microbes by manipulating their genes—contend that genetically engineered food is unproven and may be unsafe. The city of Chicago has responded to these critics with an ordinance requiring grocers to post signs informing shoppers that particular foods have been genetically engineered.[1]

The U.S. biotech industry worries that a misinformed public will confuse *genetically altered* foods—some of which, like tangelos and NutraSweet, have been around a long time— with *chemically contaminated* products. They suspect that the true purpose of such signs in grocery stores is not to inform consumers but rather to scare them away from new food products. If that happens, they fear, there will be a decline in

investment in R&D-driven biotech stocks that will result in the United States losing its leadership in bioengineering, an international growth industry.

Biotechnology, potentially a multibillion-dollar industry, employs genetic engineering to try to develop products ranging from drug treatments for cancer and Alzheimer's disease to computers that "think" like a human brain. Because of the huge costs required to develop such products, the industry is particularly sensitive to public fears that may affect stock prices and the availability of R&D money.

What would you do if you saw a sign in your grocery store informing you that the apple you are about to buy was developed through genetic engineering? Would it make you pause? Would you put it back? Or would you say that every apple in the store has been improved in some way through genetic engineering, so what's the big deal? ■

In this chapter we will consider the development of new products—goods and services—for both consumer and industrial markets. First we analyze the definition of new products and the strategies behind their development. Then we look in detail at the new-product development process, which includes everything leading up to product introduction—the beginning of the product life cycle.

THE CONCEPT OF NEW PRODUCTS ●

Just what is a "new" product? Is a Campbell soup that is simply reformulated to reduce the salt content "new"? If the Bank of Montreal begins offering a thirty-year home mortgage in addition to its standard twenty-five-year mortgage, is the thirty-year mortgage a "new" product? If a soft-drink company introduces a diet version of its brand after other brands have had diet products on the market for years, is this a "new" product? Can a product billed as "old-fashioned," like the Maxwell House coffee in Exhibit 13-1, be simultaneously a "new" product? What about Camay soap? Procter and Gamble introduced the concept of brand management with this product in 1928. Recently it has been split into three different variants but the brand has endured.

HOW NEW IS "NEW"?

new product
A product being introduced to the market for the first time as a result of invention, innovation or improvement.

Most marketers define a **new product** as one that must be "introduced" to a market—that is, distributors and consumers are not aware that the product exists. New-product development, the subject of the first objective for this chapter, generally takes one of three routes. A new product may be: (1) an *invention* (an entirely new type of product); (2) an *innovation* (a significantly better product); or (3) an *improvement* (a gradually changed existing product or product line). Inventions include the compact disk, the felt-tip pen, and the personal computer. Innovations include Nintendo, tangelos (a biotech innovation), and portable personal computers. Improvements include Liquid Tide,

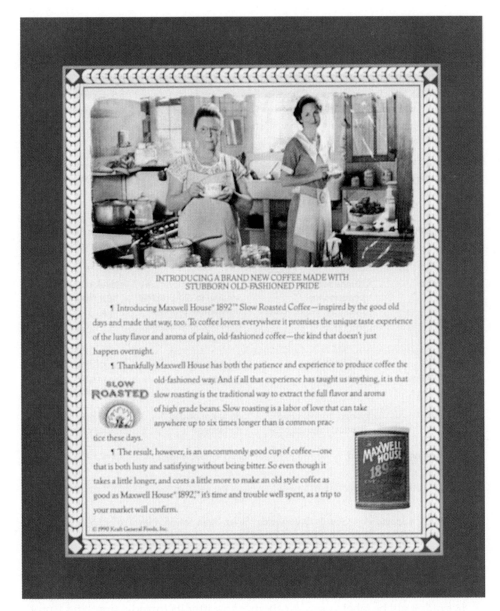

Exhibit 13-1
When Is an Old
Product New?

Maxwell House introduced a new version of an old product and used a nostalgic theme to emphasize the old-fashioned formulation. Is this a "new product"?

Diet Coke, and tartar-control Crest. About two-thirds of all new products are improvements, while only 10 percent are inventions.[2] Table 13-1 outlines the decisions and strategies involved in each of these three approaches.

Product "newness"—the topic of the second chapter objective—has three dimensions: *difference, customer perception,* and *legal requirements*. A new product must *differ* in significant ways from products already being offered in a particular market. It must also be *perceived* as new by a group of customers. Thus a product that is well established in one place may be a new product when first introduced elsewhere. For example, fast-food restaurants are old hat in North America but new in Eastern Europe and China. To what degree must a current product be changed in order to be legally advertised as "new"? One of the best defenses a company can present is research findings (based on professionally acceptable methodology) showing that a majority of potential

TABLE 13-1   NEW-PRODUCTS PLANNING MODEL

	Approach		
	Improvement	**Innovation**	**Invention**
Decisions			
Focus of strategy	Existing product	New product in existing category Competitive advantage product	New product New category
Objectives	Maintain, build brand franchise category	Increase market share in existing category	Enter and dominate new markets
Tactics	Change form, performance, package, price/value, distribution	Create new entry, new solution to old problem, devise new problem solution, fill new need, create line extension	Develop entirely new marketing mix
Profit potential	Hold/increase sales levels	Major increase in sales level	Major new source of corporate revenues
Cost	Funded from existing product revenue base	Short-term added investment	High; new money required
Development time	Short	Short to medium	Long
Risk	Small	Small to medium	Great

Source: Adapted from George Gruenwald, "Seven Steps Toward New Product Success," *Advertising Age*, April 27, 1981, p. 52.

customers perceive the product as significantly different. In Canada, a product may only be labeled *new* for six months after its introduction, and a product may only stay on retail shelves for up to one year with the "new" label. Similar laws exist in the United States. Elsewhere, in Britain for example, brands such as Persil have been advertising that they are "new" and "improved" for generations.

Inventions may require formal government approval. New food additives and pharmaceuticals, for example, have to be approved by the Health Protection Branch of Health Canada before they can be marketed. HPB approval can be a lengthy process. It can also be expensive because of all the special tests, reports, and demonstrations required. Legal approval not only delays market entry but can also influence the product-development process. For instance, since all biotech improvements and innovations are subject to HPB review, the industry strives to proceed in ways that will satisfy the HPB and alleviate the types of public fears we discussed in the opening story.

Some new products are protected by a **patent**—the right to exclude others from making, using, or selling an invention. In Canada patents last for

patent
The right to exclude others from making using, or selling an invention.

twenty years, after which other companies are free to use the patented product without paying a fee. Patents can be taken out on original inventions or on innovations in existing patented products. For example, Gillette holds two patents on its Sensor razor, which has twin movable blades mounted on molded plastic springs, allowing each blade to move independently and follow body contours. The words "patent pending" are often used to ward off counterfeiters but the actual likelihood of a patent being granted is another matter, and for how long. Patents are awarded to protect original designs and have more recently been extended into the domain of intellectual property and computer software.

IMPORTANCE OF NEW PRODUCTS

New products are the lifeblood of many businesses. Many companies today are dependent on products and brands that did not exist say five years ago. Today, with technology changing at an accelerated pace and global marketing becoming a pressing concern of medium and even small companies, firms must continue to improve their current products and look for new ones in order to survive. As chapter objective three indicates, there are two important reasons for developing new products: to compensate for declining brands and to safeguard or improve a company's standing in the financial community. The odds of failing with any new product are high, but falling behind the competition by not introducing products that meet changing consumer needs and wants is an even riskier course for a company.

There are four ways in which companies use new products to defend as well as increase a brand's share. First, new products can give a company a foothold in a new-category segment. For example, when Procter & Gamble transformed Pert shampoo into Pert Plus, creating a combination shampoo-conditioner, it increased its U.S. market share from 2 percent to 12 percent. This formula is now sold around the world under various names—Rejoice in Hong Kong, Vidal Sasson in England, and Pert Plus in North America and the Middle East. Second, new products can preempt a market segment, as when Apple, a late-comer in the computer industry, built the personal computer market right under IBM's nose. Third, they can maintain a firm's position as product innovator: AT&T, for example, continues to come out with new phone-related services such as "call waiting" and "code ringing" to identify callers and is also aggressively merchandising the hardware that is required to enable you to take advantage of these services. In this way it is maintaining a technological edge and market share in those products and services which also carry the higher value added. Finally, new products can keep overall corporate sales up when other products or categories fall. For example, in the 1980s recording companies introduced cassette singles and music videos, and killed off the vinyl LP in favor of the digitally produced CD. Technology push was not the answer behind this move as much as a desire to cream profit from a new product, the CD, which would also accompany sales in CD players. Technologically, the analogue record players produced by Linn Electronics, a small unheard of company in Scotland are acoustically superior to the flat notes produced by digitally remastered sound.

Because the continuous introduction of new products has become the hallmark of corporate success, the ability to produce new products is one of the criteria used by the financial community in evaluating a company. Thus a company with a good new-product image usually has a higher stock value and a better credit rating than similar companies that do not have such an image. One of the most highly regarded companies in the North America, 3M, gets 37 percent of its sales from products that have been developed only within the last five years.[3]

The Big Idea Generally, for a new product to make a significant contribution to a company's profit picture, it must be a *big idea,* meaning it must appeal to a large market segment and be significantly different from anything offered by the competition. A big idea usually produces economies of scale. Thus in the magazine industry the production facilities of major publishers work most efficiently when running a million or more copies at a time, but it requires a big idea for a new magazine to generate such high circulation. A good example is *People* magazine, a Time, Inc., publication. When research showed that one of the most popular features in *Time* magazine was its "people" section, Time developed *People* to satisfy this interest more fully (and profitably). Today *People* magazine has a huge sustainable circulation, proving it was a truly big idea.

There are many unmet consumer needs, but finding one that exists in a large segment of the population is difficult. Some new ideas are so needed by so many people that they virtually sell themselves: if you discover a cure for cancer, you probably won't need to promote it. Most, however, need to be marketed: if you discover a new method for people to stop smoking, your product will probably need a push from marketing communication.

From the diffusion of innovation literature comes a model for evaluating the adoption rate for new ideas. This model, which is based on the work of Everett Rogers[4] and depicted in Figure 13-1, suggests that the rate or ease of adoption of a new idea depends on the following elements:

Relative advantage: the degree to which the idea is perceived as better than the one it supersedes. The greater the relative advantage an idea has, the faster it will be adopted.

Compatibility: the degree to which the idea is perceived as being consistent with existing values, past experiences, and needs of potential adopters. The more compatible a new idea is, the faster it will be adopted.

Complexity: the degree to which the idea is perceived as difficult to understand and/or use. The less complex a new idea is, the faster the rate of adoption.

Figure 13-1
Locating the "Big Idea"

A truly "big idea" for a new product is created only when five crucial qualities come together: relative advantage over other products, compatibility with existing consumer needs and values, lack of excessive complexity, ease of trial, and ease with which the benefits of the new product can be envisioned. It is because this happens very rarely that the area in which the "big idea" occurs appears very small.

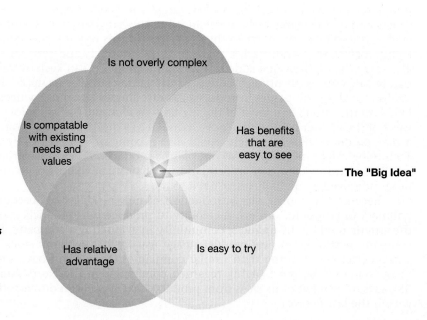

Is not overly complex

Is compatable with existing needs and values

Has benefits that are easy to see

The "Big Idea"

Has relative advantage

Is easy to try

Trialability: the degree to which the idea can be tested. The easier it is to experimentally test a new idea, the faster it will be adopted.

Observability: the degree to which the results of an innovation are visible to others. The more observable these results, the faster the idea will be adopted.

Why New Products Fail   About 90 percent of the ideas for new products never even get off the ground. Moreover, the president of New York City's New Products Workshop estimates that the overall failure rate of new products is close to 85 percent. Even among new products that actually hit the shelves, some 50 percent fail.

As you will see in the next section, many new products fail. Why? The most important reason is the product cannot be produced and marketed profitably. After doing a series of "autopsies" on new-product failures, one major consulting firm concluded that the number-one killer of new products was *market misjudgment,* which includes such things as bad timing, mistargeting, mispositioning, and misestimating sales potential. Even though most marketing executives acknowledge the benefits of having new products, many hesitate to invest heavily in new-product development because they know there are many situations and decisions that can cause failure[5] (see Table 13-2).

TABLE 13-2   **WHY NEW PRODUCTS FAIL**

1. *Bad Concept*   The product does not meet a consumer need or does not offer a good value.

2. *Insignificant Difference*   A difference exists but isn't significant enough to warrant changing from a current brand; many failures here are "me-too" products.

3. *Poor Execution*   The product never actually duplicates the original, proven concept.

4. *Inadequate Budget*   Underestimating the investment needed to launch a new product and move it into profitability can adversely limit development at every step from initial R&D through promotion.

5. *Insufficient Market Size*   The market is not big enough to generate the volume necessary to produce a profit.

6. *Bad Timing*   The product may be tested or introduced at the wrong time of year or in the wrong cultural or economic environment.

7. *Mistargeting*   A good product may be offered to a group that doesn't want or need it.

8. *Mispositioning*   A product designed to do one thing may be positioned as something different or marketing communications explaining the product may be unclear.

9. *Misjudging the Competition*   A company may fail to read the exact nature of the competitive situation and lack adequate planning for competitive counterstrikes.

10. *Misestimating*   Forecast sales may be overstated or costs may be underestimated.

11. *Market Changes*   The market environment may change between testing and launch.

12. *Wearing Blinders*   A company may become so committed to making a concept come alive that it subconsciously overlooks or downplays all "bad news" as it goes through the developmental steps.

FLOPS

Big companies with big budgets can afford all the research they need to guarantee success for their new products, right? Wrong, if you

consider such monumental flops as Ford Motor Company's Edsel (estimated loss $250 million), RCA's VideoDisc player ($500 million), and Time, Inc.'s, TV-Cable Week ($47 million). Other costly historical failures are New Coke, Pepsi A.M. and Jolt cola, dry beers, milk beers, clear beers, R. J. Reynolds' Premier cigarette, and the Cadillac Allante.[6]

Robert McMath, president of Marketing Intelligence Service, Ltd., which tracks new products in test markets, has a storeroom overflowing with more than 80,000 products that flopped. His collection includes Singles (baby food for adults) by Gerber, Instant Baby Food Flakes (dehydrated) by Heinz, Great Loaf (breaded mix for meat loaf) by General Foods, Salvo detergent tablets by Procter & Gamble, and Smithers Love Boats (chocolate "boats" to be filled with dessert toppings) by Alberto-Culver.

Some Come to Laugh But Stay to Learn

Nestled among the hills of Ithaca, New York, is Robert McMath's New Products Showcase and Learning Center, where more than 80,000 failed products have found a final resting place. McMath, a former Colgate-Palmolive executive, consults for marketers who want to review past efforts in particular product categories, for he can tell them why the flops flopped and, often, why competitors succeeded.

One marketing research company estimates that little more than half (56 percent) of all products that get launched are still on the market five years later. Since most ideas never make it to the test-market stage, the failure rate of new-product ideas is much, much higher. Producing flops seems to be part of doing business. Many people argue that in our highly competitive age improving on this failure rate is the last frontier of marketing. So despite the risky nature of new-product development, it is one of the most exciting and challenging aspects of marketing.

NEW-PRODUCT STRATEGIES

Before developing a new product, a firm should weigh the risks involved against the potential benefits. Only then can it intelligently decide if it should proceed and determine the best strategy for doing so.

WEIGHING THE RISKS AND BENEFITS

In Chapter 2 we noted that corporate cultures differ in attitude toward risk. A firm's attitude toward risk is often most visible when it considers new-product development. Although the risks of developing new products are often great, new-product introduction hit an all-time high in North America, in the late 1980s, when no less than 10,558 items were recorded in Gorman's *New Product News*. The number of new-product introductions continues to climb in the 1990s, but the rate of growth is slowing. One explanation for the slowdown is that retailers have been demanding significant increases in "slotting" allowances, or the amount of money they receive from manufacturers to stock and display new products (see Chapter 16 for a detailed explanation of slotting allowances). This has raised the price of market entry and had a somewhat chilling effect on new product launches.

STRATEGY OPTIONS

Firms that have opted to launch new products have generally used one of three major strategies: duplication of what competitors have done successfully ("me-too" products); attempts to gain competitive advantage through product improvement; and new-product ventures. These strategies are the focus of the fourth chapter objective.

As Figure 13-2 shows, me-too products generally involve the lowest amount of risk and R&D investment, whereas new ventures usually involve the highest. Not all products fit this pattern, however. The Georgia pharmacist who concocted and sold the first Coca-Cola at the soda fountain in his drugstore was risking little and had spent virtually no money developing his product. In contrast, the major automobile makers have spent billions of dollars designing luxury cars that are fundamentally me-too products and seen by the buying public as "me-too" products. The result is that the manufacturers then have to sell these products by bundling the benefits, seeking to offer a value package. The alternative would be to research and produce a product that the market exactly wants which would then, of course, be less price sensitive as well.

Me-Too Strategies Products that basically duplicate ones already introduced and proved successful by another firm are called *me-too products*. For example, forty years ago most bicycles had fat balloon tires, fenders, and one speed. Then came lighter-weight, three-speed, thin-tired bikes, still with fenders. Next came ten-speed racing bikes without fenders. They were followed by

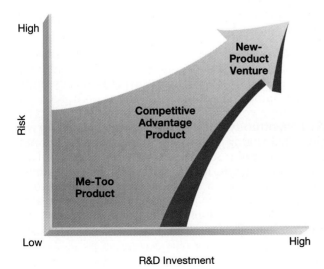

Figure 13-2
Relationship of Risk to R&D Investment

bikes with 18 to 21 speeds, and most recently by cross-country or mountain bikes. During this evolution nearly every bike manufacturer made the kind of bike that was fashionable at the time. Not until a new style proved itself did most bike manufacturers jump on the bandwagon and start making several variations of that particular type.

Letting other firms come up with an idea and test-market it saves a company the considerable amount of money and time needed to invent and sell a new-product concept. However, the first brand, if properly marketed, may well position itself as *the* brand and build strong brand loyalty. Coca Cola was the first major cola, and with sound marketing over the years, the brand has maintained its leadership position despite the Pepsi challenge. If the first company to market a product obtains a patent that keeps others out of the market for years, the disadvantage of a me-too approach is even greater. The second brand into the market usually gets only half the share of the first brand, the third brand only half that of the second brand, and so on. In other words, the longer a company waits to enter the market with a me-too product, the less sales potential its product will have.

Me-too product strategies can be highly profitable, however, if the innovator does a poor job of marketing and fails to ensure that it will maintain its leadership position. When that happens, another firm can take the same product concept and become the category leader. IBM didn't invent the computer; Sperry Rand did. But IBM outmarketed Sperry Rand and established itself as the dominant computer company.

The most typical way of being successful with a me-too product is to have a competitive advantage in another marketing area, such as distribution, customer service, pricing, or extremely creative marketing communications. Anita Roddick's The Body Shop sells body lotions and similar products that have few, if any, physical competitive advantages other than that the very basic "no frills" packaging further endorses the image of Body Shop and its customer profile. The chain owes its success to its positioning and mission—as a socially and environmentally conscious organization that does its sourcing in third world companies, encourages recycling, and promotes the rights of indigenous peoples.

Competitive-Advantage Strategies These strategies also call for watching the competition to identify viable product concepts. But firms adopting a competitive-advantage strategy don't merely *duplicate* what is already on the market; they make significant improvements or innovations on it. Some improvements result from testing a competitor's product and finding a major weakness or an overlooked opportunity. For example, Nintendo came up with superior graphics and more challenging games than Atari and nearly put Atari out of business. Then in the early 1990s Sega went from having less than a 10 percent share of the 16-bit video game market to nearly tying Nintendo, which had owned the market ever since it overtook Atari. Sega significantly increased its share by having a competitive advantage in two primary areas: technology, which made its games more sophisticated than Nintendo's; and marketing communications (especially advertising) that had more appeal to teens than Nintendo's.

In the service arena one of the most spectacular examples of creating a competitive advantage is a brand we have cited several times before, Saturn. Saturn's physical product is good, but most agree that the car merely matches the Japanese imports in its price class. It has been Saturn's service that has given it a competitive advantage over both foreign and domestic competition. Not only service *after* the car has been sold, but service in how *potential* buyers are treated (no high pressure) when they first come into a Saturn show room and all through the selling process, especially the no-haggling pricing strategy that makes customers feel more confident about their buying decision.

New-Venture Strategies When a firm or individual invests in a totally new product (or even product category), it stands to reap tremendous profits—if the product succeeds. As we noted in Chapter 2, such ventures may come out of the company's research and development department and/or from "intrapreneurs" within the corporation. The hand-held Newton personal communications assistant was an intrapreneurial development. An intrapreneurial attitude and structure are also responsible for the huge number of inventions that come pouring out of 3M every year. 3M's commitment to product innovation is expressed in the ad reproduced in Exhibit 13-2.

When development costs are very high, companies may join together to spread the costs and the risk. Motorola, one of the few major U.S. competitors left in the Japanese-dominated computer chip market, has found its $750 million R&D budget inadequate in an industry where new products are the lifeblood. Accordingly, its R&D staff has joined a semiconductor consortium with several of its major customers' R&D staffs. Motorola has even teamed up with a major competitor, Toshiba, in order to speed up product development. Toshiba drives its new-product engine with these kinds of partnerships: it has similar alliances with Apple Computer, United Technologies, Time Warner, Sun Microsystems, Siemens, Samsung, and Olivetti, among others.[7]

More often the high risks associated with new-product undertakings make established firms opt for one of the other two strategies. Many new-product ventures, therefore, involve new companies that must struggle not only to develop the product and a marketing plan for it but also to construct the systems necessary to make the marketing plan work.

NEW PRODUCTS FOR GLOBAL MARKETS

Strategically, new products can be developed for national, regional, or global markets. A product can be developed for the home country and then extended into markets in other countries, or it can be developed for the global market and then adapted to meet the precise requirements of each country. The Sony Walkman, for example, was developed specifically for the global market, and Technomed International was formed to undertake the global marketing of a machine that uses sound waves to break up gallstones and kidney stones in the human body, thus avoiding the need for surgery.

Developing a new global product (or global adaptations of a product), the subject of chapter objective five, is complex. There are many more external factors to consider than in national or regional marketing, particularly the laws and regulations of the various countries. Also, consumption patterns tend to reflect cultural differences. Interestingly, however, new products are sometimes easier to market globally than old ones, at least when the new items reflect the use of new technologies. Perhaps people of all cultures re-

NEW PRODUCTS

Exhibit 13-2
3M's Road to
Innovation

One of the most
innovative
companies in the
world, 3M,
continues to refine
its products.

spond more freely to a product in an area none of them have had any experience with than to a product in an area where they have preformed attitudes and beliefs.

Firms attempting a new-product venture can draw on research among far more customers, suppliers, and distributors than can firms that limit their marketing to one nation. But organizing this feedback poses a problem in some cases, especially in firms that are organized along country-specific operating divisions.

Global new-product development leverages the effort of the product-development group and concentrates the firm's resources. When a sound basic idea is combined with strong research input from the specific countries targeted, a global product can be adapted to meet the needs of each market. As you'll see in the section that follows, however, global development of new products can pose considerable problems.

RISKS AND GAMBLES
THE HIGH RISK OF HIGH DEFINITION TV

Japan's Sony Corporation made a big breakthrough on high-definition television (HDTV) in the 1980s. Sony believes that this system will create a demand not only for the new television sets but also for a new nationally *integrated services digital network* (ISDN) to handle high speed telecommunications.

Just what is "high definition" in a television set? Standard TVs use 525 parallel lines to produce an image. The HDTV system uses 1,125 lines, which provides four to five times as much detail. The result is a high-quality, cinemalike screen image that conventional TVs cannot achieve. The American Electronics Association estimates that by the year 2010 sales of HDTVs and compatible VCRs will total U.S. $40 billion a year worldwide. How will this system be built and who will build it?

Clearly the Japanese companies are in the lead. Unfortunately, North American companies may be left without a piece of this new electronic market since most of its TV companies—Philco, Quasar, Magnavox, RCA and GE—are now owned by foreign firms. Zenith is the only exception, and most of its TV sets are now made in Mexico. While Japanese companies enjoy the support of their government in financing the huge costs of developing HDTV, North American governments have been slow to get involved.

In contrast, the French government identified HDTV as a goal in 1986 and, after resisting a Japanese

High-Tech Video

The Space System TV introduced by the French-owned Thomson Consumer Electronics is a panoramic stereophonic marvel. As a forerunner of futuristic HDTV, it's ahead of its time. In order to recoup a part of its hefty R&D investment while waiting for HDTV to become a reality, Thomson sells some of the Space System's exclusive (and expensive) features—like its state-of-the-art 34-inch screen—as specialty goods for use in other products. Thomson hopes to generate both enthusiasm for its own products and eventual demand for HDTV later in the 1990s.

proposal for a uniform global analog-based HDTV standard, led other European governments in funding research for a European HDTV system based on the French analog communication model.[8] Unfortunately for both the Japanese and the French, communication scientists determined in the early 1990s that a digital-based system was more practical than analog. It is estimated that by 1992 the Thompson-CSF company had lost U.S. $1.3 billion trying to keep its analog system afloat, though most of the loss was borne by the French government.

A new consortium of North American and European companies is now working on a digital TV standard for the new generation of HDTV. In North America, there is some deliberation on the idea of establishing a single HDTV standard. Experts fear that such a standard will lock broadcasters into single uses of their channels rather than leaving them free to provide whatever electronic products they think will best serve their local markets—for example, digital HDTV, standard television, E-mail, fax, paging systems. The development of HDTV is surely one of the biggest new product dramas in international business.

THE NEW-PRODUCT DEVELOPMENT PROCESS ●

We have said that new firms are more likely than established ones to risk bringing out inventions instead of innovations or improvements. They also tend to take a different approach to the new-product development process, the subject of the sixth chapter objective. As depicted in Figure 13-3, there are nine steps in the *new-product–development process* used by firms that manufacture goods or provide services: idea generation, screening, business analysis, concept testing, product and strategy development, product testing, marketing-mix planning, test marketing, and product launch. Entrepreneurs and some Japanese firms often skip certain steps, such as business analysis, concept testing, and test marketing, which speeds the process but heightens the risks.

Although this model is a useful generalization, keep in mind that no two products have ever been developed in exactly the same way. Some products take as little as a few weeks to develop; others require ten years or more. How long the process takes depends on the complexity of the product, management's commitment and expertise, the firm's attitude toward risk (companies willing to take more risks proceed faster), and what the competition is doing. For example, microwaveable french fries were under development for years, and many companies had given up when Golden Valley Microwave Foods, Inc., maker of Act II microwave popcorn, found a complicated solution to the problem of soggy nonfried "fries." By pulverizing the potatoes and packaging the final product in a special box lined with thin metalized polyester heater strips, Golden Valley has been able to make microwave fries that approach the quality of McDonald's. However, the company still hasn't figured out how to keep the price down to McDonald's level, and the safety of Golden Valley's heating strips is still under investigation.

STEP 1: IDEA GENERATION

Idea generation—whether it results in improvement, innovation, or invention—is a process that demands creative thinkers. Who are these creative

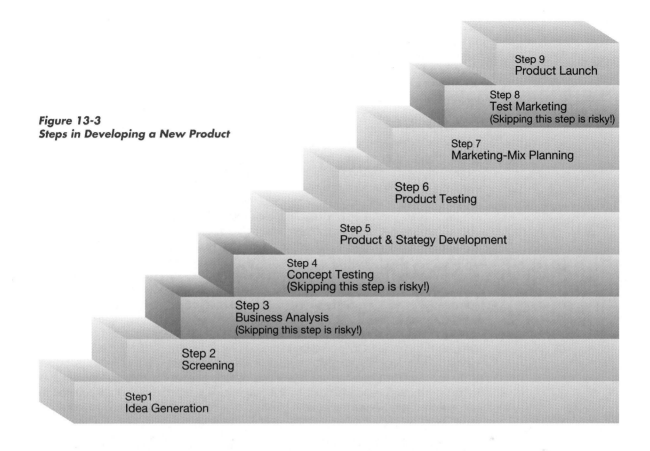

Figure 13-3
Steps in Developing a New Product

Step 9
Product Launch

Step 8
Test Marketing
(Skipping this step is risky!)

Step 7
Marketing-Mix Planning

Step 6
Product Testing

Step 5
Product & Stategy Development

Step 4
Concept Testing
(Skipping this step is risky!)

Step 3
Business Analysis
(Skipping this step is risky!)

Step 2
Screening

Step1
Idea Generation

thinkers? A few companies have new-product development teams responsible for thinking up and developing new-product ideas. Creative thinking is valued throughout business, but it is particularly important in new-product development. Books and seminars on creativity in business are big sellers today, but the pioneer in this area is the course at Stanford University taught by Michael Ray, who, with Rochelle Myers, wrote a book on how to encourage creativity in business.[9]

The sources of new-product ideas are either *internal* (R&D and the sales force), or *external* (suppliers, and customers). One research study found that while the source of ideas for most industrial products was research (internal), the source of ideas for consumer goods tended to be competitive products (external).[10]

Internal Sources *Market research* can provide clues to new-product opportunities. Dunkin' Donuts' research picked up the need for low-cholesterol foods that spurred the company to develop a profitable new line of doughnuts. New-product ideas can also come from *engineering*, *production*, and *distributors*. Aspartame, the key ingredient in NutraSweet, was discovered when a scientist working on something else inadvertently put the white crystals to his mouth and discovered their

431

intense sweetness. Because it gets direct feedback from distributors and/or customers on a product's performance, including suggestions for improvement or innovations, the *sales force* is an excellent source of ideas. Salespeople are often the first people in the company to learn about a competitor's new product and its strengths and weaknesses. The idea for Millennium's rechargeable battery system came from an analysis of the inadequacies of competitors' products.

The most important source of new-product ideas, however, is the research and development department. Athletic shoes, for example, are computer designed, and any maker that wants to be competitive has to have a large R&D staff. Converse, which fell behind in the R&D foot race, is now catching up with a new lab that includes a "foot morphology platform" that uses computerized X-ray equipment, a "stomp measurer" known as the "bio-lab force plate," and a robotic device called "the whole shoe flex tester" that puts Converse prototypes through their paces.[11]

It is essential that R&D departments work closely with marketing. Unfortunately, there is often friction between the scientists and engineers in R&D and the marketing department over questions of authority and budget. Studies have found that one of the most significant causes of new product failure is the lack of integration of R&D and marketing early in the new-product development process.[12]

The high R&D costs in some industries can be a major barrier to innovation, as the Ampex Corporation found when it invented the VCR but didn't have the financial resources to market it. Monsanto, which has so far put over $800 million into biotechnology, is still waiting for its payback. Upjohn has increased its R&D spending from 9.4 percent of sales to around 14 percent in order to get new pharmaceutical products out of its lab and into the market more quickly.

External Sources Firms that sell equipment, ingredients, parts, and other raw materials to manufacturers have good reason to suggest new products and new uses for existing products: both generate sales for them. *Suppliers*, because they deal with many different manufacturers, are in a position to know the competitive situation and can provide information about trends and breakthroughs in related fields. In some cases, new-product ideas are as easy as asking potential *customers* what they want or observing people shopping and identifying a need that is not being filled. For example, many people have feet of two different sizes, but no shoe manufacturer has yet devised a way to sell single shoes so customers can mix and match to get a better fit—a real, but unmet, consumer need.

Simply asking customers about their needs may not elicit a sufficiently detailed picture of the desired good or service. On the surface this may sound inconsistent with the marketing concept that says companies should be customer driven, but when it comes to generating new product ideas, consumers should not be expected to be too creative. That is why companies use indirect approaches to discovering new consumer needs, such as monitoring consumption trends. Identifying lifestyle trends—for example, the current move toward plush bathrooms that look like health clubs—may require formal consumer marketing research. Four years of "habits and practices" research on consumer product usage at Procter & Gamble found that people no longer wash everything in hot water. The result was "all-temperature" Cheer. Industrial customers normally have a better idea of what they want than individual consumers do, and can describe it exactly. As we noted in Chapter 7, many new industrial products like subway and mass transit systems are made to customer-designed specifications (see Exhibit 13-3).

Exhibit 13-3
Traveling into the Future

A German company that is a leader in new mass transit systems ties its products to the theme of making in the present products that are designed for the future.

STEP 2: SCREENING

Successful companies generate a great many ideas for new products because they know that most new ideas will not survive the development process. The process of systematically eliminating less viable ideas is called *screening*. Most companies screen new-product ideas by rating them against certain characteristics the firm deems important: for example, market size, potential competition, fit with existing products and capabilities, and compatibility with known consumer needs. Marketers rate ideas on these characteristics and assign to these ratings relative values depending on corporate goals, as illustrated by the screening scale in Table 13-3. The result is a number for each new idea. Ideas with the highest number are pursued, while lower-rated ideas are dropped.

STEP 3: BUSINESS ANALYSIS

Screening may tell you if an idea will appeal to potential buyers, but new products must be profitable as well as in demand. Sophisticated companies evaluate new-product ideas against various financial criteria such as sales estimates and forecasts, required capital investment, and projected profit and loss statements. The goal of a **business analysis** is to help managers weigh the potential profitability of a new-product idea and then decide what level *of investment spending*, if any, to commit to develop the product. As we noted earlier, new-product development can be very expensive. That is why many firms choose to limit their outlay by following a me-too strategy.

A new product that can be produced using a company's current facilities will generally be more profitable since it doesn't require investment in new buildings and equipment. This is particularly true if the company's current products are seasonal and the new product can be produced out-of-season. A good example is a local lawn care service company that does snowplowing during the winter. Managers also have to decide how much time to commit to developing a product. Procter & Gamble spent nine years developing Pampers

business analysis
Weighing the potential profitability of a proposed new-product idea in order to decide whether to invest in developing it and at what level of expenditure.

TABLE 13-3	SCREENING A NEW PRODUCT

Rate the new-product concept using a ten-point scale. Score a "1" if the concept fails the question altogether and a "10" if it meets the criterion perfectly.

Relative Advantage
1. Does the product offer a cost advantage compared to substitutes?
2. Does the new product or service have value-added features?
3. Is your innovation directed at neglected segments of the marketplace?

Compatibility
4. In the business/industrial arena, is the product compatible with corporate practices, cultures, and value systems?
5. Is the product compatible with the buyer's work flow?
6. Is the new product compatible with the market's physical environment?

Perceived Risk
Note: on the following questions, it is absence of risk that should receive a higher score.
7. Does the customer perceive an economic risk if he or she adopts the new product?
8. Does the customer perceive a physical risk in adopting the product?
9. Does the market fear the new technology won't perform properly?
10. Does the new product offer a social risk?

A bottom-line score of 100 (10 points for each question) suggests a new-product winner. For most companies, a score of 70 or better signals a "go" decision on the new-product concept. A risk-oriented company would probably consider anything that scores 50 or higher. A score of 30 or less identifies a concept that faces many consumer obstacles.

Source: Adapted from Bob Donath, "Can Your New Product Pass This Test?" *Business Marketing,* July 1984, pp. 66–68.

disposable diapers and even longer developing Crest toothpaste. Today, with management often under severe pressure to produce short-term returns, companies often don't have the "financial patience" it takes to develop a Crest or Pampers.

When making time and money investment decisions, marketers forecast potential sales volume at various prices, and then run a *breakeven analysis* to find the point where a quantity sold at a given price equals the start-up costs. Breakeven analysis sets the stage for later pricing decisions. (The calculation of breakeven points is explained in more detail in Chapter 16 and Appendix B.) Even Broadway shows operate with a business analysis. Reaching the breakeven point is a concern for every producer—and very unpredictable. It costs between $6 million and $7.5 million to put on a show like *Will Rogers Follies*, *Kiss of the Spider Woman*, and The Who's *Tommy*, and it can take several years of nearly full houses to recoup that investment and begin making a profit. Unfortunately, only a few Broadway shows last that long.

The breakeven point also depends on the firm's size and profitability requirements. Hearst Corporation, a large publisher of consumer magazines, is not interested in new magazines with circulation potentials of less than 750,000. But the publisher of *Rocky Mountain Sports and Fitness* was pleased to acquire *Women's Sports and Fitness*, which had a circulation of only 250,000. Because RMS&F has a considerably lower overhead than Hearst, it can make money on a circulation of 250,000, while Hearst cannot.

Toyota conducted an extensive business analysis before it launched Lexus, its entry into the superluxury car category. Because the Lexus was so different from Toyota's regular line, the company had to completely reevaluate potential consumers, determine what type of management organization would be required, and rethink components down to the tiniest screw. Even after all this analysis, Toyota ended up investing more time and money—six years and over $500 million—than anyone had originally imagined.

BEHIND THE SCENES

GLOBAL JOINT VENTURES IN BIOTECHNOLOGY

Biotechnology, discussed in the opening story, is a big area of international new-business development, and one in which it is very difficult to project costs and revenues because of the immense amount of R&D investment needed. For this reason biotech companies engage in joint ventures on a large scale. The development of new drugs, for example, often takes so long and carries such a high price tag that even companies with $5 billion in revenues are seeking mergers to help cover their costs.[13]

The United States has long been ahead in biotechnology, with companies like Genentech, Biogen, Cetus, Genex, and Amgen enjoying the status of acknowledged international leaders. American researchers have concentrated their efforts in two major areas: pharmaceuticals and agriculture. For example, Amgen has produced a gene-spliced drug that helps combat the infections patients on chemotherapy often contract, while Genentech has developed a heart drug that breaks up blood clots.

Even though both these companies have made a great deal of money on their inventions, R&D in this field has become so expensive that they and other North American biotech companies now routinely join forces with European and Japanese firms to finance the development of potentially lucrative products. When Genentech became a 60-percent-owned subsidiary of the giant Swiss-based pharmaceutical company Roche Holdings Ltd., the merger made it possible to invest $30 million in three projects that originated in small, innovative North American start-up companies. Other mergers in which North American firms join with international companies with deep pockets to form ventures to develop new products will materialize. Japanese companies have yet to enter the international joint-venture arena on the same scale as North American and European companies like Roche, but they are showing an interest in international collaboration.

Although small R&D firms see this trend as a window of opportunity for creating new international business, they are cautious. "We terminated one possible joint venture," explains an official of Genetics Institute of Cambridge, Massachusetts, because "we didn't feel very comfortable giving away proprietary information and scientific know-how." For many companies, biotechnology is a very expensive game of roulette. The stakes are high, the potential winnings are high, but the losses can be equally high.

STEP 4: CONCEPT TESTING

Ideas that survive the business analysis may next be subjected to **concept testing**, a form of market research that evaluates a new product *idea* (not an actual product, which doesn't yet exist) by describing it and its proposed benefits to potential consumers in words, pictures, or both. The more complex and expensive the product is likely to be, the more sophisticated the concept testing must be. Most concepts are first tested in focus groups, but if it is difficult to form a focus group of potential consumers (as it can be with industrial products), interviewing is done one-on-one. Experts recommend several rounds consisting of two or three focus groups each.

It's risky to subject an invention to concept testing because competitors may find out about the product and begin developing it themselves. But skipping such testing—or doing it poorly—is even riskier. A firm can easily wind up with an innovation in search of a market, rather than the other way around. Three-dimensional cameras are a case in point.

STEP 5: PRODUCT AND STRATEGY DEVELOPMENT

If the business analysis says an idea could be profitable and concept testing confirms there is a demand for the proposed product, the company moves on to develop the actual good or service and its basic marketing strategy. What it is, how it will be produced, and how it will be positioned are all interwoven decisions; therefore the competitive strategy, targeting decisions, and positioning strategy must evolve hand-in-hand with the design, production, and operations decisions.

As noted in Chapter 10, the design for any product must take into account function, aesthetics, and ease of production. This step is usually handled by industrial designers, engineers, and scientists in the R&D, design, engineering, and production departments. Development often includes the preparation—usually in the R&D lab—of a **prototype**, or a model of the new product made in limited numbers for testing purposes only. Union Carbide constructed hundreds of disposable diapers by hand in its labs in order to have something to consumer-test when it tried to enter this market several

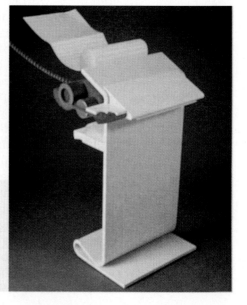

New-Product Designs

Product designers search for aesthetically pleasing designs as well as functionally improved ones: (A) an abstract answering machine, designed by Design Logic & Details and Dictaphone Industrial Design Group; and (B) the free-flowing Elaine Printer, designed by Technology Design.

years ago. Similarly, car companies build prototypes by hand so they can test new ideas in a variety of ways. The Knight-Ridder newspaper publisher chain has a "newspaper of the future" lab in Boulder, Colorado, that has developed a prototype electronic newspaper using a hand-held portable computer-generated electronic tablet. In this case, the prototype is used to guide the refinement of both the hardware and software systems that will make such a product feasible.[14]

In the case of a one-of-a-kind product, such as a building or space station, the prototype may be a miniature model or mockup. Many companies now design new products using computer modeling systems, such as Predictive Cost Modeling (PCM), that analyze alternative designs and also predict costs throughout the life cycle of a product.[15]

STEP 6: PRODUCT TESTING

One reason for the popularity of prototypes is that they can be used to test a product before it goes into full production. Testing at this stage often asks the same questions as concept testing, but it relates these questions directly to an actual product prototype rather than to a product concept. In seeking answers, marketers may use both internal testing such as lab tests and in-house test groups or external test groups such as outside consumer and government tests. Actually, the type of testing depends on the budget for product development and the risks involved. Risky products are more likely to receive extensive internal and external testing. Minor extensions of a product line may get only internal tests.

Internal *lab tests* mark the first stage of product testing. Thus Union Carbide tested the absorbency of its diapers in its own labs. Makers of food products often conduct lab tests of cooking times, shelf life, and color stability. As soon as R&D has developed a product (often in several variations), marketing managers are given a chance to examine it. Some food companies screen management and staff employees for their ability to discern small differences in taste and texture, then train them on what to look for and how to describe their findings. These individuals serve on *in-house testing groups,* sampling new products and passing on their judgments.

Once a new product meets internal standards, it may be consumer-tested. Besides evaluating the product's practicality, consumer testing tells marketers consumers' *psychological reactions* to the prototype and which of its *critical features* they use to judge it. For example, car manufacturers have learned that consumers use the sound of a car door being shut as an important cue in selecting a car.

Most new products are *blind-tested*—that is, the respondents in the test sample aren't told what company made the product. Goods that can be evaluated quickly—prepared foods, ballpoint pens, hairbrushes—are often tested by *intercept* methods (see Chapter 5): potential customers are asked to try the product and answer questions about it in public settings such as shopping

Butter as a New Product

To counter the consumer perception of butter being less healthy than margarine, the dairy industry has repositioned butter as a pure and natural product.

437

centers. Because most of these interviews are one-on-one, they allow the interviewer to ask probing questions about specific aspects of the product.

Products that require more extensive use before they can be evaluated—dish detergents, disposable diapers, weed killers—demand different testing methods. Marketers of such goods often opt for *home placement*—providing free samples of the new product to a portion of target segment homes. The samples come in a plain container (a blind test) with only the ingredients and instructions for use printed on the package. In-home tests are particularly important for food companies which want to test products in the environment where they would normally be consumed.

Product tests can be very helpful to marketers. But to be accurate—and thus useful—they must meet three conditions:

1. The product tested must be the version that will be marketed.
2. The product must be tested under normal use conditions.
3. Sufficient time must be allowed for participants to use and reuse the product.

Government-Required Tests Products subject to *government regulations* or *licensing* may have to be tested by outside agencies. For example, the Food Safety and Quality Division of Health Canada examines many products containing meat (such as pizza, frozen dinners, soups), and some service providers (such as doctors, realtors, and beauticians) must pass special exams to obtain a license before they are allowed to offer their services to the public.

STEP 7: MARKETING-MIX PLANNING

If product tests go well, the company must settle on other aspects of the marketing mix. Pricing strategies must be determined. Plans for effective marketing communications—advertising, sales promotion, packaging, personal selling, and public relations—must be drawn up. Arrangements to distribute the product must also be set in motion. These topics are covered in more detail in later chapters of this book, but keep in mind that they are part of the new-product development process. Timing and scheduling of all these activities are particularly important.

STEP 8: TEST MARKETING

Unlike product testing at earlier stages, test marketing, which we discussed in Chapter 5, allows marketers to try out all aspects of the marketing mix by offering a new product *for sale* to a limited market before spending the time and money needed to introduce that product regionally, nationally, or globally. The objectives of a test market are:

◆ To make a final check on product performance—to determine how intermediaries and customers react to and use the product

◆ To determine the number of trial and repeat purchases, and the frequency of purchase, in order to get an indication of potential sales volume

◆ To evaluate the effectiveness of marketing communications

Although determining the number of first-time or *trial* buyers is important, it is even more important to know the percentage who become *repeat* buyers. Because of the high cost of developing and distributing a product, informing consumers about it, and motivating them to try it, most firms do not start to make a profit from repeat purchases of a new product until it has been on the market for two or three years.

Consumer-goods producers are the most frequent users of test marketing. Industrial products usually get their final test as demonstrations in trade shows or dealer show rooms. Not all consumer-goods makers use market testing, however. Most fashion items would be out of style before they made it through the typical test market, and me-too products seldom warrant the time and expense of test marketing.

How much money and time a firm decides to spend on test marketing depends in part on how risky the product is. Two markets and six months are generally considered *minimum*. If actual sales are significantly below forecast, most companies will either delay introduction while they determine what went wrong or do additional test marketing.

Types of Test Markets   Consumer test markets are described as standard or controlled. In a *standard test market* the company selects a small number of representative cities and exposes them to the full marketing mix. This type of test market requires a complete introductory marketing plan and the ability to get adequate distribution for a limited area. It is also very expensive (the average cost is $3 million) and can take a long time (up to three years) to complete.

In contrast, a *controlled test market* involves a selected sample of stores that agree to carry the product for a fee. This form of test marketing is usually done by research companies that have established store panels in representative test cities, handle distribution of the product to the stores, and orchestrate the pricing, shelf space, and in-store promotions called for by the maker.

In some controlled test markets selected households in test cities receive cards that they present at the checkout counter when any member of the household buys a packaged good from a local retail store. Each of these panel households also has a tracking device on its television set that records which programs (and consequently which commercials) household members are exposed to. In addition, panel households report on the magazines and newspapers to which they subscribe. The resultant *single-source data* (see Chapter 5) give the manufacturer a fairly accurate reading of consumer response to a new product. These data can also help the firm fine-tune its marketing mix.

It is easier, cheaper, and less time-consuming to obtain extensive information from a controlled test market than from a standard test market. However, the small samples that are involved mean there is an increased risk of research error.

STEP 9: LAUNCHING THE PRODUCT

Finally, after months or years of development and testing, the product is ready for full-scale production and marketing. The official **product launch** involves formally introducing the product to the market. The product now starts to "flow" through the distribution channels. If a brand in this product-launch stage has no competition, the marketer must educate consumers about the product category as well as establish its own brand image, as Apple did when it introduced the new category of personal computers. It must also find the *innovators* and *early adopters* we discussed in Chapter 6, those risk takers who generally provide the initial trial and response. If the category is one that is already growing or developed—such as the bicycle market—then the new brand must focus on showing customers how it is better than established brands. Obviously, the greater the brand's competitive advantage, the easier this is to do: me-too brands tend to die quickly in the introduction stage.

product launch
The introduction of a product to the market.

| TABLE 13-4 | DECIDING WHETHER TO GO NATIONAL OR GLOBAL |

Decision Factor	Example
Risk	If a wholly new product needs heavy marketing communication spending, it may have to be started locally and in stages. But if a well-known brand like Smucker's wants to offer a new jam or jelly flavor, going national or even global immediately may pose very little risk.
Production capacity	If a new product requires different and complex production equipment, a company may not want to invest in the expanded facilities needed for national and global marketing until local experience indicates that the product will sell well.
Timing	Some season-dependent products, like swimsuits should generally be introduced widely because by the time local sales mount up, the season may have passed in other market areas. In fashion, timing also must take account of changing trends; Catalina, for example, might find that a "new" line had become obsolete if it waited too long to introduce it in some areas.

The launch stage can be costly, especially if the company must build new facilities to manufacture a good or supply a service. But for most firms it it the first opportunity to generate a positive cash flow. Having decided *what* and *when* to offer, the firm must now decide *where* (distribution) and *how* to offer it (marketing communications).

Rollout and Sell-in Some firms may have the confidence and financial ability to introduce a product to a national or even global market all at once. Most companies, preferring to minimize their risks and initial launch expenditures, opt to **roll out** new products: that is, they introduce the new product in limited geographical areas and then gradually add more markets as production capacity, management time, budget, and product success permit. Whether a firm decides to roll out or go national or global all at once will depend on the factors listed in Table 13-4. The decision to roll out a product calls for a rollout strategy. Markets with the greatest potential for success—because the competition is weak or the firm's brand or distribution system is strong—are usually the first to receive the product.

Once a firm knows where it wants to introduce its new product, it must persuade distributors to sell it. This **sell-in** generally occurs in several steps. First, the marketing staff prepares a sales kit and briefs the sales force on the target market, on what makes the new product better than competing brands, and on what the company intends to do to help create consumer demand for the new item. Then, together, the marketing and sales forces seek to persuade distributors to carry the product. With consumer packaged goods, getting retail distribution—called **brand authorization**—can be extremely difficult because there are so many more products available than retailers have room to carry. Retailers demand not only that new items be supported with consumer advertising and promotions but also that manufacturers offer them

roll out
To introduce a new product in limited geographical areas, with new markets added as capacity and budget permit.

sell-in
Educating and "selling" the sales force and distributors about a new product.

brand authorization
Persuading distributors to carry the good; in consumer packaged goods, getting retail distribution.

special introductory *slotting allowances* as "insurance" against the high failure rates of new products. (We will discuss these issues further in Chapters 15 and 19.)

Marketing Communications Advertising and promotion costs are usually at their highest levels during the launch period. Packaged-goods manufacturers often spend nearly 50 percent of their promotional budget during the first three months of a new product's entry to create awareness.

Advertising is good for building awareness, but other tools like merchandising can also be effective. Compaq spent $240,000 for a "monitor hood," a cardboard frame printed with information about the new computer's features, and sales of the model increased 11 percent.[16]

Many low-priced industrial goods—tools, adhesives, chemicals—can be launched nationally with a marketing communications cost of less than $25,000 if carefully targeted to qualified prospects. With an additional page in the company's catalog, a four-page brochure, and one or two ads in trade magazines, such products can even be introduced globally. In contrast, the cost of promoting highly competitive consumer goods can easily exceed $100 million and take months of advance negotiations with national television and radio networks and magazines. Even a simple direct-mail campaign takes time and money to organize.

Tracking Progress Marketing does not stop when the new product rolls out. Rather, marketing is an ongoing process of refining old products and seeking new ones. Thomas Kuczmarski says that establishing a tracking system (see Figure 13-4) is critical, and that this system should measure the company's effectiveness and efficiency overall, not only with the new product.[17]

One way to check on the progress of a new product and make needed adjustments to both product and marketing mix is through *tracking studies*. For consumer goods, such studies usually take the form of phone surveys of selected households to measure whether consumers are aware of the product's existence, whether they have tried it, and, if so, whether they have bought it two or more times. Tracking studies usually begin during the test marketing stage of the new-product development process, but they are also heavily used after the new product is launched.

Figure 13-4
Factors in Implementing a New-Product Tracking System

Source: Adapted from Thomas D. Kuczmarksi, Managing New Products: The Power of Innovation (Englewood Cliffs, N.J.: Prentice Hall, 1992), p. 100.

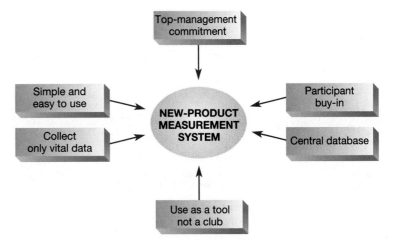

A "NEW WORLD" MEANS NEW PRODUCTS

If you are skeptical about the importance of new products, read the following excerpt from the opening of a recent *Fortune* magazine cover story titled "Welcome to the Revolution":

Revolution, says Webster's is "a sudden, radical, or complete change . . . a basic reorientation." To anyone in the world of business, that sounds about right. We all sense that the changes surrounding us are not mere trends but the workings of large, unruly forces: the globalization of markets; the spread of information technology and computer networks; the dismantling of hierarchy, the structure that has essentially organized the work force since the mid-nineteenth century. Growing up around these is a new, information-age economy, whose fundamental sources of wealth are knowledge and communication rather than natural resources and physical labor.

Each of these transformations is a no-fooling business revolution. Yet all are happening *at the same time*—and fast. They cause one another and affect one another. As they feed on one another, they nourish a feeling that business and society are in the midst of a revolution comparable in scale and consequence to the Industrial Revolution.[18]

The Industrial Revolution spawned more new products more quickly than any other period of history. And as you just read, current business conditions suggest a repeat of the Industrial Revolution. All of the changes that are now taking place will translate, directly or indirectly, into the need and/or desire for new goods and services.

Take the "dismantling of hierarchy"—which means a complete restructuring or reengineering of how firms are organized. It requires new methods of internal communication, and dozens of companies have sprung up to respond to this need, supplying computer networks, databases, and E-mail software that provides nearly everyone in an organization with the same information at the same time. One result of these new organizational structures made possible by the new software and hardware is employee empowerment, which, in turn, has allowed such companies as 3M, Apple, and General Electric to develop new products quicker.

Another change the article notes—the "globalization of markets"—has resulted not only in more new markets in which to sell goods and services (remember, a product is "new" to people who have never heard of it) but also in more sources of new-product ideas. Companies such as Procter & Gamble are using a strategy called "search and reapply," meaning they look all over the world for new ideas and then use these ideas in geographical markets unfamiliar with them. ▼

KEY POINTS SUMMARY ▼

1. A product is *new* if it represents a significant difference from other offerings, is perceived as new by potential customers, and meets certain legal requirements.

2. New products can be developed through one of three routes: by the *invention* of something totally new; by making an existing product significantly better through *innovation;* or, by im-

provement, gradually altering a product to heighten its desirability.

3. New products are important to most firms because they help compensate for declining brands: without the introduction of new products, a firm's market position often deteriorates. Producing successful new products is also one of the criteria the financial community uses in evaluating a company's health. Although the profit potential of many new products is great, so is the potential for failure, making new-product development one of the riskiest activities in marketing.

4. There are three major new-product strategies and they have different risk/benefit levels: me-too (low risk/benefit) strategies rely on duplicating other firms' products that have already proved successful; competitive-advantage (moderate risk/benefit) strategies seek to improve on another firm's product; and new-venture (high risk/benefit) strategies depend on introducing a totally new product or product category.

5. Strategically, new products can be developed for national, regional, or global markets. Global new-product development leverages the effort of the product development group and maximizes the firm's resources, but it is the most complex undertaking of the three. Consumption behaviors may reflect cultural differences, and while global markets provide huge quantities of market research information, the ability to organize and analyze the data is often lacking. Also, global marketing is challenged by the variety of laws and regulations that have to be met.

6. The nine steps in the new-product development process are: idea generation, screening, business analysis, concept testing, product and strategy development, product testing, marketing-mix planning, test marketing, and product launch or commercialization. Each step influences the others. Entrepreneurs and Japanese firms often skip steps to speed the process, but this increases the risk.

DISCUSSION QUESTIONS ▼

1. What makes a product "new"? Brainstorm and see if you can develop three new-product ideas using the three approaches of invention, innovation, and improvement.

2. Explain the differences between me-too, competitive-advantage, and venture new-product strategies and find examples of each in ads for a newly introduced good or service. Analyze how the ads positioned the products.

3. Where do ideas for new products generally come from? If you were the new-products manager for Celestial Seasonings tea, where would you look for new ideas?

4. You are the marketing manager for a new line of hand-crafted, old-fashioned children's toys. What testing methods would you use at the product testing stage?

5. Distinguish among improvement, innovation, and invention. Pretend you are the new-products manager for Celestial Seasonings tea and give an example of a new product that might evolve in each of these three ways.

6. Interview the manager of a local company and describe the firm's new-product strategy and its approach to risk.

7. Design a test-marketing plan for a new line of frozen Japanese foods to be sold in Canada.

8. Identify two new products that might become available as a result of the changes brought on by the new "Industrial Revolution" discussed in the chapter closing story. Then analyze each of these products in terms of Rogers' rate of adoption factors that were discussed in this chapter.

9. A new product available in the produce section of many supermarkets is a hybrid vegetable combining cauliflower and broccoli. Interview shoppers to determine if this product carries any negative connotations because it is genetically engineered. Consider yourself the brand manager for a major produce distributor who has been assigned to brand this product and introduce it to a new metropolitan market with a major product launch. Write a new-product introduction plan using the nine steps in the new-product development process.

The Body Shop*

1. How does new-product development at The Body Shop differ from the process described in the chapter?

Harley-Davidson

1. What constitutes the bulk of Harley-Davidson's new products?

The Millennium Power System

1. Millennium plans to introduce a new one-hour charger. How could it test-market that product to determine the best price to charge?

*The three cases at the back of the book—"The Body Shop," "Harley-Davidson," and "The Millennium Power System"—illustrate topics discussed in all chapters of this book. Your instructor will tell you when to read a particular case and when to answer the discussion questions on it that appear at the end of each chapter.

1-800 Marketing

You've seen those 1-800 TV ads telling you to buy some new product at $14.95. What you don't see are the dramatic stories of entrepreneurs behind those products, staking all on those few seconds of late night TV time. Everything rides on how many people are convinced to pick up the phone. Yes, real operators are standing by, and that is the instantaneous test of whether or not the product will be a success.

Dr. Larry Frydman, a chiropractor, felt he had developed the ultimate home massage unit. Dr. Frydman was motivated by a classmate friend who had made millions by being the inventor of the Abdominizer, a marketing success story that sold 4 million units. The Abdominizer, as you may recall, was "not available in stores," just through the 1-800 outlet. 1-800 marketing combines the advertising and retailing functions of marketing in one operation. It's a tough, highly competitive business that accounts for $5 billion in annual sales in North America. And recently, retail stores specializing in "You've Seen It on TV" merchandise have begun to appear, increasing the sales figures even more.

Dr. Frydman spent $100,000 developing the unit, a roller massager that can be put in the freezer or heated in the microwave for either hot or cold messaging. After test marketing the product with a local low-budget TV commercial, he became convinced there was demand. Soon, he ended up on the doorstep of Quality Records. Their direct mass marketing division has the expertise to rack up $23 million in annual sales in Canada and products like Don Cherry's RockEm Sockem, Ginsu knives, and Topsy Tails. But for every TV product that scores, dozens more are yanked off the air. And the life of a hit can be as short as three months. Knock-offs appear fast, especially if the product is not patentable.

In the case of *La-Sagge*, Dr. Frydman's massager, Quality bought 10 days worth of air time on broadcasters like TSN for a cost of $19,000. This generated only 200 sales, partly the result of poor air times for the TV spots. They revamped the advertisements and tried again. In spite of getting much better air times, two events reached out to grab them. First, their best time slot ended up being during a lengthy rain delay at the U.S. Open Tennis tournament. Hardly anybody was watching. And the next day, Kim Campbell called a federal election and all extra TV time was quickly gobbled up by the political parties. Only 13 units got sold, at a promotional cost of over $30 per unit sold. Really bad, considering that target figures in this industry are for $6–8 per unit.

Quality records quickly shifted their strategy to the retail side. After all, they had 20,000 of these in stock. However, they still were taking a risk, as stores would only take them on consignment. Discussions were held to try to add some value to the package by giving away a free towel or selling a second unit at half price. Nothing seemed to work, and Quality decided to end their losses.

QUESTIONS

1. What went wrong? If this method worked for the Abdominizer, why does it not work for La-Sagge?
2. Is there anything Dr. Frydman, the inventor, could have done differently?
3. What do you do now with all of the units packaged and ready to sell?

Source: This case was prepared by Ray Friedman and is based on the *Venture* series episode "1-800 Ads," which was originally broadcast on July 3, 1994.

445

Chapter 14

Marketing Channels and Physical Distribution

OBJECTIVES

AFTER COMPLETING THIS CHAPTER, YOU SHOULD BE ABLE TO:

1
DESCRIBE THE FUNCTIONS OF MARKETING CHANNELS

2
COMPARE THE FUNCTIONS OF THE MOST COMMON TYPES OF CONSUMER- AND INDUSTRIAL-GOODS CHANNELS

3
EVALUATE THE STRATEGIC IMPLICATIONS OF VARIOUS DISTRIBUTION ALTERNATIVES AND EXPLAIN THE MAJOR CONSIDERATIONS IN DESIGNING MARKETING CHANNELS

4
IDENTIFY THE MAJOR VARIABLES MARKETERS MUST TAKE INTO CONSIDERATION WHEN MANAGING AND DEVELOPING INTERNATIONAL DISTRIBUTION CHANNELS

5
ANALYZE THE INFORMATION TECHNOLOGY CONTRIBUTION TO CHANNEL MANAGEMENT

6
DESCRIBE THE VARIABLES IN THE PHYSICAL DISTRIBUTION OF A PRODUCT AND THE OPTIONS AVAILABLE TO MARKETERS

BROKEN BIKE THREATENS BREAK

It's one day before spring break. In just twenty-four hours you and several others will be flying off to Ireland to start the biking adventure you have been planning for a year. But this morning you discover the front frame of your high-performance mountain bike is cracked!

No problem. A front frame can be replaced in an hour. You call the one bike shop in the city that sells and services your make of bike. "Sorry," they say, "we just sold the last frame an hour ago. We have several on order and they should come in tomorrow afternoon, but I can't promise."

No way, you say. By tomorrow afternoon, your plane will have left. Even if they call in the order and the part is sent overnight express and arrives tomorrow morning, that won't leave enough time to get your bike fixed and drive to the airport. Do you buy a new bike, take a chance on renting one in Ireland, or cancel

your trip?

In the early afternoon you are still trying to decide what to do when the phone rings and the bike shop says the part is in. Magic? No, EDI! Your upscale bike shop has an *electronic data interchange* with your bike manufacturer. This computer database lets the factory know the exact status of each of its customer's parts invento-ries. Spotting that your bike shop had only one front frame for your particular model left, it had automatically shipped three of these frames four days earlier. Is this future shock—or today's reality? ■

MARKETING CHANNELS

In this chapter we discuss the role of distribution—how products move from the manufacturer to the end user and the types of strategic decisions that need to be made to make this happen. We also consider the overall structure of marketing channels and physical distribution systems, the focus of chapter objective one. In the next chapter we will look more closely at the wholesaling and retailing operations that make the system work.

The individuals and companies that make up the distribution channel are basically service companies called **intermediaries.** To better understand the complexity of the intermediary role, let's look at a scenario for moving a new product through the distribution channel. When a new product enters the market, one of the most important marketing strategies involves "filling the pipeline." Typically, the product leaves the manufacturing plant, is transported in large lot sizes (packaged in bulk for shipment—often in truckloads or railroad carloads) to the manufacturer's warehouse, then moves to a wholesaler's distribution center, where the lot is broken down and repackaged for sale to the wholesaler's organizational customers—individual stores or industrial buyers. The product is then sent to a retailer's distribution center or to retail outlets, where it is placed on a shelf or rack for final sale to the customer.

For established products, a manufacturer must continually manage the physical distribution, how products are handled and protected both in storage and in transport, where and when they are stored, and who physically moves them and in what manner. Because manufacturers prefer to produce in large quantities and in just a few locations while consumers like to buy in relatively small quantities at a convenient local store, distribution is an essential element of the marketing mix. For example, McCain's processes potatoes in its french fry factory in Florenceville, New Brunswick, before making french fries available in stores across Canada.

Here's another simple example of the benefits of distribution. Hershey's produces millions of cases of chocolate syrup at a plant in Pennsylvania. Ault Foods produces millions of gallons of ice cream at a plant in Ontario. Planters produces millions of cases of nuts at a plant in California. All three of these companies know that you and a lot of other people love chocolate sundaes. But they also know that not even the most fanatical sundae lover is going to go to the trouble and expense of traveling to each of these plants to collect the necessary sundae ingredients. They know the only way to sell you their items is to make them available, in the size you want, at your favorite food

intermediaries
Businesses that assist producers in the performance of distribution tasks; if intermediaries take title to the product, they are called *resellers*.

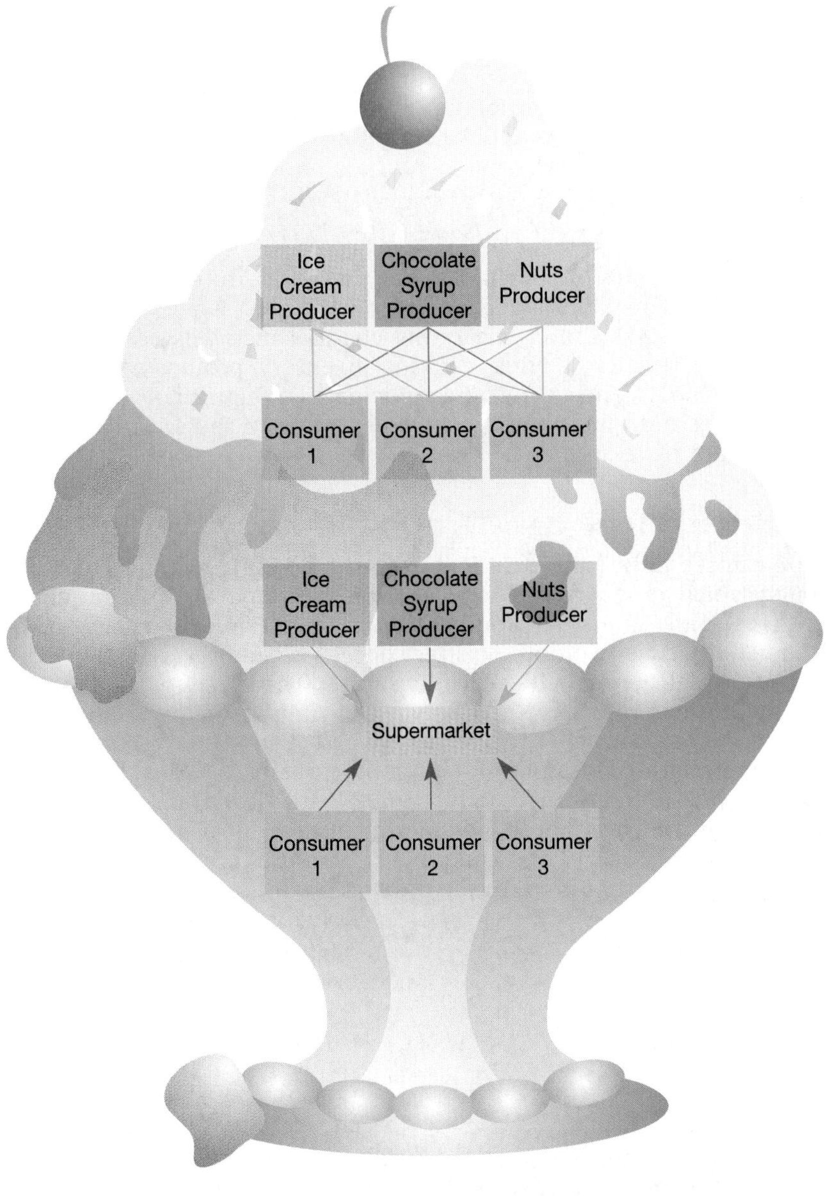

Figure 14-1
How Intermediaries
Improve Channel
Efficiency

Ice Cream Producer | Chocolate Syrup Producer | Nuts Producer

Consumer 1 | Consumer 2 | Consumer 3

Ice Cream Producer | Chocolate Syrup Producer | Nuts Producer

Supermarket

Consumer 1 | Consumer 2 | Consumer 3

449

MARKETING
CHANNELS AND
PHYSICAL
DISTRIBUTION

store or fast-food outlet (see Figure 14-1). The actual cost of making your sundae may be higher at both the food store and the fast-food outlet than it would be if you were able to buy each ingredient from the plant that made it. But as you are quick to realize, the extra cost of transportation, time, and so forth would push the total cost of the sundae out of sight. The bottom line of all this is: marketing channels help reconcile the needs of the consumer (convenience and small purchase size) with the needs of the producer (high production levels and efficiency of producing in few locations).

Distribution is the physical flow of goods through channels. **Distribution channels** are the internal and external organizational units that direct the flow of products to customers and perform functions that add value to a product. Distribution channels are complex and require a number of independent firms playing a variety of roles. The process begins with the manufacturer, who can either handle its own distribution or assign it to whole-

distribution
The flow of products through distribution channels.

distribution channels
The internal and external organizational units that direct the flow of products to customers and add value to these products.

salers, agents, and brokers. Other types of distributors that function as intermediaries between the manufacturer and the ultimate customer are retailers,
dealers, and bottlers. The drivers who deliver products to retail stores and stock
the shelves perform another important function in the distribution channel.
UPS delivery service, whose cellular tracking system is reproduced in Exhibit
14-1, provides a distribution channel for both businesses and individuals.

DISTRIBUTION CHANNEL FUNCTIONS

Distribution channels provide more than just a way to bring buyers and sellers together and make products available when and where customers want
them. As Table 14-1 shows, marketing channel members accomplish their
goals through research, buying, carrying inventory, promoting, negotiating,
financing, selling, transporting, and servicing.[1] Through all of these functions
intermediaries add value to a product, and the cost of these services is relative
to the amount of value added.

DISTRIBUTION CHANNEL TYPES

As you can see from Figures 14-2 and 14-3, marketing channels are systems
through which products and services flow. Although distribution channels
for consumer and industrial products show a similar overall pattern, there are,
as chapter objective two notes, distinct differences between the two. For one
thing, industrial channels are generally shorter. The length of the channel denotes the number of intermediaries between the manufacturer and the final
customer. Japan is found to have the longest distribution channels in the
world, not because of efficiency level but because of traditional business practices. Channels for consumer products handle the flow of products from producers to consumers. Channels for industrial products handle the flow of
products (materials, parts, and equipment) from producers to other industrial
firms or organizations for use in the production of their products or for daily
operations. While the diagrams in
Figures 14-2 and 14-3 are useful
for depicting the most common
types of channels, you should remember that an almost infinite
number of channel configurations is possible, particularly in
the industrial marketing arena.

The river metaphor evoked
by the term *channel* is extended in
the terms used in the industry to
describe where one channel
member is relative to another.
The producer is the farthest *upstream* channel; the retail outlet is
the farthest *downstream* channel,
the one closest to the customer.

Consumer Product Channels
Some consumer product channels
are very simple, while others are
multilayered, as Figure 14-2
demonstrates. The first channel is
called a *direct channel* because the
product moves directly from the
producer to the consumer with

*Exhibit 14-1
TotalTracking Your
Shipment*

*In 1993 UPS, a major
provider of
transportation,
launched a cellular
tracking system to
make it easier for
customers to check on
the status of their
shipments. Late the
same year, it added
computer software
with which customers
could track their
shipments themselves,
even accessing the
company's own
information systems
around the clock.*

Introducing TotalTrack. It's like getting live
broadcasts from the scene of your package.

Despite what you may have seen on TV, the world's largest staff of on-the-spot
reporters isn't at CBS, NBC, ABC, or even CNN. They're at UPS.

Because we've just launched a nationwide cellular tracking system: TotalTrack.
Our 55,000 drivers now carry hand-held computers, while our vehicles are
equipped with state-of-the-art cellular technology. So now you can find out the status
of any air or designated ground package at any time. We can even confirm delivery in
seconds. And only UPS TotalTrack digitally captures the recipient's signature.

Which means that now there's just one thing that travels faster than
a UPS package. And that's news of it. **The package delivery company more companies count on.** **UPS**

TABLE 14-1	DISTRIBUTION CHANNEL FUNCTIONS ADD VALUE TO PRODUCTS

Function	Description
Research	Channel members gather information about target markets
Buying	Channel members purchase an assortment of goods from suppliers
Carrying Inventory	Channel members maintain sufficient inventories to match supply-and-demand cycles
Promoting	Channel members distribute communications about offerings
Negotiating	Through mutual interaction, channel members determine final prices
Financing	Channel members provide funds needed for channel activities
Selling	Channel members perform activities necessary to sell products to consumers and other channel members
Transporting	Channels arrange for the shipping of goods
Servicing	Channel members provide such services as customer credit and return handling

Source: Based on Louis W. Stern and Adel J. El-Ansary, (Englewood Cliffs, N.J.: Prentice Hall, 1989), pp. 7–17.

MARKETING CHANNELS AND PHYSICAL DISTRIBUTION

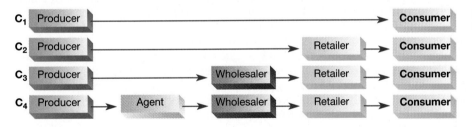

Figure 14-2
Consumer Channels

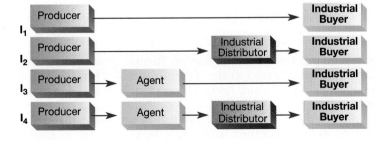

Figure 14-3
Industrial Channels

few or no stops in between. When you buy Taber corn from a farmer's roadside stand in Taber, Alberta, you are using a direct distribution channel. The farmer produced (grew) the corn and is selling it directly to you, the customer.

Direct marketing, a major growth area today, is discussed in more detail in Chapter 20. Many food manufacturers are beginning to sell specialty products through direct channels. For example, General Foods markets a line of gourmet coffees and distributes it to consumers through the mail. Services, by their nature, are suited to direct marketing. When you need a haircut, for example, you go directly to a barber or hair stylist.

The remaining three consumer product channels are all *indirect*: the product goes through one or more intermediaries before it reaches the consumer. An intermediary, sometimes called a *reseller*, is a business that handles one or more distribution tasks. In the second channel in Figure 14-2 the product goes from the producer to the type of reseller that is most familiar to us— a *retailer*—and from there to the customer. For example, Whirlpool produces washing machines and sells them to Sears, which in turn sells them to private consumers. Sears adds value by displaying and demonstrating the washing machine and by providing delivery and credit. Many large retailers use this type of channel configuration. Moreover, as retailers merge and consolidate, they do more and more buying directly from manufacturers.

The third consumer channel includes both a wholesaler and a retailer. Many perishable products—for example, fresh fruits and vegetables—are sold by producers to wholesalers, who then sell them to supermarkets where customers purchase them. Book retailers are increasingly using this type of channel. Wholesalers obtain books from a large number of big and small publishers, then channel desired books to individual book sellers, saving these retailers from having to locate and deal with publishers individually.

In the fourth consumer channel a product is handled by agents, often called *brokers,* who sell the goods to wholesalers. Agents perform many of the same functions as wholesalers and, in addition, offer certain technical and financial services. We will discuss the function of the agent/broker in greater detail in the next chapter.

Industrial Product Channels Figure 14-3 shows four of the more common types of industrial distribution channels. Notice that marketing channels for industrial products are generally shorter than those for consumer products. The first channel, again, is a direct channel of distribution. It is often used by manufacturers of expensive equipment such as aircraft or computers—industrial goods that have a limited number of customers who need technical assistance—and by service providers of almost all kinds.

As the number of customers increases and the average purchase size decreases, it is less efficient for producers to sell directly to customers and more efficient to involve a distributor. The second industrial channel in Figure 14-3 shows such a situation. A producer that has too many customers to sell to directly, but too few to use a distributor, may select a distribution channel like the third one in Figure 14-3. In this case, producers contract with regional agents, who sell the product to firms that use it. For example, many Florida orange juice companies sell their excess pulp to food processors, who use it to make orange flavoring. The pulp is often sold in railroad tank cars through agents who contact food processors in their region. The use of an agent is also typical of some kinds of services sold to the trade. In the travel industry, for example, agents buy large lots of rooms and seats on planes for resale as packages to tour operators.

The fourth industrial channel is most often used by small producers whose customers need to replenish their inventories frequently. For example, a supplier of small electronic components that does not have its own sales force would use an agent to sell large quantities of these parts to regional distributors, who in turn would sell them to manufacturers that make such things as power mowers and vacuum cleaners.

Multiple Channels   When producers target their products to diverse target markets, they often find it efficient to use *multiple channels*, or several different channel configurations simultaneously. In competitive markets micromarketers who are trying to market one-on-one are designing "distribution portfolios" with innovative distribution schemes to reach individual market niches.[2]

IBM uses a multiple channel design. It sells its large mainframe computers and large computer networks directly to manufacturers and other large organizations. But it supplies replacement parts, components, and software through company-owned distributors in the local area. At the same time, it sells its PCs and components to consumers and small businesses both direct through its own sales organization and through computer stores. By using multiple channels, IBM is able to offer optimal service to both large industrial buyers and individual consumers—that is, its several channel structures meet the needs of all its target markets.[3]

In summary, intermediaries perform varied functions for both consumer and industrial marketing and add value in a variety of ways. Coca-Cola has an interesting relationship with its bottlers. The bottlers fulfill a variety of intermediary functions and they are particularly important in helping to develop Coke's dynamic European market.

BEHIND THE SCENES
COKE SERVES A NEW EUROPE

Coca-Cola believes that by 2000 the world's carbonated beverage lovers, led by Europeans, will be drinking twice as much Coke as they do today.[4] Coke has a long-term strategy to take it to the year 2000, and it depends on making its European distribution operations more efficient.

Coke on the Continent

Coke's international strategy is to add its own merchandising skills to the local merchandising mix. This merchandising partnership is crucial in Europe, as retailers consolidate and gear up for the changes the new European Union is expected to bring about. As the market grows in size, Coke bottlers need to satisfy inventory demands and improve delivery schedules in order to maintain a competitive advantage in service.

The company took a big step toward realizing its long-range goal in 1989, when after a two-year legal battle it forced its French bottler of forty years, Pernod-Ricard, to sell its operations to the parent company because of disappointing sales performance. Coke still insists that it prefers joint ownership or independent local bottlers even in troubled or in new markets. So why did the company decide on the aggressive strategy of taking over the French bottling operation?

To answer this question requires an understanding of Coke's relationship with its bottlers. Coke bottlers purchase from the parent company everything from trucks and bottling equipment to packaging and promotional material. Most importantly, they purchase the prized secret-ingredient concentrate on which Coke makes gross profits of 85 percent. In combining and packaging ingredients, bottlers are manufacturers responsible for quality control. In storing and delivering Coke products, they are warehousers and distributors. But their most crucial function is to get Coke's products onto retail shelves. In this respect, they are Coke's merchandisers.

When Coke wrested control of its French bottler, it installed William Hoffman, an Atlanta bottler, as head of operations. Hoffman went straight to his strength—merchandising Coke at the store level—by hiring 350 special "merchandisers" to travel to over 15,000 retail outlets per month and by launching a variety of promotional activities. Under his leadership, results have been impressive. The consumer-products manager for the giant Auchan hypermarket chain (hypermarkets are large retailers that are a cross between supermarkets and discount stores) reports an increase in Coke sales of 40 percent. And the soft drinks buyer at Cora, another hypermarket chain, says: "It's much better now than with Pernod-Ricard. There's more contact with the bottler, more promotions, and more money to spend." Unit volume rose 23 percent in France the year after the takeover—the biggest sales increase Coke registered on the Continent—and the sales continue to build as the year 2000 approaches.

EXPORTING AND IMPORTING

Participation in foreign trade and international marketing generally depends on a country's level of economic development. Some countries, such as Japan, play primarily the role of **exporter**—that is, they sell mainly high value-added products to other foreign markets while importing only low value added commodities such as food and fuel. Others, including many third world countries, play primarily the role of the **importer**—they mainly buy from other countries but there the problem is a different one. The capacity to consume is self-evident but the capacity to pay may be in doubt.

Most marketing strategy is concerned with exporting, which is part of international marketing. The physical distribution of an exported product requires inserting the product into the distribution system of another country. Because of their knowledge of local languages, customs, laws, and business practices, intermediaries are particularly important in exporting. They may or may not take ownership of the product. Table 14-2 describes the various intermediaries in international distribution.

exporter
One who sells products to foreign markets.

importer
One who buys products from other countries for sale at home.

TABLE 14-2	TYPES OF INTERMEDIARIES IN INTERNATIONAL DISTRIBUTION

Export specialists, also called *expediters*, find markets in other parts of the world for their home country's products.

Import specialists find products in other parts of the world to bring into their home markets. It is almost impossible to enter the complex Japanese market without the help of import agents, and in Saudi Arabia you are required by law to use agents to import industrial goods.

Export trading companies, the most common type of intermediary, have been around since the time of the East India Company in the sixteenth century and the Hudson Bay Company in the seventeenth. A trading company handles merchandise from a number of suppliers, transports the merchandise, and negotiates trade in one or a number of foreign countries.

Freight forwarders, who focus on physical distribution, handle the details of getting the merchandise out of the home country, through the international distribution and transportation channels, into the foreign country, and then into the appropriate retailing or sales environment.

Export-management companies, or *agents*, operate in several ways. They may take title to the product and then resell it, or they may market it under an exclusive contract with the exporting firm. These companies tend to specialize by product categories and frequently have tremendous resources and knowledge to offer in a specialized area.

CHANNEL STRATEGY ●

The decisions a firm makes relative to the use of direct sales, wholesalers, and retailers are a crucial element of its *distribution strategy*. These decisions and their strategic implications are the focus of the third chapter objective. Whether a firm uses one channel or many, its choice is crucial to the success of the firm's marketing. Each channel must be evaluated as an entity and each element in the channel—each agent, distributor, wholesaler, and/or retailer—must be carefully considered.

CHANNEL OBJECTIVES AND DESIGN

When no channels currently exist or existing channels need modifications, marketers must develop an appropriate *channel design*. Channel design should receive the same kind of strategic attention as decisions about other important elements of the marketing mix: price, product, and marketing communications. In designing marketing channels, managers need to consider four questions:

1. What are the distribution objectives?
2. What is the nature of the product and how does it affect channel requirements?
3. What are the nature and needs of the target market and which channels will best satisfy these needs?
4. What channel(s) and intermediaries will most efficiently and effectively satisfy all these considerations?

Channel objectives describe what part the channel is expected to play in the achievement of the firm's overall marketing objectives. Thus channel objectives should be stated in terms of the desired level of service to the relevant target market. Here are some examples of different types of channel objectives:

◆ For a manufacturer of personal computers, *response time* is important: to have computers available within forty-eight hours at any authorized European Union dealer.

◆ For a manufacturer of diet products, *market coverage* is important: to have product displayed in 80 percent of all supermarkets in Canada and in 95 percent of supermarkets in high income areas.

◆ For a manufacturer of vending machines, *quick repair service* is important: to make replacement parts and repair service available within twenty-four hours of any request.

◆ For a grower of oranges, *perishability* is important: to have product on retail display no more than seventy-two hours after being picked.

To determine which channel system is best for meeting objectives like these, a manufacturer needs to consider market coverage, target-market characteristics, the nature of the product, and cost efficiencies.

Market Coverage Implicit in setting consumer-goods distribution objectives is determining the type of market coverage desired. In general, the larger the number of customers, the greater the need for channel agents regardless of the stage of market development. Market coverage can be achieved by one of three major types of distribution: intensive, selective, or exclusive.

Intensive distribution is a good distribution strategy for convenience goods and services like fast food and other widely used products. For example, Canada's largest processed meat marketer, Maple Leaf Meats, uses an intensive distribution strategy as part of its overall marketing strategy for its core bacon, wiener, and sliced meat products. Since certain goods and services are purchased frequently and require little or no service, they sell on the basis of availability and impulse—the more frequently consumers see them, the more likely they are to buy such things as candy bars and soft drinks. Gasoline stations now successfully sell batteries, razors, bread, milk, and beer because consumers buy these items from the most convenient outlet and because most consumers regularly visit gas stations.

Selective distribution is strategically used for shopping goods and durable goods such as major household appliances, stereos, and automobiles. Selective distribution is also appropriate when a product needs some special handling or service, for example, appliances which require retailers to provide repair service and replacement parts.

Exclusive distribution is a good strategic choice for specialty goods and luxury items. Products distributed in this channel are usually purchased infrequently and consumed over a long period of time—an example is luxury watches. Some have a very exclusive image which the producer wants to maintain, as in the case of Rolex watches, Rolls-Royce automobiles, and designer hair stylists. Exclusive distribution is also appropriate where very spe-

456

cialized service or training is needed to sell or handle a product. Since where a product is sold says something about that product, it is strategically wise to put luxury items and services in stores and shopping areas that reinforce the upscale price and quality of the item or service. Bernard Callebaut chocolates, for example, are sold in upscale retail centers, not in the average neighborhood shopping mall.

A fourth type of strategy, called *local distribution,* is used primarily by local producers selling within a community or neighborhood. It is an important method of distribution in many parts of the nonindustrialized world.

Target Market Characteristics To design an effective channel, marketers must look at the size and density of the target-market population and purchase frequency. *Market size* refers to the number of customers in the relevant target market. Generally speaking, the more customers, the more likely the use of intermediaries. A special tool used by only a small group of artists will probably be sold directly to the artists. In contrast, a new breakfast cereal must be sold through wholesalers and retailers if it is to reach a very large targeted market.

The concentration of the target market in a particular area is called the *market density.* Market-density issues are particularly important in industrial goods markets, where certain industries tend to concentrate in the same geographic areas. The rule of thumb for market density is that the denser the market, the more direct the distribution channel. For example, a manufacturer of specialized equipment for microchip production may sell directly to microchip makers since they are grouped together in small geographic areas such as Silicon Valley in California. But a manufacturer of solvents that are used for machine maintenance in many different industries may well prefer to involve agents and/or distributors to increase contacts with users everywhere.

Channel strategy also considers the frequency and quantity of purchase and the services customers will require. Generally, the smaller the purchase quantity and the more frequent the purchase, the longer the channel. To efficiently supply items which are purchased frequently and in small quantities, producers must sell these items through wholesalers and retailers. However, if an item is likely to require considerable after-sale service, technical advice, or updating and alteration, the channel will be shorter.

Nature of the Product Product characteristics important to the choice of a direct or indirect channel include product size and weight, perishability, level of producer control, and input required. Since the larger and bulkier an item, the greater its handling and storage costs, it is usually more efficient to sell items like large machinery and furniture through more direct channels.

The more perishable an item, the more important it is to get it directly into the hands of end users. (As the ad in Exhibit 14-2 shows, Westinghouse's Thermo King subsidiary has specialized in refrigeration transport for over fifty years.) Direct channels minimize the time the product spends in the system and decrease the probability that an item will spoil or become obsolete before it reaches consumers. The Limited distributes products made under contract with other firms. This approach has allowed The Limited to speed up the movement of fashion items to its stores, ensuring that these items get to market while still in demand.

When a product requires a lot of producer input and control, such as custom manufacture, installation, or training, a shorter channel is in order. Also, when a product is new to the market or when the producer feels that an advantage can be gained by pricing, presenting, and promoting the product in a certain way, a more direct channel may be used. For example, Frito Lay

THE BEST-KNOWN, UNKNOWN COMPANY IN AMERICA.

Westinghouse. People rely on our transport refrigeration in over 80 countries around the world.

The next time you're enjoying farm-fresh produce or a juicy steak, remember this unexpected name—Westinghouse.

Our Thermo King subsidiary is the world leader in transport refrigeration technology and products for trucks, trailers, and containers. Thermo King invented transport refrigeration in

1938, revolutionizing the way perishables were delivered.

Today, Thermo King-equipped vehicles transport all kinds of perishables—everything from produce and film to chemicals and pharmaceuticals—in more than 80 countries around the world. Controlling cargo temperatures within one degree to ensure freshness.

And Thermo King is backed by the industry's largest dealer support network.

Thermo King technology. Just one more reason why the best-known unknown company in America is a company you should get to know better.

You can be sure...if it's Westinghouse

Exhibit 14-2
Delivery When Time Counts

Westinghouse has been an international leader in developing technology needed for the fast delivery of perishable products.

Corporation employs its own route drivers and delivers its product directly to retailers so that it can be sure of proper shelf placement, rotation, and stocking. When a product is subject to what may be monopoly control, as in the next case, the channel itself may be open to question.

OPEN TO DEBATE

SEEING THROUGH THE FOG

In the United States, if you want to replace your contact lenses, you can go back to the eye-care professional where you had your eye exam and order a new pair. Or you can order a replacement pair through a mail-order company. The only problem with the second choice is that your optometrist may refuse to release your prescription so you can order directly.[5]

The issue is: Can eye-care professionals legally restrict how eye-care products are sold? Various state attorney generals and the Federal Trade Commission are investigating possible antitrust violations, particularly by manufacturers who won't sell to direct marketing companies. In Canada, however, patients may demand to receive their prescription as part of their medical records, and contact lenses are only sold in stores with resident optometrists, who can fit lenses.

The manufacturing costs of contact lenses have decreased so much that consumers are viewing lenses as commodity products that can be sold by anyone, including discount stores like Kmart and direct-mail outlets. Because the optometrists and opticians who once monopolized distribution have maintained such high markups, they are highly vulnerable to this kind of competition. They are fighting back, however, by trying to get legislation passed that would protect their monopoly of what they claim is "a medical device."

Is this attempt to shut out competition just good business practice or is it pure greed and a conflict of interest? Would you support the availability of contact lenses from mail-order services and discount stores in Canada?

Cost Efficiencies As in every marketing decision, cost is a factor in channel selection. Table 14-3 describes some of the functions of marketing channels. Each impacts on the total cost of distribution in different ways. If the channel manager determines that certain functions add too much to the cost, these functions may be dropped as a channel responsibility. Using the cheapest channel is not always the right solution either: if the cheapest channel does not provide necessary services, it may result in customer dissatisfaction and lost sales. The goal is to find the most *efficient* channel—the one that best balances costs as it accomplishes necessary channel objectives.

TABLE 14-3	SOME COST CONSIDERATIONS IN DESIGNING MARKETING CHANNELS

Function	Cost Factor
Order processing/customer service	Handling and processing of all customer orders
Carrying inventory	Carrying inventories when demand and supply do not match
Warehousing	Warehousing products that need to be kept closer to the point of sale
Marketing communications	Communicating the nature of products and their availability to potential customers
Profit margins of channel members	Each organization in the channel needs to make a profit
Opportunity costs	Customer dissatisfaction or lost sales if intermediaries provide poor service

Note: Costs can be absorbed by producers or shared with channel intermediaries.

INTERNATIONAL DISTRIBUTION CONSIDERATIONS

Distribution channels in markets around the world are sometimes among the most highly differentiated aspects of marketing programs. Developing and managing global channels, the subject of the fourth chapter objective, is one of the most challenging and difficult components of international marketing. The Japanese market, for example, is seen as a special challenge by foreign firms seeking entry because the Japanese commonly use exclusive distribution agreements which lock competitors out of existing channels.

The distribution channels available in foreign markets are often the product of cultural characteristics that have evolved over long periods of time, and these characteristics affect channel relations. For example, in Japan and China, firms must first establish a trusting social relationship with a channel partner before expecting a business commitment. Firms marketing outside their home country must also contend with strong local competition for distribution: local producers that have long-established ties with intermedi-

Avon Calls in Budapest

In Hungary as in North America, the Avon representative calls on her customers in their homes. As you'll see in Chapter 20, Avon had to overcome some special difficulties in adapting its distribution methods to Japanese ways.

aries in their home countries often receive priority. Another problem is that manufacturers from many nations frequently vie for the services of the same established local intermediaries.

If the distribution system is complicated or difficult to penetrate, a producer may be better off selling its product to an intermediary and then allowing the intermediary to sell the product as it pleases or to use direct marketing.[6] This is a viable solution if the product does not require a great deal of producer input (information, assembly) or after-sales service. For example, Avon uses intermediaries in Africa and the Middle East, but employs its familiar direct-sales approach in Latin America, Europe, and the Pacific.[7]

Governmental control is another major obstacle confronting marketers planning international distribution channels. When Federal Express decided to enter the Japanese market, for example, it took three years of negotiations before the company got permission to make four flights a week from Memphis to Tokyo. Japanese regulators also took steps to protect local express companies. Just days before FedEx was due to begin service to Japan, they informed the company that no packages weighing more than 70 pounds (31.8 kg) could be flown into Tokyo, even if they were already en route. As a result of all these obstacles, Federal Express lost over $1 million a month on the Tokyo route during its first year of operation.

Sometimes simple geography presents an obstacle to reaching global customers and clients. As Exhibit 14-3 shows, DHL offers worldwide express service to obscure places by employing local deliverers.

CHANNEL MANAGEMENT ●

No company can effectively manage its marketing program without an effective distribution strategy. But channel strategies aren't the end of the process. A distribution system must be managed as well as designed, and effective management depends on information and coordination, the focus of chapter objective five.

ELECTRONIC DATA INTERCHANGE (EDI)

One major area of change in channel management is electronic inventory control, which uses the rapidly growing computer technology called *electronic data interchange* that we first discussed in Chapter 5. This electronic system of data management allows channel members to share information about product movement and sales and to transact business. Working closely together, the manufacturer and the various members of the channel create an information network through which channel members share critical data about distribution volume.

Inventory management is an extremely important factor in marketing because it affects the size of a company's physical plant, its ability to respond to market changes, and its performance in terms of sales and return on investment. Bar codes on shipping cartons make it possible to use hand-held scanners to quickly and easily record inventory flow both into and out of warehouses, distribution centers, and wholesalers' and retailers' receiving departments. In retail stores the scanning of bar codes on each individual package as it is stocked and sold provides an even more precise measure of current inventories. Retailers and wholesalers that connect their inventory control systems to suppliers through EDI can automatically create instant orders and billing. It's this technology that saved the biker's vacation in the story at the beginning of this chapter.

electronic data interchange (EDI)
An electronic means of collecting and recording data about product movement and sales which permits channel members to share information and transact business.

461

just-in-time inventory control
An operations management system that, by means of constant electronic communication between retailer and supplier, permits the retailer to carry just enough inventory to meet immediate demands, yet ensures rapid and automatic order processing as inventory is depleted.

EDI permits a **just-in-time inventory control** system. In this operations management program only enough product inventory is carried to meet immediate demand, but replenishment stock is constantly being ordered and delivered as the product is sold. EDI works like this: A retailer's inventory is electronically linked to an automatic ordering process. When the information system determines that the stock has reached a certain minimum level, it initiates a predetermined order and relays it to the appropriate distributors who then fill and deliver the order.

Hallmark supplies its retailers with hand-held CrownLink EDI terminals, on which they transmit merchandise orders to Hallmark's headquarters. The retailers like the system because their orders are acknowledged in seconds, are

Distribution by Satellite

Wal-Mart's Bentonville, Arkansas, "satellite room" is the company's distribution nerve center. Wal-Mart is the retail industry leader in warehousing technology and information distribution, especially in its relationships with suppliers and retailers. Through computer networks, Wal-Mart works with suppliers to fill orders and to adjust production schedules when necessary.

filled faster than they were through traditional ordering methods, and cannot get lost in the mail; as a result, they run out of stock less often. Eaton's now has about 500 of its 3,500 suppliers connected to its EDI system, and Kmart Canada is one-third of the way through its EDI program.

Wal-Mart's just-in-time system is an example of state-of-the-art operations management. Computer terminals in Wal-Mart stores connected to the company's local distribution centers monitor sales and automatically order and ship new supplies as a store needs them. Wal-Mart's computer system is also connected to the systems of 200 vendors—a fact that ensures a steady stream of the most needed products to Wal-Mart distribution centers, most of which are within a day's drive of the stores they serve.

COORDINATING MARKETING CHANNELS

For a marketing channel to be effective, each member must fulfill its responsibilities in a way that complements the activities of other channel members. Unfortunately, since channels consist of independent individuals, there is always the threat of disagreement over issues such as who should perform what function, who should make what decision, and what products should be handled by which channel members.[8] Often the dominant member, or *channel captain,* discussed later in this section, is expected to mediate conflict.

One common conflict occurs when a manufacturer like Levi Strauss decides to open up its own stores and sell direct to customers rather than using its traditional network of wholesalers and retailers. Table 14-4 shows some other potential conflicts in the distribution channel along with some possible solutions. Notice that many of these solutions depend on doing a better job of communicating the corporate vision.[9]

Two examples will make the notion of channel conflict less abstract. Lotus Development Corporation discovered that some of its distributors were

TABLE 14-4	SOME DISTRIBUTION CHANNEL PROBLEMS AND SOLUTIONS

Problem	Possible Solutions
Manufacturer bypasses intermediaries to sell direct	Agreement never to sell direct Identify accounts for direct sale and negotiate agreement with intermediaries Sell direct but pass on profits to appointed intermediaries to appease them
Manufacturer gives products to new types of channels, broadening the products' availability	Partition markets, using different channels for different markets Develop different brands for different intermediaries
Manufacturer appoints more intermediaries per geographic region—in the incumbent intermediaries view, oversaturating the area with too many resellers	Appoint a set number of intermediaries based on the region's potential and communicate this policy to the intermediaries Appoint "master distributors" who sell to dealers; keep such designations for select high-performing intermediaries Encourage existing intermediaries to build another branch in an area with unrealized market potential
Intermediaries dispute the fairness of the way profits are split among different intermediaries along the channel	Tie margins to functions performed by the intermediaries regardless of each intermediary's position in the channel
Manufacturers contend that intermediaries are disloyal and give minimal support to manufacturers' products and offer few programs of assistance to them	Design programs more in keeping with intermediaries' views; listen to channel members Make sure the manufacturer's "house is in order" in terms of service levels to the intermediaries
Intermediaries refuse to share end-user account information considered important by the manufacturer for purposes of marketing	Pay the channel for such data Jointly sponsor paid market research with intermediaries Gain resellers' trust so they will share such data with the manufacturer

Source: Kenneth G. Hardy and Allan J. Magrath, *Marketing Channel Management* (Glenview, Ill.: Scott, Foresman, and Company, 1988), p. 109.

selling its famous 1-2-3 spreadsheet package to mail-order retailers, who then priced the package up to $200 lower than Lotus's suggested retail price. This situation caused strong dissension because Lotus felt that its distributors' actions were lowering the value of a product it had worked to develop and market as unique. When Domino's Pizza Corporation decided to test selling its pizza through Burger King restaurants, Domino's franchisees were enraged because they believed that Domino's corporate office was using Burger King to steal their retail business. In the first example, it was the manufacturer who felt aggrieved; in the second, it was the distributors who felt betrayed.

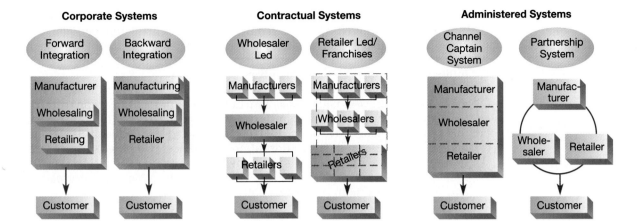

Corporate Systems

Forward Integration

Backward Integration

Contractual Systems

Wholesaler Led

Retailer Led/ Franchises

Administered Systems

Channel Captain System

Partnership System

Figure 14-4
Vertical Marketing Systems

Vertical Marketing Systems One way to minimize channel conflicts is to own or control the entire channel, an arrangement known as a **vertical marketing system.** In a vertical distribution system a marketing channel is controlled by a single channel member and professionally managed for efficiency and better coordination.

There are three types of vertical systems: corporate, contractual, and administered. Studying Figure 14-4 as you read the next few paragraphs will help you understand how these systems and some of their subsystems work. To compare the vertical marketing system with a common traditional channel arrangement, look back at the third channel (C_3) in Figure 14-2.

Corporate Systems. A corporate system combines production and distribution functions under the ownership of the manufacturer or retailer. In *forward integration* the manufacturer owns its own wholesaling and retailing operations. Paint producer Sherwin Williams, for example, owns its own retail paint stores. In *backward integration* a retailer or wholesaler purchases its own production facilities. An example of backward integration is Southland Corporation (7-Eleven) which operates its own gasoline refineries (Citgo).

Contractual Systems. A contractual system integrates the efforts of production and distribution firms on a contractual basis. These systems, currently the most popular form of vertical marketing, fall into three categories: wholesaler-sponsored voluntary chains, retailer-sponsored cooperatives, and franchises.

In *wholesaler-sponsored voluntary chains* (so-called because retailer members join in the chain voluntarily) like Western Auto, a wholesaler contracts with small independent retailers in order to standardize and coordinate buying practices, merchandising programs, and inventory management. By contractually organizing a large group of small independent retailers, the wholesaler-sponsored voluntary chain is able to take advantage of distribution economies and volume discounts when purchasing, often from more than one manufacturer. In *retailer-sponsored cooperatives* like Associated Grocers, retailers contract with one another to operate a wholesale facility; they may also engage in producing some of the goods they sell. Cooperatives allow the retailers to concentrate their buying power and plan collaborative promotional programs. *Franchising*, which involves a contractual relationship between a parent company and an individual or firm that owns and operates a local outlet, is common not only in the fast-food industry (McDonald's, Domino's) but also in other service industries such as hotels (Holiday Inn and Days Inn) and tax preparation (H&R Block).

vertical marketing system
An arrangement in which a set of marketing channels is managed and controlled by a single channel member.

465

Administered Systems. In the third type of vertical marketing system, the administered system, channel members remain independent but agree to work together. The channel is administered by a channel member, sometimes referred to as the *channel captain*, who generally has more size and influence than other channel members.

Another type of administered system that is developing in relationship marketing is the *partnership system* in which two or more firms come together to create more business opportunities for everyone in the channel.[10] Through this type of *channel integration*, IBM has contracted with Federal Express to handle parts and supplies for all its after-sale services, which guarantees that IBM service representatives will have any supplies they need within twenty-four hours. IBM and FedEx have worked together to design an information and distribution system that meets both their needs.

Warehousing: Storage for Future Demand

Due to uneven customer demand, manufacturers will generally produce and store a surplus in warehouses so as to be able to meet customer demand whenever and wherever it arises.

PHYSICAL DISTRIBUTION MANAGEMENT ●

The smooth operating of a marketing channel requires a workable system of *physical distribution*—the storage, handling, and movement of goods to make them available when and where customers want them. Such a system can be a major expense, though costs for physical distribution vary widely from firm to firm. For example, Sears, which operates a rather antiquated distribution system, has distribution costs equal to 8 percent of sales. In contrast, Wal-Mart, with its national network of distribution centers, manages to hold distribution costs to about 3 percent of sales. Controlling costs and keeping a product's physical distribution moving smoothly requires coordination of the four primary components of the system—order processing, warehousing, inventory handling, and transportation. The options available to marketers in managing these components are the focus of the sixth chapter objective.

ORDER PROCESSING

The receipt and transmission of sales order information is called *order processing*. The more efficiently orders are processed, the less time it will take for delivery and the greater will be the satisfaction of customers. Order processing consists of three steps: order entry, in which the order is received from the customer or department; order handling, which includes all the operations involved in locating, assembling, and moving the products ordered into distribution; and order delivery, the process by which the products or services are made available to the customer. Today, many companies use hand-held electronic order processing machines which the salesperson can download via a modem and telephone line to the head office, thus minimizing order processing time.

WAREHOUSING

The storage of goods while they are waiting to be sold is known as **warehousing**. Manufacturers produce goods in large quantities at fairly constant rates. Since demand typically fluctuates and manufacturers generally prefer to produce a surplus in order to cover peak demand periods, some product must be stored. Warehousing balances the quantity with the level of demand. When looking at warehousing costs, marketers must weigh the faster-service advantage of numerous warehouse locations against the higher costs of maintaining multiple locations.

In addition to warehouses, which are used to *store* goods for moderate to long periods, many companies also have **distribution centers**, which are designed to *move* goods. These large, highly automated facilities receive goods from various suppliers and then quickly and efficiently fill orders for individual stores. Distribution centers are such a high-tech business today that many companies are outsourcing this element of distribution, although, as you will see in the next section, Wal-Mart chooses to handle its own distribution. Federal Express's Business Logistics Services Group, for example, has taken over product handling, warehousing, and distribution not only for IBM, as we mentioned, but also for Sun Microsystems and a number of other companies that can't afford or don't want to construct and manage their own high-tech automated centers.

warehousing
The physical storage of goods that are ready to be sold.

distribution centers
Highly automated facilities designed to receive goods from a variety of suppliers, assemble the merchandise, and process and deliver orders quickly and efficiently.

BEHIND THE SCENES

HOW WAL-MART WORKS

Wal-Mart owns and manages its own distribution channel, and that, along with location, has been its most important competitive advantage. It operates twenty distribution centers in the United States, as well as its own trucking fleet. A typical center occupies 1 million square feet, or about as much floor space as 23 football fields, and is filled to the rafters with the 80,000 different items that Wal-Mart stores carry.

Because Wal-Mart is so good at moving merchandise, it is far more profitable than its competitors. Kmart, which owns twice as many stores, registered U.S. $37.7 billion in sales and a profit of U.S. $941 million in 1993. That same year Wal-Mart had sales of U.S. $55.5 billion and a profit of U.S. $2 billion.

On one side of a Wal-Mart distribution center is a shipping dock with loading doors for around thirty trucks; on the other side is the receiving dock, which may have as many as 135 doors for unloading merchandise from suppliers. As the goods move in and out of the trucks and the warehouse on some 8½ miles of laser-guided conveyer belts, the lasers read the bar codes on the cases and direct them to whatever truck is filling an order for that product. To the naïve observer, this sophisticated operation is a blur of boxes and crates flying down the belts, with red lasers flashing everywhere.

A little more than half of the chain's inventory is put on shelves in the warehouse; the remainder of the inventory, the high-volume/high-turn merchandise, moves through the distribution center on conveyers in continuous transit. (*High turn* means that the merchandise sells fast in Wal-Mart stores.) Wal-Mart calls this continuous transit operation its "assembly system" because the merchandise (referred to in-house as "assembly products") is not warehoused, but rather constantly assembled into orders.

Most of Wal-Mart's stores have a distribution center no more than a day's drive away. The centers run twenty-four hours a day and directly replenish almost 85 percent of the inventory from stocks on hand, compared to about 50 to 65 percent for the competition. By locating its distribution centers close to its stores, Wal-Mart can speed delivery and achieve more flexibility in inventory management. The average interval between the time a store places a computer order and the time it receives a shipment is only about two days, and some stores receive service overnight. In contrast, the interval between order and delivery is five or more days for many of Wal-Mart's competitors, who contract out most of their trucking.

The financial implications of this distribution system are highly favorable to Wal-Mart. Most suppliers bill retailers every thirty days, and their invoices request payment within a thirty-day period. Wal-Mart may sell an "assembly product" thirty days before the bill is due, which provides the company with an accelerated cash flow. In a sense, the speed of its distribution system allows Wal-Mart to use its suppliers' cash to finance its operations without paying interest.[11]

Wal-Mart entered the Canadian market in March 1994, and six months later there were 123 Wal-Marts across Canada. Although there were no Canadian distribution centers as of late-1994, it is expected that distribution practices in Canadian Wal-Marts will soon match their U.S. counterparts.

INVENTORY MANAGEMENT

The control of inventory levels, or the amount of product on hand either in storage or on retail shelves, is referred to as **inventory management**, and management always involves making some difficult decisions. Once again, as in the just-in-time discussion, we encounter the paradox of distribution: managers must balance the risk of running out of stock and not satisfying a customer (and potentially losing that customer) against the costs of carrying too much stock and incurring excess storage costs. Managers also must balance order-processing costs against inventory-carrying costs. The more often a product is ordered, the higher the order-processing costs (unloading, stocking, order placing, and so forth). The less often a product is ordered, the higher the inventory-carrying costs, since more product must be kept in inventory to cover the longer period between orders.

To help control inventory costs, many producers now use a new concept called *total system inventories*. In these systems the inventory of a particular product is monitored throughout the channel. Thus the producer as well as the retailer knows what inventory is in wholesale and retail warehouses, how much is in transit, and how much is in retail outlets.[12] To take one example, hospitals now have a computer link with major suppliers such as Baxter Healthcare. The supplier may provide the computer link. For the hospital, an out-of-stock situation may mean the loss of life. The criticality of supply is more important than cost of the system which may even work out cheaper than out-of-stock situations where special delivery has to be arranged for economic order quantities for the supplier. Economic order quantity features greatly in the operations management literature and is another consideration that has to be borne in mind. Not all customers are profitable or may be serviced profitably. There may be an 80/20 ratio in that 80 percent of business is derived from 20 percent of customers. This requires a restructuring of the customer base as well as range and levels of inventory to be maintained.

TRANSPORTATION

Decisions about transportation also have a significant effect on overall distribution costs. There are five basic transportation methods available for moving a company's products—rail, truck, water, pipeline, and air—as well as intermodal methods that combine different types of transportation.

Rail is still the largest carrier in North America, accounting for over 37 percent of all cargo moved. The advantages of railroads are that they are very cost-effective for moving large quantities of merchandise long distances and they are capable of carrying the widest range of products.

Trucks have steadily increased their share of cargo transport in recent years and now account for about 25 percent of all cargo moved in North America. Trucks are not only an excellent choice for moving products short distances, especially within cities, but are also the most flexible form of transportation for routing and time schedules. Because trucks have the best point-to-point capability, most items shipped long distance by other methods usually wind up on trucks in the final lap of their journey.

Shipping goods by *water* is extremely low in cost, but water travel is quite slow and more susceptible to weather-caused delays than any of the other transportation methods. Still, the low cost of water transport makes it the first choice for moving relatively high weight goods, such as coal, iron ore, steel, autos, and heavy machinery, and for international distribution.

Air is the fastest means of transport, and thus the carrier of choice for perishable merchandise, but it is also the most expensive. Companies moving fairly lightweight expensive items with high value added—diamonds, watches and telecommunications equipment, for example—may choose air. Companies that urgently need replacement parts also may find it worthwhile to foot the air freight bill. In addition, direct marketing employs air transport through its package delivery services.

Pipelines meet only very specialized routing demands. They are particularly popular among petroleum and chemical producers—the Trans Canada oil pipeline is a well-known example. Pipelines are more expensive than water but less expensive than rail.

Channel strategy looks at each method of distribution to determine how a company can best use one or multiple methods to maximize efficiency. Combining several different methods—a common practice in international marketing—is called *intermodal transportation*. To take advantage of more than one method of shipping goods, companies are turning to containerization.

Containerization means using trailers or boxes of standard sizes that can easily be transferred from one mode of transportation to another to ship products. Containers, which range from 20 to over 50 feet in length, are constructed of steel. Deciding whether to use this method of transport requires knowing the costs of shipping a container of a particular size, that has specific contents, from point A to point B.

In summary, the computer and electronic information systems have given managers not only JIT systems but also computer controlled air/sea/surface transport modules. In planning distribution channels, managers must balance the values provided by a distribution method—for example, speed, direct service, convenience—against the added cost of that method.

containerization
The practice of placing products for shipment into large steel boxes or trailers of standardized sizes; these containers can then easily be transferred from one mode of transportation to another.

469

MARKETING POSTAL SERVICES

Speaking of balancing costs, what do you think about privatizing Canada Post? Canada Post handles about 10 billion pieces of mail per year (or an average of 40 million pieces per day), and employs 54,000 full- and part-time workers, many of whom earn more than non-postal workers doing comparable jobs. But with any other service, do you think you could send a letter from Vancouver to Halifax in just three or four days and for about 45 cents? At present, labor accounts for approximately two-thirds of costs, but Canada Post is trying to reduce costs further.

Although courier companies (such as Federal Express, Canpar, DHL, the United Parcel Service, and even local bicycle couriers) compete with the Canadian postal service, The Canada Post Corporation Act gives Canada Post the exclusive privilege delivering letters. Right now, however, numerous private companies compete with Canada Post for publications and advertising mail distribution.

Many people believe that increased competition in postal services would keep costs from rising by increasing efficiency. Also a private service would greatly reduce the likelihood of strikes.

Do you think that Canada should privatize its postal service? Would privatization decrease costs for mailing between major urban centers, while increasing the cost of service for rural and remote areas? Does permitting alternative delivery services to distribute magazines and promotional material seriously threaten Canada Post? What other methods could help make Canada Post more competitive?

Interview managers at a company in your town that does a lot of bulk mailing and get their opinions on using Canada Post versus private delivery. Pretend you are starting a new local magazine for your chamber of commerce, and estimate the difference in costs between regular mail and a private delivery service serving your community. ▼

KEY POINTS SUMMARY ▼

1. Distribution channels direct the flow of products to users. Members of the distribution channel perform many functions—research, buying, carrying inventory, promoting, negotiating, financing, selling, transporting, and servicing—that add value to the product.

2. Channels for consumer products guide the flow of products from producers to consumers. Channels for industrial products guide the flow of products (materials, parts, and equipment) from producers to other firms for the production of other products or daily operations.

3. Decisions concerning the use of direct sales, wholesalers, and retailers have strategic implications. In designing a distribution channel, managers must consider market coverage, target market characteristics, product characteristics, and costs. The best design is the most efficient and cost effective, but the channel must also meet the firm's distribution objectives.

4. Although global channels are similar to domestic channels in many ways, managing them successfully often poses specific requirements and makes special demands on mar-

keters. The role of the intermediary in global marketing channels is particularly important, for it is usually the intermediary who speaks the local language and who is familiar with local business practices, laws, taxation, and customs.

5. The effectiveness and efficiency of channel management depend on the quality and timeliness of the data available for decision making. Channel members' activities must be coordinated and channel conflict minimized. Coordination can be achieved through channel leadership or vertical marketing systems.

6. The four principal components of physical distribution are order processing, warehousing, inventory management, and transportation. Today electronic data information systems can speed order processing, but managers must weigh the costs of such systems against their benefits to the firm and to the customer. Similarly, managers must choose among alternative warehousing options, including the new high-tech distribution centers, and must balance costs against convenience. Efficient inventory management requires deciding how to balance such things as the costs of storing large quantities of goods against the costs of frequent order processing. Finally, managers have many transportation options from which to choose, each at a different cost level. For some goods, intermodal transport can effect cost savings.

DISCUSSION QUESTIONS ▼

1. What is a marketing channel? How does it help marketers to satisfy consumer needs?

2. Identify the functions of distribution channel members and explain how they help meet consumer needs and add value to the product.

3. What are vertical marketing systems and how do they help channel coordination?

4. Identify the four major components of a physical distribution system and explain why each is important to the effectiveness of the marketing channel.

5. What important factors must be considered when designing global channels? Explain why each of these is a concern.

6. For each of the four marketing channels for consumer goods described in this chapter, give two examples not found in the text.

7. If you were designing a channel for a new type of dog food, what factors would you have to consider? Plot the channel from your factory to the customer. If you were designing a channel for a new high-priced specialty wine, what would it look like?

8. Why does channel conflict occur? Give three examples of channel conflict situations and describe how you would resolve them.

9. What are the five principal modes of transportation? Choose a product that you think would be most appropriate for shipment on each of the five modes, and explain why you chose that mode.

10. Interview the manager of a local company and determine the nature of the marketing channel(s) used for the firm's primary product, the manner in which the channel is coordinated, and the systems used to handle that product's physical distribution.

Integrative Case ● Discussion Questions

The Body Shop*

1. How would you classify The Body Shop's distribution system? Could Anita have built the kind of social-responsibility image The Body Shop now has with another kind of distribution system?

*The three cases at the back of the book—"The Body Shop," "Harley-Davidson," and "The Millennium Power System"—illustrate topics discussed in all chapters of this book. Your instructor will tell you when to read a particular case and answer the discussion questions on it that appear at the end of each chapter.

2. What types of conflict are likely to arise in this system?

3. How might physical distribution be better managed in The Body Shop system than in a more traditional system?

Harley-Davidson

1. What sort of vertical marketing system does Harley-Davidson have?

2. Compare Honda's and Harley's dealer networks: Are they intensive, selective, or exclusive? Support your answer.

3. What does Harley expect of its dealers?

The Millennium Power System

1. What sort of distribution—intensive, selective, or exclusive—is appropriate for the Millennium System?

2. Millennium sells private label brands of batteries as well as its own name-brand batteries to retailers. How might that affect the distribution of Millennium brand battery systems?

Mail-Order Pharmacy

■n today's marketplace, we see lots of creative ideas for alternate methods of getting products and services to consumers. One of the most original that has appeared is mail-order drugstores. Toronto's MediTrust and Newfoundland's PharmEx are two such operations. Mail-order pharmacies are getting ready acceptance by consumers and especially by group health plan administrators. But they are getting stiff opposition from the established store owners. Is it just a case of protecting turf, or is there more to it?

Rose Fischman, Vice President of MediTrust, used to own two Shoppers Drug Mart franchises. According to her "Pharmacists have gone from the old apothecary shop of being that dispenser of knowledge, that gatekeeper of healthcare; to shoving it to the very back of the store. You're paying for franchise fees, you're paying for advertising, for insurance, you're paying for a mall location, you're paying for all that front shop inventory, millions of dollars worth of tobacco and cosmetics that's really expensive to keep on your shelves; you're paying all that extra overhead." Most drug stores today look more like the old *general* store than the old *drug* store. Is that a good thing or is it bad? Here's how it is supposed to work, ideally. Mail-order companies use automated equipment to process the order and deliver via priority post. They are fully computerized, and are able to cross check a patient's files for things like allergies and incompatible medications. Order processing can be done for a flat dispensing fee of $5, compared to the national average of $7–10. Qualified pharmacists are available 24 hours a day for counseling or crisis.

Traditionally, most people get their prescriptions filled at the local pharmacy. Why? Is your local pharmacist in a better position to deal with you on a one-to-one basis? They are intended to be the last safety valve to check for errors in prescriptions. But can all pharmacists provide this care? Can it be done by mail-order operations? In the end, it comes down to the definition of "convenience" by different groups of consumers. Some define convenience as face-to-face contact, and the ability to get what they want immediately. Others define convenience as a caring voice, available 24 hours per day without having to leave the house. A key issue for many is the privacy afforded by the phone that cannot be obtained with others standing around overhearing their questions and personal advice.

Consider this case to be a wake up challenge to all other "traditional" routes of distributing goods.

QUESTIONS

1. Describe the profile of alternate groups of consumers for whom convenience in drug purchasing is defined differently.
2. What other industries are likely ripe for changes such as this?

Source: This case was prepared by Ray Friedman and is based on the *Market Place* series episode "Mail-Order Pharmacy," originally broadcast on January 25, 1994.

● Chapter 15

Wholesaling and Retailing

WHO'S IN CONTROL HERE?[1]

You're excited because you just came back from the discount store with an automatic camera that cost about half what your local camera store would charge. A good deal, right! . . . But is it?

One of the most startling changes in the distribution field in recent years is the shift in power from manufacturers to retailers. This shift in channel control, referred to in Chapter 14, has occurred because retailers have been consolidating into huge chains that are able to control the entire distribution channel. The chains have become so powerful, in fact, that in some cases they can dictate marketing strategies to the manufacturers who supply the products they carry. This tension between manufacturers and retailers has become a major topic of discussion in the industry and in trade journals.[2] "The retailer has the leverage in the relationship," a column by two financial analysts in *Brandweek* stated.

The result for consumers, in most cases, has been lower prices.

This is because the large discount chains can virtually tell manufacturers what prices they will pay for merchandise and under what terms, based on their own market information and on estimates of what price levels will sell best. The manufacturer can either take a smaller profit margin or reformulate its product so that it can be sold at the lower price and bring in the same profit. Because these large chains often do 20 to 40 percent of all business in a particular metropolitan area, manufacturers—even those as large as Procter and Gamble—are often reluctant to resist their demands.

Some manufacturers, however—especially producers of small appliances, apparel, and computers—have begun to fight back by using other forms of distribution such as direct marketing (see Chapter 20) and their own factory outlet stores. In fact, factory outlets have become a growth segment in retailing.

Although you are currently benefiting from the lower prices powerful retailers have been able to set, in a few years some of the higher priced brands you now buy in your local stores may only be available through direct marketing How do you see the Information Superhighway changing the way you order and pay for things. In general, how can you—the consumer—come out the winner in this battle for control between manufacturers and retailers? ▪

THE ROLE OF INTERMEDIARIES ●

In the vast consumer goods market customers rely on the retailers to provide availability of most of the products they buy and on the wholesalers to get the products from the manufacturer to the store. This is a complex arena of shifting responsibilities and interrelationships. Chapter 14 discussed the entire distribution channel. This chapter focuses on two key functions of that channel: retailing and wholesaling.

Understanding the objectives of wholesalers and retailers can be confusing because both are members of the distribution channel and they both compete, just as manufacturers do. Therefore, explanations of "distribution" objectives and strategies will differ depending on whether we are looking at things from the perspective of the manufacturer, the wholesaler, or the retailer. Sometimes, as the opening story in this chapter suggests, the objectives of these key players are not only different, but in direct conflict.

wholesalers
Intermediaries who link manufacturers with other intermediaries like retailers and industrial stocklists and add value to a product by means of services like speedy shipment of small order quantities.

THE WHOLESALING SCENE ●

As we noted in the preceding chapter, **wholesalers** link manufacturers with other intermediaries such as retailers and industrial stocklists and add value by providing such services as product availability and speedy shipment of small order quantities. Retailers can take over the role of wholesaling, which lets them control the entire distribution channel from the factory to the store, as the opening story explained. It is possible for a retailer, for example,

merchandise, in return for which they receive a commission from the manufacturer. Some 3,544 agents and brokers account for $37.4 billion worth of trade in Canada. The most common types of **agents** are *manufacturer's representatives* who sell two or more related product lines from noncompeting manufacturers in a specific geographic territory. *Selling agents* sell the full product line of a single small producer and are responsible for all aspects of marketing of that product. *Commission merchants* take possession of goods on consignment in small local markets and resell them in larger regional or national markets. They are often found in agricultural markets.

In contrast, **brokers** are not affiliated with any particular manufacturers. Rather, they specialize in certain product lines, bringing buyers and sellers together and negotiating contracts, for which they collect a commission. Although there has been a decline in the number of manufacturer's representatives in recent years, the number of brokers has grown phenomenally, particularly in the food industry. A typical broker represents fifteen to twenty-five noncompeting brands in a major metropolitan area. The main strength of brokers is their close personal relationship with local retail buyers. The Klondike ice cream bar has been around for fifty years. Thanks to food brokers, the bars became widely available in supermarkets, and during the 1980s, sales increased by over 600 percent.

INTERNATIONAL WHOLESALING

The distribution channels in markets around the world are among the most highly differentiated aspects of national marketing systems. For this reason, channel strategy is an extremely challenging and difficult component of any international marketing program. Smaller companies trying to export internationally are often blocked by their inability to establish relationships with intermediaries. And larger multinational companies find that making arrangements for the intermediaries is the element of the marketing mix that is least likely to be controlled by headquarters and most likely to be left to the discretion of the local marketing management group.

Japan is a particularly difficult market to enter. Wholesalers and retailers are very specialized, and focused on product categories. This specialization is made possible by the clustering of various types of stores at major street intersections or stops along commuter rail lines. Because of Japan's tremendous number of small shops and small wholesalers, as well as its limited and very costly physical storage space, the Japanese retailing system is one of the most complex in the world—which makes the role of intermediaries even more important than elsewhere. Japan has the longest distribution channels in the world at a time when elsewhere in the world these channels are becoming shorter. Longer channels means higher costs and more product tied up in the distribution channel.

Trading Companies   Distribution and wholesaling are handled by trading companies like the Mitsubishi Corporation, which launched Cannondale's products in Japan. **Trading companies** are responsible for both imports and exports and act as both purchasing and sales agents for the companies they represent. They generally represent a variety of categories and may even represent competitors within the same category. They are an important factor in the business success of Japanese firms.

Trading companies are nothing new in history. British, French, Dutch, Belgian, and German trading companies played an important part in the European exploration of Africa, Asia, and the Americas from the seventeenth through the nineteenth centuries. In certain markets and regions of the world they continue to be well-embedded, often as the key to acquiring market access.

agents
Intermediaries who do not take title to goods, but rather sell them and receive a commission on the sale from the manufacturer.

brokers
Intermediaries who specialize in certain product lines and bring buyers and sellers together, negotiate contracts, and collect commissions.

trading companies
Companies in Europe and Japan primarily, which handle all aspects of distribution and wholesaling and are responsible for both imports and exports; they act as both purchasing and sales agents for the companies they represent. They often specialize in certain regions of the world or country markets.

THE RETAILING SCENE

retailing
The activities involved in
the direct sale of prod-
ucts or services to cus-
tomers who are the end-
users of the products or
services in question.

The activities involved in the direct sale of goods or services to consumers are called **retailing**. Retailers are businesses which manage the exchange at the point where the customer makes the purchase. In effect, they are purchasing agents for customers. The act of *buying* is thus one of the retailer's most important functions. Indeed, an old retailing maxim holds that "a product well bought is half sold." The *buyer*—this is an official job title in most retail operations—must know the market well enough to be able to predict what consumers want and what price they will pay for it. Retailing is an important element of business around the globe. In 1992, total retail sales were $184.9 billion in Canada.

Retailers' knowledge of their customers' buying patterns has given them increasing clout in the distribution channel, as illustrated in the opening story, and much of this knowledge comes from data acquired at the point of sale through scanner systems. Manufacturers and other intermediaries are trying to gain access to this information by creating more valuable marketing relationships with retailers.

The newest concept in this struggle for control over distribution is *ECR*, which stands for *efficient consumer response*, a retailer/manufacturer partnership program that aims to cut costs out of the distribution pipeline.[3] In ECR programs manufacturers give promotional allowances to retailers based on what the stores actually sell to their customers during the promotional period rather than on what they buy from the manufacturer. ECR programs also try to cut unnecessary costs in the replenishment cycle and look at packaging design efficiencies, uniformity in case packing, and variety and duplication in product sizes.

For ECR programs to work, retailers must share their scanner data with manufacturers so they can be compensated for the changes and programs that succeeded in moving merchandise. ECR is important for manufacturers who are trying to win back some of their lost influence in the battle for shelf space, but ultimately, it will be good for both sides because it creates a relationship based on trust and accurate information.

In this section we'll look first at the value which retailers add to products. Then we discuss the classification of retail operations by product and price, including the important concept of the wheel of retailing. This is followed by a description of ownership categories. We conclude the section with some remarks on the changes going on in international retailing today. For a graph of the product life cycle of retailing, see Figure 15-1.

THE ADDED VALUE OF RETAILING

Most supermarkets, as well as gasoline stations and video stores, carry the same brands and their prices are nearly the same. So why do some consumers shop at one store rather than another? The answer is *added value*, the topic of chapter objective three. Added value is what each store offers consumers besides its boxes of detergent, its gasoline, or the latest movie video release. As Table 15-3 shows, the retailer adds something—cheaper prices, personal assistance, a wide selection of products, a convenient location—to the exchange that the consumer values. For that reason, retailers (as well as some types of wholesalers) are referred to as *value-added resellers* or *VARs*.

PRODUCT AND PRICE CATEGORIES

There are several ways to classify today's complex retailing industry, and these classifications are the focus of the fourth chapter objective. One common sys-

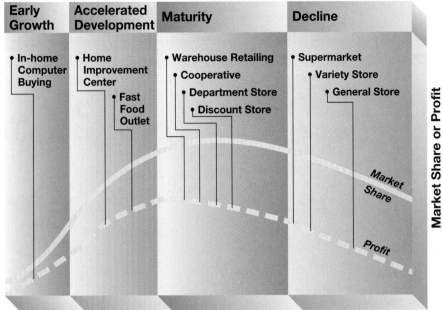

Early Growth

- In-home Computer Buying

Accelerated Development

- Home Improvement Center
- Fast Food Outlet

Maturity

- Warehouse Retailing
- Cooperative
- Department Store
- Discount Store

Decline

- Supermarket
- Variety Store
- General Store

Market Share

Profit

Market Share or Profit

Stage of Life Cycle

FIGURE 15-1
The Retail Life Cycle

Source: Berkowtz, Kerin, and Rudelius, *Marketing,* 2nd ed. Richard D. Irwin Inc., 1989.

tem classifies retailers by the breadth and depth of the product lines they handle. Another uses price as the criterion. In addition, the retail business can be described in terms of store location, ownership, and various aspects of retail strategy. Product and price categories are discussed here in the context of the changing retailing and wholesaling scene. The other three classifications are discussed in subsequent sections of the chapter.

For a particular purchase, consumers look either for retailers with an extensive selection within a product line—*depth*—or for retailers with a wide selection of products—*breadth* (see Figure 15-2). It is difficult for most stores to offer a merchandise mix that is both broad and deep, although we will discuss some newer types of stores that are trying to do just that. Selection is the first consideration in deciding where to shop, and it is second only to price as a purchase motivator in most buyers' decision making. It is stores' selection or

TABLE 15-3	THE ADDED VALUE OF RETAILING
Retailing Function	**Value to Customer**
Locations and parking	Convenience
Storage and inventory	Availability
Selection	Choice
Bulk buying	Lower prices
Display of merchandise	Opportunity to examine
Dressing rooms	Trial
Ambiance and atmosphere	Pleasurable experience
Store image	Familiarity, predictability
Sales clerks	Information, assistance, courtesy
Credit	Immediate purchase
Advertising	Product information

A Discount Store

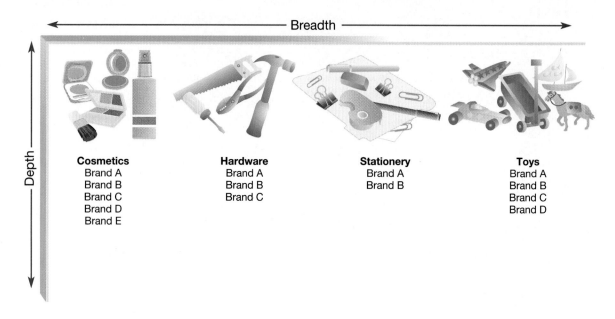

Breadth

Depth

Cosmetics
Brand A
Brand B
Brand C
Brand D
Brand E

Hardware
Brand A
Brand B
Brand C

Stationery
Brand A
Brand B

Toys
Brand A
Brand B
Brand C
Brand D

B Specialty Store: Athletic Shoes

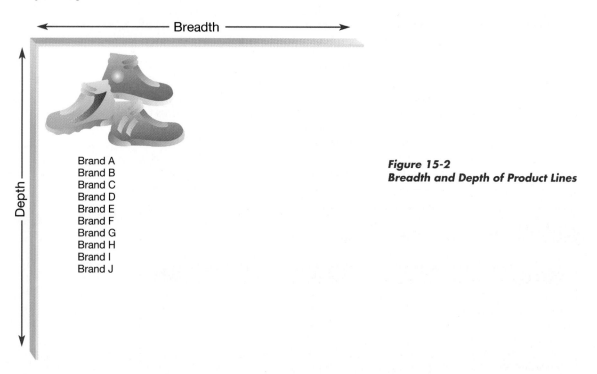

Breadth

Depth

Brand A
Brand B
Brand C
Brand D
Brand E
Brand F
Brand G
Brand H
Brand I
Brand J

Figure 15-2
Breadth and Depth of Product Lines

merchandise mix
The selection or assortment of products carried by a store.

assortment of merchandise—what retailers call their **merchandise mix**—that helps consumers distinguish one store from another.

Single-line stores, such as Mmmuffins, and *limited-line* stores that carry several related product lines, such as Tie Rack and Foot Locker, offer deep selection within a few product lines. In contrast, department stores like The Bay

	Store Type	Product Line		Pricing Strategy	Customer Service	Product Quality	Desirability of Location	Store Image
		Breadth	Depth					
Traditional Retailing	Department Store	Broad	Deep	Moderate	Moderate/High	Moderate	Moderate	Moderate
	Discount Store	Broad	Shallow	Low	Low	Low/Moderate	Low/Moderate	Low
	Specialty Store	Narrow	Deep	Moderate/High	Moderate/High	High	High	High
	Superstore	Narrow	Very deep	Low/Moderate	Low	Moderate/High	Low	Low
	Off-Price Store	Moderately broad	Deep	Low	Low	Moderate/High	Moderate	Low
	Hypermarket	Broad	Deep	Low	Low	Low/Moderate	Low/Moderate	Low/Moderate
	Supermarket	Broad	Deep	Moderate	Low	Moderate/High	Low	Low
	Convenience Store	Narrow	Shallow	High	Low	Moderate	Moderate	Low
Wholesale Retailing	Warehouse Store	Very broad	Moderately deep	Low	Low	Low/High	Low	Low
	Factory Store	Narrow	Deep	Low	Low	Low/High	Moderate	Moderate/High

Figure 15-3
Retailing Strategies (Retailing Mix)

and Eaton's, supermarkets like Safeway, and discount stores like Kmart offer broad selections.

Some retailers have broadened their selection in recent years through *scrambled marketing*—carrying a wide mix of unrelated items whose only point of similarity is high-volume sales. Thus, in addition to prescription and over-the-counter drugs, many drugstores now carry garden implements, cosmetics, personal-care products, some groceries, hardware, housewares, records and tapes, photo supplies, and small appliances. The only thing holding this merchandise mix together is the expectation that the unrelated product lines will produce both high sales volume and high profit. Figure 15-3 shows the breadth and depth of product lines in discount and specialty stores.

Department Stores Traditional **department stores**—large retail firms that handle a variety of general product lines organized into departments such as appliances, clothing, cosmetics, furniture, housewares, hardware, and jewelry—are being attacked from all sides in today's highly competitive retailing climate. Many department store chains are in serious financial trouble. Some that were legendary have already disappeared—such as Vancouver-based Woodward's, which offered a very high level of customer service.

The remaining department stores have devised various strategies for survival. After decades of catering to affluent older customers who can afford Chanel suits and $800 Valentino shirts, the elegant Holt Renfrew has been compelled to broaden its appeal. Sears has repositioned itself as a "value merchant" in an effort to compete with the dynamic growth of chains like Wal-Mart and Zellers. So far its *everyday low-price (EDLP)* strategy has had only mixed results. Decades ago New York's venerable Ohrbach's tried this type of strategy: it downgraded to appeal to the value-oriented customer, and in the process lost its original loyal upscale customers. The strategy did not attract enough new customers, and now there is no Ohrbach's.

Another survival strategy used by some big department stores is the specialty store approach. Harrod's in London, England, for example, is no longer a department store but a collection of specialty shops. This "galleria" ap-

department stores
A retail store which is large in sales area square footage and is departmentalized, selling a wide variety of product lines grouped by product class.

proach came in from Europe. Sears has experimented with specialty departments, including Mainframe for juniors and McKids, a joint venture with McDonald's that opened in 1988 and closed in 1991. Since the late 1980s, American discount giant J. C. Penney's strategy has been to widen its apparel selection to include higher-fashion merchandise and to eliminate electronics, sporting goods, and photography equipment. This strategy has made Penney's the largest fashion-oriented department store chain—or, some would say, specialty chain—in the United States.

Department store retailing is in flux elsewhere in the world. GUM, Moscow's state-run turn-of-the-century retail shopping arcade with arched glass roofs, central fountain, and balconies, is now seeking to shake off the effects of the last seventy years of state management. Under elegant roofs it is no more than a bazaar rather than the showpiece department store of a superpower. It has yet to address the demands of the twentieth century.

Successful department stores all over the world are those that are able to identify a merchandising strategy that appeals to today's customers. Bloomingdale's is known for turning the shopping experience into theater. Nordstrom's has taken the concept of customer service to the limit. The largest department store chain in Japan, Mitsukoshi, has been bringing Zen culture to the art of shopping as it expands around the world. Harrod's in London, the largest department store in the world, offers a wide array of merchandise from around the world in its 25 acres of retail space and is now opening outlets in airport shopping locations around the world.

discount stores
Retailers that offer reduced services and lowest possible prices on a wide array of branded goods.

wheel of retailing
The retailing cycle in which new types of retailers enter the market at the price scale's low end and, as they develop more services, offer more upscale products, and raise their prices, new stores replace them at the low end.

Discount Stores Kmart and Zellers have been attracting so many traditional department store customers in recent years, and recently, Wal-Mart has expanded into Canada. A broad product mix—everything from apparel to appliances to automotive supplies—is typical of **discount stores**. In order to offer the low prices that attract their clientele, discount stores have to trade off some other aspect of retailing—usually service. Most discounters use self-service and do not provide delivery. To further reduce overhead, discounters may operate in spartan quarters in low-rent areas. However, since they draw customers from a wide area, good parking facilities are usually crucial.

Price, an important element in positioning any retailer in the minds of consumers, is crucial for discount stores. As Figure 15-4 shows, a study of 120,000 consumers covering 11 retail categories found that price was the single most important determinant of consumer store choices. Discount stores have been charging ahead of the field because of their low prices, but, interestingly, an opposite trend is also at work. Kmart, for instance, has been moving upscale by refurbishing its stores and adding quality brand merchandise, a strategy that is making it look more like a department store.

A theory called the **wheel of retailing**—illustrated in Figure 15-5 and the focus of chapter objective five—describes this pattern in which stores move upscale. The theory of retailing life cycles holds that new types of retailers tend to enter the market at the low end of the pricing scale and then, as they develop more services and offer more upscale products and more services, they gradually increase their prices. As their expenses and prices rise, they vacate the space at the low end of the retailing wheel, which new retailers move into. This experience is repeated until the original retailer becomes a full-service store and confronts the kind of competitor it was when it originally entered the market.[4]

Wal-Mart has built its spectacular success on being the first retailer to bring discount stores to rural North America, where it also put many small mom-and-pop stores out of business. There is a backlash to Wal-Mart in many

Figure 15-4
Reasons for Choosing a Store

Source: Based on Judith Graham, "Walking the Slippery Retail Tightrope," Advertising Age, April 24, 1988, p. 36.

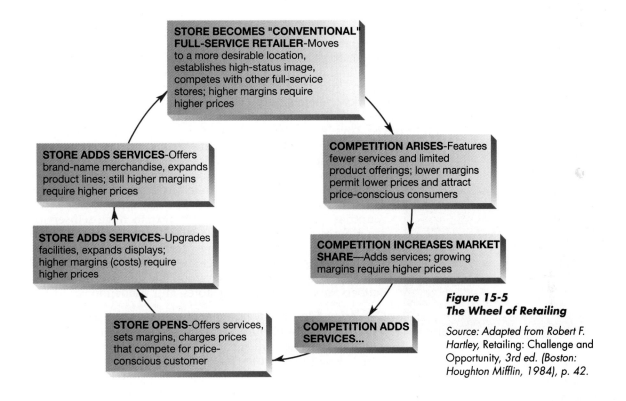

STORE BECOMES "CONVENTIONAL" FULL-SERVICE RETAILER-Moves to a more desirable location, establishes high-status image, competes with other full-service stores; higher margins require higher prices

STORE ADDS SERVICES-Offers brand-name merchandise, expands product lines; still higher margins require higher prices

STORE ADDS SERVICES-Upgrades facilities, expands displays; higher margins (costs) require higher prices

STORE OPENS-Offers services, sets margins, charges prices that compete for price-conscious customer

COMPETITION ADDS SERVICES...

COMPETITION INCREASES MARKET SHARE—Adds services; growing margins require higher prices

COMPETITION ARISES-Features fewer services and limited product offerings; lower margins permit lower prices and attract price-conscious consumers

Figure 15-5
The Wheel of Retailing

Source: Adapted from Robert F. Hartley, Retailing: Challenge and Opportunity, *3rd ed. (Boston: Houghton Mifflin, 1984), p. 42.*

communities, whose leaders feel that when these giant stores move in and dominate local markets, they destroy the downtowns of small towns.[5]

Specialty Stores The most common type of retail store is the **specialty store**, which focuses narrowly on one product or line. Specialty stores are "hot" in shopping malls, where they often occupy 60 to 70 percent of total mall space. Fashion-oriented specialty stores are often called *boutiques*. Some well-known specialty stores are Louis Vuitton, Baskin Robbins, Purdy's, The Gap, and, of course, Benetton.

specialty store
A store that focuses narrowly on one product or line.

Specialty stores have entered virtually every category of goods offered by the traditional department store, including apparel, which is the most profitable department in the traditional department store. In fact, retail analysts report that mass merchandisers like department stores have been losing market share to specialty stores since the early 1980s. But specialty stores have to work to keep ahead of the market. Fairweather is a good example of the processes depicted in the wheel of retailing. Building on its early success as a small outlet geared toward teens, Fairweather transformed itself into a polished store with the ambiance of a European boutique that woos older, more affluent fashion-conscious customers. Surprisingly, the largest retail menswear store in the world, according to the Guinness Book of Records, is Slater's in Glasgow, Scotland. Slater took over a large textile warehouse and has no retail window space and is not in a mall. Word of mouth about quality and keen prices more than compensated for a weak promotion budget.

Superstores Large specialty **superstores** like Toys 'R' Us and Office Depot, which sell toys and office furniture, have taken much business away from department stores. Sears is trying to counter superstore competitors with Brand Central, a department that features a collection of brand-name appliances and electronics selling alongside Sears' venerable Kenmore label. So far

superstores
Large-scale, high-volume specialty stores.

487

supermarket
A moderately large, fairly focused retail food store that stresses self-service and low prices.

convenience stores
Small retail stores offering a limited selection of convenience items at a convenient location that are open longer hours and so charge for that added convenience.

Sears has had some success in competing with appliance and electronics superstores with this strategy.

These new superstores are breaking old retailing rules by featuring both tremendous breadth and depth of merchandise. They are able to do this by tackling one category, such as electronics, toys, or furniture, and serving it with exhaustive stocks of merchandise. They are called *category killers* because they tend to destroy smaller competitors, who simply can't compete on either selection or price.[6] Toys 'R' Us, one of the first and most successful category killers, stocks some 15,000 items in the toy category alone. IKEA, the huge contemporary Scandinavian furniture retailer, already has stores in the 155,000-square-foot range, and is planning new stores with as much as 250,000 square feet—which is equal to five football fields. Ikea's 119 stores in 24 countries feature large showrooms next to huge self-service warehouses. Sportmart, a Chicago-based sporting goods chain, offers 70 models of sleeping bags, 265 styles of athletic socks, and 12,000 varieties of shoes. One element of Kmart's growth strategy is to create its own group of superstores such as Builders Square, Payless Drug Stores, and Waldenbooks.

Off-Price Stores   By bringing discounting to brand and designer fashions and other consumer-goods markets, off-price retailing is hitting hard at the very market on which the traditional department stores have lately become so dependent. Off-price retailers like Winners buy designer labels or well-known brands at prices below wholesale and pass the savings on to customers. Because the merchandise is usually excess production or overstock, inventory is unpredictable and changes rapidly. The stores provide a minimum of services. At Loehmann's, for example, customers must try on clothes in a common room rather than in a private dressing room.

Supermarkets   The grocery industry equivalent of the department store also on a stage of product life cycle maturity is the **supermarket**. These low-margin, high-turnover, self-service retail stores offer an average of 15,000 food and non-food items in a variety of departments—meats, baked goods, cleaning products, beauty supplies, fresh flowers, and so forth. Suburban supermarkets are characterized by large size—the average is 25,000 square feet—and expansive parking lots that accommodate the many customers who come from beyond the store's immediate neighborhood. Checkout is centralized and located at the main entrance.

Convenience Stores   Often open seven days a week and twenty-four hours a day, **convenience stores** such as 7-Eleven usually serve a neighborhood clientele or a high-traffic area, such as a busy intersection, where they offer easy access and parking. They provide rapid checkout and a limited range of high-turnover convenience items that are purchased for emergency needs, fast meals, or on impulse.

Hypermarkets   A contemporary trend in retailing is the move toward bigger stores that carry a wider and wider range of merchandise, often combining the kinds of items sold in discount stores with those found in supermarkets. In the 1970s European retailers came up with the *hypermarché* in France and *verbrauchermarkts* in Germany—enormous self-service combination food and general-merchandise stores occupying as much as 250,000 square feet of space. The concept has recently been introduced into North America in the form of **hypermarkets**.

OWNERSHIP CATEGORIES

Another way to classify retail operations is by store ownership. Originally, retail stores were independently owned and operated. In recent years, however, the worldwide trend has been toward multiple store ownership and control. Today many retail stores belong to chains or are franchises or cooperatives.

Chain Store A group of retail subsidiaries with many locations is termed a **chain store**. Chain stores often have lower costs than other retailers because they can take advantage of economies of scale obtained from centralized decision making and volume purchasing. The chain offers consistent merchandise, store policies, promotional activities, and staff training. Global retail chains are beginning to appear. Toys 'R' Us, for instance, now has stores in West Germany, the United Kingdom, Singapore, Hong Kong, and Japan in addition to its U.S. and Canadian stores. Kmart is in Australia, McDonald's in Moscow, The Gap and Esprit in London, Kentucky Fried Chicken in Beijing, and Red Lobster in Japan.

Although some chains remain quite successful as they expand, others that grow to dozens of stores become bureaucratic. In acquiring many layers of management, these stores because of their centralization become slower at decision making and often lose touch with their customers.

Franchises Today, franchising is common not only in the fast-food industry but also in such other industries as hotels (Holiday Inn and Days Inn) and tax preparation (H&R Block). A **franchise** is a contract between a franchiser (parent company) and a franchisee (an individual or firm) that gives the franchisee the privilege of operating a business of a certain type that was developed by the franchiser in return for a fee plus royalties on sales and an agreement to adhere to certain franchise-wide policies and practices. The agreement spells out the duties and responsibilities of franchiser and franchisee.

The contract stipulates that certain marketing functions must be standardized and coordinated without duplication. In addition to the initial fee, the franchisee pays royalties on sales and rental or lease fees for franchiser-provided equipment, and, in some cases, purchases supplies from the franchiser. In return, the local franchisee gets a recognized brand name backed up by management systems, national advertising, complete operations manuals, and ongoing assistance in site selection, building plans, store setups, and staff training.

Franchises are a very popular way of owning a small business today, but prospective franchisees should beware because there has lately been an increase in fraudulent franchises. Unsuspecting entrepreneurs can lose a lot of money by signing up for a business opportunity that turns out to be far less attractive than described.[7]

More than any other policy or practice, ensuring *consistency* in all the major things each retail unit does is what keeps a franchise system successful. McDonald's, probably the world's best-known franchiser, is fanatical about maintaining a consistent level of quality in every McDonald's restaurant. Consumers know that they can order a consistently reliable Big Mac the world over, and it is that consumer confidence, plus all the systems and procedures behind it, which franchisees buy into when they sign on with McDonald's. However, like other franchisers that operate internationally, especially in the food and hotel industry, McDonald's has learned to adapt in some ways to local cultures. In Germany, for example, you can get a beer with your Big Mac and in France, wine.

One of Kentucky Fried Chicken's most successful franchisees is in Malaysia. In addition to having good distribution through its stores, this franchisee raises and processes its own chickens to maximize the quality of its

489
WHOLESALING
AND RETAILING

hypermarkets
Large stores with broad product lines that often combine the merchandise of discount stores with that of grocery supermarkets.

chain store
A group of stores offering many different locations.

franchise
A contract between a franchiser (parent company) and a franchisee (an individual or firm) that allows the franchisee to operate a business developed by the franchiser in return for a management fee, royalties on sales and adherence to franchise-wide policies and practices.

product. This vertical integration of operations and sourcing eliminates a lot of intermediaries in addition to providing extra quality control. The Maylaysian franchisee recently opened a chain of chicken delis where fresh chicken, along with salads and other KFC extras, can be bought.

cooperative
A business owned by the customers it serves.

trade cooperative
A group of independent businesses which join together to facilitate centralized volume buying and distribution.

Cooperatives Consumers sometimes join together to form **cooperatives** that purchase and sell products (for an example, see the case in Chapter 5). Some retail stores lso group themselves into what are called **trade cooperatives**. The Independent Grocers Association, is a good example. All member stores of IGA are independent, but they do certain things together, like cooperative buying to obtain volume discounts and collaborative promotions.

INTERNATIONAL RETAILING

International retailing is retailing activity by an organization that crosses na-

BEHIND THE SCENES

A MARRIAGE OF CONVENIENCE[8]

Innovations in Customer Service

Japanese customers can pay household bills at their neighborhood 7-Eleven. Recent merchandising innovations include "Shop America"—a catalog service specializing in imported luxury goods like Rolex watches and a variety of items from Tiffany and Cartier.

It's not the first American idea that the Japanese have borrowed, modified, and shipped back to the United States in better shape than they found it. That is precisely what 7-Eleven Japan is doing for Dallas-based Southland Corporation, the chain that virtually invented the business of serving on-the-go consumers.

Ito-Yokado, Japan's most profitable retailer, purchased the rights to franchise Southland's 7-Eleven convenience stores in 1973. It now has over 4,300 stores in Japan and 57 in Hawaii. Not surprisingly, Ito-Yokado runs its stores a little differently. Some of those differences, of course, reflect culture—in addition to magazines and milk, Japanese 7-Elevens offer sushi and dumplings, boiled tofu, and sliced octopus.

Unquestionably, though, 7-Eleven Japan's most important innovation is its computerized inventory-control system. Using a sophisticated point-of-sale (POS) system, managers can make extremely precise decisions about what to stock and how much to charge. In any given store, the manager can punch up full-color graphs detailing sales patterns for every item sold there, including the sex and age of buyers. With a portable terminal, the manager can stroll down the aisles preparing next week's purchase orders and taking inventory at the same time.

Naturally, all of this valuable marketing information is relayed directly to company headquarters, where a finely tuned *just-in-time inventory* system allows the company to distribute supplies precisely when and where they're needed. Its POS system has helped Ito-Yokado transform retailing into a very profitable information business. Although 7-Eleven Japan outlets are one-half the size and carry one-third the inventory of their American counterparts, they sell twice as much.

490

Even more important, Ito-Yokado's POS system has freed up an immense cash flow for expansion. This has allowed Ito-Yokado to purchase a 70 percent share of Southland Corporation—once its parent company. It remains to be seen how well the American franchisees will adapt to the Japanese system of retail-distribution management. It also remains to be seen how well Ito-Yokado's management system will adapt to the American retail environment. In the United States, where 7-Eleven stores are spaced out over a much larger area, the new Japanese partner will find it harder to maintain the heavy distribution schedules that pose few difficulties in densely populated Japan.

tional boundaries. The biggest change in international retailing today involves the gradual dissolution of the old colonial retailing structure and its replacement by new global retailers who are extending their business across national boundaries.

Basically, a retailer has two things to offer to consumers: a selection of goods at certain price points, and the overall manner of offering these goods in the store setting. Many retailing practices are tied to local cultures. However, innovations can spread to international markets if they serve a broad need. For example, supermarkets, which were a product of the post-World War II suburbanization of North America, exist today in virtually all industrialized countries and are rapidly spreading in newly industrialized countries. Similarly, the French innovation of hypermarkets has spread worldwide. The next major thrust may arise out of online computer shopping, when location of outlet is no longer an important variable.

RETAIL STRATEGY

Retailers make many of the same strategic decisions that manufacturers make—segmenting, targeting, and positioning—as well as determining the best retailing mix. In addition, contemporary retailers are involved in complex business processes that demand a high level of management sophistication. These are the elements of retailing referred to in chapter objective six.

An owner of a truck stop, for example, must make decisions on all of the previously mentioned strategic factors as well as determine what types of retail services and service levels will be provided at what competitive price points. The ubiquitous truck stop, in fact, is an incredibly complex business that does a lot more than sell gas. Typically, it has a restaurant and snack bar, a gift shop, a convenience food store, and services such as sleeping rooms and showers. The more farsighted establishments maintain service departments, parts shops, and tire stores, all of which are profit centers and may be run as separate businesses. Some truck stops also lease space to supporting retailers, such as Radio Shack franchisees.

THE RETAILING MIX

Retailing mix describes how *price* and *selection* are traded off against other retail factors—*service, location, store personality and ambiance, marketing communication,* and *quality*—to form an overall store image, create value for the customer, and produce profits for the retailer. Figure 15-5 shows how different types of stores vary in the strategic areas of price, service, product quality, location, and store image, as well as in the breadth and depth of their product lines.

Service   In retailing, the word *service* describes the personal attention and amenities a store provides to its customers. Most stores offer at least some services. The help of a trained sales staff, for example, adds value for consumers buying cars or men's suits. Other types of retail services are credit, gift wrapping, installation, and tailoring. Some major stores and shopping centers even offer child care services so parents can shop without distraction.

But more service isn't always better service—especially if consumers view it as adding to the price. As the rise of self-service stores attests, consumers are in many cases willing to forgo services in order to obtain lower prices. In short, service is generally not a primary factor in selecting a store. Still, it can be the tie-breaker that prompts a customer to choose one retailer over another, otherwise similar retailer. It is also critical for building customer loyalty.

Location   Even though today's consumer is highly mobile, the convenience of location is still one of the top criteria people use in choosing where to shop. This is especially true for food, drug, gasoline, and discount stores that sell primarily mass-consumption products.

Retailers have learned that when stores are grouped together, there is a synergistic effect: the complex of stores attracts more people than any one store would in a stand-alone location. This is the underlying idea of shopping malls, which are now successfully spreading around the world.

Because mall owners have found that people can be lured from farther away and stay three times longer in malls where there are amusement facilities, many malls are adding rides, magic shows, exhibits, and special-interest shows. The largest mall in the world is still the West Edmonton Mall at 5.2 million square feet and over 800 retail stores, eleven major department stores, over 150 restaurants and kiosks, the world's largest indoor amusement park with 25 rides, a seven acre waterpark, an NHL-size ice arena, four seaworthy submarines, an exact replica of the Santa Maria ship, a dolphin show, world class aquarium facilities, an aviary, a 360 room hotel, a miniature golf course, 19 movie theatres, a casino, original art and sculpture, 58 entrances, and parking for 20,000 vehicles.

Location is not important for nonstore retail operations. Products offered house-to-house through personal sales such as Electrolux vacuum cleaners and Mary Kay cosmetics (see Chapter 21), as well as retail services such as plumbers, electricians, and carpet cleaners, can be located anywhere, since the service itself is performed at the customer's location. Direct marketing is another type of nonstore retailing that operates independently of location (see Chapter 20). Although we have used the term *retail store* through much of this chapter, remember that retailing is a much broader concept than a business location.

Personality and Ambiance   Most successful stores have distinct images—store "personalities"—that are a result of many factors besides price and quality.[9] Retailers often talk about *atmosphere* or *ambiance*, when describing their image. Atmosphere reflects the environment both outside and inside the store; it includes window displays, signage, decor, furniture, store layout, lighting, sounds such as music, and even scents. Contrast the image you have of Laura Ashley stores with the image you carry of the women's clothing section at Kmart. The differences are partly tangible—the arrangement of merchandise, the signs and banners, the materials and textures of counters and displays. Some differences, however, are intangible—the feeling of warmth and friendliness, excitement, or haughtiness—and these are as much a part of the store's personality as its physical ambiance.

Marketing Communication   A store's image—as well as other information about merchandise for sale—is communicated largely through advertising and in-store promotional materials. The ad in Exhibit 15-1 shows how advertising can enhance the image of a store like Sainsburys British supermarket chain. True, most retail advertising is geared toward price and sales promotion, but keep in mind that *every* ad makes an image statement. In an interesting twist on retail store design, Nike and other companies are using their stores to push their brand image rather than their products. The Nike Town store on Chicago's Magnificent Mile has been described in *Forbes* as half art gallery and half walk-in ad.[10]

Another objective of most retail advertising is to generate *store traffic*. Retailers know that if they can lure customers into their stores by advertising extremely low prices on a few items or by promising free samples, their odds of making a sale of something else are good. Stores' **loss leaders**—products with special reduced prices, often below profit margins—attract customers but usually, once inside, customers find themselves trading up to a higher priced product than the one which brought them in the first place.

Quality   Service, location, marketing communication, merchandise selec-

loss leader
A product with a special reduced price, often below the profit margin, that is used to draw customers into a store where usually, customers will trade-up to a higher priced product.

In Italy this fine olive oil is only sold by one long established family business. Just like in Britain.

The Archibusacci's have much in common with Sainsbury's.

Both businesses, for example, are run with the sort of care that only comes with generations of tradition.

But while Sainsbury's is 122 years old, the Archibusacci family has been making and selling olive oil since 1700.

Continuing a tradition in the village of Canino near the Tuscan border that dates back to Etruscan times.

The Canino Olive is small and matures slowly. And Sainsbury's Extra Virgin Olive Oil Di Canino comes from olives grown on the thousands of trees surrounding the village. (Some are over 300 years old.) It is made from the first cold pressing of the olives which takes place within 24 hours of picking.

Nothing is added to it at any stage.

It is a rich dark green colour. And intensely fruity in flavour.

Perfect in salad dressings or as a marinade.

The same oil, in fact, that's been enjoyed for hundreds of years by families all over Italy.

Thanks to Sainsbury's, it can now be enjoyed by yours.

Good food costs less at Sainsburys.

Exhibit 15-1
Tradition Travels Well

This ad ties Sainsbury's long-established reputation for high-quality foods to the 200-year-old family-owned Tuscan business that produces Sainsbury's finest Italian olive oil.

493

Nike's Brand Art Gallery

In a new program of image making, companies like Nike are using their stores to attract customers and showcase their goods as art.

tion, and price all come together when consumers make a decision about quality and what to buy. As we have noted repeatedly throughout this text, consumers generally try to get the best quality they can afford. In other words, quality is relative—it is evaluated in relation to price, and the best value is maximum quality for minimum price. In developing a retailing strategy, then, firms must consider all aspects of what they offer—and what they propose to charge customers. For example, The Bay offers high-quality products in a very pleasant atmosphere with high service levels; Kmart offers lower-quality products in a less pleasant atmosphere with limited service and lower prices.

BEHIND THE SCENES

BENETTON'S TOTAL MARKETING

In the early days Benetton sold directly to small specialty shops. Now this total marketing company sells its merchandise directly to Benetton shops and knows exactly what is selling and who is buying it. Shop owners are not Benetton employees—they are franchisees. The hand-picked store owners, however, must agree to sell only Benetton products. In this way, the family-owned company maintains control over information, inventory, and distribution.

Benetton subcontracts about 80 percent of its manufacturing work to regional factories in Europe, Asia, and North and South America. So Benetton isn't really a manufacturer or a retailer; it *directs* the manufacture of its goods and their sale. In other words, what Benetton does is pure marketing—that is, it controls product design, the information needed to keep its fashion ahead of trends, pricing, and promotion. Most of all, it controls distribution.

Although they are not employees, both factory subcontractors and shop owners are considered part of the Benetton family. Luciano Benetton explains: "We work with people on a human level, people we like. Our rapport is one of trust in the handshake, of faith in each other and what we're doing. That's the secret of our company strength." That company strength has been tested at times, particularly in recent years as Benetton retailers have questioned the wisdom of the stances the company has taken on social issues in its controversial advertising (see Chapter 18 box on "Advertising that 'Makes a Statement'"). In the United States the number of Benetton stores dropped from 700 in 1986 to 250 in 1993, with many store owners citing the controversial advertising as the reason they lost business and were forced to close up shop. The number of Bennettons in Canada has also declined recently. In the first half of 1994, the number of Canadian Bennettons dropped from 30 to 27.[11]

COORDINATION AND CONTROL

Sometimes wholesaling and retailing are separate functions, but sometimes, as we saw in Chapter 14, the manufacturer, retailer, or wholesaler controls the entire process, an arrangement called a vertical marketing system. Within such a system a process of *vertical integration* enables a firm like Benetton (see the previous section) to control all of its business functions—manufacturing, distribution, retailing—and even the services of its outside suppliers. Benetton's high-tech electronic information network has revolutionized the clothing industry, and as a result of its great success in international fashion the company has been called a "total marketing company."

Factory Outlets To counter the growing power of retailers that we discussed in the chapter opening story, some manufacturers have created a special form of off-price store called a *factory outlet*. A **factory outlet** is a retail operation that is owned and stocked by a manufacturer. Originally, manufacturers used these outlets to carry discontinued lines, overstocks, and second-quality goods. Today they are serious retail stores for other forms of sale merchandise and highly profitable for the manufacturer, who can control both retail and distribution expenses.

Burlington Coat Factory and Polly Flinders Factory Stores are two prominent factory outlet store chains. These stores frequently cluster in "factory outlet malls" that are near tourist destinations.

Warehouse Retailing Wholesalers have also moved into the retail arena. Computerland and Radio Shack are two merchant wholesalers that specialize in a product area but also operate their own retail outlets. The biggest and most visible type of warehouse retailer is the members-only **warehouse**

factory outlet
A retail store owned by and selling the goods of a particular manufacturer, usually seconds and overstocked items.

warehouse club
A low-price retail store that sells only to members.

shelf management
Getting maximum sales from every square foot of shelf and display space in the store.

shelf facings
The numbers of units of a product visible at the front of a retail store shelf.

club, where customers must acquire membership (for which requirements vary) in order to shop at the store. Products as varied as furniture, office supplies, auto supplies, and food are stacked high and piled deep in a warehouse-like room as big as several football fields. High-volume purchasing is encouraged, particularly in the categories of groceries and packaged goods. A spartan environment, a low-rent location, and a de-emphasis on national brands keeps costs and prices low.

The boom in "members only" warehouse clubs—like Price Club/Costco, Kmart's Place, and Wal-Mart's Sam's Club—is stealing customers not only from department stores but also from supermarkets. Some analysts predict that North Americans will become accustomed to making large grocery purchases at these warehouse clubs, with traditional supermarkets filling the role of convenience stores.

RETAIL INVENTORY MANAGEMENT

Wholesaling and retailing are increasingly dynamic components of the distribution channel. Since the 1990s, the push has been to improve productivity and cut costs by doing a better job of managing inventory and shelf space and by developing partnerships with others in the distribution channel.

Shelf Management   The basic concept of **shelf management** is to get maximum sales from every cubic foot of shelf and display space in the store. Many larger stores now use advanced EDI systems (discussed in Chapter 14) for shelf management. Hypermarkets, for example, would be unmanageable without computerized systems.

Every store that carries physical products must consider how much inventory it needs to have within the store (a combination of what's on the display shelves and what's in the back room), how much should be out on the "floor" (displayed in the area open to customers), and when reorders should be made and in what quantity. In supermarkets, superstores, and hypermarkets, which may carry 20,000 to 35,000 products, stocking shelves is a complex and time-consuming staff function. Space is valuable, and although stores can't afford to overstock an item, they also can't afford to be out of stock. There's an old saying from the days of the horse-and-wagon peddler that's still apt: "You can't sell from an empty wagon."

Shelf Facings   Manufacturers who supply supermarkets and discount stores are particularly concerned about the number of their packages that a customer can see at one time—that is, the number of **shelf facings**. If Heinz has three bottles of its family-size ketchup showing, it has three facings (though there may be a dozen more bottles behind these three). The more facings, the larger the "billboard effect."

High-volume categories such as soft drinks and cereal get many facings, with how much space each brand within the category receives generally determined by the brand's market share. Stores that have their own *private labels* (see Chapter 10), on which gross margins are

Get It for Yourself, Wholesale

The American-based Costco first opened in October 1985, and now there are 43 Costcos across the country. Through buying and selling in bulk and spending almost nothing on advertising, Costco keeps its prices extremely low, but customers must purchase an annual membership (at $35 plus G.S.T.) to shop there. In total, Costco sells 3500 different products, including groceries, automotive supplies, hardware, and office supplies.

generally higher, often give these brands slightly more and better space than they would deserve based on their market share.

Because shelf space is so important, most retailers charge manufacturers a special fee for agreeing to display a new item. As we noted in Chapter 13, these fees, called *slotting allowances*, are very common when new products are introduced. Their function is to assure retailers that they will not lose money by carrying an untried product. Critics charge that slotting allowances keep the new products of small companies out of the market. (For more on this subject, see the case at the end of Chapter 14.)

The Cost-Control Battle As we have seen in this chapter and in Chapter 14, in an age of shrinking profit margins, the pressure is on wholesalers to form "partnerships" with producers and sellers of products to help everyone become more competitive. Hughes Aircraft, the big defense contractor, has narrowed its list of suppliers of electronic components from twenty-two to seven. The advantages of these partnerships for surviving suppliers are more business and a more important position on the Hughes team. The advantage for Hughes is a lot more leverage on costs. Many other companies involved in quality programs are taking the same route. The ad in Exhibit 15-2 describes IBM's efforts to arrange partnerships in the computing industry.

Manufacturers and retailers are also under pressure to work together despite the tug-of-war between them for control of the shelf. As mentioned earlier, retailers who used to bow to the demands of big manufacturers like P&G for prime shelf space now find themselves able to charge slotting fees for access to that valuable space. In highly competitive environments retailers are in the "retail real estate" business of selling valuable shelf space (directly and indirectly) to manufacturers.

With 1,800 stores and more than $50 billion in sales, Wal-Mart is a channel captain *par excellence* and can engage in *category management* activities. The company raised a storm in 1993 when it demanded customized marketing plans and detailed information on all brand strategies from a small trial group of manufacturers who wished to do business with the retailer.

Exhibit 15-2
Building Inter-Species
Relationships

**Creating partnerships
is an important part of
relationship
marketing. This ad
explains how IBM
hopes to bring
suppliers, distributors,
and technologies
together.**

Although Wal-Mart eventually dropped its demand, the trend is still toward closer partnerships between marketers and retailers, whether forced or voluntary.[12]

On a more positive note, P&G is experimenting with TV advertising that will let it customize commercials to include local retailers' names. Called The Bonus Media Program, the plan's objective is to boost brand sales while increasing the retailer's store traffic. Kraft General Foods and Borden are also revamping their operations to develop retailer-specific promotions that build the retailer's brand image as well as the product's.

BOTTOM LINE REALITIES

IS THERE HOPE FOR SEARS?[13]

It's no secret that department stores that try to function as mass merchandisers selling a variety of products to a variety of customers are a dying breed. The major reason is that the retail marketplace in North America has changed. Older people, who are loyal department store customers, tend to make fewer shopping trips and visit fewer stores, while younger people, who value selection and low prices, are more likely to shop in specialty stores, superstores, and discount stores.

Perhaps the most troubled department store today is Sears, the largest retail chain in the world—though no longer the largest retailer in the United States since it was overtaken by Wal-Mart in the early 1990s, at least partly because of Wal-Mart's superior distribution system. For years, Sears has been losing market share to specialty and discount stores, and since the 1970s, it has given up 15 percent of the worldwide retail market to its largest competitors. Many analysts refer to Sears as a "department store dinosaur."

One problem is that its expenses are higher than those of its rivals. According to *The Wall Street Journal*, 30 cents of every dollar from Sears' retail sales has been eaten up by expenses—compared to 23 cents at Kmart and 16 cents at Wal-Mart. Another problem is that just as the superstores have been making inroads into Sears' electronics and hardware lines, the specialty stores have been hurting its apparel lines. Sears has long had great brand names in its Craftsman and Kenmore lines, but it has been very slow to emphasize brand marketing.

Sears has also shown great weakness in inventory management. While its competitors were installing state-of-the-art computerized systems to minutely manage their inventories. Sears' corporate-wide buyers were finding it impossible to tell how certain products were selling in various regions. As a result of this sloppy inventory tracking system, Sears was slow to react to sales patterns and consumer trends.

Struggling to Find a Strategy

In the early 1990s Sears tried to engineer a turnaround by jumping on the everyday low price (EDLP) bandwagon. But it wasn't enough to stop the flow of red ink.

In order to improve sales and profits, Sears Canada has made several changes, including improved customer service training, a new concentration on apparel and cosmetics, new management team members, a 1-800 line for catalog orders, new advertising programs, new marketing techniques aimed at specific market groups, and reduced costs throughout all of the company's operations. Also, Sears began accepting third-party credit—VISA, Mastercard, and American Express—in addition to Sears and Discover Cards.

Sears is engaged in a desperate struggle for survival in which it has stripped itself of unprofitable businesses, undertaken much-needed store renovations, and drastically changed its marketing strategy. What other strategies might the company consider to restore itself to a healthy operation with a strong market position? ▼

KEY POINTS SUMMARY ▼

1. Wholesalers add value to a product by acting as representatives for manufacturers, by offering technical assistance to customers, by providing manufacturers with market information, and by splitting large quantities of goods into smaller lots and making stocks of goods available on short notice.

2. There are three types of wholesalers, and they differ from one another mainly in degree of independence and whether or not they take title to the goods they handle. Manufacturer wholesalers maintain their own distribution and sales offices for the products they produce. Merchant wholesalers, both full-service and limited-service, take title to and ship goods. Agents and brokers merely arrange for sales and have goods shipped directly to customers.

3. Retailers add value to products by acting as purchasing agents for customers and by adding something of importance to the exchange, such as personal assistance, convenience, or cheaper prices.

4. Retail operations may be classified according to product line, price, store location, ownership, and retailing strategy.

5. The wheel of retailing describes a pattern in which new firms offer few services and low prices, then gradually add services and raise prices in an upscale move until a new firm takes their old place at the low end of the pricing scale and the cycle repeats itself.

6. In developing a retail strategy, marketers must balance price and selection against store personality and ambiance, marketing communication, location, service, and quality to create an overall store image, value for consumers, and profits for the retailer.

7. In the battle for control over distribution costs and shelf space, new partnerships—as well as new retail forms—are being developed among retailers, wholesalers, and manufacturers.

8. Two significant trends in wholesaling and retailing today are the tendency of many wholesalers to move into retailing and the growing power of retailers to control the manufacturers who supply them. These and other changes are exerting pressure on manufacturers, on wholesalers and other intermediaries, and on sellers to work together in partnership.

DISCUSSION QUESTIONS ▼

1. How does wholesaling add value? How can the added costs of wholesaling be justified?

2. Distinguish between merchant wholesalers and brokers, and between manufacturers who handle their own wholesaling and agents.

3. Why would a manufacturer want to handle its own distribution and wholesaling? What are the trade-offs in doing so?

4. How does retailing add value? Why do you pay more to shop in a supermarket rather than

buying foodstuffs from roadside stands? When does it make sense to buy from a roadside stand? From a store? Why?

5. Select a retail store you use frequently and describe it in terms of its product lines, price, location, and ownership.

6. Find a local store that stresses price advertising and one that mainly uses image advertising. Compare them on image and atmosphere.

7. What do you think is the most important change in retailing today? Why?

8. If you were marketing manager for HDTV (high-definition television) sets, what would your distribution opportunities be? What distribution and retailing strategies would make sense for launching this new product?

9. Visit a local shopping center and describe it in terms of ambiance, features, and price of the goods found there. Also describe the target market you think its designers had in mind.

10. Choose two local retailers—one that you think is well positioned and well targeted and one that you think is not. Explain why you feel one is strategically more sound than the other.

11. Interview the owner or manager of a local retail store and determine how that firm interacts with wholesalers, how it adds value for its customers, and how it combines elements in the merchandising and retailing mixes.

Integrative Case ● Discussion Questions

The Body Shop*

1. What type of retailer is The Body Shop?
2. Contrast The Body Shop's approach to retailing cosmetics with that of Estée Lauder or Revlon. How does each of these approaches add value to its product lines?

Harley-Davidson

1. What type of retailer is a Harley dealer?
2. How do Harley dealers add value to Harley products?

The Millennium Power System

1. Describe the ways in which Millennium makes the retailer's job easier. Do you think this encourages retailers to carry the Millennium line?
2. Do you agree that Millennium should increase its sales in hardware and home centers?

*The three cases at the back of the book—"The Body Shop," "Harley-Davidson," and "The Millennium Power System"—illustrate topics discussed in all chapters of this book. Your instructor will tell you when to read a particular case and answer the discussion questions on it that appear at the end of each chapter.

Franchising

Tired of being on the employment merry-go-round, you feel it's time to strike out in business as one of Canada's self-employed entrepreneurs. There's just one catch: you really have little idea of where to begin. After reading several "start your own business and be a millionaire overnight" manuals, you realize that you need some kind of assistance. After talking to friends, you discover that everyone seems to know of someone who has been successful in running one of Canada's hundreds of franchised business operations.

Operating a franchise seems to be right up your alley, big potential with little risk, with an industry publicized success rate of at least 80 percent, compared to an 80 percent failure rate amongst independent businesses. Franchisers will supply you with a great business concept, a "cookbook" business operations manual and plenty of knowledgeable support, you can capitalize on group buying power and large distribution channels when sourcing your supplies, you can share advertising costs, and obviously, franchisers would only select the most choice location for the operation. All this for only the franchise fee and the sweat off your back. You are an instant entrepreneur on the way to financial independence! Or are you?

Once touted as the lowest risk type of business venture, industry experts are taking a much harder look at the franchising industry, and in many cases, not liking what they see. It seems that the commonly touted 80 percent success rate figure has absolutely no substance. Only the franchisers in the industry like to use the figure, and even they cannot explain its origin. In fact, a small independent U.S. study recently concluded that franchises have had a higher failure rate than independent operations in recent years.

Upon searching, you discover some literature on franchising that does not necessarily applaud the concept. You discover that many franchisers make all their money selling and reselling failed franchises, many of which are in low-cost, horrible locations; that franchisers often have significant legal rights related to the volume and price of supplies and equipment that franchisees must purchase directly from them; that the franchiser often has legal direct access to the franchisees' bank account and can withdraw weekly cash sums equal to whatever they feel they are owed; and that worst of all, the franchiser can give you a "song and dance" with little in the way of legal repercussions, as Alberta is the only province that currently has any laws regarding full disclosure of information between franchisers and their franchisees. In fact, in any other province, you may be purchasing a franchise' location that has failed numerous times, while you are given the direct impression that you are only the second owner, the previous owner having retired early on all the profits!

You quickly realize that you must proceed with caution if you intend to invest in any form of business franchise. You promise yourself that you will take your time, arm yourself with knowledge and information, and be one of the smart entrepreneurs who manages to sort out the ethical franchisers from the sleazy types.

501
WHOLESALING AND RETAILIING

QUESTIONS

1. What might be some of the advantages related to marketing your own independent business operation rather than franchising?
2. Do you think that you could effectively re-position a franchise in the marketplace on your own? How would you go about it?
3. Do you think franchisees or independent business operators have the advantage when it comes to niche marketing? Why?
4. What aspects of a franchised operation, which are largely determined by your potential legal relationship with a franchiser, do you feel require intensive consideration?

Source: This case was prepared by Byron Osing and is based on the *Venture* series episode "Franchising," which was originally broadcast on April 3, 1994.

● Chapter 16

The Basics of Pricing

OBJECTIVES

AFTER COMPLETING THIS CHAPTER, YOU SHOULD BE ABLE TO:

1
EXPLAIN HOW PRICE, VALUE, AND QUALITY ARE INTERCONNECTED AND WHY PRICE IS AN IMPORTANT ELEMENT IN THE MARKETING MIX OF ANY FIRM

2
DISTINGUISH AMONG THE FOUR C'S OF PRICING—COSTS, CONSUMER DEMAND, COMPETITION, AND CONTROLS

3
DESCRIBE THE WAY FIXED AND VARIABLE COSTS ARE ANALYZED AND DISCUSS THE ROLE THEY PLAY IN DETERMINING PRICE

4
DESCRIBE HOW PRICE ELASTICITY WORKS AND HOW CUSTOMER PRICE SENSITIVITY AFFECTS DEMAND

5
EXPLAIN HOW PRICING IS AFFECTED BY DIFFERENT TYPES OF COMPETITIVE SITUATIONS

6
ANALYZE THE EFFECTS OF GOVERNMENTAL CONTROLS AND INTERNATIONAL TRADE AGREEMENTS ON PRICES

7
EXPLAIN HOW TO ANALYZE COSTS, USING REVENUE ANALYSIS, COST ESTIMATION, MARGINAL ANALYSIS, AND BREAKEVEN ANALYSIS.

THINK ABOUT IT!

THE STORY BEHIND TEXTBOOK PRICES

You are staggering out of the bookstore at the beginning of the semester—less under the weight of the six bulky textbooks you just bought, than under the shock of the bill, which came to $180. And three of the books were *used*. Why do textbooks cost so much?

Publishers began pushing textbook prices up in the 1960s to cover spiraling inflation. Then, in the 1970s it became important that many textbooks—particularly those used in

large introductory courses—be in full color with lots of graphics. These books are very expensive to produce, but students liked them better, and professors tend to adopt books they think their students will want to read. Publishers who still opted for no-frills black-and-white books found there wasn't much of a market for their low-cost products. The game got still more competitive when professors insisted that textbooks be more current. To oblige, publishers went from four-year to three-year revision time tables on major books.

The numbers of books published annually for every introductory course taught in colleges and

505

universities increased astronomically in the 1980s. This increasingly intense competition made publishers up the ante on the big books by producing expensive support packages of teaching aids—everything from instructor's manuals, overheads, slides, videos, and test item banks with answer keys and computer grading discs to computer simulations and CD-ROM discs. Today, the costs of everything in the publishing industry are rising and profit margins on textbooks are much thinner. The markup is now smaller on textbooks than on other books, such as regular fiction and nonfiction works.

The high cost of new textbooks has been a bonanza for the used-book business. When this market got started in the mid- to late-1950s, the idea was to make textbooks available at low prices to students who couldn't afford new books. Today a large proportion of textbooks sold are used. Even students who would like to hold onto their textbooks after they finish a course to build up their personal and professional libraries are feeling forced to sell them back.

Although publishers are criticized for issuing new editions so frequently, it's necessary in order to remain competitive. Many professors stop using a book when they feel it has become dated, so publishers risk losing market share if they stretch out the revision time frame beyond three years. Not too long ago, publishers were able to amortize their upfront costs on a textbook over this three-year revision cycle. Now, because of the used-book business, there is a 40 to 50 percent drop in sales on the new book from year to year. Thus publishers are forced to get most of their revenue out of the equivalent of the first year and a half of sales. Textbook prices reflect this need to recoup the investment fast. Heightened compe-

tition—more and more books vying for a place in classrooms—means that publishers have to cover all their costs with smaller printings of each book. Shorter press runs reduce cost efficiencies.

The end result is that students are out a lot of money and feel compelled to sell their books, publishers are sharpening their pencils to try to break even on a shortened amortization schedule, and both publishers and authors earn less because they receive nothing from used-book sales. Does anyone win in this scenario other than the used-book sellers? Do you think this scenario can be changed? How would you go about making the returns to the different players more equitable while still offering the consumers—students and teachers—a reasonable deal? Tax library copies which contribute nothing beyond the initial sale? ■

textbook, the bookstore takes $12.50 and the publisher and authors receive $37.50. The author makes 10 to 15 percent of the *wholesale price* of the book—the price the bookstore pays, which in this example is $37.50. On a big introductory book selling for $50.00, then, the authors would get between $3.75 and $5.63 and the publisher between $31.87 and $33.75.

It can take three years or longer for a book like this to be developed. That's three years of planning and writing for the authors (although not full-time, since most textbook authors are also professors) and editing and production for the publishers. When the book moves into revised editions, the development time is approximately one and a half years, with one year of planning and writing time for the authors.

Although the publisher's $32–$33 may sound like a lot of money, it has to cover the costs of market research, art and design, production, and distribution, as well as the costs of copyright permission fees for reproducing any borrowed materials plus the supplemental teaching materials. The publisher must also pay its sales force (who sometimes have to make many calls to professors before they secure a book's adoption), produce and distribute promotional materials, and maintain staff who manage the project and edit the manuscript. Finally, it must meet its overhead costs—such as offices, computers, and warehouses.

As you can see from Figure 16-2, the biggest cost category in the college textbook industry is manufacturing expenses—which comes to a little more than 25 cents (25 percent) of the textbook dollar's total costs. Next are the costs associated with the bookstores, whose personnel and operations account for 21 percent of the total cost.

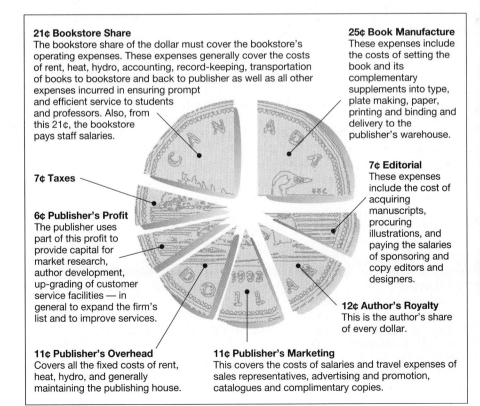

21¢ Bookstore Share
The bookstore share of the dollar must cover the bookstore's operating expenses. These expenses generally cover the costs of rent, heat, hydro, accounting, record-keeping, transportation of books to bookstore and back to publisher as well as all other expenses incurred in ensuring prompt and efficient service to students and professors. Also, from this 21¢, the bookstore pays staff salaries.

7¢ Taxes

6¢ Publisher's Profit
The publisher uses part of this profit to provide capital for market research, author development, up-grading of customer service facilities — in general to expand the firm's list and to improve services.

11¢ Publisher's Overhead
Covers all the fixed costs of rent, heat, hydro, and generally maintaining the publishing house.

11¢ Publisher's Marketing
This covers the costs of salaries and travel expenses of sales representatives, advertising and promotion, catalogues and complimentary copies.

25¢ Book Manufacture
These expenses include the costs of setting the book and its complementary supplements into type, plate making, paper, printing and binding and delivery to the publisher's warehouse.

7¢ Editorial
These expenses include the cost of acquiring manuscripts, procuring illustrations, and paying the salaries of sponsoring and copy editors and designers.

12¢ Author's Royalty
This is the author's share of every dollar.

**Figure 16-2
Where Does the College Textbook Dollar Go?**

Source: *College Textbook Pricing*, Canadian Book Publishers' Council, 1984.

The great advantage the used-book market has is low risk. The publisher takes a risk in putting out a new book; the product may not sell. The used-book store has only to buy the already-manufactured product, stock it, and resell it. If bookstores know a book is going to be used in a course the coming semester, they will usually pay students 50 percent of the original price. If the book will not be used in a course that semester, its price will drop. Bookstores then put the books back on the shelf at approximately 75 percent of their original price, which means they make a 25 percent gross profit, with nothing going back to the publisher or author. Although bookstores' profit margins are probably not as high as many people think, it is also true that these stores do not have to face investors who, having taken a sizable risk, expect a high return. Still, according to some writers, the used-book industry has grown 500 percent since the early 1980s and is now a $500 million annual business.

What do you think? Do you see any price-gouging in these figures? If you were the manager of a textbook publishing firm, where would you apply pressure to reduce costs? Would you seek any opportunities for increasing royalty revenue (e.g., a library borrowing fee for authors)?

CUSTOMER DEMAND

The second major influence on pricing is *demand* for the product. How many potential customers are there, how affluent are they (that is, what price can they afford), and how often do they use the product (e.g., do they use it evenly year round)? Consumers and industrial buyers shape pricing policies through the amount of a good or service they need or want and their ability and willingness to buy it at a given price.

Tastes and preferences also affect demand, especially concerning fad- and fashion-related products. This is demonstrated nearly every Christmas season when one or two toys are the "hot" items that every child has to have. The toy manufacturer lucky enough to have a hit may not have enough production capacity to meet demand, and therefore can increase the price, knowing that scarcity will motivate consumers to pay more than they normally would. This produces high profits for the manufacturer. Marketers attempt to influence fashions, tastes, and preferences through marketing communications, but it is difficult to predict what items will be "hot."

Elasticity of Demand Sales of some products are much more affected by changes in price than others. We describe these variations of price influence in terms of price elasticity, the topic of chapter objective four. *Price elasticity* shows to what extent a change in price affects the number of units sold. This is different for every product category and, in some cases, even for brands within a category. Where there is a direct relationship between prices and quantities sold, the product is said to have an **elastic demand**. This means that when the price is reduced, demand increases, and when the price is increased, demand decreases.

elastic demand
A measure of the sensitivity of demand to changes in price; when demand is elastic, it is quite responsive to changes in price—in general, increasing as price declines.

Take strawberries, which most large grocery stores now carry nearly year around. In the fall and winter months strawberries are scarce and have to be imported; consequently, the price is relatively high and sales are low. As shown in Figure 16-3a, when a store drops the price per quart from $2.50 to $1.00, however, sales per store can increase from 10 to 50 cases per week. The price of strawberries, therefore, is said to be elastic. Here is why. For many product categories, like strawberries, there is a group of potential buyers.

However, the people within each of these groups have different levels of interest in buying. A small proportion just have to have strawberries at any price, a larger proportion would like to have strawberries but can live without them. As the price drops, strawberries (and other elastic-demand products) become more attractive to people with only a modest or a low interest in the product, and as a result sales increase.

For other products, buying decisions are not affected by changes in price, and these products are said to have an **inelastic demand**. Textbooks have an inelastic demand because students have to buy what their professors assign. Medical products are another example of inelastic demand. Suppose a doctor gave you a prescription for a drug for migraine headaches. You would probably pay whatever it cost if you thought it would save you from the suffering of migraines (Exhibit 16-1). In general, the price of a prescribed drug has to rise a great deal before people consider not buying it. Substitutions are already possible where there is a generic pharmaceutical product available as an alternative to a presented brand name at a considerable cost saving. As Figure 16-3b shows, dropping the price of a medicine from $25 to $5 has only a

inelastic demand
A measure of the sensitivity of demand to price changes; in a price-inelastic situation, a price decrease has minimal effect on total demand.

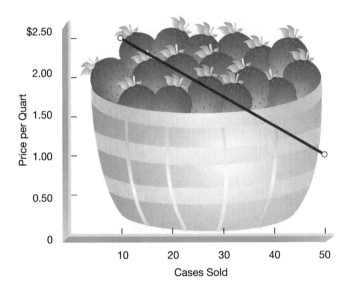

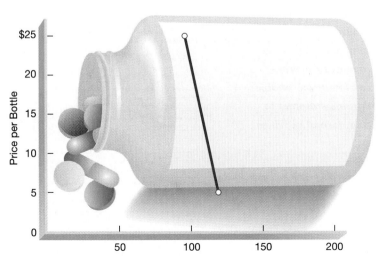

Figure 16-3
Example of Elastic and Inelastic Demand

(A) When demand is elastic, as it is for strawberries, a decrease in price may cause an increase in demand.
(B) When demand is inelastic, as it is for prescription medicines, neither an increase nor a decrease in price has much impact on demand.

slight effect on the quantity sold. This is a strong case of inelastic demand: people who need a drug are going to buy it regardless of price (assuming there is no comparable substitute, such as a generic version of the drug), and those who don't need it aren't going to start buying it simply because the price has been lowered.

Knowing the elasticity of demand for a product is important to marketers because it tells them how price-sensitive consumers are, and price sensitivity is an important factor in price-setting. Price-setting depends on how easy it is for customers to go without a product and how much of a factor price is in the buying decision. People can live without dining in restaurants (elastic demand, price-sensitive consumers), but if they get hit by a car, health care (inelastic demand, price-insensitive consumers) is literally a life-and-death necessity. Marketers use market research to estimate both demand and price sensitivity.

Note that many industrial products are more price-insensitive (inelastic) than consumer products. For example, a category decrease in the price of airplane engines will not convince Boeing to buy more of these components than the number it needs to fill current orders. The fact that the cost of one of the plane's components—engines—has decreased will probably not motivate Boeing to build, or other airlines to buy, more planes at this particular time. Some industrial and business-to-business categories *are* price-sensitive (elastic). For example, many companies buy supplies in relatively large quantities. A ten-cent-per-kilogram drop in the price of chicken will probably motivate Swanson, which makes many types of frozen chicken entrees, to increase its purchase of chickens. It knows it can freeze these and use them in the future when the price of chicken rises again. (However, if the cost of freezing the excess chickens outweighs the savings at today's price per kilogram, Swanson will probably not buy more chickens than it normally does.)

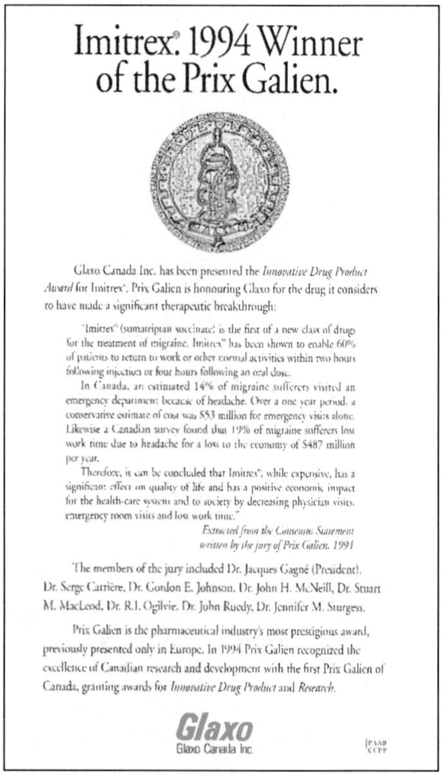

Exhibit 16-1
Inelasticity and Medications

An effective new medication usually results in inelastic demand if there are no comparable substitutes. Glaxo Canada Inc. developed Imitrex®, a drug for the treatment of migraines and the 1994 winner of the Prix Galien. One dose of Imitrex® enables 60 percent of migraine sufferers to return to work and normal activities within two hours.

MAKING A PROFIT ON BABIES?

The pricing of baby formula is based on inelastic demand, and some people consider this unethical. Several million babies are born in North America every year, and many of them—perhaps most, in this day of two-career families—consume formula to some extent. Many babies are put on the formula recommended by their pediatricians in the hospital, and most mothers stick to that brand. The three largest makers of infant formula, who manufacture almost 90 percent of all the infant formula sold in North America, operate as an oligopoly. They have raised prices in virtual lockstep almost every year since 1981. Although the cost of milk, formula's main ingredient, rose only 25 percent during the 1980s, formula prices increased almost 250 percent.[5]

Consumer advocates believe that a cozy relationship between formula makers and pediatricians lies at the heart of this highly profitable closed market. Pediatricians are rightly concerned that newborns begin life with the most nutritious diet available. In general, they oppose advertising of formulas because, although it might make mothers more aware of the relative advantages of lower-priced formulas, they fear it would open up the market to dangerous competition. For if companies were to cut costs and reformulate their products to make them cheaper, physicians believe, this could endanger the health of many babies.

Although formula makers defend their pricing practices, critics feel they are making excessive profits at the expense of babies and their trusting parents who, regardless of their income levels, are not particularly price sensitive about something as critical as their baby's food.

What might pediatricians have to gain from supporting high-priced baby formulas? Consumer advocates suggest that there may be something unethical going on here—some sort of payoff arrangement between companies and doctors. Or are formula makers simply taking advantage of physicians' legitimate concerns for the physical health of their patients? What do you think?

Pricing Influences on Demand Just as customers, costs, and competition influence how a product is priced, price influences customer buying behavior. To understand this, we'll start with one of the fundamental principles of economics, the demand curve. A **demand curve** shows how a change in price affects the number of units sold, assuming all other conditions remain constant. (Note that a "curve" in economics is often a straight line.) You've already seen two demand curves in Figure 16-3. Now let's look at another example of how the demand curve works.

Have you ever considered the factors that may affect the price of an admission ticket to a movie? Time of day is one; popularity of the film is another. Because most people prefer to go to the movies in the evening, theaters generally charge a much lower price during the day to attract customers

demand curve
A graphic representation of the effect of a change in price on the number of units of a product sold.

515

during these "off" hours. As demonstrated by line A in Figure 16-4, if a movie theatre charges $8 during the day, it will attract only a few people per showing (50 in this hypothetical example). But by lowering the price to $5 during the day, it may attract as many as 200 per showing. The only thing that has changed to create this difference in ticket sales is the price of the ticket.

Lines B and C demonstrate the principle of *shifting the demand curve*. This is done by changing the conditions relating to the product and how and when it is sold. Line B illustrates that during the evening, when most people prefer to attend movies, our theater can attract 300 people even though it charges $8 a ticket. But if the theater lowered its evening price to $5, it could sell over 500 tickets which would be more people than the theater can accommodate. Line C shows another way the theater can shift demand—by showing a big hit movie, for example, such as 1993's *Jurassic Park*, when it was a box-office sellout. In the evening the hit movie continues to attract more customers than the theater can seat, even without lowering the $8 admission fee. Another instance of shifting demand is the recent history of oat bran. Before the 1980s, demand for oat bran was limited. But after medical studies indicated that eating oat bran might reduce people's chances of having a heart attack, demand for the product—at all prices—shot up. Demand then declined somewhat in the wake of a report in the late 1980s that concluded the link to heart attacks was not clearly substantiated.

Figure 16-4
Shifting Demand
Curves

In this example of shifting demand, the two factors of time of day and popularity of a film interact with price to determine the numbers of tickets sold by a movie theater under different conditions. See text for further discussion.

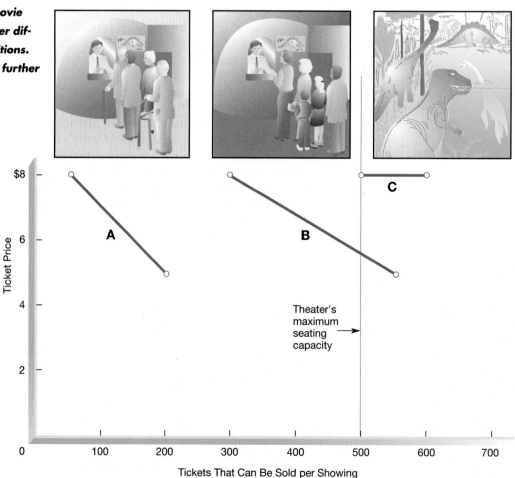

COMPETITIVE INFLUENCES

Competition, the subject of chapter objective five, is another important factor in determining pricing strategy. Because substitute products decrease the demand (and therefore acceptable price) for a product, marketers try to *differentiate* their products—that is, they strive to make people feel there are no "real" substitutes.

The maximum amount it makes sense to charge for a product, called its *price ceiling,* is often determined by the competition's prices. In the 1980s Caterpillar, the leading maker of earthmoving equipment, paid a price for failing to watch the competition. For fifty years, Caterpillar had record sales growth and profits. But when Komatsu, a Japanese firm, entered the market with prices only 40 percent as high as Caterpillar's, the U.S. firm was slow to respond. Before Caterpillar realized it would have to find ways to cut costs so that it could lower prices, Komatsu had walked off with an 11 percent share of the global market in this category. Caterpillar has since adjusted its pricing (following changes in product design) as well as its marketing communications, in which it more persuasively points out why its products are worth more than Komatsu's. Like Caterpillar, more and more firms have come to realize they need a systematic approach to pricing that includes an analysis of the competitive situation as well as consumer demand.

As the North American car industry has learned, global competition has widened the perspective that marketers must take when setting price objectives. For example, in high-income nations many labor-intensive industries—including shoes and clothing—are unable to compete on price alone against manufacturers in nations where wages are much lower. That is why the North American clothing industry has created advertising to persuade North Americans that buying domestic-made goods at somewhat higher prices also provides extra benefits—a higher-quality product and the positive feeling of keeping North Americans working. However, there is the less visible problem of domestic retailers subcontracting manufacturing, sourcing from abroad and receiving products under the store's own label.

Catnapping Can Be Risky

Caterpillar dominated the heavy earthmoving machinery market for years but was caught napping when Komatsu entered the scene with lower prices and lower costs. Caterpillar trimmed down quickly, however, and regained its world leadership.

Market Structure The degree of competition—and thus its influence on pricing—depends somewhat on the structure of the market in which a firm operates. In Chapter 1 we noted four common market structures: *pure monopoly, oligopoly, pure competition*, and *monopolistic competition*. A company that has a monopoly—meaning it has no direct competitors—can price its products without consideration of competitive actions, although in some cases (for example, Canada Post) substitute products (UPS, DHL, Federal Express) provide some competition. Although competition exists within oligopolies, it is not unusual to find producers in this kind of market acting in concert to raise prices. Thus when OPEC, the Organization of Petroleum Exporting Countries, decides the price of crude oil should rise, all OPEC members generally are free to raise their prices.

Following the leader in price cuts is generally necessary in a purely competitive market, where the only difference in brands is price. Whenever customers view the brand of one producer as identical to the brands of other producers, they make decisions almost exclusively on the basis of price. The extent to which a firm in a monopolistically competitive market will follow the pricing policies of its competitors depends on how many direct competitors it has and how similar their brands are to the firm's own. The more differentiated its brand, the more likely it is that the firm will behave like a monopoly; the less differentiated its brand, the more likely the firm's pricing strategy will follow strategies used in oligopolies or even pure competition.

Table 16-1 summarizes these different types of competitive situations.

Competitive Pricing Policies A marketing manager who is pricing a firm's products must keep in mind the pricing activities of competitors and their likely reactions to a price change. When competing marketers are unable to significantly differentiate their brands—for example, Shell, Esso and Texaco gasoline—they will generally *match their competitors' prices*. Customers view such undifferentiated products as *commodities* (see Chapter 10) that are mutually substitutable, and they are very sensitive to prices when selecting a particular brand. They will reject brands priced much above the competition unless those brands offer obvious additional benefits.

When firms set a price at the low end of the price range in order to discourage competition, they are creating a *barrier to entry*. An established firm can afford to do this if it has lower costs because of patented technologies it developed or because its high market share and production levels give it greater economies of scale than a new firm can achieve initially. However, this policy can backfire if the low cost firm cannot achieve the volume of sales necessary to make a profit at the low price or if the price is set artificially low and is therefore considered to be predatory pricing, which is illegal. (We discuss predatory pricing and other illegal pricing activities below.) The strategy decision in a new-product situation involves determining whether to set a high price initially and profit from the competitive advantage or set a lower price in order to maintain market domination as long as possible. In oligopolies and mature markets, firms may compete on a nonprice basis. In that situation, they have a pricing policy of *maintaining a price position relative to the competition*.

The competitive situation, like product categories, has an inherent level of price elasticity. For example, if you own the only store that sells tires in Grand Falls, New Brunswick, the prices you charge will not affect the quantity you sell as much as they would if there were two other competing tire stores in Grand Falls. If you raise prices too high, however, potential customers may be willing to spend the time and energy necessary to drive 60 km to Edmundston where there are several tire stores that have lower prices. Generally, the more competitive the product category, the more price elasticity there is.

TABLE 16-1

Features	Pure Competition	Oligopoly	Monopolistic Competition	Pure Monopoly
Number of sellers	Very large number	Few	Substantial number	One
Product	Undifferentiated perfect substitutes	Differentiated products with close substitutes		No close substitute for unique good
Price	No control over price—seller must accept market price	Pricing in concert is strong tendency; firms mutually interdependent	Some price competition can prevail; price control depends much on degree of differentiation	Much control over price—but can sell only what market will take at his price
Entry of new firms	Easy	Usually difficult because of size of firms and high costs	Somewhat easy— but depends on technology and size of firms	No entry as resource access is blocked
Marketing effort	Price promotions	Very large amount of nonprice promotion with heavy emphasis on brands and product differentiation; wide use of advertising and any marketing activity to build market share		Little, but can enjoy benefits if less product elasticity is created

Source: Robert J. Holloway and Robert S. Hancock, *Marketing in a Changing Environment*, 2nd ed. (New York: Wiley, 1973).

GOVERNMENT CONTROLS

In addition to costs, consumers, and competition, a number of laws and regulations control how firms set prices. Furthermore, prices on products sold internationally are sometimes determined by *trade agreements* between countries. Government controls and international trade agreements are the focus of the sixth chapter objective. Most nations impose restrictions of some kind on the pricing of various product categories. In some cases, governments may temporarily or permanently set prices for products (and all the materials that go into them, including labor) through wage-price freezes. More common are restrictions on specific types of price-setting. Canadian laws generally forbid *price-fixing, price discrimination, predatory pricing,* and *deceptive price advertising.*

Price-Fixing Under the 1986 Competition Act, price-fixing or what is referred to as price maintenance is illegal. **Price-fixing** is an agreement among most or all of the major firms in a market (usually an oligopoly) to set prices for a product at a given level. Court cases involving the Competition Act have resulted in rulings stating that *any* conspiracy to fix prices is illegal, regardless of the reason for or level of such price-fixing. For example, on September 6, 1991, Canadian Oxygen Limited and Union Carbide Canada Limited pleaded guilty to conspiring to fix the price of compressed gases sold or supplied in

price-fixing
An agreement, illegal in Canada, whereby most or all of the major firms in a market (usually an oligopoly) set prices for a product at a given level.

Does Nintendo Play Fair?

Despite some accusations of price fixing, Nintendo Entertainment Systems continues to lead the video game market. Championship competitions for young players, boost sales and win new customers.

bulk liquid form, and were fined $700,000 and $1.7 million respectively. On September 17, 1991, Canadian Liquid Air Limited and Liquid Carbonic Inc. pleaded guilty to similar charges and were fined $1.7 million each.[6]

Agreements among competitors are called *horizontal price-fixing*. Another type of price-fixing—*vertical price-fixing*—involves agreements among channel members to set minimum resale prices. Such practices—also called *resale price maintenance*—protect small retailers from being underpriced by large retailers. In Canada, it is illegal to attempt to induce a supplier to engage in price maintence.

THE HIGH PRICE OF PRICE-RIGGING

In the ongoing trade conflicts between the United States and Japan, one of the biggest obstacles to peace has been the long-established practice of *dango*, whereby construction companies in Japan decide secretly and in advance which one will submit the winning bid and how much of the resulting business it will then divide up through subcontracts to other companies. To the Japanese, *dango* is a customary business practice; to Westerners, it is bid-rigging.[7]

According to U.S. trade officials, *dango* cartels have effectively prevented American builders from competing for a portion of the $500 billion-a-year construction market in Japan. Recently, however, the U.S. government has acted to force some changes in this system. In a closely watched case, the Department of Justice hired a Japanese law firm to press for about $35 million in damages against 140 companies accused of rigging bids on projects at the American Yokosuka Naval Base near Tokyo between 1984 and 1987. To put teeth into its claims, the United States threatened to sue the Japanese companies and to deny them future contracts with the U.S. government if they refused to pay up.

The time was ripe to strike, Justice Department officials felt, because the Japanese Fair Trade Commission had ruled in 1988 that the 140 companies had colluded to rig the bids. Also, the United States has received some support from within Japan itself. Besides being anticompetitive and costing the country billions yearly, these critics argued, *dango* was embarrassing the Japanese government, which had for years vigorously contended that Japanese business is not only noncollusive but welcomes foreign companies.

This combined assault from within and without encouraged 99 of the 140 companies sued to sign a consent agreement in which they agreed to pay $32.6 million to settle the accusations against them. Still, the dispute over *dango* is far from over. Japan's powerful construction industry, now recovering from a decade of austerity, will no doubt fight to keep its large share of the building pie. The 520,000 Japanese builders are understandably afraid of foreign competition within their domestic market.

Nevertheless, the U.S. assault on *dango* is beginning to pay definite dividends. The U.S. Air Force and the Justice Department have been investigating charges that another *dango* association overcharged the Air Force and the Navy about $96 million for communications contracts during the last decade. Says Arthur Williams, former chief of the contracts law division at Yokota Air Base: "I don't think any big firm has defrauded us like that before."

Price Discrimination The 1986 Competition Act prohibits most forms of **price discrimination**—charging different customers different prices for the same product. These laws specifically forbid such pricing when *commodities are of like grade and quality*. The primary objective of the Competition Act is to prevent a manufacturer from giving one buyer a competitive advantage—such as a lower price—over another buyer.

Price discrimination may be legal if the differences are based on the perceived value of branding or the actual costs of serving different groups of customers. Thus a customer who buys a small quantity of individually packaged items that must be shipped by expensive private trucking firms may legally be charged more than the giant firm that buys a railroad car of the mass-packaged product. A more familiar example is airline seating: first class costs more than coach, and business flyers who travel frequently often receive the special benefits of business class by paying only a few dollars more than the cost of a coach class ticket.

price discrimination
When a supplier charges different prices to competitors who purchase similar volumes of an article.

Predatory Pricing **Predatory pricing** infractions fall into two categories in Canada. The first is selling products in one region of Canada at prices lower than in another region (after taking into account transportation costs) for the purpose of lessening competition substantially or eliminating a competitor. The second category is setting an artificially low price for the purpose of containing or driving a competitor out of the market. Predatory pricing is illegal under the 1986 Competition Act. Opponents of this practice note that it restricts competition, and thus gives the predatory firm more control over the price of its products.

predatory pricing
The practice, illegal in Canada, of setting an artificially low price for the purpose of restraining a competitor or driving competition out of the market.

dumping

Dumping means more than cheap imports. There are two criteria to be met. First, these imports are lower-priced than in the country of origin. Second, they are injurious to local industry.

Selling a product abroad for a price below that charged in the country of origin—a practice called **dumping**—has been the subject of a number of investigations in recent years, including a case involving the "dumping" of automatic transmission springs by a Canadian firm. However, aside from establishing a competitive, lively cost structure, it has to be established that these imports are injurious to local industry. This is the approach followed both by the U.S.A. and by the E.U.

Deceptive Pricing   There are many forms of deceptive price advertising that may lead to government intervention. For example:

1. Setting a fictitious "original" higher price on a product in order to claim that the one now being offered is a substantial reduction is deceptive.
2. Claiming a phony "retail value" that one's own price undercuts is deceptive unless a reasonable number of competing retailers are selling the product at that higher price.
3. Claiming that a product's price is below the manufacturer's suggested retail price is deceptive unless the latter price is regularly charged by principal outlets within the trading area.

Other illegal pricing practices are: advertising a retail price as wholesale; advertising "factory" prices when they are not; offering seconds at reduced prices without disclosing that the higher comparative price refers to perfect merchandise; and offering an "advance sale price" or "limited time price" when the product will be offered at that same price in the future.

One other form of deceptive advertising merits special discussion. **Bait-and-switch pricing** attracts customers by offering a low-priced model with the intention of persuading customers to "trade up" to a higher-priced one when they arrive at the store. As long as a store has the low-priced model available in at least reasonable quantities, it has committed no crime. But if the advertised item is not available—a situation too frequently found in appliance shops, car dealerships, and furniture retail outlets—the Federal Bureau of Competition Policy (part of Consumer and Corporate Affairs, Canada) can step in and impose penalties on the advertisers.

bait-and-switch pricing

The practice of attracting customers by offering a low-priced model with the intention of persuading them to "trade up" to a higher-priced model. In Canada this practice is illegal if the store does not carry reasonable quantities of the lower-priced good.

International Regulatory Issues   Many pricing practices regulated in Canada and the United States are also subject to regulation in other countries. Price-fixing, for example, is outlawed by the European Union under Section 80 of the Treaty of Rome. Of particular concern to global marketers, however, are the conflicting price policies of different governments. For example, IBM, which was then leasing its computers in the United Kingdom, was once threatened by the U.S. government with antitrust action if it did not offer its equipment for purchase as well as lease. In the process of developing purchase prices, IBM had to raise its lease prices. The British government saw these increases as a violation of its price guidelines at the time and forced IBM to roll them back in the United Kingdom.

Trade agreements are becoming much more important in determining price levels. Historically, countries have used tariffs, which can dramatically increase prices, to restrict the flow of international products into their local markets. Today the trend is toward free trade. The ongoing GATT (General Agreement on Tariffs and Trade) negotiations among most of the countries engaging in *international* trade are intended to discourage protectionist practices like tariffs and promote unrestricted trade. Other trade agreements—most notably the continuing negotiations among members of the North American Free Trade Agreement (NAFTA) concluded in late 1993 to establish free trade among Mexico, the United States, and Canada—seek to eliminate trade barriers within a *region*. Free trade agreements usually result in greater flexibility in pricing so that pricing strategies reflect actual demand rather than the artificial limitations created by trade restrictions. Tariffs on products imported into Mexico, for example, averaged 13 percent before NAFTA.[8]

PRICE AND PROFIT ANALYSIS ●

Customer perceptions of a firm's brand and the price of competitive brands together impose a ceiling on how much the firm can charge for its brand; the total cost of producing and selling the brand establishes the minimum price at which it should be sold. Although consumers, the competition, and government controls are important factors in determining the price range, the primary factors used to set the exact price are *costs* and *estimated revenues*.

A *cost analysis* is the process used to study these two factors together to arrive at a selling price. A *breakeven analysis* determines the minimum level of sales needed to cover costs at a particular price point. In other words, a breakeven analysis will show you how many units you have to sell before you can begin making a profit. To gauge the wisdom of trying to increase sales beyond the original sales plan, a *marginal cost analysis* is done to determine if additional revenues will exceed additional costs.

This section discusses the various ways to analyze costs and determine what it takes to make a profit, the focus of chapter objective seven. In the long run, if a firm wishes to stay in business, it must make a profit. And to make a profit, it must have more revenue than costs, for

$$\text{profit} = \text{total revenues} - \text{total costs}$$

As you can see, when costs exceed revenues, the company loses money.

DETERMINING REVENUES

Marketers measure revenue in three ways: as total revenue, average unit revenue, and marginal revenue. *Total revenue* is simply total income from sales. It is determined by multiplying the average unit price by total units sold. *Average unit revenue* is the amount of revenue received on average for each unit sold or service performed. It is determined by dividing the total revenue by the total number of units sold (or services performed) within a given period of time. For example, if a car rental office has 2,000 rentals within a month, and the total revenue generated from these rentals is $170,000, the average revenue per unit or transaction is $85 ($170,000 ÷ 2,000 = $85). In the restaurant industry, average unit revenue is called "cheque average," and one of the marketing objectives of most restaurants is to increase the "cheque average"—in other words, to sell more items or a higher priced item to each customer. *Marginal revenue* is revenue generated by additional sales over those originally budgeted minus the additional costs necessary to generate the additional sales. (Marginal revenues are discussed in more detail at the end of this section.)

These three types of revenue can be stated in equation form, which may make it easier for you to understand and remember them:

$$\text{total revenue} = \text{unit price} \times \text{quantity sold}$$

$$\text{average unit revenue} = \frac{\text{total revenue}}{\text{quantity sold}}$$

$$\text{marginal revenue} = \frac{\text{additional revenues over those budgeted}}{\text{additional costs over those budgeted}}$$

In the short run, managers can influence profits in three ways: (1) by selling more units (increasing quantity sold) at the same price and maintaining costs; (2) by selling the same amount of units at the same price and reducing costs; or (3) by using a combination of 1 and 2—that is, by selling more units at the same price while reducing costs. In the long run, however, managers must focus on the level of sales that causes the greatest difference between total revenue and total cost. Such a focus requires that they understand the concepts of *cost estimation* and *marginal analysis*.

margin
The difference between the selling price and total unit costs for an item.

Margin Marketers frequently use the term **margin** or *gross margin* when talking about the difference between costs and selling price. In general, a margin is the difference between selling price and the total unit cost of an item. However, the precise meaning of these widely used terms can differ by type of business, by product category, and sometimes even by division within a company. This is because the concept of *total cost* and how it is computed varies dramatically.

In most retail operations, for example, gross margin is the difference between what a store pays for an item and the price for which it sells that item. If a grocery pays $2 for a box of Wheaties and sells it for $3, the gross margin is $1. From that gross margin the store subtracts what it pays for labor, utilities, advertising, and other expenses; the remainder is profit.

In manufacturing, gross margin often refers to the direct cost of making a product (ingredients, labor, packaging). From that gross margin the company subtracts selling costs and overhead, and what is left over is profit. Some companies use the concept of *divisional* or *departmental margins*. Take a truck stop that has several different departments—gas and oil sales, a restaurant, a garage where repairs are made, and a convenience store—each set up as a profit center. Each of these profit centers would have a departmental margin, which is its sales minus the expenses it takes to run that particular department. Overall building costs, utilities, insurance, and administrative expenses are often not included in these departmental expenses. What all of these examples suggest is that to understand what people mean when they refer to *margins* or *gross margins*, you need to know what business they are in and how that business attributes costs.

profit margin
The percentage of revenue that remains after both fixed and variable costs have been subtracted.

Profit Margin Companies aren't in business for the thrill of the exchange. They are in business to make a *profit*, the amount of revenue above costs that goes back to the company and its owners. The most important margin, then, is the **profit margin**, which is the percentage of revenue that remains after the variable and fixed costs. Like the concept of margin, profit margin (also called *gross profit*) is difficult to define because different companies include or exclude different factors. Taxes, for example, may or may not be factored into the computation of gross profit.

markup
The amount by which the price of an item exceeds its total cost. The percent of increase represents the desired profit margin.

The most basic way to determine a profit margin is *cost-plus pricing*, in which a desired percentage—representing the profit margin—is added to the total cost for each unit produced or forecasted. This percentage is commonly referred to as a **markup**. To calculate it in dollars and cents, marketers first determine the *average total cost (ATC)*—that is, the total of all fixed and variable costs divided by the number of units produced—and multiply it by the desired percentage:

$$\text{average total cost (ATC)} \times \text{desired percentage} = \text{markup}$$

Then the markup is added to the ATC to obtain the selling price. Thus, if a firm has an ATC of $80 per unit and wants a profit margin of 50 percent, the result will be a unit selling price of $120:

$$\$80 \times 50\% = \$40 \text{ markup}$$
$$\$80 + \$40 = \$120 \text{ price}$$

The opposite of profit is *loss,* and losses occur when total revenues are less than total costs. Sometimes pricing at a loss is a strategic decision. Price reductions, or **markdowns**, are based on the same kind of calculation used for markups, but the goal in this case is to stimulate demand. If an item has a selling price of $80 and the store runs a sale offering "25% off," the sale price of that item will be $60:

markdowns
Reductions from the original retail or selling price of a piece of merchandise.

$$\$80 \times 25\% = \$20 \text{ markdown}$$
$$\$80 - \$20 = \$60 \text{ selling price}$$

For most products, especially consumer goods, a chain of markups determines the final retail price. Traditionally, these markups are expressed as a percentage of the ultimate selling price set by a particular member of the distribution channel—not, as you might think, as a percentage of the cost to that channel member. For example, Nike may contract to have a pair of running shoes made in China and pay $15 for the finished goods. It may then sell these shoes to wholesalers for $25, which means that Nike is taking a $10 or 40 percent markup (40% × $25 = $10). Nike's wholesalers may sell the shoes to The Running Room for $33—an $8.25 or 25 percent markup (25% × $33 = $8.25). The Running Room in turn may price the shoes at $60—a $27 or 45 percent markup (45% × $60 = $27). Figure 16-5 shows all these markups.

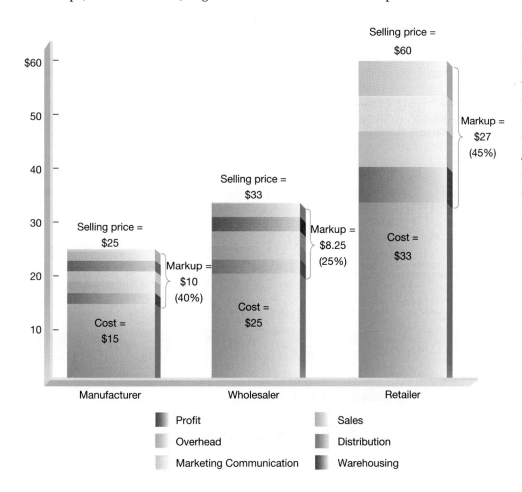

Figure 16-5
How a Price Is
Built

Markups for the manufacturer, wholesaler, and retailer on a hypothetical pair of running shoes sold to the end user for $60.

Markups reflect the additional costs and profits for each member of the distribution system: the value their activities add for consumers and the profit they earn by adding this value. For example, The Running Room must maintain its store and inventory of sizes and styles, it must pay its sales clerks, and it must advertise. On top of all these costs it adds its profit margin. The Running Room customers, in return, gain the convenience of shopping nearby and being able to see the product and try it on instead of chasing across the country to a distributor or buying it by direct mail from Nike.

The formula for doing a markup, using as an example Nike's desire to have a 40 percent markup on an item for which it paid $15, is:

$$\text{markup price} = \frac{\text{cost of unit}}{100\% - \text{desired markup}}$$

$$\text{markup price} = \frac{\$15}{100\% - 40\%} = \frac{\$15}{60\%} = \$25$$

BREAKEVEN ANALYSIS

breakeven (payback) analysis
A mathemetical technique that attempts to find the point at which total revenues are equal to total costs of a particular product.

In attempting to achieve profitability, marketing managers use **breakeven** (or **payback**) **analysis**, a mathematical technique whose purpose is to determine the price point of which the total cost of producing a good or service exactly equals the expected revenue from the product's sale. The *breakeven point* is the sales level at which total revenues equal total costs. Managers naturally want to set prices high enough and generate enough sales to more than cover costs—that is, total revenues need to be higher than total costs if a profit is to be made. Figure 16-6, the breakeven chart for a hypothetical firm, shows the point at which a loss turns into a profit. It also breaks costs down into variable and fixed costs. The breakeven point occurs where the total revenue and total costs lines intersect—in this case, where 30,000 units of the product sold produce $45,000 in revenue. Below this point, the firm incurs a loss because total costs exceed total revenues. Above the breakeven point, the firm earns a profit.

You can also find the minimum number of units you need to sell in order to break even by dividing total fixed costs by the unit price minus the unit variable cost. In the following breakeven analysis, total fixed costs are $20,000, the selling price per unit is $1.50, and the average variable cost per unit is $0.83.

$$\text{breakeven point (in units)} = \frac{\text{total fixed costs}}{\text{selling price per unit} - \text{average variable unit cost}}$$

$$\text{breakeven point (in units)} = \frac{\$20,000}{\$1.50 - \$0.83}$$

$$= \frac{\$20,000}{\$0.67}$$

$$= 29,851 \text{ units}$$

To calculate the breakeven point in dollars instead of in units, you would use the following formula:

$$\text{breakeven \$ sales} = \frac{\text{total fixed costs}}{1 - (\text{average variable cost} \div \text{unit price})}$$

$$= \frac{\$20,000}{1 - (\$0.83 \div \$1.50)}$$

Figure 16-6
Breakeven Analysis

At the breakeven point, where 30,000 units of product are sold and sales revenues of $45,000 exactly cover, but do not exceed, total costs. Below and to the left of the breakeven point (in the portion of the diagram marked off by dashed lines) the company operates at a loss. Above and to the right of the breakeven point, as units sold and sales revenues climb, the company makes a profit.

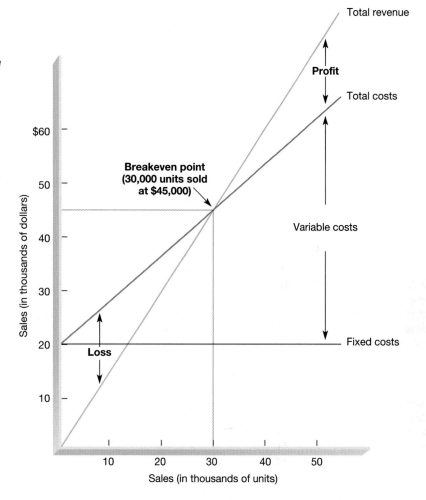

$$= \frac{\$20,000}{.44}$$

breakeven $ sales = $45,455

Since each *price point* (the price at which an item is sold) has its own breakeven point, a breakeven analysis can be used to evaluate how changes in price will affect profits. That is, a manager may conduct an analysis assuming different levels of costs and revenues to determine how many units must be sold in order for the firm to reach a targeted profit objective. For example, if the hypothetical firm in the above example desires a profit of $10,000, it would have to sell 45,000 units, calculated as follows:

$$\text{sales objective} = \frac{\text{total fixed cost} + \text{desired profit}}{\text{unit price} - \text{average variable cost}}$$

$$= \frac{\$20,000 + \$10,000}{\$1.50 - \$0.83}$$

$$= \frac{\$30,000}{\$0.67}$$

$$= 44,776 \text{ units}$$

527

If the manager wants to know what the breakeven unit volume would be at a 10 percent increase in unit price, the following calculation would be done:

$$\text{breakeven in units} = \frac{(\$20,000 + \$10,000)}{(\mathbf{\$1.65} - \$0.83)}$$

$$= \frac{\$30,000}{\$0.82}$$

$$\text{breakeven in units} = \mathbf{36,585} \text{ units}$$

Notice the difference in results: a $1.65 unit price instead of $1.50 means that only 36,585 units must be sold to break even instead of 44,776 units.

Breakeven analysis, which is discussed in more detail in Appendix B, is important because it lets the marketer evaluate price options in terms of price points, unit sales, and sales objectives. It is not as simple in real life as it looks on these pages because a lot of the data used in the calculations are gathered through estimates that vary in accuracy and actual revenues and costs are rarely the straight lines we have depicted. Nevertheless, breakeven analysis is a very useful tool when combined with the other forms of analyses we discussed in this chapter.

BOTTOM LINE REALITIES

SATURN'S BREAKEVEN PROBLEM

In 1990 General Motors introduced a brand new car that changed the way cars in North America are priced and sold. To the auto industry, Saturn was a moonshot gamble, and involved about the same level of investment—roughly $3.5 billion to get the line up and running. The question is: Will GM recoup its investment?[9]

A generation ago, the common practice in the automobile industry was to price a line of cars by starting with a *base*

model sold with minimal equipment and a long list of optional features. Once buyers had checked off their choices, however, they often had to wait weeks for the car of their dreams to be assembled. To accommodate buyers who didn't want to wait, savvy dealers maintained inventories of "loaded" cars based on their instincts about what people wanted.

When Japanese auto companies moved into the North American market, they did away with base model pricing. Instead, they divided model lines into *trim levels*—a sort of low, medium, and high

approach—and offered relatively few options. This practice greatly simplified production, reduced inventories, and generally made life easier for dealers. (This is not to say that it always made dealers happier—the old long-lists-of-options technique was extremely profitable.) Consumers loved the new approach, and in some parts of North America, Japanese cars began to account for 50 percent of sales.

In the fall of 1990, after nearly eight years in development, General Motors unveiled its new Saturn automobile with a *fixed price, no-haggle* pricing strategy. The *no-dicker sticker* has now become so popular that other dealerships are moving in that direction, although some industry analysts warn that the policy is harder to transfer to existing nameplates.

GM surprised many people in the industry by announcing a first-year price of only U.S. $7,995* for its Saturn SL sedan—about $1,000 less than the least expensive Toyota Corolla. According to new GM President Lloyd E. Reuss: "The market has been waiting for Saturn for some time, and these prices put us at a distinct competitive advantage against imports." A fancier sports sedan carried an initial price of $8,595. At the high end of the Saturn line, prices for the SL 2 touring sedan started at $10,295—about $1,600 less than the rival Toyota Camry. Topping out the line was a two-door sports coupe selling for $11,775.

Within two years of introduction, Saturn's sales were the bright spot in the North American market. In 1991, however, Saturn was also thought to have lost $800 million. By May of 1993, it reached its first profitable month, and 1993 was considered to be the breakeven year, which means Saturn was finally matching its costs with its revenues. But how long will it take GM to recoup its investment, which had reached $4.5 billion by 1993? Although low prices made Saturn's launch extremely successful, was this pricing strategy good business? If you had been managing Saturn's launch, would you have begun with prices that low? What would you do now that Saturn has proved an important competitor? Would you begin raising prices? ▼

---

* All dollar amounts in this box are given in U.S. dollars.

KEY POINTS SUMMARY ▼

1. Pricing is important to the firm because it represents the opportunity to recover costs spent developing, distributing, and promoting the product. Value (benefits divided by price) depends on consumer perceptions. Such factors as quality and brand image enable a firm to compete on a nonprice basis.

2. Although *costs* are the first and most important factor in pricing, three other factors—*consumer demand*, the *competitive situation,* and *government controls*—have to be factored into the pricing decision.

3. Cost factors are analyzed in terms of two categories: *fixed costs*, or costs that are not tied directly to production—such as rent, utilities, property taxes, and executive salaries; and *variable costs*, or costs directly related to making the physical product or providing the service—such as ingredients, parts, labor, packaging. In the short run, a firm incurs the same fixed costs whether it makes a million units of the product or no units at all. Variable costs, however, increase as the number of units produced increases.

4. Consumer demand for products may be described as either price-elastic or price-inelastic. With price-elastic products, demand responds strongly to price; thus, consumers are described as price sensitive. The more price-elastic the demand for a product is, the less opportunity a firm has to charge a premium price. With inelastic products, consumers are not price-sensitive. Producers can charge more for price-inelastic products without affecting demand.

5. A firm's ability to set prices is affected by the structure of the market in which it operates, which may be a monopoly, an oligopoly, a purely competitive, or a monopolistically competitive market. The more competitive the market, the more price-sensitive customers are. Competitors' pricing policies also have a direct effect on the price a firm can set for its products.

6. Every nation has laws regulating the pricing of at least some products in some ways. In Canada the government specifically forbids price-fixing, price discrimination, predatory pricing, and deceptive price advertising in most circumstances. Trade agreements like GATT and NAFTA further affect the pricing of products sold internationally.

7. In order to make a profit, a firm must price a product above its costs. In a *cost analysis*, rev-

enues are first determined, followed by cost estimation, which identifies fixed and variable costs. Then *marginal cost analysis* is used to compare revenues with costs. Finally, a *breakeven analysis* is conducted to determine at what different price points and sales levels a profit can be achieved.

DISCUSSION QUESTIONS ▼

1. Find a product, service, or store that has changed its value equation (value = benefits/price) recently. Explain how it manipulated the price, quality, and benefits to shift the perception of value. How important was price in driving the change?

2. Describe how the monopolistic, oligopolistic, purely competitive, and monopolistically competitive nature of an industry can influence pricing.

3. Define price-fixing, price discrimination, predatory pricing, and deceptive price advertising, and explain the rationale for outlawing these practices in Canada.

4. At which stage of the product life cycle would you expect to find the highest prices? The lowest prices? Why?

5. Explain under what circumstances a firm might price its products below cost.

6. A beauty shop has a $100,000 annual overhead (fixed cost). The average variable cost per customer visit is $3. If the average price

charged is $6, how many customers must the beauty shop attract in a year to break even?

7. Select a high-quality sweatshirt in your college or university bookstore and describe how competitive forces, consumer demand, the distribution chain, and the product costs have probably influenced its price. Using library research and local interviews, compare the pricing of this sweatshirt with the pricing of a typical textbook for a big introductory course. If you were to go into business, would you rather market sweatshirts or textbooks?

8. Develop a cost analysis for used textbooks for your bookstore. How much profit does the distributor make? How much does the bookstore make? What are their costs? Working with your student government association, develop a consumer education program on buying used books. What guidelines would you draw up for both buying and selling used books? At what price points (considering original cost and the book's condition) are students getting fair prices?

Integrative Case ● Discussion Questions

The Body Shop*

1. If price equals perceived value, what factors constitute perceived value for Body Shop products?

2. Anita never wants to discuss profits, and she wouldn't understand a breakeven analysis. What factors do you think determine prices at The Body Shop?

Harley-Davidson

1. What constitutes value for a loyal Harley owner?

2. Is demand for Harley products price-elastic or price-inelastic? Explain your answer.

3. What sort of competitive pricing strategy does Harley use?

*The three cases at the back of the book—"The Body Shop," "Harley-Davidson," and "The Millennium Power System"—illustrate topics discussed in all chapters of this book. Your instructor will tell you when to read a particular case and answer the discussion questions on it that appear at the end of each chapter.

The Millennium Power System

1. If the rechargeable battery industry were oligopolistic, how would that affect pricing of Millennium Systems?

2. If the industry were monopolistically competitive, how would that affect Millennium Systems pricing?

Auction

What determines the price to charge for the product or service you are about to market? Some standard cost plus markup scheme? Do you check out your direct competition and set your prices accordingly, perhaps slightly underpricing them? Or do you draw on experience and simply charge what you know your consumer market will bear? Study various sales catalogs or shop around in competing retail outlets. Does the disparity in pricing strategies surprise you? How can those merchants seemingly overpricing their products and services hope to survive? However, experience has taught you that the lowest-priced competitor does not necessarily garner the lion's share of the market, even in recessionary times. Pricing is indeed a complex issue, and a critical element of any overall marketing strategy, as the pricing strategy must mesh with the balance of the strategy.

Price is a central aspect of the overall value sought by consumers when procuring goods and services. A good rule of thumb used by many businesspeople is that "value" is the combination of absolute price, product or service quality, and the subjective consumption experience. Individual consumers each possess their own personal notions of what constitutes value, and what they are satisfied to exchange their hard-earned cash for. Combine consumer subjectivity with your own marketing strategy, which addresses issues further complicating the appropriate pricing of your products or services, such as market positioning, target markets, location, service levels, and a host of additional marketing-related factors, and you end up with a real three-Tylenol headache!

Perhaps the best example of the volatility of consumer product pricing is presented by the auction industry, with auction customers willing to pay whatever sum they personally feel constitutes good value for a given article. Many auctioned-off items only command a fraction of what experts feel their market value should be, while on the right day, with the right crowd, perhaps with the planets in proper alignment, numerous auctioned-off articles will command sums vastly exceeding their appropriate "market value."

Who, you ask, determines market value or price anyway? To a very significant degree, it is the consumer, not the marketing organization. There exist price points on which most industries operate, years of industry experience dictating that when prices rise above certain cutoff points, consumers are not willing to spend the sums of money required to acquire those goods. This is referred to as price elasticity in purely economic terms, numerous and complex price elasticity formulas being applied to various product groups and industries by exuberant economists. In reality, price elasticity is impacted by such a variety of "confounding" market-related factors that such theories are seldom accurate.

How then does the marketer arrive at the appropriate market price for a product or service? Through precise market and consumer research, diligent competitive analysis, and a scientific product costing formula? Not always. If this method fails, the marketer can always fall back on common business sense and experience, as there are no guarantees that any product or service will command the expected price.

QUESTIONS

1. Which marketing strategy elements significantly impact pricing strategy and in what manner?
2. What additional difficulties might be involved in pricing an intangible product or service?
3. When is a "skimming" strategy more suitable to an overall marketing strategy than a "penetration" strategy?
4. Why do you think some consumers shop in higher-priced specialty stores instead of low-priced "box" stores such as Wal-Mart or Costco/Price Club?

Source: This case was prepared by Byron Osing and is based on the *Venture* series episode "Auction," which was originally broadcast on May 29, 1994.

533

Chapter 17

Pricing Objectives and Strategies

WILL PRICING STRATEGIES BRING DOWN BRANDS?

In classical economic theory, philosophers worry about market leaders who become so strong that they can dominate the market and set prices as high as they like. Strong brands have traditionally been able to get premium prices in return for their brand's credibility and image —a practice some called price *skimming*. What's happening with Marlboro cigarettes and IBM computers in the 1990s is providing a test of pricing and the product life cycle.

The trade press carried big headlines in 1993 when the world's number-one-selling cigarette, Marlboro, announced the unthinkable—it was cutting its price by 20 percent.[1] Analysts applauded the action as a way for the troubled cigarette marketer to regain market share lost to discount cigarettes. During the 1980s Marlboro had instituted double-digit price increases, and by the early 1990s, its cigarettes were priced 30 percent higher than store brands—a difference customers began refusing to honor. In spite of the enormous power of its brand equity, Marlboro confronted serious market share losses. So Marlboro changed its pricing strategy from a *market leader strategy* to the strategy of *lowering prices to gain market share.*

Meanwhile the once-unsinkable IBM struggled to keep its bottom line above water by jettisoning business units and tossing employees overboard. For years IBM had dominated the mainframe market, and because its customers were locked into the IBM system once they had made a major investment in mainframes, IBM could charge whatever it wanted to for its products. On some products margins were over 50 percent. IBM's leadership in the computer market was seriously challenged, however, when the technology changed and high-powered minicomputers became available at cheaper prices from competitors. No longer

able to depend on mainframes and its price leadership strategy, IBM saw its stock lose two-thirds of its value over eighteen months in the early 1990s. Still, as the ad in Exhibit 17-1 shows, IBM continued to defend its mainframe strategy to the financial community.

Analysts say that the most important strategy for a market leader is to avoid any action that could erode the profitability of the category—because strong brand equity supports premium prices and cre-

ates customer demand. But how much can a market leader charge on the basis of a strong brand? Will such companies inevitably have to sacrifice category profitability to maintain market share in highly competitive industries? Are market leaders just "price bandits" who are finally getting their just desserts? Or is it just that the day of the market leader concept is waning, and with it the power of branding to command premium prices? ■

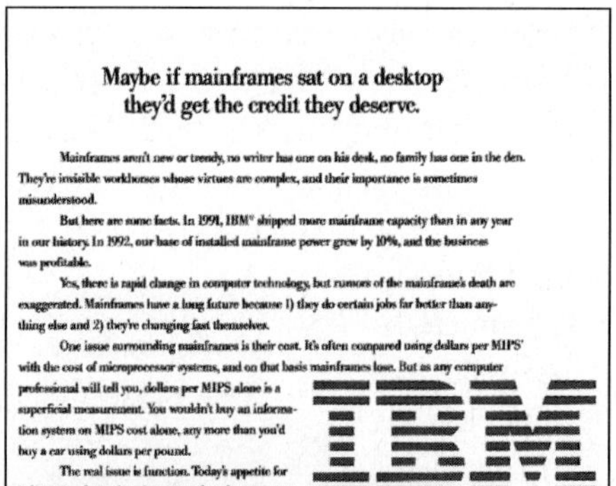

Maybe if mainframes sat on a desktop they'd get the credit they deserve.

Exhibit 17-1
Don't Forget the Mainframe
Oriented toward the financial community, this IBM ad defends the company's leadership in mainframe computers, a market that some analysts say is declining.

SETTING PRICING OBJECTIVES ●

Because pricing has a direct impact on revenues and profits, it is very important to corporate planners and top management and plays a highly visible role in strategic planning. Pricing is the point where a number of the issues in contemporary marketing intersect. The battle between big retailers and manufacturers over control of the distribution channel is played out largely through pricing strategies. Furthermore, as we discussed in the last chapter, in today's highly price-conscious environment, it is far tougher for name brands to maintain the price premium they have long enjoyed.[2]

The last chapter introduced the basic concepts of pricing. This chapter focuses on pricing objectives and strategies. *Pricing objectives* are those goals a company wants to accomplish in order to protect and increase its profits. They depend directly on—and must be coordinated with—the organization's overall corporate and marketing objectives. We'll start by looking at corporate objectives and then explore the way three of the four C's of pricing that we discussed in Chapter 16—cost, consumer demand, and competition—influence the formation of marketing pricing objectives. The fourth C, that of government controls, does not shape a company's pricing objectives, although in the general pricing endeavor marketers must take into account the restrictions imposed by various government agencies and regulations.

CORPORATE DIRECTIONS

All the other elements in the marketing mix—the product itself, its distribution, and its promotion—create costs for the firm. Pricing allows the firm to recover the cost of the value these marketing activities have added to the product. It is the element of the marketing mix that most directly addresses the firm's profitability.

At the corporate level, the pricing objective is to cover costs and achieve a targeted rate of return that will ensure the firm's desired return on investment. **Return on investment (ROI)** is a measure of profitability based on a comparison between the firm's net income and the sum of all moneys invested in the firm by the owners, including shareholders' purchases of stock. Until Komatsu entered the North American earthmoving market, for example, Caterpillar averaged a healthy 27 percent ROI, a rate that was seriously eroded by the aggressive Japanese competitor.[3] (For more on ROI, see Appendix B.)

The major drawback to the target-rate-of-return objective is that it focuses on short-term profits and neglects both the competitive marketing environment and the customer. For example, many cable-TV companies use target-rate-of-return as an objective. But a Wall Street Journal/NBC News poll showed that 37 percent of cable-TV subscribers were dissatisfied with service prices and believed rates were not fair and reasonable. Only automobile insurance prices received a worse rating from respondents.[4]

MARKETING PRICING OBJECTIVES

In addition to considering corporate profitability objectives, organizations develop pricing objectives that will enable them to develop a *cost advantage*, stimulate *customer demand*, and increase *competitive market share*, attempting as they do this to choose the most favorable options allowed them by *government controls*. Pricing objectives also usually specify two factors—geography and timing. Examples of pricing objectives are given in Table 17-1.

Return on investment (ROI)
A ratio that estimates a firm's profitability in terms of how its net income compares with its total equity, or the sum of all moneys invested in the firm.

Profits and the Efficiency Paradox

Efficiency—on the simplest level, minimizing resources in order to maximize profits—is generally a key advantage in economies of scale. In 1989, however, H. J. Heinz discovered that new high-speed slicing machines were dicing the spuds for a popular potato snack too finely. As a result, quality, sales, and profits suffered. Heinz decided to sacrifice efficiency (slowing down the equipment produced more uniform morsels) for the sake of effectiveness—the reward for doing what is appropriate to meet objectives.

TABLE 17-1	SAMPLE PRICING OBJECTIVES

Achieve Cost Advantage
To increase prices in British Columbia in order to capitalize on high levels of demand during strong tourist months in a resort area, and to lower prices off-season to stimulate demand.

Stimulate Customer Demand
To decrease prices in regions with lower sales levels in order to stimulate demand and build a stronger brand presence.

Increase Market Share
To maintain an average 10 percent price advantage over leading competitors in all markets in the eastern region.

Costs Although achieving a certain level of sales at a price that more than covers costs would seem a logical way to establish a *cost advantage* over competitors, lowering costs in order to meet or beat a competitor's price is another common method. Reformulating the product so that it is less expensive to produce is one way to lower costs. Reducing the size of the product, which is what the candy-bar industry has done recently, is another. Product costs, although primarily a concern of production rather than marketing, are often the most important building block for a cost-based pricing strategy.

The second type of cost objective aims at survival. This may involve *stabilizing prices* in a market where they tend to fluctuate, either because of cost changes or competitive actions. A firm in financial trouble may have little choice but to make survival a pricing objective by *raising or lowering prices.* Since price is a flexible strategic variable, marketers can usually change prices more quickly than products, distribution channels, or marketing communications. However, price may be *too* easy to change for the long-term good of the company. A firm with profitability problems may be tempted to raise prices because it is quicker and easier than trimming production costs, yet raising prices under conditions of slack demand will only compound its problems. Lowering prices is an alternative form of survival pricing. In order to generate enough cash to stay alive, the firm sells at cost or—if inventories are high—even below cost. In recessionary times "value" brands have become a popular survival tactic. For example, Coors successfully introduced Keystone and Keystone Light as "value" brands with a quality image.

In 1993 the technology companies of the former Soviet Union did something they never dreamed of doing five years earlier.[5] They held a trade show in England to sell the technology of the old Russian military industry to buyers from around the world. On display were the discoveries and inventions resulting from the investment of hundreds of billions of rubles and decades of development—the guts of the nation's military hardware.

The question that stumped the Russians, however, was: How do you price such technology? In trying to answer it, the new marketers got a crash course in capitalistic pricing strategies. While many of the technologies they were attempting to sell were no longer state-of-the-art, they did have one major competitive advantage: because of Russia's low labor costs, as well as R&D costs that had been paid by the Soviet government which were therefore "sunk" costs, the Russians could afford to sell their technological products for far less than the prices charged for similar products made in the West.

The Russians are putting behind them the old Soviet production mentality. They are learning how to listen to customers and adapt their products to market needs in the West and in developing countries. Some Russian capitalists are even learning how to corner the market for certain types of technological developments, a move that will enable them to move beyond price-based strategies.

Consumer Demand   Sales can be increased by stimulating the levels of consumer demand, an objective that calls for *manipulating the price-value ratio*. For example, making the product more affordable (price) to a particular target can also make it more desirable (value). Another way to stimulate demand is to increase benefits relative to price. Another consumer-oriented pricing objective is increasing product turnover in order to increase sales.

Since consumers often compare substitute products largely on the basis of price, consumer-oriented pricing strategies are important for undifferentiated or commodity products.

In some industries demand is highly seasonal. For that reason, industries as diverse as ski resorts and long-distance phone services usually consider pricing objectives that will shift some demand to off-peak periods. Ski resorts offer low-priced summer vacations to attract clients at a time when rooms would otherwise be standing empty but charge a premium price in the winter when demand is highest. Long-distance phone companies offer special low rates during non-peak hours and charge a premium for calls during peak hours (8 A.M. to 5 P.M. Monday through Friday).

These pricing objectives are intended to *balance fluctuations in demand*: when demand is strongest, prices are highest; when demand is weakest, prices are lowest. They offer firms an opportunity to spread fixed costs over a broader base. A ski resort has virtually the same fixed costs for mortgage, insurance,

The more rapidly a seller's inventory can be turned over, the more likely that prices can be marked down. If a store that stocks products costing $1 million has a stock turnover rate of once a year, its average inventory cost is $1 million; if it turns that stock over four times a year, its average inventory cost goes down to $250,000, and it can afford to reduce its markups and lower prices. Some supermarket items turn over thirty, forty, or fifty times a year.

and maintenance whether its rooms are full or empty. Thus the resort must attract as many guests as possible all year long to offset these costs.

Competition   Many objectives can be designed around the goals of beating the competition on price or discouraging competition by establishing a low base price. Saturn used the latter strategy in its assault on Japanese imports.

Firms often try to improve their profitability by adjusting their prices to *increase their market share.* In general, a larger market share means higher production levels, greater economies of scale, and thus lower costs. *Establishing a price advantage* over a competitor is one objective that can lead to an increase in market share. Studies support the validity of using market share as a pricing objective. For example, the Strategic Planning Institute, which conducts a program called the Profit Impact of Marketing Strategies (PIMS), has found market share to be highly correlated with profitability. Businesses with market shares greater than 50 percent had ROI's more than three times higher than businesses with market shares of less than 10 percent.[6]

PRICING STRATEGIES

Three of the pricing C's that affect pricing objectives are key to the formation of pricing strategies. Thus pricing strategies may be *cost-oriented, customer-oriented,* or *competition-oriented.* Again, although government controls, the fourth C of pricing, do not dictate strategies, marketers must consider the limitations they place on pricing in implementing their pricing strategies.

COST-ORIENTED STRATEGIES

A firm's need for profits or cash flow and its cost structure may motivate marketers to adopt strategies based solely on the internal needs of the company. As the second chapter objective notes, there are three cost-oriented pricing strategies: *cost-plus, target-return* and *experience-curve pricing.* Many firms use one or more of these strategies.

Cost-Plus Pricing This pricing strategy was mentioned in Chapter 16, where it was used to explain profit margins, markups and markdowns. Cost-plus pricing is one of the simplest strategies because it merely requires adding a set amount—a *markup*—to all costs. This strategy is widely used by construction firms, government contractors, and manufacturers of custom-made goods. Military and aerospace contractors use a version of it called *cost-plus/fixed-fee pricing*, in which the government reimburses the contractor for all agreed-upon costs and also pays the contractor a fixed fee. This method is common when firms are reluctant to bid on government contracts because they fear that many uncontrollable factors could wipe out all their profits.

Target-Return Pricing In the **target-return pricing** strategy, marketers set a specific profit objective and then determine a product's price based on both fixed and variable costs and the number of units they expect to sell. The target-return price is calculated as follows:

target-return pricing
Pricing a product by setting a specific profit objective and then calculating price on the basis of fixed and variable costs and number of units expected to be sold.

$$\text{target return price} = \frac{\text{fixed costs} + \text{target return}}{\text{sales volume in units}} + \text{unit variable cost}$$

For example, a firm with demand of 5,000 units, a target return of $200,000, fixed costs of $400,000, and variable costs per unit of $90 would set the price as follows:

$$\text{target return price} = \frac{(\$400,000 + \$200,000)}{5,000} + \$90$$

$$= \$120 + \$90 = \$210$$

In addition to ignoring customer needs, the primary weakness of target-return pricing is its reliance on estimates of market demand. If demand is lower than expected, fewer units are sold. Thus there are fewer units over which to spread fixed overhead costs, which could result in a loss.

Experience-Curve Pricing **Experience-curve pricing** depends on achieving a predetermined sales volume. Firms using this strategy make assumptions about the relationship between their average total cost and total sales volume. Costs drop often by 30 percent each time that production doubles because the firm's experience enables it to find greater efficiencies and its higher volume gives it greater economies of scale. Electronics products like hand-held calculators and digital watches were sold according to experience-curve pricing. So are such newer technological devices as fax machines.

experience-curve pricing
Pricing a product according to the relationship between its average total cost and its total sales volume. This strategy assumes that costs will fall as volumes rise (creating economies of scale) and manufacturers become more experienced and efficient producers.

Firms adopting experience-curve pricing often price very aggressively—sometimes even below current costs—in order to target more price-elastic segments of the market more rapidly. These firms are betting that they will achieve enough volume at their low prices to earn a profit in the future. They are also trying to create a barrier to competitors by forcing them to accept equally low prices without the volume savings they enjoy.

CUSTOMER-ORIENTED STRATEGIES

Marketers who adopt *customer-oriented pricing strategies*, the topic of chapter objective three, focus on customer tastes and preferences, lifestyle, purchasing behavior, and price sensitivity. The relationship between price and the perception of quality is one of the most important factors in these strategies. With parity or undifferentiated products, price is often the most important cue of product quality: many buyers believe that a higher price means higher quality, and a lower price means low quality.

Diamonds in the Rough

Exploring for diamonds takes long hours of searching the soil for mineral signs of the presence of diamond ores. South African fields like this one have paid off handsomely for DeBeers, which has held a virtual monopoly of the diamond market since the 1870s, but Canada's Northwest Territories are thought by some to be the leading 21st-century source of these precious stones. [William J. Broad, "Clues Emerge to Rich Lodes of Diamonds," The New York Times, February 15, 1994, C1.]

skim pricing
The practice, often used in introducing a new and innovative product, of setting a high price in order to take advantage of the relative price insensitivity of some market segments.

penetration pricing
Setting a low price in order to penetrate a price-sensitive market.

Marketers who decide to use a customer-oriented approach have 4 strategies to choose from: *skim pricing, penetration pricing, psychological pricing*, and *value pricing*.

Skim Pricing Setting a high price in order to take advantage of the relative price insensitivity of some market segments is called **skim pricing**. This is how "cash cows" are created. It is also the pricing strategy referred to in the opening story about the troubles of market leaders Marlboro and IBM. Skimming is most often used in pricing new products, especially inventions. In such cases, the firm may be the only producer of the product and thus does not have to fear being undercut by competitors when it sets a high price to recover its development costs. Some customers are also willing to pay a premium price to be among the first to own a new item.

As the novelty wears off and competitors enter the market, however, prices generally have to become more competitive. For example, hand-held video cameras were introduced to the market at a price of over $2,000; today similar cameras sell for $600. Likewise, copying machines were high-priced when the target market was largely professionals and office managers; when it became feasible to sell copiers for the home, prices came down.

How long can a company maintain a price-skimming strategy for a new product? The answer depends on the product and the *barriers to entry* that the initiating firm sets up. Without such barriers as patents and copyrights, control of vital raw materials, dominance of distribution channels, strong brand equity, and the ability to mount massive advertising campaigns, initiators will soon have competitors. With such barriers, the skimming strategy can work well for long periods. For example, DeBeers, the South African diamond monopoly, has long controlled the supply of gem-quality diamonds entering the world market. It has expanded its market through advertising, and it continues to command premium prices.

Penetration Pricing The objective of a new-product or a new-market strategy is to quickly gain buyer trial and acceptance. If the product has an element of actual newness or distinct differences, then a nonprice-based strategy is appropriate, particularly if there are few direct competitors. But if the category is already established and highly competitive, then the easiest entry strategy may be **penetration pricing**. By offering a product at a reduced price or using coupons or rebates, the producer hopes to encourage trial of the product and to *penetrate* the market. Once the product is established in the market, the producer will raise prices. In general, the more competitive the product category, the more likely a newcomer will use penetration pricing to establish a foothold. This was the pricing strategy Saturn used in introducing its new line of cars.

Penetration strategies are also effective for existing products in highly competitive markets such as fast food and airline tickets for high-traffic routes. Such strategies are designed to appeal to price-sensitive customers and to keep out competition.[7] Only firms that can generate enough sales to produce massive quantities of the product—and thus realize economies of scale (see Chapter 1)—can compete effectively in these situations.

Psychological Pricing   Psychological pricing strategies such as *image pricing* and *reference pricing* recognize that a buyer's psychological reaction to a given price can play an important role in the purchase of a product. In many instances, buyers use the price of a product as a signal of its image and quality. Marketers use **image pricing** to capitalize on this kind of perception by pricing goods at high prices so they will be perceived as high quality. This kind of pricing strategy isn't used, however, for high-status goods. The marketing psychology for these goods downplays price as the Porsche advertisement reproduced in Exhibit 17-2 demonstrates.

Image pricing is most often used when the target audience is not knowledgeable. For example, most purchasers of jewelry know little about precious gems and metals, so they are also inclined to judge quality by price. Businesses, too, often equate premium prices with the quality of a law firm, investment banker, or management consultant. By contrast, when customers are knowledgeable about a product or indifferent toward its prestige, they are less likely to associate high price with high quality. Industrial components such as machine parts are judged by how well they meet technical specifications, not by their price.

Reference pricing is often used for retail merchandise for which customers have built up an idea of what the price generally is—that is, they have a "reference price" and are price-sensitive to any difference between that and the stated price. One type of reference pricing, **price lining**, is used primarily by retailers whose customers differentiate goods on the basis of price. For instance, men's suits are commonly sold at a specified number of *price points* such as $129.95, $179.95, and $249.95. Because of consumer reference prices, a number of regularly purchased inexpensive products such as candy and chewing gum are subject to *customary pricing*. "Correct prices" for these goods

image pricing
Setting a high price to convey an image of high quality.

price lining
Pricing groups of products at set points relative to nearest competitive offerings.

Exhibit 17-2
The Power of Fantasy

High-status image products are not sold on price, as this ad for Porsche demonstrates.

Old cars go to scrap yards.
Old Porsches go to museums.

OUR FIRST PORSCHE: 1948 TYPE 356 ROADSTER.

PORSCHE

Promotional Prices Are Relative

Promotional prices exist only in relation to other prices. When consumers are exposed to a promotional price, they often judge its value on the basis of their own idea of the marketplace or "usual" price of the product in question. This internal reference price, which plays an important role in the buyer's perception of value, tends to fluctuate, and one of the influences on it is the difference between the regular and promotional prices in a given situation. Promotional pricing strategy must thus consider the buyer's internal reference price carefully.

odd or reverse pricing
Pricing products slightly below the dollar in order to make them appear to be lower-priced than they are.

everyday-low-price (EDLP) strategy
A retail pricing strategy that emphasizes the lowest prices possible on all merchandise rather than artificially low promotional prices on selected items and higher prices on the rest of the merchandise.

value-in-use pricing
Pricing products based in part on their lifetime operating costs.

are so firmly fixed in customers' minds that producers have little leeway to change a price, so, they offer a smaller package instead.

Another type of psychological pricing is **odd or reverse pricing**, which is pricing products a few cents below the dollar to make them appear to be lower-priced than they are. For instance, a product priced at $4.99 appears cheaper than one priced at $5.00—and a $499 item looks like a better deal than a $500 item. In New Zealand, products are usually priced at five cents below the dollar because that country has no one- or two-cent pieces.

Value-Based Pricing Increasingly, marketers are basing pricing on customers' *perceived value*. Such value-based strategies call for increasing perceived value and then setting the price at a level compatible with that value. Perceived values may be either tangible or intangible. For example, Frito Lay is trying to expand its profits by building up its market with less expensive offerings. Dropping the price of its large bags of chips to under $2 from $2.39 increased unit sales and earnings by more than 10 percent. The company also introduced small 25-cent bags, which pumped up volume among its smaller vendors.

Discount stores, supermarkets, and some other retailers manipulate markups and markdowns to build store traffic. In a strategy called *high-low pricing*, they offer weekly specials on selected items and higher prices on everything else. In contrast, other stores have moved to an **everyday-low-prices (EDLP)** policy, which better regulates distribution and promotion costs (Exhibit 17-3). In this strategy, stores offer the lowest prices possible on all goods all the time rather than putting low promotional prices on selected items from time to time.

Value-in-use pricing incorporates a product's lifetime operating costs into the pricing decision. For instance, energy-saving appliances often cost more than those that use more electricity. Over their lifetimes, however, these products save money through lower energy usage. The savings constitute an increase in value that can be factored into a higher initial price.

Some industrial-goods producers use **economic-value-to-the-customer (EVC) pricing.** With this strategy, the supplier determines the maximum amount that customers will pay if fully informed about both its own offering, product X, and the product currently in use, product Y. The EVC for product X is then computed as the purchase price of product Y (the reference product) plus or minus the difference in value between products X and Y.

Figure 17-1 illustrates this process. Note that here reference product Y has $100 more ($200 versus $100) in start-up costs and $100 more ($500 versus $400) in postpurchase costs than does product X. In addition, product X offers the buyer $100 more value over the product life cycle so it follows that customers should be willing to pay $300 more ($200 in cost savings plus $100 in additional value) for product X. Adding this $300 to the $300 the customer is currently paying for the product gives a maximum EVC price of $600. To induce customers to switch to product X, however, marketing managers for the firm may opt to price the good at $475—sharing $125 of the firm's competitive advantage with the buyer.

Sometimes companies offer two or more products as a "package deal"—usually at a special price that is lower than the sum of the individual products' prices. This practice is known as **price bundling**.[8] Travel agencies, for example, offer vacation packages that include airfare, lodging, and ground transportation, while law firms often give businesses lower prices on legal services in return for a promise to use the law firm for all of their legal work. The logic behind bundling is that it offers the

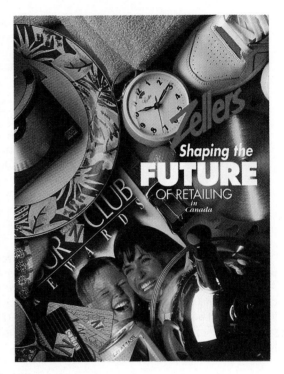

Exhibit 17-3
"The Lowest Price is the Law"

As Canada's most successful discount store, Zellers has always stressed the importance of everyday low prices. Zellers now operates 276 stores across Canada.

economic-value-to-the-customer (EVC) pricing
Setting a product's price at the maximum amount customers will pay if they are fully informed about both the product and competitive offerings.

price bundling
Combining two or more related products or services as a "package deal"—usually at a special promotional price.

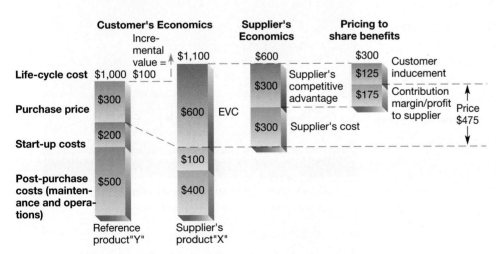

Figure 17-1 The EVC (economic-value-to-customer) concept
Source: Brenda Forbis and John L. and Nitri T. Mehta, "Value-Based Strategies for Industrial Products," Business Horizons, May–June 1981, pp. 32–41.

customer increased value and simpler decision making. The marketer benefits if the greater attractiveness of the package increases volume and lowers marketing costs. Bundling is a common strategy in the sale of cars, new houses, batteries, light bulbs, bars of soap, and six-packs of soft drinks and beer.

COMPETITION-ORIENTED STRATEGIES

In general, marketers use *price-based strategies* in highly competitive markets where there is little but price to differentiate the products and *nonprice-based strategies* when they can achieve their marketing objectives through product differentiation (which may consist of either actual physical differences or perceived differences such as those created by branding). *Competition-oriented strategies* are adopted primarily to increase or protect market share. The three major types of competition-based strategies, the focus of chapter objective four, are *competitive-advantage pricing, promotional pricing, and market-entry strategies.*

Competitive-Advantage Pricing Some marketers set their prices according to how well their product matches up feature by feature with competing products. If the firm feels that its product has a strong competitive advantage over competitors—or that it can create such an advantage through a strong marketing communication program—it may elect to become a **price leader** and charge a *premium price* for the product (see Exhibit 17-4). Maytag uses this strategy successfully in the consumer appliances market.

price leader
A firm that is able to charge a premium price for its product because customers view it as offering greater benefits.

Exhibit 17-4
Paying for Top Quality

Emphasizing quality, prestige, and status, the Range Rover commands a premium price. This ad points out that no other 4-wheel drive vehicle comes close to matching the luxury and performance of a Range Rover.

You've never seen an interior like this before.

RANGE ROVER

Other firms, after assessing their product and their market, decide that they do not have a strong enough competitive advantage to justify a higher price. Instead, they opt to be *price followers* and meet the competition. College textbook producers often use this form of pricing in well-established markets. Pharmaceutical companies, under attack from many sides for their past pricing policies and threatened by the spreading popularity of generic drugs, are altering their pricing strategies. Although some have elected to hold the line on prices and give up market share, others are lowering their prices in order to compete and protect their share. In the latter situation, a price leader may become a price follower.

Finally, firms whose products offer fewer features than those of their competitors and firms that haven't made large R&D investments may decide to price their goods *below the competition*. For instance, companies making IBM-PC–compatible "clones" price their machines below IBM's, and Hyundai positions its midsize cars as "cars that make sense" by pricing them generally lower than other imports.

For much government and construction work, sales are made through **competitive-bid pricing**. Firms submit sealed bids stating prices that meet the customer's technical specifications and volume requirements. As a rule, the bids are all opened at the same time and the contract is awarded to the lowest qualified bidder. Engaging in competitive-bid pricing is difficult and risky because the price setter must try to find a price that will both undercut competitors and be high enough to cover costs and generate a profit.[9]

Promotional Pricing Setting temporarily low prices on selected items in order to build market share quickly at the expense of competitors is called **promotional pricing.** One example of promotional pricing is **loss-leader pricing;** in this strategy, retailers price some goods at close to cost, or wholesale price, hoping to increase store traffic and, they hope, sales of other goods that they sell at regular, marked-up prices.

As noted in Chapter 16, in oligopolies and mature markets a promotional price cut by one firm may force price cuts by others, and the result may be a *price war* that damages the profits of all firms in the market. In times of economic recession like the early 1990s, promotional pricing may be man-

competitive-bid pricing
A practice in which several firms submit sealed bids stating prices for items that meet customers' technical specifications and the volume requirements, with the contract being awarded to the lowest qualified bidder.

promotional pricing
Setting temporarily low prices on selected items in order to buy market share.

loss-leader pricing
Pricing a product at or below cost in order to attract customers to a retail store, where they may then buy other, high-margin products.

Can Kellogg Keep Its Customers?

Despite the advancing army of store-brand cereals, Kellogg CEO Arnold Langbo raised prices of Corn Flakes and other popular brands 6% in 1993. The company makes heavy use of couponing, and it was planning, early in 1994, to increase its advertising budget. Langbo says Kellogg has "very loyal customers" and that "it's stayed there. According to D'Agostino Public Affairs Director Mary Moore, every product in this line is of excellent quality, and some products, like the cookies, are simply better than anything else at any price.

dated because lower-priced products sell better than their higher-priced counterparts. When the economy moves out of recession, as happened in North America during 1993 and 1994, higher priced items tend to sell better because of the pent-up demand and the increase in consumer confidence.

WHY ARE THERE PRICE WARS?

Times are tough. You're barely balancing the books when your competitor suddenly cuts prices to steal market share. What do you do? Ride out the challenge and hope the damage to your sales volume isn't too bad? Or do you match the price cuts and hope the damage to your bottom line is recoverable?

Both responses, of course, are based on the premise that the price cut is temporary—which isn't always true, as the fast food industry found out when Taco Bell cut its prices 1989 and started a price war that is still in progress. Before 1989, fast-food outlets offered discounts only when business was slow, but in the last several years discounting is a year-round practice and EDLP has become an important strategy.

But even if price cuts do tend to lure customers—especially during the winter doldrums—and energize slumping menus, they may also be a dangerous sales strategy. One potential problem is that they can permanently decrease the value of products for consumers—certainly a factor in McDonald's hesitation to match Taco Bell's price cuts. Another is that although discounting usually brings in more people, the stores have to serve 15 to 20 percent more customers just to stay even. This makes it harder for a local franchise to remain afloat. They are, in effect, doing extra work to give away food.

Tough times, a weak economy, flat sales, and killer competition—that's the situation facing many companies in the 1990s.[10] In the television set industry prices have been steadily dropping from year to year, and analysts have declared that no companies are making money today on color TVs. In the computer industry the prices fall every day, particularly for laptop computers. Price cuts are the rule even in such esoteric service industries as training, where Career Track made its reputation by pricing $400 seminars at $49.

Since big companies have investments with large established overheads, such as plants, they are forced to protect market share at all costs. In marketing theory, that's known as a *barrier to exit*. Companies can't exist on low revenues forever, though, no matter how huge their investments. Sometimes they fold, sometimes they are acquired by someone with deeper pockets, and sometimes they operate in a state of bankruptcy with their debts on hold, which establishes an artificially low pricing floor. Bankruptcy has deeply distorted pricing in the airline industry. Between the mid-1980s and the mid-1990s, several North American airlines went out of business, while many of the remaining airlines continued operating unprofitably.

In consumer products price-cutting takes a different sort of toll. Here price wars erode brand equity, the differentiation factor that is so costly and painstaking to build. When that happens, products become commodities. A hamburger is a hamburger is a hamburger . . . so why go to McDonald's when there is a discount fast-food outlet on the next corner? Brand equity has always been the antidote to price-cutting, but it doesn't seem to be working so well anymore.

In the marketing battleground of the 1990s, companies are forced to maintain share, even if that means cutting prices below their profitability levels. And no one is predicting that this trend will stop any time soon.

Market Entry Pricing Strategies Whether you move into a new market or move a new product into an existing market, your pricing strategy must focus on opening up a market. New products in a new category may use market-skimming pricing strategies because they are innovative and have few competitors. Competitive categories, however, may demand a *penetration pricing strategy*. A low initial price may be set to undercut competition and penetrate the market quickly. The objective is to build market share by attracting many customers as quickly as possible.

In order for a penetration strategy to work, the market must be price elastic; as you'll recall from Chapter 16, this means a market in which lower prices will attract large numbers of new customers. Furthermore, the product market must be susceptible to economies of scale (see Chapter 1) that can offset the initial losses on the low price. An example might be a new entry by Weight Watchers into the diet-drink category dominated by Ultra Slim-Fast. The category is moderately price sensitive—a lower price might get consumers to switch brands—and the production and distribution costs will decrease as the volume increases. Conceivably a new product could successfully enter this market by undercutting Ultra Slim-Fast prices.

ARRIVING AT THE FINAL PRICE ●

In addition to pricing objectives and strategies, marketers must estimate all the costs and other consumer- and market-related price factors when setting prices. But before we discuss that last step, we will consider specific pricing situations and various types of price adjustments that affect how the final price is set.

SPECIAL PRICING SITUATIONS

So far, we have discussed concepts that may be applied in one degree or another to goods and services as well as to both domestic and international marketing situations. However, both services and global marketing have some peculiar characteristics that complicate price-setting.

Services The special nature of services has some important implications for pricing, and these are the focus of the fifth chapter objective. For instance, when a buyer purchases a service to cover a period of time, the producer often quotes a single price that is charged for the service over that period. University tuition, automobile insurance, cleaning services, and software support fees fall into this category.

The same is true in the car-rental industry, although, car-rental pricing is very complicated. Competition is based almost entirely on market-specific prices. Each firm tries to match or better competitors' prices, and low prices are emphasized. Quoted prices may or may not be adjusted according to such auxiliary features as mileage charges, insurance waivers, and availability. Quality may be emphasized as a feature (Alamo and Avis emphasize the availability of Cadillacs), as may facilitating services like the advantage of using a particular credit card. In addition, there are special pricing arrangements for frequent users.

Other services are also priced to reflect usage rates. Phone customers in many parts of the country may choose a fixed price for unlimited local service or a measured service that ties charges to the number and type of calls made. People who make few calls save with measured service, while those who make many calls benefit from fixed prices. For other services, the best solution is often a mixture of both approaches. The Canadian Automobile Association, for example, provides basic road emergency service, trip planning, and maps and tour books for a fixed annual fee but charges members for insurance and travel bookings.

Global Pricing Considerations Pricing strategies in global markets, the topic of chapter objective six, are affected by several factors. The most important is the value of money relative to a country's standard of living. A hamburger priced at $1 is cheap in Canada, but when that price is translated into rubles, the same hamburger may become very expensive in Moscow. The valuation of currency and changes in exchange rates can play havoc with firms' pricing schedules, as can inflationary or recessionary periods resulting from national fiscal policies.

Most global companies have developed a transfer pricing procedure to guide how goods will be priced and how these costs will be transferred through the company's international distribution channels. Establishing a final price for a product that is sold in various countries can be extremely complex, but the need to do so is growing as regional trading blocks bring pressure to equalize prices in such areas as Europe and North America. Developing a coordinated pricing policy for the European Union will be particularly difficult since the markets in the various member countries are dramatically different. One 1993 study found that a box of Kellogg's Corn Flakes cost 243 percent more in Italy than in Britain and a can of Coke cost twice as much in Ireland as in France.[11]

Taxes, particularly duties and tariffs (which are discussed in Chapter 16), are another factor that must be considered in global pricing strategies. Since there are differential rates of income taxation throughout the world, companies have an incentive to minimize income in high-tax environments and maximize it in lower-tax environments. This leads into transfer pricing controversies where it is in the power of a multinational corporation to transfer goods across countries so as to choose selectively where it pays taxes, preferably in a low-tax country.

PRICE ADJUSTMENTS

In arriving at a final price, marketers must also consider specific price adjustments that are standard business practice in various markets. These adjustments, the subject of chapter objective seven, include *allowances, discounts,* and *geographical adjustments.*

Allowances To encourage distributors to perform some activity, manufacturers often extend various *allowances* to the wholesalers and retailers who carry their products. New-car dealers and appliance dealers often give *trade-in allowances* to customers—that is, they buy back a customer's used model for an amount that is credited against the cost of a new model. Businesses receive trade-in allowances on everything from trucks and agricultural equipment to industrial machinery. Manufacturers use **promotional allowances** to encourage distributors (wholesalers and/or retailers) of their products to sell their products more intensively. Promotional allowances may take the form of advertising allowances or of additional products supplied at no cost to the distributor. For example, a distributor may get one case of a product free whenever it orders twelve. Wholesalers and/or retailers may then pass on some of these savings to their customers in order to build sales volume.[12]

Discounts It is common practice in industrial sales (see Chapter 7) to quote a list or base price for a product and then offer *discounts,* or reductions from that price. Firms offer *quantity discounts* to get customers to purchase larger volumes of a given product and *cash discounts* to get them to pay quickly for what they buy. Cash discounts allow a customer to take a certain percentage off the bill if it is paid by a certain date. In consumer products, probably the most common example of a cash discount is the "cash price" offered by some gasoline stations. Cash discounts allow these firms to reach price-sensitive customers with lower prices, while getting higher prices from customers who are less price-sensitive and more inclined to want the convenience of using a credit card.

From time to time, firms offer their distributors various types of *trade discounts*—temporary reductions from the list price designed to promote higher sales volumes. These discounts are used to promote slow-selling brands or to encourage customers to buy more cases or units of a product than they normally would. Some manufacturers offer *seasonal discounts* to encourage wholesalers and retailers to stock up prior to the prime selling season or during the off-season. Seasonal discounts help manufacturers even out peaks and valleys in production volume. In contrast, *functional discounts* are offered to distributors at various levels for work they save the manufacturer. For example, wholesalers warehouse goods and break large quantities into the smaller ones demanded by retailers.

Geographical Adjustments Whether the seller or the buyer pays the cost of transportation is another decision that affects the final price of a product. Since costs can be high, whoever does *not* pay these charges realizes substantial savings. In exporting, quotations employ Incoterms such as F.O.B. and C.I.F. These can be explained further by saying that a seller would welcome F.O.B. as it minimizes responsibility for freight and handling at the earliest possible agreed-upon location which may even be the factory gate. From a buyer's point of view, price comparison is important and so a C.I.F. (cost, insurance, freight) quotation will typically involve shipping to a named port in the buyer's country of origin and allow direct comparison with other quotations as we now have a landed cost in the foreign country. Incoterms are internationally agreed-upon and administered by the International Chamber of Commerce in Paris, France. Situations in which the seller pays the cost of freight and handling to some specified location is called **F.O.B. pricing** (short for "free on board"). Two common forms of F.O.B. pricing are F.O.B.-origin pricing and F.O.B.-delivered-pricing. In *F.O.B.-origin pricing* also called *(F.O.B.-plant pricing)*, the location is the *seller's* factory or warehouse. In *F.O.B.-delivered pricing*, the seller holds title to the goods until they arrive at the *buyer's* warehouse.

promotional allowance
An attempt by a manufacturer to encourage wholesalers and retailers to sell its product by supplying distributors with extra, free units of the product or by providing cash allowances or financial support for advertising.

F.O.B. pricing
This from the seller's point of view, minimizes responsibility for freight and handling to the earliest possible agreed location.

Some sellers use *zone pricing*, a form of delivered pricing that charges an average freight charge to all buyers within a specified geographic area. Freight charges are lowest in zones close to the manufacturer and become progressively more expensive in zones that are farther away. For example, a manufacturer in Mississauga might divide Canada into four zones. Since Vancouver, B.C., and Saint John's, Newfoundland, are roughly the furthest points from Mississauga, they would be in zone four, the most expensive. This pricing method standardizes final delivered prices within zones, making for fewer price points and simplified freight calculations. Most firms opt for multiple zones, but in some circumstances a firm will choose to view the entire market as one zone and use *uniform delivered pricing*, or one set delivery price regardless of the customer's location. An example is a mail-order house that reminds all customers, wherever they are, to "be sure to add $1.50 to cover shipping and handling."

To implement *basing-point pricing*, the seller specifies one or more locations to act as *basing points*. A basing point is then used as the point of origin for charging freight to *all* customers, regardless of where the goods are actually shipped from. For example, if the basing point is Brandon, Manitoba, the buyer is in Moncton, New Brunswick, and the factory is in Montreal, the buyer will pay freight as if the product were actually shipped from Brandon instead of Montreal. If freight from Brandon to Moncton is $100 and from Montreal to Moncton $40, the seller keeps the difference of $60, which is called *phantom freight*. If the freight from Montreal to Monction is $100 and the freight from Brandon to Mocton $40, the seller swallows the $60 difference, a process called *freight absorption*.

SETTING THE PRICE: THE PRO FORMA ●

The tool marketers use in aggregating all the pricing factors and determining profit margin is called a **pro forma**—a breakdown of all the costs involved in producing and selling a product. To complete a pro forma, marketers must first forecast customer demand for the product, taking into account competitive factors (see our discussion of forecasting, in Chapter 8).

In Figure 17-2 we show a hypothetical pro forma for frozen pizza. If the company making this pizza can sell two million cases at a price of $12.50 each, and the total cost of making and selling each case is $11.50, it will have a profit margin of $1.00 per case.

Using a pro forma, managers can quickly see the impact of any cost or sales volume change. For example, if distribution costs to our pizza manufacturer were to rise by $.25, the company would either have to accept $.25 less per case in profit (a less desirable alternative for the retailer and one that might risk loss of market share), or find a way to save $.25 in some of the costs of producing or promoting the pizza (the option most producers prefer). Although for simplicity's sake we show only one set of numbers in the pro forma in Figure 17-2, it is common practice to prepare this financial statement for several forecasted levels. For example, if a company could achieve a better profit margin by projecting higher sales and if its assessment of the competitive environment suggested that such a risk might be worth taking, it would want to see how things would cost out at that level.

Bear in mind that a pro forma is only as good as the forecasting information behind it. If sales fall short of the forecast, economies of scale will not be realized (causing variable costs per unit to rise), and overhead-per-unit will rise (because each unit must take a bigger part of the overhead), resulting in less profit.

pro forma
A breakdown of all the costs involved in producing and selling a product that is used by marketers to determine profit margin. Pro formas often compute profit margins at various forecasted cost and sales levels.

Pro Forma for Frozen Pizza
(Based on sales of 2,000,000 cases at $12.50 per case)

	Per Case Costs	% of Sale Price
Cost of Goods		
Raw materials	$2.75	22
Labor	3.00	24
Totals	$5.75	46
Marketing Costs		
Volume discounts	.25	2
Returns	.25	2
Distribution	.50	4
Sales Commissions	.75	6
Advertising	1.50	12
Sales Promotion	1.75	14
Totals	5.00	40
Overhead	.75	6
Profit Margin Before Taxes	1.00	8
Totals	$12.50	100

Figure 17-2
Hypothetical Pro Forma

BOTTOM LINE REALITIES

THE BATTLE OVER EDLP

When in the fall of 1991 the giant Procter & Gamble began switching to an everyday-low-pricing strategy (EDLP) it caused a lot of discussion in supermarket, discount, and drugstore chains. Actually, a manufacturer can't introduce EDLP, only the retailer can. What P&G was trying to do was to use its market-leader power to force retailers to switch from a high-low strategy to an EDLP value strategy.[13]

The weapon a manufacturer like P&G uses to try to force this sort of change is trade allowances. By cutting back on its trade allowances, the package-goods manufacturer hoped to make the industry establish more efficient pricing and distribution programs and offer consistently lower prices on all merchandise. This would allow P&G to reallocate dollars from promotion to building brand loyalty. This is not a small change in the way P&G does business; it involves total change throughout every aspect of P&G's marketing and the marketing programs of every company that does business with it. One analyst called it the most important strategic decision P&G has ever made.

The switch made sense to P&G, but it didn't make much sense to many retailers that depend upon trade allowances to either support their promotional budget or increase their general revenues. Furthermore, it discourages *forward buying*—that is, stocking up on discounted products for future sale. Forward buying, however, plays havoc with manufacturing operations, causing overtime production schedules followed by costly lulls. One retailer that was pleased with P&G's announcement was Wal-Mart, which has based its growth on a value strategy. And Wal-Mart is P&G's largest customer.

P&G's sales results in 1993, after eighteen months of EDLP, weren't encouraging: analysts reported that the company's market share declined in virtually every category as competitors like Lever Brothers moved in with substantial trade deals. For P&G's competitors, it was a feeding frenzy as unhappy retailers got even by reducing their P&G orders and switching to competitors' products.

P&G, however, maintains the strategy is working and that consumers are paying 14 percent less on most P&G's products. The company was surprised at retailers' resistance but says initial losses during the changeover were expected. P&G's data also show that market shares in late 1993 were beginning to regain their earlier levels. The company says its national volume the first year of EDLP fell 7 percent with wholesalers and 16 percent with drug chains, but rose 11 percent with mass merchandisers, 19 percent with club stores, and 6 percent with grocery chains.

Further complicating the picture is a 1993 research project that reported the EDLP approach may not work as well for everyone as it works for Wal-Mart. This study found that value pricing doesn't match the profits generated from most grocers' traditional *high-low approach*; stores featuring everyday low pricing rang up slightly more sales but a lot less profit than the high-low stores. In fact, the study found that some of the EDLP stores weren't actually offering the lowest prices.

Will P&G's strategy work and will it ultimately be good for business? Is it possible for a market leader to force a change like this or will the market leader lose its leadership? These are the questions the industry is debating. If you were in charge of this program at P&G, how would you analyze the advantages and disadvantages of EDLP? Would you recommend that the company stick with this strategy? If you worked for a competing company like Colgate-Palmolive or Johnson and Johnson, would you follow the leader on this strategy? ▼

KEY POINTS SUMMARY ▼

1. The major types of pricing objectives are tied to corporate and marketing objectives. At the corporate level, pricing objectives are established to cover costs and achieve a targeted level of return. At the marketing level, pricing objectives are developed in terms of three of the four C's of pricing. *Cost*-oriented objectives are designed to set a price based on adjusting the cost of making or providing a product in order to achieve a cost advantage over the competition or to survive. *Consumer*-oriented objectives rely on stimulating consumer demand by manipulating the price-value ratio and balancing demand fluctuations. *Competition*-oriented objectives are designed to meet, beat, or prevent competition and increase market share. Government *controls*, the fourth C of pricing, are taken into account in formulating the three types of pricing objectives.

2. Cost-oriented pricing strategies seek to meet a firm's internal needs. Cost-plus pricing consists of adding a markup to all costs. Target-return pricing uses demand estimates and fixed and variable costs to calculate a price that will meet a stated profit objective. Experience-curve pricing assumes that a new product will generate enough sales volume to create cost-lowering production efficiencies and economies of scale.

3. Customer-oriented pricing strategies focus on the relationship between price and consumer perceptions of quality. Skim pricing—setting a high price—is used for innovative products to keep out the competition and for products with strong brand images. Penetration pricing—setting a lower price—is used to build market share for a new product. Psychological pricing uses price as a signal of high quality (image pricing), to conform to consumers' ideas of correctness (reference pricing), or to make a product appear lower-priced than it is (odd pricing). Value-based pricing is based on consumers' perceptions of value.

4. Competition-oriented pricing strategies seek to protect or increase market share by differentiating the firm's product from those of the competition. The major types of competition-oriented strategies are competitive-advantage pricing (price leading, price following, or pricing below competitors), promotional pricing (temporarily low prices), and market-entry pricing (penetration of new markets).

5. Service pricing differs from the pricing of goods by taking into consideration the pricing of a service performed over a period of time. Service pricing also reflects usage rates.

6. Special factors to consider in the pricing of global products are the value of a country's currency and the taxes, duties, and tariffs involved in intercountry transactions.

7. In setting an item's final price, marketers must include trade-in and promotional allowances, any type of discount, and geographical adjustments related to freight charges.

DISCUSSION QUESTIONS ▼

1. Which of the pricing objectives described in this chapter would you expect to yield the best long-term results for a firm? Why?

2. You are the marketing manager of a newly invented product. Describe the product briefly and identify the pricing objectives you would pursue for it. Explain your rationale.

3. Why do firms sometimes introduce products using skim pricing and then shift to penetration pricing later in the product life cycle?

4. Your company has just invented a new patentable technique for making tires that will provide 35 percent more miles than current tires in the same category. What pricing strategy would you, as marketing manager for this new product, recommend using? Why?

5. You are the marketing manager for a product that is not doing well and you cannot permanently lower your price because your profit margins are already very thin. How might you stimulate a short-term sales increase?

6. Interview the marketing manager for a local company and determine the pricing strategies the company uses for its primary product line and how it fine-tunes those prices.

7. What other mature brands besides Marlboro might be categorized as "price bandits"? Pick one and analyze its pricing strategy. Is it a market leader and will its strong brand equity continue to support a premium price? If you were the brand manager for this product, what pricing strategies would you recommend for the short term and long term?

8. Interview the manager of a store in your community about how and why the store's EDLP strategy was implemented. What data does the store have comparing profitablity before and after EDLP? Interview customers to see if they are aware of and understand the EDLP approach. Do they agree that the store's prices are generally lower than those in other stores selling similar products?

The Body Shop*

1. What kind of pricing strategy does The Body Shop use?

2. Is price a primary concern to Body Shop customers? Why or why not? Is this good or bad from the firm's point of view?

Harley-Davidson

1. What would happen if Harley used penetration pricing; that is, if the company dropped the price of its cycles?

2. Does Harley make most of its earnings and profits from motorcycles? parts? accessories?

3. Which firms in the motorcycle industry use experience curve pricing?

The Millennium Power System

1. What type of pricing strategy does Panasonic employ? What type does Millennium use?

2. Does Millennium use price bundling?

3. Why would Millennium offer advertising allowances only at certain times of the year?

*The three cases at the back of the book—"The Body Shop," and "Harley-Davidson," and "The Millennium Power System"—illustrate topics discussed in all chapters of this book. Your instructor will tell you when to read a particular case and answer the discussion questions on it that appear at the end of each chapter.

Industries Competing Head On

The northeastern United States was once the most lucrative market for Canadian hydro producers. No longer! Due to fierce price competition from another sector in the energy industry, U.S. power producers are switching suppliers. The three provinces generating hydro power are Ontario, Quebec and New Brunswick. Ontario Hydro and Hydro Quebec are two of Canada's largest corporations. But, the cost of exporting hydro power to the eastern seaboard is expensive, particularly in light of alternative energy sources.

What is a bust for Canada's hydro power producers is a boom for western Canada's natural gas producers. The gas pipeline system into the United States has expanded, opening new markets for natural gas. The new Iroquois Pipeline into upper New York state has pitted one Canadian industry against another.

Selling power to the U.S. is worth $1.5 billion a year to hydro producers. Unfortunately, labor problems and debt burdens have put hydro power into a high price bracket. Alberta's natural gas suppliers are now North America's lowest cost supplier of energy. With export sales to the U.S. at $5.5 billion in 1993, gas suppliers are responding to this new access with low prices. This new demand has stimulated a sagging oil and gas industry with increased exploration activity. Gas suppliers are estimating that 4,000 new gas wells will be drilled over the next few years and industry analysts are expecting the business to grow between 15 and 20 percent in total exports next year.

Hydro producers in Canada did not expect their customers to switch energy sources, but since 1989, there has been a decrease in hydro consumption as independent power producers developed the technology to convert natural gas to electricity. Even major institutions, like hospitals, are investing in their own power plants as they see the benefit in reduced costs.

New York Energy Commission, which used hydro power, is now switching to natural gas. The Commissioner compares the cost per kilowatt and sees an advantage of using natural gas at 2 cents versus 6 cents per kilowatt with hydro power.

Until the gas pipeline was installed along the eastern United States, the utilities had few energy choices. Now that there is a low cost alternative, Canada's hydro producers need to consider their strategy for surviving.

557

QUESTIONS

1. What strategic mistake did Canada's hydro producers make in terms of their understanding of the players in their market? Is there anything Canada's hydro producers can do to recover their market share in the eastern U.S.?
2. Do Canada's hydro producers have any unique characteristics which would help them to compete with a low-cost producer?
3. What long-term pricing strategy should Canada's natural gas suppliers consider?

Source: This case was prepared by Deborah Andrus and is based on the *Venture* series episode "Natural Gas vs. Hydro Sales," which was originally broadcast on March 13, 1994.

● Chapter 18

Marketing Communication and Advertising

OBJECTIVES

AFTER COMPLETING THIS CHAPTER, YOU SHOULD BE ABLE TO:

1
DEFINE MARKETING COMMUNICATION AND LIST THE COMPONENTS OF THE MARKETING COMMUNICATION MIX

2
DESCRIBE THE COMPONENTS OF THE MARKETING COMMUNICATION MODEL

3
EXPLAIN THE PROCESS OF INTEGRATED MARKETING COMMUNICATION AND HOW IT CAN BE USED TO COORDINATE THE COMMUNICATION MIX

4
UNDERSTAND HOW TO DEVELOP A ZERO-BASED MARKETING COMMUNICATION PLAN

5
IDENTIFY THE TYPES OF ADVERTISING USED IN MARKETING COMMUNICATION

6
DESCRIBE THE SEVERAL FUNCTIONS OF ADVERTISING

7
DIFFERENTIATE BETWEEN ADVERTISING STRATEGY AND ADVERTISING EXECUTION

8
DISCUSS THE NEED TO DEVELOP GLOBAL MARKETING COMMUNICATION THAT IS ACCEPTABLE OUTSIDE THE HOME COUNTRY

9
IDENTIFY THE FIVE BASIC DECISIONS THAT DRIVE MEDIA STRATEGY

10
EXPLAIN MEDIA OBJECTIVES AND MEDIA SELECTION STRATEGIES

THINK ABOUT IT!

COMMUNICATING THE SATURN DIFFERENCE

The first Saturn car rolled out of its new assembly plant in Spring Hill, Tennessee, in October 1990. Since then, Saturn's marketing communication program has been a model for the auto industry. Using an integrated communication approach, Saturn has brought its nontraditional corporate philosophy to life. The "Saturn difference" is now a textbook case of how to build a brand through a single-minded focus on creating strong customer, employee, and community relationships.[1] The opening photo for this chapter, which was used in a Saturn advertisement, features a satisfied customer, Cheryl Silas, who bought her second Saturn coupe after walking away, unharmed, from her first Saturn when it was totalled by another car.

In 1993 Hal Riney & Partners, Saturn's advertising agency, was

named Agency of the Year by *Advertising Age* largely because of its work on the launch of the car. The agency's campaign reinforced Saturn's corporate phi-

559

losophy with the slogan "A Different Kind of Company and a Different Kind of Car." Two years earlier, Saturn had received two Silver Anvil Awards from the Public Relations Society of America for excellence both in internal communications and community relations.

Saturn's total communication program consists of more than advertising and public relations. It also includes word of mouth by satisfied customers, employees who participate in consensus management and are committed to their product, a sales training program and a philosophy that breaks with the hard sell tradition used in the auto industry, suppliers who are considered partners, and an environmental advisory council made up of Saturn employees and local Spring Hill residents. The Saturn factory itself was sited and designed to minimize the visual impact of a large assembly plant on a rural landscape.

Recognizing that all areas of the marketing mix send a message, Saturn emphasizes customer relationships by offering long-term guarantees on its cars. That's why you will never find an unhappy Saturn owner. People who are unsatisfied are encouraged to return their cars after 30 days or 1,500 miles and get their money back. The company doesn't want anyone owning a Saturn who doesn't love it. Local dealers have the option to provide support services such as free oil changes, car washes, and a loaner car during repairs for the lifetime of the car.

Shopping at a Saturn showroom is entirely different from the usual buying experience at car dealerships: there is no haggling over price, no confusing rebate deals, no high-pressure sales techniques. Saturn "sales consultants" help customers purchase the right car rather than attempting to *sell* them one just to get a commission.

And the sticker price is the actual price. Actually, it is the price that sends the most important message. Saturn prices start at a fraction of what a Lexus or an Infiniti costs—the only other North American cars that rival Saturn in quality.

There have been two serious hitches in Saturn's marketing. In 1991 the manufacturer announced it would replace all 1,836 cars sold to that date because of a defective coolant installation. Then, in 1993, an electrical flaw that causes engine fires prompted the recall of 352,000 cars.

Has Saturn successfully transformed the image of North American cars, making it possible for them to compete successfully with Japanese imports on both quality and price? Or have recalls undermined Saturn's quality image? What is your image of Saturn? Would you buy one? ∎

As the opening story demonstrates, all the different ways in which an organization makes an impression—everything written, said, or pictured that contributes to the company's image and that of its products—is a form of *communication.* This includes every element of the marketing mix that carries meaning and communicates value to customers and stakeholders—from the firm's letterhead, signs, and trucks to its receptionists and even its shopping bags. We begin this chapter with an overview of marketing communication, including a discussion of the concept of *integrated marketing communication.* In the second half of the chapter, we focus on one of the most visible tools of marketing communications—*advertising.*

MARKETING AND COMMUNICATION

Marketing communication, the focus of the first chapter objective, encompasses all the elements in the marketing mix that establish meaning and communicate value to customers and other stakeholders of an organization. The marketing communication section of a marketing plan focuses on such primary components of the marketing communication mix as advertising, public relations, sales promotion, packaging, direct marketing, and personal selling. Advertising is discussed in this chapter, the other topics in Chapters 19–21. To gain a better appreciation of the complexity of marketing communication, let's first look at the theory behind the messages.

marketing communication
All the elements in the marketing mix that establish meaning and communicate value to customers and stakeholders.

THE MARKETING COMMUNICATION MODEL

The traditional *communication model* provides the basis for all marketing communication. In Figure 18-1 we have translated this model into a marketing context. As you read the following descriptions of the model's components—the topic of chapter objective two—you'll see that they are actually steps in the communication process:

◆ *Sender:* The source of the message—that is, the marketer (a company or an organization).

**Figure 18-1
The Marketing
Communication Model**

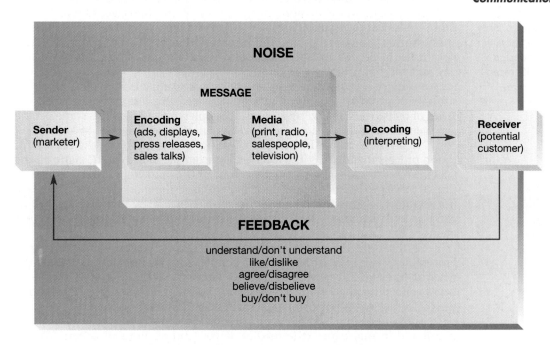

◆ *Encoding:* The process of putting the idea of the message into a form that will both be understood by and have the desired effect on the receiver. This step embodies the *creative strategy* or the selling proposition—the promise that the company makes to a customer about a product or about the company itself.

◆ *Message:* The message is the *execution* of the creative strategy. The message may be expressed in different ways—including words (spoken or written), diagrams, pictures, and dramatizations—and may take various forms—such as a sales presentation, a publicity release, a package label, or an advertisement designed for newspapers, magazines, or television.

◆ *Media:* The channel or channels through which the message is communicated. Channels include radio, television, the print media, telephone, fax, electronic mail, and direct contact between salespeople and consumers or, as in word of mouth, between consumers.

◆ *Decoding:* The interpretation of the message by a receiver. The same message may be interpreted quite differently by different receivers, each of whom has a unique set of experiences, knowledge, and circumstances. As in the traditional communication model, the decoding component here precedes the receiver component on the grounds that a message is not fully received until decoding is completed.

◆ *Receiver:* The one who receives the message—a business, consumer, or other stakeholder the sender wants to influence in some way.

◆ *Feedback:* The receiver's response to the message, which marketers hope will be either a change in attitude or behavior or a request for more information. For example, the receiver may test-drive a new car, visit a retail store, call an 800 number, or—best of all—simply buy the company's product. Feedback tells senders whether they have accomplished their purpose. Note that not to respond is to respond! If you throw out a piece of "junk mail" without opening it, you have given the sender of the mail an answer.

noise
Anything, physical or psychological, that interferes with the design, transmission, or reception of a message.

Throughout the entire communication process, "noise" may interfere with the design, transmission, or reception of the message. **Noise** is anything—physical or psychological—that gets in the way of the successful creation, transmission, reception, and interpretation of the marketing message. First, it has to be said that people receive literally thousands of messages each day and will pay attention to very few. When they do, it will be due to product or service need awareness or emotional stimulation which is either strongly positive or negative. Benetton falls into this last category with their series of controversial advertisements. Examples are the conflicts some people experience when they see a controversial Benetton ad (see page 581).

Noise can also be other, unrelated things going on during the communication process that distract the receiver. For example, noise can be static on the television set or radio during the broadcast of the marketer's advertisement. It can be messages from competitors that confound the marketer's own message (for example, claims that "knock-offs" of the marketer's product are just as good at half the price). It can even be information stored in the receiver's memory (for example, bad past experiences with the marketer's product).

To illustrate the real-life workings of the marketing communication process, let's use Levi Strauss as an example. Levi Strauss acts as the sender when it hires an advertising agency to determine what it should say about Levi's (encoding the selling proposition) in order to convince you to buy them. The agency then comes up with clever ads that persuasively demonstrate the benefits of Levi's 501 jeans (the message) and runs these ads on television and in magazines (the media). If you and millions of others (the receivers) see the ads and decide that you like the image you perceive (decoding) enough to buy a pair (feedback), Levi's marketing communication will be considered a success. Even though you may not have heard the entire message because of noise, enough of it came through to influence you to make a buying decision.

TYPES OF MARKETING COMMUNICATION MESSAGES

Marketing communication is far more pervasive than most people imagine. Most people think of "marketing communication" as advertisements and sales promotions. But as more and more marketing managers are coming to realize, *all marketing is communication.* That component of the communication model called the "message" includes much more than press releases and print and television ads. There are four different types of messages—planned, inferred, maintenance, and unplanned—that most organizations send all the time. As Table 18-1 illustrates, these messages vary both in the amount of impact they have on consumers and in the degree to which marketing can control or influence that impact.

Planned messages are regularly used marketing tools such as advertisements, publicity releases, and package labels. *Inferred messages* are implied by other parts of the marketing mix—price, distribution method, the product itself. For example, a high price usually implies that the product is high in both quality and status. *Maintenance messages* are delivered to consumers by the quality of customer service the marketer offers. For example, if the manual for a bread-making machine fails to state clearly when to add specific ingredients or how to set the baking timer, the customer will probably get the message

| TABLE 18-1 | MARKETING MESSAGE TYPOLOGY |

Message Type	Description	Relative Impact of Message	Degree of Marketing Management Control
Planned	Marketing communication tools such as advertising, public relations, packaging, sales promotion, direct response, event sponsorships, signage, stationery, letterhead	Low-moderate	High
Inferred	Impressions sent by the product's design and performance (e.g., customer's experience with the product), as well as by such things as the product's price, where and how it is distributed, and the cleanliness of company trucks and cars	Moderate	High
Maintenance	Quality of customer service offered by such employees as receptionists and salespersons, by product-usage instructions, and by service and repair programs	Low-moderate	Moderate-high
Unplanned	External communications such as news stories, consumer advocate group activities, product recalls, employee gossip	High	Low

that the company's designers and manual writers are incompetent and that the company itself doesn't care much about satisfying its customers. *Unplanned messages* are those that "just happen." An investigative reporter may write a story about a defective product; an employee may tell people at a party about the dirty conditions inside his company's plant; a consumer interest group may protest the way a manufacturer is making or promoting its products.

Control over messages varies greatly, as does their impact. Marketers have total control over the content of most planned messages, since they are created by or under the direction of marketing managers. But they have less success in controlling their impact, since given the high daily bombardment of messages, people have become very good at screening out marketing communication messages. Furthermore, although marketing communication is good at building long-term brand images, only certain kinds of messages are capable of creating an immediate sales response. In short, the impact of planned marketing messages on a buying decision may not be as high as marketers would like.

On the other hand, unreliable distributors (inferred message), a surly sales clerk (maintenance message), or a television report on a questionable manufacturing process (unplanned message) can have tremendous impact on customers' attitudes and buying decisions. Marketers have a good deal of control over inferred messages (they can manage distributors better or change them) and a fair amount of control over maintenance messages (they can train their sales clerks to give good customer service). And they are not helpless when it comes to unplanned messages: a company that has a good public relations program—that is, maintains good relations with the media by being scrupulously honest with reporters at all times—may well be given the benefit of the doubt by the media when trouble strikes.

CONTACT POINTS

The marketing message typology in Table 18-1 encompasses all the various kinds of messages delivered at all the different customer and stakeholder *contact points*, which are situations where consumers encounter a brand or corporate message.[2] Although some contact points arise naturally—you go into a store and there is the product—others are created—a company, for example, sponsors a sports event. Remember, every time and place where a customer or potential customer sees, hears, and/or experiences something about your product or brand is a contact point and a communication opportunity. Table 18-2 shows the results of a *contact point analysis* for Vaseline Intensive Care hand lotion.

By knowing all the contact points for its product, a company can design and deliver its planned messages more effectively and efficiently. In this chapter and the next three, we discuss marketing communication in terms of the primary communication tools used to produce *planned* messages. But before we describe the major marketing communication tools, you need to understand the process that is used to determine to what extent each of these tools is used. That process is known as *integrated marketing communication*, and it is the focus of chapter objective three.

INTEGRATED MARKETING COMMUNICATION (IMC) ●

Until the late 1980s, most organizations thought "functionally" about their marketing communication: they assumed they were doing a good job if they

564
CHAPTER 18

TABLE 18-2   CONTACT POINT ANALYSIS

Participants in a corporate seminar were asked to brainstorm the question: Where do people come into contact with messages about Vaseline Intensive Care hand lotion? The following are just some of the contact points listed by the seminar participants.

- Retail settings: shelf, point-of-sale messages, special promotions
- Advertising: newspapers, magazines, coupon inserts
- Professional endorsements
- Home: bathroom, kitchen, bedroom, laundryroom, nursery/child's room
- Someone else's home
- At the office; lockers at school or gym
- Articles/stories: consumer, trade publications; newspapers; TV
- Store demonstrations
- Health-care settings: doctors' offices, hospitals, clinics
- Beauty parlor/barber shop
- Massage therapists
- Conversations, word of mouth
- Trade show exhibits and booths
- Hand bag, gym or golf club bag
- First-aid kits
- T-shirts, mugs, other specialty items
- Sales and distribution vehicles
- Corporate facilities
- Receptionist, employees' uniforms
- Trash

had memorable advertising, effective public relations, attention-getting packaging, good sales-promotion programs, and salespeople who met their sales objectives. Because each of these different functions requires special skills, each was handled separately. Consequently, the functional approach created industries of communication specialists—advertising agencies, public relations firms, packaging-design firms, direct-response specialists, and sales-promotion agencies—largely working independently of one another (Figure 18-2A).

Today, however, more and more firms recognize the need to coordinate these functions, and **integrated marketing communications (IMC)** is the key to such coordination. IMC is the process of strategically developing and controlling or influencing all messages that customers and other stakeholders use in forming an image of, and nourishing a relationship with, a brand or company. In contrast to the traditional functional approach, Figure 18-2B shows the IMC process in which marketing communication objectives and strategies are collectively decided—ideally, not only by the firm's own marketing communication specialists but also by the outside communication agencies that will be working with the firm. At this time a coordinated schedule of the various marketing communication programs is also determined. Both internal and outside marketing communication specialists then begin their work, keeping in close communication (represented by dotted lines in Figure 18-2B) as they move forward with their projects. The main difference between the traditional and the IMC process is that the strategic thinking is centralized rather than individually determined for each marketing communication function.

Integration can occur on several levels. At the most basic level, it means all the messages say the same thing—as Pepsi's "one voice, one look" youth

integrated marketing communications (IMC) The strategic development and coordination of the messages and media used by an organization to enhance the value perception of the organization and its brands.

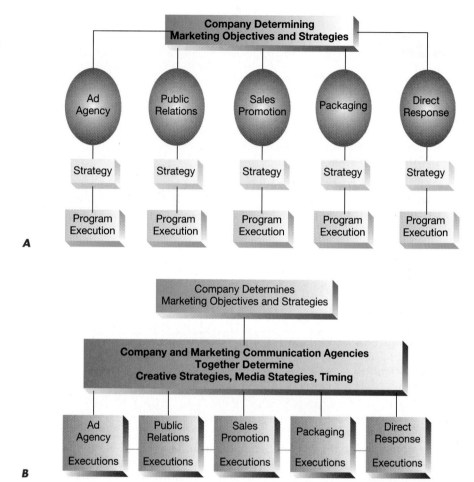

generation advertising does—or say different things to different audiences but with a consistent theme—as Coca Cola's "Always" campaign does, with its differing images and styles for MTV viewers and their grandparents. At a higher level, IMC refers to the use of two-way communication to create a dialogue between marketers and their stakeholders that leads to a mutually beneficial relationship. Saturn's IMC program is an excellent example of relationship marketing: it encourages buyers to talk to dealers and it has successfully convinced many buyers that they are part of a special group of people. Saturn drivers wave to one another on the highways, and some owners have even volunteered to participate in Saturn displays at auto shows.

At the most sophisticated level, IMC means "mission marketing." The firm's mission—and its sense of social responsibility—are integrated into all facets of marketing communication by such companies as Ben and Jerry's Homemade, Benetton, and Anita Roddick's Body Shop.[3] (The Body Shop is discussed at some length in a case at the back of this book.) Companies practicing IMC at this level believe product satisfaction is not enough. They are determined to offer social and/or moral satisfaction as well to purchasers of their products. As technology enables companies to quickly match their competitors' offerings, product differences will be minimized. Therefore customers will base their brand selections on things other than product differences, such as the reputation of the company making the product. This has been the "secret" of The Body Shop. Anita Roddick is quick to admit that most of her products have no physical competitive advantage. Many customers patronize The Body Shop because they like the socially responsible things the company does, such as sourcing from Third World countries and paying its employees to take two weeks off annually to do volunteer work.

THE IMC MIX

The marketer's objective is to make all elements of the marketing communication mix—advertising, direct marketing, public relations, packaging, personal selling, and sales promotions—work together *synergistically*—that is, so that their total effect is greater than the sum of the individual messages would be. In comprehensive IMC programs the objective is to identify all message sources and then (1) strategically *manage* those that the firm controls (planned and maintenance messages) and (2) positively *influence* those the firm cannot control (inferred and unplanned messages).

All paid mass-media messages—whether in print, on radio or TV, or on posters or blimps—are considered to be *advertising*, a communication element we discussed in the second half of this chapter. *Public relations* (discussed in Chapter 19) is the systematic effort to obtain favorable nonpaid attention in the media and the community through press releases, articles, video news releases, special events, and public service, and create favorable relationships with other stakeholders such as employees, the financial community, and the government. *Packaging* (Chapter 19) is the last "ad" a customer sees before buying a product. *Sales promotions* are short-term inducements for customers and dealers to buy; they include trade performance allowances, coupons, premiums, retail sales events, sales contests, and sweepstakes. Other promotion efforts include trade shows, exhibits, sponsorships, and special events. (All forms of promotion are discussed in Chapter 19.) *Direct marketing* (Chapter 20) uses the mass media, electronic media, and mail to deliver messages that communicate offers and benefits to prospective customers, who then respond directly to the company without going through a store or sales agent to make the transaction. *Personal selling*, as the name implies, is one-to-one selling; it is particularly critical in retailing and business-to-business marketing (Chapter 21).

Exhibit 18-1, taken from a Millennium sales piece developed for retailers, summarizes all the different types of marketing communication messages that were developed for the Millennium rechargeable battery power system product launch. The foldout includes a panel on the left depicting the product line, then a panel on the company's advertising and public relations efforts. Next is a panel on special features, such as the recycling logo and the warranty, as well as special promotions, including television show tie-ins, rebates, and gift packs. The last panel depicts promotional activities of particular interest to retailers, such as the Good Housekeeping seal, merchandising programs, booklets that explain rechargeable batteries, an 800 number that locates the nearest Millennium salesperson, and sales support materials. Note that the materials in the fourth panel have several design elements in common, which helps integrate Millennium's selling effort.

ZERO-BASED COMMUNICATION PLAN

Formal IMC planning begins with a clean slate, not with last year's plan.[4] This is known as developing a *zero-based marketing communication plan*, the subject of the fourth chapter objective. The types of communication activities

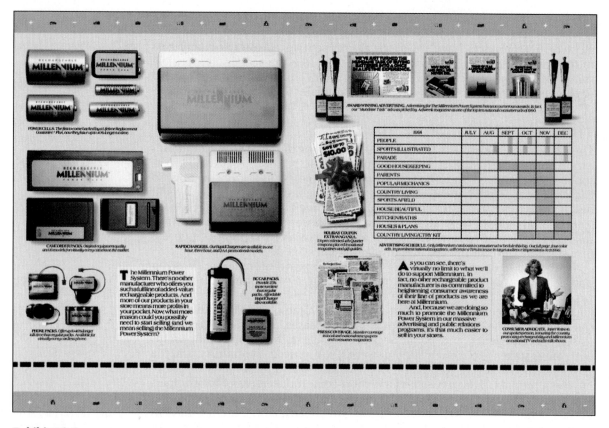

selected depend on what message problems need to be solved. The IMC planning process is a continuation of the SWOT analysis explained in Chapter 4. Once the SWOT analysis has been completed and the SWOT findings prioritized, the next steps in the zero-based planning approach are:

◆ Determining target audiences (see Chapter 8).

◆ Using the prioritized SWOT findings to determine IMC objectives by identifying attitudes and behaviors that need to be changed in order to (a) leverage the organization's most significant strengths and opportunities and (b) address its weaknesses and any threats it confronts.

◆ Selecting the communication area or areas (advertising, public relations, etc.) that are best suited to accomplish the IMC objectives.

◆ Determining the creative and media strategies that will accomplish the IMC objectives and drive the total communication program.

◆ Assigning message and media responsibilities to the various communication functional areas based on their ability to contribute to the IMC objectives.

◆ Coordinating the execution in each functional area, making sure each functional specialist (ad agency, packaging agency, event sponsorship agency, etc.) is aware of how the other specialists are executing the agreed-upon strategies.

Targeting Nearly every organization has more than one *target* or *stakeholder audience* with whom it must communicate. These target audiences—

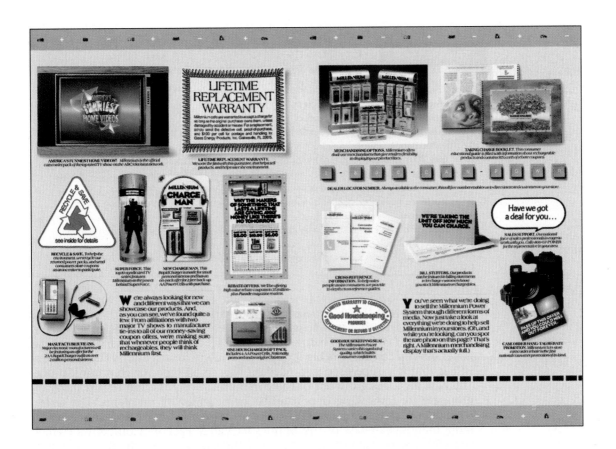

customers, users (if different from the people who actually buy the product), suppliers, government regulators, local community leaders, the mass media, and the trade press—all need to be identified when the marketing communication plan is being developed. Specifying target audiences leads to determining which communication specialists will be addressing which targets, thus ensuring that each audience will be reached in the most effective and efficient manner. For example, Millennium targets the *trade market* (major discount, drug, catalog, photo/camera/electronics, and food stores and key decision makers in corporate offices, buyers, and merchandise managers) with the positioning statement "One Brand Fits All." It targets the *consumer market* with the position "The Power to Last a Lifetime."

IMC Objectives   The challenge to marketing managers is to determine precisely what needs to be accomplished to meet the overall marketing objectives. Setting marketing communication objectives is a crucial task. For example, if it is found that the brand's low awareness is a significant weakness, then one of the objectives may be to generate 50 percent brand awareness by the end of the fiscal year. If customers are aware of a brand and have a favorable impression of it but nevertheless are not trying it, then an appropriate objective is to generate trial among 35 percent of the target market by year end. If product claims are not believed, an objective might be to increase believability in the brand's superiority by 10 percentage points within the year. For some other possible marketing communication objectives see Table 18-3.

IMC Strategies   Once the IMC objectives are determined, the strategies to accomplish them must be selected. An integrated campaign requires a "big

---

TABLE 18-3   EXAMPLES OF TYPICAL MARKETING
COMMUNICATION OBJECTIVES

- Generate 50% brand preference among target audience.
- Generate 35% trial of new product among target audience.
- Have 65% of target audience able to accurately describe the company in terms of the new desired image.
- Have 80% who are aware of the brand associate it with an outdoor lifestyle.
- Generate awareness of product improvements among 100% of sales force, 80% of trade currently carrying brand, and 65% of current brand users.
- Counter competitive activities by maintaining a 50% brand preference among current brand users.
- Introduce brand into the region by generating a 50% brand awareness among targeted category users.
- Have 85% of trade buyers rate company as number one in service vs. the competition.

---

idea"—a concept that is broad enough to provide continuity through all the communications that will be used. Examples of big ideas are the Jolly Green Giant, Apple's concept of being "user friendly," and Benetton's focus on social issues. As you can see, the big idea can take many forms, but its key characteristic is that it can be used in a relevant way in all types of communications. The best big ideas grow out of the communication function that is most appropriate for leveraging opportunities or neutralizing problems. The Green Giant is an advertising big idea that was developed to answer the need for more brand awareness of the Minnesota Valley Packing Company's canned vegetables. It became so successful that the company eventually changed its name to the Green Giant Company.

We said that different types of communication functions do different things, and therefore marketers have the task of deciding which communication functions are most likely to accomplish the IMC objectives. For example, public relations (or product publicity) messages often have more credibility than advertising because they appear in the editorial part of the media. Direct marketing uses highly targeted personalized messages that motivate specific behaviors (request more information, order a product, request a sample). Sales promotion adds tangible value and stimulates short-term sales increases. Packaging designs call attention to a product and make a sales pitch at the point of purchase. (With services, such as restaurants and accounting firms, the "packaging label" is their physical facilities, signage, and letter heads.) Table 18-4 lists the strengths and weaknesses of the major marketing communication functions.

At the heart of all marketing communication strategies lies the need to decide whether to "push" or to "pull" the product. A push strategy, as we explained in Chapter 4, is designed to motivate the middleman (wholesaler, distributor, retailer) to buy the product. Manufacturers know that once intermediaries own a product, they will try hard to resell it as soon as possible in order to recover their costs and make a profit. Marketers, particularly those with new products like Millennium, "push" products through the channels of distribution with personal selling and promotion incentives to channel members. A pull strategy, also explained in Chapter 4, is designed to motivate customers to demand that the distribution channel members—usually a local store—carry the product. Marketers "pull" products through the channels with advertising, sales promotions, and public relations programs. Different

TABLE 18-4	STRENGTHS AND WEAKNESSES OF MAJOR COMMUNICATION FUNCTIONS

This list, which is not exhaustive, is intended to stimulate thinking rather than provide a formula for choosing among marketing communication functions.

ADVERTISING

Strengths

Creates identity and focus for a brand or cause

Reaches a large mass audience

Creates brand awareness, builds long-term brand image

Positions brand

Increases brand knowledge

Provides message repetition

Serves as reminder

Weaknesses

Expensive and with long time lags, difficult to establish success rates

Perceived as intrusive; elicits high level of audience avoidance

Clutters message environment

Reaches high percentage of nonusers

PUBLIC RELATIONS

Strengths

Adds credibility/believability

Establishes corporate-citizen role

Editorial-type messages can break through "ad" clutter

Low media costs

Reaches hard-to-reach targets, such as upscale opinion leaders

Reaches stakeholders other than consumers—employees, community leaders, legislators and regulators, financial community

Proactive—can plan for crises, head off special interest groups' moves

Fewer legal restrictions

Weaknesses

Subject to gatekeeper approval

Bottom line impact is difficult to determine

SALES PROMOTION

Strengths

Adds tangible value to product offering

Gives sense of immediacy to purchase

Adds excitement, spectacle

Stimulates trial

Stimulates continuity of purchase or support, repeat purchases

Increases purchase frequency and/or quantity

Balances inventory, helps clear overstocks

Motivates trade support

Builds database

Adds involvement/participation

Weaknesses

Clutter

Can set false retail price

Can undercut brand image

(continued)

Russia and Its Miners On the Way Up

According to some analysts, the booming economies that have been developing in the formerly less advanced countries are outperforming the industrial nations. For example, coal, nickel, magnesium, and other minerals and metals are pouring out of Russian mines. In 1992, Russia sold as much as a million metric tons of aluminum, the reason, Alcoa says, it laid off 750 workers and let a quarter of its facilities lay idle in mid 1993. How can a global economy adjust to these new players? [Christopher Farrell, Michael J. Mandel, Bill Javetski, and Stephen Baker, "What's Wrong? Why the Industrialized Nations Are Stalled," Business Week, August 2, 1993, pp. 54–59.]

Global advertising can work well provided marketers understand the need to make certain cultural adjustments. For example, Levi Strauss bent a long standing policy against celebrity endorsements by using American movie stars in advertisements designed to attract Japanese consumers. Up to that point the Japanese had seen "Levi's" as "less American" (and thus less desirable) than Japanese brands with Western names like "Big John." Exxon, on the other hand, had to give up its "Put a tiger in your tank" slogan in Thailand, where the tiger is not symbolic of strength.

To help companies build global brands, international advertising agencies have been setting up shop around the world. Young & Rubicam and Ogilvy & Mather, for instance, have offices in Moscow that are busy with public relations, consumer research, trade shows and exhibits, and packaging design. These activities do not produce much revenue today because Russia's market economy is in its infancy in comparison with the North American, Western European, and Japanese economies, but they do allow the agencies to build contacts with the growing Russian private sector. Both agencies are betting that Russia will soon become a profitable market-based economy, and thus need more sophisticated marketing communication programs.

574

The Marlboro cowboy is used throughout the world to create a strong brand identity for the world's best-selling cigarette. A truly global brand, Marlboro is sold everywhere in the same red-and-white package—and represented everywhere by the archetypal character of the cowboy. Only the language changes.

The cowboy, of course, is quintessentially North American, and the values communicated by this symbol may seem curious in cultures as different as those of the Far East. After teaching in Malaysia, an advertising professor, Katherine Frith, wondered if the Marlboro cowboy wasn't a form of *cultural imperialism*. She observed, for example, that the cowboy signifies Western individualism—a notion at odds with the Far East's general concern for community, group, and family.[5]

Classic imperialism—the practice of one nation extending dominion over another nation by direct territorial conquest or by gaining control of the nation's political and economic institutions—is a waning phenomenon in the late twentieth century. But the issue of cultural imperialism—the forcing of the values of one culture upon another—is very much alive today. As countries modernize, they traditionally develop along Western lines—which means they change from a "production ethic" to a "consumption ethic." In a consumer culture, according to social critics, people measure their worth by the size of their homes, the make of their cars, and the possession of the latest household equipment, clothes, and gadgets. In Southeast Asian cultures, Frith explains, "the fulfillment of family, group, and community needs is more highly esteemed than the gratification of individual consumption goals."

The determination to protect traditional values has been apparent in Asia in recent years. The government of Indonesia, for instance,

banned television advertising in 1981 because it found it too Western. India regulates the way women are portrayed in commercials, and Malaysia has created a national advertising code to ensure that advertisements will project the Malaysian culture and identity and be filmed locally with Malaysian talent.

If it is true that the Marlboro cowboy symbolizes Western values that clash with Asian values, he is still very effective in selling cigarettes to Asians. If the advertising speaks with an alien tongue, why does it sell the product so well? How should Western products be advertised in non-Western countries? Should Western images be modified for Eastern cultures?

ADVERTISING ●

advertising
Any paid form of non-personal presentation or promotion of ideas, goods, or services by an identified sponsor using mass media.

Advertising, one of the most highly visible areas of marketing communication, is any paid form of communication that is broadcast, published, or otherwise displayed in public and in which an identified sponsor promotes ideas, goods, or services. (Table 18-5 lists Canada's top 20 advertisers of 1993.) In order to accomplish its primary objective of getting people to buy a particular

TABLE 18-5	CANADA'S TOP 20 ADVERTISERS OF 1993	Total ($000s)
1.	General Motors of Canada	113,048.4
2.	Procter & Gamble	84,499.5
3.	The Thomson Group	70,159.3
4.	BCE	53,972.9
5.	John Labatt Ltd.	50,036.0
6.	Eaton's of Canada	47,582.1
7.	Sears Canada	46,582.1
8.	Government of Canada	43,928.7
9.	The Molson Companies	42,873.6
10.	Chrysler Canada	41,171.5
11.	Paramount Communications	36,476.8
12.	Kraft General Foods Group	36,293.5
13.	Imasco	35,625.2
14.	McDonald's Restaurants of Canada	35,475.8
15.	UL Canada	35,198.9
16.	PepsiCo	35,157.8
17.	Nestlé Enterprises	34,304.2
18.	Vycom Electronics	33,863.7
19.	Ford Motor Co. of Canada	33,282.4
20.	Kellogg Canada	33,195.2

Source: Marketing Magazine, May 2, 1994, p. 21.

product, advertising must get people's attention and it must be remembered. A little later in the chapter we will discuss the strategies and tools of advertising, and in Chapter 22 we will consider the difficult task of evaluating the impact of advertising on consumers. We begin this section by exploring the several types of advertising and then discuss the way advertising actually works. We conclude the section by examining advertising management and budgeting methods. (For more information on advertising standards in Canada, see Appendix 18.)

TYPES OF ADVERTISING

On the broadcast scale, advertising can be categorized as global, national, or local. The kinds of global and national advertising commonly discussed in a marketing plan are brand, corporate, and business-to-business, or trade, advertising. Local advertising includes retail and cooperative advertising.

As we saw in Chapter 10, **brand advertising** helps establish an individual personality or image and builds brand equity over time. The opening story about Saturn discussed the company's attempt to project its mission—a new kind of company, a new kind of car—through advertising and other marketing communication activities. Most national advertising seeks to establish brand identity and reinforce product image. Over 29,000 different brands are advertised nationally in North America.

Advertising used by a company to create and nurture positive attitudes toward the company itself is called **corporate advertising**. It is this kind of advertising that an organization uses when it wants to influence the opinions of consumers and other important groups such as suppliers, stockholders, government, and employees. *Advocacy advertising*, a type of corporate advertising, communicates a company's views on environmental, social, business, or other issues, again seeking to influence public opinion.

Sometimes called *trade* or *industry* advertising, **business-to-business advertising** is directed at people and companies in or associated with a particular industry who buy or influence those who buy products for use in that industry. Although personal selling is generally the most common method of communicating with business buyers, business advertising is used to make announcements about products, create product awareness, enhance a firm's reputation, and support its sales staff.

Just as advertising is part of the marketing mix for nationally and internationally promoted products and services, it also plays an important role in the marketing mix for local retailers—most of whom serve a geographically limited area. The primary differences between national and **retail advertising** are geography, timeliness, store focus, and an emphasis on price. Whereas national advertisers are primarily interested in creating brand awareness, retailers are more concerned with attracting customers to their stores. Because the number-one objective of most retail advertising is to increase store traffic, retail advertising is more price-focused. It frequently announces sales or discounted prices, and has more short-term objectives than national advertising. Moreover, although a national ad may be used for an extended period of time, most retail ads run for only a few days.

Most manufacturers have ongoing promotional programs to provide retailers with advertising support in the form of money and materials. Funds for this sort of **cooperative advertising** of a product are often based on a percentage of sales to the retailer. Co-op funds, sometimes called *promotion allowances*, have become so widespread and significant that most retailers won't even consider taking on a new brand without receiving advertising support.

brand advertising
Advertising that establishes individual personality or image and builds brand equity over time.

corporate advertising
Advertising used by a company to create and nurture positive attitudes toward the company itself or to advocate views important to it.

business-to-business advertising
Advertising directed at people and companies within or related to an industry who buy or influence the purchase of products for use in that industry.

retail advertising
Advertising that is designed primarily to attract customers to stores; usually geographically delineated, store-focused, price-focused, and short-term.

cooperative advertising
Advertising in which the manufacturer of a product provides advertising materials to or reimburses a retailer for part or all of the retailer's advertising expenditures for a brand.

PURPOSE AND FUNCTION OF ADVERTISING

People buy more than a product—they buy the benefits, results, and satisfaction communicated by the advertising for that product. For example, although you might think that people would take a particularly rational approach to buying an automobile, in actuality people rely very much on their *feelings* in making this major and often costly purchase. People feel very differently about buying a car that's advertised as an economy sedan than they do about purchasing a sports or other luxury-type car. Although they all have four wheels, use gas, and can go as fast as speed limits allow, a Mercedes costs two to three times as much as a Firebird and four to five times as much as a Cavalier. If people didn't perceive the advertised attributes of these cars as different in a major way, they would purchase solely according to price. Thus advertising's overall purpose is to *add value* to products; it is this added value that, in the hearts and minds of consumers, becomes the often intangible differences on which purchases are based. Adding value by appealing to people's feelings can be used for a wide variety of products. In Exhibit 18-2, the Ballygowan ad evokes feelings of innocence and nostalgia.

How Advertising Works Advertising uses a number of methods to create value for consumers. In this section we discuss a group of closely interrelated and very basic activities: stimulating demand for a product, building brand awareness, and differentiating brands by, when possible, showcasing competitive advantage. In subsequent sections we will explore several other tasks in which advertising can be very effective: positioning and repositioning brands, preempting positions, and opening the door for personal sales.

Exhibit 18-2
Longing for the Past

This ad for
Ballygowan Irish
Spring Water is selling
not just a product—but
also a feeling. The
ad's copy and visual
presentation makes
people think of
childhood, innocence,
and nostalgia.

Most consumer advertising is based on a *pull strategy*—it stimulates consumer demand that, in turn, convinces retailers that it would be profitable to offer a particular good or service.[6] Advertising stimulates two types of consumer demand—primary and selective. *Primary-demand*, or generic, advertising sells a category rather than a specific brand and is often mounted by an industry association. For example, the cattle and dairy associations pay for the advertising campaigns that urge consumers to buy and consume beef and milk. Sometimes a company whose brand dominates a category will use a primary or generic selling strategy. For example, the Campbell Company, which dominates the soup industry, has used "Soup is good food" and "Never underestimate the power of soup" in its advertising. Campbell's can afford to make such general statements because with a 60 to 70 percent share of the soup market, it will get the majority of business its ads generate. Campbell's also knows that people often pay attention to primary-demand advertising because they see it as less self-serving than other media campaigns.

Selective-demand advertising stresses brand differentiation and tries to convince consumers to choose one brand rather than another—for example, to buy Seven Seas salad dressing rather than Kraft. As we saw in Chapter 10, brands are based on product features and images that add value to the product, features and images that are established in consumers' minds and reinforced primarily through advertising.

Building brand awareness is an important advertising function. Even after the brand has been established, brand advertising is needed to remind consumers of the image, personality, and features of the good or service. Although marketers may hope to win new customers with brand advertising, research has found that such advertising is probably better at retaining brand loyalists than at getting people to switch brands.[7]

Another function of advertising is to *differentiate brands* in a competitive market. When a product has a strong feature that is both important to the target audience and lacking or weak in competing brands, marketers can differentiate it and create competitive advantage by building an advertising strategy around the product's strength. However, because so many products are clones of market leaders, a competitive-advantage strategy may not always be possible, and a marketer may focus instead on differentiating brand images. Exhibit 18-3 reflects British Airways' effort to turn its first-class service into a competitive advantage.

Positioning and Repositioning One of the tasks advertising handles well is positioning. You will recall from Chapter 9 that a *position* is the psychological niche in the marketplace owned by a product. Advertising can both position a product and reposition it. In a fast-changing marketplace, maintaining a strong competitive advantage is difficult because product innovations are quickly copied by competitors. The basis, then, for competition among many brands is image and position—which are created largely by advertising.

One way to stake out a claim for a product that is really not different from competing brands is to use **preemptive advertising**, which establishes a position for a product before anyone else can claim it. The "Pepsi Generation" campaign, for example, says that Pepsi is for people who think young. This notion is not a feature of the product—it's an image planted in the minds of consumers. Nevertheless, Pepsi so "owns" that position through its advertising that no other soft drink company can attempt to use the "youth" strategy without reminding consumers of Pepsi. The next section describes what we might consider a variant of preemptive advertising—the ads in which a company establishes its position on one or more social issues.

preemptive advertising
Advertising that stakes out a position for a product before anyone else can claim it; it is based on a unique image rather than a distinctive product feature.

WE'VE MANAGED TO CONFOUND SOME OF THE WORLD'S TOP DECISION-MAKERS.

Cognac or Cabernet. Mozart or Mendelssohn. The Times or the Tatler. British Airways' First Class offers an extraordinary range of amenities, courtesies and comestibles—in an atmosphere both responsive and refined. Choose First Class. And discover how enchanting indecision can be.

BRITISH AIRWAYS
The world's favourite airline:

BEHIND THE SCENES

ADVERTISING THAT "MAKES A STATEMENT"

Benetton, the Italian fashion company that targets the international youth market, has built its image on advertising that makes statements about social issues like racism and AIDS (Exhibit 18-4). The controversial advertising routinely attracts more attention than its relatively modest budget would suggest. Benetton ads and in-store posters have featured a rainbow of colored condoms, as well as tamer images like the one of colored leaves floating on a polluted sea to illustrate the chain's United Colors of Benetton theme and reinforce its commitment to the global environment. Some feel a corporate stance in support of environmentalism is appropriate since Benetton is an international retailer with 7,000 stores around the world.[8]

Images in the company's advertising campaign against intolerance, however, have stirred up a storm. One is of a black woman nursing a white baby, another of a priest and nun kissing, a third of a black man and a white man bound together by the same handcuffs. Benetton's magazine *Colours* has run a double-page spread of nude young men and women of different races and colors to reinforce the idea that underneath it all, we're all the same. Other controversial photographs by Benetton's (former) photographer/art director, Oliviero Toscani, show a newborn baby with its umbilical cord still attached and a family gathered around the bedside of a dying AIDS victim. Toscani's AIDS bedside photograph has been likened by some people to Michelangelo's famous *Pieta* sculpture in which Mary grieves over the body of the dead Jesus. Others see it as commercial exploitation.

Can such images build a retailer's image as a socially conscious company? Do they speak to young people in a way that more conventional ads don't? In a review of the Benetton campaign in *Rolling Stone*, Spike Lee pointed out that Benetton had rejected what he called the low road of selling its clothes with pretty faces and bodies in favor of using riskier images that make people think.

What do you think? Is there a market—an international market—for such statements and do they sell clothes? Is Benetton practicing "mission marketing"? Or is it just being sensational to draw attention to itself? In Spike Lee's terms, is Benetton's advertising on the high road or the low road?

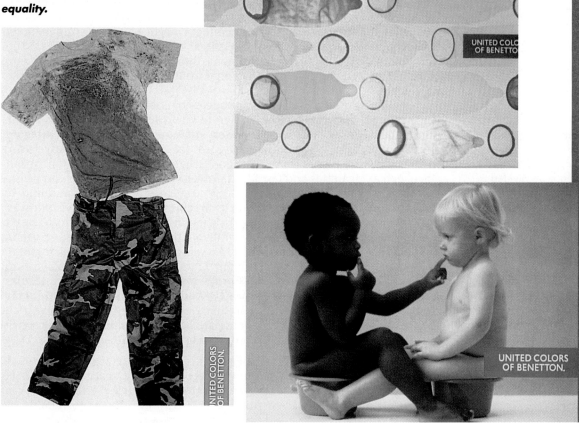

Supporting Sales Another function of advertising is to support other areas of the marketing communication mix. Most special events and sales promotions use advertising to announce the activity or offer and intensify excitement about it. Advertising also creates a *reputation platform*—an established image that supports sales efforts. An established brand with a national or international image created by advertising has more prestige and commands more respect. This reputation is invaluable to the salesperson trying to make a first contact, especially in business-to-business marketing.

ADVERTISING MANAGEMENT

The executive in charge of the advertising function in a marketing program is usually called an *advertising manager* or *director of advertising*. The principal responsibilities of this position are managing the budget and the schedules, helping to set objectives for the marketing communications program, coordinating the advertising with the other elements in the marketing communications mix, and monitoring the work of the advertising agency.

An important management decision is whether to go outside the company for advertising help or to build in-house expertise. Advertising agencies provide highly trained specialists to write, design, and produce advertisements and place them in the media. However, some companies like large retailers need close control over the advertising function and fast response, and as a result they have their own internal advertising departments. Some manufacturers also handle their own advertising. Called AdCom, the Quaker Oats Company's internal agency operates as both a full-service agency and a *profit center*, which is a kind of mini-SBU.

Developing the Advertising Budget Advertising budgets are established in the marketing plan. A firm approaches most budgeting decisions by looking at the total market for the product category and assessing its potential for growth based on different levels of advertising expenditures.[9] Typically, a firm's advertising expenditures are 3 to 5 percent of its total marketing costs, but advertising can take anywhere from 0.5 to 25 percent of a marketing budget.

Marketers analyze advertising budgets by looking at how much money is spent by product category in relation to sales in that category. This calculation, called the **advertising-to-sales ratio**, is the brand's or category's annual advertising expenditure divided by its total sales. Advertising-to-sales ratios are higher for durable goods, games, and toys than for consumables such as cigarettes and fast foods. Advertising-to-sales figures can be used to compare competing brands within a category. Generally speaking, the leading brand doesn't have to spend as much to maintain high visibility as a challenger does to build visibility.[10] Although because it is relatively easy to use, the advertising-to-sales ratio is probably the most widely used budgeting method, it is not necessarily the best. As we explained in our discussion of the SWOT analysis in Chapter 4, different brands have different problems and opportunities, and a single brand's problems and opportunities are continually changing. Therefore, a better way to budget is often the **task-objective method,** in which marketers set specific objectives for the coming year and then rely on their own past experience and the advertising agency's expertise in order to determine how much advertising is required.

Other Advertising Costs Other costs of advertising are primarily media expenditures—the amount of money needed to buy space and time. For years, advertising agencies were compensated by receiving a 15 percent *commission* on all media placements. For this commission, major clients like Kodak and Campbell received "full service," meaning all the other services

---

advertising-to-sales ratio
Annual advertising expenditure divided by total sales.

task-objective method
Advertising budget that is directed by specific marketing objectives.

the agency provided—creative design, strategic planning, and research—were done at no extra cost. Today the practice is to charge a much lower commission for media placement and then bill separately for the other services. This practice, called *unbundling*, came about because more and more clients choose one agency to create their ads and another to handle the media placements. Some agencies that provide services other than media placement and creative design—for example, public relations and package design—do this work on a project basis, meaning they give the client an estimate of the total cost for the job and then do the work for that agreed-upon price.

ADVERTISING STRATEGY AND EXECUTION

The differences between advertising *strategy*—decisions about *what* to say—and advertising *execution*—*how* to say it—are the topic of the seventh chapter objective. Strategy and execution work hand-in-hand to create effective advertising.[11]

Planning advertising involves five critical decisions: (1) whom to talk to; (2) what you want them to do or believe; (3) what to say; (4) how to say it; and (5) how to reach the audience. The targeting decision—"whom to talk to"—was discussed in Chapter 8. "What you want them to do or believe"—which involves setting advertising objectives—and "what to say" and "how to say it"—which involve developing copy strategies and advertising executions (the actual ads)—are discussed in this section of the chapter. "How to reach the audience"—which is the responsibility of media planners and buyers—is discussed in the next major section of the chapter.

ADVERTISING OBJECTIVES

Advertising objectives state what target audience responses the marketer hopes to elicit with an advertising message. Whereas marketing objectives are framed in terms of both specific amounts of sales and market share, advertising objectives set communication goals and describe the desired impact of the advertising message.

A number of formulas for setting advertising objectives have been derived from the consumer information-processing literature.[12] Traditionally referred to as *hierarchy-of-effects* models, these formulations describe the levels of impact that a message might have on consumer decision making and are designed to help advertisers structure their objectives. For example, although Cadillac has high brand awareness, fewer and fewer consumers have much interest in this particular car. Knowing this, Cadillac is likely to bypass the steps proposed in the first column of Table 18-6, which focus on creating brand awareness, and to concentrate instead on the processes described in the remaining columns of the table—for example, arousing consumers' interest, educating them about the product, and persuading, or motivating, them to visit Cadillac showrooms.

As we discuss in Chapter 22, because there are so many other elements in the marketing mix besides advertising, advertising professionals are often reluctant to measure the effects of advertising—especially image advertising for nationally distributed products—strictly by sales results. There are, however, some types of advertising that can be measured by sales results because advertising is the primary variable. Local retail ads announcing a fourteen-hour sale and direct-response ads (see Chapter 20) with an immediate-response mechanism such as an 800 number are good examples. Still, advertis-

TABLE 18-6	HIERARCHY-OF-EFFECTS MODELS

AIDA

Attention	Interest	Desire	Action

DAGMAR[1]

Awareness	Comprehension	Conviction	Action

Lavidge/Steiner Model[2]

Cognitive (Thinking)	Affective (Feeling)	Conative (Doing)
Awareness	Liking	Conviction
Knowledge	Preference	Purchase

Moriarty's Domains[3]

Perception	Education	Persuasion
Arousal (Attention)	Comprehension	Attitudes
Retention (Memory)	Learning	Behavior

[1] Russell H. Colley, *Defining Advertising Goals for Measured Advertising Results* (New York: Association of National Advertisers, 1961).
[2] Robert C. Lavidge and Gary A. Steiner, "A Model for Predictive Measurements of Advertising Effectiveness," *Journal of Marketing* 25 (Oct. 1961): 59–62.
[3] Sandra E. Moriarty, "Beyond the Hierarchy of Effects: A Conceptual Model," *Current Issues and Research in Advertising* (1983): 45–56.

ing experts regard most advertising as an investment because most advertising objectives focus on brand awareness and the creation of positive images, and the return on these objectives is indirect and long-term. For example, one of Millennium's most important objectives is to create national awareness of the Power System as well as develop an image as the dominant brand in the rechargeable category.

COPY STRATEGY

copy strategy
The means by which advertisers plan and develop the logic of sales messages.

selling premise
A statement of the logic behind a sales strategy.

The term **copy strategy** refers to the means by which advertisers plan and develop the logic of the sales message. The **selling premise** is the carefully crafted statement of this logic. A Leo Burnett agency memo described the selling premise as "the one competitive premise that will have the most influence on changing or reinforcing the target consumer's belief or perception of our brand in the desired way."

The relationship between product features, benefits, and claims is important in advertising strategy because most products are sold according to what they can do for the consumer. A *feature* is a product attribute such as size or color; a *claim* is an assertion regarding the product's performance; and a *benefit* is what the product promises to do for the user—it is the advantage you will derive from the various features of a particular product. Suppose you are shopping for a pair of shoes. You probably look first for the shoes' features: you want your size, a particular style (for example, low or high-heeled, brogan or loafer), and a particular color. Next come the manufacturer's or advertiser's claims: you want the shoes to be durable and to protect your feet from rough surfaces and bad weather. But in addition, you're likely to be equally concerned about the fashion statement that the shoes make; this is the largely psychological benefit the shoes offer you.

Advertising that presents features, claims, and benefits in especially effective ways and that can be shown to have had a significant effect on sales or market share sometimes wins the recognition of the American Marketing Association. In 1993, the AMA's annual Effie (for "effectiveness") Advertising Award went to the Isuzu Rodeo, for its "Going Outside the Lines" advertising campaign. Isuzu created a rugged, sporty, adventurous off-road image to rival that of the Rodeo's bigger-selling competitors, the Toyota 4-Runner and Nissan Pathfinder. Its campaign identified the Rodeo with people who, from their childhood, took unconventional routes to get where they were going (Exhibit 18-5). This advertising strategy increased sales by 65 percent, and in 1992 the Isuzu Rodeo became the number-one import in its class.

ADVERTISING EXECUTION

All the details and decisions involved in the production of an advertisement—how the ideas are expressed and what they look like—constitute the ad's **execution**. The challenge is to translate the selling proposition into an attention-getting and memorable execution built on a strong **creative concept**. An example of what we mean by a creative concept is the soap opera-like series of romance commercials that have been running for Nestlé's Taster's Choice in Canada and the United States and for Gold Blend in the United Kingdom. In each country—but particularly in Britain, where the series began—the ads have become a national obsession. A spinoff novel inspired by the ads, *Love over Gold*, made the London *Sunday Times* paperback best-seller list within two weeks of its release in 1993. That's the kind of creative idea power that most advertisers would die for. Even where there have been comedy sketches on the coffee-lovers' romances, this has only reinforced further the awareness of this brand.

Packaging the pieces of an advertisement is a complex process that involves manipulating a tremendous number of elements, all of which can have an impact on the perception of the message. In print, these elements include source credibility and attractiveness, psychological appeal, tone and style,

Exhibit 18-5
Rodeos Aren't Just for Ropin'

One message sent by this ad is that adventurous people will go through anything to get where they're going and that kind of rugged individualist drives a Rodeo. The name itself suggests strength, skill, and control in a dangerous situation.

585

MARKETING COMMUNICATION AND ADVERTISING

message structure, and such mechanical factors as ad size, picture size, color, type of art, and typefaces. In television, the important elements are the setting, action, characters, costumes, dialogue, sound effects, and lighting.[13]

Saturn's advertising, which has been created by Hal Riney & Partners since the car's launch, uses a tone and style unique in the annals of car advertising. A feature in *Advertising Age* attributed the ongoing success of the car to its advertising, which it described as "so understated that industry followers at first badly misread its power, over time, to stand out from the amorphous blur of ads using worn-out adjectives to boast about one unremarkable feature or another."[14] Another thing this advertising agency did for Saturn was to integrate its advertising with all of its other marketing communications. For this work, Hal Riney & Partners was named agency of the year in 1993 by *Advertising Age*, underlining the importance of integrated campaigns.

OPEN TO DEBATE

ARE NORTH AMERICAN ADS ETHNIC ENOUGH?

It has been said that some of the contemporary race problems in North America might never have happened if Ozzie and Harriet, characters in a popular family-based situation comedy of the 1950s, had had black neighbors. The point is that television is the most influential medium of our time and, as such, is presumed to shape social behavior. But does television shape our behavior or merely mirror it?

Television advertising is part of this shape/mirror debate. Many people believe that advertising definitely has an impact on social practices, and they want to see positive images of women and minority subcultures in ads. Although some marketers have recognized the multicultural nature of our society today, not much has changed in the way entertainment and advertising reach these diverse markets.

Statistics compiled in 1992 and 1993 by the *Asian American Quarterly* indicated that only 2 percent of the people who belong to the Screen Actors Guild and only 1 percent of members of Actors Equity were Asians. As illustrated in Table 18-7, of the 660 ads studied for this report, Calvin Klein, Estée Lauder, Giorgio, Armani, Gucci, and Perry Ellis did not feature one African, Latino, Asian, or other ethnic minority member. This suggests that minorities are presumed not to be part of the target market for most upscale clothing ads nor considered to be attractive models.[15]

On the other hand, there are a few companies that celebrate diversity. Nike ran a 30-second ad entirely in Spanish during the 1993 baseball All-Star game. Filmed in the Dominican Republic, the ad was titled "La Tierra de Mediocampistas" or "Land of the Shortstop." Nike's director of advertising admitted that airing a Spanish-speaking spot, even one with English subtitles, was risky, but added: "It's high time that advertisers had the courage to speak directly to Hispanics for something that is important to them."[16]

Companies in Canada that are putting "ethnic faces" on mainstream creative ads include Best Foods, Procter & Gamble, Bell Canada, Knorr, Ultramar, the Royal Bank, and North American Life.[17]

Because blacks have as much spending power as other North Americans, are more avid shoppers, and are far less brand-loyal than most marketers realize, failing to pitch advertisements at black customers is clearly poor marketing practice.

What do you think? Is there a positive social value in depicting diversity in advertising and is it good for business?

TABLE 18-7	PEOPLE OF VARYING ETHNIC BACKGROUNDS SHOWN IN ADVERTISEMENTS	
	Ethnic Minorities Represented	
	Percent	**Number**
In Magazine Ads		
Mademoiselle	2.6	NA
Vogue	2.5	NA
Seventeen	3.5	NA
In Ads for Product Lines		
Cover Girl	0.4	1 out of 226
L'Oréal	0.8	1 out of 131
Georges Marciano	1.0	2 out of 195
Clairol	1.5	1 out of 67
Gianni Versace	2.7	2 out of 73
Ralph Lauren	2.9	4 out of 138
Calvin Klein, Estée Lauder, Giorgio Armani, Gucci, Perry Ellis	0.0	0 out of 660

Source: "Numerically Speaking." The Asian American Quarterly 1 (Spring 1993): 7.

GLOBAL STANDARDIZATION AND ADAPTATION

Like other forms of international marketing, advertising strategy may be standardized—that is, an extension of the home-country strategy—or it may be adapted to local conditions. In some cases, marketers have to create separate strategies for each different national market they enter. Even those that are quite standardized on a macro level must often adapt local executions. For example, S. C. Johnson uses the same basic message worldwide for Edge shaving cream—the idea that Edge gives a very smooth shave. But while having a man scrape a credit card down both the Edge-shaved and the non-Edge-shaved sides of his face works well in industrialized countries, the scarcity of credit cards in developing nations calls for a different demonstration. Even Pepsi Cola, which prides itself on the universality of its strategy of "one sight, one sound, one sell," recognized that the high-spirited nature of the typical Pepsi ad posed too great a contrast to the reality of life in Eastern Europe to work. The selling proposition may be that the product brings fun and pleasure. But it may be necessary, in different parts of the world, to vary the types of people in the execution and the way they have fun.

campaign
A series of ads for a
product run in one or
more media under a
common theme.

ADVERTISING CAMPAIGNS

Advertisers can create a "single-shot" ad that stands alone, or they can devise a **campaign**—a series of thematically related advertisements run in different media over an extended time to intensify message memorability. An advertising campaign pushes essentially the same message, but with different executions to ensure that the audience remains involved and the message doesn't *wear out*. The Saturn launch campaign, for example, focused first on employees and their values. As the car moved through the initial sales phase, the campaign's focus shifted to buyers, their experiences with Saturn, and the reasons they were satisfied with the car.

Campaigns are developed using *continuity* devices such as slogans, design formats, music, typefaces, and characters like the pink Energizer Bunny. The heart of a good campaign, however, is a continuing emphasis on a strong feature or position. For example, Speedy Muffler King (see Exhibit 18-6) has relied on a consistent message for many years: "At Speedy, You're a Somebody."

MEDIA PLANNING AND BUYING ●

When you buy media, you buy access to an audience a certain number of times. From television to radio, you buy time; from newspapers and magazines, you buy space. What you do with that time and space is up to you (as long as it's legal). The percentage of readers, listeners, or viewers who pay attention to your ad will depend on how well your ad is executed.

For products that rely heavily on advertising, media buying is one of the most crucial steps in the marketing communication process for two reasons. First, even the greatest advertising campaign in the world will be worthless if the target audience never sees or hears it. Second, the media budget is frequently the biggest expense in the marketing communication mix, especially for consumer products advertised on television.

MEDIA DECISIONS

Media Strategy Good media planning ensures that media dollars will be spent wisely. The first step in planning is to determine a formal *media strategy*, which is based on the five key decisions that are the focus of the eighth objective for this chapter.

◆ *Who?* The target audience should be described as accurately as possible on the basis of demographic data. Most media vehicles—newspapers, magazines, television channels—have specific audience profiles, and unless a brand is trying to enter a new market, the audience profile should match that of the brand's current users.

◆ *Where?* Here the choice of media depends on the geographic area in which the product is distributed and thus available. For example, if a product is available only in Eastern Canada, it does not make sense to advertise it in the *Vancouver Sun*.

◆ *When?* Some products are seasonal and others have weekly sales peaks. Ads should be scheduled to run with these fluctuations in mind.

◆ *How?* Media choice is generally dictated by the type of creative message marketers want to communicate. For example, if the advertising involves action or demonstration, TV is a logical choice. For many food products, which are sold on appetite appeal, magazines are used because they can reproduce colorful ads that appeal to taste.

Exhibit 18-6
Always a "Somebody"

Canadian-owned Speedy Muffler King was founded in Toronto in 1956 and now has over 870 locations worldwide. Speedy's famous slogan "At Speedy, You're a Somebody" has always played an important role in its advertising.

◆ *To what extent?* Repetition of the campaign message is important to ensure that it is received by the target audience. Marketers must determine how much they will spend in which media vehicle. As part of media planning, the media budget is allocated according to such considerations as media categories, geography, and time periods. Certain types of media, areas, or parts of the schedule will be emphasized and thus need more of the budget. This practice is called *weighting*.

In IMC planning, discussion about the use of media is even more complex because the concept of customer contact points introduces a much wider range of message opportunities. IMC campaigns typically use a variety of alternative media, as well as traditional media. For example, Hal Riney & Partners agency used an informercial to help launch Saturn, "Spring in Spring Hill," that ran on Arts & Entertainment and VH-1 cable networks. An **infomercial** is an advertisement, usually on television or radio, that runs as much as 30 minutes and tries to educate consumers about a good or service. In format, it often resembles an interview or news show. The Riney media department also suggested linking Saturn with bicycling sponsorships because research found that people who drive imports, Saturn's target market, also ride bicycles and are interested in environmental and health issues.

infomercial
A lengthy advertisement, usually on television or radio, that attempts to educate consumers about a good or service; its format often resembles an interview or news show.

Media Objectives The next step in media planning—and a topic of chapter objective ten—is to determine media objectives. Because most brands have limited media budgets, advertising executives must decide how much advertising is needed to create the impact specified by the marketing communication or advertising objectives. Most media planners believe that if you don't spend enough to achieve minimum audience-awareness levels, you'll have no impact at all, and also that too much splintering of the media buy will mean the message may not be seen enough times to be remembered. In determining media objectives, there are two primary considerations: *reach* and *frequency*.

reach
The average percent of the target audience exposed to an advertising message at least once within a given period of time.

Reach is the average percent of the target audience exposed to the advertising at least once within a given period of time. **Frequency** is the average number of times within that period that an advertising message for the brand is seen by those who have been reached. For example, a media plan could have a four-week reach of 70 percent and a frequency of seven—meaning that in a four-week period 70 percent of the targeted households in the viewing area, on average, will be exposed to the advertisement seven times.

frequency
The average number of times within a given period of time that advertising for a brand is seen by those who have been reached.

There is seldom enough budget to satisfy both, so media planners must decide whether to emphasize reach or frequency. Because wide awareness is a must for new brands, advertisers for new products generally try to maximize reach. In highly competitive product categories, particularly for mature products that are purchased frequently, frequency is usually more important. Coke and McDonald's must keep their brands "top-of-mind" among targeted customers; these image campaigns require a great deal of repetition. Media planners have a rule of thumb that, on the average, it takes at least three exposures to a message to make an impression on an audience.[18]

One way to maximize reach is to use a variety of media. To maximize frequency on a national level, marketers can focus on one medium and increase repetition. On the local level, radio is one of the best frequency-building media because each radio station tends to have its loyal listeners.

Media Selection The third step in media planning—and the second topic of chapter objective ten—is media selection. In most countries there are three ways to buy media—*local, spot,* and *national*. Most magazine advertising in North America, for example, is bought on a national basis. Larger-circulation magazines such as *Reader's Digest* and *TV Guide* have regional and, occasionally, individual market editions. When buying national TV, agencies make *national buys* from national networks such as the CBC. Buying TV time in just a few markets is called a **spot buy**. Newspapers, radio, and outdoor billboards are primarily local media, with most of their revenue coming from locally owned or managed businesses. There are a few national newspapers in Canada, such as *The Globe & Mail* and the *Financial Times*.

spot buy
Buying TV time in a few selected markets.

The Millennium media plan (Chapter 4) for the trade audience includes ads in trade magazines such as *Discount Store News* and *Photo Business*. For consumers, the plan calls for a combination of network TV (American Thanksgiving Day: the parade and NFL Football), national cable TV (The Family Channel, USA Network, A&E, CNN, and Nickelodeon), network radio (CBS NFL Football), and national print (*USA Today* and consumer magazines with toy-related advertising).

The media buy is based on three other factors in addition to reach and frequency: *media strengths, audience size,* and *rating points*. Table 18-8 compares various media in terms of their general patterns of strengths and weaknesses. For each buy, the media planner must weigh these strengths and weaknesses in terms of advertising strategy and objectives. Knowing how to make this evaluation is essential for anyone with responsibility for spending media dollars.

TABLE 18-8

MEDIA VEHICLE STRENGTHS AND WEAKNESSES

Strengths	Weaknesses
Newspapers	
• Timely (2–4 days leadtime), most publish daily	• Not target-selective
• Good one-time reach (55–75% metro-area coverage)	• Teens and lower socioeconomic groups not reached
• Local	• Readership relatively low
• Good for detailed copy	• Builds reach slowly
• Low production costs	• Poor reproduction, especially color
Magazines	
• Excellent color reproduction	• Long leadtime (2–3 months)
• Special interest means good targeting	• Low reach
• Pass-along readers, readership may exceed bought circulation many times	• Production relatively expensive
• Long life	
• High credibility, prestigious	
Radio	
• Target-selective	• Message can't be "reread" if missed
• Good frequency builder	• Average station has low reach
• Short leadtime	• Background medium, low attention level
• "Free" merchandising	• No illustrations
• Relatively low production costs	
Television	
• Combines sight, sound, and motion for best impact	• Not too selective
• Local and national	• Production expensive
• Low CPM	• Long production leadtime (but local "quick and dirty" in a few days)
Direct Mail	
• Fast response	• Most expensive per impression
• Most selective	• Mailing lists not always up-to-date
• Message can be in wide range of sizes, configurations	• Bad reputation ("junk mail") of misdirected direct mailings
• Demands attention, consideration	• Lots of clutter
• 2–4 times more coupon redemptions than with newspapers	
• Can be personalized	

In print media, the size of the audience is determined by *circulation*—the number of people reached by the copies distributed. In broadcast media, it is determined by the *rating* of the program during which the advertising is scheduled. A **rating** is the percent of the total broadcast-area households tuned to a station when a commercial runs. The larger the newspaper or magazine circulation, the more an ad will cost; the higher the broadcast rating, the more the commercial will cost.

In order to determine the *weight* of a total media schedule, the reach is multiplied by the frequency. The result is the *gross rating points (GRPs)*. This is how a marketing manager compares different media-mix plans. In the example

rating
Percentage of total broadcast-area households tuned to a station when a TV or radio advertisement runs.

591

mentioned earlier, the four-week media plan contained 490 GRPs (70 percent reach × 7 frequency = 490).

Global marketers must also consider the availability of different media on which to carry their messages. Over 85 percent of advertising in Peru, for example, is done via television, in part because of Peruvians' high illiteracy rate. At over 35 percent, Nepal leads the world in the percent of advertising done through radio, partly because of the unavailability of television and the difficulty of reaching that mountainous nation's far-flung residents in other ways. Denmark, Sweden, and Norway have banned television advertising in the past, and many other European countries limit the amount of television advertising per day. Advertising in Saudi Arabia must be done through print media.

MEDIA COSTS

cost-per-thousand (CPM)
A method of stating the costs of a particular media buy that is based on the cost of reaching 1,000 households.

When buying media, the "buy" should be based on the number of GRPs—the number of households reached—not the number of ad units. For example, five ads (a "5-spot package") scheduled to run during the "morning drive" time on radio station CHUM, which normally has a relatively high rating, may reach four times as many consumers as a 10-spot package that runs between 10 P.M. and midnight. To quantify such alternatives, advertisers depend on cost-per-thousand comparisons. Both print and broadcast costs are quoted in **CPMs**—industry shorthand for **cost-per-thousand**—which establish the cost of the buy in terms of reaching 1,000 households (HHs). For example, if a full-page ad in *The Toronto Star* costs $110,000 and the circulation is 5,000,000, the cost of reaching each 1,000 of *The Toronto Star*'s households would be $22:

$$\frac{\text{cost of ad} \times 1{,}000}{\text{circulation}} = \text{CPM}$$

$$\frac{\$100{,}000 \times 1{,}000}{5{,}000{,}000} = \$22$$

A cost of $22 to reach 1,000 households seems quite cheap—only about 2 cents per household. But what if only a small number of *The Toronto Star's* readers are interested in your product? Then you are paying to reach a lot of people who won't even look at your ad. That is why more sophisticated marketers talk in terms of *TCPMs*, or *targeted cost-per-thousand*. For example, suppose Chrysler wants to run an ad in *The Toronto Star* that is pitched to households that have cars that are four or more years old—perhaps 1,000,000 out of *The Toronto Star*'s 5,000,000 total circulation. Following our formula, Chrysler would compute its TCPM as follows:

$$\frac{\$110{,}000 \times 1{,}000}{1{,}000{,}000} = \$110$$

area of dominant influence (ADI)
A geographic area surrounding a television broadcasting center, which is usually located in a city; the ADI may have a radius of 40–60 miles. Also referred to as a *designated marketing area (DMA)*.

As you can see, TCPM gives marketers a better idea of what they are getting for their money. The Chrysler marketer finds he is actually paying five to six times as much as he would have thought had he used the simpler CPM formula.

Although newspapers still generate more advertising revenue than any other medium, it is television that determines the geographic description of markets. TV signals are received 40 to 60 miles from a city center, so TV advertisers are buying more than just coverage of consumers inside the metro area. Because many consumer product companies have set up sales operations that are based on these TV markets—generally called **areas of dominant**

influence (ADIs), but sometimes referred to as *designated marketing areas (DMAs)*—they have become the standard geographic markets.

INTEGRATED MARKETING ●

Marketing communication—especially integrated marketing communication—is a powerful marketing tool. But communication is just one element in the marketing mix and can be undermined by other marketing-mix elements. A price may be perceived as too high; customers' past experience with a product may have been negative; or the product may be unavailable in stores in large parts of the nation or the world. In such cases, sales will be low no matter how good the marketing communication program is.

There's an old saying in marketing that the fastest way to kill a bad product is to give it good advertising because such communication will generate extensive trial—and disappointing product experiences. Even with a good product, marketers must be careful not to overpromise in their advertising. When customers buy a product, they have expectations—usually acquired from marketing communications—about its performance. If these expectations are not met, sales may suffer, regardless of the product's quality.

For example, when the poultry industry first started making hotdogs and lunch meat to compete with traditional pork and beef processed-meat products, ads claimed that poultry products tasted just like traditional hotdogs and lunch meat. Not only was this untrue, but many of the poultry products were made by grinding up the bones along with the meat, which gave the products a slightly gritty texture. Consequently, few consumers repurchased. But when the nutritional craze hit, the poultry industry switched from a "taste" to a "nutritional" message that could be well documented, and sales increased significantly. The poultry processors were able to deliver on the "nutritional" promise more effectively than on the "taste" promise.

Without question, how a company communicates its message determines its corporate image and that of its brands. And, as we noted in earlier chapters, a strong brand image can translate into competitive advantage and greater market share and profits. The challenge to the marketing manager is to use marketing communication in all of its varieties to create both maximum marketplace impact in the short run and a strong brand image for the long term. Consistent messages produce a synergy that benefits the brand.

BOTTOM LINE REALITIES

NIKE SETS THE PACE

Nike's advertising regularly wins acclaim from consumers and awards from the advertising industry. But Nike is more than just an excellent advertiser, it is a case study in integrated marketing and integrated marketing communication. For example, it has three different lines of shoes aligned with different basketball stars: Air Jordan represented by Michael Jordan; Force represented by David Robinson and Charles Barkley; and Flight represented by Scottie Pippin. The idea is that not every player has the same appeal for every consumer, so the basketball market was sliced up to reflect the personalities of its stars.

593

Nike's women's campaign has been getting rave reviews from women who are tired of being treated as either fashion dingbats or superjocks. The sensitive campaign, which was written by women, speaks to women in real language about real concerns relating to health, fitness, and attitudes (Exhibit 18-7). Nike has also moved into retailing, setting up its own stores called Nike Town. One objective is to make the retailing of sports clothing and shoes more friendly to women (most sporting goods stores have small or nonexistent fitting rooms and male salespersons). Another objective is to enhance its own image by making retailing a form of entertainment.

Nike's integrated philosophy goes beyond its advertising: it is woven into all phases of athletics. Besides sponsoring events and hiring athletes to endorse products, Nike has entered the sports management business. It has management contracts with NBA players Alonzo Mourning and Harold Miner that guarantee them salaries in return for handling all aspects of their careers, including NBA contracts and endorsements. Mourning, in fact, considers himself an employee of Nike rather than the Charlotte Hornets, the team that holds his NBA contract.

Nike has also signed a deal with CAA, Hollywood's largest talent and literary agency. Together, Nike and CAA will create live sporting events and programming for broadcast and cable TV. Such programming, of course, will spotlight Nike's star athletes and products, as well as CAA's celebrity clients. By generating a new income stream from these sports marketing events, Nike hopes to advance toward its goal of being a broadly defined sports and fitness marketer.

These ambitious schemes take Nike to a new level of marketing and marketing communication. What do you think about Nike's moves into such areas as celebrity product lines, management contracts, retailing, and sporting event management? Are there risks here that might backfire, or are these strategies brilliantly visionary? ▼

Exhibit 18-7
The "Shock of Recognition"

For years, Nike's advertising has had incredible success reaching people with powerful images and moving stories. In this ad for the Magazine Publishers of America, another creative director from a different agency explains what she likes about an ad that is part of the Nike women's campaign.

KEY POINTS SUMMARY ▼

1. Marketing communication encompasses all the elements in the marketing mix that establish meaning and communicate value to customers and other stakeholders of an organization. The marketing communication mix includes advertising, direct marketing, public relations, packaging, personal selling, and sales promotions.

2. The marketing communication model, which resembles the traditional communication model, has the following components: the sender or source of the message—the marketer; encoding of the message, or putting the creative strategy or selling proposition into a form that is understandable and effective; the message itself, which is the execution of the creative strategy; the media, or channels through which the message is communicated; decoding, the interpretation of the message by the receiver; the receiver—the business, consumer, or other stakeholder the sender wants to influence; and feedback, the receiver's response to the message, which may be a change in attitude or behavior or disregard of the message.

3. Integrated marketing communication (IMC) is the process of strategically developing and controlling or influencing all messages that customers and other stakeholders use in forming an image of, and maintaining a relationship with, an organization. Specialists in all the different communication functions work together to coordinate the communication mix for maximum message impact.

4. A zero-based marketing communication plan is one that starts with a clean slate rather than with last year's plan. After doing a SWOT analysis, marketers identify the target audiences, determine the IMC objectives, and select the communication areas and creative and media strategies that will best accomplish those objectives.

5. The broadcast categories of advertising used in marketing communication are global, national, and local advertising. Global and national advertising includes brand, corporate, and business-to-business or trade advertising. Local advertising includes retail and co-op advertising.

6. Advertising's functions are: adding value; stimulating demand; building brands; differentiating brands by providing information about competitive advantages; positioning, repositioning, and preempting positions; and supporting sales.

7. Advertising strategy, which focuses on *what* is said, sets communication objectives and identifies selling premises. Advertising execution, which is concerned with *how* the message decided upon is communicated, includes developing a creative concept, finding the appropriate message approach, and handling the production details.

8. Global communications programs are complicated because although the selling propositions in such programs may travel well from nation to nation, the executions of these may encounter problems when firms attempt to apply them locally.

9. Media strategy decisions are driven by five questions—who, where, when, how, and to what extent. The answers to these questions determine the most effective and efficient ways of reaching consumers.

10. The two most common media objectives are reach and frequency. Media selection involves decisions about global, national, local, and spot buys, as well as comparisons of media costs and weighting strategies.

DISCUSSION QUESTIONS ▼

1. Explain the basic marketing communication model and identify the points at which communication breakdowns can occur. Give specific marketing communication examples.

2. Identify your favorite cosmetic product and explain how elements of the marketing mix besides the traditional marketing communication areas send messages and contribute meaning to the product.

3. Interview a local marketer and determine the degree (if any) to which the firm has integrated its marketing communications. What factors do you think have helped/hurt integration efforts at this company?

4. What are some ways that advertising affects demand for products? Can you think of a product that you have bought as a result of advertising?

5. How does advertising add value to a product? What products do you own that you value because of their image or what they contribute to your own self-image?

6. Find a print ad that you like and:
   (a) Analyze the difference between its strategy and its execution.
   (b) Develop proposals for two different copy strategies for that product—in other words, what else might the marketer say or focus on strategically in the advertisement?
   (c) Develop proposals for two different executions of the marketer's original strategy—in other words, in what other ways might the original strategy be presented?

7. Analyze Benetton's advertising strategy as described in this chapter. Is it appropriate for a fashion retailer to take controversial stances? Are Benetton's ads thought provoking and ideologically courageous, or are they exploitative and in poor taste?

8. In your library find an international men's or women's magazine that competes with a magazine you read and find a brand that is advertised in both (or product category, if you can't find a specific brand). Analyze how global marketers cope with the fact that selling propositions "travel" well internationally, while exe-

cutions may not? Does your brand follow or depart from that maxim?

9. Analyze the issue of cultural imperialism. Is it possible for some products to trade on their Western "cachet" without offending local cultures? Should cultural imperialism be of concern to multinational advertisers, and should they modify their advertising strategies to minimize it? Develop a "white paper" (a report that views both sides of an argument, then takes a position and provides justification for that position) for an international jeans marketer with a decidedly Western product image.

10. Explain how advertising objectives can be derived from hierarchy-of-effects models. Find four ads that clearly are trying to do different things—each one representing one of the four levels (columns) of the AIDA model.

11. Build an argument supporting *or* opposing the inclusion of sales response in a set of advertising objectives for (a) a soft drink and (b) a local copy center.

12. You have been asked to do the media buying for ads for a new cellular phone store in your town. List the five key questions you would ask in developing a media plan for this store and speculate on how you would answer them.

Integrative Case • Discussion Questions

The Body Shop*

1. Anita claims that The Body Shop does not advertise. Do you think that's true? Support your answer.

Harley-Davidson

1. What is/are the primary purpose(s) of Harley advertising?

2. How did Harley's and Honda's advertising objectives differ in the 1960s?

The Millennium Power System

1. Do you agree with Melvin that the magazines selected for consumer advertising are not appropriate? Why or why not?

*The three cases at the back of the book—"The Body Shop," "Harley-Davidson," and "The Millennium Power System"—illustrate topics discussed in all chapters of this book. Your instructor will tell you when to read a particular case and answer the discussion questions on it that appear at the end of each chapter.

Radio Shack Commercials

Every day in Canada, there are a thousand radio and TV commercials produced, all with the same aim. The creators want to make something that will make you want to see the ad, remember the ad, and buy the product. To do that, they must stand out from the clutter of the crowd. Vaughn Whelan is the head of a new independent advertising agency. He has a reputation for advertising that gets attention. After years of working with established agencies in Canada, he has ventured out on his own, and must now prove to the industry that he is capable of not only surviving, but also creating the images that make his clients thrive. Radio Shack has hired him to produce an off-the-wall set of commercials for their Christmas campaign. Radio Shack has lost considerable image and focus over the pas ten years. A lot of their business has gone to discount stores and big boxes. First, they had to start stocking the national brands people were asking for. Now, they need a campaign that will remind the consumer of the full assortment of products that are available, that the price points are good and that there are 800 stores all across the country.

Whelan has concocted the idea of using comic Pete McCormick to integrate a mix of improvised comedy with a chosen sample of products available at Radio Shack. The series will be shot in an 18 day period during a cross-Canada production trip covering 27 different cities and the line that will link them all together is "This place is completely wired." That line needs to be said in as many different ways and situations as possible. It's up to Whelan and McCormick to improvise as they go, as no scripts or storyboards are being used. All they have planned is a list of places and the products that will be featured. This is a $3.5 million campaign, including production and air time, so a lot of risk is riding on every decision in the shoot and the post production editing. It has to look real, but zany enough to be remembered. Sure, there are lots of laughs, but will it translate into sales?

As they proceed through the production, they encounter a number of unexpected situations. Some they can take advantage of. In other cases, it's a good thing they came prepared with a Plan B. Watch the video that accompanies this case and you will get some of the feeling of what goes into these simple creative productions we consumers love to hate.

QUESTIONS

1. Why does humor work?
2. Could they have turned out better advertisements if they had done more pre-planning? Would storyboards and scripts have helped?
3. Put yourself in the shoes of the marketing manager from Radio Shack that hired Whelan. In hindsight, was it a good decision?

Source: This case was prepared by Ray Friedman and is based on the *Venture* series episode "Radio Shack," originally broadcast on January 16, 1994.

Appendix 18

The Canadian Code of Advertising Standards

ADVERTISING'S SELF-REGULATORY PROCESS

The *Canadian Code of Advertising Standards* has been developed to promote the professional practice of advertising. The Code's clauses set the criteria for acceptable advertising and form the basis upon which advertising is evaluated in response to consumer or trade complaints. The Code is generally endorsed by advertisers, advertising agencies, media which exhibit advertising, and suppliers to the advertising process. (See Appendix 18A.)

The Code is the principal instrument of self-regulation for the advertising industry in Canada, supplemented by the standards set by individual media and by other advertising-related associations. The Code does not supersede municipal, provincial or federal regulation affecting advertising. (See Appendix 18B.)

The Code is administered by the Advertising Standards Council, le Conseil des Normes de la Publicité, and by regional councils located in Vancouver, Edmonton, Calgary, Regina, Winnipeg and Halifax. The Council/Conseil and the regional bodies are supported and coordinated by the Standards Division of the Canadian Advertising Foundation. (See Appendix 18C.)

DEFINITION OF ADVERTISING

For the purpose of this Code, "advertising" is defined as any paid message communicated by Canadian media with the intent to influence the choice, opinion or behaviour of those addressed by the commercial messages.

APPLICATION

The Code applies to advertisers promoting the use of goods and services, to corporations or institutions seeking to improve their public image, and to governments, government departments and crown corporations, provided such advertising meets the criteria set forth in the definition.

EXCLUSIONS

The Code does not govern or restrict the free expression of public opinion or ideas through advocacy advertising, or election advertising.

SCOPE OF THE CODE ●

The Code deals with *how* products or services may be advertised, not with *which* products or services may be advertised. Thus, the authority of the Code applies only to the content of commercial messages and does not prohibit the promotion of legal products or services or their portrayal in circumstances of normal use. The content of the advertisement and audience reached or intended to be reached by the message are relevant factors in assessing its acceptability.

THE CODE ●

The *Canadian Code of Advertising Standards* has been approved and is supported by all participating organizations, and is designed to help set and maintain standards of honesty, truth, accuracy, fairness and taste in advertising. The principles underlying the Code and more detailed descriptions of its application are presented in the Manual of General Guidelines for Advertising.

No advertising shall be prepared or knowingly exhibited by the participating organizations which contravenes this Code of Standards.

The clauses should be adhered to both in letter and in spirit. Advertisers and advertising agencies must be prepared to substantiate their claims promptly to the Council upon request.

1. ACCURACY, CLARITY

(a) Advertisements must not contain inaccurate or deceptive claims, statements, illustrations, or representations, either direct or implied, with regard to price, availability or performance of a product or service. In assessing the truthfulness and accuracy of a message, the concern is not with the intent of the sender or precise legality of the presentation. Rather, the focus is on the message as received or perceived, that is, the general impression conveyed by the advertisement.

(b) Advertisements must not omit relevant information in a manner which is deceptive.

(c) All pertinent details of an advertised offer must be clearly stated.

(d) Disclaimers or asterisked information must not contradict more prominent aspects of the message and should be located and presented in such a manner as to be clearly visible.

2. DISGUISED ADVERTISING TECHNIQUES

No advertisement shall be presented in a format or style which conceals its commercial intent.

3. PRICE CLAIMS

(a) No advertisement shall include deceptive price claims or discounts, unrealistic price comparisons or exaggerated claims as to worth or value. "Regular Price", "Suggested Retail Price", "Manufacturer's List Price", and "Fair market Value" are deceptive terms when used by an advertiser to indicate a savings, unless they represent prices at which a reasonable number of the item was actually sold within the preceding six months in the market place where the advertisement appears.

(b) Where price discounts are offered, qualifying statements such as "up to", "XX off", etc., must be in easily readable type, in close proximity to the prices quoted, and, where practical, legitimate regular prices must be included.

(c) Prices quoted in advertisements in Canadian media, other than in Canadian funds, must be so identified.

4. BAIT AND SWITCH

Advertisements must not misrepresent the consumer's opportunity to purchase the goods and services at the terms presented. If supply of the sale item is limited, or the seller can fulfill only limited demand, this must be clearly stated in the advertisement.

5. GUARANTEES

No advertisement shall offer a guarantee or warranty, unless the guarantee or warranty is fully explained as to conditions and limits and the name of the guarantor or warrantor is provided, or it is indicated where such information may be obtained.

6. COMPARATIVE ADVERTISING

Advertisements must not discredit, disparage or attack unfairly other products, services, advertisements, or companies or exaggerate the nature or importance of competitive differences.

7. TESTIMONIALS

Testimonials, endorsations, or representations or opinion or preference must reflect the genuine, reasonably current opinion of the individual(s), group or organization making such representations, and must be based upon adequate information about or experience with the product or service being advertised, and must not otherwise be deceptive.

8. PROFESSIONAL OR SCIENTIFIC CLAIMS

Advertisements must not distort the true meaning of statements made by professionals or scientific authorities. Advertising claims must not imply they have scientific basis which they do not truly possess. Any scientific, professional or authoritative claims or statements must be applicable to the Canadian context, unless otherwise clearly stated.

9. IMITATION

No advertiser shall imitate the copy, slogans, or illustrations of another advertiser in such a manner as to mislead the consumer.

10. SAFETY

Advertisements must not display a disregard for public safety or depict situations which might encourage unsafe or dangerous practices, particularly when portraying products in normal use.

11. EXPLOITATION OF PERSONS WITH DISABILITIES

Advertisements must not hold out false hope in the form of a cure or relief, either on a temporary or permanent basis, for persons who have disabilities.

12. SUPERSTITION AND FEARS

Advertisements must not exploit superstitions or play upon fears to mislead the consumer.

13. ADVERTISING TO CHILDREN

Advertising which is directed to children must not exploit their credulity, lack of experience, or their sense of loyalty, and must not present information or illustrations which might result in their physical, emotional or moral harm.

Child-directed advertising in the broadcast media is separately regulated by the Broadcast Code for Advertising to Children, also administered by the Canadian Advertising Foundation. Advertising to children in Quebec is prohibited by the Quebec Consumer Protection Act.

14. ADVERTISING TO MINORS

Products prohibited from sale to minors must not be advertised in such a way as to appeal particularly to persons under legal age and people featured in advertisements for such products must be, and clearly seen to be, adults under the law.

15. TASTE, PUBLIC DECENCY

It is recognized that standards of taste are subjective and very widely from person to person and community to community, and are, indeed, subject to constant change. Advertising must not present demeaning or derogatory portrayals of individuals or groups; must not exploit violence, sexuality, children, the customs, convictions or characteristics of religious or ethno-cultural groups, persons with disabilities or any other person, group or institution in a manner which is offensive to generally prevailing standards.

SELF-REGULATION OF ADVERTISING IN CANADA ●

The *Canadian Code of Advertising Standards* was originally sponsored by the Canadian Advertising Advisory Board, the predecessor organization of the Canadian Advertising Foundation (CAF). First published in 1963, it has since been reviewed and revised periodically to keep it contemporary, and has been supplemented by other industry Codes. Change in the provisions of the Code is an ongoing process.

The CAF-Standards Division in Toronto handles all national advertising complaints and complaints from the Ontario region, when these concern English-language advertising; complaints from Quebec and all national French-language complaints are handled by le Conseil des Normes de la Publicité in Montreal. The majority of these complaints are processed at the staff level and only unresolved complaints are referred to the Advertising Standards Council or le Conseil.

Across the country, regional councils—in the Atlantic provinces (Halifax), Manitoba (Winnipeg), Saskatchewan (Regina), Alberta (Calgary and Edmonton), and British Columbia (Vancouver)—handle local advertising complaints in their respective areas. Each council operates autonomously and, generally speaking, it is the full regional advertising council which reviews and rules on each complaint received.

Each council includes public representatives, nominated by consumer, academic or special interest groups, as well as representatives from advertisers, agencies and media.

PRE-CLEARANCE PROCEDURES ●

All English language broadcast commercials directed to children as well as English-language television commercials for feminine sanitary protection products, must be pre-cleared by special committees of the CAF prior to acceptance. Scripts and storyboards are checked by CAF staff but a final approval number is not given until the finished commercial has been viewed by the appropriate clearance committee.

Cosmetic advertising for broadcast must be pre-cleared by the appropriate government regulatory body. Broadcast scripts for cosmetic products may be submitted through the Toronto and Montreal offices of the Canadian Advertising Foundation. This service is offered in cooperation with the Health Protection Branch of the Department of Health and Welfare Canada.

A Pharmaceutical Advertising Advisory Board (PAAB) Code of Advertising Acceptance applies to advertisements for pharmaceutical products appearing in health-services magazines—directed to doctors, dentists, hygienists, nurses and pharmacists. Such messages must also be pre-cleared. Because these messages are often highly technical, they are cleared by the Commissioner of the Pharmaceutical Advertising Advisory Board, of which the CAF is a member.

ROLE OF RESPONSIBILITIES OF COUNCIL ●

The Advertising Standards Council, le Conseil and the regional councils are pledged to:

I Review and, where appropriate, resolve public complaints regarding advertisements.

II Work within the advertising industry and with consumer bodies in developing, updating, administering, and publicizing self-regulatory standards and codes.

III Counsel individual advertisers and agencies on laws, regulations, standards and codes affecting advertising.

CAF staff in Toronto and Montreal maintain a tracking process to monitor trends in advertising, trends in advertising complaints, and to bring to the attention of the various advertising standards councils new developments so that the councils can review the information gathered and consider the appropriate action to be taken.

HOW TO COMPLAIN ●

If you are exposed to advertising carried by Canadian media which you believe contravenes the *Canadian Code of Advertising Standards*, write to the Advertising Standards Council nearest you.

If it is a print advertisement, it helps if you can enclose a copy of the advertisement; with a broadcast message, identify the station, approximate time, the name of the product, etc. Give a brief written explanation as to why you think the message contravenes the Code.

HOW COMPLAINTS ARE RECEIVED AND HANDLED ●

All written complaints directed to the Toronto or Montreal office of the Canadian Advertising Foundation will be initially handled by Standards Division/le Conseil staff. Complaints to the Regional Councils are processed by the full council in that region. All written complaints will be acknowledged and reviewed and if there appears to be a Code violation, the advertiser will be notified of the nature of the complaint. The advertiser is required to respond to the enquiry and to provide the requested information so that a determination can be made as to whether the *Canadian Code of Advertising Standards* has been violated. If a violation has occurred, the advertiser is requested to amend the advertising in question or withdraw it. Once the advertiser has taken either of these two steps, the complaint will be closed and the complainant informed in writing of the corrective action taken by the advertiser.

If the complaint is not sustained, the complainant will be informed of the reasons why it has been determined that the advertising does not violate the Code.

If the advertiser or complainant disagrees with a staff or Council ruling, an appeal may be requested. The matter will be referred to, or back to, the Advertising Standards Council/le Conseil des Normes de la Publicité for a further review. If Council/Conseil sustains the complaint, the advertiser is notified, and asked to amend or withdraw the advertising. Generally, this closes the matter. Regardless of whether the complaint has been sustained or not, both the complainant and the advertiser will be notified of the outcome of an appeal. Occasionally an advertiser will be reluctant to take corrective action. When this occurs, the media involved will be notified indicating that this message has been judged to have contravened the Code. In general, this means that supporting media will not exhibit the advertising in that form.

Communications regarding the interpretation of the Code should be addressed to:

Canadian Advertising Foundation
Standards Division
350 Bloor Street East
Suite 402
Toronto, Ontario
M4W 1H5

or to:

le Conseil des Normes de la Publicité
4823 ouest, rue Sherbrooke
suite 130
Montreal, Quebec
H3Z 1G7

Appendix 18A

PARTICIPANTS

The *Canadian Code of Advertising Standards* has been reviewed and approved by the following participating organizations:

Advertising and Sales Executive Club of Montreal
Association of Canadian Advertisers
Association of Medical Advertising Agencies
Association of Quebec Advertising Agencies
Better Business Bureau of Canada
Brewers Association of Canada
Canadian Association of Broadcasters
Canadian Broadcasting Corporation
Canadian Business Press
Canadian Cable Television Association
Canadian Community Newspapers Association
Canadian Cosmetic, Toiletry and Fragrance Association
Canadian Daily Newspaper Publishers Association
Canadian Direct Marketing Association* (See list of Other Industry Codes)
Canadian Magazine Publishers Association
Canadian National Yellow Pages Association
Direct Sellers Association
Grocery Products Manufacturers of Canada
Institute of Canadian Advertising
Le Publicité Club de Montréal
Magazines Canada
Non-Prescription Drug Manufacturers of Canada
Ontario Funeral Service Association
Outdoor Advertising Association of Canada
Pharmaceutical Advertising Advisory Board
Retail Council of Canada
Society of Ontario Advertising Agencies
Telecaster Committee of Canada
Trans Ad Limited
Trans-Canada Advertising Agency Network
Welcome Wagon Ltd.

The Canadian Advertising Foundation and the regional advertising standards councils also endorse in principle the *International Code of Advertising Practice*, developed by the International Chamber of Commerce and now adopted in some 30 countries.

LEGISLATION AFFECTING ADVERTISING

Federal Acts

Broadcasting Act (Sections 5(1), (2), 8(1), (2), (3), (4), 16)

Regulations: Advertising Generally
Liquor, Beer, Wine and Cider Advertising Criteria
Food and Drugs

Circulars:

Pre-clearance of adds for food and drug commercials
Food advertising
Registration procedures for television commercials
Canadian Human Rights Act
Competition Act
Consumer Packaging and Labelling Act
Copyright Act
Criminal Code
Department of National Revenue–Customs and Excise Tariff
Items 99221-1, Schedule C, June 30, 1972
Food and Drugs Act
Canada Hazardous Products Act
Income Tax Act (Section 19)
National Trade Mark and True Labelling Act
Official Languages Act
Textile Labelling Act
Trade Marks Act

Provincial Acts

British Columbia

Trade Practices Act
Consumer Protection Act and Regulations
Closing Out Sales Act
Human Rights Act
Motor Dealer Advertising Guidelines
Liquor, Beer and Wine Advertising Regulations

Alberta

The Unfair Trade Practices Act
Consumer Credit Transactions Act
Liquor, Beer and Wine Advertising Regulations

Saskatchewan

Consumer Products Warranties Act
Cost of Credit Disclosure Act
Liquor, Beer and Wine Advertising Regulations

Manitoba

Consumer Protection Act
Trade Practices Inquiry Act
Liquor, Beer and Wine Advertising Regulations

Ontario

Business Practices Act
Consumers Protection Act
Human Rights Code
Regulation 12B (credit advertising)
Liquor Control Act

Quebec

Charter of the French Language
(under above heading) Regulations—Language of Business and Commerce
Consumer Protection Act
(under above heading) Regulation—Children's Advertising
Lotteries Act—Publicity Contests and Lotteries
Broadcast Advertising Tax Act
Agricultural Products, Marine Products and Food Act
Liquor, Beer and Wine Advertising Regulations
Pharmacy, Professional Advertising Regulations
Roadside Advertising Act
Act Respecting Class Actions

New Brunswick

Consumer Product Warranty and Liability Act
Cost of Credit Disclosure Act

Nova Scotia

Consumer Protection Act
Liquor, Beer and Wine Advertising Regulations

Prince Edward Island

Business Practices Act
Consumer Protection Act
Highway Advertisements Act
Liquor, Beer and Wine Advertising Regulations

Newfoundland

Trade Practices Act
Consumer Protection Act
Exhibition of Advertisements (Billboards) Act
Liquor, Beer and Wine Advertising Regulations

Other Industry Codes

Advertising Code of Standards for Cosmetics, Toiletries and Fragrances
Broadcast Code of Advertising to Children
Cosmetic Code for Advertising Acceptance
CBC Advertising Standards
Code of Consumer Advertising Practices for Non-Prescription Medicines
Canadian Direct Marketing Association Code of Ethics and Standards of Practice
Guidelines for the Use of Comparative Advertising in Food Commercials
Guidelines for the Use of Research and Survey Data in Comparative Food
    Commercials
Pharmaceutical Advertising Advisory Board Code of Advertising Acceptance
Telecaster Committee of Canada Guidelines
Television Code of Standards for the Advertising of Feminine Sanitary
    Protection Products

You may obtain free copies (up to 5) of the *Canadian Code of Advertising Standards*, in French or English, by writing to:

CAF-Standards Council
350 Bloor Street East
Suite 402
Toronto, Ontario
M4W 1H5

or to:

le Conseil des Normes de la Publicité
4823 ouest, rue Sherbrooke
suite 130
Montreal, Quebec
H3Z 1G7

Regional Councils:

Advertising Standards Council—B.C.
P. O. Box 3005
Vancouver, B.C.
V6B 3X5

Alberta Advertising Standards Council—Calgary
P.O. Box 2400, Station M
215-16 Street S.E.
Calgary, Alberta
T2P 0W8

Advertising Standards Council—Nova Scotia
C/O Halifax Herald Ltd.
1650 Argyle Street, Box 31819
Halifax, Nova Scotia
B3J 2T2

Advertising Standards Council—Saskatchewan
P.O. Box 1322
Regina, Saskatchewan
S4P 3B8

Advertising Standards Council—Manitoba
P.O. Box 848
1700 Church Avenue
Winnipeg, Manitoba
R2X 3A2

● Chapter 19

Public Relations, Sales Promotion, and Packaging

THE SHAKE-UP IN MARKETING COMMUNICATION

If you wanted a hot career in marketing communication, what area would you gravitate to? Advertising? Sales promotion? Public relations? That decision has become increasingly difficult because of the changes going on in the various marketing communication areas.

Although advertising is highly visible and perceived as glamorous, you might be surprised to learn that it is becoming a less important player in marketing communications. Between 1988 and 1992, spending on nonadvertising marketing communications went up nearly 30 percent, while advertising expenditures rose only about 7 percent.[1]

The reasons for the increasing impact of nonadvertising promotional activities are many. The large number of advertising messages—consumers are exposed to 1,500 to 2,000 a day—have created so much commercial clutter that customers are screening more and more of them out. Public relations is often being used in preference to advertising because of

the credibility that news stories in the media can create for a product. At the same time, the cost of using databases has dropped significantly as computers have become more economical, making it much easier to use one-to-one marketing to reach prospects directly, and this has given a real boost to direct marketing companies (see Chapter 20). Direct mail is now the fastest growing sector within promotion, and is taking this away from print media advertising.

Furthermore, in the last twenty years the long-standing ratio between advertising and sales promotion has, by and large, been reversed. Packaged-goods firms used to spend roughly 60 percent of their marketing communication budgets on advertising and 40 percent on sales promotion. Today 73 percent of those dollars go to sales promotion, including both consumer and trade promotions. Why? Because sales promotion provides an immediate response.

Advertising is feeling the pressure, as you can tell from the ad in Exhibit 19-1. This message was created by *The Wall Street Journal*'s advertising department to make the argument in support of advertising and its role in long-term brand building. It's an attack on sales promotion's short-term results.

From an advertisement like this, you can sense the tensions in the marketing communication field. Sales promotion, public relations, and direct marketing are all jockeying for increasing shares of the marketing communication budget at the expense of advertising but once one medium starts to lose its share of advertising, it has never regained it.

Change continues to go on in marketing communcation. As you read through the rest of the chapters in this part of the book, try to think of some ways in which marketing communication activities may be restructured in the months and years to come. Ask yourself which of these areas offers the most promising career. ■

Building brand relationships and sales is the principal task of marketing communication, and the question of just what proportions of the various marketing communication functions should be used in this effort is a major issue for marketers today. Although the exact mix will differ for each marketing situation, ideally all the various tools will reinforce and support one another. Like advertising, the marketing communication functions explored in this chapter—public relations, sales promotion, and packaging—all reinforce brand recognition and awareness, and also like advertising, each has its particular strengths.

PUBLIC RELATIONS

One area of growing activity in marketing communications is public relations. **Public relations**, commonly known as **PR** or as publicity, fosters goodwill and understanding between an organization and its stakeholders— customers, employees, stockholders, financial analysts, the general public (especially in areas where the organization has offices and plants), governments (local, state, national, and international when a company sells in more than one country), and suppliers. In an effort to maintain good relationships with all these stakeholders, PR undertakes a variety of "relational" activities. As Table 19-1 shows, each of these activities and programs provides benefits to the overall marketing effort.

Internationally, public relations is now growing more rapidly than any other marketing communications function—on average, 20 percent per year. In some countries PR is growing more than twice as rapidly as advertising and sales promotion.[2] One of the most important reasons for this burgeoning growth is that consumers today are more sophisticated; they want to know that the companies they buy from understand and empathize with their concerns, such as protection of the environment, health care, and job opportunities. These concerns can best be addressed through a strong public relations program.

Some major Canadian companies, however, have recently downsized or eliminated their public relations departments. For example, Trans Alta Utilities Corp. of Calgary has cast the principal communications responsibilities out to its business units across Alberta. Ontario Hydro has reduced the size of its public relations department from 210 to 106. Also, Teleglobe Canada Inc. of Montreal has completely done away with its PR department and has hired Cossette Communication-Marketing Inc. to perform the function instead.[3]

Although in some companies it is the practice to separate *marketing public relations* (MPR) from corporate public relations, the writers of this textbook agree with Thomas Harris, author of *The Marketer's Guide to Public Relations*,[4] and many others that this separation is unwise. Firms that use MPR often assign this function a rather narrowly focused role, one that stresses specific campaigns or promotions. They leave broader-based activities, which involve relations with stakeholder groups such as company employees, the community, and the government, to the PR function. However, stakeholder groups overlap: community residents know company employees, stockholders know people in the financial community. If different messages are sent to different groups, conflict and serious misunderstanding may result. Suppose that at the same time a company's ads are touting the high quality of its products, the company's managers are warning employees that if they don't improve product quality, the company will lose business. The net result may be loss of confidence in the company.

public relations (PR)
Activities that promote goodwill and understanding between an organization and its stakeholders.

611

PUBLIC
RELATIONS,
SALES
PROMOTION,
AND PACKAGING

TABLE 19-1   **THE BENEFITS OF PUBLIC RELATIONS**

Target Audience	Channel	Benefits to Marketing
Customers	• News releases to media • Events • Sponsorships	• Increased brand awareness • Message credibility (for higher sales levels)
Employees	• Newsletters • Social activities • Feedback	• Higher morale (leads to fewer product defects and less absenteeism)
Suppliers	• Trade articles • Incentives	• Preferred-customer status • On-time deliveries • Higher allocations during shortages make possible smoother production and distribution and lower costs
Community/ General Public	• News releases to media • Plant tours • Support for local community activities	• Attraction of better employees, who make higher-quality products • Fewer local conflicts—zoning, taxes, community services—make lower prices possible
Government	• Lobbying • News releases to financial publications • Direct mail • Personal calls	• Favorable legislation • Less regulation, which reduces overhead and lowers prices
Financial Community	• Briefings • News releases to financial publications • Direct mail • Personal calls	• Higher stock prices • Better credit makes leveraging easier

All marketing communications should have the ultimate objective of building good stakeholder relationships. Some organizations will doubtless continue to separate corporate PR and MPR, but what is important to remember is that no matter what internal structure an organization adopts, if it wants to be and stay on the cutting edge, it must ensure that those responsible for marketing and public relations functions work together.

HOW PUBLIC RELATIONS WORKS

Public relations is a sophisticated planned effort that focuses on creating positive images for a company, product, or brand and building relationships. One of PR's most important contributions to marketing communication is the concept of stakeholders, which we defined in Chapter 2. As we saw, there are a variety of important audiences or publics for a company's communications beyond the customers who buy its products. These groups, all of whom have a stake in the company's well-being, include suppliers, consumer and trade markets, the press, the financial community, consumer groups, regulatory agencies, and the local community and local government. All of these groups can be the target for public relations messages.

The government relationship was a focus of both critics and supporters of the North American Free Trade Agreement (NAFTA) between the United States, Mexico, and Canada. Critics charged that NAFTA would encourage U.S. and Canadian companies to shift their manufacturing operations to Mexico in order to pollute as freely as they wish and employ Mexicans as virtual slave labor.[5] In contrast, supporters of the treaty pointed to actions by the Mexican government to control polluting practices. The signs are that U.S. and Canadian companies intending to take advantage of NAFTA will have to be good corporate citizens south of the border. Engineering cross-border business opportunities will be a particular challenge for public relations professionals in coming years.

STRENGTHS AND STRATEGIES OF PUBLIC RELATIONS

As chapter objective one implies, the strengths of public relations lead to its most important strategic uses. The *publicity* aspects of MPR, for example, consist of brand messages that appear in media articles and stories. Since product publicity messages are considered news or entertainment rather than advertising, the media do not charge organizations for running them—although firms do incur costs in preparing these messages.

When PR efforts are effectively coordinated with marketing strategy, PR's contributions move beyond product publicity into the realm of managing broad-based stakeholder relations that are important to brand building. Note in the following explanations of the major strengths of PR how each of these strengths drives different kinds of PR strategies that make important contributions to a marketing program.

1. *PR adds credibility/believability.* In the past, "product publicity," or *media relations*, has meant getting the company or brand name mentioned in the mass media in as many different ways, times, and places as possible. The idea is that press mentions, because they are presented by objective news media, are more credible than other forms of marketing communication, such as advertising, which are developed and presented by the company. A 1992 study of trends in public opinion showed that 28 percent of the public has confidence in television news reports and 21 percent in newspaper news reports. However, a mere 13 percent said they had confidence in consumer information provided directly by major corporations, and only 5 percent said they had confidence in advertising.[6] *The New York Times* article on rechargeable batteries, for example, added credibility to Millennium rechargeable batteries when the line was first launched.

2. *PR breaks through advertising clutter.* As the number of commercial messages grows and customers become resolute about ignoring them, it is crucial to find other ways to reach current and potential customers (see Exhibit 19-2).

3. *PR costs less.* When the McDonald's All-American Marching Band appears in the Macy's Thanksgiving Day parade, it is seen by over 10 million TV viewers. McDonald's does not pay anything for this huge media exposure, which would cost millions if it were advertising, though it does have expenses associated with the band's appearance (such as airfare and accommodations for the 100 musicians from 50 states and their chaperons) and the time the company's PR staff and its PR agency

613

PUBLIC
RELATIONS,
SALES
PROMOTION,
AND PACKAGING

**Exhibit 19-2
Publicity That
Counts**

**The media can
contribute to a
products's visibil-
ity and reputa-
tion. This article
from The Globe
& Mail provides
an objective
view of Honda's
mini-van.**

The Globe & Mail   November 20, 1994

How Honda set minivan in motion

A late entrant into a hot market, company is spending $7-million on launch

By Timothy Pritchard
Auto Industry Reporter
Phoenix

Honda's minivan entry has been the works for five uears, but many Canadian dealers didn't get a glimpse of the Odyssey until October, when it was unveiled with much pomp at a company get-together.

In the warm morning sun of Phoenix, a clutch of Canada's best-known auto writers, wearing casual shirts and jeans, are on the job.

Pens and notebooks in hand, they mill around a new metallic-green mini-van—with one side of its body partly cut away—that sits on a patio at the Pointe Hilton, a large resort hotel in the desert hills. Most of the passenger-side roof of the minivan is missing, and so are its two right-side doors. It's been created for a show and tell, or as they say in the car business, the "walk-around presentation."

A select few from among 80 writers in the Automobile Journalists Association of Canada, the 10 critics have a coveted chore: test drive the Odyssey, **Honda Motor Co. Ltd.'s** first mini-van. They will also try out Honda's new V6-powered Accord.

The group drifts away from the peekaboo version, moving over to an intact, maroon one nearby. Here they take more tactile impressions—opening the doors and hood, trying out the seats, fiddling with the dashboard fittings.

In a few minutes, they will drive off for lunch in five of these vans, preproduction models hand-built in Japan for $100,000-plus apiece.

The writers expect a lot from Odyssey, not just ̃ause Honda has ̃ation for ̃ty good ̃

but also because it is tackling the minivan market late in the game.

A hands-on ride and drive for influential auto journalists is a critical step in any new vehicle launch—priming the sales pump, in this case, for two vehicles that are about to hit Honda dealer showrooms.

Wives have been invited on the junket, a rarity, because 80 per cent of Odyssey drivers are expected to be women, says Honda's public relations chief Dennis Manning. The Automobile Journalists Association of Canada has only three women members.

The Globe and Mail reporter's assignment is to write about a vehicle launch. The paper has a "no freebies" policy and has paid air fare and hotel costs, but its reporter is being fed and watered with the others by Honda Canada.

In vehicle launch jargon, this trip is a "short-lead" preview. That means ̃porters can ̃pictures and ̃

An alternative format is the "long-lead" preview ab early opportunity for evalution they may take a month or two to get articles written and into print.

During the summer, writers and photographers from the U.S. "buff books"—Automobile, Motor Trend, Car and Driver—were taken to Japan for Odyssey test runs. Their reviews were under embargo until the November issues.

———◆———

Honda's minivan entry has been in the works for five years, which "seems like an eternity to many dealers," admits Jim Miller, Honda Canada's senior vice-president of sales and marketing.

Over the past decade, minivans, Jeep-like vehicles and small trucks have won over mil'ions of b·vers. Honda dealers h? ̃ had ̃n-tende ̃heir li ̃

spend on the project, but the cost is still much less than a comparable amount of advertising.

4. *PR reaches hard-to-reach audiences.* Upscale and well-educated audiences, such as business executives, are often difficult to reach with traditional advertising. They can be reached, however, with articles in newspapers and special interest magazines. MPR can also get around the "road-blocks" (for example, secretaries and answering machines) that hinder sales calls.

5. *PR reaches other stakeholders besides consumers.* Good public relations people know how to reach employees, community leaders, legislators and regulators, consumer groups, and the financial community. Since all of these groups are important to an organization and its marketing program, it is vital that two-way communication exist between them and the organization in order to get feedback.

6. *PR takes a proactive approach.* Keeping lines of communication open between the organization and all stakeholder groups can often prevent

special interest groups from harming the organization. Like some other railways, British Rail has had many employee strikes. Unlike most of the other airlines, Southwest Airlines has not had an employee strike. One reason is the former's weak communication with its employees, which prevents the company from addressing complaints and problems before they become serious.

7. *PR establishes a corporate-citizen image.* As we noted in Chapter 18, when a company reaches the "mission marketing" level of communication, it has maximized its relationship building program. Ben & Jerry's and The Body Shop have relied exclusively on public relations to create their image as concerned "corporate citizens."

8. *PR faces fewer legal restrictions.* Sometimes you can say things in a press release that you can't say in advertising.

Targeting The concept of targeting is very important to public relations. In corporate PR, the focus is on targeting a variety of stakeholders. In marketing PR, however, the targeting strategies are more concerned with markets. Marketing PR is very useful for reaching important but hard-to-reach *customer targets*—for example, Nike reaches the young and active consumer segment by placing stories in such media as *Sports Illustrated* and by sponsoring sporting events.

PR releases and events also contain strategic messages or themes that reinforce or complement other marketing communication messages. A good example is Campbell Soup's use of a video news release in which Olympic ice-skating stars talk about the nutritional value of soup during their workouts. This MPR program was particularly valuable to Campbell because it also used the same skaters in TV spots and print ads stressing nutrition.

Gatekeepers We saw in Chapter 7 how certain individuals within a firm act as "gatekeepers" to limit and focus the flow of information to buyers of industrial goods. We use the term *media gatekeeper* to describe the editors and other decision makers in the media who decide not only what stories will be printed or aired but also when they will run, how much space or time they will occupy, and what they will say.

For marketing publicity to get past media gatekeepers, it must have enough news or human interest to justify publication or broadcast. For example, Heinz once made the "world's largest salad" by filling a portable swimming pool with salad makings and then covering it with gallons of a new Heinz dressing. Both TV and print editors ran a human interest story on the event.

PUBLIC RELATIONS PROGRAMS AND TOOLS

Public relations programs, the focus of the second chapter objective, are grouped into specific categories that reflect traditional ways of identifying stakeholders, such as media relations, government relations, community relations, financial relations, and employee relations. Strategic planning determines the specific messages appropriate for each of these various stakeholders. However, a common set of tools is used for the tactical implementation of all these programs, and we discuss each of these tools in this section.

Among the variety of publicity tools used to execute PR strategies, news releases, press kits, press conferences, and media tours are the most important. A **news release** is any form of usually professionally prepared print, visual, or broadcast announcement an organization makes available to the media about its activities. News releases range from a one-page story on a

615
PUBLIC
RELATIONS,
SALES
PROMOTION,
AND PACKAGING

news release
A form of publicity in which an organization makes available to the media some form of professionally prepared print, visual, or broadcast announcement about its activities.

brand improvement to a 90-second video clip, called a video news release (VNR), on some aspect or activity of a company.

The value of the video news release was demonstrated by McDonald's astute use of this tool when it cosponsored the 1993 Superbowl. Because Superbowl sponsors often make elaborate new commercials specifically for the Superbowl, the commercials themselves have become news. McDonald's made special commercials featuring NBA stars Michael Jordan and Larry Bird having a basketball shooting contest. A few days before the 1993 Superbowl, McDonald's PR agency sent the spot, along with the extra footage (outtakes) shot during the making of the commercial, to all major TV stations in the United States. The stories that these stations ran during their sports news segments, including the spot and/or some of the outtakes, were seen by more people than saw the actual Superbowl spot for which McDonald's paid $1 million.

A **press kit** is a packet of information that includes pictures of the product or the service being marketed, maps, histories, and background facts plus several different stories that focus on such topics as the product's history, development, or testing. Food, sports, news, and entertainment editors on large daily newspapers and nationally circulated magazines receive over a hundred news releases and press kits each week. To break through this clutter, some firms have been including free samples or premiums (such as a pair of wine glasses and a bottle of champagne to "celebrate the birth" of a new product or innovation) in their press kits.

On those rare occasions when there is a major news announcement, a company may hold a **press conference,** in which corporate officials meet with media representatives to inform them about some major company-related news event. When Coca Cola involved Hollywood deal maker Michael Orvitz and his cast of producers and actors in the company's big "Always" campaign, the press conference announcing the campaign received major coverage in advertising industry publications.

In a **media tour** a spokesperson for a firm travels to selected cities and meets with as many newspaper and magazine representatives and local radio and TV show hosts as possible. The goal is to get the media to run stories about the firm or its product or to invite the spokesperson to be interviewed on the air. Although it is more costly to send someone on the road than it is to mail out press kits, it may be cost-effective because reporters are more likely to use a company's publicity materials when they have had personal contact with the company's representative.

Publications   Besides press releases and press kits, public relations offices produce all kinds of literature, including brochures, fliers, posters, calendars, newsletters, magazines, and annual reports. Sales literature, sometimes referred to as *collateral materials*, is also an important part of the MPR toolkit. Exhibit 19-3 shows part of a brochure produced by Millennium to keep various audiences informed about its promotional activities.

Special Events   One time-honored way to create a publicity opportunity is to put on an event that is newsworthy, complete with dignitaries. Traditional PR events include groundbreaking ceremonies and ribbon cuttings, grand openings, christening boats with a bottle of champagne, and celebrations of anniversaries and centennials. The bigger the event and the more dignitaries involved, the more likely the media will cover it.

Public Service Programs   As part of their corporate-citizen mission, companies often engage in activities that support the community or the arts. This is another way to ensure positive press coverage of a firm and its employees. Research conducted by Goldfarb Consultants of Toronto indicates that Canadians judge the credibility of a company more by its research funding and special event sponsorship than by its advertising or its media play.[7]

press kit
A package of publicity information that includes such materials as press releases, background histories, schedules, maps, pictures of the product, and stories that focus on the product's development or testing.

press conference
A meeting held by a corporate official or officials with representatives of the media to announce, explain, or bring the media up to date on some major news event related to the company.

media tour
A form of publicity in which a spokesperson for a firm travels to selected cities and meets with as many press representatives as possible.

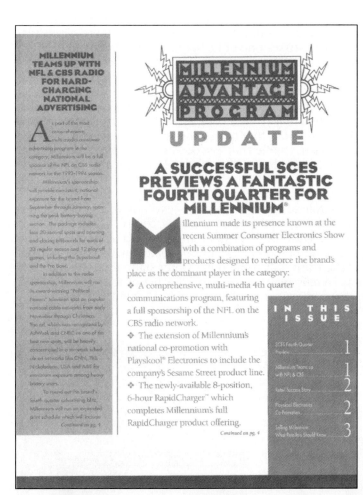

Continued on pg. 4

Continued on pg. 4

Exhibit 19-3
Advantage Program Newsletter

The Millennium Advantage Program is designed to keep the trade involved and informed about the product and its promotional activities.

617

PUBLIC
RELATIONS,
SALES
PROMOTION,
AND PACKAGING

Business Sponsoring Charities

The CHUM/CITY Christmas Wish collects money and distributes toys to needy children in Metro Toronto at Christmas. It is a non-profit event and CHUM Limited absorbs 100 percent of administrative costs.

Crisis Management Every company should have a public relations plan in place for when disaster strikes one of its brands or the company itself. All companies make mistakes, and companies that make mistakes often make the news. Marketers need to be proactive instead of reactive—to think of major things that can go wrong and then develop a general plan for handling such events. This is one area where marketing and PR concerns definitely overlap, since many of the disasters that strike a company relate to production, distribution, or promotional activities that have gone awry.

Public relations experts agree that a successful crisis management plan must not only be developed before a crisis occurs but must also be rehearsed so that all parties involved will know what to do. Furthermore, the plan should reflect the company's values and basic approach to doing business. A crisis plan outlines the role of top management—executives, lawyers, security specialists, financial experts, and public relations counsel—and designates who the primary news media contact will be and how a crisis center near the site will be set up.[8] The number-one principle in dealing with a crisis is to accept the fact that "the truth will come out." Don't stall, don't speculate. Be candid and honest. *Fortune* magazine compiled a list of fourteen suggested ways to deal with the media when a crisis occurs (see Table 19-2).

Soap Wars

Media battles carried out by corporate rivals can leave consumers wondering what they should believe. In Europe, Unilever and Procter & Gamble are archrivals in the laundry detergent market. Unilever developed a new version of its Persil brand that contained a manganese-based accelerator, which meant that clothes could be washed at lower temperatures, and thus users could save energy. Despite claims from Procter & Gamble executives that the new detergent was "defective," Unilever chose to launch the revolutionary new detergent anyway. Shortly after, a report appearing in a Rotterdam newspaper revealed that in tests of the Dutch equivalent of the new Persil, the detergent destroyed clothes in fewer than 25 washes. This research, however, was commissioned by Procter & Gamble (makers of Ariel, Persil's chief competitor).

TABLE 19-2

FOURTEEN WAYS TO DEAL WITH THE MEDIA

- **Make the CEO responsible for press relations.** That means he or she must often speak for the corporation, both routinely and in times of crisis, and delegate enough authority to make the PR spokesperson a credible source.
- **Face the facts**. If you screw up, admit it candidly. Avoid hedging or excuses. Apologize, promise not to do it again, and explain how you're going to make things right.
- **Consider the public interest in every operating decision**. Your reputation depends far more on what you do than on what you say. Act accordingly. Try giving your senior PR expert a seat at the table when decisions are made.
- **Be a source before you are a subject**. The time to make friends with reporters is long before trouble hits. Get to know the people who cover your company, educate them, help them with their stories, and give them reason to respect you. Determine which journalists deserve *your* respect and trust.
- **If you want your views represented, you have to talk**. Reporters are paid to get stories, whether you help or not. When you clam up, they must depend on other sources—often people like that marketing VP you fired last month.
- **Respond fast**. You can't influence a story once its deadline has passed. Nor will you appear credible if you seem to be stalling. In a crisis, figure you have a day to get your story out.
- **Cage your lawyers**. They will always tell you to keep your mouth shut. But in many crisis situations your potential legal liability may be trivial compared with the risk of alienating your customers, employees, or regulators.
- **Tell the truth—or nothing**. Nobody likes a liar.
- **Don't expect to bat 1.000**. PR is a game of averages, so be content if you win most of the time. Even the most flattering story will likely have a zinger or two, and even the best companies get creamed now and then.
- **Don't take it personally**. The reporter is neither your enemy nor your friend: he or she is an intermediary between you and the people you need to reach. And forget about your ego—nobody cares about it but you.
- **Control what you can**. Release the bad news yourself—before some reporter digs it up. Use your selective availability to reporters as a tool. Set ground rules every time you talk. If the public isn't buying your message, change it.
- **Know whom you're dealing with**. The press is not monolithic. TV is different from print, magazines are different from newspapers, and the Globe and Mail is different from *The Wall Street Journal*. Within a news organization will be a normal mix of individuals, some honorable and competent, some not. Do your homework on journalists before you talk to them, reviewing their past work and talking to other executives they have covered.
- **Avoid TV unless you feel free to speak candidly**. Even then, learn to present your views in the 10-second sound bites that are the building blocks of TV stories. Use simple declarative sentences and ignore subtleties. Whenever possible favor live T V shows over those that can edit your remarks.
- **Be human**. Reporters—and the public—usually will be more sympathetic to a person than to a corporation. If you can do it without lying or making an ass of yourself, reveal yourself as a person with feelings. Your mistakes will as likely be forgiven as criticized. Insist on being judged on a human scale, with normal human fallibility taken into account. Remember that people love to root for underdogs.

BEHIND THE SCENES

HOW TO HANDLE (OR NOT HANDLE) A CRISIS

If you were a fast-food chain, how would you handle a food poisoning epidemic traced to your product? What type of crisis management plan would you implement and where would you begin? As we mentioned in the branding discussion in Chapter 10, the outbreak of food poisoning at Jack-in-the-Box restaurants in 1993 left two Seattle children dead and as many as 450 people ill in Washington, Idaho, and Nevada, to say nothing of what it did to the firm's stock prices. This incident illustrates how a crisis can turn into a public relations disaster.[9]

The chain threw away 20,000 pounds of affected meat, changed its meat supplier, instructed its employees to cook all hamburgers at a higher temperature, and established an 800 number to handle consumer questions. Unfortunately, however, the restaurant waited almost a week to take responsibility for the poisoning. Jack-in-the-Box executives refused to comment at the outset of the crisis, which is the worst thing you can do. When the president did speak to the media, he faulted state health officials for not telling the company about new cooking regulations when they had, and also tried to pass on the blame to the company's meat suppliers.

Jack-in-the-Box eventually ran apologetic ads—but only in a few affected areas, despite the fact that the entire nation had been exposed to news about the crisis. Furthermore, the ads didn't run in Los Angeles, the chain's biggest market. Worse, news stories about some children who died during the crisis were linked to Jack-in-the-Box even though these children had not eaten at the chain. Finally, the company waited over two weeks to announce to ill customers that it would pay their medical bills.

Because Jack-in-the-Box and its parent company, Foodmaker, failed to convey their concern to the public early in the crisis, the initial steps they took to handle the crisis appeared halfhearted. If Jack-in-the-Box had been operating with a well-thought-out crisis plan, what do you think its first actions would have been when it learned of the crisis? What actions would you have recommended? Think about that for a minute before we move on to another case.

Also during 1993, reports of foreign objects being found in Diet Pepsi cans started pouring in from around the United States. During the week-long crisis the escalating claims included finding pins, needles, loose screws, bullets, a crack vial, syringes, and a blob of mysterious brown goo.[10]

Pepsi immediately brought together a team of twelve company executives to handle the complaints. In less than a week, Pepsi's president made the rounds of newsrooms and distributed several video news and press releases to explain how the bottling process works and why it is impossible to insert foreign objects during the process. Second, Pepsi brand worked closely with the FDA, and the FDA commissioner went so far as to assure customers and retailers that the tampering reports were a hoax. The FDA involvement added immense credibility to Pepsi's crisis management campaign. The company also established an 800 number to take consumer calls and faxed daily morning updates to its 600 offices, distribution centers, and bottlers across the nation. A week later, after it was clear that the claims were hoaxes, the company ran an ad thanking consumers and retailers who "stood with us."

Even though all the reported incidents of finding foreign objects in Diet Pepsi were proved false, and many of those who perpetrated the hoaxes were arrested and assessed large fines, Pepsi still lost $35 million in sales. However, Pepsi's quick reaction and effective crisis management helped it maintain its public image and prevented much greater monetary losses.

What did Pepsi do right that Jack-in-the-Box did wrong? What can you learn about crisis management from a comparison of these two cases?

SALES PROMOTION

The word *promotion* is sometimes used in textbooks as an umbrella term for all aspects of marketing communication. In business, however, the word is a short form of the phrase **sales promotion**, which refers to any consumer or trade program that adds immediate tangible value to the brand (such as an incentive to buy) in order to stimulate trial, increase consumer demand, or increase product availability. We will follow business practice and use *sales promotion* or *promotion* to refer to such specific activities or programs.

In this section of the chapter, we explore the controversy about the usefulness of sales promotion versus advertising (the focus of the third chapter objective) and discuss the strengths and strategies of sales promotion (the topic of the fourth chapter objective). While advertising creates the psychological environment for selling, sales promotion provides an extra reason for the customer to buy or respond, which is why it became so popular during the recession of the early 1990s and the uncertain recovery. Recognizing this important difference, most marketers agree that both advertising and sales promotion are needed. Keep in mind, however, that a sales-promotion offer can have no impact unless the target audience knows about it, which usually requires some advertising support.

The type and scale of sales promotion varies from product to product and from company to company. There are two types of sales promotions: trade and consumer promotion. **Consumer promotions** are incentives aimed directly at the ultimate user of the good or service, while **trade promotions** are incentives aimed at wholesalers, distributors, dealers, retailers, and other members in the distribution channel. We explore these two types of incentive programs later in this section.

THE GROWTH OF SALES PROMOTION

Until the late 1960s and early 1970s, promotion industry veterans estimated that up to 80 percent of consumer goods companies' marketing communication budgets went to traditional media advertising. "Promotion used to be the stepchild," says Bud Frankel, a respected sales promotion expert. Advertising continued to be the marketing tool of choice through the '70s and early '80s because of its power to build strong brands. But in the mid-1980s something significant happened in the world of marketing communication—sales promotion beat out advertising. Advertising's share of the marketing-mix budget has been declining ever since, a situation alluded to in the opening chapter story.[11]

Sales promotion has overtaken advertising in most marketing mixes because its results are immediately discernible, and that is particularly important in troubled economic times. Paralleling the switch in emphasis from advertising to sales promotion was a strategic shift from stressing long-term brand building to emphasizing short-term bottom line sales responses. Advertising experts decried the shift and developed ads like the one in the opening story (Exhibit 19-1) to remind marketers of the value of brand equity. The

---

sales promotion
Any consumer or trade program that adds immediate tangible value to products in order to stimulate consumer purchasing and foster trade cooperation.

consumer promotions
Incentives aimed at the ultimate user of a good or service in order to increase demand.

trade promotions
Incentives directed at the sales force as well as wholesalers, distributors, and retailers in order to stimulate both selling activity and demand.

conflict between advertising and promotion intensified recently, when sales-promotion programs, historically used for short-term marketplace impact, started to be used to contribute to long-term brand building.

The shift from advertising to sales promotion also reflects tensions in the distribution channel. Trade promotion spending increased over 15 percentage points in less than ten years, reflecting manufacturers' efforts to *push* their products through the channels of distribution. Because retailers were being offered larger trade incentives more frequently, they began to run more and more sales. The end result is that consumers have been conditioned to look for the best deal, and both retailers and manufacturers are lamenting the decline of brand loyalty.

Today manufacturers are beginning to change their spending strategies to favor brand building once again. The amount of money they allocated for trade promotions decreased by 4.6 percent in 1992, while marketing communication funds increased by 2.8 percent and even advertising spending gained 1.8 percent.[12] These statistics suggest that even though trade promotion will retain the largest share of the marketing communication mix for some time to come, the percentage of spending it will claim compared to the other types of promotion may shrink as manufacturers and retailers seek to regain the long-term relationship they once enjoyed with their customers.

STRENGTHS AND STRATEGIES OF SALES PROMOTION

The reason sales promotion is such a growth area is that it has certain strengths that impact directly on sales. In economic downturns sales promotion is a particularly effective tool in the marketing communication mix. There are certain things it can do more effectively than any other marketing communication function. The following nine strengths *apply to all types of sales promotion*—consumer, trade, institutional, and business-to-business—and provide the framework for a set of universal sales promotion strategies.

1. Sales Promotion Adds Tangible Value In Chapter 18 we learned that advertising adds value to products and services. Basically, sales-promotion tools are also designed to *add value* to something that we already want or need. How, then, do advertising and sales promotion differ? The difference is this: While advertising adds *psychological* value—an image or feeling of status, sexiness, quality, or dependability—sales promotion adds something *tangible*, such as a 20 percent price reduction, a free coffee mug, or a chance to win a million dollars. A trade sales-promotion program may offer the soft drink wholesaler or retailer $1 off per case, $2 off per case if the brand is advertised in the retailer's ad, or a free vacation trip if a certain volume of the product is ordered within a specified time period.

A key factor in the concept of adding tangible value is the incentive. *Incentives* are inducements that motivate action and this is true for the trade as well as for the consumer market. Incentives are something extra beyond the benefits and features inherent in the product, and they can also be a reward for achieving a high level of performance (see Exhibit 19-4). There are three basic kinds of incentives:

  a. *Price reductions:* a percent or actual dollar/cents off the regular price.

  b. *Free goods or services:* additional product free or a different product (good or service) free.

  c. *Experiences:* a trip, party, or participation in a contest or sweepstakes (chance to win something).

Because of the increased emphasis on sales promotions over the last ten years, consumers and the trade have been conditioned to look for—and in many instances, demand—special incentives before buying. An example is the increasing use of a sale on top of a sale, such as "take an additional 20% off the already reduced price."

2. Sales Promotion Reduces Risk One of the reasons that customers, both industrial and consumer, hesitate about buying a new good or service is the *risk* that they won't like it, it won't work, or it won't sell. Most customers are concerned about getting good value for their money. Sales promotion is one important tool that marketers use to decrease *perceived risk* and thus reduce buyer resistance. For example, to allay the risk involved in trying Rogaine, the baldness remedy, Upjohn offered consumers a $5 rebate on each of the first four bottles of the product they purchased.

3. Sales Promotion Stimulates Immediate Response Most sales promotions create a sense of immediacy by adding extra value to a brand for a limited time. For example, most coupons carry expiration dates, trade incentives are good for only a certain number of days, and most rebates must be sent in by no later than a specified date. Although generating immediate sales increases is often desired, as companies take a more strategic approach, they are beginning to place more emphasis on sales-promotion activities that contribute to long-term brand relationship building. In 1993, manufacturers of packaged goods distributed 4 billion coupons to Canadian consumers. Canadian consumers redeemed 174 million direct-to-consumer coupons, or approximately 17 coupons per household.[13]

4. Sales Promotion Adds Accountability   Because sales promotions can have a definite time frame and can provide immediate results, they have a relatively high level of *accountability*. This is a key reason for the shift away from advertising toward sales promotion. A brand manager set to spend $500,000 on a marketing program needs to have an idea of what the return to the company will be. Because sales promotion is designed to affect behavior directly, it is easier to measure and therefore predict results of sales-promotion spending than of advertising spending.

5. Sales Promotion Adds Continuity of Purchases   As technology enables competing firms to quickly match most of one another's innovations and other competitive advantages, brands often need help in maintaining brand loyalty. One of the most successful continuity programs is the airlines' frequent-flyer offers. These programs require a customer to make multiple purchases before the incentive is awarded.

6. Sales Promotion Increases Purchase Frequency/Quantity   Closely related to the continuity strategy is the strategy of getting customers to increase their rate of purchase or quantity of purchase. In the selling of advertising space and time, the media will often offer discounts to those who advertise every week (frequency). Soft-drink and beer bottlers often offer a "pick a pair of six-packs" incentive to motivate people to buy two rather than one six-pack (quantity). The strategy here is to motivate those who have already been sold on your good or service to use it more.

7. Sales Promotion Builds Databases   Sales promotions are being used more and more to collect information about customers. This is done by requiring customers to complete some kind of form when taking advantage of a promotional offer. For example, when you buy an Apple computer, if you fill out a "customer profile" card, telling when and where you bought your computer and answering several demographic questions, Apple will send you a free mouse pad. In return, Apple now has a complete buyer profile it can use to sell you additional Apple products.

Rewarding Repeat Business

Frequent-buyer programs like this one for Subway's "Sub Club" are designed to increase loyalty and keep satisfied customers coming back.

8. Sales Promotion Adds Excitement   For a long time, Eckrich (a brand of processed meat) didn't use any type of consumer promotions. When it finally did use one—offering a Louisville slugger bat for several proofs of purchase plus cash—sales went up 40 percent. The strange thing was that less than fifty bats were requested. It turned out that what made the promotion so successful was the excitement the consumer bat offer created in the sales force and the trade. The salespeople worked much harder, and the trade was willing to give the brand additional space and additional features in their grocery ads. So, even though most consumers did not find the promotion that motivating, the extra advertising and display resulted in a significant sales increase.

9. Sales Promotion Adds Involvement   Because sales promotions generally require some type of behavioral response (rather than just a change of attitude), the customer actively interacts with the brand. This involvement helps increase brand awareness and recall, and also helps build a strong relationship with the brand. How did your own personal relationships develop? By interacting with someone and getting to know and trust that person. The same is true of people's relationships with brands and companies.

TRADE VERSUS CONSUMER STRATEGIES

As we mentioned before, the special strengths of sales promotion are linked to strategies that can be used when selling to consumers, other businesses, and institutions. However, as the fifth chapter objective points out, the objectives and tactics for each of these targets vary, the most important difference being between consumer and trade promotions.

Most manufacturing companies use both consumer and trade promotions. Because of the importance of channel members, producers may devote considerable resources to trade promotions. While most consumer promotions are distributed by mass media and in-store devices (displays and signs), trade promotions are more often presented through direct mail and sales kits delivered by the sales force. Although trade and consumer promotions have different targets, they work most effectively when they work in tandem.

Push and Pull Promotions   As we discussed in Chapter 4, in consumer packaged-goods marketing a perennial strategic question is how much emphasis should be placed on selling to the trade and how much on selling to the consumer. In other words, should the manufacturer use sales promotion to *push* the product through the trade channel or *pull* it through by increasing consumer demand?

A retailer's decision on which brands to carry and feature is a bottom line decision—one based solely on which brands will generate the highest rate of return. This decision, of course, is greatly influenced by the bottom line value of the trade incentive. The primary disadvantage of push promotions is that expanded shelf space or distribution can be lost to a manufacturer offering better incentives. Trade promotions also do little to build brand loyalty.

A pull promotion offers the consumer an extra incentive—a coupon, a rebate, "20% more free"—to choose the brand. For new products, a pull promotion is designed to create demand—buyers for chains often say that when their stores get enough consumer requests for a product, they will start carrying it. A pull promotion used by Upjohn for Rogaine was a toll-free 800 number that consumers could call for referral to a doctor who could treat hair loss. Upjohn also promised a payment of $10 to callers who actually visited a doctor.

One advantage of a pull promotion is that once a brand has developed consumer demand, that demand will last as long as the brand remains competitive. Furthermore, once a brand has created a strong brand franchise (see Chapter 10), such as Coke or Campbell soup, it can spend less on trade

625

PUBLIC
RELATIONS,
SALES
PROMOTION,
AND PACKAGING

promotions.[14] A disadvantage of using a pull promotion is that most discounts apply to everyone who buys—regular brand users who would have bought the brand without the discount benefit as well as new buyers.

CONSUMER PROMOTION OBJECTIVES

Deciding what consumer sales promotion objectives should be set for a certain brand requires a review of the brand's SWOT analysis and marketing objectives (see Chapter 4). Although sales promotions are extremely effective at creating short-term results, good marketers look for both short- and long-term results that are image- and relationship-building as well as response based. Typical objectives of consumer sales promotions are *intensifying demand*, *stimulating trial*, *stimulating impulse buying*, *differentiating the brand*, and *countering competitive offers*.

Intensifying Demand Increased demand can be achieved by accomplishing one or more of the following objectives: increased *penetration* (expanded user base due to more people buying the brand); increased *continuity* (higher rate of repeat purchase); and increased *loading* (current users using more).

penetration
The percentage of the target market that buys a given brand.

    Penetration refers to the percentage of households or target consumers who use a product at least once during a given period of time. Consumer diary panels and household scanner data are the best sources for determining penetration (see Chapter 5). When use percentage is low—particularly when a product has recently been improved—a good promotion objective is running sales promotions that are aimed at getting more people to try the brand.

continuity programs
Promotional activities that encourage repeat purchasing and brand loyalty.

    For products that are used frequently—car washes, soap, soup, gasoline—a good sales-promotion objective will encourage continuity of purchase and brand loyalty. For example, Kraft, Del Monte, and Campbell Soup use **continuity programs** in order to evaluate their brand franchise—that is, their segment of repeat buyers. Airline frequent-flier programs and preferred-customer programs like Zellers' Club Z are longer-term promotional tools that help build brand loyalty.

loading
Encouraging consumers (or the trade) to purchase more of a product than they normally do.

    Another sales-promotion objective that increases demand is **loading**, or encouraging customers to purchase more of a product than they normally do. Loading recognizes that people tend to use more of certain products, such as soft drinks and snack foods, if they have them on hand. Consumers may be encouraged to stock up by, for example, an offer of two two-liter bottles of soda as a "bonus pack." Loading also ensures that, with a supply of one brand on hand, consumers will be less likely to buy a competing brand. Manufacturers of seasonal products often run promotions ahead of their competitors in order to "load" consumers before the seasonal buying peak.

    Many promotions that intensify demand are very successful. A risk in this type of promotion, however, is that the company may not be logistically capable of handling the demand the promotion produces. Hoover found this out in its ill-fated airfare promotion.

OPEN TO DEBATE

A PROMOTION THAT CRASH LANDED

What happens when you offer a premium for buying a product and the premium turns out to be worth more than the product? How do you deal with an overwhelming consumer demand that will cost your company millions of dollars? And how do you handle a great idea for a sales promotion that becomes an issue of consumer fraud? At what point do you pull the plug on a promotion that's backfired—and how do you handle the aftermath? These are some of the questions that confronted Hoover when its airfare promotion went awry.[15]

Hoover, a subsidiary of Maytag that markets appliances like vacuum cleaners, ran its ill-fated promotion in 1993. It was a simple offer. Customers in the United Kingdom and Ireland were offered two free airline tickets to the United States or Continental Europe when they purchased at least $200 worth of Hoover products. The promotion was such a success that Hoover sold tens of thousands of appliances—many more than anticipated.

How did the promotion turn into a catastrophe? Hoover had planned to use the commissions it made from land arrangements, such as hotel reservations and car rentals, to help pay for the airline tickets. Unfortunately, the commissions were less than anticipated, while the ticket demand was far greater than expected. Because the 200,000 responses were much more than Hoover had budgeted for, its travel agents began attaching unreasonable demands to the free tickets, such as expensive extras, inconvenient airports, and undesirable departure dates, in an effort to discourage acceptance of the offer. This turned happy winners into complaining customers.

One promotion agency president commented: "This shows that if you encourage people with the right offer, you can get an enormous response. But it also shows that you need more than a big idea. You need good management and attention to details and logistics." Reacting to the promotion's poor management, Hoover fired three top executives. The company also had to set up a $30 million fund to pay for the airline tickets.

627

PUBLIC
RELATIONS,
SALES
PROMOTION,
AND PACKAGING

Stimulating Trial and Impulse Buying   One of the most important sales-promotion objectives is motivating nonusers of your brand to try it—in other words, stimulating *trial*. The faster customers can be convinced to try a brand, the better the chance of building a brand franchise (see Chapter 10). The most difficult sale is the first one. After that—assuming a product delivers what it promises—the customer becomes more familiar with the brand and thus perceives less risk in purchasing it.

For products which are relatively low-priced and have extensive distribution, a common sales-promotion objective is to have a penetration strategy and thus increase the level of *impulse buying*. Manufacturers recognize that they must influence consumers at the *point of purchase*, particularly in self-service stores such as supermarkets and discount stores. This is why off-shelf and point-of-purchase displays and special offers on packages have become so important. Research on purchasing decisions indicates that impulse buying has increased in recent years.

Differentiating and Countering   Because some product categories (such as soft drinks and cereals) are so competitive, demand is heavy enough to support *parity* brands—that is, brands with no significant physical or image difference. Fighting to differentiate brands, marketers have resorted to "buying" consumers, either by reducing prices or by offering incentives to motivate brand selection. A good example is the frequent price promotions used by soft-drink manufacturers.

Sales promotion is also used to counter competitive promotions. If your offer is as good or better than your competitor's, then you may be able to neutralize the impact of your competition's sales-promotion efforts. In fact, you may even be able to ride the excitement created by your competitor's offer. American Family, for example, publishes its sweepstakes announcement at the same time and with the same deadlines as Publishers Clearing House.

TRADE PROMOTION OBJECTIVES

One of the biggest challenges faced by packaged-goods brands is obtaining trade cooperation. The trade channel members—sales force, wholesalers, retailers—act as "gatekeepers" between manufacturers and consumers. To make things even more difficult, a company's own sales force may have more than one brand to sell. P&G's soap division, for example, sells Ivory, Tide, Cheer, Camay, Lava, and other brands, so a brand manager needs extra incentives to mobilize the company sales force behind a special promotion.

Chain-store merchandise buyers are offered dozens of promotions every day, but their stores have only so much space and their ads can carry only so many items. Consequently, they participate in just a small percentage of the promotions offered to them. The company's sales force must not only inform trade members about a promotion, it must also "sell" them on accepting the promotion. The main objectives for trade promotions, then, are *securing authorization*, *advertising support*, and expanded or *off-shelf display space*.

Securing Authorization and Support The most important trade sales-promotion objective may be getting (and keeping) brand **authorization**—which means a store agrees to carry a brand, stock it, display it, and promote it. The growth of giant chain retailers like Wal-Mart, Canadian Superstore, Kmart, Sears, and Safeway has affected the way sales-promotion dollars are spent. As we explained in Chapter 14, getting a brand authorized by major chains can significantly affect the brand's success because these retailers are so large. Consequently, *trade allowances*, which are special price deals offered to intermediaries and retailers, have become an important part of the cost of introducing new products, as well as of maintaining the authorization of existing products.

There are also costs associated with getting a brand promoted by the retailer. When a brand is featured in a retailer's ad, its sales can increase anywhere from five to ten times its normal sales. *Co-op advertising* programs, which were discussed in Chapter 18, provide funds to support the cost of store advertising that features the manufacturer's brand names.

Almost as important as getting into the retail ad is getting expanded display space in the retail store. A typical sales-promotion display objective is to get a certain percent of displays set up during a promotion period. For example, when cookies are stacked prominently at the end of a shelf (*end-aisle display*), more store customers see the product, particularly if the display is accompanied by signage and other promotional materials such as tear-off coupons.

Efficient Consumer Response A trade practice that manufacturers particularly dislike is *forward buying*—meaning that retailers use trade price promotions to stock up on large quantities of goods, then sell the product later at its regular price and pocket the difference. The objective of the new efficient consumer response (ECR) programs that were discussed in Chapter 15 is to provide electronic information to manufacturers so they pay only for promotions that are actually used to draw in consumers. Although this restricts re-

authorization
Getting a retailer to agree to carry a brand, stock it, display it, and promote it.

tailers' ability to do forward buying, most retailers realize that being an integral part of the manufacturer's just-in-time electronic information system is of more value to them, so they generally agree to participate in ECR programs.

PROMOTION TOOLS

A variety of tactics are available for use in sales promotion. Some are strictly consumer tools, such as rebates and refunds, coupons, sweepstakes, and sampling; some are strictly trade tools, such as trade allowances, dealer loaders that encourage retailers to support a promotion, and merchandising materials such as displays and point-of-purchase materials. Other tools, however, can be used in both consumer and trade promotions, such as price reductions, contests and games, and specialties.

Today a maze of regulations affects sales promotion in Europe, as Table 19-3 shows. In the Scandinavian countries, where broadcast advertising is tightly controlled, sales promotion has long been an important marketing tool. However, Denmark and Sweden, along with Finland and Germany, have the most stringent sales-promotion regulations in Europe. Nevertheless, the market for pan-European promotions is expected to double in the mid-1990s as these regulations get ironed out with the implementation of the European Union and the creation of a pan-European marketplace.

PROMOTIONAL PRICING TACTICS

As chapter objective six points out, the most common sales-promotion tactics used to accomplish trade and consumer objectives involve some kind of price manipulation. Consumers benefit from *price reductions*, *rebates and refunds*, *sampling*, and *coupons*. According to annual surveys by Donnelley Marketing, the most common consumer sales promotion, after the basic price reduction,

629

PUBLIC
RELATIONS,
SALES
PROMOTION,
AND PACKAGING

Products on Display

Usually large and attracting high customer traffic, end-of-aisle displays focus customer attention on the promoted product relative to competing brands.

is couponing, followed by money-back offers. Trade promotion is also driven by monetary deals in the form of *trade allowances*, which marketers offer in return for support of a brand promotion.

Price Reductions   The most common type of consumer sales promotion is a price reduction—a *sale*. Although sale prices can generate tremendous response, they can also have a negative effect on a brand's overall pricing strategy. When a product is frequently on sale, both the trade and consumers may get into the habit of waiting to buy until the next sale. Continuous price promotion, in fact, sets a *false retail price*: that is, the consumer tends to consider the promotional price to be the regular price and refuses to buy at the higher (regular) price. Sears has faced this problem and tried to turn the sale mentality of its customers around with an emphasis on everyday low prices. So far, this strategy hasn't been particularly successful.

An indirect price reduction is the *price pack*, which provides the consumer with multiple units priced less per unit than they would be if they were individually purchased. Bar soap is often sold in price packs. *Bonus packs* contain additional amounts of a product for free when a standard size is purchased at the regular price. Shampoo, for example, may be packaged in larger than normal bottles with the announcement "20 percent more FREE." Some retailers dislike price packs because they require different shelf configurations and constitute new stock-keeping units—which means more inventory and bookkeeping work.

Coupons   After price reductions, the most common price incentive is the **coupon**—a certificate offered by either manufacturers or retailers that grants specified savings on specific brands when presented for redemption at the point of purchase. Because coupons are legal certificates, the company that issues them assumes a financial liability, an obligation that must be taken into consideration when budgeting. *Manufacturer-sponsored coupons* can be redeemed at any outlet distributing the manufacturer's brand. *Retailer-sponsored coupons* must be redeemed at the sponsoring retail store or chain.

coupon
Legal certificate offered by manufacturers and retailers that grants specified savings on selected products when presented for redemption at the point of purchase.

| TABLE 19-3 | PROMOTIONAL REGULATION IN EUROPE |

Promotion	U.K.	Spain	West Germany	France	Italy
In-pack premiums	●	●	○	▲	●
Multiple-purchase offers	●	●	▲	●	●
Extra product	●	●	▲	●	●
Free product	●	●	●	●	●
Mail-in offers	●	●	○	●	●
Purchase-with-purchase	●	●	○	●	●
Cross-promotions	●	●	○	●	●
Contests	●	●	▲	●	●
Self-liquidating premiums	●	●	●	●	●
Sweepstakes	▲	▲	○	▲	▲
Money-off coupons	●	●	○	●	▲
Next-purchase coupons	●	●	○	●	▲
Cash rebates	●	●	▲	●	○
In-store demos	●	●	●	●	●

● Permitted   ○ Not permitted   ▲ May be permitted

Source: David Murrow, "Europe Remains Mixed Bag," *Advertising Age*, August 7, 1989, p. 45.

In 1993 the number of coupons distributed in Canada was over 4 billion. Consumers redeemed 174 million, or approximately 17 coupons per household. Americans receive about eight times more coupons per household than Canadians, and Americans redeem about four times as many coupons. Like rebate program, however, coupons are losing favor with some marketers who wonder if their extensive use isn't making a certain segment of consumers more loyal to coupons than to brands.

Electronic information will make couponing even more efficient. US Narrow Network, a company partly owned by NBC, is developing a coupon dispenser that can target consumers so precisely that it will be able to challenge, say, their coffee-brand loyalty with a significant enough coupon to make them want to switch. USNN is experimenting with a television set attachment that can print coupons. It works by laying its signal over that of an existing broadcast or cable network, making it accessible to virtually any household.[16]

Sampling One of the most effective—and costly—forms of price promotion is **sampling**, which allows the consumer to experience the product or service either free or at a reduced price. For example, private liquor stores in Alberta now provide free samples of some drinks for customers. The primary tool for new-product introductions because it *stimulates trial*, sampling is also effective for introducing modified products, for dislodging an entrenched market leader, and for demonstrating brand superiority. Packaged-goods and food marketers maintain that sampling can boost sales volume as much as five to ten times, so it more than repays its expenses. Sampling is even more effective when it is reinforced with product coupons. Samples, which usually come in miniature packages, are distributed to consumers through the mail, door-to-door, or in stores. An interesting news report by *Wall Street Journal Europe* described how large multinational corporations like Procter & Gamble were being bombarded with "thank-you" letters from grateful consumers in Poland. The report went on to detail how these large companies which had the distribution network to deliver free samples in Poland had no organizational response to these thousands of grateful consumers. The irony is that these people who took the time and trouble to write in with their thanks would make an ideal database for any company. Clearly, organizational inertia is not a product solely of Eastern Europe and the former Soviet Union.

Refunds and Rebates A sales promotion that reduces price after the purchase is made is known as a **refund** or **rebate**. The marketer promises to return a certain amount of cash or high-value coupons to the consumer who purchases a product. Most refunds and rebates encourage product purchase by a given time, thereby creating a sense of immediacy and limiting the manufacturer's period of liability. Rebates are not as popular with retailers as they are with manufacturers. In fact, some retailers refuse to participate in mail-in rebates, contending that they are troublesome for customers as they usually involve long delays in settlement, which is exacerbated by a slow mail service.

Trade Allowances To achieve the authorization objective explained above often requires *slotting allowances*, which were mentioned in Chapters 13 and 15. These are fees paid to a retail chain to stock the brand in its warehouses and make it available in its stores. Originally, slotting allowances were modest sums meant to cover the costs of physically placing the product on the shelves and entering it into the chain's computer ordering system. Today, however, the major chains use slotting allowances as a profit center, charging a manufacturer as much as $5,000 *per store* for merely agreeing to stock its product.

sampling
The practice of allowing the consumer to try a product or service free of charge or at a reduced price.

631

PUBLIC
RELATIONS,
SALES
PROMOTION,
AND PACKAGING

refunds and rebates
Promotions that promise money or coupons to the buyer after the purchase is made.

Off-invoice allowances, such as $1 a case, are similar to consumer price reductions. They are used periodically by most brands to keep retailers buying and displaying their products. This allowance sometimes takes the form of free goods—"buy six cases and get one free." *Performance allowances* are given when a wholesaler or retailer promises to do, or "perform," some additional activity to help sell or "move the brand." A retailer, for example, may order twenty-five cases of Heinz ketchup and be promised $1.50 per case purchased in return for giving the item end-of-aisle display space or for featuring the item in its ad. These invoicing tactics would have the benefit of conceding the price actually paid by the purchaser so it would maintain the semblance of premium price integrity.

The downside to trade allowances is that they merely put money in retailers' pockets; except for some kinds of performance allowances, they do little to encourage consumer buying. For this reason, Procter & Gamble began to cut back on trade allowances in 1991. Instead, the health and beauty care giant decided to increase its advertising budget to *pull* its products through the distribution channel.

OTHER SALES-PROMOTION TOOLS

The non-price-related sales-promotion tools referred to in chapter objective six are used to create excitement in the marketplace as well as involvement. In consumer markets these tools include *sweepstakes, contests and games,* and *premiums and specialties.* At the trade level the most important of these tools are *dealer loaders* and *merchandising materials.*

Contests, Sweepstakes, and Games   The growth of contests and sweepstakes during the 1980s attests to the power of tools that generate excitement by promising "something for nothing." Although contests and sweepstakes are considered low-level motivators because people know that the odds are against them, many companies favor them because they are highly visible inducements to participation and don't cost as much as coupons.

In most trade contests a sales quota is set and the store, chain, or salesperson that exceeds it by the largest percentage wins. Exhibit 19-4 advertises the use of a gourmet food program packaged by a sales-promotion company as an incentive for a sales contest. Contests can provide a short-term boost in sales. They can also improve the manufacturer-reseller relationship and provide merchandising excitement for everyone involved.

Premiums and Specialties   An offer of merchandise, either free or at a reduced price, for responding in some way (visiting a store, taking a test drive) is called a **premium**. Many companies also use premiums to encourage consumers to switch brands or to reward customer loyalty. When Maxwell House coffee offers a free mug to customers who purchase its 32-ounce can of coffee, the premium not only attracts users of competitive brands but also rewards faithful Maxwell House customers. Premiums can be classified as *in-pack premiums,* which are inserted into the package by the manufacturer; *on-pack premiums,* which are placed on the outside of the package at the factory; or *container premiums,* which are special packages, such as decorative coffee canisters, that have extended use after the product contents are gone.

Premiums are also good for reinforcing an advertising campaign or image. It is important that premiums reflect the image of the product. One novel premium that did just that was a two-day racing course offered by Porsche. The promotion was successful because it appealed to fantasy, and because it had a *high-value perception*—it was something that consumers knew was worth thousands of dollars.

Much like premiums, **specialties** are free gifts or rewards ranging from pencils to cellular telephones. The difference is that the customer doesn't

premium
An offer of either free or reduced-price merchandise as a reward for some behavior such as purchasing a product or visiting a store.

specialties
Free gifts or rewards requiring no purchase and carrying a reminder advertising message.

have to purchase anything to get them. The items carry a promotional message that reminds users of the name of the brand or company. The objective of specialties is to create long-term reminders of companies, stores, or brands.

Business-to-business specialties are becoming particularly popular. High-value *business gifts*, such as VCRs, videotape players, and small portable televisions, can also be considered specialty promotions. These promotional items are expensive and usually tightly targeted to a few key decision makers.

Dealer Loaders   To help encourage the retailer to put up a special display for a promotion, the marketer will sometimes design a display to include an attractive item of value to the retailer. This is known as a **dealer loader.** For example, a soft-drink bottler might have a springtime picnic theme display that features a large cooler. The store manager knows that if he uses the display, he can have the cooler when the promotion is over.

dealer loader
An item of value to retailers that encourages them to support a promotion and use promotional display materials.

Merchandising Materials   Every promotion needs communication support if customers are to know about it. Such merchandising materials include banners, signs, window posters, shelf strips and tags, racks, stack cards, end-aisle displays, shelf risers, and shelf extenders. There are also *shelf talkers*—small signs attached to the shelf on which the product is displayed that carry information like coupons, recipes, and premium offers for the displayed brand. Restaurants and bars are also provided with signs, banners, and *table talkers*—small tent-shaped signs promoting a certain brand of food or drink that are placed on tables to encourage patrons to order that brand.

A display provided by the manufacturer and distributed to retailers to promote a particular brand or group of products is called a **point-of-purchase (POP) display also known as a Point of Sale (POS) display.** Checkout counter and other POP displays are designed to attract attention and increase impulse purchasing. According to the Point-of-Purchases Advertising Institute (POPAI), two-thirds of North Americans' purchase decisions are made in the store; for some impulse-driven categories like candy and dessert items, the rate is 80 percent.[17] POPAI also estimates that more than $15 billion is spent on POP displays.[18] Retailers, however, are highly selective about using manufacturer-supplied displays, first, because they are offered many more displays than they can accommodate at one time, and second, because many modern retailers have invested heavily in designing store interiors and are reluctant to detract from their decor with splashy displays.

point-of-purchase (POP) display also known as Point of Sale (POS) display
A display designed to give a brand or product line extra in-store exposure.

COMBINATION PROMOTIONS

Some promotional activities, such as cross-promotions and tie-in promotions, involve a number of marketing communication areas, such as advertising and PR, as well as sales promotion. These wide-ranging programs, as chapter objective seven notes, are only truly effective if they are coordinated with the other marketing communication functions. The sponsorship of events, for example, is an integrated marketing communication activity that involves all forms of communication. Exhibits and trade shows are also unusual promotional efforts that cross the lines between marketing communication categories.

TIE-INS AND CROSS-PROMOTIONS

The **tie-in**, which promotes two products together, is an increasingly popular sales-promotion tool. Disney is a dream tie-in for many companies, including General Motors, which has been using Disney cartoon characters in its sales promotions and advertisements. General Motors has also allied itself with Visa (see Exhibit 19-5), which will benefit both companies.

tie-in
A sales-promotion tool that promotes two products together in order to increase both brands' visibility.

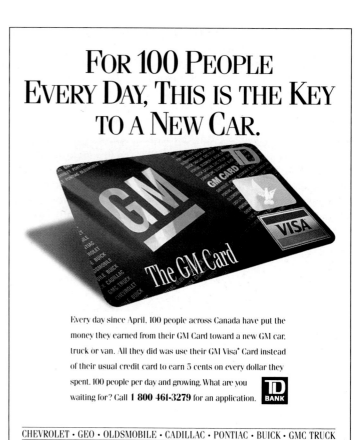

FOR 100 PEOPLE EVERY DAY, THIS IS THE KEY TO A NEW CAR.

Every day since April, 100 people across Canada have put the money they earned from their GM Card toward a new GM car, truck or van. All they did was use their GM Visa* Card instead of their usual credit card to earn 5 cents on every dollar they spent. 100 people per day and growing. What are you waiting for? Call **1 800 461-3279** for an application.

TD BANK

CHEVROLET · GEO · OLDSMOBILE · CADILLAC · PONTIAC · BUICK · GMC TRUCK

Offer is redeemable as credit on any new GM car, truck or van. Up to $500 per Cardholder Year or maximum of $3,500 over 7 years. Subject to GM Card Program Rules. *TD and GM are licensed users of Marks. **Registered Trade Mark of General Motors Corporation. TD licensed user.

In 1992 McDonald's entered a tie-in promotion with Orion Pictures. Orion gave McDonald's the exclusive rights to sell *Dances With Wolves*, *Dirty Rotten Scoundrels,* and *Babes in Toyland* during the holiday season. McDonald's offered the videos for $7.99 each with the purchase of a sandwich. McDonald's sold an estimated 10 million videos.

Sometimes one brand is used as a "carrier" to promote another, noncompetitive brand. This strategy is called **cross-promotion**. Packages of Keebler crackers, for example, may carry coupons for Cracker Barrel cheese or a cake mix may contain a coupon for icing. In the highly successful undertaking by Nabisco and CBS discussed in the next section, each partner promoted the other, and both won.

cross promotion
A sales promotion that uses one brand to promote another, noncompeting brand.

BEHIND THE SCENES
COOKIES, CRACKERS, AND TV

At first glance, Nabisco and CBS make strange marketing bedfellows. What does selling cookies and crackers have in common with selling people on watching a certain TV network? However, the two corporate giants combined their efforts in a highly successful integrated marketing communication strategy in the fall of 1993. Nabisco used its vast distribution of packaged products to promote CBS shows, and the network provided Nabisco with TV time at a reduced price. Nabisco hoped to build consumer awareness and trade enthusiasm for a new product line, while CBS hoped to increase its promotional reach in promoting its new fall television lineup.

To achieve these goals, Nabisco and CBS created the America's Favorites Giveaway, a sweepstakes with prizes ranging from Nabisco cookies and crackers and 10,000 Walt Disney World family vacations to the grand prize of $1 million. Nabisco offered numbered game cards in its advertising supplements and in-store displays, telling people to watch CBS for the winning numbers. CBS aired the winning sweepstakes numbers during commercials broadcast between episodes of its new fall shows.

The companies cross-promoted the sweepstakes through broadcast and print advertisements, in-store displays, trade incentives, retailer tie-ins, promotional "flags" on packaging, and local publicity. The promotion was a complete success. Nabisco's sales increased, and CBS won the TV ratings war that fall. There were over 10,000 consumers who won prizes, with one lucky consumer walking away with $1 million.

EVENT SPONSORSHIPS

Specially created and sponsored events that create publicity opportunities are growing in popularity. RJR Nabisco spends an estimated U.S. $60 million a year for sports sponsorships, second only to Philip Morris's U.S. $85 million, and more than 100 companies sponsor cars in the Indianapolis 500 race each year. Millenium is an NFL sponsor and runs radio commercials in conjunction with the games that feature coaches Bart Starr and Bum Phillips. IBM, Labatt's, and Reebok, along with the government of British Columbia and Canada, were sponsors for the 1994 Commonwealth Games in Victoria.

Why do major firms sponsor special events? Volvo estimates that its U.S. $4 million investment in tennis sponsorships results in over 1.7 billion consumer impressions (an impression is one person's exposure to anything connected with the Volvo name). This exposure is worth an estimated U.S. $24 million in advertising.[19] Because the demographic profile of Volvo car owners closely matches that of tennis fans, it is a highly targeted promotional effort. Similarly, tobacco firms use events such as the Virginia Slims Tennis Tournament to attract young adults, whom they cannot reach through radio and TV ads because of government regulations against such advertising.

As sponsors of these events, companies receive free tickets and special event privileges. The events therefore become a good way to reward high-performing salespeople and entertain good customers. Not only do these people get to attend the events, they often get to meet the participating performers and athletes.

For global companies, such sponsorship is a great opportunity, especially in Europe, where advertising media is more limited due to a number of government restrictions in place. For the launch of its Allante model in Europe, Cadillac ignored traditional media and used selected sporting events instead. Corporations also sponsor major international events to gain global visibility. For example, 3M has used its worldwide Olympic sponsorship to integrate the marketing efforts of its diverse product groups on a global basis.

TRADE SHOWS

Manufacturers, suppliers, and vendors in a particular industry gather to display and review new product developments at **trade shows**. Manufacturers have exhibits or booths where they can demonstrate the product, provide information, answer questions, and write orders. In addition to promoting and selling products, manufacturers use trade shows to gather competitive information and note customer reactions and suggestions regarding their product. Table 19-4 gives the most popular reasons for attending a trade show.

Because of the tremendous importance of trade shows in industries like electronics and computers, some companies spend several hundred thousand dollars each year planning and staging their exhibits. For some firms, especially highly specialized and smaller ones, trade shows are the primary marketing communication program. A study from the Trade Show Bureau revealed that trade shows reduce the cost of generating leads and closing sales: the average cost to close a sale is ordinarily U.S. $1,080; at a trade show the cost is only U.S. $419.[20]

PACKAGING

A product's *packaging*, especially for consumer goods, is a major communication vehicle. Its front panel or its label defines the product category, identifies the brand, and is the "last ad a customer sees" before buying a brand. In other words, a package is much more than just a physical container for the product, a function we discussed in Chapters 11 and 13. It is also a complex *message* about the product, the brand, its image, and its selling points. How packaging works as marketing communication is the focus of chapter objective eight.

A package is both a *medium* of communication and a *message*. For the package as advertising medium, for example, it is possible to calculate the number of impressions generated by different shelf arrangements. The message should be considered a part of the brand's integrated marketing communications effort, which means it should have the same "look" and personality that is communicated in all other brand messages. For example, Celestial Seasonings' packaging uses delicate illustrations, unusual names, soft colors, and quotes about life to help create a positive image and reinforce its positioning as a New Age tea.

Not surprisingly, packaging became more important as the self-service concept in retailing took hold. Prior to the advent of self-service retailing, most ads instructed shoppers to *ask* for a product; now they are told to *look* for it. Thus the package takes the place of the salesperson. As shoppers move through a crowded supermarket, they scan shelves at the rate of 300 items a minute.[21] Which items will a consumer notice and consider? Which ones will they actually place in their shopping cart and purchase?

Contemporary packaging has come in for its share of criticism, primarily for wastefulness. Over-packaging—using multiple layers of packaging materials—is putting stress on landfills and waste management but it is seen also as a means of signalling a luxury product. An example of the overpackaged product might be Nestlé's "After Eight" mints, which go beyond protection and information to form an image for the product.

Labeling is another area of concern to consumers, particularly in bilingual Canada.

HOW PACKAGING COMMUNICATION WORKS

What do you think of when you consider certain product categories such as soft drinks, juice, and coffee? In many cases, what comes to mind is a visual

TABLE 19-4   **WHY GO TO THE SHOW?**

Respondents in seven industries rank factors in their decisions to attend trade shows on a scale of 1 = little importance; 5 = great importance

Factors in Decision	Health Care	Industrial	Communication	Transportation	Computers/ Electronics	Food & Beverage	Banking/ Finance Insurance
General curiosity	2.7	2.4	2.8	2.8	2.2	3.1	2.3
Interest in speakers/topics	3.7	2.3	3.5	3.4	2.6	3.1	3.5
Have always attended show in past	2.3	2.7	2.3	2.7	2.4	2.8	2.7
To gather information for purchase	3.3	3.2	3.3	3.2	3.0	3.9	3.3
Professional education	4.0	3.2	3.9	3.7	2.9	3.5	3.5
Interest in specific exhibitors/demonstrations	3.6	3.8	3.5	3.7	3.8	3.8	3.6
To purchase products	2.2	2.4	2.1	2.1	1.9	3.5	2.7
To meet other industry professionals	3.6	3.4	4.0	4.0	3.7	3.9	3.5
New-product introductions	3.6	4.2	4.0	3.9	4.0	4.2	3.7

Source: Trade Show Bureau, as cited in Kate Bertrand, "Survey Finds Trade Shows Influence Buying Decisions," *Business Marketing*, March 1990, p. 34.

image of a brand's package. One study by a marketing design and research center asked consumers to name the brands they felt had the best beverage packaging. The winners were:

Soft drink:	Coca-Cola
Beer:	Budweiser
Fruit/vegetable juice:	V-8
Fruit juice:	Minute Maid
Water:	Perrier
Coffee:	Maxwell House
Tea:	Lipton

L'eggs Go Everywhere

One of the best examples of a product with strong visual equity is the L'eggs brand of pantyhose. Familiar to super-market shoppers and to visitors to discount drugstores and other retail outlets, this product's distinctive container was a highly successful packaging innovation. The offbeat play on words caught on immediately, and the product continues to sell well.

Consumers picked these packages not necessarily because of their superior design, but because they have a *familiarity* and *consistency* of design that creates high levels of consumer awareness. As the research director explained: "We found that consumers are most familiar with the brand that has been on the market the longest. Consumers in our study visualize the product that is considered as 'the standard' in the category."[22] In other words, this study was a measure of the strength of a brand's *visual equity.* A brand builds visual equity through a continuity of imagery in packaging that creates an enduring impression. For example, even though the glass Coca-Cola bottle is rarely used now, its distinctive shape is still recognized as Coca-Cola's by many consumers worldwide and a plastic facsimile of the famous glass bottle is now available in certain markets. Even new products, if launched with a distinctive package—as L'eggs and Mrs. Butterworth's syrup were—can have instant impact because of the communication power of the package symbolism.

PACKAGING STRENGTHS AND STRATEGIES

From a marketing communications perspective, there are eight ways in which packaging works to effectively and efficiently build brand relationships and sales.

1. Packaging Is the Last Message Before the Purchase Decision

Over 50 percent of all purchases are impulse items—this is especially true in the snack, ice cream, and cookie categories—and impulse purchases are highly affected by well-designed packaging that has "shelf impact" and creates appetite appeal. Expectations shape packaging as well. An own-label must be seen to be economical in packaging. Packaging is particularly important for brands that do little or no advertising or would not otherwise readily sell themselves. Many grocery items use photographic illustrations as their labelling to entice the customer. Dehydrated soups do not show dust and dried peas but hot inviting soup. Packaging offers a visual promise as to how the product may perform.

For consumer packaged goods sold in food, drug, discount, and other self-service stores, products are usually grouped together. This means consumers must choose from among several brands competing simultaneously for attention. It is at this critical point in the buying decision process—the "action" step—that the package has the greatest opportunity to influence the decision.

2. Packaging Is Highly Targeted

The package is exposed to those consumers who are specifically looking for a brand or type of product—in other words, people who are definitely *in the market.* This self-selection makes the package audience the most valuable group of people a marketer can target.

3. Packaging Provides Decision Information

A package's message may be designed to provide specific information the customer needs to make a decision. Well-designed packages help consumers quickly identify a brand's unique selling points with phrases like "caffeine free," "cottony soft," or "cleans hard water stains." When more than one product in a line carries the same brand, consumers rely on packaging to make clear such vital information as the flavor or type of product. However, words such as "Lite" lack definition. In a nutritional sense it denotes that this product contains slightly less fat, cholesterol, or carbohydrate than its established sister brand.

4. Packaging Is a Low-Cost Brand Reminder

For some products, package shape and design communicate brand identity even faster than the product's name or logo. Mrs. Butterworth's distinctive brown bottle reinforces

639

PUBLIC
RELATIONS,
SALES
PROMOTION,
AND PACKAGING

the personification of this brand of syrup. Marketing research has found that consumers often can't remember the brand name of products they use, but they can describe the package.

Packaging works like a billboard, particularly on the shelf at supermarkets and discount stores, where massed packages can create tremendous visual impact and contribute to "brand power." Today a package in the typical food, drug, or discount self-service store must also have "stopping power." Thus an important objective of packaging communication is to reduce *find time*—the amount of time it takes to "find" a favorite brand when it's displayed among competing brands. Packaged goods that are used from the package—like cereals, detergents, and milk—serve as mini-billboards for the brand after purchase. At each use they remind the consumer of the brand's name and its key benefits—all at no additional cost to the brand.

5. Packaging Showcases Promotional Reminders If the brand is involved in other major promotional activities, a tie-in message is often designed for the front of the package to serve as a reminder. Most package front panels (the side that faces the customer as the package sits on a shelf) provide space for promotional *flags*. These "interrupters" call attention to current sales-promotional offers and advertising themes, such as "free toy inside" or "official sponsor of the Olympics" (a message usually reinforced by using the Olympics rings logo).

6. Packaging Reinforces Advertising For heavily advertised brands, packaging provides the *link* between advertising and the product. (The next time you see a soft drink commercial, notice how much of the time the can is shown.) Advertising extols a product's benefits, but the packaging shows customers what to look for to get these benefits. Even radio copy sometimes describes a package, especially for a new product—for example, "Look for the package with the red and blue stripes."

7. Packaging Makes a Strong Visual Statement Think of the type of visuals packages of ice cream, cereals, cake mixes, and pizzas have on them—most are extremely appetizing shots of the product. Or think about packages containing appliances such as food mixers or hand drills—these often show dramatic shots of the product in use. This visual impact is an important form of persuasive nonverbal communication.

8. Packaging Can Add Value From the turn-of-the-century printed flour sacks used by mothers to make children's clothes, the physical package can add value to the product it contains. For some products, packaging creates the brand—as, for example, with Toilet Duck, its distinctiveness being in a conspicuous design shape. Liquid detergent bottles that have a special nondrip spout, for example, provide an extra value. Some products, especially during holiday seasons, use specially decorated packages that can be reused. This extra feature can be the focus of a brand's advertising. Packaging can also be like a fifth "p" to the marketing mix. Packaging solution, can create new conditions of use for mature products. Wine used to be sold in bottles but now is in wine boxes, cans, and resealable styrofoam containers. Each packaging form is designed for a different condition of use. Similarly, toothpaste packaging added value for manufacturers with the introduction of the pump dispenser. Many parents today will remember days when hair shampoo was available only in sachets and when the oil can was actually metal. Convenience and cost are two factors which explain packaging substitution, but packaging still holds the ability to create distinctive products and enlarge markets for existing products. Packaging is a highly competitive industry drawn from the glass, paper, plastics, and aluminum industries; they cross compete for business. Dried soup is sold in sachets made of paper, aluminum and plastic film as well as glass jars. Packaging forms change over time but so too does the technology employed. As with coffee packaging, first there was the vacuum pack of fresh ground filtered coffee, then the value pack was introduced, which meant the coffee did not have to be fully dried before packaging. Being able to smell the coffee freshness can easily be a competitive advantage of sophisticated packaging.

THE TOTAL PROMOTION PACKAGE

Event marketing is big business, but it is one with a puzzling problem: The higher the costs, the greater the number of corporate sponsors that are needed; but unfortunately, the more corporate sponsors there are, the harder it is for any individual sponsor to maintain a useful level of visibility. This is a problem that faces the event organizers, the media that cover the event, and the companies that use event sponsorship as part of their promotional programs.[23]

The *Hallmark Hall of Fame* is an example of a television program that is totally "owned" by its sponsor. The sponsorship of such a program lends credence to Hallmark's quality image. Bowling games and many other sporting events are sponsored by companies that assume all or a major part of the costs of putting them on in return for attaching their name to the event. The Virginia Slims tennis tournament is an example. For major sporting events, such as the Super Bowl, however, the television network assumes the risk and sells ads to spread the cost.

The Olympics is another example of an event far too costly to be borne by any one sponsor. Worldwide sponsorships for the 1996 Atlanta Olympics cost as much as U.S. $40 million. For that amount of money, the sponsor gets to advertise that it is the official sponsor within a category (car, bank, credit card, film, breakfast cereal, camera, coffee, peanut butter, beer, etc.) and use the Olympic logo of five interlocked gold rings in its advertising. This kind of corporate sponsorship promotes a company's good-citizen image. It can also be a valuable promotional tool if the sponsor manages to leverage the event to achieve maximum visibility.

The concept of sponsorship for the Olympics is complicated by the fact that large advertisers on the network coverage are also allowed to use the Olympics tie-in symbols, and this can be confusing to consumers. For instance, McDonald's may be the official fast-food sponsor, but Wendy's may buy enough commercial time to entitle it to also use the Olympic logo.

It is easy for a sponsor to get lost amid the glamour of the Olympics. The year Sanyo was an official sponsor, it redesigned its packages, linked its advertising and promotions to the Olympic theme, sent dealers to the games as rewards, and offered Olympic pins as premium items. After all that effort, however, the company was disappointed in the level of brand awareness it achieved.

Another problem with event marketing is shallow participation across a variety of sports. Marketers that take this shotgun approach usually fail to create much visibility for themselves. As a Budget Rent-A-Car marketing VP explained, the company found that being designated the official rental car for a bunch of events like Nascar racing, football, baseball, and water skiing wasn't having much of an impact. Budget's new strategy is to concentrate its sports marketing budget on women's golf and target the 40 percent of business travelers who are women. As part of a database-driven promotional plan, Budget offers golf tournament tickets, personal appearances by women golfers, and discount coupons to its best customers. Its advertising also stresses its concern for women's issues. The program is an effective marriage of event sponsorship and media buying that eliminates the clutter of competitive sponsorship messages.

Other companies have taken up this strategy of developing an integrated promotional package around a particular type of sporting event that relates to an important target market, and then using all possible marketing communication tools in a coordinated way to maximize the impact.

Some executives hope a similar approach can be designed for the Olympics, only on a larger scale. Both the networks and the Olympic Association are worried that they are going to drive advertisers away unless they can provide better control over the message environment and deliver a more unified package.

If you were a marketing director, would you approve an Olympics sponsorship given its huge costs and highly cluttered environment? If you were a marketing consultant to the Olympics committee, how would you design a more integrated and totally coordinated promotion package for the Olympics and its sponsors? ▼

KEY POINTS SUMMARY ▼

1. Public relations focuses on creating positive images and building relationships with all stakeholders. It adds credibility to communication; breaks through advertising clutter; reaches hard-to-reach audiences and other stakeholders besides consumers; takes a proactive approach; establishes a good-citizen image for a company; and costs less and has fewer legal restrictions than other forms of marketing communication.

2. Public relations programs are grouped into the specific categories of media relations, government relations, community relations, financial relations, and employee relations. The tools used for the tactical implementation of these programs include publicity, publications, special events, public service programs, and crisis management plans.

3. Sales promotion, which has a greater immediate short-term impact on sales, has displaced advertising as the marketing tool of choice. Advertising is still considered better for building brand equity, but corporate preoccupation with short-term results and retailers' demands for trade incentives have favored the use of sales promotion in recent years. The resulting decline in brand loyalty has sparked controversy about the usefulness of promotion versus advertising over the long term.

4. There are certain things that sales promotion does better than any other marketing communication function. Most importantly, it adds tangible value to a product and provides an incentive to respond immediately. Other strengths include reducing risk and increasing accountability, as well as increasing purchase continuity, frequency, and quantity. In addition, sales promotion can help with database building and add excitement and involvement to a marketing program.

5. Consumer promotions are aimed at the ultimate user of the good or service and use pull strategies. Trade promotions are incentives aimed at distributors and retailers and push a product through the distribution channel. The primary objective of consumer promotion is intensified demand, which is created by increasing penetration, repeat purchases, and the rate of consumption. Other consumer objectives are stimulating trial and impulse buying, creating brand differentiation, and countering competitive activities. The primary objectives of trade promotion are to secure authorization of the product, advertising support, and expanded display space.

6. Price promotions lead to immediate sales responses, which is sales promotion's greatest strength in both the consumer and the trade market. The most common consumer promotions related to pricing are temporary price reductions such as sales, bonus packs, refunds and rebates, and coupons. Other consumer-

promotion tools are contests, sweepstakes, premiums, sampling, and specialties. The most
common price-related trade promotion is the
trade allowance. Other trade promotions are
dealer loaders, contests, merchandising materials, and trade shows.

7. Wide-ranging promotions have to be coordinated with a variety of other marketing communication areas to be effective. These combination promotions include cross-promotions,
tie-ins, event sponsorships, and trade shows.

8. Packaging works as marketing communication
through visual equity: it makes a strong visual
statement that creates familiarity and symbolic
impact. Its major strengths are its position as
the last message before the purchase decision
is made and its ability to target people who are
in the market and provide them with information they need to make a decision. In addition,
packaging is a low-cost brand reminder, a
showcase for promotional reminders, and a
link with the product's advertising. It can also
add tangible value to the product.

DISCUSSION QUESTIONS ▼

1. You are planning to open a new restaurant in
your city. What public relations tools would
you use and how would you use them?

2. What should have been Jack-in-the-Box's first
crisis management step in the food-poisoning
tragedy? What should have been the first public statement the company issued? What
should Jack-in-the-Box do to prepare for any
future crisis?

3. Interview the public relations director for a
local company and try to determine if that
firm operates with a marketing PR or a corporate PR philosophy.

4. If you were a marketing manager and under a
lot of pressure to show good "numbers" in
each quarterly sales report, would you use all
the sales promotion tools available to you to
increase those sales? Do you think the increasing use of sales promotion deemphasizes
brand equity and brand loyalty?

5. Interview the manager of a local car dealership
to find out what methods the dealership uses
to get people to come into the showroom to
see and test-drive new cars.

6. Find four ads with sales-promotion offers and
describe the sales-promotion objective behind
each ad (besides buying the product).

7. You have just been hired by a sales-promotion
agency as its new director of local business
promotions. Identify a local business you feel
is not using sales promotion adequately or effectively. Explain how and why you feel the
company could benefit from a sales-promotion
program and what types of sales promotions it
should consider.

8. Develop a coupon offer for a local store. Interview the manager to determine what the probable response would be. Estimate the cost of
the coupon offer and the return it would be
likely to generate.

9. Analyze a product category in an aisle of a supermarket, drugstore, or discount store:
a. Pick one brand and explain how the package functions as both medium and message.
b. Within that product category, which brands
have the strongest and weakest visual equity? Explain why.

Integrative Case ● Discussion Questions

The Body Shop*

1. How does The Body Shop use packaging as a
communication tool?

2. Describe the sales-promotion tactics used by
The Body Shop.

3. Why is The Body Shop's promotional strategy
effective?

*The three cases at the back of the book—"The Body Shop," "Harley-Davidson," and "The Millennium Power System"—illustrate
topics discussed in all chapters of this book. Your instructor will tell you when to read a particular case and answer the discussion
questions on it that appear at the end of each chapter.

Harley-Davidson

1. Describe Harley's marketing public relations.
2. What is Harley's visual equity?
3. What sorts of sales-promotion techniques are used in the motorcycle industry?
4. Are motorcycles sold by a push or pull strategy?
5. What is Harley's most powerful form of promotional communication?

The Millennium Power System

1. How is Millennium using marketing public relations? For brand awareness? Brand positioning? Targeting?
2. What are the advantages of a rebate from the company's point of view? From the consumer's point of view?
3. Why would Millennium prefer a tie-in with Playskool to one with Sony? Is such a tie-in appropriate, given Millennium's preference for locating its products in the electronics section of a retailer's store?

Canada's Public Image Abroad

Tourism is one of the fastest growing industries in the world. Canada has created a good image with which to attract tourists. Recently, though, the Canadian tourism industry has been experiencing some difficulties.

Canada's image is connected to freshness, cleanliness, and safety. The outdoor experience is one of the reasons tourists are attracted to Canada as a vacation destination. Canada's reputation as a clean, safe environment is portrayed in brochures with photographs of breathtaking scenery and beautiful landscapes that are found coast to coast.

Why, if Canada has a positive image, is the tourist industry not performing as well as it is in other countries? Is Canada's pristine image beginning to tarnish?

In the tourism industry, image and reputation are important ingredients in attracting visitors. According to the World Tourism Organization, in 1980, Canada was the sixth most visited location in the world. By 1992, Canada dropped out of the top ten list and is now in eleventh place. Over that time period, even with an international recession, competition for the tourist dollar has increased.

Exotic competition comes from camel rides in Egypt to visiting the tigers in India. Compared with this competition, a canoe trip in Canada may not be enough to attract a more discriminating tourist. Americans no longer come to Canada as much as they used to. The advantage of a lower dollar is not helping to bring Americans to Canada's attractions as it did a few years ago. Canada is now attracting more overseas tourists. This is not necessarily a negative trend as overseas visitors spend, on average, three times more than what Americans spend each visit.

Canada needs more than a good image. It needs a focused strategy and strategic alliances with all the actors in the tourism trade. Other countries have taken unique approaches to enhancing their images and provide a specific package of attractions to promote themselves to international tour operators. Mexico's strategy is driven by the government and it has now reached the top ten list. Australia took a different strategic approach and involved private as well as public money in the promotion of its best qualities.

Tourism promotion consists of a range of techniques to create a positive international image. Reputation is an important ingredient in a successful destination marketing program.

645

QUESTIONS

1. What role does public relations, sales promotion, and packaging play in tourism marketing?
2. What does the reputation of a destination mean to international tour operators?
3. What is Canada's reputation and how could it be used to promote tourism to Europeans?
4. What does the Canadian tourism industry need to do to successfully take advantage of Canada's image?

Source: This case was prepared by Deborah Andrus and is based on the *Venture* series episode "Tourism," which was originally broadcast on May 29, 1994.

● Chapter 20

Direct Marketing

THE FINE LINE ON PRIVACY

Suppose you received a letter from a company you had never heard of, offering you a product perfectly tailored to your interests, your income level, even your personal habits. Suppose the letter made it clear that the company offering the product knew a great deal about you. How would you react? Would you feel that your privacy had been invaded?

Porsche, the German automobile manufacturer, took just such an approach in a direct-marketing effort in the early 1990s that invited some 300,000 carefully screened affluent prospects to test-drive its new sports car.[1] Porsche considers the effort to be the most sophisticated direct marketing program ever used in the auto industry.

The two-page letters on watermarked stationery were mailed in hand-stamped, personal, letter-size envelopes. Although the message was relatively straightforward, the details about the recipients' lives—which were accessible through the latest computer technology and database

management—raised a few upscale eyebrows. For example, one version of the letter read as follows: "Your preeminent position in society and your success as a doctor demonstrate that you pursue excellence in all things. . . . Since you already own a luxurious European car, I would like to introduce you to another—the Porsche." Some of the 300,000 prospects were quite surprised to find out just how many intimate details of their lives were known to this company.

A senior VP at Porsche's direct-marketing agency explained how successful it was in obtaining information about prospects, such as profession, income range, the types of cars they drive (and used to drive), where they live, and what type of neighborhood they live in.

There is nothing illegal about accumulating this kind of information, and Porsche insists it acted within government regulations regarding direct marketing. Still there remains the question of privacy. As Porsche's marketing database manager acknowledged: "We have access to a lot more information . . . than we can legally use in an unsolicited communication."

Porsche admits that it is treading a fine line. Would you be flattered to receive such a letter or would you feel the marketer had invaded your privacy? Do you think there should be controls on the way direct marketers obtain and use such personal information? ■

WHAT IS DIRECT MARKETING? ●

direct marketing
A system of marketing that integrates ordinarily separate marketing-mix elements to sell directly to both consumers and other businesses, by-passing wholesalers, retail stores and personal sales calls.

A complete buying and selling process, **direct marketing** is a "microcosm" of the entire marketing process—it requires the integration of previously separate marketing-mix elements like targeting, distribution, and marketing communications. Said another way, direct marketing is a way of selling to consumers without using a retail store or of selling to businesses and institutions without using a traditional sales force that makes personal calls on customers. In other words, it combines *demand creation* and *demand fulfillment* in one operation. For these reasons, direct marketing, as the first chapter objective points out, is different from all other forms of marketing communication.

Figure 20-1 outlines the operations of the direct marketing industry. The foundation of all successful direct-marketing efforts is the *database*, an extensive computerized list of information about prospects that is used to personalize and individualize the marketing process. Because of the advances in computer technology, the cost of storing and retrieving a single name and address has dropped from approximately $1.50 to 2–4 cents in the last twenty years. This drastic drop in cost has made it feasible to do one-on-one marketing for a wide range of products and made direct marketing one of the fastest-growing areas in marketing. In 1992, revenue from direct marketing in Canada was estimated to be $8.5 billion, up by 7 percent in 1991. The average Canadian now spends approximately $307 per year through direct marketing channels.[2] Table 20-1 shows revenue from direct marketing by sector in Canada in 1992.

Because the unique characteristic of direct marketing is that the customer responds directly to the company making the offer, it is sometimes called direct-response marketing. In this chapter, however, we will use the term *direct marketing* to refer to the overall business function and *direct response* to identify types of advertising that are used by direct marketers.

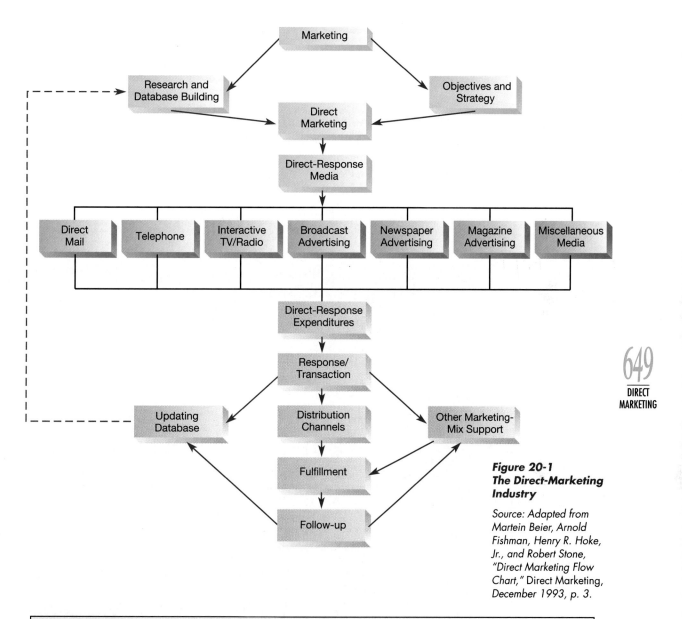

Figure 20-1
The Direct-Marketing Industry

Source: Adapted from Martein Beier, Arnold Fishman, Henry R. Hoke, Jr., and Robert Stone, "Direct Marketing Flow Chart," Direct Marketing, December 1993, p. 3.

TABLE 20-1	REVENUE FROM DIRECT MARKETING BY SECTOR IN CANADA, 1992	
		$ million
Business-to-business (non catalogue)		$2,310
Catalogue		$1,990
Consumer Services		$1,960
Charities, non-profit organizations		$1,170
Consumer goods		$ 828
Broadcast		$ 220

Source: The Globe and Mail, Tuesday, February 15, 1994. p. B29.

USES OF DIRECT MARKETING

Direct marketing is used in virtually every consumer and business-to-business category. IBM, Digital Equipment, Xerox, and other manufacturers selling technical and trade products use direct marketing, as do many banks, insurance companies, and retailers. Service industries, including airlines, hotels, cruise lines, restaurants, resorts, and government tourist agencies, also use direct marketing. Nonprofit organizations employ direct marketing, as do political groups in their membership drives and fund-raising campaigns. In Exhibit 20-1, the Royal Alexanda Theatre in Toronto uses direct marketing in a pamphlet for a musical production.

Types of Users More than 12,000 firms use direct marketing to sell products and services directly to buyers. (This figure doesn't include retail stores that use direct marketing as a supplemental marketing program or organizations that use direct marketing to reach members.) In North America the

Exhibit 20-1
Direct Marketing for the Arts

This pamplet for the Royal Alexandra Theatre's production of "Crazy for You" uses direct-response advertising—note the 1-800 number—to generate interest in the musical. Using the toll-free number, customers can find out about times and prices, as well as order tickets.

product most commonly ordered through direct marketing is clothing; magazines are the second most popular product. Other consumer-product categories that heavily use direct marketing are book and record clubs, insurance companies, collectibles, packaged foods retailers, and gardening firms. Among the largest direct marketers, both retail and service, are Time Inc., and American Express.

Many firms in the financial services industry also use direct marketing extensively. Toronto Dominion, the Bank of Montreal, and the Royal Bank are just a few that employ this method to sell mutual funds, mortgages, RRSPs, GICs, credit cards, and other financial products. According to figures from the Canadian Direct Marketing Association, more than $1.9 billion worth of financial products were sold through direct-response marketing in 1992. This figure represents a 19 percent increase over 1991 figures.

Business-to-business marketers are also very active in direct marketing. A large part of IBM's marketing communication efforts, for example, are focused on direct-response programs aimed at current customers as well as prospects. Direct response makes it possible to maintain a business relationship with busy customers and keep them informed about new products and new uses for products in a way that is largely unintrusive and respectful of their time.

Types of Transactions   Direct marketing is a specific type of *transaction* that can be useful in a wide range of *product categories*. As Figure 20-2 shows, there are three basic types of transaction situations. The first two are the typical retail transaction (see Chapter 15) and the personal-selling transaction (Chapter 21). The third type—a sales message delivered by one or more types of media, with the product then delivered by mail or some other delivery system—is used exclusively by direct marketing. A given company may use all three types of transactions.

In many cases, direct-response advertising supports all three types of transactions. One of the most successful international direct-mail campaigns was developed by British Aerospace, which used direct marketing to open the door to the North American market. When a ban on the use of small aircraft for domestic shuttles was lifted in North America, British Aerospace suddenly found a huge new market for its forty-four-seater airplane, a top-seller elsewhere around the world. The company developed an image campaign to precede its North American sales tour. The package, mailed from the United Kingdom to 500 executives at U.S. domestic airlines, contained an elegantly designed booklet about its 748 model with a reply card offering fine-art prints of internationally famous aircraft. A quarter of the addressees responded immediately; and another 20 percent responded after a follow-up mailing. The mailings helped set up the demonstration tour that displayed the actual aircraft, and the total effort produced orders totaling $50 million. The entire cost of the direct-mail campaign was less than $10,000.

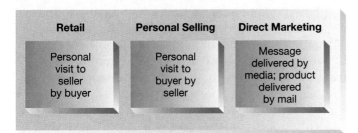

Retail	Personal Selling	Direct Marketing
Personal visit to seller by buyer	Personal visit to buyer by seller	Message delivered by media; product delivered by mail

Figure 20-2
Types
of Transactions

Global Uses of Direct Marketing The direct-marketing industry is growing fast in many Far Eastern and European countries—in some places, even faster than in North America. The global trend is fueled by the same technological forces driving the growth of direct marketing in North America: the increasing use of computer databases, credit cards, and toll-free phone numbers, plus lifestyle changes. In addition, the growth of direct marketing can be attributed to the measurability of direct response and the drive for accountability in the marketing function.

This rapid growth is not limited to consumer marketing. As direct marketing catches on around the world, especially in Europe, a brisk international traffic in business-to-business direct mail is developing. The direct-mail trend across the Atlantic has been accelerated by the introduction of trans-Atlantic bulk electronic mail through Western Union and British Telecom.

Because of the proliferation of computers, systems that combine computers and video are also going global. For example, Minitel Services, an outgrowth of French Telecom's Minitel system, allows access to some 5 million worldwide users, including strong customer bases in France and Japan. In the United States, Minitel is interconnected with most of the Bell companies and has local-dial access in 150 cities. Advertisers pay a monthly fee to be on the network. Computer based services such as Unitel, Compuserve, Delphi, Genie, Prodigy, and America-On-Line enable American Airlines, for example, to make all of its flight schedules available to service users who make reservations through their own PCs.

Direct marketing is particularly important in marketing programs in countries that have tight restrictions on advertising and other forms of marketing communication.

BEHIND THE SCENES — SWEDEN'S DIRECT CONNECTION

If there is such a thing as a direct marketer's paradise, it must be Sweden.[3] Sweden has efficient postal and telephone services and only minor restrictions on direct-marketing activities. The government has compiled a vast amount of computer data about Swedish citizens, and basic information about the population is available to corporate clients for a fee. It is thus quite easy to pinpoint target groups using demographics. To encourage the growth of direct marketing and thus boost its own revenues, the Swedish Post Office has for thirty years operated a database service that provides information on businesses and occupational groups.

Sweden also has the highest employment ratio in the industrialized world, and two-income households are common—which means scarce time for shopping out of the home for many families. For all of these reasons, direct marketing is Sweden's fastest-growing marketing tool.

But perhaps the greatest reason for the popularity of direct marketing is that it provides a way around Swedish advertising regulations. Sweden tightly controls media advertising, particularly the promotion of liquor, which is banned in virtually all mass media except satellite TV (a medium beyond the reach of Swedish regulators).

The Canadian beer Moosehead became the first foreign beer to gain significant share in Sweden in many years by using a direct-response push campaign in a situation where conventional advertising was impossible. The launch was announced by mailing postcards to 4,000 bars and restaurants with the slogan "Warning: The Moose Is Loose," followed two weeks later by a brochure from the beer's local distributor detailing point-of-purchase and merchandising materials built on that slogan. This push direct-mail campaign was supported by consumer ads in a free entertainment specialty magazine, the only place where such advertising is permitted. Moosehead's direct-response campaign was so successful in Sweden that the beer will be launched throughout Europe using the same approach.

STRENGTHS AND STRATEGIES OF DIRECT RESPONSE

There are a number of reasons why direct marketing is a growth area in marketing, and these are the subject of the second learning objective for this chapter.

Convenience Because of social trends and technological developments, direct marketing makes consumer buying easier. *Convenience* is the *added value* motivating more consumers to respond to this type of marketing. Marketers find that appealing to consumers' need for convenience is a very efficient way of selling. For example, Domino's Pizza has become the fastest-growing company in the $12 billion pizza market because of the convenience of its home-delivery service.

Precision Targeting Although *precision targeting*—developing a highly select target audience for a marketing communication—can be quite expensive per impression (person or household reached), it can also be the most

653

economical tool for reaching a small audience. Precision targeting is particularly efficient for reaching business-to-business and niche markets.

Through an efficient use of computerized information and lists of names, the marketer can identify serious prospects—that is, people who are more likely to be in a given market for a given product. As we saw in the opening story for this chapter, upscale auto makers find direct marketing an effective tool for reaching precisely those people who are able to afford expensive cars. According to the marketing manager for Toyota's Lexus: "We know the waste percentage on direct-mail targeted to a luxury car audience is very, very low. More than 90 percent of the audience we're mailing to is truly a prospect." Cadillac, another upscale car maker, spends about 15 percent of its marketing budget on direct marketing.[4]

Interactivity   As the emerging information highway fuses telephone, television, and computer, customers' ability to interact quickly and easily with business is greatly improving. The TV home-shopping shows we discuss in the text of this chapter as well as in the case "The Battle over Home Shopping Stations" are one example of how this interactivity works. Many cable TV systems are now "addressable," meaning individual messages can be sent to, and received from, individual subscribers. Thus interactive media both make immediate purchases possible and encourage other types of feedback. As interactive media continue to develop, reaching customers on a one-on-one basis will become less expensive and therefore more attractive to marketers.

Measurability   Direct marketing communication is more easily *measured* than most of the other communication functions. Because a direct marketing *offer* is itself the primary variable that generates direct-marketing *sales*, a company can easily test a selling message by comparing marketing communication costs to sales generated. From a research standpoint, direct marketing communication is also a good way to conduct a quasi-confidential market test because you expose the product, message, package, or whatever is being researched to a limited number of people. Thus you minimize the likelihood that your competition will become aware of what you are testing.

Because direct marketing is a "self-contained" marketing process, it is easy to determine the exact cost of each response (whether an inquiry or an actual purchase). For example, when Eddie Bauer or Consumer's Distributing sends out a catalog, it knows precisely what it costs to produce and mail it. Because each catalog is coded, every order received from that particular catalog can be identified. If the production and mailing costs were $700,000 and 35,000 orders were received, the average cost-per-order would be $20 ($700,000 ÷ 35,000 = $20). If the average order were $80, the $20-per-order cost would be 25 percent of the total sale.

Marketing-Mix Efficiencies   Direct marketing is used by both consumer and business-to-business companies for a number of reasons, all of which create greater marketing efficiency: *lower media and selling costs, alternative distribution channels,* a *second sales force, inventory management,* and *lead generation.* Accurate targeting is important because media costs are often a major part of the marketing budget, and paying to reach only those people most likely to buy reduces media costs (see Chapter 18).

Another reason that direct marketing can achieve *lower selling costs* is that it avoids many of the major expenses faced by the average retailer such as maintaining an attractive store, a large parking lot, and an army of sales clerks. Most direct marketing operations are located in low-cost areas like industrial parks; in general, they operate out of warehouse-type facilities, and they lack expensive decor and elaborate merchandising displays. In addition, most businesses do not offer the amount of training to direct-market employees that they would give to sales personnel who would be making personal calls on customers or working in retail stores. In other words, direct marketers enjoy low overhead expenses, even though the cost of generating each purchase is relatively high. Furthermore, in business-to-business selling, where the average cost of an industrial sales call is about $500, direct marketing can often replace or at least reduce the number of these very expensive personal sales calls.

Second, direct response provides companies with *alternative channels* of distribution into areas where traditional channels are either unavailable or unprofitable. For example, Mountain Equipment Co-op sells outdoor equipment out of several successful retail stores in such cities as Yellowknife, Northwest Territories. It would be unprofitable for the company to open a store in Yellowknife, Northwest Territories, where the customer base would be too small to support a retail operation. With direct response, however, Mountain Equipment Co-op sells to small and medium-sized markets throughout the country, and even abroad, for just the cost of some catalogs and postage. In addition, direct response allows retail store customers to make additional purchases without coming to one of its stores.

Third, in industrial sales a direct-marketing operation can be like adding a *second sales force*. For example, A. B. Dick, which sells duplicating machines and supplies, found that its sales force was spending most of its time selling duplicating machines and giving little attention to supplies, because copiers paid them a lot higher commission. Not wanting to distract from its primary business of selling copiers, the company decided to let the sales force concentrate on these and to set up an in-house direct-marketing operation to sell office supplies. Often direct response is also an inexpensive way to test or launch new products, especially minor items that do not generate enough volume to warrant serious attention from a sales force or distributor.

Better *inventory management* is another source of efficiency. Some direct-marketing operations have arrangements with suppliers that permit them to order only on need. Using the just-in-time inventory management system we discussed in Chapter 14 lets them maintain *minimal levels* of inventory on certain items (especially those that are expensive or slow-moving) and keep in daily communication with suppliers and order additional merchandise as their own orders come in. Another advantage of this control of distribution and inventory levels is that it gives companies the ability to manage *cash flow* effectively. A direct-marketing company's customers pay for an order before it is sent out. A retail store, in contrast, must buy quantities of each item and store and display the merchandise in the hope that customers will eventually come in and buy it. In other words, direct-marketing customers pay at the beginning of the distribution process and retail customers at the end. Because convenience is one of the major reasons people buy from direct-marketing companies, these companies are also able to *pass on* distribution costs (the cost of packaging and mailing) to the customer by simply adding them to the price of the merchandise.

Finally, in both business-to-business and consumer marketing, direct marketing can generate the *sales leads* that make personal selling so much more targeted and efficient. In this type of selling, marketers employ a two-step process. First, customers are extensively educated about a product, and then the sales force attempts to make the sale. Direct marketing programs are used to make that initial educational step more efficient by identifying high-potential prospects and moving them through the initial awareness stage—a strategy called **lead generation**. The prospects are then passed on to the sales force for follow-up calls or sent additional information and/or samples designed to motivate purchase.

lead generation
The process of identifying customers who are highly likely to purchase a given product.

SOME DISADVANTAGES OF DIRECT MARKETING

The primary disadvantage of direct-response marketing is its relatively high cost per prospect reached. Direct-mail efforts, for example may have costs per thousands (CPMs) that reach $400 when you add up the expense of designing and printing the materials, buying the mailing lists, and stuffing, addressing, and mailing the envelopes. By comparison, because of economies of scale, regular mass-media advertising can cost as little as $7 per thousand. The trade-off is that direct marketing can be tightly targeted and thus have far less wasted reach than conventional advertising.

From the buyers' standpoint, there are four primary disadvantages to direct marketing. First, there is the privacy issue raised by the use of computer-based lists of consumers with detailed characteristics that was the focus of the story at the beginning of this chapter. According to a survey released by Toronto-based Equifax, 62 percent of Canadians show a "medium" amount of concern for privacy issues—but much greater concerns were expressed about the collection of excessively private information. Second, buyers have no opportunity to see, touch, or test products before buying. Third, they are dealing with businesses they never see—their only contact is through an ad, a computer, or a phone. Finally, they pay more for items because the costs of shipping and handling products sold this way are added to their price. Consequently, there will always be a *segment* of buyers who will not respond to this type of selling either because they don't want to tell marketers their credit card number, they don't want to buy products without examining them and risk the hassle of having to return them by mail if they don't like them, they don't like dealing with marketers who are so remote, or they don't want to pay the extra costs for shipping and handling.

There are also certain *types* of products that do not lend themselves to direct marketing—for example, fresh foods (for obvious reasons) and mass-distributed convenience items that cost a few dollars or less (ball-point pens, toothpicks, and candy bars) and whose packaging and mailing costs would be as much or more than the price of the items themselves. For some products, such as cigarettes and liquor, there are legal restrictions on sale through the mail. Finally, for industrial products that need to be customized, the best that direct marketing can do is generate sales leads.

It should be noted that although it is much less expensive to reach primary customers with catalogs and other types of direct marketing, such impersonal selling messages are not nearly as effective as a salesperson for *closing* a sale. So before a business replaces its salespeople with direct marketing, it should determine if the loss in sales—resulting from lower percent of sales per customer contacted—will be offset by the reduction in selling costs.

HOW DIRECT MARKETING OPERATES

In this section we look at the organization and operation of the direct-marketing process, the topic of chapter objective three. First we examine the various stages in the direct-marketing function, and then we explore some of the elements, such as a reliance on databases, that distinguish direct marketing from other forms of marketing communications.

THE DIRECT-MARKETING PROCESS

Unlike advertising or pricing, which are single-function processes, direct marketing is a process that integrates three functions—communication, selling, and distribution. There are five basic steps in direct marketing: (1) strategic decisions (targeting, segmenting, prospecting); (2) the communication of an *offer* by the seller through the appropriate *medium*; (3) *response*, or customer ordering; (4) *fulfillment*, or filling orders and handling exchanges and returns; and (5) maintenance of the company's database and customer *relationships*. Figure 20-3 outlines these steps.

Strategy begins with marketing research, targeting, and setting objectives. The basics of marketing research and setting objectives have already been covered, and we will examine targeting in more depth later when we discuss databases. Here we will focus on the other basic steps of direct marketing: the offer, the response, fulfillment, and maintenance or relationship building.

The Offer   Making an offer means more than advertising a particular product for a particular price. An **offer** involves everything, both tangible and intangible, involved in the exchange between seller and buyer. A typical example is an offer that Sears once made for a stereo system. It included the product's price, notice of savings over the regular retail price, a fifteen-day free trial, a money-back guarantee, credit terms, an 800 number for convenient ordering, a time limit on the offer, and finally, a set of stereo headphones for only one cent (a premium). Premiums and coupons (see Chapter 18) frequently accompany direct-marketing offers.

A good offer not only minimizes perceived risk for consumers who cannot personally inspect the product but also generates a sense of immediacy—

offer
A term for everything that is involved in the exchange between buyer and seller, including tangible items such as the product itself and intangibles such as credit terms and guarantees.

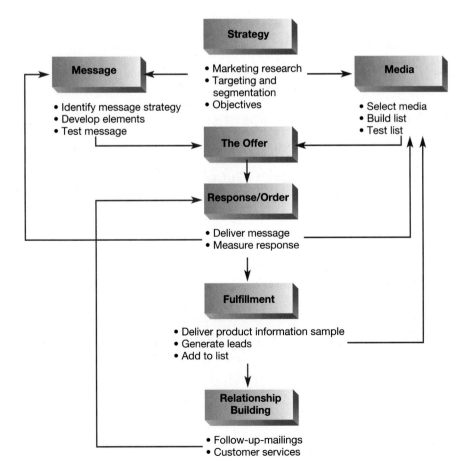

Figure 20-3
The Direct-Marketing Process

Home Shopping on the Move

Today, home shopping networks require rows upon rows of personally attended computers to handle incoming orders. Tomorrow, will these too be gone? Will the customer, by pushing the right buttons, send his or her order direct to a warehouse or shipping center?

the offer is generally good for only a limited time. Direct marketers know that if a consumer doesn't respond shortly after receiving an offer, the likelihood of response decreases dramatically.

The Response Unlike advertising, whose primary objective is to generate a *psychological* response like brand awareness, direct marketing aims to generate a *behavioral* response. Consumer response may be in the form of direct action—purchase, donation, subscription, membership—or in the form of behaviors that precede purchase—attending a demonstration, participating in a taste test, test driving a car, or asking for more information about a product. To motivate people to take the next step—action—direct marketing often uses strong motivational devices such as prizes, awards, and emotional appeals.

Fulfillment As we said earlier, direct marketing is a selling process that includes distribution or fulfillment—that is, getting the product to the customer. In direct marketing, the term **fulfillment** refers to more than just distribution: it covers all the *back-end* activities that take place both in anticipation of orders and after orders are received. Back-end activities include manufacturing or ordering; receiving product inventory; warehousing; receiving, opening, reading, and sorting customer orders; order entry; contacting customers when orders are unclear or when merchandise cannot be shipped on schedule; inventory control; packing, metering, shipping, and customer service.

The goal of fulfillment is making sure that customers get what they ordered for the price they ordered it within a reasonable period of time. An effective fulfillment program can reduce returns by 20 to 40 percent. Returns normally range between 15 and 20 percent, depending on the company's reputation and the type of goods it offers. Returns require restocking and crediting customers, which are costly procedures. It takes nearly as much staff time to receive, credit, and restock a return as it does to process the original order, so a well-managed fulfillment program that minimizes returns is cost-effective.

A well-managed fulfillment operation also minimizes problems with regulatory groups such as the Better Business Bureau. By law, direct-marketing companies must either fill an order in a specified time period or notify the consumer that the order will be delayed and extend the right to cancel for a full refund.

Relationship Building Direct marketing experts Stan Rapp and Thomas Collins describe an approach to marketing that they call maximarketing. Maximarketing uses highly targeted messages built on customer databases and multifunctional advertising to open up buyer-seller dialogues.[5] This type of marketing builds long-term relationships—similar to the building of a brand franchise—and strengthens the link between customer and marketer. While computers and databases help identify heavy users and prime prospects, *interactive media* make it possible for customers and marketers to have dialogue much quicker than through the mail. Also, the real-time dialogue faciliated by interactive media increases the customer's involvement, which creates a desirable selling situation.

The Millennium rechargeable battery campaign has used direct marketing to build customer relationships through its Compare and Save programs. For example, consumers who buy rechargers are offered a rebate if they return the product registration cards, and the information obtained from these cards is used to build a list of users. In addition to the rebate, users are sent coupons for discounts on other products in the line; this helps establish continuity of purchase. Consumers who purchase a Millennium Cordless Phone Pack can apply for the Millennium Calling Card, which has an 800 number on it with their own personal code. The card does not require the consumer to be linked to any particular long-distance company. It supplants the phone company relationship and helps Millennium keep the user plugged into its data bank.

DIRECT-MARKETING OPERATIONS

Three types of firms offer direct-marketing service: full-service direct-marketing agencies, advertising agencies, and special-service firms. *Full-service* direct-marketing agencies specialize in determining the best ways for clients to reach target customers. Their services include creating and placing direct-response advertising. Unlike full-service advertising agencies, however, full-service direct-marketing agencies specialize in selecting and testing mailing lists. They are knowledgeable about the fulfillment end of direct marketing, often serving as consultants in this area. Many of these agencies, although

659

DIRECT
MARKETING

operating independently, are quite large, and many are affiliated with advertising agencies.

Some *advertising agencies* have departments that specialize in direct-response advertising. Many agencies that provide integrated, full-service marketing communications programs have bought smaller direct-marketing agencies or created their own in-house departments.

Because direct marketing has become such a large industry, it now has its own set of *special-service firms*—companies that specialize in certain direct-marketing services, such as collecting, verifying, and selling mailing lists; handling the customized printing of direct-marketing mailings; stuffing and addressing envelopes; and handling the fulfillment function. ADVO-System in the United States, for example, focuses on grouping advertising from various companies in shared mailings, thereby cutting postal expenses for clients by as much as 60 percent. Its database of 98 million households is one of the most comprehensive lists of individual households in the United States.

THE DATABASE

You will recall from the discussion in Chapter 5 that a *database* is an extensive collection of information compiled, stored, and accessed by computers. Customer information can be retrieved in a number of different ways—by name, by address, or by other demographic, psychographic, or purchasing characteristics. **Database marketing**, the subject of the fourth chapter objective, allows marketers to use extensive lists of prospects and relevant information to narrow their target to serious prospects and customize their offer to the interests of this group (see Exhibit 20-2).

This information also makes it possible to ascertain specific brand usage by individual and household—that is, to identify people who use a company's own brands as well as those of its competitors. It is possible, for example, to send a certain set of promotional materials for a specific brand and type of dog food only to owners of Great Danes and another promotional offer to owners of poodles.

Building the list is one of the more difficult tasks in relationship marketing. In the past, databases were built from company records and credit card lists. Now marketers are using innovative and creative sales promotions to compile lists. Pepsi Cola, for example, as part of its move into integrated marketing, has been building an extensive database of frequent customers. A Diet Pepsi Convert a Million campaign attempted to convert Diet Coke drinkers by mailing sample cases to 1 million Coke households. These people were identified from a prior mailing that invited cola drinkers to call a toll-free contest number. As part of their response, they were also asked for additional demographic and soft-drink purchase data.

Another example is TTS Meridian Systems (a Northern Telecom Company based in Montreal) who recently used database marketing for customized seminar selling. It put together a program to sell a specific call center management software targetted at five particular customers. Two sales were made and total revenue generated was over $75,000.[6]

Eventually, direct-marketing databases may help manufacturers identify types of consumers such as innovators—people who lead in the product-adoption sequence (see Chapter 6). By targeting innovators with coupons and samples, marketers may be able to stimulate word-of-mouth testimony for new products. As database management gains in efficiency, even one-to-one marketing is becoming feasible. *Solo mailings*—customized marketing pieces that appeal to individual interests—are being used today by direct marketers like American Express.

database marketing
Marketing that uses extensive lists of prospects and relevant information to narrow the target to serious prospects and customize the offer to their interests.

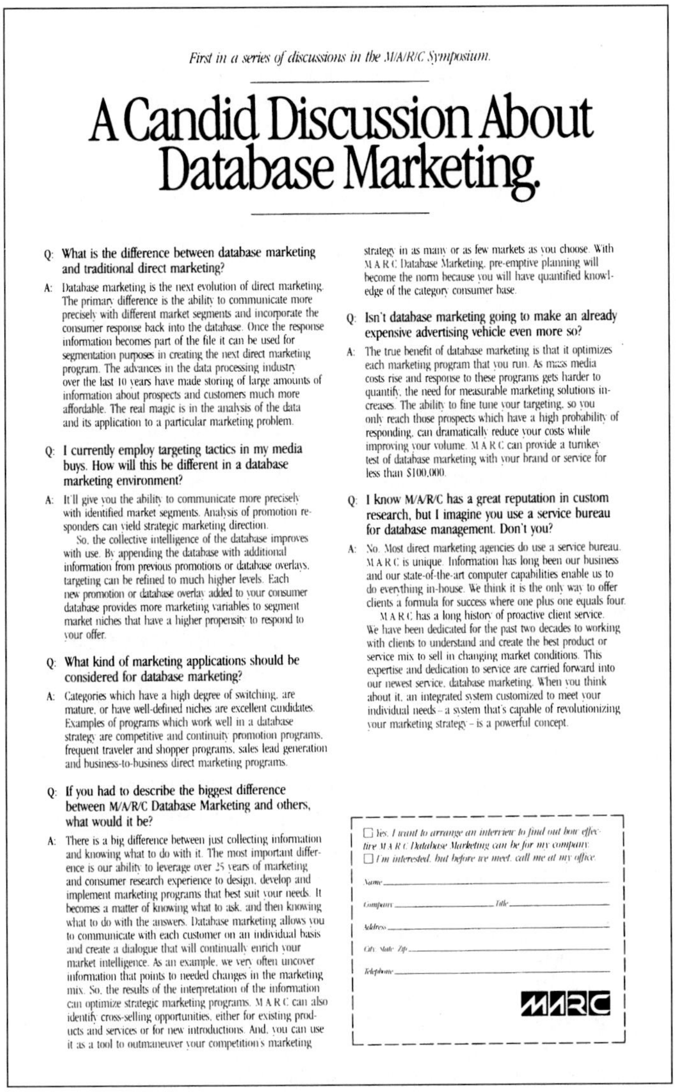

Exhibit 20-2
Advances in Direct Marketing

In this ad M/A/R/C Database Marketing, a database service provider, explains the uses and value of database marketing.

As the prices of computers have come down and computer software has become more sophisticated, the cost of operating a database has dropped significantly. In the early 1970s, for example, it cost over $7 to access one person's name, address, and purchase record. By the early 1990s, Rapp and Collins tell us, it cost about 1 cent. Consequently, large databases are now affordable for even small companies.

List Management There are three primary kinds of lists—*house, response,* and *compiled.* The *house list* is made up of a company's current customers. Because the best customers are current customers, this list is the most productive, accurate, and least expensive to obtain. A *response list* is made up of consumers who have already responded to a similar direct-marketing offer. A *compiled list* contains names from sources like phone directories and organizational membership directories. Not surprisingly, response lists are more expensive (on a cost-per-thousand basis) than compiled lists.

List brokers have thousands of lists classified by common demographic, psychographic, and geographic categories (see Chapter 8). Canada's households are classified by census data, postal codes, and even postal-carrier routes. List brokers obtain names and addresses from a variety of sources, including government records, organizational membership directories, magazine subscription lists, and various company customer lists. Some businesses, such as Sears and American Express, maintain lists that number in the millions. For these firms, the customer list is an extremely valuable asset. About 2,000 lists are available for rent in Canada. Ossie Hinds, president of Toronto-based Cornerstone List Brokers Inc., one of the largest list brokers in Canada, estimates that there are about four Canadian-based list brokers and 20 U.S.-based brokers active in Canada.

Screening Criteria   There are four criteria that direct marketers use in evaluating mailing lists:

1. How *frequently* targeted customers have made a direct-response purchase.
2. How *recently* they have made such a purchase.
3. How much they *spent* on their last direct-response purchase.
4. From what product *category* they purchased (for example, gardening, sports, literary).

These four characteristics are important because they indicate how likely it is that a prospect will respond: the more recent and the more frequent the direct-response purchases, and the more money the prospect has spent on merchandise within a certain product category, the more likely it is that person will buy a similar product again. Also, new credit card holders are more likely to respond, as are established credit card holders who have unpaid balances. In fact, the larger the unpaid balance, the more likely the card holder is to buy.

Not surprisingly, the development of such information about so many Canadians has led to concerns about consumer privacy. Such concerns have surfaced often in The Canadian Direct Marketing Association, the Office of the Privacy Commissioner, and the Canadian Radio-Television and Telecommunications Commission. The primary complaint is that information collected for a single specified purpose, such as a credit application, is being sold and used for the various activities of direct marketing and that this disclosure of personal information without the consumer's consent constitutes a "breach of confidentiality." As people learn more about these activities, they are seeing them as a threat to personal privacy. For example, an American Express study found that 90 percent of consumers believe that companies should disclose more about how they use their mailing lists and 80 percent feel that information collected for one purpose should not be used for another.[7]

Manipulating Lists   The secret to the success of direct marketing today is the power of the computer to manage the incredible wealth of descriptive data being accumulated. Computers can compile lists by sorting for such key variables as age and income and recency, frequency, and type of purchase in terms of quantity and value.

The problem is that the same potential customer often appears on more than one list, and it is a waste to send the same person two or more of the same offers. To eliminate these extra mailings, direct marketers use a process called *merge-purge*. When a catalog marketer of garden equipment, for instance, wants to base a mailing on several different customer lists rented from several different large retail florists, it will combine the lists (merge) and then eliminate (purge) all duplicated names. In this way the marketer avoids sending several catalogs to one household.

Standard lists now rent for $40 to $50 per thousand names. Custom-designed lists—such as neurosurgeons or households with annual incomes over $1 million—may cost up to $400 per thousand. The additional cost is usually worthwhile because precision targeting reduces mailing and production costs and then produces a larger return.

For the Porsche direct-marketing effort we described at the beginning of this chapter, the agency spent more than $250,000 over eight months in developing the mailing list. Starting with a universe of 80 million names of car owners, the agency filtered the list by matching it with a composite of recent Porsche buyers, which reduced the number to 15 million households. The agency then applied demographic, psychographic, and lifestyle attributes to the list, which brought it down to 2 million. At that point, it ranked prospects and arrived at its prime list of 300,000 names.

THE MEDIA OF DIRECT MARKETING ●

Although direct mail is still the primary method of direct marketers, this form of marketing uses a variety of media. The conventional mass media used to deliver direct response offers—newspapers, magazines, television, radio—are the focus of chapter objective five. Less conventional are the one-to-one media—E-mail, telephones, and fax systems. Figure 20-4 outlines the different ways in which offers can be delivered, ranging from these personal one-on-one methods to the impersonal "mass" methods. Frequently, direct marketers use media in combination. A mail offer, for example, is preceded by a week or two of heavy TV advertising. Publishers Clearing House—a company that sells magazine subscriptions and also conducts sweepstakes—does this each year.

MASS-MEDIA ADVERTISING

The primary difference between mass media and one-to-one media is *specificity* of targeting. The people marketers reach when they use mass media such

Figure 20-4
The Media of Direct Marketing

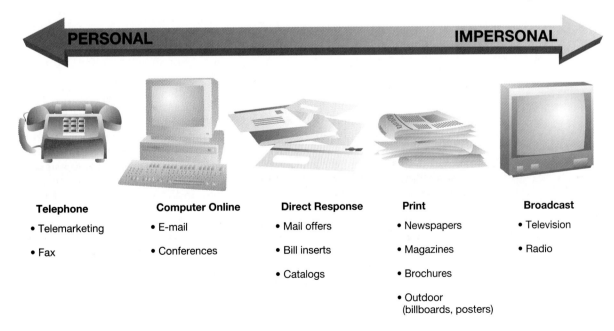

Telephone	Computer Online	Direct Response	Print	Broadcast
• Telemarketing	• E-mail	• Mail offers	• Newspapers	• Television
• Fax	• Conferences	• Bill inserts	• Magazines	• Radio
		• Catalogs	• Brochures	
			• Outdoor (billboards, posters)	

as TV, magazines, and newspapers are those who tune in or subscribe to a particular station or publication. Because these media reach a broad range of consumers with varied needs and wants, response rates are much lower—but then, too, are costs when compared in terms of CPM impressions.

Offers made on television commercials may use an 800 number or an address for response. But a lot of the direct-response advertising that appears on late-night TV falls in the category of *infomercials* (see Chapter 18), the lengthy ads that look like talk or news shows. Originally hawking vegetable choppers, real estate opportunities, and study courses, the genre has moved upscale. Ross Perot, 1992's maverick U.S. presidential candidate, spent millions during the election campaign to air his eight half-hour prime-time "infomercials," which, among other things, solicited money for his campaign and signed up supporters.[8] Similarly, Mike Harris, leader of the Ontario Progressive Conservative Party, has a monthly cable phone-in show, allowing people to find out about polices and to offer the party support.

Although newspapers and magazine ads are not as well targeted as direct mail, such as catalogs, they are used to carry direct-response messages because their CPM is so much lower than direct mail's. As the ad for Precision Marketing Associates in Exhibit 20-3 points out, newspapers and magazines compete directly with direct mail. Local retailers and communications companies like AT&T and MCI, which sell widely used products, use newspapers for direct-response offers because newspapers have good reach and short lead times. This strategy helps build name awareness even among people who do not respond immediately. The typical direct-response ad in a newspaper or magazine carries an order form, telephone number, and/or coupon (see the Doubletree ad in Exhibit 20-4).

An example of a successful television direct-response offer was the effort by Shearson Lehman Hutton to sell zero-coupon U.S. Treasury bonds during an Andy Williams Golf Classic. The company gave away a zero-coupon bond worth U.S. $40,000 each day of the tournament to the player with the best score. It also ran spots describing the bonds, along with an 800 number for requesting more information or placing orders. As Shearson's vice president of advertising reported: "The phones were ringing off the hook."

HOW TO CONTROL THE RISING COST OF DIRECT MAIL WITH DIRECT RESPONSE PRINT ADVERTISING

PRINT ADVERTISING is one of the most targeted...cost effective... & responsive Direct Marketing media available!

Sound incredible? If you've been listening to the prevailing mythologies about the unique powers of Direct Mail...it probably does. Most Direct Mail proponents have cast print as a decidedly second class media...that's too untargeted to be truly effective.

Frankly, this is just untrue. At PMA we've been using print as an integral part of a balanced media mix for our clients for over 10 years with *consistent* success! Here's how...

The Cost Advantages of Print Advertising Are Serious.

If you are concerned about the rising cost of Direct Mail...it is hard...very hard...to argue with the incredible cost efficiencies of print advertising. Simple arithmetic tells you that if you can reach 1,000 prospects for $12/M in print...and $425/M in the mail...print has a very powerful cost advantage.

Plus...keep in mind that most publications...and the ads they carry... have an active life of 4-6 weeks, and many have an average readership of *twice* the circulation.

Factor that advantage into the base CPM and print becomes almost impossible to beat!

Print Ad Targeting *Can* Be Precise.

Direct Mail is a precise medium, to be sure...but it is *not* the only precise medium!

The explosion in special interest publications has revolutionized print advertising for Direct Marketers. Currently there are more than 2,000 publications serving specialized markets from sports all the way to organic gardening and farming.

In addition many publications offer regional, state, or even city buying opportunities. And that's just the beginning! Product positioning...ad size...use of color...specialized response devices...ad placement and timing *all* play a critical role in successful Direct Response print advertising.

Does *this* sound like an untargeted medium to you?

The "Brand Awareness" By-Product.

"Brand Awareness" is a concept that's alien to traditional direct marketers. It smacks of the fuzzy, unmeasurable advertising of the "general" agencies. It lacks *action & accountability*.

But, "Brand Awareness" really isn't *all* bad...particularly when it's a *FREE* By-Product of solid Direct Response Advertising.

Print is better at taking advantage of this powerful "Brand Awareness" than any other media. It's out in the open...it's public...it circulates and it *lasts!* It may never be the only reason to advertise in print...but "Brand Awareness" is clearly an invaluable windfall in building for future sales.

The Power of Lead Generation.

Print advertising can be a powerful selling medium...using single or multi-page offers to sell *right off the page!*

A lesser known, but equally powerful, print opportunity is getting your best customer prospects to *self activate.* Instead of going directly for the sale, use print ads to create *interest & involvement* with your product. Then create *action* by motivating prospects to "raise their hands" and request *more information.*

This method...often called *lead generation*...puts your best prospects into *immediate action*...and creates an *immediate relationship* with you and your product.

The result. A *super* qualified customer file who will buy now...and keep on buying over time.

Call PMA...For Complete Direct Response Services.

Needless to say we believe in Direct Response Print Advertising...and are anxious to talk further about its potential for *You!*

But, keep in mind that PMA is more than a Print Advertising shop... much more! We have extensive experience in every Direct Response medium including Direct Mail, Television, Catalog & Package Insert Programs...even Radio! We've run successful Lead & Order generation programs for a broad spectrum of products ranging in price from $100 to well over $1,000.

With a staff of 50 full time Direct Response Professionals in every key discipline we have the knowledge and capacity to handle any Direct Marketing challenge.

Call us TODAY at 518-235-6302 for a FREE information package on our complete Direct Response Services.

FOCUS YOUR PRINT ADS ON *ACTION!*

STOP BURGLARY BEFORE IT STARTS. CALL 1-800-645-8900 TODAY!

Tiller Users **Discover TROY-BILT's CAST-IRON Quality!**

There's no room for vague approaches in Direct Response print advertising. Stop your prospect with a compelling promise... *follow with a clear* benefit *story...and finish with an irresistible call to* ACTION!

PMA | Office of the President
Precision Marketing Associates
20 Gurley Avenue Troy, New York 12182. 518-235-6302

☐ Please send me details on your complete Direct Response services...
including *Print Advertising!*

Name _____
Company _____
Title _____
Address _____
City, State, Zip _____
Phone ( ) _____

CALL 1-518-235-6302 TODAY!

**Exhibit 20-3
Cutting Coupons Cuts Costs**

Precision Marketing Associates handles many different types of direct marketing. This ad explains the advantages of reaching consumers through print direct-response advertising.

DIRECT MAIL

The predecessor of today's direct-marketing industry, direct mail dates back to the late 1800s and the early catalogs of Montgomery Ward and Sears Roebuck. The mail order business emerged in Canada in 1953 when Simpsons' catalog was developed to cater to Canada's many rural residents who had few options as to where to shop. The first Simpson-Sears (now Sears Canada) produced more than 12 million copies of its catalogs, each offering approximately 20,000 items. Direct mail produces the highest response rate of all the mass media used by direct marketers, but it is also the most expensive. **Direct mail** is an advertising medium that delivers the message by mail. **Mail order** is a form of direct mail that distributes the product to the buyer by mail. Because direct mail is the primary way direct marketers make their offers, many people refer to direct marketing as direct-mail advertising. As we have explained, however, this is misleading because today so many other types of delivery systems are also being used.

Direct mail or as Canada Post calls it: "addressed admail," has increased steadily since 1989, increasing from $246 million to $343 million, while at the same time, publications have decreased over the same period from $290 to $190 million. Media have life cycles and this is evident from an examination

direct mail
An advertising medium that delivers the message by mail.

mail order
A form of retail distribution that delivers the product to the buyer by mail.

One smart business call.

That's all it takes to put you in touch with over 60 Doubletree Hotels from coast to coast, where you'll enjoy the luxuries you like at rates that will let you rest easier.

And at every Doubletree, you'll find the kind of personal service and special attention that will bring you back again and again. And it begins the very first night with our welcoming chocolate chip cookies.

So. You don't have to give up the great restaurants, swimming pools, and health clubs that make business trips bearable. Because now, you've got the right connection. Doubletree Hotels. It's a smart call.

When your travels take you to Canada, consult your travel professional or call us for reservations at any of 26 Canadian Pacific Hotels & Resorts.

of the volume of mail by segment: addressed admail has increased from 1,103 million to 1,321 million pieces, and publications have decreased frim 592 million to 451 million pieces. This reflects shifting trends and the dollar value of addressed admail which now represents 16 percent of revenue and 21 percent of volume, compared to 10 percent of revenue and 71 percent of volume for the unaddressed advertising mail, popularly known as "junk mail"—although some would argue that there is no such thing as junk mail, only direct mail that has been poorly targeted. To meet the increasing demand in direct mail, Canada Post has opened a CONNEXIONS Direct Marketing Resource Centre in Toronto's business and financial center which has been specially designed to oversee the preparation of mailings for major admail customers.

Why is direct mail used so extensively if so many people consider it "junk" and never respond? Because it takes only a small percentage of responses for most mailings to be profitable—on average, 2 to 4 percent. So, if only one person out of twenty-five responds, chances are the mailing will be profitable.

Another important consideration is speed. Unlike advertising which has long time lags in origination, and printing and publication which is indirect with the producer, direct mail is readily measurable, and the effect of a mailout can be readily assessed in terms of the responses received. In other forms of advertising it takes usually two sightings of an advertisement to move a consumer to action and to buy and, as they generally buy the product or service from a retail outlet, it usually involves another time lag before this information is received by the producer.

CATALOGS

A *catalog* is a publication that displays a variety of merchandise available from a manufacturer or retailer. Over 40 billion catalogs are distributed in North America annually—that's roughly a catalog for every person in North America every week of the year. In 1992, revenue from catalog selling was $1.99 billion.

Catalog selling is very profitable elsewhere in the world. At the beginning of the 1990s, of the ten largest catalog marketers in the world, only two were North American—Sears and Penney's (although Sears no longer continues to operate a mail order catalog in the United States, it still flourishes in Canada). Four of these top ten companies were German, and three were based in the United Kingdom.

You can buy almost anything from catalogs—from a golf cart equipped with stereo and sun roof (Austad's, $8,500), to a $6,000 eighteenth-century French Provincial armoire or a $10,000 Chinese screen (Horchow), to a one-person hot-air balloon (Neiman-Marcus, $18,000). Although virtually every type of product can be found in a catalog, consumers say they prefer to use catalogs for buying things like books, compact disks, and tapes rather than expensive jewelry and major appliances.

Regal Greetings and Gifts Inc. of Toronto is Canada's second largest mail-order catalog company—with sales of $80 million in 1993. Traditionally Regal just sold gifts and cards, but recently it decided to sell children's clothing through an agreement with Walt Disney Co.[9]

There are three major types of catalogs: *retail mail-order, consumer-specialty*, and *business*. Although many variables determine the cost of producing a catalog, the four primary factors are the number of pages, page size, the use of color, and the number of catalogs printed.

Retail Mail-Order Catalogs Historically, the biggest catalogs were produced by retail giants, such as Sears and Eaton's, that also operated hundreds of retail stores. Because of increasing competition from smaller and more specialized companies, Sears was forced to kill its annual U.S. catalog in 1993 after ninety-seven years of publication. Eaton's stopped publishing their catalog in Canada for the same reason. Other retailers, however, like Holt Renfrew, Neiman Marcus, and L.L. Bean, have been quite successful at extending their in-store sales revenue by producing and distributing catalogs. At the other extreme is Spiegel, a big U.S. catalog merchandiser that sells everything from furniture to kitchen utensils. Though Spiegel has only a few retail stores, it is one of the most successful catalog retailers. Besides large glossy catalogs mailed two times a year to active buyers and prospects, the company produces ten specialty catalogs, each of which is mailed twice a year. The typical Spiegel buyer spends an average of U.S. $116 every time he or she orders.

Retailers like Regal Greetings and Gifts Inc. is primarily a catalog merchant that also operates 38 stores across Canada. Some retailers are exclusively catalog merchants—for example, Lillian Vernon, Hanover House, and Horchow do not maintain retail stores. Some merchandise is relatively inexpensive: Hanover's items are usually $10 or less. Others are much more upscale: Neiman Marcus, Holt Renfrew, Steuben, and Tiffany all offer items priced in the thousands of dollars. Exhibit 20-5 shows the covers of two Sears' catalogs. Covers like these are cues to the organization's personality and merchandise.

Canada Post Corp. (a federal Crown Corporation), Regal Greetings and Gifts, and Livingston Group Inc. have teamed up to form Catalogue Services International (CSI), a company that brings together delivering, warehousing, and database marketing skills. CSI offers U.S. catalog marketers expertise on the key differences between the Canadian and U.S. markets.

Specialty Catalogs   One noteworthy area of growth in the catalog field is *specialty catalogs*. There are now catalogs for every hobby, as well as for a great variety of general interests, such as sporting goods, housewares, gardening, and electronics. There are catalogs for purses, rings, cheese and hams, stained-glass supplies, garden benches, and computer accessories. Laura Secord is evaluating the use of catalogs to sell their range of upscale chocolates.

Business Catalogs   Although almost every technical and professional area is served by catalog merchants, catalog selling is used most frequently for routine products purchased in large quantities like office supplies. The Inmac catalog, for instance, serves the computer *aftermarket*—that is, supplies needed to run computers once they've been purchased. Inmac offers computer disks and disk filing boxes, user-friendly desks, printer stands, printer paper, and other accessories. It is AT&T's largest mail-order supplier. Other large-volume Inmac customers are NYNEX, Bell Communications, Boeing,

Exhibit 20-5
Sears—Yesterday and Today

The design of a catalog plays an important role in attracting the attention of a target market. Note the different styles for the Sears' catalogs for the 1950s and the 1990s.

and Eastman Kodak. Inmac has annual sales of U.S. $165 million and leads the industry.

Dell Computer has also created a strong niche for itself as a direct marketer of computers. When Compaq tried to catch up with Dell in 1993 by launching its own DirectPlus catalog operation, it succeeded in gaining only 3 percent of the sales in this market, which was significantly less that its 10 percent objective. Analysts say that Compaq erred by limiting its catalog to items aimed at small-business customers. It probably forfeited sales by leaving out some of its new computer products, like the Presario, that are also sold to consumers. In this industry the business user and consumer tend to cross over and buy from the same sources.[10]

TELEMARKETING

Telemarketing is the solicitation of sales by telephone. This type of direct marketing is the focus of the sixth chapter objective.

There are two types of telemarketing. The first is the *straight personal sales call*. As we will see in Chapter 21, although this method is not effective with some people, a fairly large group of consumers is responsive to it. The second type, called *automatic dialing*, calls potential customers and delivers a recorded message. Many consumers consider automatic dialing very intrusive. In fact, consumer complaints to the Canadian Radio-Television and Telecommunications Commission (CRTC) about automatic dialing increased to 40 percent of the telecommunication complaints in the first half of 1993, up from 3 percent in 1987.

The CRTC has established some tough rules to limit the invasion of privacy by telemarketers. For example:

1. Computerized and prerecorded telephone promotions, sales, or fundraising calls by Automatic Dialing-Announcing Devices (ADADs) are prohibited.
2. Use of ADADs is allowed for uses such as emergencies or surveys.
3. Organizations using "line" people to make telemarketing calls will have to comply with a consumer's request not to be called again for three years. (This applies in Bell Canada's territory for now.)[11]

The use of the *fax machine* in telemarketing is generating a great deal of controversy because of the volume of messages some people receive. Although unsolicited fax messages don't take you away from what you're doing or force you into unwanted conversations like telephone calls, they can pile up on your desk or your floor and add significantly to your fax paper costs.

Despite these less appealing uses of the telephone in marketing products, the phone has long been an important medium for both outgoing and incoming marketing messages. It is important to the salesperson in making sales contacts and appointments and in taking customers' orders; it is important to the customer in gathering information about a product, contacting sales personnel, and placing orders. In fact, more direct-marketing dollars are spent on telephone solicitations than on any other marketing-communication medium. Business-to-business marketing accounts for about 81 percent of all telemarketing. The secret behind a successful telemarketing effort is the compilation of a targeted, accurate database, and as we have seen, this takes a great deal of careful and continuous work by marketers, salespeople, and other corporate personnel.

General Electric uses telemarketing to manage small accounts and to generate sales among existing customers as well as in customer service. More than forty GE sales centers—almost all of which serve the business-to-business

telemarketing
The solicitation of sales by telephone.

669

DIRECT
MARKETING

sector—also use telemarketing to identify leads. 3M combines telemarketing with direct mail to create product awareness and to generate sales leads. "I don't think there's a division at 3M," observes a company direct-marketing consultant, "that doesn't use some kind of direct mail with tele-marketing." FNA Financial of Richmond Hill, Ontario, uses telemarketing to sell its financial services to women. After identifying prospects, telemarketers call to set up appointments for the company's financial advisers who meet homeowners in their homes. The telephone combines personal contact with mass marketing. In fact, the primary advantage of telemarketing is that it is *personal*: the human voice is the most persuasive of all communication tools.

As we will see in Chapter 21, in-person sales calls are quite expensive, averaging about $500 each whether or not a sale is made. Nevertheless, such one-to-one contacts are very persuasive. Telemarketing is the way to make a personal sales call to large numbers of people at a much lower cost. A telemar-keting firm can put a salesperson on the phone for an hour for approximately $65. If this person can reach five decision makers—people with the authority to make a purchase—within that hour, the average cost per contact is only $13. This is the point GTE makes in the ad displayed in Exhibit 20-6.

Depending on the targeted audience, however, the number of contacts per hour can vary greatly. For example, buyers in major retail chains are much more difficult to reach by phone than are owners of small independent oper-ations. In addition, although telemarketing is *less* expensive per contact than personal selling, it is *more* expensive than mass-media advertising—which, you'll recall from Chapter 18, may cost as little as a few cents to reach a thou-

Exhibit 20-6
The High Cost of Time

Sales calls made by telephone are much less costly than those made in person, in large part because they save time, the point made in this GTE ad.

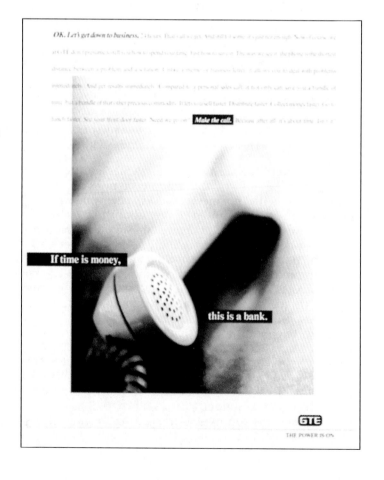

sand households. If the medium can be so expensive, why use it? Quite simply, the *returns* tend to be much higher. For many products, telemarketing definitely pays off.

About one-third of North Americans are telephone shoppers and respond favorably to telemarketers. However, that leaves two out of three consumers who regard unsolicited telephone calls as annoying. In order to surmount this irritation factor, telemarketers are devising creative techniques to make calls more appealing—for example, using taped celebrity voices in phone solicitations. As you can see in the next section, telemarketing is less successful in other countries, particularly Japan.

BEHIND THE SCENES
CROSSING BORDERS WITH DIRECT MARKETING

Entry into international markets is a strategic necessity for direct-marketing companies that want to keep growing. Day-Timer, Inc., for example, began selling executive appointment books internationally after saturating the North American markets. In 1993 over 15 percent of its sales came from licensing agreements in the United Kingdom and Australia.[12]

Marketers are also finding that direct-marketing techniques developed in one country often work in other countries. For example, at American Express, "card-member acquisition models are becoming global models," according to the president of AmEx's direct marketing agency. Catalogs make up 25 percent of AmEx direct-mail revenue and constitute a booming side of the business. AmEx catalogs always feature expensive, sometimes exclusive, merchandise from around the world. The Christmas Catalog is AmEx's largest annual direct-marketing effort, with a mailing of 5 million and an average order of U.S. $500. Other international specialty catalogs offer furs, business items like cellular phones, computers, fax machines and copiers, and high-quality art reproductions. Electronics and health-and-fitness catalogs are also popular.

The language of finance is also understood around the world. The New York–based Chase Manhattan Bank is a large global financial institution that uses direct marketing for international business accounts. A sophisticated three-part business-to-business direct-mail campaign was designed to reach some of Chase's most demanding customers in Europe: international bankers needing highly specialized currency exchange services. The campaign had the extraordinary response rate of 14 percent.

Japan, however, is considered a difficult market for global marketers to enter. Of the top fifty direct-marketing companies in Japan, only three are non-Japanese. Another problem for international marketers is that mailing lists are not as plentiful as they are in North America. One reason for this is that less than 10 percent of magazines are sold through subscriptions; the great majority of sales are from newsstands. Despite these limitations, the Japan Direct Marketing Association says Japan is the second-largest mail-order market in the world, topped only by the United States. Furthermore, many large marketers, such as automobile manufacturers, have begun supplementing their mass-media advertising with direct mailings to potential and current customers.

Because most Japanese resent phone solicitations, telemarketing has not gained a foothold in Japan. Catalog selling, however, has been quite successful. The Austad Company, a U.S. firm that sells golf equipment and clothing, has formed a partnership with a Japanese company in its direct marketing venture. The Japanese firm researches local pricing and competition, gets materials translated into Japanese, and handles customer service. Interestingly, although the catalog is printed in Japanese, its headlines appear in English to underscore its U.S. origin.

ALTERNATIVE MEDIA

The continuing development of new technologies in video, computers, and telecommunications has given rise to a variety of new media that can be used for direct marketing. These alternative and interactive media, as chapter objective seven points out, will become increasingly important in direct marketing in the future.

Video Catalogs   Some retailers have developed video catalogs to display products in live-action color. Sears, for example, has used a Christmas video catalog for exclusive toys that feature state-of-the-art electronics. Cadillac developed a video brochure for the introduction of the Allante. Air France, Soloflex, and Royal Silk have also used videos for in-home promotions. Video cassettes mailed to the home let marketers compete with shop-at-home broadcasts and cable TV programs while achieving precise targeting.

audiotext
A system of 800 or 900 number "hotlines" that consumers can call to hear a recorded message about a particular product.

Audiotext   A growing form of alternative advertising is **audiotext**—phone-in hot-lines with recorded messages that are reached with an 800 or 900 number. In contrast to telemarketing, which involves outgoing sales messages, audiotext is an incoming system—buyers contact sellers. Calls to an 800 number are free; the caller pays for calls to 900 numbers (charges range from 50 cents to $2.50 per minute). A 900 number can handle thousands of simultaneous calls to a single number without sending out a busy signal. Although it costs a company up to $100,000 to obtain a 900 number, the revenue the number produces can pay for this charge many times over. The cost of 800 numbers depends on the volume of calls received, but generally the rate is significantly less than a regular long-distance call and only a fraction of the cost of a collect call.

Computer Data Disks   Some marketers have developed sales material on disks that can be sent directly to computer owners. Auto makers particularly like this format. Both General Motors and Ford have put high-tech sales brochures on computer disks, and they run direct-marketing ads in computer trade magazines for the disks. Buick's initial pilot program for Macintosh users received 67,000 requests for its animated presentation—more than triple the anticipated response—and it has given away more than a million computer disks to consumers since it started the program in 1986. On its 1994 disk Buick offers prospective customers a round of video game golf at renowned Warwick Hills Country Club in Grand Blanc, Michigan, home of the Buick Open, as they learn more about the new Buick products. Customers can even "watch" a car being built. Promotional disks, available through mail order, are usually free.[13]

INTERACTIVE MEDIA

Most *electronic marketing* systems use computer or television to transmit information. As marketing systems, computer-aided home and office shopping are still in their infancy. A related industry, *electronic publishing*, started in the 1980s as **videotext**, a database system of information that was transmitted to personal computers or television via phone or TV cable lines. To date, no companies have been able to make a profit offering this system. In any case, the more advanced technologies that send video and provide interactive capabilities have made videotex unattractive.

The most recent new media technology, called **interactive media**, offers customers an opportunity to participate in two-way communication.[14] As we've noted, the telephone—which is the simplest interactive communication medium—has been used for years in direct marketing, with telemarketing becoming even more common since the advent of 800 and 900 numbers and home shopping networks. The computer-driven new technology, however, makes it possible for consumers to interact with programs, companies, and large compilers of information—Dow Jones, AP/UPI, and the Library of Congress, as well as educational and entertainment sources such as cable channels, Nintendo and Sega, and Time-Warner and merchants such as Sears—or simply order a pizza to go from Pizza Hut.

Using a *modem* (a computer accessory that ties a computer into a phone line), most people with personal computers can access these databases. For years, users have had to buy the modem separately, but since 1994 nearly all the computers made by Apple and many other manufacturers contain built-in modems. Modems allow users to receive information and respond immediately, either with a comment, a question, or a purchase. Purchases can be made by merely punching in a credit card number or, where credit has been established, signaling the company should bill you at a later time. The electronic data interchange (EDI) system discussed in Chapters 14 and 15 allows businesses to place an order and receive an invoice from a supplier, both transmitted electronically.

In Chapter 3 we referred to these developments as the "Information Highway." What such linkages bring to the consumer is choice and a feedback vehicle. This new media configuration, a case of technology called *convergence*, physically brings together a computer, a TV set, and a telephone. This will allow people to do videoconferencing, process digital data, and, eventually, receive digital video.

Although subscriber bases are still relatively narrow, new-technology demographics are appealing to marketers. The market size today is estimated at approximately 5 million PCs with modems. Subscribers tend to be male (more than 90 percent), young, affluent (average income is more than $50,000), college educated, and comfortable with technology—a group that is difficult to reach with traditional media. The IBM-Sears joint venture called Prodigy is a good example of an older on-line interactive information system.

See the Palm Trees Waving

Video catalogs can be an excellent way to sell vacation travel, hotels, and tours. It's hard to resist pushing a free video into your VCR, and when it shows you an island paradise with everything you want but just haven't had the time to plan for, you may be hooked.

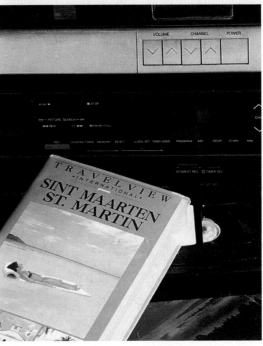

videotex
A database system of information in text and graphic form that is transmitted to personal computers via phone lines.

interactive media
Media systems that make it possible for individual or business customers to participate in two-way communication with sellers by means of combined computer, television, and telephone line hook-ups.

There are more specific uses of interactive media in marketing. For instance, a kiosk at a trade show might have a touch-screen run by a laser disc (CD-ROM) that contains a tremendous amount of information on a particular subject. Since at least 5 percent of the PCs purchased in 1993 have CD readers (and that percentage is increasing significantly each year), direct-mail campaigns can include CD-ROMs or even just floppy discs with in-depth product information that can be searched by the user. Other direct-marketing uses for interactive media are product demonstrations, sales presentations, interactive catalogs, and polling.

Interactive retailing will allow you to call up a menu of restaurants, pick one, and talk to the chef about items on the menu that interest you. In the electronic mall you will be able to enter a brand-name store from your computer and use your remote control to see a full-motion video of a model wearing a high-fashion sweater. You will zoom in closer for details on the stitching, while checking the accompanying text for size, color, fabric, and cleaning instructions. If you order the sweater and pay for it with your credit card, it will be delivered the next day. These are just some of the things you should soon be able to do with your home computer and remote control.[15]

Is all this a high technology fantasy? The Earth Share nonprofit group, which raises funds for thirty-nine environmental groups, was invited by the Prodigy computer service to promote its environmental fund-raising group on-line. During a nine-month run in 1993, Earth Share brought in more than $54,000 in pledges. In the first month alone, the ad drew more responses than the group's public service TV spots got in a year.[16]

Traditional media are also being rerouted to the information highway. News bulletins may be selected in the future from a computer or television service and from a wide choice of international, national, or local. This will affect newspapers and radio as well as television journalism, for control over selection will pass from editors to the consumer with the keypad or keyboard who is now in full control. In addition to offering more choice in story selection, on-line newspapers will allow readers to communicate with reporters, editors, and advertisers as well as with each other. Newspapers aren't the only print media to be affected by the new technology. *Newsweek* is available quarterly on CD-ROM disks with full-motion sound and video and is considering going on-line, as is Time Inc. with its magazine properties. Time Warner has also developed a partnership with Hewlett-Packard to develop an in-home color printer tied to the TV set that will allow viewers to receive coupons, maps, magazine articles, and other printed materials through their TV sets.[17]

BOTTOM LINE REALITIES

IS THERE A MARKET FOR HOME SHOPPING TV?

Home Shopping Network combines two of America's greatest loves:

watching television and shopping. As Bud Paxson, president of HSN, puts it: "We have created a romance." Do you live in one of the estimated 1.5 million RCD (remote control device) households?[18]

Buyers from more than 62 million homes agree with Paxson and pour in anywhere from $2.5 million to $3 million daily. These shows sell products ranging from jewelry to telephones that look like tomatoes to teddy bears that play "Love Me Tender" when squeezed. A recent study found that 65 percent of home shoppers purchased jewelry via TV; this is by far the biggest category. Next came clothing (26 percent), then collectibles and consumer electronics (both at 15 percent each). Home Shopping Network ships out about 70,000 packages of merchandise every day.

On the twenty-four-hour-a-day show, products appear on the screen accompanied by a lot of hoopla like ringing bells and clapping hands to grab attention. They are presented by an enthusiastic announcer/salesperson whose pitch is designed to stimulate impulse purchasing. Calls to HSN come in to a large computer-filled room, where the orders are entered and processed.

About 70 percent of HSN's viewers are women thirty-five to fifty-four years old who are watching, HSN believes, while going about their work at home. Originally, the founders thought that the show would appeal primarily to rural dwellers because of the conve-

nience factor, but they found that there is no difference in response between urban and rural areas. A recent study showed that the home-buying audience includes the college-educated upscale professional in the market for the latest consumer electronic device. According to this study, home shopping channels are beginning to rival catalog selling and traditional retailing.

Some critics wonder just how long viewers will keep watching once the novelty wears off. Nevertheless, HSN continues to build momentum as it maneuvers to corner the market on home shopping. Meanwhile, two major competitors—Quality Value Convenience Network, which sells Sears products, and the Cable Value Network—are challenging HSN's growth. Recently Spiegel joined with Time-Warner to create two new home shopping cable services. Time-Warner's Catalog Channel will feature products from several catalog companies, including Spiegel. The second service is described as an interactive "video mall" and

will go on-line in Time Warner's test market in Orlando, Florida. This Full Service Network is an interactive information highway system. US West is testing a similar system in Denver, Colorado.

QVC is preparing to launch a new network, called Q2, that will combine television with a specialty store. Instead of round-the-clock product pitches, Q2 will package its merchandise in 30-minute television shows that the company intends to be intelligent, informative, and entertaining. A show on gardening, for example, would conclude with a pitch for products used in the program. Q2 is targeted to a younger audience—people in their mid-twenties to mid-thirties—with incomes of $40,000 and up.

If you were a marketer, would you want your products featured on HSN? If you were an investor, would you put your money into this operation? What kind of future do you see for this type of marketing? ▼

KEY POINTS SUMMARY ▼

1. Direct marketing is a highly targeted buying and selling process that requires the integration of previously separate marketing-mix elements like targeting, distribution, and marketing communications. By combining both the marketing and the selling processes, it both creates and fulfills demand in one operation. Through its sophisticated database manipulation, it combines the *target audience* with the *sales prospect*.

2. Direct marketing is growing because it offers convenience, precision targeting, interactivity, measurability, and marketing-mix efficiencies. The primary disadvantage of direct marketing is its relatively high cost per prospect.

3. The basic steps in the direct-marketing process are: (1) the development of the message strategy; (2) the communication of an offer by a seller through the appropriate medium; (3) the response or customer order; (4) fulfillment, or

filling orders and handling exchanges and returns; and (5) maintenance of the customer relationship.

4. Database marketing employs advanced computer programs to build, store, and retrieve information about potential customers. Using database lists, marketers can identify prime prospects and personalize a sales message.

5. The traditional media used by direct marketers are newspapers, magazines, television, radio, direct mail, and catalogs.

6. Telemarketing accounts for more of the direct-marketing dollars spent than any other form of marketing communication. Its primary advantage is that it provides personal interaction between seller and buyer at a much lower cost than in-person contacts. Its principal disadvantages are that it is still more costly than mass media advertising and that a majority of people resist it.

7. The new media technologies are providing such alternative media as video catalogs, audiotext, and computer data disks to direct marketers. Interactive media like computer on-line networks are opening up new opportunities for marketing by combining the computer with television, linking both through telephone lines or cable TV. Such systems offer the promise of interactive communication in which consumers can examine, select, and order products through electronic marketing.

DISCUSSION QUESTIONS ▼

1. Analyze the privacy issues raised in the opening story and mentioned throughout the chapter and balance them against the advantages direct marketing brings to consumers. Do you think there should be government restrictions on direct marketing? If you think this form of marketing should be regulated, what restrictions would you propose? Why?

2. Interview a local businessperson who uses direct marketing. Describe the program. What is the marketer's most important reason for using direct marketing? Who is targeted and how is the list obtained and maintained?

3. Collect two catalogs that have arrived at your home or the home of a friend or relative. Analyze them in terms of their targeting strategy and the personality and tone they establish with their graphics and merchandise selection. In each case, decide if the catalog reached the right consumer.

4. Explain videotex and interactive media. Do you know anyone who uses these new technologies? Build a profile of that person. What products might that person be interested in that could be marketed through a computer network?

5. College students are frequently the target of database marketers. Analyze a piece of direct-response marketing that you have received recently in terms of its targeting strategy, its objectives, and the development of the sales message. Do you think it is successful? Why or why not?

6. Find a friend who watches a home shopping network. Interview that person about his or her viewing behaviors—ask such questions as: Do you watch it a little or a lot? Do you watch it continuously or occasionally when flipping channels? Have you ever purchased anything from a television shopping program? Why or why not? Analyze the purchase decision.

Integrative Case • Discussion Questions

The Body Shop*

1. How does The Body Shop engage in direct marketing?

2. What are the advantages and disadvantages for consumers of The Body Shop's direct marketing effort? What are they for The Body Shop?

Harley-Davidson

1. How has Harley used direct marketing over the decades?

The Millennium Power System

1. What is the purpose of the Compare and Save direct mail program?

2. What other uses could Millennium make of the database created from rebate and product registration cards?

---

*The three cases at the back of the book—"The Body Shop," "Harley-Davidson," and "The Millennium Power System"—illustrate topics discussed in all chapters of this book. Your instructor will tell you when to read a particular case and answer the discussion questions on it that appear at the end of the chapter.

Direct Response—Immediate Results

Dr. Larry Frydman and his invention was introduced in the video case for Chapter 13. Dr. Frydman had a new product and used a unique medium to introduce that product to the market. He tried direct response advertising, advertising designed to encourage the audience to order immediately and directly from the marketer. Direct response advertising is direct marketing—dealing directly with the ultimate consumer, bypassing wholesalers and retailers.

Quality Records is one of the largest mass marketers in Canada. They look for new ideas and products which they turn into lucrative ventures by creating ads to stimulate interest in purchasing a product directly, using a telephone. If done well, direct response advertising can generate sales of millions of dollars in Canada and the United States for the inventor and the mass marketer, like Quality Records.

Companies choose direct response advertising for a number of reasons, only one of them being profit. A mass marketer is driven to get to the market and reap profits before competitors can imitate their products. Direct marketing provides instant feedback through the 1-800 number. Within hours of a product launch, Quality Records and their partners know if the product will sell and where it is selling. They can quickly change their strategies according to their initial results. The key to winning this game is immediate results.

Direct response advertising has grown into a $5 billion industry in North America over the past five years. There are a number of reasons why mass marketers find direct response advertising a blessing. Changes in technology and production techniques make it easy to copy a product, reducing development time. As well, selling directly to the target market is a more efficient means of operation. Intermediaries are not necessary. Finally, it does not take long to find out if a product or idea will not sell.

There are some disadvantages to direct response which need to be considered in the decision to use this method. Timing is critical. The time slots for the airing of the ads dictates the audience profile and can make or break a product introduction. As Dr. Frydman learned, there are a number of uncontrollable events which can interfere with the introduction of a product. Quality Records sets very high expectations for the products it promotes. When products do not perform according to plan, little time is spent trying to repackage it. Within 10 days of a product introduction, a product may see the end of the trail.

QUESTIONS

1. What did Dr. Frydman learn about the advantages and disadvantages of direct response advertising?
2. Are there other factors Quality Records should consider before deciding to drop a product from its promotion list?
3. What types of products and what product categories best fit with direct response marketing?

Source: This case was prepared by Deborah Andrus and is based on the *Venture* series episode "1–800 Ads," which was originally broadcast on July 3, 1994.

● Chapter 21

Personal Selling

THE CHANGING IMAGE OF A "SALESMAN"

Would you be interested in working in sales? Are you clear now on the difference between marketing and sales, which we discussed first in Chapter 1? And what is your image of a salesperson? Do you immediately think of the stereotyped used-car salesman? Or maybe of Herb Tarlek, the sales manager in *WKRP*? Or perhaps of Willy Loman, the traveling salesman so pathetically portrayed by Arthur Miller in his play *The Death of a Salesman*?

Or do you think of independent, entrepreneurial businesspeople (both women and men) who are in charge of their own lives, set their own schedules, and often, as *telecommuters*, work out of their own homes (and cars)? Do you think of modern sales representatives who generate new business and maintain customer relationships with the aid of such tools as computers, fax machines, modems, databases, and MIS programs? Do you think of stockbrokers, insurance agents, and real estate brokers? Do you think of

company presidents who've traveled the fast track to the top?

The world of the salesperson is changing, and so are the job and its image. Before computers

681

and fax machines, the world of sales—although it could be high-pressure—was a business of personal relationships. It was built on warm and friendly personal contacts—and on trust. Today, because of the push for efficiency and the need to lower the cost of sales calls, fax machines, E-mail, and video conferences are replacing personal sales calls. People in the business are wondering what these changes will mean to the human side of sales. Will the live sales call become as much of an anachronism as Willy Loman? ■

In this chapter we consider the nature and technique of personal selling, the way a sales force is selected, organized, and managed, and the objectives, strategies, and sales tactics used in actual practice. As you study this material, you may be pleasantly surprised: there are many attractive aspects to personal selling, including the potential for a high income.

PERSONAL SELLING: ITS STRENGTHS AND WEAKNESSES ●

Selling is universal. Literally everyone "sells" something. People must sell themselves in order to land a job or obtain a bank loan. Politicians, ministers, and United Way volunteers all sell their ideas. And many people "sell" business products without knowing it. In a sense, everyone working for a business is a salesperson for that business. The corporate lawyer who ensures that the company's trademark is not misused is selling the firm's image. The recruiter interviewing a prospective employee is selling the firm. The plant supervisor who brags to her biking group about her company is selling its products.

Personal selling can be defined as a two-way flow of communication between a potential buyer and a salesperson that is designed to accomplish several tasks:

◆ Identify the potential buyer's needs
◆ Match those needs to one of the firm's products

personal selling
A two-way flow of communication between a potential buyer and a salesperson that is designed to identify the customer's needs, match those needs to one of the firm's products, and convince the customer to buy the product.

Modern Selling Techniques: The Video Conference Presentation

The sales presentation made by video conference hookup is becoming increasingly common and is highly cost effective. "A traditional sales call these days," says the media-center manager at Texas Instruments, "can cost from a few hundred to a few thousand dollars. Doing it by satellite costs about $40 per person reached, and the net effect is the same—increased sales and better service."

◆ On the basis of this match, convince the potential buyer to buy the product.

In most cases, this communication between buyer and seller takes place face-to-face and involves a personal relationship.

As the first chapter objective indicates, personal selling has both strengths and weaknesses as a form of marketing communication, and we will consider some of these in this section. Despite its occasional pitfalls, however, personal selling is a very important function in a company, and sales personnel are generally paid well. Moreover, in many companies it is former salespeople who are selected for the highest executive positions. According to one survey, about 30 percent of CEOs at the largest North American firms started in sales.[1] At IBM, for example, a company founded by veteran salesman Thomas Watson, Sr., there is a long tradition of choosing CEOs with sales backgrounds. Because of this trend, the field of personal selling has acquired a strong sense of professionalism, and both college textbooks and professional articles dealing with this field are focusing on such topics as leadership styles, power, and influence.[2]

THE PERSONAL TOUCH

Assuming excellent product knowledge which is the reason why most of us would turn to a salesperson, perhaps personal selling's greatest strength is its *personal touch*. Of all the marketing communication functions, personal selling involves the most human contact and interaction, qualities that are indispensable to building lasting relationships between buyers and sellers. A related strength is the *flexibility* of personal sales: sales agents can tailor their presentations to the specific needs of each potential customer, highlighting the characteristics of a product that are most likely to meet those needs.

Personal selling is also more likely to *persuade* someone to buy a product than are other marketing communications tools. The one-to-one situation facilitates *instant feedback*, with the result that the salesperson can address customers' objections and allay any concerns on the spot.

RELATIONSHIP BUILDING

Of all the marketing communication techniques we have discussed, clearly personal selling involves the most direct personal contact between sellers and buyers. Another of personal selling's strengths is its ability to quickly build a *relationship* with a customer. As we have emphasized throughout this book, companies are increasingly emphasizing relationship marketing, and because the sales force is the primary link between the company and its customers, sales representatives play a major role in this new form of marketing. Theodore Levitt of Harvard Business School did more than just refer to this need. He, in effect charted it in "The Marketing Imagination" whereby he laid out clearly the steps that had to be followed from a traditional perspective to where the company wanted to be vis à vis the buying public. A long-term customer relationship is the only solution.

It is important that relationships be built both upstream and downstream. *Upstream*, you will recall, refers to all those activities that take place before a tangible product leaves the plant or before a service is provided. In a manufacturing business upstream activities include the company's contacts with all the different sales forces that provide it with the parts, equipment, and services (such as legal and accounting advice) that enable it to make and market a product. *Downstream* relationships are those a company's sales force builds with the company's distributors (wholesalers, resellers), retailers, and

Figure 21-1
The Flow of Sales
Relationships

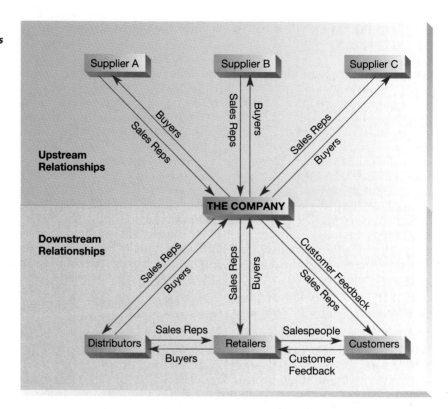

customers. A smart company is just as concerned with maintaining good relationships with its suppliers and their sales forces as it is with maintaining good relationships with its own customers.

Figure 21-1 depicts this network of reciprocal relationships. One of the advantages of nourishing all of these relationships is that they are important channels of communication for information and feedback. The better the relationships, the better the information the company obtains.

Salespeople are part of the corporate team, and their relationships with other areas and functions within their own company are important factors affecting the company's image and, ultimately, its sales. When a new piece of equipment breaks down, for example, customers are as likely to call their sales reps as they are to contact the company's service manager. The sales rep then makes sure the customer's problem is handled quickly. Clearly, if the salesperson does not have a good relationship with the company's customer service department, the customer may be kept waiting and become dissatisfied.

A weakness of personal selling is that one person can sometimes spoil a relationship between a company and one or more of its customers. Because the salesperson is the company's main representative to customers, anything this person does that is out of line will reflect negatively on the entire company. Another weakness is that if a salesperson leaves the company to work for a competitor, he or she takes along all the company's selling strategies and other inside information.

COMPARATIVE COST

Because it is so labor intensive, personal selling is very costly, and this is its biggest weakness. Many firms, especially those selling business to business, require to spend more money on personal selling than on any other element in the marketing communications mix. On average, it costs almost $500 for one sales representative to make one personal call on one customer, and one call is seldom enough to close a business-to-business sale.[3] A highly qualified professional salesperson calling on corporate headquarters and selling high-tech products (computers) or large-volume products (cereal) can make only a few calls a day because customers are rarely geographically close. This type of selling can also require large travel budgets. For example, in 1993 IBM spent over $600 million on air travel, most of which was undertaken for the purpose of assisting customers.

Even if a salesperson never leaves the showroom floor, each contact made with a **prospect**, or potential customer, may cost $10 or more. The need for one-on-one communication also means that the number of prospects with whom any sales agent can speak in a day, week, month, or year is severely restricted. Even a busy retail salesclerk is likely to assist fewer than 100 people in a day. Compare this with the potential to reach millions of people with a single 30-second television commercial at a cost per viewer of pennies, not dollars! It is for these reasons that in recent years more and more companies have turned to the direct-selling techniques that we discussed in Chapter 20. A good advertising campaign together with a good product will presell the brand to the buying public turning the role of the salesperson into that of an order taker.

Another weakness of personal selling as a marketing communications tool is its poor reputation with many people, particularly in the retail trade. Consumers often complain about high pressure and dishonesty among salespeople, an image that competent salespeople are continually trying to dispel. In fact, in one study nearly two-thirds of those surveyed held negative attitudes toward sales agents. When you read the opening story in this chapter, were you among this group, or the one-third that, presumably, did not harbor such ill will toward salespeople?

THE SELLING PROCESS

There are basically two selling processes: one for new customers and another for current customers. These processes are the focus of chapter objective two. As you will see in this section, both processes share several steps, or stages.

SELLING TO NEW CUSTOMERS

The process of selling a new good, service, or idea is generally broken down into seven stages: *prospecting, problem solving, approaching, presenting, handling objections and questions, closing,* and *following up.* These steps are outlined in Table 21-1.

Prospecting The process of looking up and checking out leads is called **prospecting** and involves the *continuous* search for and qualification of individuals and/or organizations that might be in the market for the firm's products. As any salesperson can tell you, there is a world of difference between *leads* and *qualified prospects*. A **lead** is a person or organization that may need or want the seller's product or that might benefit from buying it. By contrast, a **qualified prospect** is someone who not only needs and can benefit from the product but who also can afford it and can make the decision to purchase it.

How do you qualify a prospect? One of the best places to start is with your established accounts. If a buyer you have worked with can refer you to another buyer in a different department of the same company, you will have more credibility and your contact may even turn into your advocate. In addition, most organizations maintain active customer lists that are categorized in

prospect
In personal selling, a potential customer.

prospecting
The continuous search for and qualifying of leads, or potential customers.

lead
A person or organization that may need or want the seller's good or service or that can benefit from buying it.

qualified prospect
A person or organization that not only needs and can benefit from a product but that can afford it and is able to make the decision to purchase it.

TABLE 21-1   THE SELLING PROCESS

Stage	Purpose	Example: A Stock Broker
Prospecting	To identify qualified prospects	Broker telephones a list of investor prospects to qualify their purchasing power.
Problem solving	To gather information on a prospective customer's problem areas and prepare to show the customer how a product can solve these problems	Research department analyzes various industries, selects promising company, and does in-depth analysis of that company and its performance.
Approaching	To establish a good impression and build a relationship with the prospect	Broker calls prospect, introduces self and firm, and asks permission to call if a special investment opportunity arises.
Presenting	To provide information about a product and persuade the prospect to buy it	Broker calls prospect and presents "stock of the month."
Handling objections and questions	To overcome any remaining resistance to buying the product	Broker answers questions about the firm issuing the stock.
Closing	To get the order from the prospect	"Can we put you down for 1,000 shares?"
Following up	To assure customer satisfaction and thus ensure repeat business	Broker calls prospect to discuss new opportunities for investment.

various ways. Commercial databases can also be very useful sources. Many salespeople collect the names of leads when they attend exhibits, conventions, and trade fairs. And so too, do the management of the trade fairs and conventions. They ask for a visitor profile card to be completed usually on entry. This then is used to compile a profile of the visitors to the show or exhibition at the end. There is also a database that has been created. They acquire other leads from current customers (these are called *referral leads*), trade journals, newspapers, professional organizations, and social contacts. Exhibit 21-1 shows how 3M generates leads and qualifies prospects by getting people to respond with a direct-reply coupon.

Problem Solving   With a list of qualified prospects in hand, the salesperson must next find out how *problem solving* can help him or her make a sale. By putting together such information about a potential customer as what the customer needs and what product the customer currently uses, salespeople try to identify problems that their own products may solve. For example: What is the customer doing that is costing more than it should? Why is this company not getting more people to try its products? Why does it have more product complaints than the industry standard?

In industrial sales problem solving may take quite a long time. Often the salesperson prepares an elaborate sales presentation and information package before even crossing the customer's threshold. In retail sales, of course, advance problem solving is seldom possible. Retail salespeople have to assess a

Exhibit 21-1 Coupons as Lead Generators

Coupons can be used for a number of purposes other than sampling. 3M can use the coupon responses from this ad to build a database of users and generate leads for sales calls to corporate buyers.

687
PERSONAL SELLING

prospect's needs and wishes by observation—clothing, manners, even the car someone drives—and by asking specific questions.

One of the things that makes selling so challenging is figuring out whom to approach at a given firm, for the real decision makers differ from company to company. Although most businesses have official purchasing agents, it is sometimes important—particularly in selling such things as production equipment or parts—to make the sales presentation to a group that includes the production supervisor or the head of R&D or that constitutes a *buying center* (see Chapter 7). The salesperson needs to identify the appropriate decision makers before approaching a prospect, which is the next step.

Approaching The first *approach* to a prospect can make or break a sale. The salesperson must be well groomed, friendly, knowledgeable about the products, and confident. Handling this meeting well will enable a salesperson to gain the prospect's attention and to acquire additional insights about that individual's or organization's needs. In industrial sales, where several calls must generally be made before a sale is transacted, the aims of the first call are to build a favorable image of the sales representative and of the firm and to begin building a relationship between the sales representative and those people in the organization who form the buying center.

Handling the approach depends a great deal on the situation. In retail sales, for example, sales personnel must decide which is more appropriate—allowing the customer to browse for a while or offering assistance right away. In industrial sales the approach often varies according to whether the salesperson has an appointment or is making a **cold call**—a sales call without an appointment or prior knowledge—and whether sales representatives have called on the prospect before in connection with other products.

Presenting The formal *presentation* can take many forms. Usually presentations are made one-on-one to a key decision maker, but as we've said, they are sometimes made to groups. Most presentations are live, whether in person or by means of video conferencing; others are made on (delayed) video tape.

cold call
A personal sales call that is made without a prior appointment or prior knowledge.

Whereas the approach takes about 5 minutes, the presentation itself is generally about three times that long. The time required will vary, depending on the situation, on what is being presented, and on the prospect's interest in the offering. For example, presentations that include a product demonstration or give the prospect the opportunity to try the product (often very effective sales tools) generally take longer than purely verbal presentations.

Although some consumer-goods makers—especially those that sell door-to-door—require their sales agents to have a prepared presentation down word for word, most sales agents have a great deal of latitude in shaping their presentations. Increasingly, some use notebook computers for a graphic presentation. This works well where a spreadsheet would be useful to answer "what if" type questions. For larger audiences, a notebook can be coupled to an LCD display and simply beamed via an overhead projector onto a wall or screen. Presentations for highly technical products are often made by a sales team and usually include a written prospectus which is often customized with the company name that prospects can study after the sales representatives have left.

Sales materials range from simple one-page leave-behind fliers to complex books or sets of brochures. For example, Millennium's sales support material, "The Advantage Program,™" is contained in a large, glossy three-ring binder encased in a hard box (see the opening photo for Chapter 4 and Exhibit 21-2). The binder offers sections on product selection, power merchandising ideas, dealer advertising, consumer advertising and public relations, consumer promotions, market research, and ways to customize the "Advantage" sales materials.

Handling Objections Many professional salespeople feel that a good presentation involves only 25 percent talking and demonstrating and 75 percent listening. The salesperson needs not only to anticipate questions that a prospect may raise but also to listen carefully to the questions and/or objections that the prospective customer actually does raise. Prospects' questions can help sales representatives hone their knowledge of the customer's needs so they can point to the benefits and advantages of the product in meeting those needs. A useful sales technique is to plan your presentation to elicit specific questions that you are prepared to answer convincingly.

Exhibit 21-2
The Millennium
Advantage™
Program

The sales-support
literature for the
Millennium launch
contained infor-
mation about the
product line and
marketing re-
search, as well as
merchandising,
advertising, public
relations, and
promotion support.

689

PERSONAL
SELLING

Salespeople should encourage prospects to express any objections they have. Whether a buyer's objections are of a *business nature*, reflecting a real concern to know how the product will affect the firm, or of a *personal nature*, reflecting the buyer's uncertainty or insecurity, if the buyer does not express these concerns in some way, the salesperson has no opportunity to explain why the objections are not valid or to offer concessions that will overcome the objections. Table 21-2 identifies some common objections and possible ways to overcome them.

Again, *active listening* is one of a salesperson's most important tools. *Rephrasing* objections as questions that the salesperson can answer is another tool, as is a systematic approach to identifying and then *removing* obstacles. *Testimonies* and referrals to other satisfied customers can also be useful in in-

| TABLE 21-2 | COMMON OBJECTIONS AND STRATEGIES FOR OVERCOMING THEM |

Objection	Strategies
"Your price is too high."	Don't even try to compete on price alone. Talk to the prospect only about value, quality, satisfaction, profit, prestige, or service.
"I can't afford to buy it at that price."	If you qualified the prospect properly as to ability to buy, his objection simply means that you have not made the prospect want or desire your offering. Show why the prospect needs or should want it and how it can be obtained most easily.
"Your price is out of line. I can buy something like it for less money."	Very few products are exactly the same. Avoid argument and concentrate on distinguishing features.
"The cost is far over our budget allowance."	Walk the buyer through facts and figures, demonstrating how your product will solve a problem, increase profits, or cut costs, and point out how much it could cost not to have it.
"We're really doing fine with our current version."	Point out how much better the buyer can do with the new version.
"I don't like the color (or style or quality or features) of your product."	Acknowledge concerns and express willingness to convey these thoughts to development staff, but steer conversation back to features the buyer does seem to like.
"We aren't looking to change suppliers at this time."	Note that your firm is just looking for an opportunity to show that it can deliver equally good service and with a better product.

creasing credibility and answering objections. There is still no form of advertising stronger than word of mouth. Once a salesperson has answered a question or objection, he or she can often turn a prospect's positive response immediately into a reason for a *trial close*—that is, he can try to get a quick, favorable decision.

Closing the Sale Getting the prospect's agreement to buy the product, or **closing**, is the payoff, and it can come at any time throughout the selling process. It's the most challenging part of the process and it is also the most rewarding.

Prospects rarely volunteer orders—they must be *asked* for their business. Many salespeople are uncomfortable asking for an order because they're unsure they've built agreement and are afraid the prospect will turn them down. Getting a *yes* answer means knowing *when* and *how* to close and people will become hostile if they feel they are being manipulated. There are many mo-

closing
Getting a prospective customer's oral or signed agreement to buy the product being offered.

ments during sales interviews when prospects may be prepared to buy. A yes response may follow any believable and compelling reason the salesperson gives, and may be reflected not only in oral speech but also in other *buying signals* such as a pleased facial expression or the act of picking up an order form and glancing over it. For this reason, most salespeople are trained to try to close as often as possible during the course of the sales interview.

The stall comes when a prospect says: "I'd like to think it over." Successful salespeople know that a **stall**—defined as evasive behavior by a customer designed to avoid or delay a decision—generally means you've only a small chance of getting the prospect back to the decision point. Some 95 percent of the time, you've lost them. They also know that a stall means either there's a conflict in the person's mind or the person sees no good reason to make a decision at this time. The way out of the stall is to uncover the conflict and deal with it or give the prospect a compelling reason for deciding now.

Following Up   A sale does not end when the order is signed because the ultimate aim of personal selling is to gain a satisfied customer who will continue to buy the firm's products. One way to ensure follow-up sales is to call or send a written thank-you to the buyer. Another way is to make telephone or personal calls to check on delivery and installation (if any), product operation (and training of operators) where necessary, and whether the customer wants to change the size or some other aspect of the order or buy additional units. In addition, salespeople can help build long-term business relationships by asking customers for leads. Strong follow-up not only cements relationships but also provides an opportunity for sales personnel to gather information about creative uses of existing products and needs for new products.

One of the authors bought a Citroen and after buying it received a letter from the dealer introducing by name the entire team of people working at the dealership. Every six months there was another letter asking whether everything was satisfactory. In between times postcards arrived which made provisional dates for oil and filter changes. Christmas cards always arrived. When a major service was called for there was a "loaner" available. This Citroen dealer may or may not have been representative of them all but the extremely positive image that it leaves with the customer has to be imagined.

Even if a customer decides not to place an order, many successful salespeople continue to stay in touch in order to pave the way for future sales. People prefer to deal with salespeople and firms that show an interest in them and their business, and they generally remember how well a salesperson took defeat. It costs a salesperson only a little time or effort to follow up a failed presentation with a sincere "thank you for your time" by telephone or letter.[4]

As you think through this outline of the sales process, remember that not every sales response is *yes*. Even the best sales professionals encounter a *no* from time to time. The important thing is to know whether the *no* can be prevented or turned around.

SELLING TO CURRENT CUSTOMERS

Especially in business-to-business selling, once a new customer has been acquired, the salesperson moves on to the second type of selling, which focuses on maintaining and nourishing the relationship that has been established. Five of the seven steps we discussed in selling to new customers—problem solving, presenting, handling objections and questions, closing, and follow-up—are also used in current-customer selling. All of them fall under the umbrella of *relationship building*.

As salespersons continue to sell to a particular company, they will usually learn a good deal about the company's operations and problems, sometimes more than the buyers with whom they deal. For example, as we mentioned earlier, a firm may be having more problems in a certain area than is common throughout its industry. The sales rep, by virtue of relationships with other customers, may have a better feel for this difference than people within the company, and if he or she can suggest an improvement—even if there is no product to sell in that context—the customers are likely to be very appreciative. Clearly, however, a salesperson should *not* tell one company about specific procedures being used by one of its direct competitors. Discretion, particularly in the business-to-business salesperson, is a very important quality.

Because most companies are continually adding, replacing, or improving products, the salesperson often has something new to present to a current customer. Presentations of such products are made easier and less formal by the fact that the sales representative and the buyer or buyers all know one another.

The ultimate in relationship building is *partnering*, in which a customer and a supplier team up to develop a new product. In such a relationship the customer may agree to cover some of the supplier's R&D costs in exchange for the promise of exclusive access to the newly developed product for a certain period of time. The salesperson is often pivotal in a partnering relationship; a company may assign him or her to the account full-time, and the customer may even provide office space.

COMPUTERIZING THE SELLING PROCESS

The increasing use of electronic communication, computers, and databases is changing the traditional selling process. For example, Chicago's Leo Burnett advertising agency has two teleconferencing facilities in its main office. Rather than send a group of account managers and creative people to New York City to sell a new Marlboro advertising campaign to Philip Morris and incur the cost of a two-day business trip for an entire team, Burnett can now show the new campaign to Philip Morris and discuss it through teleconferencing at a cost of two hours' online time.

In Denver a Boyd's Coffee's sales representative, Chris Geyer, carries a hand-held computer into each of his customer's stores. He checks the store's inventory and immediately enters the amount of coffee needed into the computer. Back in his truck, he fills the order and prints out an invoice that he gives to the store manager along with the order. Every evening, by modem, he transmits the day's sales and any future orders to Boyd's corporate headquarters in Portland, Oregon. With a push of a button on his computer, which stores all his sales for the year to date by account, the salesperson can quickly review any account, see which items are selling best, and figure the sales commission for that particular month.

A manufacturer of mops, Roll-A-Matic, can determine on a daily basis exactly what inventory each of its Wal-Mart customer stores has on hand. Using an electronic system that links Roll-A-Matic and Wal-Mart, the company can tell when a particular product is needed in a certain region. It then sends a message to its manager for that district, the manager approves the order, and Roll-A-Matic ships the order and bills Wal-Mart. The entire selling process has been completed and invoiced by electronic communication, without any personal contact. Roll-A-Matic has not eliminated personal selling, however. When sales in some Wal-Mart stores begin to fall off, the company sends salespeople to those areas to talk personally with the Wal-Mart area manager or local store managers to try to determine the reasons for the sales decline.

ORGANIZING AND MANAGING THE SALES FORCE

In order to get the most out of a sales force, companies must manage sales operations well. As with all other areas of marketing, managing a sales force begins with overall goal-setting by top management. Such management requires a firm to set sales-force objectives, manage a sales-force organization that can meet those objectives, develop and implement a sales plan, and evaluate the end results.

Sales positions can be described in several ways—by type of customer, by type of employer, or by sales objectives. Table 21-3 displays these three classifications and gives some examples under each. The *detailer* and the *afterseller* are somewhat unusual sales positions in that the salesperson sells the *idea* of something and provides information about it, rather than the product itself. One type of detailer, the pharmaceutical sales rep, contacts doctors to persuade them to prescribe the company's drugs but does not get or take orders. An automobile afterseller does not sell cars, but offers service to a customer after a sale.

SELECTING A SALES FORCE

The all-important starting point for successful sales-force development is selecting and hiring the right people, the focus of the third chapter objective. The personal characteristics and human qualities found to be most desirable in salespeople are self-confidence, self-motivation, enthusiasm, and a drive to achieve. (For some other desirable qualities in sales personnel, see Figure 21-2.) Many surveys have shown that in nearly every sales force, about 20 percent of the salespeople consistently produce about 80 percent of total sales, while another 10 to 30 percent do not even pay their own way. Among the second group, many are either dismissed or leave the selling field of their own volition. Why do so many people fail at sales? The most often cited reasons are lack of ambition, drive, or desire to succeed; lack of ability to plan and manage one's time; lack of resourcefulness or of "an eye" for sales possibilities; and lack of self-confidence.

ORGANIZING A SALES FORCE

In establishing a sales force to meet its objectives, a firm must decide how large a sales organization it needs and whether to maintain its own salespeople or use an independent sales force. In addition, it must weigh the benefits of a large sales staff against the attendant expenses: the larger the sales staff, the more thoroughly reps can cover a market and the more likely it is that

Selling Pharmaceutical Expertise

Pharmaceutical sales representatives do not actually sell their companies' drugs; they provide physicians with detailed information about their products in the hope that they will prescribe them for their patients. As in other technical sales fields, some special training or expertise is generally a qualification for the job; for example, a pharmaceutical rep may need to have a science major or training in medicine or a related field.

TABLE 21-3	CLASSIFYING SALES POSITIONS

By Type of Customer

Industrial, or business-to-business, sales representative
Institutional or governmental sales agent
Trade sales representative (wholesaling and retailing)

By Type of Employer

Manufacturer's or wholesaler's sales representative
Manufacturer's agent or sales broker (independent)
Retail sales clerk

By Sales Objective

Order getter (a salesperson who uses active, persuasive tactics)
Order taker (e.g., a waiter or a supermarket cashier)
Detailer (e.g., a pharmaceutical sales rep)
Afterseller (e.g., automobile postsale rep)

some salespeople will be able to specialize in particular products or customers. Here we consider the organization of both domestic and global sales forces, the topic of chapter objective four. We look first at the function of independent agents, and then at the in-house sales force.

Independent Agents The use of independent sales agents, whose role we discussed in Chapters 14 and 15, is especially popular with small firms because it saves them the expense of maintaining a full-time sales force and allows them to tie selling expenses directly to sales through the commission system. The drawback to using independent agents is that it limits both the producing firm's control over sales and its ability to respond flexibly and aggressively to market growth. Thus most businesses prefer to have their own sales forces as soon as they grow large enough to afford them.

Consumer goods are also sold by independent agents. For example, the salespeople for Amway, a nutritional products company with thousands of

Figure 21-2
Desirable Qualities in Salespeople

Ambition
Self-discipline
Persistence
Dependability
Initiative
Stability
Thoroughness
Loyalty
Empathy and Tact
Sincerity
Positive mental outlook
Willingness to cooperate

representatives throughout North America, are all independent agents, as are the sales representatives for Avon (see the feature titled "Avon *de Gozaimasu*") and Mary Kay (see "Bottom Line Realities: Mary Kay Sales Reps Are in the Pink"). Throughout the world, **direct selling**, in which independent sales agents sell a product directly to end users, adds up to big business. By some estimates, direct selling in 1990 accounted for over U.S. $35 billion in retail sales made by nearly 9 million people on six continents.

direct selling
Sales of a firm's products by independent agents who sell the product directly to end users.

Company Sales Forces There are three basic models for structuring a company's sales force. Sales management and the sales force can be organized by *geographic region*, by *product line*, or by *market* or *customer type*. Figure 21-3 shows each of these types of organization side by side in one diagram with a few representative titles so you can compare these three organizational structures. Of course, if this were a chart for an actual company that was organized by, say, geographic region, it would have sales managers for an

**Figure 21-3
Structuring a Sales
Force Along
Geographic, Product,
or Market Lines**

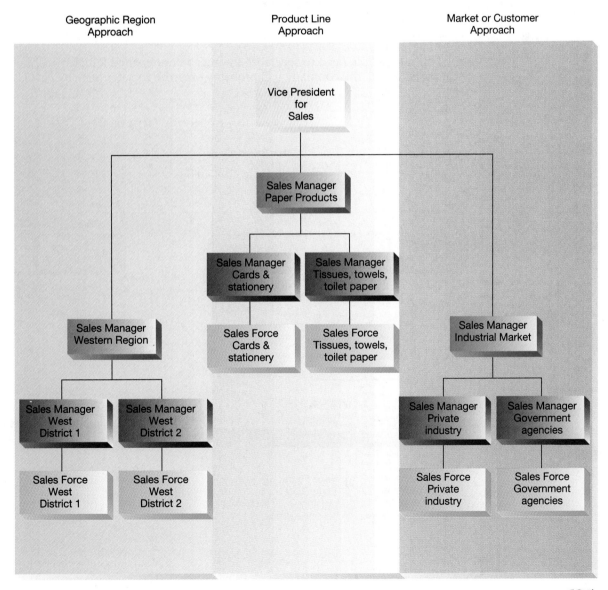

695

eastern region and a western region, with corresponding subordinates for different districts.

A fourth possibility is to organize a sales force by some combination of these three categories. Figure 21-4 shows how a firm making paper, soap, and cosmetic products might organize its sales staff along both product and geographic lines. Factors such as diversity of product line, technical complexity of the product line, and the extent of geographical distribution determine the choice of organizational approach. For example, a company that makes five supercomputers a year may need only a few people to sell its one product line worldwide. IBM, on the other hand, requires a sales force in the thousands, most of whom specialize in certain product lines and sell in certain regions.

To understand these various ways of organizing a sales force, let's look at the models in greater detail. The simplest form of sales force organization is along *geographic lines* (left panel of Figure 21-3). Sales territories can range in size from a few city blocks to an entire province, state, or country. A geographic approach keeps travel times down and turns a sales agent into a territory "manager" who sees customers often and thus can easily cultivate close relationships. However, a geographical organization assumes either that the product line is limited or that it is not so technical as to require more than one salesperson.

Figure 21-4
Combined Product and Geographic Organization of a Sales Force

If salespeople need to specialize in order to understand a highly technical product line, the company will probably organize its sales force by *product*

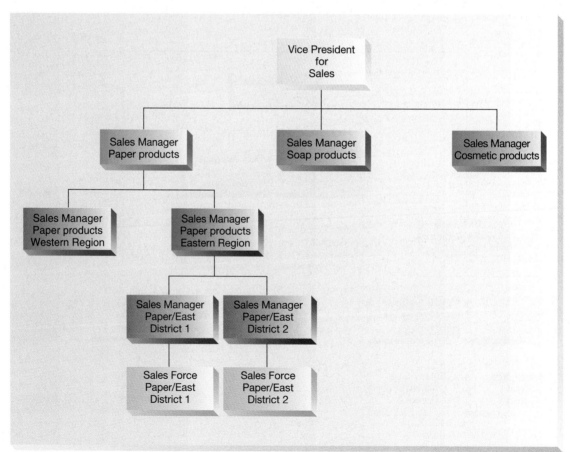

lines (middle panel of Figure 21-3). The advantage of this structure is that salespeople can develop in-depth knowledge about their products; the disadvantage is that they will probably have to cover a larger geographical area. Moreover, if a producer has several product lines, each with its own specialized sales force, different salespeople from the same company may call on the same prospects, perhaps causing customers to feel that their time is being wasted through duplication of selling efforts.

A variation on the product-line organization is an organization structured around specialized *markets* (right panel of Figure 21-3), commonly classed by industry, size, or channels of distribution. In this structure sales personnel sell only to a specific industry or to subdivisions of allied industries. A major advantage of this form of sales specialization is that salespeople get to know market or customer types thoroughly; the disadvantage is that they may have to handle a variety of product lines and cover a much larger geographical base.

A fourth variation, which can only work for large companies, is to organize the sales force by either product line or market and then add a regional breakdown at the level of the individual salesperson. The sales force specializes in a product or market, but within a smaller geographic area (Figure 21-4).

Unisys, a giant in the computer industry, decided to reorganize its sales staff along customer lines when it realized that software buying is no longer the exclusive province of computer departments. The new organization is based on six "clusters": (1) industrial and commercial markets, (2) financial services, (3) communications and airlines markets, (4) the public sector, (5) the federal government, and (6) the defense market. Each of these clusters is further segmented according to the kinds of products it requires. Sales and profit increases have proved that Unisys's decision to reorganize was correct.[5]

Some firms have organized their sales forces along more innovative lines, such as selling teams, technical sales groups, or special task forces. A *selling team* assigned to a specific large account might consist of a sales engineer, a marketing expert, and other specialists needed to handle all customer requirements, from selling through after-sale service.[6] Special *technical sales groups* are assigned in the same manner. And in order to introduce a new product quickly to all accounts or prospects within a given area, an organization may set up *special task forces*. Sometimes such a task force includes the entire sales force, which concentrates on nothing but the one new product. For example, two or three times a year Bell and Howell pulls its entire consumer product sales force off the road for its highly effective "telesell" campaigns, in which salespeople "telesell" key dealers from their homes.

The Global Sales Force Despite variations among countries in such things as income level, stage of development, language, and cultural practices, many of the basic principles of personal selling and sales-force organization apply equally to all nations. The best-managed companies take advantage of this fact and apply their experience worldwide. For example, IBM Italy decided to reorganize its sales force around industry groups instead of territories. When the shift in focus proved highly successful, IBM reorganized its sale forces worldwide along the Italian industry-group lines.

Sometimes, however, differences between markets do require adaptations in sales strategies. A case in point is the cosmetics giant Avon, noted for the success of its personal-selling approach in North America and Europe. When the firm tried to apply the same sales techniques to sales in Japan, however, it initially met with failure. As the feature titled "Avon *de Gozaimasu!*" shows, it took a very new approach to win Japanese market share.

"AVON DE GOZAIMASU!"

In 1968, when Avon wanted to enter the Japanese market, the Japanese government would only permit the company to establish a branch office. Avon executives decided that this branch would run like any other, with the same line of cosmetics that the firm sold in North America and Australia, the same pricing structure, and the same use of representatives in assigned territories selling products door-to-door. Avon ladies began ringing doorbells, announcing "It's Avon (Avon *de gozaimasu*)!"

Five years later, the firm had little to show for its efforts: it had just 2,500 sales representatives (a very small number in relation to the overall population); it had trouble finding new representatives and keeping old ones; and many representatives turned in only small or infrequent orders. To identify the source of the problem, the firm hired George Fields of ASR Research, who found three difficulties. First, the Japanese do not like to have strangers calling on them door-to-door. Second, Japanese women were wary of Avon products because they were not advertised as other (Japanese) cosmetics were. Third, the Avon product did not satisfy Japanese demands for high quality and effectiveness, especially in skin-care products.

Developing new formulations and running some advertising were relatively easy. Considerably harder was rethinking the nature and operations of the sales force that is Avon's lifeblood. One change the company made was to eliminate assigned territories so that salespeople could call on any household; thus the sales reps were often able to deal with people they knew. The company also took a more flexible approach to the hiring and management of salespeople. In the words of Louis Consiglio, an Avon vice president: "Rather than trying to find people who would 'qualify' to be good salespeople, we really opened it up wide and said, 'Why don't you just join this wonderful world of Avon and cosmetics? Buy the products, buy them for yourselves, buy them for your friends. Earn 10% commission, earn 50% commission. Do it your way. Go for the golden ring or just be a nice friendly saleslady." As a result, Avon soon built up a sales force of over 100,000 in Japan.

The next move was to make the reconstituted sales force more profitable. The company realized that it now had three overlapping sales forces, each requiring a different type of management. The first contained true salespersons, and people who would gradually become salespersons; the second group contained customers who had evolved into saleswomen; and the third group consisted of mostly customers. The first group turned in larger and more frequent orders; the third group turned in small, infrequent orders. Avon decided to devote most of its time and training to the women who were anxious to be salespersons and to treat any sales from the other women as a bonus. Like many other successful global businesses, Avon found that it could adapt successfully to local situations and prosper.

OBJECTIVES AND STRATEGIES OF PERSONAL SELLING

Sales objectives, the subject of the fifth objective for this chapter, are often set at the corporate level and expressed in units, cases, or, in the case of services, number of services performed (such as number of cars rented). Corporations set sales objectives in order to meet their profit and return-on-investment (ROI) objectives. A sales objective without a profit objective is of little value—if you don't make a profit, you'll soon have nothing to sell!

Sales Quotas Individual salespeople at various levels are judged by their success or failure at meeting their assigned **sales quota** for a given period of time. This quota encompasses individual objectives that usually specify (1) *units* or *volume* of a product; (2) total *value* or worth in *units of currency*; and sometimes (3) *number of sales calls* to be made. Managers at all levels must remember that objectives should be measurable and include a time frame for achievement. Without sales quotas, there is no way to evaluate the success of either the sales plan or the sales staff.

Communication Objectives Other objectives for the sales force are related to communications. Communication objectives may include providing feedback about customers and information about the competition. Salespeople are also expected to generate the enthusiasm needed to push sales promotions and special merchandising activities through the distribution channels and into retail stores. Some product-line salespeople are expected to join in the ongoing battle to improve the company's products and to acquire more points of distribution and more shelf space in retail stores.

In terms of relationship marketing, the salesperson's ultimate objective—regardless of whether the product is computer chips, satellite glass panels, or refrigerators—is a *satisfactory buying decision*. Customer satisfaction is what establishes long-term relationships and makes customers recommend a company's product to co-workers, family, and friends.

Sales Strategies and Tactics Chapter objective six asks you to distinguish between sales strategies and tactics. A *strategy* is an overall plan for accomplishing objectives; a *tactic* is a specific action taken to advance the strategy.

Planning is as important to sales as it is to marketing. Success in meeting objectives most often comes to those who follow these three steps:

1. Develop a written sales plan to manage sales volume, costs, and profits in such a way as to achieve the required sales volume and profit objectives.

2. Recruit, organize, train, lead, motivate, and manage members of the sales force to accomplish the sales plan's objectives.

3. Decide on specific sales tactics: for example, develop sales assignments, sales literature, and timing schedules.

Because of its link with distribution and retailing, personal selling has some unique strategic characteristics. Whereas advertising is the critical driver of a "pull" strategy, personal selling drives a "push" strategy. Its primary strategic contribution is to get the product into the channel and, particularly, into the stores that will try to sell the product by promoting and displaying it. Because retailers have limited storage space and cannot make money when products sit on shelves, manufacturers know that retailers will make an effort to sell a product they've bought to recoup their costs and make a profit.

Individual sales representatives use a variety of sales tactics. In the *feature-advantage-benefit (FAB)* approach, salespeople build their presentations around *features*, the characteristics of a product or service; *advantages*, the way

sales quota
The sales objective for an individual salesperson within a given period of time; usually expressed in units or volume of product and in value or units of currency, but may also be expressed in number of sales calls to be made.

699
PERSONAL SELLING

the features work or what they do better than competing products; and *benefits*, the advantages offered to the prospect by the features.

Selling to organizational buyers often has some peculiar dimensions. For one thing, whereas persuasion is basic to most selling, selling to large institutions often requires considerable managerial and interpersonal skills. Often the salesperson must work out complex *negotiations* that involve devising partnerships and concession strategies among different groups within the organization before a formal sales presentation is even made.[7]

The cornerstone of good relationships with all customers is a *nonmanipulative* sales strategy. Most successful salespeople know that this approach is the best way to build mutual respect between buyer and seller and that it is in line with quality programs and the thrust toward customer satisfaction that have been adopted by many companies around the world.

MANAGING A SALES FORCE

Good communication between sales managers and members of the sales force is essential to maintaining morale and motivation. One-on-one consultations, sales meetings, sales contests, telephone calls, newsletters, and memos are among the many techniques that sales managers use to keep open the lines of communication with their salespeople. Managers and sales staff are increasingly using computer software and electronic data interchange services such as those offered in the GE ad in Exhibit 21-3 to communicate with one another and to manage leads, calls, and follow-up strategies as well as corporate reporting systems.

The major issues involved in sales management—the topic of the seventh chapter objective—are compensation, motivation, training, and salesforce monitoring and evaluating. We discuss each of these in turn.

Compensation A firm's compensation policies play a crucial role in recruiting and selecting sales people and are vital for motivating and holding on to top performers.[8] The money salespeople earn depends on the following factors: (1) the type of selling area; (2) the salespeople's educational background and skill level; (3) the country, region, or area in which they work; (4) their level of experience; (5) what competitors are paying; and (6) employers' compensation plans. In some industries experienced salespeople can earn $100,000 or more per year.

Compensation is often lower in retail operations, where it is important to minimize labor costs. In discount stores particularly, where gross margins are relatively low, both the number of salespeople and their pay are kept to the absolute minimum. (Now you know why it's so difficult to find someone to wait on you when you shop at these stores.) Management at most large retail chains regards sales jobs as "revolving doors." Employees come and go as managers fill positions that take relatively little time and effort to learn. As one manager notes: "We offer just a job—a way for people to earn some extra money. It's not a career." Some well-known large retail chains, however, do offer excellent compensation plans, especially when personal selling is considered essential. Wal-Mart rates very high among retailers for its outstanding concern for employees, all of whom participate in generous profit-sharing and stock-purchase plans.

There are three general compensation plans in selling. Under the **straight-salary** plan, the salesperson is paid a fixed annual salary, although an annual bonus based on the company's overall performance may also be paid. The **straight-commission** plan pays the employee either a fixed or a variable percent of his or her actual sales. In other words, the more salespeople on straight commission sell, the more they earn.

straight salary
A form of sales compensation in which sales personnel are paid a fixed salary regardless of the volume of sales they achieve plus, sometimes, an annual bonus.

straight commission
A form of sales compensation in which a salesperson's total income is a fixed or variable percentage of his or her total sales.

**Exhibit 21-3
Moving the Sales
Force onto the
Electronic Highway**

*Personal selling
involves more than
a sales pitch and a
handshake. In
today's high-tech
marketplace sales
representatives
need productivity
tools, such as infor-
mation manage-
ment systems, to
increase their
efficiency.*

PERSONAL
SELLING

The third method of sales compensation is a combination of the first and second methods. Called the *combination salary-and-commission* approach, it is the most widely used. In fact, nearly three-fourths of all North American companies use some form of this plan. A combination plan provides a fixed base salary plus a commission or bonus that is directly related to the employee's sales or profits. In the case of a variable commission, the percentage will change (generally increasing) the more one sells. For example, a person may receive 10 percent on sales up to $25,000 and 12 percent on sales over $25,000. Often commission is paid only on sales above a certain minimum level.

Each of these plans has advantages and drawbacks. The greater the fixed-salary portion of a salesperson's compensation, the more secure his or her income is and the more likely that this person will be able to keep clients abreast of new product developments. On the other hand, the greater the commission portion, the more motivated he or she may be to perform well—and the more potential for increasing income, but the attention span may be focused only on those products which perform well in terms of bonuses for the salesperson. In addition to the earnings from salary and/or commissions, sales personnel are generally reimbursed for travel and entertainment expenses they incur in the line of business. Many firms also provide their sales force with fringe benefits such as medical plans, profit sharing, and the use of a company car (which they may also use for personal purposes). Some companies offer incentive programs that give salespeople the chance to earn extra cash, merchandise, or expense-paid trips.

Motivation Incentive programs are designed to motivate salespeople to produce the highest possible level of sales. Motivation, of course, is something within an individual—an idea, desire, wish, or need—that incites action. Managers can stimulate motivation by learning each salesperson's particular needs, wants, and interests. For example, some salespeople are motivated by the opportunity to advance into a management position. Some care more about raises and frequent bonuses. Others desire a pleasant working environment and occasional recognition of their efforts. Still others are more interested in job security or in trips to exotic places. To the degree that it is possible in a given company, a good manager will identify the varying needs and interests in the sales force and attempt to match them with appropriate incentives.

All salespeople like to be praised. Recognition of good performance, in fact, is key to generating the enthusiasm essential to an effective sales force. As we will see in the discussion of Mary Kay Cosmetics at the end of the chapter, singling out highly successful sales representatives at special awards ceremonies is one of the most effective motivators in a **sales-incentive program,** which normally also includes rewarding high sales performance with prizes such as cash bonuses, merchandise gifts, and, increasingly, free trips.

Free trips to such exotic places as Tangier, Sydney, Bangkok, Moscow, and Marrakesh now account for 40 percent of all sales incentives and have created a $2.3-billion-a-year business. More than 3 million North Americans annually enjoy this kind of incentive travel, for which corporations spend about $2,000 per winner ($4000 for a winner and spouse). Free trips like the one described in "A Trip to Remember" are thought to generate a 20 percent increase in sales. Since only half of this increase goes to pay for the incentive programs, companies that offer them come out well ahead.[9]

sales-incentive program
A system of motivating salespeople to achieve record sales by offering them praise and recognition as well as such rewards as cash bonuses, merchandise, and free trips.

BEHIND THE SCENES

A TRIP TO REMEMBER

The CEO of an insurance company wanted to devise a truly spectacular incentive program for his sales agents. He decided to reward his top salespeople with a five-day trip to Hong Kong and a surprise sidetrip to China. The trip took an enormous amount of planning and cost the company $600,000, but it was a great success.[10]

Based on earlier contests, the CEO anticipated that from among a combined sales force of 11,000 brokers and agents, about 130 winners would achieve the goal of earning between $40,000 and $150,000 in commissions from new accounts. Counting spouses and a small group of company executives, he expected that some 300 people would make the trip.

Starting a year and a half ahead of time, an independent meeting planner designed the trip, striking deals with United and Cathay Pacific to fly two groups, one from Seattle and one from San Francisco. Next, the travel broker had to find a modern hotel in Hong Kong that fronted on the water, as well as a company to handle the local entertainment and restaurant arrangements.

A year before the trip, a company vice president flew to Hong Kong to evaluate the suggested itinerary, accommodations, entertainment activities, and restaurants. At about the same time, the insurance company launched an intense campaign to promote the contest. The entire sales force received brochures about Hong Kong and a series of small gifts, including Chinese fans, wind chimes, chopsticks, and fortune cookies (all of which prophesied a trip to the Far East!). Each month, two newsletters were mailed to salespeople's homes, carrying news about the event to the sales representatives' families. Headquarters staff frequently called agents and brokers around the country to keep the excitement high. Some 135 winners, who collectively sold more than $1 billion in new policies, eventually qualified.

On the fourteen-and-a-half-hour flight a violinist wandered up and down the airplane's aisles serenading the winners; four movies were shown; and games of bingo and Let's Make a Deal were piped over the public address system offering sixty-five prizes ranging from Sony Walkmans to bottles of wine. Once ensconced in the Hong Kong hotel, each couple received a new gift every day—such as a porcelain tea set, a bottle of Grand Marnier, and embroidered Chinese silk robes. Daily entertainment included a private fashion show, a sampan tour, a tram ride 1,308 feet up to the top of Victoria Peak, and tours of Hong Kong's fabled jewelry markets and tailor shops. The surprise trip to China carried the group across the South China Sea by jetfoil to the Chinese province of Zhongshan.

At one banquet the group watched lion dances. The final night was a black-tie president's dinner at which the top fifteen sales reps were awarded Baccarat crystal sculptures. The top five winners and their spouses were given a choice of fur coats for the women and gold-and-diamond Rolex watches for the men, along with enough cash to cover the import duties. When the group left for home, each winner carried a brass-bound album containing eighty photographs taken throughout the trip. Video tapes arrived two weeks later. For this company's star salespeople, it was a trip to remember.

Training Many sales failures can be avoided with proper training. The amount of time and money allocated to developing training programs will depend on the nature of the firm's business, its specific training needs, and company policy. It can cost a firm anywhere from $10,000 to $100,000 (including salary) to put a new industrial-products salesperson through an intensive orientation program that may last as long as thirteen weeks.

Worldwide Selling

Training for global sales positions includes practices unique to a particular country. In Japan, for example, you must present your business card first to the most senior person, and you must read the card given you in exchange carefully lest you insult the giver.

In addition to training in sales, salespeople working in technical areas may also need technical or scientific degrees. Salespeople who are product engineers or designers, for example, are often able to relate to their customers more as consultants than as salespersons. This is excellent for relationship building. At a bare minimum, every business-to-business salesperson needs to know the product line, the industry, and the consumer needs that drive sales.

In contrast, new salespeople at retail stores often receive as little as two days' "training," which is largely aimed at teaching them to write up orders and use the cash register. Recently, however, in an effort to meet customer demand for more effective service, a number of department, appliance, and jewelry stores have increased the length and sophistication of their training programs.

Sales-force training and development in most business firms is normally carried out at three levels: (1) initial indoctrination and training, (2) advanced continuing training, and (3) management-development training. The *initial indoctrination* and training stage normally covers four major areas:

◆ Knowledge of the company, its products, policies, and promotional-support activities

◆ Knowledge of the marketing environment and the competition

◆ Fundamental selling skills

◆ Principles of time and territory management

Advanced continuing training programs normally provide refresher training in the same areas, but the training is more sophisticated, personalized, and problem-centered.

Management-development training programs seek to perfect selling skills, develop teaching and coaching skills, facilitate a change in viewpoint from salesperson to manager, and develop administrative, decision-making, and leadership skills. Sales training may take place at company facilities, in the field, or at educational institutions. In some cases, senior salespeople and/or sales managers serve as instructors; in other cases, professional consultants and educators are called in.

Monitoring and Evaluating In order to motivate sales personnel, sales managers need to know just what their staff is doing and how well things are going. To keep managers abreast of such information, many companies require salespeople to fill out daily, weekly, monthly, quarterly, or yearly reports or summaries of their activities. Sales agents are also responsible for conveying customer comments and/or suggestions to the home office.

Among the most common types of reports completed by sales representatives are *quantitative reports*, such as work plans of each day's scheduled activities, and daily or weekly *call reports* that chronicle actual activities for the time period covered. By comparing these two types of reports, managers can judge how effectively salespeople are sticking to plans. Sales staff or sales managers may also be required to summarize the information they receive in these daily and weekly reports in the form of monthly, quarterly, or semiannual reports. In addition, some companies require *qualitative reports*—the sales representative's personal assessments of such things as customer reactions to a new product or marketing campaign.

Managers' periodic assessments of the overall performance of their sales staff—generally performed on an annual basis—are both quantitative and qualitative. Besides reviewing and summarizing specific sales figures assembled for shorter periods, managers must compare each salesperson's performance with the objectives the individual has set for him- or herself for the period of time under consideration. Managers may also compare a salesperson's current performance with his or her performance the preceding year or with the performance of other salespeople in similar settings. Managers must also take stock of such subjective elements as a salesperson's attitude, appearance, communications skills, and product knowledge. All of these judgments will weigh in the manager's decision to recommend a raise, a promotion, a disciplinary warning, or additional training. Training courses should not be viewed as either purely remedial or as a perk for those who have performed splendidly well. Instead, selection should be made with a view to raising the median level. Those personnel who are "average" but have some potential could be encouraged through further training to develop skills which then allow them to outperform their peers and raise total aggregate sales for the company as a whole.

BOTTOM LINE REALITIES

MARY KAY SALES REPS ARE IN THE PINK[11]

For Mary Kay Ash, the brilliant founder of Mary Kay Cosmetics, selling is more than a job—it's a relationship. Ash has built a highly successful organization on the strengths of personal selling—the personal touch, direct interaction, immediate feedback, and the nurturing of long-term relationships both within the company and between sales representatives and their customers.

Twenty-five years of successfully selling products for a variety of firms had left Mary Kay Ash feeling frustrated and discriminated against as "a woman in a man's job." These experiences convinced her that there had to be a better way to organize and manage a sales force, one built on communication and the power of employee recognition.

It was a gamble. Few believed it was possible to build a successful company

with a cadre of housewives who had little business experience and virtually no sales training. But it was a gamble that paid off big: Mary Kay Cosmetics went from sales of $198,000 in 1963 to over

$600 million in 1993, and the company has been hailed as an "opportunity-generating machine" by John Kotter, Matsushita Professor of Leadership at the Harvard Business School.

Recognition Builds Success at Mary Kay

Whether a "consultant" given a first award for record sales or a sales director rewarded for turning hardworking waitresses or homemakers into high-earning directors, every Mary Kay agent at the company's annual convention radiates the pleasure of being recognized as a successful businessperson. Pink Cadillacs may seem a bit silly to you, but they're secondary to that recognition—that admiration, that confirmation that a sales representative is a winner. [Alan Farnham, "Mary Kay's Lessons in Leadership," Fortune, 9/20/93, 68–77.]

The Body Shop*

1. Describe the "selling process" that Body Shop sales people use. How is this different from that of most sales techniques?

2. What are the distinguishing characteristics of The Body Shop's method of sales management?

Harley-Davidson

1. Describe Harley's sales follow-up procedures.

2. How can Harley sales people engage in relationship marketing?

The Millennium Power System

1. In what type of selling might Millennium salespersons engage?

2. Distinguish between national account representatives and other sales people.

*The three cases at the back of the book—"The Body Shop," "Harley-Davidson," and "The Millennium Power System"—illustrate topics discussed in all chapters of this book. Your instructor will tell you when to read a particular case and when to answer the discussion questions on it that appear at the end of each chapter.

Reward and Recognition

A critical issue for sales managers is motivating their sales force or their distributors. There are monetary and non-monetary methods to motivate people. An entire industry exists to help sales managers and human resource professionals deal with this issue. This industry is referred to by a number of names. Terms such as specialty promotion, incentives, and awards and rewards can all be used to describe the business of recognizing and motivating sales representatives.

Using incentives to recognize outstanding sales performance has become big business. This industry, however, is experiencing a slight slump. Since the last recession and the weak recovery, corporate budgets for incentive programs have not returned to the levels reached in the early eighties. No longer do sales people see cars or exotic trips in a sales force contest or trade promotion designed to stimulate sales revenue.

At the Incentives 94 show in Toronto, some of the items displayed by suppliers of awards and rewards are not as glamorous as they once were. How about a $5 plastic bubble watch embossed with a company logo? Has this replaced the once envied gold watch for loyal employees?

The most popular items used in incentive programs these days are computer games or pool tables. Bell Canada and other large corporations are expanding the use of incentive gifts. They are no longer only used for sales representatives or distributors. They are used in employee motivation programs, replacing annual raises. Motivation programs consist of a scheme where employees can earn points towards a pre-selected range of gifts. Items such as a cordless drill may find their way into a corporate catalogue.

Incentive gifts can be used to reward outstanding achievement. One of the most enduring and popular items used by Canadian corporations is still the lapel pin.

709

QUESTIONS

1. Corporations spend thousands of dollars in purchasing incentive items. How do these items motivate a sales force?
2. How can a sales manager evaluate the success of an incentive program?
3. What other methods can a sales manager use to motivate a sales force or a dealer network?

Source: This case was prepared by Deborah Andrus and is based on the *Venture* series episode "Incentives 94," which was first broadcast on March 13, 1994.

● Chapter 22

Leading the Marketing Effort

OBJECTIVES

AFTER COMPLETING THIS CHAPTER, YOU SHOULD BE ABLE TO:

1
IDENTIFY THE CRITICAL LEADERSHIP RESPONSIBILITIES OF A MARKETING MANAGER

2
DISCUSS THE USE OF SCHEDULING AND TIMING IN MARKETING PLANNING

3
UNDERSTAND THE DIFFERENCE BETWEEN REENGINEERING AND BUSINESS AS USUAL

4
DESCRIBE HOW MANAGERS CONTROL MARKETING OPERATIONS THROUGH BUDGETING AND THROUGH A FOCUS ON PROFITS AND PROFITABILITY

5
IDENTIFY AND DISCUSS THE MAJOR METHODS FOR EVALUATING THE EFFECTIVENESS AND EFFICIENCY OF MARKETING OPERATIONS, INCLUDING THE MARKETING AUDIT

6
UNDERSTAND THE IMPLICATIONS OF GLOBAL MARKETING FOR MARKETING LEADERSHIP

THINK ABOUT IT!

ULTRASOFTS WERE ULTRA-EXPENSIVE

Having a great idea for a product is no guarantee of success. Poor planning and management can kill a product before it is able to establish itself in the market, as Weyerhaeuser learned to its sorrow when it tried to enter the baby diaper market with UltraSofts.[1] Weyerhaeuser was convinced that it could take on Procter & Gamble and Kimberly-Clark with a premium diaper that had a unique clothlike cover instead of the plastic one typical of the leading premium brands.

UltraSofts, priced 10 percent below the competition, got off to a good start: surveys showed that consumers preferred UltraSofts by two to one over the leading brands. Then manufacturing problems arose, forcing Weyerhaeuser to increase its price to retailers by 22 percent. With the price hike, consumers lost interest. Rather than risk the investment necessary to fix its manufacturing problems, Weyerhaeuser chose to pull UltraSofts from the market. Clearly, the company's marketing plan underestimated manufacturing and marketing realities—investment necessary to produce the diaper efficiently and the need to price the product according to consumers' willingness to pay. Do you think they did enough to communicate the advantages of their brand? ■

management
The process of achieving a company's desired goals through the most efficient use of resources and strategies, requiring managers to plan, organize, implement, lead, control, and evaluate all aspects of the process.

After the marketing vision, mission, and objective comes action, and action entails **management,** the process of achieving a company's goals through the most efficient use of resources and strategies. Management involves the functions of planning, organization, implementation, leadership, control, and evaluation. Throughout this book, beginning with Chapter 4 on the marketing plan, we've discussed the first three of these functions in some detail. In this chapter we turn to the last three.

We cannot repeat too often that the challenge to marketers today is to create a mutually beneficial relationship with their customers. Within this relationship, customers must be satisfied and marketers must make a profit. Responsible and responsive leadership guides marketing activity, and effective methods of control and evaluation give support to every marketing function.

LEADING ●

The responsibility for marketing programs lies with management. Successful marketing managers are highly involved to create value for customers. A product's features, its cost, the channels of distribution, and the communications about the product are all important elements of this effort. As you just saw in the opening story, however, brilliant ideas are worthless without the right follow-through. Successful marketers both do things right (efficiency) and do the right things (effectiveness). Specifically, they research the market to stay on top of changing customer and marketplace needs, operate under the future concept of marketing, practice a strategy of stretch and leverage, and provide focus and direction for the firm's marketing activities. These are the critical leadership responsibilities referred to in this chapter's first objective.

CHANGING CUSTOMER NEEDS

Throughout this book, we have talked about the importance of meeting customer needs. The successful marketing manager is one who understands what people want and what they are willing to pay for it. This understanding is often the result of a "gut instinct" based on years of experience in a market. But savvy managers verify their instincts with market research.

For example, when Philips introduced a line of pastel-tinted light bulbs in 1989, many in the marketing community wondered if there was a market in North America for such a product. The pastel bulbs, which are designed to enhance a room's color scheme, were a big hit for Philips in England, and the firm's management thought that they would capture the imagination of

North American consumers, too. About 95 percent of American women interviewed in focus groups said that they would buy the product. A year after the pastel bulbs were launched, they accounted for 8 percent of the company's sales in a category in which decorative bulbs have traditionally been responsible for only 7 percent of all consumer sales.[2] Thus instinct blended with market research and experience enabled Philips to transfer a European success to the United States.

Managers need to identify changing customer needs early in order to get a jump on the competition. For example, today's consumers are increasingly demanding multipurpose products: combination shampoo-conditioners, fabric softener sheets that contain stain resisters, combination allergy and sinus formulations, disposable razors with built-in strips that release moisturizers. These combination products create new ways to differentiate products while giving consumers more convenience.

Consumers are not the only buyers demanding changes. Industrial customers also find their needs changing. For example, rising fuel prices have led many companies to demand more fuel-efficient equipment and truckers and airlines to demand vehicles that get better mileage. Environmental concerns are also reshaping industrial demand. Airlines need planes that will meet the more stringent noise pollution standards being set in world markets.

CHANGING MARKETPLACE NEEDS

We have already discussed market dynamics in terms not only of buyer and supplier power but also substitutes and the threat of new entrants in the market. Technological convergance was discussed earlier in Chapter 20 and shows, for example, how telephone, television, and computer technology are converging to bring new products to the consumer. Sometimes an entire market changes. When this happens, the marketing plan has to be changed as well. Markets are continually evolving, and product managers today need not only a vision of the marketplace but also the flexibility to adapt to changing opportunities and threats. The alternative is to be left behind.

Fashion products are notoriously vulnerable to fast changes in the market. L.A. Gear, for example, made its reputation as a trend-setter—a hard position to maintain. Known for its pastel sneakers, silver and gold lamé workout shoes, fluorescent fashions, and other products geared to young teens, the company lost market share rapidly when this fickle market latched onto other trends. Now management is trying to make L.A. Gear America's number-one family brand in clothing and fashion watches as well as athletic footwear. This is a tricky transition that requires managers to come up with products that attract adult men and women, while at the same time continuing to create new styles that appeal to teenagers. The company also intends to make an impact overseas. Analysts wonder if it is possible for L.A. Gear to sell adult men's athletic shoes without destroying its trendy image among adolescents—and simultaneously go global.

IMPLEMENTING THE FUTURE CONCEPT OF MARKETING

Since Chapter 1, you have been reading about the future concept of marketing—the shift in focus from sales to the creation of a mutually beneficial relationship between marketer and buyer. This is, you might agree, a wonderful concept, but does it work? Is anybody actually using it? The answer is definitely yes. Even companies in mature industries with well established practices are gaining competitive advantage by implementing this exciting new concept of marketing.

Relationship Marketing

Spar Aerospace, maker of the Canadarm, is one of many companies that have embraced the concept of relationship marketing.

Recently, one of the authors of this book bought a new Saturn. Under the old marketing approach, the name of the game at an auto dealership was to maximize profitability by selling options and negotiating price. Most consumers found all these negotiations an ordeal. Saturn decided to reinvent automobile marketing by establishing a fixed-price policy and putting salespeople on straight salary instead of commission. In fact, Saturn hired people without prior experience in auto sales to ensure a fresh approach.

Because they were operating with fixed margins, dealers were able to offer services that until then only luxury automobile dealers had provided. The author's dealer, for instance, offered free oil changes for the life of the car, a free car wash with every oil change, and free roadside towing service in the event of a breakdown. One particularly creative element all Saturn dealers offer is a thirty-day money-back guarantee if the customer does not like the car for any reason. This return policy is a creative way of strengthening the word-of-mouth support for the product—it practically guarantees that everyone driving a Saturn likes the car and will endorse it to others.

When the author picked up his new Saturn, the salesperson sat down with him and went over all of the car's mechanical and operating features. The service manager introduced himself and outlined the Saturn service schedule and fees, the dealer manager introduced himself, and then the entire staff of the dealership came out and serenaded the author and welcomed him to the Saturn family. In a grand finale, the salesperson handed the author a huge bouquet of flowers and rode with him to the gas station across the

Saturn Salutes All Members of the Family

Saturn purchasers keep reporting warm and friendly treatment by Saturn dealers. Do you suppose that instead of flowers the dealer presented this family with a box of Kibbles 'N' Bits?

street, where he filled the car with gas and wished the new owner godspeed! The author was enchanted.

Early results indicate that Saturn has attracted an enthusiastic and loyal customer group, but the company cannot afford to get complacent because the automobile market is intensely competitive. Already other dealerships are copying some of Saturn's innovations. And while Saturn's product is attractive, it is far from perfect. Since the line was introduced in 1991, cars have been recalled several times for defects. Moreover, although the author has a number of ideas for improving the car, he has never been contacted by the company. This is perhaps the Achilles' heel of Saturn's marketing effort. The company has done a superb job of *conquest marketing*, (attracting new customers) but may not understand aftermarketing; that is, staying in touch with customers after a sale to ensure customers' continuing satisfaction.

STRATEGY AS STRETCH AND LEVERAGE

In Chapter 4 we outlined the basic elements of marketing strategy and the marketing plan. We emphasized the importance of strategy as fit—to the opportunities and threats in the marketing environment, and to the strengths and weaknesses of the company. Fit is an important element of strategy, but it is not enough.[3] Really successful companies practice the strategic discipline of **stretch**, meaning they are willing to adopt goals that open a gap between the company's resources and its aspirations. You may have noticed that truly successful organizations (and people) have ambitions out of line with their present resources. The discipline of stretch encourages companies to come up with exciting new ways of creating value for customers.

One of the critical tasks of management is to provide leadership and vision for their organizations. No company can succeed by simply going to customers, asking them what they want, writing down their answers, and going back to the shop and producing what they asked for. Customers often don't know exactly what they want until you give it to them. One of the biggest failures in the history of marketing was the Edsel, launched by Ford in the 1960s. This new mid-sized car was the result of a product-development program that, at the time, was the largest single marketing research effort in the history of marketing.

As we pointed out in Chapter 1, the future concept of marketing has moved beyond a simple customer focus to a focus on the entire way of doing business. True, successful firms are customer driven, but they are led by executives who have not abdicated their responsibility for surprising and delighting customers with innovations they might not think of asking for but realize

stretch
The willingness to adopt goals that open a gap between the company's current capability and its aspirations.

they want when they are presented to them. Marketers must listen to customers carefully to find out what they really want, what is important to them. The company that practices the future concept of marketing knows that this information is available to everyone who has contact with customers. The tasks of management are to get this information, process it, and then act on it in ways that will delight customers.

leverage
Getting the best possible results from available resources.

The successful firm also needs a strategy that is based on **leverage**, or taking every advantage of available resources to get the best possible results. Leverage makes the difference between the successful firm and the less successful firm. The firm that spends wisely and creatively to create value will win.

Consider manufacturing. Many manufacturing firms want to be the low-cost producers in their category. The question is how to achieve and maintain this position. For example, both GM and Caterpillar invested in upgrading their manufacturing systems in recent years with the objective of becoming the low-cost/high-quality producer in their respective product categories. GM spent billions on an ill-fated effort to upgrade through automation. The company threw cash at the problem in an approach that experts agree was simple-minded and wasteful. GM continued to lose market share and operate at a deficit.

Caterpillar, in contrast, was careful not to overautomate its factories when it set itself the objective of being the low-cost/high-quality leader in earth-moving equipment. Instead, it leveraged its physical plant, equipment, and people. After it spent $2 billion on a production system it calls "the factory with a future," Caterpillar achieved world leadership in the production of earth-moving equipment.

In the 1980s Cat's archrival, Komatsu of Japan, announced its aspiration to surpass Caterpillar. One of Komatsu's first moves to try to accomplish this objective was to form a joint venture with Dresser Industries in the United States. It looked like a great fit, but Komatsu's management found that it was unable to achieve the results it had expected from the joint venture. While Cat successfully leveraged its skills and resources, Komatsu was unsuccessful in achieving any leverage by teaming up with Dresser. Today Caterpillar is stronger than ever, and Komatsu has backed off, admitting that it cannot succeed in direct competition with Cat.

One of the most powerful forms of marketing leverage is choosing to serve customers who generate the most returns and contribute to long-term growth. There is a big difference between *switchable customers*—those who are legitimately unhappy with their current brands—and happy and loyal customers. Acquisition costs for switchable customers are only one-tenth to one-fifth as high as the costs of acquiring loyal customers. When targeting, companies need to differentiate between the garage sale switchers, who always go to the cheapest source, and the customers who are looking for more value.[4]

PROVIDING FOCUS AND DIRECTION

Marketing executives incorporate the results of their research and analysis into a vision of the company that provides focus for the activities of the firm's employees and guides managers in setting objectives and strategies. Without a clear vision, a company may drift and squander its resources. Xerox, for example, lost its product vision in the 1980s when, seduced by the go-go atmosphere of that decade, it decided to pour resources into real estate investments and financial services. It apparently did not occur to Xerox managers that neither was a core competency of the company. A clearer vision would have led Xerox to create competitive advantage in business areas that fit its focus—such as the low-end small-volume copier market. Instead the company floun-

Partnering in Business-to-Business Relationships

Marketing-concept businesses are beginning to develop new kinds of relationships, not just with their customers but with their suppliers. Betz Laboratories engineers and managers work in close partnership with Allied Signal's staff, going through every inch of each plant to make sure that Betz chemicals do their job of keeping Allied pipes unclogged and machinery free of corrosion. At "Motorola University" suppliers to this electronic giant learn Motorola's TQM techniques, including cycle time reduction and customer satisfaction. [Myron Magnet, "The New Golden Rule of Business," Fortune, 2/21/94, 60–64.]

dered in businesses its managers knew nothing about. Today, under new leadership, Xerox has abandoned its ill-fated diversification into real estate and financial services and has returned to its origins by focusing on positioning itself as *the* document company.

Communicating and Coordinating   A clear vision is of no use unless it is communicated to and carried out by the firm's employees at all levels. "Nothing great was ever achieved without enthusiasm," wrote philosopher Ralph Waldo Emerson. The enthusiasm so crucial to success in business is grounded in motivation and a shared sense of vision and direction. Thus one of the critical leadership responsibilities of a marketing manager is to communicate a clear vision to employees, motivate them, and coordinate working relationships among top management, the in-house marketing staff, engineers, buyers, the sales force, outside specialists, suppliers and vendors, distributors, and retailers.

Without effective communication and coordination, people and departments lose sight of their roles within the organization and tend to pursue their own special interests—often at the expense of organizational goals. One of the biggest communication problems is ambiguity. An unclear memo from top management, for example, can lead lower-level mangers to insist upon different interpretations and therefore pursue conflicting activities under what they think is its direction. Marketing coordination depends on cooperation, so such a short-circuit in communication flow can derail an entire marketing plan.

One of the most important—and stressful—working relationships is between "inside" marketing and "outside" marketing or salespeople. When these two groups engage in a tug-of-war for resources and bigger shares of the marketing budget, it is usually because of a failure of communication.

The heart of coordination is managing the information flow from those who know to those who need to know. In many organizations the sales force would be more effective if it had more quantitative data and more information about the products, the competition, and the customer—all of which product (inside) managers amass and include in their marketing plans. Table 22-1 offers some suggestions on how inside managers can better communicate this information to salespeople. Conversely, inside marketers are missing out on a major source of information about customers and competitors if they do not tap the insights of the field sales force, the organization's "eyes and ears."

Decision Making   Communication and coordination are simplified when there is a clear delineation of decision-making responsibilities. Managers have to figure out where their responsibilities end and where the tasks of specialists begin. Advertising agencies, for example, have horror stories about marketing managers who want to write headlines and design logos. Most good managers know their time is better spent making the crucial go/no go decisions than in taking over the work of specialists hired for their unique talents. If the work isn't acceptable, then the proper management decision is to send the specialists back to do it over or to find new specialists.

Scheduling and Timing   In order to coordinate marketing activities, managers need to decide which activities to undertake and in what sequence—the topic of the second chapter objective. *Timing*—figuring out the ideal moment to implement a marketing strategy—is often a critical factor. For example, if marketers run ads for a new product before they issue public relations news releases, fewer of the media will use the releases because the advertising has made the new-product announcement "old news."

To handle the complex and intertwined nature of marketing activities, product managers rely on **flow charts,** like the *PERT* (Program Evaluation and Review Technique), which map the flow of activities in terms of what can start when, how much time is needed for the completion of each, and what must be completed before another activity can take place. PERT charts may also incorporate CPM (the critical-path method), which determines the minimum time for completing the program by identifying those activities that can hold up the project if not completed on schedule.

flow charts
Scheduling techniques that map out when critical activities start and finish, the amount of time needed to accomplish each, and the order in which each must be completed.

TABLE 22-1	HOW TO KEEP THE SALES FORCE INFORMED

- Prepare a manual that is sales and marketing oriented, listing features, benefits, pricing, and cross-selling opportunities (for example, selling financing services or alarm systems to new- and used-car buyers).

- Develop a comparison of your products with those of the competition.

- Formulate customer profiles for each product, including demographic and psychographic characteristics.

- Build a historic sales database (accounts opened and closed, dollar values of accounts). Using statistical techniques, project the historical data into the future and work directly with sales management to adjust these projections to fit the organization's objectives.

- Participate directly in sales and product-knowledge training sessions. The feedback received can be invaluable for formulating future product strategies.

Source: Adapted from Carl R. Knoch, "How Product Managers Can Help Sales Force," *Bank Marketing,* March 1989, p. 46.

Some products are seasonal; others have weekly sales peaks. Marketing activities should be scheduled with these fluctuations in mind. For example, advertising for seasonal products should begin before the selling season and continue as long as buying remains strong. Chemlawn, a lawn-care service, does most of its advertising in late winter and early spring, knowing that most of the money spent on lawn care is spent from May through August.

For products that have weekly sales peaks, marketing communications must be timed closer to the purchase point. Fast-food restaurants advertise heavily on radio during evening rush hours, when many people are driving home from work. KFC, knowing that roughly two-thirds of all carry-out fried chicken is bought on weekends, advertises heavily on Fridays and Saturdays.

Speed to Market   To gain competitive advantage, many companies are trying to shorten the amount of time it takes to respond to customer and marketplace changes, particularly in the development of new products. Speed-to-market can be risky. Many observers raised questions about Apple Computer's management when the company introduced its long-awaited Newton Message Pad. According to Stewart Alsop of *Info World*, Apple "delivered the first units with bugs, didn't build any inventory before introduction, [and delayed in delivering] key components of the system . . . all suggesting that it rushed the product to market."[5]

Nevertheless, it is often possible to reduce the amount of time a product spends in development, thereby making profits available earlier in the product's life cycle. The Yankee Group, a consulting firm that specializes in speed-to-market as a corporate strategy, emphasizes the relationship between speed and the product life cycle. The chart in Figure 22-1 illustrates how marketers implementing a speed-to-market philosophy can increase profitability by shrinking the unprofitable developmental period at the beginning of the product life cycle. As you can see, the speed-to-market program shifts the sales curve of the product life cycle to the left, cutting the time required to develop and launch a product. This program makes it possible to pursue projects that might otherwise have been rejected as too costly and time-consuming to develop.

REENGINEERING THE CORPORATION

Reengineering, a concept popularized by Michael Hammer and James Champy,[6] means beginning again. As chapter objective three notes, it means rejecting conventional wisdom and the assumptions of the past—"business as usual"— in favor of searching for new ways of organizing work. For example, a *work*

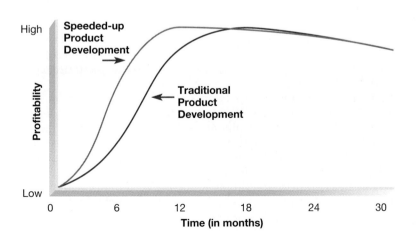

Figure 22-1
Impact of Speed to Market on Profitability

Notice that the speeded-up product-development process represented by the left-hand curve starts at the same point in time that traditional product development starts but proceeds more rapidly, reaching the point of maximum product profitability some six months before the traditional process would. Thus the speeded-up process can greatly reduce the amount of time during which a new product is not profitable for a company.

unit may become a *process team*, a group of workers who together complete a whole piece of work. The change to process teams is usually accompanied by a change in job content from simple tasks to multidimensional work. People's job roles change from simply following orders to devising and regulating their own work procedures. Performance measures shift from activity to results, and advancement criteria go from being tied to performance to being anchored to ability. Management changes from supervision to coaching, and organizational structures from hierarchical to flat. This happens because when a whole process is the work of a team, process management is part of the team's job. Finally, the job of the executive changes from scorekeeper to leader.

CONTROLLING

Effective control is crucial in keeping marketing operations in line with the marketing plan. Control systems not only identify deviations from the plan but also help managers anticipate and correct problems before they occur and make the necessary adjustments in the plan. Although managers use a variety of methods to control marketing operations—including research and testing programs and periodic reporting—fiscal management activities are the major focus of their concern. Thus this section looks principally at budgeting and the management of profits and profitability, the topics of chapter objective four.

BUDGETING

Based on the forecasts that we discussed in Chapter 8, managers develop **budgets**—formal statements of the amounts of money a firm expects to spend on specific, planned programs and activities over a given period of time. In both for-profit and not-for-profit organizations budgets are the most widely used financial tool. Because budgeting must rely on projections and estimates, it is as much an art as a science. John Wanamaker, the Philadelphia store owner who revolutionized retailing practices in the late nineteenth century, expressed his concern about the advertising budget in his often-quoted comment: "I know that half the money I spend on advertising is wasted; I just don't know which half."

A marketing budget projects the expenditures necessary to implement a marketing plan. Because budgets deal with *future* allocations of resources, they serve not only as planning tools but also as standards by which future performance is evaluated: actual expenses, sales, and revenues are compared with the budgeted figures.

Budgets are also important tools for managing the coordination of various activities and functions. For example, if the current marketing plan calls for special emphasis on advertising, a greater proportion of budgeted funds will be allocated to advertising than to other elements of the marketing communication mix.

Budgeting has a tremendous impact on staff attitude and morale. Allocation of funds is critical to the development of new programs, to a department's success, and to the careers of managers. Those who lose the "budget battle" must make do with less support (for example, secretarial assistance, equipment, R&D, advertising, and sales-promotion activities), a problem that can erode both confidence and enthusiasm.

Although all areas of the marketing mix operate with budgets, managers pay particularly close attention to marketing communication budgets—for example, the budgets for advertising, public relations, and sales promotions.

budget
A formal statement of the amounts of money an organization expects to spend on specific, planned activities and programs over a specified period of time.

These are often among the highest in a consumer product company. Let's consider the sales-promotion budget as an illustration of the complexities of budgeting for one of the functional areas of marketing.

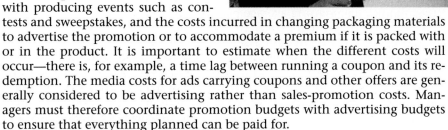

The promotion budget must include all the costs of promotion: revenue loss from price deals and coupon redemption, the cost of premiums or prizes, the costs associated with producing events such as contests and sweepstakes, and the costs incurred in changing packaging materials to advertise the promotion or to accommodate a premium if it is packed with or in the product. It is important to estimate when the different costs will occur—there is, for example, a time lag between running a coupon and its redemption. The media costs for ads carrying coupons and other offers are generally considered to be advertising rather than sales-promotion costs. Managers must therefore coordinate promotion budgets with advertising budgets to ensure that everything planned can be paid for.

In budgeting for sales promotions—or any other marketing expense—managers must bear in mind that you get what you pay for. Costs can be more than offset by an increase in sales that follows a creative and accurately targeted promotion.

MANAGING PROFITS

Most marketing controls focus on revenues, expenses, and profits. In addition, socially responsible marketers must balance bottom-line considerations with concern for the public good. The first step in marketing control is to collect financial data. The second step is to put these data into perspective, using benchmarks, indexing, and trend analyses.

Benchmarking In marketing, a single number is meaningless. If Videotron's sales are up 14 percent, is that good, average, or bad? Ultimately, it depends upon some **benchmark**—what the number is *compared* with. One type of benchmark is internal—the company's previous performance in terms of monthly averages or the same period during the previous year, or the performance of other products of the firm.

Another type of benchmark compares the firm's performance with that of competitors and the industry as a whole. Returning to our Videotron example, if the industry is up 14 percent, then Videotron is simply maintaining its position. If the market is growing at 7 percent, then Videotron is gaining on its competitors. If the market is growing at a rate of 28 percent, then Videotron is losing share.

But share of *what*? We need to define a market and its competitive structure in order to understand "market share." For example, a company that is holding its share of the domestic market but, unlike competitors, is not participating in global markets is losing share in the bigger world market. Indeed, speaking in terms of domestic market share may obscure the fact that a firm is losing position and share in a globalizing industry. When this happens, a company's domestic share, too, is generally in danger from more farsighted companies. This is precisely what happened to the former RCA, a company that in the 1960s was one of the highest of high-technology companies. RCA believed it had a leading position in the color television industry, but its share claim applied only to the U.S. market: it was number one in the United States,

Creative Budgeting

At 3M, where innovation is a key feature of the corporate culture, planning precedes budgeting as a means of managing the future of innovative products: "Plan first, budget later," advises one 3M vice president. Creative financial management practices are designed to reduce interdivisional conflict and foster cooperation. For example, when a division making newly designed industrial filters could not afford to expand globally, it negotiated extra financing from the budget of a European area-management unit.

benchmark
A known number or set of outcomes against which other numbers or sets of outcomes can be compared.

721

but only number five or six worldwide. The distinction proved to be fatal to RCA. In the late 1980s the faltering company was acquired by GE. Subsequently, GE—which remains in a business only if it is number one or two worldwide in that business—sold its newly acquired TV business to Thompson of France and quit the industry.

The use of benchmarks has led to the practice of **benchmarking**, in which a company identifies the practice or practices in other companies that have produced excellent results, studies those practices, and then makes the changes necessary to achieve equal or better results.

Indexing To quickly compare the relationships among several numbers, marketing managers use **indexing**. In indexing, 100 is generally used as the base number representing average performance: a number below 100 means less than average, a number over 100 better than average.

Indexes are easy to calculate. For example, let's evaluate consumer awareness levels of a hypothetical new CD player, model ABC. Marketing research has determined that, on average, 40 percent of people around the world are aware of this product; the lowest awareness level is 20 percent in Japan, the highest is 50 percent in France. Awareness in the Canada is about 44 percent. In order to construct indexes from this data, we must calculate ratios between each country's level of awareness and the average level.

Multiplying by 100 produces a meaningful whole number:

$$\text{Index} = \frac{\text{number for individual country}}{\text{average number for all countries}} \times 100$$

Thus the index for Japan is 50 ($20/40 = .50 \times 100 = 50$); for France, it is 125 ($50/40 = 1.25 \times 100$); and for Canada, 110 ($44/40 = 1.10 \times 100$). Table 22-2 summarizes these calculations.

Trend Analysis Changes in an index are one indication of a shift in trends. A trend is a general direction, pattern, or tendency. A meaningful trend is one that spans a long enough period to be a reliable indicator of a pattern. **Trend analysis** seeks to predict future demand, sales, and market penetration by extrapolating from a past situation to an expected future position. Whenever possible, managers try to use at least five years of data from trend analysis, although such data are not always available.

The simplest form of trend analysis is *extrapolation*—predictions based on the assumption that a past trend will continue into the future. More sophisticated analyses look behind and beyond the trend data to determine customer motives and needs.

benchmarking
Identifying the practice or practices that have produced excellent results for a company or its competitors very often in a different industry altogether, studying those practices, and then making the changes necessary to achieve equal or better results.

indexing
Comparing numbers by putting them on the same scale. Most indexes use 100 as the base or average number and report scores in relation to 100 above or below that average.

trend analysis
A means of predicting future demand, sales, and market penetration by extrapolating from a current situation to an expected future position.

722

TABLE 22-2	INDEX COMPARISONS FOR CD PLAYER MODEL ABC	
	Awareness Level	**Index**
Average	**40**	**100**
Canada	44	110
Japan	20	50
France	50	125

MANAGING PROFITABILITY

Most product managers and marketing plans seek to lower production and marketing costs in addition to increasing sales and market share, all of which can translate into *higher profitability* for the firm. Cost-management practices and achieving economies of scale, as well as strategic implementation decisions, are particularly important to managers who are focused on higher levels of productivity.

The idea behind *managing profitability* is that a marketing organization cannot run efficiently if sales and profits are the only yardsticks. Other factors, such as market share, must also be considered. On the other hand, as we have already seen, a company can't be profitable if its only concern is market share. It also has to consider costs and revenues—*and* a sense of social responsibility.

Market-Share Analysis **Market-share analysis** is the tracking of a company's share of a defined market. It requires identifying and measuring the market as a whole and the sales of each participant in that market. Market-share analysis is a critical measure of a firm's performance and defines the firm's perception of the scale of the industry in which it competes and the markets it serves.

Market-share analysis also helps managers understand whether a disappointing sales pattern is the result of external factors or of problems with the marketing plan. If sales drop but market share remains constant, then problems in the external environment are probably affecting all firms in the industry. But if a firm's market share drops—even if its sales continue to increase—then the problem may well be in the marketing plan.

Cost Management Because profits are what is left of revenues when costs have been recouped, cost management is an important aspect of profitability. *Marketing costs* include expenditures required for all activities undertaken to determine the needs of the market, make products available, and communicate to consumers about them, as well as marketing administration and overhead. Marketing-cost analysis is the organization of marketing-cost data to determine the exact nature of all costs. It requires ferreting out all sources of expense and identifying those areas that could be eliminated or managed in more efficient ways.

IBM is struggling with the market's shift from mainframes with proprietary operating systems and processing that is distributed throughout an electronic network to personal computers. When mainframe computers were the standard, IBM was in a position of great competitive strength. The company charged high prices and generated high operating margins. Part of this high margin was used to finance a large and expensive field sales force. Customers were willing to pay IBM's prices because they liked the security of buying from the market leader and appreciated the support and service provided by the sales force.

Today, IBM is no longer the leader in the revolution that is taking place in the computer industry. There are many strong competitors, and competition is driving down prices. IBM's margins are shrinking, and the company must reevaluate the role of its expensive sales force. What made sense with high margins is a costly drag in a business where customers are price sensitive and feel they do not need the support of a sales force. IBM's slowness in responding to these changes has damaged the company's competitive position. Part of IBM's challenge is to learn how to compete in the marketplace with much smaller margins.

market-share analysis
Calculation of a company's share of a particular market; requires identifying and measuring the market as a whole and the sales of each participant in that market.

Most marketing managers believe that in order to achieve profitability, a firm must achieve the "critical mass" of product sales that makes economies of scale (see Chapter 1)—and greater profits—possible. Reaching critical mass can be difficult, however. Quaker thought it was on the right track when it bought Anderson Clayton Company to get its Gaines Foods division, a leading pet-food maker. Quaker was already a major presence in the highly profitable semimoist dog-food category. Gaines and Quaker products together would have 75 percent of this category—doubling the size of Quaker's pet-food business. Managers believed that consolidating the two businesses would lower production and marketing costs, giving the firm a low-cost competitive advantage.

Quaker's hopes were dashed because managers overestimated the benefits of combining the two businesses. Gaines had three distinct brand names (Gainesburgers, Cycle, and Gravy Train) and Quaker had two (Ken-L-Ration and Kibbles 'n' Bits). Merely assembling all of these brands under one corporate umbrella did not make any of them stronger. Quaker still had to present five different marketing messages to consumers, while competing giant Purina had to present only one.[7] Quaker learned that **brand proliferation**—allowing the number of brands to expand excessively—results in a costly spread of resources. It dilutes marketing forces, which is essential for success.

brand proliferation
Allowing the number of brands to expand excessively. Proliferation dilutes marketing focus, which is essential for success.

Recall from our discussion in Chapter 8 that General Motors has suffered from the same problem. The company's segmentation of the auto market just after the First World War resulted in five separate auto divisions: Chevrolet, Pontiac, Oldsmobile, Buick, and Cadillac. This approach was insightful and accurate at the time, and it worked for some thirty years. But nothing is forever. The market changed: consumers began to see the auto as an expression of lifestyle rather than as a simple (uniform) status symbol. GM's competitors each had only one brand (Mercedes, BMW, Volvo) or two (Toyota and Lexus, Nissan and Infiniti, Honda and Acura). GM needed to reduce the number of nameplates to compete successfully. Instead it added a new division: Saturn. By 1994, GM was facing the world market with twelve different brands! This brand proliferation is a major structural problem for GM as it struggles to compete in the 1990s and into the next century. Too many brands dilute both economies of scale and the leverage that can come from a concentration of effort and resources.

EVALUATING ●

Managers must evaluate all aspects of a marketing program so they can make better decisions next time. This important part of marketing, the subject of the fifth chapter objective, is too often neglected, resulting in the repetition of mistakes.

Evaluation includes periodic reporting and specific testing. Marketing managers work closely with sales and distribution in gathering information for reports, and with R&D in designing and carrying out research and testing. They use a wide variety of mathematical measures to evaluate a program's effectiveness and efficiency.

Collecting information about a product's continuing performance is critical for daily decision making as well as for long-term planning. Managers often maintain a reporting system for this purpose as part of a comprehensive management information system (MIS; see Chapter 5). An information system that provides reports on a regular (weekly, monthly, quarterly, and yearly) basis keeps managers informed about their product's market position.

THE MARKETING MIX

Although managers are concerned with evaluating all elements in the marketing mix, some of the most serious and costly evaluation efforts focus on marketing communications. Let's look at the evaluation of advertising, a major expense for most packaged-goods companies and one of the most difficult programs areas to assess. Our approach involves selecting measurable criteria by which to judge the program's effectiveness, collecting the necessary data, and comparing these data with some benchmark. This general approach can be used by business-to-business advertisers, who are just as interested as consumer-products advertisers in assessing buyer awareness (see Exhibit 22-1), and it applies equally well to all areas of the marketing mix.

Exhibit 22-1
Expanding Awareness

New Equipment Digest *targets the industrial, or business-to-business market. Here, an industrial contributor of the* New Equipment Digest *highlights a number of advantages to print advertising including the development of "awareness" of a company or product outside its original market. According to Jim Steele, his company's initial market now makes up only 16 percent of total sales; through advertising, the company's message reached markets it hadn't been able to tap before.*

In evaluating the impact of advertising on the targeted audience, managers want to know three things:

1. Is the advertising message memorable?
2. Does it deliver the intended message?
3. Does it achieve its objective? That is: Does it persuade people to buy a product? Improve or change or create an image? Create awareness of a product or service?

In order to be memorable, the ad must get the prospective customer's attention. Attention is a serious problem in television advertising, for viewers are bombarded with commercials and have learned to avoid them by leaving the room, changing the channel, or turning their attention elsewhere. Two words that strike terror in advertising executives are *zipping* (skipping past the commercials on a recorded videocassette) and *zapping* (changing channels when the commercial comes on). The call in the TV industry is for "zap-proof" ads—ads that are so interesting that viewers won't want to zap them.

The best way to be memorable is to be *relevant*. Advertising messages that speak directly about something the viewer cares about are more likely to have an impact. In **copytesting**, marketers check the memorability and effectiveness of ads by surveying consumers and assessing their *recall* and *recognition* of a brand and its message as well as the success of the message (did the consumer get it?). Copytesting answers such questions as: Who has seen the ad? How did they feel about it? Did it affect their feelings about the product? Is the approach worth pursuing or should the advertiser adopt a new strategy? Would those who have seen the advertising buy the product?

The most widely used tests measure *memorability*. A study of the advertising featured during Super Bowl XXIII found that average total recall for its commercials was 49 percent—almost twice the prime-time average. However, 57 percent of the respondents also found these commercials to be more interesting than most television spots, which may explain the high recall.[8]

Companies also need to evaluate the *effectiveness* of an advertisement at *delivering the intended message*. One study found that 96.5 percent of its 2,700 respondents exhibited some degree of misunderstanding of ads. But it also found that advertising generally tends to produce lower misunderstanding rates than other types of marketing communications. Only about 30 percent of the core information content in selected television commercials and 21.4 percent of magazine advertisement content was misunderstood.[9]

Assessing the *persuasiveness* of advertising is the most difficult task of all. Most studies of advertising effectiveness have focused on recall. Yet researchers have found little relationship between persuasiveness and recall.[10] A major study of 1,069 commercials tested over 150 elements with hundreds of consumers. The study found that some commercials succeed at being memorable without managing to persuade viewers, while others are persuasive without being memorable. The single most powerful element in TV commercials appears to be a brand-differentiating message.[11]

Tests that measure buying behavior resulting from advertising are costly largely because so many other variables affect the actual purchase decision—for example, distribution, availability, pricing, and the competition's activities. The growing use of *single-source data* (see Chapter 5) should make it easier to track advertising effectiveness in terms of household purchases.

MARKETING AUDITS

Yet another way to assess the effectiveness of a marketing program is through a marketing audit. A **marketing audit** is a formal, systematic review of the

copytesting
Evaluating completed advertising in terms of target-audience recall and recognition.

marketing audit
A formal, systematic review of an executed marketing strategy and plan; may be carried out by either internal or external experts.

executed marketing strategy and plan. It may take the form of an external audit by independent experts or an internal audit by members of the marketing organization.

Audits examine records and management procedures and identify problems in the marketing environment, within the organization itself, and between the marketing department and other departments and suppliers. Auditors evaluate the extent to which managers and programs meet objectives, use resources well, and follow plans. The goal is to see how well the firm is applying the marketing concept—creating meaningful value for its customers—as well as generating profits.

Marketing audits enable top management in large firms to look beyond routine sales reports and market-share estimates for various brands, products, and product lines.[12] Managers use an audit's findings to improve the effectiveness of marketing planning and market program operations. As the price of competing keeps rising, many marketers are using audits to question the productivity of their marketing dollars. At Campbell Soup marketing managers are looking at the "return on marketing investment" in terms of a concept the company calls "value management." Campbell's philosophy is that any product, person, or function that doesn't ultimately add value to its brands needs very close scrutiny.[13]

Types of Audits   Periodic *internal audits* carried out by members of the firm or department provide reasonable assurance that the marketing programs are being operated efficiently. These audits are used to pinpoint problems, illuminate hidden trouble spots, and uncover potential dangers before they become serious. Audits by outside experts are performed less frequently and are usually major checkpoints in the evolution of a marketing program's direction and management. These external audits generally have greater credibility because they are conducted by people without a vested interest in the operation and are therefore assumed to be more objective. Note, however, that external auditors may lack in-depth knowledge of the industry.

Audit Procedures   Table 22-3 is a partial outline of a marketing audit checklist. By ensuring that an audit is done in a *systematic* way, such an outline increases the effectiveness and reliability of the information assembled. Although the outline shown here may seem long, any one of its questions can, and should, be expanded in an actual audit. For example, question 7 under Strategy asks: "Are marketing resources allocated optimally to prime market segments, territories, and products of the organization?"

In an actual audit we would explore each element in this question in detail. For example, with regard to territories, we would need to ask such questions as: "How do the domestic and global marketing mixes compare? What is the allocation of effort to high-, upper-middle, lower-middle, and low-income countries? What is the company's position in each major world region, and what is the company's strategy vis-à-vis China, Eastern Europe, the European Union, North America, and so on.

An audit is valuable even if it does not uncover major new directions, for small improvements often make a big difference. That is why the effective marketing manager puts periodic marketing audits at the top of his or her list.

EVALUATION OF PROFITABILITY AND PERFORMANCE

In addition to assessing the overall performance of a marketing program, managers need to evaluate the fiscal performance of specific brands, products, and product categories. Investors often want to compare the profitability and performance of one company with another. Sales figures, profit margins, and

---

TABLE 22-3   **MARKETING AUDIT CHECKLIST**

Macroenvironment

Economic

1. What is the projected growth rate for the economy? The inflation rate? Credit availability? Cost level? Savings rate? Buyer confidence?

Demographic

1. What significant demographic trends will have an impact on the company?

Ecological

1. What is the impact of the company's current operation on the environment? Is this consistent with government policy, market expectations, and management aspirations and goals?

Technical

1. What significant changes are taking place in the technological environment? How will these changes affect the company's operations?

Political/Regulatory

1. What changes are developing in the political and regulatory environment, and how will these affect the company? What specific new laws and regulations should the company be preparing for?

Cultural

1. What are the cultural attitudes and values of the markets served by the company? How are these attitudes and values changing?

Task Environment

Markets

1. What are the most significant characteristics of the company's markets?
2. What changes are developing?

Customers

1. How do the company's customers rate the company vis à vis its competitors?
2. How do customers make their buying decisions?

Competitors

1. Who are the company's competitors, and what are their major strengths and weaknesses?
2. What are competitors doing right that should be emulated, and what are they doing wrong that opens an opportunity for the company?

Channels of Distribution

1. What changes are taking place in the channels? What are the implications of these changes for the company?

Suppliers

1. How well are the company's suppliers performing? What can the organization do to strengthen supplier performance?

(Table 23-3 continued)

Marketing Strategy

Objectives
1. Is the company's overall objective to create mutually beneficial relationships with its customers?
2. Are the corporate objectives stated clearly, and do they lead logically to the marketing objectives? Are the marketing objectives stated clearly enough to guide marketing planning and subsequent performance measurement?
3. Are the marketing objectives appropriate, given the company's competitive position, resources, and opportunities? Is the appropriate strategic objective to build, hold, harvest, or terminate this business?

Strategy
1. What is the core marketing strategy for achieving the objectives? What is the deep need that the organization satisfies?
2. Is there a good fit among the environment, the organization, and the values of the organization's stakeholders?
3. Does the marketing strategy include the use of stretch and leverage? Where is the stretch, and how does the strategy leverage the organization's assets?
4. How are markets segmented? If the segmentation is more than five years old, is it still valid?
5. What is the organization's and the product's positioning in the marketplace? What does the product do? What does it not do? Who is the product for? Who is it not for? With which products/companies does it compete?
6. Are enough (or too few) resources budgeted to accomplish the marketing objectives?
7. Are marketing resources allocated optimally to prime market segments, territories, and products of the organization?
8. Are the marketing resources allocated optimally to the major elements of the marketing mix—that is, the quality of the product, whether a good or a service; pricing mechanisms; distribution; and marketing communications such as advertising, promotions, and public relations?

Organization

Formal Structure
1. Is there a high-level marketing officer with adequate authority and responsibility over those company activities that affect the customer's satisfaction?
2. Are the marketing responsibilities optimally structured along functional, product, end user, and territorial lines?

Functional Efficiency
1. Are there good communication and working relations between marketing and sales?
2. Is the product-management system working effectively? Are the product managers able to plan profits or only sales volume?
3. Are there any groups in marketing that need more training, motivation, supervision, or evaluation?

Interface Efficiency
1. Are there any problems between marketing and manufacturing that need attention? Between marketing and R&D? Between marketing and financial management? Between marketing and purchasing?

continued

similar measure, *return on equity,* divides net income by total equity—the sum of all investments in the company. Thus it is a measure of how well the firm is meeting its goal of providing value for shareholders.

In using ROI and return on equity as measures of profitability, marketers must take account of both internal and external factors that may contribute to unexpected ROI results. Internal influences include the firm's marketing philosophy and service orientation. Premier Industrial, a distributor of industrial parts, carries some 250,000 parts. Although these parts may seem inconsequential, the breakdown of a single $10 electrical relay can force an entire assembly line to shut down, making the afflicted firm more than willing to pay Premier's premium prices for fast delivery from a large selection of parts in stock. This focus on meeting customer needs has enabled Premier to earn a healthy return on equity: 28 percent on sales of over 600 million. An important external influence is changing customer trends. McCormick & Company, for instance, the largest North American producer of spices, has been hurt by the fact that today fewer people cook from scratch. McCormick's profits in the late 1980s were no higher than they were in 1981, and the company's return on equity dropped to 11 percent from a 1984 peak of 22 percent.

Because inventories are important to most firms, *inventory turnover*—the number of times during a given period (usually a year) that the average inventory has been replaced or the number of times that the average inventory has been sold—is another important financial ratio. As we saw in Chapter 15, inventory turnover is expressed as the cost of goods sold divided by the average value of the inventory.

MANAGING GLOBAL MARKETING PROGRAMS

Global marketing, the subject of chapter objective six, presents formidable problems for managers responsible for marketing control. Distance and differences in language, customs, and practices create problems that affect many aspects of marketing-program management.

ORGANIZATIONAL ISSUES

Communicating with and coordinating employees scattered around the globe has become far easier in recent years because of major developments and improvements in communications technology. The challenge for managers is to create an organization able to adapt to each market, yet adept at leveraging the company's particular strengths and advantages. In this type of organization all managers are powerful. Successful global organizations are efficient, creative, and responsive.

CONTROL AND EVALUATION

Irrespective of corporate size and geographic distance a subsidiary's performance strongly affects how much control its parent will try to exert over it. Normally a subsidiary that achieves its budget objectives is left alone. A negative difference between budgeted and actual performance, however, triggers intervention by headquarters.

The greater the specialization of a headquarters staff, the more extensive and penetrating its control over subsidiaries and other operating units. In smaller-country markets the control process must be streamlined and simplified because the expertise and time required to generate and evaluate data are not available.

The product itself also affects the type of marketing controls used. A product that is technically sophisticated can be more extensively controlled because its use is highly similar around the world. This similarity creates opportunities to apply international standards of measurement and evaluation. For example, a process-control computer for the petrochemical industry is the same in Rotterdam as it is in Saskatoon.

Other products are more "environmentally sensitive"—that is, they are used in different manners in different parts of the world. In such cases, it can be difficult to apply international standards. Drugs and packaged foods are two examples of environmentally sensitive products that often require adaptation to meet the preferences of different eating cultures and different systems of medical practice. For example, for the same drug and the same dosage, North Americans take pills, while the French like suppositories. The Japanese *have* credit cards, but they only use them for international travel. At home, they prefer cash (it is quite safe to carry cash in Japan).

Clearly, then, global management of marketing programs is an arduous task. But, as Exhibit 22-2 points out, there are at least two ways to look at the challenge of the global marketplace. The success of companies ranging from McDonald's to Coca-Cola, from Benetton to British Airways, underscores the rewards awaiting those willing to take the risks and apply sound marketing techniques to lead, organize, plan, control, and evaluate marketing programs.

Exhibit 22-2
Private Banking in the Global Marketplace

In this ad, Credit Suisse explains that while operating on a global scale, it still provides all the services of a private bank.

▬▬▬▬
▬▬▬▬
▬▬▬▬

BOTTOM
▼ **LINE** ◄
REALITIES
▼

MANAGING CREATIVITY—THE MOUSE THAT ROARS

Disney, the world's most valuable entertainment company, transformed itself from a moribund has-been in the early 1980s into a dynamic giant that analysts now herald as one of the best-run companies in the world. Disney's secret? Imagination. Many of the business management methods used at Disney could make up a textbook for other managers who are eager to exploit creative ideas but can't manage the risk of developing them.[14]

The man behind the ideas is Michael Eisner, who, with the help of President Frank Wells and Walt's nephew, Roy Disney, woke up the Sleeping Beauty company when they took it over in 1984. The latest ideas include the new Disney-MGM movie studio's theme park at Disney World and theme parks in Japan and Europe. The addition of the Touchstone production company has resulted in highly successful films for adults like *Who Framed Roger Rabbit?*, *Honey, I Shrunk the Kids*, *Dead Poets Society*, *Dick Tracy*, *Three Men and a Baby*, and *Good Morning, Vietnam*.

Not to fear, however: Disney has not abandoned children's films. *Aladdin* was one of the highest-grossing films of 1993. And Buena Vista, the company's home video marketer, has developed some highly creative marketing plans for Disney videos with unusual tie-ins like Crest and M&M/Mars as well as a rebate program to promote the 1993 *Bambi* re-release. Disney's new chain of retail stores has fast become one of the hottest concepts in retailing. With half of the market, the Disney label dominates children's records. In Italy the third most popular magazine (after *TV Guide* and *Vatican*) is *Topolino*, the Italian-language version of *The Mickey Mouse Magazine*. Disney consumer products blanket the world—over U.S. $1 billion in Mickey Mouse watches, sweatshirts, stuffed animals, and crib linen is sold annually in Japan alone.

Disney's creativity comes from having a creative executive in charge—a rational notion in the entertainment business, where a new product line must be created from scratch every year. Eisner, who was previously president of Paramount and has held creative posts there and at ABC, tosses out ideas like a kid rummaging through a trunk in an attic—ideas for new pavilions in the theme parks, new copy lines for the advertising, a new kind of health-food restaurant, a new type of record company, a gag for a new movie.

However, Eisner and Disney balance creative ideas with strict financial controls and a strategic planning group that reviews project ideas to see if their economics make sense. This process includes innovative group meetings and decision-making practices that let Disney move fast enough to steal the lead on its competitors. The result? Since 1984, when Eisner took over, net income has increased from 23 to 50 percent annually, while the company's return on equity has jumped from 8 percent to 22 percent. In the kind of dramatic turnaround rarely seen, Eisner's team has transformed Walt Disney Studios from little more than a break-even operation with 3 percent of the market into an enterprise that leads the market with a 19 percent share. In the volatile world of movies, twenty-nine of Disney's last thirty-six films have been profitable—the best winning streak on record. The one blip on the Disney screen is Euro Disney, which hovered on the edge of bankruptcy until creditors came up with a cash infusion in early 1994 and which is not expected to show a profit until the late 1990s. Like so many other successful companies, Disney failed to recognize critical differences in the European market. This failure has been costly to Euro Disney investors and embarrassing to Disney's reputation for marketing savvy.

Disney management operates with a set of principles that ensure that the creativity will turn into pots of gold. They are:

◆ Exploit the most profitable niches.

◆ Stay ahead technologically.

◆ Cut costs ruthlessly.

◆ Be financially creative.

◆ Find efficient ways to stretch the marketing budget.

◆ Add a touch of class.

Disney is an impressive success story. As Walt Disney noted, "It all began with a mouse." A mouse that roared. ▼

KEY POINTS SUMMARY ▼

1. It is the marketing manager's responsibility to manage all aspects of the marketing program. This means researching the market for changing customer and marketplace needs, creating a mutually beneficial relationship between company and customer (the future concept of marketing), practicing a strategy of stretch and leverage, and motivating and coordinating people in the various marketing functional areas.

2. In scheduling and timing marketing activities, managers must understand what activities can begin at what time and what activities must be completed before others may take place. A useful tool in this task is a flow chart, such as the PERT, that maps the flow of activities. The critical path method can identify crucial activities that will hold up the project if not completed on time.

3. Leadership in marketing also involves reengineering the marketing function as needed. This means rejecting traditional ways of organizing and performing work and searching for innovative work methods and patterns.

4. Budgeting, a critical function of the marketing manager, is both an art and a science. Based on projections and estimates, budgets are the most widely used financial tool in all kinds of organizations. They serve both as plans to be followed and as standards against which performance is measured. Marketing communication budgets are often among the highest in a consumer packaged goods company, and are thus subject to careful scrutiny.

   Marketing managers must monitor and manage both profits and profitability. Profits are weighed against some benchmark figure in the industry, over time, and against indexes of various kinds. Changes in an index may indicate a trend that marketers must heed in order to maintain or improve profit levels. Profitability control often involves market-share considerations and always depends on cost management and economies of scale.

5. The successful marketing manager uses management information systems, reporting systems, program evaluations, marketing audits, and other measures to determine the overall effectiveness and efficiency of a marketing program and the degree to which members of the marketing team are adhering to the marketing plan and its standards. Reporting systems generally operate on a regularly scheduled daily, weekly, or monthly basis, while program evaluations occur as programs are put into place.

   The marketing audit provides a formal examination of a marketing plan's performance, examining such things as developments in the company's external environment; the behavior of the company's market, its customers, and its competitors, particularly changes in any of the behaviors that may present threats and/or opportunities to the firm; the firm's current marketing objectives and strategies and any need for changes in these; the company's internal functioning and any conflicts among marketing groups; the adequacy of the firm's information and new-product development systems; and the overall profitability and cost effectiveness of the marketing program.

6. Differences in culture, language, and location make management of a global organization a complex task. Technological advances make it much easier to communicate with employees,

suppliers, and customers around the world today, but deciding how and when to adapt products and communications to local markets to play to a company's particular strengths is still a difficult challenge. Highly sophisticated products may be marketed very similarly in widely different countries and cultures, but food and many other products require considerable adaptation to local preferences.

DISCUSSION QUESTIONS ▼

1. Interview the marketing vice president or marketing manager of a firm in your area and determine how that person sees his or her role as leader of the firm's marketing program. How much time does the person devote to each management function? How important does the person consider each function to be?

2. Assume that your current or most recent employer invites you to head a project to reengineer the organization. Where would you begin? Why? How would you begin? Explain your approach and the rationale behind it.

3. Select a local business on campus, such as the campus newspaper or bookstore, and analyze its approach to budgeting. Develop a marketing budget for this business for next semester.

4. Why do marketers need benchmarks? Select a product that you use regularly and identify a potential benchmark for it.

5. Suppose you have been hired to advise a new company founded to offer tutoring services to athletes at your university or college. Develop a program for a reporting system for this company. What data should be routinely gathered and how should they be used to monitor profitability?

6. Describe a marketing audit and the way managers use its data.

7. Interview a retailer in your community about inventory turnover. What is the store's turnover rate and how is it measured? Does the store monitor turnover effectively?

8. Go to the library and research a company with dealings in a number of countries. What organizational challenges would you expect it to encounter in managing its marketing programs? What planning challenges? What controlling challenges? Identify ways in which the firm might cope with these challenges.

Integrative Case ● Discussion Questions

The Body Shop*

1. How does The Body Shop headquarters control the firm's franchisees?

2. What additional criteria might the firm use in evaluating franchise performance?

Harley-Davidson

1. Why is Harley Davidson a market leader?

2. What control measures might Harley-Davidson use? Explain your answer.

The Millennium Power System

1. How are market needs changing in this industry? How should Millennium respond?

2. What measures could Millennium use in evaluating the brand's profitability?

*The three cases at the back of the book—"The Body Shop," "Harley-Davidson," and "The Millennium Power System"—illustrate topics discussed in all chapters of this book. Your instructor will tell you when to read a particular case and when to answer the discussion questions on it that appear at the end of each chapter.

Information Highway: Changes

Everyone's heard of the imminent arrival of the "information highway," but is the general public as eager to embrace the concept and the technology as large corporations or the limited "techno-jock" market? While concept, technology, and infrastructure developers, as well as the media, have eagerly hyped the information highway's benefit potential, the potential using public may not necessarily share in the optimism, as dramatic change is not always an easy pill to swallow. But perhaps the real danger lies in creating too great an expectation among potential users, then not possibly being able to live up to advance billing.

Many typical Canadians admit that they are "technophobes," or in plain English, afraid of computers and new technology. To them, the apprehension felt toward the information highway, only accentuated by the complex, technology-laden terminology bandied about by those conveying information to potential new users, presents a very significant obstacle, complicating acceptance of the service. The typical Canadian seems more than happy to shy away from complex technology, preferring instead to stick to tried and true methods which apparently work well enough.

Given this, an issue begging for an answer is: Are the services and potential benefits promised to information highway users, hinging largely on marginal added conveniences, viewed by the average potential user as offering enough value to justify the cost of the service? Typically, services accessible via more traditional means may be accessed on the information highway for an additional average markup on the service cost of approximately 15 percent. Depending on the cost of the service or product, this can be a substantial amount. At what point are consumers unwilling to pay for an additional marginal element of convenience? Another factor deserving of mention relates to the notion that most benefits derived by using the information highway are related to the provision of services, a realm in which personalization and the human touch have traditionally been highly valued by consumers. Will the marginal addition of convenience be enough to justify to consumers the loss of human interaction?

The impact, and the ultimate success of the information highway, is at best unpredictable, simply because human nature is unpredictable. Potential users must be convinced to overcome their initial hesitation in accepting a new technology; they must be convinced to undertake a first trial of the technology; they must be willing to pay a premium for what is, in many cases, an insubstantial element of additional convenience; and their fears of losing their privacy must be abated. This is a critical issue. Providers of the information highway service will be hard pressed to convince potential users that they, and only they, have access to confidential information. Public distrust of government and big business may prove extremely difficult to overcome.

QUESTIONS

1. Do you feel that the Canadian public is willing to accept the new technology presented by the information highway in order to enjoy the additional convenience benefits?

2. Do you feel that the consuming public is willing to pay a 10–20% premium on services in exchange for the additional convenience promised by the information highway given current economic and social conditions?
3. List as many barriers to the public acceptance of a new concept and new technology, such as that inherent in the information highway, as you can think of.
4. What do you think is the critical role of marketing in the information highway venture?

Source: This case was prepared by Byron Osing and is based on the *Venture* series episode "Information Highway," which was originally broadcast on February 6, 1994.

The Body Shop:
Promoting a Beautiful Business

I hate the beauty business—Anita Roddick

Those are strange words coming from someone who became one of the richest women in England by selling cosmetics, but Anita means them. She will tell you forcefully that the cosmetics industry is dominated by firms using outdated notions of glamor to sell women overpriced products. According to Anita, the industry lies and cheats by promising purchasers youth and beauty—claims that their products can't possibly deliver. But what really enrages Anita is that the cosmetics industry has no sense of social responsibility.

So why did she get into the cosmetics business and how has she managed to succeed so spectacularly when she goes against all the established ways of doing business?

Business Philosophy

> When I opened the first Body Shop in Brighton in 1976, I knew nothing
> about business; my sole object was simply to survive. . . . Today The Body
> Shop is an international company rapidly expanding around the world.
> . . . my passionate belief is that business can be fun, it can be conducted
> with love and be a powerful force for good.

Although she began without any business training, business philosophy, or a traditional vision of what her business should be, Anita was able to create a unique global company in a highly competitive industry because she passionately believes in what she is doing, is willing to attack the establishment, and learned her mother's life philosophy: "Be special, be anything but mediocre." Anita devotes herself wholeheartedly to what she believes in.

Anita's business idea came out of her travel and employment experiences. After finishing college, she interspersed traveling—frequently by hitchhiking—to Greece, Israel, Panama, the South Seas, Australia, Madagascar, and South Africa with teaching and working as a researcher at the United Nations. During her travels she saw women using natural products such as rhassoul mud and pineapple to clean their hair and bodies and to soften their skin. This is what gave Anita the idea to make cosmetics from natural ingredients.

Since her experience at the UN had convinced her that giving money to impoverished peoples would never solve their problems, she worked out trade programs whereby in exchange for the raw materials she needed for her company's products, native peoples received enough income to maintain their culture and their dignity.

Anita's background as a social activist led her to use her business as a powerful voice to speak out on behalf of such issues as world hunger, acid rain, the destruction of the rain forest, animal rights, and human rights. Under her guidance, every Body Shop disseminates information on global and local causes.

Because she had no sales training, Anita developed a sales approach that consists of treating customers as she herself wanted to be treated in a store. Since she always wanted to try products, in her shops there are testers for almost every product. Because she wanted to be an informed consumer, she makes sure that every product she sells is carefully explained to consumers on labels, on shelf facings, by salespeople, and in company literature. And she never claims that her products will restore youthful skin or erase lines. The Body Shop's products are meant to cleanse and protect the skin, not make it look twenty years younger!

As a traditional businessperson or entrepreneur, Anita was over her head. At the same time, she was a hard worker; she was willing to learn; she was (and is) sincere, honest, outspoken, aggressive, and unconventional; and her ideas were in step with the times. Her products, her approach to selling, her management style, her causes, and her shops are appealing because they show that a business that is socially responsible can be viable. Today Anita is an articulate spokesperson for her business philosophy, but like most of us, she had to learn the hard way. To understand The Body Shop, one must know how and why it was founded.

Origins of The Body Shop

> Passion persuades, and by God, I was passionate about what I was selling.

In 1976, when her husband, Gordon, wanted to fulfill his lifelong ambition of traveling from Buenos Aires to New York on horseback, Anita decided to open a cosmetic shop to support herself and their two daughters while he was gone. In the early 1960s, before settling down and starting a family, Anita had traveled extensively and observed women using natural "cosmetics" to take care of their skin and hair. For example, she remembered that Tahitian women, who spent the bulk of their lives in the hot sun, had beautifully soft skin because they rubbed cocoa butter on their bodies. In Sri Lanka, she saw women rub pineapple on their skin to clean and tone it.

To make her cosmetics and open a shop, Anita needed a bank loan of £4,000 (about $8,000). Because she and her husband owned a small hotel in Littlehampton, she envisioned no difficulty in borrowing the money, but much to her surprise and disgust, the bank loan officer turned her down. He was not impressed by the passionate young mother clad in a Bob Dylan T-shirt who had appeared in his office with both of her small children in tow and announced she had this unusual idea for a business. He wanted to see a business plan. Before Gordon left for South America, he drew up the plan and made Anita buy and wear a suit on her return visit to the loan officer. Anita was angry about having to make these concessions, but she got the loan.

Anita initially approached some large cosmetics manufacturers to make her products, but they weren't interested in producing small quantities for her, and besides, they thought the ingredients she wanted in her products were ridiculous. Finally, through the Yellow Pages, she located a young herbalist she could work with. Together, they drew up a list of twenty-five possible products that would use such natural ingredients as jojoba oil, rhassoul mud, and aloe vera.

Next, she looked for a location for her first store. Deciding Littlehampton was too small to support the kind of store she envisioned, she went to Brighton, which had a more upscale population, and hunted until she found an inexpensive shop close to the town center. Even though Anita was inexperienced, she realized that location is crucially important in retailing—that a good site is more important than the physical condition of the shop.

She painted the walls dark green to disguise the dampness and cracks and hung garden fencing over them to hide the dripping water. A local art student designed a logo for £25 (about $50). (This stylized laurel wreath is still used today on The Body Shop product labels.) Because she had traveled in the United States and been amused that Americans call certain types of auto repair places "body shops," she named the store The Body Shop. Unfortunately, her shop was close to some morticians, who threatened to sue her because, they claimed, bereaved relatives would not want to hire a funeral director whose premises were close to a "Body Shop."

Perplexed by their logic and lacking the money to hire an attorney, Anita retaliated by calling the Brighton *Evening Argus* and telling them that a gang of businessmen were attacking a defenseless woman who was simply trying to support herself and her children by going into business. After the newspaper printed the story, Anita never heard from the morticians again. The experience taught her the value of publicity: it's effective and it's free. Since then, The Body Shop has made extensive use of publicity, but has never used traditional advertising and, according to Anita, never will.

To package her products, Anita used the cheapest containers she could find— which happened to be urine specimen bottles. Despite their cheapness, she lacked the capital to continue buying them, so she offered customers a discount if they brought their bottles back to be refilled.

Since she didn't yet have a sufficient variety of products to cover the shelves, Anita bought five different sizes of bottles and put multiple sizes of every product on display. She was especially concerned to offer small sizes of products because, as a consumer, she had been very annoyed at having to buy large containers. Because she couldn't afford to prepackage different sizes of perfumed products, she stocked the fragrance oils separately and encouraged customers to mix the oils they liked with unscented items like hand lotion or shampoo. Both of these practices continue in Body Shops today.

When the first Body Shop opened on Saturday, May 27, 1976, it was so mobbed with customers that Anita had to call in her husband for help. According to their financial plan, the shop had to make £300 pounds a week. In the first day of operation, it took in £130. They were elated and thought they were well on the way to success.

Anita loved being in her shop, talking to customers, rearranging displays, and cleaning up. To her, educating customers was far more important than persuading them to buy. Hand-lettered signs throughout the store explained all the products and their uses. She rarely pressured customers to buy. Instead, she encouraged them to try before buying, and at times even tried to convince them to buy smaller sizes if she thought they couldn't afford a larger size. Customers found The Body

Shop a charming cottage industry, and that was a large part of its attraction.

The first few months were far from easy, however. Anita and her friends worked long hours hand-lettering labels, transporting heavy supply bottles, and filling or refilling customers' bottles. When business was slow, Anita took to loading up her truck and peddling her goods wherever she could find customers. She even left trails of strawberry essence on the sidewalk to entice customers into the store.

Although by fall the shop was not yet a financial success, a friend of Anita's wanted to open another Body Shop in Chichester. Again they needed £4,000, and again, the bank (yes, the same one) wouldn't lend it to them. Fortunately, another friend, Ian McGlinn, came up with the money. In return, Anita gave him a 50 percent stake in the business—an arrangement that has made him a multimillionaire.

Within a year, two important events occurred: Gordon came home earlier than expected, and another friend opened a Body Shop in Hove and still another in Bognor Regis. Anita allowed her friends to use The Body Shop name, logo, and colors in these two new stores so that she could sell more of her product. As more people approached the Roddicks about opening Body Shops, Gordon realized that he and Anita needed some control over the stores selling their products. He hit upon the idea of franchising to grow their business and asked their attorney (who had the unsettling name of Mr. Careless) to draw up a simple supply and distribution agreement that would require franchisees to sell only products made by The Body Shop. The first formal franchise opened in Brussels in 1978 in a kiosk. A businessman bought it for his wife as a present!

Growth of The Body Shop

A true key to success is knowing what features set you apart from the competition.

By October 1993, 1,100 Body Shops had opened in 45 countries, and the plan was to open 150 every year for the next three years—60 a year in the United States alone. The product line had expanded from skin- and hair-care products to include a complete line of cosmetics and aromatherapy products. The only standard beauty products not sold by The Body Shop are nail polish and polish remover. Total worldwide retail sales for 1993 were expected to be over $266 million and profits of about $34 million were anticipated. (Table 1 offers some additional Body Shop sales statistics.) To illustrate its success, the company publishes fact sheets containing such information as: A branch of The Body Shop opens every 2.5 days worldwide,

TABLE 1	**WORLDWIDE STATISTICS**						
	1984	**1986**	**1989**	**1990**	**1991**	**1992**	**mid-1993**
Total number of Body Shops worldwide	128	232	367	457	n.a.	794	1,100
Pretax profits (in millions of U.S. dollars)	$1,044	3,451	11,232	14,508	36,100	45,400	n.a.

Source: Harvard Business Case, "The Body Shop International," prepared by Christopher A. Bartlett, 1991.

and someone buys something from The Body Shop somewhere in the world every 0.57 seconds.

Today a Body Shop franchise is expensive—about $300,000 in Canada. The company maintains strict control over the store's layout, product selection, and merchandising. Body Shops in the 1990s still look like the original in Brighton, even down to the same dark green paint. The company chooses the store locations.

To get a Body Shop franchise takes more than money and the patience to fill out long, strange application forms. It requires approval by Anita Roddick. She personally interviews applicants at least once, and her interviews, like her personality, are highly unconventional. She may ask: "How would you like to die?", "Who is your favorite literary heroine?", "What car do you have?", and "What car do you want?" to see how candidates respond when caught off-guard and to find out what interests them. According to Anita, "If they have a Golf and want a Mercedes, we are going to have real trouble with them." Applicants who don't meet her standards don't get a franchise, period. Even though this is widely known, when The Body Shop decided to enter the U. S. market, the company was flooded with so many calls for applications that it had to use a telephone recording to provide prospective investors with instructions for applying. It is still behind in processing applications.

Once they are accepted into The Body Shop family, shop owners are inundated with information. There is a newsletter published by Anita's brother, Bruno, for which she personally writes the copy (unlike most CEOs, who generally use ghost writers). There are video tapes, brochures, posters, and training programs. And there is a training center in London where both franchise owners and salespeople are accepted free. Instead of being taught how to sell or how to make money, attendees are instructed in the nature and uses of The Body Shop's products. The goal is to equip them with the knowledge necessary to answer any customer query.

Most employees pick up some of Anita Roddick's enthusiasm for the business. Traditional incentive plans such as equity participation and stock option plans encourage it, as do company-run day-care centers with sliding charges adjusted to income. But most employees are enthusiastic because they were carefully chosen for their comfort with the company's socially conscious business philosophy and their willingness to put educating customers ahead of racking up commissions. In Canada, shop staff spend about 16 hours per month volunteering at a community project of their choice, and are paid for it.

To meet the needs of customers, the company barrages them with information when they enter the store. There are posters on the wall; a very large reference book called *The Product Information Manual* which lists every product and its uses; and signs under every product explaining its ingredients and uses, and frequently its origin as well.

Even the product names are informative. There is Peppermint Foot Lotion, Banana Shampoo, Mango Body Butter, Cucumber Cleansing Milk, and Carrot Moisture Cream. There are brochures and T-shirts with slogans supporting company-endorsed social causes such as animal rights. Instead of putting products in their windows, Body Shops display posters and banners supporting organizations like Amnesty International and causes like preservation of the rain forest. Stores frequently run videos showing the company's trading ventures in such places as Nepal and Brazil. Catalogs with extensive information and colorful pictures are sent to consumers several times a year. These are especially important for reaching people who do not live near a Body Shop but want to order products by mail or phone.

The result is a reputation as a caring company. Customers and employees want to support it because it speaks to their consciences and their hearts. According to Anita, her customers are turned off by extravagant advertising claims. They have been overmarketed, and they've grown indifferent to or outright cynical toward selling efforts. The Body Shop sells cosmetics with a minimum of hype and promotes health and well-being. There are no fantasy pictures of impossibly glamorous models on the walls of these stores. Anita frequently claims that no skin product can do more than cleanse, polish, and protect the skin, that nothing other cosmetic companies have come up with will really eliminate wrinkles, that no matter how much the customer spends, she still isn't going to look like Cindy Crawford.

With this kind of sober philosophy, you might think The Body Shop has dull stores. Absolutely not! The typical Body Shop is awash in color, sounds, and smells and offers a bazaar of unusual products like Viennese washing grains. Customers feel free to explore the store and its merchandise because everything is displayed on open shelves. Nothing is under glass or hidden away. Products have clearly marked testers, so customers can smell and feel the exotic potions. Because Anita spends months each year scouring the globe to find new and exciting products, there is a constant flow of unusual product items. Indeed, this feature is one of The Body Shop's keys to success because it encourages customers to come into the stores frequently. In addition, all Body Shops are arranged the same way and sell the same products, so regular customers are immediately at home in any Body Shop anywhere in the world.

To maximize consumer appeal, product quality is equal to that of high-end cosmetics, but prices are considerably lower (though they are higher than discount prices). All fancy packaging is eliminated; The Body Shop still uses those plain urine-sample-type bottles Anita began with. The company not only encourages recycling of containers but also urges customers to bring their own bags. Anita is proud of the fact that three out of every ten of her customers say no to a shopping bag.

And there is something for everyone. While most of The Body Shop's products were originally aimed at women, the company has added the Mostly Men line, which includes Passion Fruit Cleansing Gel and shaving brushes, creams, and aftershave lotions. There is a Mama Toto line of cosmetics for mothers-to-be, mothers, and babies that includes Neroli facial wipes, baby hairbrushes, and baby powder. For children, there are endangered-species soaps, T-shirts, and back packs. In addition to cosmetics, the Body Shop sells baskets, paper products, loofah scrubs of all kinds, washcloths, and hairbrushes.

Helping Brazil's Kayapo Tribe

Late in 1988 Anita and her younger daughter Samantha were instrumental in raising funds to support the Kayapo and other indigenous tribes in their struggle to preserve the rainforest, their villages, and their way of life.

Customers and employees wax enthusiastic about this company's sincerity, lack of sales pressure, and informative approach that cuts through the hype and cynicism endemic in the cosmetic field. Because The Body Shop is so clearly differentiated in the consumer's mind, copycat efforts are unlikely to succeed. Given the company's devoted customers and employees and its two decades of successful marketing and sales, even Wall Street skeptics believe The Body Shop is capable of maintaining its rapid growth for the forseeable future. There are 112 shops in Canada and the chain continues to expand. The company's global goal is 3,000 shops. Although it has saturated the market in England, it has room for considerable expansion in the rest of the world.

Helping Others Help Themselves

The Body Shop believes trade—not aid—offers a positive solution to economic hardship in the developing world.

Anita Roddick defines business as essentially trading, with a little bit left over for her. And she loves to trade. To provide her stores with a flow of new products, she travels for several months each year, meeting new peoples and discovering their solutions to body care and health. As she points out, "All women are interested in looking after their skin, and that is why one woman can go up to another, without any hesitation and ask, 'How come your skin's so soft?' "

She finds that native peoples want to share their knowledge, and in exchange for their "product ideas," she establishes trade programs with them. In Brazil the Kayapo Indians harvest Brazil nuts, which they sell to The Body Shop for use in Brazil Nut Oil Conditioner; the women of the tribe make beaded bracelets, which are also sold in the shops. In India the company set up a factory to make Footsie Rollers—tubes of grooved acacia wood to roll under one's tired feet. Factory workers are orphaned boys, who are paid above-market wages that enable them to leave the orphanage with some capital to start adult life with. In Nepal the Bansbari Paper Project employs fifty-three people to produce handmade paper products from water hyacinths and banana fiber. Baskets come from Bangladesh, scrubs from the Aztec Indians in Mexico, and Blue Corn products from the Santa Ana Pueblo Indians in New Mexico. In Africa the Body Shop buys honey and beeswax from the Tabara Honey Cooperative in Zambia, and shea butter from women's cooperatives in northern Ghana. Providing these peoples with employment enables them to remain on their lands and preserve their culture.

Not all The Body Shop's "trade" programs are among foreign peoples. In Glasgow's slums The Body Shop provides employment for 100 people at the Soapworks, which produces one-third of the Body Shop's soaps. Twenty-five percent of the factory's profits are plowed back into the community for projects such as playgrounds. For this effort, the Confederation of British Industry in Scotland commented:

Mrs. Roddick is to be congratulated for converting a thousand speeches into a million pounds worth of positive investment. This belies the myth that nothing can be done. This business leader is about to prove otherwise. We welcome this imaginative venture and hope it will be the first of many such enterprises which will bring money and jobs to deprived city areas.

Supporting Entrepreneurship in Nepal

In 1988 Anita began buying the paper used with her products from a small Kathmandu business owned and operated by Milahn Battahria and his family. Using the water hyacinth, an environmental predator, as raw material, the handmade paper business also helps preserve its own environment.

The Embodiment of Social Consciousness

> In a society in which politicians no longer lead by example, ethical conduct is fashionable, and the media does not give people real information on what is happening in the world . . . what fascinates me is the concept of turning our shops into centres of education.

In 1986, with ninety shops and a successful company whose shares were now publicly traded, Anita and Gordon Roddick were trying to decide what to do next when they hit on the idea of using their business to do good. As children of the 1960s, they were fascinated by the idea of using a corporation to foster social change. They knew their company had a soul and a good sense of values, but how could they communicate these things to people?

They started by sponsoring posters for Greenpeace to lobby against the dumping of hazardous wastes in the North Sea and later promoted the Save the Whale campaign. The latter campaign fit well with their business, since their jojoba oil has many of the same properties as spermaceti, the oil from sperm whales that is used by cosmetic companies in many creams.

Their next effort was undertaken with the environmentalist group Friends of the Earth. Together, they produced a surreal poster showing a dead tree sprouting from a decomposing human head against an industrial background of smoking chimneys. The headline read: "Acid Reign." This effort failed because it was not only quirky and unpleasant; it was also too sophisticated. Consumers did not understand it and were repulsed by it. Their next effort, a poster showing a child in a desert holding an umbrella for shade with the headline "Ozone or No Zone," was much more successful at communicating their message to consumers.

Later campaigns have involved Amnesty International, FREEZE (a group against weapons), the Brazilian rain forest (Stop the Burning), voter registration projects in the United States, civil rights (Dr. Martin Luther King's birthday), animal rights, and the preservation of endangered species. In addition, The Body Shop supports orphanages in Romania and Albania. The Body Shop U.S. unveiled an HIV/AIDS awareness campaign in September 1993. It may raise some eyebrows, however. It involves hanging pictures of AIDS victims in Body Shop display windows and passing out lubricants, educational pamphlets, and advice on how to avoid this disease. While many customers don't mind campaigns to save endangered species of the rain forest, they may find this latest social campaign ambitious—especially since so many of The Body Shop's customers are very young. For the month of March, The Body Shop Canada ran a national campaign to "In the Name of Love—STOP Violence Against Women." They raised $100,000 for campaign partners violence prevention programs.

Two years ago The Body Shop began taking an environmental audit that examines every aspect of the company, from waste management to energy efficiency. The results are verified independently and released each year along with the company's financial report. And the Roddicks are planning to introduce another audit, called the Social Performance Audit, to examine The Body Shop's corporate giving, community projects, progress against animal testing, and Trade Not Aid projects.

What Next?

> I think the leadership of a company should encourage the next generation
> not just to follow, but to overtake.

As The Body Shop matures, it faces a number of problems. Competition is growing. Other companies are copying their stores. For instance, Leslie Wexner, founder of The Limited, has started the Bath and Body Shops, which closely resemble The Body Shops. Other companies are producing all-natural, "organic" cosmetics in both discount and upscale lines. Estée Lauder, for example, has created Origins, packaged in recycled containers and marketed in stand-alone stores, while Revlon has New Age Naturals, a line of cosmetics with names reminiscent of Body Shop products.

In 1991 The Body Shop was attacked by a television program that claimed the company had misled consumers into thinking that its products were not tested on animals. In fact, the company had changed its labeling from "Not Tested on Animals" to "Against Animal Testing" in 1989, after the Roddicks found out that some of their suppliers did use ingredients that had been tested on animals. At that time, the company instituted a five-year rule—it will not use ingredients tested on animals in the last five years. Because The Body Shop had made these changes as soon as the Roddicks realized that some ingredients had been tested on animals *and* before the show was aired, it was able to sue the show's producers successfully. But this controversy illustrates the vulnerability of companies that have a high profile on social consciousness: The media and others will look hard for evidence of any mistake on that company's part.

In 1992, Anita Roddick appeared in several ads for American Express. She had been reluctant to do the commercials in the beginning, but finally consented because Amex allowed her to talk about her Trade Not Aid program. The response was overwhelming, and brought home to her how powerful advertising can be—especially in the United States, where consumers are conditioned to very heavy advertising exposure. Some observers believe that The Body Shop should advertise in the United States to create brand awareness and to respond to the promotional efforts of competition. They argue that Americans expect to learn about products through advertising and that competitors who are making heavy use of advertising are attracting customers who might prefer to shop at The Body Shop if they knew about it. So far, Anita has resisted their arguments.

In 1992 there were also some signs that the company's sales and profits might be slowing down. Although some observers judged the sales slump only natural for a company that had grown so fast, others were more skeptical. Several "green" funds—that is, funds that buy only the stocks and bonds of companies that are environmentally concerned and/or support animal and human rights—eliminated The Body Shop from their portfolios, thereby lowering the company's stock price. In October 1993 during the first half of the fiscal year, however, Anita announced an increase in profits of 20 percent over the preceding year. This was far ahead of the 9-10 percent increase that had been forecasted.

What concerns the Roddicks most at this point is not their company's stock price but the lack of promising leaders coming up from the ranks. Neither of their children appears to be interested in leading the company, so where will the enthusiasm, stamina, and constant flow of new ideas come from when Anita Roddick finally steps down? Will this highly distinctive firm then lose its vitality and join the rest of the corporate pack?

Sources: The Body Shop Press Releases, March 1992; Body Shop Catalogs; "The Body Shop: One Woman's Soothing Potion for the Planet," *Greensboro News and Record,* August 18, 1993, p. D1; Bo Burlingham, "This Woman Has Changed Business Forever," *Inc.,* June 1990, pp. 34–45; Jennifer Conlin, "Survival of the Fittest," *Working Woman,* February, 1994, pp. 29–31, 68, 69, 72, 73; Robert Dwek, "Body Shop Rethinks Promos with Danone," *Marketing,* May 6, 1993, p. 3; Mary Gottschalk, "Think Green Cosmetics," *Fort Worth Star-Telegram,* November 28, 1991, pp. 1, 9; Jeff Haggin, "Show Your Customers Respect!", *Catalog Age* 9(10):91–92; Rachel Jacob, "What Selling Will Be Like in the '90s," *Fortune,* January 13, 1992, p. 63; Valerie Latham, "Body Shop Splits Hairs with Rival," *Marketing,* January 28, 1993, p. 6; Martha R. Moore, "Body Shop: Profits with Principles," *USA Today,* October 10, 1991, Section E; Tom Peters, "Body, Soul and Profit," *Rochester Business Magazine,* March 1992, p. 72; Anita Roddick, *Body and Soul,* New York: Crown, 1991); James R. Rosenfield, "In the Mail: The Body Shop, Institute of Noetic Sciences," *Direct Marketing* 55(3):14–16; Paul Southgate, "Own-label: The Next Great Step," *Marketing,* November 19, 1992, pp. 28–29; Laura Zinn, "Whales, Human Rights, Rain Forest—and the Heady Smell of Profits," *Business Week,* July 15, 1991, pp. 114–15; Alex Pentland of The Body Shop Canada.

Integrative Case

Harley-Davidson: HOG Heaven

I must have died and gone to heaven! . . . I am at the Northeast Regional Harley Owners Group Rally—I spend two solid days in this parking lot. . . . "What," you might ask, "are you nuts?" No, not really, for you see, the highlight of a HOG rally [is] . . . the Harley Demo Ride Program—thirty or so brand-new Harleys, there for the taking! Just stand in line in front of the bike of your choice, wait your turn (5 to 30 minutes) and hop on the Harley of your dreams. And when you're done with that one, get in another line and do it again. Over and over and over. . . . You think Harley might sell a motorcycle or two to the people who stand in line and ride these bikes on a scenic, twisty road, only to return grinning from ear to ear? The most ingenious marketing tool I've ever seen.*

Everyone knows the Harley brand name. It's famous: There are HOG fanatics (Harley Owners Group) who tattoo "Harley" on their arms. It's also infamous: Where there are Harleys, there may be Hell's Angels. Whether loved or condemned, Harley is one of the most powerful and internationally recognized U.S. brands—so much so that the company cannot satisfy demand for its motorcycles at home or abroad.

To achieve this global prominence, you might think that Harley spent its nine decades of existence cleverly crafting, shaping, and managing its macho image. Not so. Harley started with the idea of creating silent motorcycles in the hope of making motorcycling socially acceptable. It produced motorcycles for racers, U.S. soldiers, and the police. Then Hollywood taught us that Harleys are the vehicles of choice of Hell's Angels and other outlaws. And today? The Harley-Davidson Motor Company wants everyone to think of Harley as the cycle for clean-cut, upscale members of society—your father, your plumber, and your stockbroker. Obviously, something went awry in image management at this company.

Richard Kolbe, Harley's Information Services director has joked that the Harley buyers of today are so affluent and law-abiding "the only things they carry in their tool kits are their chequebooks." Waiting lists now exist for these bikes. Kane's Motorcycle Shop, a Harley dealer in Calgary often lends Mayor Al Duerr a machine to cruise away an hour or two. Company officials say that for every Harley owner there are dozens more like Duerr who want to be, and so Harley has a network of specialty stores, including one in Calgary, and another in Banff to make the firm's logo on a growing list of high priced items including jackets, T-shirts, boxer shorts, lingerie and watches. There are also cookie jars shaped like motorcycle gas tanks for $109.95. Sales of this merchandise now accounts for one-third of the firm's total sales revenues. As to the bikes, 15-20% of Harley-Davidson sales are to men in their 40's, a new class of rich urban bikers willing to spend $17,000 on average for a bike.

*Webb Collings, personal communication, November 24, 1993.

How did the product of a well-meaning small company from Milwaukee, Wisconsin, become both an international symbol of outlaws and the prized possession of Japanese businessmen, college professors, and stockbrokers? To understand the twists in Harley's image saga and the company's strategy for success, we have to start at the beginning.

The First Four Decades

The first step in creating the Harley image was taken in 1903 when the company's founders, the three Davidson brothers (William, Walter, and Arthur), and their friend Bill Harley, decided to put Harley's name first on the door of their "factory" (a 10-by-15 foot building in the Davidson backyard in Milwaukee) because he had actually designed their first motorcycle. They could not have guessed how important the name *Harley* would be to their company—that someday their motorcycles would popularly be called "Harleys" or that customers would form Harley Owners Groups or "HOGS." The latter term is crucial to the Harley mystique. Think what might have happened had the name *Davidson* come first: Davidson Owners Groups forms the acronym DOGS. The Harley Owners Group have 250,000 members worldwide, including 13,000 in Canada.

As sales grew rapidly from three motorcycles in 1903 to 150 in 1908, the company's prospects looked good. Its success back then depended on several factors. First, the founders insisted that only high-quality machines would bear the Harley-Davidson name—another step in creating a strong brand image. Second, they published a product catalog, which had the advantages of being less expensive than other advertising forms and of giving the company complete control over the presentation of its brand. Third, they sold motorcycles for police duty. Usage by the police enhanced the image of Harleys as durable, reliable, fast machines and made the brand name familiar to Americans.

Fourth, and probably most important, they introduced the 45-degree V-twin engine, which displaced 61 cubic inches and produced 7 horsepower—a big improvement over the previous 4-horsepower engines. The twin-cylinder engine has since become a Harley trademark. It inaugurated the Harley tradition of producing ever-larger engines and cycles (or *bikes,* as some riders prefer to call them).

In 1908 Harley began its long domination of American motorcycle racing when Walter Davidson entered the Federation of American Motorcyclists Endurance Run in the Catskill Mountains in New York. Although not expected to do well, he turned in a flawless performance, which netted him a perfect score of 1,000 points plus 5 more for outstanding consistency of both rider and machine.

Although most of the company's actions in the early years led to an image of big, powerful cycles, the Harley-Davidson cycle was nicknamed the "Silent Gray Fellow" because the company used gray as the standard color and refused to open mufflers to increase exhaust noise—a practice common in that era. The founders believed that promoting motorcycling as a quiet activity rather than a boisterous one would make it more acceptable to the populace.

The company gained points for patriotism when it converted its production entirely to military use during World War I. Heavy production for the military— over 20,000 cycles—coupled with the need for in-the-field maintenance and repair led to the establishment of the first Harley-Davidson Service School. After the war, Harley continued the school because it realized that good repair service would reinforce the company's quality image.

Harley-Davidson shifted into high gear in the Roaring Twenties as its motorcycles won more and more racing titles and pent-up demand from the war years boosted sales. To perpetuate its machines' reputation for racing prowess, the company built bigger, faster cycles. In 1921 it produced the first cycle to go more than 100 miles per hour, and in 1922 it introduced the 74-cubic-inch V-twin—a giant machine designed to pull two passenger sidecars. Harley also introduced the teardrop gas tank and the first hand brake—two features that would also become Harley trademarks.

Unfortunately, the era of motorcycling exuberance skidded to a halt in the Great Depression. Production dropped from 32,000 cycles in 1929 to just over 6,000 in 1933 as the role of the motorcycle changed. Initially, cycles were considered less expensive than cars and less arduous to use than bicycles. Then, in the 1920s, they were considered recreational vehicles for racing, leisure-time sport, and off-the-road riding. In the 1930s, economically depressed Americans could no longer afford recreational motorcycling.

To stimulate consumer demand, the company began restyling its machines. It added colors to make them more attractive in 1933. The army-green that had been retained after World War I was replaced with two- and three-tone paint jobs. Artdeco decals and other special touches were added, and in 1936 the company redesigned its big cycle. By 1939, Harleys looked quite different. They were sleeker, more powerful, more visually appealing, and more aerodynamic than they were in 1929.

During World War II Harley-Davidson began to build an international reputation when its motorcycles were supplied to British troops because British factories had been severely damaged during the German air attacks known as the Blitz.

All This and Elvis Too

After the war, Harley introduced the Hydra-Glide, the first of the classic heavy Harleys. This machine and its companions were ridden by Marlon Brando and his gang in the movie *The Wild Ones,* which introduced the motorcyclist-as-outlaw stereotype to Americans. The movie simultaneously made Harley a household name. The larger public now viewed the Harley rider as a black-leather-jacketed, asocial, violence-prone undesirable, even though only a minority of Harley riders fit this image. Most were just motorcycling enthusiasts. Even the King rode a Harley—an article in the 1956 *Enthusiast* (Harley's in-house publication) showed Elvis with his Harley.

Unfortunately, Harley's tradition of developing ever-bigger and more powerful cycles not only reinforced the outlaw image but also overshadowed the company's production of smaller motorcycles. In the late 1940s Harley introduced a 125-cc single-cylinder lightweight cycle designed for those who wanted something smaller and less expensive than the V-twin. Later, in 1960, Harley joined with Aeronatica Macchi S.p.A. in Varese, Italy, to produce light- and middleweight machines that ranged from 50 cc upward and had names like Shortster, Legera, Baja, and Z-90.

Despite its negative image in many quarters, Harley prospered during this period. Other motorcycle manufacturers did not. At one time, there were over 150 motorcycle manufacturers in the United States. By 1953, there were only two large, well-known U.S. manufacturers: Harley-Davidson and Indian—and in that year, Indian closed its doors, leaving Harley as the lone survivor.

Booming Sales and Kawa-What?

The decade of the 1960s vastly changed the motorcycle market. Sales jumped from 500,000 cycles in 1960 to over a million in 1974 because of demographic and product-use changes. The size of the population aged fourteen to twenty-four—the big target market for cycles—rose from 27 million to 41 million, and in North America disposable income nearly doubled. Some younger consumers—the motorcycle hobbyists—wanted off-the-road machines like trail bikes, motocross, scramblers, and desert bikes for fun and daring. Other consumers, who relied on their motorcycles for transportation, wanted bigger bikes. Sales of superbikes—those over 750 cc—grew at an annual rate of 47 percent. These were the cruising bikes popularized by Peter Fonda and Dennis Hopper in the movie *Easy Rider.* Although Fonda and Hopper were outlaws of a sort, they were much less menacing than Brando and his pack were in the 1950s. The image of the biker began to soften.

The typical motorcycle buyer in this era was a male under twenty-five years of age with a median income of $12,720*. In purchasing a cycle, this consumer shopped extensively (usually for eight weeks) and gathered a lot of information. Over 80 percent of buyers consulted other motorcycle owners; 82 percent visited several dealers; 69 percent read motorcycle magazines; 52 percent read manufacturers' literature; 39 percent studied competition results and test-drove cycles. The average buyer considered 3.7 makes or models before purchasing and was less brand loyal than buyers in previous eras (only a third repurchased the same brand).

The combination of increasing sales and extensive shopping behavior by consumers spurred an increase in the number of franchised dealerships, which more than tripled in ten years. Franchisees were expected to carry a full line of the manufacturer's merchandise and to provide knowledgeable sales personnel and good service facilities. As motorcycle engines and parts became more complex, discount houses and service stations were no longer able to service these machines. Thus dealer service became paramount in selling cycles, and Harley's service school gave its dealers a competitive edge in providing superior service.

Then, in the early 1970s, motorcycle sales stagnated and dealers started to push accessories and the notion that the buyer should customize his cycle. Harley-Davidson broadened its accessories lines. Since these were promoted through the Harley catalog, dealers were relieved of the need to carry all these parts and accessories. As a result, cycles began to sport more luggage packs, sheepskin seats, and sheepskin backrests. Styles of riding gear mushroomed, and the Harley image was now dressed up.

The biggest change in the motorcycle market in the 1960s was the reintroduction of competition. With the collapse of Indian, Harley-Davidson's share of the U.S. market grew to over 60 percent by 1960. Although European manufacturers had exported cycles to the American market for decades, their individual market shares had been small until the demise of all U.S. manufacturers but Harley. From then on, their share of sales increased so that three British firms—BSA, Triumph, and Norton—plus the Italian brand Moto-Guzzi accounted for 40 percent of industry sales not owned by Harley.

This comfortable competitive situation was disrupted when another formidable European competitor, BMW, entered the U.S. market. Known for its high quality and outstanding engineering, BMW was considered the "Rolls-Royce of the motorcycle world." Worse yet from Harley's perspective, BMW was especially well known for big machines. Even with a minuscule dealer network, BMW's sales in just the 750-cc market quickly grew to 5 percent by 1974.

While Harley worried about BMW, the Japanese—Honda, Yamaha, Kawasaki, and Suzuki—were entering the U.S. market. At first, the American and European companies welcomed the Japanese because they produced mostly light- and middleweight bikes that didn't compete with the big Harleys and BMWs. U.S. and European manufacturers viewed the small Japanese cycles as a means of enticing more Americans into riding motorcycles. Once these new riders learned something about cycles, Harley and the European manufacturers reasoned, they would trade up to a big machine—a Harley or maybe a Norton or a BMW.

Even after the Japanese began to produce larger cycles, they were not seen as a threat. The chairman of BSA wrote: "Personally, I do not think the Japanese Motor Cycle industry will eclipse the traditional type of machine that the British motorcyclist wants and buys . . . [but] they are bound to make some impact on our home market by virtue of the high quality of their product and low prices." That comment sums up

*All monetary figures in this case are given in U.S. dollars.

the dangerously complacent attitude of both U.S. and European producers, who assumed that their hold on the market was irrevocable because anyone who learned anything about cycles would naturally want an American or European cycle as soon as they could afford one. These companies completely underestimated the Japanese.

Since the turn of the century, the British had had a reputation for producing some of the finest hand-crafted and -machined motorcycles on the market. In less than a decade, however, the Japanese proved they could produce equivalent-quality machines more cheaply. They invested in more efficient production technologies to reduce labor costs, and they used lighter-weight materials, which meant the average rider could lift a cycle. As the Japanese moved along the experience curve, the cost of their cycles consistently declined. In addition, they invested heavily so that they could introduce major technological changes more quickly.

While U.S. and British companies were raising prices, the Japanese held their price levels constant, although demand was so good they could have reduced prices. They also expanded their dealer network and spent more on promotion and advertising. By attacking the Hell's Angels image of Harley with promotional messages such as "You meet the nicest people on a Honda," the Japanese hoped to expand the market by making motorcycling a socially acceptable pastime that was fun and safe—a move that was reminiscent of Harley's early image building. As a result of heavy advertising, lower prices, and readily available financing, sales at Japanese dealerships skyrocketed, which enabled these dealerships to discount their motorcycles and thereby achieve even greater volume.

What happened to Harley and the European firms in the late 1960s and early 1970s? Harley diversified into building gasoline- and electric-powered golf carts. The British firms went through a succession of mergers, but these moves failed to save them. By the end of the 1970s, all of them except Triumph were extinct.

Sometimes Up, Sometimes Down

In the mid-1970s demand for motorcycles slowed as the industry approached market saturation; only a fourth of motorcycle buyers now were first-time purchasers. In addition, legal changes threatened to diminish demand as environmentalists worked to restrict off-the-road riding and noise and to implement emission regulations that might lead to reduced-power machines and riding enjoyment. Safety regulations such as mandatory crash helmets tended to emphasize the danger of motorcycling and turn off would-be buyers. In Europe and Japan sales slowed as motorcycles became more recreational vehicles than necessary transportation. Only in less developed countries, where motorcycles were still considered a primary means of transport, did sales continue to grow.

How did Harley-Davidson fare in this period? To counteract inroads by the Japanese in the lightweight segment of the market, H-D introduced a line of lightweight machines, which gave it the widest range of engine displacements: from a 90-cc minicycle to the 1200-cc Electra Glide. It also introduced cycles, such as trail bikes, for specialty uses and modernized the styling on many of its bikes. To enhance its big bike/serious bike status, H-D sponsored and/or participated in many motorcycle races.

Harley also moved its advertising from a Milwaukee agency to a major Chicago agency "to avail itself of greater media buying efficiencies" and increased its ad spending to $1.15 million in 1972. The resulting campaign with the slogan "The great American freedom machine" was a big success and added a patriotic spin to Harley's appeal and image. Harley ads appeared in a broader range of print media, such as *Sport, Sports Illustrated,* and even *Time* and *Newsweek*. Successful though this effort was, it was dwarfed by Honda's $3.5 million promotional campaign.

Thanks to the Arab oil embargo in 1973, sales of motorcycles temporarily spurted. Without orders from the military and police departments, though, Harley would have been in deep trouble. Its total market share was a mere 5 percent; its share of heavy bikes declined from 99.6 percent in 1972 to 40 percent in 1976 because of competition from BMW and the Japanese; sales of lightweight Harleys had dropped; and the recession had slowed total motorcycle industry sales.

Given the slowdown in sales, manufacturers should have reduced production in the early 1970s, but the Japanese companies chose not to. As a result, they had excessive inventories, which they moved by using aggressive sales-promotion techniques. Honda offered $80 rebates and Yamaha announced discounts of $300 to $1,200. Other manufacturers offered dealers free inventory and delayed payment options in order to get cycles on the dealers' floors. Yamaha even copied the auto industry by introducing yearly models to justify discounts on last year's models and to entice buyers with "new" models. As the Japanese used temporary price reductions to sell their products, U.S. and European companies felt forced to increase prices because of higher labor and production costs, especially for meeting new emission standards in a more environmentally conscious age.

Harley fought the competition by increasing advertising and promotional campaigns and by moving into radio and television advertising—especially late-night TV. The company also stepped up its sponsorship of racing and exploited its grand national championship in advertising. Although the primary targets of these efforts were the enthusiast and the repeat buyer, dealers also benefited from the increased advertising as ads stimulated buyers to visit showrooms.

Harley developed a computerized file of dealers so that it could adapt and improve its services to the individual dealer. In addition, it established new inventory- and production-control systems to lower costs and increase operating efficiencies. Also, it had set up Harley-Davidson International in 1975 to develop markets outside the United States.

The biggest change for Harley, however, was a change in ownership. In 1965 Harley had become a publicly traded company, and four years later it merged with American Machine and Foundry Company (AMF). The merger proved a mixed experience for Harley. While AMF supplied millions of dollars for capital improvements at Harley-Davidson and enabled the company to increase marketing expenditures, it failed to support extensive R&D. The result was that Harley stayed with its two-cylinder engine, which was by then outmoded. Worse, AMF was production oriented—more interested in getting greater numbers of Harleys out the door than in maintaining quality. (Table 1 shows Harley's percentage of AMF's total sales.) So Harley's prices remained high even as its styles failed to keep up with the times, and the Harley image was tarnishing as new lightweight models produced in Italy were added to the line. These were unsuccessful because of poor product quality and poor service from the Italian manufacturer. Quality overall deteriorated.

The year 1978 provides a good example of the fluctuating fortunes of Harley-Davidson. Because this was the seventy-fifth anniversary of the company's founding, the president of the firm and other executives toured the United States—on motorcycles, of course—visiting dealers to show that everyone enjoys motorcycling. The tour garnered the company a lot of free publicity. Sales of heavyweight bikes turned up, partly because the declining U.S. dollar reduced the price spread between Harleys and Japanese bikes, and partly because Harley introduced a new 1,340-cc Electra Glide to complement the Low Rider it had brought to market in 1977. The Low Rider was so popular that dealers sold their entire allotment of the 1978 model by June. The company's market share rose to nearly 7 percent and profits were up by nearly 10 percent. (Table 2 shows changes in Harley's market share throughout the 1970s.) But even as sales of heavyweights went up, sales of lightweight bikes went down, so Harley was forced to close its plant in Italy.

On Their Own Again

In 1981 AMF decided to sell Harley-Davidson because of its declining profits. However, there wasn't much buyer interest in a capital-intensive company in a deteriorating

TABLE 1	SELECTED FINANCIAL DATA, 1971–1976 (IN MILLIONS OF U.S. DOLLARS)					
	1971	**1972**	**1973**	**1974**	**1975**	**1976**
Revenues, motorcycles	$ 97.2	$126.7	$143.0	$152.6	$190.8	$189.1
Total corporate income	762.6	938.0	976.8	1,026.9	1,004.7	1,111.4
Net income (after taxes)	43.5	56.0	59.0	22.6	31.4	38.2

Source: Harvard Business School Case, "Harley-Davidson/Marketing Strategies for Motorcycles—1977," by Robert D. Buzzell, 1983.

TABLE 2	SELECTED MARKET SHARE STATISTICS, 1971–1976 (IN PERCENT)					
	1971	**1972**	**1973**	**1974**	**1975**	**1976**
Harley-Davidson	3.6	4.3	5.0	5.7	6.9	6.8
Honda	51.8	47.7	42.1	43.0	40.2	37.9
Yamaha	15.4	17.9	20.3	20.3	16.2	20.4
Kawasaki	8.7	9.3	12.1	12.8	17.2	17.1
Suzuki	10.4	12.4	12.9	10.7	12.8	11.7

Source: Harvard Business School Case, "Harley-Davidson/Marketing Strategies for Motor-cycles—1977," by Robert D. Buzzell, 1983. *Note:* Because other brands' shares were not estimated, columns do not sum to 100.

industry that was losing sales to the Japanese. Honda and Kawaski were now effec-tively penetrating the super heavyweight motorcycle markets that previously be-longed entirely to Harley. Quality was deteriorating and the plant and equipment at the Milwaukee plant was old and unreliable. A move was planned to York, Pennsylva-nia, and that introduced labor union problems on top of mounting Harley dealership complaints. On top of all this, there was no capital for expansion. In June Vaughn Beals and a dozen other Harley managers, including Willie Davidson, a grandson of one of the founders, purchased Harley-Davidson for $75 million in a buyout leveraged by loans against the company's assets, one of the most leveraged buyouts in U.S. history.

In 1981 and 1982 operating losses mounted at Harley owing to declining sales and market share and the company experienced a shortage of funds. To deal with all its problems, H-D responded in six ways.

First, management attacked the quality problem. They surveyed customers, and were shocked by the volume and vociferousness of consumer complaints about quality, which had slipped greatly during the AMF years. As many as half the bikes coming off the production line had defects, and Harleys were widely known for leaking oil. Management negotiated a $100 million line of credit to improve production processes and facilities. As an example of the new dedication to quality, CEO Beals decided to make the Cafe Racer—a new Harley product—the kind of high-quality product the company would henceforth stand for. He sent a group of engineering, service, and manufacturing managers to the Racer plant with instructions to make the Racer come out right. It cost $100,000 to fix the first 100 machines, but that set the tone for reviving Harley's quality image.

To transform the manufacturing process from a production to a quality orientation, H-D implemented just-in-time manufacturing, statistical operator control, and employee involvement. Employees were empowered to take action whenever they thought quality was being threatened—even if that meant stopping the entire production line.

Second, Harley introduced a new line of cycles based on customer demands for beautiful customized bikes. The company redesigned the V-twin powerplants and developed the Heritage Series—a line of cycles that re-created the classic big Harleys of the 1950s.

Third, Harley revved up dealer support through extensive training of dealer salespeople and modernizing and decorating of dealerships.

Fourth, Harley cut costs drastically by eliminating executive perks like luxury hotels and first-class airfares, laying off 426 workers, cutting officers' salaries by as much as 12 percent, freezing other salaries, and negotiating lower wages with its union.

Fifth, Harley went after bootleg manufacturers of goods bearing the Harley name and/or logo. Many of these products, such as drug paraphernalia and T-shirts bearing swastikas or obscenities, propagated the "bad boy" image the company was determined to eradicate. After numerous sting operations, most Harley bootleggers were put out of business and the company was once again in control of the goods bearing its logo. It used its new control to promote a more upscale image of its products: Along with the T-shirts and coolers, it produced $700 Harley gold rings, $130 leather boots, sheets and towels for kids, and a men's cologne.

Sixth, Harley asked the International Trade Commission for protection from Japanese motorcycle imports, charging that Japanese companies were dumping cycles on the U.S. market at prices lower than those charged in Japan. In January 1983 the ITC ruled that motorcycle imports posed a threat to domestic producers (actually, there was only one domestic producer: Harley-Davidson), increased the 4.4 percent import duty on foreign cycles to 49.4 percent, and ruled that this high duty would be gradually lowered over the next five years. Thus Harley had until 1988 to improve its market position enough to face renewed unfettered competition from the Japanese. Few believed it had much of a chance. In fact, H-D's prospects still looked so dim that the Japanese even offered to help the company! H-D turned them down, but clearly, the once-proud American corporation had hit bottom.

The Harley Eagle Soars Alone

By 1987, Harley had come roaring back. It now had 45 percent of the domestic heavyweight market and profits were up. (See Table 3 for Harley's revenue and income in selected years between 1985 and 1993, and see Table 4 for Harley's market share in Canada in relation to other motorcycles.) Harley's contracts from police departments and highway patrols were recovering, and the company had purchased Holiday Rambler, a maker of recreational vehicles. Things looked so good, in fact, that the company asked the Reagan Administration to drop the protective tariffs a year early. But Harley was unwilling to take this remarkable comeback for granted. H-D executives continued to tour the country, participating in rallies and talking to customers.

The good news continued into 1988, when Holiday Rambler increased sales by bringing out new products, motorcycle contracts with law enforcement units increased,

TABLE 3	SELECTED FINANCIAL DATA, 1986–1993 (IN MILLIONS OF U.S. DOLLARS)							
	1986	**1987**	**1988**	**1989**	**1990**	**1991**	**1992**	**1993**
Revenues, motorcycles	$295.3	$646.0	$709.4	$791.0	$864.6	$939.9	$1,105.3	$1,217.4
Net income, motorcycles	4.9	21.2	23.9	32.9	37.8	37.0	54.2	70.0
Foreign revenues, motorcycles	—	324.6	397.8	496.0	595.3	678.5	n.a.	n.a.
Net income, motorcycles	—	29.4	49.7	60.9	87.8	85.6	n.a.	n.a.

Sources: Data for 1986 to 1991 from Harley-Davidson, Inc., annual statements. Data for 1992 and 1993 from Value Line, Edition 12, March 4, 1994.

TABLE 4	1992 MARKET SHARE IN CANADA
BMW	— 1%
Honda	— 27%
Yamaha	— 26%
Suzuki	— 17%
Harley-Davidson	— 16%
Kawasaki	— 13%

and Harley won a $9.8 million contract to make 500-pound bomb casings for the Department of Defense. In late 1988 H-D announced record earnings; sales had reached $559,823,000 in the first nine months of the year alone.

These gains were amazing considering that the Japanese had been blatantly copying Harley's big bike designs and had raised their advertising expenditures to dizzying levels. Harley owed its new success to the loyalty of its customers. By the late 1980s, an amazing 75 percent of Harley buyers were repurchasing Harleys.

There are several reasons for this loyalty: high quality standards, constant design and style improvements, the "Buy American" movement, and buyers' identification with the company. This is not a corporation run by Mercedes-driving executives who have little first-hand contact with their market. Harley execs continue to meet Harley owners when they ride to rallies to conduct seat-of-the-pants market research. To strengthen the owner-company tie, they founded the Harley Owners Groups (HOG) and a bi-monthly newsletter to group members.

A HOG rally is overwhelming. It usually lasts two to three days, and the parking lot fills up early with trucks towing Harleys. Many attendees come from too far away to ride their Harleys to the rally, while others have so much invested in their "show" machines that they are reluctant to risk damaging them on the highways. Many bring more than one cycle to a rally. For several days, HOG members talk to fellow bikers, look at cycles, get ideas for new designs for their machines, tell stories and jokes about "rice grinders" (slang for Japanese bikes), and polish their own cycles to dazzling beauty. There are different kinds of wax for most parts of a motorcycle, and it may take more than five types to polish a bike to show standards.

A wide range of socioeconomic groups attend HOG rallies and ages range from the teens to the seventies. Some HOG members are blue-collar workers, others are affluent professionals. Married, single, with kids and without, they meet old friends and make new road acquaintances. This is essentially a family affair where heavy drinking and boisterousness are frowned on.

On the last night of the rally, there is often a show of lights. Harleys decorated with flashing, pulsating lights of red, white, and blue or maybe green, yellow, and pink slowly pass by the spectators. Everything on the bike can be lit up—handlebars, engine parts, spokes and wheels to create Ferris wheel effects, seats, luggage packs, and license holders. Some owners invest as much as $35,000 to dress up a machine. The effect is awesome, and the crowd oohs and aahs over each machine.

Part of this buyer loyalty stems from Harley's status as a cultural icon. Many of you can probably close your eyes and easily visualize the Harley logo or the Harley eagle. You've seen these symbols in so many places because Harley is so popular. Harley's Super Glide cycle is thought of as the archetypal big bike—*the* American motorcycle. To most people, "big bikes" means Harley, not Honda.

A new sort of rider has been appearing on Harleys in recent years: Rubbies, or Rich Urban Riders. In Canada NHL stars Theoren Fleury and Doug Gilmour, Calgary Stampeders' owners Larry Ryckman, and Calgary mayor Al Duerr are among the celebrities who own and enjoy riding Harleys. These riders buy Harleys the way they once bought time shares in fashionable vacation homes. These Rubbies, who have done so much to make weekend cycling a major pastime, are known generically to dealers as "Attila the Stockbroker" because they are ruthless about quality. They don't want oil leaking on their Gucci loafers.

Harleys have also become popular among the distinctly nonwild and nonaffluent. There is a thriving group of Christian bikers who belong to the Christian Motorcyclists Association (CMA). At CMA rallies, many of the Harleys sport Bible scenes or quotes such as "Narrow Is the Road That Leads to Life." Most rally participants are married couples: some attend with their children and pets. (Spice, a schnauzer, has logged over 130,000 miles sitting on the sheepskin cover of his owner's gas tank.) Rallies feature bike shows, preaching, praying, and good clean fun.

Harleys have a special mystique in Japan, where they are associated with being "wild." While the technologically sophisticated Japanese cycles actually go faster and are easier to handle than Harleys, they don't have the thrill of the untameable American machine. Harleys are major Japanese status symbols, which explains why members of the All-Japan Harley-Davidson Owners Association spend as much as $50,000 to fully equip and customize their bikes. Like their American counterparts, Japanese riders like to sit back and enjoy the Harley experience. As the CEO of Harley says: "Harley-Davidson doesn't sell transportation, we sell transformation. We sell excitement, a way of life."

HOGS Abroad

In the late 1980s Harley began targeting foreign markets to offset flat sales in the United States, where the company already had 70 percent of the domestic heavyweight cycle market. In 1989 H-D established a wholly owned distribution system in Japan, which generated sales of over 3,000 machines by 1993. It also sells a line of Harley apparel that has proved quite popular with the Japanese. In Australia, the

An Informal Rally

Diane Peirano, Business and Economics Supervisor at Prentice Hall, and a group of friends on a recent HOG ride in Connecticut.

United Kingdom, and other European countries, Harley dealers have trouble keeping up with demand and buyers frequently have to wait six months or more to get their cycles. Harley's share of the worldwide heavyweight market rose from 21 percent in 1986 to 31 percent in 1992, with 7 percent of the increase coming from Europe and a little over 2 percent from the Pacific Rim.

Some of Harley's success abroad derives from its determination to customize its marketing package for foreign cultures. H-D establishes HOGs in foreign countries, publishes Harley magazines in foreign languages, and stages beer and band fests all over. Sometimes the company makes a cultural misstep, however. For example, at a rally in southern France, where the people keep later hours than Americans, rally attendees were extremely upset when Harley closed the bar and ended the music at the early hour of midnight. To oblige its loyal French customers, Harley reopened the bar and convinced the band to play on until 3 A.M.

In Europe as in the United States, Harley execs bike around the countryside. After discovering that in Germany Harleys are frequently ridden at more than 100 miles per hour, they explored ways of creating a smoother ride and pushed the sale of safety options. While some analysts think that foreign sales will soon fizzle, Harley's European manager believes that all the goodwill created by HOGs and rallies will last, and he may be right. By May 1993, all European-bound Harleys were sold and dealers could not get any more machines until 1994.

On the Home Front

Unsatisfied demand for Harleys is also a big problem in Canada and the United States. Manufacturing facilities limit production to 70,000 per year, and roughly one-fourth of these are sold overseas. As a result, Harley dealers in the United States have been able to sell all the machines they can obtain—usually before the bikes are in the shop. Even used Harleys are in short supply because as the price of the new cycles has risen, less affluent buyers have turned to second-hand sources in droves. Now that most of those have been purchased, it's a good thing that a well-maintained Harley can stay on the road for decades!

In the meantime, Harley has a new product: credit. Dealers can enter into joint venture with Harley-Davidson to finance their inventories and can even resell credit to bikers. Next on the list is a black Harley credit card.

Harley CEO Richard Teerlink is adamant that Harley will not make the mistakes it made in the late 1970s when it got sloppy with success and allowed quality to slip. Despite dealer and owner pressure, he refuses to open overseas plants, stop selling abroad, or increase production in the United States until he thinks the company is ready to handle expansion without sacrificing quality.

Some industry observers suspect that Teerlink's policy is based on the recognition that scarcity generates demand just as well as quality, and has the fortuitous side effect of maintaining high prices. Part of the Harley owners' willingness to pay a high price is the knowledge that the bikes are a good investment. If kept long enough, in fact, their resale value becomes greater than their original price—and the owner has all the enjoyment of riding the Harley in the meantime.

Industry observers also suspect that H-D refuses to increase supply because a glut of Harleys could damage the product's exclusive image, reducing both sales and resale prices. From the company's perspective, then, the smart thing is to restrict supply. That philosophy seems to be working, as Harley's 1993 total sales were estimated to be roughly $1.2 billion, up from $791 million in 1989.

Meanwhile, customers look through catalogs to pick out the Harley of their dreams, and dealers sell Harley parts, accessories, and other merchandise such as baby bibs and *The Holy Ranger—Harley-Davidson Poems* by Jack Rosenblum.

Sources: *The Harley-Davidson Story* (Harley-Davidson, 1982); "AMF Unit Charges Japanese Motorcycles Are Dumped in U.S.," *The Wall Street Journal*, June 8, 1977, p. 42; "Motorcycle Officials Hail Firm's Birthday with a Mighty Roar," *The Wall Street Journal*, June 2, 1978, p. 4; "Harley-Davidson: A Revival as Macho Motorcycles Take Off," *Business Week*, August 21, 1978, p. 110, 111; "Cash in on U.S. Companies That Are Hammering the Japanese," *Money*, April 1992, pp. 69–72; "Marketer of the Month: Willie G. Davidson," *Sales and Marketing Management,* April 1991, pp. 26, 28; "Going Whole Hog to Provide Stakeholder Satisfaction," *Management Review,* June 1993, pp. 53–55; "Harley-Davidson, Inc., Division Chief Takes New Marketing Role, " *The Wall Street Journal,* August 5, 1990, p. B5; "BMW, the Motorcycle, Gears Up for a Big Run," *The New York Times,* October 11, 1990, p. D19; "Mind My (Motor) Bike", *The Economist*, July 2, 1977, p. 82; "The Power of Cult Brands," *Adweek's Marketing Week,* February 24, 1992, pp. 18–21; "That Vroom You Hear Is Harley," *Business Week,* August 17, 1987, p. 78; Robert D. Buzzell and Nancy Jackson, "Note on the Motorcycle Industry," *Harvard Business School Case,* 1978; Robert D. Buzzell, "Harley-Davidson/Marketing Strategies for Motorcycles," *Harvard Business School Case,* 1983; Susan Caminiti, "The Payoff from a Good Reputation," *Fortune,* February 10, 1992, pp. 74–77; Claudia H. Deutsch, "Now Harley-Davidson Is All Over the Road," *The New York Times,* April 17, 1987, pp. F12, 13; Claudia H. Deutsch, "Selling Bikes After the Wild Ones Have Settled Down," *The New York Times,* December 22, 1991, p. 4F; Art Pine, "Stiff Motorcycle Duties to be Aimed at Spurring Japan-U.S. Cycle Industry," *Wall Street Journal,* April 4, 1983; David Handelman, "Heck's Angels," *The New York Times Magazine,* November 18, 1990, pp. 48–50ff.; Kevin Kelly, "The Rumble Heard Round the World: Harleys," *Business Week,* May 24, 1993, pp. 58, 60; Steve Kichen, "More Than Motorcycles," *Forbes,* October 3, 1988, p. 193; Michael Kneebone, "No Apologies Needed . . ." *Road Rider,* October 1991, pp. 18, 19, 22; Gary Levin, "Awash in Awards," *Advertising Age,* November 17, 1986, pp. 46, 48; Carolyn Lochhead, "Still Made in Milwaukee After All the Rivalrous Years," *Insight,* August 10, 1987, pp. 38, 39; Bob Marich, "Motorcycles Push Harder Despite Rough Terrain," *Advertising Age,* January 12,1981, pp. 20, 56; Mark Marvel, "The Gentrified Hog," *Esquire,* July 1989, pp. 22, 26; Clifford D. May, "Rising Sun Meets Rising Temple and Riding Capitalists," *Forbes,* November 3, 1986, pp. 235–38, 240ff.; Harley-Davidson Seeks U.S. Protection From Japanese Imports," *Wall Street Journal,* 8/26/82; Stephen Phillips, "That 'Vroom!' You Hear Is Honda Motorcycles," *Business Week,* September 3, 1990, pp. 74ff.; Julie Schlax, "Ode to a Hog," *Forbes,* December 24, 1990, p. 109; James Schnepf, "How Harley Beat Back the Japanese," *Fortune,* September 25, 1989, pp. 155ff.; Gary Slutsker, "Hog Wild," *Forbes,* May 24, 1993, pp. 45–46; Bernie Woodall, "Hog Wild!" *Greensboro News and Record,* October 16, 1993, pp. D1, D6; Jeff Adams, "Harley Heaven" *Calgary Herald* July 23, 1994, p. B1-B2; Randell Scotland, "Aging boomers kick start bike sales," *Financial Post*, November 12, 1992, p. 16; David Grant, "Harley-Davidson: A case study of a corporate turnaround using Logistics and Marketing" unpublished case study, University of Calgary Faculty of Management, 1994.

The Millennium Power System:
Marketing For The Millennium

Dilemma at 8:17 P.M.
Friday Night

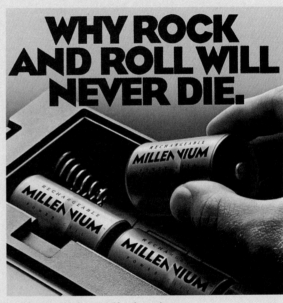

DANNY: Dad, do we have batteries? The ones
in my tape player
are shot.

DAD: No. I used the last
ones in my flashlight.

DANNY: Can we go get some? I
want to listen to this
awesome tape.

DAD: Tomorrow. I just started watching a
video.

DANNY: Aw, Dad . . .

A Solution

Sound familiar? Ever put on your earphones, press
"Play," and nothing happens? Then you know how Danny feels. Well, there's a
simple solution—rechargeable batteries. Maybe you're thinking that it takes too
long to charge batteries, and anyway, even rechargeable batteries can only be
reused a limited number of times before they have to be thrown away and replaced.
Those complaints were justified in the past, but they're not any longer.

The Industry

With the rapid growth of sales in the 1990s, competition among firms in the
rechargeable battery business has produced many improvements aimed at increasing customer satisfaction. Although rechargeables still claim only 8 percent of the
total battery market, their sales are growing more than 20 percent annually, so that
total rechargeable battery sales are expected to rise from $600 million* in 1990 to
$1 billion in 1995.

Producers are vigorously attacking the three barriers to the purchase of
rechargeables: their long charge times, high cost, and short run times. Industry
leader Eveready has a one-hour rechargeable battery system called Generator that
will shut down if a nonrechargeable battery is inserted into it *and* it has a rechargeable alkaline battery line. GE has a one-hour charger that can be used with non-

*All monetary figures in this case are given in U.S. dollars.

rechargeable batteries, although it can only handle AA batteries. Ray-O-Vac's Power Station can charge batteries in three to five hours, while Panasonic's chargers take between six and fourteen hours. Both Ray-O-Vac and Panasonic offer AAA to D size batteries, but Ray-O-Vac's batteries are alkaline and Panasonics' aren't. On the other hand, Panasonic's chargers cost only about half what other charging systems cost. Gates Energy Products of Gainesville, Florida, introduced the Millennium Power System, which has both three-hour and six-hour chargers and a full line of rechargeable battery sizes.

All these firms have chose different marketing strategies. Eveready and GE have concentrated on speed in charging and providing a full product assortment of chargers and batteries to consumers. In addition to lower prices, Panasonic has produced the smallest charger—the SlimCharger—which fits into an audio cassette. It is portable, which makes it appealing to teenagers, but it only charges AA and AAA batteries. The Millennium System has touted its 33 percent longer run time, full line of batteries and chargers, and lifetime replacement guarantee to grab the consumer's attention.

Millennium Plans for 1995

From its introduction in the fall of 1991 until the summer of 1994, the Millennium System's sales grew annually by over 15 percent. Only Eveready (whose market share was declining), GE, and Panasonic were ahead of Millennium in sales. In the meantime, Ralston Purina, looking to strengthen its presence in the battery market, purchased Gates Energy Products to complement its Eveready Battery Division, which dominated the alkaline nonrechargeable battery market.

Prior to the purchase, the Millennium marketing team had begun work on their marketing plan for 1995. As late fall approached, they set aside an afternoon to review the structure of the plan to date. Larry Scott, the head of marketing, asked each team member to describe a different part of the plan.

To start the session, he reminded everyone of the company's major goal and strategy: Millennium needed to increase sales by 50 percent, which would necessitate repositioning the brand, expanding distribution, and increasing communications both with the trade and with consumers.

The first person to speak was Kelly Meyers, Larry's assistant, who described Millennium's marketing to the final consumer market. "There are five aspects of the consumer marketing program that I should mention. First, we're using a lifestyle positioning with the tagline 'The Power to Last a Lifetime,'" Kelly began. "This positioning emphasizes the lifetime guarantee and longer playing time of our batteries. We want consumers to think of Millennium as the highest-quality, most technologically advanced products available. As proof of our advanced technology, we will introduce a one-hour charger next year.

"Second, we will make two packaging changes. The first involves the statement on your handouts (Figure 1), which is now required by the Portable Rechargeable Battery Association. To beef up our environmental image, we're going to add a recycling logo to the package as well and let consumers know that they can return the batteries to us for recycling.

"The other packaging change is a new design for the Charge Man—a picture of a set of headphones with the recharger positioned between the earphones. That should catch the consumer's attention while playing off the Charge Man name.

"Third, to increase awareness in our target market, we'll increase media spending up to 40 percent. This will make us look like a key industry player. Television advertising will start with the Thanksgiving Day NFL game and Thanksgiving Day Parade and be followed by six weeks of cable advertising on The Family Channel, USA Network, A&E, CNN, and Nickelodeon. On radio, we'll sponsor CBS NFL Football throughout the season, the Super Bowl, and the Pro Bowl. Print ads will

NICKEL-CADMIUM (OR SEALED LEAD-ACID) RECHARGEABLE BATTERY. MUST BE RECYCLED OR DISPOSED OF PROPERLY.

appear in *Working Mother, Parents, Good Housekeeping, Country Living, Popular Mechanics, Sports Afield, House Beautiful, Kitchens/Baths, Home Building,* and *Home Remodeling.*

"Each month of the year will have a different product publicity theme," Kelly continued. "I won't go over all of them, but some of them are: environmental concerns in April for Earth Day; 'Dadgets'—which is power tools for Dad—for June; sporting events in September; and gift giving in November and December. And we'll have a lot of publicity releases built around our "garbologist" to emphasize the environmental benefits of rechargeables.

"Fourth, to stimulate purchase, we'll give a $3 rebate on six-hour Rapid Chargers. This will feed into a direct-mail Compare and Save (C&S) Program, as we'll send other rebate offers to purchasers who get the $3 rebate as will as to those who send in their product registration card. Through the C&S program, we'll build a data base of names for future offers and marketing research.

"Fifth—and the best part of the plan, I think—Millennium will become the 'official rechargeable battery' of Playskool Electronics. This tie-in will give us exposure in Playskool advertising and through inserts in selected Playskool Electronics such as Kids First Walkie Talkie and Kid Keys Electronic Keyboard. It should get the attention of parents, who will then continue to buy Millennium products as their children grow up. To make sure that happens, our insert will inform parents that an additional $20 worth of rebates are available on purchases of Millennium products. That's it for the consumer market summary."

"Well, Kelly, do you think there are any problems with the consumer program, or is it fine the way it is?" Gifford Wu, a recently hired college graduate in the management training program asked.

"I really don't see any major problems, Gifford," Kelly responded.

At that point, Melvin Scales of sales interrupted Kelly. "I'm not sure that we should jump into this recycling-environmental issue. It's a two-edged sword, you know. While it's true that none of our batteries contain mercury, which is bad for the environment, they do contain cadmium, which is also bad for the environment. Every time we call the consumer's attention to the problems of disposing of batteries, we're really reminding them that batteries are not good for the environment. What we're really saying is that we'll help clean up the mess that our products make if we recycle."

"Well, you've certainly got a point," Kelly responded, "but we have to put the statement from PRBA on the package, so we might as well make our package recyclable and do what we can to reassure consumers."

"Maybe so," Melvin conceded. "But I see another issue with the magazines you listed. Do those really reach our target market? I thought the target was males over twenty-five years old with incomes above $50,000. Do those guys read *Country Living?*"

"Probably not," Kelly responded, "but all the magazines other than *Working Mother* and *Parents* are part of a Hearst package, where you get advertising in all eight books. Notice that we will reach men through *Popular Mechanics* and *Sports Afield.* By using the package, we'll get more ads for our budget, and we will certainly reach young men with some of them. Besides, most of our television and radio advertising is aimed at men. For women who buy batteries, we'll have the magazine ads."

MILLENNIUM POWER SYSTEM – OFFICIAL RECHARGEABLE BATTERY OF PLAYSKOOL ELECTRONICS

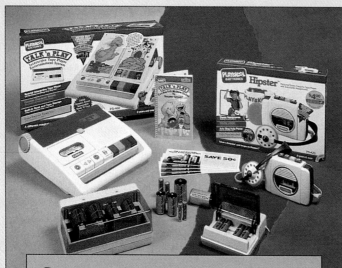

Consumers who purchase Playskool Electronics products closely match the Millennium customer profile, a similarity which allows both brands to extend the reach of their marketing and merchandising efforts.

- Offers retailers opportunity to cross-merchandise two high-margin product categories with similar consumer purchase profiles
- More than 1.25 million select Playskool Electronics products will feature Millennium promotion violators on-pack and $15 Millennium rebate coupons in-pack, good on Power Cells and RapidChargers
- Coupon insert shows parents how to save money using rechargeable power, and delivers an environmental message
- More than 500,000 RapidChargers will feature Playskool promotional product brochures
- Playskool and Millennium national print advertising in fall of 1993 will feature co-promotion details

A Valuable Tie-In

A tie-in with Playskool should prove highly beneficial to the Millennium Power System.

At this point, Gifford broke. "If we want to reach men, shouldn't we use television rather than radio for the football games?"

"Radio is a better medium for us because people put batteries in their radios. Advertising on radio relates to our product better than does advertising on television," Kelly commented. "Besides, with television, we could afford fewer spots. We actually get more for our dollar with radio."

Maybe we should hear about our trade program before we launch into changing the consumer program," Larry said. "So, Melvin, why don't you summarize the trade program for us?"

"Sure thing, Larry. Our new positioning for the trade is 'One Brand Fits All,' which communicates that Millennium is the brand that fits all of customers' battery needs—whether for electronics, toys, housewares, or cameras. This positioning presents us as a leader in the industry and stresses the importance and profitability of the partnership between us and the retailer.

"And next year we will really enhance the value of our partnership with retailers. First, we have devised the Millennium Advantage Program—or MAP, as we call it. That's a good name for it because it really is a map of how retailers should market our products. It includes video aids for developing selling skills and knowledge of the product and easy-to-understand educational information and features about product benefits. Most importantly, it contains a comprehensive buying system in a step-by-step guidebook that helps retailers with product selection, merchandising, promotion, advertising, and tracking market trends.

"To distinguish ourselves from the competition, we will continue to emphasize cross-merchandising by suggesting that retailers place our batteries close to the equipment they are used with. To facilitate this, we're going to offer two types of countertop display units to retailers. One will be circular, and the other, intended for displaying higher-priced Camcorder and cellular products, will be lockable in order to prevent theft. Both displays will come with cross-reference headers. We are also distributing plan-o-grams that position the Charge Man and RapidChargers at the top of the display with batteries below them. Positioning them at eye level will communicate their importance in the charging system. In addition, we are going—"

"Excuse me, Melvin," Gifford interrupted. "I'm afraid I don't understand what cross-reference headers and plan-o-grams are."

"Oh, sorry, Gifford. Cross-reference headers are plastic-coated flip charts for each of our Millennium Power Pack product lines. With a cross-reference display, consumers can check information independently when sales assistance is unavailable. That's why we think it's important to have these display units that retailers can position in various locations. They give us a sales voice even when there is no salesperson available.

"The plan-o-grams are layouts of possible retail displays. The rectangles on the layout represent products—batteries and chargers. By moving the rectangles around, the retailer can design a layout that maximizes his display space without actually having to physically move the goods."

"That sounds like a really good idea, Melvin," Gifford commented. "Sorry I interrupted."

"No problem, Gifford. If you don't ask, you won't learn. Now, where was I? Oh, yeah. Our promotional efforts will increase this year as we will offer lucrative advertising and merchandising allowances of 10 percent and 5 percent at different times during the year. And we will advertise in *HFD (Home Furnishings Daily)*, *Twice*, *Discount Store News*, *Dealerscope Merchandising*, *Photo Trade News*, and *Photo Business* in issues with editorial content on rechargeables or coverage of important trade shows. The shows are especially important to us, so we will be at all the major ones: the Winter Consumer Electronics Show in Las Vegas, the Consumer Electronics Show in Chicago in June, and the National Hardware Show in August. Besides booths at the shows, we'll have morning television ads aimed at the audience as they prepare to leave for the show, poster ads on shuttle buses and airport walls, and ads in trade show publications. In addition, we'll have personnel stationed at key locations at the shows to direct participants to the Millennium booth.

"While all of that is important, I guess the biggest change in our selling effort is the move to penetrate hardware and home centers, drug, and photo trade channels. To do that, we will hire national account representatives with selling experience in those channels."

"Excuse me, Melvin, but I don't understand why we are making a push in those channels," Gifford commented. "The stats I've seen indicate that most batteries are sold at mass merchandisers—food and drug stores. It makes sense to me to make a greater push in drugstores, so why would we go after hardware and home centers and photo outlets when less than 10 percent of batteries are bought in those outlets?"

"Good question, Gifford," Melvin responded. "You're right that drugstores are a major outlet, and we aren't represented there, so we have got to get space in those outlets. But we think hardware and home centers are also important because that is where men shop, and they're our target market. We want them to use Millennium rechargeables in all those hand-power tools. We have a slight toehold in that market that we should be able to increase."

Millennium is Multipurpose

Moving into more varied outlets, Millennium hopes to expand its customer base.

"Oh, I hadn't thought of those stores in terms of our market," Gifford replied.

At this point, Larry commented: "Well, that's the summary. Are there any other questions or issues that we need to address?"

"After listening to this presentation, I am beginning to think that we are putting too much of our effort into a push strategy," Kelly said. "I think we should build awareness in the consumer market. After all, Millennium isn't a familiar brand name like Eveready, GE, or Panasonic. Sure, we've had a lot of experience making rechargeable batteries under private labels for the last twenty years, but consumers don't know that. We're asking them to spend more than $20 on most of our systems, and they want to be reassured that they are buying a reputable product. The countertop displays are helpful, but they don't create the brand image that we need."

"But, Kelly," Melvin said, "what's the point of a lot of advertising if our product isn't available in a wide variety of stores? Consumers aren't going to shop around for battery rechargers. They'll probably buy what they consider to be the best product on the display. So what we really need is in-store merchandising, which is why we'll give away all those countertop displays and provide all those retailing aids. By helping retailers, we'll get much better shelf and counter placement."

"Uh, speaking of placement, Melvin," Gifford interrupted. "I wonder if we would be better off to place our batteries near the checkout counter rather than near the electronics products in our cross-merchandising strategy. Most of the competitive products are displayed together near the checkout counter. Shouldn't we be in the same location as the competition?"

"Gee, Gifford, that's a tough question. We discussed it before and decided that being next to the competition isn't always advantageous. Sometimes we're better off by ourselves—then customers don't even consider the competitive brand when they see us. They concentrate on us 'cause we're the only team in the park."

"Melvin, that's true only if they are already familiar with Millennium," Kelly said. "Otherwise they might not be interested in an unknown brand."

"Which is why we focus on getting those retailer salespeople to sell our brand," Melvin countered. "What do you think, Larry?"

As Larry looked at his team, he commented: "You've all given me a lot to think about. You've raised some important issues here about a push versus a pull strategy, the need for more different media, the cross-merchandising strategy, and the effort to penetrate different distributive channels.

"One issue that I'm very worried about is the environmental one. Melvin made a good point about the problems with ni-cad batteries. Did you guys realize that Duracell, Toshiba, and Varta have joined together to research nickel-metal hydride rechargeable batteries to replace the ni-cads? Nickel-metal hydride batteries perform much better and can run 50 percent longer, depending on how they are used."

"If they're so good, why aren't we into nickel-metal hydrides?" Gifford asked.

"Well," said Larry, "nickel-metal hydrides can't be recharged as many times, cost more to produce, and worse yet, the demand for nickel-metal hydride outstrips the world's known supply. Even so, we will have to work toward a cadmium-free battery by the late 1990s, which is going to cost a lot of money in research and development. That's why it is so important to increase our sales next year."

"What should we do, Larry?" Kelly asked. "I don't know right now, and it's getting late."

"Why don't we think about this over the weekend and meet again on Monday morning?" Larry responded.

After Kelly, Melvin, and Gifford left, Larry swiveled around to look out the window. While he knew that the issues they had just discussed were important, his mind was really on the recent purchase of Millennium by Ralston Purina. He was uncertain what would happen to Millennium in the future. "Why would a company with the number-one battery brand in both the disposable and rechargeable battery markets buy the fourth-place rechargeable brand?" he asked himself for the hundredth time. Although the Ralston Purina people had assured Larry that they would support Millennium, that they viewed it as an attractive acquisition and thought that an additional brand would increase their total market share more than they could ever achieve with just the Eveready brand, Larry was still uncomfortable about competing in-house with Eveready. For the next half-hour, his thoughts revolved around the disadvantages Millennium faced vis-à-vis Eveready. Finally, he concluded: "No matter what Ralston Purina has in mind, one thing's for sure. If we don't succeed in building market share, we won't fit into their long-run strategy. Whatever we decide on Monday, it had better build market share!"

Saturday 2 P.M.

Danny and his Dad were wandering through the aisles of a discount store when Danny spotted a display of batteries. This reminded him that he needed batteries. He went straight to the batteries his family usually bought, but his Dad noticed the displays of rechargeable batteries.

"I am so tired of buying batteries that I think we ought to buy rechargeables and reuse them instead of throwing away old batteries," he commented.

Danny looked at him and said: "Yeah . . . at school we learned that batteries containing mercury are really hazardous when placed in landfills and that several states have banned them. So, it's environmentally good to use rechargeables, Dad. You know—reduce, reuse. Besides if we had had rechargeables, I wouldn't have had to wait until today to listen to my tapes."

"Well," his Dad said, "let's see what we have here."

There were three types of rechargeable systems on display. The first one they noticed was Millennium because it was the largest display and because Danny was immediately attracted to the Charge Man. Besides, he thought Millennium was a cool name. The others were the Renewal system from Ray-O-Vac and the Panasonic Rechargeable System.

The Millennium batteries stood out because they were different colors—size Ds a pinkish-gray, Cs a medium shade of purple, AAs light purple, AAAs a light blue. And, of course 9 volts, Camcorder packs, and telephone batteries were all black. The Renewal batteries were all silver and white, while the Panasonics were black and blue.

There were two chargers from Millennium that had LED indicator lights, adjustable holders to handle different-size batteries, and automatic power reduction circuitry that allowed the purchaser to store batteries in the charger. One was a three-hour charger, that cost $12.97 and could charge four batteries at one time. The other was a six-hour charger that cost $19.97 and could charge eight batteries at the same time.

The Renewal systems are called Power Stations. The smallest of these charges four AA or AAA batteries in three to five hours and sells for $14.99. The larger Power Station charges up to eight D, C, AA, or AAA batteries in three to five hours and is priced at $29.99. The smaller Panasonic charger can charge two batteries in six hours and costs $8.99. The larger one charges four batteries in fourteen to sixteen hours and costs $11.99. All of the chargers have one-year warranties.

"Gee, the Millennium chargers seem to be cheaper, Dad, because there's a $3 rebate on the six-hour charger."

"Well, that's true," Danny's father commented, "but I always forget to send for the rebates, and the Millennium batteries cost more. See, I wrote down the prices while you were looking at the Charge Man . . ."

	Size D	Size C	Size AA	Size AAA	Size 9V
Millennium	$6.97	$6.97	$5.97	$5.97	$6.97
Renewal	$4.59	$4.59	$4.99	$4.99	——
Panasonic	——	——	$4.37	$4.37	$5.14

—— means there were none on display.

"But, Dad, the Millenniums have a lifetime guarantee and it says they last 33 percent longer. Besides, you see this Charge Man? It comes with two AA batteries, and that's all we need for my tape player, and it only costs $9.97. I could plug the Charge Man in my room and you'd never be bothered with it!"

Meanwhile, Danny's father had picked up a brochure about the Renewal system and read to Danny that Renewals are alkaline batteries, which last 50 percent longer than ni-cad batteries. Also, the alkaline batteries come fully charged to begin with and can be recharged *before* they run down. According to the brochure, ni-cad batteries must be charged before the first use, and they can't be charged until they're fully discharged.

"So," Danny's father concluded, "maybe we ought to get the Renewals."

"Aw, Dad, I want a Charge Man."

Standing close enough to Danny and his father to overhear their conversation was a Millennium sales representative and the store manager. The sales rep was surprised that the battery prices made such a difference to the buyer. He had thought that the rebate and the lifetime guarantee would overcome the buyer's price resistance. He asked the store manager if most customers were that price conscious.

"Well, I'm not sure," said the manager. "A lot of buyers of rechargeables are concerned with environmental issues and very concerned with run time because rechargeables have a bad reputation for not lasting very long. We sell a lot of Millennium systems as well as the Renewals. It's kids that want the Panasonic. Mostly, I think that customers just want the easiest system to use," the store manager commented.

"Maybe I ought to tell Larry about this experience," the salesman thought.

Sources: The Millennium 1993 Sales and Marketing Plan; Dana Cervenka, "Towards a Better Battery," *Communications 28* (December 1991): 29–35; Christopher Cornell, "Nineteen Strategies in Rechargeable Battery Sales," *Dealerscope Merchandising 33* (May 1991): 26–29, 100; Karen Jacobs, "Rayovac Corp. Unveils Reusable Alkaline Batteries," *The Wall Street Journal,* June 16, 1993, Sec. B, p. 3; Julie Liesse, "Batteries Getting Greener," *Advertising Age,* February 17, 1992, pp. 1, 58; Maureen Metzger, "'Green' Rechargeable Batteries," *Appliance Manufacturer 39* (September 1991): 56–57; Renee Covino Rouland, "Batteries Have Staying Power!", *Discount Merchandiser 32* (August 1992): 72–74; "The New Business with Batteries," *Discount Merchandiser 30,* June 6, 1990: 80–83; "Rechargeables Gain Momentum," *Discount Merchandiser 29* (November 1989): 30–36; Eben Shapiro, "New Life for Rechargeable Battery, *The New York Times,* February 15, 1991, p. 1; Murray Slovick, et al., "SCES Wrapup: A Day at CES," *Dealerscope Merchandising 34,* (July 1992): 10–22.

Appendix A

Careers in Marketing

Articles focusing on marketing and careers in marketing appear frequently in Canada's business publications and marketing careers do seem to have great appeal for today's graduates. In part, business school and college graduates are motivated by the desire to deal with things they can touch rather than abstract numbers on computer spreadsheets. They are also eager to become immersed in their careers. Rita DaSilva, a student in Business Administration at the University of British Columbia, compares her summer work launching an innovative security device in private homes with her previous work as a management consultant. "In my marketing work for the home-security company I was helping to make important decisions about the way a small but dynamic company was going to develop. As a consultant I was simply not close to the action—to the decisions that made a real difference to the way things were done."

Fortunately for the thousands of students who want the excitement marketing careers offer, employment opportunities are expected to grow, often substantially, over the next decade.

This appendix will introduce you to some of the many career opportunities in marketing and will show you how to conduct a successful job search. By learning as much as you can about marketing careers and search techniques while you are still in school, you start with a competitive advantage.

WHAT FIELD OF MARKETING?

Deciding that you want a career in marketing is only the starting point in your career investigation. Your first step is to focus on specific employment opportunities. As you explore job titles, keep in mind that marketing careers employ the largest single segment of the civilian labor force. As a result, there are more opportunities than you dreamed. Whether you want to work in your own country or for a firm with offices in other countries, you will find that the job descriptions in this section apply equally well.

Each of the jobs we will examine deals with the exchange of products and services between the marketer and the customer and thus is crucial to the success of the organization. Marketing managers must understand the intricacies of the marketplace and react quickly to frequent changes. If a challenge and change are things you are looking for in a career, marketing may be for you.

Marketing jobs can be classified into eight major categories: brand and product management, marketing communication, sales and sales management, industrial (business-to-business) marketing, retailing, services marketing, marketing research, and logistics management. In exploring these categories we will focus on some specific jobs in each.[1] As you read, keep in mind that many jobs can be performed in various industries. For example, a public relations director may be a member of a brand management team or work in industrial marketing, retailing, or services marketing.

BRAND AND PRODUCT MANAGEMENT

When a company believes that a product needs special attention in order to maximize sales, it assigns the product a brand (or product) manager. For example, early in 1994 Procter & Gamble placed Beth Kaplan in charge of its cosmetics and fragrance lines with the assignment of turning such also-rans as Max Factor cosmetics into market contenders and deciding whether or not to add a cosmetics line to its Oil of Olay skin treatment products.[2]

Brand managers are strategic planners as they develop and direct the total marketing effort for their products. Areas of responsibility include basic product research and development, packaging, manufacturing, marketing research, sales and distribution, advertising, and promotion. In a one-brand or one-product company, the product manager is often the marketing manager.

MARKETING COMMUNICATION

As you recall from the discussion in Chapter 18 of integrated marketing communication (IMC), a host of internal and external marketing communication specialists work together as a team to develop and influence all messages about a company and its products that are delivered to target consumer groups. Among the professionals working in the area of IMC are specialists in advertising, public relations, direct marketing, packaging, sales promotion, and personal selling. We examine job opportunities in the first five of these areas next and discuss personal selling later, within the context of sales and sales management.

Advertising

Many different career professionals create and communicate consumer and business-to-business advertisements to targeted markets. Advertising agencies and companies with internal advertising departments hire writers and artists, account executives, marketing researchers, media specialists, production specialists, and others to create ads for television, print, radio, and other media. Some advertising management jobs include:

Account Executive
Liaison person between an advertising agency and its clients. The account executive studies the clients' marketing objectives and creates promotional programs (including message, layout, media, and timing).

Advertising Manager
Director of a firm's advertising program, this person selects an advertising agency for the firm and determines media, copy, size of budget, and advertising frequency.

Advertising Production Manager
This person arranges to have an advertisement filmed (for television), recorded (for radio), or printed (for newspapers, magazines, etc.).

Media Director (also, **Space** or **Time buyer)**
This person determines the day, time (for radio and television media location), and size of an advertisement and negotiates contracts for advertising space or air time.

Public Relations

As you recall from Chapter 19, organizations use public relations, along with advertising and sales promotion, to implement their marketing communication strategies. It is the job of public relations professionals to generate favorable publicity for their organizations through the use of such techniques as public service announcements, press conferences, and event sponsorships. A critical job in public relations is the public relations director:

Public Relations Director
Manager of a company's efforts to keep the public aware of its accomplishments and benefits to society and minimize negative reactions to company policies and activities. The director constantly measures public attitudes and seeks to maintain a favorable public opinion of the firm.

Direct Marketing

Direct response marketing attempts to reach consumers without the intervention of a retailer or personal sales and through a variety of selective media including direct mail, catalogs, various print and broadcast media, and telemarketing. Among the companies that practice direct marketing are Northern Telecom, Ford, General Electric, McCain Foods Ltd., and IBM. Specific career opportunities include:

Direct Response Copywriter
This person generates simple copy, including headlines, for a variety of goods and services. Copywriters learn to adapt to different formats, media, and creative strategies.

List Compiler
This person generates lists used by direct marketers from a variety of sources including organization membership lists, directories, and lists of trade show registrants.

Telemarketing Account Executive
On the staff of a telemarketing agency that handles a client's telemarketing program, the account executive coordinates script writing (scripts are used as the basis for telephone contacts), script testing, list preparation, and prepares client reports.

Packaging

Marketing professionals involved in packaging work either in the area of physical design or package communication. Specific careers include:

Industrial Designer

With a background in engineering, this individual chooses the type of packaging materials (box versus can, for example) that are right for product content and deals with physical distribution issues, including wrapping and shipping.

Graphic Designer

This person focuses on the communication side of package design. Graphics designers work with copywriters to create eye-catching packages that capture consumer interest.

Packaging professionals work closely with brand managers to determine design. Design decisions are often motivated by competitive pressures, as managers are forced to respond with such devices as their own pop-top cans for soft drinks.

Sales Promotion

It is generally the brand manager who coordinates the various sales promotion strategies for products, including those aimed at consumers and retailers. Working with advertising copywriters and graphic artists, brand managers create coupons, contests and sweepstakes, refunds and rebates, premiums, specialty advertising, point-of-purchase displays, trade show exhibits, and other promotional devices.

SALES AND SALES MANAGEMENT

Sales representatives identify potential customers, determine the customer's specific business problems, offer solutions via the range of products and services they sell, and close deals. This process is considered personal selling when it involves a one-on-one, face-to-face relationship between a potential buyer and a sales person. (As you recall from Chapter 21, personal selling also takes place in retailing and business-to-business marketing.) In addition, sales representatives offer sales support and handle such administrative tasks as preparing reports and completing competitive analyses.

Many mid-sized and large companies have sales training programs that move capable individuals up the ranks from sales representative to territory sales managers to district sales managers to national sales managers. In addition, sales careers are often the stepping stone to jobs in upper management. At Prentice Hall, for example, many executives start in the sales force.

Sales careers offer the opportunity for rapid advancement, independence, and compensation tied to achievement. In an increasing number of companies sales commissions are tied to evidence of customer satisfaction. Specific jobs include:

Manufacturers' Representative

This person represents several, usually small manufacturers that cannot afford their own sales force. The representative normally deals with wholesalers and retailers, determining needs and then describing and sometimes demonstrating products and services, often at the customer's place of business.

Sales Manager

This person supervises the sales force and is responsible for recruitment, selection, training, motivation, evaluation, compensation, and control.

Salesperson

Interacting directly with consumers, a salesperson may require limited or extensive skills, deal with final or intermediate customers, work from an office, in a retail store, or go out in the field, and be a career salesperson or progress into management.

INDUSTRIAL (BUSINESS-TO-BUSINESS) MARKETING

The focus of industrial (business-to-business) marketing is buying and selling activities between commercial, governmental, and institutional organizations. When Boeing sells jet engines to Canadian Airlines or Air Canada, or when Intel sells computer chips to Dell Computer, participants are engaged in business-to-business marketing. Because business-to-business buyers focus on design specifications, on-time delivery, and continuing service as conditions for the sale, industrial marketing is complex, with deals often taking years to complete.

Michèle Van Walleghem is an account manager with BBDO Calgary, a regional office of the largest advertising agency in Canada. Her varied responsibilities include writing advertising plans, interfacing with the agency staff to develop advertising campaigns, implementing advertising programs, and making presentations to clients.

A marketing graduate from the University of British Columbia, Van Walleghem was always interested in developing skills in the creative side of marketing. This led to her introduction to the advertising industry as account coordinator in 1987. The fast-paced, diverse environment gave her added enthusiasm to pursue a career in advertising.

Looking to expand her network of contacts, she became involved with the American Marketing Association, and in 1992 became president of the Calgary chapter. According to Van Walleghem, the experience "gave me the opportunity to run an organization and learn many management skills on the job. The rewards from my involvement with the AMA were many. But most importantly, I reached out to be my best and was rewarded by the Chicago headquarters of the Association with the Chapter Excellence Award for the efforts of our chapter."

At BBDO Calgary, Michèle Van Walleghem is the liaison between her clients and the agency. She spends many hours in meetings and on the telephone. She is constantly receiving information, other people's ideas, and opinions that must be distilled into an effective briefing document. She plays a key role in directing the agency team in developing and executing communications strategies for the agency's clients. "The challenge," she says, "is managing the diversity of demands in a given day and staying on top of your 'to do' list. Change is constant and the rewards of the day come from stretching your abilities and keeping your interest."

Industrial marketing jobs involve various aspects of sales, research, distribution, and dealer support. Two examples are:

Industrial Traffic Manager
This person arranges the transportation to and from firms and customers of raw materials, fabricated parts, finished goods, and equipment.

Sales Engineer
This sales representative is involved with technical products and services.

RETAILING

Through retailing, goods and services are delivered from manufacturers and wholesalers to the ultimate consumer. Career opportunities in retailing have grown in recent years along with the proliferation of new types of retail outlets, including discount houses, warehouse stores, franchises, and catalog operations. Some jobs in retailing are:

Consumer Affairs Specialist
This person handles consumer complaints and attempts to adjust the firm's policies to reflect customer needs.

Retail Buyer
This person is responsible for purchasing items for resale. The buyer generally concentrates on a product area and develops a plan for styles, assortments, sizes, and amounts of the product. The buyer must also analyze vendors on such bases as quality, flexibility, reliability, and price.

Retail Merchandise Manager

Supervisor of several buyers, this manager sets the retailer's direction in terms of styles, product lines, image, pricing, and allocates budgets among buyers.

Retail Store Manager

This person supervises the day-to-day activities of a store. All in-store personnel report to this manager.

SERVICES MARKETING

With the growing importance of the service sector in the national economy, careers in services marketing are abundant. Some fields that require the marketing of services include, finance, entertainment, telecommunications, transportation, and sports. In addition, many professionals in service careers use marketing techniques to promote business growth: Lawyers, doctors, and dentists who want to attract new customers are turning to advertising and public relations specialists.

Because of the technical nature of many service marketing jobs, companies often require jobholders to undergo special training. Several specific services marketing jobs are:

Insurance Agent (Broker)

An insurance agent may specialize in life insurance or in property or casualty insurance. An agent advises clients on policy types suited to their needs and sells policies that provide life insurance and/or retirement income and ensure against such perils as fire, burglary, and accidents.

Securities Salesperson

Salesperson involved with the buying and selling of stocks, bonds, government securities, mutual funds, and other securities.

MARKETING RESEARCH

Marketing research professionals act as support staff for key decision-makers as they collect, analyze and interpret data that affect marketing plans and strategy. Researchers frame problem statements and identify the information needed to solve a problem. They then design the research project, including the questionnaire and sampling method, tabulate and analyze data, and prepare and deliver written and oral reports after their research is complete. Marketing research professionals also run focus groups and conduct personal interviews to gather data. Marketing research consulting firms (e.g., Coopers & Lybrand), advertising agencies (e.g., J. Walter Thompson Company Ltd.), and other businesses, ranging from auto makers to publishers, hire marketing research professionals. Among the jobs in marketing research are:

Interviewer

This person conducts face-to-face and telephone interviews with subjects in order to collect data and may also run focus groups.

Marketing Research Projects Supervisor

This person develops research methodology, evaluates the accuracy of different sample sizes, analyzes data, and addresses statistical errors.

Statistician

This person is engaged in sample and questionnaire design, data tabulation, correcting statistical errors, and report writing.

DISTRIBUTION, OR LOGISTICS MANAGEMENT

Distribution or logistics professionals handle the range of functions involved in moving goods from buyers to sellers. Careers in distribution include, logistics planning, traffic management, warehouse operations, packaging, customer service, inventory planning and control, purchasing and material management. Two specific jobs are:

Industrial Traffic Manager

This person arranges transportation to and from firms and customers of raw materials, fabricated parts, finished goods, and equipment.

Warehouser

This person is responsible for storage and movement of goods within a company's warehouse facilities. The warehouser maintains inventory records and makes sure older items are shipped out before newer ones (rotating stock).

CONDUCTING A JOB SEARCH ●

With an understanding of the career opportunities open to you in marketing, you are now ready to tackle your personal job search. Searching for and finding a job in your chosen field of marketing are your first employment challenges. They are challenges that put your analytical, organizational, communication, and personal-relationship skills to the test—the same skills that will ultimately determine your success on the job. David Liu, an MBA graduate from Calgary, discovered that searching for a job requires self-discipline. "Before graduation I researched all the companies I could find that I thought would be interested in someone with my background. I tried to be systematic about it by sending out five applications each day." David was eventually successful, landing a position with a multinational food company in Toronto, but not before he had sent out almost a hundred applications.

As you will see, searching for a job involves a series of stages including a personal analysis of career objectives, a job-market analysis, writing an effective résumé and cover letter, finding sources of employment assistance, and interviewing.

ANALYZE YOUR CAREER GOALS

Although job hunting is an outer-directed effort as you contact companies, conduct research, and write letters and résumés, it should begin with a process of self-evaluation in which you catalog your interests and skills, accomplishments, strengths, and weaknesses. This evaluation will help you learn *who* you are and *what* you can offer prospective employers.

Evaluate Your Interests and Skills

Since most of us spend at least seven to eight hours a day at work, it makes good sense to match the things we like to do with a job that allows us to do them. For example, a love of travel may lead naturally to a job in international sales. Similarly, a passion for sports can lead to a career in sports and special events marketing.

Skills are the abilities and talents that are the prerequisites for a job. They involve everything from an ability to speak Japanese to the quantitative analysis skills needed to conduct sophisticated marketing research. As you evaluate your skills, evaluate your skill proficiency. For example, if you were asked by an employer to give a sales presentation in Japanese, could you do it?

Look At Your Accomplishments

All companies are results oriented, and this is especially the case in marketing occupations. Therefore, your tangible accomplishments—the things you have done in school, in part-

time and full-time work, in your community, and at home—will help you assess what you are good at and help prospective employers judge the results of your efforts. Make a list of these accomplishments as part of your career analysis and save them for later. They will become the building blocks of your résumé. For example:

- Sold magazine subscriptions for college fund-raisers and received sales award
- Organized a recycling drive for Scout group
- Helped write a diversity survey for community school board
- Wrote sales letters that brought in $4,000 in ads to college newspaper

Assess Your Strengths and Weaknesses

Just as marketers begin the marketing plan process by assessing a company's internal strengths and weaknesses (Chapter 4), you need to make a list of your own personality traits, those you consider strengths and those you consider weaknesses. Strengths might include ambition, an ability to analyze complex situations calmly, a willingness to take risks, persistence, organization, a take-charge attitude, and an ability to get along with people. Common weaknesses that affect job success are impatience, intolerance of different ideas, lack of self confidence, and being quick to anger.

By paying attention to these traits, you are more likely to choose a career that suits your personality. For example, if you have a hard time working with people, are easily angered, and impatient, retail sales is probably a poor career choice. Similarly, if you are analytical, organized, numbers-oriented, and comfortable with computer technology, you might do well in marketing research.

As part of your personality assessment, think about what you need and want in order to achieve personal happiness. As you ask yourself the following questions, remember that only honest answers will help you learn more about yourself:

- What lifestyle do I want and what kind of job would allow me to achieve it?
- Which part of life is most important to me: career, family, community, hobbies, leisure?

- What geographic location do I prefer and where will jobs be most plentiful? Canadian Business publications, such as *The Globe and Mail's Report on Business,* or *The Financial Post Magazine,* help you keep in touch with what is happening and where.

- Do I prefer to work in a large city, suburb, or small town?

- Would I like to work overseas or for a global company?

- Would I reject a position in which I would be required to work for more than forty hours a week?

- How important are money, job security, benefits, career potential, and prestige in my job choice?

This process of self-evaluation prepares you for the next stage in the job search: matching your goals with specific careers and fields.

MATCH YOUR GOALS WITH SPECIFIC CAREERS AND MARKETING FIELDS

The next stage of the job search involves market analysis, a process in which you research available job opportunities. Use the list of marketing careers presented earlier in this appendix as the starting point for your search. Then place your chosen career objective within the context of the kind of company you want to work for. Exhibit A-1 lists just some of the different types of companies in which marketing careers are pursued.

Your goal is to choose a career *and* a specific type of marketing field and then to narrow your search to specific companies. For example, even if you are sure that you are interested in sales, you must still decide whether you want a career in financial marketing, database marketing, marketing research, or even radio marketing, and whether you want to work for such varied companies as Northern Telecom, Altamira Investment Services, Global Television, or Weston Foods Ltd.

At some point in the process of matching your goals to specific careers and marketing fields, it is important to create a profile of an ideal company—one whose work environment suits your preferences. You can learn more about the work environment of various companies from a variety of sources.

WRITE AN EFFECTIVE RÉSUMÉ AND COVER LETTER

Once you target a career and perhaps a company, you are ready to write a résumé and learn how to write an effective cover letter. The purpose of a résumé is to sell your skills, personal characteristics, and background to prospective employers and to convince them to grant you an interview. Your résumé is your most important job search sales tool. With dozens and sometimes hundreds of résumés flooding their desks, most busy executives take no more than a few seconds to scan each one. Those longer than a page, those that lack a clear, crisp visual presentation that highlights important information, and those without an action-oriented writing style are lost in the shuffle. As you construct your résumé, remember that it is through this document, and the cover letter that accompanies it, that you make your first impression. Job candidates who present themselves poorly on paper are not likely to get a second chance.

The Building Blocks of a Résumé

Although the specific information in every résumé is unique, the categories of information are standard. Employers expect to see the job candidate's name, address, phone number, education, and work experience. Job objectives, community and professional activities, and employment references are optional. We will take a closer look at these categories in the order in which they appear on the résumé:

- *Name, address, and phone number*—Place this information at the top of the first page. If possible, use an answering machine during your search to ensure that you receive all messages.

- *Objective*—Many résumés state an objective, a brief description of the job you seek. For example:
    Objective—An entry-level position in a mid-size marketing research firm that draws on a background in statistics and marketing
    Objective–A sales-management position in computer software with opportunities to develop new territories and marketing programs
  Because the objective immediately tells prospective employers your job search target, it may knock you out of the race

EXHIBIT A-1	COMPANIES THAT EMPLOY MARKETING PERSONNEL IN VARIOUS OCCUPATIONS

Type of Company	Example
Consumer products companies	Weston Foods, Procter & Gamble
Industrial sales companies	Intel Semi Conductor of Canada
Retail Businesses	Ikea, Canadian Tire
Professional services	Andersen Consultants
Hotels	Four Seasons, CP Hotels
Media	Global Television, Toronto Sun Pub. Corp.
Financial services	Canada Trust, Deloitte, Haskins & Sells
Sports and special events marketing firms	Christopher Lang & Associates
Direct marketing	Vickers & Benson Direct Marketing Inc., Southam Business Information and Communications Group Inc.
Marketing research	Decima Research, A.C. Nielson Company of Canada
Telephone marketing firms	Watts Communication Ltd.
Advertising agencies	J. Walter Thompson Company, McCann Erickson Advertising
Hospitals	Vancouver General Hospital, Sunnybrook Medical Centre
Public relations	Hill & Knowlton
Moving companies	Tippit-Richardson Ltd.
Credit bureaus	Equifax Canada Inc.
Transportation companies	Via Rail, Canadian Airlines International
Real Estate companies	Royal Lepage, Richardson Greenshields

for jobs that differ slightly from your target. Therefore, it's a good idea to write different résumés with different job objectives.

◆ *Education*—If you are just completing school, list your educational background next. List the names and locations of all colleges, universities, technical schools, and training programs you attended, the dates you attended, and the degrees you received or expect to receive. Include grades, awards, projects, reports, and extracurricular activities if they relate to your career objective. As you gain work experience, you'll list education *after* "Work Experience," which then becomes your résumé's central focus.

◆ *Work Experience*—Next, list all the jobs you have held. Include each company's name and location, dates of employment, and job titles. As you will see later, the way you list and explain what you did at each job varies according to

the type of résumé you use. In general, however, describe the job in terms of your specific achievements (for example, "Developed campaign that increased subscriptions by 90 percent"), and list your skills and responsibilities.

◆ *Activities*–List community, student, and professional activities next, especially if they are tied to your job target. Include student and professional organizations and any offices you held in these organizations as well as volunteer projects. For example, if you are applying for a job in database marketing, highlight your participation in a community program that targeted companies interested in moving to your area. List non-job related activities as well. Writing that you were a volunteer fund-raiser for your local hospital or sports team demonstrates your initiative and willingness to work as a member of a team. This section may be especially important if you are entering the job market for the first time and have little paid work experience.

♦ *References*–Many résumés end with the line "References available upon request." References are previous employers, college professors, and community leaders who can vouch for your experience and abilities. Provide at least two references who can attest to your ability at work or school as well as one character reference.

Type the names, titles, organizations, addresses, and phone numbers of your references on a separate sheet of paper and give it to employers when requested. And don't forget to inform each reference before including him or her on your list. In addition, discuss your job objective so that your references will focus on information that relates to your employment goal.

Creating the Résumé

How you present yourself in your résumé— your writing style—is almost as important as your past accomplishments. In addition, the document layout affects whether or not your résumé will be read.

Writing Style. Résumé writing uses brief, action-oriented phrases that focus on results. For example, "Created business-to-business client database that increased sales leads by 50 percent." Use personal power verbs, like those in Exhibit A-2, for impact and emphasis.

Layout. Nowhere is an effective layout more important than in a résumé. If your résumé contains dense, difficult-to-read paragraphs, chances are it will not be read. All of the following suggestions to help you improve the look of your document are incorporated in Exhibit A-3.

♦ Surround important information with plenty of white space.

♦ Use headings consistently and emphasize their importance with upper-case letters.

♦ Create bulleted lists of specific accomplishments.

♦ Use consistent indenting to arrange key blocks of information on the page. For example, all dates should line up under one another on the left margin.

♦ Eliminate all errors from the final copy. Your final résumé should be free of spelling, grammatical, and punctuation errors. Verify the spelling of all individuals and company names.

♦ Finally, print your résumeé on white or off-white, high-quality paper.

Organizing Your Résumé

The two most popular résumé formats are functional and chronological. Choose the format that will maximize your strengths, minimize your weaknesses, and allow you to present your background in the best possible light.

Functional Format. This format, illustrated in Exhibit A-3 focuses on your accomplishments and abilities instead of your specific work history. It is ideal for recent college graduates with little work experience and for people with gaps in employment, modest career growth, and a history of hopping from job to job. Functional résumés are not recommended when you want to show a progression of steady job growth.

Ideally, your résumé should include no more than five functional headings that are consistent with your job objective. Examples of functional headings are database management, sales, advertising, and public relations. List the

EXHIBIT A-2	PERSONAL POWER VERBS ADD IMPACT TO YOUR RÉSUMÉ		
	achieved	generated	presented
	analyzed	implemented	researched
	budgeted	introduced	sold
	coordinated	launched	supervised
	devised	negotiated	trained
	formulated	prepared	wrote

EXHIBIT A-3	A FUNCTIONAL RÉSUMÉ

MARK STRUNK
173 Pacific Avenue
Vancouver B.C. V6M 2B9
(604) 555-1234 (home)
(604) 555-4321 (messages)

Career Objective   Corporate Public Relations Manager for a company that develops innovative, highly visible promotional campaigns.

PROFESSIONAL SKILLS

Writing/Editing
*Created award-winning brochures on current environmental issues.
*Wrote monthly newsletter distributed to 5,000 employees
*Used state-of-the-art desktop publishing systems to design and produce print materials

Media Contact
*Conducted numerous telephone interviews with print and electronic media concerning federal and provincial transportation questions
*Wrote daily press releases
*Helped formulate corporate response to community complaints about increases in trucking
*Acted as deputy spokesperson

WORK EXPERIENCE

1992 - present   Trans Solutions, Inc., Vancouver, B.C.
Deputy Public Relations Manager
Summer 1991   Committee to Re-elect Mayor Julie D'Abruzzo
River Falls, B.C.
Media relations assistant

EDUCATION

1987-1991   University of Calgary
Bachelor of Arts degree in Marketing
Cum Laude

ACTIVITIES

Summer 1988   Fund-raiser for Save the Children
Raised $5,000 in contributions
1988-1990   Vice President, Public Relations for student newspaper

References available upon request

---

function that is closest to your job objective first, even if your experience in the field is limited.

Depending upon your job history, you can choose to close a functional résumé with a chronological list of employment and education. Forego the employment section if you are applying for your first job or if you have a history of job hopping.

Chronological Format. This format lists your activities in chronological order, starting with the most recent information in each category. Use this format when you have a steady job history with few employment gaps or job changes. Included in a chronological résumé are the names of employers, dates of employment, specific job titles, and a description of major responsibilities. Because of its emphasis on past work experience, the chronological format is generally not recommended for first-time job applicants.

THE JOYS OF BRAND MANAGEMENT

Mary E. McPherson's career in brand management at consumer products giant Procter & Gamble has been developing impressively over the past five years. After graduating from the Commerce program at Queen's University in Kingston, Ontario, in 1990 (and after a summer internship working on promotions for Oil of Olay), McPherson joined Procter & Gamble as a brand assistant for Pringles Potato Chips. She was responsible for event marketing, consumer promotion, market research, and business analysis.

In 1991, she was promoted to assistant brand manager for Crisco Oil, where she was responsible for advertising, public relations, ethnic marketing, and many other activities. As she headed into her second year on the brand, she was given the responsibility of developing and presenting the brand's strategy, marketing plans, and budget.

In March of 1993, McPherson was promoted to brand manager on Institutional Cleaning Products and Foodservice Shortenings and Oils in P&G's Commercial Service Products department. This assignment gave her the opportunity to learn about an entirely new type of consumer—namely foodservice establishments. Six months later, she was appointed brand manager of Crisco Shortening, Crisco Oil, and Foodservice, and a year after that she was given additional responsibility for Duncan Hines Baking Mixes.

Most recently, in December 1994, McPherson became the brand manager for Crest Toothpaste.

What are Mary McPherson's feelings about working in brand management at Procter & Gamble? "The advantage of working in brand management at a large company like P&G is that you get to feel like you run a small business," she says, "but you have all of the resources and support groups that only a large company can provide. Project teams involve representatives who are experts in their respective functions, such as product development, finance, sales, and manufacturing. Since each team member has responsibility for only a few brands at any given time, they are really committed to achieving success on each project."

According to McPherson, there is no "typical" day in brand management, and no "typical" assignment, but she says, "that's what makes this career so exciting and challenging."

Accompany Every Résumé with an Effective Cover Letter

An effective cover letter sells your value and prepares the reader for the information in your résumé. Cover letters are targeted sales tools aimed at convincing a specific employer that you can handle a specific job. They demonstrate your knowledge of the company to which you are writing and communicate ways in which you can help the employer.

Cover letters usually contain between three and five paragraphs. The first paragraph should capture the reader's attention in some way, for example, by mentioning a mutual contact or an aspect of company operations, or by complimenting the company. The last sentence in this paragraph should state your interest in employment. The middle paragraphs describe how you can help the employer by meeting a specific need. You may also choose to summarize a particular aspect of your background that is targeted to the job. The closing paragraph is action oriented as it requests an interview or tells the employer

EXHIBIT A-4   A SAMPLE COVER LETTER

12 Somers Street
Regina, Sask. S3P 2A4
(306) 555-7654

June 10, 1995

Ms. Paula Devere
Vice President, Account Services
Davis, Singh and Associates
10673–75 Ave.
Edmonton, Alta. T4M 0B6

Dear Ms. Devere:

In the recent *Report on Business* article about Davis, Singh & Associates' advertising campaigns directed at the 50+ population, I thought that the four categories you used to describe this group made a lot of sense—it is bound to help focus marketing campaigns at the 50+ group more precisely. I am very interested in working with an agency that targets this group and I believe that I could be effective in working on your current campaigns.

For the past five years, I have worked with the Bracht & Fullerton Advertising Agency in Regina. This agency has several clients whose market focus is the 50+ age group. I helped devise marketing strategies specifically aimed at the high to middle income group and I quickly discovered the weaknesses of a campaign that spreads itself too thinly across a diverse group.

My knowledge of this market is readily transferable to your agency and I am eager to talk with you about my ideas for your current campaigns.

I will call during the week of June 24 to learn if my background interests you and to arrange a meeting in the near future.

Sincerely,

Magda Yevtusheoko

Enclosure: résumé

---

that you will call for his or her reaction to your résumé. Exhibit A-4 offers a sample cover letter.

SOURCES OF EMPLOYMENT ASSISTANCE

With a résumé and a draft of a cover letter you are ready to begin your actual job search. The most common sources of employment assistance are networking, college and university career placement services, employment agencies, and classified ads.

Networking

Networking involves contacting everyone you know for help in finding a job. Start networking your family, friends, neighbors, teachers, and business associates. Ask for concrete job leads as well as the names of people *they* know who might be able to help. This will enable you to continually develop new contacts. Conferences are also an excellent source of networking contacts.

College and University Career Placement Services

The career placement offices at colleges and universities help students and alumni find jobs by providing a number of employment-related services. These include résumeé preparation, vocational counseling, on-campus interviews with prospective employers, and publicizing job opportunities. Be aware, however, that because on-campus recruiters are typically from large companies, you will learn little about job opportunities in small companies via this route.

Employment Agencies

Private employment agencies are also a source of help. Most private agencies specialize in specific fields—computers or publishing, for example—and match your background with a list of available jobs. In many cases, the employer pays the agency's job placement fee, but in other cases the fee is your responsibility.

Classified Ads

Help-wanted ads in newspapers, such as *The Vancouver Sun* and *The Globe and Mail*, provide concrete job leads. Classified ads can also be found in specialized journals and trade publications. For specific publications check a reference source such as the *Canadian Almanac & Directory*.

THE JOB INTERVIEW

When an organization you have contacted expresses an interest in you it will invite you to a job interview. Your letter and résumé can get you this far, but only a good interview can get you a job. Employers make their final decisions based on how you impress them in person. During an interview, they judge you on a host of factors such as your experience, social skills, ability to think on your feet, personality, and communication skills. The interview is critical in determining whether you or another candidate gets the job.

Preparing for an Interview

Start by doing your homework. Thoroughly research a company *before* the interview to learn about its products, policies, financial condition, history, and culture (corporate culture was discussed in Chapter 2). Look for information about corporate restructuring, financial strengths and weaknesses, and hiring patterns. If you are interviewing with a publicly owned company, begin with the latest annual report, then consult periodical indexes for recent articles, and corporate directories, including *The Canadian Key Business Directory* and *The Canadian Trade Index*. Business and industry groups, such as trade associations, are also helpful. Your research will help you tie your abilities directly to company needs. Research also helps candidates ask intelligent questions during the interview (see Exhibit A-5).

In addition, research the salary range for the job. Ask members of your business network who hold similar jobs, check the ranges listed in newspaper ads, talk to employment agents.

As you analyze salary data, keep in mind that compensation varies by position and industry. For example, the salary of a manufacturers' representative is determined according to whether the candidate is a trainee or a middle or top-level salesperson and according to whether the job is in a consumer-goods, industrial goods, or services company.

Preparation also involves polishing your personal style. Practice your delivery to eliminate repetitive phrases such as "you know" and "um" and to emphasize eye contact. Learn the fine art of a firm handshake and the finer art of active listening (see Chapter 21). Finally,

---

EXHIBIT A-5   **QUESTIONS JOB CANDIDATES CAN USEFULLY ASK AN INTERVIEWER**

- What are the specific responsibilities of the job?
- What challenges would I face if I took the job?
- A recent article I read in [name the publication] mentioned that you are planning to increase production in this division. How will that affect the position?
- To whom would I report and where is the position in the organizational structure?
- Is there a formal training program?
- What is a typical career path for someone who takes this position?
- Do you encourage in-house transfers or tend to fill positions from the outside?
- Did any of your company's top executives start in this division?
- How would you characterize your corporate culture?

spend time thinking about your interview wardrobe. The right choice, in most cases, is a conservative suit that communicates that you are ready for business.

Kinds of Interviews

Today it is common for an applicant to face more than one interview for a particular job. There are four main types of interviews— known as screening, in-depth, multiple, and stress interviews—and each has a different purpose and a different place in the interview sequence.

The *screening interview* typically is the candidate's first interview. Normally conducted by a recruiter from the company's human resources department, its purpose is to narrow the list of candidates and present the most qualified to the person making the hiring decision. Your best bet is to be pleasant and relaxed, to answer questions specifically but succinctly, and to show your interest in the company and the job by asking one or two of the more general questions listed in Exhibit A-5.

The *in-depth interview* involves the job candidate and the person for whom he or she would be working. During the interview, the manager will explore your background and qualifications and try to learn about your personality and working style. At the same time, she or he will answer questions about the job, department, and company. To be successful in this interview, try to direct the conversation to the specific ways your experience can benefit the company.

The *multiple interview* involves meeting people in the organization other than the person doing the hiring. Included are division and department heads, peers, subordinates, and others you would work with if you got the job. Although many multiple interviews take place over lunch or in a similarly casual atmosphere, there is nothing casual about them. If you make mistakes—for example, if you appear hostile or indicate that you like to do things your own way—you are likely to be eliminated from the running.

Finally, the *stress interview* is designed to test your reactions to a difficult situation, namely the job interview itself. Interviewers may ask a series of abrasive questions that make you uncomfortable and put you on the defensive. They may be impolite and unrelenting as they try to assess how you respond to pressure. Your goal is to keep your composure throughout the interview by focusing on the content of the questions rather than the manner in which they are asked.

Handling Yourself During the Interview

Most interviews begin with a few minutes of casual conversation that allows candidates to relax and establish rapport with their interviewers. Generally, interviewers turn next to a discussion of the candidate's work experience, followed by education, activities and interests, and strengths and weaknesses.[3] Some of the questions commonly asked during interviews are listed in Exhibit A-6.

Many interviews include difficult questions designed to elicit negative information. Instead of hoping these questions will never come up and being surprised when they are asked, prepare for them by confronting them in advance. Your goal in each case is to put a positive spin on something, showing how you grew professionally or personally from a negative situation. For example, when asked about your most serious weakness, try to turn a deficit into a positive characteristic: "I want to make sure every job is done right and on deadline, so I sometimes get impatient when I see people wasting time."

A discussion of salary and benefits usually comes at the end of the interview *after* a job offer. Using the salary information you collected in your research, try to decide on a fair compensation package as well as the absolute minimum you would accept.

When interviewers start talking about money, ask for a figure near the top of the salary range and see how they respond. If they balk, ask for their best offer. If this is still too low, tell them that you would like a day to decide. As you consider the offer, try to take a long-term as well as a short-term career view. Consider what you can learn on the job and the opportunities in the company for career growth.

After the Interview

After each interview, write a letter thanking the interviewer. State clearly that you want the job and reemphasize your qualifications. This letter also gives you the chance to provide additional information and to clear up any wrong impressions.

When the interview process ends in a job offer, be sure you fully understand the nature of the deal, including compensation and benefits, working conditions, and starting date. Then take time to consider your final decision. If you decide to refuse the offer, write a

EXHIBIT A-6 | QUESTIONS INTERVIEWERS COMMONLY ASK DURING AN INTERVIEW

Work

- Describe the accomplishment you were most proud of in your last job.
- Do you consider yourself more of an independent contributor or a team player?
- What serious problems did you face and how did you handle them?
- Describe an incident in which you handled a problem involving personal interaction well. Describe another incident in which you were less effective.
- Where do you see your career in five years?

Education

- Why did you choose your major field of study?
- What courses did you like the best? Least? Why?
- If you worked during school, how did you manage your time?
- Were you satisfied with your college?
- How important were extracurricular activities to your education?
- If you were starting college all over again, what would you do differently?

Activities and Interests

- What activities are you involved in?
- Would you describe your role in these activities as more of a follower or a leader?

Strengths and Weaknesses

- Give me three reasons why you are especially qualified for this job.
- What weaknesses have previous employers identified over the years?
- What part of this job would probably give you the most trouble?

letter to the employer explaining your reason for not taking the job. Be gracious and express your appreciation for the offer so as to leave the door open for future contact at a later stage in your career.

SELECTED SOURCES OF MARKETING AND CAREER INFORMATION ●

Use this appendix as the starting point in your search for information on marketing careers. Then consult the following references for more detail:

MARKETING CAREERS

Career Opportunity News (Published by Garrett Park Press, PO Box 190C, Garrett Park, MD 20986-0190).

The Employment Kit: Your Career Advantage, ed. by Ginny Shipe. Chicago: American Marketing Association, 1992.

Explore Your Future: A Career in Life Insurance Sales (National Association of Life Underwriters, 1922 F St., NW, Washington, DC 20006)

Michael David Harkavy and the Philip Lief Group. *The 100 Best Companies To Sell For.* New York: John Wiley & Sons, 1989.

International Employment Hotline (Monthly newsletter published by International Employment Hotline, PO Box 3030, Oakton, VA 22124)

Robert Levering and Milton Moskowitz. *The 100 Best Companies To Work For In America.* New York: Plume, 1993.

National Business Employment Weekly (Published weekly by Dow Jones).

Perterson's Job Opportunities for Business and Liberal Arts Graduates. Princeton: Peterson's, 1991.

NOTHING FEELS QUITE AS GOOD AS WINNING

Patti Arneson, Senior Marketing Manager for Marketing, Economics, and Finance at Prentice Hall, is responsible for the annual marketing of approximately $20 million in college textbooks. Her varied responsibilities include "writing marketing plans, implementing advertising programs, working with the editorial staff in acquiring and developing books, planning Prentice Hall sales convention programs, making presentations to the sales force, and working with sales reps" in her areas of specialization.

Arneson, for whom being a marketing manager was always a career goal, started out as a sales rep. She believes that her initial experience in the field gave her "an invaluable understanding not only of the different markets in which we compete but of the needs that drive customers' decisions." After three years she was promoted to district sales manager, and five years after that moved into her present position.

The rewards of her job are many, says Arneson: "It is really gratifying to see your work come to fruition, whether it's playing a role in getting a sought-after author to sign with us, realizing that I've had some significant influence on the success of a book, finding that a direct mail piece has had real impact, or seeing a suggestion I've made for a book's content or pedagogy become a particularly effective sales feature."

According to Arneson, it's the challenges that "stretch your abilities and keep you interested." In today's corporate world, she points out, mergers and downsizing are reality, and "learning how to win in mature and highly competitive markets like college publishing takes well-thought-out strategic planning."

Arneson, who lives with her husband and young son in Illinois, is representative of a rapidly growing trend in business today. She is a telecommuter, with regular travel between her Illinois office and Prentice Hall headquarters in New Jersey.

Sales Managers. Moravia, NY: Chronicle Guidance Publications, Inc. 1991.

U.S. Department of Labor, Bureau of Labor Statistics, *Occupational Outlook Handbook: 1992-93 ed.* Washington, D.C. U.S. Government Printing Office, 1992.

GENERAL REFERENCES

Richard H. Beatty. *The Perfect Cover Letter.* New York: John Wiley, 1989.

Arthur H. Bell. *International Careers.* Holbrook, MA: Bob Adams, 1990.

Richard N. Bolles. *How to Create Your Ideal Job or Next Career.* Berkeley: Ten Speed Press, 1990.

Richard N. Bolles. *What Color Is Your Parachute?* Berkeley: Ten Speed Press, 1994.

Careering and Re-Careering for the 1990's (Published by Consultants Bookstore, Templeton Road, Fitzwilliam, NH 03447).

Tom Jackson. *The Perfect Résumé.* New York: Doubleday, 1990.

Paul Kaponya. *How to Survive Your First 90 Days at a New Company.* Hawthorne, NJ: The Career Press, 1990.

William J. Morin and James C. Cabrera. *Parting Company: How to Survive the Loss of a Job and Find Another Successfully.* San Diego, CA: Harcourt Brace Jovanovich, 1991.

Ed Rushlow. *Get a Better Job!* Princeton: Peterson's, 1990.

NOTES

1. Specific job descriptions from Bradley J. Morgan, *Marketing and Sales Career Directory,* 4th ed. Detroit: Visible Ink, 1993, pp. 1–102; *The Employment Kit: Your Career Advantage,* ed by Ginny Shipe. Chicago: American Marketing Association, 1992, pp. 35-38.

2. Gabriella Stern, "P&G Hopes Kaplan Can Bring Some Zip To Its Cosmetics and Perfume Business," *The Wall Street Journal,* March 25, 1994, p. B1.

3. Interview sequence described in William J. Morin and James C. Cabrera, *Parting Company: How To Survive the Loss of a Job and Find Another Successfully.* San Diego: Harcourt Brace Jovanovich, 1991, pp. 278–286.

A-17
CAREERS IN
MARKETING

Marketing-Data Analysis and Mathematics

This appendix offers a brief introduction to the analysis of marketing data and the mathematical calculations necessary to create and implement a successful marketing plan. There are many different ratios that can help marketing managers in this task; the manager's choice will depend on the product, target market, and marketplace with which she or he is dealing.

With limited space, we can present only a few analyses and calculations that have fairly broad application. You'll recall that in Chapter 22 we outlined the method of indexing, which gives the marketer a quick handle on how a set of marketing data compare with similar data from other areas. Here we introduce you to somewhat more complex analyses of marketing data. We begin with the business-performance ratio and two of its primary varieties—the operational-marketing ratio and the profitability ratio. Then we discuss two methods of breakeven analysis that will add to the basic method you acquired in Chapter 16.

BUSINESS-PERFORMANCE RATIOS

Business-performance ratios measure company performance in such general terms as brand profitability or in specific areas like inventory turnover. These ratios are used in comparing the firm or its products with:

◆ *Company goals*
◆ *Past company performance*
◆ *Industry averages or standards*

We focus our discussion in this section on two important types of business performance ratios: operational marketing ratios and profitability ratios. We will use the retail income statement in Exhibit BI-1 and balance sheet (Exhibit B1-2) to anchor our illustration. An *income statement* is a summary of both revenue and expenses for a particular business over a specified period of time, usually one month or one year. A *balance sheet* is a summary of the firm's assets, liabilities, and owners' equity or capital as of a specific date, usually the last day of a month or the last day of the firm's fiscal year.

Revenue

Gross Sales	$ 1,832,450
Less Returns and Allowances	$ 98,500
Net Sales	**$1,733,950**

Less Cost of Goods Sold

Beginning Inventory (at cost)	$ 200,000
Plus Net Purchases	$ 850,000
Total Goods Handled	$ 1,050,000
Less Ending Inventory	$ 160,000
Gross Cost of Goods Sold	$ 890,000
Less Cash Discounts	$ 60,000
Total Cost of Goods Sold	$ 830,000

Gross Margin   **$ 903,950**

Less Operating Expenses

Administrative	$ 409,883
Research and Development	$ 18,000
Depreciation	$ 20,000
Advertising	$ 83,230
Selling	$ 200,000
Total Operating Expenses	$ 731,113
Operating Income	$ 172,837

Less Other Expenses

Interest	$ 26,500
Total Other Expenses	$ 26,500
Net Income Before Taxes	$ 146,337

Less Provisions for Taxes

Taxes	$ 62,887
Total Taxes	$ 62,887
Net Earnings, or Profit Margin	**$ 83,450**

Definitions of selected terms:

Gross Sales:	Total Sales
Allowances:	Reductions in gross sales resulting from markdowns, employee discounts, and/or theft
Inventory:	For manufacturers, raw materials, goods in process or finished goods; for retailers, merchandise
Gross Margin:	The difference between net sales and total cost of goods sold; sometimes also referred to as gross profit
Depreciation:	The prorated cost of using an asset over its lifetime

---

EXHIBIT B1-2   YEAR-END BALANCE SHEET

ASSETS
Current Assets

Cash and Short-Term Securities	$	15,500
Accounts Receivable	$	195,300
Inventories	$	737,700
Total Current Assets	**$**	**948,500**

Fixed and Other Assets

Property, Plant & Equipment (at cost)	$	449,500
Less Accumulated Depreciation	$	134,900
Net Property, Plant and Equipment	$	314,600
Goodwill, Patents, Trademarks	$	194,000
Total Fixed and Other Assets	**$**	**508,600**
Total Assets		**$1,457,100**

LIABILITIES
Current Liabilities

Accounts Payable	$	142,100
Accrued Expenses	$	16,400
Federal Income Tax Payable	$	42,300
Total Current Liabilities	**$**	**200,800**

Long-Term Liabilities

Notes Payable	$	393,200
Total Long-Term Liabilities	**$**	**393,200**

Stockholder's Equity

Capital Stock	$	447,500
Preferred Stock	$	11,100
Paid-in Capital	$	248,200
Retained Earnings	$	156,300
Total Stockholders' Equity	**$**	**863,100**
Total Liabilities and Stockholder's Equity		**$1,457,100**

OPERATIONAL MARKETING RATIOS

Before we discuss profitability ratios, which focus on the firm's total profitability, we will examine *operational marketing ratios,* which focus on specific parts of the business. We look at two kinds of operational marketing ratios: the *inventory-turnover ratio* and the *sales-efficiency ratio.*

Inventory-Turnover Ratio In many businesses, inventory is the largest part of the asset base. Therefore, it is often worthwhile to isolate inventory in order to determine if it is being managed properly.

Inventory turnover is the number of times during a given period—usually one year—that the *average* inventory has bee.n replaced. We can also define this ratio as the number of times that a product must be sold, replaced in inventory, and sold again in order to produce a given amount of net sales during the specified period. Inventory turnover, which can be figured either for the entire inventory or for specific merchandise lines, is often calculated by dividing net sales (gross sales less returns on allowances) by average inventory on hand.

Average inventory is defined as beginning inventory plus ending inventories divided by the total number of inventories. Assume, for example, that a store's T-shirt department had a beginning inventory of $8,000 on June 1 and ending inventories of $7,200 on June 30 and $7,800 on July 31. Sales for June and July totaled $5,600. What is the average inventory rate for the two-month period of June and July, what is the turnover ratio for that period, and what is the projected turnover rate for the year? We can calculate these rates as follows:

Where:

$$ICPs = \text{Inventory Check Points (\$8,000, \$7,200, \$7,800)}$$
$$S = \text{Sales for period (\$5,600)}$$
$$N = \text{Number of inventory check points (3)}$$

Then:

$$\text{average inventory on hand} = \frac{ICP_1 + ICP_2 + ICP_3}{N}$$

$$= \frac{\$8,000 + 7,200 + 7,800}{3}$$

$$= \$7,667$$

Now we can calculate the inventory turnover ratio for the store. The formula is

$$\text{inventory turnover} = \frac{\text{net sales}}{\text{average inventory}}$$

Thus,

$$\text{inventory turnover} = \frac{\$5,600}{\$7,667}$$

$$= .73$$

Projecting 7/10 of one turnover for a two-month period over 12 months, we calculate as follows:

$$\text{annual turnover rate} = .73 \times \frac{12}{2}$$

$$= .73 \times 6$$

$$\text{annual turnover rate} = 4.38 \text{ times per year}$$

Once calculated, the turnover rate must be compared to company goals, past annual results, and industry standards. Unsatisfactory results are usually one of two types and suggest one of the following corrective tactics:

1. *Increasing net sales relative to average inventory on hand.* For example: Consider promotional tactics; improve personal-selling effectiveness; take markdowns on price-elastic products and markups on inelastic products; examine inventory shortages.

2. *Decreasing average inventory relative to net sales.* For example: Avoid duplication of product styles and brands; eliminate slow-moving lines; purchase goods in less quantity but more frequently; adhere to purchase cancellation dates on seasonal merchandise.

Sales-Efficiency Ratio The sales-efficiency ratio compares gross sales with net sales. Gross sales are total sales recorded. Net sales are gross sales less returns or allowances; the latter are reductions due to markdowns, employee discounts, or theft. A sales-efficiency ratio of 1 indicates no returns or allowances; thus a ratio of less than 1 tells a marketer that sales efficiency may be improved by more effective management of returns and allowances. The sales-efficiency ratio is calculated as follows:

$$\frac{\text{net sales}}{\text{gross sales}} = \text{sales efficiency ratio}$$

Based on the income statement in Table B-1,

$$\frac{\text{net sales}}{\text{gross sales}} \quad \frac{\$1,733,950}{\$1,832,450} = 94.6\%$$

This result indicates that 5.4 percent of the firm's sales go to covering returns and allowances. In order to determine if corrective action should be taken, this figure would be compared to the figures for the company's previous years, to expected ratios, and to industry standards.

PROFITABILITY RATIOS

Whereas operational marketing ratios focus on specific aspects of a business, *profitability ratios* focus on the firm's overall profitability. We will examine three of the most important kinds of profitability ratios: *gross-margin ratio, profit margin,* and *return on investment.*

Gross-Margin Ratio The *gross-margin ratio* shows the percentage of sales revenue that remains after deducting the cost of goods sold and that is available for operating expenses, taxes, and profit. This ratio is calculated as follows:

$$\text{gross-margin ratio} = \frac{\text{gross margin}}{\text{net sales}}$$

From Table BI-1:

$$\begin{array}{ll}
\$1,733,950 & \text{net sales} \\
- \$830,000 & \text{cost of goods sold} \\
\hline
\$903,950 & \text{gross margin}
\end{array}$$

$$\frac{\text{gross margin}}{\text{net sales}} \quad \frac{\$903,950}{\$1,733,950} = 52.1\%$$

Thus we see that over 52 percent of net sales remain to cover operating expenses, taxes, and profits.

Profit Margin As Table BI-1 indicates, profit margin, or net earnings, represents the balance of total revenues after cost of goods sold, operating expenses, other expenses such as interest, and taxes are deducted. Note the difference between net earnings and net sales: the latter represent the balance of gross sales after returns and allowances are deducted.

Marketers compare the profit margin both to the firm's profit margins in previous years and to average profit margins recorded by other firms in their industry. A shrinking profit margin indicates either that operational and marketing expenses have increased in relation to sales or that sales have declined without an accompanying reduction in these kinds of expenses.

The profit margin ratio is the percent of net sales represented by net earnings. This ratio is calculated as follows:

$$\text{profit-margin ratio} = \frac{\text{net earnings}}{\text{net sales}}$$

Again, based on Table BI-1:

$$\text{profit margin ratio} = \frac{\text{net earnings}}{\text{net sales}} \quad \frac{\$83,450}{\$1,733,950}$$

$$= 4.8\%$$

Return on Investment The *return-on-investment* ratio uses a firm's net earnings, total assets, and net worth to provide an overall picture of financial health. Total assets, as you can see from Table BI-2, are the sum of cash, accounts receivable, inventory, property, and good will. Net worth is equal to total stockholders' equity. Return on investment is calculated as follows:

$$\text{return-on-investment ratio} = \frac{\text{net earnings}}{\text{total assets}} \times \frac{\text{total assets}}{\text{net worth}}$$

The first part of this equation is the firm's *return on assets*—that is, the ratio of profits to the investment needed to make them. The second part is the firm's *leverage ratio.* A high leverage ratio means that the firm is dependent on borrowed funds. If the leverage ratio is quite low, the firm is probably being financed by the owner's equity rather than by borrowed funds. A low ratio suggests that the firm's ownership is fairly conservative and uncomfortable with risk. Although this strategy is viewed as generally positive, keep in mind that owner's equity is basically more expensive than borrowed capital. Firms that are financed by owner's equity forgo the chance to "leverage" the owner's funds by borrowing at *going rates,* thereby gaining the higher return afforded by cheaper dollars. In other words, most firms should be able to generate a greater rate of return than the cost of the money they need to operate.

All of this, however, assumes that owners are in business for long-term profit margins that are greater than the cost of either owner funds or borrowed capital. If this were not true, businesspeople would be better off investing their equity in money markets or some other similar investment vehicle. If you own a business, you are assuming that, *over the long term,* your money will produce a greater rate of return by being invested in your business than by being invested in a vehicle that may generate greater *short-term* return.

From Table BI-1 and BI-2, we insert the appropriate numbers to calculate return on investment for the company in our illustration:

$$\frac{\$83,450}{\$1,457,100} \times \frac{\$1,457,100}{\$863,100} = .06 \times 1.69$$

$$= .10, \text{ or } 10\%$$

This ratio determines the return generated by the company on its invested funds. A low ratio, whether in terms of past performance, budgeted return, or industry standards, may be the result of an unfavorable business environment, improper or inefficient use of borrowed funds, over-investment in assets, distribution or marketing weakness, or financial mismanagement.

PRICING BREAKEVEN ANALYSIS ●

We discussed *breakeven analysis* in Chapter 16. Here, we will go into a little more detail and present two common methods for determining price on a breakeven basis.

METHOD 1

The purpose of this method is to provide a guideline for ensuring that expenditures do not exceed sales. The result is a pricing structure that will cover costs and provide a basis from which to estimate expected profit. In addition, this method takes into direct account the effect of both past demand and price sensitivity on current pricing decisions.

The following formula is the basis for this calculation:

$$AP(U) - AVC(U) = FC$$

Where:

AP = *Average Price:* the average amount for which a product is sold
FC = *Fixed Costs:* costs that do not change with fluctuating sales or production
AVC = *Average Variable Costs:* average cost per unit, which varies according to the volume of production or sales
U = *Volume of Units produced at the breakeven point:* the number of units that must be sold in order to break even.

For example: A game store has an average unit sale of $40. Fixed costs are $15,000 per month, and variable costs are $20 per unit sold. The retailer is selling above breakeven if he sells 2,000 units per month. If we know this much, we can determine the breakeven point in terms of number of the units sold and projected profits. First, let's calculate the breakeven point *from the standpoint of number of units sold per month:*

$$\$40(U) - AVC(U) = FC$$
$$\$40(U) - \$20(U) = \$15,000$$
$$\$20(U) = 15,000$$
$$U = 750$$

The breakeven point in units is thus: 750 units.

Following up on this illustration, let's determine the profits generated from the sale of 2,000 units at an average price per unit of $40. We can determine profits according to the following formula:

Number of units sold = 2000
Total sales   = 2000 × $40
     = $80,000
Total costs   = $15,000 (fixed) + $20(2000)
     = $55,000
Profit   = $80,000 − $55,000
     = $25,000

Now, let's assume that through past experience, the retailer estimates that a reduction on the selling price per unit from $40 to $30 will result in a 20-percent increase in business. From this information, we can determine if profits will increase and if the price reduction is warranted:

Number of units sold = 2400 [2000 + 20%(2000)]
Total sales   = 2400 × $30
     = $72,000
Total costs   = $15,000 (fixed) + $20(2400)
     = $63,000
Profit   = $72,000 − $63,000
     = $9,000

Based on these calculations, our retailer would *not* place his entire stock on sale because profits would fall from $25,000 to $9,000.

METHOD 2

Method 2 is more "static" than Method 1 because it does not consider *price elasticity* (a product is *price-elastic* if a reduction in price results in an increase in sales and/or an increase in price results in a decrease in sales; see Chapter 16). However, it is a common method for determining the breakeven point in certain product categories. As an example, let's project the following figures for a hypothetical company:

Net Sales	$1,200,000
Cost of Goods	–$620,000
Gross Margin	$580,000

The following table shows our company's operating expenses and net profit:

Operating Expenses		Nature of Expense	Fixed Expenses	Variable Expenses
Wages & Salaries	$300,000	Semi-variable	$150,000	$150,000
Rent	$30,000	Fixed	$30,000	
Advertising & Promotion	$55,000	Variable		$55,000
Miscellaneous	$100,000	Semi-variable	$50,000	$50,000
			$230,000	$255,000
Totals				
Net Profit	$95,000			

Method 2 uses three ratios to determine the breakeven point:

variable-expense ratio = variable expenses divided by net sales
gross margin ratio   = gross margin divided by net sales
marginal-income ratio = gross-margin ratio less variable-expense ratio (the percent of sales volume available to cover fixed expenses, the remainder being profit)

A breakeven point *in dollar sales* is then determined by dividing the fixed expense by the marginal-income ratio. We begin with the following formula:

breakeven point in sales = fixed expenses ÷ marginal-income ratio

Then we insert the appropriate numbers:

variable-expense ratio = $255,000 ÷ $1,200,000 = .21
gross margin ratio   = $580,000 ÷ $1,200,000 = .48
marginal-income ratio =   .48   –   .21   = .27

Our breakeven point in dollar sales can thus be calculated as follows:

230,000 ÷ .27 = $851,852

In summary, then, 27 percent of our store's sales volume can be used to cover fixed expenses.

Notes

Chapter 1

1. Peter D. Bennett, *Dictionary of Marketing Terms* (Chicago: American Marketing Assoc., 1988), p. 115.
2. Regis McKenna, *Relationship Marketing* (Reading, Mass: Addison-Wesley, 1991), p. 5.
3. Richard C. Morais and Michael Schuman, "Hong Kong Is Just Around the Corner," *Forbes*, October 2, 1992, pp. 50–58.
4. R. C. Bennett and R. G. Cooper, "The Misuse of Marketing: An American Tragedy," *Business Horizons*, November–December 1981, pp. 51–60.
5. "Mail Order Firms Putting Shoppers First," *The Globe and Mail*, Monday, August 8, 1994.
6. Neil H. Borden, "The Concept of the Marketing Mix," *Journal of Advertising Research*, June 1964, pp. 2–7.
7. Benson Shapiro, "What the Hell Is 'Market Oriented'?" *Harvard Business Review*, November–December 1988, pp. 119–25.
8. Theodore Levitt, "The Globalization of Markets," *Harvard Business Review*, May–June 1983, pp. 92–102.
9. Thomas Hester, "Into Europe," *Marketing*, July 30, 1988, p. 31.
10. *The Globe and Mail Report on Business Magazine*, September, 1994.
11. John C. Reid, "This Is Not Niche Marketing: Coke Exec," *Advertising Age*, June 29, 1992, pp. S8–S9.
12. Tracy Kett, "Cutting Package Waste Becomes More Difficult," *The Globe and Mail*, May 11, 1994, p. B20.
13. Adrian Cadbury, "Ethical Managers Make Their Own Rules," *Harvard Business Review*, September–October. 1987, pp. 69–73; Kenneth R. Andrews, "Ethics in Practice," *Harvard Business Review*, September–October 1989, pp. 99–104; and Shelby D. Hunt, Van R. Wood, and Lawrence B. Chonko, "Corporate Ethical Values and Organizational Commitment in Marketing," *Journal of Marketing 53* (July 1989): 79–90.
14. John McCormick and Marc Levinson, "The Supply Police," *Newsweek*, February 15, 1993, pp. 48–49.
15. This discussion is based on Michael Janofsky, "P&G, the Diaper Leader, Strikes Back," *The New York Times*, April 15, 1993, p. D1: Carl Lehrburger and Rachel Snyder, "The Disposable Diaper Myth," *Whole Earth Review*, Fall 1988, pp. 60–67; Annette Miller, "A Pitched Battle for Baby's Bottom," *Newsweek*, March 6, 1989, p. 44; Alecia Swasy, "Procter & Gamble Hopes to Recycle Disposable Diapers," *The Wall Street Journal*, June 21, 1989, pp. B1, B6; Laurie Freeman, "BioDegraded?" *Advertising Age*, June 26, 1989, p. 66; Dan Koeppel, "P&G's New 'Whole Earth' Approach," *Adweek's Marketing Week*, June 26, 1989, p. 2; Rose Gutfeld, "Even Environmentalists Still Use Disposable Diapers," *The Wall Streeet Journal*, December 26, 1989, pp. B1, B2; and Kathleen Deveny, "States Mull Rash of Diaper Regulations," *The Wall Street Journal*, June 15, 1990, pp. B1, B6.

Chapter 2

1. John Smale, "Behind the Brands at P&G," *Harvard Business Review*, November–December 1985, pp. 79–90.
2. "Selling is Dying," *Sales and Marketing Management*, August, 1994, pp. 82–84.
3. Robert W. Ruekert and Orville C. Walker, Jr., "Marketing's Interaction with Other Functional Units: A Conceptual Framework and Empirical Evidence," *Journal of Marketing*, January 1987, pp. 1–19.
4. "Executive Stereotype Still Reigns," *Sales & Marketing Management,* February 1989, p. 23.
5. Laurie Freeman, "The House That Ivory Built," *Advertising Age*, August 20, 1987, p. 1.
6. William J. Holstein, "The Stateless Corporation," *Business Week*, May 14, 1990, pp. 98–105.
7. J. A. Pearce, "The Company Mission as a Strategic Tool," *Sloan Management Review 23* (1982): 15–24.
8. Theodore Levitt, "Marketing Myopia," *Harvard Business Review*, July–August 1960, pp. 45–56. See also Irving D. Canton, "'Marketing Myopia' Revisited," *Marketing News*, March 13, 1987, p. 1.
9. Rohit Deshpande and Frederick E. Webster, Jr., "Organizational Culture and Marketing: Defining the Research Agenda," *Journal of Marketing*, January 1989, pp. 3–15.
10. Nigel Piercy and Neil Morgan, "Internal Marketing: Making Marketing Happen," *Marketing Intelligence & Planning 8* (1990): 4–6.
11. David Norburn, Sue Birley, and Mark Dunn, "Strategic Marketing Effectiveness and Its Relationship to Corporate Culture and Beliefs: A Cross-National Study," *International Studies of Management and Organization 18* (1988): 83–100.
12. John Burgess, "IBM's Magazine Mirrors Company's New Direction," *Business Plus*, October 26, 1993, pp. 9–11.
13. Robert Haavind, *The Road to the Baldridge Award* (Stoneham, MA: Butterworth-Heinemann, 1992), p. xii; Barnaby J. Feder, "At Motorola, Quality Is a Team Sport," *The New York Times*, January 21, 1993, p. D1.
14. Shelby D. Hunt, Van R. Wood, and Lawrence B. Chonko, "Corporate Ethical Values and Organizational Commitment in Marketing," *Journal of Marketing*, July 1989, pp. 79–90; A. Parasuraman and Rohit Deshpande, "The Cultural Context of Marketing Management," in *1984 AMA Educator's Proceedings*, Series 50, Russell W. Belk et al., eds. (Chicago: American

Marketing Association, 1984), pp. 176–79; and Thomas V. Bonoma, "Making Your Marketing Strategy Work," *Harvard Business Review*, March–April 1984, pp. 69–72.

Chapter 3

1. Andrei Illarionov, Richard Layard, and Peter Orszag, *The Conditions of Life* as quoted in "Poverty of Numbers," *The Economist,* July 10, 1993, p. 40; Anders Aslund, "Runaway Rubles," *The New York Times,* November 24, 1993; and Peter Galuszka, "BMW, Mercedes, Rolls-Royce—Could This Be Russia?" *Business Week,* August 2, 1993, p. 40.
2. Noel M. Tichy, and Stratford Sherman, *Control Your Destiny or Someone Else Will: How Jack Welch Is Making General Electric the World's Most Competitive Corporation* (New York: Currency, 1993).
3. Keith J. Tuckwell, *Canadian Marketing in Action*, 2nd ed., (Scarborough, Ontario: Prentice Hall Canada, 1994), p. 52.
4. "Predatory Pricing Issue Is Due to Be Taken Up in American Air's Trial," *The Wall Street Journal*, July 12, 1993, p. 1.
5. Theodore Levitt, "The Globalization of Markets," *Harvard Business Review*, May–June 1983, p. 92.
6. Amar Gupta and Hoo-Min D. Toong, "Bringing Everyman into the Computer Age," in *Insights into Personal Computers*, ed. Amar Gupta and Hoo-Min D. Toong (New York: IEEE Press, 1985), p. 1.
7. Stewart Brand, "The Media Lab: Inventing the Future at M.I.T. (New York: Penguin, 1988), p. 9.

Chapter 4

1. James Pollack, "Kmart Readies for Battle," *Marketing*, August 1/8, 1994, p. 21.
2. Gary Hamel and C. K. Prahalad, "Strategy as Stretch and Leverage," *Harvard Business Review*, March–April 1993, pp. 75–85.
3. Dana Wechsler Linden, "The Bean Counter as Hero," *Forbes*, October 11, 1993, pp. 46–47.
4. Gary Hamel and C. K. Prahalad, "Strategic Intent," *Harvard Business Review*, May–June 1989, p. 65.
5. Peter D. Bennett, *Dictionary of Marketing Terms* (Chicago: American Marketing Association, 1988), p. 195.
6. Sharon Moshavi, "Please Deposit No Cents," *Forbes*, August 16, 1993, p. 102; Dinah Zeiger, "Battle of 'Smart' Cards," *Denver Post*, July 11, 1993, p. 61.
7. Roman G. Hiebing, Jr. and Scott W. Cooper, *The Successful Marketing Plan* (Lincolnwood Ill.: NTC, 1990), p. 2.
8. Malcolm H. B. McDonald, *Marketing Plans* (London: Heinemann, 1984), p. 92.
9. Donald R. Lehmann and Russell S. Winer, *Analysis for Marketing Planning*, 2nd ed. (Homewood, Ill.: Irwin, 1991), p. 159.
10. J. I. Moore, *Writers on Strategy and Strategic Management* (London: Penguin Books, 1992), pp. 47–51.
11. Mark Stevenson, "The Store to End All Stores," *Canadian Business*, May 1994, p. 20.

12. Nils-Erik Aaby and Anthony F. McGann, "Corporate Strategy and the Role of Navigational Marketing," *European Journal of Marketing 23* (1989): 18–30; John R. Darling and Raymond E. Taylor, "A Model for Reducing Internal Resistance to Change in a Firm's International Marketing Strategy," *European Journal of Marketing 23* (1989): 34–50; Nigel Piercy and Kenneth J. Peattie, "Matching Marketing Strategies to Corporate Culture: The Parcel and the Wall," *Journal of General Management 13* (Summer 1988): 33–48.
13. Joseph Weber, "Campbell: Now It's M-M-Global," *Business Week*, March 15, 1993, pp. 52–54.

Chapter 5

1. "New Marketing Research Definition Approved," *Marketing News*, January 2, 1987, p. 1.
2. Thomas Arenberg, "Tombstone Pizza Marketing Basics Spice Up Growth," *Quick Frozen Foods*, July 1983, pp. 40–44.
3. Lisa Fortini-Campbell, *Hitting the Sweet Spot: How Consumer Insights Can Inspire Better Marketing and Advertising* (Chicago: The Copy Workshop, 1992).
4. Dick Harvey, "Coke Changed Formula to Break from Old Habits," *Advertising Age*, June 24, 1985; "Two Cokes Really Are Better Than One–For Now," *Business Week*, September 9, 1985, p. 38.
5. Alan R. Andreasen, "'Backward Market' Research," *Harvard Business Review*, May–June 1985, pp. 61–72.
6. David A. Weiss, "Syndicated Studies Appeal to Marketers in a Hurry," *Marketing News*, September 11, 1989, p. 46; and "Findex 1989," *Adweek's Marketing Week*, June 12, 1989, p. 48.
7. Sean Milmo, "Export Data Banks Boom in Europe," *Business Marketing*, October 1988, pp. 27–35.
8. Stan Rapp and Thomas L. Collins, *The Great Marketing Turnaround: The Age of the Individual—and How to Profit from It* (Englewood Cliffs, N.J.: Prentice Hall, 1990), p. 5.
9. Mary Connors, "A Research Odyssey," *Adweek*, December 1, 1986, p. F.K. 4.
10. Lisa Fortini-Campbell, *Hitting the Sweet Spot*, 1992.
11. Betsy Sharkey, "Put to the Test," *Adweek*, December 7, 1992, pp. 28–32.
12. Carol Moog, *"Are They Selling Her Lips?" Advertising and Identity* (New York: William Morrow, 1990).
13. Andrew M. Tarshis, "The Single Source Household: Delivering on the Dream," *Aim*, premier issue 1989, pp. 15–16.

Chapter 6

1. Natalie Perkins, "Zeroing in on Consumer Values," *Advertising Age*, March 22, 1993, p. 20; Betsy Israel, "Lost in the Name Game," *The New York Times*, February. 14, 1993, Sect 9, pp. 1, 9; Scott Donaton, "The Media Wakes Up to Generation X," *Advertising Age*, February 1, 1993, pp. 16–17.
2. Mark Stevenson, "Global Gourmet," *Canadian Business*, July 1993, pp. 22–33.

3. This model is built on work by Kurt Lewin, described in his *A Dynamic Theory of Personality* (New York: McGraw-Hill, 1935). Two other prominent models of consumer behavior are those described by John A. Howard and Jagdish N. Sheth in *The Theory of Buyer Behavior* (New York: Wiley, 1969); and by James F. Engel, Roger D. Blackwell, and Paul W. Miniard in *Consumer Behavior*, 6th ed. (Chicago: The Dryden Press, 1990).

4. Philip Shenon, "Lining Up for Shares in Singapore," *The New York Times,* May 16, 1993, p. 15.

5. Thomas R. Duncan, "Standardized Global Marketing Communication Campaigns," *American Marketing Association Educator's Conference Proceedings* (Chicago: AMA 3, 1992) pp. 352–58.

6. Excerpted from Keith J. Tuckwell, *Canadian Marketing in Action,* (Scarborough, Ontario: Prentice Hall Canada, 1994) pp. 172–173. Adapted from Barbara Wickens, "Cultural cross talk," *Maclean's,* October 28, 1991, p. 42; Ken Riddell, "New study shows visible minority groups growing," *Marketing,* June 8, 1992, pp. 1, 4; Don Hogarth, "Marketers set sights on Asian-Canadians," *Financial Post,* September 16, 1991, p. 2; and Gillian Pritchard, "Polyglot profits," *Canadian Business,* February 1988, pp. 47–50.

7. Henry Assael, *Consumer Behavior and Marketing* (Boston: Kent, 1981), 351.

8. Richard P. Coleman, "The Continuing Significance of Social Class to Marketing," *Journal of Consumer Research,* December 1983, p. 265; Richard P. Coleman and Lee P. Rainwater, *Social Standing in America: New Dimension of Class* (New York: Basic Books, 1978).

9. Lawrence F. Feick and Linda L. Price, "The Market Maven," *Managing,* July 1985, p. 10; Lawrence F. Feick, Linda L. Price, and Robin A. Higie, "People Who Use People: The Other Side of Opinion Leadership," in *Advances in Consumer Research,* ed. Richard J. Lutz (Provo, Utah: Association for Consumer Research, 1986), pp. 301–05.

10. Thorstein Veblen, *The Theory of the Leisure Class* (New York: New American library, 1953 reprint of 1899 original).

11. Jon Berry, "Consensus on the New Census—A Key Demo Plummets in Numbers," *Brandweek,* December 7, 1992, p. 8; Patricia Orsini, "Spotlight 50 Plus: Wild at Heart," *Adweek,* July 22, 1992, p. 21; Diane Crispell and Willima H. Frey, "American Maturity," *American Demographics,* March 1993, pp. 31–42; Richard Halverson, "Core Shopping Group Shrinking as Baby Busters Grow Up," *Discount Store News,* May 18, 1992, pp. 193–94; "Billions of Boomers," *American Demographics,* March 1992, p. 6; Marcy Kornreich, "A Generation of Caregivers," *Adweek's Marketing Week,* July 22, 1991 p. 18–19.

12. Abraham H. Maslow, *Motivation and Personality,* 2nd ed. (New York: Harper & Row, 1970), pp. 35–58.

13. Marian Burros, "Eating Well," *The New York Times,* March 31, 1993, p. 21; Kathleen Deveny, "Putting It Mildly, More Consumers Prefer Only Products That Are 'Pure,' 'Natural'," *The Wall Street Journal,* May 11, 1993, p. B1.

14. Ralph Westfall, "Psychological Factors in Predicting Product Choice," *Journal of Marketing,* 26 (1962): 34–40.

15. John Dewey, *How We Think* (Boston: Heath, 1910).

16. Calvin P. Duncan and Richard W. Olshavsky, "External Search: The Role of Consumer Beliefs," *Journal of Marketing Research 19,* February 1982, p. 32–43.

17. See B. M. Campbell, "The Existence of Evoked Set and Determinants of Its Magnitude in Brand Choice Behavior," in *Buyer Behavior and Empirical Foundations,* ed. John A. Howard and Lonnie Ostrom (New York: Knopf, 1973), pp. 243–44.

18. The concept of *cognitive dissonance* was originally formulated by psychologist Leon Festinger to describe the situation in which a person has two contradictory "cognitions"–that is, two contradictory pieces of knowledge–at the same time. See Festinger, *A Theory of Cognitive Dissonance* (Evanston, Ill: Row, Peterson, 1957).

19. Everett M. Rogers, *Diffusion of Innovations,* 3rd ed. (New York: Free Press, 1983); Ashok K. Gupta and Everett M. Rogers, "Internal Marketing: Integrating R&D and Marketing Within the Organization," *The Journal of Consumer Marketing 8,* (Summer 1991): 5–18; Everett M. Rogers, *Communication Technology: The New Media in Society* (New York: Free Press, 1986).

Chapter 7

1. Howard Schlossberg, "Makers of Organic Clothes Find Mainstream Outlets," *Marketing News,* March 1, 1993, p. 1.

2. Carl McDaniel and William R. Darden, *Marketing* (Boston, Allyn & Bacon, 1987), p. 165.

3. U.S. Department of Commerce, Bureau of Economic Analysis, *Survey of Current Business 67* (April 1987).

4. Todd M. Helmeke, "Customer Satisfaction Is a Myth for Many Companies," *Marketing News,* June 7, 1993, p. 4; Gail Gilbert, "Customer Satisfaction Measurement Is Core of Firm's Quality Improvement," *Marketing News,* January 4, 1993, p. 18.

5. "The Time Is Right for ISO 9000," TIA/Technical Information Associates, Inc., *Docu-Mentor 8* (1993).

6. Patrick J. Robinson, Charles W. Faris, and Yoram Wind, *Industrial Buying Behavior and Creative Marketing* (Boston: Allyn & Bacon, 1967).

7. Bob Donath, "We Need Equitable Bix-to-Biz Marketing Measurements," *Marketing News,* April 27, 1992, p. 15.

8. Bob Donath, "Probing Buyers in This Post-Yuppie Age," *Marketing News,* October 14, 1991, p. 4.

9. Cyndee Miller, "Cessna's New Marketing Tool Is a 311,000 Square-Foot Campus," *Marketing News,* March 1, 1993, p. 2.

10. "Kings of the Hill," by Jenefer Curtis, *Canadian Business,* September 1994.

11. C. A. Marken, "Marcom Departments Trimmed as Businesses Adopt Outsourcing," *Marketing News,* June 7, 1993, p. 8.

Chapter 8

1. Shelby D. Hunt and John J. Burnett, "The Macromarketing/Micromarketing Dichotomy: A Taxonomical Model," *Journal of Marketing 46* (Summer 1982): 9–26.
2. Zachary Schiller, "Stalking the New Consumer," *Business Week,* August 28, 1989, pp. 54–62.
3. Gary Levin, "JWT Researches Stages, Not Ages," *Advertising Age,* June 26, 1989, p. 30; Joanne Lipman, "Thompson's Game Plan Maps Attitudes, Not Age," *The Wall Street Journal,* June 22, 1989, p. B4; Ron Gales, "Next Research Wave? Lifestages, Says JWT," *Adweek,* June 26, 1989, p. 6; and Christine Donahue, "JWT Charts Consumer's Lifestages," *Adweek's Marketing Week,* June 26, 1989, p. 3.
4. Peter F. Drucker, "The Big Three Miss Japan's Crucial Lesson," *The Wall Street Journal,* June 18, 1991, p. 18.
5. Cathy Madison, "New Illinois Lottery Spots Target Player Personalities," *Adweek,* April 3, 1989, p. 8.
6. Tim Cornwell, "Coke's New OK Brand 'For People with Holes in Their Jeans'," *Marketing Magazine,* June 20, 1994.
7. "Find the Lady," *The Economist,* July 1, 1989, p. 68.
8. William Taylor, "Message and Muscle: An Interview with Swatch Titan Nicolas Hayek," *HBR 71* (March–April 1993): 99–110.
9. For an excellent discussion of the theory of forecasting, see Bertrand de. Jouvenel, *The Art of Conjecture* (New York: Basic Books, 1967).
10. "Dell Programs New Products, Sales Strategy," *The Wall Street Journal,* August 2, 1993, p. B-1.

Chapter 9

1. Peter D. Bennett, (ed.), *Dictionary of Marketing Terms* (Chicago: American Marketing Association, 1988), p. 3.
2. Michael E. Porter, *Competitive Advantage: Creating and Sustaining Superior Performance* (New York: The Free Press, 1985).
3. William Taylor, "Message and Muscle: An Interview with Swatch Titan Nicolas Hayek." *Harvard Business Review 71.* March–April 1993, p. 100.
4. Tom Peters and Robert Waterman, *In Search of Excellence* (New York: Harper & Row, 1982), p. 174.
5. Joann Lublin and Craig Forman, "Going Upscale: Ford Snares Jaguar, but $2.5 Billion Is High Price for Prestige," *The Wall Street Journal,* November 3, 1989, pp. A1, A4; Bradley A. Stertz, "Trying to Crack the Luxury Car Market," *The Wall Street Journal,* August 7, 1989, p. B1; Joseph B. White, "Luxury-Car Makers Scrambling to Stand Out in Crowded Market," *The Wall Street Journal,* February 17, 1988, p. B25; John Templeman, "Infiniti and Lexus: Characters in a German Nightmare," *Business Week,* October 9, 1989, p. 64; Bradley A. Stertz, "Chrysler Planning to End Purchases of TC Convertible," *The Wall Street Journal,* November 17, 1989, p. B8; and Paul C. Judge, "Cadillac's Bid to Recapture Youth," *The New York Times* May 7, 1991, pp. D1, D5.
6. "Slow Growth Spurs Shakeup in Computer Sales," *The Wall Street Journal* April 19, 1991, p. B5.

7. Russell Mitchell, "The Genius: Meet Seymour Cray, Father of the Supercomputer," *Business Week,* April 30, 1990, p. 80.
8. James Lardner, *Fast Forward: Hollywood, the Japanese, and the VCR Wars* (New York: New American Library, 1987), p. 1.
9. Gary Hamel and C. K. Prahalad, "Strategic Intent," *Harvard Business Review,* May–June 1989, p. 69. See also Hamel and Prahalad, "The Core Competence of the Corporation," *Harvard Business Review,* May–June 1987, p. 88.
10. *Source:* W. Edwards Deming, "Improvement of Quality and Productivity Through Action by Management," *National Productivity Review* 1 (Winter 1981–1982): 12–22; Tom Peters, *Thriving on Chaos: Handbook for a Management Revolution* (New York: Alfred A. Knopf, 1988); and Susan E. Kuhn, "Eager to Take On the World's Best," *Fortune,* April 23, 1990, pp. 71, 74.
11. Hamel and Prahalad, "Strategic Intent," p. 35.
12. If it seems that we are focusing too much on Japanese companies, remember that Japanese approaches to marketing strategy have radically altered the competitive situation and the process of establishing competitive advantage. Although many of these ideas are American in origin, their application has been distinctly Japanese. The discussions that follow attempt to dissect these new approaches to competitive advantage in order to learn from them.
13. Hamel and Prahalad, "Strategic Intent," p. 35.
14. Stanley L. Jacobs Research Inc.
15. Adapted from James Lardner, *Fast Forward: Hollywood, the Japanese, and the VCR Wars* (New York: New American Library, 1987), pp. 41–46.
16. Al Ries and Jack Trout, Positioning: *The Battle for Your Mind* (New York: Warner Books, 1982), p. 8
17. The following discussion and some of the examples are adapted from David A. Aaker and J. Gary Shansby, "Positioning Your Product," *Business Horizons,* May–June 1982, pp. 56–62.
18. James B. Stewart, "The Vodka Challenge," *The Wall Street Journal,* December 12, 1989, p. A12.
19. Joseph B. White, "New Ads Give a Boost to the Olds Image but Don't Help the Olds Sales Woes Much," *The Wall Street Journal,* June 19, 1989, p. B1.
20. Phipps Arabie et al., "Overlapping Clustering: A New Method for Product Positioning," *Journal of Marketing Research* 28(1981): 310–317; and Hugh J. Devine, Jr., and John Morton, "How Does the Market Really See Your Product?" *Business Marketing,* July 1984, p. 70–77.
21. "How Honda Slipped from Its Perch," *The New York Times,* June 16, 1993, p. D-1.

Chapter 10

1. Giep Franzen and Freek Holzhauer, *Brands* (The Netherlands: BBDO College, 1989).
2. Regis McKenna, *Relationship Marketing* (Reading, Mass: Addison Wesley, 1991).
3. Stuart Elliott, "Advertising" *The New York Times,* January 28, 1993, p. D20.

4. Marieke de Mooij, *Advertising Worldwide* (London: Prentice Hall, 1994).
5. James A. Taylor, "Brand Equity: Its Meaning, Measurement and Management," and Joel N. Axelrod, "The Use of Experimental Design in Monitoring Brand Equity," ESOMAR seminar on "The Challenge of Branding Today and in the Future?" Brussels, October 1992.
6. Max Blackston, "The Levers of Brand Power," *Admap*, March 1993, pp. 29–33; and Christine Restall and Wendy Gordon, "Brands—The Missing Link: Understanding the Emotional Relationship," *Marketing and Research Today*, May 1993, pp. 59–67.
7. William D. Wells, "How Advertising Works," speech presented to the St. Louis AMA, September 17, 1986.
8. Carrie Goerne, "Disney Rated Top U.S. Brand," *Marketing News*, April 27, 1992, p. 1; and Chris Macrae, *World Class Brands* (Workingham, U.K.: Addison-Wesley, 1991).
9. David Short, "Coke Surpasses Marlboro as Most Valuable Global Brand," *Marketing*, 1994, p. 6.
10. Marsha Lindsay, "Establish Brand Equity Through Advertising," *Marketing News 22* (January 1990): 1.
11. Allan J. Magrath, "A Brand by Any Other Name," *Sales & Marketing Management*, June 1993, pp. 26–27.
12. Franzen and Holzhauer, *Brands*, p. 4.
13. Paul Ingrassia and Gregory A. Patterson, "Is Buying a Car a Choice or a Chore?" *The Wall Street Journal*, October 24, 1989.
14. Michael Janofsky, "Discount Brands Flex Their Muscles," *The New York Times*, April 24, 1993, p. 37.
15. Julie Skur Hill, "World Brands: Asians See World as Their Oyster," *Advertising Age*, September 21, 1989, pp. 1–78.
16. "A Rose by Any Other Name . . . ," *Sales & Marketing Management*, January 1989, p. 78.
17. Jack Alexander, "What's in a Name? Too Much, Said the FTC," *Sales & Marketing Management,* January 1989, p. 75–78.
18. Wells, "How Advertising Works."
19. Stuart Elliott, "Advertising," *The New York Times*, April 22, 1993, p. D24; Michael Janofsky, "Discount Brands Flex Their Muscles," *The New York Times*, April 24, 1993, p. L37; Laurel Wentz, "Saatchi: Brand Building Requires Ad Investment," *Advertising Age*, June 14, 1993, p. 4; and Stuart Elliott, "Advertising," *The New York Times,* May 11, 1993, p. D22.
20. Larry Light, "At the Center of It All Is the Brand," *Advertising Age*, March 29, 1993, p. 22.
21. Aaker, David. *Managing Brand Equity: Capitalizing on the Value of a Brand Name* (New York: Free Press, 1991).

Chapter 11

1. William M. Weilbacher, *Brand Marketing* (Chicago: NTC, 1993).
2. Christopher Lorenz, "How Ford Used Intuitive Design to Break Free of Committee Cars,'" *Financial Times,* September 29, 1988, p. 24.
3. Dick Alberding, "A Company Study: Exploiting Your Competitive Edge," *Journal of Business and Industrial Marketing*, Spring 1987, p. 37–46; and Yunus Kathawala, "A Comparative Analysis of Selected Approaches to Quality," *International Journal of Quality & Reliability Management 6* (1989): 7–17.
4. Tom Eisenhart, "Spring the Quality Gospel," *Business Marketing*, February 1990, pp. 34–38.
5. Steve Lohr, "Recycling Answer Sought for Computer Junk," *The New York Times*, April 14, 1993, p. A1.
6. Louis P. Bucklin, "Retail Strategy and the Classification of Consumer Goods," *Journal of Marketing 27* (January 1963): 51–56.
7. Damon Darlin, "Korea's 30 Biggest Firms Told to Shrink," *The Wall Street Journal,* April 23, 1990, p. A21.
8. Mary Lambkin and George S. Day, "Evolutionary Processes in Competitive Markets: Beyond the Product Life Cycle," *Journal of Marketing 53* (July 1989): 4–20; and John E. Smallwood, "The Product Life Cycle: A Key to Strategic Marketing Planning," *MSU Business Topics*, Winter 1973, pp. 29–35.

Chapter 12

1. James Brian Quinine and Christopher E. Gagman, "Will Services Follow Manufacturing into Decline?" *Harvard Business Review*, November–December 1986, pp. 95–102.
2. Regis McKenna, *Relationship Marketing* (Reading, Mass: Addison-Wesley, 1991); Frank K. Sonnenberg, *Marketing to Win* (New York: Harper & Row, 1990); and James W. Gentry, Gerald Macintosh, and Jeffrey J. Stoltman, "Reconsideration of the Structure of the Marketing Core Curriculum: Implications of the Trend Toward Relationship Marketing," in *Enhancing Knowledge Development in Marketing*, 1993 AMA Educators' Proceedings (Chicago: American Marketing Association, 1993).
3. Peter M. Mudie, "Internal Marketing: Cause for Concern," *The Quarterly Review of Marketing*, Spring–Summer 1987, pp. 21–24.
4. Mary C. Martin and Ravipreet S. Sohi, "Maintaining Relationships with Customers: Some Critical Factors," and Pratibha A. Dabholkar, "Customer Satisfaction and Service Quality: Two Constructs or One?" in *Enhancing Knowledge Development in Marketing*, 1993 AMA Educators' Proceedings (Chicago: American Marketing Association, 1993).
5. Amanda Bennett, "Making the Grade with the Customer," *The Wall Street Journal*, November 12, 1990, p. B1.
6. Stephen W. Brown, "Perceptual Gaps Hamper Professionals' Efforts," *Marketing News 31* (July 1989): 13.
7. Joan C. Szabo, "Service=Survival," *Nation's Business*, March 1989, pp. 16–24.
8. Leonard L. Berry, Valarie A. Zeithaml, and A. Parasuraman, "Quality Counts in Services, Too," *Business Horizons*, May–June 1985, pp. 44–46.
9. Kate Bertrand, "In Service, Perception Counts," *Business Marketing*, April 1989, pp. 17–20.
10. A. Parasuraman, Valarie Zeithaml, and Leonard Berry, "A Conceptual Model of Service Quality and Its Implications for Future Research," *Journal of Marketing 49* (Fall 1985): 41–50; "SERVQUAL: A Multiple-Item

Scale for Measuring Customer Perceptions of Service Quality," *Journal of Retailing 64* (Spring 1988): 12–40; and "Refinement and Reassessment of the SERVQUAL Scale," *Journal of Retailing 67* (April 1991): 420–50.

11. Dorothy Riddle, "Designing a Culturally Sensitive Service Requires Staff Flexibility," *Marketing News*, January 17, 1994, p. 14.

12. Julian Yudelson, "The Four Ps of Nonprofit Marketing," *Nonprofit World*, November–December 1988, p. 21.

Chapter 13

1. T. J. Howard, "'Jurassic Park' Gives Biotech Firms a Scare," *Business Plus*, September 14, 1993, pp. 7–8.

2. John R. Rockwell and Marc C. Particelli, "New Product Strategy: How the Pros Do It," *Industrial Marketing*, May 1982, pp. 49–60.

3. Tim Davis, "Creativity, Autonomy, and Evaluation Are Keys to New Product Success," *Marketing News 27* (March 1989): 16.

4. Everett M. Rogers, *Diffusion of Innovations*, 3rd ed. (New York: Free Press, 1983).

5. Christopher Power, "Flops," *Business Week*, August 16, 1993, p. 76–82; and Barry Feig, "Adapt and Adopt," *Food & Beverage Marketing*, October 1989, p. 14.

6. Christopher Power, "A Smithsonian for Stinkers," *Business Week*, August 16, 1993, p. 82.

7. Brenton R. Schlender, "How Toshiba Makes Alliances Work," *Fortune*, October 4, 1993, pp. 116–120.

8. Paul Klebnikov, "Les Folies HDTV," *Forbes*, July 19, 1993, pp. 65–69; Bob Davis, "Proponents of HDTV Fight Back," *The Wall Street Journal*, June 13, 1990, p. B1; Neil Gross, "Japan's HDTV: What's Wrong with This Picture?" *Business Week*, April 1, 1991, pp. 80–81; and Andrew Kupfer, "The U.S. Wins One in High-Tech TV," *Fortune*, April 8, 1991, pp. 60–64.

9. Michael Ray and Rochelle Myers, *Creativity in Business* (Garden City, N.Y.: Doubleday, 1986).

10. Claudio A. Romano, "Identifying Factors Which Influence Product Innovation: A Case Study Approach," *Journal of Management Studies 27* (January 1990): 75–95; and Leigh Lawton and A. Parasuraman, "So You Want Your New Product Planning to Be Productive?" *Business Horizons*, December 1980, pp. 29–34.

11. Glenn Rifkin, "The Machines of a New Sole," *The New York Times*, February 10, 1993, p. D7.

12. Ashok K. Gupta and Everett M. Rogers, "Internal Marketing: Integrating R&D and Marketing Within the Organization," *The Journal of Consumer Marketing 8* (Summer 1991): 5–18.

13. T. J. Howard, "'Jurassic Park' Gives Biotech Firms a Scare," *Business Plus*, September 14, 1993, pp. 7–8; Joan O'C. Hamilton, "Genentech Is Climbing Down from Its High Horse," *Business Week*, Feb. 11, 1991, p. 79; Thane Peterson with Larry Armstrong, "Roche's Big Buy May Set Off a Shopping Frenzy," *Business Week*, February 19, 1990, p. 38; Armstrong, "Can Amogen Follow Its Own Tough Act?" *Business Week*, March 11, 1991, 94–96; Neil Gross, "Japanese Biotech's Overnight Revolution," *Business Week*

March 12, 1990, p. 69, 72; and Jonathan B. Levine with John Carey, "Cutting the Heart Out of European Biotech?" *Business Week*, June 18, 1990, p. 177–78.

14. Patrick M. Reilly, "Publishers Design Electronic Newspapers to Keep Control of Information Delivery," *The Wall Street Journal*, April 26, 1993, p. B1, B7.

15. Bart Huthwaite, "The Power of Cost Measurement in New Product Development," *National Productivity Review 8* (Summer 1989): 239–48.

16. Stephanie Losee, "How Compaq Keeps the Magic Going," *Fortune*, February 21, 1994, pp. 90–92

17. Thomas D. Kuczmarksi, *Managing New Products: The Power of Innovation* (Englewood Cliffs N.J.: Prentice Hall, 1992), p. 100.

18. Thomas A. Stewart, "Welcome to the Revolution," *Fortune*, December 13, 1993, pp. 66–68

Chapter 14

1. These channel functions are primarily adapted from Louis W. Stern and Adel I. El-Ansary, *Management in Marketing Channels* (Englewood Cliffs, N.J.: Prentice Hall, 1989), pp. 7–17.

2. David Perry, "How You'll Manage Your 1990s 'Distribution Portfolio,'" *Business Marketing*, June 1989, pp. 52–56; see also Martin Everett, "When There's More Than One Route to the Customer," *Sales & Marketing Management*, August 1990, pp. 48–56.

3. Frank V. Cespedes and E. Raymond Dorey, "Managing Multiple Channels," *Business Horizons*, July–August 1990, pp. 67–77.

4. Patricia Sellers, "Coke Gets Off Its Can in Europe," *Fortune*, August 13, 1990, pp. 68–70+.

5. Mark Maremont, "Contact-Lens Sellers Just Don't See Eye-to-Eye," *Business Week*, July 12, 1993, pp. 28–29.

6. Lisa Petrison, Masaru Ariga, and Paul Wang, "Strategies for Penetrating the Japanese Market: A Comparison of Traditional and Direct Marketing Distribution Channels," working paper, Integrated Advertising/Marketing Communication Program, Northwestern University, 1993.

7. Saul Klein, Gary L. Frazier, and Victor J. Roth, "A Transaction Cost Analysis Model of Channel Integration in International Channels," *Journal of Marketing Research*, May 1990, pp. 196–208; and Erin Anderson and Anne T. Coughlin, "International Market Entry and Expansion via Independent or Integrated Channels of Distribution," *Journal of Marketing 51* (January 1987): 71–82.

8. Allan J. Magrath and Kenneth G. Hardy, "Avoiding the Pitfalls in Managing Distribution Channels," *Business Horizons*, September–October 1987, pp. 29–33; George H. Lucas, Jr., and Larry R. Gresham, "Power, Conflict, Control, and the Application of Contingency Theory in Marketing Channels," *Journal of the Academy of Marketing Science*, Summer 1985, pp. 25–39; and Janet E. Keith, Donald W. Jackson, and Lawrence A. Crosby, "Effects of Alternative Types of Influence Strategies Under Different Channel Dependence Structures," *Journal of Marketing 54* (July 1990): 30–42.

9. Marty Jacknis and Steve Kratz, "The Channel Empowerment Solution," *Sales & Marketing Management*, March 1993, pp. 44–49.

10. Joseph Weber, "Getting Cozy with Their Customers: 'Partnerships' Are Transforming Wholesaling," *Business Week*, January 8, 1990, p. 86.

11. Sam Walton, *Made in America: My Story* (New York: Doubleday, 1992); and Sally Johnson, "Vermonters Are Up Against the Wal-Mart," *Insight*, January 10, 1994, pp. 12–15.

12. Shashi K. Shah, "Designing an Integrated Distribution System," *Journal of Systems Management*, August 1989, pp. 27–32.

13. "Private Couriers and Postal Service Slug It Out," *The New York Times*, February 14, 1994.

Chapter 15

1. The information in the opening story is adapted from Michael McLaughlin and Cortney Kingston, "A 4-Point Reform Plan for Service Merchandising," *Brandweek*, January 3, 1994, p. 16; and Zachary Schiller and Wendy Zellner, "Clout! More and More, Retail Giants Rule the Marketplace," *Business Week*, December 21, 1992, pp. 66–73.

2. Rita Koselka, "Distribution Revolution," *Forbes*, May 25, 1992, pp. 54–62.

3. Matt Nannery, "Making Promotions Pay Off," *Supermarket News*, November 15, 1993, pp. 14, 16 Doug Adams, "Are Brand Managers Ready for the ECR Revolution?" Nielsen Marketing Research Report, December 1993; and Matt Nannery, "Keeping the 'C' in ECR," and "Going With the Flow," *Supermarket News*, November 15, 1993, pp. 12, 16.

4. Malcolm McNair, "Wheel of Retailing," *Competitive Distribution in a Free High-Level Economy and Its Implications for the University* (Pittsburgh: University of Pittsburgh Press, 1958), p. 17.

5. Edward O. Wells, "What to Do When Wal-Mart Comes to Town," *Inc.*, July 1993, pp. 76–88; Sally Johnson, "Vermonters Are Up Against the Wal-Mart," *Insight*, January 10, 1994, pp. 12–15.

6. Michael J. McDermott, "Killers Stalk a Shifting Landscape," *Adweek's Marketing Week*, October 28, 1991, p. 24.

7. John R. Wilke, "Fraudulent Franchises Are Growing," *The Wall Street Journal*, September 21,1990, p. B1.

8. This section is based on James Sterngold, "New Japanese Lesson: Running a 7-11," *The New York Times*, May 9, 1991, pp. D1, D7; and Robert Neff with Kimberly Blanton, "You Can't Get Sushi at the Local 7-Eleven—Yet," *Business Week*, November 12, 1990, p. 59.

9. Adapted from David Mazursky and Jacob Jacoby, "Exploring the Development of Store Image," *Journal of Marketing 62* (Summer l986): 145–65.

10. Elizabeth Comte, "Art for Shoes' Sake," *Forbes*, September 28, 1992.

11. Elaine Underwood, "Benetton Blinks: Product Ads Are Due," *Brandweek*, March 8, 1993, p. 2; "More Controversy, Please, We're Italian," *The Economist*, February 1, 1992, p. 70; and Spike Lee, "United Colors of Benetton," *Rolling Stone*, November 12, 1992, special insert on inside front cover.

12. Gary Khermouch, "Wal-Mart Plan Hits Snags," *Brandweek*, May 10, 1993, p. 3; Seema Nayyar, "Manufacturers Get New Set of Rules," *Adweek*, February 15, 1993, p. 10; and "Wal-Mart Move Confirms Shift in Retailer-Marketer Ties," *Brandweek*, February 15, 1993, p. 8.

13. The information in this story is taken from the following sources: Michael J. McDermott, "Only Downsizing Can Save Sears," *Adweek's Marketing Week*, October 29, 1990, p. 32; Isadore Barmash, "Big Change Is Expected for Sears," *The New York Times*, January 28, 1991, p. C1; Francine Schwandel, "Fashion Statement: Its Earnings Sagging, Sears Upgrades Line of Women's Apparel," *The Wall Street Journal*, May 9, 1990, pp. A1, A4; Francine Schwandel, "Sears's Glitzy Ads Target Buyers of Stylish Fashions," *The Wall Street Journal*, August 15, 1990, p. B1; and Stephanie Strom, "Sears to Spend $4 Billion to Remake Itself as Retailer," *The New York Times*, February 12, 1993, p. D1.

Chapter 16

1. Kent B. Monroe, *Pricing: Making Profitable Decisions* (New York: McGraw-Hill, 1990).

2. Leslie de Chernatony, Simon Knox, and Mark Chedgey, "Brand Pricing in a Recession," *European Journal of Marketing*, 26: (1992): 5-14.

3. Thomas Nagle, *The Strategy and Tactics of Pricing* (Englewood Cliffs, N.J.: Prentice Hall, 1987), p. 12.

4. This section is based on Katherine Farrish, "Students Trying to Sidestep Spiraling Cost of Textbooks," *The Hartford Courant*, September 30, 1992, p. A1. David Hoh, "Used Textbooks Are Big Business," *Camden Courier-Post*, March 11, 1993, p. 4; Patti Doten, "Text Book Buying and Crying," *The Boston Globe*, September 25, 1989, p. 27.

5. Gregory Spears, "Infant Formula Price Hikes a Rip-Off, Some Say," *The Denver Post*, July 10, 1993, pp. 2A, 10A.

6. *Annual Report for the Year Ended March 31, 1992*, Director of Investigation and Research, Minister of Supply and Services, Canada.

7. Jay Peterzell, "Penetrating the World of Dango," *Time*, January 15, 1990, p. 48; and David E. Sanger, "Settlement by Japanese Builders," *The New York Times*, November 24, 1989, pp. D1, D7.

8. Geoffrey Brewer, "New World Orders," *Sales and Marketing Management*, January 1994, pp. 59–63.

9. Jim Mateja, "Profit, Higher Output Raise Saturn Hopes," *Chicago Tribune*, June 15, 1993, p. 1; Lindsay Chappell, "Dealers Return Profit to Raise Saturn's Total," *Automotive News*, June 14, 1993, p. 1; and "Saturn: Enjoys Robust Sales, but Continues to Lose Money," *Economist*, July 3, 1992, p. 80.

Chapter 17

1. Gary Levin, "PM Shores Up Marlboro," *Advertising Age*, April 5, 1993, pp. 1, 44.

2. Gabe Lowy, "Suppliers and Retailers: Partnership for Profits," *Brandweek,* January 10, 1994, p. 14; and Patricia Sellers, "Yes, Brands Can Still Work Magic," *Fortune*, Feb. 7, 1994, p. 133.
3. Allan J. Magrath, "Eight Timeless Truths About Pricing," *Sales & Marketing Management*, October 1989, pp. 78–83.
4. "Why Viewers Would Like to Zap Their Cable Firms," *The Wall Street Journal*, March 19, 1990, pp. B1, B10.
5. Richard W. Stevenson, "Russia's Bargain Basement in Technology," *The New York Times*, May 26, 1993, pp. D1, D5.
6. Robert D. Buzzell and Bradley T. Gale, *The PIMS Principles: Linking Strategy to Performance* (New York: Free Press, 1987).
7. Gerard J. Tellis, "Beyond the Many Faces of Price: An Integration of Pricing Strategies," *Journal of Marketing 50* (October 1986): 146–60.
8. Thomas Nagle, *The Strategy and Tactics of Pricing* (Englewood Cliffs, N.J.: Prentice Hall, 1987).
9. Pam Weisz, "Not Software, Not Hardware: It's Profits in Gizmoland," *Brandweek*, January. 10, 1994, p. 18.
10. Bill Saporito, "Why the Price Wars Never End," *Fortune*, March 23, 1992, pp. 68–78; Julie Liesse, "Price War Bites at Pet Food Ad $," *Advertising Age*, April 5, 1993, p. 12; Richard Gibson, "Super-Cheap and Mid-Priced Eaters Bite Fast-Food Chains from Both Sides," *The Wall Street Journal*, July 22, 1990, pp. B1, B6; Joan E. Rigdon, "Fast-Food Chains in Hungrier Times Concoct Menus to Lure Penny Pinchers," *The Wall Street Journal* January 7, 1990, pp B1, B8; and Udayan Gupta and Jeffrey A. Tannenbaun, "Casualties in the Fast-Food Price Wars," *The Wall Street Journal,* October 23, 1989, p. B1.
11. Hermann Simon and Eckhard Kucher, "The European Pricing Time Bomb—and How to Cope with It," *Marketing and Research Today*, February 1993, pp. 25–36; and "So Much for Predictable Pricing of International Brands," *Adweek*, January 25, 1993, p. 18.
12. Paul W. Farris and John A. Quelch, "In Defense of Price Promotion," *Sloan Management Review*, Fall 1987, pp. 63–69.
13. Jennifer Lawrence, "Supermarket Tug of War," *Advertising Age*, April 19, 1993, pp. 1, 42–43; Richard Gibson, "Broad Grocery Price Cuts May Not Pay," *The Wall Street Journal*, May 7, 1993; and Jon Berry, "It's Closer Than You Think: Two Studies Show Marketers and Retailers Are Moving Toward EDLP," *Brandweek*, October 26, 1992, pp. 26–28.

Chapter 18

1. Raymond Serafin, "The Saturn Story," *Advertising Age*, November 16, 1992, pp. 1, 13.
2. Don E. Schultz, Stanley I. Tannenbaum, and Robert F. Lauterborn, *Integrated Marketing Communications* (Chicago: NTC, 1992).
3. Tom Duncan, "To Fathom Integrated Marketing, Dive!" *Advertising Age*, October 11, 1993, p. 18.
4. Tom Duncan, "Integrated Marketing: It's Synergy," *Advertising Age*, March 8, 1993, p. 22.

5. Katherine T. Frith, "More Than We Bargained For: The Impact of Consumer Culture in Southeast Asia," Advertising Division, Association for Education in Journalism and Mass Communication Annual Conference, Portland, Ore., July 1988.
6. See David Jacobson, "ARF/ABP Panel Set to Choose Three Field Test Advertisers," *Business Marketing*, May 1989, p. 30.
7. Jeffrey L. Seglin, "The New Era of Ad Measurement," *Adweek's Marketing Week*, January 23, 1989, pp. 23–25.
8. Christina Lynch, "The New Colors of Advertising: An Interview with Luciano Benetton," *Hemispheres*, September 1993, pp. 23–26; and Noreen O'Leary, "Benetton's True Colors," *Adweek*, August 24, 1992, pp. 27–31.
9. William D. Wells, *Planning for R.O.I.* (Englewood Cliffs, N.J.: Prentice Hall, 1989).
10. Esther Thorson, "Consumer Processing of Advertising," *Current Issues and Research in Advertising 12* (1985): 197–230.
11. Betsy D. Gelb, Jane W. Hong, and George M. Zinkhan, "Communications Effects of Specific Advertising Elements: An Update," *Current Issues and Research in Advertising 12* (1985): 79–98.
12. Herbert E. Krugman, "What Makes Advertising Effective?" *Harvard Business Review*, March–April 1975, pp. 96–103.
13. Ivan L. Preston, "A Review of the Literature on Advertising Regulation," *Current Issues and Research in Advertising 10* (1983): 2–37.
14. Raymond Serafin, "Riney Media Strategy Gets High Marks," *Advertising Age*, November 16, 1991, p. 13.
15. Statistics in this feature are from: Laura Bird, "Marketers Miss Out by Alienating Blacks," *The Wall Street Journal*, April 9, 1993, p. B3; Diana Putterman, "Three Examples of What Hispanic Marketing Can Do," *Brandweek*, October 18, 1993, p. 26; and "Numerically Speaking," *The Asian American Quarterly I* (Spring 1993): 7.
16. Kevin Goldman, "Nike to Run Ad in Spanish with Subtitles," *The New York Times*, July 12, 1993, p. B3.
17. James Pollock, "Ethnic Marketing: The New Reality," *Marketing Magazine*, 1994.
18. Herbert E. Krugman, "Why Three Exposures May Be Enough," *Journal of Advertising Research*, December 1972, pp. 11–19.

Chapter 19

1. Scott Hume, "Trade Promotion Share Dips in '92," *Advertising Age*, April 5, 1993, p. 3.
2. Paul Homes, "Public Relations," *Adweek* ("Marketing to the Year 2000" Special Report), September 11, 1989, pp. 234–35.
3. Tamsen Tillson, "PR Departments Take New Shape in Downsizing Era," *The Globe and Mail*, July 19, 1994, p. B22.
4. Thomas L. Harris, *The Marketer's Guide to Public Relations* (New York: John Wiley & Sons, 1991).
5. "Free Trade's Communication Challenge," *Inside PR*, March 1993, pp. 42–43.

6. Saul Bennett, "PR Is the Answer to Advertisers' Prayers," *Inside PR*, January 1993, p. 7

7. Ann Kerr, "Image Makers Get New Respect," *The Globe and Mail*, Tuesday, July 19, 1994, p. B22.

8. Marcus E. Servoss, "Planning for That Crisis You Dread," *A&M Review*, May 1993, p. 25.

9. "Jack In The Box's Worst Nightmare," *The New York Times*, February 6, 1993, pp. 35, 37; and Ronald Grover, "Boxed in at Jack In The Box," *Business Week*, February 15, 1993, p. 40.

10. "Pepsi Panic: Plaudits Pour In," *Inside PR*, July 1993, pp. 5–6

11. "Advertising vs. Promotion: A New Game with New Rules," *Potentials in Marketing*, January–February 1993, p. 7.

12. Hume, "Trade Promotion Share Dips in '92."

13. Wayne Mouland, "Canada vs. the U.S.: A World of Difference in Couponing," *Marketing Magazine*, 1994, p. 24.

14. Scott A. Neslin and Robert W. Shoemaker, "An Alternative Explanation for Lower Repeat Rates After Promotion Purchases," *Journal of Marketing Research 26* (1989): 205–13.

15. "Marketing Madness: An Ingenious Giveaway Scheme by Hoover Backfires by Working Too Well," *Time*, April 12, 1993, p. 21.

16. Elaine Underwood, "NBC Uplinks for Niche Markets," *Brandweek*, January 17, 1994 p. 6.

17. J. Max Robbins, "Making Point-of-Purchase More Pointed," *Adweek*, November 10, 1986; and David Kalish, "Supermarket Sweepstakes," *Marketing & Media Decisions*, November 1988, pp. 33–38.

18. Kerry J. Smith, "P-O-P Outlays Remain Steady," *Promo*, January 1994, pp. 62–63.

19. Michael Hiestand, "Volvo Plays It Safe with Tennis," *Adweek's Marketing Week*, June 12, 1989, p. 61.

20. Graig Miller and Paul Nolan, "Promotion Marketing: Withstanding the Test of Time," *Potentials in Marketing*, January–February 1993, pp. 5–6.

21. Lori Kesler, "Successful Packages Turn Medium into Message," *Advertising Age*, October 13, 1986, p. 72.

22. "Stop! Don't Can That Can," *Madison Avenue*, August 1985: p. 6.

23. Gary Levin, "Sports Play Integrated Marketing Game," *Advertising Age*, March 1, 1993, p. 12.

Chapter 20

1. Cleveland Horton, "Porsche 300,000: The New Elite," *Advertising Age*, February 5, 1990, p. 6.

2. *The Globe and Mail*, Tuesday, February 15, 1994, p. B29.

3. David Bartal, "EC, Sweden Clash over Alcohol," *Advertising Age International*, September 20, 1993, pp. I–6; Leslie Gilbert, "OM Takes Direct Route to the Top," *Advertising Age*, May 15, 1989, pp. S12–S13; and David Bartal, "Moosehead Defies Odds in Sweden," *Advertising Age International*, October 11, 1993, pp. I–14.

4. Janice Steinberg, "Exhaustive Research Lines Up Infiniti, Lexus Prospects," *Advertising Age*, July 24, 1989; p. S6; Janice Steinberg, "Direct Mail Becoming Hottest Incentive Conduit," *Advertising Age*, July 24, 1989, pp. S4–S6.

5. Stan Rapp and Thomas L. Collins, *MaxiMarketing* (New York: McGraw-Hill, 1987).

6. Paul LePage, "Marketing Databases Mean Business," *Marketing Magazine*, June 6, 1994, p. 41.

7. John Osborn, "Abuses Draw Congress' Fire," *Advertising Age*, September 25, 1990, pp. S8–S9.

8. David J. Jefferson and Thomas R. King, "'Infomercials' Fill Up Air Time on Cable, Aim for Prime Time," *The Wall Street Journal*, October 22, 1992, pp. 1, 7.

9. *The Globe and Mail*, "Mail Order Firms Putting Shoppers First," Monday, August 8, 1994.

10. Stephanie Losee, "How Compaq Keeps the Magic Going," *Fortune*, February 21, 1994, pp. 90–92

11. *The Globe and Mail*, Tuesday, June 14, 1994, pp. A1-A2.

12. Lisa A. Petrison, Masaru Ariga, and Paul Wang, "Strategies for Penetrating the Japanese Market: A Comparison of Traditional and Direct Marketing Distribution Channels," unpublished paper, Medill School of Journalism, Northwestern University, April 1993; "Direct Marketing Makes International Waves," *Advertising Age*, October 17, 1988, pp. S8–S9; Judith Graham, "Filling Down Time for Globe Trotters," *Advertising Age*, August 1, 1988 pp. S10–S12; "Mail Order Top 250 +," *Direct Marketing*, July 1989, pp. 30–31; and Claire Wilson, "Chase Mailer Chases New Business Accounts," *Advertising Age*, January 12, 1987, pp. S4–S5.

13. Leah Rickard, "Buick Goes Golfing with Car Shoppers," *Advertising Age*, December 6, 1993, p. 18; and Patricia Strand, "Carmakers Take Spin with Computer Discs," *Advertising Age*, February 8, 1988, p. 30.

14. Andrew Batkin, "Don't Dawdle: Time to Go Interactive Is Now," *Advertising Age,* September 20, 1993, p. 28; and David C. Churbuck, "The Digital Press," *Forbes*, September 27, 1993, pp. 136–37.

15. Debra Aho, "ICTV Squares Off Against Giants," *Advertising Age*, December 13, 1993, p. 12.

16. Debra Aho, "Earth Share Finds Prodigy a Good Environment," *Advertising Age*, October 18, 1993, p. 26.

17. Christy Fisher, "'Washington Post' Outlines Technology Plans," *Advertising Age*, November 22, 1993, p. 10; and Scott Donaton, "Time Warner's Levin: Explore, Explore," *Advertising Age*, October 18, 1993, pp. 24, 27.

18. Elaine Underwood, "Queen of the Superhighway: Carpenter Takes QVC Upscale," *Brandweek*, January 24, 1994, p. 26; Scott Donaton, "Home Shopping Audience Widens," *Advertising Age*, November 22, 1993, p. 19; Wayne Walley, "Strategical Spiegel," *Advertising Age*, October 18, 1993, p. 26; "Couch-Potato Paradise," *The Economist*, June 17, 1989, pp. 83–84; Paula Schnorbus, "Sold!" *Marketing & Media Decisions*, March 1987, pp. 53–57; Judann Dagnoli, "Home Shopping Net Expands Its Game Plan,"*Advertising Age*, June 22, 1987, p. 18; Judann Dagnoli, "Home Shopping Beams to Japan," *Advertising Age*, January 19, 1987, p. 20; Thomas King, "Family Circle, Home Shopping Set Link," *The Wall Street Journal*, October 18, 1990, p. B6; and Laura Zinn and Antonio Fins,

"Home Shoppers Keep Tuning In—But Investors Are Turned Off," *Business Week*, October 22, 1990, pp. 70–72.

Chapter 21

1. *Chief Executive Officer* (Chicago: Heidrick and Struggles, 1987), p. 7.
2. Paul Hersey, *Selling: A Behavioral-Science Approach* (Englewood Cliffs, N.J.: Prentice Hall, 1988), pp. 15–27.
3. Clarke Caywood, "Marketing and Integrated Marketing Communications," IABC IMC Seminar, Kansas City, March 14, 1994.
4. See Leonard L. Berry, A. Parasuraman, and Valerie A. Zeithaml, "The Service-Quality Puzzle," *Business Horizons*, September–October 1988, pp. 35–43; and Joan C. Szabo, "Service-Survival," *Nation's Business*, March 1989, pp. 16–21.
5. Kate Bertrand, "Unisys: Lining Up Business Targets," *Business Marketing*, October 1988, pp. 41, 44, 46.
6. Jim Rapp, "Team Selling Is Changing the Sales Trainer's Role," special report, *Training*, May 1989, pp. 6–10.
7. Allan L. Reid, *Modern Applied Selling* (Englewood Cliffs, N.J.: Prentice Hall, 1990), pp. 353–55.
8. See William Strahle and Rosann L. Spiro, "Linking Market Share Strategies to Salesforce Objectives, Activities, and Compensation Policies," *Journal of Personal Selling & Sales Management*, August 1986, pp. 11–18.
9. Leslie Aldridge Westoff, "As Incentive, Anything Goes," *The New York Times Magazine*, April 2, 1989, pp. 60, 80–81; and Ronald B. Marks, *Personal Selling*, 4th ed. (Boston: Allyn and Bacon, 1991), p. 33.
10. Westoff, "As Incentive, Anything Goes."
11. This section draws on Alan Farnham, "Mary Kay's Lesson in Leadership," *Fortune*, September 20, 1993, 66–77.

Chapter 22

1. "Diaper's Failure Shows How Poor Plans, Unexpected Woes Can Kill New Products," *The Wall Street Journal*, October 1990, p. B-1.
2. Warren Berger, "Philips' Decorator Bulbs Light Up a Dull Market," *Adweek's Marketing Week*, November 6, 1989, pp. 20–21.

3. Hamel, Gary, and C. K. Prahalad. "Strategy as Stretch and Leverage." *Harvard Business Review*, March–April 1993, pp. 75–85.
4. Slywotzky, Adrian J., and Benson P. Shapiro, "Leveraging to Beat the Odds: The New Marketing Mind-Set." *Harvard Business Review*, September–October 1993, pp. 97–107.
5. Stewart Alsop, "Newton's Just a Party Favor Today, but a Work Saver in the Future," *Info World*, September 13, 1993, p. 4.
6. Michael Hammer and James Champy, *Reengineering the Corporation* (New York: HarperCollins, 1993).
7. Bill Saporito, "How Quaker Oats Got Rolled," *Fortune*, October 8, 1990, pp. 129–38.
8. Donald Pom, "Liking vs. Remembering," *Marketing & Media Decisions,* June 1989, pp. 109–12.
9. See Jacob Jacoby, Wayne D. Hoyer, and David A. Sheluga, *Miscomprehension of Televised Communications* (New York: American Association of Advertising Agencies, 1980); and Jacoby and Hoyer, *The Comprehension and Miscomprehension of Print Communications* (Hillsdale, N.J.: Erlbaum, 1987).
10. See Jack B. Haskins, "Factual Recall as a Measure of Advertising Effectiveness," *Journal of Advertising Research,* March 1964, pp. 2–8; Calvin L. Hodock, "Predicting On-Air Recall from Theater Tests," *Journal of Advertising Research,* December 1976, pp. 25–32; and Shirley Young, "Copy Testing Without Magic Numbers," *Journal of Advertising Research*, February 1972, pp. 3–12.
11. David W. Stewart and David H. Furse, *Effective Television Advertising* (Lexington, Mass.: Lexington Books, 1986), p. 23.
12. John A. Quelch, Paul W. Farris, and James M. Oliver, "The Product Management Audit," *Harvard Business Review,* March–April 1987, pp. 30–38.
13. Herbert Baum, "Marketing Dollars Must Become More Productive," *Marketing News* September 3, 1990, p. 24.
14. See, for example, Christopher Knowlton, "How Disney Keeps the Magic Going," *Fortune*, December 4, 1989, pp. 111–32; and Wayne Walley, "Disney Double-Bill," *Advertising Age*, June 12, 1989, p. 4.

Glossary

added value Marketing's contribution to the value of a product, which may take the form of special features, extra quality, durability, or reliability.

advertising-to-sales ratio Annual advertising expenditure divided by total sales.

advertising Any paid form of non-personal presentation or promotion of ideas, goods, or services by an identified sponsor using mass media.

aftermarketing The servicing by a company of a customer's needs related to the purchase and use of the company's product.

agent An intermediary who does not take title to goods, but rather sells them and receives a commission on the sale from the manufacturer.

area of dominant influence (ADI) A geographic area surrounding a television broadcasting center, which is usually located in a city; the ADI may have a radius of 40–60 miles. Also referred to as a *designated marketing area (DMA)*.

audiotext A system of 800 or 900 number "hotlines" that consumers can call to hear a recorded message about a particular product.

authorization Getting a retailer to agree to carry a brand, stock it, display it, and promote it.

bait-and-switch pricing The practice of attracting customers by offering a low-priced model with the intention of persuading them to "trade up" to a higher-priced model. In Canada this practice is illegal if the store does not carry reasonable quantities of the lower-priced good.

benchmark A known number or set of outcomes against which other numbers or sets of outcomes can be compared.

benchmarking Identifying the practice or practices that have produced excellent results for a company or its competitors very often in a different industry altogether, studying those practices, and then making the changes necessary to achieve equal or better results.

benefit segmentation The process of grouping customers into market segments based on the benefits people seek from the product.

bid A proposal made by a seller to a buyer in which the seller offers a product that meets a set of formal specifications at a certain price.

brand A complex bundle of images and experiences in the customer's mind that communicates a promise about the benefits of a particular product manufactured by a particular company.

brand advertising Advertising that establishes product personality or image and builds product equity over time.

brand authorization Persuading distributors to carry the good; in consumer packaged goods, getting retail distribution.

brand equity The goodwill value attached to a brand because of the relationship that has been developed with customers and other stakeholders over time.

brand image The sum of impressions that affect consumers' perception of a brand, including identification elements, product personality, and benefits promised.

brand licensing The practice whereby a company with an established brand "rents" it to another company.

brand loyalty A consumer's tendency to have a consistently positive attitude toward a particular brand and to purchase it repeatedly over time.

brand manager An executive who is much like a product manager, but who manages only one particular brand.

brand proliferation Allowing the number of brands to expand excessively. Proliferation dilutes marketing focus, which is essential for success.

breakeven (payback) analysis A mathematical technique that attempts to find the point at which total revenues are equal to total costs of a particular product.

broker An intermediary who specializes in certain product lines and brings buyers and sellers together.

budget A formal statement of the amounts of money an organization expects to spend on specific, planned activities and programs over a specified period of time.

business analysis Weighing the potential profitability of a proposed new-product idea in order to decide whether to invest in developing it and at what level of expenditure.

business-to-business advertising Advertising directed at people and companies within or related to an industry who buy or influence the purchase of products for use in that industry.

buying center The group of people assembled to make a particular buying decision in an organization. The buying center is usually temporary but may also be a permanent team.

campaign A series of ads for a product run in one or more media under a common theme for a period of time.

capacity management Balancing the number of staff in a service organization with the amount of demand for the organization's service.

capital good Expensive, long-lasting industrial good used in the production of other goods and services.

chain store A group of stores with many different locations.

closing Getting a prospective customer's oral or signed agreement to buy the product being offered.

cognitive dissonance Self-doubt which has crept in after the purchase of a high-value item is quite common. Advertisers of cars, for example, build reassurance into their advertisements which will be reread by new buyers.

cold call A personal sales call that is made without a prior appointment or prior knowledge.

commission A percentage of the cost of a transaction paid to an individual or firm instrumental in providing a service.

commodity goods Undifferentiated products, like raw materials, with little difference between supplier offerings, that are purchased frequently and in large quantities.

competitive advantage An advantage over the competition gained by offering either greater perceived value or a lower price or a combination of both.

competitive-bid pricing A practice in which several firms submit sealed bids stating prices for items that meet customers' technical specifications and the volume requirements, with the contract being awarded to the lowest qualified bidder.

concentrated marketing. Targeting just one or two market segments with the same marketing mix.

concept testing Testing an idea for a new product by describing it to potential consumers in words and/or pictures.

consumables Products purchased frequently and used up in a relatively short period of time.

consumer The user of a product.

consumerism A movement seeking to protect consumers against dangerous products and unethical or deceptive business practices.

consumer promotion Incentives aimed at the ultimate user of a good or service in order to increase demand.

containerization The practice of putting products for shipment into large steel boxes or trailers of standardized sizes; these containers can then easily be transferred from one type of transportation to another.

continuity program A promotional activity that encourages repeat purchasing and brand loyalty.

controlled-market system An economic system that relies on a government economic plan to decide what to produce.

convenience sample A form of *nonprobability* sample in which the easiest people to find are selected.

convenience store A small retail store offering a limited selection of convenience items at a convenient location that is open for long hours and so charges for that added convenience.

cooperative A business owned by the customers it serves.

cooperative advertising Advertising in which the manufacturer of a product provides advertising materials to or reimburses a retailer for part or all of the retailer's advertising expenditures for the product.

copy strategy The means by which advertisers plan and develop the logic of sales messages.

copytesting Evaluating completed advertising in terms of target-audience recall and recognition.

corporate advertising Advertising used by a company to create and nurture positive attitudes toward the company itself or to advocate views important to it.

corporate culture The pattern of shared values and beliefs that structures the way an organization's employees work and interact.

corporate mission A formal statement that defines a firm's business values and usually includes the types of products or services it offers and the markets it serves.

cost-leadership advantage A strategy of gaining a competitive advantage by being an industry's lowest-cost producer.

cost-per-thousand (CPM) A method of stating the costs of a particular media buy that is based on the cost of reaching 1,000 households.

coupon Legal certificate offered by manufacturers and retailers that grants specified savings on selected products when presented for redemption at the point of purchase.

creative concept A "big idea" that gets attention, is memorable, and dramatizes the selling premise.

cross promotion A sales promotion that uses one brand to promote another, noncompeting brand.

culture A way of living that distinguishes one group of people from another. Culture is learned and transmitted from one generation to the next.

customer The buyer of a product, often someone with whom a seller deals on a regular basis.

database marketing Marketing that uses extensive lists of prospects and relevant information to narrow the target to serious prospects and customize the offer to their interests.

databases Large, often computerized, collections of information.

dealer loader An item of value to retailers that encourages them to support a promotion and use promotional display materials.

demand The amount of a product consumers are willing to purchase at a particular price.

demand curve A graphic representation of the effect of a change in price on the number of units or a product sold.

demographic environment Objective, measurable population characteristics such as size, geographic location, age, gender, race, income, and education.

demographics Statistical measures of a population in terms of such characteristics as age, life stage, gender, ethnicity, income, education, household size, and socioeconomic status.

department store A retail store which is large in square footage and is departmentalized, selling a wide variety of product lines grouped by product class.

depression A period of economic contraction in which consumer income and purchasing power decline.

deregulation The practice of relaxing or eliminating laws and regulations governing specific industries.

derived demand Demand in organizational markets that arises, or is derived from, demand in consumer markets.

differentiated marketing Identifying multiple market segments and developing a unique marketing mix for each.

direct competition Products or brands in the same category as a company's product.

direct mail An advertising medium that delivers the message by mail.

direct marketing A system of marketing that integrates ordinarily separate marketing-mix elements to sell directly to both consumers and other businesses, bypassing retail stores and personal sales calls.

direct selling Sales of a firm's products by independent agents who sell the product directly to end users.

discount Any reduction from the list price given to a customer by a manufacturer, wholesaler, or retailer.

discount store A retailer that offers reduced services and lower prices on a wide array of branded goods.

discretionary income Money that consumers have left after paying taxes and making essential personal and household expenditures.

disposable income The balance of all income that consumers have left after paying taxes.

distribution The physical flow of products through distribution channels.

distribution centers Highly automated facilities designed to receive goods from a variety of suppliers, assemble the merchandise, and process and deliver orders quickly and efficiently.

distribution channels The internal and external organizational units that direct the flow of products to customers and add value to a product or service.

distribution leadership A strategy of gaining a competitive advantage through innovative or superior product distribution.

dumping Selling a product in foreign markets for less than in the home market.

durable goods Major high priced purchases that last for three years or more.

economic environment The economic factors and forces that affect both the production and availability of goods and services and the willingness and ability of buyers to purchase them; includes the economic system, factors of economic growth and stability, consumer income levels, and foreign exchange rates.

economic-value-to-the-customer (EVC) pricing Setting a product's price at the maximum amount customers will pay if they are fully informed about both the product and competitive offerings.

economies of scale The principle that as the size of a production run grows, per-unit production costs decrease because of gains in efficiency.

elastic demand A measure of the sensitivity of demand to changes in price; when demand is elastic, it is quite responsive to changes in price—in general, increasing as price declines.

electronic data interchange (EDI) An electronic means of collecting and recording data about product movement and sales which permits channel members to share information and transact business.

entrepreneur A person with novel but often risky ideas who organizes, operates, and assumes the risk for a start-up business venture.

everyday-low-price (EDLP) strategy A retail pricing strategy that emphasizes the lowest prices possible on all merchandise rather than artificially low promotional prices on selected items and higher prices on the rest of the merchandise.

evoked set In consumer purchase decision making, the relatively small set of alternatives that one actually considers in making a final choice.

exchange A marketing transaction, often called a *sale*, in which a buyer gives something of value to a seller in return for goods or services.

execution All of the details and decisions involved in the production of an advertisement.

expense good Inexpensive industrial good used regularly and rapidly.

experience-curve pricing Pricing a product according to the relationship between its average total cost and its total sales volume. This strategy assumes that costs will fall as volumes rise (creating economies of scale) and manufacturers become more experienced and efficient producers.

exporter One who sells products to foreign markets.

external marketing environment All the forces outside a firm that affect market opportunities or pose threats to marketers.

F.O.B. pricing The payment by the seller of the cost of freight and handling a product to some specified location.

facilitating service An activity or task performed by a seller in order to enhance the value of a service product.

factory outlet A retail store owned by and selling the goods of a particular manufacturer, usually seconds and overstocked items.

feature analysis Comparing a product's features with the features of competing products and analyzing the perceived importance of each to consumers.

features The distinctive physical characteristics and perceived service advantages of a product.

fixed cost A cost that does not change in proportion to a change in production levels.

flow charts Scheduling techniques that map out when critical activities start and finish, the amount of time needed to accomplish each, and the order in which each must be completed.

focus group An in-depth group interview with a small number of people who engage in intensive conversation about a particular product or advertisement for a product.

forecasting The estimation of the future based either on the analysis of hard data or on expert judgment or intuition.

foreign exchange rate The value of a country's currency in another currency, or the price of a currency quoted in another currency.

four Ps The four major types of activities included in the marketing mix: activities revolving around the product's development; pricing; placement, or distribution; and promotion, or marketing communication.

franchise A contract between a franchiser (parent company) and a franchisee (an individual or firm) that allows the francisee to operate a business developed by the franchiser in return for management fees, royalties on sales, and adherence to franchise-wide policies and practices.

franchising The practice whereby a company permits its name, logo, design, and management systems to be used in establishing a new firm or store.

free-market system An economic system in which private individuals or businesses own the resources needed to produce goods and consumer demand determines what will be produced and how products will be distributed.

frequency The average number of times within a given period of time that advertising for a brand is seen by those who have been reached.

fulfillment A term for the entire group of activities involved in getting a product to a customer; fulfillment includes maintaining inventory, filling orders, shipping, billing, and handling complaints and adjustments.

generic product A product sold without a brand name, and using just a category label.

geodemographics A measure that combines geographic and demographic data to identify residents of a particular area with similar demographic traits.

global marketing Applying the fundamental concepts, tools, and practices of marketing on a worldwide basis and focusing an organization's resources and objectives on *both* international and domestic market opportunities.

goods Tangible products that are grown, produced, or manufactured.

gross national product (GNP) The value of all goods and services produced by factors of production owned by a country's citizens, regardless of where the goods and services are produced. GNP is differentiated from *gross domestic product (GDP)*, which is the value of all goods and services produced by factors of production within a country.

guarantee A general assurance that a product can be returned if its performance is unsatisfactory.

hierarchy of needs Abraham Maslow's five-level theory of needs in which the need at each successive level must be essentially fulfilled before the person will attempt to fulfill higher-level needs.

hypermarket A large store with broad product lines that often combine the merchandise of discount stores with that of grocery supermarkets.

image pricing Setting a high price to convey an image of high quality.

importer One who buys products from other countries for for sale at home.

indexing Comparing numbers by putting them on the same scale. Most indexes use 100 as the base or average number and report scores in relation to 100 as above or below that average.

indirect competition A term for products that are in a different category from a company's product but that serve as alternative purchase choices.

industrial market The aggregate of all firms in an industrial sector which buy goods and services to produce other goods and services.

industry environment The character of the industry in which a particular firm is a member.

inelastic demand A measure of the sensitivity of demand to price changes; in a price-inelastic situation, a price decrease has minimal effect on total demand.

inflation An increase in the price levels of available goods and services caused by an imbalance of supply and demand.

infomercial A lengthy advertisement, usually on television or radio, that attempts to educate consumers about a good or service; its format often resembles an interview or news show.

information processing The procedure by which individuals receive, interpret, and retain information.

integrated marketing communications (IMC) The strategic development and coordination of the messages and media used by an organization to influence the value perception of the organization and its brands.

interactive media Media systems that make it possible for individual or business customers to participate in two-way communication with sellers by means of combined computer, television, and telephone line hook-ups.

intermediaries Businesses that assist producers in the performance of distribution tasks; if intermediaries take title to the product, they are called *resellers*.

inventory management The control of inventory levels of finished product. Inventory may be held in storage or on retail shelves.

involvement The degree to which a consumer believes that a buying decision is important. In deciding whether to purchase a high-involvement product, the individual generally goes through all five stages of the buying decision-making process.

just-in-time inventory control An operations management system that, by means of constant electronic communication between retailer and supplier, permits the retailer to carry just enough inventory to meet immediate demands, yet ensures rapid and automatic order processing as inventory is depleted.

lead A person or organization that may need or want the seller's good or service or that can benefit from buying it.

lead generation The process of identifying customers who are highly likely to purchase a given product.

leverage Getting the best possible results from available resources.

lifestyle An individual's set of values and tastes that determines the conduct of his daily life, as well as how time, energy, and money are allocated or spent.

line extension The addition of new, related products to an existing line with the same brand name.

loading Encouraging consumers (or the trade) to purchase more of a product than they normally do.

logo The distinctive way in which a brand name is written, symbolized and incorporated in a design.

loss leader A product with a special reduced price, often below the profit margin, that is used to draw customers into a store where usually, customers will trade-up to a higher priced product.

loss-leader pricing Pricing a product at or below cost in order to attract customers to a retail store, where they may then buy other, high-margin products.

lot splitting (also known as "breaking bulk") Buying large quantities of a product and selling it to retailers in smaller lot sizes.

mail order A form of distribution that delivers the product to the buyer by mail.

management The process of achieving a company's desired goals through the most efficient use of resources and strategies, requiring

managers to plan, organize, implement, lead, control, and evaluate all aspects of the process.

margin The difference between the selling price and total unit costs for an item.

marginal revenue The change in total revenue resulting from the sale of additional units of a product.

markdown A reduction from the original retail or selling price of a piece of merchandise.

market A group of potential buyers who need and want a particular product and who are both willing and able to buy it.

market challenger A firm seeking to displace the market leader by means of an innovative marketing strategy.

market follower A firm that allows other firms to introduce innovations into the market and waits to verify market response before making any changes in its own marketing offerings.

marketing The process of planning and executing the various activities that are involved in selling goods, services, or ideas and that lead to an exchange between a seller and a buyer.

marketing audit A formal, systematic review of an executed marketing strategy and plan; may be carried out by either internal or external experts.

marketing communication All the elements in the marketing mix that establish meaning and communicate value to customers and stakeholders.

marketing communication leadership A strategy of gaining a competitive advantage through innovative use of marketing communications.

marketing concept The philosophy that marketing activities should focus on consumer needs and wants.

marketing information system (MIS or MkIS) An integrated companywide information program that collects, stores, and processes both internal and external data to provide appropriate staff with the information they need to make sound marketing decisions.

marketing mix The tools and techniques for implementing the marketing of a product, sometimes referred to as the *four P's*.

marketing plan A document that summarizes a coordinated and focused program for managing the marketing mix in order to meet consumer needs at a profit for the company.

marketing research A systematic process of identifying the information needs of marketing decision makers, designing and implementing procedures for gathering and analyzing the relevant data, and reporting research findings.

market leadership The competitive advantage enjoyed by a company that has twice the market share of its closest competitor and successfully defends that position against all competitors.

market segment A group of customers who make up a subcategory within a larger target market.

market share The percentage of the total market held by a particular company or brand.

market-share analysis Calculation of a company's share of a particular market; requires identifying and measuring the market as a whole and the sales of each participant in that market.

markup The amount by which the price of an item exceeds its total cost. The percent of increase represents the desired profit margin.

mass marketing Selling the same product to a variety of people in a variety of geographic areas through a variety of outlets and using the same marketing mix to do so.

matrix system An organizational system that uses functional departments simultaneously with project teams created to handle special assignments.

maximarketing The use of customer databases and multifunctional advertising to create highly targeted messages that reach and build long-term relationships with specific groups of customers.

media tour A form of publicity in which a spokesperson for a firm travels to selected cities and meets with as many press representatives as possible.

merchandise mix The selection or assortment of products carried by a store.

merchant wholesaler An independent seller who purchases from the manufacture, takes title to the inventory, then ships and sells to retailers perhaps also offering credit, collaborative advertising and warranty servicing.

mixed economic system A system combining elements of the free-market and controlled-market systems.

modified repurchase A type of buying situation in which a firm makes some change in the specifications for a product that it has bought before.

monopolistic competition A competitive environment in which a reasonably large number of sellers compete on the basis of differentiated products.

monopoly A competitive structure characterized by a single seller in a market.

narrow-focus advantage A strategy of gaining a competitive advantage by studying the needs and wants of a narrowly defined target market and creating greater customer value for this segment.

need A real lack of something that people consider necessary and desirable.

new product A product being introduced to the market for the first time as a result of invention, innovation or improvement.

new purchase A type of buying situation in which a firm purchases a good or service for the first time. As there is no prior experience to provide guidance, this is accompanied by a high level of risk.

news release A form of publicity in which an organization makes available to the media some form of print, visual, or broadcast announcement about its activities.

niche market A small, tightly defined group of customers who share

certain characteristics that make them a target market for some specialized product.

noise Anything, physical or psychological, that interferes with the design, transmission, or reception of a message.

objective A goal; a statement of what the firm wants to accomplish.

odd or reverse pricing Pricing products slightly below the dollar in order to make them appear to be lower-priced than they are.

offer A term for everything that is involved in the exchange between buyer and seller, including tangible items such as the product itself and intangibles such as credit terms and guarantees.

oligopoly A competitive environment in which each of a small group of sellers has substantial market share and influence on price.

operating margin The difference between the cost of a product and its selling price.

parity product A product that is equal in features, performance, and quality to its competition.

patent The exclusive legal right to make, use, license, and sell an invention.

penetration The percentage of the target market that buys a given brand.

penetration pricing Setting a low price in order to penetrate a price-sensitive market.

perceived risk The risk that a customer believes is involved in any given purchasing decision.

perceptual map A diagram that indicates how consumers rate various brands in terms of their most important decision-making criteria.

perfect competition A competitive environment in which there are so many competitors that none holds an advantage over the others in price, quality, or size.

personal selling A two-way flow of communication between a potential buyer and a salesperson that is designed to identify the customer's needs, match those needs to one of the firm's products, and convince the customer to buy the product.

physical environment The geologic, atmospheric, and biological world in which we live.

point-of-purchase (POP) display A display designed to give a brand or product line extra in-store exposure.

population A defined group of people or organizations about which a researcher wants to know something.

portfolio analysis The assessment of needs, allocation of resources, and balancing of risk across a corporation's separate business units so that all SBUs can contribute to the achievement of corporate objectives.

positioning The act of formulating a marketing mix that locates a product in the mind of the customer in relation to alternative products or services offered by competitors with the aim of achieving competitive advantage.

predatory pricing The practice, illegal in Canada, of setting an artificially low price for the purpose of restraining a competitor or driving competition out of the market.

preemptive advertising Advertising that stakes out a position for a product before anyone else can claim it; it is based on a unique image rather than a distinctive product feature.

premium An offer of either free or reduced-price merchandise as a reward for some behavior such as purchasing a product or visiting a store.

press conference A meeting held by a corporate official or officials with representatives of the media to announce, explain, or bring the media up to date on some major news event related to the company.

press kit A package of publicity information that includes such materials as press releases, background histories, schedules, maps, pictures of the product and stores that focus on the product's development or testing.

price The statement of value put on goods or services by a seller.

price bundling Offering two or more related products or services as a "package deal"—usually at a special promotional price.

price-fixing An agreement, illegal in Canada, whereby most or all of the major firms in a market (usually an oligopoly) set prices for a product at a given level.

price leader A firm that is able to charge a premium price for its product because customers view it as offering greater benefits.

price leadership A strategy of gaining a competitive advantage by initiating a price change in a given product category and stimulating other companies to follow suit.

price lining Pricing groups of products at set points relative to nearest competitive offerings.

primary data Data obtained from original research by the firm itself or by professional researchers hired by the firm and that answer a specific research question.

private brand A brand that is sold exclusively by one retailer even though the actual product is generally made by another company to the retailer's specifications.

privatization The conversion of a government-owned firm to private ownership.

pro forma A breakdown of all the costs involved in producing and selling a product that is used by marketers to determine profit margin. Pro formas often compute profit margins at various forecasted cost and sales levels.

proactive market follower A firm that seeks competitive advantage by refining or improving on a market leader's innovations.

product Any good, service, or idea that can be offered to a market and that satisfies consumer wants or needs.

product category The collection of branded products against which a particular product must compete.

product differentiation advantage A strategy of gaining a competitive advantage by offering products with unique customer benefits or features not available from competitors.

product launch The introduction of a product to the market.

product leadership A strategy of gaining a competitive advantage by being the first to launch an innovative product or to add new product features and benefits.

product liability The reality that firms are responsible for any damage or injuries caused by their products.

product life cycle The set of stages through which a product passes in the marketplace over time.

product line A group of related products that are similar in one or more ways and that are manufactured by the same company.

product manager An executive who controls all business and marketing efforts, including profit and loss, for a particular product, product line, or brand.

product mix The assortment of products and product lines available from a given manufacturer.

profit The return that a company receives on a transaction after costs have been subtracted.

profit margin The percentage of revenue that remains after both fixed and variable costs have been subtracted.

promotional allowance An attempt by a manufacturer to encourage wholesalers and retailers to sell its product by supplying distributors with extra, free units of the product or by providing cash allowances or financial support for advertising

promotional pricing Setting temporarily low prices on selected items in order to gain market share.

prospect In personal selling, a potential customer.

prospecting The continuous search for and qualifying of leads, or potential customers.

prototype Model of a product made in limited numbers for testing.

psychographics The study and classification of differing lifestyles, based largely on the analysis of people's attitudes, interests, and opinions.

public relations (PR) Activities that promote goodwill and understanding between an organization and its stakeholders.

pull strategy A marketing strategy that stimulates customer demand by communicating directly with potential customers, leading them to seek out and purchase a product.

purchasing power The potential ability of consumers to buy goods and services at prices set by marketers.

push strategy A marketing strategy that emphasizes product distribution and that creates an incentive for retailers and other distributors to sell or "push" a product to customers.

qualified prospect A person or organization that not only needs and can benefit from a product but that can afford it and is able to make the decision to purchase it.

qualitative research Research that typically uses open-ended data-collection methods in order to gain insight into consumers' motives and reasons.

quality control The process of testing products in production to detect and correct defects in structure or function.

quantitative research Research that seeks quantifiable data and usually employs some form of statistical analysis.

quota sample A form of *nonprobability* sample in which the population is divided into categories based on certain characteristics and then a number (quota) is assigned for each category that mirrors the percentages of people found in that category within the total population.

random sample A form of *probability* sample in which names are selected according to a specific formula that ensures the randomness of their selection.

rating Percentage of total broadcast-area households tuned to a station when a TV or radio advertisement runs.

reach The average percent of the target audience exposed to an advertising message at least once within a given period of time.

reactive market follower A firm that "clones" the products of market leaders.

recession A period of economic contraction with little or no economic growth.

reference group Any set of people whose views and behavior are modeled by others in developing their own attitudes and actions.

refunds and rebates Promotions that promise money or coupons to the buyer after the purchase is made.

relationship marketing An approach to marketing in which a company endeavors to build continuing relationships with its customers that promote both the company's long-term growth and the customer's maximum satisfaction.

resellers Organizations that buy goods and services and resell these products, without alteration, to end users, both individuals and businesses.

retail advertising Advertising that is designed primarily to attract customers to stores; usually geographically delineated, store-focused, price-focused, and short-term.

retailing The activities involved in the direct sale of products or services to customers who are the end-users of the product or services in question.

return on investment (ROI) A ratio that estimates a firm's profitability in terms of how its net income compares with its total equity, or the sum of all moneys invested in the firm.

role The set of actions (including purchasing decisions) that society expects an individual to perform under certain circumstances.

roll out To introduce a new product in limited geographical areas, with new markets added as capacity and budget permit.

sales forecast An estimate of the total sales of a product that a company expects to achieve during a specified period of time with a specified marketing mix and a specified level of marketing activity.

sales-incentive program A system of motivating salespeople to achieve record sales by offering them praise and recognition as well as such rewards as cash bonuses, merchandise, and free trips.

sales potential The maximum percentage of market potential that a given firm can expect to achieve based on certain assumptions about the market and the behavior of customers.

sales promotion Any consumer or trade program that adds immediate tangible value to products in order to stimulate consumer purchasing and foster trade cooperation.

sales quota The sales objective for an individual salesperson within a given period of time; usually expressed in units or volume of product and in value or units of currency, but may also be expressed in number of sales calls to be made.

sample A portion of the population that the researcher selects for a particular study. A sample must be representative of the population from which it is drawn.

sampling The practice of allowing the consumer to try a product or service free of charge or at a reduced price.

scanner A hand-held computer that reads UPC bar codes on products and records other information about a sale.

secondary data Published sources of information that are usually in the public domain but are often very general and lack timeliness. Government is the largest provider of such data.

segmentation Identifying groups of people who have common needs.

self-regulation Activities on the part of an industry to police itself.

sell-in Educating and "selling" the sales force and distributors about a new product.

selling premise A statement of the logic behind a sales strategy.

service Time and expertise provided or activities performed on the customer's behalf by an individual or firm.

service attitude The degree of effort exerted by an employee to make a customer's buying experience easier and more satisfying.

service product A task or action, usually performed by a seller, that offers some benefit to a buyer.

service sector Those businesses and other organizations whose product is a service rather than a good.

set fee A charge for services rendered; a specific amount based on a schedule of charges for specific activities.

shelf facing The number of units of a product visible at the front of a retail store shelf.

shelf management Getting maximum sales from every cubic foot of shelf and display space in the store.

shopping goods Relatively high-value branded products.

single-source data Information about individual household purchases often derived from a number of sources but notably from a combination of supermarket scanner data and household consumer panel data.

situational analysis A summary of the conditions and situations that can positively or negatively affect marketing objectives, strategies, and tactics.

skim pricing The practice, often used in introducing a new and innovative product, of setting a high price in order to take advantage of the relative price insensitivity of some market segments.

sociocultural environment The beliefs, attitudes, values, and social institutions of the society and culture in which marketing activities take place.

specialties Free gifts or rewards requiring no purchase and carrying a reminder advertising message.

specialty store A store that focuses narrowly on one product or line.

spot buy Buying TV time in a few selected markets.

stakeholders All the people who have an interest in the success or failure of a firm—its employees, suppliers, stockholders, distributors, legislators and government officials, consumer advocates, and people in the community.

stall Evasive behavior by a prospective customer to avoid or delay a buying decision.

Standard Industrial Classification (SIC) system A system of classifying industries and firms according to the types of products they produce.

stock-keeping unit (SKU) An individual product item and its identifying inventory number.

straight commission A form of sales compensation in which a salesperson's total income is a fixed or variable percentage of his or her total sales.

straight repurchase A type of buying situation in which a firm buys the exact same item that it has purchased in the past.

straight salary A form of sales compensation in which sales personnel are paid a fixed salary regardless of the volume of sales they achieve plus, sometimes, an annual bonus.

strategic business unit (SBU) A division, product line, or brand that operates independently of other units in the corporation, with its own mission, objectives, and marketing plan.

strategic planning The systematic setting of objectives and establishment of strategies that enable the organization to make operational decisions in the light of probable consequences over time.

strategy A plan of action designed to accomplish a stated objective.

stratified sample A form of *probability* sample in which a population is divided into predetermined categories and then selected at random from within those categories.

stretch The willingness to adopt goals that open a gap between the company's current capability and its aspirations.

supermarket A moderately large, fairly focused retail store that stresses self-service and low prices.

superstore A large-scale, high-volume specialty store.

supply The amount of a product producers are willing to provide at a particular price.

SWOT analysis An analysis of the *s*trengths and *w*eaknesses in a firm's internal environment and the *o*pportunities and *t*hreats in its external environment.

tactics Specific short-term actions designed to accomplish longer-term objectives.

targeting Focusing a marketing effort on a market group that has significant potential to respond.

target market The group of people most likely to buy or influence the purchase of a given product.

target-return pricing Pricing a product by setting a specific profit objective and then calculating price on the basis of fixed and variable costs and the number of units expected to be sold.

task-objective method Advertising budget that is directed by specific marketing objectives.

technological environment Those forces of innovation that contribute to improvements in the ways in which human beings and machines accomplish tasks.

telemarketing The solicitation of sales by telephone.

test marketing A form of field experimentation in which a new product or new marketing strategy is given an initial trial in one or two selected market sites.

tie-in A sales-promotion tool that promotes two products together in order to increase both brands' visibility.

Total Quality Management (TQM) A type of quality program that demands total commitment by the firm to the idea of customer satisfaction and defect-free products.

tracking study A survey that monitors top-of-mind awareness as well as trial and repeat purchases of a particular product.

trade cooperative A group of independent businesses that join together to facilitate centralized volume buying and distribution.

trade promotion Incentives directed at the sales force as well as wholesalers, distributors, and retailers in order to stimulate both selling activity and demand.

trade show A meeting and exhibition for manufacturers, suppliers, and distributors at which firms display their products and provide information to potential trade buyers.

trade-in allowance A credit against the price of a new model of a product offered by a seller to a buyer who "trades in" an old model.

trademark A legally registered symbol that a company has the exclusive right to use.

trading companies Companies in Europe and Japan, primarily, that handle all aspects of distribution and wholesaling and are responsible for both imports and exports; they act as both purchasing and sales agents for the companies they represent. They often specialize in certain regions of the world or country markets.

trend analysis A means of predicting future demand, sales, and market penetration by extrapolating from a current situation to an expected future position.

undifferentiated marketing An alternative term for *mass marketing*.

universal product code (UPC) Vertical barcodes printed on packages that allow stores to identify the product's SKU number and price electronically.

usage rate A measure of the amount and frequency with which a particular group of individual consumers buys and uses a specific product. Assesses whether they are light, heavy, or committed loyal users to the brand in question.

user status A measure of a market segment that reflects members' past, present, and possible future purchase and use of a product; categories include potential users, nonusers, ex-users, regulars, first-timers, and users of competitors' products.

value The power of a good to command other goods, such as money, in an exchange; the importance of a product to its potential consumer.

value chain Marketing activities whose cumulative effect is the creation of value for customers.

value equation An expression of value as the relationship between benefits and costs of a product to the consumer.

value-in-use pricing Pricing products based in part on their lifetime operating costs.

variable cost A cost that changes in direct proportion to a change in production levels.

vertical marketing system An arrangement in which a set of marketing channels is managed and controlled by a single channel member.

videotext A database system of information in text and graphic form that is transmitted to personal computers via phone lines.

want The manner in which individuals seek to satisfy a need; influenced by individual tastes and societal factors.

warehouse club A low-price retail store that sells only to members.

warehousing The physical storage of goods that are ready to be sold.

warranty A formal statement of expected product performance and of the manufacturer's liability for replacement or repair of defects.

wheel of retailing The life cycle of retailing in which new types of retailers enter the market at the low end of the pricing level and, as they develop more services, offer more upscale products, higher prices, and more service, new stores enter at the low end.

wholesaler An intermediary who links manufacturers with other intermediaries like retailers and industrial buyers and adds value to a product by means of services like shipping and storage.

Illustration Credits

Chapter 1

3 Canadian Airlines International Ltd.; **6** J. Higby's Gourmet Frozen Yogourt/Ryde Industries Inc.; **7** Courtesy of Rubbermaid; **11** Shell Canada Limited Photographic Services (Neg #86-004-0040; Calgary Research Centre, 86/05/29); **12** Canadian Diabetes Association; **13** Gamma-Liaison, Inc.; **21** Paul Lieberhardt; **23** First Calgary Savings and Credit Union; **25** Will McIntyre; **26** Knowaste Technologies

Chapter 2

31 Stock Boston, Inc.; **36** James Schnepf; **37** Matrix; **38** Courtesy of IBM Corporation; **43** Courtesy of Daewoo Securities (America) Inc.; **46** Courtesy of Toshiba America, Inc.; **47** Hewlett-Packard Canada Ltd.; **49** Courtesy of Hamilton Avnet Electronics; **51** Canada Awards for Business Excellence/Industry Canada; **53** Contact Press Images

Chapter 3

59 Matrix; **62** Superstock; **64** Courtesy of Swatch, a division of SMH(U.S.) Inc.; **66** Sygma; **68** The Granger Collection; **71** Gamma-Liaison, Inc.; **75** AECL CANDU; **77** Courtesy of American International Group, Inc.; **80** The Granger Collection

Chapter 4

95 Frank La Bua; **102** Monkmeyer Press; **107** Courtesy James Kilkelly; **113** Barry Levy; **115** Holiday Inn Express/DAL Holdings Ltd.; **116** Courtesy of Steelcase Inc.

Chapter 5

169 Pillsbury, Inc.; **172–73** Courtesy of Mediamark Research, Inc.; **173** Superstock; **174** Photoedit; **180** Matrix; **184** Courtesy of Infomix Software, Inc.; **187** Stock Boston, Inc.; **188** Lester & Partners Inc.; **195** Courtesy of Catalina Marketing Corporation

Chapter 6

205 Tony Stone Images; **206** Schwinn; **207** Canada Wide; **212** Tony Stone Images; **218** Courtesy of Land Rover North America, Ltd.; **221** The Royal Bank of Canada; **224** Courtesy of Pioneer Electronics (USA) Inc.; **227** Werner Jo Schmid; **229** The Image Works

Chapter 7

237 Stock Boston, Inc.; **239** Courtesy of Millennium Power" Systems', a brand of Eveready Battery Company, Inc.; **240** The Royal Bank of Canada; **244** Courtesy of Mobium and R. R. Donnelly; **246** Dare Foods/Marovino & Associates Inc.; **248** Courtesy of Lee Printwear, a division of Bassett Walker VF Company, Fallon McElligott (Advertising Agency) and Marry! Advertising Photography; **251** Stamp reproduced courtesy of Canada Post Corporation; **252** Monkmeyer Press; **255** Ed Rosenberg, Center for Engineering Design, University of Utah/Sacros Research Corporation; **256** Courtesy of National Defence; **257** Onyx

Chapter 8

263 Picture Cube; **265** FPG International; **268** Courtesy of Safety 1st; **269** Robyn Craig/Prentice Hall Canada Inc.; **273** JB Pictures; **275** Ontario Ministry of Health; **277** Courtesy of Tiffany & Company; **279** Courtesy of Dataradio Inc.

Chapter 9

293 The Image Bank; **297** Courtesy of Citicorp; **299** Courtesy of Compaq; **302** Courtesy of Maytag; **306** The Image Works; **307** Courtesy of 3M Corporation; **308** Courtesy of Solvay Automotive; **311** Dilmah Tea/MJF Group; **314** Copyright © by Mercedes-Benz AG/ Courtesy of Nissan Motor Corporation; **317** Beef Information Centre; **318** Matrix

Chapter 10

327 Canadian Airlines International Ltd.; **330** Canadian Tire Corporation, Limited; **331** Canadian Imperial Bank of Commerce; **333** Chaumeil-Jerrican; **337** Courtesy of Nestlé USA, Inc.; **339** Courtesy of The Coca Cola Corporation; Stock Boston, Inc.; **345** Unitel; **346** Courtesy of Xerox Corporation; **348** Courtesy of General Mills, Inc.

In suppliers, 246
In-depth interviews, 187–88
In-store testing, 194–95
Incentives, 622
Income, 68
 NFP-generated, 407
 segmentation by, 269
Independent agents, 694–95
Indexing, 722
Indirect competition, 298
Indirect distribution channels, 452, 453
Indirect price reduction, 630
Industrial goods, 368, 369, 370
Industrial market, 8, 239–40
 segmentation, 276–79
Industrial product channels, 452
Industrial Revolution, 17, 442
Industries, related and supporting, 293, 294
Industry Canada, 364
Industry environment, 85
Inelastic demand, 513–14, 515
Inept set, 228
Inert set, 228
Inferred messages, 563
Inflation, 67–68, 209
Influencers, 250
Infomercial, 589
Information, 174
"Information highway," 88–89, 673
Information processing, consumer behavior and, 222–23
Information search
 by resellers, 255
 in consumer decision-making model, 227
 in organizational buying decision process, 251
Innovation, 230
 competitive advantage through, 310–15
 competitive-advantage strategies and, 426–27
 corporate culture and, 46–48
 and market leadership, 307
 See also Technological
Innovators, 230, 378
Inseparability of service and employee-provider, 391, 393–94
Institutional market, 8, 242
Intangible of services, 390, 391
Integrated marketing, 119–20, 593–94
Integrated Marketing Communication (IMC), 564–76
 defined, 565
 function of, 566
 global marketing communication, 573–74
 and integrated marketing, 593–94
 message execution and coordination, 573
 mix, 567
 objectives, 569
 strategies, 569–70, 572–73
 targeting, 568–69
 zero-based communication plan, 567–68
Intensive distribution, 456
Interaction Model, 252, 253
Interactive media, 673–74
Intermediaries, 8, 448–50, 452, 570
 bottlers as, 453
 defined, 448
 in international distribution, 455
 See also Retailers; Wholesalers
Intermodal transportation, 469

Internal organizational environment, 43–52
 corporate culture and, 46–47
 corporate mission and, 44–45
 expertise of employees and, 45
 financial resources and, 43–44
 technology and, 43
Internal strengths and weaknesses, analysis of, 52
International direct marketing, 671–72
International distribution channels, 460–61
International expansion, 374–76
International market, 8
International regulatory issues on pricing practices, 522–23
International retailing, 491
International Standards Organization, 244
International strategies, 113–14
International wholesaling, 481
Interviews, 187–88
Intrapreneur programs, 48
Intrapreneurial development, 427
Invention, 418–19, 420, 427
Inventory management, 461–63, 468–69, 655
Involvement
 in buyer orientation model, 69, 368
 level of, 230
ISO 9000 certification program, 244

J

Japan
 adaptation of personal selling in, 698
 consumer behavior in, 212, 270–71
 direct marketing in, 672–73
 distribution channels in, 450, 460, 461
 domestic market of, 481
 domestic rivalry in, 294
 Fair Trade Commission, 521
 keiretsu in, 243
 low-cost producers, 301
 Ministry of International Trade and Industry (MITI), 315
 mixed economy of, 64
 quality standards in, 311, 396–98
 retailing system in, 481
Japan Direct Marketing Association, 672
Japanese construction industry, 520–21
Japanese firms, approach to competitive innovation, 311–15
Judgement, as forecasting method, 285
Junior Achievement, 408–409
Just-in-time dyeing process, 197–98
Just-in-time inventory control system, 462–63, 490

K

Kaizen, 310
Keiretsu, 243

L

Labor costs, 281, 301, 312, 393, 470, 517
Labor intensity, 395
Laggards, 230, 378
Late majority adopters, 230, 378
Law of supply and demand, 13
Lead, 685
Lead generation, 655
Leader, market, 305
Leading, 712–15
Learning, 223
Legal environment, 76
Legal and regulatory environments, 76–84
 and business property, 82
 and competition, 80–81

consumer protection, 81–82
 and deregulation and privatization, 82–84
 regulatory protection in Canada, 77–79
 and trade policy, 84
Leverage, 97, 716
Leverage pricing, 349
Life cycle, 214
 brand, 335
 product, 376–79
Life stage
 and consumer behavior, 217–19, 272
 segmentation, 267–68
Lifestyle, and consumer behavior, 220, 221
Limited-line stores, 484
Limited-service wholesalers, 480
Line extensions, 112, 338, 373–76
List management, 661–62
Loading, 628
Lobbyists, 256
Local distribution, 457
Location, retailing strategy and, 492
Logo, 331
London Chamber of Commerce, 179
Long-distance telephone services, deregulation in, 83
Loss, 525
Loss leaders, 493
Loss-leader pricing, 547
Lot splitting, 478
Loyalty. *See* Brand loyalty

M

McKinsey-GE model, 99
Mail order, 473, 665
Mail-order catalogs, 667–68
Maintenance messages, 563
Makers, 274
Management, defined, 712
Management information system (MIS), 171
Management-development training programs, 704
Managers
 brand, 41–42
 category, 42
 product, 41
Managing Brand Equity (Aaker), 350
Managing profitability, 723
Manufacturer-wholesaler, 478, 480
Manufacturers, 364, 477, 478
 tension between retainers and, 475–75
Manufacturing, gross margin in, 524
Manufacturing process, quality in, 362, 363
Margin, 524
Marginal analysis, 524–26
Marginal cost analysis, 523
Marginal revenue, 523
Markdowns, 525
Market challengers, 305, 308
Market coverage, 456, 457–58
Market demand, 284
Market density, 457
Market development approach, 112
Market diversification, 113, 120
Market entry pricing, 548
Market entry pricing strategies, 549
Market expansion strategy, 112, 120
Market follower, 309
Market forecast, 285; *See* Forecasting
Market leader, 305
Market penetration approach, 112
Market potential, 284
Market restriction, 79

Global Issues
Index

The following index lists substantial discussions of global matters; it does not include every single reference to a global company or issue in this text. Global concerns are also addressed throughout the book in illustration captions.

Ethical Issues
Index

The following index lists substantial discussions of ethical, social, and environmental responsibility in marketing. These kinds of concerns are also addressed throughout the book in illustration captions.